10284 **Liturgy.** A Collection of Tracts on the REFORMATION of the LITURGY, and on the Episcopate, including the rare first edition of the Puritan Prayer Book, 1644, with remarks on it, printed at Charles I's press at *Oxford*, 1645, and a number of other rare pieces, from 1640 to 1711, all in excellent sound preservation, bound in 4 vols. sm. 4to. *Cambridge calf*, £10. 10s 1640-1711

Contents:—Certaine Considerations touching the Pacification of the Church of England, 1640; an humble Remonstrance to the High Court of Parliament, 1640; Answer to "the humble Remonstrance," 1641; R. Bayly's Parallel of the Liturgy with the Mass-Book, and other Romish Rituals, 1661; L. Wemocke's Beaten Oyle for the Lamps of the Sanctuarie, 1641; The Bishop of Armaghe's Direction in 1642, concerning the Lytungy, and Episcopall Government, 1660; Certain Grievances, or the Errors of the Service Book, 1643; Directory for the Publique Worship of God, 1644, **First Edition** of the Puritan Prayer Book, *rare, fine copy*; View of the New Directory, and vindication of the ancient Liturgy, *Oxford, Lichfield*, 1645; Advice of the Assembly of Divines on a Confession of Faith, 1647; Pearson's No Necessity of Reformation of the Public Doctrine of the Church of England, 1660; The Old Nonconformist, touching the Common Prayer, 1660; Gauden's Considerations touching the Liturgy, 1661; T. Bolde's Rhetorick Restrained, or Gauden's Considerations considered, 1660; the Liturgical Considerator considered, a view of Gauden, *with Epistle by Z. Crofton*, 1661; Discourse on the just Antiquity and Pedigree of Liturgies, 1661; Freeman's Reasonableness of Divine Service, 1661; V. Powell's Common Prayer-Book no Divine Service, 1661; Grand Debate between the Bishops and the Presbyterian Divines, Commissioners for the review and alteration of the Common Prayer, 1661; Petition for Peace, with the Reformation of the Liturgy, presented by the Divines, 1661; W. Prynne, on some Ceremoniall Appurtenances to the Common Prayer, 1661; Common Prayer-Book Devotions, Episcopal Delusions, 1666; Arguments for Concessions in the Common Prayer and Rites of the Church of England, 1689; Vox Cleri concerning alterations in the established Liturgy, with an account of the present Convocation, 1690; Answer to the Vox Cleri, 1690; Vindication of two letters relating to Convocation and alterations in the Liturgy, 1690; Answer to Scots Cases against Dissenters, 1700; Irwin's Discourse concerning Publick Prayer, 1711; and others.

CHARLES I.—Eikon Basilike, the Pourtraiture of his Sacred Majesty in his Solitudes and Sufferings, with His Majesties Praiers, etc., *portrait of Charles II.*, 32mo, in the old and well worn Velvet Jacket, gilt edges, 8s 1649

411 GAUDEN (John, *of Bocking*, Essex) Tears, Sighs, Complaints, of the Church of England, with probable Cures of her Distempers, thick sm. folio, 2 *very curious folding plates*, fine impressions, *clean in old calf neat*, 16s 6d 1659

On Innovations, Vulgar neglect of Ancient formes in the Decalogue, Lord's Prayer, Bickerings with anabaptists, Infant Baptism, etc. The writer was author of Eikon Basilike.

Tracts on and by Non-Conformists, and on the Oath of Allegiance, etc. 1 vol. sm. 4to. *old calf*, 36s 1643-60

Contents: Z. Crofton St. Peter's Bond abide: a consideration of Gauden's sence of the Covenant, relating to Episcopacy, 1660—Queries concerning Tithes 1639—Jesu-Worship confuted, 1660—Gobert's Character of a Communicating Church-Member, 1650—Bakewell's Answer to the Anabaptists, 1649—the Arraignement of Persecution, by yongue Martin Mar-Preist (*no title, ca.* 1650)—and several other controversial pieces.

SEVENTEENTH CENTURY RITUAL.

Sir,—I have before me a pamphlet of four pages, entitled "A Letter from a Dissenter to the Divines of the Church of England, In Order to a Union." At the end it is stated to have been "printed" and "to be sold by Randal Taylor, near Stationers' Hall, MDCLXXXVII." On page 2 I find the following:—

"You know what has hinder'd us hitherto from joyning with your Church: We have always suspected you for Papists in Masquerade; The many Ceremonies you have retain'd, your Crosses, and Altars, and Tapers, and Surplices, and Bowings; Your Confessions and Absolutions, and Mass-Forms of Prayer, &c., have oblig'd us to these Thoughts; and that tho' you pretend to have left Babylon, yet by the Rags and Livery you have brought along with you, we could not but still suspect you of her Retinue."

Have we not here evidence that in the year 1687 "tapers" were "retained and in use" in the Church of England?

W. F. CLEMENTS.

Kentish Town, Festival of St. Nicolas, 1875.

144 CHARLES I.—Eikon Basilike, The Portraiture of his Sacred Majestie in his Solitude and Sufferings, 8vo, *first edition, portrait, old calf neat*, 4s 6d 1648

CHARLES II.—*EIKON BASILIKE DEYTERA*, The Pourtraicture of his Sacred Majesty King Charles II, with His Reasons for turning Roman Catholick, published by King James, Found in the Strong Box, *portrait*, sm. 8vo, calf, 4s 1694

WORDSWORTH (C., *D.D.*) "Who Wrote Eikon Basilike?" Considered and Answered, 8vo, calf neat, 3s 6d 1824

Gauden is said to have
been Author of
"Εικων Βασιλικη"
Formerly Rector of Mayfield became 1st Bp
of Exeter — He became Bp of Worcester afterwards
In youth he was a scholar at King Edward's
school (1623) Bury St Edmunds
Vide J. Toland Amyntor,
1699
Nazarenus 1718

"Analogy" 109
Apology 57

Engraved frontispiece by Thos Cross [illegible]
Wm. Marshall.

The King is Charles I

"The Minister" Gardner?
The author [illegible] before the Directory came out

1645 The Solemn League & Covenant forbid
the Sacrament to any who had not sworn it"

Which things the Angels desire to looke into 1 Pet. 1
The gates of Hell shall not prevaile
The Sun of righteousnes with healing in his wings
I will bee with you to the end of the World
The Lord God is a Sun & Sheild
HIERASPISTES
A DEFENCE of the Ministry and Ministers of the Church of England by JOHN GAUDEN D.D.
for the defence of the Gospel. Phil. 1.17
Woe bee to me if I preach not the Gospel
Oliua Charitatis
Gentium Tutela
στυλος και εδραιωμα της αληθειας
MAGNUM PIETATIS MYSTERIUM
S. APOSTOLI
LEX et PROPHETÆ
α: IESVS CHRISTVS: ω
Armed prudence
Magistratus Polit.
Learned Pietie
Minister Eccl.
London Printed for Andrew Crooke. 1653.
Tho. Cross Sculpsit.

HIERASPISTES:

A

DEFENCE by way of APOLOGY

FOR THE

Miniſtry and Miniſters

OF THE

CHURCH of *ENGLAND*:

HUMBLY PRESENTED

To the Conſciences of all thoſe that excell in *VIRTUE*.

By *JOHN GAUDEN*, D.D.
and MINISTER of that Church
at *BOCKING* in *ESSEX*.

Mat. 28. 19. Goe ye therefore, and teach all Nations, baptizing them, &c.
20. And loe, I am with you alway, even to the end of the world.
Tit. 1. 5. That thou ſhouldſt ordain Presbyters in every City, as I had appointed thee.
Heb. 13. 17. They watch for your ſouls, as they that muſt give an account, &c.
Ἕκαστος ὑμῶν ἐν τῷ ἰδίῳ τάγματι εὐχαριστείτω θεῷ. ὁ λαϊκὸς ἄνθρωπος τοῖς λαϊκοῖς προστάγμασι δέδεται. Clem. Pauli diſ. Ep. ad Corinth.
Presbyteris qui ſunt in Eccleſia obaudire oportet, qui ſucceſſionem habent ab Apoſtolis, & cum ſucceſſione Chariſma veritatis certum acceperunt ſecundum Patris beneplacitum; Qui vero a principali abſiſtunt ſucceſſione, quocunque loco colliguntur, ſuſpectos habere oportet, vel hæreticos & malæ ſententiæ, vel ſcindentes & elatos, & ſibi placentes: Omnes hi decidunt a veritate, Sophiſtæ verborum magis eſſe volentes, quam diſcipuli veritatis. Irenæ. l. 3. c. 40. & l. 4. c. 43.

Printed for *Andrew Crooke*, and are to be ſold at the *Green Dragon* in St. *Pauls-Church-yard*, 1653.

Prudens simplicitas.

To the Reader.

THE ensuing *Apologetick defence of the Ministry and Ministers of the Church of England*, can hardly expect more *Readers* than severe *Censurers*; of whom some will be wearied with the length, others offended with the freedome: some despisers of the manner, others contradicters of the matter: In sum, it lookes for not many, or any friends; but such as are humble, judicious, and impartiall; And not a few enemies, of those that are proud, ignorant and biassed by secular interests. So prevalent are our enemies grown even in matters of Religion, that few can bear, either their diseases, or their remedies. Albeit the age extreamly wants, yet it can hardly endure a plain and faithfull stile; though it keeps the *medium* between severity and flattery, bitternesse and dulnesse, morose antiquity and petulant novelty. It is some mens Religion to have none setled by education or profession; Others cavill at all that hath been taught or established: Many esteem their *Levity* in opinions, and inconstancy in profession to be a kinde of *Empire* and *Soveraignty* in Religion; Never thinking themselves to be, what they should be, till they are, what they list: judging that Liberty, which is *Lawlesnesse*, and that freedome, which is without fear of God, or reverence of man: calling that piety with peace, which is the dissolving and desolating of all publique society, order, unity, and polity in Churches; crying up their later fragments, and broken meats; being all those loaves and fishes, with which Christ hath for so many hundred of years fed his Church and people in all the world.

Others of deeper reaches taking the advantage of such popular easinesse and credulity, which is lesse separable from the vulgar, than shadowes are from grosse bodies, study to variate and shift the extern forms and models of Religion, untill the sacred and eternall interests of Gods glory, and mans salvation are drawn to stoop to, or forced to comply with temporary designes, and secular policies; where *Christ* must be made to serve *Belial*; *God* to bow down to *Mammon*; the *Ark* must become captive to *Dagon*; piety turn page to avarice; and Religion be onely entertained as a *lackey* for Ambition; Where there are such abasings, distortings and deformings of the beauty and rectitude of Christian Religion, (sowring the *wine* of *Primitive verity*, simplicity, and charity, with the *vinegar* of worldly jealousie, craft and cruelty) what can be expected, as to any thing written, in behalf of *Religion*, and its holy *Institutions*, with a plain, free, and upright genius, but onely such *fate and doome*, as the severall humors, parties, prejudices, and worldly interests of men will afford: which being so divided, and thwarting each other, it will be hard to please any one, without displeasing many.

The Author therefore (who writes as addicted to no faction:) nor personally *injured*, or *obliged* by any novel parties, but studying only to discharge a good conscience, as to men, so chiefly toward God; (the assistance of whose *Heroick Spirit*, and free grace he humbly begs through all this work) neither seeks, nor hopes to please any men; whose passionate adherence to any *sidings* either in civill or religious concernments, lesse inclines them to that calm, judicious, and charitable temper, which is *Scripturall*, *Catholick*, and truly *Christian*; This he onely studies, this he preacheth, for this he prayes, this he commends, this he admires: Not doting upon any *rust* or *drosse*, which ancient and venerable *Episcopacy* might in many hundred of years easily contract; and from which it may as easily be cleared, if men impartially sought the things of

Jesus

Jesus Christ, and his Churches prosperity, without gratifying any passion in themselves or others. Nor yet doth the *Author* any whit admire those *rigid Reformations*, which some rash, envious, or ambitious *Presbyters* drive on; who know not how to shave their *Fathers* beards without cutting their throats; nor to pair their nailes without cropping off their hands. They are unskilfull Chymists, who cannot refine from drosse without consuming what is pretious: And they are pitifull Empiricks, who cannot purge without casting into Bloudy Fluxes. Nor in the last place doth this *Apologist* so far temporise, as in the least kinde to magnifie the *violent breakings*, and hotter meltings of any bolder Independents; who make Religion and Reformation run to any new moulds, which they fancy, to *Separating*, to *Seeking*, to *Shaking*, to *nothing*; that ownes any Ordinance, order, publique establishment, Christian communion, or holy profession; being wholly resolved into these two principles; the pleasing of themselves, and the confounding of others.

Amidst these sad distractions and various confidences of men in their *opinions*, and *undertakings*, there is no wise man, but discerns the *pulse* of mans Ambition equally beating in *spirits* Monarchicall, Aristocraticall, and Democraticall: as in *civill policies*, so also in *religious administrations*; some are for *primacy* and priority, others for paucity and parity, a third sort for popularity and vulgarity: where as indeed the best constitution in any government, is rather from the harmonious temperament and proportionate mixture of all three, than from the *predominance* of any one, so as to oppresse the other two. Men of eminent parts are prone to affect to govern alone; without any *flatnesse* or allay from inferiours: Men of *moderate* abilities are content to goe in a joint stock, mutually supplying those defects, to which singly they are conscious: Men of *low* and mean endowments are for *huddles*; *one and all*; where no one man is so much *confident* of himself, as indeed he is *envious* at all others; and impatient to see any thing done without him: Whereas in true wisdome, the *eminency* of the first, the *mediocrity* of the second,

 and

and the *meanneſſe* yet multitudinouſneſſe of the third, ſhould be fairly modelled and *compoſed*, as the head, hands, and other members of the body are, to the common welfare. And certainly they did of old (in the beſt times and tempers of Chriſtians) all meet in a moſt happy harmony, Church-order, and conſtitution; no leſſe than the humours, bloud, and ſpirits doe in healthy and vigorous bodies: All experirience tels us that the diſorder of any one of them, cauſeth *ſickneſſe*, weakneſſe, or diſſolution of Chriſtian charity, ſociety, and ſweet communion, as to their extern polity and profeſſion of Religion.

Which ſad effects, or ſymptomes at leaſt of them in this Church, this Author with grief and ſhame beholding, hath endeavoured with the *greateſt ſerenity and expediteneſſe* of ſoul (before he leaves this *Bacha* and *Aceldama*, this *valley of tears*, contention, and confuſion) to aſcend himſelf, and lead others, as much in him lies, to the height, and top of that *Primitive verity*, *unity* and *charity*, which made Chriſtians ſo much admired, and venerated, even when they were moſt cruelly perſecuted. From which free and *un-ingaged proſpect*, both *he* and they, may with a clear and full view behold the later and worſer changes in extern matters of Religion; wherein various opinions, and different deſignes of Chriſtians have either ſtrayed from, or quite croſſed the great road of *pious and plain hearted Antiquity*, which no doubt beſt knew, beyond all the cenſorious Criticks, and factious Noveliſts of after times, what was the minde of the *bleſſed Apoſtles*, of the Primitive Martyrs and Confeſſors: who moſt exactly followed thoſe methods, which the Apoſtolical wiſdome and piety had preſcribed to thoſe Churches they planted, watered and preſerved, chiefly aiming at the *Catholick* good, and common benefit of all Churches.

From which, *private fancies*, aims and intereſts, afterward varying, both in opinion and practiſe, occaſioned thoſe many uncomfortable ſchiſms, and uncharitable factions, which (in all times, and now as much as ever) ſo divide the *unity*, deſtroy the *charity*, and deform the *beauty* of Chriſtian Religion;

To the Reader.

That many, if not most Christians, doe not onely *read*, and *hear*; *write*, and *dispute*; *pray*, and *preach*; but they *believe*, and *repent*; love, or hate; damn, or save; *communicate* with, or *excommunicate* one another, most-what, out of their naturall *constitutions*, as they are of more calm and cholerick *tempers*; or out of those *prejudices* and prepossessions, which *custom* and *education* have formed in them; or from *adherence* to parties and mutuall *agitations*, whereby they hope to drive on some worldly and secular concernments; rather than from true and *impartiall principles* of right *reason*, Scripturall *precept*, and Ecclesiasticall *practise*; which threefold cord, twisted into one, is not easily broken: And which, beyond all disputes, affords, both in doctrine and discipline, in opinion and practise, as to *inward piety*, and *outward polity*, the surest measures of Religion, and bounds of conscience; which are then most *pure* and *unblameable*, when they look directly to those great designes and ends of every wise man and good Christian, the glory of God, the honour of Christ, the peace of the Church, and Soules eternall welfare; without any sinister *squintings* to secular ends, or *warpings* to worldly designes, which are the *moths* of Religion, the pests of society, the overlayings of charity, and the *Incubusses* of Conscience; easily seising upon Christians of weak judgements, and strong passions; for which we need not goe far to see many and unhappy *instances*.

For, what serious and well advised Christian sees not; how vehement *drawings* and *impulses* in matters of Religion are made upon men by weak, and at first scarse perceptible, *byasses* of *opinions*, and *hopes* of advantages: How, want of *solidity* or *sincerity* is the greatest motion of violent affections in most men: How, the lesse they weigh those things, they call *Religion* and *Reformation*, the more eagerly they pursue and extoll them: (The most wise and *gracious* men being alwayes the most grave and calm, the most serious and constant) *Vulgar devotion* and *heats*, like weak fires, and dubious flames, are usually kindled by *light fewell*, and fomented with fear materials; Blazing, like *Comets*, the more prodigiously, by how much they have more of grosse and earthly vapours.

Hence, not onely the glory of *outward successes*, and worldly *prosperities*, attending the number, policy, or prevalency of any faction, makes many Christians, (ere they are aware of it) turn *Turkes*, and secretly subscribe to *Mahumetanism*; (which for many *centuries* hath outvived Christianity in point of *victorious progresses*, military advantages, and latitude of *Empire*) The current of worldly *events*, like *quick-tides*, easily and undiscernibly carrying many Christians from that course of pious *strictnesse*, and conscientious *exactnesse* in truth, justice, and charity, which they ought alwayes to steere without any variation, according to the clear and fixed *Word of God* in Scripture; and not according to his dark permissions, or unsearchable *workings* in *providence*; which are alwayes just and to be admired, as from the divine wisdome and justice; but not alwayes to be approved or imitated, as from mans wickednesse and folly; which like poysonous drugs are in themselves deadly and to be abhorred: however the skill of the great and good Physitian, God, knows how to attemper and apply them as Physick and Theriacals, to purge, or punish; to cure, or correct the distempers of his Church and people.

Nor is it this *temptation* onely of *events*, (in which is a *strong delusion*, able, if *possible, to deceive the very elect*; which none but *steddy* judgements, and *exact* consciences can resist;) But even the *smallest differences*, the most easie and triviall considerations, which are but as *the dust of the balance* in Reason or Religion, in piety or prudence, these, like *motes*, falling into some mens *eyes*, presently appeare as *mountaines*; and so possesse their sight, that they will owne nothing for *Religion* in any men, or any Church, which appears not just after that colour, figure and notion, which they are taken withall.

How many peoples Religion consists much in the very extern modes of *dressing* themselves, or others, in the *fashion* of their own or others *clothes*, for their plainnesse, or costlinesse; for

for their novelty, or Antiquity: yea in the length, or shortnesse; in the laying out, or hiding of their *hair*: Hence their censures, scandals, or approbations of others; their confidences, and ostentations of themselves, even as to *piety*, *purity*, and *holinesse*; (which are indeed seldome seen in *ruffianly* and *dissolute fashions*; yet, often in those proportions of *elegancy* and *decency*, as to the *outward garb*, and fashion, which some mens rusticity, severity, or slovenliness cannot bear:) Because they doe not understand, that, in things of this kinde, not *Scripture*, but Nature gives rules to the *Religion* of them; which is their usefulnesse and their comelinesse, 1 *Cor.* 11. 3,14. And this, not by any *morall innate principles*, but by those (*mores gentium*) *customes* of Countries, and dictates of *sociall nature*, which not by written Lawes, but by *tacit consent and use* doe for the most part prescribe what is agreeable to humanity, modesty, and civility; which customary measures and civill rules of ornament and *outward fashions* in any countrey, are not *scrupulously* to be quarrelled at; nor *cynically* neglected, nor *morosely* retained; but may with *freedome*, and *ingenuity* be *used*, and *altered*; according to the *genius* of all things, of extern *mode* and *fashion*, as cloathing, dressing, building, planting, fortifying, speaking, &c. which depend much upon the *fancies* of men; and so are *mutable*, without any sin, or immorality; as all things are, within the compasse of mortality.

How many mens *Religion* lies in their *admiration* of some mens persons, gifts, piety, and supposed zeal, in their being of his sect, way, *body*, fraternity, and *confederacy*? when yet many times they have but an *Idol* for their God, though they glory to have a *Levite* to be their *Priest*: Able men may have great infirmities; and learned men grosse errors; foul diseases oft attend fair faces: Doting sectaries will worship the *pudenda* of their Priests, and magnifie what is most dishonest, and uncomely in their ringleaders. Yea, many *silly souls* we see are every where much taken with other mens *ignorance*, set off meerly with *impudence*; where the want

of

of all true worth for ability and authority is attended with the want of all *shame* and *modesty*; Factious spirits in poor people makes them content to have their *Religion* hatcht under the wing and feathers of any *foolish and uncleanbird.*

In how many Christians is their Religion *blown* up, (as the paper kites of boyes) meerly with their own *breath*, or other mens applauses; setting off all that is done in *their way* with the Epithites of *rare*, *pretious*, *holy*, *gracious*, *spirituall*, *sweet*, *divine*, *Saint-like*, *&c.* when yet *wise men*, that weigh their *boastings*, evidently finde, much of these mens Religion to be deformed with *Mimicall affectations* of words and phrases, with studied *tones*, scurrilous *expressions*, antick *gestures*, and ridiculous *behaviours*: Much in them is *fulsome* by the length, lowdnesse, tumultuarinesse, unpreparednesse and confusednesse even of those *duties*, which they count religious, holy, and spirituall: which are so far scandalous, and suspected to sober Christians, as they finde them not onely full of faction, but also *destitute* of that common sense, order, comelinesse, gravity, discretion, reason and judgement, which are to be found in others: from whom they separate not out of scruple so much as scorn; not out of conscience, but pride and arrogancy; when yet they bring forth, after all their swelling and tympanies, nothing comparable to what others in an orderly way have done, either for the *soul* and essence of Religion, which is *truth* and *charity*; or for the *body* and *ornament* of it, so far as it appears to others in *order and decency.*

Many have little that they can *fancy*, or call *Religion* in them, but onely a *fiercenesse* for that *side*, to which they take, a morosenesse, censoriousnesse, and supercilious indifferency towards all, but those whom they count *theirs.* Vehemently *opposing*, what ever *Adversary* they undertake; abhorring all they doe, or hold in *piety or prudence*; branding all they like not with the *mark of Antichrist*; and crying downe what ever by any Christians is diversly *observed* in the fashion of their Religion: Hence many of the *lowest form* of Christians, place much of their Religion, in *innovating*

Church-

Church government; contending for *discipline*; disputing against all *Liturgies*: in scuffling with *ceremonies*; in beating the air, and fighting with the *shadows* of Religion: the measure of all which, as to piety, prudence and conscience, stands in their *relation* to the main *end*, Gods *glory*, the Churches *peace*, and the salvation of *soules*; which, where-ever they are with truth, holinesse, order, and charity carried on in *any Church*, Christians need no more scruple the extern *form* and manner, wherein they are decently set forth; than they need quarrell at the *roome*, *table*, or *dish*, where *wholesome meat* is handsomely presented to them; whether in a plainer or more costly way.

Others of more airy and *elevated fancies*, are altogether in *Millenary dreams*, religious *fantasms*, Apocalyptick *raptures*, *Prophetick* accomplishments; not caring much how they break any moral precept of Law or Gospel, if they thinke, thereby they may help to *fulfill a Prophecy*; which every *opiniaster* is prone to imagine strongly portendeth the advancement of his opinion, party, and way in Religion; untill they come to such a soveraignty, as may be able to govern and oppresse others; their Mopsicall humors being never satisfied, but in fancying themselves as Kings, and reigning with Christ; Not in the inward power of his grace and spirit (which is a Christians commendable ambition) joined with an holy and humble subjection to God and man; which makes them conquerours over the lusts in themseves, and their love of the world; whence flows the greatest peace both to Churches and States: but in that extern worldly power and policy which enables them to rule others, after the same bloudy arts and cruel methods of government, which *Zimri*, or *Herod*, or *Alexander*, or *Cæsar* exercised: and not the Lord Jesus Christ, who was meek and lowly, as one that served and obeyed. And herein not onely the weak, illiterate and fanatick vulgar are oft observed to act mad and *ridiculous prankes* in Religion; but even men of some learning and seeming piety, oft lose themselves in their wild, and *melancholy rovings*; which make all *Pro-*

phecies found to their *tune*, and to be for their party and opinion; though never so novell, small and inconsiderable: Nothing is more easily abused even by easie wits, than *Prophetick emblemes*, and allusions, which like soft waxe are capable of severall shapes and figurations, by which, no doubt, the *Spirit of God* aimed at the *generall aspect* and *grand proportions* of the Catholick Church in its visible profession and outward estate: for whose use all Scripture is written, and to whose elevation, or depression, either in the Orthodoxie, or corruption of doctrine; in its integrity, or schismes; in its peace, or persecution, prophecies are generally calculated; and in no sort to those lesser occasions, obscurer events, or alterations, incident to particular persons, *countries*, or Churches. It is hard to discerne the *Star of Prophecy* so over any one man, or place, or time, as that was over the house where Christ was in *Bethlehem*; Hence many *meteors*, falling *Stars*, and fatuous fires, are frequently discovered in the writings of fancifull and factious men; as if all they did, or desired, or approved, were evidently foretold and commended in the *Revelation*; In whose Visions one sees this Princess; another sees that learned man; a third, that State or Kingdome; a fourth, that *Commander* and Conqueror, &c. according as men list to fancy themselves, or flatter others; whose sparks are far extinct, and their glory presently vanisheth, as no way proportionable to that fixed light and ample glory, which the spirit of prophecy holds forth, chiefly to the Christian world, in opposition to Heathens, Jews, or Antichrists. After the way of these *Prophetick fancies*, and *passionate methods* of some mens misinterpreting, and misapplying Prophecies; *great Religion*, we see, hath been placed by small mindes, in pulling down and extirpating the ancient order and government of Episcopacy, (which was in all Churches, as here in *England*, from the first plantation of Christianity:) Also in setting up the *supremacy* of an headlesse Eldership and *Presbytery*; or in dashing both of them into *sheards*, and small pieces by the *little stone* of *Independency*;

dependency: How doe ſome glory in their dividing and deſtroying the ancient goodly frames of Churches, that they may new *modell* them to their popular way of calling, chuſing, and ordaining of *Miniſters*: Many boaſt much in their forſaking the calling and communion of all former Miniſters and religious aſſemblies; in their deſpiſing and demoliſhing the very places of publique meeting to ſerve God; (which, not conſcience of any divine particular precept, but *common reaſon* and civility have preſented Chriſtian Religion withall, for its honour and its profeſſors conveniency.)

Some, here with us in *England*, (a place whoſe *Genius* much diſpoſeth people to *prophecies*, novelties, and varieties) are (as *Pygmalion* with his Image) ſo inamoured with their (Corpuſculo's) the little *new bodies* of their gathered Churches; that they deny any *Nationall Church* in any larger *aſſociatings* of Chriſtians, by *harmonies* of confeſſion, and peaceable ſubordinations; yea, and many will allow no *Catholick Church*; nor any religious ſenſe to that *article of our Creed*; denying any true Church at all to be now in the world. Some place all *Church power* in paucities, in parities, in popular levellings, and Independencies; others contemn all thoſe *broken bodies*, as *ſchiſmaticall ſlips*; having nothing in them of that goodly beauty, ſtature, ſtrength, and integrity, to which the Church of Chriſt was wont to grow; and wherein it flouriſhed and continued conſpicuous ſo many hundred of years; before theſe novelties were broached or brewed, either in *England*, or any other countrey.

The height of ſome mens Religion and Reformation is, to have neither *Biſhops*, nor *Miniſters*, of the *ancient authority, ſucceſſion*, and *ordination*; Others refuſe theſe alſo of the *new Presbyterian ſtamp*; (which is not much older here in *England*, than the figure and ſuperſcription of the *laſt coin*) A third will have no *Miniſter*, but ſuch as the common people ſhall try, chuſe, conſecrate, and judge. Some will have no Miniſter at all, by office, or divine miſſion: others will have any man a Minister or Prophet that lists to make, or call himself one. In like manner some will allow *Baptism* to no Infants; others to none but such, whose parents they judge to *be Saints*; a third baptize the children of all that professe they beleive the truth of the Gospell; a fourth sort deny the use of any *water Baptism* at all; By a *Catabaptisticall boldnesse*, or blindenesse, magisterially contradicting, and sophistically disputing, against the expresse letter of the *Scripture*; against the *command of Jesus Christ*; against the *practise* of all the Apostles; and against the custom of all Christian Churches: Pretending, as a rare and *warm invention*; that the *Baptisme of fire and of the Spirit*, (which they now at last hold forth) will both supply and explode that *colder ceremony* of sprinkling or dipping in water. It is strange *these Rabbies* and Masters in *Israel* should be so silly, as not to know, that long before their brain brought forth any such blasphemous brood against baptizing by water, all judicious Christians ever esteemed baptism by water to be an *extern sign* and *meanes*, by which the wisedome of Christ thought fit to administer to his Church on earth, not onely that *distinctive mark* of being his Disciples, but also the representation of his *bloud*, shed for their redemption, and the *obsignation* of that *Baptismall grace*, which his *Spirit* confers on those that are his by the cleansing of the conscience, and renewing of the inward man: 1 *Pet.* 3. 21. Christians, must not after the short and more compendious methods of their fancies, therefore neglect the sign or ceremony, because they presume of the thing signified; but rather with humble obedience doe the duty and use the meanes divinely instituted, that they may obtain the grace offered. On the same grounds, all outward *Ministrations* among Christians may be despised and abolished, by those that pretend to the Spirits inward efficacy; which is never in any man that doth not obey the Gospell in its outward mandates, as well as the Spirit in its inward motions: Proud, idle and ignorant fancies are dayly finding shorter wayes to heaven than the wisdome of Christ hath

laid

laid out to his Church; in following of which no good Christian can judge, that there is either piety, peace, or safety.

Some boast much of their popular and plausible *gifts*, for knowledge, utterance, prayer, &c. others slight all, but *inward grace*, and the Spirits *dwelling in them*. Some dote much upon their *select fraternities* and *covenanting congregations*; others are onely for *private illuminations*, solitary seekings, sublime raptures, and higher assurances. Some admire themselves in their tedious *strictnesses*, and severer rigors, by which they gird up the *loins* of their Religion so strait, that it can hardly take civill *breath*, or the air of common courtesie: others joy, as much, in the Liberty they fancy themselves to have attained both of opinions and actions. Some make every thing a sin and errour, which they like not; others count nothing a sin, to which they have an impulse, and are *free* as they call it. Some *tolerate* all wayes of Religion in all men, till it comes to be private *Atheisme*, and publique confusion; others crack all *strings*, which will not be wound up to their pitch; damning and destroying all, that are not of their particular mode and *heresie*, though never so novel, and differing not onely from the Catholick practise of the primitive Churches, but also from the expresse rule of the Scriptures.

Whom would not these *monsters of novelties*, varieties, and contradictions among Christians in their Religion, as it is Christian, and *reformed* too, even amaze and greatly astonish: ready to scare all men from any thing, that wee in *England* call Religion, Reformation, Church, or Conscience; if judicious, choise and well grounded Christians did not (as they doe) seriously consider these things, which may establish them in that holy profession of this Church, wherein they have been baptized and educated:

First, the *naturall levity* and instability of mens mindes; which can have no fixation (like the *magnetick needle*) but onely in one point, or line; where it is in conjuncture with its *Loadstone*, the *Truth of God*; from which, while the

the minde is wandering, and *shaking*, it is prone to love *noveltie with lies*, and detriment, rather than wonted things of religion with *truth*, and benefit. The *itching* humors of mens *lascivient* fancies and lusts, chuse to *scratch* themselves to *bloud* and sorenesse, rather than enjoy a *constant soundnesse*; which distempers among those of the reformed Churches, never want vigilant and subtill *fomenters*; whose design is, to spread any *infection* among *Protestants* to the most pestilent *contagions*; that so they being sick and ashamed of themselves, under the scandals, and *madnesses* of that profession, they may, at last, seek to *Rome* for cure; and entertain *forain Physitians*; who will easily perswade such *diseased Protestants*, that those old sores and lingring maladies (with which the *Romish party* hath a long time laboured, and with which it is justly charged, however it refuse to be healed) are much safer for *soules*, than these new *quick feavers*, pestilent *Agues*, and desperate *Apoplexies* among us; which threaten utterly to kill all piety, to destroy all Christianity, to extirpate all charity, and dissolve all society both as men, and as Christians: while neither *morals*, nor *rituals* of Christianity are observed; neither the superstructure of Catholick customes, nor the foundation of Scripture commands; neither truth, nor peace, things of piety, or Christian polity, are inviolable: but all old things must be dissolved and passe away, that some men may shew their skill to create *new heavens* and *new earths*, in which, not order and righteousnesse, but all injuriousnesse and confusion must dwell.

2. Secondly, besides this innate *fondnesse* of men, which is alwayes finding out new (evill, or vain) *inventions*, (as unwholesome bodies are ever breaking out) there are also *crafty colourings*, and *politick affectations of piety*, which grow as *scurfe* or *scabs*, over those *prurient novelties* of opinion: by which unwonted formes (as with severall *vizards* and plaisters) hypocrisie seekes as to amuse the vulgar, so to cover, and hide its *cunning*, and *cruelty*; its *avarice*, *ambition*, *revenge*, and *sacriledge*: still avoiding the

 discoveries

discoveries of its deep plots and *wicked designes*, by specious pretensions of serving God in some more *acceptable* way, and better manner, than others have done; when indeed every true *factionist*, who is Master of his Art, at last, winds up the thread of that Religion he spins, upon his own *bottom*, so as may best serve his own *turn*; nor is he ever so modest, so mortified, or so self-denying, with his pious *novelties*, but that he will possesse himself, and his *party* of any places for worldly profit, power or honour, to which he can attain; though it be by the violent and unjust ruining and outing of others: which is no very great symptom of an amended or heightned Christian.

Lastly, sober Christians doe, and ought to consider those *just judgements of God*, either as *diseases*, or *medicines*, usually falling upon Christians, (as here in *England*) when they are *surfeited* with peace and plenty; *cloyed* with preaching and praying; wantonly weary of wonted duties, and wholesome formes of sound *religion*, though never so holy, and comely; Burthened with the weekly and daily importunities of *Ministers* doctrine, and examples, (where the sin and misery was; not that people had no *true light*, or no *true Church*, and no *true Ministers*, but that, *having all these*, they *rejoiced not in them*, they neglected them, and sinned the more provokingly against them;) Hence it is, that squeamish, nauseating, and *glutted Christians*, easily turn, as foul stomachs and wanton appetites, all they take, (though never so *wholesome*) into *peccant* and morbifique humors, to pride and passion; to self conceit, and scorn of others; to ambitious lusts of disputing, contending, and conquering in matters of Religion; endeavouring to destroy all, that they and their way may alone prevail and govern: which is the last result of all unwarrantable and unjustifiable commotions in Church or State. Nor doe men ever intend that such victories (which begin with the *tongue* or *pen*, and end in the *hand* and *sword*: commencing with piety and religion, but concluding with soveraignty and dominion) shall be either inglorious or fruitlesse; 3.

lesse; Seditious and schismaticall *Champions* for Religion will be sure (as soone as they have power) to carve out their own *crowns* and rewards; the determination of scruples in conscience, and differences in opinion, must end, not onely in *imperious* denying others, the *liberties* of conscience (at first craved or contended for) but in the outing others of different mindes, from their places, callings, profits, and enjoyments: which is very far from that taking up the crosse of Christ and following him; from being crucified to the world in its lusts, pride and vanity, as becomes those that will be Christs Disciples, in verity, justice, and charity: To such *mountains of changes* and *mighty oppressions* doe little *mole-hils* in Religion usually swell, when the justice of God suffers piety to be both poysoned with policies, and Religion perverted with humane passions. *Little differences* in Religion, (like Crocodiles egs) bring forth *prodigies*; which are ever growing greater, till they dye; adding *fury* to faction; *passion* to opinion; *cruelty* to novelty; *Self-interests* to Conscience: *Divine vengeance* oft punishing sin with sin; extravagancies of judgements, with exorbitancies of deeds; suffering the greater lust, or stronger faction (like pikes in a pond) to devoure the lesser; and one *error* to be both executioner and heir to another; Because men *obeyed not the Truth in love*, nor practised what they knew, with a pure heart, in an humble, meek, and *charitable* conversation, which alwayes chuseth rather to suffer with *peacefull* and holy *antiquity*, than to triumph with turbulent and injurious novelty.

From which have risen those many *Church-Tragedies*, as of ancient, so of later times, which make the *bloud* of Christians, (yea of Jesus Christ too) so *cheap and vile* in one anothers eyes: Hence those *unstanched effusions*; those unclosed *wounds*; those irreconcilable *fewds*; those intractable *sores*; those wide gaping *gulphs* of faction and division, malice and emulation, war and contention, which are enlarged and deep *like hell*, threatning to swallow up and exhaust whole kingdomes, flourishing Nations, and famous Churches:

Churches; sometimes professing *Christian*, and reformed Religion, with order, peace, and truth. Where now *countreymen*, and neighbors, kindred and brethren, Ministers and people, teachers and disciples, are so far from that *charity*, *sympathy* and *compassion* becoming *beleivers in Jesus Christ*, (so as to *weep with those* that *weep*, and to *rejoice* with those that *rejoice*) that contrarily, there is nothing almost to be heard or seen, but such a *face of cruelty and confusion*, as a shipwrack, a troubled Sea, or Scarefire is wonted to present: The *teares* of some mingled with their owne, or others bloud; the cryes and *sighes* of some with the *laughter* of others: smiles with sorrowes, hopes with despaires, joyes with terrors, *Lamentations* of some with the *triumphs* of others. The insolency of any prevailing faction hardly enduring the *underling* or suppressed party, to plead their cause, either by law or prepossession: to deplore their losses, defeats, poverties, and oppressions; which they either feel or fear; nor yet to enjoy the liberty of their private consciences: And all this strugling, fury and confusion both in Church and State meerly to bring forth, or to nourish up some *Pharez* or *Esau*; some opinion or faction, which must come in by a breach, and prevaile by violence. After this horrid *scene* and fashion, and on such *Theaters* (of mutuall massacrings, fightings and wars) are divided Churches, broken factions, and uncharitable Christians always ready to act their sad and *sanguinary parts* of Religion; (if there be not wise and powerfull *Magistrates*, to curb and restrain them.) Some mens spirits are ever dancing in the *circles* of Reformations; trampling on the ruines of Churches and States, of charity and peace; lost in *endlesse disputes*, and wearied with *restlesse* agitations; starting many things, and long pursuing nothing: Ever hunting for *novelties*, and following with eagernesse and lowdnesse the *game* they last sprang, or put up, till they light on another: Still casting away all that is old, though never so good and proper, for any thing that is new, though never so *bad* and impertinent: being better pleased with a *fooles coat* of yesterdayes making, though never so fantastick and ridiculous; than with the ancient *robes* of a wise and grave Counsellour, never so rich, and comely; preferring a rent or piece of Christ coat before the whole and entire garment.

Thus, *ever learning*, fancying, cavilling, contending, disputing, and, if they can, destroying one another for matters of religion, poore mortals and *consumptionary Christians* tear others, and tire out themselves, untill (having thus wasted the *fervor* of their spirits, and more *youthfull* activity of their lives) at length the *dulnesse of age*, or the burthen of infirmities, or the defeat of their designes, or the decline of their faction, or the wasting of their estates, or the conscience of their follies, or the *summons* of death, so dispirit and appale these sometimes so great *Zealots* and *sticklers*, for what they call Religion, that they appeare like very *Ghosts*, and *Carkases of Christians*; poor, blinde, naked, withered, deformed, and tattered in their Religion, both as to *Conscience* comfort, and credit; Far enough (God knowes) from that *soundnesse* of judgement, that setlednesse in the *faith*, that sobernesse of *Zeal*, that warmth of *charity*, that constancy of *comfort*, that sincerity of *joy*, that saint-like *patience*, that blessed *peace*, and that lively *hope*, which becomes and usually appeares in those, that have been, and are sincerely religious and truly *gracious*; that is, *knowing*, *serious*, and *conscientious Christians*; who have, a long time, been entertained, not with splendid fancies, and specious novelties, wrested prophecies, and rare inventions; touching government of Churches, modelling of Religion, and Saints reigning: but with the treasures of *divine wisdome*; with the rivers of spirituall *pleasures*; with the fulnesse of *heavenly joyes*; with the sweetnesse of *Christs love*, and Christians communion: with the feasts of *faith unfeigned*; with the *banquets* of well *grounded hope*, with the marrow and fatnesse of *good works*; of an usefull Holy life: which are to be had not in *fantastique novelties*, and curious *impertinencies*, in unwarrantable and self-condemning practises; but in the serious study of

the

the *Scriptures*; in the diligent attending on the Ministry of the Word, and all other holy duties; in fervent and frequent *prayers*; in Catholick communion with charity towards all that professe to be Christians; in a patient, meek, orderly, just, and honest conversation toward all men whatsoever.

From which, whoever swerves, though with never so specious and *successefull aberrations*, which vulgar mindes may think gay and glorious *novelties* of Religion, like the flying of *Simon Magus*, or *Mahomets* extasies; yet they are to be pitied, not followed, by any *children of true wisdome*; which is from above, both pure and peaceable, *Jam.* 3. 17. Whose lawful progenie, the professors of *pure Religion*, and undefiled, have in all times been, as in worth far superiour, so in number and power oft inferiour to the *spurious* issues, and *by-blowes* of *faction* and *superstition*; which, as easily fall into *fractures* among themselves, as they naturally confederate against that onely true and legitimate *off-spring* of Heaven, *True Religion*: which is (as the Poets feigned of *Pallas*) the *daughter* of the *Divine minde*; the *descent* and *darling* of the true God; For, as it hath been *wonderfully* brought forth, so it hath alwayes been *tenderly* brought up, by that *power*, *wisdome*, and *love*, which are in those eternall *relations*, infinite perfections, and essentiall endearements, wherewith the *Divine Nature* everlastingly happy, recreates and enjoyes it self; which are set forth to us under the familiar names, yet mysterious and adorable Persons of *Father*, *Son*, and *Holy Ghost*; in whom is an *holy variety* with an *happy Unity*; a reall diversity, yet an essentiall identity: Who have taught the Church *true Religion* in a few words: *Know and doe* the will of God: Beleive and repent; Live in *light*, and *love*; in *verity* and charity; in righteousnesse and true holinesse: without which all Religion is vain; either fanstaticall, or hypocriticall; unprofitable, or damnable.

From which plain paths and grand *principles* of true Christian Religion the *Author* of this defence, having obſerved the great and *confuſed variations* of many Chriſti-ans, as in all ages, ſo never more than in this; his intent in this work muſt be, and is, (as he ſaid) Not to *gratifie* any ſide or faction, never ſo *ſwoln* with plauſible preten-ſions, with pleaſant fancies, with gainfull ſucceſſes; or o-vergrown with ſplenitick *ſeverities*, and *melancholy* diſcon-tents: but onely to make good by the *impartiality* of clear *Scripture*, ſound *Reaſon*, and pureſt *Antiquity*, that *ſtation*, and *office*, wherein the providence of God hath placed him, (and many others, far his betters) in the *publique Miniſtry* of that Religion, which as Chriſtian and reform-ed, was eſtabliſhed and profeſſed here in the *Church of England.* Which, of any Reformed Church, hath ever ſince the *Reformation* had the *honor*, of being, both much *admired*, and mightily *oppoſed:* So that its miraculous peace, and proſperity for ſo many years paſt, as they were the effects of Gods indulgence; and of the great wiſdome of governours in Church and State; ſo they were alwayes ſet off and improved by thoſe many and *ſmart* oppoſiti-ons, both forain and domeſtick, which were made againſt it, both as to its truth and peace, its doctrine and di-ſcipline.

All which, men of *excellent learning*, and *lives* in this Church, have valiantly ſuſtained, and happily repelled; to the great advancement of Gods glory, the proſperity of this Nation, the honour of this reformed Church, and the comfort of all judicious Chriſtians; And this was chiefly done by the able and accurate *pens* of the godly and *learned Miniſters*; who needed (in thoſe times) no other *defence* on their part, either for order, government, maintenance, Miniſtry or doctrine; All which were then preſerved from *vulgar injuries* and inſolencies by the ſame power and ſword, which defended thoſe civill *ſanctions* and lawes, which eſtabliſhed and preſerved all things of *ſa-cred* and *Eccleſiaſtick*, as well as of civill and *ſecular* con-cernment.

Untill theſe laſt *fatall times*, which pregnant with civill wars and dissensions, have brought forth such great revelations and changes in Church and State; wherein *Scholars* and *Churchmen*, in stead of *pens* and *bookes*, have to contend with *swords* and *pistols*. Which weapons of *carnall warfare*, were unwonted to be applyed either to the planting, propagating, or reforming of Christian Religion; onely proper to be used for the preservation of what is by law established, from *seditious* and *schismaticall perturbations*; (For it was not the *vinegar*, but the *oil* of Christian Religion; not its fierinesse, but its meeknesse; not its force, but its patience, that ever made its way through the hardest *rocks*, and *hearts*.) And by these strange *Engines*, these new *armes of flesh*, we have hitherto onely seen acted and fulfilled with much *horror*, misery and confusion, those things in this Church and Nation, which were foreseen and *foretold* by two eminent, and learned persons, yet of different opinions, as to the extern matters of *Ecclesiasticall polity*; Mr. *Richard Hooker*, and Mr. *Thomas Brightman*; the one in the preface to his *Ecclesiasticall polity*: the other in his comment on the third chapter of the *Revelations*. Who many years agoe in times of peace, and setlednesse in this Church of *England foretold*, not by any infallible spirit of *prophecy*, (for then the *later* of them would not have been so much mistaken in the *fate* of his dear *Philadelphia* of *Scotland*) but meerly out of *prudence*, conjecturing, what was probable to come to passe, according to the fears of the one, and the hopes of the other: in case the then spreading, though suppressed *differences* and parties in Religion, (which they then saw made many *Zealously* & boldly discontented) came to obtain such power, as every side aims at, when they pretend to carry on *matters of Religion*, and Reformation; wherein, *immoderation* being usually stiled *Zeal*; and *moderation*, *lukewarmnesse*; it was easie for sagacious men to foresee and foretell, what *excesses*, the transports of inferiours would in all probability urge upon *superiours*; if ever these *managed power* so weakly and unadvisedly, that any *aspiring* and discontented *party* might come to gain *power*, in a way not usuall; which at the very first *rupture* and advantage, would think it self easily *absolved* from all former ties of obedience, and subjection to governours in Church or State; without which liberty and absolution, it is not *possible* to carry on by force any Novelties and pretended amendments of Religion contrary to what is established in any Church or Nation.

Indeed, we see, to our *smart* and *sorrow*; that the *deluge* foretold would break in, hath so overflowed this and the neighbour Churches; that not only Mr. *Brightmans* blear-ey'd *Leah*, his odious *Peninnah*, his so abhorred *Hierarchy*, (the *Episcopall* order and eminency) but even his beloved *Rachel*, his admired *Hannah*, his *divine Presbytery* it self; yea & the whole function of the Ministry feels, and fears the terror of that *inundation*, which far beyond his *divination*, hath prevailed, not only over his so despised *Laodicea*, which he made to be type of the Church of *England*, (truly) not without passion and partiality, (as I think with far wiser men) He not calmly distinguishing between the constitution and execution of things: between the faults of persons, and the order of places: between what was prudentiall, and what is necessary; what is tolerable, and what is abominable in any Church, as to its extern form and polity: but also over his *darling* and so *adored Philadelphia*; which he makes to answer to the *Scottish*, *Palatinate* or *Geneva form of Presbyterian government* and *discipline*; as if that Church of *Philadelphia* in its primitive constitution under the presidency and government of its Angell, had any thing different from, or better than the other neighbour Churches; which is no way probable, nor appears either in Scripture or Ecclesiasticall histories; However, it might be commendable in its Angell or President, for its greater zeal and exacter care to preserve that doctrine, discipline, and order, which it had lately received from the Apostles; and which, no doubt, was the same in each Church, who had their severall Angels or Overseers alike; which all Antiquity owned for those Pastors, Presidents, or Bishops, to whose charge they were respectively committed.

As

As for that *evomition*, or Gods *spewing this Church of England out of his mouth*, which Mr. *Brightman* so *dreadfully threatens*; It must be confessed that the sins of all sorts of Christians in this Church, and of Ministers as much as any, have made them *nauseous* and burthensome to the *Divine patience*; both in their *luke warm* formalities, and *fulsome affectations* of Religion; in their empty *pompes*, and emptier *popularities*: So that Gods *patience* once turned into *just fury*, hath indeed terribly powred out his *vengeance* on all degrees and estates in this Nation: by suffering *flouds of miseries*, and *billows of contempt* to overwhelm (for a time) the face of this Church, (as of old wars, heresies, and schisms wasted the *Asiatick*, *African*, and *Latin* Churches) not more, it may be, upon the account of *Ministers* weaknesse and unworthinesse, than upon that of peoples levity, pride, and ingratefull inconstancy; which hath been a great means to bring on and continue these overflowing streams: Which nothing but the mighty *power* of God, by the help of good and wise men, can *rebuke* and asswage; so that the face of this Church and its Ministry may yet appear in greater beauty and true Reformation, after its so *great squalior*, and deformity: which is not to be despaired of, through *Gods mercy*; yet in a farre other way than ever Mr. *Brightman* foresaw.

But when, and by what means this shall be done, the Authour of this Apology doth not, as a Prophet, undertake to foretell; onely he observes the usuall *methods* of Gods Providence, in the *midst of judgement to remember mercy*: and after he hath sorely afflicted, to *repent of the evill*, and *return* to an humble *penitent people*, with *tender mercies*; so that we may hope his *wrath will not endure* for ever; nor that he hath quite *forgotten* to be gracious, or shut up his loving *kindenesse in displeasure*. Also hee considers the *wonted vicissitudes* of humane affairs, arising from the changes *incident to mens mindes*, who weary of those *disorders* and *pressures* necessarily attending all forcible changes in Church or State; and long frustrated with vain expecta-

tions

tions of enjoying those better conditions in things civill and religious, which are alwayes at first liberally promised and expected; at last they are prone with the same *impetuosity*, to retire, (as the ebbing Sea) from those fallacious or pernicious *novelties*, to which the breath of some politick or *passionate* spirits had raised them, so much above the ordinary *mark* of true Christian religion, as to *drown* or threaten to carry away all those many happy enjoyments of truth, peace, order, government, and Ministry, which formerly they enjoyed: Not wholly (it may be) without; but yet with fewer and more *tolerable grievances*; which humble Christians ought to look upon in any setled Church and State, rather as exercises of their *patience*, duty, and charity; than as *oppressions* of their spirits: Knowing that *impatience* usually punisheth it self, by applying *remedies* sharper than the *sufferings*; easily and hastily running down the *hill*, as from health to sicknesse, from peace to war, from good to bad, from bad to worse; but very slowly *returning* from evill to good, or recovering up the hill, from *worse* to better.

It is true, the *Ministers of the Church of England*, of all degrees, seem, now, to have an *harder part* to act, for their honor and wisdome, than ever they had under *any Rulers*, professing to be Christian and reformed. But they may not therefore weakly disclaim, or meanly *desert* their Ordination and holy function; nor may they *despair* of Gods (if they have not mans) protection, who can soon make their very *enemies to be at peace with them*; and stir up many friends unexpectedly for them. It may be through the *Lords mercy*, this *winters flood* shall be for their mendment or fertility, and not for their utter vastation and ruine: This *fire* shall not consume them, but refine them; this *winnowing* will be their *purging*; and this *shaking* their *setling*: (As *oppositions* of old gave the greatest *confirmations* and polishings to those *Truths*, which were most exercised with the *hammer*, or file of *heriticall pravity*, or *schismaticall fury*.)

If

If it be the *mending*, and not the *ending*; the *reformation*, and not the *extirpation* of Ministers, which their severe censurers and opposers seek for: why should not time of *triall* be given; and all honest industry used to improve these well grown and flourishing *fig trees*, before they be *hewed down* and *stubbed up*; which heretofore have not been either barren or unfruitfull to God and man?

If either Papall, or Anabaptisticall and Levelling enemies must at length after severall windings and turnings be gratified with their utter ruine and destruction, (which God forbid) yet while Ministers have leave and liberty to pray, to preach, to print, to doe well, and worthily, God forbid they should so farre *injure God*, good men, and so *good a cause*, as not Christianly to endeavour its *defence*; which at worst is to be done by *comely suffering*: And who knows but that when these *witnesses* both against superstition and confusion in the Church shall seem to be slain, cast out, and buryed, they may live again, to the astonishment both of friends and enemies?

But if the *sins* of this Nation, and the decrees of *divine Justice*, doe indeed hasten an utter overthrow here of the reformed Ministry, and the reformed Religion: If *Ministers* of the *ancient Ordination*, lawfull heirs of the true Apostolick *succession*, are therefore accounted *as sheep for the slaughter*, because they are better fed, and better bred, than others of *leaner soules*, and meaner spirits: If they are therefore to the *men of this world*, as a *savour of death unto death*, because they hold forth the *Word of Truth*, and Life, to the just reproach of a *lying*, dying, and self-destroying generation: If we must at last *perish* and *fall*, with our whole function and fraternity, after all our studies, charges, labours, and sufferings: Yet, it is *fit* some of *us* (and the more the better, lest our *silence* may argue *guilt*) give the world both at present, and in after ages some account; why, and how in so *learned*, valiant, wise, and religious a Nation as this of *England* hath been, wee as *Ministers* have stood so long; what *pious frauds*, and holy *arts* we had, whereby to *impose* so many hundreds of years, upon so many *wise Princes*; so many *venerable Parliaments*; so many pious *professors* of Christian and reformed Religion: And lastly, upon so quick and high *spirited a people*, as these of *England* generally are; neither so grosse, as to be *easily deluded*, nor so *base*, as patiently to suffer themselves in so high a nature to be abused.

That so, at least if the world can lesse discern, for what cause the Ministry and Ministers are now to be destroyed, they may see upon what grounds of piety, or policy they were so long preserved in *peace*, *plenty*, and *honour*: And for what reasons they now seek (as their pious predecessors did) to maintain not their *persons* so much, as their *office* and function, in its due *order* and *authority*; that so they might have transmitted it in an holy and *unblameable succession* to posterity; as that, which in their consciences they verily think to be a most divine and *Christian Institution*: Beneficiall for the good of the Church, and of all mankinde; which in former ages, was ever esteemed the *glory*, and blessing of this, or any other Nation; The setter forth of the *light*, wisdome, power, and *love* of the *eternall God* in his Son Jesus Christ for the *salvation* of sinners; and which thousands of Christians in all ages and places have experienced, and approved to be to their soules the *Savour of life unto life*, the mighty power of God to salvation.

The Author easily observes the present *face of our heavens*; which are much darkned by those black, and *lowring clouds*, which chiefly hang over constant, true, and faithfull *Ministers heads*; menacing them above any rank or calling of men; Nor is he ignorant of the *touchinesse*, and roughnesse; the *jealousies*, and *timorousnesse*, of many mens spirits in these times, whose highest pretentions to piety are set forth, either by fierce oppositions against the *Ministry*; or by such a weak pleading for, and *wary owning* of their succession and ordination, their *calling* and persons, as ra-rather invites opposition, *contempt*, and insolency, than any

way

way gives credit or countenance to them and their function; whose remaining branches of Presbytery will *hardly thrive* by the watering of those hands which have been, and are destroyers of its root, the *Primitive* Apostolicall *Episcopacy*; they are pitifull defenders of that, who are passionate opposers of this: who, of all men, have given the greatest advantages to those that seek to abrogate the whole function and calling, or to arrogate it to vulgar ignorance and impudence.

The *grim* and sad *aspect* on all hands upon Ministers, makes the Authour out of charity to himself and others, as willing to give a fair account of his *profession*, so loath to offend any sober and judicious Reader, or to contract the *enmity* of any others of ruder tempers, by any rash stroke or inconsiderate dash of his pen, to which he may be subject, and for which he begs pardon, both of God and man, if any have escaped; which yet may be so far *venial*, as its *innocent sharpnesse* aims at no *mens person*, but onely at their supposed errors, which are grown in some so rough and insolent, both in words and deeds, against poore *Ministers*, that they had need to meet with something, that hath good metall and usefull sharpnesse; and not with that phlegmatick and sanguine softnesse, which impudent men easily baffle and put both to the blush and silence: yet hee meddles not, save with great respect and tendernesse, with any thing of Civill Power; which no man may wisely dispute, that is not able to resist, (it is foolish to shake the pen *against the sword*, or oppose *armed Legions* with flocks of Geese;) No man may discreetly offend, while, as he must necessarily, so he may *honestly* and safely be *subject*: Prudence commands *private men* to leave the accounts of *Ruling power* to mens *own consciences*, and to the *Supream Over-ruler*; who best knowes, as by what *means* they obtain it, so to what ends, and in what *manner* they use it. It is enough for private persons at convenient distances to *warm* themselves by the light and heat of prevailing power; neither *scorching* themselves by too neer *approaches*; nor consuming themselves by indiscreet contestations with it: *Modesty* also forbids such as are in *subjection* to *dispute* the actions, or *disparage* the *counsels* of any that are above them; who being many and so stronger, are commonly by esteem supposed wiser than any one man: and being successefull are usually esteemed blest and happy. Although it is most certain, That *the many* beginning from one, and combined strength or counsell being but the *twisting* of single *feeblenesse* (as so many hairs together) the *united many* may be mistaken, as wel as the *divided unites*; Yea, one sick man may infect many whole: especially if *his disease* hath something catching and pleasing in it. But if there happen, by the *Divine displeasure*, pestilent airs, and noxious breaths in any countrey, the *strong*, the *wise*, the great and the many, are as liable to contagion and *destruction*, as the weak, the few, and the foolish: yea to Epidemicall and *contagious* diseases, pestered *cities*, and *crowds* of *men* are more subject, than cels, and solitudes. No men are so wise, but they may have *errors*; And the sooner they see them to *amendment*, the wiser they will be: Nor is it the least part of wisdome in inferiours to shew to superiors their misapprehensions and failings, rather by obliquely intimating than directly thwarting; by great reflexions, than rude affronts: Especially in those things wherein a private man may be competently versed, both by study and education; yet no way trenching upon that tender point of civill power and dominion, which is not a fit subject for a pen and inkhorn.

Therefore this Author presumes, that the fair and free vindication of so publique an interest, as this of the Ministry (which is his proper sphear and calling) can displease no men, that have candor, wit, honesty, honour, good conscience, or true Religion in them: Nor will it anger sober men to be shewed what is amiss, and how it may be mended; which possibly they may be as unable, as willing to doe; Diseases may sometimes exceed the Art of Physitians; violent Paroxysms are sometimes better left to spend themselves, than provoked and encountred with medicines. As for others of vain, violent, and foolish tempers, it is better to offend than to *flatter* them; and to suffer from them (if God will have it so) is more *honorable*, than to be *rewarded* by them.

The greatest danger indeed is, from those, that are (*stolidè feroces*) full of those boisterous, rude and brutish passions, which grow, as bristles upon hogs backs, from ignorance, pride, rusticity, and prejudice; which make men, either unable to read, or impatient to bear, or unwilling to understand, the *words of truth and sobernesse*; trusting more to *bestiall* than rationall or religious *strength*: which most unmanly, and unchristian disorders in mens soules, how prevalent and epidemicall soever they may be, yet they must not be here either flattered, or fomented: By calling their *darknesse light*, or their evill good; their presumptions, inspirations; their duller dreams high devotion; their dissolute licentiousnesse, Christian liberty; their sillinesse, sanctity; their fiercenesse, zeal; their self-confidence and intrusion, a *divine call*; their disorderly activity, speciall abilities; their jejune novelties, pretious rarities; or their old errors, and rotten opinions, extraordinary and unheard of perfections.

When, indeed, their *root* is for the most part nothing but an illiterate and illiberall disposition; neither learned to morality, nor polished to civility; neither softned nor setled by good education or true Religion: being full of levity, *vulgarity*, unsatiate thirst and desire of *novelties*; their *fruit* also is little else, but malice, cruelty, avarice, ambition, worldly policy, hypocrisie, superstition, loosenesse, and profanenesse; all conspiring, as upon *untrue* and unjust *pretentions*, so to evill ends; namely to abase and *destroy* the true and *ancient Ministry* of the Gospell in this Nation, and to bring into contempt all holy *duties*, and *divine Ministrations* in this Church of Christ; to cry down all *good learning*; to corrupt the mindes of men with *error* and ignorance; to *debauch* their manners by licentiousnesse, or superstition; to bring shame upon the reformed Religion here professed; to *wilder* the judgements, to *wast* the comforts, to shipwrack the conscience, and to damn the soules of poore people.

Where the Apologist meets with this black guard, these *factors* for error and sin, these agitators for the Prince of darknesse, these *enemies* to God, to Christ Jesus, to all good Christians, and to mankind, God forbid he should give place to them, or not charge them home, and resist them to their *face*: His duty and design is to *detect* their frauds and wickednesse; to *countermine* their deep projects; to frustrate their *desperate* counsels; to *fortifie* the mindes of all good Christians against their *strong delusions*, and oppositions; to pull down their *high imaginations*; to demolish their self-conceited *strong holds*; to maintaine the honour of this Nation, the glory of this reformed Church, and the worth of its godly, learned, and *industrious Ministry*, against their envious *cavils* and ungratefull *calumnies*.

If any men, apart from *fanatick presumptions*, *secular interests*, *popular applauses*, rusticall clamors, and ignorant confidences, shall, upon rationall, prudent, and religious grounds, propound any thing in a more excellent way, either for kinde, or degree, whereby to advance the *glory* of God, the *honour* of Jesus Christ, the reall propagating of the *Gospell*, the exercise of usefull *gifts*, and graces of Gods Spirit in this Church; for the encrease of *charity*, or comforts among Christians; for the encouragement of learning, vertue and godlinesse; for the welfare of this Nation, or the serious reforming of Religion, and the Ministry of it, beyond what hath been, still is, and ever may be had, from the gifts and graces, the order and office, the labours and lives of those, that are the *chief* professors, preachers, and pillars of learning and religion in this Nation; which are the *able*, and *faithfull Ministers* of a due succession and right Ordination;

God forbid they should not, with all candor and impartiality be heard, with all chearfulnesse *accepted*, and with all uprightnesse be *entertained*; No good man or worthy *Minister* is so vain, as to fancy he may not be *mended*, and happily *improved*: But first let those *alterations* and novelties, which beare this title of reformation, and amendment,

ment,

ment, be publiquely set forth; duly, seriously, and impartially be weighed in the *balance* of sober demonstrations, and sound reasonings, so, as becomes the honour, wisdome, and piety of this Nation; before they be *injuriously* concluded, and forcibly obtruded upon *conscientious* Ministers, or people. The *English* world (as other *Protestant* Churches) hath had enough of the Apes and *Peacocks*, which crafty *Merchants* have ever sought to *vend* to the vulgar: if they have any *gold* and *spices*; any commodities that are of reall use and worth; it is pity, the worlds *wants* have not been sooner supplyed, and their *expectations* satisfied; which being so long *deluded*, and oft *frustrated*, hath made sober Christians to suspect the whole fraight of some mens religious novelties, to be nothing else but far fetcht and dear bought toyes, variating so much from the *uniform* judgement, and universall practise of all *ancient* and *modern Churches*, of the best note and account, no lesse, than from the worthy *constitution*, and wise frame of this reformed Church of *England*, whose honor and renown was justly great in the Christian world, for its piety and peace, its order, and its proficiency in all good learning, sound doctrine, and holy manners: which owed as much, as any *Church* under heaven, to the wisdome, piety, and impartiality of its Ministers and *reformers* (under God) as also to its establishers and defenders.

Nor have the effects of later offers and *endeavours* to mend or change their *work*, been yet so excellent or blest, as to give any cause to preferre these, before them; who no doubt could easily have reached those later seeming *heights* and *raptures* of Religion and Reformation, which some men so much boast of, in their *hotter*, yet *looser tempers*; but those learned, grave and godly men considered, in the *extern polity* and frame of Religion, what was then most necessary, and convenient for men and times, what latitudes of prudence and graines of charity are to be allowed by Christian piety: Not prescribing their *plat-formes*, then fitted to the publique good, as the *Non ultras* of Reformation; but giving

posterity

posterity a pattern; that, if we would indeed attain *to further perfection*, we should imitate their wise and charitable moderation; and tread in their humble, easie, and even steps; which were not *slippery* with bloud, nor rough with *insolencies*, nor unequall with *factions*, nor dark with *policies*, nor *extravagant* with varieties; but fairly laid out, and freely carried on by *due authority*, with publique and impartiall counsels, in a peaceable way, to a general *uniformity*, and satisfaction of both the most, and the best.

Whereas, among the many *specious offers*, and earnest importunities, either formerly, or lately made by some men in reference to *Religion*, and the *Ministry* of it in this Church, little hath hitherto appeared to have any uniform or well-formed face of *further edification*, or future bettering of Religion, in doctrine, government, discipline, or manners. Some few, it may be, of honest hearts have taken to themselves a liberty to serve God in that way they best fancy and most affect; But thousands have run to errour, ignorance, atheism and licentiousnesse, under that colour of freedome; which besides the laxation and confusion brought among the bad, hath occasioned great heart-burning and distance and uncharitablenesse among those that seemed to be good. In some things indeed sober and wise men have offered *good counsell*; and propounded some things fit to be considered of and *embraced*; but the noise and violence of other (mens passions and interests) suffer not those mens *calmer voices* to be heard; Their *rougher* work seemes to be all with *axes* and *hammers*; not for building or repairing the *Temple of God*, without *noise*; but for *beating* all down, with the greatest stir, and clamour they can make; All is for demolishing *Schools* and *Universities*; for despising all learning and *sciences*; for taking away all order, society, larger communion, subordination, and government in the Church; for casting away all ancient *Ordination*, and authoritative *Ministry*; that we may be left in the next age, like the *Tohu* and *Bohu* of the Chaos, void of *light* and full of *confusion*; without good learning or true Religion,

gion, without any form, or power of godlinesse; So far are those lines, which the *Antiministeriall* fury and folly drawes, from running *parallel* to piety, or Christianity, to right Reason or true Religion; that they are most *diametrically opposite* to all civility, prudence, policy, sense of honour, and principles of humanity: Of which *deformities* and defects none are lesse patient to hear, than they that are most guilty; whose *preposterous activity*, rather than sit still, must needs imploy it self in *pulling all down*; which is indeed the work of plebeian hands, and *pragmaticall* spirits; but to *build* or repair either Church or State, is the businesse onely of *wise* and *well advised persons*, such as having publique and generall consent, to deliberate of such things, may also have an universall influence in the reason and authority of their determinations: But such able men are hardly found in *Countrey crowds*, and illiterate heaps; nor are they very forward to obtrude themselves upon publique works, without a very fair call *from God*, and man; which they doe not think to be the either countreymans *whistle*, or the armed mans *trumpet*.

From neither of which, as this *Author* hath any invitation to this work; so he hath no temptation in it, to captate favour with the giddy and *uncertain vulgar*; by seeming to adore their *Diana's*, or admire their many *new masters*, and their *rarer gifts*; which make them worthy indeed of such *soft* and sequacious *disciples*.

Nor yet hath he any design to *ingratiate* with *supercilious*, and *self-suspecting greatnesse*; or to comply with the more *solemn errors*, and *graver extravagancies* of those, who study *safety*, more than piety; who think to flatter *Magistrates* by crying down Ministers, being more a fraid of that sword, which can but kill the body; than of that, which proceeds out of the *mouth of Christ*, and is able to slay both soul and body.

He bespeaks no men further, than the truth, justice, and merit of *this cause* of the Evangelicall Ministry, made good by Scripture, Antiquity, and good experience among us

 here

here in *England*, may perswade them to look favourably, and friendly on the Authour and his endeavour: wherein, albeit every one, that ownes himself to be a Christian in this Church, is highly *concerned*; yet the undertaking seemes to have very little *tempting* in it, or inviting to it; as (now) the face of the *Ministry of the Church of England* seemes to appear *besmeared*, and disguised with infinite odious aspersions; *loaden* with unmerited injuries and indignities; a *wonder to its enemies and friends*; a sad spectacle to all good men and good *Angels*; (whom it cannot but afflict to see those that are the *Brethren of Angels* in heaven, *Revel.* 19. 10. and the fathers of Christians on earth, 1 *Cor.* 4. 15.) thus treated and threatned by some men, who have this onely of *proportion* and *equity* in them, to pursue the *greatest vertues*, with the *greatest hatred*.

The Apologist therefore hath purposely declined to bring the *odium* or envy of *Dedication* upon any one particular person; lest this *defence* should seeme like a *blazing Star*, threatning with malignant influence any mans greatnesse, and honour, either of ancient or modern edition; which may be jealous, lest the *patronising*, or pleading for the distressed, and *despised Ministry*, should be the next way to their *diminution*; lest the dust and *rubbidge* of the so much battered and *defaced Clergy*, should deform or bury them. Besides, he thought it in vain to single out any *one Patron* to this book, and its Subject: For first how few persons of more ample conditions, *splendider fortunes*, and higher quality in civill estimation, doe much lay to heart the *afflictions* of these *Josephs*, godly Ministers and good scholars: Most are intent to their policy, *profit*, or pleasure; or to their sufferings, revenges, and reparations: Nothing costs a *grosse spirited Gentleman*, who lives like a great earth-worm in a fat dunghill, lesse, either as to his *purse*, or his *care*, than the *interests of Learning or Religion*; The ignorance and dissolutenesse of many makes them indifferent, if not enemies to piety and good education; as lights that reproach their *deformities*, or bonds that restrain

their

their *exorbitancies*; Some are best pleased when least molested by any *morall* or *gratious importunities*: esteeming those their best friends, who suffer them to degenerate to *beasts*, or to *devils*; or to both, at once, in being *Hypocrites* or *Atheists*: who have the stupidnesse of the beast, and the malice of the devill.

Not that I would diminish the honour of the *Nobility* and *Gentry* of this Nation, the good and gallant sort of whom none in the world exceeds for civility, fidelity, justice, constancy, and piety. Though some be the shame of honour, and the stain of Gentry, as bags of chaffe, puffes of airy vanity, *illiterate vice*, insolent ignorance, and folly well fed: who have nothing to boast of but empty names of reproached ancestors and undeserved titles, which are comely when inscribed on the Escucheon of vertues, but deformed and ridiculous, when usurped by pultroones, and such, whom no worth redeems from being vile and despicable to wise and serious mindes. Yet there are not a few eminent persons of *true honour* and reall worth (which consists in *just valour*, *judicious piety*, usefull *virtues*, both to private and publique relations) whose *purses* have been as *cruses*, and their houses *sanctuaries* to many godly and learned men in the distresses of these times. Yet in stead of paying a respect and honour to any of these truly noble and generous persons it might be but an injury to *single out* any one of them, in the *cloud* and *jealousies* of these times, to be as a publique *refuge* and *Asylum* to this work and its cause; which carries with it something more *immense* and *ponderous*, than ordinary occurrences in the world: And besides its high concernment to Church and State; to the *temporall* and *eternall* good of men; it hath vast difficulties attending it; *rough oppositions*, *implacable odiums*, and incorrigible malices to contend with: In the midst of all which there must needs be a very great deadnesse, and almost despair, for any one man never so worthy and well-affected, to advance beyond honest desires, and *sincere*, but *ineffectuall* endeavours.

Furthermore to take aright scantling of things; what one mans shoulders, I beseech you, how potent soever, can bear the *burthens*, which are now cast upon the Ministry and Ministers of this Church of *England*? What hands can raise their *declined state*; what arms can support, or stay their tottering and threatning *ruines*? Alas, what *private influence* can be so benign, as to oversway, or counterpoise that *malignity*, which some men pretend to discover, not onely in the mindes of men on earth, but even in the very *Stars* and *constellations* of heaven, which, some say, fight against the *Ministry* now, as they sometime did against *Sisera*? If these Western wise men (who seem to be of a different strain and way from those Eastern *Magi*, that came to worship Christ in the Manger, with their persons, and *presents*) if I say they had not daily *intelligence from heaven*, and sat neer to the *Cabinet Councell* of that *High Court*; truly good Christians would hardly beleeve, or regard their reports; It being very improbable, that the *Stars*, either fixed or *planetary*, should be *enemies* to those, who bear their *name* in the Church; as Ministers doe, being called both Stars and Angels, *Revel.* 3. 1. And who have ever been, as much brighter in their light, so more necessary to the Church; and more *dear* to God; than those are in the *Firmament* or visible *heavens*; by how much the intellectuall and eternall light of mens soules exceeds that which is onely sensible and momentary to their eyes: by how much *reason* and *truth* are above the beames and lustre of the Sun; which is infinitely short of the *divine glory of Christ*; and those spirituall benefits, which by his healing wings (the *Ministers* and Ministrations of his Church) are derived to the world.

Although the study, and knowledge of the *Stars* be very worthy of a wise and Christian man, because in their beauty, lustre, and numberlesse number, in their vast magnitude, and height, in their admirable motion, and various influences, the *wonderfull* glory of the Creators power and wisdome is eminently set forth, beyond what vulgar eyes discern: yet,

yet, experience tels the truly learned and religious *Astronomer*, (for such there are) that nothing is so blinde and bold as an hungry Astrologaster: who must *flatter*, that he may *feed* (starveling wisards like witches, threaten all that doe not give to them, or approve them:) But if wise men by their *moral* liberty of virtue and grace, may over-rule the *Stars naturall* inclinations upon them; sure they may (as the wisest of men, both Christian and heathen, ever did) despise those *sorry Star-gazers* and silly *divinators*, of whom *Tacitus* in the first book of his history writes; That they were oft *banished* from *Rome*, and yet could never be *kept out*; a verminly generation (ever *destroyed*, yet ever *breeding*) who owe their best education to their *bellies*; their wit and *science*, to the sense and knowledge of their *wants*: Who pretend to get their *harvest* out of heaven, and glean their food from among the stars, when indeed they have their greatest influence upon the spirits, and harvest from the purses of credulous and simple people. They are alwayes *fawning* and *unfaithfull* to great men; *Deceivers* of all, that expect any great, or good matters from them; thus he, a learned Heathen: So that the insolency among Christians must needs be great and intolerable, to see *Almanacks* dashing against their Bibles, and some Almanackmakers casting a generall and publique scorn upon their Ministers and Ministry: imputing both unjustly and indignly the folly and ridiculous impotency of some Ministers passions and actions, which may be but too true to the whole function, venerable order and learned fraternity, without limitation or distinction of the wise from the foolish.

But the *badnesse* of the times, or madnesse rather of any *men* in them, makes this *cause* never the worse; Indeed it is so great and so good, having in it so much of Gods glory, and mans welfare, that it merits what it can hardly finde in secular greatnesse, a *proportionate patron*; who had need to be one of the best men; and the *boldest of Christians*; And therefore is the addresse so generall, that besides our great *Master the Lord Jesus Christ* (the *founder* and protector of our order and function, this work might finde some pious and excellent *Patrons* in every corner; whither so great a Truth hath of late been driven to hide it selfe, by the boldnesse and cruelty of some; the *cowardise* and inconstancy of others: This book requires not the cold, and *customary formality* of *patron-like* accepting it, and laying it aside; but the reality of serious *reading*, generous *asserting*, and conscientious vindicating.

Who ever dares to countenance this *Apology* in its main Subject, The *true and ancient Ministery of the Church of England*, must expect to adopt many *enemies*, and it may be, some *great ones*: Whom he must consider, at once, as *enemies* to his *Baptism*, his Faith, his Graces, and Sacramentall seals to his spirituall comforts, his hopes of heaven; to his very being being a *Christian*, or true member of this, or any other sound part of the *Catholick Church*: Enemies also to his friends, and posterities *eternall happinesse*; The means of which will never be truly found in any Church, or enjoyed by any Christians, under *any Ministry*, if it were not *in that*, which hath been *enjoyed*, and *prospered* in *England*; not onely ever since the *reformation*, but even from the first Apostolicall *plantation* of Christian Religion in this Island.

Of which blessed priviledge, ancient honour, and true happinesse, no *good Christian*, or honest *English* man, can with patience or indifferency suffer himself, his Countrey, and posterity to be either cunningly *cheated*, or violently *plundered*: Certainly there is no one point of *Religion* merits more the *constancy* of Martyrs, and will more bear the *honour of Martyrdome*, than this of the divine Institution, authority, and succession of the *true Ministry of the Church*; which is the onely *ordinary means* appointed by Jesus Christ, to hold forth the *Scriptures* and their true meaning to the world; and with them all saving *necessary truths*, duties, means, and Ministrations; wherein not onely the foundation, but the whole fabrick of Christian Religion is contained, which in all ages hath been as a *pillar of heavenly fire*, and as a ſhield of invincible ſtrength; to plant and preſerve, to ſhine and to protect, to propagate and defend the *faith*, name and worſhip of the true God and his Son our Lord Jeſus Chriſt.

This makes the *Authour* not deſpaire to meet with ſome *Patrons* and *Protectors* of this Defence in *Senates*, *Councels*, *Armies*, and on the *houſe top*, no leſſe, than in cloſets, and private houſes; To whom it cannot be unacceptable to ſee thoſe many *plauſible pretenſions*, and *potent oppoſitions* made by ſome men againſt the *Divine authority*, and *ſacred Office*, and peculiar calling of the *Miniſtry*, ſo diſcovered, as they ſhall appeare to be not more *ſpecious*, and ſubtill, than *dangerous* and deſtructive, to the *temporall* and eternall welfare of all true *Proteſtants*, ſober Chriſtians, and honeſt hearted *Engliſh* men; who, certainly, next the *pleaſing of God*, and the *ſaving* of their ſouls, have nothing of ſo great concernment to themſelves and their poſterity, as this, The *preſerving*, and *encouraging* of a *true and authoritative Miniſtry*, which is the great *hinge* on *which all learning* and *civility*, all piety and charity, all gracious hopes and comforts, all true Religion and Chriſtianity it ſelf depends, as much, as the light, beauty, regular motion, and ſafety of the body, doth upon its having eyes to ſee.

But if this freer and *plainer*, Defence ſhould neither merit nor obtaine ſuch *ample meaſure* of favour, and publique acceptance in the ſight of *judicious Readers*, as it is ambitious of, and (at leaſt) may *ſtand in need* of; yet hath the *Author* the comfort of endeavouring with all uprightneſſe of heart to doe his *duty*, though he be but as an *unprofitable ſervant*.

And (poſſibly) this great and *noble Subject*, the *neceſſity*, *dignity*, and *divine authority* of the *Miniſtry of the Church of England*, ſo far carried on by this *Eſſay*: (which ſets forth, 1. The Scripture grounds eſtabliſhed by the authority of Chriſt and his Apoſtles. 2. The Catholick conſent and practiſe of the Church in all ages and places. 3. The conſonancy,

sonancy to reason and order observed by all Nations in their Religion, and specially to the Institutes of God among the Jewish Church. 4. The Churches constant want of it, in its plantation, propagation, and perfection. 5. The benefit of it to all mankinde, who without an authoritative Ministry would never know whom to hear with credit and respect; or what to beleive with comfort. 6. The great blessings flowing from this holy function to this Church and Nation, in all kindes;) These and the like grand considerations and fair aspects which this subject affords to learned, judicious and godly men, may yet *provoke* some nobler pen, and abler person to undertake it with more gratefull and successefull endeavours: whose charitable eyes finding the sometime *famous* and *flourishing Ministry of this Church*, thus exposed in a *weeping*, floating, and *forlorn condition*, to the *mercy of Nilus*, and its Monsters, (the threatning, if not overflowing streames of modern violent errors) may take pity on it; and from *this Ark of Bulrushes*, which is here suddenly framed, may bring it up to far greater strength and publique honour, than the parent of this *Moses* could expect from his obscurer gifts and fortunes.

To which although he is very conscious, as being of himself altogether *unsufficient* for so *great a work*, and so *good a word*; yet the confidence of the *greatnesse* and *goodnesse of the cause*; the *experience* of Gods, and (generally) all *good Christians*, *attestation* to it, in all former ages of the Church: The *hopes* also of Gods gracious assistance, in a work designed with all humility and gratitude wholly to his glory, and his Churches service: These made him not wholly *refractary*, or obstinate against the *intreaties* of some persons, whose eminent merit in all learning, piety, and virtue, might incourage by their command so great *insufficiencies* to so great an undertaking: Which is not to *fire a Beacon* of faction or contention; but to establish a *pillar of Truth*, and certainty; Also to hold forth a *Shield* of defence and safety; such as may *direct* and *protect*, stay

and

and secure the mindes of good Christians in the midst of *straying*, *backsliding*, and *Apostatizing* times; wherein many seek to *weary* God, his Ministers, and all men but themselves, with their *variating wickednesse*.

The weight and worth of this *great Subject*, the *Ministry* of this, and so of all true Churches, in which, as in *Noahs Ark* all that we call *Religion*, all that is *sacred*, Christian, and reformed, is deposited and embarqued, would have (indeed) required a more *proportionate assertor*: who might, out of the *good treasure of his heart*, have given more strength, and ornament to so divine and necessary an *Institution*.

But who sees not the *methods* and *choices* of Gods wisedome and power; who (*oft-times*) makes his light and glory to shine clearest through the darkest *Lanternes*? He appears in a *bush*, when he purposed the great redemption of his Church out of *Egypt*: The skilfull *hand* of *God* can write as well with a *Goose quill*, as with a Swans or Eagles. The self-demonstrating beams of *sacred Truths* need no borrowed reflexions: By soft and easie breathings the Lord hath oft dispelled the *grossest fogs* and *blindest mists*, which rose in his Church; His fair and most *orient pearles* are frequently found in *rough and unpolished shels*; The excellency of his *heavenly Treasure*, and power doth best appeare in *earthen vessels*. The plain and main Truths of Christian Religion (among which this of *an holy ordained Ministry* is one) like *soverain* and *victorious Beauties* lose nothing by the *meannesse* of their dresse, or unaccuratenesse of their habit; it is enough if they can but freely appeare like themselves.

This fashion of writing by way of Apology (which requires a diffused and *pathetick* stile) was, indeed, judged the best and fittest, as for the Subject and the times, so also for this *Author*; considering the little leisure, the short time, the great variety of *other businesse*, and distractions upon him; besides the *terror* and *precipitancy* of the ruine, daily threatning the Ministry and Ministers; if God by the justice, wisdome, and piety of some men did not defend them and divert that mischief. For the preventing of which some others have wrote in vindication of the Ministry after a more succinct and Syllogistick way of argumentation; But the Antiministeriall disease, having seised not so much the heads, as the hearts of men; and depraved affections having swerved many from the judgements; it was thought necessary to apply some remedy at once to both, setting Christians in the Truth, and exciting them to such a love of it and zeal to it, as may best encounter the heady boldnesse of those which oppose it.

If the Authour have in this larger way done any thing worthy so *excellent a Subject*, it must be first imputed to Gods *gracious* assistance, and the blessing of prayers, more *than of studies*; wherein it may be the *charitable flames* of many worthy Christians have greatly helped his infirmities; Next, it must be ascribed to the *sacrednesse*, *dignity*, and *amplenesse* of the matter, or Subject handled, which (as Orators of old observed) like rich soile, and good ground raiseth to *generous productions* the weaker spirits of any thing *sown*, or *planted* in them.

It is true, the *Authors ambition* is in nothing more than to excell in the discharge of his duty, as a *Minister* of this Church; that he might *finish his course* with joy; and also to have *equalled* with height of abilities and industry, the *excellency* of this Cause, which is of so high concernment, to the glory of God; to the honour of his Saviour; (to the salvation of so many soules) to the happinesse of this *Church*; to the blessing of this Nation; to the *preservation* of so many worthy men, his Fathers and Brethren of the Ministry, who make conscience not onely to discharge their duty, but also to preserve the divine authority, and holy succession of their heavenly calling as Christian Ministers; whom the blessing of God hath as much honored and confirmed in this Church of *England*, as in any other under heaven; having made them in every place, where they were planted, as the trees of knowledge and of life; bringing the

desolate

desolate and barren wildernesses to become as the garden of God, by their good husbandry, their learned and godly industry; which meriteth all incouragement and protection of all good men; to whose vindication and assistance if this Author hath come in either too late, or too weak, it will be his great grief.

And if he have not been able to adde any *strength* or honor to *this cause*, (which some others before him, have either fairly touched, or somewhat fully handled); yet he may adde to the *number* of the *witnesses*, who have or shall give *testimony* to this great Truth, holy Order, and happy *Institution of Jesus Christ*; who must not cease to *prophecy*, though they be clothed *in sack-cloth*, *Revel.* 11.3.

To conclude; Nothing seemed, in *honor* and *conscience*, to him more *vile* and *uncomely*, than to see this *Reformed Church of England*, which hath brought up so many *learned* and *valiant* sons; which lately was so much *praised* and extolled by them in her prosperity; to be now so much *deserted* by many of her *children*, both Ministers and others, in this day of her great *agony* and *calamity*; wherein ignorant, *mechanick* and *meritlesse* spirits, think it not enough to endeavour to *strip her* of her *ornaments*, to rob her of her *garments*, to deprive her of her *dowry*, to divorce her from her *best friends*, and faithfullest servants; but they must also cast *dirt* in her face; spitefully *scratching* her, wanonly rending her, cruelly wounding her, and most scornfully *destroying* her, as if she were an *impure prostitute*, a most abhorred *Adulteresse*; when indeed shee was, and is, a fair Daughter of heaven, and the fruitfull *Mother of us all*: Iustly esteemed by all learned, sober, and godly men, *both at home*, and abroad, as *wise*, *grave*, *chast*, and *venerable* a *Matron*, as any, in all the Christian, or *reformed world*. Nor doth shee cease to be *comely*, though she be now black and *scorched*; There appeares *beauty* amidst her *ashes*, and lovelinesse amidst her scratches: the Spirit of *glory* shines through her *Sackcloth*; still meriting, and therefore not despairing of the *love*, favour, *pity*, and protection of all worthy persons who are

considerable

considerable either for counsel or in power, and commendable either for honesty or Religion: Suffering indignities, and dayly fearing more from none but those that are *enemies*, as to all learning, order, and religion, so to all honesty, modesty, and humanity; Her sad, deplorable fate and (by such men threatned) if this Author cannot hinder or help to recover, yet he shall, with *Jeremie*, heartily pity, deeply lament, and most passionately *pray for her*, and her *children*, so long as he lives; as thou wilt (O Christian and *compassionate Reader*) if thou beest of his minde, who bids thee Farewell.

HIERASPISTES:

OR A

DEFENCE

BY WAY OF

APOLOGY;

FOR THE

Miniſtry and Miniſters

OF THE

CHURCH

OF

ENGLAND.

Humbly Preſented

To the Conſciences of all thoſe that excel in Virtue.

I Am neither afraid, nor aſhamed to preſent to your view and patrociny, in whom is a more *Excellent Spirit*, this *Apology*: For which, as I have no *encouragement*, ſo I expect no *acceptance*, or thanks from any men, who carry on other deſigns, than thoſe of Glory to God, Peace to their own Conſciences, welfare to this Nation, and Love to this and other Reformed Churches of *Chriſt*. I know, That *Secular Projects*, and *Ambitious Policies*, have (for the moſt part) ſuch jealouſies, partialities, and unevenneſſes in their Counſels and Motions, as can hardly allow or bear that * *Generous Integrity* and *Freedom*, which is moſt neceſſary, as well as moſt comely, for the *Cauſe*

1. *The Addreſs.* Dan. 6. 3.

* Ἐχθρὸς τῆς Παῤῥησίας ἡ κολακεία. *Chryſ.*

Cauſe of Chriſt, which I in my Conſcience take to be this of his *Faithful and true Miniſters*, of this *Church*, and of the *Reformed Religion*: Of which, in no caſe, and at no time, any true Chriſtian, leaſt of all a *Miniſter* of that *ſacred Name and Myſtery*, may without ſin be * aſhamed, or afraid, to own before men, in the place where God hath ſet him, and after that maner which becomes *Heavenly Wiſdom*, when ſhe is juſtified by any of her Children. It is your *Honor*, and happineſs to *Excel*, not onely in that *Wiſdom*, which can diſcern, but alſo in that *Candor*, which cheerfully accepts, in that *courage*, which dares publikely own what ſhall appear to be the *Cauſe of God*, the *Inſtitution of Chriſt*, and his *Churches Concernments*, amidſt the Contempts, Calumnies, and Depreſſions, which they meet with, from the Ignorance, Errors, Paſſions, Prejudices, Luſts, Intereſts, and Jealouſies of the World.

* Ὦ παῖ, φοβηθεὶς μὴ ἐν αἰσχύνῃ ἢ τιμιωτέρα πρίμοντα ... καὶ ὀνειδιζόμενοι ... H. Steph. Mark 8, 38.

2 Cor. 4. 5.

The excellency of the knowledge of our Lord Jeſus Chriſt (which you have attained by the bleſſing of God, upon *his*, and, for Chriſts ſake, *your ſervants*, the able, faithful, and true Miniſters of the Goſpel, in this Church of *England*,) hath taught you *to eſteem all things in compariſon, but as loſs, and dung*; to chuſe to be with Chriſt in his *ſtorms*, (if the will of God be ſo) rather than enjoy the worlds *calms*. There was never, I think, any time, or cauſe, ſince the Name of Chriſt had place upon Earth, wherein your *real and commendable excellencies*, had more opportunities to ſhew, or greater occaſions to exerciſe themſelves, than now: This being the firſt adventure of ſome mens *impudent Impiety*, attempting at once to annul, and abrogate, the whole Function and Office, the Inſtitution and uninterrupted Succeſsion of the *Evangelical Miniſtry*: Which prodigious attempt, no antient Hereticks, no Schiſmaticks, none that ever owned the name of Chriſtians, were ſo guilty of, as ſome now ſeem to be: So that now, if ever, you are expected, both by God, and good men, to appear worthy of your ſelves, and your holy Profeſsion, either in Piety to God, and Zeal to the Name of your *Saviour Jeſus Chriſt*; or in juſtice and gratitude to thoſe your true Miniſters, who have Preached to you *the true way of eternal life*; or in Pity and Charity, not ſo much to them, as to your ſelves indeed, and your poſterity (the means of whoſe Salvation is diſputed, and endangered;) or in any other Chriſtian Affections, and heroick Motions; ſuch as are comely for thoſe that are filled with *holy Humanity*; being therefore the beſt of men, becauſe they have in them *the moſt of Saints*.

Phil. 3. 8. *Tutiora ſunt Chriſti pericula, quàm mundi ſecuritates. Jer.*

2. *True Saints Characters.*

Saints, I ſay, Not becauſe great, but good men; not as applauded by men, but approved of God; not as Arbitrators of outward, but enjoyers of inward Peace; not becauſe Conquerors of others, by the arm of fleſh, but more than * *Conquerors of themſelves*, by the Graces of Gods Spirit; not as violent Rulers of others, but voluntary ſubduers

* τὸ νικᾷν αὐτὸν αὑτὸν πασῶν νικῶν πρώτη τε καὶ ἀρίστη. *Plat. de Leg. Dial.* 1.

Rom. 8.

ducers of themselves; not because prospered, and encreased in Houses, Lands, Honors, and Vain Glories, by the ruine of others, but by being mortified in Desires, crucified in Enjoyments, cautious in Liberties, modest in Successes, impatient of Flatteries, (which turn *proud* Herods *into noysom Worms*,) full of Self-denyings, where they most excel; coveting nothing so much, as to be nothing in their own eyes; to enjoy Christ in and above all things; to abound in every good word and work; to be humble in heights; poor in plenty; just in prevalencies; moderate in felicities; compassionate to others in calamity: Ever most jealous of themselves, lest prosperity be their snare, lest they grow blackest under the hottest Sun-shine lest they should have their portion and reward in this world; lest they should not turn secular advantages, to Spiritual Improvements, to holy Examples, to the ornament of Religion, to the good of others, to the peace and welfare of the Church of Christ.

Acts 12. 23.

Secundæ res acrioribus stimulis animum explicant, Tacit. hist. 1.

Such *living and true Saints*, I may humbly and earnestly supplicate (without any Superstition) who affect least, but merit most, that *title* upon Earth; who are Gods visible Jewels; the Darlings of *Jesus Christ*; the Lights and Beauties of the World; the regenerate Honor of degenerate Humane Nature; the rivals and competitors with Angels, yet their *care and charge*; the candidates of Eternal Glory, and Heirs of an Heavenly Kingdom; the *crown* and *rejoycing* of every true Minister; the Blessed Fruit of their Labors, and happy Harvest of their Souls: The high Esteemers, the hearty Lovers, the liberal Relievers, the unfeigned Pitiers, the faithful Advocates, and the earnest Intercessors, for the distressed Ministers; the so much despighted, and (by many) despised Ministry of this Church. You, in whom is the *Spirit of the most Holy God*, shining on your *mindes*, with the *setled wisdom* of sound Knowledge, and saving Truths; captivating all wandring fancies, and pulling down all *high imaginations*, which exalt themselves beyond the *written Rule of Christ*, and the *Analogy* of that Faith, which *was once delivered to the Saints*, in the *holy Oracles* of the Scriptures, and continued to this day, by the Ministry and Fidelity of the Church; which is the *pillar and ground of Truth*; both propounding and establishing it, against all unbelief, and opposition. You, whose *wills* are redeemed from the servitude of sinful lusts, slavish fears, secular factions; whose *Consciences* and *Conversations* are bound by the silver Cord of the Love of God and Christ, to all Sacred Verity, real Piety, unfeigned Charity, sincere Purity, exact Equity, comely Order, holy Policy, and Christian Unity; from all *prophane novelties*; seditious Extravagancies, licentious Liberties, fanatick Enthusiasms, pragmatick Factions, and hellish Confusions. You, that are strengthned with all holy and humble Resolutions, which become the sober courage, and calm magnanimity of *true Christians*, either

Mal. 3. 17.
Heb. 1. 14.
Phil. 4. 1.
Rom. 8. 11.
2 Cor. 10. 5.
Rom. 12. 6.
Jude 3.
1 Tim. 3. 16.
2 Tim. 2. 16.
Βεβήλους κενοφωνίας, & κενοφωνίας.

to speak and do, what honestly you may, for Christ and his Church, for his and your *true Ministers*, or else to chuse with *Moses*, rather to suffer with them, than to be any way assistant to, rejoycing in, or compliant with, the ruine of them; that so in all things you may *adorn the doctrine of Christ*, and honor the true Reformed Christian Religion, established and professed in this Church of *England*.

Heb. 11. 25. Tit. 2. 10.

To your judicious Zeal, sincere Piety, unbyassed Charity, holy Discretion, which have no leaven of sinister ends, or unworthy policies, (being got above the vain hopes, fears, diffidences, and designs of meer men,) I do in all Christian Charity and Humility, present this *Apology*, in the behalf of those *Pearls*, the *true Ministers* of this Church of *England*, whose worth is not abated, though their lustre be obscured; nor are they less precious when *trampled* by *Swine under their feet*; nor less *Stars in Christs right hand*, and fixed in the Firmament of the true Church, when they are clouded by these Fogs and Vapors, which ascend from the Earth, or from the *bottomless pit*, from the malice and rage of men or devils.

Math. 7. 11. Rev. 2. 1. Rev. 9. 2.

Godly Ministers sufferings are their Glory.

Nothing more adorned and perfected Christs divine Person, and meritorious Patience, than his being blinded, buffetted, scourged, mocked, reviled, stripped, crowned with Thorns, and Crucified; * nor was he less a *King and Saviour*, when his *Purple Robe* was taken off, and his own *Garments* divided *among the soldiers*: He was not less the *Messias*, the *sent*, and *anointed of God*, the *Great Preacher*, and *fulfiller* of Righteousness, when he was the *scorn* and *outcast of men*; nor a less *precious Foundation*, and *corner Stone*, when refused by *foolish builders*, who dashed themselves against him, instead of building and resting by Faith upon him.

Heb. 5. 9. & 2. 10. Luke 22.

* *Inglorii & deformes esse non possumus, quocunque modo ad Christi imaginem conformamur; cujus nunquam magis enituit gloria quam quæ sputo & sanguine & vibicibus operiebatur.* Chrys.

In like sort, the *true Ministers of this Church*, (whom the pride and wantonness of some men glories to account, as the *filth and off-scouring of all things*, to speak and do all maner of *evil against them falsly* and injuriously;) if they may be so far blest of God, and honored, as to *suffer after Christs* example, and to *make up* (to their measure) the *remainder of the sufferings of Christ* in his Body, the Church; there is no doubt, but the *Spirit of Glory* will more rest upon them, the power of Christ be more *perfected* in them, and the light of Gods countenance be more shining on them, than when their *Corn, and Wine, and Oyl increased*; their faces will then appear most, as *Angels of God*, when with Saint *Stephen*, they are beset with *showres of stones*; overwhelmed with all maner of *hard speeches*, and rude indignities. Thus it becomes the proud and petulant world to act; and thus it becomes learned, able, and humble Ministers to suffer. Who have then least cause to be ashamed, when they are most opposed, and oppressed for Christs sake: For, troden in

Isai. 53. 2 Pet. 2. 6. 1 Cor. 4. 13. Matth. 5. 11. Phil. 1. 29. Col. 1. 24. 1 Pet. 4. 14. Psal. 4. Acts 6. 15. Jude 15. σκληρῶν.

in the *wine-press* of mans displeasure, they may then yield the noblest juyce, and most generous expressions of their Zeal, Courage, and Constancy.

Wherefore I have adventured, although the weakest and unworthiest among many of my Fathers and Brethren, the Ministers of this Church of *England*, so far to satisfie the worlds curiosity, as to give them some prospect, and view of the Ministers of *England*, in their present distresses, fears, and afflictions; that men may see, with how *stedfast countenances*, they can look upon their adversaries, while they *stop their ears* against them, *gnash their teeth* at them, and threaten utterly to destroy them; that their *causeless and implacable enemies* may behold, with what divine comfort and assurance, they can walk, both cheerfully and uprightly amidst their *fiery furnaces*; into which they are therefore cast, because they will not fall down and worship, * those *Idol-shepherds*, those *False-prophets*, those *Meer-images* of *Ministers*, which have set up themselves as *gods* in the Church of God; such, as neither they, nor their *Fore-fathers*, nor any Church of Christ for One thousand six hundred yeers, ever knew, or heard of; who were ever blessed, and thankfully contented in all times, either of persecution, or peace, with those *true Ministers*, who in a right *way of due Ordination*, descended from, and succeeded in the place, and ordinary power of the Apostles, and the other Disciples which were first sent and ordained by Christ: Which the true Ministers of the Church of *England*, being conscious to themselves, (as I shall after prove) that they have rightly received, they have this confidence still, That they are neither so *forsaken* of God, nor destitute of good Consciences, nor despised by good men, nor do they despair, but that they may have leave, be able, and permitted, with just freedom, and modest courage, to plead their cause, before any *Tribunal* of men; not doubting, but they may have so fair an hearing, as St. *Paul* (their Great Predecessor, both in Preaching and Sufferings) hoped from *Felix*, *Festus*, *Agrippa*, or *Cæsar*: Of whose piety the Apostle having no great perswasion, yet he charitably presumed to finde so much equity, and common humanity in them, as not to be *condemned* by them, being *unheard*; or to be acquitted, as to any crimes falsly laid to his charge; if he had but the favor of a fair Trial, and impartial Hearing. So *hard it is for a good man ever to despair in a good cause*.

3. *Reason of this Address.*

And however my confidence be just, and wel-grounded, as to the merit of that Cause which I have (by *Gods help*) undertaken; yet when I consider my strength, which is small; my infirmities, which are many; my defects, which are manifest; my interest with men of place and power, which is very little; and the prejudice, against whatever I, or any other Minister can do in this kinde (which may be

Acts 6.15.

Dan. 4.

Zach. 11.17.

* As Idols, so are false Teachers, *Dolores, Vanitates, Labores, Stultitiæ, Abominationes,* אלילים אל אלים *Mordii. Res vana, nihili.*

Mark 3.14. And Jesus ordained twelve, that they should be with him, and that he might send them forth to Preach.

Acts 25.11.

Toto cælo distant benè operari & desperare.

—Sibi conscia virtus Dat animos.

Quod deest viribus, habent cautelâ.

Acts 27.

be great and many) I have (as feeble *Creatures*, conscious to their weakness, are wont to do) fled to the *refuge* and *assistance*, first of Gods grace (which is *sufficient* for me, and which in the midst of threatnings, storms, and shipwrack, bids me *be of good chear.*) Next, to that of *your mediation*, (*O excellent Souls*) who are every where dispersed in this Nation; whose *soundness* of minde, and *uncorruptedness* of maners (yet remaining) hath hitherto preserved this *backsliding* and *unsavory* age from utter *rottenness* and *putrefaction*: Possibly *your mediation* may so far prevail among all estates of men, as to allay those asperities, abate those animosities, remove those prejudices, satisfie those jealousies, under which, the *Ministers* and *Ministry* of this *Church*, do now lie in many mens mindes; and, it may be, in some of theirs, who are become *men of power and renown*.

Humble Monition to those in Power.

In sublimitate positis tam descensus quàm ascensus perpendendus: Nec minus est quod terreat, quam quod placeat. Ambr.

τὰ ἀνθρώπινα πάντα ῥύσινα. *Chrys.*

Whose *eminency*, I hope, will not be offended, if I humbly put them in minde, That their glory and greatness is not more evident to others (who are prone to measure their hopes and fears, by the beams or shadows which they cast upon them) than most of all to be seriously considered by themselves; since, from those *ruines*, on which they are raised, and from that *height*, to which they are exalted, they may easily look down, and learn, in how *slippery* a station, and how tottering a posture all, humane glory, and *excellency* doth consist. That, the *triumphs* of such *poor mortals* carry their own deaths after them, as well as other mens before them; that, as *bubbles*, they have the same principles of frailty in them, by which others have suddenly disappeared, who lately swelled as big, and swam as high above the waters, as these now do. All religious experience tells the most *subtile* and *elated spirits*, the *profoundest projectors*, and the most *potent actors*, That they can have but a short time here, may have a sudden change or period, and must give a *severe account* of all actions they do, and all advantages they enjoy, in this present world: Of all which, they shall carry no more comfort with them, than they have made conscience to do the *work of God*, according *to his will*, revealed to mankinde in the *sure and sacred Oracles* of his written Word.

Zach. 11.

*1 Chro. 22. 8. Thou shalt not build an House to my Name, because thou hast shed much blood upon the Earth in my sight.

It is manifest, That some men have been a *staff of Bonds* in Gods left hand, to punish the sins, or exercise the Graces of many in these three Nations; whether they shall be a *staff of Beauty* in his right hand, for the support of Piety, Peace, Order, and true Religion, the event will best shew. They have acted many things as *Men*, with great policy and power; it is now expected, they should act as truly *Reformed* and wisely *Reforming Christians*, with Piety and Charity; (if, at least, that may be hoped in the time of the Gospel, which was denied to *Davids zeal* under the Law: That such as have * *shed much blood* in Civil Wars, should be instrumental *to build* the

House

House of God :) Peradventure they may be means, if not to repair its great decayes, yet to hinder it from that total ruine, and utter vastation, which by many and bad men are threatned ; but, we hope by more and better men (with Gods help) will be prevented.

And truly, if I knew, how I might most acceptably make my Address, and fairly plead my excuse with men in *place and power* ; if I understood what might most merit to Apologize before all great, good, and ingenuous men, for the boldness of now publishing this *Apology*, I would in the most soft words, and comely terms, bespeak their favor, and deprecate their offence, for so it becomes Candidates and Petitioners : But my *integrity* is beyond all oratory ; and my *plainness* beyond all artifice or study ; I having no design, but onely this, (which I take to be, as pious and just, so not altogether misbeseeming the station wherein God hath set me) That from the Country obscurity (wherein I am not wholly buried) I may crave leave to use *honest Christian Liberty* in this one thing, which relates, not so much to my Person, as to my Profession and Function ; And in this, to appear in publick not as a Counseller, or Dictator, or Threatner, but as an humble Client and Suter, among those many, which always attend those who have power to *save*, or to *destroy*, to *do good or evil*. Nor in this am I pragmatically suggesting, what I might foolishly imagine fittest to be done in State affairs, (from which, as from Pitch and Birdlime, I am most willingly a stranger ;) but onely propounding, in all humble and due respect, what is by many men, much wiser and worthier than my self, conceived as most necessary for this particular *Church of God* in *England* : And wherein the fears of very many *Excellent Christians* are so urgent upon them, that it were better to offend by speaking in love, than by silence to act the part, both of an Enemy and a Coward. Yet in this *freedom*, I would not willingly offend any, that really are, or esteem themselves, my Betters, and Superiors, so, as to exasperate them by any rash or rude expressions. I earnestly deprecate all such failings in my self, and such suspitions in others. This restraint and caution, I have, not so much out of fear of men, (yet do I *fear men*, as far as *fear* is due ;) but rather out of that fear of God, which is the *beginning of Wisdom*, and that *reverence* I ow to my self, and my Profession, as a Christian, and a Minister ; whom nothing less becomes, than the badge and livery of Passion ; or the jaundice of *Cholerick Diffusions*, evident in the face of their writings. I love not (if they were safe) affectations of Language, which power may interpret Seditious, Turbulent, or Treasonable : I have learned to be patient under hard things, thankful for moderate ; hopeful for better : Nor do I disdain to beseech mans favor, whose *fury God can restrain*, and *turn the remainder of wrath*, to his praise and his Churches good. Let others complain of their *Civil Burthens*, which

πολλῷ μᾶλλον ἄξιον ἐν βασιλείαις ἀκούειν λόγον ἐλεύθερον. Synes. de Reg.

The design of this Apology.

καλοῦ παῤῥησίας τῶν λόγων ἐγχειρήσεως. Vocat. Synes.

Δεῖ τοίνυν ἐγὼ βούλομαι τῶν σωφρονούντων εἶναι καὶ μάλιστα [illegible] ἐπὶ τῆς συμπαθείας. Synes. ad Arcad. Imper.

πάντων μάλιστα αἰσχύνεο σεαυτόν. Pythag.

(which I feel, as well as they.) Let them agitate *secular Interests*, which never want their vicissitudes, crosses, and defeats: My *sense* and *address* in this *Apology*, is chiefly for those things which concern the true Ministry, and the Reformed Religion established in *England*; (In which, not custom, and education, but judgement and conscience, I hope, hath confirmed me by Gods grace,) And for those men especially, whose office and duty I think it is, by Preaching, doing and suffering, as Christian Ministers, *according to the Will of God*, to vindicate and preserve true Christian Religion, and to transmit it as Reformed, in an unblemished, and unquestionable succession to Posterity.

4. *Why in way of Apology.*

Your *Virtuous Excellencies*, upon whose favor, chiefly, I have adventured this Address, to the view of the supercilious, and more untractable World, are not ignorant what *noble Precedents* may be alleged for my writing in this maner of *Apology*, (which is or ought to be a * twisting of Logick and Rethorick together; a Checquer-work of Arguments and Oratory; studying to cloth the Bones and Sinews of Syllogisms, with the smoothness and beauty of Eloquence) seeking at once, both to convince the Understanding, and to excite the Affections: For besides those lesser and obscurer pieces recorded by the Antients, of *Aristides, Melito, * Quadratus, Apollinaris, Methodius, Johannes Gram. Themistius*, and *Apollonius*; (this last, being a *Roman* Senator, wrote and recited in the Senate, his *Apollogy for the Christians*, and was after crowned with Martyrdom;) We have also extant those famous *Apologies* of *Justine Martyr*, who dedicated his first to the *Roman* Senate, and his second to *Antoninus Pius Augustus*; also that of *Tertullian*, who in the time of *Severus* the Emperor, seeing Christians persecuted onely *for the * Name*, as a sufficient crime, (as many Ministers now are by some men) wrote his Learned, large, and accurate *Apology*, dedicating it to the Emperor and his Son. Saint *Hilary* also, wrote a Defence for the Orthodox, against the *Arrians*, presenting it to *Constantius* the Emperor. And of later times (in its kinde, inferior to none) is that *Apology* of the Learned, Pious, and incomparable Bishop *Jewel* *. The former wrote their Learned, Modest, and Eloquent *Apologies* for *Christian Religion*, as it then stood (like the *Lilly among the Thorns*) baited, persecuted, and condemned on all sides by the Heathen, who wanted neither numbers, nor arts, nor power to oppress; yet was it boyed up and preserved by Gods blessing on the learned Courage, and industrious Constancy of those, and other Holy Men: This last (our Renowned Countryman) vindicated the *Reformed Churches* (and particularly this of *England*,) for their not complying with, and submitting to the Councel of *Trent*; and for their necessary receding from the Church of *Rome*; so far onely, as this did in Doctrine or Maners from the Scripture Rules, and from

* *Apologeticum scribendi genus est mixtura quædam oratoris disputantis & Dialectici deprecantis.* Eras.

* *Quadratus Apostolorū Discipulum Atheniensis Pontifex Ecclesiæ, Adriano principi, librum pro Christiana Religione tardidit. Et tantæ admirationis omnibus fuit, ut persecutionem gravissimam illius exellens sedaret ingenium.*

Cant. 2. 2.

Jeron. ad Mag. de Aristide & aliis doctis Christianis.

* *Vel solo nomine, & ex præjudicio damnantur Christiani.* Ter. Apol.

*Bishop *Jewels* Apology.

from the Primitive Judgement, Canons, and practise of the Fathers, the first Councils, and the Primitive purest Churches: That excellent Prelate, no doubt, would have then fully asserted (as he did other points then in dispute) the Order, Honor, Office, and Authority of the Ministry of the Church of *England*; if either the ignorance, or malice of those times had been so far guilty and ingenious, as to question or oppose it, which some men now do; who dare any thing, but to be wise, honest, and humble.

5. *Why by this Author.*

I know my self unworthy to bring up the rear of so gallant a Troop of Worthies, in all Ages; nor is it from the ignorance of my own Tenuities, or other mens Sufficiencies, that I have thus far adventured to *list my self in the Army of Christian Apologists*, or to *march under the Banner of this Apology*: Onely in some respects, I seemed to some men (if not to my self) to be signed out by providence to this duty (or endeavor, at least) in as much as I may be thought redeemed somewhat beyond the ordinary, from that *grand prejudice*, which is like a *beam* in many Readers eyes; or like a *dead Fly* ready to viciate the sweetest Confections, made by any Minister in this kinde: As if all were done, onely for that *livelihood* and *estate* which their *Church-Livings* afford them, that any Ministers so stickle, and contend to uphold their Function and Ministry, either by speech or writing.

Few men stand freer from the *dashes* of this suspition, than my self; in regard of either present benefit, or future expectation, by any imployment in the Ministry; which is such, as neither an idle man would undertake the work, nor a covetous man much envy the reward: Yet, I thank God, I want not either abilities or opportunities to exercise Piety and Charity among a company of poor (for the most part) yet good and orderly people; whose love, respect, and peaceable carriage to me in these times hath merited, that I should prefer the good of their souls, before any private advantages, so long as I am over them, in the Lord. I thank God, I have far less temptations of private interest, than would be required to put any discreet man upon so rough an adventure in a tempestuous Sea, where silence with safety were to be chosen, rather than publickness with peril; if I did not consciously and charitable look much more upon the publick; where taking a general view of the state and condition wherein most of my Brethren *the Ministers*, either are, or are like to be in this Church, (if some men may have their wills.) I cannot but with shame and sorrow behold in all corners of the Land, to how low an ebb, not onely their persons, but the *whole profession of the Ministry*, now is, or is like to be brought; for Government, Maintenance, Reputation, Authority, and Succession, in these Churches, through the *dissentions* of these times.

And truly in the midst of our dust and ashes, we the *Ministers* of *England* must confess, That *with no less justice, than severity, the Lord hath poured upon us this shame and confusion of face*, as well as upon other ranks and orders of men; since our many great spots, and foul stains, both in Doctrine and Maners, could not but be the more remarkably offensive to God and man, by how much, in the *sacredness* and *eminency* of that Calling, more exact holiness was expected from us, and pretended by us.

1. *Whence the lapse of Ministers in the love and reputation they had?*

And here, I hope, I shall not give any my Betters, or my Brethren, any offence, while I *humbly prostrate* my self in the *Porch* and *Threshold* of this *Apology*; giving *glory to God*, and taking shame to my self, as well as others; Not by an uncharitable censuring of any man, but by a penitential searching and discovering the true cause, for which I think the Lord hath poured this contempt upon the Ministers of this Church: Herein to begin aright with God, and our own Consciences, may best relieve us with men; the disburthening of a ship, is half buoying it up, when sunk or aground. *Ingenuous confession* is a good part, and a great pledge of future amendment: Some diseases are half healed, as soon as well searched and discovered. It may be, we may finde the same readiness both in God and man, to forgive our failings, as *David* did; who, no sooner had confessed, *I have sinned against the Lord*, but he heard that gracious reply, *The Lord hath put away thy sin, thou shalt not die.*

Μέγα φάρμακον κακίας ἡ τῦ πταίσματος ὁμολογία. Naz. orat. 15. *Quicquid defuit pietati aut charitati confessionis humilitas suppleat.* Bern. 2 Sam. 12. 13.

1. *Peccator celando non facit nescium, at confitendo facit propitium Deum.* Aug.

In the first place, this for certain we may conclude; That it is not the galling and stinging of these *flesh flies*, (now our *busie and bitter enemies* of the *Antiministerial* faction) that first brought this sore and rawness upon us; but it is some foul and corrupt humor from within us, which first brake out to such putrified sores and wounds, which have invited those to feast upon our ulcers and deformities.

Confessio fallax periculosior est quā procax & obstinata defensio. Nonnulli dolosa confessione se subtilius defendunt. Bern. de Humil.

In a matter then most fit for *deep and serious repentings*, I cannot be so *superficial*, as some have been; who like Lapwings, cry out loudest, when furthest from their Nests; being severe censurers of all men, but themselves; loth to see and confess *their bosom sins*, or to own the deformitids of their darlings; hardly perswaded to cast away to the * *Moles* and *Bats* (to the dark and deformed crew of *Heretical novelties*, and *Schismatical vanities*) these specious and gilded *Idols*, *Teraphims* of their own imaginations, which their fancies have forged, and with *Micahs* devotion, set up to themselves as *Divine*.

* Isa. 2. 20.

2. *Former due Conformity, not the sin of the Clergy.*

Sure, it is but a very poor and pitiful account (the product of Passion, not of Reason) which some men give; while they, with a *vulgar vehemency*, accuse all the *Clergy* and *Ministers* of *England* for their former *conformities* and *subjections* to Authority, in things

to

to some men disputable for their nature and use; yet, then, according to Law; that is, approved, established, and enjoyned by the * publick consent, wisdom, and piety of all estates, in this Church and State. And which things, very holy and learned men generally used; accounting them, if burthens to weaker *consciences*, yet to *wise and stronger men*, as lawful as it was for St. *Paul* to sail in the ship, whose sign was *Castor* and *Pollux*, *Acts* 28. 11. Yea, and so far necessary, as (being agreeable to their judgements) the use and extern observation of them was enjoyned in the Church by due Authority, and approved by their own personal subscriptions; being no way destructive to any thing of Christian Faith, or Holy Life: Certainly, a sober and good Christian must not tear in pieces, or cast away his *Bible*, because it is not so neatly bound, as he would fancy: Nor would, I believe, any humble Primitive Martyr, or Confessor, have despised Salvation by *Jesus Christ* alone, duly exhibited in the Word and Sacraments, as they were in this Church; nor have refused Communion, with this, or any part of the Catholike Church, truly professing *Christ* Crucified, although the * nails of the Cross had been much sharper and heavier, than any thing was in the stablished Order and Ministry of the Church of *England*; which few Churches since the first hundred years, wherein the Apostles lived, ever enjoyed with more Purity, Order, and Simplicity, as to the main, than the Reformed Church here in *England* did.

In quibus nihil certi statuit Scriptura divina, mos populi Dei vel instituta majorum pro lege tenenda sunt. Aug. ep. 86.

Rom. 14. 1, 5. Let every man be fully perswaded in his own minde; and whether they act, or act not, both are accepted of God in those things, whereof there is no precise command.

So 1 Cor. 10. 30.

Master *Hooker* (ὁ γλυκυσυμφοσ-μένος) in his *Ecclesiastical Policy*, with incomparable Learning, and gravity of Judgement, hath beyond any Reply, vindicated both the integrity of his own Conscience, and the honor of this Church, in things of extern order; Μέσον σοφίας πρᾶγμα. * *Ipsa mutatio consuetudinis etiam qua adjuvat utilitate, novitate perturbat.* August. ep. 19.

So that many wise, and good men, begin now to think (since these unhappy disputes have by attrition been kindled, and far driven on *to fire and sword*, seeming heretofore to have risen from humble, meek, and charitably tender spirits) That the greatest sticklers against those things (which were oft declared to be, *not any part of piety, duty, or devotion in themselves*; but onely as *matters of extern order, decency, and circumstance*.) were rather *curious* (for the most part) than * *conscientious*; Dissenters being either very *weak*, or very *wilful*. And some have since sufficiently appeared, rather wantonly nice, loose, and *given to change*, than any way grave, setled, or seriously solicitous in matters of Religious Order, and Publick Ministrations. Possibly, it was not the least of our follies and sins, that we did not with more thankfulness enjoy the many rich

* *Disciplina nulla est melior gravi prudentiq; viro, in his, quæ liberas habent observationes, quam ut eo modo agat, quo agere viderit ecclesiam ad quamcunq; fortè devenerit. Quod enim neq; contra fidem, neq; contra bonos mores injungitur, indifferenter est habendum, & pro eorum inter quos vivitur societate servandum est.* August. ep. 118. ad Jan. *Cavendum est ne tempestate contentionis serenitas charitatis obnubiletur.* August. ep. 86.

Hinc in bella civilia præcipitamur, quod mala mitiora nimium cavemus. Eras.

* *Qui in levibus à quotidiana recedit consuetudine, Magnus licet vir sit certis tantum horis illum sapere noris.* Verulam.

mercies, we then had; instead of that *regret and querulous impatience*, which was so loth to bear any such defects or burthens, as some men imagined; wherein (for the most part) ignorance, or easiness, or vulgarity of mindes and maners, made * *greater out-cryes, and aggravations*, than either truth of judgement, or tenderness of well-informed Consciences. The after-instability in some men mindes, and stupidness of their maners, shews the *Vertigo* and *Lethargy* of their Brains: For many men, who, when it began to be in fashion, strained at those *gnats*, which formerly for many years, they had digested, yet afterward made no bones to swallow *Camels* of *grosser innovations*, such as no distinctions can mince or chew small enough for a good Conscience. And it is confessed by those, that have now attained their *after-wits*, that those *former conformities* enjoyned by Law, were but *motes*, in comparison of those *beams*, which now threaten to eclipse the lights of this *English World*, and to put out the very eyes of the *Seers* and *Watchmen* of this *Church*.

4. Many excellent Ministers, for Learning, Piety, and Industry, (besides innumerable other Christians) did in former times, grow up, to great thrift in sound knowledge, and all beauties of holiness, even amidst those so much suspected and decryed *weeds of Conformity*; which if they were not, as sweet *Marjoram*, very savory; yet sure, they were not as (*mors in olla*) *Colloquintida* or *Hemlock*, very hurtful, or death in the pot; being judged by the wisdom of the Church and State here, and by the most learned Divines abroad, to be within the liberty and compass of those things, of *Order and Decency*, which by that *one grand charter*, 1 *Cor*. 14.40. are allowed by God to be ordered by the prudence of any particular National Church; And in which, all Churches, in all ages and places, have esteemed their several *Customs*, as *Laws* to them, without any breach of Charity, or prejudice of Christian Liberty, or blemish of the Faith; yet never (perhaps) without the offence of some particular Members in the Churches, whose fancies easily finde fault with any things, whereof themselves are not *Fathers*, or at least *Gossips*. Humble Christians will thank God for moderate enjoyments; nor are they bound to contend for what they think best, to the perturbance of the publick Peace. *Patience* is a remedy always near, easie, and safe; nor is it likely, that the state of any Church on Earth will ever be so happily compleated, as to have nothing in it, which may displease any good man, or which may not exercise his tollerancy, and charity; which are generally more commendable and unsuspected virtues, than those of *zealous activity*, and *publick opposition*, which commonly draw somewhat upon the *dregs of self*, either as to Passion or Interest, Party or Concernment: For, who is so mortified, that doth not hope to get something of credit, profit, or honor, by adhering

εὐσχημόνως καὶ κατὰ τάξιν: *ut ordinata acies*, As an Army with Banners, in Rank and File, where nothing may be deformed by being disorderly.

Cato optimè sensit sed nocet interdum reipublicæ. Tacit.

Et multis utile bellum. Luc.

adhering to any side or new faction, against the former setlings?

How many learned and godly men are, and ever will be (till better grounds be produced, from Scripture, Reason, and practise of the Primitive Church) unsatisfied with the *parity* and *novelty*, yet pretended *Divine Right*, of the *sole-headless-Presbytery*; which chalenges to it self, as from *Christ*, such a supreme power, as is exclusive and destructive of all *Episcopacy*; that is, of the constant Presidency of one, among other *Presbyters*; so placed by their own choice and consent?

And no less unsatisfied are thousands of learned, and good Christians, with that power of *Lay Elders*; (for so they are best called, for distinction sake; and not *Ruling Elders*; lest by that *title* of Ruling, they should fancy and usurp the *sole power* of *rule* to themselves; which undoubtedly, is equally, if not eminently due to the *Preaching Elders*, who labor in the Word and Doctrine:) Touching which point of *Lay Elders* in the Church, I have read two Books written above thirty years since, by a very learned, godly, and impartial Divine, Master *Chibald* of *London*: In the first of which, he proved these *Lay Elders* to have no place, office, use, power, or maintenance assigned them by Scripture; nor ever in any Church of Christ; which he demonstrates in the second Book (which is full of excellent reading) as to the Fathers, Councils, and Histories of the Church: In none of which he findes them to have any footing, as to office and power, upon any *Divine Right*, ever owned in the Church; nor can they now have in every little Parish, or private Congregation; where the Country plainness may afford careful *Over-seers* for the Poor, and *Church-wardens*; but not fit men to match with the Minister, and to sit as Rulers to govern their other Neighbors; who will hardly believe they have authority from Heaven to rule them, unless they see more abilities in them, than usually can be found. What use may be made of such Elders, in the way of Prudence among greater Representations of the *Church*, as in *Synods* and *Councils*, he leaves to the wisdom of those, that have power in such *Conventions* to call and regulate them: But he denies any thing, as of *Divine Right*, belonging to them; so, as to binde every *Parish* or *Congregation* to have them, which would be ridiculous, and most inconvenient. Both these Books being seven years since committed to the hands of Master *Coleman*, as then a Licencer, were unhappily, either smothered and embezzled, or carelesly lost; to the great detriment of truth in that particular: For, truly, in my best judgement, and in other mens of far better, to whom I imparted them, never any thing was written, of that subject, more learnedly, more uprightly, more copiously, or more candidly; especially, considering

Mr. *Chibalds* two Books of *Lay Elders*.

sidering the Author was one that scrupuled some things of *Conformity*.

In like maner, how few *Christians* in any *Reformed Church* are satisfied with those new, and strange *Limbs*, rather than *Bodies of Independent Churches*; (which word of *bodying* into small *Corporations*, is as a novel, so a very gross expression, and hath something of a Solecism; not onely in *Religion*, which owns properly but *one Body of Christ, which is his Catholike Church*; whose *communion* with *Christ*, the onely Head, and one another, as Members in several Offices and Operations, is by the same Faith, the same Scriptures, the same Ministry, the same Ministrations, and as to the main and substance, the same Christian Profession:) But it is also incongruous and absurd in ordinary significancy of Language; while by such a singular *Bodying*, they mean a *Spiritual Union* of those, that pretend to be most *Spiritual Christians*: Which names, and novel inventions, about constituting and compleating Churches, in so many fractions, parcels, and places, apart from all others, by the means of an *explicit Church Covenant*, (as they call it;) how *unscriptural*; how *unconform* to the examples of all antient Churches; how *impertinent* as to Piety; how *dangerous* and *destructive* to the Truth, Union, Harmony, and Dependance (which ought to be among all Christians, and all Churches, to avoid Schism in that one Catholike Body of Christ,) do they seem to many judicious and gracious Christians? who think themselves, and all others, that profess to be Christians, sufficiently added, and united to the Church, as the *Primitive Believers*, being once baptized, were without any more a do, yea, and declaredly bound by their * *Baptism* and *Profession*, to all *Christian conversation*, *charitable communion*, and *holy walking*, by these *Publick Bonds*, and *Sacraments* of *Religion*, which they owned; and of which, they were publickly *partakers* and *professors*.

> Rom. 12. 5. We being many, are one body in Christ. 1 Cor. 12. 13. By one Spirit we are all baptized into one Body, which is Christs.

> 1 Cor. 12. 25. That there be no schism in the body. (*i.e.*) In that one Body of Christ, the Catholike Church.

> * Acts 2. 41. They that gladly received the word, were baptized; and the same day there were added (to the Church) about 3000. soul .

So that, not onely in these, but in many other things, we see the *remedies*, which some men apply to former seeming *distempers*, do (to many men) seem worse than the *diseases* ever were: The *little finger* of grievances, scruples, disorders, and scandals, being far heavier than the *loyns* of the Law were in former-times; where, if there was less liberty by the restraints, which men had by *Laws* laid on themselves; yet there was also far less ignorance in mindes, fewer errors in judgements, blasphemies in opinions, brokenness in affections, dissolutions in discipline, undecencies in sacred administrations, and licentiousness in the ordinary matters of men? So that if those times were not the *golden age* of the Church, sure these cannot brag to be beyond the *iron*, or *brazen*.

> 5. *Other weak conjectures of the causes of Ministers abating in their honor.*

No less superficial and unsearching are those Conjectures or Censures, which a late Writer makes of Ministers ostentations of reading,

reading, and humane learning in their Sermons, (of which, many men cannot be guilty, unless it be of making shews of more than indeed they have:) Also, he allegeth, as an occasion of Ministers lapse in their love, and respect among the people, their *small regard*, and *strangeness* to *godly people*: When it is evident, many mens and womens *godliness*, brings forth now no better fruit, than, first, quarreling with; then neglecting; afterward, despising; next, separating from; after that, bitter railing against; and lastly, stirring up faction, not onely against that one *Minister*, but his whole *calling*. Certainly, some are become such *godly brambles*, and *holy thistles*, as are not to be conversed with more than needs must, and are never to be treated with bare hands. But in case some *Ministers*, by many indignities provoked, grow more teachy and morose to these mens thrifty, inconstant, and importune godliness; If they fortifie what they assert, by the *testimonies* of *learned men*, (which is no more than is sometimes needful, among captious, curious, and contemptuous auditors;) yea, if they seem to some severer censor, something to exceed, in these particulars, those bounds of gravity, and discretion, which were to be desired; yet, what wise man can think, that such fleebites or scratches (in comparison) can send forth so great corruption, or occasion so ill a savor in the nostrils of God and man, that, for these things chiefly, Ministers should be so much under clouds of obloquy and disrespect; that, although they have every *seventh day*, at least, wherein to do men good, and to gain upon their good wills, yet many of them are so lost, that there are but few can give them so much as a good word.

But, some men are willing to mistake the *Image* and *Goats-hair* for *David*, and pretend with *Rachel*, *infirmities*, when they sit upon their *Idols*. Alas, these cannot be the symptomes of so great conflicts and paroxisms, as many *Ministers* now labor under, who were sometimes esteemed *very pretious men*, and highly lifted up on the wings of popular love and fame: In which respects, no men suffer now a greater ebb, than those that were sometime most active, forward, and applauded. The *sticks* and *straws* of lesser scandals, and common failings among Ministers, might kindle some flashes to singe and scorch some of them; but these could not make so *lasting flames*, so fierce and consuming a fire, as this is: In which, many, or most Ministers, that thought themselves much refined, and undertook to be refiners of others, are now, either tried, or tormented. Who sees not, that the *fire* and *wood* of this *Tophet*, which God hath prepared, is not (as some conceive) onely for *Princes* and *Prelates*, for *Archbishops*, and *Bishops*, &c. (In some of whom, what ever there was of want of zeal for Gods glory, of sincere love to the truth, of charity to mens souls, I cannot excuse, or justifie, since they could not

1 Sam.19.12.
Gen.31.34.
Isai.30.33.

not but be as highly displeasing to God and man, as from both they enjoyed very great and noble advantages above other men, of glorifying God, advancing Christian Religion, and incouraging all true holiness: Nor was the having of *Dignities* and *Revennes* their sin, but the not faithful using of them; no wonder, if of them, *to whom* Luke 12. 48. *much was given, much be required*, either in duty, or in penalty.) But this *Tophet* is also (we see) *enlarged*, for the *generality of Presbyters*, and such as disdained to be counted the *inferior Ministers*; nor is this fire thus kindled in the *valley of Hinnom*, nourished onely by the bones and carkases of ignorant, profane, and immoral Ministers Jude 12. (who are as *dry sticks*, and *trash*; *twice dead*, to *conscience*, and to *modesty*; fit indeed to be *pulled* up by the *roots*;) but even *those greater Cedars of Lebanon* have added much to this *pile*, *and fewel*, who sometimes seemed to be *Trees* of the *Lord*, tall and full of *sap*; very able and useful in the Church; and, while within their due ranks and station, they were faithful, flourishing, and fruitful; whose very Children, and Converts, (their former disciples, followers, favorers, Gen. 19. 22. and beloved ones,) now in many places, turn *Chams*, pointing and laughing at their *Fathers* real or seeming *nakedness*; Who drinking perhaps too much of the *new wine* of *state policies*, *opinions*, and *strange fashions* of *reformations*, possibly may have been so far overtaken with the strength of that thick and heady liquor, as to expose something of *shame* and *uncomliness* to the view of the wanton world; where, not strangers, open enemies, proud, and profaner aliens, but even Protestants, Professors, Domesticks, and near Allies, sit in the *highest seat of scorners*; inviting all the enemies of our Church, our Ministry, and our Reformed Religion, to the *theatre* of these times; Where, among other bloody and tragical spectacles, this is by some prepared for the *farce* and *interlude*; to expose by *Jesuitical engines* and *machinations*, the *learned* and *godly Ministers*, together with the whole *Ministry* of this Church of *England*, to be baited, mocked, and destroyed, with all maner of *irony*, *injuries*, and *insolency*: And alas, there are not many, that dare appear, to hinder the project; or redeem, either the persons, or the function; yea, many are afraid to pity them, or to plead for them.

Micah 6. 9. Θεὸς ἀεὶ μεμετρεῖ. The merciful hearted, and tender handed God, who smites us, (whose hand we should all see, and return to him, *who hath appointed this rod and punishment*) doth not use to make so deep wounds and incisions for little corruptions, which are but superficial and skin-deep; nor to shoot so sharp and *deadly arrows*, in the faces of those that *stand before him, as his Ministers*; unless they first provoke him to 1 Sam. 2. 22. his face, by their *grosser follies* in *Israel*, as *Eli's* sons did. Wherefore, I conceive, a further penitent search and discovery ought to be made of *Ministers' sins and failings*, for which the *Lord* hath brought

this

this great evil upon them; which although it be a *just punishment*, yet it may prove a *fatherly chastisement* to us all; and at once, both purge us, as fire from our dross, and by exciting those gifts and graces, truly *Christian* and *Ministerial* in us, it may prepare us, both for greater service, and ampler mercies, than ever yet we enjoyed, as *Ministers* in this Church; who have always lain under, and contended (since the *Reformation*,) not onely with the burthen of our own infirmities and defects, but also with the *evil eyes*, the *envious hearts*, the *sacrilegious hands*, the *prophane maners*, the *superstitious* and *factious humors* of many men, both open *enemies*, and *seeming friends*: Some mens innate leudness and pravity endures any thing easier, than an able and faithful *Minister*; others Cynical sourness grudges at any thing less, than to see *Ministers* enjoy either honor, or estate, beyond the vulgar: Both are ready to be severe censurers of *Ministers faults*, that so they may justifie their hatred or envy; but neither are likely to *judge righteous judgement*, nor shall we, I hope, ever stand to these mens sentence.

For my particular, I desire, both my self, and others of my minde and Profession, may by an *ingenuous acknowledgement* of our failings, be fitted for Gods and mans absolution, both in present and after ages; that it may not be said, The *Ministers* of *England* erred greatly, and were punished sharply, yet knew not how to repent humbly, and truly; every one palliating their own errors, and transferring the blame and guilt still upon others, when themselves were in somethings more blamable than any men, and merited, in their own censure, to be esteemed the chief of sinners. 6. *What is conceived the true cause.*

Nihil pudori esse debet pænitenti nisi non fateri. Ambr. de Pœn.

Of true Honor.

You then, O excellent Christians, know (in general) That all *true honor* from man, is but the *agnition* or *reflexion* of those Virtues and Graces, by which men are, or appear likest to God; that is, truly good and useful to others: From God, *honor* bestowed on any men, is a testifying before men (in some way of his providence) his approbation of those graces and endeavors in us; by which we draw neerest to that resemblance of the *Divine goodness*, and *holiness*, which is lively set forth in the Word of God, and the example of Jesus Christ; who is the visible *express image of the fathers glory*: By the gracious imitation of which glory, *human nature* attains and partakes somthing of the *divine*; and by a kinde of transfiguration both of minde and maners (as *Moses* and *Elias* in *Christs* company on the Mount) both Christian Magistrates and Ministers, acting in holy and good ways, cannot fail by sincere honoring of God, to attain that *honor* which *God hath promised*; which consists, not so much in those preferments and applauses of the world, (which are for the most part vain, like it self;) but in that *holy wisdom*, *gravity*, and *constancy*, which becomes a Christian, either in wel-doing, or in comly suffering,

Θεῖον ἀγαθὸν τιμή. Plato de leg. Dial. 5. τῶν καλῶν ἕπεσθαι τίμιον. Id.

τοῦ ἀξιώματος τὴν ἀρετὴν ὁρῶν. Plat. Heb. 1. 2 Pet. 1. 4.

1 Sam. 2. 30. Those that honor me, I will honor.

according to the clear will of God in his Word; which gives both precepts and paterns of all true excellencies. The robes of *true honor* are not made of the slight and thin Cob-webs of popular opinions and practises; but are (*tela crassiore*) of more solid and substantial virtues, as *Gonsalvo* said. Worthy actions do always, not onely joy the soul, calm the conscience, and strengthen the heart; but also they make the face of good men to shine; conciliating such a *majesty to virtue*, and such *beauty* to *true holiness*, that even those who hate, and persecute them, (as to the interests of their worldly lusts) cannot in their judgements, but approve, reverence, and esteem them, even in the midst of their sufferings; which do not less honor and adorn them, than their wel-doings: For nothing discountenanceth a Christian, but the conscience of *vile actions*, and *Gods displeasure*. In the judicious and constant way of holy walking, and honorably *suffering*, no man can *lightly speak evil of another*, without a secret shame, and reproach to himself; nor injure, or despight them, without some inward regret and pain.

Phil. 1. 29. ὑμῖν ἐχαρίσθη; To you it is given, as a free favor; not onely to believe, but to suffer.

Pati pro Christo, honorarium Christiani. Ber.

And certainly, the Christian World here in *England*, (which owed and owned as much to their *Ministers* heretofore, and esteemed them as highly, and treated them as honorably and ingenuously, as any people under Heaven could do their *Teachers in Religion*) would never have so much opened their mouths, and withdrawn their love and respects from many, if not most Ministers; nor would some men have dared so far to meditate, and endeavor their total ruine and extirpation; if we Ministers had not in some things (beyond the *venials of common infirmity*) either much exceeded, or come very short of those due bounds, wherein true Christian virtues, and especially Ministers excellencies do consist.

7. *The ordinary failings of Ministers, not the cause of their lapse.*

Nor is it to be thought here, that the eyes of men are so severely fixt, onely, or chiefly, upon the *ordinary defects* of Ministers, either in gifts or industry, proper to their calling; Although (God knows) even herein too many of us may be justly blamed, and without injury despised; as either wanting those ministerial abilities, which we might by prayer and study attain; wherewith competently to discharge, and adorn that sacred Work, and redeem it from vulgar invasion, which brings the highest contempt of it. The *ignorance, idleness, indiligence*, and *needless non-residency* of some of us, from our charges, is not to be concealed. In others, the neglect of our studies, both in Divinity, and in all kindes of good learning, by which our *profiting might appear to all men*, is to be deplored: It is not expectable, that Ministers should increase in *favor with God and man*, unless (as Christ did) they grow in *wisdom* too, as well as in age or stature: And alas, what fruit of honor to Ministers, or glory to God, or good to mens souls, can be reaped, either from those that

1 Tim. 4. 15.

Luke 2. 52.

Preach

Preach and Pray, chiefly for applause and popular air; taking much pains to little or no purpose; or yet from that contrary descending of others in their preaching to such a *popular flatness*, which stretcheth forth *dead sermons*, and *spiritless prayers*, meerly to an excessive length, (as if the *Pulpits* were their *Coffins*;) with so much *insipidness*, *vain repetitions*, *vulgar flattery*, *senseless oratory*; yea, and sometimes with strange *figures of Blasphemies*, which maner of some mens preaching hath given (we see) the very meanest sort of hearers (who heretofore were wonted to more *useful*, and more *sober preaching* and *praying*;) if they have any thing of parts, or *pragmaticalness* in them, not so much a *presumption*, as a *just confidence*, that they can both preach and pray, as well or better, than such *lazy*, *supine*, *superficial*, and empty *Ministers*; whose *duller plainness*, and *ruder fervency*, is not that *demonstration of the spirit*, which sets forth *divine truths* in their *native Scripture-simplicity*; which is their greatest strength and beauty (as the Sun's, when it shines freest from all mists and cloudings;) Nor are those mens *rebust* and *deformed heats*, that *judicious zeal*, which becomes grave Ministers, both as *sober men*, and *holy Orators* from God to the Church: For expressions ought always to be proportioned, in true *oratory*, to the weight of the matter in hand: Yea, where the unaffected quicknings of a Ministers own *spirit*, or the *dulness* of his *Auditors*, requires more than ordinary vehemency; yet still it must be carried with very comly heats and emotions, either for voice or gesture; but all the whole *Pageantry* of some mens preaching is, onely a gratifying their own fancies and passions, or else a miserable way of *mocking God*, and cheating the poor peoples souls; who (some of them) are as well content with chaff, as with good corn, or the *bread of life*; and if the flail be still going, they care not what grist ariseth: Others thirsting for the pure and wholesom waters of life, the *idleness* and *poverty* of these men, gives them to drink, onely of that ([illegible]) water, which is at their doors; in the shallow *plashes* and *foul puddles* of their own dull inventions; where their sudden and confused thoughts are oftentimes sooner out of their mouths, than in their mindes: And this for want of either ability, or industry, to dig to the depths of those *sacred springs*, the *Scriptures*; which chiefly afford that *living water*, which can refresh thirsting, wash polluted, and save sinful souls; which are not to be wrought upon by flat, or fine notions, by soft expressions, or by feminine insinuations; but by *sound demonstrations*, *learned arguings*, *serious convictions*, and *masculine ways of expressions*; such as become the *Embassie* and *Embassadors of God to man*.

Bonorum ingeniorum insignis est indoles in verbis verum amare non verba. August.

Planctum malo, quàm plausum.

2 Cor. 2. 4.

Conciones sacræ nec rudes esse debent, nec delicatæ, nec cincinnatæ, nec impexæ: Simplex quædam gravitas & subtilis soliditas adsit, quæ pondus & ornatum deferat. Zanch. Orat.

Sermonis vis & actionis vehementia materiei pondere æquanda. Quint.

Lucens putrido, Scenæ in cathedram translatio.

Multi tædio investigandæ veritatis ad proximos divertunt errores. Min. Fæl.

2 Cor. 5. 20.

But, as not these *Ministerial defects*, in their peculiar *Function*; so neither are they the *private immoralities* of their lifes (which usually attend the negligence of their *calling*, and bring many scandals upon both their persons, and their function. These are not the *spots*, or that kinde of *leprosie*, which could have thus made the whole body of their profession to be esteemed by many as unclean: For under these personal failings and deformities, (wherein some, and it may be too many of us, have been blamable in all times,) yet still, that abilitie, soundness, and diligence, which was found in many other worthy Ministers, both as to their *learning* and *piety*, was sufficient to preserve the dignity and venerableness of the function, from general obloquy, and contempt; nor ever was it brought to that *precipice*, where now it seems to stand, both as to disrespect, and danger.

8. *The main cause, as some conceive.* Until, that those *thick clouds*, and *grosser vapors* (heretofore unknown among *Protestant Ministers* in *England*) like a *Scotch mist*, or *Egyptian darkness*, came over the whole Firmament (almost) of this Church; *darkning*, and *turning into Blood*, even many of those Stars of the second and third magnitude, at least; which formerly shined, without blemish, in the soundness of their judgement, welguided zeals, meekness of their spirits, and diligence in their places, to all exemplary holiness; who (good men) probably did not know, while their *nails* were pared, and kept short, by the Laws and Government above them, how much they could scratch (even till the blood came) if once the liberty of times suffered them to grow so long, that some mens secular projects might use them, as the Ape did the Cats paw. Then indeed it soon appeared, that though *Ministers* might be *well-gifted*, and *well-affected men*, as to the *Reformed Religion*, to the Laws, and all publick Relations, yet they were *but men*; yea, though they were able and useful, while *fixed* in their *Ecclesiastical* orb and sphere; yet when they came to be *planetary* and *excentrick* to that duty and modesty, which the Laws of God and man most exactly require of them, as *lights* and *paterns* to others, than did their *beams* and *influences* begin to grow *malign*, *fiery*, and *combustive*.

Hence too many *Ministers* are looked upon, (how justly God knows; and the World, with their *own consciences*, not I, must judge) as *great incendiaries*; full of violence, immoderation, tumultuary heats, and passionate transports; beyond, what was either comly, or just for grave men of their calm and sober profession; into which high distempers, it was as easie for men of learned parts, of zealous spirits, and little experience in humane publick affairs, especially that of a Civil war, to fall; as for *constitutions* of *high colour*, and *sanguine complexion*, to lapse into *Feavers* or *Calentures*; which by degrees, if not allayed, bring the wisest and strongest men to ravings, and fits of distraction: Such did those *violent fits* and

inordinate

inordinate activities seem to be (upon the second thoughts and cooler reflexions of people) wherein many Ministers, so much, and so busily, appeared in *Senates* and *Armies*; in *Conventicles* and *Tumults*; more like *Statesmen, Politicians*, and *Soldiers*; or what became onely light and vain persons, than like *learned, grave*, and *godly men*; such as were called to a *spiritual, holy*, and *unbloody warfare*: This forwardness in sanguinary motions, rendred *Ministers* vile, and contemned, even to those, who were content to use their uncomly activities. The sound of Trumpets, the clashing of Swords, the thundring of Canons, were not a newer and greater terror to mens ears in *England*, than were those *bold Philippicks*, those *bitter Orations*, those *sharp Invectives*, those *cruel Railings*, used by some Ministers, even in their *Prayers* and *Preachings*, against those, to whom they formerly shewed a fair compliance and subjection: Who, if they had deserved *evil language*, and *railing accusations*, yet of all men these did not become the mouths of *Ministers*; who should in publick appear, as the *Angels of God*; with such modesty, light, and beauty, as sets them farthest off from any passionate darkness of minde, or deformity of maners, or undecency of expressions. Since Christ hath commanded them most eminently to bless those that curse them; to pray for those that persecute them, &c.

λόγος χαριεντισμοῖς, ὀχλικοῖς καὶ παρέργου βωμολοχίας πλήρης. Plat. *in Pericle.*

After these, followed other *vials of wrath*, (poured forth from those, who should have been onely *Pitchers* with *Lamps*, filled with *holy oyl*, and fired onely with *holy fire*,) *strange and new prodigies of opinions*, in *doctrine, government*, and *maners*; *sudden* and *violent changes* (like wilde-fire) running even to all extremes; greater *jealousies* and *impatiences* of *sufferings*, than of *sinning*: *Fierceness* to be revenged upon any, by whom they sometimes thought themselves injured in the least measure, when it may be, it was not the man, as the Law, by which they suffered. (Judges 7. 20.)

Yea, when some *Ministers* were gratified with such *measures of revenge*, as might move even *envy* it self to pity those persons, who suffered indeed justly from God for their sins; yet from man, they chose affliction, rather than sin: Yet still many Ministers followed with severe censures, and harsh declamings, even the miseries of those their Brethren, or Fathers; (who were in all true worth, equal to them, and in many things, as well as in an envied *authority*, above them;) Yet in those *sad ruines* of some *learned, grave*, and *godly men*, they seemed to *glory*; casting *faggots of calumnies* into their fires; shewing so little pity, and so much severity to them in *calamities*, That it will be no wonder to see many of their own *Thumbs and Toes cut off*; and themselves brought to creep under, even enemies tables, for their Bread; who helped or joyed so cruelly in maiming others, and bringing them even to a morsel of bread: Shewing (Judges 1. 7.)

 less

less pity and humanity to their destroyed Brethren and Fathers, than
Judges 21. 2. the *Israelites* did to the *wasted Benjamites*; more rejoycing in the victory of a party, than deploring the sin, disorders, and miseries of the whole.

The *mean complyings* also of some *Ministers*, with those *weaknesses* and *extravagancies* of some *mens opinions* and *practises in Religion*, which they then knew, or suspected to be evil and dangerous; of which, they have since been forced oft to complain with bitterness of soul, for want of *timely reproving*, and *resolute opposing*: Adde to these, what is frequently observed, and with great scandal, Their *shiftings* and *variatings* from one *living* to another, under pretence of *Gods*, or the *peoples call*, (where the greater *benefice* is always the *louder voice*, and most *effectual call*) being always deaf to any thing, that may in any kinde diminish their *profit*, or *preferment*: Still seising (like *ravenous Birds* and *Beasts*, or cunning *Woodmen*) on any prey they can espie; upon which they gain by a thousand windings, and wily ambushes, though never so injurious to the true owners, even their *Fellow Ministers*, and their whole Families.

These, and such like frequent publick passages, together with some *Ministers* most imprudent neglects of opportunities, sometimes offered, and much in their power, by which, to have brought differences to an happy composure, especially in matters of Religion; which were neither great nor hard to have been reconciled by men of *true Prudence* and *Christian moderation*; (which *virtues* have great influence in things of extern form and policy in the *Church of Christ*:) The fatal omissions and rejections of fair offers; those cruel defeats also which have followed after, and the unsuccessful blastings of all those plausible projects, and specious designs, which many of them had, for some time, driven on (as *Jehu*) very furiously, and as they thought very *triumphantly*; These, I say, and the like notorious imprudences, if not scandalous impieties, seem to many *sober men*, to have been among the chief *mists* and *clouds*, both of *folly* and *infamy*, which have risen from too many *Ministers lives* and *maners*, and so much eclipsed the glory and face of their whole Function, which they have rendred too many men suspected, as having more of the Jesuitick cunning and activity, than of that meek and quiet spirit which was so eminent in *Jesus Christ*; That from a *pragmatical fierceness* (which sought to have an Oar in every Boat) many *Ministers* are by many thought so superfluous, both in *Church* and *State*, that they are ready to throw them all over-board; as thinking there is no use of them, neither in the *sad solemnities* of *Christians burial* (who beyond all men, dying in the *Lord*, and in hope of a *blessed Resurrection*, ought not to be buried with the burial of an *Ass*, or an *Infidel*) nor in the joyful celebrities of *mariage*, where there needs not onely much of *humane prudence*, as to choice; but more of *divine benediction*, as to the holy use, and happy successe of *mariage*, which among *true Christians*, ought to be *in the Lord*; and so may, very well, bear the *publick benediction* of those, who are to *bless* the people *in the name of the Lord*; yea, even in matters peculiar to their office, and ever so esteemed, and used in the Church of Christ, both as to the Church-Government, Discipline, and holy Ministrations, of Prayer, Preaching, and Sacramental Celebrations, are Ministers, by many, thought more easily to be spared, and dispenced withal, as to any *publick necessity*; than any *Bailiff* in an Hundred, or a *Constable* in a Village: And no wonder, for nothing is more ordinary, than for the most excellent things, once degenerated to abuses, so far to lapse in the opinion and esteem of *vulgar* and *passionate mindes*, that they are ready, foolishly to wish, and greedily to welcome, the *total disuse* and *abolition* of them.

Preceps est vulgi animus, &c. insano impetu à rerum abusu, adversus usum ipsum propellitur, Petrarch.

9.
The dishonor cast by some upon the Ministers of England.

I cannot write it, and I hope no good *Protestant*, or true *English heart*, will read it, without grief and shame, That I have lived to see that verified and fulfilled in too great measure, which * *Campian*, an *Eloquent railer*, sometimes wrote (not with more malice, than apparent falsity, at that time, when the *state of the Ministry in England* had not more of *publick favor*, than of *true honor and merit*, both for *learning*, *piety*, and *order*,) *Nothing* (saith he) *is more putid and contemptible, than the English Clergy*. O that this reproach were with *truth* now to be *contradicted*, or *confuted*; which hath so heavily befaln us, and so justly; since too many Ministers became so *pragmatick*, so *impertinent*, so *unsuccessful in State policies*, in *worldly projects*, in *secular agitations*, in *counsels and actions* of *war and blood*, which they have agitated more intensively, than *Church affairs* and matters properly *religious*. How odious must it needs be, when they are publickly seen so vastly differing from that *Spirit of the Gospel*, which they Preach? So disguised in their *Habit*? so degenerating from their *Calling*? so different from the *rule and example of the Lord Jesus Christ*, of the *holy Apostles*, of the *blessed Martyrs*, of the *primitive Bishops*, *Presbyters*, and *Confessors*? These might be seen (possibly) after the patern of their *Saviour*, *riding meekly on an Ass*, or, as *Ignatius*, on some *vile beast*, to be *crucified*; but they were never met, on *red, and pale, and black horses*; threatning blood, and war, and famine, and death, to the *Ages*, and *Churches*, in which they lived: By the imitation of whose *wisdom from above*, *which was pure, and peaceable, and gentle, and easie to be intreated*; by walking in the *good old ways of meekness, patience, gentleness, and Christian Charity*, *Ministers* were heretofore so highly esteemed, in this

* *Campian.* 10. Ratio. *Nihil Clero Anlicano putidius.*

Rev. 6.

Jam. 3. 17.

Church-men, by Civil and Canon Laws, were forbidden to have any thing to do in matters of blood, though but in a way of Civil Judicature. Among the *Romans*, *Pontifici non licuit quenquam occidere*. Suet. in Vespas.

this Church, That nothing was thought too much, or too dear for them: But, when by *worldly passions* and *secular engagements*, they are found *too light for the balance of the Sanctuary*, (where onely learned humility gives weight, and an holy gravity to them;) when these *sons of God* court the *daughters of men*, and disguise themselves into the forms of *Politicians*; when they carry on vain and violent projects, and opinions, by pride, choler, fierceness, tumultuariness, faction, and sedition; or by rusticity, grossness, levity, and credulity, or in ways of scurrility, popularity, and cruelty; when to advance themselves to some shew of power, they cry up the *Scepter* and * *Kingdom of Jesus Christ*, to be carried on, *after the fashions of this world*, with Arms and Engines of War, to be erected upon the Bones and Skulls of their Brethren and Fathers; when Reformation of Religion must be squallid, and besmeared with the blood of Christians; when they make the Throne of *Christ* to be supported, as *Solomons* on both sides, with Lyons, or Tigers, Bears and Wolves, instead of Lambs and Doves: As if *Ministers* had changed, or lost, their meek, humble, patient, silent, crucified *Messias*, and had got some *Mauzzim*; a *Mahumetan God of forces*; who is to be served in * *Buff-Coats*, and *Armor*, with the (*Opima spolia*) the goodly spoils and victims of slain Christians, their Neighbors, Brethren, and Fathers.

Alas, who is so blinde as not to see; who so dull, as not to consider, how destructive such distempers are (even in the justest secular conflicts) to the dignity; how contrary to the duty of true Ministers of the Gospel: Whose honor consists, in *meekness, patience, humility, constancy, diligence, charity, tenderness*, and *gravity* in their *Preaching, Praying*, and *Living*, joyned to *good learning*, and *sound knowledge*? The want of these *holy deportments* conjured up those evil *spirits of sacrilege, sedition, perjury, cruelty, contempt*, and *confusion*, against them, and among them, which are not easily laid again: No man, ordinarily, being ashamed to offer that measure of *scorn, evil speaking, ruine*, and *oppression*; which they see, even some *Ministers* themselves have offered liberally to their Brethren, and Betters: Who can make conscience to destroy those, that make so little, to consume and devour one another? And this, at length, with the greater *odium*, because with the greater defeat: Honest meaning Christians expecting nothing less than such conclusions from the specious premises of zeal for *Religion*, and a *through Reformation*; when it is too evident, how much, not onely the mindes and maners of men, but the general form and face of the *Christian* and *Reformed Religion*, was never tending to more deformity, either in *Doctrine, Government*, or *true Discipline*, than now it is; as other where, so in *England*, through the miscarriages of many *Ministers*, as well as *people*.

* John 18. 36. My Kingdom is not of this world; (*i. e.*) After the way and forms of the Kingdoms of the World. Luke 17. 21. The Kingdom of God is within you. Rom. 14. 17. For the Kingdom of God is not meat and drink, (much less, the flesh and blood of Christians) but righteousness and peace, &c. Dan. 11. 38.

* *Laudant Deum in tympano non in Choro. Classicum canunt non pacem prædicant. Janum aperiunt, quo clauso Christus natus: Bellonæ sacerdotes non ecclesiæ; Martis faces & titiones non Evangelii lumina; Cometæ infausti, pestes & dira omina; non stellæ salutares Christum prænunciantes:* Greg.

people. No wonder, if ordinary men (who naturally love not a Minister of Gods truth) do easily *disesteem* those, who so little *reverence themselves*, and their *holy Function*: No marvel, if men make so little conscience to hear, or believe them, whose actions so contradict, and palpably confute, their former doctrine and maners: Yea, many now make *conscience to neglect*, *despise*, *forsake*, and *separate* from them; yea, some seek utterly to depose and destroy them; not onely as *useless*, but as *dangerous* and *pernicious creatures*, who seem to have more of the Wolf and Fox, than of the Sheep and Lamb. Thus from *Ministers* of *Gods truth*, *peace*, and *salvation*, they are too much faln to be esteemed as *State-firebrands*, and by some as *vessels of wrath*, onely fitted for destruction: What was sometime cryed up as a commendable zeal (and who but *Phinehas* with his Javelin, was then thought fit to be a *Priest to the Lord!*) is now looked upon, as either *miserable folly*, or *detestable fury*.

10. *Ministers duty in civil dissentions.*

And certainly, (in the calmest representation of things) if some warmth of natural zeal, and sparks of humane affections, were allowable to *Ministers* (who are still but men) in *civil and secular affairs*; relating (as they thought) to the good and safety of their *Country*, their *Laws*, *Religion*, *Liberties*, *Estates*, and *Governors*; yet should these warmer *gleams in Ministers hearts*, rather have vented themselves *in soft dews and sweet showres*, than *in lightnings and hot thunderbolts*, or *coals of fire*: Their *politick Preaching*, their *earnest Prayers*, their *unfeigned Tears* should have attempered, both their own and other mens passionate heats and propensities to civil flames: They should, as * *the Priests of the Lord*, have stood and wept between the *Porch* and the *Altar*; crying mightily to *Heaven*, that God would *spare his Church*, and *people*; And with men on *Earth*, they should have interceded, that they would pity themselves, and one another. *Ministers* of all men, should have *studied*, *preached*, *prayed*, *wept*, and *fasted*, all sorts and degrees of men in this *Nation*, (who were so many ways neerly related to one another) into *calmness*, *moderation*, *Christian temper*, *forbearings*, *mutual condiscendings*, and *proneness to reconciliation*: If this would not do, they should have * *stood in the gap*, or lain prostrate (as *Cæcina* did) in the unhappy breach, and rather chose to be trodden under the feet of *Armies*, *Men*, and *Horses*, than to see the *woful day*, in which their *King*, and *Country-men*, and *Fellow Christians*, and *Brethren*, should rush into an *unnatural war*, to cut one anothers throats.

This I say, godly and tender-hearted Ministers should rather have done, than in the least kinde, have kindled or fomented such

Vide Joel 2. v. 3, 10, 11, 13, &c.

* V. 17. Let the Priests, the Ministers of the Lord weep: Let them say, Spare thy people, O Lord, &c.

* Ezek. 22. 30. I sought for a man, among them that should make up the hedg, and stand in the gap before me for the Land, that I should not destroy it, but I found none. Cæcina *cùm militet, nec autoritate, nec precibus, nec manu retinere possit, projectus in limine, miseratione demum, quia per legati corpus eundum erat, clausit viam.* Tacit. An. l. 1.

unnatural flames, and *unchristian fewds*; rudely intruding themselves into all Councels; full of restless sticklings, State agitatings, politick plottings, cunning insinnatings, putid flatterings, secret whisperings, evil surmisings, uncomly clamors, and rude exasperatings of fears to fewds, of jealousies to enmities, of misapprehensions to irreconcilable distances, especially in matters wherein their proper interests (as in those of *Church-Government* and *Discipline*) might seem any stop or difficulty to *peace*, or any occasion to *war*: Who concludes not, that in such violent deeds and demands, Ministers forgat and forsook the greatest honor and duty of their Function! which is, to be *blessed peace-makers*, to *beseech men* to be *reconciled to God*, and *for Christs sake* to one another; by whose *pretious blood*, they, above all men, should shew they are *redeemed* from those *fierce wraths*, and *cruel angers*, which cannot but be cursed; and merit to be *seriously* and *deeply repented*, lest for them, Ministers be divided in *Jacob*, and scattered in *Israel*. And however, many *hotter spirited Ministers*, might have honest hearts to God and man; yet it appears they had but weak heads, and were not aware, That *secular policies* and *worldly interests*, though they begin never so plausibly, and ascend like vapors from fair grounds, yet they presently thicken like mists into black clouds, drawing on jealousies and fears like strong winds: These drive men to new counsels; after they plead necessities; and from necessity obtain what indulgences and dispensations soever, either prosperity, or adversity require, in order to that great *Idol Self-preservation*; which even in the Church of Christ exalts it self above all that is called *God*; far different from *primitive practises*, which were in ways of *self-denial*, *Christian patience*, and *civil subjection*, *losing* their lives to *save them*; following of *Christ*, in taking up his *cross*, * when they wanted not numbers. All which holy Christian arts, by the unnecessary designs, precipitant counsels, and rash adventures, of some passionate, weak, or self-seeking men, are oft forced to vale, and give place to that, which is falsly called *Reason of State*; which loves not to be too straight-laced with any ties of *true* and *self-denying Religion*; whose passiveness is the best preservative, both of the Church, and of any true Minister whatsoever.

Matth. 5. 9. 2 Cor. 5. 20.

Gen. 49. 7.

* Tert. Apol. de Christianis, cap. 37. *Omnia vestra implevimus, urbes, insulas, castella, municipia, castra, palatium, senatum, forum, &c. Et tamen libenter trucidamur.* Et Cap. 30. *Precantes sumus semper pro omnibus Imperatoribus, &c.*

II.

Ministers much ow to themselves their shame.

All true and wise Ministers teach, (and so they should practise) That it is better *patiently to suffer* * some *deformities in Church*, and *pressures in State*, than to be *violent actors* of any new ones, as a means to reform the old. And since the mindes of men are generally prone to measure counsels, and purposes, by the events, they do easily conclude, That God never leaves a good cause (wherein his glory, and Churches good were said to be so highly interessed, so in the loss and lapse,) (as now the *Presbyterian* cause seems to be,)

* *Multa tolleravimus quæ non probamus*. Aug.

unless

unless it were carried on by *impure hearts*, or *unwashen hands*; either *hypocrisie* levening the *end*, or *iniquity* defiling the *means*: Truly it is seldom, that God waters good *plants* with so salt *streams*, as he hath done that, which some Ministers sought so resolutely to *plant* in the *Garden* of this *Church*, what *pains* or *perils* soever it cost them, or the publick.

So that the present dangers, distresses, and complaints of many Ministers seem to most people to be, but as the just *retributions* of *vengeance* upon the rude frowardness, and factious forwardness, of many of them in *civil troubles*, which was far different from the tender and wise charity of the good *Samaritan*. For these men finding this Church and State *much wounded*, as it was going from the *Jericho* of some *grievances*, to the *Jerusalem* of a *through Reformation*, (as was pretended) were too liberal of their *vinegar*, and too nigardly of their *oyl*; by *rash infusions*, by *undiscreet* and *unskilful searching* the *wounds*, they made them deeper, wider, more festred and incurable: (Clergy-mens hands usually poysoning those light hurts in State, which they touch, or undertake to cure, with neglect of their *Spiritual cures* and *callings*.) Luke 10. 30.

Thus justly, and usually there follows the black shadow of *shame* and *confusion*, when Ministers of the Church had rather appear *cunning active Statesmen*, than *honest quiet Churchmen*; studying *matchiavel*, more than the *Gospel*; as if they were ashamed of the still * *voice* and *quiet spirit* of *Jesus Christ*; which descended upon his *Apostles*, not in the *shape of flaming* and *dividing swords*, but off * *fiery cloven tongues*: And this, not to set the world on fire, or to scorch and burn men, but softly to enlighten them; and by variety of *gifts* and *graces*, sweetly to warm them to a love of God, and mutual charity: Which is far from bringing in, either *Christian Religion*, or any *Reformations*, with *wilde-fires*, *whirl-winds*, and *earth-quakes*; wherein *Christians* had rather quite cast off the *cross of Christ* from their shoulders, than bear it with any thing, which they count a *civil burthen*; and wherein the meanest *Ministers* are more ambitious to wear a peece of the *Popes Triple Crown* on their heads, in an imaginary parity of *power*, than either that of *thorns*, or that of *olive branches*; the one an embleme of their *patience*, the other of their *peaceableness*: When the very *Novices* and *Beardless striplings*, in the Ministry, which have but lately been manumitted from the *rod* and *ferula*, are more eager to *rule* and *govern* all in an *absolute community*, and *Country parity*, than either able to rule themselves, or patient to be ruled, even by those that are worthy to be their Fathers, as every way their Elders and Betters; whom *Age* and *Nature*, *Custom*, *Law*, *Reason*, *Religion*, all *order* and *polity* among men, would have set as over-seers over them; (howsoever,

* Mat. 12. 19. He shall not strive, nor cry, neither shall any men hear his voice in the streets.

Acts 2. 2.

* *Linguâ Evangelicâ propitiis ignibus, & mollissimo fervore, potenter at suaviter illuminare & perpurgare debent mentes ac mores hominum.* Greg.

 to

to some uses and ends, those, the yonger Preachers, may be fit to be set over others, as *Ushers* of *lower Forms*:) When the passions and exorbitancies of some *Ministers*, shall punish other mens failings and sins, with greater of their own; and exceed what was most blamable in others, by such defects of charity, or excesses of cruelty, as are most condemnable in such as hold forth the *love of God*, and *mercies of Christ* to the World. What stability can be hoped in mens esteem and love, to such as are of so *variable tempers*, that

Jam. 1. 8.

they are not *double, but treble minded men?* sometimes *Episcopal*, then *Presbyterian*, after *Independents*, next *nothing at all*, unless it be something of an *hobling Erastian*; who runs like a Badger, with variating and unequal *motions*, yet still keeping where the *ridg of secular power* goes highest; who is ashamed, not to seem a *Christian*, but yet afraid to be *taught* and *governed*, as *Christians* were in *primitive times*, when they had not the support of *Civil Magistrates*; whose *protection* in *Government* and *duties religious*, the *Church* willingly and thankfully embraces; but it cannot own the derivation of either its *Institutions*, or its *Discipline*, from *secular Powers* and *Laws*.

12.
Of changes in Ministers.

Not, that all *mutation* is the *companion* of *folly* or *weakness*; there are happy *inconstancies*, and *blessed Apostacies*; from *Error* to *Truth*; from *Heresie* and *Schism*, to *Verity* and *Catholike unity*; from *factious pride*, to *obedient humility*; from *impotent desires* of *governing*, to *patient submissions* under due and setled Government; from * the *Devils camps*, to *Gods Tents*. But then *truth*, and not *faction*; *piety*, and not apparent *self-interest*; a change of *maners* to the better, as well as of *side*, and *principles*, will follow; and not the least appearance once of *evil*. From which, *Ministers* of all men, must abstain. There must be no shew or shadow of worstings and decays in *holiness*; of greater indifferencies in *Religion*; of any licentiousness and immoralities in *maners*; any of which, discover their *bellies*, or this *world*, to be their god, more than *Jesus Christ*, or the *true God*.

* *A castris Diaboli ad Dei tentoria; Felix transfuga, & beatus Apostata.* Luth.

1 Thes. 5. 22.

Phil. 3. 19.

And (which is most ridiculous and intollerable) many *Ministers* in their greatest *ramblings* and *shiftings*, and *separatings* from themselves, and from all *gravity*, *order*, and *modesty*; deserting their former *Station*, *Ministry*, and *Ordination*; or taking it up upon some fanciful new way; some easie account of popular calling to any place; yet still they are many times *eager declamers* against *Sects* and *Schisms*, *Heresies* and *Separations*, *Errors* and *corrupt Opinions*, &c. that is against all that are not of their *party*, *way*, and *faction*: Not considering, that like *Gehazi*, the *leprose* of those *Syrians*, cleaves to many of their own foreheads, who carry their heads full high.

Now after all this, (which I reckon up, not in *bitterness*, but

in

in charity, not for a reproach *, but for a motive to repentance, in my self, or any other, that may be guilty of any thing, unworthy and scandalous to our *holy Profession* ;) It cannot seem strange, if Ministers are generally looked upon, as *naked* and *ashamed* of themselves ; since many of them, have wantonly *sinned* themselves out of that *innocency* and *protection* (together with that *love, respect, estate,* and *honor*) which formerly they enjoyed ; when *publicks Laws and Authority* compassed them about ; keeping them, as in *subjection* and *due obedience*, so in *plenty, safety, love,* and *respect*. Which last, (preserving them from irreverence, affronts, and vulgar insolency) is easily obtained; when once the common people see that *Power* stands Centinel, and *Civil Favor* keeps a Guard, on any Men, or any Calling. Indeed, with the common sort of people, it matters not much, what *straw* and *clouts* the *Scare-crow* be made of, so it be set upon a *Pole*.

* *Dum peccata aliorum confiteor, ipse compatiar, nec superbè increpo, sed lugeo ; & dum alium fleo meipsum defleo.* Ambr. de Pœn. l. 2. c. 8. Νόμ☉ κύριον, ἔστω καὶ φυλακὴ τοῖς ὑπηκόοις. Stobæus.

13. *Ministers way of recovery.*

By these *secular* and *worldly temptations*, hath the *Devil*, in great part, beguiled the *Ministers* and the *Ministry* of *England*, of that *favor*, and those *blessings* which they once enjoyed ; which to recover, by Gods help, must be the *work*, not of *weak, heady, popular, passionate, factious,* and *clamorous men* , who are resolved never to confess any * error or transport, but to continue in that troublesome and rugged path of *novel opinions, State projects,* and *secular ambitions* ; wherein they see they have lost themselves past all recovery, without ingenuous *retractation* and speedy *amendment*. The rashness and obstinacy of such *Uzzahs*, is not fit to stay the *tottering Ark*, who have almost quite overturned it ; nor ever will they be able to bring back the *pristine honor* of the *Ministry*, or the *majesty* of the *Reformed Religion* : Their *penitence, publick, real,* and as *bold* as their sin and error, will more recover and recommend them, than all those murmurings and complaints, by which they scratch one anothers *itch* ; and confirm each other in their *erroneous obstinacy,* and *defeated novelties*. * Ingenuous confessings and forsakings of their *follies, facilities, superstitious heats* and *immoderations*, will best reconcile them, not onely to God and man , but also to themselves : Who can have little peace, while they are pertinacious in their errors, and are impatient to recant any thing, either in opinion or practise, although never so much amiss and blasted, both by the disfavor of God and man. This opiniativeness and restiveness in extern *Forms* of *Religion*, is likely to be the greatest *obstruction*, which will hinder the recovery of *Ministers* to *unity , order,* and *honor* ; which was ever greatest, when for their painful *preaching*, and peaceable *living*, they were persecuted by others, *Heathens*, or *Hereticks*, or *Schismaticks* ; who never wanted will to vex the *Orthodox Christians*, when ever they had power ; were their beginings

* *Incidere in errorem imperiti est animi, at perseverare, postquam agnoveris, contumacis est.* Salvia. l. 5.

* *Verè pœnitentes pudoris magis memores, quàm salutis, esse non debent.* August.

ings never so gentle, and their pretensions never so specious: But then is the regard to Ministers least, or none at all, when they turn *Pragmaticks* instead of *Preachers*; *Persecutors* instead of *Peace-makers*; and *sticklers* for, and with the world, rather than sufferers with, and for *Christ*. Since, being Ministers of *Jesus Christ*, the *Lamb* slain for the sins of the World, they are more comly on *the rack*, and at *the stake*; in the *prison* and *dungeon*, with *bolts* and *chains*, with *wounds* and *brands* for Christs sake, than with *Buff-coats* and *Belts*, and *Banners*, and *Trophes*, dipped in and defiled with the * blood of their *People*, and *Neighbors*, and *Governors*, in any case whatsoever. Sure, it is hard for Ministers of the Gospel, to pick out *Letters of Mart* from the Gospel; or to have any *Commission* to kill and slay, from *Jesus Christ*; in order to reform Religion, or to plant any of his clearest Institutions; much less to pull down any antient good *orders* in the *Church*, or to set up any new ones; which have so much of mans *vanity* and *passion*, that they cannot have any thing of *Christs* divine appointment.

* πολεμικώτερον τοῖς ἱερεῦσιν ἐνθύμημα, καὶ λογικῶς ἐστ' ἐκ ὁπλιτικῶς, τὸ γὰρ καὶ χεῖρας ἀντιτυπεῖν στρατιωτῶν ἔξω τῆς ἀμετέρας αὐλῆς. Naz. Orat. 40.

Nor is this meek and passive temper, requisit in a true Minister, any softness and cowardise, but the greatest valor and magnanimity; which, having least of *revenge*, *passion*, *self-seeking*, *humane faction*, and *worldly interest*, (which are always dubious in their rise, and prone to be exorbitant in their progress, and most injurious in their success) have most of *Love*, *Patience*, and *Christian Charity*; which are indisputably commendable in the Christian, though they be to the mans own *hinderance*.

Psal. 15. 4.

It will not be asked of *Ministers of the Gospel*, at the last account, who fought, and slew, and spoiled, &c. but who fasted and prayed, and mourned, for the sins and judgements on the Nation, and Church; nor will they easily be found in *Gods Book of Martyrs*, who died upon disputable quarrels in *Civil Wars*, while they neglected the indisputable duty of their *Office and Ministery*.

Levit. 19. 19. Thou shalt not sow thy field with mingled seed. *Incongruam non probat mixturam Deus, & bonitate simplicissimus & simplicitate optimus.* August.

Ministers never reap less crops of love or respect from men, than when they sow that forbidden *mislane*; the *Tares* and *Cockle* of passionate novelties, unproved opinions, and civil dissentions, among the *seeds of Religion*, and *essays of Reformation*: From which mixtures, those Ministers, whose *gravity*, *wisdom*, and *humility*, have most withheld, or soonest withdrawn their hearts and hands, are the likeliest men, by their *piety*, *moderation*, *patience*, and *constancy*, in *holy* and *justifiable ways*, to recover and restore the dignity of their *Calling*; Who in the midst of those great and wide inrodes, which have much broken down the *fence*, and occasioned the letting in all sorts of *wilde beasts* upon the *Lords Vineyard* of this *Church*; while others, like *dead stakes*, formerly making a great shew in the *hedg*, are found rotten, weak, and unsound: These are evidenced to all

true

true Christians, to be as *living standards*; well rooted in their pious principles, and not easily removed from that *stedfastness*, and *meekness* of their practises in ways of *judicious constancy*; which they have hitherto with patience maintained, in the midst of those tempests, which have not so utterly overwhelmed them, but that in many places they appear fixed and unmoved in their *pious integrity*, and *patient charity*; which makes them looked upon with some eye of pity, love, and honor, by all ingenuous spectators; while yet, they generally reflect with scorn and laughter, on many others; who in the *publick storm*, thought themselves *gallant sailers* and *skilful steersmen*; yet having made great waste of their *patience*, *obedience*, and *discretion*, they seem also much crackt in their *conscience*, *credit*, and *reputation*; For seeking, inconsiderately, to pull down, or to possess themselves of others *Cabins*, (who as *Pilots* had a long time safely steered the *Ship*) they have almost split, and sunk the whole *Vessel*, wherein they and others were embarqued: Nor will they any way be able to buoy it up again, or stop the daily increasing, and threatning leaks, till forsaking those soft and shameful compliances with factious novelties, and immoderate ways of vulgar reformings, they return to that *primitive firmness*, and *indisputable simplicity* of the *Antient* (which were the purest and best formed) *Churches*, both as to *Doctrine*, *Discipline*, and *Government*; which no *learned* and *unpassionate man* needs go far to finde out, either in *Scripture paterns*, or in the *Churches after-imitation*; by which the *dignity* of the *Ministry*, and *Holy Mysteries* of the *Gospel*, always preserved themselves, amidst the hottest persecutions, both in the *love*, and *obedience* of all *sound* and *sober Christians*.

So that in my judgement, who know how hard it is to play an after-game in point of *Reputation*, and who have no design but a *Publick* and *Common good*, (writing thus freely, as under the favor, so without the offence, I hope, of any good man) The *Ministers* of this Church will never be able to stand before those men of *Ai*, their many adversaries; who are daily scattering them into many feeble factions, and pursuing them every where (so divided) with scorn; and afflicting them with many affronts and injuries; until having taken a *serious review* of their late extravagancies, and making a serious scrutiny into their consciences; and finding (as they needs must, if they be not wilfully blinde, or obstinate) some *accursed thing*, some *Babylonish garment*, and *wedg of Gold*; something wherein proud, or ambitious, or covetous, or revengeful, or injurious emulations; or other more venial errors have tempted them to offend; they cast them quite away; and so humbly re'ally themselves, to that *Primitive Harmony*; that *Excellent Discipline*, *Order*, and *Government*, wherein was the honor, beauty, and consistency

of

of the Church and Christian Religion, even when least protected and most opposed by secular powers: Of whom Christian Bishops, Ministers, and People, never asked leave, either to believe in *Jesus Christ*, or to live after that *holy form* and *publick order*; wherein *Jesus Christ*, and the *blessed Apostles* after him, established and left them, which obtained *universal imitation*, and use in all *Churches*, for many hundred of years, from *true Christians*, both *Pastors* and *People*, in the midst of persecutions.

14. Out of which *old* and *good way* of *Primitive Unity, Order, Government, Discipline*, and *holy Ministrations*, if those *immoralities* be kept, (as they may most easily) to which (we see) the lusts and passions of men are prone to run; even in all * *novel forms*, and *inventions*, (pretend they never so much, at first, to *glorious Reformations*;) Nothing can be a more present and soverein restorative for this Church, and the true Reformed Religion, to settle with truth, and peace among us; both to the comfort of all able Ministers, and the satisfaction of all sober Christians; who study the *truth*, and *unity* of the *Faith*, not the *power* and *prevalency* of any *faction*: We need not go far to seek the root and source of our miseries present or impendent, which have brought forth so bitter fruits; whereby God at once would shew and satisfie vain men with their own *delusions* *. In which, heady and high-minded men, trusting more to their own wits or tongues, and to the * *arm of flesh*, in politick machinations, than to the *living God*, in holy and humble ways of truth and peace, have soon found them to be, both *vain* and *cursed things*.

Jere. 6. 16. Thus saith the Lord, Stand in the ways and see, and ask for the old paths, where is the good way, and walk therein, and ye shall finde rest for your souls.

* *Non datur reditus ad unitatem nisi per veritatem, nec ad veritatem nisi per vetustatem; Quum illud est antiquissimum, quod verissimum.* Cypr.

* Isai. 66. 4. * Jere. 17. 5. Cursed be the man that trusteth in man, and maketh flesh his arm, and whose heart departeth from the Lord.

As it is evident at this day in the sad fate, which some Ministers folly, presumption, and precipitancy, together with other sinful frailtiles, and excesses, have brought upon themselves, and their whole Function in this Church. Who, first despising, then destroying the *Antient* and *Catholike conduits* of their *Order* and *Ministry*, (which, derived from *Christ*, by his *Apostles*; went on in an after constant succession of *true Ministerial Power* and *Authority*,) have *digged to themselves, empty, broken cisterns*, of novel and divided ways, which can hardly hold any water; but *like wandring clouds without water*, affecting Supremacy, or Parity, or Popularity in Church power; they have almost brought it to a nullity; through the incroaching and over-bearing of *Plebeian Insolence*; who finding Ministers thus divided among themselves, and scrambling for *Church power* in common, without any order or distinction, either of *age*, or *gifts* and *parts*; the common people (being the most) begin to conceit and

Jere. 2. 13.

Jude 12.

and challenge to themſelves, firſt a ſhare, next the ſupremacy and original of all Church power; as if in the illiterate heads, illiberal hearts, and mechanick hands of the common ſort of Chriſtians, (and, without reproach, the moſt part of them, and the forwardeſt of them, againſt the Function of the Miniſtry, have been and ever will be of no higher rank, breeding or capacity,) *Jeſus Chriſt* had placed the *Keyes of Heaven*, the power eminent and paramount of all *Church* authority, and holy adminiſtrations; which *Chriſt* eminently, and his *Apoſtles* miniſterially had, and exerciſed; afterward committing them to able and faithful men; ſuch as (doubtleſs) were many degrees raiſed above the vulgar, and diſtinguiſhed in gifts and power Miniſterial, both ordinary and extraordinary.

Thus from the head, and ſhoulders, and arms, (*Jeſus Chriſt*, the *Apoſtles*, the ſucceeding *Biſhops* and *Presbyters*) which were of Gold and Silver, *Church power* is by ſome forced to deſcend to the *belly, thighs*, and *feet of the people*, which are part of Iron, and part of miry-clay: Moſt of whom, ſo much ſtickling to be *controlers of Chriſts houſhold* (the Church) are not in any diſcreet and ſober mans judgement, fit to be *ſtewards*, or ſcarce in any degree of ingenuous ſervice, in a well ordered family; They may make good *Gibeonites* for the houſe of God, but very ill *Levites* or *Prieſts*. **Dan. 2. 32.**

Thus I have ſhewed how the ſparks of many Miniſters paſſionate opinions, and violent practiſes, flying up and down in their many diſorderly breathings and extravagant *Motions*, both in *Church* and *State*; they at laſt, lighting upon the *thatched houſes*, the combuſtible ſtuff of common peoples mindes, and maners, have ſet their own houſes on fire, to the deformity, diſcontent, and danger of all that dare own themſelves, and their holy Function, as delivered to them from a better and *diviner hand*.

And indeed it is of the *Lords mercies*, that we have not been, ere this, utterly conſumed both *root and branch*, for our follies and ſtrange fires, by the malice, cruelty, and deſpight of thoſe, to whoſe rage, as to the Seas, the Lord hath hitherto ſet bounds; who are our enemies, not for our *ſins* and *failings*, but for the *reformed truths*, and *Goſpels* ſake, which we *preach* and *profeſs*. Amidſt the *ſequeſtrings, plunderings, ſilencings, waſtings, affronts, calumnies, indignities*, and *diſcouragements* caſt upon, or threatned by ſome, againſt thoſe of the Miniſtry, above any other calling; as if the Croſſes taken down from Steeples and Churches, were to be laid on the necks and ſhoulders of Miniſters; It is a wonder, that any *remnant* of godly, able, and true Miniſters, hath hitherto eſcaped, through the indulgence of God, and the favor or moderation of ſome in *power*; who know not (it ſeems) how to *reprobate* all thoſe as *Antichriſtian*, by whoſe *Miniſtry*, they may hope, themſelves and others, either are, or may be 15.

brought to the *saving faith* of *Jesus Christ*; and to the *hope of Gods elect*. Nor can they yet be perswaded, to act as *Pharaohs*, that knew not *Joseph*.

Exod. 1. 8.

So that we cannot, but wonder (with thankfulness to God, and to those who now exercise *civil power* amongus) that, the *Reformed Ministers* and *Ministry* in this *Church*, have not been made like *Sodom* and *Gomorrah*; when we consider, how many showres of *fiery darts*, from *violent* and *cruel men*, like thick clouds (pregnant with *thunders* and *lightnings*) hang over our heads. Who like *Julian* the Apostate, are impatient of nothing so much as this, That their should be any true *Ministers* or *Ministry*, in *due order*, *holy Authority*, *Evangelical succession*, and *setled maintenance*, continued in this, or any other Reformed Church. Who seeking to joyn the *Lyons* skin to the *Fox's*, would fain leven *Military spirits* against the *Ministry*, that so the Soldiery might use, or rather abuse, their *Helmets* as *Bushels* *, under which they may put the *Candles* of the *Ministry*; thereby to overwhelm and extinguish those *lamps* of *true Religion*; pretending, that some *Troopers flaming swords*, as the *guard of Cherubims*, will be more useful to keep *the way of the tree of life*, than all those *burning* and *shining lights* of the true *Ministers*, who are rightly *called* and *ordained* in the *Church*; whose *learned labors*, and *patient sufferings* in all ages, from the *Apostles* times, have undoubtedly planted, watered, propagated, and (under God) preserved the *true Christian Religion*; either from *Heathenish ignorance*, *Idolatry*, *Atheism*, *Prophaneness* and *Persecution*, on the one side; or from *Antichristian Errors*, *Superstitions*, *Corruptions* and *Confusions*, on the other.

Julian took away from the Clergy, all immunities, honors, and provisions of corn formerly by Emperors given to them; he abrogated all Laws in favor of them. *Sozomen. l. 5. c. 5.*

* Matth. 5. 15.

16. *Politick and Atheistical Engines used by some against the Ministry.*

Yet are there now, not onely *secret underminings*, but *open engines* used, by which some men endeavor utterly to overthrow these great boundaries, firm supports, and divine constitutions of Christian Religion; the Authority, Office, Power, and Succession of the true Ministers, and Ministry of the Gospel: Which plots and practises can be nothing else, but the *devils high-way*, either to utter *Atheism*, *Irreligion*, and *Prophaneness*; or to the old *grosser Popery*, *Error*, and *Superstition*; or, at best, to those detestable and damnable *formalities* in matters of Religion, which our late *Seraphick Sadduces*, or *Matchiavellian Christians* have learned, and confidently profess. Some of whom (like *Jezebel*, that made her self a *Prophetess*, or like the old * *Gnosticks*, *Montanists*, *Maniches*, *Carpocratians*, *Circumcellians*, *Valentinians*, and the like rabble of wretches) have their *wilde speculations*, beyond what is written in the holy Scriptures, or ever believed and practised in the Churches of Christ; who

Rev. 2. 20.

* Irenæus l. 1. c. 35. *Carpocratis & Gnosticorum doctrina, per fidem & operationem salvari homines; reliqua indifferentia secundum opinionem hominum bona aut mala vocari; cum nihil natura malum sit.*

teach

teach men to think, say, and write, That *God*, *Christ Jesus*, the *holy Spirit*, good *Angels* and *Devils*; the *Scriptures*, *Law*, and *Gospel*, *Ministry* and *Sacraments*; the *Souls immortality* and *eternity*; the *Resurrection* and *Judgement* to come; all *Virtue* and *Vice*; *Good* and *Evil*; *Heaven* and *Hell*, all are but meer fanciful forms of words, fabulous imaginations, feigned dreams, empty names; being nothing without us, or above us. That all this, which men call Religion, is nothing else, but the issues of *humane inventions*; which, by the cunning of some, the credulity of others, and the custom of most men, serves, where seconded with power, to scare and amuse the world, so as to keep the vulgar in some aw and subjection.

And in their best and soberest temper, they hold, That no Religion is, or ought to be other, than a *lackey* and *dependant*, on *secular power*; that *piety* must be *subordinate* to *policy*; that there the people serve God well enough, where they are kept in subjection to those that rule them: From whose politick dispensations and allowances, they are humbly and contentedly to receive what *Scriptures*, *Law*, and *Gospel*, *holy Institutions*, *Ministry*, and *Religion*, those, who govern them, think fittest, whereby to preserve themselves in power, and others in peace under them. That, where the *principles* of *Christian*, or *Reformed Religion* (which hath so far obtained credit in these Western parts of the World) do cross, or condemn the designs, and interests of those in Sovereinty, (how unjustifiable soever they are for *righteousness* or *true holiness*;) yet are they, by *Reasons of State*, and the *supposed Laws of Necessity*, first to be dispensed withall, and actually violated: Next, by *secret warpings*, *variations*, *connivencies*, and *tollerations*, they are to be *ravelled*, *weakned*, *discountenanced*, and *decryed*. Thus gradually, and slily introducing *new parties* and *factions* in *Religion*; which, cryed up by men of looser principles, profaner wits, and flattering tongues; also set off and sweetned with novelty, profit, and power, will soon bear down, and cast out, with specious shews, of easier, cheaper, freer, and safer modellings, all true *Religion*, and the true *Ministry* of it; and all the antient, (if they seem contrariant ways) though never so well setled, and approved, not onely by the best and holiest of men; but, as to their constant preservation, even by God himself.

17. *Ambition: the Moth of true Religion.*

Indeed, all experience teacheth us, That no passion in the soul of man is less patient of sober, just, and truly religious bounds, than * *Ambition*; which will rather adventure, as it were, to *countermand*, and *over-rule God himself*, than fail to rule over man. Nor

* *Luctanter & ægrè fert humana ambitio Christi jugum, aut Dei Imperium; nec libenter crucem gestant qui sceptra captant & diademata aucupantur.* Parisiens.

hath any thing caused more changes, tossings, and persecutions, in the Church, than this forcing *religious rectitudes*, and the *immutable rules* of *divine Truth*, *Order*, and *holy Institutions*, to bend to, and comply with, the * crookedness of ambitious worldly * interests. Insomuch, that very *Reformations pretended*, and by well meaning men *intended*, have oftentimes degenerated to great *deformities*; through the immoderations, and transports of those, who cannot in *reason of State* (as they pretend) subject themselves to, or continue to use those severer rules of *righteousness*; or follow those primitive examples of holy *Discipline* and *Religious orders*, which Christ and his Church hath set before them; but they must so far wrest and innovate *Religion*, formerly established, and remove the *antient Landmarks*, which their forefathers observed, as they finde, or fancy necessary to the interest of that party or power, which they have undertaken.

* *Cupido dominandi cunctis affectibus dominantior.* Tacit. An. l. 15.
* *Regnandi causa violandum est jus, cæteris æquitatem cole.* Jul. Cæs. Suet.

Hence inevitably follows by those *unreasonable* * *Reasons of State*, (which, not the Word of God, nor his providence, nor any true prudence, but onely some mens fancies, passions, lusts, and follies, make *necessary*,) That the antient established Ministry, and true Ministers, be they never so able, worthy, useful, and necessary, must either be quite removed, and changed; or else, by degrees drawn to new *Modellings* and *Conformities*; which can never be done, without great snares to many, injuries to others, and discouragements to all, that have any thing in them of *Religious setledness*; whose pious and judicious constancy in their holy way and profession, chusing rather to *serve the Lord, than the variating humors of any men and times*, shall be judged pertinacy, faction, and the next step to *Rebellion*; how useful, peaceable, and commendable soever their gifts, and mindes, and maners be, in the Church of Christ.

* Pope *Pius* the fifth, could not with patience hear of *Ragioni di Stato*, counting those pretensions to be against all true Religion, and Moral Virtues. *L. Verul.*

18\. To this *Tarpeian* rock, and precipice, by Gods permission, and the *English* worlds variation in *Civil and Ecclesiastical* affairs, doth seem to be brought (as to some mens designs and purposes) the whole frame and being of the *Reformed Religion* in this *Church* of *England*, as to its formerly established *Doctrine*, *Discipline*, *Government*, and true *Ministry*: Not, but that I know, the *Lord Jesus Christ* can withdraw this his Church and Ministers (as he did himself) from their malice, who sought to *cast him down headlong* from the browe of that *Hill*, on which their City stood: I know he is as willing, able, and careful to save his *faithful servants*, as himself. And who knows, how far God may be pleased to use (as he did the relation of the * *captive maid*, in order to his mercy, both for *healing* and *converting Naaman*) this *humble Intercession* and *Apology* of

Luke 4. 30.

2 Kings 5.

* *Sermonem ancillæ sequitur heri sanitas; per servulam captivam liberatur leprosus Dominus: De parvo momento pendent res magni momenti; ne vel minima Dei aspernemur.* August.

the

the meaneſt of his ſervants? who ows all he is, hath, or can do, to his bounty and mercy. God oft hangs great weights on ſmall wires, and ſets great wheels on work by little ſprings. We know, that *words ſpoken in due ſeaſon*, before *the * decree be gone forth*, may be acceptable and powerful, even with God himſelf; how much more ſhould they be *as * Apples of Gold in Pictures of Silver*, to ſober and religious men; and in the behalf of thoſe, who (at leaſt) have deſerved to be heard, before they be condemned and deſtroyed?

Zach. 2. 2. * *Monet Deus de propoſito ut prævenïamus decretum; quaſi à nobis pœnitentibus pœnitentiam diſcat dominus.* Fulgent. * Prov. 25. 11. *Verba tam ſplendida quàm pretioſa, & pietate bona, & tempeſtivitate grata.* Bern.

I have read of *Sabbacus*, a King of *Ethiopia*, who being by * dreams admoniſhed, that he could not poſſeſs himſelf of the Kingdom of *Egypt*, otherways than by *Sacrilege*, and the ſlaying of the * Prieſts; he choſe rather to lay aſide his claim, and advantages of War, which he had gotten, and to refer the Government of that Kingdom to twelve Wiſemen; who erected to the memory of that Princes piety, one of the ſtatelieſt *Pyramids* of *Egypt*, which yet remains: How much more will it become Chriſtians in any way of Power and Magiſtracy, not to make their way upon the ſpoils, nor lay the foundations, or to carry on the fabrick of their greatneſs and dominion, upon the carkaſſes and ruines of ſuch as are able, true, and faithful Miniſters of the true God, and the Lord Jeſus Chriſt?

* *Herodoti Clio.* * *Servil. de Mirandis. l. 1.*

However my own private comforts of life might other ways be, either ſecure, or ſatisfactory; yet how can I with ſilence, or as *Nehemiah* without ſadneſs, behold the miſeries of many my *Brethren* and *Companions*? For whoſe ſakes, I cannot but have great *compaſſion*, even in worldly regards; well knowing, that many, if not far the moſt of them, *have born the heat and burthen of the late days*, or *years rather, of great tribulation*, beyond any ſorts of men; to whom have been allowed ſome ways, either for reparation, or compoſition, or reſtitution, or oblivion: But not ſo to any Miniſters; from ſome of whom hath been exacted the whole *tale of Bricks*, as to the neceſſary *labors* of their Miniſtry, and *charges*, when the *ſtraw of maintenance* hath, in great part, been, either denied to them, or ſome way exacted from them; nor was ever any publick eaſe, or relief granted to them in that regard.

Nehe. 2. 2.

But it becomes neither them, nor me, in this particular, to plead or complain, as to any private intereſts, preſſures, or indignities, already ſuſtained. The *Lord is righteous and holy*, though we be waſted, impoveriſhed, and exhauſted; yea, though we be accounted, as the *off-ſcouring* of all things (1 Cor. 4. 13.) and as *unſavory ſalt* fit to be caſt on the *dunghil*, (Math. 5. 13.) While there are ſo many * *haſty intruders, and confident undertakers* of the work of the Miniſtry,

* *Vel in hoc uno maximè; inidonei, quòd ſibi idonei videntur tam tremendo Miniſterio.* Jeron.

Ministry, yet the best and ablest of us all, desire before the majesty of God, in all humility to confess, That we are *less than the least of his mercies*; that none of us are, as to *Gods exactness*, or the weight of the work, *sufficient* for that *sacred Office* and *Ministry*.

2 Cor. 2, 16.

2 Cor. 4. 7. *Non thesaurus dehonestatur vasculo, sed vas decoratur thesauro.* Prosp.

Yet since this *heavenly treasure* hath been duly committed to such *earthen vessels*, who have wholly devoted, even from their youth, their studies, lives, and labors, to the service of *Christ*, and his *Church*, in this work of the Ministry; since the *publick wages* and *rewards* for that *holy service*, have by the order of *humane Laws*, by the piety, bounty, and justice, of this *Christian Nation*, been hitherto conferred upon them, and they rightly possessed of them; I cannot but present to the considerations of all men, that have *piety*, *equity*, or *humanity* in them, That there are no objects of *pity* and *compassion*, more *pitifully calamitous* and *distressed*, than those many *learned* and *modest men*, the *godly and faithful Ministers* of this *Church* of *England*, either are already, or are shortly like to be, if the malice of their *adversaries* be permitted to run in its full scope and stream against them; which will be like that flood, which the *old Serpent*, and great *red Dragon*, cast out of his mouth after the *woman*, (the *Church*) which would carry away both *mother* and *childe*, *old* and *yong*, the *sons* with the *fathers*, *true piety* with the whole *profession*; the present *Ministers* with all future *Succession*, as to any right *Authority*, and lawful *Ordination* or *Mission*.

Rev. 12, 15.

19. *The cunning and cruelty of some against the Ministry.*

What I pray you (O excellent *Christians*, all whose other excellencies are most excelled in your Christian pity and compassion) can be more deplorable, than to see so many persons of ingenuous education, good learning, honest lives, diligent labors, (after so much time devoted chiefly to serve God, their Country, and the Church of Christ, and the souls of their Brethren, with their Studies, Learning, and Labors) to be turned, or wearied out, of their *honest* and *holy employment*; to be so cast out of their houses and homes, together with all their nearest relations; to be forced to begin some *new methods of life*, in some mean imployment or dependance; and this in the declining and infirmer age of many? wherein they must either want their bread, or beg it; or, at best, with much contention, against the *armed man*, *Poverty*, in *labor* and *sorrow*, *night* and *day*, they must mingle their *bread with ashes*, and their *drink with weeping*; when they shall be deprived of all those *publick rewards* and *setled incouragements*, (which God knows, were neither very liberal in most places, nor much to be envied, if * *charity did not grow cold, and iniquity abound*) wherewith the whole labor of their lives, their

Prov. 24. 34.

* Matth. 24. 12. *Deficiente charitate necesse est abundare nequitiam, quum non auferantur iniquitatis stercora nisi per charitatis fluenta, & mentem, & gentem, & rempublicam, & ecclesiam validissime purgantia.* August. *Tepente charitatis fervore frigescunt & rigescunt conscientiæ.* Bern.

learning,

learning, and chargable studies, besides their industry, humility, and other vertues, were but meanly, yet, to them, contentedly recompensed, by those Laws of *publick piety* and *munificence*; which invested Ministers in their places and livings, after the same * *tenure* for life, and good behavior, that any man enjoys his *free-hold* in house or land; keeping himself within the compass of the Law.

* Ministers have the same Right to their Ecclesiastick estates by *Magna Charta*, as others have to their Temporalities. *Concessimus quod Ecclesia Anglicana libera sit in perpetuum, & habeat omnia jura sua integra, & omnes libertates suas illæsas.* Magna Charta, c. 1. See the Statute of 2. *Edw*. 6. and 19. for treble damages in case of not paying Tithes, where due.

And that the * *barbarity*, *impiety*, and *monstrosity* of the *injury*, may seem the less with the common people, all these *sufferings of poverty* and *necessity* (which either have faln upon some, or threaten other *true Ministers* in this *Church*,) must be attended with the *black* * *shadows* of all *evil speaking* and *reviling*; such as was used to their *great master* and *institutor Jesus Christ*; when he was to be thus crucified with contempt, *lest the Romans come and destroy the City* (though there was nothing found in him, by his Judge, *worthy of death*.) That so the proud mockers of the Ministry, may say with scorn, *Behold, these men of God*; these that *pretended to preach salvation* to others, let them now come down, and save themselves from that *Jesuitick*, *Socinian*, and mechanick *Cross*, to which they are with all cruel petulancy, either now, or shortly (as their malicious enemies hope and boast) to be fixed.

* *Pereuntibus (Christianis sub Tiberio) addita ludibria, ut ferarum tergis contecti laniatu canum interirent, & ubi defecisset dies in usum nocturni luminis flammati urebantur.* Tac. An. l. 19. Luke 23. 34. Joh. 11. 48. & 18. 38.

O what would the enemies of this *Reformed Church* and *State*, 20.
whatever they are, have wished more to crown their envious desires, and consummate their malicious designs; than to see, that *woful day*, wherein *this abomination* (which threatens to make the *Reformed Religion* desolate, in this Church of *England*,) being set up, the whole *Function* and *Succession* of the *true and lawful Ministry* here, should be questioned, cashiered, triumphed over, and trampled upon, by the foot of *Ignorance*, *Error*, *Popery*, *Jesuitism*, *Atheism*, *Profaneness*, and all sorts of disorderly mindes and maners?

Hoc Ithacus velit, & magno mercentur Atridæ. Virg.

All which heretofore felt the powerful restraints, the mighty chains, the just terrors and torments cast upon them, by the convincing *Sermons*, learned *Writings*, frequent *Prayers*, and holy *examples* of many excellent *Ministers* in *England*; before whom the *devils of ignorance*, *error*, *profaneness*, *schism*, and *superstition*, were wont to fall as *lightning* to the ground, from their *fanatick Heavens*.

Luke 10. 18. *Vera fulgente luce flaccessit fulguris coruscatio, terrore magis quàm lumine conspicua.* Chrysost.

Have all these *Sons of Thunder* and of *Consolation* too; (who were esteemed heretofore by all Reformed Christians in this Church, to be as *Angels of God*, *Embassadors from Heaven*; *Friends of Christ*, *the*

the Bridegroom of their Souls; more pretious than fine Gold; dearer, to humble and holy men, than their right eyes; the beauty of this Church, and blessing of this Nation,) Have they all been hitherto, but as *Mahumetan Juglers*, or *Messengers of Satan*, or *Priests of* Baal, or as the *cheating Pontifs* of the *Heathen gods and oracles?* Have they all been found lyers for God, and born false witness against the Truth, and Church of Christ? Have they arrogantly and falsly * *taken too much upon them, in exalting themselves above their line and measure?* Or magnifying their *Office and Ministry*, above the *common degree* or *sort of Christians?*

* Numb. 16. 3. Ye take too much upon you, since all the Congregation is holy, every one of them, *&c.* Wherefore lift ye up your selves above the Church of the Lord? Thus *Korah* and his company against *Moses* and *Aaron*.

And why all this *art, fraud,* and *improbity of labor in Ministers?* (Sure, with the greater sin and shame *learned* and *knowing men* should *weary themselves* in their *iniquity*, when they had so *little temptation* to be, either false or wicked, in so high a nature:) Alas, For what hath been, and is, all this *pompous pains*, and *hypocritical sweat of Ministers?* Is it not for some *poor living*, for the most part; for a *sorry subsistence*, a *dry morsel*, a *thred-bare coat*, a *cottagely condition?* In comparison of that *plenty, gallantry, superfluity, splendor,* and *honor*, wherewith *other callings* (which require far less *ability* or *pains*) have invited and entertained their *professors* in this plentiful Land? Are not the *gleanings of the grapes of* Ephraim, *better than the vintage of* Abiezer? Are not the *superfluities* * of any *ingenuous calling*, beyond the necessaries of most *Ministers?* And all this, that after infinite studies, pale watchings, fervent prayers, frequent tears, daily cares, and endless pains, exhausting their *Time, Spirits, Estates,* and *Health*, they might, through many *vulgar slightings, reproaches,* and *contempts*, with much patience condemn themselves and their relations, first to * *poverty*; which is no light burden, where a good conscience is wanting, or an evil one attending (as in this case *malice* doth suppose.)

Quò minor tentatio eò majus peccatum. Aquin.

Judges 8. 2.

* *Merito à secularibus negotiatoribus & lucro, & praemio superamur, quum caelestia & aeterna à Christo expectamus munera.* Jeron.

* *Grave est paupertatis onus ubi deest bonae conscientiae levamen; quâ sublevante gravescit nihil, quâ dulcante nihil amarescit.* Petrach.

And, now at last, (after more than One thousand five hundred years, and one Century and half since the *Reformation*) in all which time this Nation hath more or less enjoyed the inestimable blessing (for so our pious *Ancestors* esteemed the *lights of this World*, the *true Ministers of the Church*, in their *Prayers, Preaching, Writings, holy Offices,* and *Examples*,) they should by some men be thought unworthy of any further *publick favors* or *imployment*, and to have merited to be counted as *sheep for the slaughter* *, in their persons: And as to their *Function* or *Calling* (which was ever esteem-

* Rom 8. 36. For thy sake are we counted as sheep for the slaughter, and killed all the day long; *Lanista diaboli Christi victima.* Leo. They are Christs Lambs, whom the Devil delights most to butcher.

ed

ed *sacred* among true Christians) to be wholly laid aside and outed with all disgraceful obloquies ; as if they had been, but *pious Impostors, devout Usurpers,* and *religious Monopolizers*, of that *holy Ordination, divine Mission, Power,* and *Authority* , which Christ gave personally to the *Apostles* ; and both by declared intent, and clear command, to their due and rightful *Successors*, in that ordinary *Ministry* which is necessary for the *Churches* good : Or at best they must be reputed, but as *superfluous, burthensom,* and *impertinent*, both in *Church* and *State* ; *chargeable* to the *publick purse* ; *dangerous* to the *publick peace* ; *useless* as to any *peculiar power* of *holy Administrations* ; which some think may be more *cheaply, easily,* and *safely*, supplied by other *forward pretenders* ; who think themselves endued with greater *plenitude of the Spirit*, with *rarer gifts*, with *diviner illuminations*, more *immediate teachings*, and *special anointings* ; by which, without any pains or studies, they are suddenly invested into the *full office* and *power Ministerial* : And as they are themselves *led*, so they can infallibly *lead* all others, *into all truth* ; with such wonderful advantages of *ease*, and *thrift*, both for mens pains and purses , that there will be no need to entertain that antient form, and succession of *ordained Ministers*, as any *peculiar calling* or *function*, amidst so gifted and inspired a *Nation*. So much more sweet, and fruitful, do these self-planted *Country Crabs* , and *Wildings*, now seem to many, than those *Trees of Paradise*, which, with great care and art, have been grafted, pruned, and preserved by most skilful hands ; which these *new sprouts* look upon, and cry down, as onely full of *Moss* and *Missletow*.

In this case then, O you excellent Christians, such *freedom*, as I now use, I hope may seem not onely pardonable, but approvable, and imitable to all good Christians, who fear God, and love the Lord Jesus Christ ; who have any care of their own souls, any charity to the Reformed Churches , any pity to their Countrey, any tenderness to the religious welfare of *posterity* : And in a matter of so great and publick importance, it is hoped, and expected by all good men, That none of you, either in your private places, or publick power and influences, will by any *inconsiderate*, and mean *compliance*, gratifie the evil mindes of *unreasonable men*, in order to compass the Devils most *Antichristian designs* ; who seeks by such devices, first to deceive you, next to destroy, and damn, both you and your posterity : Your * silence or reservedness, in such a cause, and at such a time, as this, *will be your sin* ; as it would have been mine : How much more, if you use not your uttermost endeavors , in all fair and Christian ways, to stop this *Stygian stream* ; but most of all, if you contribute any thing of that power you have, whereby to carry on this *poysonous* and *soul-destroying torrent*. Words are never more due, than in

* *Blasphemiæ proximum est Christiani silentium, ubi Christi causâ agitur, & negligitur ; quam silendo æquè prodimus ac Judas salutando, aut Petrus abnegando.* Jeron.

Christs behalf, who is the *Incarnate Word*; and for his Ministers, who are the Preachers of that Word.

22. *The sense of the best Christians, as to the Ministers case.* Nor is this my private sense and horror alone; but I know you (O excellent Christians (who are (truly) men of pious and publick; not of proud, or pragmatick spirits,) cannot but daily perceive, That it is the *general fear and grief* of honest and truly reformed Christians, in this *Nation*; Who with *one mouth* are ready to say to those in *place and power*, as *Abraham* did to the King of *Sodom*, or *Mephibosheth* to *David*; Let those cunning, cruel, and covetous *Zibas* (whose treacherous practises, and ingrateful calumnies, seek to deprive us of our *Houses, Goods, Lands,* and *Liberties*,) let them take all, so as our *David*, the beloved of our souls, our Christ, our true Religion, our glory, our true Ministers and Ministry, may be safe; Let others *take the spoils and booties of our labors*, onely give us *the souls of our selves*, and our *posterity*, for a prey; which are like to perish for ever, unless you leave us those holy means, and that sacred Ministry, which the *wisdom and authority of Christ* onely could (as he hath) appoint; which the Churches of Christ have always *enjoyed*, and *faithfully transmitted* to us for the saving of our sinful souls. This request, the very *Turks* unasked, do yet grant in some degree to the poor Christians, who live under their dominion.

2 Sam. 19. 30.

Gen. 14. 21.

And if it may seem to be *our error* and *fondness*, thus to prise our *true and faithful Ministers*, and that *onely divine Authority*, which is in their Ministry; yet vouchsafe to indulge us in the midst of so many *epidemical errors*, this one *pious error*, and *grateful fondness*; which not custom and tradition, but conscience and true judgement have fixed in us; since we esteem, next * God, and our blessed Saviour, and the holy Scriptures, the *true Ministry of the Church*, as that holy necessary *ordinance* which the *divine wisdom* and *mercy* hath appointed, whereby to bring us to the *saving knowledge* of God, and our Lord Jesus Christ, by the Scriptures; That, as we ow to our *parents*, under God, our Natural and Sinful Being (whom yet we are bid to honor;) so our Christian, Mystical, and Spiritual Being, we ow to our true *Ministers*, as our holy and spiritual *Fathers*; by whose care we have been truly taught, and duly Baptized, with divine Authority, in the Name of the *blessed Trinity*; both instructed, and sacramentally confirmed in that *faith*, which is the onely true *way of eternal life*.

Illos nimis diligere non possumus Christiani, quorum Ministerio & Deum diligimus, & à Deo diligimur. Cypr.

* *Unicus est modus diligendi Deum nescire modum.* Aug.

1 Cor. 4. 15. Though you have ten thousand teachers in Christ, yet you have not many fathers; For in Christ Jesus I have begotten you through the Gospel.

By their *study, pains, love*, and *diligence* (when we would have been otherwise *willingly ignorant*, and *wholly negligent* of our souls good) our *darkness* (by Gods grace and blessing on their labors (chiefly) hath been dispelled; our *ignorance* enlightned; our *deadness* enlivened; our *enmity* against God, and our Neighbor, removed; our *hardness* softned; our *consciences* purged; our *lusts* mortified;

our *lives* (as to an holy purpose, prayer, and endeavor) reformed; our *terrors* scattered; our *ghostly enemies* vanquished; our *peace* and *comforts* obtained; our *souls* raised and sealed to a *blessed hope* of eternal life, through the mercies of God, and the merits of our *Redeemer*; whose *Embassadors*, our true *Ministers* are: And indeed, we have no greater sign, or surer evidence of our faith in Christ, and love unfeigned to God, than this, That we love and reverence those, and their calling, as men who onely have authority in Christs name to *administer holy things* to us.

23. *Of Pretenders to the Ministery.*

And however others (who have lately sought to come in, not in * *by the door, but over the wall*; who seek also like * *theeves* and *robbers* to lead us plainer people out of the right way, that they may the better rob and spoil us,) pretend they are so rarely gifted, that they will teach us the same, or higher truths; and administer the same holy things in a new and more *excellent way*, than ever the best ordained Ministers of this Church have done: Yet truly, (saving the confident boasting of these *new masters*) we could never, hitherto, discern in any of them, either by their much speech, or writing (with which they may make a great sound, and yet be very empty) any such *sufficiencies* as they list every where so much to boast of: Muchless have they ever produced any shew of *Scriptural power*, *Divine authority*, *Mission from Christ*, or footstep of *Apostolical succession* in the Church; in which, every one that can speak tollerably, we cannot think is presently *sent of God*, for a publick Minister of *holy things*; no more than every well-spoken *Traveller*, or diligent *Factor*, or *Carrier*, is a *Publick Agent*, *Herauld*, or *Embassador* to any *Prince*, or *State*, or *City*; although they may know their *Princes*, *Masters*, or *Neighbors* minde, in many things. We know it is not, *what waters men fancy*, but *what God appointeth*, which will cure the blinde or leprous.

* *Seducunt è via incautos viatores, ut securius ipsos perdant lenocinantes latrones.* Greg.

* John 10. 8. All that came before me, (i. e. as Messias, or Christ) are theeves and robbers. John 10. 1. He that entereth not by the door into the sheepfold, but climbeth some other way, is a thief and a robber. Vers. 7. I am the door of the sheep. We can neither come to be of the sheep of Christ, but by faith in him; nor shepherds of those sheep, but by that door of authority, which Christ hath set open in the Church by Ordination. Bishop *Downam* Serm.

And we finde by daily sad experience, that they, whose *pride* or *peevishness* forsakes, or scorns to use the waters of *Jordan* (the means which Christ hath instituted, and the Ministers, which by his Church he hath ordained) do commonly get no * more good by their *padling*, or *dipping* in other *streams*, (which they fancy better) than *Naaman* would have done if he had gone to his so much extolled Rivers of *Damascus*, and had forsaken *Jordan*: They may a little wash over, and for a while seem to *hide mens leprosies* of Ignorance, Error, Pride, Levity, Schism, Licentiousness, and Apostacy, but they cannot *heal*

2 Kings 5. 12.

* *Sacra mysteria non vi naturali, sed voluntate dei supernaturali perficiuntur.* August. *In sacris, sine mandato Divino vel maxima virtus deficit; cum illo vel minima valescit.* Jeron.

 them;

them; yea, rather they provoke the *itch of novelty*, and increase the *leprous scurff of obstinacy*; by which men refuse to be healed, and glory in their despising, and conquering all remedies: **Strange fires* we know (of old) would burn, as well as *holy*, in a natural force; but it was neither *acceptable*, nor *safe* to be used in the *solemn service of God*; nor did it *consume* the *sacrifice* so much, as * *kindle* the wrath of God, to *blast* and *destroy* the *presumptuous offerers*: However, good men might use it *lawfully* in their *private hearths* and *houses*, yet not at the *Publick* * *Altars*, or in the *Temple*.

* Levit. 10. 1. They offered strange fire before the Lord. V. 2. And there went out fire from the Lord and devoured them.

* *Illorum temeritas irâ divinâ meritò castigatur, quorum autoritas sacro ordine non consecratur.* August. * *Tutus est in privatis ædibus pietatis & charitatis ignis; quô nec rite nec tutò in publicis Dei officiis uti possumus, quia non sine peccato, & ideo non sine peccato, quia sine Dei mandato.* Zanch.

So that indeed we cannot hope, that those whom *the Lord hath not sent* by his authority (which hath been commited to, and derived always by the hands of the *Governors and Pastors* of his Church) either can, or will take care to guide, or keep us and our children, in that *true*, *holy*, and *good way* of *reasonable* and *acceptable serving God*; since themselves are (for the most part) such *unreasonable persons*; of so *silly*, *blinde*, *weak*, *wandring*, *vain*, and *various spirits*; abounding in nothing so much, as in their *ignorance*, *pride*, *confidence of themselves*, and *contempt of others*: And what they pretend to do, as to any *holy Ministrations*, is not, as of any duty, conscience, necessity, (as St. *Paul*, (who applies that) *Wo to me if I preach not the Gospel, &c.*) but meerly, as of *courtesie*; as arbitrary and spontaneous; as of novelty and curiosity, when, where, what, how, and as far, as their own sudden fits, humors, and interests; or others flatteries and vulgar applauses move them; while the novelty, curiosity, and admiration of these mens boldness, more than of their rare *gifts*, works upon the *itching ears*, not the *humble hearts*, of their *gaping*, or *giddy hearers*.

Rom. 12. 2. λογικὴ, ϗ δεκτὴ δουλεία.

1 Cor. 9. 16. *Væ negligenti officium, quod debuit, & arroganti, quod non debuit.* Bern.

2 Tim. 4. 3. They will not endure sound doctrine, but after their own lusts shall they heap up to themselves Teachers, having itching ears.

Such *Ivy* and *Country Garlands*, as these men hang out in their private *Cells* and *Conventicles*; or in their more *Publick Fairs*, and *Taverns*; are no temptations to us, to think their unseasoned *new bottles*; or their *flatuous and unrefined Wines*, (which have fumed so much into their own, and their auditors weak heads, that many of them every where reel and stagger, and vomit out their own shame, and wallow in their filthiness, like *drunken men*) are any way comparable to our *old bottels*, * and *veterane Wines*; which are sound, sweet, well-refined, and full of spirits. Nor will these *new patches* of *gifted*, but *unordained Preachers*, ever be suitable with, or comparable to our *good old Garments* *, the *learned*, *ordained*, and *true Ministers*, either

* Math. 9. 17. *Vetus vinum mulso longè defæcatius; & gustu suavius, & spiritu lenius, & ætate mollius, & sanitate salubrius, & cerebrum minus movet, & cor magis reficit.* Greg. * Matth 9. 16. *Ecclesiæ vestem (ordinem scilicet & decoram politiam) & deformi novitate lacerant, & turpiter lacerando magis deformant novatores.* Prideaux.

for

for durableness, comliness, or comfort; being heavier in the Summer of *prosperity*, and colder in the Winter of *adversity*. So that they are rather a shame, an oppression, and deformity to us, to our reformed Christian Religion, and to our Church, and Nation; as if we had chose, rather to be clothed with a ridiculous *pybald fools-coat*, or a *beggars cloak*, checquered with infinite *rents* and *patches*, than with that *holy* and *comly Garment* of *order* and *unity*, which *Christ* left to his *Church* and *Ministers* (like his own) *without any rent or seam*: That is, An *uniform, compleat, constant way*, and *order* of *holy Ministerial power*, derived in a right and successive *Ordination*: These new *short jumps* of *unordained Teachers*, are to the *Churches* and *Religion's* proportions, like the *coats* of *Davids* Messengers, 2 *Sam*. 10. 4. when they had been shamefully and spightfully treated by ungrateful *Hanun*; exposing indeed our *Nation*, and our *Religion*, to all * *reproach and scorn*; when all round about us shall see such *feeble* and *uncomly parts*, as indeed these gifted men, for the most part, are, in the body of our *Church*, thus *discovered*, which were far better *concealed* and *hidden*.

John 19. 23. *Qualis Christi vestis inconsutilis, inconscissa, talis esse debet ecclesiæ constans ordo & politia uniformis:* August.

* *Quantum deest autoritati, tantum adest pudori, aut inverecundiæ*; *Nihil enim impudentius, quàm injussum muneri, aut officio cuicunque sese immittere.* Gerard.

Yea, although they may (with truth) in somethings justly tax and reprove, some failings, or faults in some, yea, all our Ministers; yet we do not think presently they are to intrude into their places, and Ministry; no more than *Balaam's* Ass might presume to become, presently, a *Prophet*; because it sometimes spake and reproved its *masters madness*. Nor do we see any reason, that men should wait upon the *lips of such animals* for *Instruction*, who cannot justifie their speaking without a miracle; no more indeed, than these new *Teachers* can their chalenging the publick *place*, and constant *office* of *Christs Ministers*, to which they have no ordinary *Call* or *Mission*. 24.

Boldness of unordeined Teachers.

Num. 22. 28.

2 Pet. 2. 16.

Indeed we have rather cause, greatly to suspect these *intruders*, as for many other things, so for their *boldness and forwardness*: Since, such as have been *ablest for that great service*, have always been * *modestly slow*, and *humbly reserved*: That these mens undesired promptitude is like that *malicious readiness of Satan*, who, uncall'd, presents himself among the *sons of God* *; so are the *ministers of Satan* most prone to *transform themselves* by their *hypocrisies*, into *angels of light*; in order to advance *hellish darkness*, and *damnable doctrines*. And the times are much injured by reports, if it be not in some degree true, That many of these *Mushroom Ministers*, the most forward *Teachers* of this *new race* and *mechanick extraction*, are such

So *Moses*, *Isaiah*, *Jeremiah*, *Ezekiel*.

* St. *Jerome* tells of *Nepotianus*: *Eò dignior quo se clamabat indignum, fugiebat, dum populus quærebat; Humilitate superabat invidiam.* Ep. ad Heliod. So *Socrates* of *Ammonius*, when he was sought to be made a Pastor of the Church. *Lib*. 6. *c*. 30. * Job 1. 6. & 2. 1. 2 Cor. 11. 13.

Nunquam periculosius fallit tenebrarum & mendaciorum pater, quàm cùm sub lucis & veritatis specie delitescit. Jeron.

persons in disguises of *vulgar plainness*, and *simplicity*, who have had both their learning and their errand from the vigilant *Seminaries* beyond Sea: Out of which *Galliles* can come little good to our *Reformed Church* and *Nation*. *Satan* is not less a *Devil*, when he will seem a *Doctor*; nor more a dangerous *tempter*, than when he would appear a zealous *teacher*. Whence soever they are, sure we are, That many of these, who are so suddenly started up into Pulpits, are not ashamed to vent by word and writing, such *transcendent blasphemies*; That they teach whatever they think or say, of the *Majesty of God*, of *Christ*, of the *holy Spirit*, of the *Divine Nature*, though never so *irreverent*, *profane*, and *ridiculous*, yet it is no *blasphemy*, but *sublimity*; no *profaneness*, but getting above, and out of all *forms*; Whatever they contradict of the clear literal sense, and rational scope of the Scriptures, though it seem, and be never so gross a lie and error, in the common significancy of the words, yet it is a *truth in the spirit*; Whatever they act, never so disorderly, brutish, horrid, obscene and abominable, yet it is no *sin*, but a *liberty*, which God, and Christ, and the Spirit exercise in them; who cannot sin.

So *Ireneus*, l. 1. *Tertul.* de præ. ad Hæ. *Austin.* de hær. & de unitate Eccles. c. 16. Tells us of the *Portentiloquia Hæreticorum*. Vid. p. 204.

Nor is this the least cause we have to suspect, beware of, and abhor these *new Modellers* and *Levellers* of the *Ministry*; That, how different soever their faces and factions are, one from another, (though they go one *East*, and the other *West*; whether they *separate*, or *ram*, or *seek*, or *shake*;) yet still they meet in this one point, No *Ordination*, no *Function*, or peculiar *Calling* of the *Ministry*: The Serpents tail meets with his head, that he may surround truth with a circle of malice; As *Herod* and *Pilate*, they agree to crucifie Christ; as *Samsons* Foxes, though their *wily-heads* look several ways, yet their filthy tails carry common *fire-brands*; not onely to set on fire the sometime well-till'd and fruitful Field of this Church; but also to consume the very *laborers* and *husbandmen*. Their *eyes* and *hands* are generally bent against the best and ablest *Ministers*; and their *spirits* most bitterly inconsistent, with that *holy Ministry*, which *Christ once delivered*, by the *Apostles*, to the *Church*; and which, by the *fidelity* of his Church, hath been derived to us; of which, we and all the *true Churches* of *Christ*, have in all ages had so great, and good experience; which no malice of devils, or personal infirmities of men, have been hitherto able so to hinder, as wholly to interrupt; much less so to corrupt it, that it should be, either just, or any way necessary to abolish it, according to those *tragical clamors*, and *tyrannick purposes* of some unworthy men; whose *malice* and *cruelty*, (as our modern *Hamans*) doth hope, and daily with eagerness expect, when the whole *Function* and *Calling* (*which is from God, though by man*) of the *ordained* and *authoritative*

In hoc uniformes esse solent errantium deformitates, quod rectè sententes odio habent. August.

Esther 5. 9.

tative Ministry (which hath succeeded the *Apostles* to our days) shall be *trussed up that fifty footed Gallows*, which *malicious* and *ungrateful envy*, or *sacrilegious covetousness*, or *vulgar ambition*, or *Jesuitick policie*, hath erected for the whole Nation of the *antient* and *true Ministers*; And all this, because (like *Mordecai*) they will not; nor in any Reason, Law, and Religion, can *bow down*, or pay any respect (such as the *pride* and *vanity* of some men expect) to those high and self-exalting gifts, whereto their *Antiministerial adversaries* pretend; and which they seek to cry up in their *meetings* and *scriblings*; with which they say, (and onely say) They are *divinely called*, and more *immediately inspired*, not onely above *their fellows* and *brethren* (who are still modestly *exercised* in their first *mechanick occupations*) but even above those, that are much their betters, every way; and, who merit to have been, (and possibly have been to many of them) as *Fathers* in Religion; by whose pains and care, with Gods blessing, the true Christian Religion in all ages hath been planted, propagated, and preserved, or (where need was) reformed, and restored to its *essential lustre* and *primitive dignity*.

So that the cruel contrivances and desperate agitations, carried on by some men against the true Ministers and Ministry in this Church, (like the looks of the great *red Dragon*, upon the *Woman* of the *Revelation*) have a *most dire* and *dreadful aspect*; not onely upon all *good learning* and *civility*, but also upon all true *Religion*, both as *Christian*, and as *Reformed*. Threatning at once to devour the very *life*, *soul*, *beauty*, *honor*, *joy*, and *blessing* of this *Nation*; on which we may well write *Ickabob*, the *glory is departed from our Israel*; so soon as the fury of these men hath broke the hearts and necks of our *Elies*, the *Evangelical Priests of the Lord*, the true *Ministers of Christ*, who are as the *chariots and horsmen of our Israel*.

25. *Sober mens greatest sense.* Revel. 12. 4. 1 Sam. 4. 21.

Civil changes and *secular oppressions* have their limits, confined within the bounds of *things mortal* and *momentary*, with which, a wise and well setled Christian is neither much pleased nor displeased, because not much concerned, nor long: (For no wind from the four corners of the Earth, can blow so cross to a good mans sails, but he knows how to *steer a steddy course to Heaven*, according to the *compass of a good Conscience*.) But what relates to our *souls eternal welfare*, to the *inestimable blessing* of *present times* and *posterity*; What more concerns us in point of being true Christians, (that is *rightly instructed*, *duly baptized*, and *confirmed* in an *holy way*) than any thing of *riches*, *peace*, *honor*, *liberty*, or the very *being men* can do; (for without being true Christians, it had been *good for us*, *we had never been men*;) what evidently portends, and loudly proclaims

Quadratus cùm sit vir bonus ad omnem fortunæ jactum æquabilis est & sibi constans. Sen. *Tanto satius est esse Christianum quàm hominem, quanto præstat non omnino esse hominem quàm non & esse Christianum.* Bern.

Darkness, Error, Atheism, Barbarity, Profaneness, or all kinde of *Antichristian tyrannies* and *superstitions*, to come upon us and our children; instead of that *saving truth*, *sweet order*, and *blessed peace*; instead of those *unspeakable comforts*, and *holy privileges*, which we formerly enjoyed, from the *excellency* of the *true knowledge* of our *Lord Jesus Christ*, declared to us by the labors of our *true* and *faithful Ministers*: We hope it can offend no good Christians to see us, more piously passionate, and more *commendably impatient* against those who seek to deprive us of all those *divine blessings*, than *Micah* was against those, who *stole away his gods*, and *his Priests*; in as much as our *true God*, and *true Saviour*, and *true Ministers*, infinitely exceed his *Teraphins*, his *Ephod*, his *Vagrant*, and idolatrous *Levite*, who yet was as a *father* to him: Who can wonder! if we, or any other, who have any *bowels* of *true Christians*, or *tenderness of Conscience* for our *Reformed Religion*, do (as the *true Mother* did) passionately yern within themselves, and earnestly cry to others, lest by the *seeming liberty* of every ones *exercising his gifts*, in *Preaching* and *Prophecying*, their eyes should behold the *true and living childe of Religion* reformed, cruelly murthered and destroyed, under pretence of equable dividing it; to gratifie thereby the cunning designs of an impudent and cruel Harlot. It is the least, that we as true *Protestants* in this Church of *England* can do, *earnestly by prayers to contend with God and man, for the faith once delivered to the Saints*; that we may neither craftily be cheated, nor violently robbed, of that onely *heavenly treasure* of our souls; nor of those *earthen vessels*, which the *Lord* hath chosen and appointed, both to preserve it, and dispence it to us; namely, *the truly ordained and authoritative Ministers*; the original of whose *office and power*, as of all *Evangelical Institutions*, is from our *Lord Jesus Christ*, and not from the will of man, in any wanton, arbitrary, and irreligious way.

Sancta & laudabilis est in religionis negotio impatientia. Jeron.

Judges 18. 24.

1 Kings 3. 26. *Viscera genuinam matrem indicant: Ex vero dolore verus amor dignoscitur. Fictitius & meretricius animus facilè patitur infantem dividi.* Greg.

Jude 2.

2 Cor. 4. 7.

26. Thus then may your *Virtuous Excellencies* easily perceive, That it is not as *mine, or my Brethren, the Ministers, private sense alone*, but it is as the *publick eccho of that united voice*, which with sad complaint and doleful sound, is ready to come from all the *holy hills of Zion*; from every corner of the *City of God* in our Land; through the prayers and tears, sighs and groans, of those many thousands judicious and gracious Christians, who are as the *remnant that yet hath escaped*, the blaspemies, extravagancies, seductions, pollutions, and confusions of the present world; occasioned by those, who *neither fearing God, nor reverencing man*, seem to have set up the design and trade of *mocking both*. None bear the true *Ministry* with less patience than they, whose deeds will least endure the touch-stone of *Gods Word*: Whose violent projects against this Church and State, (being wholly inconsistent with any rules of righteousness and godliness)

Who are the Antiministerial adversaries most, and why.

Luci nimium adversantur meritò, qui tenebrarum opera operantur. Aug.

lineſs) makes them moſt impatient to be any way cenſured, croſſed, or reſtrained, by thoſe precepts and paterns of juſtice and holineſs, which the *true Miniſters* ſtill hold forth out of Gods Word, to their great reproach and regret; no more able to bear that freedom of truth, than the old world could bear *Noahs*, or *Sodom Lots* preaching of righteouſneſs. To theſe mens aſſiſtance comes in (by way of clamoring or petitioning, or writing ſcandalouſly againſt the Miniſters, and Miniſtry of this Church) all thoſe ſorts of men, whoſe *licentious indifferency, profane ignorance*, and *Atheiſtical malice*, hath yet never *taſted*, and ſo never valued the bleſſings of the *learned labors* and *holy lives* of good *Miniſters*; both theſe ſorts are further ſeconded by that *ſordid and ſelf-deceiving covetouſneſs*, which is in the earthy and illiberal hearts of many ſeeming *Proteſtants*; who either ingratefully grudg to impart any of their *temporal good things* to thoſe of whoſe *ſpirituals they partake*; or elſe they are always *ſacrilegiouſly gaping* to devour thoſe remains of *Bread* and *water*, which are yet left, as a conſtant maintenance to ſuſtain the *Prophets* of the *Lord* in the *Land*. Rom.15.27. 1 Cor.9.11.

And laſtly, not the leaſt evil influence falls upon the *Miniſters* and *Miniſtry* of this *Reformed Church*, by the cunning activity of thoſe *pragmatick Papiſts*, and *Jeſuitical Politicians*, (for all of the *Roman Profeſſion* are not ſuch) who make all poſſible advantages of our *civil troubles*, and ſtudy to fit us for their ſumation, and a recovery to their party, by helping thus to caſt us into a *Chaos*, and ruinous heaps, as to any ſetled *Order* and *Religion*: The moſt effectual way to which, they know is, To raiſe up rivals againſt, to bring *vulgar ſcorn* and *factious contempt* upon, to foment any *ſcandalous petitions* againſt *Miniſters*, and the whole ſupport of the *Miniſtry*, that ſo they may deprive that *function*, of all the *conſtant maintenance*, and thoſe *immunities*, which it hath ſo long and peaceably enjoyned, by the Laws, (which are, or ought to be, as the reſults of free and publick conſent, ſo the great preſervers of all eſtates in this Land.) Thus by *ſtarving*, they doubt not, ſpeedily to deſtroy the *holy function, divine authority*, and *due ſucceſſion* of all *true reformed Miniſtry* in *England*; Solicitouſly inducing all ſuch deformities, as are moſt deſtitute of all *ſober* and *true grounds*, either of *Law, Reaſon, Scripture*, or *Catholike* practiſe in the *Church of Chriſt*; Thus ſhortly hoping, that from our *Quails* and *Manna* of the *Learned* and *Reformed Miniſtry*, and *true Chriſtian Religion*, we may be brought back again to the *Garlick* and *Onyons* of *Egypt*, to praying to *Saints*, to worſhipping of God, in, or by, or through *Images*, to ſuch implicite *Faith* and *Devotion*, to truſt in *Indulgences*, to the uſe of burthened, or maimed *Sacraments*, to thoſe *Papal Errors, Superſtitions*, and *Uſurpations*, which neither we, nor our *Forefathers*, of later ages have tasted of; which, however somewhat better *dressed* and *cooked* (now) than they were in grosser times; yet still they are thought (and most justly) both *unsavory* and *unwholsome*, to those serious and sounder Christians, who have more accurate palates, and more reformed stomachs: With whose *judgements* and *consciences*, nothing will relish, or down, as to *doctrine*, and *rule* of *Faith*, or *Sacramental Administrations*, and *duties* in *Religion*, which hath not *Scripture* for its ground; to which, no doubt, the *primitive* and *purest Antiquity* did consent: To whose holy rule and patern, this Church of *England* in its *restitution* or *reformation* of *Religion*, did most exactly, and with greatest deliberation, seek to conform both its Ministry and holy Ministrations, using *liberties* or *latitudes* of *prudence*, *order*, and *decency*, no further, than it thought might best tend to the *edification* and *well-governing of the Church*, 1 *Cor.* 14. 40. Wherein it had (as all particular *National Churches* have) an allowance from God, both in *Scripture*, and in *Reason*.

Si canonicarum Scripturarum autoritate quidquam firmatur, sine ulla dubitatione credendum est: Aliis verò testibus tibi credere vel non credere liceat. August. ep. c. 12. *Hoc prius credimus, non esse ultra Scripturas quod credere debeamus.* Tertul. de præ. ad Hæ. l. 3. *Sacris Scripturis non loquentibus quid loquetur?* Ambr. voc. Gen. l. 2.

27. *Things of Religion ought first and most to be considered by Christian Rulers.*

But, as if nothing had been reformed and setled with any wisdom, judgement, piety, or conscience in this Church, nor hitherto so carried on by any of the *true and ordained Ministers* of it; infinite calumnies, injuries, and indignities, are daily cast upon the whole Church, and the best Ministers of it: The cry whereof (no doubt) as it hath filled the Land, so, it hath reached up to Heaven, and is come up to the *ears* of the *most high God*.

And therefore, I hope, it will not seem rude, unseasonable, or importune to any *excellent persons* of what *piety* or *power* soever, if it now presseth into their presence; who ought to remember, that they are but as *Bees* in the same Hive; as *Ants* on the same Mole-hill; and as *Worms* in the same clods of Earth, with other poor inferior Christians, whom they have far surmounted in civil and secular respects. The swarms and crowds of worldly counsels and designs, we hope, have not (as they ought not) overlaid or smothered all thoughts, care, and conscience of preserving, restoring, and establishing, *truth*, *good order*, and *peace*, in matters of *Religion*: Which are never by those publick persons, who pretend to any thing of *true Christianity*, to be so far despised and neglected, that those above all other matters of publick concernment, should be left, like *scattered sheaves*, to the wastings and tramplings upon by the feet of the *Beasts* of the people; ungathered and unbound by any *civil sanction* and *power*, agreeable to *holy order*, *divine method*, *Christian charity* and *prudence*. Possibly it had fared better with all estates in this Church and State, if they had learned and followed, that *divine*

Meritò à Deo negliguntur qui res Dei secularibus postponunt negotiis. Cypr.

divine direction, and *grand principle* in *Christian politicks*; *First seek the Kingdom of Heaven, and the righteousness thereof, and all these things shall be added to you*: The neglect of *Gods house*, (the Church) and its *beauty*, *holy order*, and *ministry*, hath been a great cause of overthrowing so many *seiled houses*, which were covered with *Cedar*, and decked with *Vermilion* and *Gold*.

τὸ ὅσιον ὡς πάντων πρῶτον. Primum quod sanctum. *Plat.*
Matth. 6. 31.
Hag. 1. 4. Is it time for you to dwell in your ceiled houses, and this house lie waste.
V. 5. Now therefore, saith the Lord of hosts, consider your ways.

Certainly no men employed in publick power or counsel, have any business of so *great concernment*, or of so urging and crying necessity as this, *The preservation of the true Evangelical Ministry*, in its due power and authority; Upon which, without any dispute among sober and truly-wise men, the very life, being, weight, honor, and succession of our Religion doth depend, both as Christian, and as reformed: For it is not to be expected, that the *ignorant prating*, and *confident boasting* of any other *voluntiers*, will ever *soberly adorn*, or *solidly maintain* our *Religion*, which hath so many very *eloquent*, *learned*, and *subtile enemies*, besides the *rude* and *profaner rabble*, besieging it; both *learned* and *unlearned* oppose *true Religion*, as the right and left-hand of the *Devil*; the one out of *ignorance*, the other out of *crookedness*; the one as *dark*, the other as *depraved*; the one cannot endure its *light*, nor the other its *straitness*. Against neither of them can these afford help, any more than the *confused cackling* of a *company of Geese*, could have defended the *Roman Capitol*: Which noise is indeed, but an *alarm* to sober and good *Protestants*, intimating the approach or assault of enemies; and should excite the *vigilancy* and *valor* of all *worthy Magistrates*, *conscientious Soldiers*, and *wise Christians* of this *Reformed Church*, to resist the invading danger; as by other fit means, so chiefly by *establishing* and *incouraging* a *succession* of *learned*, *godly*, and *faithful Ministers*.

ἐκ Διὸς ἀρχώμεσθα. Arat. Phainom.

Anserum clangore crepituque alarum excitus Manlius capitolium propugnat, Gallos deturbat, &c. Livi. Dec. 1. l. 5.

Nor in any reason of State, or of Conscience, should those who exercise *Magistratick power* in this Church and State, so far neglect him, who is *Higher then the highest* *; by whom all power is dispenced; or so far gratifie the irreligious rudeness, the boisterous ignorance, and violent profaneness of any, (who are but *Gods executioners*, the *instruments* of his *wrath*, and *ministers* of his *vengeance*;) as for their sakes, and at their importunity, to despise and oppress those who are by Christ and his Church appointed to be *Ministers* of *Gods grace*, and *conveyers* of his *mercy* to men: The meanest of whom, (that do indeed *come in* his name) the proudest mortal may not safely injure or despise; because not without sin and reproach to Christ and God himself. For *he that heareth you, heareth me; and he that despiseth you, despiseth me, and him that sent me*; is signally and distinctly spoken in favor to *true Ministers*, and for terror to those that are prone to offer insolency to their worldly weakness,

* Eccles. 5. 8. He that is higher than the highest, regardeth; and there be higher than they.
John 19. 11. Thou couldst have no power, except it were given thee from above. *Christ to Pilat*
1 Cor. 12. 1.
1 Pet. 4. 10. Stewards of the manifold grace of God.
Luke 10. 16.

weakness, and meanness. Such as despise and oppose the Ministers of Christ, are more rebellious than the devils were; for of these, the seventy returning testifie, *Luke* 10.17. *Lord, even the devils are subject to us in thy Name.*

If then we have *immortal souls* (which some *mockers* now question,) sure they are infinitely to be preferred before our *carkases*; and the *instruments* which God hath appointed, as means to *save them*, are proportionably to be esteemed beyond any, that are oft the *destroyers*, at best, but the *preservers* of *mens bodies*, and *outward estates*.

1 Cor. 1. 21. It pleased God by the foolishness of preaching, to save them that believe.

Who can dissemble, or deny, That the *banks of equity, piety, modesty*, and *charity*, yea, of *common humanity*, are already by some men much *demolished*, through the *pride, presumption, insolence, scurrility*, and *profaneness* of some *spirits*, who are set against the *Reformed Religion*, the *Ministers* and *Ministry* of this *Church*? Who sees with honest and impartial eyes, and deplores not, to behold; how the deluge of *Ignorance, Atheism, Profaneness*, and *Sottishness*; also of *damnable Errors, devilish Doctrines*, and *Popish Superstitions*; together with *Schismatical fury*, and *turbulent Factions*, are much prevailed (of later years) both in Cities and Countreys here in *England*: And this, since men of *Antiministerial tempers*, have studied to act the *Devils Comedy*, and this *Churches Tragedy*; endeavoring to render, not onely the *able, godly*, and *painful Ministers*, but the *whole Ministry* it self, and all *holy Ministrations* (rightly performed by its *Authority*) *despised, invalid, decryed*, and *discountenanced*: In many places affronting some, vexing and oppressing others, menacing all every where, with *total extirpations*: For, they who pretend to have any man a Minister that lists, intend to have none, such as should be; (As they that would have every man a Master or Magistrate, mean to have none, in a Family or State;) but onely, by *specious shadows* of *New Teachers* and *Prophets*, they hope to deprive us of those *substances*, both of *true reformed Religion*, and the *true Ministry*; which we and our Forefathers have so long happily enjoyed, and which we ow to our posterity.

Gaudet in malis nostris diabolus, lætatur in miseriis, dilatatur angustiis, delectatur angoribus, triumphat ruinis. Bern.

28. *The great and urgent causes of complaint.*

Nor is this a feigned calumny, or fictitious grief, and out-cry: Your *piety* (O excellent Christians) knows, That the *spirits* of too many men, are so desperately bent upon this design against the *Function of the Ministry*; that they not onely *breathe out threatnings against all of this way* (the *duly ordained Ministers*;) but daily do (as much as in them lies) make *havock* of them; and in them, of all good *maners* and *reformed Religion*; while so many *people*, and whole *Parishes* are void and desolate of any *true Minister*, residing among them: I leave it to the *judgements* and *consciences* of all *good Christians* to consider, how acceptable such projects and practises

practises will be to any sober and moralized *professor*; to any *gracious* and *true Christian*; to any *reformed Church*, or to *Christ*, (the *Institutor* of an *authoritative* and *successional Ministry*) or, last of all, to *God*, whose mercy hath eminently blessed this *Church* and *Nation*, in this particular, of *able* and *excellent Ministers*; so that they have not been behinde any Church under Heaven; That so exploded Speech then, *Stupor mundi clerus Anglicanus*, The *Ministers* of *England* were the admiration of the *Reformed World*, had not more in it of crack and boasting, than of sober Truth, if rightly considered; onely it had better become (perhaps) any mans mouth, than a *Ministers* of this *Church*, to have said it; and any others, than *believers* of this *Church*, to have contradicted and sleighted it: Since to the *English Ministers* eminency, in all kinde, so many forein Churches, and Learned Men, have willingly subscribed; as to *Preaching*, *Praying*, *Writing*, *Disputing*, and *Living*.

On the other side, How welcome the disgrace of the Ministry will be to all the enemies of *Gods truth*, of the *Reformed Religion*, and of all *good order* in this *Church* and *State*, it is easie to judge, by the great *contentment*, the ample *flatterings*, the unfeigned *gloryings*, the large and serious *triumphings*, which all those that were heretofore professed enemies to this *Church* and our *Reformed Religion*, (either such as are factious and politick *Factors* for another *Supremacy* and *Power*; or such as carry deep *brands* of *Schism* and *Heresie* on their foreheads; or such as are professedly *Atheists*, *profane*, *idle*, and *dissolute mindes*) discover, in this, That, they hope, they shall not be any more *tormented by the prophecying of these witnesses*, the true and faithful Ministers of the *Church* of *England*; Than whom, none of that *order*, in any of the late *Reformed Churches*, and scarce any of the *Antients*, have given more *ample*, *clear*, and *constant testimony*, to the *glory of God*, and the *truth* and *purity* of the *Gospel*, by their *Writing*, *Preaching*, *Praying*, *Sufferings*, and *holy Examples*, *Living*, and *Dying*; which I again repeat, and justifie against those, who swell with *disdain*, and are ready to *burst* with *envy*, against the *real worth*, and *undeniable excellency* of the *Ministers* of the *Church* of *England*.

Revel. 11.10. They that dwell on the earth, shall rejoyce (over the dead, and unburied bodies of the witnesses) and make merry, because these two Prophets tormented them that dwelt on the earth.

All which makes me presume, That you (O excellent Christians) can neither be ignorant, nor unsatisfied in this point of the *Evangelical Ministry*, both as to this, and all other *Churches* use, benefit, and necessity; as also, to the *divine right of it*, by *Christs institution*, the *Apostles derivation*, and the *Catholike Churches* observation, in all times and places; as to the *main substance* of the *duties*, the *power*, and *authority* of the *Function*; however, there may be in the succession of so many ages, some *Variation*, in some *Circumstantials*: The *peculiar office*, and *special power*, were seldom, (as I have said) if ever questioned, among any Christians, until of late; much less, so shaken, vilified, and traduced, as now it is by the *ungrateful wantonness*, and *profane unworthiness* of some; who, not by force of reason, or arguments of truth, but by forcible sophistries, armed cavillings, violent calumnies, and arrogant intrusions, have (like so many *wilde Bores*) sought to *lay waste* the *Lords Vineyard*; Pretending, That their *brutish confidence* is beyond the best *dressers* skill; that their *irregular rootings* are better than the *carefullest diggings*; that their *rude croppings* and *tearings* are beyond any *orderly prunings*, or *wary weedings*; that their *sordid wallowings*, and *filthy confusions*, are before any *seasonable manurings*; that there needs no *skilful Husbandmen*, or *faithful Laborers* of the *Lords sending*, the *Churches ordaining*, or the *faithful peoples approving*; where so many *devout swine*, and *holy hogs*, will take care to plant, water, dress, and propagate the *Vine* of the *true Christian Reformed Religion*; to which, the hearts of men are naturally no *propitious soyl*. Nor is the event, as to the happiness of this Church, and its Reformed Religion, to be expected other (without a miracle,) (if once those *unordeined, unclean*, and *untried spirits*, be suffered to possess the Pulpits, and places of true and able *Ministers*) than such, as befel those *forenamed cattel*, when once *Christ* permitted the *devils* to enter into them: All truth, order, piety, peace, and purity of Religion, together with the Function of the Ministry, will be violently carried into, and choaked in the midst of the Sea, of most *tempestuous errors*, and *bottomless confusions*.

Psal. 80. 13. The Boar out of the wood doth waste it, and the wilde Beast of the field doth devour it.

Et atroces insidiatores, & aperti grassatores, Ecclesiam divastare contendunt, tam marte quàm arte. Aug.

Matth. 9. 38. Pray ye the Lord of the harvest, that he would send forth laborers into his harvest.

Matth. 8. 32. The whole herd of swine ran violently down a steep place into the Sea, and perished in the waters. *Immundi illi Ministri, & inordinati Doctores, per ignorantiæ, temeritatis, & superbiæ præcipitia feruntur in* (τὰ βάθη τοῦ σατανᾶ) *profunditates Satanæ* (Apoc. 2. 24.) *in errorum, blasphemiarum, & confusionum omnium abyssum.* Chemnit.

29. *Absurdities* The *impious absurdities*, *enormious bablings*, and *endless janglings*, whereby some men endeavor to dishonor, and destroy the whole Function of the reformed and established Ministry in this Church; and to surrogate in their places, either *Romish Agitators*, or a *ragged Regiment* of new and necessitous *voluntiers*, (whosoever lists, not to consecrate, but desecrate himself, by an *execrable boldness*; or else is elected and misordained by that *zealous simplicity*, *schismatical fury*, and *popular madness* after any novelty, which is ever, in any meaner sort of people.) These no doubt are sufficiently known to you, together with those learned solutions, those sober, and to wise men, satisfactory answers, which have by many worthy Pens, both long since, and lately been made publick, both as to the calumnies of the

1 King. 13. 33. *Jeroboam* made of the lowest of the people, Priests; whosoever would he consecrated him, and he became one of the Priests.

V. 34. And this thing became sin to the house of *Jeroboam*, to cut it off, and destroy it from the face of the earth.

adversaries, and the vindication of this Church, and its Ministry; Which is conform, not onely to our wise, excellent, and antient Laws; but to all right reason; common rules of order and policy; dictates of humane nature; practise of all Nations: Also, to the Precepts, Institutions, Paterns, and Customs of God, of Christ, of the Apostles, and of all the Churches; and ever was so esteemed and reverenced, until the *sour* and *unsavory dregs* of these perilous, last, and worst times, came to be stirred and drawn forth: Wherein, under pretences of (I know not what) *special calling, gifts*, and *privileges*, (but really to advance other *fruits*, than those that use to grow from the *Spirit of truth, peace, holiness*, and *order*,) some men are resolved to ascend to that desperate height of *impiety*, which counts nothing a *sin*, a *shame*, or a *confusion*. 2 Tim. 3. 1.

I shall not so far distrust the *knowledge, memory*, or *consciences*, of *wise* and *worthy Christians*; as to abuse their leisure, by a large, exact, and punctual disputing every one of those *Particulars, Arguments*, and *Scriptures*, which have been well and learnedly handled by others; who have put the *heady rabble* of their opponents, to so great disorders; as from *Arguments*, to threaten *Arms*; from shews of *Reason*, to flie to *Passion*; from sober *Speaking*, to bitter *Railings, Scoffings*, and *Barkings* at that *Light*, which they see is so much above them.

30. *Ministers unheard, ought not to be condemned.*

Quod rationibus non possunt fustibus satagunt; deficientibus scripturis succurrant gladii. Aug. de Circumcel.

Lunam è cælo quum non possunt deducere, allatrant canes. Sen.

Onely I cannot but suggest in general, to all good men, That it seems, not to me onely, but to many, much wiser and better than my self, a very *strange precipitancy*, which no Christian wise Magistrates will permit, (more like *tumultuary rashness*, and *schismatical violence*, than either *Christian zeal*, or *charitable calmness*) That the whole Order and Function of the Ministry of the *Gospel* in this Reformed Church, so long owned by all good men, both at home and abroad; so long, and largely prospered here with the *effects* and *seals* of *Gods grace* upon it; so esteemed necessary to the very Being of any Church, and Christianity it self, by all sober and serious Christians; (For, there can be no true Church, where Christ is not; who promised to be with his Ministers to the end of the World: So, that where no true Ministry is, there can be no presence of Christ, as to outward Ordinances, *Matth.* 28. 20. which is spoken to those that were sent to *Teach* and *Baptize, &c.*) Lastly, This Calling so never opposed by any, but erroneous, seditious, licentious, or fanatick spirits of later times; That (I say) this *antient*, and *holy Function*, should without any *solemn publick conference, impartial hearing*, or *fair consultation*, even among *Professors of Reformed Christianity*, be at noon day, thus *vilified, routed*, and sought to be wholly outed; by persons, whose *weavers beams*, or *rustick numbers*, and *clamorous crouds*; not their *reason, learning, piety*, or *virtue*, renders them, either

either formidable, or any way considerable; further, than to be objects of wiser, and better mens, pity, and charity, or fears, and restraints.

Is it that there are no *Ministers* of the *true* and *good old way*, worthy to be heard, or comparable to those plebeian pieces, who by a most imprudent apostacy, becoming *haters* and *desertors* of their former *holy orders*, and *authority Ministerial*, have taken a new Commission upon a popular account? Are none of the *antient Ministers* fit to be advised with, or credited in this matter, which concerns not themselves so much, as the publick good, both of Church and State? Are they all such friends to their own *private interests* (some poor living, it may be) as to have no love to God, to Christ, to the Truth, or to the Souls of men? Have they no learning, judgement, modesty, or conscience, comparable to those, who being *parties*, and *enemies* against them, hope to be their onely judges, and to condemn them? Is wisdom wholly perished from the wise, and understanding hidden from the prudent? Is Religion lost among the Learned; and onely now found among simple ideots? Or rather, are not the *Antiministerial adversaries*, so conscious to the *true Ministers learned piety*, and their own *impudent ignorance*, that they are loth, and ashamed to bring the one or other, to a publick test and fair trial; resolving with the *Circumcellions* with more ease to drive them, than to dispute them out of the Church; aiming not to satisfie any by their reason, but to sacrifice all to their passion, if they can get power? Who doubts, but that if the *learned* and *godly Ministers* in this sometime so famous and flourishing Church of *England*, who seem now in the eyes of their enemies, (as if they had been taken by *Pirates* or *Picarooms*) onely fit to be so thrust under Hatches; not worthy to be spoken with, to appear, to be trusted or regarded, if they might have so much *publick favor*, (which they despair not of, and do *humbly intreat*) as by *solemn tryal* and *dispute*, to *assert* their *Station* and *Function*, against their *adversaries*, (as some have in private ways done,) Who doubts, (I say) but by Gods assistance, (whose mercy hath not, will not, ever forsake them) they would make the *halting* and *ungrateful people* of this *Church*, to see, whether the *Lord* or *Baal* be *God*? Whether (I say) the *Primitive Order*, and *Divine Constitutions* of *Christ*; (which have on them, the *Seal of the Scripture*, the *Stamp of Authority*, and carry with them all the *beauties of holiness*. For *right reason*, *due order*, *decency*, *peaceableness*, and *proportionableness*, to the great ends of *Christian Religion*; together with their *real usefulness*, confirmed by the happy experience of the *Primitive times*, the *purest Saints*, the *best Christians*, the *constantest Confessors*, *holy Martyrs*, and most flourishing *Churches*;) Whether (I say) these should continue in their place and

Et osores & desertores sui ordinis. Sulp. Sev.

Circumcelliones inter Donatistas furiosiores, cùm ἐγκρατεῖς, i. e. Continentes se vocitabant, jus fasq; omne evertentes sacerdotibus & Ministris Catholicis vim inferebant, omnia diripientes, &c. Calcem cum aceto in oculos piorum ingerebant. Vit. August. c. 9.

1 King. 18. 21.

and power, wherein God hath set them, and our pious Predecessors have maintained them in this *Church* and *Nation*; or these *yesterday-novelties*, the *politick whimseys*, and *Jesuitick inventions* of some *heady*, but *heartless men*, should usurp and prevail in this *Church*, after sixteen hundred years prescription against them; and which are already found to have in them (besides their *novelty*,) such emptiness, flatness, vanity, disorder, deformity, and unproportionableness to the great end of right ordering *Christian societies*, or saving of souls, by edifying them in *truth and love*; that they have been already productive of such *dreadful effects*, both in *opinions* and *practises*, that they make the *Protestant* and *Reformed Churches* stand amased, to see any of their kinde bring forth such *Monsters of Religion*, as seem rather the fruit of some *Incubus*, some foul and filthy spirits, deluding and oppressing this *Reformed Church*, than of that *blessed* and *promised Spirit*, whose power, whose rule, whose servants, have always been the most exactly and constantly, *holy*, *just*, and *pure*. For any true Christians then, to allow and foster such prodigies of *Protestant Religion*, as some are bringing forth, seems no less preposterous, than if men should resolve, to put out their eyes, and to walk both blindfold and backwards; or to reverse the body by setting the feet above the head: Indeed it is putting the *Reformed Religion* to the *Strapado*, and crucifying *Christ* again, as they did Saint *Peter*, after a new posture, with his head downwards; As if in kindness to any men, they should take away their souls, and make them move (like Puppets) by some little springs, wyars, and gimmers; or by the Sorcery of some Demoniack possession.

Eph. 4. 10, 11, 12, 13.

Mirabatur & ingemuit orbis se tam citò fieri Arianum. Jeron. cont. Lucif.

John 14. 16. The Comforter, even the Spirit of Truth, he shall abide with you for ever.

31. *Therefore this Apology endeavors the Ministers defence.*

For want of the favor of such a *publick tryal* and *vindication* of the *Ministry*, I have adventured to present to the view of all Excellent Christians in this Church, this *Apology*; By which I have endeavored to take off from the *Josephs* and *Josedecks* of this Church, those *prisons* and *filthy garments*, wherewith some men have sought to deform them; and to wash off from their *grave countenances*, and *angelike aspects*, the chiefest of those scandals and aspersions, under which (for want of solid reasons, or just imputations against their persons and calling) by some mens unwashen hands, and foul mouths (whose restless spirits cast out nothing but dirt and mire against them) they are now so much *disfigured* to the world; That so, *odious disguises* (as of old to the Christians) may render them less regarded, and more abhorred by vulgar people: This art of evil tongues, and pens, serving to colour, excuse, or justifie the injustice,

Gen. 41. 14. Zach. 3. 4.

Isai. 57. The wicked is as a troubled sea, when it cannot rest; whose waters cast up mire and dirt. *Tertul. Apolog.* 2 Cor. 10. 10. His bodily presence is weak, and his speech contemptible; so the false apostles, the ministers of Satan, 2 Cor. 11. 13. The deceitful workers reproached St. *Paul* behinde his back.

cruelty, barbarity, unthankfulneſs, and irreligion of thoſe, who ſeek firſt to *bait them* in the *Theatre* by all publick diſgracings, and then to diſpatch them. For againſt theſe Beaſts (as Saint *Paul* ſometime at *Epheſus*) whom no reaſon, learning, gravity, merit, parts, graces, or age doth tame or mitigate, the *true Miniſters* of the *Goſpel*, even in this *Reformed Church* of *England*, have now to *contend*, for their *Calling*, *Liberties*, and *Livelihood*; yea, for their *lives* too, if the *Lord*, by the favor and juſtice of thoſe that have *wiſdom*, *courage*, and *piety*, anſwerable to their places and power, do not reſcue and protect them.

Veri criminis defectus falſis ſupplet calumniis; & factis innocentes, verbis deturpat malitia. Sulpit. *Donatiſtarum anteſignani B. Auguſtinum ſeductorem & animarum deceptorem clamitabant; & ut lupum occidendum; & tale facinus perpetranti remiſſionem peccatorum obventurum.* Poſſid. vit. Auguſt.

32. *What Miniſters I plead for.* If in any thing, as weak and ſinful men, any of the *true Miniſters* of this *Church*, are (indeed) liable to *juſt reproaches*, either of *ignorance*, or *idleneſs*, *factiouſneſs*, *ſedition*, any *immorality*, or *ſcandalous living*, (and what *Church of Chriſt* can hope to be abſolutely clear, when even in *Chriſts family*, and the *Apoſtles* times, there was *droſs* and *chaff* in the *floor*, by *Judas*, and *Demas*, *Simon Magus*, *falſe Apoſtles*, *deceitful workers*, *Miniſters of Satan*, *&c*?) I am ſo far from excuſing, or pleading for them (as to their perſonal errors and diſorders) that I ſhould be a moſt *ſevere advocate* againſt them, (if after two or three admonitions, they ſhould be found incorrigible.)

2 Cor. 2. 17. Not as many which corrupt the Word of God.
2 Cor. 11. 13.
Tit. 3. 10.

And this, upon the ſame ground, on which now I write this *Apology*; namely, in behalf of the honor of the *Goſpel*, the dignity of the *true Miniſtry*, and the glory of the moſt *ſacred name* of the *Chriſtians God*, and *Saviour*; which, *idle*, *evil*, *unable*, and *unfaithful Biſhops*, and *Miniſters*, beyond all men, cauſe to be *blaſphemed*; when they pull down more with the *left hand of profaneneſs*, than they build with the *right hand* of their *preaching*; betraying *Chriſt with their kiſſes*, and ſmiting the *Chriſtian Reformed Religion under the fift rib*, when they ſeem with great reſpect to ſalute and embrace it. Confuting what they ſay, by what they do; and hardning mens hearts to an unbelief of that doctrine, which they contradict by the *Solecíſm* of their *lives* and *maners*; either *rowling great ſtones* upon the *mouth* of the *Fountain*; or poyſoning the emanations of *living waters*; or *perforating* the *mindes* and *conſciences* of their *hearers*, to ſuch *liberties* and *hypocriſies*, that they retain no more of true Religion, and ſerious holineſs, than *ſieves* can do of *water*. As

Nihil deformius eſt ſacerdote claudicante; qui non æquis & rectis pedibus incedit in viis Domini. Greg. *Plus deſtruit ſiniſtra pravæ vitæ, quàm aſtruit dextra ſanæ doctrinæ.* Bern. *Non confundant opera tua ſermonem tuum. Proditores ſunt non prædicatores Chriſti, quibus factis deficientibus vita erubeſcit.* Jeron. ad Nepot. *Niſi præſtes quod prædicas mendacium non Evangelium videbitur.* Lact. Inſt. lib. 3. cap. 16. *Exemplum operis eſt ſermo vivus & efficaciſſimus.* Bern. *ut ſumenti cibum & non digerenti perniciofum eſt; ita docenti & non facienti, peccatum eſt.* Id. *Animata virtus eſt quæ factis honeſtatur: Cadaveroſa, quæ verbis tantum macreſcit.* Leo. *Myſterium Theologiæ non ut olim Philoſophiæ, barba tantum & pallio celebratur: Sed doctrinæ ſanitate & vitæ ſanctitate.* Lact.

Salvian, lib. 4. de Gub. sometimes complained of *Preachers* and *Professors* too in his time.

No, I beseech you to believe, That I am the most rigid exactor of all *holy exactness* from *Ministers* (of all degrees) beyond all other sorts of men; That they who are the *Evangelical Priests* to the *Lord*, should have no *blemish from head to foot*, *Levit.* 21.17,18,19. Neither defective in intellectuals, nor deformed in morals; sound in doctrine, sacred in deeds; the want of which, makes them, (as *Eunuchs, Levit.* 21. 20.) forbidden to serve before the Lord; as unfit for *spiritual generation*. That they bear on their brests before God and all men, the *Urim and Thummim, Light and Perfection, Truth and Charity*; in both *Integrity*. That none of this *holy Ministration*, be either incurably blinde, or incorrigibly lame; that they may be worthy to stand before God, as to their sincerity; before men, as to their unblamableness; and between both, as to their unfeigned fervent love, both of God and man. For I well know, That not onely *gross offences* in them, as in *Eli*'s sons which made people to *abhor* the *offerings* of the Lord, 1 *Sam.* 1.17. must be avoided; but the very *flies of common frailties*, must be kept off from their *sacrifices* (as *Abraham* did the *fowls of the air* from his *oblations, Gen.* 15. 11.) And as the *Jews* affirm, That natural flies were never seen on any *sacrifices* of the *true God*, or in his *Temple*; which infested all other Temples of the *Beelzebuls, gods of flies*. *Ministers motes*, as well as *beams*, must be kept out of the worlds eyes; which are prone to look with a more prying curiosity, and pitiful censoriousness, on Ministers smaller infirmities, than on other mens grosser enormities: This being one of *our happinesses*, That being compassed about with many *sinful frailties*, which easily beset us, we have as many *severe censurers*; which may help to keep us in a greater exactness, both before God and man: In whose account, *drunkenness* and *riot*, which in all men, is a sin; in *Ministers*, is as sacrilege: Rash and vain oaths in them, are as so many perjuries: Any profaner levity in them, is as the blaspheming that God, whose Word they Preach, whose Name they invocate, whose holy Mysteries they celebrate: Their illiterateness, is barbarity and brutishness; their factiousness, and

Facta & verba sibi occinant; Ambr. de Bo. m.

Verba vertas in opera. Jeron. ad Paulinum.

Quæ docuit Christus præceptis, firmavit exemplis. Chrysost.

Factis ostende te possibilia docere. Chrysost.

Catholici in prædicando, hæretici in operando. Bern.

Salvian. l. 4. Gub. *Scientia nostra nihil aliud est quàm culpa; quod lectione & corde novimus, libidine & despectione calcamus, &c.*

Honorius the Emperor is commended by *Theodoret*, for removing those from being Bishops and Presbyters, whose lives were not agreeable to the dignity of their calling, and exactness of their duty. *Theod. l.* 5. *c.* 28.

Non loquamur magna, sed vivamus. Cyp. de Bo. Patien. *Honor sublimis & vita deformis.* Ambr. Ἀξιόπιστος ἐστιν ὁ λόγος τῷ βίῳ συμφωνούμενος. Nis. de Perf. οὐδὲν σοφίας ἀπαιδεύτου μὲν ἦν πάντα χαλεπὸν, χρῆσθαι δὲ παγχάλεπον. Socrat. in Plato. Phile. ὁ μὲν λέξις ἐστὶν ὥσπερ ἐπὶ σώματος, τὰ δὲ πράγματα σαρκές εἰσι καὶ νεῦρα. Cl. Al. Strom. 215. *Et quotidianæ incursiones, & vastantia conscientiam facinora à sacerdote Christiano evitanda.* Bern. בעל לבול *Musca Dominus in* *Moreh. Nebuchim. Rambam.* Ambr. offic l. 2. c. 2. & c. 12. & 17. ὁ ταὐτὸν τοῖς λαοῖς ἁμαρτάνων καὶ ἴσα μεῖζον γίνεται ἁμαρτία, οὐ τῇ φύσει ἀλλὰ τῇ ἐξουσίᾳ τοῦ δρῶντος. Isi. Pel. l. 2. Who observes out of *Levit.* 4. There is as great a sacrifice for the Priest, as for the whole people. *Ebrietas in quovis vitium à sacerdote sacrilegium.* Chrys. *Præceptis Christi detrahit pondus sacerdotum levitas.* Lact. Luke 6.46. Why call ye me Lord, and do not the things I say?

fury in secular motions, is such a madness of pride, and vain-glory, as possessed him, who in all things else very obscure, set the Temple at *Ephesus* on fire; that he might be remembred for something; their laziness and negligence in their *studies* and *preaching*, is supine slothfulness, and sinful slovenliness; while they content themselves with any *raw and extemporary hudlings*; in which, is nothing of *holy reasonings*, and *Scripture demonstrations*, mightily convincing; nor of right method, duly disposing; nor yet of any grave and pathetick oratory, sweetly converting, and swasively applying; but onely a *rudeness*, and *rambling* next door to *raving*; which hath partly occasioned (indeed) so many *new undertakers* to preach; who, thinking some Ministers stocks of divinity quite broken and spent, by their so little *trading* and *improving* in any *good learning*, or *solid preaching*; have adventured to serve the Country credulity with their *Pedlars packs*, and small *wares*; not despairing to preach and pray, at that *sorry rate*, and *affectated length*, which they hear from some that go for Ministers; resolving (at worst) to colour and cover over those real defects of *parts* or *studies*, to which they cannot but be conscious, by *excessive confidences*, *loud noises*, *immoderate prolixities*, and theatrick shews of *zealous activity*; (even as *Country Fidlers* are wont to do, when they play most out of tune,) Abusing the *vulgar simplicity*, with their bold, yet unharmonious melody.

2 Tim. 1. 15. Study to shew thy self a workman, that needs not to be ashamed. *Non impudentem vult, ut non erubescat; sed diligentem (ἀνεπαίσχυντον) ut non mereatur verecundari.* Amb.

1 Tim. 4. 15. ἐν τούτοις ἴσθι. Give thy self wholly to these things, that thy profiting may appear to all men; so 16.

παιδαγωγία. *Quò longius aberrant, eò vehementius agitantur.* August.

What can be more fulsom and intollerable, even to the worst, as well as the best of Christians, than to see *Clergymen* study more the gain and pomp, than the *life* and *power* of *godliness*? To content themselves, and delude others with the *husk and shells* of Religion? What more unreasonable, than for *Shepherds* to starve, or tear and worry the *flocks*? For *Physicians* to infect their *patients*, by not healing themselves? for *Builders* to pull down the holy Fabrick of *Truth* and *Charity*? or to build with the *untempered morter* of *Passion*, *Fancy*, and *Faction*? For *Embassadors*, either through idleness to neglect, or through baseness to corrupt, or through cowardise not to dare to declare and assert the message and honor of their *Soveraign* sender? which should with all courage, fidelity, and constancy, be discharged, even to utmost perils; so as to be ready with St. *Paul*, not onely to be bound for Christ, but to lay down his life also. *Acts* 20.

Sicarii animarum. Naz. or. de Sacerd.

πῶς ἄλλους ἁγιάζεις ὁ ἐναγής, πῶς καθαίρεις ὁ ἀκάθαρτος, πῶς υἱοὺς Θεοῦ κατασκευάζεις, ὁ [illegible]. Isi. Pel. l. 2. Zosimen. profano Presbytero.

I know that in *Ministers* any spot of *pride*, *levity*, *affectation*, *popularity*, *pragmaticalness*, *timorousness*, or other *undecencies*, below a *wise*, *holy*, *grave*, *constant temper*, and *carriage* of a *worthy minde*,

Unicus rectoris lapsus par est totius populi flagitio. Chrys.

Levit. 4. 3, 14. The sacrifice for the sin of the Priest, is as much as for the sin of the whole Congregation.

is

is a foul deformity, a putid futility, a pueril vanity, scarce a venial madness; so much the worse in them, by how much the *contagion* of their *folly* is prone to infect all that look upon them; for the *plague* and *leprosie* of a *Ministers* life, cannot be kept within his private walls. There is nothing more delicate and abhorring all sinful sords, than the *Ermine of Christian Religion*, and its *true Ministry*, which sets forth the *Lamb of God*, without spot or blemish, who came to take away the sinful stains of mens souls, by the effusion of his *pretious blood*. The care of all good Ministers, is so to live, as shall not need the impotent severities of those *Reformers*, who joy as much to finde faults in others, as to mend none in themselves, and are always eloquent against their own sins in other men. Allow us onely to be, as *Ministers* of the *Gospel* for the *Churches* good, we desire no indulgences, farther than the duty and dignity of our *Calling* doth allow, and the strictest *Conscience* may bear: No men shall more welcome mens *favors*, than we shall do their just *severities*; nor do we desire greater testimonies of mens loves to us, than such, as we use for the greatest witness of ours to them; by never *suffering* them to sin, through our silence or flatteries. Let the *righteous smite us*, and it shall be a kindness; let them *reprove us*, and *reform us*, and it shallbe a balm, which shall not break our heads; but our prayer shall ever be, That we may *not taste of the new dainties* of those *supercilious censurers*, and *envious reformers* of *Ministers*; who are their enemies, because they tell them the old truths; and make *them offenders for a word*, because they will not forbear to reprove their wickedness; who heretofore seemed to hear them gladly, till they touched their *Herodiasses*.

Non solum ipse cùm malè agit dignè perit, sed & alios secum indignè perdit. Ambr. de Sa. dig.

Præpositorum vitia imitari obsequii genus videtur ne scelera ductoribus exprobrare viderentur, si piè viverent. Lact. Inst. l. 5.

Psal. 141. 5.

Isai. 29. 21.

Mark 6. 20.

The less scandalous Ministers are, the more that *Hypocritical generation* (who have set themselves against them) are bent to destroy them: I intercede onely for such, whose *greatest offence* is, That they give *lest offence* to any good Christians, and do most good to this Church; preserving still the *purity* and *honor* of their *Calling*, and the *Reformed Religion*, against the many policies of those, who lie in wait to destroy it; who are honored with, and are an honor to the Function of the Ministry; whose competent, and (in some) excellent *learning*, and *holy lives*, makes them still appear like *bright stars* in a dark and stormy night, amidst the thick and broken clouds of envy and calumny, which rove far beneath them; however they are sometime darkned by their interposing.

Eò acriores sunt odii causæ quò magis iniquæ. Tacit. An. 1.

Eò gratiori lumine, quò spissiores tenebræ. Tert.

If, as to these mens *holy Function, Ordination*, and *Authority*, I may be happy to give you (O excellent Christians) or any others, any satisfaction; as a *Calling* useful, and necessary to the *Church*; as of *Divine Institution*, and *Catholike practise* in all setled *Churches*, I shall then leave it to any men of *good conscience* to infer, how *barbarous* and *Antichristian* a design it is; how *bad* and *bitter consequences* it must needs produce, by any arts and ways of *humane power* and *policy*, to destroy and exautorate these men, and their Ministry; in whose *lives* and *labors*, the *glory of God*, the *honor of Jesus Christ*, and the good of *mens souls* are so bound up, that they cannot without daily miracles be separated, or severally preserved. And for the persons of the *Ministers*, which I plead for, I hope to make it appear, That for their casting thus into the *fiery furnace* of *mechanick scorn*, and *fanatick fury*; or into the *Lyons den* of *publick odium* and *disfavor*, there will be found, by *impartial Readers* of this *Apology*, no more cause, than was against *Daniel*, or the *three children*; no more than for beheading *John Baptist*, or stoning St. *Stephen*; for beating and imprisoning the *Apostles*, and charging them *to speak no more in that Name of Jesus*; or for the *Galatians* hating St. *Paul*, or the Beasts *slaying the witnesses*; or the *Jews* seeking to stone, and after crucifying the *Lord Jesus Christ*.

Acts 4. 18. Gal. 4. 16. Am I therefore become your enemy because I tell you the truth.

33. *Ministers infirmities do not abrogate their Authority or Office.*

Not, but that the *very best Ministers* of this *Church* own themselves still to be but poor sinful men; and so not *strangers* to the *common passions* and *infirmities of humane nature*: Men must not be angry, that *Ministers* are not *Angels*, or such *Seraphins* and *flaming fires*, as admit no *dross* or *defects*, incident to sinful mortality: Though they oft fail, as men, yet have they not *forfeited* the Authority of their Calling as Ministers; though they have dispenced the *Gospel* in weakness, as *earthen vessels*, yet hath the *Treasure* of *Heaven*, and *Power of God*, been manifested by them, and in them: Take them with all their *personal failings*, yet they will hardly be matched, or exceeded by any order of men, or any Clergy in any Church under Heaven; for they have not been behinde the very chiefest of *true Ministers*; and far beyond any of these *new pretenders*: Insomuch, That I have oft been ashamed to see the *necessity of this Apology*, and such like *Vindications* of the Ministry, which *ungrateful* and *impudent men* extort from the *Ministers* of *England*; when indeed (as St. *Paul* pleads for himself; instead of thus being compelled to an unwelcome, yet just *glorying*) they ought rather to have been *commended* and *encouraged* by others.

Pro defensione famæ licita est laus propria. Reg. Jac. 2 Cor. 12. 11.

Truly, it is to me a great trouble to finde out by any of their confused *Pamphlets* and obscure *Papers*, what these *Modellers* of a *new Ministry* would be at, in any reason of *piety* or *prudence*, more to the advantage of this *Church*, or the *Reformed Christian Religion*, than hath been heretofore, and may still be effected and enjoyed, by the *true* and *antient Ministry*: Would they have better *Scholars* in all kindes of *good learning*? *Acuter Disputants* in *controversies*? *Clearer Interpreters* in *Commentaries* upon the *Sacred Texts*? Better *Linguists*? More *solid Preachers*? More *pathetick Orators*? more *fervent Pray-*

ers; higher *Speculatists* in all *true Devotionals*? Exacter *Writers* in all kindes of *Divinity*? Would they have more *grave*, *comely*, *prudent*, and *consciencious dispencers* of all *holy Mysteries*? Or *nobler examples* of all *piety* and *virtue*, than those, which have every where abounded in the *Ministers* of the *Church* of *England*, according to the several *measures* of their *gifts* and *graces*?

No, I finde their enemies *envy*, is more than their *pity*; For one *century of scandalous Ministers*, (which, I fear, was not so made up by *exact sifting* the *pretious* from the *vile*; but that it hudled up, and kneaded some finer flowre with some bran;) How many hundreds were there then, and are still of unblamable, of commendable, of excellent, and most imitable Ministers in this Church? As weighty, as fair, and as fit every way, yea, far beyond what any *new stamp* is likely to be, for all *holy admistrations*: But I finde, it is not any *new Truth*, or *Gospel*, or *Sacraments*; or *Gifts*, or *Graces*, or *Virtues*, or *Morals*, or *Rationals*, or *Reals*, which these *new Ministers* require; or can with any *forehead* pretend: All is but an affectation (for the most part) to have the same things, in a *new*, and *worse way*; which because it is of their own invention, they so eagerly quarrel at the former order, maner of our Church and Ministry. Many would have the same *meat* (else they must *starve*, or *feed upon the wind*) onely it must be *new dressed*, and *disked* up to the mode of *Familistick hashes*, and *Socinians* (*Quelques choses*) *Keckshoes*; by more plain and popular hands, than those of the *learned Ministers*: They would have a generation of Teachers rise up *unsown*, out of the *dust*; whose *father should be corruption*, and whose *sister*, *confusion*: More vulgar, submiss, precarious, facile, dependent Preachers; who should more consider an act or ordinance of man, than a command of Scripture, or dictate, and stroke of Conscience; be more steered by the events and various successes of Providence, than by the constant *precepts* and *oracles* of Gods written Word: Whose *common places* of divinity must fit any *Eutopian Commonwealth*, what ever any *power* and *policy* shall form to their *new fancies*, and *interests*; whose *Preaching* and *Praying*, shall make *Christ*, and the *Scriptures*, and the *Sacraments*, all *holy things*, and the *Ministry* it self of the *Church*, meanly servile and compliant to any *State design*, and *secular projects*; Just as the sorry *Almanack-makers* do, who command the *Sun*, and *Moon*, and *Stars*, and the whole host of *Heaven*, to assist any party whom they list to flatter, or hope to feed upon: Such *planetary Preachers*, all *true Ministers* abhor to be; and such their enemies deserve to have, or to be; who observing the *winds* of *worldly* and *State variations*, shall never sow the *good seed of true Religion*; nor ever serve the *Lord*, while they slavishly and sinfully serve the times: Not, but that all good Ministers know,

Non laudabili pietatis æmulatione, sed improba virtutis invidia feruntur, qui virtutem aspiciunt intabescuntq; relicta. Casaub.

Multi novitatis amore in veritatis odium & præjudicium feruntur. Quum illud pulcherrimum quòd verissimum; id verissimum, quòd antiquissimum. Tert.

ἐσθλοὶ κακίονες τ' ἀτυχέστεροι. Eurip. Hel.

Eccles. 11. 4.

know, as wise and humble men, how to be content in what *State* soever they are; and to be subject to *civil powers* in all *honest things*, with gratitude and due respect; yet not so, as to prostrate God, to level Christ, to subject Conscience, to debase the glorious Gospel, its due *Reformation*, and its true *Ministry*, and *divine Authority*, to the *boundless lusts*, and *endless designs* of *violent* and *restless mindes*.

Phil.4.11. Rom. 13.5.

Against all which, and chiefly against those *plots* and *practises* which aim to overthrow the Reformed Christian Religion of this Church, and its Ministry, I desire this *Apology* may be as a *Pillar* and *Monument* to posterity of my *perfect abhorrency*, That when I am dead (if it hath any spark in it of an *immortal spirit*, or *living genius*) it may testifie for me, and my Brethren, the Ministers of my minde, in after ages; that, as *Joseph* of *Arimathea*, we neither gave counsel, nor consent to those wilde or wicked projects, which the ages will afterward see, attended with most sad and deplorable effects; either of Atheism, Profaneness, Ignorance, and Barbarity; or of Popish superstitions, Heretical oppressions, and Schismatical confusions, which will follow the alteration and rejection of the antient, true, and Catholike Ministry of this Reformed Church; which cannot but be attended with the subversion of many souls, as to all stability or soundness in true Religion; with the unsatisfaction of many, and with the unspeakable grief and scandal of all those good Christians, who love and wish the prosperity of this Church; which I shall now endeavor to prove to be of a most *Christian* and *Evangelical constitution*; chiefly by answering what is alleged by those, who look upon both Church and Ministry as reprobate; and would fain have power to *damn* them both, without redemption: And this they endeavor with as much *justice* and *truth*, as *Satan* accused *Job*, and would have provoked God to destroy him without a cause.

Luke 23.50.

Job 1.

OBJECT.

OBJECTION I.

That we have no true Ministry, because no true Church-way in England.

I Finde there are many and great things objected, by the *Anti-ministerial party*, through *ignorance, weakness, mistake*, or *malice*; not onely against the *Ministers*, and the peculiar office of the Ministry; but also against the *whole frame* of our *Religion*, especially as to the extern social maner of our *holy Administrations*: Some of them *deny* us to be any *true Ministers*, because not in any way of a *true Church*; not having any *true Religion* owned or established, and exercised among us, *in any right Church-way*, as they call it. So that it is not onely the *main pillars of Christianity*, the *learned* and *godly Ministry*, which they would change: But the whole *model* of our *Church*, and *frame* of our *Religion*, is that, which these men would remove, either pulling it down by force, or undermining by fraud: Therefore, I have thought it necessary, in the first place, to countermine against these *Moles*, and to establish against these *Shakers*, and *Subverters* of the very foundations of our *Church* and *Religion*.

Answ. 1.

Here I must crave leave of you, to whose *favor* I have dedicated this work (whose *highest excellency* is your *Christian Reformed Religion*; who esteem it your *greatest glory*, with the Emperor *Theodosius*, That you are *Members* of this *Reformed Church*, and in this of the *true Catholike Church*,) to give these *fanatick*, and *cavilling disputers* against our *Ministry*, some account of that *Religion*, which we profess; and of that so much disputed, and by some despised *Church-way*, wherein we take our selves to be; as upon surer grounds of *divine truth*, so with much more order and decency, as to antient patern and prudence, than themselves: That so, as good Christians may be comforted and confirmed in their *holy Profession*, so the world may see, That we are neither ignorant our selves, nor willingly deceivers of others, in so great a matter as *Religion* is, which we publickly have *professed* and *preached* in this *Church*, both with *science* and *conscience*, with *judgement* and *integrity*.

Of true Religion.

Vera est religio, quæ uni vero Deo animas nostras religat. Aug. de Relig.

Micah 6.8.

James 1.27.

First then, We esteem *True Religion* to be the *right performance* of those duties, which we ow to the *One onely true God*; or to any Creature for his sake; That is, upon such grounds, to such ends, and after such maner, as God requires them of us, in the several relations, wherein we stand obliged to him, or them.

K

This

Internal.

Lux est religionis in conscientia, lumen in conversatione. Bern.

1 Cor. 2. 11.

1 John 1. 3. & 3. 19.

Nec deest Christus ubi est fides, nec ecclesia ubi Christus, nec societas ubi charitas, nec templum ubi cor sanctum. Cypr.

Heb. 1. 1.

Prov. 20. 27.

Lucerna Domini: Scintillans in intellectu, radians in voluntate, ardens in affectu, fumans in desiderio, flammans in amore, scrutans in conscientia, exhilarans in virtute, torquens in facinore. Bern.

2 Tim. 3. 16.

2 Pet. 1. 19.

Matth. 10. 26.

Gal. 6. 1.

Et solidè fundanda, & ad amussim Scripturâ ædificanda, & veritate stabilienda, & charitate consummanda religio. August.

Eò pulchrior est anima, quo ad summam Dei pulchritudinem propius accedit. Bradward. [illegible] Greg. N.s.

This *Religion* is discharged by us; first, *Internally*; in the *Receptions* and *Motions* of an enlightned and sanctified *Soul*; to which none can immediately be conscious, but onely God, and a mans own spirit: Herein, we conceive the very soul, life, and quintessence of true *Religion* doth consist, so far as it is to be considered apart, from all outward expressions, visible Form, Society, or Church Communion; onely as having spiritual inward *converse* and *fellowship* with God and Christ, by the *graces* of the holy Spirit; although Christians should be in desarts, dungeons, prisons, solitudes, and sick beds; amidst all forced sordidness, disorders, and dissolutions of any *shew* and *profession* of Religion, as to the outward man. This *sincerity* wants nothing of extern fashion, or ornament to compleat its *piety*; but is satisfactory both to God, and a mans own conscience, by that integrity of a judicious, holy, and devout heart; which hath devoted all its *powers* and *faculties*, to the *knowledge*, *meditation*, *adoration*, *imitation*, *love*, and *admiration of God*; according as he was pleased in *various times* and *maners* to reveal himself to it: As, partly (yet, but darkly) by the *light of reason*, in *rational* and *moral principles* seconded with fears and strokes of Conscience, which is a *beam* and *candle* of the *Lord* in the soul of man; but more clearly by *supernatural manifestations*, in *dreams* and *visions*, in *audible voices*, *prophetical revelations*, or *angelical missions*: By all which, *religious light* was onely *occasional* and *traditional*; but now most evidently, compleatly, and constantly, in that *declaration of his will* to mankinde, which is contained in the *lively oracles* of his now written and perfect Word; the onely infallible rule of a good Conscience, and foundation of true Religion: According to which, onely, we measure it; both as to its internals, which are summarily comprehended, in the love of God; and its externals, which are compleated in that charity, which for Gods sake, we bear, and really exercise toward all men; but chiefly to the *houshold of faith*, that is, the Church, or Society of those, who profess to believe in *Jesus Christ*, as the onely *Saviour* of sinners.

This well-grounded and well-guided Religion (as it is then an *Internal*, *Judicious*, and *Sincere devoting* of the *whole soul to God*, as the *supreme good*, offered us in *Jesus Christ*) We esteem the highest *honor* and *beauty* of the reasonable soul; the *divinest stamp* or *character* on mans nature; the *noblest property* and *capacity* of the *immortal* spirit in us; demonstrating, not onely its common relation to the *Creator* (which all things have,) but the Creators peculiar favor, and indulgence to man; whom he teacheth to fear, enableth to serve, and encourageth to love him above all: As also *mans capacity*,

to

to attain that knowledge of the *divine wiſdom*, and that fruition of the *divine love*, which onely can make it *truly*, and *eternally happy*.

For true Religion, thus ſeated in the ſoul of man, is not barely a *ſpeculative knowledge* of God, according to what his wiſdom hath revealed of *himſelf*, in his *works*, and *word*; As, that he is; what he is not, as to any defects; what he is, in all poſitive *excellencies* in himſelf, (which yet is a great and divine light, ſhining upon mans underſtanding from experience, and from the hiſtorick parts of the Scripture.) But further, it alſo ſhew us, what *God is to us*, in *Nature*, *Grace*, *Law*, *Goſpel*, *Works*, *Word*, *Creation*, and *Chriſts Incarnation*; what *we are to God* in *Chriſt*, for duty and dependance; what *all things are to us*, as they are in God, (that is, in his *wiſdom*, *will*, *power*, *providence*, &c. either making, or preſerving, or diſpoſing them for our good and his glory.) According to which light, we come to deſire, to love, to enjoy God in all things, and all things in him; that is, within thoſe bounds of honor, order, and thoſe leſſer ends, which he hath ſet in reference to the *great ends* of our good, and his glory, which are as a leſſer circle in a greater; having both the ſame centres. At length God becomes the *joy*, *life*, *beauty*, *exaltation*, and *happineſs* of the *believing ſoul*; by its often contemplations of him, and ſincere devotions to him; whence we come to have an *humble ſight*, *ingenuous ſhame*, *penitential ſorrow*, and *juſt abhorrence* of our *ſinfulneſs*, *vanity*, *deformity*, *vileneſs*, and *nothingneſs*, compared to God, and apart from him.

2. *True Religion not barely ſpeculative, but alſo practical.*

χτιανισμὸς ἐστι τῆς θείας φύσεως μίμησις. Niſſ. de prof. Chriſtiana.

Eph. 1. 23.

After this our *wills* come to be *enclined* to him (as the moſt excellent good and perfecting *Beauty*) drawn after him, and duly affected with him; to fear him for his power and juſtice; to venerate him for his excellent majeſty and glory; to admire him for incomprehenſible perfection; to love him for his goodneſs in himſelf, in all things, and in Chriſt above all; (in whom his *love*, *grace*, and *bounty* is moſt clearly diſcovered, and freely conveyed to us;) We come to *believe* him for his *veracity* or *infallible truth* in his *Law* and *Goſpel*; to be *guided* by his *unerring wiſdom*, and *directions*, which are diſcerned in the *mandates* of his *Word* to us, and agreeable *motions* of his *Spirit* in us (which are always conform to each other:) We come alſo to *obey* him in all things for his *ſoverein Empire* and *Authority*; to *truſt* in him at all times for his *faithfulneſs* and *immutability*; to *hope* in him, and to wait patiently for the conſummation of his *rich and pretious promiſes*, 2 *Pet*. 1. 4. both in grace and glory. All which we believe upon the *divine teſtimony* of the written Word; however we cannot by bare humane reaſon, comprehend or demonſtrate them;

Virtus Spiritus ſancti in motibus, & veritas verbi in mandatis ſuaviſſimo & inſeparabili nexu conjuncta ſunt; nec magis ab invicem diſtrahi poſſunt quàm calor ſolis à nativo lumine: Quum à Spiritu ſit veritas, ut in veritate ſit Spiritus neceſſe eſt. Auguſt.

oftentimes *praying* to God, as all sufficient, omniscient, omnipresent, and omnipotent: supplicating for that, from his *grace*, *power*, and *bounty*, which we have not, deserve not, nor can attain otherways, in this *lapsed*, *corrupted*, and *cursed estate* of our *nature*.

Eph. 2. 5. By grace ye are saved.

Blanda violentia, victrix delectatio. Aug.

Which owes all its reparations onely to the free *grace* of God, manifesting himself in his *works* and *words*; also in those secret inward operations of the Spirit upon the *conscience*, and whole *soul*, by illuminations, restraints, terrors, convictions, conversions; sweet, yet powerful, attractions; victorious, yet delectable prevailings, agreeable to the *nature* of the *soul*, and the *liberty* of the *will*; which then recovers its *true liberty*, when by the cords of Gods love, its unwillingness is bound up; and its chains of violent lusts are taken off: Whence such *great impressions*, and *real changes*, are made upon every rational faculty in the soul; as those from *darkness to light*, from *captivity to freedom*, from *death to life*; according to the several representations of Gods excellencies in *nature*, in *morals*, and in *mysteries*; wherein, the *exceeding great riches of his free-grace, and love to us in Christ*, *Ephes.* 1. 9. & 2. 7. hath the most softning, melting, and transforming influence; which, fully received upon the soul, the *whole-man*, in *minde* and *spirit*, in *fancy*, *understanding*, *judgement*, *memory*, *will*, *appetite*, *affections*, *passions*, and *conscience*, becomes partaker, through grace, of a *divine nature*, 2 *Pet.* 1. 4. (compared to what he was) and becomes a * *new creature*, not as to its essence; but as to all ends, principles, motions, and actions; which are begun and continued, designed and ended in *holiness*; that is, in *humble* and *unfeigned regards* to the *glory of God*, and exact purposes of *conformity* to the *will of God*, in his written Word. *New creatures* by a newness of *grace*; in which, we remain what we were, *Men*; but are made, what we were not, *Saints*.

Quò strictius ad Deum ligamur, eo perfectius liberamur, & à peccatorum pondere, & pravitatum vinculis; nec reatu, nec terrore, nec infirmitate amplius detinemur, aut opprimimur. August.

Non dii facti sumus sed divini; non in Dei essentiam transmutamur, sed in sanctam, hoc est, divinam naturam reparamur; quantum satanæ lapsi, tantum Deo reparati, confirmamur. Prosp. * 2 Cor. 5. 17.

3. *Scripture the only rule of true Religion.*

1 Tim. 3. 15. Heb. 4. 12. Acts 7. 38. Rom. 3. 2.

To which Word of God in the Scriptures, we being guided and directed by the *constant* and most *credible testimony* of the *Church* of *Christ*, (that *pillar* and *ground of Truth*) so as to receive, and regard them, They at length, by Gods grace on the heart, demonstrate themselves (by their *native* and *divine light*) to be the very Word of God; those *lively oracles*, which set forth most *divine precepts*, *paterns*, *prophecies*, *histories* and *mysteries*; *proffers* also and *promises* of such good things, as the soul would most desire, most wants, and onely can truly delight in living and dying; and to eternity.

Religion consists in no fond fancies.

* *Hæc prius cre-*

Beyond * these Scriptures, which we justly call *The Word of God*, understood in their true sense and meaning; we do not own any thing *for a ground*, *rule*, or *duty* in *Religion*: Nor are we at all moved, by those *bold triflings*, and *endless janglings* about *Religion*,

Grace,

Grace, *Spirit*, and *Inspirations*, which weak and vain men, (looking to their own *foolish fancies*, and not to the *divine Oracles*) do scatter too and fro, as *chaff*, to blinde the eyes of simple and credulous people; which would make *Religion*, a matter of *novelty* and *curiosity*; of cavilling meerly and contending, of censuring and condemning others of self-confidence and intollerable boastings, of sequaciousness and feminine softness, of custom onely and paternal example, or of ease and idleness; where, out of a lazy temper, neglecting all ordinary *means*, *Ministry*, and *duties*, some men expect by *special inspirations* and *dictates*, to have their defect of pains and industry supplied: Or else they place their *Religion*, in the adhering to some *party* and *faction*; in *popular* and *specious insinuations*, and *pretensions*; or in admiration of mens persons, and gifts; or in the prevailencies of *power* and *worldly successes*; or in *unjust gain* and *sacrilegious thrift*; or in great *zealotries* for some *new form* and *way* of *constituting*, *disciplining*, and *governing Churches*; or in *boldness* to affirm, to deny, and to do any thing; or in meer *verbal assurances*, and *loose confidences* of being *elected* and *predestinated* to *happiness*, of being called to be *Saints*, and *Preachers*, and *Prophets*, in a new and extraordinary way; to advance such *opinions* and *practises*, as no holy men of old, ever knew, acted, or owned for Religious; or lastly, in railing upon, despising, and seeking to destroy all those, that approve not, or follow not those *self-conceited confidences* and *violent extravagancies*, which some men affect in their rude and unwarrantable undertakings. Such were the fanatick, mad, and at last, sad, Religion of those *Circumcellions* of old, and those *Anabaptists*, and other later Sects in *Germany* *, who wanted nothing but constant successes and continued power to have made all men, as wilde and wicked as themselves, or else to have destroyed them.

dimus; non esse ultra Scripturas, quod credere debeamus: nobis curiositate non opus est post Christum, nec inquisitione post Evangelium. Tertul. de præs. ad Hæ.

κάνονες ἡ θεία γραφὴ πιστευέτωσαν, ἢ τῆ ἀμορφίας, ἢ τῆ εἰς κόσμον ἀμήχανον μετατίθεσθαι δίκαιον. Niss.

Ζωῆς ἀϊδίου ἐφόδια αἱ θεῖαι γραφαί. Cl. Al. ςρω. 1.

Nos tantum Scripturas sacras habemus, plenas, inviolatas, integras; eas vel in purissimo fonte, vel in pura translatione bibimus. Sal. de Gub. l. 5.

Tantummodo sacris Scripturis canonicis hanc ingenuam debeo servitutem, quâ eas solas ita sequar, ut conscriptores earum nihil omnino in eis errasse, nihil fallaciter posuisse non dubitem. August. ep. 19. ad Jeron. *Si canonicarum scripturarum authoritate quidquam firmatur, sine ulla dubitatione credendum est: Aliis verò testibus tibi credere vel non credere liceat.* August. ep. cap. 12. * Sleidan. Com. l. 10. ad an. 1535.

Alas, who sees not, how far different and much easier to sinful flesh and blood, to vain ambition, and proud hypocrisies, these pretty *soft fallacies*, these *froths* and *fumes*; those great *swelling words*, and *titles of vanity*, That *God is their Father*, that they are *Saints*, and *spiritual*, inspired *Prophets*, sent of God to call the World to repentance; to reign with *Christ*; Those *rotten sensualities* of *Religion* (as some blasphemously call it;) those *libidinous excrescencies*; those *lying prophecies*, *&c.* How much easier (I say) these are, than those *humble*, *sober*, *exact*, and *constant tyes* of *Conscience*, and *duties* of 2 Pet. 2. 18.

true Religion; by which holy men and women, in all ages, have given all *diligence to make their calling and election sure*, to *work out their salvation with fear and trembling*; by hearing, reading, searching and meditating on the *Scriptures*; by repenting, fasting, praying, watching, and weeping; by examining, trying, judging, and condemning their sinful self, even in the most specious and successful actions. Thus by *mortification* and *self-denial*, coming to the *Cross of Christ*; taking it up; bearing it, and fastning themselves to it, as to all *just strictnesses*, *holy severities*, and *patient sufferings*; still endeavoring to abound in all exactness of *justice*, *charity*, *meekness*, *temperance*, and *innocency*, before *God* and *man*. Thus going with some *holy agony*, through many difficulties the narrow way; true Christians (having *done all*) enter in *at the strait-gate*, which *leads to life*, and are scarcely saved.

These were harder *disciplines*, and rougher *severities* of *piety*, than our delicate *novelists*; our gentle *Enthusiasts*; our smiling *Seraphicks*; our triumphant *Libertines*; our softer *Saints* can endure; which makes them so impatient (as *Ahab* to *Eliah*, and *Micaiah*) to hear, and bear the words of faithful and true *Ministers*; which seem as hard sayings; when they recommend and urge these *Scripturals* and *Morals* of *truth and holiness*, *justice*, *mercy*, *and humility*, *Micah* 6. 8. to be the onely reals of Religion: In which, the duty, rule, end, comfort, and crown of true Religion, do consist; whose greatest and surest enjoyment, is *self-denial*; bringing the lost soul, to finde it self lost, and to seek after God; and having found him, to follow him with all obediential love; with a pious, impatient, *panting* and *thirsting* after happiness in him, by the ways of holiness; as having *none in Heaven or Earth comparable to him*; still earnestly pressing toward him; as always, and onely wanting him, in the fullest enjoyments of all things here; unsatiably satisfied with his unsurfetting-sweetness; ever filled with him, yet ever longing more to partake of him: The soul in this its excessive thirst, and spiritual feaver, being confident, it can drink up that *Jordan*; *that ocean of divine fulness*; which alone, it sees, can give it an happy satisfaction to eternity.

2 Pet. 1. 10. *Non est vera aut firma certitudo gloriæ, sine diligenti industria gratiæ?* Chrys.
Phil. 2. 12.
1 Cor. 15. 32. I die daily. *Verè Christum sequi, est omnia perpeti, indies crucifigi, jugiter mori.* Prosp.
2 Pet. 1. 6.
1 Pet. 4. 18.
Non vult Deus ut delicato itinere ad cœlum perveniamus. Jeron.
Aut hoc non est Evangelium aut hi non sunt Evangelici. Luth.
Vana est religio quæ sceleri locum facit. Æn. Syl.
Vana est religio quæ vera non est; nec vera esse potest nisi certa sit, & firma, & æquabilis, & sibi semper constans, & in omnibus una. Tertul.
Hoc primum invenimus, quod perditissimi sumus; nec nisi quærendo Deum salvari possumus. August.

4.
The Souls search after, and discoveries of God.

The *devout and pious Soul*, thus *intent to God*, and *content* with him, is not always *sceptically* wandring in endless mazes and labyrinths of Religion; either groping in obscurities, or guessing at uncertainties, or grapling with intricate disputes, or perplexed with various opinions, or shifting its parties, or doubting its profession, or confounding its morals, or dazeling its intellectual eye; by looking to *prospects of immensity*, and *objects of eternity*; (which are so remote

mote from it, and far above it, that it onely sees this, That it can see nothing of that *transcendent Good*, which we call *God*. (Who is indeed, that *superexcellent excellency*, which we can least know as he is ; and can no way comprehend in his ineffable essence , and most incomprehensible perfections.)

[illegible] ουσία. Dionys.

Quod est omni creaturâ melius, id Deum dicimus. Aug. Retract.

But, the Soul in its religious search after, and devout applications to, this *supreme Good*, which it esteems, as its God, stayes and solaces it self (as Miners do, who still follow and chiefly intend the richest Vain) with those lesser grains and sparks of *divine goodness* and *beauty* , which it findes every where scattered in its passage among the *Creatures* ; which are as little essays, pledges, and tokens of that *divine glory* and *excellency*, which must needs be infinitely more admirable, and delectable in *God* himself.

The *pious* (which is the onely wise and well advised) *Soul*, so soon as ever it seriously searcheth after God, findes him in some kinde or other, every where present ; and in every thing lovely, yea, admirable, both within and without it self ; yet still it conceives him to be infinitely above it self, and all things. Something of God it discovers, and accordingly admireth, adoreth, praiseth, loveth, and exalteth him, in the order, goodness, greatness, beauty, variety, and constancy of his works, which are every day visible ; something it perceives of his *sweetness* and *delectableness* in the *sober* , *moderate*, and holy *delectations*, which our senses afford us, when they enjoy those objects, which are convenient, and fitted for them ; something it observes of *divine wisdom*, *power*, *benignity*, and *justice*, in the experiences of Gods *providence*, *bounty*, and *patience*, which the histories of all times afford ; something it discerns of God, in those common beams and principles of *reason*, which shine in all mens mindes, and are evidenced in the consent of all *Nations*. Sometime also in the reflexions, terrors, or tranquilities of its own, and other mens *consciences* ; which, are as the first Heaven or Hell, rewarding the good, or punishing the bad *intentions* and *actions* of every man : More fully it sees God in the *manifestations* of the *divine Word* ; in the exactness of the *Moral Law* ; in the *rules* of *Justice* given to all men ; of which, their own reason and will is the measure and standard. Being commanded *to do to other men, as we would have them do to us*, *Matth*. 7. 12. yea, and to do to God also ; in the relations whereby we stand obliged to him, for *duty*, *love*, and *gratitude*, as we would have others do to us ; when we are as *fathers*, or *masters*, or *friends*, or *benefactors*, or *well-willers* ; against which, to offend, is by all men thought most barbarous, unjust, and wicked ; how much more against God, who hath the highest merit upon us ? Yet further, the Soul searching after God, findes his *wisdom* and *prescience* in all those *prophetical predictions* , and many *prefigurations* of things to come ;

Habet Deus testimonia totum hoc quod sumus & in quo sumus. Tert. l. 1. adv. Mar.

Psal. 111. 2.

Psal. 8.

Dei opera sunt quotidiana miracula, consueta vilescunt. Aug.

Rom. 1. 20.

Amplissima merx est bona conscientia. Hic murus aheneus, &c.

—*Prima est haec ultio quod se Judice nemo nocens absolvitur, &c.* Juv.

Matth. 1. 6, 8.

If I be a father, &c.

Offer it now to thy Prince, &c.

Tam pater, tam pius, tam beneficus nemo. Tert. de Deo.

Idoneum est divinitatis testimonium veritas divinationis. Tert. Apol. c. 20.

come; which, from several hands, and at several times derived, have yet punctually been fulfilled; chiefly in the coming of the *Messias*, the sum, center, and consummation of all prophecies and promises; which setting forth the *nature, love, life,* and *death of Jesus Christ*, were all most exactly accomplished in him, and by him; on whom were those notable *signatures* and *characters* of the *divine wisdom* and *power*, that *his glory* appeared to men, as *the glory of the onely begotten Son of God, full of grace, and truth.* John 1.14.

The *freeneß* and *fulneß* of this *Evangelical grace* and *truth* by *Jesus Christ*, the faithful Soul further discerns in the *sacred emblems* and *seals* of the *holy Sacraments*; by which the *divine goodneß* is represented and conveyed to us under the *notions* and *efficacy* of those things, which are most necessary to our lives; either for Being, or Ornament; to nourish us, to cleanse us, and to chear us. Moreover, the pious Soul sees God in the exemplary patience of the *holy Martyrs*; in the miraculous constancy of the *heroick Confessors*; in the humility of *true Penitents*; in the purity and amendment of *real Converts*; in the contentedness of *true Believers*; in the mercifulness and charity of *true Christians*; in the mortifyings, and self-denyings (as to this world) of all *true Saints*, which are *followers of Christ*; and lastly, in that holy ordination and succession of the *Evangelical Ministry*; which as *Christ instituted* for the *Churches* good, so he hath through all the vicissitudes of times, amidst all oppositions, preserved it to these days; and by it, the knowledge of God, and the faith of Christ in the World.

The *devout Soul* still guided and going on by the light of the *Ministry*, discerns something of God; which is yet more *retired, secret,* and *ineffable*, in the *enlightnings, softnings, serenities, enlargements, calmings,* and *comforts*, which are made by a *divine power* and *supernatural influence* upon it self; where it beholds the *brightest glimpses* of *divine glory*, through the face of *Jesus Christ*, and by the *efficacies* of his most *sweet* and *holy Spirit*, who is both *God* and *man*; subject to our *infirmities*, sensible of them, and victorious over them: Him the *Soul* answerably loves; as *man*, with a love of *union* and *complacency*; as *God*, with the love of *admiration* and *extasie*; as both *God* and *man*, with a love of *adherence* and *satisfaction*: As one, that hath undertaken, and is able to *save* it to the *uttermost*; reconciling it with preparing it for, and uniting it to, the supreme Good, God. Heb. 7. 25.

All these excellencies of *Christ*, it sees diffused and derived to it by convenient means, instituted and continued in the *Church*; which as pipes laid into the *Oceans* unexhaustible fulness, draw from it, not to what measure it can give, but to what we want, and can receive.

At

At length this *devout Soul*, by this daily confluence of many heavenly *Meditations*, holy *Motions*, and happy *Experiments*, flowing (like lesser *rivolets*) from all parts of the *Creation*, from *Scripture*, and from its own, with others experiences, to this *stream* of the knowledge of God; It findes it self by degrees advanced, like *Ezekiels* waters, from vulgar and shallow conceptions, and answerable affections, to mighty and profound *contemplations*; which, gathering strength by their daily increasings, like an imperious, and irresistible *torrent*, carry away the *devout Soul* in its holy *propensities*, and *impetuous fervencies* toward God: Impatient of any stop or hinderance, till, at last, it comes (as all *Rivers* into the *Ocean*) to be wholly resigned, and happily resolved into its *Alpha* and *Omega*, its *principle* and *perfection*, its *fountain*, and its *fulness*, God. Ezek. 47.

So then, when the *Soul* in ways of *true Religion* comes to *know*, and *love*, and *serve* God, it is not conversant in *vagrant fancies*, in uncertain *speculations*, in in-significant *notions*; but it so far really enjoys him, as it loves him; and loves him, as it sees him; and sees him, as it seriously and deliberately observes him; (there being nothing of *true Religion* in *volatile spirits*, and *transient glances*;) which it doth most evidently, though not perfectly; darkly, yet truly, in those *glasses* of the *Creatures*; in the *Scriptures*, and in its own *Conscience*; in all *ways* of Goodness, Truth, and Holiness; in *lights* Natural, Moral, and Evangelical; by all which, the *Soul*, as the *Eye*, sees somewhat of the *divine glory* of that *invisible Sun*, in the *descents*, *scatterings*, and *aptitudes of its beams*; whose infinite, and intire *brightness* it cannot, without injury to it self, fully, and immediately, behold. 1 Cor. 13. 12. Exod. 33. 20.

So that herein (we see) true and solid *Religion*, both by its light and holiness, its truth and practise, abundantly discovers, the *fancifulness*, *levity*, *pride*, *vanity*, *fondness*, and *futility*, of all those *giddy opinions* and *pretensions*, by which some men seek to amuse the world, and to abuse honest hearts: And also it shews its own real worth, beauty, dignity, fulness, usefulness, wisdom, and power; by all which it fits and fills the *Souls various faculties* and *vast capacity*: And in so doing it gives the *devout Soul*, the greatest evidences and surest demonstrations of its own immortality, beyond what any arguments drawn from ordinary reason and philosophy can do: All which the *Atheistical impudence* of some men easily elude, having no experimental knowledge of God; and living without God in the world, they are content to imagine an utter extinction of their souls.

Malunt impii extingui, quàm ad supplicia reparari. Mi. Fæl.

Souls immortality discovered in true Religion.

Whereas the *sanctified Soul* concludes, and glories in its *immortality*; which it endeavors to improve to a *blessed eternity*; when it

considers seriously, and alone; whence can those high and holy *enlargements*, *desires*, and *designs* arise, so far above, and beyond all worldly *objects* and *enjoyments*? whence that *unsatisfiedness*, which carries the soul of man, with ambitious impatiencies, to this height of
Rom. 2.7. coveting after a blessed *eternity*, and the supreme *Good*, *God blessed for ever*? Whence this magnetick *tendency* and divine *traction of love* to God, and to his *infinite goodness*; but onely from the *Father* of our spirits, and *Fountain* of our souls, God? And why all these *meditations*, *desires*, and *motions*, planted in us by so *good* and *wise* a *Creator*, if never to be enjoyed by us, in those *satisfactions*, which onely can flow from some *divine* and *perfective object*? Sure it is all one to *omnipotent goodness*, to fill us with the *perfect good* desired; as to endue us with the *desires* of that *good*; which are but our *torments* and *imperfections*, if never to be in completion: Our very desires of Heaven, would else be our Hell; and our longings after happiness, our misery. Nor is it agreeable to the methods of *divine wisdom* and *goodness*, to *plant frustaneous* and *vain desires*, or *Tantalising tendencies* in mans nature, which he hath done in no other Creature; who attain whatever they naturally covet, or have innate propensities to. The same *divine power* having prepared the *object*, hath also implanted the *desire*. This unproportionableness of the *Creators* dealing with man, is less to be imagined, when we consider in the *sacred story*, That man had most of *divine counsel* and *deliberation*
Gen. 1. 26. in his *Creation*; (not as needful to God, who can work by *omniscient* and *omnipotent power*, in an instant) but, implying to us, those most *exact* and *accurate proportions* observed by the *great* and *allwise Creator*, in his *formation* of man: All other Creatures rising up, as *bubbles* on water, so soon as the *formative Word* of *God*, in its several commands, fell like distinct drops from Heaven, on the *face of the great deep*, the *Chaos*, or *Abyss*; But man, as a *signet* or *seal*, was graven by a special hand, and deliberate method of God, with the *marks* and *characters* of his own holy *image*, in *spirituality*, *wisdom*, *righteousness*, *purity*, *liberty*, *eternity*, and a proportionate capacity to enjoy whatever felicity he can understand and desire.

5. That, if we raise man to the highest glory and perfection, which
Mans improvement. he covets, and is capable of in this world of *vanity* and *mortality*; we shall see something in him of a *little god*, like the *figure of a great monarch* expressed in a small *model* or *signet*: For, bring him from
τίμιον ζῶον ἄνθρωπος ὅτι θεῖον. Plat. the *sords* of his *nativity*, from his *infant infirmities*, from his *childish simplicities*, from his *youthful vanities*; redeem him, by the politure of good *education*, from his *rustick ignorance*, his *clownish confidences*,
Stolida feritia. Tac. his *brutish dulness*, his *country solitude*, his *earthy ploddings*, his *beggarly indigences*, or *covetous necessities*; rack him off further, and

refine

refine him from the *lees of sensual* and *inordinate lusts*, from *swelling* and *surly pride*, from *base* and *mean designs*, from *immoderate affections, violent passions, unreasonable impulses*, and *depraved temptations*, from within or without: Then furnish him with *health, procerity*, and *beauty*; fortifie him with competent *strength*, both single and social; endue him with all wisdom, both *divine* and *humane*, which the minde of man is capable of; compass him with all fulness and plenty; invest him with that publick honor, which (as beams of the Sun, concentred in a Burning-glass,) arising from the *consent* of many men, to unite the honor of their *protection* and *subjection* in one man, makes up the lustre of a *majesty*, something more than *earthly* and *humane*; coming neerest to the resemblance of what is *divine* and *heavenly*. Adde to these *endowments* of *power, opportunity*, and *place* to do good; those *real* and *useful graces*, those *charitable* and *communicative virtues*, which enlarge the *nobler soul*, to a *love* of the *publick good*, and a *zeal* for the *common welfare* of mankinde, in works of *humanity, gentleness, pity, patience, fortitude, justice, mercy, benignity*, and *munificence*: What can more lively express to us a terrene *visible Deity*? whom we may (without *Idolatry*) own and reverence so far, as, without *blasphemy*, we may call such a man a God; while he *wisely teacheth* and *instructeth* others (a work worthy of a *Parent*, a *Prince*, a *God*;) or he powerfully *protects*, or he bountifully *rewards*, or justly *punisheth*, or mercifully *pardoneth*, or graciously *loveth* others, and rejoyceth in their *well-doing* and *happiness*, without any design or interest of his own. Yea, what do we ordinarily wish, and expect, or fancy more from God, than all these *excellencies* (of which, we see there are some *sparks* and *beams*, even now in mans nature) *sublimated* to *infinite perfections*; and extended to us, with *eternal durations*? is not this, that estate of *full enjoyment*, which we call *Heaven*? Wherein we hope never to want those *divine* and *immediate communicatings*, with the *all-sufficient bounty*, and *unenvious benignity* of God, is, as well able; so, no less, well pleased, to impart to the soul, than its necessities do require, and its desires ambitiously, and unsatiably covet to be supplied by them: Not onely in order to this *natural* and *politick Being*; which as men we have with men, for a moment (which is daily pressed upon with the fatal and inevitable necessity of dying, which is a ceasing to enjoy God, by the *mediation* of the *Creatures*, in this visible world) but also, in reference to that *rational, religious, spiritual, gracious, perfect*, and *unchangeable Being*, whereto we naturally aspire; (for, who would not be ever happy?) by *enjoying himself*, in the *wisdom, strength, beauty, fulness, love*, and *sweetness*, flowing for ever from the *excellencies* of the *Creator*: The fruition of whom, is onely able to exclude all *defects*, and *fears*; to satisfie all *desires*, to

Ἀφαιρετέα μὲ τὰ ἀπέρατα, ἃ ἐφ λυπήσαι ἀγέλαν δόξα ἐσόντα. Plat. de Cupiditat.

ὡς χαρίεν ἐστ᾽ ἄνθρωπος ἂν ἄνθρωπος ᾖ. Clem. Alex. è Menandro. How goodly a creature is a man, while he continues a man?

Exod. 22. 28. Psal. 82. 6. John 10. 34. Magistrates are called gods.

Paternum est docendi munus. Psal. 34. 11. Jer. 9. 34.

Beatitudo est interminabilis vitæ perfecta possessio. Boet.

reward all *duties*, to requite all *sufferings*, to compleat all *happiness*, to crown and perfect all true *Religion*; which in *Heaven* shall be no other, than what we desire it to be here on *Earth*; that is, a *right knowledge*, and a *willing performance* of that *duty*, which the *reasonable creature* (Man) ows for ever to God: First, as his *Creator*, *Conservator*, and *Redeemer*, by *Jesus Christ*.

6. *True Religion internal instates the Soul in Christ, and in the true Church.*

This then we look upon, as the *Religious frame* and *temper* of a *reasonable Soul*, in its *internal dispositions* and *private devotions* toward God, it self, and others: By which it is daily preparing for a *glorious* and *blessed immortality*; of which *holy frame*, it self onely can be conscious, with God; and the greatest evidence is, That *sincerity of heart*, which hath no other *rule*, but Gods Word; no other end, but Gods glory; and no other comfort, but in the constancy of this disposition; which is the fruit of Gods holy *Spirit* in it. Certainly, such a *Soul* cannot, but be in, and of the *true*, and to man, *invisible Church of God*; so far as it hath a *mystical*, *spiritual*, and *invisible life*; which consists in the *union* to *Christ*, as the *head*, by *faith*, *love*, and all other *obediential graces* of his *Spirit*, which are common to every *true believer*. Out of this Church, its most true, There is no *revealed salvation*, possibly to be had for any that live to be mastets of their own *reason*, *will*, and *actions*.

1 Cor. 2. 10, 11. John 15. 5. He that abideth in me, and I in him, &c. 2 Tim. 2. 19. The Lord knoweth them that are his. *Extra ecclesiam non est salus.*

Yea further, such a *religious soul*, hath a capacity of, and right unto that *external*, *visible*, *politick*, and *social communion* with the *Church of Christ*, where ever *Christians* enjoy *outward fellowship*, with one another, in *publick profession*: Which *communion*, however such a *soul*, solitary it may be, and sequestred from all *Christian* company, may not actually enjoy; being forcibly denied that happiness (of which, many do *wilfully* and *peevishly* deprive themselves by *proud* or *peevish*, and *uncharitable separations*,) through *banishment*, *prison*, *captivity*, *sickness*, &c. Yet, that *Christian belief*, *love*, and *charity*, which such an one bears to *Christ*, and to the *Catholike Church* of *Christ*, *scattered* in many places, and *different* in many *ceremonial rites*, and *observations*; These (I say) do infallibly invest this *solitary Christian*, in *communion* and *holy fellowship* with the whole *Church of Christ*, in all the World; as *brethren* and *sisters* are related as *near kinred*, when they are never so far a sunder in place; which owns the same God, believes the same *common salvation* by the same *Lord Jesus*; useth the same *seals* of the *blessed Sacraments*; professeth the same ground of *faith*, and rule of *holiness*, the written *Word of God*; and bears the like *gracious* and *charitable temper* to others, as sanctified by same *Spirit* of *Christ*, which really unites every *charitable* and *true believer* to *Christ*, and so to every Member of true Church; however it may want opportunities to express this *communion* in actual, and visible *conversation*, either *civil* or *sacred*; by enjoying that

Ephes. 4. 5. Jude 2.

society,

society, as men, or that ordinary *ministry*, as Christians, which is by *Christ* appointed in the Church; as well for its outward *profession*, *distinction*, and *mutual assistance*; as for its inward *comfort*, and *communion* with himself.

The *willing neglect* of all such *extern communion*, and the *causeless separation* from all Church-fellowship in *Word*, *Sacraments*, *Prayer*, *Order*, and charitable *Offices*, must needs be inconsistent with any comfort; because against *charity*, and so far against *true Religion*, and the *hopes of salvation*: For, those *inward graces*, wherein the *life* and *soul* of *Religion* do consist, are not ordinarily attained or maintained, but by those *outward means* and *ministrations*, which the *wisdom of God in Christ* hath appointed for the *Churches social good*, and *edification* together: In the *right enjoyment* of which consists that *extern*, and *joynt celebration* or *profession* of *Christian Religion*, which gives *Being*, *name*, and *distinction* to that *society*, which we call *The Church of Christ on Earth*. And this indeed is that Church properly, which is called out of the World; which as men, we may discern; and of which, both in *elder* and *later times*, so many *disputes* have been raised, which we may describe to be,

An *holy company* or *fraternity of Christians*, who being called by the *Ministry of the Gospel*, to the *knowledge of God in Christ*, do publickly *profess* in all *holy ways* and *orderly institutions*, that inward sense of *duty* and *devotion*, which they ow to God, by believing and obeying his Word: Also that *charity*, which they ow to all men, especially to those that *profess to be Christs Disciples*, and hold *communion* with *his Body*, the *Catholike Church*.

Herein I conceive, That the *social outward profession* of *Religion*, as it is held forth in the *Word of God*, in its *Truths*, *Seals*, *Duties*, and *Ministry*, makes a true Church among men: And the true Church as Catholike, yea, any part or branch of this true Catholike Church, (whose *Head*, *Foundation*, *Rites*, *Seals*, *Duties*, and *Ministry*, are for the main of the same kinde, in all times and places,) cannot but make a *right profession* of *true Religion*; as to the *main essence* and *fundamentals*; which consists in *truth*, *holiness*, and *charity*: However there may be many *variations*, *differences*, and *deformities* in superstructures, both of *opinion* and *practise*: For however particular Churches, which have their *limits* of *time*, and *place*, and *persons*, (*circumstances* which necessarily *circumscribe* all things in this world) are still, as distinct arms and branches of a great Tree, issuing from one and the same root *Jesus Christ*;

7. *Of the Church as a visible society of Professors believing in Christ.*

Ea est Catholica ecclesia, quæ unicam & eandem semper & ubique fidem in Christo veram & Scripturis fundatam profitetur. Vin. Lyrin. Eph. 2. 9. As Fellow-Citizens of the Saints, and of the houshold of God; Ye are built upon the Foundation of the Apostles and Prophets, Jesus Christ being the chief corner stone, &c.

and have the same *sap* of *truth* and *life* conveyed in some measure to them, by the same way of the *right Ministry* of the *Word, Sacraments,* and *Spirit,* (so that in these respects, they are all of one and the same *Catholike Body, communion, descent* and *derivation* ;) yet, as these have their *external distinctions* and *severings* in time, place, persons, and maners ; or any outward *rites* of *profession,* and *worship* ; so they usually have *distinct denominations,* and are subject to *different accidents,* as well as *proportions* : Some *branches* of the same Tree may be *withering, mossy, cancred, peeled, broken,* and *barren,* yea, almost dead ; yet, old, and great, and true : Others, may be more flourishing, fruitful, clean, and entire, though of a latter *shooting* for time, and of a lesser *extension* for number and place ; yet still of the same Tree ; so far, as they have really, or onely seemingly, and in the judgement of *charity,* communion with, relation to, and dependance on the Root and bulk ; being neither quite broken off, and dead, by *Heretical Apostacies,* denying the *Lord* that bought them, or *damnable errors,* which overthrow the *Faith* ; nor yet *slivered* and *rent,* by *Schismatical uncharitableness, proud,* or *peevish rents* and *divisions* : Which last, although they do not wholly *kill,* and crop off from all *communion* with the Church of Christ ; yet they so far *weaken* and *wither Religion,* in the *fruits* and *comforts* of it ; as each *Schism* pares off from its *sect* and *faction,* that *Rinde* and *Bark* (as it were) of Christian love, and mutual charity, through which (chiefly) the *sap,* and *juyce* of *true Religion,* with the *graces* and *comforts* of it, are happily and most thrivingly conveyed to every *living branch* of the *Catholike Church* ; so as to make it live, at least, and bring forth some good fruit, however it be not so strong, fair, and ample, as others may be : As the Church of *Sardis,* which had a * *name to live, and was dead in some part and proportion* ; yet is bid to *watch,* and *strengthen* the things *that remain,* which are ready to die, &c.

1 Cor. 3. 12. If any man build upon this foundation gold, &c. stubble, &c. V. 15. If his work be burnt, he shall suffer loss, but he himself shall be saved. Eph. 4. 4. There is one Body, and one Spirit, one Lord, one Faith, one Baptism, &c. V. 16. The whole body is fitly joyned together, according to the effectual working in the measure of every part, &c.

Unam Deus unam fidem tradidit, unam ecclesiam toto orbe diffudit ; hanc aspicit, hanc diligit, hanc defendit : Quolibet se quisque nomine tegat, si huic non societur alienus est, si hanc impugnet inimicus est. Oros. 7. c. 35. Joh. 15. 2. Every branch in me that beareth not fruit, my Father taketh away. 2 Pet. 2. 1. 2 Tim. 2. 18. 1 Cor. 12. 25. That there should be no schism in the body. 2 Joh. 9. Whosoever transgresseth and abideth not in the doctrine of Christ, hath not God : He that abideth in the doctrine of Christ, hath the Father and the Son. * Rev. 3. 1.

8. *Of the Church, as called Catholike.*

See learned Dr. *Field* of the Church. Τοιαῦτ' ἀντιλέγειν ἀρμαι.

In this point then, Touching the true Church of Christ, in regard of outward profession, and visible communion (to the touch of which part, my design thus leads me) I purpose not so far to gratifie the endless, and needless janglings of any adversaries of this Church of *England* ; as to plunge my self, or the *Reader,* into the wide and troubled Sea of *controversie,* concerning the Church : Considering, that many good Christians have been, and still are, in the true *Catholike Church,* by profession of that *true faith,* and holy *obedience,* which

unite

unite to the *Head*, *Jesus Christ*; and by *charity*, which combines the *members* of his *Body* together; although they never heard the dispute, or determination of this so driven a *controversie*; As many are in health, and sound, who never were under *Physicians* hands, or heard any *Lecture* of *Anatomy*: Yea, although they may be cut off, and cast out of the particular *communion* of any Church, by the *Anathemaes*, and *excommunicating sentences* of some *injurious* and *passionate Members* of that Church; yet may they continue still in communion with Christ, and consequently with his *Catholike Church*; that is, with all those, who either truly have, or profess to have communion with *Christ*.

My purpose is, onely to give an account, as I have done of *true Religion* in the *internal power* of it; so also of the *true Church*, as to the *external profession* of *Religion*: That thereby I may establish the *faith*, and *comforts* of all sober and good Christians, in this Church of *England*: That they may not be shaken, corrupted, or rent off, by their own instability, and weakness; or by the *fraud* and *malice* of those, who glory more in the *proselytes* they gain to *fanatick factions*, by uncharitable *rendings* from this Church, than in any communion they might have in *humble* and *charitable* ways, with the *Catholike Church*; or any of the greater, and nobler parts of it; which they (most *impertinently*) deny to be any Churches, or capable of any order, power, joynt authority, larger government, or ampler communion.

For the *Catholike Church* of *Christ*, (that is, the *universality* of those, who profess to believe in the name of *Jesus Christ*, according to the *Scriptures*;) That this is primarily and properly called a *Church*, often in *Scripture*, there is no doubt: As the whole is called a *Body*, in its integrality or compleatness of *parts* and *organs*; whose every *limb* and *part* is corporeal too, and of the *Body*, as to its *nature*, *kinde*, or *essence*. This *Church*, which is called *The Spouse and Body of Christ*, is (as its *Head*) but one; in its integrality or comprehensive latitude; as the *Ark* containing all such, as profess the true faith of Christ: And to this are given (as all *powers* and *faculties* of *nature* to the *whole man*) primarily and eminently those *powers*, *privileges*, *gifts*, and *titles*, which are proper to the Church of Christ; however, they are orderly exercised by some particular *parts* or *members*, for the good of the *whole*. The essence, integrality, and unity, of this Catholike Church consists, not in any *local convention*, or *visible communion*, or *publick representation*, of every part of it;

Ignat. ep. ad Phil. Cypr. de unitate Eccl. *Solis multi radii, unum lumen.* August. lib. de unitate ecclesiæ. *Et omnes patres.*

Eph. 1. 22. Christ the Head over all things to the Church.

1 Tim. 3. 15. The Church of the living God; the pillar and ground of truth. Heb. 12. 23. The Church of the first born. *Tot ac tantæ ecclesiæ una est illa ab Apostolis prima, ex qua omnes.* Tertul. de præ. ad Hæ. c. 30. Eph. 3. 10, 21. & 5. 23. Christ the Head of the Church, and the Saviour of the Body. V. 32. Christ and the Church. Col. 1, 18. Christ the Head of the Body, the Church. 1 Cor. 12. The Body is not one Member, but many, &c. *vide.*

but in a *mysterious* and *religious communion* with the same God, by the same Mediator Jesus Christ; and to this Mediator Jesus Christ, by the same Word and Spirit, as to the *internal part* of *Religion*; also by profession of the same Truth and *common Salvation*, joyned with obedience to the same *Gospel*, and *holy Ministry*, with *charity*, and *comly order*, as to the *external*.

In this so clear an *Article of our Faith*, I need not bestow my pains, since it is lately handled very fully, learnedly, and calmly, by a godly Minister of this Church of *England* *; to whose Book I refer the Christian Reader.

Ecclesia in universum mundi disseminata unam domum habitans, unam animam & cor & os habet. Iræn. l. 1. c. 3. Eph. 4. 4, 5. Jude 2. πιστὶς ἐν ἐν χριστῷ πιστεύοντες, ὡς μία ψυχῇ, μία συναγωγὴ, καὶ μία ἐκκλησία. Just. M. Dial. cum Tryphone. * Mr. *Hudson* of the Catholike Church. *Tot & tantæ ecclesiæ una est illa ab Apostolis prima, dum unam omnes præbent veritatem.* Terr. de præ.

9.

Of a National Church, or distinct and larger part of the Catholick.

This name of *Church*, being evidently given to the *universality* of those, who by the *Ministry of the Gospel*, are called out of the way of the World; and by professing of it, and submitting externally to its *holy Ministry, Order, Rules, Duties*, and *Institutes*, are distinguished from the rest of the World: It cannot be hard for any sober understanding to conceive, in what aptitude of sense, any part of this Catholike Church, is also called a *Church*; with some additional distinctions, and particular limitations, visible and notable among men, and Christians; by which some are severed from others in *time, place, persons*, or any other *civil discriminations* of *policy* and *society*: Which give nearer and greater conveniences, as to the enjoyment and exercise of *humane* and *civil*; so of Christian communion, and the *offices* or *benefits* of religious relations.

The *Spirit of God* in the *Scripture* gives sufficient warrant to this stile, and language; calling that a Church (as of *Rome, Ephesus, Corinth, Jerusalem, Antioch, &c.*) which consisted of many Congregations, and Presbyters in a City, and its Territory, or Province: So the Apostle *Paul* in his Epistles to several Churches, distinguisheth them by the *civil* and *humane distinctions* of *place*, and *Magistracy*; and the Spirit of Christ to the *Asiatick* Churches, calleth each a Church distinctly, which were in great associations, of many faithful, under many Presbyters: And these under some chief *Presidents, Apostles, Angels*, or *Bishops*, residing in the prime or Mother Cities; where Christianity was first planted, and from whence it spred to the Territories, or Provinces about.

One would think, besides *common speech*, among all Christians, (which is sufficient to justifie, what word is used to express our meanings to others,) That this were enough to confute the *simplicity* or *peevishness* of those, who, to carry on new projects, dare aver, That

1 Cor. 1. 2. To the Church of God, which is at *Corinth*. Acts 13. 1. The Church of *Antioch*. κατ' ἐκκλησίαν. Acts 14. 23. Tit. 1. 5. κατὰ πόλιν. Rev. 2. & 3. *Ecclesiam apud unamquamque civitatem condiderunt Apostoli, à quibus traducem fidei & semina doctrinæ cæteræ ecclesiæ mutuatæ sunt.* Tertul. de Præ. c. 20. *Consuetudo est certissima loquendi norma.* Quintil.

they

they know no such thing as a *National Church*; and with much coynels, disdain to own, or understand any relation of *order, duty, subordination*, or *charity*, they have to any such Church: Of which, they say they know no *virtue*, no *use*, no *necessity*, no *conveniencies*, as to any Christian and Religious ends. Which so *wilful* and *affected ignorance*, was never known, till these *latter* and *perilous times* had found out the *pleasure of Paradoxes*; by which, men would seem wiser, and more exact, both in their *words* and *fancies*, than either pious *antiquity*, or the *Scriptures*: Hoping by such gross and unexpected *absurdities*, (which would fain appear very shie and scrupulous in language) to colour over *Shismatical* and *Anarchical* designs; and under such *fig-leaves* to hide the shame and folly of their *factious agitations* and *humors*; which makes them unwilling to be governed by any in Church or State, without themselves have an oar in the Boat, and a share in the Government. This *poor concernment* of some mens small ambitions, makes them disown any Church, but such a *conventicle* or *parcel* as some men fancy to *collect* and *call*; which they infect with the same fancies of sole and full Churchship, and separate Power. Whereas the *Lord Jesus Christ* always first called men by his *Ministers* to his Church; and by Baptism admitted them; and by *meet Governors*, whom he *sent* and *ordained*, ruled them, as his flock, in greater, as well as lesser parties; as *Jacob* did his distinct flocks in the hands of his sons.

1 Pet. 2. 9. Ye are an holy Nation, a peculiar people; may be said of any Christians.

Gen. 32.

By the same *Cynical severity*, these men may deny, they have relation to any other men, being themselves *compleat* men; or at most that they are to regard none, but their families where they live; and so cast off all observance to any greater Societies in Towns, or Cities, or Commonweals; yea, and all sense of humanity to the generality of mankinde, whom they shall never see together, or be acquainted with. Who doubts, notwithstanding this *morose folly*, but that, as in all right reason, equity, and humanity, every man is related by the common *nature* to all mankinde; so also, to particular polities and societies of men, greater or smaller; according to the distinct combinations, into which providence hath cast him with them, either in Cities, or Countreys? With whom, to refuse *communion*, and disown *relation*, is to sin against the common *principles* of *society, order*, and *government*, which are in mans nature; which God hath implanted, Reason suggests, and all wise men have observed, for the obtaining of an *higher* and more *common good*, by the *publick* and *united influence* of the counsel, strength, and authority of many, than can be obtained, in *scattered parcels*, or *small* and *weaker fraternities*.

Communis societatis vinculum mutua indigentia.

In like maner, to be *in* and *of the Church*, is not onely to be a *true believer* (which gives *internal* and *real union to Christ*, and to all true Christians in the *Church Catholike*,) of which, no man can judge, because he cannot *discern* it, save onely in the *judgement of charity*) But it implies also *to have and to hold*, that profession of Christian Religion, in such *external polities*, and *visible communion* with others, as the providence of God, both offers and requires of us; according to the time, place, and opportunities, wherein he sets us; so as we may most promote the common good: Which study and duty we own in *humanity*, as men, and more in *charity*, as Christians to any Church, or society of Christians; To whom our counsel and power, or our consent and subjection, may adde a further authority, a more harmonious and efficacious influence, than can be from small or *ununited parcels*: So that a *National Church*, that is, such a *Society of Christians*, as are distinct by *civil limits* and *relation*, from other *Nations*, may not onely own, and accordingly act, as they are men related in things *civil*; but also as Christians, they may own and wisely establish such a Church power, relation, and association in matters of *Religion*, as may best preserve themselves in true Doctrine, holy Order, Christian peace, and good maners, by joynt counsel, and more vigorous power; The *neerness* which they have, affording greater opportunities to impart, and enjoy the benefit of *mutual counsel* and *charity*, and all other *communicable abilities*, to a *nobler measure*, and *higher proportion*, than can be had in lesser *bodies* or *combinations*. This *joynt*, *publick*, and *united authority* of any Church, in any *Nation* or *Kingdom*, is so far from being slighted, as some *capricious mindes* do, that it is the more to be venerated and regarded by all good Christians; who know, that *duty* enlarges with *relations*; and a greater *charity* is due from us to greater *communities*, both of men, and of Christians.

Ecclesia una est quæ in multitudinem latius incremento fæcunditatis extenditur. Cyp. de Eccl. unit.

1 Cor. 2. 11. What man knoweth the things of a man, save the spirit of man which is in him.

The greatest vexation of these new *Modellers*, is, That they have so little with *truth*, *modesty*, or *charity*, to say against this famous *National Church* of *England*, and its *Ministry*: For they daily see, notwithstanding all their *specious pretensions*, and *undefatigable agitations*; the more, as *winds*, they seek to shake and subvert *well-rooted* Christians; the more they are confirmed, and setled in that Christian communion, which they have upon good grounds, both of *Reason* and *Religion*, *Polity* and *Charity*, with this Church of *England*, as their *Mother*: Which blessing, *all wise* Christians, and *well ordered* Churches, ever owned and enjoyed among themselves, as parts of the *Catholik*, in their several *distinctions* and *society*.

Odia quo iniquiora eo magis acerba. Tacit.

9. *Charity necessary in any true Church and Christians.*

In these points of the true Church, and true Religion (however I covet to be short) yet I shall be most serious, and as clear as may be; writing nothing to other mens Consciences, which I do not first read in mine own; and of which, I know account must be given by me, at Christs tribunal. And truly, I am as loth to deceive others,

τὸ κελευσμὸν εἰς τ. συνείδησιν ἀποβλέπων. Camer. de Melan.

as to erre my self, in matters of so great concernment, as *true Religion*, and the *true Church* are: Both which, every *Sect* and *Party* of Christians chalenge to themselves; and those, no doubt, with most right and truest comfort, who do it with most *charity* to any others, that have for the *foundation* of their *faith*, the *Scriptures*, and the *Sacraments* for the *seals*, and a *true Ministry* for the ordering and right dispensing of *holy things*; professing such latitudes of *charity* always, as exclude no such Christians from communion with them: (Notwithstanding, they have many and different superstructures in lesser things.) Without this *Christian charity*, it is evident, all ostentations of *true Religion*, of *Churches purity*, and of *Reformation*, though accompanied with *tongues*, *miracles*, and *martyrdoms*, are in *vain*, and *profit men nothing*.

Nulla erroris secta jam contra Christi veritatem nisi nomine cooperta Christiano ad pugnandum prosilire audet. August. ep. 56.

1 Cor. 14. 1, 3, &c.

As it is not enough to make men of the true Church, to say, *They are the onely true Church, and in the onely Church-way*; or to *censure*, *condemn*, and *exclude* all other Christians, who may be in the same *path-way* to *Heaven*, though the paving be different; of *grass*, or *gravel*, or *stone*, &c. So it is enough, to *exclude* any party, sect, or faction of seeming Christians, from being any *sound part* of the *true Church*, to say, in a *Schismatical pride*, and *uncharitable severity*, That they are *the onely true Church*; (as the *ring-leaders* of the *Novatians* and *Donatists* did;) excommunicating by *malicious*, *proud*, and *passionate principles*; or in any other *novelizing ways*, vexing and disturbing the quiet of those Christians, and Churches, who have the *true Means* and *Ministry*; the *true Grounds*, and *Seals of Faith*; with other *holy* and *orderly Ministrations*, though with some *different rites*, yet professing *holiness of life*, and this, with *Christian charity* to all others; which is *the very bond of perfection*: The want of which, cannot consist with those other graces of *true faith* and *love*, *repentance* and *humility*, by which men *pretend* to be united to Christ. The ready way, not to be any *part* or *true Member* of the *Catholike Church*, is, To *chalenge to be the onely true Church*, and to *separate* from all others; both by *non-communion* with them, and a *total condemning* or *abdicating* of them: As the way for any *branch* to wither, and come to nothing, is, To *break it self off* by a rude Schism, or violent fraction from the Tree, that it may have *the glory to grow* by it self; and to say with a *Pharisaick pride* to all others, stand by, *I am holier than you*; Thus parting from that Root and Body, Christ and the Catholike Church; in the communion with which, by Truth and Charity, its Life and Beauty did consist.

Excidisti ab ecclesia, ubi à charitate excideris; quum à Christo ipso inde excidisti. Aug.

Col. 3. 14.

Isai. 65. 4. They eat abominable things; yet they say, Stand by thy self, come not neer me; for I am holier than thou. These (saith the Lord) are a smoke in my nose, and a fire that burneth all the day.

However then, the *unholy love of novelty*, *proud curiosity*, *cold charity*, and *distempered zeal* of some men, dare *cast off*, *unchurch*, and *anathematise*, not onely single persons and private Congregations, but even greater associations of Christians; bound together, by the bonds of *civil*, as well as *Church societies*, in *Nations* and *Kingdoms*; yea, and to despise that Catholike form of all the Churches in the World, of antient, as well as present times: Yet this *vain-glorying*, through a *verbal*, *ignorant*, *proud*, and *uncharitable confidence* of themselves, and *contempt* of all others, seems to have more in it of *Belial* and *Antichrist*, than of *Jesus Christ*; more of *Lucifer*, than of the *Father of Lights*; who also is the *Father of Love*; who hath therefore shined on men with the *light of his grace*, and *love of Christ*, that he might lead them by this powerful patern of *divine love*, to love one another, as men and as Christians, with all *meekness* and *charity*; withall *good hope*, *forbearance* and *long-suffering*; toward those, especially, that profess to be of the *houshold of faith*; who hold the foundation, Christ crucified; though they may have many *additions* of *hay*, *straw*, and *stubble*; since, *Those may save*, though *these suffer loss*. God will easily discern between *his gold*, and *our dross*, between the *errors* rising from *simplicity*, and the *truths* joyned with *charity*, and *humility*; He will easily distinguish between the *humble ignorance* of many *upright-hearted Christians*, who are seduced to *wandrings*; and the *subtilty*, *pride*, or *malice*, of *Arch-hereticks* and *Schismaticks*; who seduce others for sinister ends.

2 Cor. 10. 12. They measuring themselves by themselves, and comparing themselves among themselves, are not wise.

1 Cor. 3. 15.

All *wise*, *humble*, and *charitable Christians*; should so order their *judgements*, and *censures*, if at any time they are forced to declare them, that they must above all things take heed, that they *nourish* not, nor *discover* any *uncharitable feuds*, or *distances*, and *antipathies*, against any Churches or Christians, after the rate of those *passions*, which are the *common source* both of *Schisms* and *Heresies*; whose *ignorance* and *pride*, like *water* and *ice*, mutually arise from, and are resolved into each other: Therefore *proud*, because *ignorant*; and the more *ignorant*, because so *proud*. Nor yet may they follow those *defiances* and *distances* in *Religion*, which *Reason of State*, or the *Interests of Princes*, or *Power* of *Civil-Factions*, or the *Popular fierceness* of some *Ministers*, and *eager Sticklers* for *sides and parties*, do nourish; and vulgarly commend, as high *expressions of zeal*, and the onely ways of *true Religion*; Where there is scarce *one drop of charity* in a *sea of controversie*, or *one star of necessary truth* in the whole *clouded Heaven* of their *differing opinions* and *ways*; which set men as far from *true Christian temper*, as *burning Feavers* do from *native heat*, and *health*.

Tantum distat à vera charitate quorundam zelotarum praeceps & intemperatus ardor, quantum malignae febricitantium flammae à nativo & vitali corporis calore. Cas.

10. *Extremes touching the Church.*

I know no point hath used more *liberal* and *excellent Pens*, than this, concerning the *true Church*, as it is *visible*, or *professional* before men; which is the proper *subject* of this *dispute*. Some mens *Pens* flow with too much *gall* and *bitterness*; as the *rigid Papists* on the

the one side; and the *keener Separatist* on the other: Denying any to be in a *right Church-way*, save onely such, as are just in their particular *mold* and *form*: Either joyned in communion with the *Roman profession*, and being subject to its head, the *Pope*; pleading *antiquity*, *unity*, *universality*, *visibility*, *&c.* or else *embodied* with those new and smaller *Incorporations*; which count themselves the *onely true*, and *properly so called Churches*; pretending more absolute Church-power, more exact *constitution*, and more compleat *Scripture-Reformation*, than any *antient*, *National*, dilated, and confederated Churches could, or ever did attain too.

Herein, there is a strong excess on both sides, both *Papal* and *Popular*: First, The *Romanists* extend the cords of their Churches power, and its head or chief Bishop, so far, as if it were properly Catholike, and Oecumenical; that is, by *divine appointment* invested with *soveraign Authority*, to extend and exercise *Ecclesiastical polity* and *dominion* over all other particular Churches, in all ages, and in all parts of the World: *So that it is* (say they) *necessary to salvation to be under this Roman jurisdiction, &c.* Whereas it is certain, That the *Roman Church*, antiently was, and still is (properly speaking) distinct from others in place, as well as name, and had antiently its *limited power*, and *jurisdiction*, extending to the *suburbicanian Provinces*; which were Ten, seven in *Italy*, and three in *Sicily*, *Corsica*, and *Sardinia*: According to those (like) bounds, which occasionally from *civil titles*, both named and distinguished all other Churches from one another; in both the *Asiaes*, in *Africa*, and in *Europe*; as the *Gallican*, *German*, *British*, *&c.* Nor hath ever any thing, either of *Reason*, or *Scripture*, been produced by any (more than of *true Antiquity*) whereby to prove, That we are bound to any communion (that is, (in the true meaning of *proud* and *politick Romanists*) *to that subjection to the Pope, and his party*; which may be most for his and their *honor* and *profit*) with the Church of *Rome*, further, than the rule of *Christian charity* obligeth every Christian, and every part of the *Catholike Church*, to communicate in *truth* and *love*, with all those, that in any judgement of *charity*, are to be counted true Christians, so far, as they appear to us, to be such.

1. *By the Romanists.* Baron. Anno Christi 45. p. 376. *Hæreticum esse qui à Romanæ Cathedræ communione divisus sit.* So Bellarm. de Rom. Pont. l. 2. 12. *Vetusta consuetudo servetur; ut hic (Episcopus Roma) suburbicaniarum ecclesiarum solicitudinem gerat.* Ruffin. hist. l. 1. c. 6. Concil. Nicen.

Nor is it less evident, That many Churches and Christians have scarce ever known, much less owned, any *claim of subjection* upon them, by the *Roman Church*: Which, however they had antiently a priority of *order* and *precedency*, yielded to it, and its chief Bishop, for the eminency of the City, the honor of the Empire, and the excellency of the reputed *Founders* and *Planters*, Saint *Peter*, and Saint *Paul*; also for the renown of the *faith*, *patience*, and *charity* of that Church, which was *famous in all the World*; Yet, all this *Primacy* or, Rom. 1. 8.

or *Priority* of *Order*, which was civilly by others granted, and might modestly be accepted by the chief Bishop in the *Roman Province*, as to matter of place and precedency, or Votes in publick *Councis* and *Synods*. This, I say, is very far from that * *Antichristian Supremacy* of *usurped power*, *tyrannick dominion*, and *arbitrary jurisdiction*; the very *suspition* and *temptation* to which, the *holy* and *humble Bishops* of *Rome* were ever jealous of, and avoided; especially *Gregory* the Great; who was in nothing more worthy of that title, than in this, That he so greatly detested, protested against, and refused the *title of Universal Bishop*, when it was offered to him by the Councel of *Chalcedon*: Which both name and thing was in after times gained and chalenged by the *pride*, *policy*, *covetousness*, and *ambition*, of those *Bishops* of *Rome*, who by some of their own sides confession (as * *Baronius*, * *Genebrard*, and others) were sufficiently degenerated from that *Primitive humility* and *sanctity*, which were eminent in the first *Bishops* of *Rome*, in those purer and primitive times; who never thought of any one of those Three Crowns, which *flatterers* in after ages have fully hammered, and set on the heads of the *Bishops* of *Rome*; in a *Supremacy*, not of *Order*, but of *Power*, and *plenary Jurisdiction*, above all Christians, or Churches, or Councils in the Christian World; which hath justly occasioned so many parts of the Catholike Church, in that regard, to make a necessary separation (not from any thing that is Christian among them, but) from the *usurpation*, *tyranny*, and *superstition* of those *Bishops* of the *Roman* Church, and their Faction, who unjustly claim, and rigorously exercise *dominion* over the Consciences and Liberties of all other Churches, and Christians: With whom, the *Roman* pride now refuseth to hold such peaceable communion, as ought universally to be among Christians, (in respect of *order* and *charity*) unless they will all submit to that *tyranny* and *usurpation*, which hath nothing in it, but secular pride, vain pomp, and worldly dominion: Yet still those of the *Roman* Church know, That all the *Reformed Churches*, as well as we of *England*, ever did, and do hold, a Christian communion in charity with them, so far, as by the Word of God we conceive they hold with the *head* or *root* of the *Church*, *Christ Jesus*; with the *ground* and *rule* of *Faith*, the *Scriptures*; and with all those *holy Professors*, in the *purest* and *primitive Churches*; Of whose faith, lives, and deaths, having some *Monuments* left us, by the writings of eminent *Bishops*, and others; we judge, what was the tenor both of the *Faith*, *Maners*, and *Charity* of those *purer times*, which we highly venerate, and strive to imitate.

* Greg. Mag. ep. 30. ad Mauri. Aug. *Fidenter dico, quia quisquis se universalem sacerdotem, vel Episcopum vocat, vel vocari desiderat, in elatione suâ Antichristum præcurrit; quia superbiendo se cæteris præponit. De Cyriaco, Constantinop. Episcopo, hunc frivoli nominis & superbiæ typhum affectante.* Greg. M. l 4. ep. 32, 36.

*Baronius, an. 912. tom. 10. *Fœdissima nunc Romanæ ecclesiæ facies, cùm Romæ dominarentur potentissimæ ac sordidissimæ meretrices.*

* See Genebrard. ad Sec. 10. *Pontifices per an. 150. à virtute majorum prorsus defecerunt.*

Possibly we might now subscribe to that Letter, which the *Abbot* and *Monks* of *Bangor* sent to *Austin*, (whom some report to

be

be a proud and bloody *Monk*) when he came to this *Nation*, and required obedience of them, and all Christians here, to the *Pope*; (which Letter is thus translated out of *Saxonick*, by that *grave* and *learned Gentleman*, Sir *Henry Spelman*, a *lover* and *adorner* of this Church of *England*, by his *life* and *learned Labors*.) *Be it known to you, without doubt, that every one of us are obedient, and subject to the Church of God, and to the Pope of* Rome, *and to every true godly Christian; to love every one in his degree, in perfect charity; and to help every one of them, by word and deed, to be the children of God; and other obedience, than this, we know not due to him, whom you call* Pope; *nor do we own him to be* Father of Fathers. *This obedience we are ever ready to give, and pay to him, and every Christian, continually: Beside we are under our own Bishop of* Caerleon *upon* Usk, *who is to oversee us under God, and to cause us to keep the way spiritual.*

Sir *Henry Spelman*, Concil. Brit. Anno Christi 590. out of the *Saxon* Manuscript.

Isca, one of the three *Metropolis* in *Britain*, *Caerusk*, in *Monmouthshire*, Antiq. Brit.

Nor will this benefit of the *Popes* pretended *Infallibility*, (for *deciding controversies* of *Religion*, and *ending* all *Disputes* of *Faith*, in the Church Catholike) countervail the injury of this his *usurpation*, and *oppression*: Considering, that nothing is more, by Scripture, Reason, and Experience, not so much disputable, as fully to be denied by any sober Christians, than that of the *Popes Infallibility*; which, as the Church never yet enjoyed; so, nor doth any Church, or any Christian indeed want any such thing as this *infallible judge* is *imagined* to be; in order to either Christian course, or comfort: If indeed, the Bishop of *Rome*, and those learned men about him, would, without *faction*, *flattery*, *partiality*, and *self-interest*, joyn their *learning*, *counsels*, and *endeavors*, in common, to reform the *abuses*, to compose the *rents* and *differences* in the Christian World, by the rule of Scripture, and right Reason, with Christian humility, prudence, and charity, (which look sincerely to a *publick* and *common good*) they would do more good for the Churches of Christ, than any *imaginary Infallibility* will ever do; yea, and they would do themselves no great hurt in civil respects; if they could meet and joyn, not with envious and covetous, but liberal and ingenuous Reformers; who will not think as many, the greatest *deformities* of any Church, to be the riches, and revenues of Church-men.

11. *The pretended Infallibility in the Pope or Church of* Rome.

Primatum suum non objecit Petrus, nec inerrabilitatem, sed Paulo veritatis assertori cessit: Documentum patientiæ & concordiæ, Cyp. ep. 71.

Certainly, in points of true Religion, to be believed, or duties to be practised, as from *divine command*, every Christian is to be judge of that, which is propounded to him, and embraced by him; according to what he is *rationally* and *morally* able to know and attain; by those means which God hath given him, of Reason, Scripture, Ministry, and good examples: Of all which, the *gifts* or *graces* of God in him, have inabled him seriously, and discreetly to consider. Nor is he to rest in, either *implicite*, or *explicite dictates*, *presumptions*,

and

Magnum ingenium magna teutatio. De Orig. & Tert. Vin. Lirin.
1 Cor. 8. 7. Knowledge puffeth up.
2 Pet. 2. 19. βεβαιότερον λόγον.
Rom. 6. 17. Ye have obeyed from the heart that form of doctrine which was delivered to you.
Eph. 4. 15. ἀληθεύοντες ἐν ἀγάπῃ.
2 Thes. 2. 10. Because they received not the love of the truth, that they might be fayed.

and *Magisterial determinations* of any frail, and sinful men, who may be as fallible, as himself: For, whereas they may exceed him in *gifts* of *knowledge*, they may also exceed him in *passions*, *self-interests*, *pride*, and *policy*; so that he may not safely trust them on their bare word, and assertion; but he must seek to build his faith on the more sure Word of God, which is acknowledged (by all sides) to be the surest *director*, what to believe, to do, and to hope in the way of *Religion*. Nor may any private Christians *unletteredness*, that cannot read; or his weaker intellect, that cannot reason and dispute; or his many incumberances of life, that deny him leisure to read, study, compare, meditate, *&c.* These may not discourage him, as if he were a *dry tree*, and could neither bear, nor reap any fruit of *Christian Religion*, because he hath no *infallible guide*, or *judge*: Since the *mercy of God* accepts *earnest endeavors*, and an *holy life*, according to the power, capacity, and means a man hath; also he pardons *unwilling errors*, when there is an *obedience* from the heart, to the *truths* we know; and a *love* to all *truth*, joyned with *humility*, and *charity*.

In order therefore to relieve the *common defects* of men, as to the generality of them, both in Cities and in Countrey Villages (where there is little learning by the Book, or Letter; and great dulness with heavy labor) the Lord of his *wisdom* and *mercy* hath appoint d that constant *holy order* of the *Ministry*, to be always continued in the *Church*; that so *learned*, *studious*, and *able men*, being duly *tryed*, *approved*, and *ordained* to be *Teachers* and *Pastors*; may by their *light*, *knowledge*, and *plenty*, supply the *darkness*, *simplicity*, and *penury* of *common people*; who *must every man be fully perswaded in his own minde*, *Rom.* 14. 5. in matters of conscience; and be able to give a reason of that *faith and hope which is in him*, beyond the credit of any meer man, or the opinion of his infallibility, 1 *Pet.* 3. 15.

However they may with *comfort* and *confidence* attend upon their lips, whom in an *holy succession* of *Ministry*, God hath given to them, as the ordinary and sufficient means of Faith; And however a *plain-hearted* and *simple Christian* may religiously wait upon, and rest satisfied with those *holy means* and *mysteries*, which are so dispenced to him by *true Ministers*, (who ought above all, to be both able and faithful; to know, and to make known *the truth, as it is in Jesus*;) Yet, may he not savingly, or conscientiously relie, in matters of Faith, nor make his last result, upon the bare credit, or personal veracity of the *Minister*; but he must consider and believe every truth, not because the *Minister* saith it, but because it is grounded on the *Word of God*; and from thence brought him by his *Minister*; which *doctrine* he judgeth to be true, not upon the infallibility of

any

any *Teachers*; but upon that certainty which he believes to be in the *Scripture*; to which, *all sorts of Christians* do consent; And to which, the *Grace* and *Spirit of God* so draweth and enclineth the heart, as to close with those *divine truths*, to believe and obey them; not for the authority of the *Minister*, but of *God the Revealer*; whose excellent *wisdom*, *truth*, and *love*, it discerns in those things which are taught it by the Ministry of man. So that, still the simplest Christian doth savingly believe, and conscientiously live, according to what himself judgeth, and is perswaded in his heart, to be the *Will of God*, in his *Word*; and not after the *dictates* of any man: Which either *written*, or *spoken*, have no more authority to command or perswade belief, as to *Religion*, than they appear to the *believer*, (and not to the *speaker* onely) grounded on the sure *Word of God*, and to be *his minde* and *will* to mankinde.

And as it is not absolutely necessary to every Christian, in order to *Faith* and *Salvation*, to be able with his own eyes to read, and so to judge of the Letter of the Scripture; so it is the *more necessary*, that the reading and preaching of the Word should be *committed to able and faithful men*; not, who are infallible, but who may be apt to teach, and worthy to be believed: Of whom, the people may have great perswasion, both as to their abilities, and due authority, to teach and guide them in the ways of God. We read in *Irenæus*, that in One hundred and fifty years after Christ, many Churches of Christians, toward the *Caspian* Sea, and Eastward, were very sound in the *Faith*, and setled against all *Heretical* or *Schismatical insinuations*; when yet they never had any *Bibles* or *Scriptures* among them; but onely retained that Faith which they at first had learned, and were still taught by their *Orthodox Bishops*, and *Ministers*; which they never wanted in a due *succession*: Of whose *piety*, *honesty*, and *charity*, they were so assured, as diligently to attend their *doctrine*, and *holy ministrations*; with which the blessing of God (opening their harts, as *Lydia*'s) still went along; so as to keep them in *true faith*, *love*, and *holy obedience*.

2 Tim. 2. 2. διδακτικοὶ καὶ ἀξιόπιστοι.

Irenæus, l. 3. c. 4.

Since then, no man or men can give to others, any such sure proofs, and good grounds of their *personal infallibility*, as the *Scriptures* have in themselves, both by that more than *humane lustre* of *divine truths* in it; which set forth most excellent precepts, paterns, and promises; excellent morals and mysteries; excellent rules, examples, and rewards, beyond any *Book* whatsoever: Also, from that *general credit*, *regard*, and *reception*, which they have, and ever had with all (and most with the best) Christians, in all ages; as the *Oracles of God*, delivered by *holy* and *honest men*; for a rule of *faith*, and *holy life*; also for a ground of *eternal hope*: Since that from hence onely, even the Pope, or any others, that pretend to any *infallibility*, or *inspirations*, do first seek to ground those their *pretensions*, of which, every one that will be perswaded, must first be judge of the *reasons* or *grounds* alleged to perswade him; It is necessary, that the (ἀξιοπιστία) *infallibility* of the *Scriptures*, must be first received, and believed by every Christian; in order to his being assured of any truth, which thence is urged upon him to believe, or do: Which great principle setling a believer on the *certainty* or *infallibility* of the *Scriptures*, as a *divine rule* of *Faith* and *Life*, is never to be gained upon any mens judgements and perswasion (be they either *idiotick* or *learned*) unless there be such an *authoritative Ministry*, and such *Ministers* to *preach*, *interpret*, *open*, and *apply* the *Scriptures*, by strong and convincing *demonstrations*, which may carry credit and power with them. The *succession* then of rightly *ordained Ministers* is more necessary to the Church, than any such *Papal infallibility*; in as much, as it is more necessary to believe the *Scriptures* authority, than any mans testimony, which hath no credit but from the *Scripture*: Which while the Pope, or others, do seek to wrest to their own secular advantages and ends, they bring men at length to regard nothing they say; nor at all to consider, what they endlesly wrangle, and groundlesly dispute about *true Religion*, or the *true Church*.

12. *An able and right Ministry, is beyond any pretended Infallibility.*

... So absolutely necessary and sufficient in the way of ordinary means, is a right and duly ordained *Ministry*, which *Christ* hath appointed to continue, and propagate true Christian Religion; which ever builds true *Faith*, and the true *Church* upon the *Scriptures*; That, as there is no *infallibility* of the *Pope*, or other man, evident by any *Reason*, *Scripture*, or *Experience*, so there needs none, to carry on that great work of mens salvation; which will then fail in any *Church* and *Nation*, when the *right Ministry* fails, by force or fraud: If we can keep our true Christian Ministry, and holy Ministrations, we need not ask the *Romanists*, or any other arrogant *Monopolizers* of the *Church*, leave to own our selves true *Christians*, and a part of the true *Catholike Church* of *Christ*; which cannot be but there, where there is a *profession* of the *Christian Religion*, as to the main of it; in its *Truths*, *Sacraments*, *holy Ministrations* and *Ministry*, rightly ordained; both for the ability of the *ordained*, and the authority of the *ordainers*; although all should be accompanied with some humane failings.

Where the now *Roman* Church then, doth (as we conceive) either in their doctrine, or practise, vary from that Catholikely received rule the *Scriptures*, which are the onely infallible, certain, and clear guide in things *fundamental*; as to *faith*, or *maners*; we are forced so far, *justly* and *necessarily* to leave them, and their infallible fallibility in both; yet charitably still, so as to *pity* their errors; to pray for their

their *enlightning*, their *repentance* and *pardon*, which we hope for: Where no *malice* or *corrupt lusts* makes the *additional errors* pernicious; and where the *love* of *truth* makes them pardonable, by their consciencious obeying what they know, and desire to know, what they are yet ignorant of. Yea, and wherein they are conform to any *Scriptures*, *doctrine*, and *practise*; or *right reason*, *good order*, and *prudent polity*; there, we willingly run parallel with, and agreeable to them, both in *opinion* and *practise*: For we think we ought not in a heady, and passionate way, wholly to separate from any *Church*, or cast away any *branch* of it, that yet visibly professeth Christian Religion; further, than it rends and breaks it self off from the *Word*, *Institution*, and *patern* of *Christ*, in the *Scriptures*; and so either separates it self from us, or casts us out from it, uncharitably violating that Catholike communion of *Christs Church*, which ought to be preserved with all possible *charity*. The constancy and fidelity of the *Church* of *Christ* is more remarkable in its *true Ministry*, holding forth in an *holy succession* the most Catholike and credible *truth* of the *Scriptures*; which at once shews both the innate *divine light* in them; and the *true Church* also, which is built by them, and upon them. The *truth* of which *Scriptures*, while we with *charity*, believe and profess, both in *word* and *deed*, we take it to be, the surest and sufficientest evidence to prove, That we are a part of the *true Church*, against the *cavils* and *calumnies* of those learneder *Romanists*; upon whose *Anvils*, others of far weaker arms, have learned to *forge* the like *fiery darts* against this Church of *England*.

For, on the other side, the new *Models of Independent*, or *Congregational Churches*, (which seem like small *Chapels of Ease*, set up to confront and rob the *Mother Churches* of *Auditors*, *Communicants*, *Maintenance*, and *Ministry*) winde up the *cords*, and fold up the *curtains* of the *true Church*, too short, and too narrow; Shrinking that Christian communion, and visible polity, or society of the Church, to such *small figures*, such *short* and *broken ends*, of *obscure conventicles*, and *paucities*, that by their *rigid separatings*, some men scarce allow the whole *company of true Christians*, in all the world, to be so great, as would fill one *Jewish Synagogue*: Fancying, that no Church or Christian, is sufficiently reformed, till they are most diametrically contrary in every use and custom to the *Roman fashion*; abhorring many things as *Popish*, and *Superstitious*, because used by the *Papists*: When indeed, they are either pious, or very prudential; yea, many count it a special mark of their true *Churchship*, to *separate* from all, to *cry down* every thing, to *rail at*, and *despise* (with as little *charity*, as much *passion*, and no *reason*) all *Churches* and *Christians*, as *Antichristian*, and not yet

13. *The contrary extreme reducing all Churches to small and single Congregations.*

ἀμετρία τ' ἀνθολκῆς Naz.

In vitium ducit culpæ fuga si caret arte. Hor.

yet *sufficiently reformed*, which are not of their *new Bodying*, and *Independent fashion*.

Which *novel practises* seem nothing else, but the *effects*, either of *secular polity*, or *prejudicating* and *preposterous zeal*; by which, some men, for their *interest*, or their *humor*, seek to bring back the Churches of Christ, to that *Egypt* and *Babylon* of *strife*, *schism*, *emulation*, *sedition*, *faction*, and *confusion*, to which they were running very early, as the Apostle *Paul* tells us; and St. *Clemens* in his Epistle to the *Corinthians*: From the rocks of which inconveniencies, Saint *Jerom* by express words, and all Churches, by their antient Catholike practises, do assure us, That the *wisdom* of the *Apostles*, and *Apostolike-men* in the *Primitive times*, even from St. *Mark* in *Alexandria*, and St. *James* in *Jerusalem*, redeemed and brought the Church; by setling those *large* and *publick combinations*, by *Episcopal Government*; and in ways of *ampliated communion*, and *Catholike correspondencies* (as much as might be) by *Synods* and *General Councils*; which might best keep *particular Congregations*, from *scattering* and *crumbling* themselves into such *Factions* and *Schisms*; which all *wisdom* foresaw, and *experience* fulfilled, would be the onely means, First, to break the bond of *Christian charity*, and the *Churches communion* (which consisted much, as in *the verity of the Faith*, so in those *larger fraternities*, *holy confederacies*, and *orderly subjections*,) and afterward to overthrow the very *foundations* of *Faith* and *Truth*: As those every where did, who at any time corrupted any part of the Church, *affecting singularities*, and chosing rather to *fall*, by *standing alone* in a *separation of Opinion* or *Government*, than to seem to have any *support* by the *association* with others, in a more *publick way* of *common relation*, *unity*, and *subjection*: Which undoubtedly carry the greatest strength and safety with them, both in *Ecclesiastical*, and *Civil polities*; twisting many *smaller strings* into one *cord*, and many *cords* into one *cable*; which will best preserve the *Ship of the Church*, as well as the *State*, from those *storms* and *distresses*, which are prone to fall upon it, in lesser *bottoms*. The good effects of which *larger communion* among men, and Christians, all *reason* and *experience* demonstrate to us in *civil societies*, which are the *conservatories of mankinde*, by way of *mutual assistance* in *publick combinations*; while single persons, which alone are feeble, and exposed to injuries, grow strong by making one family, and many families grow into a Village, Town, or City: Many Villages, Towns, and Cities, arise to one potent *Principality* or *Commonwealth*; which as a threefold cord, is not easily broken.

St. *Paul*, 1 *Cor.* c. 3.
Clem. ad Cor. epist. Thirty years after.
Postquam unusquisque eos quos baptisaverat suos esse putabat, non Christi, in toto orbe decretum est, ut unus de Presbyteris electus superponeretur cæteris, ad quem omnis ecclesiæ cura pertineret; & schismatum semina tollerentur. Jeron. in Tit.

It is in all Church Histories most evident, That, as soon as the *Gospel* spred from Cities, where it was generally first planted (there being the greatest conflux of people) and from thence derived to the

Territories,

Territories, and Countreys adjacent, which were called the several (παροικίαι or διοικήσεις) *Parishes* or *Diocesses*: So, those Christians, which grew up in the Countreys and Territories about, to small Congregations, continued still in a *fraternal subjection*, and a *filial submission*, both *Presbyters* and *People*, to that *Bishop* and *Presbytery*, which were in the *Mother City*; who, there residing, (where the *Apostles* or *Apostolike-men* had placed them) took care so to spred the *Gospel* to the Countreys about, as to preserve *Religion* once planted, in *peace*, *unity*, and *order*. Nor did those particular Congregations in Cities or Villages, turn presently *Acepalists* or *Independents*; nor set up any (αὐτοκρατία) *heady* or *headless bodies*, in every corner and meeting-place: For, however Christians in some places, might at *first* amount to but so small a number, as would make but one convenient *Society*, or *Congregation*, under one *Bishop*, or *Presbyter*, with the *Deacons*; and so might for a time continue in *private bounds*, not corresponding with, or depending on any other company of Christians, as to lesser concernments, which might easily be managed among them: Yet, where the number of *believers increased*, as in *Antioch*, *Jerusalem*, *Ephesus*, *Corinth*, *Rome*, *&c.* both in the Cities, and their Territories, all Histories of the Church aver; That, as by those *dictates* of *religious Reason*, which first guided the *Apostles* or *Apostolike-men*, to cast themselves and believers, into such *lesser bodies*, and *distinct societies*, as might best serve for the convenience of *meeting* together in one place, according as neighborhood invited them: So still (as growing parts of the same *body*, and increasing *branches* of the same *Tree*) they *preserved* the first, great, and common relation, of *descent* and *extraction*, from the *Mother City*; So as to *correspond* with, to *watch* over each other; yea, and to be *subject* (in every *particular Congregation*, as well as *families*) to those, who were the original of their *instruction* and *conversion*; and who by a kinde of *paternal right*, together with *Apostolical* appointment, and common consent of Christians, had the *chief power* and *authority* for Inspection and Government over them, within such precincts and bounds; yea, all Christians were thus subjected, and united in greater and diffused Churches, not by any *civil necessity*; such as compels men by the sword and force; but by that *necessity* of *gratitude*, *sense* of *priority*, *prudence* and *charity*; which bound by *love*, *humility*, and *wisdom*, particular Christians first to one *Society* or *Convention*: And these particular Congregations to *greater fraternities*; and these to a more ample and *Catholike communion*; for the *mutual peace*, and *good order* of the whole Church of Christ; which sought to preserve it self, even in the eye of the world, as one *entire body*, *under one head*, *Christ Jesus*. 1 Cor. 12. 25, &c. Eph. 4. 4, &c.

So that the *imaginary patern in the Mount*, the primitive practise which

which some men love to talk of (by which they would force all large and ampliated Churches, (which have now received (as they did at first) distinctions and denominations by the Cities, Civil Jurisdictions, Kingdoms, or Nations, wherein they are) to those lesser Forms, wherein they fancy (and not unlikely) a single Congregation of Christians, in any place, at first enjoyed themselves under some *Apostle*, or one of *Apostolike* appointment, who was their Bishop or Overseer over them,) This, I say, seems to be so childish a fancy, so weak, and unreasonable an imagination, That it is all one, as if they would needs reduce themselves to their *infant coats*, now they are grown men.

And what I pray doth hinder (save onely the *novel opinions* and *humors* of these men,) that, Christian Religion (which *sanctifies reason*, to serve God and the Church, in all *comely ways*) may not use those *principles* and *rules*, for *order*, *unity*, *peace*, and *mutual safety* of Christians, in their multiplied *numbers* and *societies*; which we are taught, and allowed to use in all *civil associations*? Yea, and not onely allowed, but enjoyned to observe in *Ecclesiastical polity* and *Government*, by that *great* and *fundamental Canon* of the *Apostle*, *Let all things be done decently, and in order*; which must hold,

1 Cor. 14. 40.

not onely in *private* and *lesser parcels*, but in the more *large* and *integral parts* of the *Church* of *Christ*.

But *Reason* then, and *Religion* sufficiently discover, the *vanity* and *impertinency* of those *novel fancies*, which are obtruded, as necessary for all *private Congregations*; when indeed they are, and ever have been, and will be *destructive* to the more *publick* and *general good* of the Church; whose *tranquillity*, *honor*, and *safety*, consists in such dependencies and subordinations, which may be furthest remote from those *fractions* and *disunions*, which arise from that *Church-dividing* and *Charity-destroying* principle of *Independent Congregations*; which was never used in any times of the Church, further than the *minority* and *infancy* of the *first planting*; while either Christians were not encreased much in number, or not enlarged in place: But when the first small company of *believers* multiplied from a Church in one Family, to a Church in many Congregations, (which could not now with conveniency all meet together in one place,) they yet as *branches*, still continued both united to the *root*, *Christ Jesus*; and also to the main *body* and *bulk* of the *visible Church*, by *union* to that part whence they descended, and to which they related; and they were not as Colonies or Slips, so transplanted and separated, as to grow *Independently* of themselves, apart from all others: Of which, there is no example in Scripture or Antiquity.

Rom. 16. 5. Greet the Church, which is in their house.

1 Cor. 16. 19. The Churches of *Asia* salute you.

14. *The Church of* England, *not blamable for its National communion.*

It follows then; That what was setled in this or other like Christian Churches, was no whit blamable, as any thing of *meer*

humane

humane invention, or any *superfluous* and *corrupt addition* to any *precept*, *patern*, or *constitution*, either of *Christs* or the *Apostles*; who never prohibited the ordering of Churches in *larger associations* or *Governments*; extending to Cities, and their Territories, to great Diocesses, Provinces, and Nations; Since there is no precept or practise, limiting Churches power, and society, to private and single Congregations: Yea, there are such general directions, and examples in the Scripture, as command, or at least commend rather than condemn those *analogous* or *proportionable applyings* of all *orderly* and *prudential means* for *union* and *communion*, according as the various state, and times of the Church may require; which still aym at the same end, the peace and welfare of the Church, both in the *lesser* and the *larger extents*; which are justly so carried on by the wise *Governors* and *Protectors* of the Church, according to the *general principles* and *rules*, or *paterns* of *pious* and *charitable prudence*, set down in the Scriptures; beyond which, in this case of the Churches outward *order* and *polity*, there neither is, nor needs, other directions; no more, than on what *Text* and *Subject*; or in what method and place; or how long time, and how often a *Minister* must pray, or preach; and people must hear *Sermons*, or attend *holy duties*.

That antient and excellent frame then, of this Church in *England*, which in a *National union*, by *civil*, *religious*, and *sacred bonds*, was so wisely built, and for many ages compacted together, and which hath been lately so undermined, so hackt and hewn, with *passionate writings*, and *disputings*, and *actings*, that it is become not onely a *tottering*, but almost a quite *demolished* and *overthrown frame*; This Church, I say, hath suffered this *hard fate*, rather through the *iniquities of times*, *malice of men*, and *just judgements* of *God* on the *Governors* and governed, (who we may fear improved not so great advantages of *union*, *order*, *power*, *peace*, and *protection*, to the real good of the Church, and furtherance of the Gospel) rather, I say, by these *personal failings*, than for any, either mischief, deformity, defects, or Antichristian excess in the way and frame it self, as to its grounds and constitutions: Which were setled and long approved by very *wise*, *holy*, and *learned men*; carrying with them, (as much, as any Christian, or Reformed Church did) the lineaments, feature, beauty and vigor, of those famous Primitive Churches; which in the midst of *heresies* and *persecutions* kept themselves safe, as to *truth* and *charity*, not by the *shreds* of *Independent Bodies*, but by the sutures of Christian Associations; in *Provincial*, *National*, and *Oecumenical enlargements*: Such ample and noble platforms of religious reason, and sanctified wisdom, as not *ambitious policy*, but *Christian charity*, and *prudent humility*, embraced; which, as our new *models* and *projections* will never *mend*, so they much commend those antient happy models, and paterns, by those *multiplied mischiefs* ensuing inevitably upon the *presumptions of posterity*; which have rashly adventured thus to remove and change the antient *limits*, *marks*, and *orders* of the *Church*, which *Primitive Fathers* and *Apostles* had recommended and setled.

15. *Seekers thence.*

The *Eutychian* Hereticks refusing to subscribe the Catholike Faith, confirmed by the Council of *Chalcedon*, called themselves Διακρινόμενοι, *Ambigentes*, *Dubitantes*; and after run out to all corrupt opinions. *Aug. de Hære.*

Nobis qui jam credimus aliud non quærendum. Si enim semper quærimus, nunquam inveniemus, nunquam credemus. Tert. de Præs. ad Hæ. c. 10.

Quemadmodum Atheorum pars maxima, non tam credunt quam cupiunt non esse Deum. Min. Fæl.

Non facile invenient veram ecclesiam, qui illibenter quærunt. Melancth.

Which *temerity* of thus *mincing* and *crumbling*, or *tearing* any *Church National* (being the issue of no *Synod*, or *Council* in the *Church*, but onely of private fancies, and most-what *mechanick adventures*) hath, we see, made some poor *souls* turn *Scepticks* and *Seekers* after *true Religion*, and a *true Church*; being wholly unsatisfied, either with the abolition of the *old way*, or the various inventions of *new ways*. These profess, whether out of *weakness*, *pure ignorance*, *passion*, or *policy* (God knows,) That they are *Christians* no further, than to see, that all *Christian Churches* are now, and have been, ever since the *Apostles* times, *adulterous*, *impure*, *deformed*, and *Antichristian*; That, they are wholly to *seek* for any *true ground*, or *way* of *Christian Religion*, *Church*, and *Ministry*, even among so many *Christians*, *Ministers*, and *Churches*: That is, they cannot see wood for trees, nor light for the Sun at noon-day. And this may easily be, either by reason of wilful blindness, or for want of that *charity* and *humility*, which keeps the hearts and eyes of *Christians*, open and clear; or from that *darkness*, and *blear-eyedness*, which *prejudice* and *perverseness* carry with them; hindring *Christians* from discerning even those objects, that are round about them; yea, it is to be feared, That some men, from *Atheistical*, *profane*, *ranting*, and *licentious principles*, *seek* for a *true Church*, as *Hypocrites* do for *their sins*, and *cowards* for *their enemies*, loth to finde them, and studying most to be hidden from them. They complain of this, and other *Churches*, as *defective*, as *impure*, as none; when indeed, it may be feared, they are sorry there are any such; and wish there were none of these *Christian societies*, *Ministers*, or *godly people*, in the world; whose *doctrine* and *examples* are their *restraints*, *reproaches*, and *torments*; being most *cross* to their *evil designs*, and *immoderate lusts*. They complain they cannot finde a *true Church*, when they are unwilling so to do; and satisfie themselves (as the *Cynick* in his Tub) morosely to censure, and Magisterially to finde fault with all *Christians*, that they may conform to none in an *holy*, *humble*, and *peaceably way*; but rather enjoy that *fantastick* and *lazy liberty* of *mocking* God, and man; till they finde such a way of *Church* and *Religion*, as shall please them: Which they would not be long in finding, as to *extern polity* and *profession*, if they did but entertain that *inward life*, and *power of Religion*, which I formerly set down; which, by a principle of *charity*, as well as of *truth*, strongly flowing from belief of Gods love in Christ

to

to mankinde, and specially to the Church; doth powerfully binde, and cheerfully encline every humble *believer*, to have peace and communion (as much as may be) with all Christians; as *internal*, in judgment and good will, so *external* and *social*; both *private* and *publick*; *amicitial* and *political*, in regard of *example*, *comfort*, and *encouragement*; as also of *Order*, *Subordination*, and *Government*; so far, as we see they have any fellowship with *Christ Jesus*, in those *holy mysteries* and *duties*, which he hath appointed; whereby to gather and preserve his Church, in all Ages, and places, and Nations.

1 Cor. 14. 33. God is not the Author (ἀκαταστασίας) of unsetledness, commotion, or confusion, but of peace, as in all Churches of the Saints.

Heb. 12. 14. Follow peace with all men, and holiness, &c.

Rom. 12. 18. If it be possible, as much as lieth in you, live peaceably with all men.

Thus we see some mens Pens serve onely to *blot the face*, even of the *Catholike Church*, and all parts of it in their *visible order* and *communion*; affecting to write such *blinde* and *small Characters*, in describing *new Church ways*, and *forms of Religion*, that no ordinary eyes can read their meaning, either in their *shrinking* and *separating* into *small ruptures of Bodies*; when they were related to, and combined with, *Churches large* and *setled*; or in their *Seraphick raptures*, strange *Enthusiasms*, *secret drawings*, and *extraordinary impulsions*, which they pretend to have in their ways, above, and without; yea, in the neglect, and contempt of all ordinary means; and setled *Ministry* in any Church: Their many *high imaginations*, and *fanatick fancies*, are (no doubt) above their *Authors* own *understandings*, no less than above all *wiser*, and *soberer mens capacities*; twinckling much more like *gloworms*, under the *hedges* of *private Conventicles*, and *Factions*; than shining with *true* and *antient light* of the *judgement* or *practise* of any Churches. Therefore they need no further confutation from my Pen, having so little, yea, no confirmation from any grounds of *Scripture*, or arguments of *common Reason*, or custom of *Christians*; nothing indeed worthy of any rational, godly, and serious mans thoughts; who list not to dance after the *Jews-trump*, or *Oaten-pipe* of every Country fancy, rather than listen to the best touched *Lute*, or *Theorbo*,

These *Syrens*, wise *Christians* may leave to sing to themselves, and their own melancholy, or musing thoughts; no sober man can understand them, further than they signifie, that *ignorance*, *illiterateness*, *idleness*, *pride*, *presumption*, *licentiousness*, and *vanity*; which some like *spiritual Canters* affect. The *rarities* which they boast to enjoy, are without any discreet mans envy, that I know: However, they carry it with a kinde of scornful indignation against others; every where pitying (as they say) the *simple diligence*, and *needless industry* of those poor Christians, who are still attending on those *thred-bare forms* (as they call them) of *old readings*, and *catechisings*, and *preachings*, and *prayings*, and *Sacraments*, &c. in the *publick Liturgies*, and *orderly assemblies* of *Christians*:

Despising as much the antient and true way of Ministry and Duty, as they would the *moldy bread*, and *torn bottles* of the *Gibeonites*; abhorring to own any relation to other Christians, or Church, or Ministry, or Governors, in any Catholike bond of *communion* and *subjection*; nor can they endure any Christian subordination, or prudent, and necessary *restraint* of *just Government*.

Which makes them look very like the *old Circumcelliones*, a company of *vagrant Hypocrites*; of whom, Saint *Jerom*, and *Isidore Hispalensis*, make large and satyrical descriptions: The first sayes, they were *impudent straglers*, whose mouths were always full of *barbarous and importune reproaches*; The other tells us, that they every where wandered in their *mercenary hypocrisie*, fixed no where; feigning *visions* of what they never saw: Counting their *opinions* and *dreams* for *divine*; and protesting to have received those *eminencies*, which they have not: Impatient to be *confined* to any *place*, *order*, or *way*; but had rather like *vagabonds* continue in their *beggarly liberty*, than fix to a *sober industry*, and enjoy a *setled competency*.

Jeron. Ep. ad Eustoch. *Quibus os barbarum & procax, & in convicia semper armatum.* Isid. Hispal. lib. de offic. eccles. c. 15. *ubicunque vagantur venalem circumferentes hypocri. sinusquam fixi, nusquam stantes, nusquam sedentes; quæ non viderunt confingunt: Opiniones suas habent pro Deo. Honores quos non acceperunt se habuisse protestantur, &c.*

These *unstable spirits*, who turn round, till they are *giddy*, and fall from all *truth* and *charity*, into all *error* and *faction*; who shut their eyes, that they may say, they *grop in the dark*; and complain of all mens blindness, but their own; These (I say) have of all others, least cause to blame the *Religion*, and *Ministry* of the *Church of England*; since they own themselves to be in no *Church-way*: Which, of all sides, is most blamed and condemned, and so need not to be confuted any more.

2 Pet. 2.14. Beguiling unstable souls.

16. *Several quarrels against the Church of Englands frame.*

Some others there are, who flatter themselves to be less *mad* than these *seeking fellows*; who glory most in this, That they have *broken* all the former *cords*, and *shaken off* all *bonds*, of any *National Government*, *Order*, and *Discipline*, whereby they were formerly restrained in this Church: Which, first, they deny to be any Church, purely, and properly so called; or in any way and frame of *Christs institution*; but onely such an establishment as ariseth from meer *civil polity*, and *humane constitution*. Secondly, These charge us, that we fail in the *matter of a Church*, the *faithful* and *holy*. Thirdly, In the *essential Form*, an *explicite Covenant*, or *Church agreement* to serve the *Lord* in such a way. Fourthly and lastly, In our *chusing*, *ordaining*, and *appointing Ministers*, and other *Church Officers*: In whom (they say) Church power is onely executively, (as to the *exercise* or *dispensation*) but it is primarily and eminently in that *Body* of the people, never so small, which is so combined together:

Yea,

Yea, they complain, that we in *England* have neglected, and deprived the people of that *glorious power* and *liberty*, by which, every Christian is to shew himself, both *King*, and *Priest*, and *Prophet*.

Psal. 83. 6, 7, 8.

Nunquam deerunt hostes ubi adest ecclesia, nec inimici ubi veritas agnoscitur. Tert.

Thus the *Tabernacles of Edom*, and the *Ismalites*; of *Moab* and the *Hagarenes*; *Gebal*, and *Ammon*, and *Ammaleck*; the *Philistims*, and they of *Tyre*, *Assur* also, Men of our own Tribes; all conspire against the *true Religion*, the *antient orders*, and *holy Ministry* of the *Church* of *England*: And finding this Church *sorely torn*, *bruised*, and *wounded*, they either leave it, and its Ministry, to die desolate, by *separating* wholly from them; or else they seek by their *several instruments of death*, wholly to dispatch it, as the *Amalekites* did King *Saul*; But blessed be God, though this Church, and its true Ministers, be thus afflicted and persecuted; yet are they not quite *forsaken* of God, or of all good Christians; Though *we be cast down*, yet *we are not quite destroyed*. There want not many *sons of Sion*, to mourn with their *Mother*, and to *comfort* her, if they cannot *contend* for her, Although, the *Lord is righteous*, who hath smitten us, and to whom we will return, and *wait till he be gracious* to this Church: Yet these *sons of Edom*, our unnatural Brethren, are very injurious and uncharitable; who seek to *enflame the wrath* of God more against her; rejoycing in *her calamities*, and crying, *now she is faln, let her rise up no more*. But the *Lord will remember* his *compassions* of old, which have not failed, and will *return to build her up*; nor shall this *furnace of affliction* be, to consume this Reformed Church, but onely to *purge her* from that *dross*, which she had any way contracted.

2 Cor. 4. 8, 9.

Lam. 1. 2.

Isai. 30. 19.

Micah 7. 8, 9, 19.

17.

Of Religion as established and protected by Laws in England.

As to these mens first quarrel, against the *frame of our Church and Ministry*, as setled and defended by *Civil Laws* and *Politick Constitutions*; They seem in this, rather offended at the *clothes* and *dress*, or the *defence* and *guard*, than at the *body* and *substance* of the *Church*: Possibly, they are angry that they had not *power* or *permission*, sooner to *deform* and *destroy* that flourishing *polity* of this Church, which by the *princely piety* of *nursing fathers* and *mothers*, hath been so long preserved to the *envy of enemies*, and *admiration of friends*. We never thought, that any *civil sanctions* (which were in favor of our Reformed Church, Religion, and Ministry) ever constituted the Being of our Church; which is from Christ, by the Ministry; but they onely established and preserved it, in its Ministry and polity, from those *abuses* and *insolencies*, to which, we see them miserably exposed; if they should want *Magistrates* to be protecting *fathers*, and indulgent *mothers* to them: Every rude and unclean *beast* delights to break in, and waste the *field* of the Church; when they see the fence of *civil protection* is low.

But this *defence* and *provision* made for this Church and its

Ministry, by *Humane Laws*, doth no more lessen the *strength* and *beauty* of it; than the *Laws* for *property* and *safety* do diminish any *mans wisdom*, *valor*, or *care* to defend his own: Christians, as men, ought to be *subject to Magistrates*, as men; although they were *Heathens*, *Hereticks*, or *Persecutors*; that so, in honest things, they might merit their *civil protection*: How much more (as Christians) ought they to be *subject to Christian Magistrates*, that are *Patrons* and *Professors* of *true Religion*: Whose *civil protection* and *government* is so far from being a *blemish* to it, that is the *greatest temporal blessing*, that God hath promised, or the Church can enjoy in this World; as it was in *Constantine* the Great's time, and some others after him.

Rom. 13. 1 Pet. 2. 13. Tit. 3. 1. Isai. 49. 23.

And however, we see, that oft-times this *sweet wine*, of *civil favor*, is prone to sowre to the *vinegar of factions*, even among Christians; And the *honey of peace*, *plenty*, and *prosperity*, easily turns to *pride*, *envy*, *anger*, *ambition*, and *contention*, through the pravity of mans nature; who, (contrary to the temper of the most *savage beasts*) grows most fierce and offensive to God, when he is *best treated* by him; * as *Eusebius*, and *Sulpitius Severus*, tell in their times; Yet we must not refuse or cast away all good things, because evil mindes abuse them; much less may we mistake the *Being* of a Church, for its well-being; That cannot turn, in any reason, to this Churches reproach, which was the *favor* of good men, and Gods indulgence to this Church: Nor do we think these *querulous Objecters*, are therefore like to be, by so much the sooner, weary of their *new ways*, by how much they more enjoy *connivance*, *protection*, or *countenance* from any men; The obtaining of which, is the thing they so much *court* and *solicite*: Sure the shining of the warm Sun on men, need not make them therefore ashamed, or weary of Gods blessing.

* *Omnia complebantur factionibus, seditionibus, querelis, odiis, invidiis.* Sulpi. Sever. de sui tempor. Epis. & Presbyteris, Hist. *Pace ecclesiis undiq; concessâ, cœpit invidia totius orbis communis inimica in media episcoporum frequentia tripudiare.* Eus. in vit. Const. lib. 2. c. 60.

18. *The matter of a Church, Saints.*

2. As for the *matter of a Church*, which those *Objecters* say, must be onely *Saints in Truth*, as well as *shew*; denying ours to be such; I answer, We wish all our people were such Saints, as are formerly described, in *truth* and *power*; we endeavor to make them such, as far as the *pains*, *prayers*, and *examples* of *Ministers* may work with the *grace of God*; But we do not think, that these *severe censurers* of this Church of *England* do believe, That all the Churches mentioned in Scripture (which were the best that ever were) consisted onely of *true Saints*. That, in *Christs family*, did not; nor that, to which *Ananias*, *Saphyra*, and *Simon Magus*, were joyned in *profession*; nor all those in *Corinth*, *Galatia*, *Laodicea*, and the rest mentioned in the *Epistles*, and *Revelation*; who are commended, or

2 Cor. 6. 1.

John 6. 70. Have I not chosen you twelve, and one of you is a Devil? Acts 5. 3. *Peter* to *Ananias*, Why hath Satan filled thy heart, to lie to the Holy Ghost? Acts 9. 13. *Simon Magus* believed, and was baptised, and continued with the Apostles, *&c.* V. 23. I perceive thou art in the gall of bitterness, and bond of iniquity.

blamed,

blamed, not so much as to the *internal temper* of their *graces*, as to the *external peaceablenesß, order*, and *purity* of their *profession in truth* and *unity*. Neither is this real *Saintship* of every *Member*, necessary to the *Being of a visible Church*; nor is it to be concluded really of all those, whom the judgment of *charity* calls or esteems *Saints*. We charitably hope well of all those, who though they may have personal errors and failings, by reason of *frailties* or *temptations*, yet they have not renounced their *covenant* with *Christ* in *Baptism*, and who make still some *profession* of *Christianity*; who attend the *Ordinances* of the *Word* preached, and prayer; who testifie their *faith* by desiring to have their *children baptised*; which we do, as of duty to them, to whom Christ hath a *federal right*, and of whom we have a Christian hope; though we approve not their parents in all things: Much more do we esteem those as Members of the Church, who have *competent knowledge*, and lead an *unblamable life*, as many of ours do. If any be *children, ignorant*, or *profane*, yet we think them not presently to be excluded from all *Church Fellowship*; no more than such a *Jew* was to be cut off from Gods people; Since they have Gods *mark* and *seal* still upon them, and are in *outward relation* and *profession*, distinguished from those that are not of the *Israel* of God; yet we do, not willingly, or knowingly allow every *Ordinance* to these, while they appear such; but onely those, of which they have a capacity: In others, we forewarn and forbid them, when we actually know their unfitness or unpreparedness: Yet still in *Gods name*, not in our own; in a way of *charity*, or *ministerial duty*; not of *private*, or *absolute authority*; wishing, that a more *publick way* of *joynt-power* and *authority* were duly established (as in all reason it ought to be) in the Chucch; both for *tryal* and *restraint*, of those that have no right to *holy Mysteries*; yet still we endeavor to instruct even the worst in the *Spirit of meeknesß*, and to apply what remedies in *prudence* and *charity* we may: But if *piety, purity, equity, charity, humility, peaceablenesß, &c.* If these may denominate men to be *Saints* in any Church, sure, I believe, the Church of *England* can produce more of these, out of her *orderly* and *antient Professors*, than these *new Modellers* will easily do of their *own forming*; besides, many of those now gone from us, have not cause so much to boast of their *beauty* and *faces shining*, since they left us; as to cover their faces, and with their own tears to wash away those black spots, with which they appear terribly dashed; which we are sure are not the spots of Gods holy people.

19. *Of Communicants in Parochial Churches.*

What is further urged against our *Parochial Congregations*, (which are as *parts* and *branches* of this Church of *England*, standing in a *joynt relation* to the *peace, polity*, and *welfare* of the whole; and to that end, under *Publick Order*, and *Authority*) as to the use and partaking of the *Sacraments*, (specially that of the *Lords Supper*;) That our *Communions* are so mixed, as to confound the *pretious* with the *vile*; the *ignorant* with the *knowing*; the *scandalous* with the *unblamable*; the *prepared* with the *unprepared*; the *washed Lamb* with the *polluted Swine*; so that even this *holy Ordinance*, which is the *touchstone*, *sieve*, and *shreen* of true Christians, and true Churches, is profaned and polluted among us; while Congregations are as *lumps full of leaven*; and no order taken to *purge* it out: That so the *pure* and *faithful* may eat the *feast* with comfort, and *childrens bread* not be *given to dogs*.

1 Cor. 5. 7.

Answ. I answer, first in general; That, although Christians, as to their Consciences, have no right to this *Sacrament*, or comfort in it, further than they have Sacramental graces, fitting and preparing them for it; yet as to men, in *outward visible society*, every Christian hath such a right to it, as he makes a *Profession of the true Faith*; and is in such an *outward disposition*, as by the orders of the Church, for *age*, and *measure of knowledge*, and *conversation*, is thought meet: In which, there are no *precise limits* in *Scripture* expressed; either what *age*, or *how oft*, or *what measure of knowledge*, and what *preparation* is required; but much is left to the *wisdom*, *care*, and *charity* of the *Ministers*, and *Governors* of the *Church*: And in this sense, though *Judas* the Traytor had no *internal gracious right* to the *Sacrament of the Passover*, or *Supper*; yet he had a *professional right*, which our *Saviour* denied not to him, and which is all that mans judgment can reach to.

Luke 22. 14. Christ sate down, and the twelve Apostles with him. V. 19, 20. He took the bread and the cup, and gave it to them. V. 21. Behold the hand of him that betrayeth me, is with me on the Table.

Secondly, As to some mens practise in the *Church* of *England*, we deny not, but that many and personal abuses may have been in that *holy Mystery* (which the antients justly called *dreadful*, *venerable*, *adorable*, *most holy*, *admirable*, *divine*, *heavenly*, &c.) through negligence both of some *Ministers* and *people*; much less do we justifie them; we rather mourn for them, and pray heartily, they may be reformed every way; yet, as to the *constitution*, *order*, and *designation* of the *Church of England*, in the celebration of that holy *Sacrament*, we affirm,

Veneranda, sacra, tremenda, mysteria. φρικωδεστάτην τράπεζαν Chrys. ad Oly. ep. 2. μυστήριον ἁγιώτατον, ἀπόῤῥητον, θαυμάσιον. Basil.

1. That the *piety*, *wisdom*, and *charity* of this *Church*, did take care, and by express order declared, That no such *ignorant*, *profane*, *impenitent*, or *unprepared person* (though not known to the Minister, or people to be so,) should come to the *Sacrament*; as in *Conscience* he ought not: And, together with these (thus onely conscious to themselves) all others, if known and notorious, were by

ἐπίσταις, ἐπουράνια, ἀγγελικά. Clem. Al. ἱερὸν ἱερῶν. N. S. τὸ τῆς ἀθανασίας φάρμακον. Ignat. ep. ad Eph. τῆς σωτηρίας τύπος, ἱερὰ καὶ ἄνω φέρουσα μυσταγωγία. Naz. or. 14. If any of you be a blasphemer, and adulterer, in malice or envy, or any other grievous crime; bewail your sins, and come not to this holy Table, &c. See the *Exhortation* before the Communion.

the

the Minister publickly, and solemnly forbidden, *in the name of the Lord Jesus Christ*, not to presume to partake of those *holy things*.

Every Minister was commanded by *preaching*, *catechising*, *examining*, and *praying*, to prepare (as *much as in him lay*) the *Receivers:* Which every *good Minister*, as he ought, did, in some sort endeavor; yea, and he might refuse any young or old, that offered to receive, if they had not some good assurance of their *competent knowledge* in the *Mysteries*; or, if he found them *defective* in those *fundamentals* which the *wisdom* of the *Church* thought necessary, and whereof it set forth a *Summary* in the *publick Catechism*. So that a Minister in *England*, both *in the name of the Church*, and *in the name of Christ*, and by *the highest authority of God*, did prohibite, denounce against, and, as it were, *excommunicate* (by that part of the *power* of the *Keys*, which is denunciative and declarative) both from the *comfort*, and *grace* of the *Sacrament*, and from the *outward partaking* of it, every one, that *presumed* (being unworthy in any kinde) to offer himself to it: If after this, any one unworthy, did adventure to come, yet (sure) the Minister had done his private duty, as far as God, or man required it of him; having both vindicated the *honor of the Sacrament*, as to the *divine Institution*, and *intent*; also declared the *care and order of the Church*; and so freed both the *Congregation*, and his own soul, from *stain* or *blame*. Who so came after this *prohibition unworthily*, came at the *peril of his own soul*, and not at the sin of either *Minister* or *people*, that were worthy; whose *work and duty* is, not by force of arms, to thrust men out by head and shoulders; which is a *military* and *mechanick power*; but by the *sword of Christs mouth* to smite them; and *in his name* to cast them out from any right to, or comfort in, the *Sacrament*; which is the *power*, properly *ministerial*, *spiritual*, and *divine*. Where either *ignorance* or *scandal* were gross, and notoriously known to the Minister, in any that offered to come, The Minister might, and oft did, not onely privately, but publickly, and personally admonish, reprove, forewarn: And in some cases, if the *impudence* of the *offender* obtruded himself, the Minister might refuse to give him the *Sacrament*; yet this not with *passion* and *roughness*, as by *empire*; but with *meekness* and *discretion*, as in *charity*: Which present *denial*, or *abstention* of such an one from receiving the *holy Sacrament*, might afterward be examined by *publick* and *lawful authority* (which was setled in this *Church*) in case that *party* had cause or confidence to complain, as of an injury.

Communio malorum non maculat aliquem participatione Sacramentorum, sed consensione factorum. Aug. ep. 152.

See the *Rubrick* before the Communion, concerning scandalous offenders.

1 Cor. 11. 29. He that eateth and drinketh unworthily, eateth and drinketh damnation to himself; not to any other, who having examined himself, Verse 28. is bid to eat and drink, *&c.*

See the *Rubrick* before the Communion, The Minister may admit the penitent, but not the obstinate, in cases of private offences, *&c.*

But

20. *Good Ministers not defective in their duty, if they make not themselves Judges.*

But where such *authority* is not setled, or not suffered to be exercised in any *Church*, which might and ought to judge in such cases best The *party* denied, and the *Minister* thus denying, (upon *pregnant*, and to him *notorious causes*, not upon *probabilities*, *suspitions*, or *general complaints* from others onely,) There, *matters* of *publick debate* requiring audience, and proofs, and witnesses, and judge; and all these, *due authority*; It cannot be expected from any *private Minister*, that he should do more than God hath commanded, and due authority empowred him; which is onely to *instruct*, *admonish*, *forbid*, and in some cases to *deny*, *&c.* according to the duty of his *place*, and the *authority* he had, both from the *Church*, and from the *Word of God*: But he hath nothing to do, to *assume* the *publick place* of a *Judge* among his Neighbors; or to *deny Communion* to all those that are by any accused, as *unworthy* or *scandalous*: No *Reason* allowing, or *Religion* commanding every *private Minister*, or any *private Christians* to be *Judges* in those cases, wherein they may be *parties*; and through *passion* do injury, and by *faction* oppress any man.

Luke 12. 14. Who made me a judge, or a divider over you?

A right Discipline, and due Authority in the Church, most desirable.

It were to be desired indeed, that such *Authority* were restored to the *Church*, as might judge and decide all *cases* of *publike scandal*; but while this is denied, we must not deny *Ministers*, or *people*, to do their duty, in celebrating the *Lords Supper*; according to the *Institution*, though there be *defects in discipline*, as to that particular. We must not forbear *holy duties*, when we may rightly enjoy them, in point of *gracious disposition* and *claim*; because they are not so asserted and ordered in point of *polity* and *extern Discipline*, as we could wish, and as it were convenient; but is not *absolutely necessary*, so as to exclude the *Minister*, or others from it, who desire and prepare for it, by examining themselves; whom no *Reason* or *Religion* can forbid to partake of their *due comforts*, because of others faults, whereof they cannot be guilty, because they are no way accessary; not failing in any *private duty* of *charity*, wherein they stand related to another; as *teaching*, *admonishing*, *reproving*, *forewarning*,

1 Cor. 11. 28. *&c.* The same *Apostle*, who blames the *unworthy receivers*, for not *examining themselves*, and forbids them so to eat, *&c.* Commands others to *examine themselves*, and *so to eat*, *&c.* Without regard to any others *unworthiness*: The contagion of whose sin cannot have influence on anothers *grace*; any more, than *grace* can make anothers sin less. What sense can there be, That *children* should be *starved*, because there is not power sufficient to keep away all *dogs*, from the *childrens bread*? Yet all men are not presently to be called or counted *dogs*, that are not ever in *actual preparedness* for the *Sacrament*; or, who may fall into *gross sins*, as *Peter* did, whose *Faith* did not fail, when he denied *Christ* after the *Sacrament*; and since

Luke 22. 32.

they

they have still *relation* to the *Church*, and may be *penitents*.

I should be glad to see (which I heartily pray for) this *Church* so ordered by due order, power, and authority established in *fitting Church-Governors* and *Judges*, in such cases, That none might be *admitted* to the *Lords Supper*, but such as are both by the *Minister*, and chief of the *Congregation*, (who are in the *Rowl of Communicants*) *allowed* and *approved*, for *knowledge* and *conversation*; yet so, as such allowance or denial may, if need be, have further hearing, and appeal, from this *private Minister* and *Congregation*; which is but just, to avoid the *factions*, *injuries*, *partialities* and *oppressions*, which may fall, and oft do, among those *Neighbors* and *Rivals*, who are seldom meet to be *Judges* of *mutual scandals*, being so oft *parties*; and besides their weak judgments, have strong *passions*, and are full of *grudges* and *emulations* against each other; which if not soberly taken up, by other *able* and *indifferent Judges*, (who have *authority* so to do) it brings *Congregations* to those difficulties, which the *Independent bodies* finde, for want of this *prudent* and *orderly remedy* of *grievances* and *offences*; which, in a short time (as the *pitch*, and *fat*, and *hair*, which *Daniel* put into the *Dragon*) *break them in pieces*; one part rending from the other, as impatient to submit to their *censure*; and so they come to *Non-Communion*, and to make new *Colonies* of *lesser Churches*, and *Bodies*; till they break and shiver themselves to such *useless shreds*, such *thin* and *small shavings*, as have neither the *staff* of *beauty*, nor of *bonds* among them: Every one by the *light of nature* concluding, *That there can be no power over others, where there is parity among them; nor can those have authority over each other, which are in an equality.*

Exod. 18. 21. Judges ought to be able men, such as fear God; men of truth, hating covetousness, &c.

Par in parem non habet imperium. Authority supposeth an eminency.

Nothing would be more welcome to good *Ministers*, and *faithful people*, than to see that *just power* setled in the *Church*, as might by the *wisdom*, *gravity*, and *integrity* of such, as are *truly fit to govern*, best repress all *abuses* and *disorders* in the *Church*, as to matters *purely religious*: Mean time, we think it better to *bear with patience* those *defects*, which we cannot hinder or amend; and to *supply* them (what we can) with private *care*, *industry*, and *discretion*, than either wholly *to deny our selves* the comfort of this *Sacrament*, which the Lord hath afforded us; or else to *usurp to our selves* an *absolute power and jurisdiction over others*, which neither the *Lord* hath given us, nor the *Church*; and which we see men do easily despise, as a matter of *arbitrary usurpation*, not of *authoritative constitution*: And which is subject, as to many *tyrannies* and *abuses*, so to infinite *private janglings* and *divisions*; which no *Minister* hath leisure to hear, if he had abilities to *compose* and *judge them*, being oft very *spightful*, *tedious*, and *intricate*; yea, and himself, possibly, a *party*, or *witness*, and sometimes the *accused*; who being (for the most part) the ablest in a *Country Congregation* to judge of matters, must yet himself be judged according to some mens weak *Models* of *Church-Government* and *Discipline*, both as to his *doctrine* and *maners*, by his *High-shoe Neighbors*, (which he counts his body,) nor may he have any appeal from them in an *Independent way*.

21. *Of the peoples judging in the Church.* 1 Cor. 5. 12. 1 Cor. 6. 1, 2, 3, 4. Do ye not know, that the Saints shall judge the World, and Angels: How much more the things that pertain to this life.

To that grand Charter and Commission, which some plead; by which every Saint is made a *Judge* in *all things* of this life, within the pale of the Church, and is after to be *judge* of *Angels*; I answer; The *wise* and *holy Apostle* doth not give to every one in the Church any such power; nor to the majority of Christians in any Congregation; but rather *reproves* their folly, that laid any *judicative works* on those that were least esteemed in the Church, Vers. 4. Whence arose that *unsatisfaction* as made their differences greater, and drove them for remedy to go to Law *before the Civil Tribunals of unbelievers*, V. 6. to the great scandal of *Religion*, and shame of the Church of *Corinth*; where being many Christians, and (no doubt) in many distinct *Congregations*, for conveniency of *meeting*, the *Apostle* wonders they could not be so wise for their own *credit* and *quiet*, as to finde out *some wise* and *able men*, who might be fit to *judge* and *end* their *controversies*; as having both real *abilities internal*, and *outward reputation* in the Church, also a *publick consent* and *orderly appointment* to the work; all which makes a compleat and valid Authority to judge others; which can never be *promiscuous*, in whole *bodies*, or *rabbles* of simple and mean men, without both contempt and confusion; which imprudent way among the *Corinthians*, the *Apostle* counts both a fault and a shame.

Of Communicants to be admitted. 1 Cor. 5. 7. 2 Cor. 6. 15, 16.

What places are further urged for *purging out the old leaven*; for *not eating with such an one*; for *the non-communion, between Christ and Belial, light and darkness, &c.* They are all fulfilled by every private Christian, when both in *conscience* and *conversation*, he keeps himself from concurring, or complying with any *wicked and scandalous persons*, in their sins; *reproving* and *repressing* them, as much as morally lies in his place and power: But the bare view or knowledge of anothers sin, must not hinder him from doing his *duty*, or enjoying his *privilege* and *comfort* by the *Sacrament*; which depends, not on what is in anothers life, or heart, of sin; but on what he findes of *grace* and *preparedness* in his own; As to the *publick honor*, and *purity*, or *unleavenedness* of the Church, the special duty, and care executive lies on those, (not who are private Christians in common, but) who have *publick authority* in special, to do it, by *censuring*, *restraining*, or *casting* out *scandalous offenders*; whereto every Christian is not *called*, because not *enabled*, either by God or man, by *gift* or *power*, to *discern* or *judge*, and *determine cases*; which

Unumquemque alienis peccatis maculari, omnes impiæ seditionis autores solam causam separationis sibi assumunt: Contra disputat. Cypr. de unit. eccl. & August. ep. 48.

which is a matter of *polity, power,* and *order* in the Church, and not of *private piety,* or *charity:* Nor is it indeed of absolute necessity; so as to deprive good Christians of any *holy ordinance,* in case such power is *obstructed,* or *hindered,* or not *established* in the Church.

Neither Minister nor People then ought to refrain from doing their duty in the holy *celebration* of this *Sacrament,* upon any such *defects of external polity,* and *power,* for well-ordering of the Church; but rather, with the more exactness and diligence, exhort one another, and prepare by *inward graces,* for those *holy Mysteries;* whose *institution* hath no such *restriction,* either by *Christ,* or the blessed Apostle *Paul;* who enjoyns *Ministers* and *Believers* to do this, *holily* 1 Cor. 11. and *worthily,* in *point of personal preparation;* but no word of either usurping a *power* to *reject others,* as they list, which belongs not to them; or else, to abstain wholly from the duty, for want of having *their will,* as too many do, both *People* and *Ministers;* to the great grief of many good Christians, and to the exceeding slighting and disuse of that *holy Ordinance* in this Church, which was wont to be much frequented, which the words of *Christ* import, or enjoyn to be done *oftentimes* in the Church.

1 Cor. 11. 25. ὁσάκις *denotat* πολλάκις. As oft as ye drink it:

22.

Of Church-Covenant.

For that new *coyned form, image* and *superscription* of a *Church,* that *Congregational Church-Covenant,* which no *Synod* or *Council,* but onely some private men have lately invented, and in formal words *magisterially dictated* (when yet they cry down all other prescribed *forms* of *administrations, prayer,* or *devotion* in the *Church,*) By which, some men fancy they onely can be rightly made up into one *lump* or *Church-fellowship:* This they accuse us in *England* for the want and neglect, when they have set us in *every corner* so many copies of it.

I answer, We have indeed in the Church of *England,* from its first Christianity, been wholly without this *covenanting way;* and I think, both happily and most willingly we had been so still, since there appears no more ground for it in *Scripture precept,* or *Churches paterns;* nor is there any more need of it, as to the *peace* and *polity* of the true Church of Christ, than there is of *rents* and *patches* in a fair and whole Garment. Who knows not, that like *Jonah's gourd* Jonah 4. 10. it is (*filius noctis*) the *production of yesterday;* risen from the darkness and divisions of mens mindes: The *fruit of discontent, separation,* and *self-conceit,* for the most part; though, it may be, nursed up by devout and well-meaning Christians; yet it looks very like those *bastard brats* which the *Novatians* and *Donatists* of old began every where; which were like *Ismaels* to *Isaac,* mockers and contemners of the true Churches Communion, Order, and Peace.

בל לולה

VVe do not think this *Covenant* any more essential to the Being of a true Church, than *John Baptists* Leathern girdle was to his being a Man, or a Prophet: It is an *easie* and *specious novelty*, therefore pleasing to *common people*, because within their grasp and reach; which its *Proselytes*, that forsake and abhor the English Churches *Order* and *Communion*, do wrap and hug themselves in as much, as any *Papist* doth in his adherence to the *Roman party*, or in his hopes to be buried in a *Monks* Cowl. Besides, it carries this *great temptation* with it, of gratifying the *common professor* with some shew of *Power* and *Government*, which he (once *covenanted* into that Church-way) shall solemnly exercise: But (in good-earnest) to sober Christians, who have no *secret byas* of *discontent* or *interest* to sway them, this new fashion of their *Church-Covenant*, seems to have, as no *command* or *example* in *Scripture*, so no *precedent* in *antiquity*; nor is it recommended for any excellent *effects* of *prudence* or *peace*, which it produceth, either to private Christians, or the publick welfare of the Reformed Churches. Some look on it as a mark of *Schismatical confederacy*, which carries in its Bowels *viperine principles*, which are destructive to the quiet of *States* and *Kingdoms*, as well as of *Churches*.

If any finde any good or contentment in it, as a *tye*, or *pledge* of *love*, in *private fraternities*; yet they vastly overvalue it, to cry it up, as a matter, no less necessary to the *Being* of a *Church*, or *well-being* of *Christians*, than the skin is to the Body; when, alas, it is but a *cloak* lately taken up, which never fell from *Elias* his shoulders; and serves rather to cover some mens infirmities and discontents against this *Church* of *England*, than much to keep them warm, or adorn them as Christians. VVe shall give a poor account of former *Churches* or *Christians*, if this *covenanting invention* should be of such concernment to Christianity. To which it seems to many wise and good men as *superfluous*, as it were to binde a man with wisps of straw, when he is already bound with chains of gold, with more firm and pretious tyes.

For, every true and conscientious Christian knows and owns himself to have upon his Conscience, far more strict and indissoluble *tyes*, not onely of *nature* and *creation*, but of the *Law* and *Word of God*; yea, and of *Christian covenant*, and *profession*, by his *baptismal-vow*; besides, that of the other *Sacrament*; also his *private vows*, *promises*, and *repentings*, *&c.* All which strictly binde the conscience of all good Christians to all duties of piety and charity, according to the relations, (private or publick, civil or sacred) wherein they stand to God or man.

And further, we see by daily experience, That these sorry *withs* of *mans invention*, obtruded as divine and necessary upon Christians

and

and Churches, binde not any of these *new small bodies* or *bundles*, so fast, but that they continually are *breaking*, *separating*, and *scattering*, into as many *fractions* and *subdivisions*, as they have *heady mindes*, *fancies*, and *humors* among them. And this they do, without any sense of *sin* or *shame*; yea, for the most part, with an *angry glorying*, *despising*, and *defying* of one another; when, but lately, they boasted in how rare a way they were of *Church-fellowship*, and *Saintly-communion*; not, as *Members of Christs Body*, the *Catholike Church*, grounded and grown up in *truth* and *love*; but onely as pieces of wood, *finely glued* together, by reciting a *form of words*, which they call a *Church-Covenant*, which a little spittle, or wet dissolves: Nor do they make any scruple to *moulder* and *divide*, if once they come to *dispute* and *differ* in the least kinde. So hard is it for any thing to hold long together, which is compacted of *weak judgements* and *strong passions*.

Error sibi semper dispar est & discolor, quam ò magis à veritate tantum ab unitate discedit. August.

Eph. 3. 17.

Last of all, It is evident in the *experience* of all *wise Christians*, That this *narrow* and *short thong* of *private Bodying*, *Church-covenanting*, cannot extend so far, as is necessary for the *Churches general peace*, *order*, and *welfare*, in reference to its more *publick relations*, and *necessities*; which oft require stronger and more *effectual remedies*: Yea, these small *strings* and *cords* binding each *particular Congregation* apart (as if it were a *limb* to be let blood) makes them at length grow *benumed*, and less *sensible* of that *common spirit* of *love* and *charity*, by which, each Member is knit to the larger parts, and so to the whole *Body* of the *Church*; to whose common good, they ought wisely and charitably to be more intent, than to their *particular Congregations*; which are, but as the *Pettitoes* or *little Fingers* of the *Church*; Which may not act, or be considered, otherways, than as they are, and subsist; which is, not apart by themselves, nor onely in relation to an *hand* or *foot*, to which they are more immediately conjoyned; but, as in an *higher relation* to the *whole Body*, of which, they are *real parts*, servient to the whole; and as much concerned in the *common good* and *preservation* of the whole (if not more) than of themselves, or any particular part or Member. A Christian must not deal out his *charity*, by retail and small parcels onely, as to *private Fraternities*, and *Congregations*; but also by *whole-sale*, to the ampler proportions of Christs Church; according as he stands in large and publick relations; the due regard to the *peace*, *order*, and *welfare* of which, is not to be dispenced withal, nor shuffled off, by saying, I am of such a *Congregational-Body*, or *Covenanting Church*; no more, than the *hand* may say, I am not of the head, nor neer it; and so will have no care of it.

1 Cor. 12. 21.

We are therefore so far from being *admirers* of the *small talents* and *weak inventions* of those men, in so great a matter, as the constituting and conserving of a *true Church*, by so poor and feeble an *engine*, as this of *private compacts* and *covenantings*; (by which, they threaten with *severe pens*, and *tongues*, and *brows*, to *batter* and *demolish* the great and goodly *Fabrick*, and *Communion*, of this and all other *National Churches*; which are *cemented* together by excellent *Laws*, and publick *Constitutions*, so as to hold an *honorable union* with themselves, and the whole *Catholike Church*,) That we rather wonder at the *weakness* and *simplicity* of those *inventers* and *abetters*, who in common reason cannot be ignorant, that as in *civil respects*, and *polity*, so in *Ecclesiastical*, no *private fraternities*, in *families*, nor *Corporations*, (as in Towns and Cities) can vacate those more *publick* and *general relations*, or those *tyes of duty* and *service*, which each *Member* ows to the *Publick*, whereof it is but a part; and it may be so inconsiderable an one, that for its sake, the greater good of the *publick*, ought not in *Reason* or *Religion*, to be prejudiced, or any way neglected: No more ought it to be in the Churches larger *concernments*, for Peace, Order, and Government.

Nay, we dare appeal to the Consciences of any of those *Bodying Christians*, (whom charity may presume to be godly and judicious;) Whether they finde in *Scripture*, or have cause to think, That the blessed *Apostles* ever constituted such small *Bodies* of *Covenanting Churches*; when there were great numbers, and many Congregations of Christians in any City, Province, or Country; so as each one should be thought *absolute*, *Independent*, and no way *subordinate* to another? Whether ever the *Apostles* required of those *lesser handfuls* of Christians, (which might, and did, convene in one place) any such *explicite Forms*, or *Covenants*; besides those *holy bonds*, which by *believing*, and *professing* of the *Faith*, by *Baptism*, and *Eucharistical communion*, were upon them? Or, Whether the blessed *Apostles* would have questioned, or denied those to be true Christians, and in a true Church, or have *separated* from them, or *cast* them off, as not ingrafted in Christ, or growing up in him, who, without any such *bodying* in small parcels, had professed the Name of the *Lord Jesus Christ*, in the due use of *Word*, *Sacraments*, and *Ministry*? who endeavored to lead a *holy*, and *orderly life*, themselves, and sought by all means, which *charity*, *order*, or *authority* allowed them, to repress the contrary in others? No doubt the *Apostles wisdom* and *charity*, was far enough from the *wantoness* and *uncharitableness* of some of these mens spirits; who do not onely mock our Church, and its Ministers, as the children did *Elisha*, the Prophet; but they seek to destroy them, as the *she-bears* did the children. Sure enough, the *Apostles*, instead of such *severe censures*, *peevish disputes*, and *rigorous separations*, would have joyned with, and rejoyced in the

2 Kings 2. 23.

Faith,

Faith, Order, and *Unity* of such *Churches*, such *Christians*, and such *Ministers*, where-ever they had met with them, in all the World, without any such *scruple*, or *scandal*, for their not being *first broken* into *Independent Bodies*, and then bound up by *private covenantings*; which are indeed no other, than the *racking*, *distorting*, and *dislocations* of *parts*, to the weakning and deforming of the *whole*.

VVe covet not a *better* or *truer constituted Church*, than such, as we are most confident, the *wisdom* and *charity* of the *Apostles* would have approved in the *main*; however in some *lesser things*, they might *gently reprove*, and *reform them*, as they did divers *famous* and *flourishing Churches*. And such a *Church*, we have enjoyed in *England*, (by Gods mercy) before ever we knew those mens *unhappy novelties*, or *cruelties*, who seek now to divide, and utterly destroy us, unless we *conform* to their *deforming principles* and *practises*. And however, we have not been wholly without the *spots* of *humane infirmities*; yet we have professed *Jesus Christ*, in that *truth*, *order*, *purity*, and *sincerity*, which gives us comfort and courage, to claim the (ἐξουσίαν) *privilege* of being true Christians, and a true Church; that is, a very *considerable*, *famous*, and *flourishing part*, *branch*, or *Member* of that *Catholike Church*, which *professeth visibly*, or *believes savingly*, in the Name of *Jesus Christ*, the *Head* of the *whole Body*, and of every part; to whom we are united, by the same *common Faith*, and by *Charity*, to one another. Certainly, the best Churches and Christians, were antiently like the *goodly bunches* of *Grapes*, which the *Spies* brought between them (as an emblem of *Christ crucified*) hanging on a staff; so *fair*, so *full*, so *great* and *united clusters*: From which, no small *slips* did ever willingly *divide*, or *rend* to *Schism*, but presently they became, not as the *fruit* of *Canaan*, but as *sowr Grapes*, fit onely to set mens teeth on edge; whetting them to *bite*, and *devour* one another.

Col. 2. 5. Joying and beholding the order, and the stedfastness of your faith in Christ.

Numb. 13. 24.

23. *The great shield of the Church of* England.

For the maner of each particular *holy Administration* in our Church, to answer all the small cavils, which men list to make, is to encourage too much their petulancy; and to make them too much masters of sober mens time and leisure: Onely this *great* and *faithful shield*, * *Learned men* heretofore have, and we do still, hold forth, to repel all their *darts* and *arrows*, That both in the *Ordination* of our *Ministers*, and in their *celebration* of *holy things*, and in its *Government*, *Order*, and *Harmony*, the Church of *England* hath followed the *clearest rules* in *Scripture*, and the *best paterns* of the *antient Churches*; onely enjoying those *Christian liberties* of *prudence*, *order*, and *decency*, which we see the gracious wisdom of Christ hath allowed his Church; and which particular Churches have always used and enjoyed in their extern *rites* and *customs*, with variety, yet without blemish, as to the Institutions of Christ, or to the

the soundness in the *Faith*, or to any breach of *Charity*, or any prejudice and scandal to each others *liberties* in those things.

So that those *busie flies* upon the Wheels of this Chariot, the *Reformed Church* of *England*, (in which the *Gospel* of *Jesus Christ* hath hitherto been carried among us, for many years, with *great triumph* and *success*) have stirred up very little *dust*; so as might blinde any eyes (that are not full of *motes and beams*, or *blood-shotten*) from seeing clearly, and evidently, a *true Christian Church*, a *true Ministry*, and *truly religious Administrations* among us. Blessed be God, though these *sowr Momusses* finde or make some faults and flaws in lesser matters, the *mending* of which they most oppose and hinder; yet their strength cannot shake the *foundations* of our *Jerusalem*, which are of *pretious pearls*, and *solid stones*; nor can their *malice* overthrow our *grand* and *goodly pillars*; the *true* and able *Ministers*, and their *holy Ministrations*, of *Word* and *Sacraments*, among *Professors* of the *Faith*; who do, as unquestionably *constitute a true Church*, as a *reasonable soul* and *body* make a *true man*.

Essentials of a true Church in England.

1 Tim. 6. 3.

Phil. 1. 27.

1 Pet. 1. 9.

It is well, some of their *charity*, is such that they allow us (for they cannot shift it,) thus much: First, That we have the *onely true ground*, and *sure rule of Religion*, the *written Word of God*; that, beyond this, we hold nothing as a matter of *faith*, or *Christian duty*: Secondly, That we celebrate the *holy Sacraments* according to the *sum and substance* of the *divine Institution*: Thirdly, That our *conversation aims* to be such, as *becomes the Gospel* in all *maner of holiness*, to the saving of our own, and others souls. What can these *Aristarchusses* carp at in the *ground of our faith*, the *Scriptures*; the *Seals* of our *Faith*, the *Sacraments*; the *life of our Faith*, *holy conversation*; and the *end of our faith*, the *salvation of our souls*? Is it not strange, That all these *sweet* and *fair flowers* of Christs planting and watering, should grow so well in that, which some call *Babylon*? in *Antichrists Garden*? or on the *Devils dunghil*? That, it should be no *true Church* of *Christ*, which owns nothing for *Religious*, but what is according to the *truth of Jesus*; either *commanding* or *permitting*, *instituting* or *indulging*; of *pious necessity*, or of *prudent liberty*.

We should put these rigid *Catoes* too much to the blush, for their *unnatural ingratitude* to the *Ministers*, and *Church* of *England*, if we should ask them: Whence they had this *privilege*, by which they own themselves to be *Christians*? whence this *power* to cast, or call themselves into *Bodies* or *Churches*, as *Believers*? (which is by them presupposed;) whence they had (till of late years) their *instruction* (for the most part) in the *knowledge of Jesus Christ*? Sure these *holy leaves* or *fruits* grow not, but in the *Pale and Garden*

of

of the *Church of Christ*; not in our own *rude mindes* and *untill'd natures*; not among *desolate Indians*, *obstinate Jews*, or *barbarous Turks*; and not often in *private closets* and *corners*; which nourish a *neglect* and *contempt* of *Publick Ordinances*. But if these men were *self-taught* and *converted*, yet sure, not *self-baptized* too; nor their *Teachers*, *self-ordained* too: If they had nothing of their *Christianity* from the *Ministry* of the *Church* of *England*; It is no wonder they prove such *Scholars*, such *Christians*, and such *Preachers*, as some of them seem to be; having been their own *Masters*, *Ministers*, and *Baptizers*: They are indeed, onely worthy of themselves, and of wiser mens pity.

24.

Of pretensions to be above any Ministry, as taught of God immediately.

For that (κρησφύγετον) the *retreat*, or *reserve* of some men (by which, as *Eaglets* they would seem to soar out of sight, and to build their Nest on a *Rock*, that is higher than our ordinary *Reason*, *Religion*, and *Experience* can reach;) as if they were *immediately inspired*, *specially called*, and *taught of God*, *baptized by his Spirit*, without any *Minister*, or outward *Ministry*, they must give us leave, not to believe them upon their *bare word*, (which hath not always been so sure,) till they demonstrate, and prove it better, by *Gods Word*, and their *better maners*; For which, we will give them time enough. Mean while, we are sure, the best Christians among them, were made such, by the *ordinary Ministers* of this *Church*; and these made *Ministers* by no other means but that *Ordination*, derived from, and ascending up to the blessed *Apostles*; whom *Christ* first chose to be *Disciples*, and after *ordained* and *sent them* as *Publick Ministers*; not onely, as to *personal discharge*, but as to *successional descent*. These were *Eagles* indeed, who flew high in their *knowledge* and *piety*, yet stooped low in their *humility* and *charity*: Those others of a *new brood*, are more like *yong Cuckoes*, which devour the *Bird*, in whose *nest*, and by whose *fostering*, they were *hatched*. Some of them have *knowledge*; I would they had more *humility* and *charity*, they would not disdain to own the parents that begat and educated them; even this (now) so poor, desolated, beaten, torn, and wasted Church of *England*, and its (*Antichristian*) *Ministers*, as they please to call them.

Be it so; some mens tongue is no slander: If we neither adde to, nor detract from the *Scriptures*, as *Jews*, *Papists*, and *Enthusiasts* do; If we erre in no *fundamentals* of *faith*, or *maners*; if we refuse no duty *divinely required*; if we allow no *error* in our selves, or others; if we drive on no worldly designs injuriously, or hypocritically; but study to approve our selves in *all godliness* and *honesty*, with *meekness of wisdom* to all men; we need no more fear the drops of *peevish tongues*, or *dashes of malicious pens*, (as to the *honor* and *comfort* of being a *part* of the *true Church of Christ*)

than

than a cloth dyed in grain, need to fear ſtains by the aſperſions of dirt, caſt on it by unclean and envious hands.

25. *Of the power of the People in Church affairs.*

. . . 4. But it is objected againſt us in *England*, That neither *Church* nor *Miniſter* of *England*, did, or do own that *high and mighty principle* of all *Church power*, which ſome call, *The People*.

Anſw. True indeed: Although we *highly love* and *eſteem* as *Brethren*, the *faithful and humble people*, for whom *Chriſt* hath died; yet we are not of ſo *ſpungy* and *popular a ſoftneſs*, as to own any part, or Congregation, or Body of People, to be the *original*, or *conduits* of any *Spiritual* or *Church power*; which no *learned* and *wiſe men* ever eſteemed to be *Popular* or *Democratical*, but rather an excellent *Ariſtocracy*; where many *able men* were in *Counſel*, and ſome one *eminent* in *order* and *authority* among them. We do not dig, or deſcend to theſe *low valleys*, for theſe *holy waters*; nor do we ſeek for the flowings of it through ſuch *crazy* and *crooked pipes*; nor do we hope to *draw* it forth out of ſuch *broken Ciſterns*, which can hold no ſuch waters: We have them from *higher fountains*, and derive them in *ſtraiter channels*, and conſerve them in *fitter veſſels*, than the *vulgarity* of even honeſt Chriſtians can be preſumed to be: That is, from the ordinary Power, and conſtant Commiſſion, which from *Chriſt* was derived to the *Apoſtles*, and from them to their *Succeſſors* in their *ordinary Miniſtry*, and *Church power*, in after ages; who had this *peculiar power of the keys of Heaven*, to binde or remit; to *gather*, to *guide*, to *feed*, and to *govern* the ſeveral parts of the *Church* in *Chriſts ſtead*, and *name*, orderly committed to them.

Matth.28.19. Matth. 16. 19. Matth.18. 18. John 20.23.

ποιμαίνειν, *Paſcere cum imperio, & paſtor inde ut princeps.* To feed and rule. Revel. 12. 5. & 19. 15. Acts 20.28. 1 Pet. 5. 2.

People may rudely wreſt theſe *keys* out of true *Biſhops* and *Miniſters* hands, but it is evident, they were never *committed* to them, by the great *Maſter of the Houſe*, *Jeſus Chriſt*; nor do they know how to uſe them, unleſs it be to break their heads with them, whom *Chriſt* hath ſet as *ſtewards* in his houſhold: Theſe *ruſtick* and *raſh* undertakers to *reform*, and controul all, are onely probable to *ſhipwrack* themſelves, and many others, and the whole *Ship* of this *Church*, by driving the *skilful Pilots*, (the true *Biſhops* and *Miniſters*) from the *Helm*, and putting in their places every bold *Boatſwain*, and ſimple *Swobber*.

Vulgus ex veritate pauca, ex opinione multa æſtimat. Tul. pro. Roſ. Com.

Yet are the populacy flattered by ſome, to this dangerous *inſolency* and *error*; who putting fire to this thatch, inſtead of the Chimney, do but provoke the poor people to their own hurt; to *forſake their own mercies*; and to injure both their own, and others ſouls: Mean time, ſober and wiſe Chriſtians cannot but ſmile, with *ſhame*, *ſorrow*, and *indignation*, to ſee, how ſome *Plebeian Preachers*, who are new riſen, as from the *ſlime of the earth*, (in whom no *Prometheus* hath breathed any *ſpark of heavenly fire*; of *ſpiritual*,

divine,

divine, and *truly ministerial power* ;) to see (I say) how these *Teachers* have brought themselves by a *voluntary humility*, to depend on *peoples suffrages* and *charity* ; not onely for *maintenance*, but for their *very Ministry* ; being now sunk so low, as to flatter their *good Masters*, with this *paradox* or *strange principle* , That they (as the *people*, or *body*, be they never so *few* and *mean*) have a *reciprocal power*, to beget those, who are to be their *Spiritual Fathers* ; that by a more than *Pythagorean Metemphycosis*, the *Power*, *Spirit*, and *Authority* of Jesus Christ , *who was sent by his Father*, and so *sent his Apostles*, and they others, in the *same Spirit*, to be *Fathers*, *Pastors*, *Rulers*, *Stewards*, &c. That at length, this *Spirit* and *Authority*, should *transmigrate* (we know not how, nor when) into the very *mass* and *bulk* of *common people*, if they be but Christians of the lowest form ; animating them in the *whole*, and in *every part*, or *parcel* of them, with such *plenitude of Church power*, as enables them to be all *Kings* and *Priests*, *Pastors* and *Teachers*, *Prophets* and *Apostles*, if need be ; and if they list ; and if they have leisure ; or, if not to act so in their *own persons* (having more profitable employments,) yet they have *virtually*, and *eminently* in them, as much *power*, as *Christ* had, and used, or left to any men ; whereby to *consecrate* and *ordain true Ministers* ; to *try* and *teach* those that are to *teach them* ; to *rule* their *Rulers* ; to *discipline* their *Shepherds* ; to *govern* their *Governors* ; to turn, not onely *Religion* out of doors, but even all *Reason*, *Order*, and *Civility*, upside down, rather than not exercise this *imaginary power*, especially, if it serve to *secular advantages* : And all this, because they are told, they are *the Church* ; and so may erect all *Church power*, as in them, and from them. This fancy is able to make a plain *Country-Christian* stand on his *Tiptoes* ; and to bring all his *family* to see him and his *other-like members*, making up this *glorious Body*, which he calls *his Church* ; that they may be witnesses, with how much folly, and simplicity, and clamor, and confidence , he with his Neighbors, *examines*, *approves* or *reproves*, *refuseth* or *chooseth*, and *ordains* all *officers*, and some new *fashioned Minister* or *Pastor* : Who (*poor-man*) must neither *Preach* nor *Pray*, not *eat*, nor *look otherways*, than pleaseth these sad and silly, yet very supercilious pieces of *popular pride*, and *itching arrogancy* ; nor can such an *hungry* and *timorous Pastor* ever be setled, or safe in this *Pastoral Authority*, unless he have the trick of *Faction* ; which is still to ingratiate with the major part of this his *flock* ; who will (otherways) as easily *push* and *beat him out* of this *fold*, or *break* all to pieces ; as ever they *admitted him* by a *profane easiness*, and *popular insolency*.

John 20. 21.

26. *Common people not fit to manage Church power in chief.*

But I must with less *flattery*, and more *honesty*, tell this *Generation of perverse Usurpers*, this truth, (which is not unwelcome to *sober*

sober spirited Christians,) That the *weight* of Christianity doth not at all hang on this *popular pin*; which is no where to be found, but in their *light heads*, and *heavy hands*; neither *Reason*, nor *Religion*, (since men were *redeemed* from the barbarity of *Acorns*, *Nakedness*, and *Dens*,) ever thought the *plebs*, or *common people* ought to be *all in all*, if any thing at all; either in conferring or managing, either Civil or Church power; but least of all, that part of Church power which is proper for the making of a *Minister*, in the way of *due Ordination*, (of which I shall after give a fuller account;) For this is that, to which they generally have *least proportion*, either of *knowledge*, *learning*, *holiness*, or *discretion*: Besides, it would thence follow, that, so soon as any *Sect* or *Faction of people* can get but *numbers*, and *courage*, they may do what they list, in this plenitude of power, without the leave of *Magistrates* or *Ministers*, in *Church* or *State*. These are *pestilent principles*, which are not onely *pernicious* to the Church, but to any *civil Societies*; threatning not our *faith* onely, but our *purses* and *throats*.

οὐδὲ τῷ πλήθει τοῦ διδόναι μετεῖν. Naz. Or. 25.
οὔποτε ὀρεκτέον τοῖς πολλοῖς ἀρέσκειν. Clem. Al. Strom. 1.
σοφία ἐν ὀλίγοις, ἀταξία δὲ ἐν πλήθει. Id. Παιδ. 1.

Nor did ever any wise men (what ever is pretended, at any time, to *amuse the people*, and to serve an occasion) intend, or suffer the community, or vulgar people (with their *massie bodies* and *numerous hands*) *really* to attain, use, or enjoy, any such *supreme power* in *civil administrations*: If once *soverain power* be gotten, though by the means of such *credulous assistants*; yet, whatever the populacy may flatter themselves with, it never is, nor can wisely and happily be managed by them, but rather without them, above them, and many times against them.

Power precarious, that is such as depends upon a *popular principle*, or *plebeian account*, such as sometime was among the *Grecian State*, and *Romans*, is, for the most part, but an *Empire* of beggery, or flattery, or falsity; Where (at best) wise and valiant men may oft be forced to prostrate themselves to the arbitrement of the vulgar; who are injurious esteemers and ungrateful requiters even of the most *publick merits*. But (oftentimes) the peoples *pretended power*, and *interest*, is made use of in specious terms, and cunning agitations, onely to serve the turn of *turbulent*, *ambitious*, and *factious spirits* in *Church* and *State*; whose *envy* or *ambition* easily teacheth the credulous community to esteem the *over-meriting* of the *best men*, and *Magistrates*, to be their greatest oppression, and most deserving (*Ostracism*) *banishment*, or *disgrace*.

Per paucorum hominum virtute crevit Imperium. Salust.
Rom. 13. 4.

The *Life of Government*, and *Soul of Dominion*, is, that *real power* and *resolution*, which is in the hand of one or more *wise* and *potent men*; who are always intent to deserve well of the people, yet always able to curb and repress their insolency and inconstancy. Without this *authentick power of the Sword*, (which is not to be *born*

in

in vain, and against which there is *no rising up*) *Government* or *Empire*, is a meer *carkaß* without a *soul*; like *dead beer*, or *evaporated wine*, or a *rotten post*, which every one despiseth. It is indeed one point of *wisdom* and *true honor*, to deserve well of the people, so as to gain their love; but the *highest* and *safest principle* of *policy* is to command them by power to *just fear*: For their *love* is no longer to be trusted, if once they cease to fear, and revere their *Governors*. The *goodneß* and *gentleneß* of *Magistrates* must not slaken or *motheat* their power; nor their power *oppreß* and *wire-draw* their goodneß: *Princes* and *Governors* are lost, if they presume common people at any time to be such *Saints*, and so good natured, that they need not power effectual and soverain to command and restrain them, as Beasts; to set banks and boundaries to them, as to *great waters*; whose *force* is not seen, but in their *eruptions* and *disorders*; and they are then best and most useful, when kept and directed in such a *course* and *chanel*, as restrains them from shewing how great a *propensity* and *fury* they have to do *mischief*, if once they get *liberty*; which soon turns the flattering smoothneß of it former *smiles*, to threatning tortuosities, and dreadful over-whelmings. Prov. 30. 31.

And so on the other side, *Governors* are not safe, if they so apply and use *rigid force* and *severer dominion*, as if they forgat that they ruled men (and not beasts) who are sensible of *gentleneß*, and may be obliged to quietneß by *humanity*. *Rehoboam* might have continued the *heavy yoke* of his wise Fathers taxes and burthens, if he had but so lined it with *soft words*, and *courtly blandishments*, as it should not much have *galled their necks*; which *custom* will harden, and *kindneß* make unsensible of what they bear. It is not imaginable, how much *common people* will bear, if they see they *must*; nor how little they will bear, if they see they may *rebel*; their *complainings* or *tumultuary petitionings*, are *menacings*; when they declare, that they cannot longer undergo *legal burdens*, their meaning is, *they will not*; and onely want power to act. *Necessity* and *force* makes the vulgar tame, with their *strength*, and patient, as *Asses*; but wanton and presumptuous fancies makes them, as the *Unicorn*, impatient of the most honest *subjection*: No condition of *Government* ever pleased all that were *Subjects*; and most are prone to be unsatisfied with the present; whatever it is, they fancy and hope change may be better for their *interest*. Therefore, the calmest tempers of people must not be trusted; no more than the *smiles* of *Halcion* Seas. Wise *Pilots* know, there is no point of the Compaß, whence a tempest may not come; nor is there any commotion, or inclination to troubles, whose impression the vulgar will not easily receive and raise to a *storm*: They are like a weighty baody kept up with engines, on the top of a hill; if once it be free, it falls;

1 Kings 12.

Job 39. 9.

τὸ παρὸν ἀεὶ βαρὺ τοῖς ὑπηκόοις. Thucid.

and falling downward, it drives it self; Motion adding an impetu to its weight; the (πολλοὶ) many, or multitude, are always the more dangerous, by how much less *suspected*: Necessity of obeying, is in most men but the cover of *hypocrisie*; except in some few, whom
Rom. 13. 5. *conscience* makes subject; and who upon *Christian principles*, chuse rather with patience to suffer under any lawful *Magistrates*, than to *contest* with them, although they were sure to conquer: Fearing no *oppression* or *tyranny* so much, as that of sin; as no sin so much, as
1 Sam. 15. 23. that of *rebellion*, either against God, or those that are in *Gods stead*, and *authority* over them. *Factious spirits*, which possess most men
2 Kings 8. 13. (though they are not awar of it, more than *Hazael* was of his) easily make surprizes upon slackned, weakned, or *over-confident power*; whose security as to mens peaceful tempers, makes it less vigilant.

The *true temperament* is, where just and *indisputable power*, is so wisely managed, as renders *Governors*, rather *august* than *dreadful*; rather *venerable* as Parents, than *formidable* as Masters; though the *Body Politick* seem never so fairly *fleshed* with love, and *skinned* over with kindness, yet there is neither *strength* nor *safety* in it, unless the *sinews* and *bones of majesty*, *real* and *effectual power*, be maintained. It is enough, and as much as is safe for common people, to have the *fancy* and *imagination* of that *power* and *liberty*, which their *deputies*, *representatives*, or *Tribunes tongues* may take in *publick Conventions* and *Parliaments*: But it is dangerous for themselves, as well as for their *Magistrates*, ever to let them tamper at the *lock of majesty* and *sovereinty*, with the *Key of Power*; for if they cannot fairly and easily *open that door*, through *fury* and *impatience* they will break it open by violence; if they be not over-awed. There is no (*Arcanum*) *Mystery* or *Secret of Empire*, like to that of keeping such power, as evil men may fear, and good men will love; because they know it is for the *publick good*; and though it should lie heavy on subjects, yet it is not so terrible, as to be *ground* between two milstones of *rival powers* in *civil dissentions*.

σεμνότερον καταπληκτικὸν μᾶλλον τοῖς ὑπηκόοις ἢ φοβερὸν ὑπάρχειν. Muson. ap. Stobæum.

No wise Magistrate therefore, either in *policy* or *conscience*, that is once invested in due *authority sovereign*, will ask the people leave, either to have it, or to use it: The *softer formalities* sometime used to ask the peoples consent, (not in their bulk and heard) but in their *proxies* and *deputies*, is but a *complement*; and where prevalent power asks, it is never denied; nor is it ever asked, but where conquering or hereditary power knows men dare not refuse it. No personal title or pretension to sovereinty is so unjust, which people will not confirm by their consent: In which, their worldly wisdom looks more to their own safety, and the publick peace, than to any particular mans right and interest; as they are wasted and ruined by

contesting

contesting with those, that are to strong for them; so they would soon be too hard for themselves, and most their own enemies, if they should be left to arrogate, or exercise power according to their own various fancies, brutish motions, and preposterous appetites.

Therefore, *God* who is (φιλάνθρωπος) *a lover of mankinde*, hath so ordered in his providence; that, where any people are blest; some one or few men, who are wiser than the people, become also stronger, by an orderly and well-united strength; thereby preserving themselves, and the publick, from those *impetuous furies*, to which this *Leviathan*, the *people*, is as naturally subject, as the *Sea* is to *waves* and *storms*, both in *Civil* and *Ecclesiastical* affairs; for they are no whit calmer in matters of *Religion*, than in those of secular regards; every man in Church matters, being confident of his skill, or at least his *will and zeal*, thinks it a shame to seem ignorant, or if he be *conscious* to his *ignorance*, seeks to cover it over, and set it off with *forwardness*.

Therefore the wisdom of the *Lord Christ*, upon whose shoulders the *Government* of his *Church* is laid, hath set bounds to mans activity and unquietness, by another way of *Church power*; which is setled in, and derived by fewer indeed, but yet, wiser and abler persons, than the community of Christians can be presumed to be; who in all affairs of *Church* or *State*, have ever given such experiments of their *follies*, *madnesses*, and *confusions*; where-ever they arrogate power, or have much to do, beyond *ciphers* in a sum; that all wise men conclude, That people are then *happiest*, when they have least to do in any thing that is called *Government*. Nor is it to be believed, that *Jesus Christ* hath ordered any thing in his Churches polity, that is contrary to the *principles* of true *wisdom*; which in man is but a *beam* of that *Sun*, which is in *God*.

Isai. 9. 7.

28. *People not fit to judge of doctrine or scandals in Religion.*

But the *Bodying men* say, They must and ought to have a Church, not onely visible in the *profession of Faith*, but *palpable* and *maniable*; so as they may at once *grasp* it, and upon every occasion *convene* it, or the major part of it, into one place; that so they may *complain* of what they think amiss, and remedy by the power of that small *fraternity*, what ever *faults* any of them list to finde in one another, as *Fellow Members* and *Brethren*; yea, and in those too, whom they have made to be their *Pastors*, *Rulers*, and *Fathers*.

Answ. That the best Men and best Ministers may erre, and offend in *religious respects*, by *error* and *scandal*, we make no doubt: Nor is it denied, but they may and ought both by *private charity*, be admonished, and by *publick authority*, be reproved and censured. Where

this

this *Authority* is (as it ought to be) in the hands of those, whom the *Lord Christ* hath appointed, as wise, able, and authorised by the *Church*, to judge of *Doctrine*, *Maners*, and *Differences*, incident among Christians, as such. But I appeal to all *sober* and *judicious Christians*, whether they can finde or fancy almost, that *venerable Consistory*, that *judicious Senate*, that *grave* and *dreadful Tribunal* (which the antients speak of among Christians of those first and best times) which is necessary for the *honor*, and *good order* of *Religion*, and *peace* of *Christians*; Whether, I say, there be any *face* or *form* of it, among those *dwarf Bodies*, those *petty Church lets*, those *narrow Conventicles*, whose *Head* and *Members*, *Pastors* and *Flock*, are for the most part not above the *Plebeian* size; of a *meer mechanick mould*; either ignorant, or heady, or wilful, or fierce, under words and semblances of *zeal*, *gravity*, and an *affected severity*.

I make no quære, Whether these sorts of men be fit persons, to whom all *appeals* in matters of Religion must be made; and by whom they must be *finally determined*; to whose *judgements*, *prudence*, and *conscience*, all matters of *doctrine* and *scandal* must be referred: By whom *Religious concernments* must be ordered and reformed; by whom *Ministers* must be examined, tryed, and ordained, first; afterward, judged and deposed. Whether it be fit, that those, who are guilty of so little learning, or experience in divine matters, should solely agitate these great things of *God*, which so much concern his *truth*, his *glory*, and *Christians good*, every way: which matters both as to *Doctrine* and *Discipline*, are able to exercise and fully imploy the most learned, able, and holy men.

In eo quisque judex recti constituitur, in quo peritus judicatur. Reg. Juris.

Who dreads not to think, that all *saving truths* stand at such mens mercy; the honor of Christ, and the good of mens souls too; while all degrees of *excommunication*, and *censures*, are *irrepealably transacted* by them; Among whom its hard to finde two wise men; and scarce any ten of them (if they be twenty) of one minde, while they boast they are of *one Body*?

Again, who will not sadly laugh to see, that, when they differ (as they oft do) and break in pieces; yet like *quantitative substances*, they are always divisible; like water and other *homogeneous bodies*, they still drop and divide into as many new Churches and Bodies, as they are *dissenting* or *separating parties*? The miracle is, that when like *Hypolitus* his Limbs, they are *rent* and *scattered* by *Schisms* into *Factions*, yet still every *leg*, or *arm*, or *hand*, *forms* presently into a new *distinct*, *compleat Body*, and *subdivided Church*: Each of which conceives such an integrality of parts, and plenitude of power, that it *puts forth head*, and *eyes*, and *hands*; all *Church Officers*, *Pastors*, *Elders*, *Deacons*, by an innate principle of *Church power*, which they fancy to be in any two or three *godly people*. At

this

this rate, and on this *ridiculous presumption*, they run on as water on a dry ground, till it hath wasted it self; till they are in small chips and slivers, making up *Bodies* at six and sevens; and Churches of two or three Believers: These ere long losing one another in the *midst* of some *new opinion*, some *sharp subtilty*; or some *angry curiosity* (which they cannot reach,) then, and not before, this *meteor* or *blasing Star* of a *popular*, *Independent*, absolute, *self-sufficient Church power* in the people, which threatned *Heaven* and *Earth*, and strived to out-shine the *Sun*, and *Moon*, and *Stars*, of all antient combined *Churches*, *Order*, and *Government*, for want of matter, quite vanisheth and disappears, by its *Members* separating from, and excommunicating, or unchurching of each other; Then the solitary *relicts* turn *Seekers*, whose unhappy fortune is never to finde the folly of their *new errors*, nor the antient true Church way; which they proudly, or passionately, or ignorantly lost; when they so easily forsook communion with the Catholike Church, and with that part of it, to which they were peaceably, orderly, and comlily united; as was here in *England*: Whose way of serving the *true God*, was privately with *knowledge*, *faith*, *love*, and *sincerity*; publickly, with *peace*, *order*, *humility*, and *charity*: Which might still with *honor and happiness* to this *Nation*, be continued, if the *proud hearts*, and *wanton heads*, and *rude hands* of some *novel pretenders*, had not sought to make the very name of *Christian Religion*, the *Reformed Church*, and *Ministry of England*, a meer sport, and may-game, to the *Popish*, profane and looser world; by first stripping us of all those *Primitive Ornaments* of *gravity*, *order*, *decency*, *charity*, *good government*, *unanimity*; and then dressing us up, and impluming us with the *feathers of popular*, and *passionate fancies*, which delight more in things gay and new, than good and old.

29. *Of Church Discipline, in whom the Power.*

But, how shall we do (say these *Bodying-men*,) to fulfil that command *Dic Ecclesiæ*, for such a *Church* as may receive complaints, hear causes of scandal, speedily reform abuses, restore defects, execute all power of the *Keys* in the *right way* of *Discipline*? without which, there is no true, at least, no compleat and perfect Church; for these men think, Christians can hardly get to *Heaven*, unless they have power among them, to cast one another into *Hell*; to give men *over to Satan*, to excommunicate, as they see cause; to open and shut *Heaven* and *Hell gates*, as they think fit: Must all things that concern our Church (say they) lie at six and sevens, till we get such *Bishops* and *Presbyters*, such *Synods* and *Councils*, such Representatives of Learned men, as are hardly obtained; and as hard to be rightly ordered, or well used, when they are met together? They had rather make quicker dispatches in Church work; as if they thought it better for every family to *hang* and *draw* within it self;

Matth. 18. 17. Tell it to the Church.

and presently punish every offence, than for a whole Country to attend, either *general Assizes*, or *quarter Sessions*.

Answ. Truly, good Christians in this Church (at present) are in a *sad and bad* case too, as well as their *Ministers*, if they could make no work of Religion, till they were happy to see all things of extern *order* and *government* duly setled: Yet sure we may go to Church, and to Heaven too in our *worst clothes*, if we can get no better; nor may we therefore wholly stay at home, and neglect *religious duties*, because we cannot be so fine as we would be. Both Ministers and people must do the best they can in their *private spheares*, and *particular Congregations*, to which they are related, whereby to preserve themselves, and one another, as Brethren in Christ, from such *deformities* and *abuses*, as are destructive to the *power of godliness*, the *peace of conscience*, and the *honor of the Reformed Religion*; until the *Lord* be pleased to restore to this Church, that *holy Order*, *antient Government*, and *Discipline*, which is necessary, not to the *being* of a Christian, or a true Church, as its *form* or *matter* (which true Believers constitute by their *internal union* to Christ by Faith, and to all Christians by Charity;) but onely, as to the *external form* and *polity*, for the peace, order, and well-being of a Church; as it is a *visible society*, or *holy nation*, and *fraternity* of
1 Pet. 2. 9. men, professing the truth of Jesus Christ. Yea, and Christians may better want (that is, with less detriment or deformity to Religion,) that *Discipline* (which some men so exceedingly magnifie, as the very *Throne, Scepter*, and *Kingdom of Christ*) under *Christian Magistracy*, (as they may the *office* of *Deacons*, where the *law* by *Overseers* takes care for the poor) where good laws by *civil power* punish *publick offences*, and repress all *disorders in Religion*, as well as *trespasses* in *secular affairs*; Better, I say, than they could have been without it in primitive times; when Christians had no other means, to repress any disorders, that might arise in their societies; either scandalous to their *profession*, or contrary to their *principles*; of which, no *Heathen Magistrate*, or *Humane Laws*, took then any *cognisance*, or applied any *remedy* to them.

Not, but that I do highly approve, and earnestly pray for such *good Order*, *comely Government*, and *exact Discipline*, in every *Church*, both as to the *lesser Congregations*, and the *greater Associations*, (to which, all *reasons* of *safety*, and *grounds* of *peace*, invite Christian Societies in their Church relations, as well as in those of Civil,) which were antiently used in all setled, and flourishing Churches; Much after that patern, which was used among the *Jews*, both in their *Synagogues*, which they had frequent, both in their own Land, and among strangers in their dispersions; and also in their great *Sanhedrim*; which was as a constant *supreme Council*, for ordering

ordering affairs, chiefly of Religion; to one or both, which (no doubt) our *Saviour* then referred the *believing Jew*, in that of, *Tell it to the Church*; that is, after private monition, tell it to the lesser *Convention* or *Consistory* in the *Synagogues*; which might decide matters of a lesser nature; or to the *higher Sanedrim*, in things of more publick concernment; both which were properly enough called קהל, *Cœtus congregatio*, ἐκκλησία, a Church, עדה, συναγωγή. Beyond this sense, none could be made of Christs words, by his then *Auditors*, to whom he speaks, not by way of *new direction*, and *institution* of a *Soverein Court*, or *Consistory*, in every Congregation of Christians to come; but by way of referring to a *well known* use, and *daily practise*, then among the *Jews*; which was the onely and best means wherein a *Brother* might have such satisfaction, in point of any offence, which *charity* would best bear, without flying to the Civil Magistrate, which was now a forein power. When *Jews* turned Christians, its very certain, they altered not their Discipline, and order (as Christians) in Church society, from what they used before in their *Synagogues*. Proportionably, no doubt, in Christian Churches, of narrower, or larger extensions, and communion, among the *Gentiles*, the wisdom of Christ directs, and allows such *judicatories* and *jurisdictions*, to prevent or remove all scandals and offences among Christians, to preserve peace and order, as may have least of *private* or *pedantick imperiousness*, and *vulgar trifflings* of men, unable and unfit to be in, or to exercise any such *holy* and *divine authority* over others; (who are easily trampled upon, and fall into *reproach*, and the *snare of the Devil*, by reason of divers *lusts*, *passions*, *weaknesses*, and *temptations*;) but rather Christ commends such *grave Consistories*, *solemn Synods*, and *venerable Councils*, as consisting of *wise*, and *able*, and *worthy men*, may have most, as of the *Apostolical wisdom*, *eminency*, *gravity*; so of *Christs Spirit*, *Power*, and *Authority* among them: Such, as no Christian with any *modesty*, *reason*, *conscience*, or *ingenuity* can despise, or refuse to submit to the integrity of their censure; when it is carried on, not with those *heats*, *peevishnesses*, and *emulations*, which are usually among men of *less improved parts*, or *ripened years*; especially, if Neighbors. Such a way, *wisely setled* in the Church, might indeed binde up all things that concern *Religion*, in private or more publick respects, to all good behavior, in the *bonds* of *truth*, *peace*, and *good order*, by a due and decent Authority; which, for every two, or three, or seven Christians in their *small Bodyings*, and *Independent Churches* (exlusively of all others) to usurp and essay to do, is, as if, of every chip of Noah's Ark, or of every rafter of a great Ship,

Philo. Jud. calls them ὁμίλους, κοίνους συλλόγους, κοινὰς συνόδους.

Nihil hic à Christo novum præcipitur, sed mos rectè introductus probatur. H. Grot. in loc.

Ecclesiæ, *i. e.* τοῖς τῆς ἐκκλησίας πρεσβύτεροις. Theoph.

Πολιτεία δὲ καὶ κοινωνία αὐτάρχους πρὸς εὐδαιμονίαν. *Plato* Every polity hath in it power enough to preserve it happiness.

Coimus in cœtum & congregationem, Ibidem orationes, exhortationes, castigationes, & censura divina: Præsident probati quique seniores. Tert. Apol.

Solebant Judæi res majoris momenti ultimo loco ad ὁμοζῆλον multitudinem referre: i. e. ad eos qui eadem instituta sectabantur; quorum judicia & conventus seniores moderabantur, tanquam præsides. Grot. in Chrys.

ἱερὸν συμβούλιον, Ign. Bas.

they would endeavor to make up a very fit vessel to sail in any Sea and any weather.

30. *The best method of Church Discipline.* But take the true and wholesome *Discipline of the Church*, in those true proportions, which *pious antiquity* setled and used; and which, with an easie hand, by a little condescending, and *moderation*, on all sides, might have been long ago, and still may be happily setled in *England*: Nothing is more desireable, commendable, and beneficial to the Church of Christ; As a *strong case* to preserve a *Lute* or *Instrument* in; that so the Church may not be broken, disordered, or put out of *tune* by every rash and rude hand, either in its truth, or purity, or harmony; either in Doctrine, or Maners, or Order. But this is a *blessing*, as not to be deserved by us, so hardly to be hoped, or expected, amidst the pride, and passions, and fractions of our times: Nor will it be done, till *Civil powers* make as much conscience to be good, as great; and to advance Christian Religion, no less, than to enlarge, or establish Temporal Dominion.

When such Magistrates have a minde, first to know, and then to set up a right Church polity, power, and holy order, in every part and proportion of it: They need not advise with such as creep into *corners*; or seek *new models* out of little and obscure *conventicles*; nor yet ought they to confine themselves to those feeble proportions, which are seen in the *little Bodyings* of these times; which begin like *Mushrooms*, to grow up every where, and to boast of their *beauties*, and *rare figures*; when nothing is more indigested, and ill compacted, as to the *general order*, and *publick peace*, of this or any other *noble* and *ample branch* of the *Catholick Church*. Pious and learned Men, who *reverence antiquity*, and know not yet how to *mock* either their *Mother* the *Church*, or their *Fathers*, the true *Bishops*, *Elders*, and *Ministers* of it, can soon *demonstrate*, how to draw forth that *little chain of gold*, (that *charity*, *communion*, and *orderly subordination* among Christians) which at first (possibly) might onely adorn one *single congregation* of a few Christians, in the *primitive paucity* and *newer plantations*; to such a *largeness*, *amplitude*, and *extension*, as by the wisdom of Christian charity, and humility, shall extend to, and comprehend in its compass, by way of *peaceable union*, and *harmony*, or *comly subjection*, even the *largest combinations*, and *furthest spreadings* of any *branch* of the *Catholike Church*: Both as to its greater and lesser *conventions*; in several places and times; as the matters of *Religion*, and occasion of the *Churches* shall require; according to its several dispersions, and distinctions by place, or civil polity.

Math. 18. 19. Which greater, yet orderly *conventions*, must needs be as properly a *Church*; and may meet, as much in *Christs Name*; and hope for his *presence* and *assistance* in the midst of them, as any of those

those *Churches* could among the *Jews*; to which Christ properly refers in that place: Yea, they must needs be far beyond any thing imaginable in the narrow confinements of *Independent Bodies*.

Such *Churches* then, of most select, wise, and able Christians, (who have the consent and Representation of many lesser Congregations,) must needs do all things with more wisdom, advice, impartiality, authority, reputation, majesty, and general satisfaction; than any of those *stinted Bodies* of *Congregational Churches*, can possibly do; yea, in all *right reason* they are as much beyond and above them, as the power of a *full Parliament*, is beyond any *Country Committee*. Those may with comly order, and due authority (which ariseth from the *consent* of many men, much esteeming the known worth of others) give audience, receive complaints, consider of, examine, reprove, reform, excommunicate, and restore, where there is cause, and as the matters of the Church, more private or publick, require in the several divisions; extending its wings as an Eagle, more or less, as there is cause; with infinite more benefit to the community of Christians, than those *Pullets*, the short winged, and little bodied Birds of the *Independent feather*, can do: Where without any warrant (that I know) from God or Man, Religion or right Reason, Law or Gospel, Prudence or Charity, a few Christians, by *clucking* themselves into a *conventicle*, shall presently seem a compleat *body* to themselves, and presume to *separate* and *exempt* themselves from all the world of Christians, as to any *duty*, *subjection*, *order*, or *obedience*; and pitching their Tents, where they think best, within the *verge* of any other, never so well, and wisely setled Church, presently they shall *raise* themselves up some small *brest work* of absolute *Authority*, which they fancy both parts from, and defends them against all Churches in the World; planting their *Wooden* or *Leathern Guns* of *imaginary Independent power*; and casting forth their *Granadoes*, or *Squibs* rather, of *passionate censures*, *angry abdications*, and *severe divorces* against all Christians, but those of their own way and party: Afterward they turn them, it may be, against their own *body* and *bowels*, when once they begin to be at leisure to *wrangle* and *divide*; As if (alas) these were the *dreadful thunder-bolts* of *excommunication*, antiently used with *great solemnity*, *caution*, *deliberation*, and *publick consent*: The great *forerunner* of Gods terrible, last judgment, exercised with *unfeigned pity*, *fervent prayers*, and many *tears*, by those, who had due *eminency* and *authority*, as *presidents* in *chief*, or *seconds* and *assistants*, to judge and act in so weighty cases and matters. In which *transactions* and *censures*, Churches Synodical, Provincial, and National, were interessed, and accordingly being duly convened, they solemnly acted in Christs Name, as the offence, error, or matter, required remedy; either for errors

ἐπιτιμία ὑπὸ πλειόνων. 2 Cor. 2. 6. Punishment inflicted by many.

ἐνώπιον πάντων ἔλεγχε. Rebuke before all. 1 Tim. 5. 20.

Synodus Antiochena Paulum Samosetanum ab ecclesia, quæ sub cœlo est universo seperabat. Eus. hist. eccl. l. 7. c. 28.

Autoritas est eminentia quædam vitæ cujus gratia dictis factisve cujuspiam multum deferimus. Tul.

Ibidem (i. e. præsidentibus probatis Senioribus) exhortationes, castigationes & censura divina. Nunc & judicatur magno cum pondere, ut apud certos de Dei conspectu; Sumumque futuri judicii præjudicium est, si quis ita deli-

errors, or publike disorders and scandals; which it concerned all Christians and Churches to see repressed, or amended.

querit, ut communicatione orationis, & conventus, & omnis sancti commercii relegetur. Tertul. Apol.c.39. *Qui ab ecclesiæ corpore respuuntur, quæ Christi corpus est, tanquam peregrini & alieni à Deo, Dominatui diaboli traduntur.* Hil. in Ps. 118. *Inobediens spirituali mucrone truncatur, & ejectus de ecclesia rabido Dæmonum ore discrepitur* Jeron. Ep.1.

Of Excommunication and censures.

The *wise and excellent* Discipline of the Church, and the power of using and applying of it, which so many now either vainly arrogate, or ambitiously Court, was not of old as a *bodkin* put into every mechanicks hands; or as a *sword* committed to every *brawny* arm; nor yet, was it such a (*brutum fulmen*) a thunder-bolt which the confident hand of every *factionist* might take to himself and Grasp, or use to his private revenge, or to the advantage of his party and design: But *Discipline*, together with Government, in the Church, was only committed and *concredited*, after the example of the Apostolicall times, by the wisdom, humility, consent, and subjection of *all good* Christians in their severall stations, either as Princes or Subjects, to those *learned*, grave, and *godly* men, Bishops and Presbyters, who were ablest *for gifts*, *eminentest* for their labours, and *highest* in place and Ministeriall authority in the Churches of Christ; whose assemblies or convenings, were greater or smaller, and their influence accordingly obliging valid and effectuall, for the good of those Churches over which they were; ascending from the first and least Country Congregations (as the smallest yet considerable branches of a visible Church,) till it arose, like *Ezekiels* waters, from the Anckles, to the Knees, and Loyns, and Head, to such large, plenary, and powerfull an *Authority*, as represented many famous Churches; and sometimes the greatest and conversable parts of the Catholick Church throughout the whole world; as in generall Councils called *Oecumeniall.*

Præsident probati quique seniores, honorem istum non pretio sed testimonio adepti. Tertul. Apol.c.39. Theodo. Hist. Eccl.l.1.c.10. *Quod sacris Episcoporum conciliis constitutum fuerit id ad divinam voluntatem est referendum.* Const.M. dictum. Euseb. vit.Const. *Episcopi in Synodo Sardicensi. Dei amantissimi Reges adjuvante divina gratia nos congregaverunt. In illa concilia totus desiderio feror, in istis devotione immoror, amore condelector, inhæreo consensu, emulatione persisto: in quibus non hominum traditiones obstinatius defensantur, aut superstitiosius observantur, sed diligenter humiliter qui inquiritur, quæ sit voluntas Dei bona & bene placens.* Bern. Ep.19.

Of Synods and Councils.

Out of which Synods and Councils however *disorders* and *inconveniences* (as *Nazianzene* and others complain) cannot be wholy kept out (they still consisting of sinfull, and so frail men,) yet they were subject to far less evils, and Errataes, than attend the small scattered and separate bodies of these later *decimo sexto* editions: In *multitude* of *Counsellors* there is wisdom, safety and honour. *Prov.* 11.14. Nor may we cast away those goodly large Robes, which the prudence and piety of the antients made, because they are subject to be soyled, or rent, by the hands of folly. It is better for the Church to enjoy the *gleanings* of the antients Integrity, Wisdom, and

Cyp. Nazi. orat.19. Ruffin Hist l. 1.c.19. & 18. *In causa Athenasii. Factionis macula fœciavit concilium: non judicandi sed op-*

and Charity, in ordering of the Church, than to have the whole *harvest* of later mens sowings: which have large *straw* of promises and shews, but little *grain* of solid benefit; yea much cockle too, and many thistles of most *choaking* and offensive consequences. The very *rags* of true antiquity, doe better cover the nakedness, and more adorne thee body of any Church; than any of those *cobweb-garments* of later making; which are torn in pieces, while they are putting on, and fitting to these new bodies of odd shapen Churches. All reason and experience teacheth, that those *grand communicative* wayes of Christian Churches in the joynt Counsels of grave, learned, and Godly men, drawing all into union, harmony, and peace, for the publike and generall good, were far more probable (though (perhaps) not absolutely necessary means) to preserve both the doctrine of Faith and good manners unblameable among Christians, than any of those *small and broken* Potsheards of private *Independency* can be; which carry little ability, and as little authority or vertue with them: appearing like the *Serpents teeth*, sown by *Cadmus*, every where rising up *in armed parties*, divided against, and destroying one another; till they have cleared the Field, as of all such new, and angry productions; so of all those *antient* and excellent constitutions of Christian Churches; which were bound up as Bibles in greater, or lesser volumes.

primendi causa agebatur, sub Constantio. Concil. Nicæ. secundum ab Arrianis coactũ terræ motu impeditum. Theod. l. 2. c. 19.

It being so naturall to all men, to affect, what they call *liberty* and power; if once mean men can by *any arts* obtein any shadow of them, they are (out of the shew of much zeal and conscience) most *pragmaticall*; And first begin to think no Church well reformed; unless they bring them to their models; Then their modell must be new; lest their Authors should seem to have been idle; being alwaies more concerned for the *reformation of any men*, than of themselves; God grant that while temerity and confidence pretends to plant none but new and rare *flowers*, and to root up all old ones as ill weeds, in the Church, that themselves and their odd inventions, with their rash abolitions, prove not at last the most *noxious plants* that ever pestered the Garden of this Church.

31. *Of prudence in ordering the Church affairs.* Mat. 15. 13.

To what some men urge (by abusing that text against the good Orders, Canons, and Constitutions or Customs of the Church,) That *every plant, which the Father hath not planted, shall be pulled up*; therefore say they, nothing of *humane prudence* is tolerable in the ordering of any Church; I answer; first, none of those that quarrelled at the Church of *Englands Motes*, but are thought by many learned and Godly men to have *beams* in their own eyes; if Scripture, right reason, and antiquity may judge: for nothing is alleged as more different from any of these amongst us; than what may be found among the new Modellers; who as they were in

number

number and quality much inferior, so they were never thought more wise, or learned; nor so calm and composed; nor so publike and unpassionate in their Counsels and determinations; as those many excellent men and Churches were, both antient and modern; to whose examples, agreeable to the Canon of the Scriptures, the Church of *England* was *conformed*.

In his rebus in quibus nihil certi statuit Scriptura, mos populi Dei, vel instituta majorum pro lege tenenda sunt. Aug. Ep. 89.

Furthermore, The great Motor of some mens passion, zeal, and activity against this Reformed Church, was, that one Error, against the judgement, liberty, and practice of all antiquity, which is *fundamentall*, as to the Churches polity and extern Peace; namely, That *nothing may be used* in the Church as to externals, which is not expresly and precisely commanded in the word; Which yet themselves observe not, when they come to have power either to form and act; some things they take in upon prudentiall account, as their *Church-Covenant*, of the form and words of which they are not yet agreed, which they urge; so their requiring each Member to give an account, not of the *historicall* belief of the truth, but, of the work of *grace*, and conversion, which no Scripture requires, or Church ever practis'd: That of St. *Austin* hath been often inculcated by many *learned*, quiet, and *godly men* in this Church of *England*, and elsewhere, as a most certain truth; That however the Faith, Doctrine, Sacraments, and Ministry of the Church, are precisely of *divine Institution*; rising from a divine Spring, and conveyed in a like sacred *Current*, which ows nothing to the wisdom, policy, power, or authority of man; yet the extern *dispensation* of this Faith, *Sacraments, and divine Ministrations*, together with the fence and hedge of them, the necessary Government, Order, and Discipline of the Church, in its parts and in the whole, these doe fall much under the managing of *right reason*, rules of good order, and common prudence, all which attends *true Religion*; So that they neither have, nor needed, nor indeed were easily capable of such positive, precise and particular precepts or commands, as these men *fancy*; and by this pertinacious fancy they have cast *great snares* on the consciences of many; *great scandals* on the Churches, both antient and modern; and great *restraints* on that *liberty*, which *Jesus Christ* left to his Churches in these things; according as various occasions and times might require.

Disciplina nulla est melior gravi prudentiq; viro in his quæ liberas habent observationes, quam ut eo modo agat quo agere viderit Ecclesiam ad quamcunque forte devenerit. Quod enim neque contra fidem neque bonos mores injungitur indifferenter est habendum, & pro eorum, inter quos vivitur societate observandum est. Aust. Ep. 118. ad Jan. *Salvâ fidei regula de Disciplina contendentibus suprema lex est Ecclesiæ pax.* Blondel sent. Jeron. præf.

None but foolish and fanatick men can think, that when men turned Christians, they ceased to be *men*; or *being Christian men*, they needed not still to be governed, both as Christians, and as men; by reason joyned to Religion; which will very well agree; carrying on Religious ends, by such prudent and proportionate means, and in such good order, as is agreeable to right reason; and the ge-

Sumus & homines & cives, cum simus Christiani. Salv.

nerall

neral directions of *Religion*; which never abandoned, or taught any Christian to *start* at, and *abhor*, what is taught by the *very light of nature*, and those *common principles* of *reason*, and *order*, or *polity*; which teach the way of all *Government* and *subjection*; either of *yonger to the elder* (whence is the very ground of all *Presbytery*) or of *weaker to the stronger*; or of the *foolisher to the wiser*, or of the *ignorant to the learned*; or of many to some few, for the good of all: None of which *methods* can cross *Religion*; nor being observed in some due measure, can be blamed; nor ought factiously to be altered, by the *members* of any *setled Church*; in which there is, neither *Apostacy* from the *Faith*, nor recession from the *Scriptures*, nor alteration of the *substance* of *Christs holy Institution*; which this Church of *England* not being guilty of, but apparently professing, and fully adhering to the *Scriptures*, as the *ground*, *rule*, and *limit* of *Faith*, and *holy Mysteries*; We doubt not, but, however it used the *wisdom* of *learned*, *wise*, and *holy men*; and followed the warrant of the *Primitive Churches*, in the *extern maner* and *methods* of *holy Administrations*, *Government*, and *Discipline*; yet it may, and ought still, as it doth, lay claim to the *right* and *honor* of an *eminent part of the true Catholike Church of Christ*, having a *true Ministry*, and *true Ministrations*: In which, I believe, all the *Apostles*, and *Primitive Martyrs*, and *Confessors* in all *Ages*, would most willingly have owned and approved; yea, the Great *God* from *Heaven* hath attested it, and still doth to the *consciences* of thousands of excellent Christians, which have had their birth and growths to Religion, in this Church of *England*.

Naturæ lumen, & rationis radios, non extinguit sed excitat Religio, quæ non vera tantum sed & decora postulat. Aust.

Phil. 4. 8. ὅσα ἀληθῆ, ὅσα σεμνὰ, προσφιλῆ, εὔφημα, &c. εἴ τις ἀρετὴ ἔπαινος, &c. Whatsoever things are true, honest, or comly, just, pure, lovely, of good report; if any vertue, any praise, think on these things; or meditate with reason and judgement. ταῦτα λογίζεσθε.

So that the *out-cryes*, *abhorrencies*, and *extirpations*, carried on so eagerly against the main constitution, frame, and Ministry of this Church, by many, (who now appear to be men of little *charity*, and *strong passions*, and very *weak reason*,) as if we were *all-over Popish*, *Superstitious*, *Antichristian*, altogether *polluted*, *intollerable*, *&c.* Those *calumnies* and *clamors*, wanted both that *truth*, that *caution*, and that *charity*, which should be used, in any thing, tending to disturb, or discourage any true *Christian*, or *Church* of *Christ*; whose differences in some small external things from us, in *judgment* or *practice*, we ought to bear upon the account of those many great things, in which we agree with them, as Christians: Nor ought *poor men*, of private *parts* and *place* in *Church* and *State*, so to *swell*, at any time, with the thought of any *Liberty* and *Power* in common, given them from *Christ* (to reign with him, or to reform, *&c.*) as to drive, like *tipsy Mariners*, those *rightful Pilots* from the *Helm*; or to break their *card*, and *compass*, of *antient design*, *draught*, and *form*, by which they steered as they ought, or as they could, in the *distress* of times. And this onely, That these *new under-*

takers may try, how they can *delineate new carts*, or *maps* ; and how soon they can *over-whelm* or *over-set*, so fair, rich, and goodly a Vessel, as this *Church* of *England* once was in the *eye of all* the World, but our own. This *Iland* was not more *nobly eminent*, than the *Church* was great in *Britany* : The leaks, chinks, and decayes, which befal all things in time, might easily have been *stopped*, *calked*, and *trimmed*, by skilful and well-advised hands ; when once it was fairly and orderly brought upon the *Publick stocks*, and into a *Parliament Dock* ; which good men hoped, of all places, would not prove either a *quick-sand*, or a *rock* to the *Reformed Church* , or the *Learned Ministry* of *England*.

But the *Lord* is just, though *we should be confounded in our confidences of men* ; though neither *mountains*, nor *hills*, nor *valleys* can help , yet will we trust in God , who is our God in Christ ; who (we doubt not, but) in mercy will own us, with all our frailties and defects, as his true Church, and true Ministers : And if in any thing we have failed, as men ; yet we are assured, the *merciful eye of Heaven* will look more favorably on our failings, to pardon them, than some *Basilicks* do on our *labors*, to accept them ; * who seek to destroy this Church, and discourage all its true Christians and Ministers , if they could , with their dreadful aspects , and spightful looks ; if they had not the *defensative* of *Gods protection* joyned to their own innocency ; and the favor of many excellent Christians ; whom I have endeavored to settle and satisfie, as briefly and clearly, as in so short a time I could, in these many, and to me very tedious, and almost superfluous objections, against this true Reformed Church of *England* ; these *first* and *lesser calumnies*, which lay in the way of my main design, I thought it my duty to remove.

* Jere. 1. 8. Be not afraid of their faces, for I am with thee, to deliver thee, saith the Lord. V. 18. I have made thee a defenced City, a brazen Wall, and an iron Pillar, &c. Ezek. 2. 6. Be not afraid of their words, though thou dost dwell among scorpions ; be not dismayed at their looks, though they be a rebellious house.

32. *Want of Charity our greatest defect.*

Where, I see, in all our *disputes* and *differences*, so cruelly carried on, the greatest ingredient is *Uncharitableness* ; which knows not how to *excuse small faults*, to *supply lesser defects*, to *interpret well* what is good, to *allow* others their true Christian Liberty, and to enjoy its own *modestly* ; to keep communion amidst some *easie differences* , and union with *harmless varieties*. We have had on all sides *truth* enough to have *saved any men* ; and *uncharitableness* enough to have *damned any angels* . Nor is it meerly a privation, or want of charity, but an abounding of envy, malice, strife, wrath, bitterness, faction, fury, cruelty, and whatever is most contrary to the excellency of Christians, which was the excellency of *Christ* ;

In the Council of *Carthage*, *An.* 401. The Orthodox Christians send Messengers to the *Donatists* : περὶ τοῦ κηρῦξαι εἰρήνην καὶ ἑνότητα, ἧς ἄνευ χωρεῖν ἡ τῶν χριστιανῶν σωτηρία καθίστασθαι οὐ δύναται. So after, they send (*An.* 404.) Orators for unity and peace ; without which, say they, Christian Religion cannot consist.

love

love and charity. The want of which, I cannot but here deplore in a *pathetick digression*; craving the *Readers* pardon, since I cannot go further in answer of *uncharitable objections*, till I have first sought for our *lost charity*: The recovery of which *one grace* would end all the *differences*, and heal all the *distempers*, not of *England* onely, but of all the Christian World. You, O excellent Christians, will, I know, joyn with me in searching after *charity*, as they did after Christ, *sorrowing*, *Luke* 2.48. In mourning for, as some of the *devout antients* did, the *sad distances*, and *wasts* of *Christian charity*, among all sorts of Christian Churches, and Professors. Alas, we *glory*, and *swell*, and are *puffed up* one against another, in the *forms* of being called *Churches* and *Reformed*; when we lose the *very power of godliness*, the *soul of religion*, and the *peculiar glory of Christianity*, which is *charity*. Joh. 13.35. *By this shall all men know that you are my disciples*, &c.

Basil. Mag. de Sp. S. deplores, ψυχρὰν ἀγάπην ἐδάκρυσε σπλαγχνὸν χρηστὸν, ἐδάκρυον συμπαθὲς, ἀλλὰ τοσοῦτον μῖσος τοῖς ὁμοφύλοις πρὸς ἀλλήλους ὑπεκκέκαυται, ὥστε μᾶλλον πλήμμασιν ἢ κατορθώμασιν ἐπαγάλλονται. ἀλόγων γεγονάμεν ἀλογώτεροι: ἐκεῖνα μὲν ὁμόφυλα ἀλλήλοις συναγελάζεται, ἡμῖν δὲ χαλεπώτατος πόλεμος πρὸς οἰκείους. So Naz. Or. 12. λύσις στάσεως ἔκγονον, &c. Πῶς συναγάγω τὰ διεστῶτα, πῶς δάκρυσι, πῶς δὲ χερσὶ διερρωγότα τὸ σύντριμμα, σὺν τῷ ἔργῳ αἱ χεῖρες ἅγιαι καὶ συγκινήτη σὺν τῷ κατόρθωμα. Naz. Or. 28. ἡ τῶν χριστιανῶν θρησκεία τρισὶ θεμελίοις ἐδηδραστηριχθεῖσα, πίστει, ἐλπίδι, ἀγάπῃ. *Clem. Alex. strom.* 5. sayes, Religion, as a *Tripos*, hath three feet, Faith, Hope, and Charity; and cannot stand if any one be wanting.

O sweet, divine, and heavenly *beauty of Christ*, and all true Christians (*Charity*:) Whither art thou fled, from Christians brests, lives, hearts, and Churches? In which was wont to be thy Nest, thy Palace, and thy Temple: Where thou wert received, welcomed, and entertained, by wise and humble Christians, either as the *Spouse of Christ*, in thy purity; or as the *Queen of graces*, in thy *beauty*; or as the *Goddess of Heaven*, in thy *majesty*. O whither art thou gone? where art thou retired? Art thou to be found in the *cells of Hermites*, in the *Cloysters of Monks*, in the *solitudes of Anchorites*? (Probably, there may be most of thee, where is least of the world; which like full diet, begets most of *cholerick* and *foul humors*:) Dost thou reside among the *pompous Papists*? The *graver Lutherans*? the *preciser Calvinists*? the *severer Separatists*? or, the *moderater English Christians*? May we finde thee at *Rome*, or *Wittemberg*, or *Geneva*, or *Amsterdam*, or *London*? Dost thou dwell in the old Palaces, and Councils of venerable *Bishops*? or in the newer Classes of bolder *Presbyters*? or in the narrower corners of subtile *Independents*? Alas, I fear these very colours and names, which are as *ensigns* and *alarms to factions*, sound ill in the *ears* of *Charity*, and are unpleasing to its *sight*; which onely loves the first common title and honor of *Disciples*, to be called *Christians*. These *faces* and *forms*, seem as if they were divided, and set one against another; and when they want a common *adversary*, each *party* is ready to

33. *Pathetick for Charity.* ἀγάπη θεῖον ἀγαθὸν μέγα. Greg. Niss. ἐπικεχάριστος τῷ ἀφθαρσίας λογικοῦ. Clem. Al. παιδ. l. 3. c. 1. *Salvian* complains. *Quis plenam vicino exhibet charitatem? Omnes à se etsi loco non absunt, affectu absunt, etsi habitatione junguntur, mente disjuncti sunt.* Lib. 5. de Gubern. *Non Albiniani, non Nigiani sumus, sed Christiani. Hoc unum studemus nullarum partium studiis abripi.* Tertul. Acts 1.26.

to *subdivide*, and seeks to destroy it self; the hand of every *faction* in *Religion*, is as *Ismaels* against his Brother, or it self. Smiting oft with the *fist of violence*, as *Factious*; where they should give the *right hand of fellowship*, as *Christians*; and *strangling* each other, instead of *embracing*.

Or are all these *divisions*, but the *disguises* of *Charity*? and under *visords* of *factions*, a meer *pageantry* is acted of *zealous ignorance*, or *proud* and *preposterous knowledge*; both carried on with *holy partialities*, *fraternal Schisms*, *zealous cruelties*, *sacred conspiracies*; so far onely, as to destroy all other *Christians*; That each sect alone may remain, as the onely Church; which then fancy themselves sufficiently built, polished, and reformed, when they are but as heaps of *rubbish*, in their several ruptures; as unpolished *lumps* in their uncharitable sidings; so far weak and deformed *limbs*, as they are *passionatly* and *violently broken* from the *intireness* and *goodly fabrick* of the well compacted *Catholike Church*, of which they were sometime a *comly* and *commendable part*: Onely then in *beauty*, *safety*, and *symmetry*, while in *order* to, and in *unity* with the whole; which is as the *Body* and *Temple* of the *Lord*, in its various parts, making but one *goodly structure*, which was antiently the *joy*, and *glory* of the whole *Earth*. Now, nothing seems best, but deformed ruines, and desolate parcels, of battered, broken, and almost demolished *Churches*, like *Hospitals*, in which, are most-what wounded, and maimed, and halting Christians; when of old, the Foundation of one, and all Churches, was *Scripture Truth*, the *Cement Charity*, the *Beauty Unity*, and the *Strength*, *orderly* and *social Government*.

Rom. 13. 10. Love is the fulfilling of the Law.

Quicquid deficiunt aliæ, unica supplet charitatis gratia, qua in æternum non deficiet. Bern.

μία τῶν πιστευόντων συγγένεια· εἷς ὁ πατὴρ Θεός, εἷς σωτὴρ Χριστός, μία μητὴρ ἐκκλησία. Nis.

Prius chari quam proximi. Min. Fæl.

πάντες ἐν Χριστῷ πιστεύοντες εἰς μίαν ἀρχὴν, καὶ μία συναγωγὴ, καὶ μία ἐκκλησία. Just. M. Trypho.

O *thou fairest of ten thousands* (Christian Charity) which wert the *wonder of the World* in the Primitive times! Which didst so spread thy wings *over all the Earth*, like *the Spirit of God, on the face of the great deep*, the ocean of mankinde, that every man might, and every Christian did enjoy, the *vital heat*, and *diviner influence* of thy *fosterings* on their souls; So far, that what weaker Christians came short of in believing, or failed in understanding, or were defective in doing, they made up in loving of Christ, and for his sake one another: Yea, what the very enemies and persecutors of Christians wanted, of that *humanity*, (which is as the morn, and dawning of Christian Charity,) true Christians sought to relieve them by their *prayers*, and to cover their *horrid cruelties* with their own kindness to them, while killed by them; and *devotions* for them, while they were dying under them, as the blessed *Martyr Stephen* did, and the Crown of *Martyrs*, *Christ Jesus*. They forgat not to pray for those that *persecuted* them; which made Christians in their *furthest dispersions*, *greatest distances*, and *grievousest sufferings*, still *admired* by by all men, though *hated* by them; still *endeared, well acquainted,* and *united in love* to each other, before they had seen, or were personally known to each other.

O *thou potent flame of celestial fire*, which the love of Christ, stronger than death, had kindled in the souls of the first and best Christians! No Seas, no solitudes, no poverty, no pains, no sufferings, no torments, no offences, no injuries, were able to damp, or quench thee of old; but still thou didst gloe to so fresh an heat, that it warmed and melted the *hardest Rocks* of *Heathen persecutors* and *tormentors*: Who before they believed the Gospel, or love of God in Christ, coveted to be of that Christian society, where they saw men love one another so dearly, so purely, so constantly, as to be ready to die with, and for each other. Alas, now every small drop of fancy, every novelty of fashion in Religion, every atome of Invention, every dust of Opinion, every mote of Ceremony, every shadow of Reformation, every difference of Practice, damps, rakes up, buries, puts out thy *sacred sparks* and *embers*, in Christians hearts; yea, and kindles those *unholy, cruel,* and *dreadful fires* of *contrariety, jealousies, scorn, hatred, enmity, revenge, impatience* of *union*, and *zeal* for *separation*; to so great heights of *all-devouring flames*, that nothing but the *flesh of Christians* will serve for *fuel* to maintain them; and nothing but the *blood of Believers* to extinguish them: So that no Christians now love further than they conspire and contend to destroy and conquer all, but their own *party* and *faction*.

Charitas est oleum unde clara virtutũ omnium lampas sustentatur. Religio sine charitate est lampas sine oleo. Bern. ep. 42.

ὧν κοινὸν τὸ πνεῦμα, κοινὸν καὶ τὸ πάθος, εἷς ἴσον τὸ πιστεύειν, ἴσον καὶ τὸ πάσχειν. Naz. Or. 28. So *Just. Martyr*, Ep. ad Diog.

οἱ χριστιανοὶ χρηστότατοι. τοῖς ἀκοαῖς ἡμῶν ἐπιστάμεθα ταῖς κατ' ἀλλήλων ὕβρεσι, κωμῳδία τοῖς ἐχθροῖς ἡμῶν παιδιά, τὴν τοῦ θεοῦ φιλαδελφίαν τῇ ὑμῶν ἀναδελφίᾳ ἀποκλείσαμεν. Naz. Or. 14.

Thus the want of this holy *grace* of *charity*, wastes us by the *fires* of *unchristian fewds*; and even presages the approaching of those last *dreadful conflagrations*, which shall consume the world; and those *eternal flames*, which shall revenge this *sin of sins* among Christians, the *want of charity*; which sins against the love of God, the blood of Christ, the Churches peace, and our own souls: How shall we *uncharitable wretches*, not dread the coming of our Judge? or how can we love his *appearance* in *flaming fire*, who have thus singed and burnt that *livery* of Christs love, wherewith we were clothed? which was dipped and died in his own blood; that so it might stanch the further effusions of blood among Christians; and cover the stayns of that bloud, which had been passionatly shed among them? How can we hope our souls should be saved in the day of the Lord Jesus, when we spend our dayes in damming and destroying each other? and scarce suffer any to possess their *souls in patience*, or in any degree of charity, amidst the wasts and troubles of this conflicting and tottering Church; Which, like a *great* tree, whose *roots* are loosned round, and almost cut through, stagger too and fro; threatning to fall on every side; being nothing now,

now, but *weakness* over-laden with *weight*; and labouring with the burthen of it self, is ready to destroy both it self and others by the suddenness and violence of its fall: O you excellent Christians, hasten, as *Lot* should have done out of *Sodom*, to withdraw your selves from the interests, designs, zeal, devotion and Religion of this uncharitable and self destroying world; wrap your selves in the mantle of charity, peaceableness and patience, hasten to hide your selves in the *holes* of this rock, the love of Christ your Redeemer, till he come, who is at the *dore* and will not tarry.

Charitas sanctitatis custos. Chrysol. ser. 94.

O pretious and inestimable grace of Charity, the only *Jewel* of our lives; the *viaticum* for our Deaths; the greatest ornament of a Christian profession; the sweetness of our bitterness, the Antidote of our poysons, the Cordiall in our infirmities, the comforter under our dejections, the supplyer of our defects, the joy in our sorrows, the witness of our sincerity, the Crown of our graces, the Seal of our hopes, the stay and Pillar of our Souls, amidst the tears, tossings, fears and conflicts of our mortall *Pilgrimage*; In which we then only joy, when we either love, or are loved by others; but then we have most cause of pious joy, when being hated, and cursed, and persecuted by others, we can yet *love* them, and *pray* for them, and bless *them* for *Christs* sake. Thou that madest *Martyrs*, and *Confessors*, and all true Christians, *more than Conquerors*, of death, and enemies, men, and Devils; O how have we *lost thee*? how have we banished thee? how have we not *injured* thee? yea, how have we *grieved* thee more in this, that we are loth to find thee; But most in this, that we *seek* thee among *Heresies, Schisms, Apostacies, seditions, furies, perjuries, tyrannies, superstitions, sacrileges*, causeless disputes, endless janglings; yea cruell *murthers* of *bodies*, and *Anathemaes* of souls? But the highest indignity, and greater than the greatest insolency offer'd thee, is, That we boast, and proclaim we have *found* thee, in what we have most *lost* thee; that we have raised thee, by what we have ruined thee; that we are most *Churches*, when we are least *Christians*; or most Christians, when we have least of a Church; in our *preposterous* zeals, our hypocriticall *charities*, our *deformed* reformings, our *distorted* bodyings, our *distracted* communions, our *divided* unions, our *fanatick* dreams, our *blasphemous* raptures, our *prophane enthusiasms*, our licencious *liberties*, our *injurious* indulgences, our irrationall, and irreligious confusions; our cruell *toleratings* of any thing, rather than sober abiding, growing, and flourishing in *truth*, which is thy root; in *humility*, which is thy flower; and in *well doing*, which is thy fruit.

1 Joh. 3. 14.

Dilectio summum fidei sacramentum, Christiani nomini thesaurus. Tertul. lib. de Patientia.

Mat. 5. 44.

Humanum est amicos, Christianum inimicos diligere. Hilar.

Αἰδεσθῶμεν τὸ ὄνομα τοῦ χριστοῦ εἰρηνικοῦ. Naz. de Christian. diffid. or. 14.

Thou wert wont to come to us Christians, and by us to others, in the *cool of the day*, in a *still voice*, in meek *intreatings*, in gentle

Praecipuum dilectionis munus aretiosius quam

tle *beseechings*, like the *sweet dew* on herbs, or soft rain on the tender Grass; so that, however Christians might be exceeded by other men, in strength, beauty, learning, eloquence, and policy, yet none equalled them in *Charity*; which hath the greatest *courage* joyned with the *greatest kindness*; and only knows how to *crucify it self*, that it may *spare others*; to *deny* it self, that it may gratify others: Hast thou now chosen to come in *Earth-quakes*, in *Whirl-winds*, in *Thunders*, and *Lightnings*, and *Fires*, in tumults, in hideous clamors and Wars? dost thou delight to wrap thy self in the Garments of Christians *rowled* in blood? to besmear thy fair and orient face with the *gore* and dust of fratricides and patricides? Is it thy pleasure to hide thy self in the thick clouds and darkness of Religious plots, reforming pretensions, and then to break forth with *lightnings* and *hot thunderbolts*, with Hailstones and Coals of fire? As if the *inseparable* twins of the love of *God and our neighbour* were now parted, or had slain and devoured one the other; Are all thy *sweet perfumes*, thy *fragrant Oyntments*, (which were wont to be diffused from the head of *our Aaron* Christ Jesus, to the skirts of his Garments, the lowest and meanest Christians) are they now all distilled and *sublimated* by our hotter brains and *Chimicall* fires, into this one drop of *self preservation*? Hast thou lost those Characters, which the blessed Apostle sometime gave thee, for long *suffering*, for *kindness*; for not *envying*, not *vanting*, not being puffed up; for not *behaving* thy self unseemly, not seeking thine own; not easily provoked, thinking no evill, rejoycing not in iniquity, but in the truth; *Bearing all things*, *believing* all things, *hoping all things*, *enduring* all things? Is thy purity embased with the love of the world, of mony, of honour, of pleasure, of applause, of victory, through *self-love*? Thou that wert wont to be that pure Christalline and celestiall love of God, and of man for Gods sake; art thou now degenerated to *sordid*, *sensuall*, and momentary lusts? Thou that didst *feed* among *the Lillies*, on the mountains *of Spices*, in the *Garden of God*, on the tree of life, the love of God in Christ, with eyes and hands intent to Heaven, praysing God for his love to thee, and praying for the like love to others; art thou now condemned to the *Serpents curse*, to goe on *thy Belly*, to feed on the dust; to make *gain thy godliness*, and to turn even *piety* it self into the *poyson* of meer *self-preservation*, in worldly interests? How is thy voice changed from that of a *Lamb*, to the roaring *of a Lion*? thy hands from *Jacob*'s smoothness, to *Esau*'s *roughness*?

Or is this rather none of thy *voice*, which we daily hear? Are these none of thy hands, O most unchangeable Charity, who art alwaies the same in thy self, and to others? Are they not the voice and hands of thy disguised enemies, tempting us with the *Serpents* *subtilty*

agnitio, gloriosius quam prophetia. Irenæ. l.4.c.63.
Gratia est & fortissima, & mitissima; generosa suavitate omnia agit, tolerat, vincit Charitas, Semper sibi lex severissima. Bern.
Charitas est motus animi ad fruendum Deo propter seipsum, & se atque proximo propter Deum. Aust. de Doct. Christi. l.3.c.9.
1 Joh.4.8.20.
Ps.133.1.2.
φιλαυτία ἁπάντων ἁμαρτημάτων αἰτία ἑκάστοις γίνεται. Cl. Al. Strω. 6.
1 Cor.14.4.5.6.7.
Charitas est sibi maxime imperiosa. Jeron.
1 Tim.6.5.

subtilty; beguiling us with the fallacy of ravening *Wolves*, covered in *Sheeps* cloathing, and bleating instead of howling, yet with no less purpose to devour? whose *bowels* are of brass, their *hearts* of Adamant, their *Fore-heads* of Flint, their *Teeth* and *Claws* of Iron; There *Feet are swift to shed blood*, yea they are dipped in the blood of Christians? Thou that wert wont to have but one *Head*, the Lord Jesus Christ; and but two Hands, the right *Hand* of affiance, leaning on God; the left of *pitty*, supporting the weak Brother; art thou now grown monstrous like *Hydra*, with many Heads, and as many stings? like *Briareus*, with many Hands, and as many Swords? mutually fighting, though seeming to branch from, and adhere to the same body of Christianity? Is thy God now to be appeased with *humane sacrifices*, or will he drink *the blood* of Christians, who would not accept *a gift* at the altar, till the offerer had first *reconciled himself* to *his Brother*? will he now accept the heads of those that are slain by us, who would not *Crown Martyrdom* it self, if the Garland of Charity had not first adorned it on earth, and so fitted it for suffering; and by patient suffering, for glory in the Heavens?

Mat. 5.23. 1 Cor. 13.3. *Nec Martyrium absque charitate coronandū.* Ber. Ep. 7.

O let not the Christian world thus mistake thee; rather let them never speak or think of thee, than thus injure thee, while they pretend to advance thee; we know, O *blessed Charity*, that thou art wholy made up of the *love* and free *grace* of God, by the merits *of Jesus Christ*, and the liberall effusions of the *holy Spirit*; having in thee as no ingredients of humane merits, so less of humane passions, secular ends, and partiall interests; O shew thy self in thy own *innocent* sweetness, in thy pious simplicities, in thy lovely lineaments, with thy harmless hands, with thy beautifull feet, which carry the *message of good* tydings, the *Gospell of Peace*, which have the *marks of the* Lord Jesus on them; which art wholy made up of softness and sweetness; *warming* us by the light *of the Truth*, and *melting* us by the warmth of Christs love; set forth thy self in thy *sober smiles*, thy modest eyes, thy soft and silken words, thy *silent tears*, thy clean hands, thy tender steps; How can we love thee, unless we see thee, like thy self? How can we not love thee, if once we be happy to see thee, as thou art! O hide not thy self from us, though we have abused thee and mocked thee, and scourged thee, and crowned thee with thorns, and clothed thee with Purple rayment, died in the blood of Christians; though we have pierced thy heart, and almost destroyed thee, so that thou art forced to fly from us *naked* and *wounded*; Though we have not only forsaken thee, but driven thee from us; not only lost thee, but are loth to find thee, and joy in thy loss, and are afraid of thy return: yet since thou art *Charity*, that is, *all divine sweetness*, kindness

Gratia est quod vivimus, quod valemus, quod pugnamus, quod coronamur. Chrysost.

Φύσεως λόγοι.

nesse and goodnesse, doe not utterly forsake us, the scattered and torn remnant of surviving Christians; Are our distances more unreconcileable, than those were between God and Sinners? yet these thou hast composed, by that *blood of attonement*, which Christ the Son and *love* of God shed for us, to redeem us out of all Nations tongues and people; who hath given us this badge of his *Disciples*, to *love one another*; not with private and Schismaticall factiousnesse, but with publike and Catholick affections, which reach as far as the *Name of Christ is* owned: Thou art not only an *Angell* ascending up to Heaven in the love of God, but also *descending* down to men, chiefly to the fraternities of Christians; Nor is the stream of thy sweetnesse, which flows with Milk and Honey, only diffused upon the *Church triumphant*, the blessed Angels, and *Souls of just men made* perfect, who are ever *bathed in an Ocean of thy Nectar*, which is infinite love; but thou hast also received *gifts for men*; and hast *effusions* of love to soften our hard hearts, to supple our brawny hands, to clear our polluted consciences, and to chear up our *Cainish countenances*. Joh. 13. 35.

Better we had been among the slain, that are *gone down to the Pit*, and covered in darknesse, with the dust of death, than, to live without thee; whose presence makes our *moment* here to be Heaven, and thy absence makes our *after eternity* to be Hell; O let not the cruell, factious, profane, and Atheisticall world say, That thou, the *Charity of Christians*, wert never beyond a fable, a meteor in their fancies, a morning dew falling from their lips; or a melancholy softnesse, a pusillanimous pitty, a devout cowardise; As if Christians were kind no longer, than they wanted power to be cruell; and humbly obeyed no longer, than they wanted opportunity to be proudly rebellious against those, whom they feared more as slaves, than loved as Christians. *Procellæ, tenebræ, mortes, tormenta, Gehennæ in sunt animæ in qua charitas non remanet, & regnat.* Fulg.

Is there nothing in thy ingenuous wisdom (which delightest to doe best, and most, where men merit least) by which to bring back those (*Theriandri*, *Anthropophagi*, or *Lycanthropi*) those men, that are become savage of civill; those Christians, that are turned Tygers, and Lions, and Bears, and Wolves, degenerated far from the pristine shape and forms which they had, of meek Lambs and Sheep? O bring forth those excellent *eye salves*, by which thou didst of old open the eyes of the blind, and barbarous Heathens. Shew to the deformed Christians of this metamorphosed age, thy *primitive* beauties; the attractives of thy meeknesse, the charms of thy gentlenesse, the trophies of thy patience, forbearances, and brotherly kindnesse; bring forth the *Magazins of thy mercies*, bowels of pitty, tendernesse, tears; use thy *honest frauds*, thy *pious crafts*, thy Dove-like arts, thy Saint-like policies, of self denyall, courtesy, modesty, 2 Cor. 12. 16.

Quanto magis regnum cupiditatis destruitur, tanto charitatis augetur. Austin. de doct. Christiano.

τοὺς θεῷ πεπιστευκότας χριστιανοὺς αὐτοῖς τῷ κόσμῳ ὥσπερ ψυχὴν πάντας καὶ θανάτῳ κατεγνωσμένους, *de Christianis.* Just. M. ad Diog.

πολλοὶ τῶν βιαίων εἶναι ὄντες μετέβαλον ὑπομείναντες ζῆλον χριστιανῶν καταπονοῦντας Just. in Apol.

Mark. 13 22.

giving and forgiving; by which means Christians ever flourished in grace, abounded in comforts, and though they were destroyed and persecuted, yet still they were emulated and renowned; (O remove the paints, and veils, and masks, and shadows, the deceits and dawbings, which are upon the face of Christian Religion; which is indeed nothing without thee; a meer mockery of graces, a pageantry of virtue; a phantasm of courage, a delusion of zeal, a shadow of reformation; fitted only to deceive, *if it were possible, even the very elect,*) If thy torments and blood-sheds, and deaths of old, will not serve to moysten and enlarge the dryed and contracted *bowels* of modern Christians, to *mollify their* hearts, to calm their spirits, and to sweeten their looks to one another; O shew them thy later foul *scratches*, thy fresh wounds, thy grievous reproches, thy many bleedings, thy deep stigmatizings; thy prisons, thy piercings, thy dyings, thy crucifyings, all which thou hast received in the *house of thy friends*, by the hands of thy friends, even such as are called Christians, but can hardly be counted, *charitable*: which have brought thee and us to these fears, and tremblings, and paleness, and despairs, as if God, and Christ, and Gospell, and Ministry, and Heaven, and salvation, and true Religion, were all departing with thee, which are thy inseparable companions.

1 Pet. 1. 29.

Obstinati animi & adamantina corda, minis duriora, & monitis pejora, solo Christi sanguine conspersa emolliuntur. Bern.

O duri, & indurati & obdurati filii Adam; quos non emollit tanta benignitas, tanta flamma, tam ingens ardor, tam vehemens amator; quem nec agon, nec crux, nec mors terruit, quin te amaret.

Acts 3. 15. & 19.

1 Joh. 3. 16.

1 Joh. 3. 15.

If these will not move Christians to look after thee, or at least to pitty thee, and to pray for thee (or rather for themselves in thee:) yet hast thou one *holy Relique* of infinite merit, incomparable worth, and inestimable valew; set forth this to the blood-shotten eyes of the Christian world; even Jesus *Christ crucified for them*, and professed by them to be their common Saviour: Possibly his precious bloud *sprinkled* on their consciences, may (as water on lime) slake, and dissolve, that firy Spirit, and flinty Heart, which is among them; Nothing can work such miracles, as this age wants, but only the cross, and wounds, and agony, and sweats, and tears, and blood, and death of Jesus Christ; whose *love* used the malice and cruelty of his enemies, for an instrument to kill him, that he, being slain by them, might *merit life* for them; that by this act of *highest uncharitableness* in man, to kill *his Saviour*, Christ might set forth his other-wayes *unexpressible* Charity toward men, by saving his destroyers; his love *being stronger than* death; and giving us hereby *a patern* how we should be disposed to one another, not only when friends, but also when enemies; Rather to dye *for them* in a way of charity, which is a beam of divine mercy; than *to kill them*, even in a way of *equity*, which is but a stroke of *humane justice*; but least of all should we *destroy* our Brother, in a way of policy, passion, and malice, which is devillish cruelty; Since to *hate our Brother*, is murther, as he is a man, sure not only to hate,

but

but even for Religion ſake to *kill our brother*, a Chriſtian, muſt be a *crucifying afreſh the Lord of Life*; who died for his Church: So then, uncharitable deſtroyers of Chriſtians, are rather *Deicides*, than *Homicides*.

If all this move not thoſe, that are called Chriſtians, to lay down their *malice*, *factions*, and *arms*, againſt each other; for whom *Charity* and *Chriſt* bids them lay down their lives; O let it move all excellent Chriſtians, (and me, who am leſs than the leaſt) that truly love thee, and long for thee, to mourn to ſee the generality of Chriſtians ſo little moved by thee, or to thee: Let our heads and eyes, be as *Fountains* and *Rivers of Waters*, running with tears night and day, for thoſe thouſands, whom *juſtice*; and thoſe ten thouſands, whom *uncharitableneſs*, *ſchiſm*, and *ſuperſtition*, have ſlain among Chriſtians, even in theſe Nations and Churches. O let our humble hearts be thy *retirement*; our ſighs, and prayers, and tears, thy *refreſhment*, in the heat and fury of theſe times; and be thou to us, *as the ſhadow of that great Rock in a weary Land*.

1 John 3. 16. Hereby we perceive the love of God, becauſe he laid down his life for us, and we ought to lay down our lives for the brethren.

Μάλιϛ' ἔχειν δῦναι τῶν ἀτυχῦντων, δακρύσιν. Μέγα φάρμακον ἔλεος, πολὺ κουφίζει τὰς συμφορὰς τὸ γνησίως συναλγεῖν. Naz. Or. 16.

Iſai. 32. 2.

O bleſſed Bleſſing of all other bleſſings, Charity; what words, what tears, what prayers, what ſighs, what Sermons, what Writings can recover thee, or recal thee, or perſwade thee to look back, and return to theſe, and others pitifully broken, waſted, forlorn, and divided Churches? But alas, our *words are ſharp ſwords*, daily whetting, and claſhing againſt each other; our *tears* are, as the drops of revengeful and impatient *ſpirits*, which cannot have their *wills*; our *prayers* are the bitter effuſions of *hearts* troubled and diſquieted, not with *ſin*, but with *choler* and *unkindneſs*; ſo far from praying for our enemies, that we pray nothing but enmity; and are impatient that any ſhould pray for their friends, if we eſteem them our enemies; our *ſighs* are but bellows, to excite the languiſhing flames of declining *factions*, againſt their *oppoſers*; our *Sermons* oftimes are as firebrands toſſed up and down by *incendiaries*; and the breath of our *Pulpits*, are like the Eructations of *Ætna*, *Veſuvius* or *Hecla*, ſcattering coals of fire, and blaſting all things neer them with *ſulphureous exhalations*: So that many *Preachers* are, indeed, as voices *crying in the wilderneſs*; ſounding alarms to *Religious War*; and preparing a way for *zealous deſolations*, both in *Church* and *State*; And for our *Writings*, they are in great part but *Pamphlets*, which ſerve as Paper to wrap up ſquibs, or to kindle to quicker flames, thoſe *ſmoaking jealouſies* and *ſecret diſcontents*, which are ſmothered in our breſts: That even we *Chriſtians*, and *reformed* too, *ſpeak*, and *act*, and *pray*, and *Preach*, and *Print*, in great part, ſo, as if we had not one *God*, and one *Lord Jeſus*, one *Spirit*, one *Faith*, and one *Baptiſm*, &c. But, as if we had no *God*, no *Faith*, no *Word*, no *Sacrament*, no common relation to one *Saviour*, no common ſalvation in *One*, and by

Beatitudinum omnium beatiſſima beatitudo charitas. Nieremburg.

Epheſ. 4. 4, 5.

One; as if we were Christians, onely to be *crosses*, and to *crucifie* one another: As if we were all turned *Canaanites*, *scourges* in the *sides*, and *thorns* in the *eyes* of one-another.

Charitas deus est substantivus, & dat nobis deitatem accidentalem. Bern. de dil. Deo.

O thou flower and fragrancy of all graces and virtues; which hast little of a *Man*, nothing of a *Devil*, and most of *God*, of *Christ*, and of the *Holy Spirit* in thee; which carriest all sweetness, serenity, and tranquillity with thee: If thou abhorrest the *crowds* of Christians, and such as glory so much in their being gathered into *Churches* after *new* and *uncouth ways*; If thou darest not trust their *smiles* and *kisses*, their *fervors* and *reformings*, who have so oft, under the *specious pretences* of *Religion*, sheathed their *swords* in thy *bowels*; If thou art afraid, not onely of *religious rabbles*, and *zealous multitudes*, but even of *sacred Synods*, and *Armies* listed for *holy Wars*, whose faith hath often failed thee and them too; who while they thought to contend earnestly for the *truth*, have crushed thee, *O Charity*, almost to nothing, by their *violences*, and *divisions*; each *novel faction* seeming to strive for thee, *pull* and *tear* thee in pieces, ready by *violent halings* of thee to their sides *Sects*, utterly to destroy thee;

O yet prepare a place for thy self among some humble and honest hearts, some meek and quiet spirits here in *England*; that so thou maist retire and hide thy self, from thy friendly enemies, from their cruel courtesies, their dangerous importunities, their deep agitations, and designs. O disdain not the *broken hearts* and *contrite spirits*, of that remnant of *truly Reformed*, *Catholike*, and *charitable Christians*, which yet have escaped in this Church. These value thee, these long for thee, these are *sick of love* to thee, and weary of life without thee. To thy *honor* and *restauration*, to their *comfort* and *establishment*, these *lines* are chiefly consecrated: O do thou cover them, and this thy *suppliant Orator*, under the *shadow of thy wings*, (till this *calamity* be overpast): hide us from the *strife of tongues*, which are set on fire *with the fire of hell*; which burn most, when cool drops, and calm pleas for *charity*, are sprinkled on them.

James 3.6. Psal. 120.7. I am for peace, but when I speak, they are for war.

In the great and sad ruines of Churches, and dissentions of Christians, O be thou *our refuge and protection*; teach us to live by *divine love*; and so to love thee, that we may live a *divine life* with thee: Learn us that highest lesson of a Christian, *to love our enemies*, *and persecutors*; while others learn to hate their *friends*, and their *Fathers*.

1 Cor. 13. 8. Charity never faileth.

O *Sempiternal Grace*, which art fitted for *immortal souls*; let us be (as *Ruth* to *Naomi*) unseparable from thee, while we are on Earth; as thou art the *onely remaining grace* in Heaven; being the *crown* and *consummation* of all other *gifts* and *graces*; which, like *stars*, then disappear, and are willingly *swallowed* up, when thy lustre,

like

like the *Suns*, is risen to its *full strength*, and shines in an *eternal Noon*, making the soul at once infinitely happy, while it sees an object infinitely lovely, and loves it with an infinite love. Rather than we should fail of thee in this life (*O thou beloved of our souls*) carry us with thee, from *Cities*, to *solitudes*; from *company*, to *deserts*; from the *unsociable societies*, and *uncharitable Churches*, to *creeping cottages*, to *weeping solitudes*, and *howling wildernesses*; where we may enjoy thee in our own *oft sighing*, and *smitten brests*, rather than dwell in *Palaces*, and *Cities*, and *Temples*, and where we see thee daily *despised*, *profaned*, and *mangled*; *tormented*, *torn*, and *trampled* under the feet of Christians, in *Villages*, in *Towns*, in *Cities*, in *Senates*, in *Armies*, in *Seats of Justice*, and in *Pulpits*. Give us the *wings of a Dove*, even thy *wings* (*O holy Charity*) by which thou ascendest at once to *God* in love, and descendest for *Gods* sake in love to man; that we may *make haste* and *flie away*, and be *at rest* for ever; that we may ascend from this *valley* of our *confusions*, to the *mountain* of thy *felicities*; Which is the *glorious vision* of thy *self* in the great *mirror* or *glass* of *Gods perfections*; who is in himself, and to us *perfect light*, that we may see him to be *perfect love*; and is *perfect love*, that we may enjoy his *perfect light*. O *Father* of *Lights*, and *Fountain of Love*, whose *immensity* and *eternity* are filled with *truth* and *peace*, *verity* and *charity*; whose *love* hath sprinkled our souls with the *blood* of thy *beloved Son*, the *promised Messias*, our *blessed Jesus*! O let our *moment* here, be *sincere love* to thy self; *perfect charity* to thy Church; and *holy humanity* to all men; that our *eternity* may be blessed with *thine*; and our *Saviours*, and our *Fellow Saints* love for ever. 1 John 1. 5. God is light. Chap. 4. 8. God is love.

You, O *excellent Christians* (whose *excellency* is chiefly in this, that *above all things you have put on charity, which is the bond of perfection*) you will not onely excuse, but (it may be) kindly accept this *little digression*; wherein my Pen, like *Jeremies*, hath shed some *few drops* of *lamentation*, mingling *tears* with the blood of Christians, which hath been so profusely shed in these *self-desolating* Churches; *mourning* for the loss of *charity*, the *extirpations* of *unity*, and the *ruines* of *harmonious order*, which are forced to yield to *contention*, *cruelty*, and *confusions*. *Nature* teacheth you to lament the loss, or forced absence, of what you love; and *Christian Religion* teacheth you, to love all *graces* in *charity*, and this one *above all*: You have learned to suffer with patience, (and in some cases, with joy) the *spoiling* of your *goods*, the *sequestring* of your *revenues*, the *imprisonment* of your *persons*, the *scattering* of your neerest *relations*, the *withdrawings* of your *wary friends*, and the great *alterations* of *civil powers*, and *secular affairs*; These are but scenes and parts of the same Tragedy, which hath always been acting

Col. 3. 14. *Supplementum, munimentum, ornamentum omnium gratiarum una charitis.* Amb. Jer. 5. 1.

ing on the *Worlds Theatre*; in which, it is safer to be Spectators, and Sufferers, than Actors; nor may your sufferings in *secular matters* disorder your *charity*; onely, the plundrings of your *true Christian Religion*, which some men aim at; the sequestring of this Church of *England*, from its *glory* and *reformation*; the dividing, and so destroying of it; the restraining you from enjoying the *great seal of charity*, the *Sacrament* of *Christian Communion*; the scattering of your *able faithful Ministers* into corners; the changing and contemning of your *antient* and *excellent Ministry*; the underminings of your *comforts*, and the hazards of your *consciences*; the many confusions and miseries threatning your *posterity* in *matters of salvation*, if the malice of some men may be suffered to abuse your *charity*, and impose upon this credulity;

These, your *zeal* (mixed with *charity*) teacheth you, to endure with an *impatient patience*: Therefore *patient* in some degree, because you yet hope better things from *God*, and all good men; therefore *piously impatient*, because you earnestly wish better for *Gods* glory, and the good of your Countrey. Your *humble zeal* hath taught you to be *discreetly charitable*; as to your own souls, so to all others; but specially to this Church of *England*, and the *true Ministers* of it; to whom, you cannot but willingly bear that *tender respect* and *love*, which pious children are wont to do to their *distressed*, yet *well-deserving parents*; from the care and support of whom, no *Corbans*, no *imaginary Dedications* and *Devotions* of your selves to any *new Church ways*, and *forms* of *Religion*, may justly alienate your *affections*; nor dispence with that *respect*, *justice*, *gratitude*, and *charity*, which you in *conscience* ow to those, to whom in some sense you ow your own selves, and the best of your selves, your souls: Whose *divine Authority*, and *holy Calling*, I shall now further endeavor to prove, having thus first established the *truth of our Religion, and of our Church*; whose greatest waste and want, is that of *charity*; whose dying embers, and almost extinguished sparks, I have (by the way) endeavored to revive in the hearts of true Christians; that so they may without *passion* or *prejudice*, embrace that *truth* which I chiefly design to vindicate in this *Apology*: Namely, The *holy Calling*, *divine Institution*, and *Function* of the *Ministry* of this *Church* of *England*; which will best be done by answering the chief *Objections*, *Calumnies*, and *Cavils*, brought against both the *Ministers* and their *Ministry*, by their many-minded Adversaries.

OBJECT.

OBJECTION II.

Against the peculiar Office and Calling of Evangelical Ministers.

Suppose we grant (say they) *true Religion*, and a *true Church* in *England*, with some defects; yet these may be without any *distinct office*, or *peculiar calling* of *Ministers*, which you challenge, as of *divine appointment*: Where as, we conceive, every Christian may and ought to dispence, in an orderly way, all such *gifts* of *knowledge*, as he hath received in the *Mysteries* of *Religion*, to the *Churches* good. So that the *restraining* of *holy Administrations* to some persons, as a *peculiar Office* and *Function*, seems but the *fruit* of *arrogance* and *usurpation* in some, of *credulity* and *easiness* in others, and is not rightly grounded upon the *Scriptures*. 1 Pet. 4. 10.

Answ. Not that, I believe, your well-grounded and well-guided *piety*, (O excellent Christians) (who know, *in whom*, and *by whom*, you have believed,) needs other satisfaction in this, or the other following *Objections*, touching the *peculiar*, *divinely-instituted Function* of *the Ministry*, than what your own solid *judgments*, and exacter *consciences*, and clearer *experiences*, *sealing* your *comforts*, and our *Ministry*, afford you; who are no novices in matters of *Religion*, either as to the *outward form* and *order*, or the *inward power*; But onely to let you see, that neither I, nor my Brethren the *Ministers*, do plead for that, in a precarious way of meer *favor* and *indulgence*, for which, we have not *good grounds*, *clear proofs*, and *mighty demonstrations*, both *divine* and *humane*, from *Scripture*, *pious Antiquity*, and *right Reason*, I shall more *largely* and *fully answer* this first grand *Objection*, which strikes at the very Root and Foundation, both of the *Ministry*, and all *holy Ministrations*.

1. *Of Catholike testimony, and practise or custom in the Church.*

1 Cor. 9. 2. Your are the Seals of mine Apostleship.

1. I may first blunt the edge of this *weapon* (which strikes against the peculiarity of the *Ministerial Function*) by the *clear* and *constant acknowledgment* (both as to judgment and practise) of all excellent Christians, and all famous Churches, in all Ages, from the very first *birth* and *infancy* of Christianity, and any Churches, to our times: Of which, no sober or learned Christian, can with any plausible shew, make any doubt; so far as *God* in his *providence* hath continued to us any *Monuments* or *Witnesses* of the Churches estate, succession, and transactions in former times. In all which, we finde there ever was a *peculiar Office* of the *holy Ministry*, and a *peculiar Order* of *Persons*, both ordaining, and ordained to be *Ministers*; and

Illud est Dominicum & verum quod prius traditum, id extraneum & falsum quod posterius immissum. Tertul.

and both so used and so esteemed, by all good Christians, in all setled Churches. *Clemens*, in Saint *Pauls* time, after him, writing from *Rome* to the *Corinthians*, where *faction* was kindled, Exhorting people and *Presbyters* to peace, tells them, That the Apostles appointed some in all Countreys (καθίσανον τὰς ἀπαρχὰς, δοκιμάσαντες τῷ πνεύματι) trying and approving them by the Spirit, to be Bishops and Deacons, for those that after should believe, *Pag.* 54. *Edit. Pat. Jun.*

Which *Catholike practise and judgment*, as it is a great *satisfaction* to all sober Christians, who *itch not after novelties*; so it must needs be a *vehement prejudice*, with any wisemen, against those *yesterday novelties*, raised by some few men of great passions and presumptions, but of no great reputation (that ever I could learn) for either such *learning*, *piety*, or *impartiality*, as may be put into the ballance against the clear and concurrent *Testimonies* of all the *Antients*, and the *universal practise* of all *Churches*, which all *Histories*, all *Fathers*, all *Councils*, all *Learned* and *Godly men*, both *Antient* and *Modern*, do with one *Spirit*, and one *Mouth* abundantly testifie; agreeable to that of Saint *Jerom*, St. *Augustine*, *Isidore Hispal.* and many others: Who, speaking of the *Calling of Ministers*, (from those words, *Called to be an Apostle of Jesus Christ*) reckon up four sorts;

First, Some, that are sent immediately from God, and not by men; as *Moses*, many Prophets, the Twelve Apostles, and Saint *Paul*.

Secondly, Some by Gods appointment, yet by Mans hand, and Ordination; as *Aaron*, *Joshuah*, *Elisha*, *Timothy*.

Thirdly, Others in the *ordinary way*, and *succession of the Church*, (as it is appointed by *Jesus Christ*) are by men onely ordained *Ministers*, either according to *real merit*, *partial favor*, and *vulgar affection*.

Fourthly, There be some whom neither God, nor man sends, but they run of themselves.

Such (saith St. *Jerom*) *were, and are false Prophets, and false Apostles, deceitful workers, Ministers of Satan, transforming themselves into Angels of light; who say*, Thus saith the Lord, *when the Lord hath not spoken to them, or sent them.* To this sense Saint *Jerom*, St. *Austine*, and accordingly all the *Antients*, before and after them, as they have occasion to speak of the *office, duty*, and *dignity* of *Ministers* in the *Church*: Which *Catholike Testimony*, and *Tradition*, or *Custom* of the *Church*, for any *Christian* to contradict without shew of *reason*, is *intollerable impudence*; and not to believe it, is *most inhumane*, and *unchristian uncharitablenes*; to disparage, and causlesly to derogate from it, can be no other, but profane

Id sine dubio tenendum, quod ecclesia ab Apostolis, Apostoli à Christo, Christus à Deo suscepit. Reliqua omnis doctrina de mendacio præjudicanda, quæ sapit contra veritatem ecclesiæ, & Apostolorum, & Christi, & Dei. Tertul. de præ. ad Hæ. c. 21.

Omnes præpositi Apostolis Vicaria Ordinatione succedunt. Cyp. l. 4. ep. 9.

Jer. Com. in 1. cap. ep. ad Gal.

Isidor. Hispal. off. eccle. l. 2. c. 5.

Radix Christianæ societatis per sedes Apostolorum & successiones Episcoporum certa per orbem propagatione diffunditur, Aug. ep. 42.

The Lord, saith *Clemens*, will have us to perform our (προσφορὰς καὶ λειτουργίας) offerings and

profane and perverse insolence; unless there can be produced such clear testimonies from *immediate divine revelations*, confirmed by miracles; or from the received *Written Word* of *God*, to the contrary; as will easily, and ought justly to overweigh all after *inventions* or *constitutions*, which are built meerly upon *humane custom* and *authority*; as that was of giving the *Lords Supper* to *Infants*, and to the *dead* sometimes.

services (ἐκ εἰκῆ ἢ ἀτάκτως) none rashly and disorderly, but in due time and season, (ποῦ τε καὶ διὰ τίνων) where also, and by whom, his will and supreme pleasure, hath appointed. Ἕκαστος ὑμῶν ἐν τῷ ἰδίῳ τάγματι εὐχαριστείτω Θεῷ. Ὁ λαϊκὸς ἄνθρωπος τοῖς λαϊκοῖς προστάγμασι δέδεται. The Faction or Schism began in Saint *Pauls* time, then renewed, or had continued, which *Clemens* shews, citing the Apostle *Pauls* Epistle to the *Corinthians*, and telling them, That the Apostles setled approved Ministers, Bishops, and Deacons after them, and ordered for a succession to follow, when those were dead, whom they ordained immediately, *p.* 57. *Edit. Pat. Jun.* *Clemens R.* ep. ad Corinth. *Ignat.* ep. ad Hieron. & in aliis ep. *Just. Mar.* Apol. 2. *Tertul.* Apol. & lib. De Baptismo. *Cyprian*, l. 1. ep. 2, 9. l. 3. ep. 5. *Eis, qui sunt in Ecclesia, Presbyteris obaudire oportet, his qui successionem habent ab Apostolis; qui cum Episcopatus successione charisma veritatis certum secundum beneplacitum patris acceperunt: Reliquos vero, qui absistunt à principali successione, & quocunque loco colliguntur, suspectos habere, vel hæreticos, & malæ sententiæ; vel quasi scindentes, & elatos, & sibi placentes: Aut rursus ut hypocritæ quæstus gratia & vanæ gloriæ hoc operantes; omnes autem hi decidunt à veritate, ut* Nadab, & Abihu, & Koram, & Jeroboam, &c. Irenæus, l. 4. c. 43. *Agnitio vera est Apostolorum doctrina & antiquus Ecclesiæ status in universo mundo secundum successiones Episcoporum, quibus illi eam, quæ in unoquoque loco est Ecclesiam, tradiderunt*, Iren. l. 4. c. 63. *Chrysost.* de Sacerdotio. *Basil. Mag.* Symoni Mago *comparat illos, qui* παρὰ τῶν χειροτονουμένων τὰ χρήματα λαμβάνουσι, Who take money for Ordination; and calls that gain, προαγωγικὸν τὸν εἰς γέενναν, Conduct money for Hell, *Ep.* 78. And in his 181. *Epist.* challenges to himself the power of Ordination from the *Corepiscopi*. So *Epist.* 187. ὁ πολλοῦ συνέδρια, &c. The antient custom of the Church receives none to be Ministers, but with strict examination, in their Ordination. *Epiphan.* Hæ. 79. *Jeron.* Dialog. ad *Lucifer.* St. *Ambrose*. De Dignitate Sacerdotali Liber. St. *Austine*, Ep. 42. and in many places. St. *Gregory* the Great, De Cura Pastorali, lib. *Quomodo valebit secularis homo sacerdotis magisterium adimplere, cujus nec officium tenuit, nec disciplinam agnovit?* Is. Hisp. off. eccl. l. 2. c. 5. οὐδέποτε παρ' ἡμῖν τοῖς Χριστιανοῖς, &c. *Nullatenus nobis Christianis permissum est, ut quis in ecclesia, seu publicè Scripturas explanet, nisi, qui in clericatem ordinem adscitus fuerit.* Suid. in l. περὶ φιλολόγ. Greg. Thaumaturgus, *juvenum quendam pium & Philosophum sub forma carbonarii obscurum in sacerdotem ordinavit.* κατὰ τὸ νενομισμένον ἔθος, *juxta solemnes ritus*, Greg. Nis. in vita Thaum.

Which counterbalancing of *Custom* by *Reason* or *Scripture*, is not yet in the least kinde done, by these men, that are the opposers of the *Ministry* of *England*; Who, by the same *proud* or *peevish incredulity*, by which they oppose the *Catholike* consent, and practical Testimony of the Church in this great point of the *holy Ministry*, do overthrow, by a *sceptical folly*, and *disputative madness*, the very *foundation*, and all possible *means* of *Historical belief* or *faith* among men; For which, the *wisdom* and *providence* of the *Creator*, hath afforded to mankinde, no other ordinary ground or inducement, but onely that, of a *charitable* and *rational perswasion*, which we have, That neither the most, nor, to be sure, the best ablest, and worthiest men, in all Ages, and these in several places, would conspire in a *lie*, or give testimony to a *falshood*; contrary to their own consciences,

 and

and the evidence of things, as to matter of fact; whereof themselves, and their forefathers, were eye-witnesses, beyond any possibility of ignorance, or mistake: Nor can any thing be alleged, or supposed, as matter of *self-interest*, or *partiality*; there being in the first Three hundred years, no temptation of secular profit, or honor, to blinde, or corrupt their *judgment* and *testimony*; whereby they should not either fully and clearly see, what was judged, and acted in the Church; or that any thing should so bribe their tongues and pens, as not to give a *true record*, and *faithful report* to posterity: Since many of them sealed their *love* to the *truth*, and *charity* to *mankinde*, by their *blood* in *Martyrdom*.

At the same rate, of obstinate *disbelieving*, and supercilious *denying*, whatever is delivered by *writing* or *tradition* to after Ages, men may foolishly, and madly question the *works of every Author*; the *facts* and *records* of all former times, left us in *History*: Christians may doubt of their *Baptism* in their Infancy; yea, and question their own *Natural Fathers* and *Mothers*, refusing to own, or pay any duty and obedience to them; since of these they can have no other assurance, than what is *told them* by others; as also of all their *forefathers* and *predecessors*; from whom these *Sceptical Infidels* are certainly descended, although they never saw them; and (possibly) they enjoy the benefit of their *forefathers labors* and *estates* to this day, which from those is derived in an orderly succession, to these their ungrateful successors: Nor is indeed the *Series* and *Genealogy* of *Natural Parents*, more necessary and certain in *reason*, that they have been, and are gone before us (however their several names and successions may be unknown) from *Noah*, or from *Adam*; than is the constant and uninterrupted succession of *Spiritual Fathers*, and *Predecessors* in the *Ministry* of the *Church*; derived by the *holy Apostles* from *Jesus Christ*, the second *Adam*; the *Everlasting Father* of a better *Generation*: Of which, there are (besides the apparent, present succession in this Church of *England*, and all other Churches-Christian, now in all the World, which lately had or still have a peculiar order of *Bishops* and *Presbyters*, as *holy Ministers* in the Church) so clear, and constant, and undeniable *Histories*, from those that were (ἀξιοπιστότατοι) of all men or writers, the most worthy to be believed, for their love to *God*, their zeal for the *truth*, their charity to all *men*; but especially, for their care *of the houshold of Faith*, the Church of Christ.

Ubi charismata domini posita sunt, ibi discere oportet veritatem; apud quos est ea, quæ ab Apostolis successio, & id, quod est sanum & irreprobabile sermonis constat. Iren. l.4. c.45.

Edant origines Ecclesiarum suarum, evolvant ordinem Episcoporum suorum ita per successiones ab initio decurrentium, ut primus ille Episcopus aliquem ex Apostolis vel Apostolicis viris habuerit autorem & antecessorem. Tert. de præ. ad Hæ. c.32.

Wherein, however it be most true, that a bare *descent*, or *succession of persons*, following each other in time and place, be not sufficient to carry on the *being* and *honor* of a *true Church Christian*, (which title is not entailed to any place, or any race of people,) unless, withal, there be a succession in Christian *Doctrine* and *Institu-*

Non fides ex personis sed personæ ex fide sunt probandæ. Ter. lib. de præ. ad Hær. c.3.

tions,

tions, according to the Scripture; yet it is as true, that the *custody and tradition* of the Scriptures, the succession of true doctrine believed in the Church, and divine Institutions celebrated, never have been, nor ever can possibly be in Christs ordinary way to his Church carried on to after generations, but only by such a *personall succession* of Bishops, Pastors, and Ministers in the Church; such as were in the beginning of the Gospell appointed by Christ, and ever since hath been orderly and constantly derived from one to another, agreeable to the divine constitution; Nor are Christians to expect or presume of daily miracles, speciall revelations, or Angelick missions, to carry on Christian Religion; but humbly to content themselves with that once setled Ministry and holy order, which God by Jesus Christ hath given to the Church, after which example some are still duly tryed, ordained, set apart, and sanctified to this office, the dispensation of the Gospell, and those mysteries which goe with it.

Cum Episcopatus successione Charisma veritatis certum accipiunt. Iren. l. 4. c. 43. *Catholici noverint, se cum Ecclesia doctores recipere; non cum Doctoribus Ecclesiæ fidem deserere debere.* Vinc. Lirin. c. 23. *Hæretici sunt posteriores Episcopis quibus Apostoli tradiderunt Ecclesias.* Irenæ. l. 5. *Audivi à quodam Presbytero qui audierat ab his qui Apostolos viderant.* Irenæ. l. 4. c. 45. Eph. 4. 11. 1 Cor. 12. 28.

Indeed I cannot but esteem, as all good, wise, and humble Christians do, and ever did, the *constant, clear,* and *concurrent* (which is the truly Catholick) testimony of the Church (in which so much of the truth, Spirit, and grace of God, hath alwaies appeared amidst the many cloudings of humane infirmities) to be far beyond any meer *humane* record, or *authority*; in point of establishing a Christians judgement or conscience, in any thing, that is not contrary to the evident command of the written word of God: However some *mens ignorance* and self, conceited confidence (like bogs and quagmires) are so loose and false, that no piles never so long, well driven, and strongly compacted, by the consent and harmonious testimonies of the most learned writers in the Church, can reach any bottom, or firm ground in them, whereon to lay a foundation of humane belief, or erect a firm bank and defense against the invasion of *daily novelties*; which blow up all, and break in upon the antient and most venerable orders, practises and constitutions of the Church, where ever they are yet continued: which being evidently set forth to me, by witnesses of so great credit, for their piety, diligence, fidelity, harmony, integrity, constancy and charity, I know not how with any face of humanity or Christianity to *question, disbelieve*, or *contradict*.

2. *The esteem to be had of the Catholick custom in the Church.*

Vincent. Lyr. *Quod ubique, quod semper, quod ab omnibus tenetur Ecclesiis id demum catholicum.* cap. 3. *Pro magno teste vetustas creditur acceptam parce movere fidem.* Claudian. *Ratio & veritas consuetudini præponenda sunt; sed si consuetudini veritas suffragatur nihil oportet firmius retineri.* Aust. l. 4. cont. Donat. de Bapt. c. 4. *In his de quibus nihil certi statuit Scriptura divina, mos populi Dei & instituta majorum pro lege tenenda sunt: si nec fidei nec bonis moribus sint contraria.* Aust. ad Casulan. *Traditiones Ecclesiasticæ, quæ fidei non officiunt, ita observandæ ut à majoribus traditæ: nec aliorum consuetudo aliorum contrario more subvertenda.* Jeron. ad Lucian. *Si nulla Scriptura determinavit certe consuetudo*

ſuetudo roboravit: quæ ſine dubio de Apoſt. traditione manavit. Tertul. de cor. M. *Sanctæ Eccleſiæ ſacerdotes Catholicæ veritatis hæredes Apoſtolica decreta & definita ſectantes, malue unt ſe ipſos, quam vetuſtæ univerſitatis fidem prodere.* Vinc. Lyrin. c. 8. *Si quid hodie per totum orbem frequentat eccleſia hoc quin ita faciendum ſit diſputare inſolentiſſimæ eſt inſaniæ.* Auguſt. ep. 118. Ὁ κύριος οὕτως ἐδίδαξεν, ἀπόστολοι ἐκήρυξαν, πατέρες διετήρησαν, μάρτυρες ἐβεβαίωσαν: ἀρκέσθητι λέγειν, ὡς ἐδιδάχθης. Baſ. M. Cont. Arium Sabel. &c. Otherways, ἀφ' οὗ Χριστὸς περιεγράφη, καίτοι ἐν τοσούτῳ χρόνῳ τὸ Εὐαγγέλιον ἡμῶν: κενὴ δὲ καὶ ἡ πίστις ἡμῶν, καὶ μάτην οἱ μὲν μαρτυρήσαντες ἐμαρτύρησαν, μάτην δὲ τοῦ λαοῦ προέστησαν οἱ τοσοῦτοι καὶ τηλικοῦτοι προεστῶτες. Greg. Naz. de Apollinario. *Poſt ſacrarum Scripturarum canonicam autoritatem Eccleſiæ Catholicæ conſenſus tantum apud me ſemper valuit, ut quæ cunque ab hoc conſenſu confirmata videam mihi ſacroſancta & immutabilia videantur.* Biſhop Carleton. de Conſen. eccleſ. cap. 11. cap. 277.

Quod univerſa tenet eccleſia nec conſiliis inſtitutum ſed ſemper retentum eſt, non niſi autoritate Apoſtolica traditum rectiſſimè creditur. Auguſt. cont. Donat. l. 4.

In Concil. Laodic. Melito Episc. Sard. miſſus ut autographa ubique decernat, &c. Conſtabit id ab Apoſtolis traditum, quod apud eccleſias fuerit ſacroſanctum. Tert. ad Mar. l. 4.

Under which cloud of *unſuſpected witneſſes*, I confeſs, I cannot but much acquieſce, and reſt ſatisfied in thoſe things, which others *endleſly diſpute*, becauſe they have not ſo *literal* and *preceptive* a ground in *Scripture*; however they have a very rational, exemplary, analogical and conſequential authority from thence, which is made moſt clear, as to the minde of *God*, by that ſenſe, which the *Primitive Doctors* and *Chriſtians*, who lived with, or next to the Apoſtles, had of them; and by their practiſe accordingly, in the ways of Religion: Thus the *Canonical Books of the Scripture*, eſpecially thoſe of the *New Teſtament* (which no where are enumerated in any one Book, nor, as from *divine oracle*, any where commanded to be believed or received, as the writings of ſuch *holy authors*, guided by the dictates or directions of *Gods Spirit*) we own and receive, as they were after ſome time, with judgment and diſcretion (rejecting many other pretended *Goſpels*, and *Epiſtles*) antiently received by the Catholike Church, and to this day are continued. So alſo, in point of the *Church Government*: How, in right Reaſon, Order, and Religion, the Churches of Chriſt, either in ſingle Congregations and Pariſhes, or in larger Aſſociations and Fraternities ought to be governed; in which thing, we ſee that ſudden variations from the Churches conſtant patern in all ages and places, hath lately coſt the expence, not onely of much Ink, but of much blood, and have both caſt and left us in great ſcandals, deformities, and confuſions, unbeſeeming Chriſtian Religion. The like confirmation I have for Chriſtians obſerving the *Lords day*, as their *holy Reſt*, or *Sabbath* to the *Lord*, and their variating herein (upon the occaſion of *Chriſts Reſurrection*) from the Seventh day or *Jewiſh Sabbath*, which is not ſo much commanded by Precept, as confirmed by Practiſe in the Church; ſo in the *baptiſing* of the Infants of Chriſtian Parents, who profeſs to believe in Jeſus Chriſt onely for the means of ſalvation, to them and their children, which, after Saint *Cyprian*, Saint *Jerom* and *Auguſtine* affirm to have been the cuſtom of the Catholike Church, in, and before their days; ſo as no Biſhop, or Council, or Synod began it, *Cypr. ep. ad Fidum. Auſt*

ep

ep. 28. And no less, in this of the *peculiar distinct calling, order, office,* and *succession,* of the Ministry Evangelical.

In all which, if the Letter and Analogy of Scripture were less clear than it is, so that the doctrines of those particulars (which are among Christians counted *divine*) were (like Vines, and Honey-suckles) less able to bear up themselves in full *authority*, by that strength and vertue which they receive from the Scripture Precept, (where undoubtedly their root is; and from whence they have grown, shooted out so far, and flourished in all Churches;) yet the constant judgment and practise of the Church of Christ (which is called the pillar and ground of truth,) are stayes and firm supports to such sweet and usefull plants, which have so long flourished in the Church of Christ, whose custom may silence perverse disputes of corrupt and contentious minds: And indeed doth fully satisfy and confirm both my believe, and my religious observation of those particulars, as sacred and *unalterable*.

ἐν τῇ ἐκκλησίᾳ, τινὰ τάξει καὶ κανόνι κρατοῦνται, τινὰ συνηθείᾳ ἐτυπώθη. Can. Afric. in Con. Carth. 1. anno 419. Some things in the Church are setled by Canon; others by custom. φυλαχθήτω καὶ ὁ ὁρισμὸς καὶ ἡ συνήθεια. Con. Nicœn.

Nor hath any of *those things*, more clear evidence from Scripture *or Catholick practice*, than this of the calling and succession of the *Ministry of the Gospell* hath, wherein some men, after due *tryall and examination* of their gifts and lives, made by those who are of the same function, and are in the Church indued with a derivable Commission and Authority, to ordein an holy succession of men in the Ministry for the Churches use, are by *fasting, prayer,* and *solemn* imposition of hands in the presence of the faithfull people, publikely and peculiarly *ordained*, consecrated, set apart, sent and authorised in the power and name of Christ; to preach the Gospell to all men, to administer the holy Sacraments, and respectively to dispense all those holy duties, and mysteries belonging to Christian Religion, among Christian people, that is, such as profess to believe, that Jesus Christ is the only Saviour of Sinners.

Eucharistiæ sacramentum non de aliorum manu quã præsidentium sumimus. Tertul. de Coro. Mil. *Impositionem manuũ qua Ecclesiæ ministri in suum munus initiantur ut non invitus patior vocari Sacramentum ita inter ordinaria Sacramenta non numero.* Calvin. Inst. l. 4. c. 14. sect. 2. Amb. l. 5. ep. 32. ad Valentin. Commends that sentence, which the Emperours Father had wrote touching judicatories and Judges in Church matters. *In causa fidei vel Ecclesiastici muneris eum judicare debere, qui nec munere impar, nec jure dissimilis, constanter assero.*

Which holy and most necessary custom of *ordaining* some fit men, by others of the same function, to be *Ministers in the* Church, hath not only the unanimous consent and practise of the Orthodox Christians, and purest Churches in all ages, from the Apostles times; But, no *Hereticks* or *Schismaticks*, who owned any relation to the Gospell of Jesus Christ, did ever so much as dispute, or question the power and succession ministeriall, as to its calling peculiar, and divinely *appropriated*, to some men in the Church, Till of later dayes in *Germany*, and some otherwheres the pride of some mens parts, and conceit of their gifts, or the opinion of their raptures and *Enthusiasms*, mixed with other lusts and secular designs, tempted some weak and fanatick men of the Anabaptistical leaven, to adventure the invasion and vulgar prostration of the office; before ever they broached their reasons against it; which presumption and disorder the *Swenckfeldians*, who called themselves *Confessors of the glory of Christ*; afterwards the *Socinians* and others intending to introduce new and heretical doctrines with their new Teachers, studied to set forth with some weak shews of reason and Scripture. Whereas in all former ages of the Church, such as should have abrogated the *antient Catholick* way, or have broached any new way of *Evangelical power* and Ministry, would have been as *scandalous*, as if he had broached a *new Messias*, or a *new Gospel*, and made the old one of none effect; as many of those strive to do, who seek to cry down the former way of Ministers right *Ordination*, *Succession*, and *Authority*. Who if they had not met with a giddy, and credulous, and licentious age, would have needed *new miracles* to have confirmed their *new* and *plebeian ways* of *Ministry*; or to cashier the old one; which was first began, and after confirmed (as the *Gospel* was) for some years, with many *infallible signs* and *wonders*, wrought by the *Apostles*, and their *Successors*, in that *Order* and *Function*.

Confessores gloriæ Christi. An. 1543. When they after proved to be *Pastoricidæ*, Vilains which conspired to destroy all the Ministers of the Gospel in *Germany*, hanging and drowning many of them, casting them into wells, *An.* 1562. *Cl. Sanctesius de temp. decept.*

Irenæus, l. 4. c. 43. *Qui absistunt à principali successione (Episcoporum & Presbyterorum ab Apostolis) quocunque loco colliguntur suspectos habere oportet, vel hereticos, vel scindentes, vel elatos & sibi placentes. Omnes hi decidunt à veritate. Sophistæ verborum magis esse volentes, quàm discipuli veritatis.* Iren. lib 3. c. 40.

3.

What can be the design of any to go contrary, or innovate?

What can it be then, but an *exceeding* want of *common understanding*, or a *superfluity* of *malice*, or a *transport* of *passion*, or some *secular lust*, either to deny credit to the Testimony of the best Christians, and purest Churches in all times, or to go quite contrary to their judgment and practise, by seeking to discredit and destroy the Authority and peculiar Function of the antient Catholike Christian Ministry, in these or other Churches? And since in *primitive times*, it could be no matter of either profit or honor in the world, to be a *Bishop* or *Presbyter* in the Church (who were the first men to be persecuted or sacrificed;) What *motive* could there be then, but onely *Religion*, *Duty*, and *Conscience*, to undertake and persevere in that *holy* and *dangerous Calling*, that so the *Gospel* might be continued? And since, now in *England*, it can be no great *temptation* of *covetousness* or *ambition* (unless it be in very poor and necessitous man) to be a *Preacher* of the *Gospel*, upon the *new account* of the peoples, or *self-ordaining* (which is as none;) what can it be that provokes so many in a *new*, and *pitiful way*, either of *egregious ignorance*, and *popular simplicity*, to undertake to be *Preachers*?

In ea regula incedimus quàm Ecclesia ab Apostolis, Apostoli à Christo, Christus à Deo accepit. Tertul. de Præs. c. 37.

Radix Christianæ societatis per sedes Apostolorum & successiones Episcoporum certa per orbem propagatione diffunditur. August. ep. 42.

ers? Or in a more *refined way* of *devilish malice* and *deep design*, to seek to *level, cast down,* and *trample under foot* all *Ministerial power* whatsoever, (which is none, if it be common, and not peculiar to some men by *divine Sanction*:) Certainly, this can arise from no other aim, but either that of destroying us, as a Reformed Church; or desolating us, quite from being a Church, or Christians: Which our posterity will easily cease to be, as to the *very form* (as many at present are, as to any *power* and *conscience* of Religion) if once they cease to have, or begin to think they have not had, any true Ministers in this, or any Church: So that all *Preaching* of the *Gospel*, all *Sacraments*, all the *Faith* of so many *Christians, Professors, Confessors,* and *Martyrs* in all Ages, together with the *fruits* of their *Faith*, in *Patience, Charity,* and *good Works,* must be in vain. Alas, these poor revenues and encouragements which are yet left to the Ministers here, (considered with their burdens of *business, duties, taxes,* and *envy*) are scarce worth the having or coveting, even by vulgar and mechanick spirits; who may make a better shift to live in any way almost than now in the Ministry. 1 Cor. 15. 14.

The design then of *levelling* the *Ministry*, must needs be from greater *motives*, such as seek to have the whole *honor* and *authority* of the *Reformed Religion* here in *England*, utterly abolished; or else, taken up upon some such *odde, novel,* and *fanatick grounds*, which will hold no water, bear no weight, or stress; being built upon the *sands* of *humerous novelty*, not on the *rock* of *holy antiquity*, and *divine verity*: That so this *whole Church* may, by the *adversaries* of it, be brought to be a *meer shadow* of *deformed* and *confused Religion*; or else, be onely able to plead its Christianity, upon *meer Familistick*, or *Anabaptistick*, or *Enthusiastick*, or *Socinian*, or *Fanatick Principles*; Upon which must depend all our *Christian Privileges, Truths, Sacraments, Ministrations, Duties,* and *Comforts, Living* and *Dying*; all which will easily be proved, and appear, to a considerate soul, as *profane* and *null*, when he shall see they are performed, or administred by those, who can produce no *Precept, Scripture,* or *Practise* from *Antiquity*, for their ways, either of *Christianity*, or of *Ministry*, but onely their own, or other mens wilde fancies, and extravagant furies; nor can they have better excuses for their errors, in forsaking the *right* and *Catholike way*, but onely a popular levity, credulity, and madness after *novelties*.

Agnitio vera est Apostolorum doctrina, & antiquus ecclesiæ status, in universo mundo, & charactere corporis Christi, secundum successiones Episcoporum quibus illi eam, quæ est in unoquoque loco Ecclesiam, tradiderunt. Ire. l. 4. c. 63

So that, as to this first part of my answer, touching *The peculiar Function of the Ministry*, I do aver upon my Conscience, so far as I have read, or can learn, That there is no *Council* of the *Church*, or *Synod*; no *Father* or *Historian*; no other *Writer*, that mentions the affairs of the *Church*; no one of them gives the least cause to doubt, but wholly confirms this assertion, *That no* part of the *Catholike*

Church

Church of Christ, in any age, or place, *was ever setled or flourished without a constant peculiar Order, and Ordination of Ministers*; who were consecrated to the receiving and exercise of that *power* in the Church, as from Christ, although by man, which have continued to this day.

Theodoret. hist. l. 1. c. 22. *De Ædesio & Frumentio apud Indos, divina Ministeria obierunt Laicii cum erant; Frumentius postea ab Athanasio ep. factus.* Cap. 23. *Captiva mulier apud Iberos Evangelium prædicabet, & miracula edebat. His Const. M. Episcopos misit.*

There are indeed three or four examples (in cases extraordinary) of some private unordained Christians in the *Primitive times*, who occasionally trading to *Heathens*, were means first to teach them the Mysteries of Christ, so as they desired to be *baptized*, which was after done by such *Bishops* and *Ordained Ministers*, as were sent them upon their request, from other Churches. To produce particular testimonies out of each *Author, Father, Council*, and *Historian*, in every age, to prove the *constant succession*, the *high veneration*, and the *unfeigned love*, which was every where conferred upon the *Bishops* and *Ministers* of the Church; also, to shew forth that devout care and religious regard, which the *ordainers*, the *faithful people*, and those to be ordained to the *office*, had, in their several *relations* and *duties*, when Ministers were to be ordained and consecrated, such allegations were easie, being very many and obvious; but I hold the pains needless, considering, that to *learned men* they are so well known; and all ingenuous Christians will believe my *solemn asseveration*, that, as in the presence of God, what I write, is *Truth*: As for those weak or wilful men, who are in this my *onely opposers*, I know, they consider not any *heaps of authorities*, which they account onely as *humane*; which they cannot examine, nor do they value them, when convinced of the certainty, and harmony of them; were there never so sweet, and many flowers gathered from the testimony of *Antiquity* and *Authority* of the *Fathers*, these *supercilious novellers* will not vouchsafe to *smell* to them: It is well, if I can make them *savor* any thing well out of the *Scriptures*, which favors the Function of the *Ministry*.

4. *Catholike custom confirmed by Scripture, as to the Office of the Ministry.*

2. So then, in the next place, This *Defence* of the Churches *clear, constant*, and *Catholike Testimony*, in this point of the *peculiar Office* of the *Ministry* (as in any other) becomes a *brazen wall*, an *impregnable bulwark*, able to break in pieces, or to retort all *engines* and *batteries* made against it; when it appears to be exactly drawn, according to the *scale, line*, and *measure*, set down in the *holy Scripture*; which are therefore much sleighted by some, who despise the *Ministry*; because, like *well-planted Canons*, they defend the *Church*, and its constant *Ministry*; as on the other side, the *Churches fidelity and constancy*, are the *ground-work* and *platforms*, on which the *Scriptures* are planted; The Church of Christ bearing up as the ground, and holding forth as a pillar, that *divine Truth, Power*, and *Authority*, which, from God, they have in them; of which, the

1 Tim. 3. 15.

Church

Church is the *Herald* or *Publisher*, but not the *Author* or *Inditer*; Conferring nothing to their *internal Truth*, which is from their *revealer* and *inspirer*, *God*; but much to their *external credit*, and *historick reception*, which we have tendered to us daily; not as immediately from *God*, or *Angels*, or inspired *Prophets*, but by the *veracity* and *fidelity* of the Church, chiefly in its *publick Ministry*; which in this point of so *necessary*, *constant*, and *universal practise*, for the good of all *faithful people*, in all Ages and Churches, cannot be thought in any reason, either to have had no *rule divinely appointed*; or that all Churches have been wholly ignorant of it, or knowingly have so wholly swerved from it, that never any Church, either in its *Teachers* and *Pastors*, or in its *people* and *believers* were followers of the *Scripture-Precept*, and *Patern*, till these last and worst days; whereas, the clear and pregnant *light* of the *Scripture*, is in this point of a setled Ministry, so agreeing with the use and practice of the *Catholike Church*; that, as no error can be *suspected* in the one, so no obscurity can be pretended in the other, by any Christians, who will allow the *divine Authority*, and *infallible Truth* of those *Scriptures*, which we call the *New Testament*.

In all which, nothing is more evident, and *self-demonstrating* beyond any *cavil* or *contradiction*, than, That our *Lord Jesus Christ*, *the promised Messias*, *the beloved Son of God*, the *Angel* of the *new* and *better Covenant*, the *Minister of Righteousness*, the *great Apostle*, the *chief Bishop and Father of our souls*, the *Author and Finisher of our Faith*, the *supreme Lord and King*, the eternal and compassionate *High Priest*, the unerring *Prophet* of his *Church*, whose voice we are onely to *hear* and *obey* in all things he commands us; That, I say, this *Lord Jesus Christ*, was *sent by the Father*, to a *personal accomplishment* of all *Prophecies*; *fulfilling of all righteousness*; to a *visible Ministration* of *holy things* for the Churches good; That he came not in his own *Name*, as a *man*, to be *Mediator* and *Teacher*; nor did he as a *man* take this *honor* of *Prophet*, *Priest*, or *King* of his Church upon him; but had his *mission* or *appointment* from his *Father*, *God*; who gave evident testimonies from *Heaven* of him; not onely before, and at his *birth*, but afterward, at his *solemn* and *publick inauguration* by *Baptism*, into the *Work of his Ministry*, where a *voice from Heaven* was heard, and a *visible representation* of the *Holy Spirit* was seen, testifying him to be the *beloved Son of God*; the *anointed*, with the *gifts of the Spirit*, above all, as *Head of the Church*: These, after, were followed with *infallible signs* and *wonders*, while *Jesus* went about doing good; teaching the *Mysteries of the Kingdom of Heaven*; instituting holy rites, for the distinguishing of his Church from the world, and for the comforting of the *faithful* in the world; by those *seals*, *pledges*, and *memorials*

Christ sent of the Father, as a Minister of Righteousness.

1 Pet. 2. 25.
Heb. 12. 2.
Math. 17. 5
John 4. 34. & 5. 36. & 6. 57. & 7. 16.
Heb. 5. 4. No man taketh this honor to himself but he that is called of God as *Aaron*.
V. 5. So also Christ glorified not himself to be made an high priest, but, &c.
Math. 3. 17.

of his love, in dying for the Church, and shedding both *water* and *blood* upon the Cross.

Christs sending his Apostles as Ministers.
Acts 1.
Phil. 2, 9.

Christ having thus personally finished the *suffering* and *meritorious* part of his Ministry; after his *Resurrection*, being now no more to converse in a *visible humane way* of presence, with his Church on Earth, but ascending (as was meet) to that *glory of the Father*, which, as *God*, he had ever with him; as *man*, he had merited of him, by *suffering* on the Cross, and enduring the *shame*, for his Churches salvation; yet he left not his Disciples *comfortless*, but, as he *promised*, sent his *Spirit* publickly and eminently upon the

Acts 2.
John 20. 21.

Twelve principal *Apostles*, whom he had formerly chosen, and appointed, in *his*, and *his Fathers Name*, to *Preach* the *Gospel*; to whom he gave the *Keys* of the *Kingdom of Heaven*, as to the *Stewards* and chief *Deputies*, or *Ministers* of his houshold in his absence; instructing them, what to do; on what *foundation* of *faith* in

ἐδόθη μοι πᾶσα ἐξουσία, All Authority, *i.e. Legitima potentia.*
Matth. 28. 18, 19, 20.
Mark 16. 15.

him, to build his Church; by what *Sacramental seals* to confirm believers; giving them *full power* and *commission*, to go into all the world, by *Teaching* and *Baptising* to make *Disciples*; confirming this *power* to them, by *breathing* on them, and conferring farther *Ministerial gifts* of the *Spirit* upon them; promising also to be *with them to the end of the world*, which could not be meant of their *persons*, who soon died, but of their *successors* in that *Office* and *Ministry*; that the same *power*, *authority*, and *assistance*, should be with them, in that holy way, to which he thus ordeined and sent them, by a *divine charter*, and *durable commission*. After all this, for further publication of this great *Authority* and *Ministerial power*, given to the *Apostles*, and their *Successors*; and for the confirmation of it, both

John 14. 17.
Acts 2.

to their own *consciences*, and to all the world, the *holy Spirit*, as was *promised*, came upon them in the shape of *fiery cloven tongues*, filling them with *miraculous gifts*, and all *Ministerial power*, both extraordinary in their persons, and ordinary, derivable to their *Successors*; such, as the wisdom of *Christ* thought most fit, both for the first planting of the Church with miraculous gifts, attending the Ministry of the Gospel; and the after propagating of it, by the same Ministry, confirmed by the constancy of the *Martyrs* and *Confessors*, which were in stead of *daily miracles*.

This whole *frame*, *polity*, and *divine constitution*, of the *order*, *power*, and *Ministry*, that should succeed *Christ Jesus* in his Church, was no other, than the proper effects of *Christs prophetick power*, and *wisdom*, for the instructing his Church; an *act* or *ordinance* of his *Kingly power*, for the governing of it; and a fruit of his *Priestly power*, and *care*, for a *right Liturgy*, or *officiating*, to be continued in his Church; thus furnishing it with an *holy Succession* of *Evangelical Priests* and *Ministers*, in his *name* and *authority*, who might

always

always *teach*, *guide*, and *govern*; also supplicate for, consecrate and offer holy things with the faithful, and for them, namely, the *sacrifices of prayers*, *thanksgiving*, and *praises*; especially, that *Eucharistical* memorial of that one *great oblation* of himself once made, on the *Altar* of the *Cross*, for the *Redemption* of the World; which is the great *accomplishment* of the *Jewish Prophecies*, the *abolishing* of their *Types* and *Ceremonies*, the main *foundation* of the *Christians Religion*, and the chief subject of that *Evangelical Ministry*, which *Jesus Christ* himself hath thus evidently instituted and sealed in his Church; For whose sake, he hath given those *Ministerial gifts*, with a distinct *power* and *authority*; making some (not all) either *Apostles*, or *Prophets*, or *Evangelists*, or *Pastors* and *Teachers*, *For the perfecting of the Saints*, *for the work of the Ministry*, *for the edifying of the Body of Christ*, &c. And this, by as *manifest a distinction*, both for gifts, and place, and use, as is in the *parts of the body*, between the eyes and the hands, the head and the feet; So that all are not *Apostles*, nor *Prophets*, nor *Teachers*, that are *Believers*, and *Members* of the *Body of Christ* his Church; no more than every part is an eye in the natural body; however it partake of the *same Soul*, as Believers do of the *same Spirit*, yet in different manifestations; of which difference of gifts and office, those onely are to judge, whom the Spirit of Christ hath enabled with gifts, and indued successively in the Church, with power from Christ to judge *of them*, and accordingly to *invest them*, by *solemn* and *holy ordination*, into the *orderly power* of *exercising* those *gifts*, which they are judged to have received from the Spirit of Christ, for the good of the Church, both for *Instruction*, and for *Government* of it. Without which divinely-constituted Order and Office of Ministry began in Christ, by him derived to the Apostles, and by them, and their successors constantly and duly observed to these days, the Church of Christ had long ere this been a *monster made up of confused excrescencies*; a very heap and huddle of Ignorance, Heresies, Schisms, all maner of erroneous blindness, and extravagant madness; like those mishapen prodigies, which we may often see among those, who having cast off the lawful succession, the sacred and antient order of the Ministry, do in their varieties exceed, even the mixtures and productions of *Africa*.

Heb. 9. 14. & 10. 12.

Eph. 4. 11, 12. 1 Cor. 12. 4, 5, 21, 28.

Vers. 29.

1 Cor. 12. 6, 7.

1 Cor. 14. 32. The spirits of the Prophets, are subject to the Prophets. V. 33. For God is not the Author of confusion, &c.

After *Christs Ascension*, we have no less evidence of Scripture, for the undoubted *practise* of the *blessed Apostles*, when they had by a *divine lot*, first filled up that place and part of the Ministry, from which *Judas* had faln, *Acts* 1. 25. For having received power Ministerial immediately from Christ, they did, duly, conscientiously, orderly, and effectually fulfil their own Ministry; and also took care to ordain others that might do so too, both in their times, and after

5. *The Apostles ordain and command other to ordain Ministers.*

 them;

them; distributing their own labors into several Countreys, and to several sorts of people; some to the *Circumcision* of the *Jews*, others to those of the uncircumcised *Gentiles*; Among whom they exercised their *Office* and *Ministry*, not *arbitrarily* and *precariously*; but as a *trust* and *duty*, of necessity, out of conscience, and with all divine power, authority, and fidelity; as *Ambassadors* from Christ, for God; as *Heralds*, as *Angels*, or *Messengers* sent from God; as *Laborers* together with God in his *Husbandry* the *Church*; as *Woers* and *Espousers*, having *Commission* or *Letters* of credence, to treat of and make up a *marriage*, and *espousals*, between Christ and the Church; which *sacred office* of *trust* and *honor*, none without *due authority* delegated to him from Christ, might perform, any more, than *Haman* might presume to court Queen *Esther*, before the King *Ahasuerus*.

Gal. 2.7. 2 Cor. 5. 20. As Ambassadors for Christ, as though God did beseech you by us; we pray you in Christs stead, be ye reconciled to God. 1 Cor. 3. 9. 2 Cor. 11. 2. Esth. 7. 8. Eph. 4. 11.

During these *Primitive* times of the Apostles Ministry of the *Gospel*, before they had finished their *mortal pilgrimage*, we read them *careful* to ordain *Presbyters* in every City and Church, to give them charge of their *Ministry*, to fulfil it; of their *flocks* to feed and guide them, in Christs way, both for truth and orders, over whom the *Lord* had made them *over-seers* by the Apostles appointment; who, not onely thus ordained others to succeed them immediately; but gave command, as from the *Lord*, to these (as namely to *Timothy* and *Titus*) to take great care for an *holy succession* of Ministers; such as should be apt to teach; able, and faithful men; to whom they should commit the Ministry of the *Word of life*, so as the Word, or Institution of Christ, might be kept *unblamable*, *till the coming of Jesus Christ*, 1 *Tim*. 6. 14. by an *holy order* and *office* of *Ministers*, duly ordained, with the *solemn imposition* of hands; as a visible token to men of the *peculiar designiation* of them, and no others but those, to this *Office* and *Function*; who must attend on the *Ministry*, give an account of their charge, and care of souls to *God*.

Acts 14. 23. And when they had ordained them Presbyters in every Church, in *Lystra*, *Iconium*, *Antioch*, &c. Acts 20. 28. Take heed to your selves, and to all the flock, over which the holy Ghost hath made you Bishops, or overseers, to feed the Church of God, &c. *Pauls* speech to the Presbyters of the Church of *Ephesus*. V. 17.

Thus we finde, beyond all dispute, for *Three Generations* after Christ, (First, in the Apostles; secondly, from them to others (by name to *Timothy* and *Titus*;) thirdly, from them to others; by them to be ordained *Bishops* and *Deacons*,) the *holy Ministry* instituted by Christ, is carried on in an *orderly succession*, in the same *Name*, with the same *Authority*, to the same *holy ends* and *offices*; as far as the *History* of the *New Testament* extends, which is not above

1 Tim. 3. & 5. 22. Lay hands (i. e.) by way of ordination to the Ministry. 2 Tim. 2. 2. The things thou hast heard of me, commit thou the same to faithful men; who shall be able to teach others also. Tit. 1. 5. I left thee in *Crete*, that thou shouldst ordain Elders in every City, as I had appointed thee. *Non tam solicitus de cura Timothei, sed propter successores ejus; ut exemplo Timothei ecclesiæ ordinationem custodirent.* Ambr. in 1 Tim. 6.

thirty

thirty years after Christs Ascension: And, we have, after all these, the next Succession, testifying the minde of the *Lord*, and the *Apostles*. *Clemens*, the Scholar of Saint *Paul*, mentioned *Phil.* 4. 3. who in his divine Epistle testifies, That the Apostles ordained every where the first-fruits, or prime Believers, for *Bishops* and *Deacons*, *Pag.* 54. And *pag.* 57. the Apostles appointed (τὰς ἐπινομὰς) distinct Offices, as at present, (ὅπως ἐὰν κοιμηθῶσιν) That when these slept with the *Lord*, others, tried and approved men, should succeed and execute their (λειτουργίαν) *holy Ministry*; than which testimony, nothing can be more evident: After that, he blames the *Corinthians* for raising *sedition*, for one or two mens sake, against all the *Presbytery*, *Pag.* 62. And exhorts at last, *Let the flock of Christ be at peace with the Presbyters ordained to be over it*, (μετὰ τῶν καθεσταμένων πρεσβυτέρων.) So after, *Be subject to the Presbyters, &c.*

Thus the excellent methods of Christs grace, and wisdom toward his Church appear, as to this *peculiar Office*, and *constant Function* of the *Evangelical Ministry*, commanding men to work *the work of God*, that they may have eternal life, *John* 6. 29. which is to *believe in him, whom the Father hath sent, sealed, and anointed with full power, to suffer, to satisfie, to merit, to fulfil all Righteousness*; Also to declare and confirm this to his Church; constantly teaching, guiding, and sanctifying it: He hath (for this end) taken care, that *faithful, able*, and *credible* men, should be ordained in an holy, constant succession, to *bear witness* or *record* of him to all posterity; that so others might, by *hearing*, believe; without which, ordinarily they cannot, *Rom.* 10. 14, 15. Nor can they hear with regard, or in prudence give credit, and honor to the speaker; or obey with conscience the things spoken, unless the *Preacher* be such an one, as *entreth in by the door*, John 10. 1. *into the sheepfold*; such as is *sent by God*, either immediately as the Apostles, or mediately as their Successors, from them and after them; who could never have preached and suffered with that *confidence*, *conscience*, and *authority*, unless they had been conscious, that they were rightly *sent of God*, and *Christ*: At whose Word onely this *great company of Preachers* were sent into the world; who so mightily in a short time prevailed, as to perswade men, every where to believe, a report *so strange*, so *incredible*, so *ridiculous*, so *foolish* to *flesh* and *blood*, and to the *wisdom of the world*.

Rom. 10. 14, 15. Psal. 68. 11. Isai. 53. 1. 1 Cor. 1. 18.

6. *Distinct Characters and Notes of the Ministerial Office.* John 15. 19.

Thus far then the *tenor* of the whole *New Testament*, (and that one Apostolike Writer *Clemens*) witnesseth, that as *Jesus Christ*, the *great Prophet*, and *chief Shepherd*, 1 *Pet.* 5. 4. was sent, and impowred with all *power* from the *Father*, to carry on the *great work* of saving sinners, by gathering them *out of the world*, into the fold and bosom of his Church; So he did this, and will ever be doing it, till

Mat.28.20. till his *comming again*, by ordeining and continuing such means and *Ministry*, as he saw fittest, to bring men into, and to guide them in, the wayes of *saving truth*, of Religious orders and of holy lives; Investing (as we have seen) particular persons whose names are recorded, with peculiar power, to teach, to gather, to feed, and govern his Church, by Doctrine, by Sacraments, and by holy Discipline; Setting those men in peculiar relations and Offices to his Church, as *Fathers*, *Stewards*, Bishops, Shepheards, *Rulers*, Watchmen; *calling them by peculiar* names, and distinct titles, as light of the world, *Salt of the earth*, Mat.5.13. *Fishers of men*, Mat.4.19. *Stars in his right hand*, Rev.2.1. *Angels of the Churches*: Requiring of them *peculiar duties*, as to Preach the word in *season* and *out of season*; to feed *his Lambs* and Sheep; to *fulfill the work of their* Ministry; to *take care of the* flock; against grievous *Wolves*, false teachers; to stop their mouths, *Tit*.1.11. to exhort, command and rebuke with all authority, *Tit*.2.15. to do their work, *as workmen that need* not to be ashamed, 2 *Tim*.2.15. as those that must give an account of their Ministry, and the souls committed to their care and charge by God and the Church. Adorns them also with *peculiar privileges*; promises and *speciall assistances*; takes care for peculiar *maintenance*, 1 *Cor*.9.9,19. and *double honour* to be given them, by all true Christians, 1 *Tim*.5.17. and encourageth them in a work of so great pains, exact care, and consciencious diligence, which must expect to meet alwaies (as now it doth) with much opposition, and *contradiction of sinners*; promising to them speciall *degrees* of glory, and more *ponderous Crowns* of eternall rewards in Heaven.

Joh.21.15. Feed my Lambs; my Sheep. Acts 20.28. Ποιμαίνειν. To feed as Shepheards, the flock. 1 Pet. 5. 2. 1 Cor. 4. 4. Let a man so account of us as the Ministers of Christ, and Stewards of the mysteries of God, *&c.* 2 Tim.4.1,2. 2 Tim.4.5. Acts 20.29. 1 Tim 4.11. Mat.28.*ult.* Heb.13.14. Obey them that have the rule over you, and submit your selves; for they watch for your souls, as they that must give an account, *&c.* Luke 12.43. Blessed is that servant (the faithfull and wise Steward set over the house-hold) whom his Master comming shall find so doing. Dan.12.3. 1 Cor.9.17. If I do this willingly, I have a reward, *&c.*

1 Cor.12.29. Are all Apo. are all Prophets? are all Teachers? *&c.* 1 Cor.9.16. Though I Preach the Gospell I have nothing to glory of (as supererogating) for necessity is layd upon me, yea woe is unto me, if I Preach not the Gospell.

By all which, and many others which might be added, the *Demonstration* is clear as the *Sun at Noon day*, to all that are not wilfully blind, That some, and not all, in the Church; and these, not arbitrary and occasionall, but *chosen* and *ordeined persons*, are sent *in a succession* from Christ, in his name, and by vertue of this divine mission, speciall authority, and ordination, to the care, service, and work of the Ministry; they are bound in the highest *bonds of conscience*, to *the glory of God*, and the *salvation of their own*, and others souls, under a dreadfull *woe and curse* of being *guilty* of their souls damnation, who perish by their neglect, to attend diligently, to discharge faithfully, and couragiously, as in the name and authority of Jesus Christ the Lord of glory, this *great* and *dreadfull imployment of the Ministry*, which Angels would not undertake

dertake, without they were sent; nor if sent, without some horror: To which no earthen vessels are *of themselves sufficient*; but through the grace of God, they are made *able and faithfull*, 1 *Tim*.1.12. and being such are both successefull, and accepted; while they give themselves wholy to this *work*; not *entangling themselves* with other incomberances, but devoting the whole latitude of time, parts, studies, gifts, to this *business* of *saving* souls; and this, not in popular and precarious wayes, or only upon grounds of charity; but with all just confidence of having *that authority* with them, as well as *necessity upon* them, which makes them bold in the Lord; that they *cannot but speak* the things for which they have received power and commission from Christ, by the Ordination and appointment of the Governours and guides of the Church, who formerly had received the same power; To which none can, without high impudence, blasphemy, and impiety pretend, who are conscious to themselves, to have received no *such authority* from Christ; either *immediatly*, or in that one *mediate* way of successive ordination, by which he *hath appointed* it to be derived to posterity: which, I have already proved, cannot by any shew of Scripture, no more than in any way of reason and order, becomming Religion, be found to have any other way, than by those that are in orders as Ministers: neither is it intrusted with the community of people among Christians, nor left to every private mans pleasure.

Onus & opus ipsis angelicis formidandum humeris. Bern. 2 Cor.2.16. Who is sufficient for these things? i.e. to speak the word of God, as of God, in the sight of God, in Christ, *i.e.* of sincerity. 2 Tim.2.4. 2 Tim.4.13, 14,15,16. Acts 4.19.20. The Epistle of *Paul* to *Tim.* and *Tit.* are the constant Canons and divine injunctions for the succession of Ministerial power by way of tryal, imposition of hands, prayer, *&c.*

As then some men are duly invested with *power ministeriall*, both to act in this power, and to confer it to others after them; and these only are commanded by the rule of Christ, by their duty or office, and by all bonds of conscience, to make a right use of this peculiar and divine power, for the Churches good; So are all *other men* whatsoever, not thus *duly ordeined*, and impowred, (though never so well gifted in themselves) forbidden, under the sins *of lying, falsity, disorderly* walking, *proud* usurpation, and arrogant *intrusion* of themselves into an holy office, *uncalled*, and unsent, either to take this office and Ministry of holy things on themselves, or to confer the power, which they never received, on others; which neither *Melchisedeck*, nor *Moses*, nor *Aaron*, nor *Samuel*, nor any of the Prophets; nor *the Lord* Jesus Christ, nor the *blessed* Apostles, nor any *Evangelist*; or any true Bishop or Presbyter, nor any holy men, *succeeding them*, did ever take to themselves, either as to the whole, or any part of that power and Ministry, not so much as to be a Deacon, but still attended the Heavenly call, and *mission*,

7. *None can be true Ministers, but such as are rightly ordeined.*

Heb.5.1. Every high Priest taken from among men is ordeined for men in things pertaining to God, *&c.* 4. No man taketh this honour to himself, but he that is called of God as was *Aaron*, &c. 5. Christ also glorified not himself to be made an high Priest, *&c.*

eithe,

Luke 12.42. Who then is a faithfull and wise Steward, whom the Lord shall make ruler over his houshold, to give them their portion in due season? 43. Blessed, *&c.*

either *immediatly*, (which was confirmed by *miracles*, and speciall *revelations* or predictions,) or *mediatly*, in such an order and method of succession, as the Lord of the Church, who is *not a God of confusion*, hath appointed, and to this day preserved: who otherwayes would have left his Church short of that blessing, of orderly Government, and Officers appointed for holy ministrations, which is necessary in every society, and which no *wise man*, that is Master of any Family, doth omit to appoint and settle; especially in his personall absence; where he governs by a visible derived and delegated authority given to others; as Christ now doth his Church, as to the extern order and dispensation of holy things.

1 Tim. 3.15. If I tarry long, that thou mayst know how thou oughtest to behave thy self in the house of God, *&c.*

Peoples duty.

Quomodo valebit homo secularis sacerdotis magisterium adimplere, cujus nec officium tenuit, nec disciplinam agnovit? Isid. Hisp. off. l. 2. c. 5.

ὁ λαϊκὸς ἄνθρωπος τοῖς λαϊκοῖς προστάγμασι δέδεται. The Lay-man is bound up by Lay commands to keep his rank and order. *Cl. ep. pag.* 53.

Nor can, saith he, the Presbyters be cast out or degraded without a great sin. Pag. 57. ἁμαρτία οὐ μικρὰ ἡμῖν ἔσται, *&c.*

Exors officii, exors solatii, & præmii, Is. Hisp.

Matth. 16.18. Eph. 2. 20. Heb 6. 2.

The *duty of all faithfull people* (in which bounds their comforts are conteined) are no less distinct and evidently confined, in the order of Christs Church; which are, diligently to attend, *humbly* to obey, *Heb.* 13.17. thankfully to own, *respect*, *love*, esteem and honor, 1 *Cor.* 9.11. 1 *Thes.* 5.12,13. liberally to *requite* the doctrine and labors of the true and faithful Ministers, 1 *Tim.* 5.17. who are thus over them in the Lord, in a right way and succession of Ministeriall Office *divinely instituted*, and constantly derived authority. In the perpetuating of which, to so many *centuries of years*, since Christs Ascension, by *Lawfull and uninterrupted* succession in his Church, the power and providence of God is *not less* remarkably seen, than in the preservation of the *Scriptures*, amidst all persecution, confusions, and variations of humane affairs. Also the love and care of Christ to his Church, the fidelity of his promise is evident: being no less made true *to the Ministry*, than to the whole Church, to be with them to the end of the world: and by the *Ministry* that is made good to the whole Church, that *the Gates of Hell shall not prevail* against the *foundations* of the Church; which are laid upon the *writings*, and by the *labours* of the *Prophets* and *Apostles*; and after them still layed and preserved by able, faithfull, and ordeined Ministers; The consecrating or ordeyning of whom by the Imposition or laying on of hands in a continued succession for the good of the Church, is reckoned by the holy Author of the Epistle to the *Hebrews* among the principles and foundations of Christian Religion; joyned with doctrines of Faith, Repentance, Baptism, Resurrection, and eternal judgement; for other meaning of the ἐπιθέσεως χειρῶν Imposition of hands, I find not by Scripture practise, or the Church afterward, so clear and constant as this in Ordination to an holy Ministry. Nor can Confirmation be rightly done to the Baptised and Catechised, but by those who are ordeined.

That

That to deny the *Ordination* and due *succession* of Ministers, by which to carry on the work of Christ in his Church; or to seek to overthrow it in any Church, is all one, as if men should deny those grand and fundamentall points of Faith, Repentance, Resurrection, and judgement, to have been taught by Christ; or Baptism to have been instituted; that to overthrow and abolish the constant Ministry and Office in the Church, can be the design of none, but those, who care not to turn *Infidels*, and to live in all Atheistical profaness.

If then, there be any force or authority from Scriptures as the Oracles of God, to prove by precept, institution, or example, the religious necessity of any *peculiar duties*, or *holy Offices*, and divine Ministrations, by which men are made Christians, and distinguished as the Church of Christ from the world; if the Preaching the word of life, the teaching of the histories, the opening of the mysteries, the urging the precepts, the denouncing of the terrors, the offering the promises, the celebrating the Sacraments; the binding to wrath, and shutting up to condemnation, all unbelievers and impenitents; the *loosing* of penitents and opening Heaven to them, by the knowledge of Law or Gospell; if these or any other *holy ministrations* be necessary, not to the well-being only, but the *very being* of a Church Christian; Sure there there is (as I have shewed) no less strength, pregnancy, and concurrent Scripture clearness, to convince, and confirm, the *peculiar office*, divine *power* and *function of the* Evangelicall *Ministry*; Without which all those ministrations must needs have ceased long agoe, as to any notion or conscience among men, of holy, divine and Christian; that is the appointments, institutions, messages, or orders of Jesus Christ; which could never carry any such marks of divine credit and authority, meerly from vulgar credulity and forwardness of reception; or from generall common talk and tradition among men, if there had been no peculiar men appointed by God, in his name and by his Commission, to hold forth to the world this great salvation; to convince, or convert, or leave men without excuse; As there can be no valid message, autoritative *Embassie*, credible *assignment* or *conveyance*, of truth, promise, command, duty, comfort, bounty, or love to others, where there is only a *generall* fame and *unauthorised* report; without any speciall Messenger, *Embassador*, *Assigner*, and *Conveyer*; to the authority of whose speech, and actions, or conveyances, not any mans own forwardness, nor others easiness, and credulity doth suffice; but some peculiar characters, Seals and evidences, by letters of credence, or other sure and known tokens of a truly assigned and really derived authority, do give ground to believe, or *power* to validate, what any man so performeth, not in his own name, or for his own interests, but to an others; who principally *employs* him; and who only can make good, what he so far promiseth, or declareth, or sealeth, as he hath commission and authority from another so to do: No man that speaks or negotiates in anothers name, especially in matters of great consequence, of as high a nature, as life and death, can expect to be believed by *wise* and *serious men*; and that they should accordingly order both their affections, and all their affairs; unless they saw the marks of infallible authority; far beyond the confidence of a trivial *talker*, and a bad *orator*. In this point then of a *peculiar office* and *function* of the *Ministry Evangelical*, which is divinely instituted, in which, some men are *solemnly invested*; by which, all Religion is confirmed and preserved to the *Church*; We have, not onely full measure from *Christ* himself, and heaped up by *Apostolical precept* and *example*, evidently set forth in the *Scriptures*, and pressed down by *after Histories* of the *Church*, in a constant *succession*; but it is also *running over* by those necessary accumulations, which all *right reason*, *order*, and *prudence*, do liberally suggest, both in the Theory, and the Practick.

8. *The peculiar Office of the Ministry confirmed by Reason.*

For, first, no man by any *natural capacity*, or *acquired ability* as a *reasonable Creature*, is bound in conscience, to be a *Minister* of the *Gospel*, and *holy Mysteries* to others; for then, all men and women too ought to be such, or else they sin.

Secondly, Nor yet by any *civil* and *politick capacity*, as living in any *Society*, or *City*, can any man be obliged to direct, and guide others in the things of God; since, that *relation* invests no man in any *civil power*, *office*, or *authority*, until the *supreme fountain* of *civil power* calls him to the place, and endues him with such power; much less, can it put any into an authority, which is *divine*, *spiritual*, and *supernatural*; to act, as in Gods and Christs name, and to higher ends, than *humane*.

3. Nor thirdly, doth any *religious common capacity*, as a *believer*, or a *Christian*, or as endued with *gifts* and *graces*, furnish any one with *Ministerial power*, and lay that duty on him; for then every Christian, great and small, yong and old, man and woman, ought to *minister holy things* to others; to challenge the *Keys of Heaven* to themselves; to be as in Christs stead, to rule and oversee his house; which cannot avoide, as the *Apostle* proves, abominable absurdities, and detestable confusions; no way beseeming the *wisdom* of *Christ*, the *majesty of Christian Religion*, or that *order* and *decency* which ought to be in *Church-Assemblies*; being as contrary to reason, as if *every servant* in an house should challenge the power of the *Keys*, and the *Stewards* place; or every member, the office of the eyes, tongue, and hands, by vertue of that common relation it hath, (as well as these parts) to the same body, the same soul and head.

1 Cor. 12. 25, 29. Are all Apostles? are all Prophets? are all Teachers, &c. 18. All are not, nor are any such as they are Christians or gracious, &c. 1. Cor. 12.

As

As then *right reason* tells us, beyond all reply, That neither natural, nor civil, nor religious, common gifts, endowments, or abilities instate any person in the office of *Magistrate, Judge, Ambassador, Herald, Notary*, or *publick Sealer*, (which places require, not onely *personal sufficiencies* for the office; but an *orderly designation* and *induction* to it, from the *fountain* of *civil power*, either mediately or immediately:) The same *right reason* (which is most agreeable and servient to true *Christian Religion*) requires a *right derivation*, or *conveyance*, of all *supernatural, Ministerial, Church power* (which is in, and from *Jesus Christ*, as the *sole supreme head*, and *divine origin* of it) either immediately, as they and none others had, to whom *Christ* first consigned it, and both by miraculous gifts and works confirmed it to be in them; or mediately, as those *Bishops* and *Presbyters* had it, who without *force, fraud*, or any *sinister way* of *usurpation*, or *bold intrusion*, received this *power* from the *Apostles*, by *prayer* and *benediction*, with imposition of their hands, *in the name of Christ*; and from them, their *successors* have lawfully derived it (without interruption) to the true Ministers of the *Gospel*, even to this day (as I have proved;) which not onely the *Scriptures*, of undisputable *verity*, but even those other, very *credible Histories* of the *Church*, and other *Records* of *learned* and *holy Men* in all ages to these times, which the *providence* of *God* hath afforded us, do abundantly declare; all which to deny, with a *morose perverseness*, or *rustical indifferency*, is, as if a *Hog* should answer all arguments with *grunting*. And to act contrary to so strong a stream of concurrent *Authorities*, both as to the judgment and practise of the *Church* in all ages, is a work onely fit for *Ranters*, and *Seekers*, and *Fanaticks*; or for *Jews, Turks*, and *Heathen Infidels*, but not for any *sober Christian* that owns in the least kinde, the Name of *Jesus Christ*; or desires to be a member of any true *Christian Church*: In which, as all true and humble Christians have always enjoyed, and with thankfulness owned the *rightful succession* and *authority* of their *ordained Ministers, Pastors*, and *Teachers*; so the *Lord* from Heaven, in all ages, hath witnessed to them; by his *blessings* of *truth* and *peace*, on the hearts of his people, and by their means chiefly continuing the light of the *Gospel*, to these days, amidst those *Heathenish persecutions*, *Heretical confusions*, and *Schismatical fractions*, which have sought to overthrow, the *Being*, or the *Purity*, or the *Order* and *Unity* of the *true Church*.

To this judgment and testimony of *Scriptures*, and antient *Writers* (both in *right* and *fact*) I might adde a *cloud of witnesses*,

Fraus est & injuria quicquid agitur sub alterius persona, sine debita ab illo autoritate. Reg. Jur.

Matth. 28 18. All power (πᾶσα ἐξουσία) or authority is given unto me in Heaven, and in Earth; that is, in order to perfect Christs design, his Churches good.

Acts 1. 8.

Autoritas delegata, ab alterius voluntate pendet; tam quoad ipsam potestatam, quam ad derivandi modum. Reg. Jur.

1 Cor. 4. 19. I will know, not the speech of them that are puffed up, but the power. V. 20. For the Kingdom of God is not in word, but in power. *i. e.* That holy polity and orderly Kingdom, which Jesus Christ hath set up and governs in his Church, is not managed by confident praters, but by authoritative Preachers. Matth. 7. 28. As Christ Jesus, so his true Ministers teach and administer holy things, as men having authority, and not as the Scribes.

from later *reformed Divines*, which were very learned and very *holy men*, far above the *vulgar spirits*, both in other *Churches*, and in this of *England*, all agreeing with our excellent Bishop *Jewel*; That no may may intrude himself into the *Ministry* by his own will and pleasure; or by any others, who are not of that *Order* and *Calling*; but he ought to be lawfully called, and duly ordained by those, in whom the *lawful succession* of *ordinative power*, ever hath been, and still is rightly placed and continued. Agreeable to which, there is a whole *Jury* of *eminent Modern Divines*, alleged by a late industrious and ingenuous * *Author*, who hath spared me that pains.

Bishop *Jewels* Apology. *Ministrum Ecclesiæ legitimè vocari oportere, & rectè atque ordine præfici ecclesiæ Dei: Neminem autem ad sacrum Ministerium pro suo arbitrio ac libidine posse se intrudere.*

* See Master *Halls* Pulpit guarded.

9. *The Priestly order among the Jews.*

Joel 2. 17.

Θεῖόν τι χρῆμα ἡ ἱερωσύνη καὶ ἀνθρώπινον. Nissl. de vita Mos. & Aronis Virga.

τῆς θείας καὶ τῆς ἀνθρωπίνης φύσεως μέσον ἱερωσύνη. Is. Pel. l. 3. ep. 20.

Philo. Judæus, de sacerdotio Aaronis, calls it, γέρας ἐξαίρετον, οὐκ ἐπίγειον ἀλλ' ὀλύμπιον κτῆμα.

Numb. 16.
Exod. 19. 6.
2 Chro. 26 20. *Uzziah* ceased to be fit to rule as a King, being smitten with Leprosie, who usurped the office of the Priest.
1 King. 13. 33.

4. I may adde by way of confirmation of that *common equity*, and *rules of order*, which must be among men in all things; and most necessarily in things *truly religious*, The *inviolable Function*, and *peculiar Office* or *Order* of the *Priests* and *Levites*; which were the Ministers of the *Lord*, in his *antient Church* of the *Jews*; which is a most convincing instance, to prove not the *sameness* and *succession* of that *Order*, but the *equity*, *comliness*, and *exemplariness* of a *peculiar Ministry*, for holy things, among Christians under the *Gospel*; since that *Levitical Ministry* was not more holy, or honorable, nor more distinguished in power, and authority, and office from the people, than this in the Christian Church; which is more immediately derived from Christ, as clearly instituted and ordained by him, and more fully exhibitive of him, both in the Historical Truths, and in the Mystical gifts and graces of his *Spirit*: Yet we see, who so despised or violated that Order and Ministry among the *Jews*, under pretence of a *common holiness* in *Gods people*, (who were in a spiritual sense indeed called an *holy Nation* and a *royal Priesthood*) so as to confound the Functions and Offices, divinely distinguished, either the earth from beneath devoured them, or some other remarkable judgement fell upon them, as on King *Uzzah*; So long, as Gods love to the *Jews* was seconded with his *jealousie* for their good. When (indeed) their *Apostacies* and *Rebellions* had alienated Gods love from them, he then suffered those *sad* and *unsanctified levellings* to come among them, consecrating *the meanest of the people*, and who ever would relieve his worldly necessities, by being a Priest to those *Talismanick Calves*; under which *new modes* and *figurations*, the *Israelites* were for some wicked *reason of State*, perswaded by *Jeroboam* to worship their God. So *Herod* when he had got the Kingdom over the *Jews*, (*ex ima & infima plebe constituit sacerdotes*) made of the basest people Priests, *&c.* Euseb. *Hist. l.* 1. *c.* 7. Which severe indulgence of God to them, in suffering them to have

such

ſuch ſorry and unſanctified Prieſts, was no other, but a *fearful preſaging* of thoſe *deſolations*, which ſoon after befel that people of *Iſrael* for the ſins of *Jeroboam*; who by his policy of new faſhioned Prieſts, and *levelled*, that is, aboliſhed, and profaned Religion, is for ever branded with that mark of *making Iſrael to ſin*, and was the occaſion of cutting off his name, and deſtroying his poſterity from off the face of the earth. Certainly, in times, when the *Jews* feared God, if all the Prieſts and Levites, whom God had appointed to miniſter before him, had *failed by death*, or *defection*, the *Ark in the Wilderneſs* muſt have ſtood ſtill, or the *ſervice of the Temple* have ceaſed, till by ſome new Commiſſion or Authority, the *Lord* had ſignified his pleaſure to his Church and people: Nor would the devout and zealous *Jews* have thought preſently, every ſtout *Porter*, or luſty *Butcher*, would well enough ſupply the room of the *Prieſts* and *Levites*; much leſs would they have beat and crouded the true Prieſts yet living, and ſerving in their offices and courſes, out of their places, onely becauſe thoſe others had *naturally ſhoulders*, which could bear the *Ark* and the *holy Veſſels*; or *hands*, which had ſkill to *ſlay a beaſt*, and *dreſs a ſacrifice*. I ſee no reaſon, why the *Evangelical Miniſtry* ſhould be leſs ſacred or inviolable, ſince it hath as much of *reaſon*, *order*, *uſefulneſs*, and *neceſſity*; alſo no leſs expreſs *authority* from Chriſt, and *divine Inſtitution*; together with many hundreds of years holy and conſtant ſucceſſion in all Churches: That to invade this, or violate and abrogate it, ſeems no leſs to any true Chriſtian, than to croud Chriſt out of his throne; to juſtle him out of his *Prieſtly*, *Prophetick*, and *Kingly Offices*: It is like *Julian* the Apoſtate, loudly to blaſpheme, or proudly to reſiſt, and inſolently to do deſpight too that *holy Spirit* of *truth*, *power*, and *order*; by which, theſe (χαρίσματα) gifts of power, and authority Miniſterial, have always been, and are ſtill given and diſpenced to his Church, in the way which Chriſt appointed; which the holy Apoſtles practiſed, and the Chriſtian Churches have always imitated.

1 King. 13. 34.

Θεῖόν τι χρῆμα ἡ ἱερωσύνη καὶ τῶν ὄντων ἁπάντων τιμιώτατον. If. Pel. l. 4.

5. I might yet adde the *common notions* and *univerſal dictates* of all mankinde; who, by the *light of nature*, and that *innate veneration* of ſome *Deity*, which they eſteemed the *inventer* and *inſtitutor* of their *Religion*, agreed always in this; That, whatever *Gods* or *Religions* they owned, their *holy Rites* and *Myſteries* were always publickly taught, celebrated, and maintained, by ſuch as were *ſolemnly inveſted* with, and reverenced under the *peculiar name* and *honor* of that *ſacred Office*, and *ſacerdotal Function*, which they held divine, as *Herodotus* tells us; which (οὐδεὶς ἀμυηθεὶς) none not *initiated*, or not *conſecrated* by the wonted Ceremonies, might profanely uſurp:

10. *Light of Nature in the Heathens.*

Diis proximi ſunt Deorum ſacerdotes. Tul.

ἱερωσύνη τάγμα τι θεῖον. Herod. Euterp.

Plutarch tells us, both among *Romans* and *Greeks*, they generally in all Cities paid great *honor* and *respect* to their Priests and holy men; because those obtained of the gods good things, not onely for themselves, and their families, but for the whole Cities where they lived. *Tacitus* tells us, That the cheif Priests were also, by the Divine Munificence esteemed the chiefest of men, least subject to anger, envy, or other mean affections from any men: So *Aul. Gellius* sets down at large the *solemnities* and *honors* for *vestments* and other regards, which among the *Romans* was used toward the *Flamines Diales*, or *chief Priests*; whom they esteemed next their gods, whose word was always to be taken without any oath; they thought all holy things profaned, if any men unsacred presumed to meddle with them, or partake of them; much more, if such an one officiated in them.

Plutarch. Moral. p. 778. τοῖς ἱερεῦσιν αἰτοῦσι καὶ τιμῶσιν αἱ πόλεις εἰμαρμένα, ἐπὶ τ' ἀγαθὰ παρὰ τῶν θεῶν, οὐ μόνον αὐτοῖς καὶ φίλοις καὶ οἰκείοις, ἀλλὰ κοινῇ πᾶσιν αἰτεῖσθαι τοῖς πολίταις.
Tac. Ann. l. 3.
A. Gellius. l. 3. c. 15.

It cannot be any thing of true Christian piety or holiness, which makes any men in the *Church* of *Christ* degenerate from the very *principles of nature*; whose light is never despised by any, but those, that are *without natural affections*, among other their black Characters, which are proper to those, *who have a form of godliness, but deny the power of it*; The strangest prodigies that ever were indeed, of so *profane a wantonness*, under pretences of *enlarged piety*; striving to remove all bounds of duty, and respect to God or man; nor did ever sober men think themselves absolved from that honor and respect, which is due to God and his *holy Service* or *Ministry*, because of the *personal infirmities* which may be seen in those that are his *Ministers* to us: We shall neither as men nor Christians, have any to serve God or man in the way of true Christian Religion, if we will allow none with their *failings*: The *Divine* is to be distinguished from the *Man*; there may be the *power of God* with the *weakness of man*, as in Saint *Paul*; Nor need we be more choise and curious, than God himself is.

Sacerdotes è rudibus indoctis & impolitis sacrandi non sunt quibus non datum est intelligere civilia, multo magis denegatum est disserere divina. Min. Fæl.
Sacerdotes Egyptii constituebant ex optimatibus tum genere tum scientia. Clem. Alex. στρω. 5.
ἱερατικὸς βίος τοῦ πολιτικοῦ σεμνότερος. Julian. Imp. epist.
Sacerdotalis vita politica Præstantior. τοῦ μὴ καθαρῷ καθαροῦ ἐφάπτεσθαι μὴ οὐ θεμιτὸν ᾖ. Plato. Phedo. …ἵνα ὡς ἱερὰ ὦσι βέβηλοι. In bello victores cum sint, solent omnes gentes, τῶν ἱερῶν φείδεσθαι. Clem. Al. 2 Tim. 3. 3. Ἀχάριστοι, ἀνόσιοι ἄστοργοι. Unthankful, unholy, without natural affections, disobedient, &c. 2 Cor. 4. 7, 11, 12. Earthen vessels, Death worketh in us, &c.

11. *A peculiar Office of Ministry, necessary for the Church.*

6. Nor is there a greater *benefit* and *conveniency* to the *Church*, than a *necessity* of having a *special calling* and *divine institution* of the *Ministers* of the *Gospel*; For we may not in this trust to the *good natures* and *good wills* of *Christians* in common, (if personal abilities and willingness would make a *Minister of Christ*, which they will not:) Certainly, no men are so *good natured* of themselves, (without hopes of gain or some benefit) as of their own good will, to undertake, and constantly to persevere in so hard and hazardous (besides so holy) a *service*,

vice, as this, of holding forth to a *vain, proud, carnal, hypocritical, persecuting*, and *devilish world*, so despicable and ridiculous a doctrine, as this of a *crucified Saviour* at first was, and still seems to the *natural*, or onely (ψυχικὸς) *rational man*; unless there were by the wisdom and authority of Christ, such ties of duty and calling laid upon some *mens consciences*, as, onely the *mission* and *mandate* of *God* can lay upon men; who are not naturally more disposed to go on Gods errand, than *Moses*, or *Jeremy*, or *Jonah* were: And however, now the peace, warmth, and serenity of times, hath made the Ministry of the *Gospel*, a matter of *covetousness*, or *popular ambition*, or *curiosity*, or *wantonness*, to many of these new *Preachers*, who with *rashness, levity*, and a kinde of *frolickness*, undertake that work, which the best men and Angels themselves, would not without much weeping (as Saint *Austine* that day when he was ordained a *Presbyter*) or with *fear* and *trembling* undertake; yet the *rigor* and *storms* of *primitive times* (it is very probable) would have *quenched* the now so *forward heats* and *flashes* of these mens spirits: When to *Preach* the *Gospel*, and to *preside*, as a *Bishop* or *Presbyter*, in the *Church*, was to expose a mans self to the *front* of *persecution*; to stand in the gap against the violent incursions of malicious men, and cruel devils; To be a Minister of *Jesus Christ*, was presently to forsake all, and to take up the Cross and follow *Christ*; to adopt, with *holy orders, famine* and *nakedness, banishment, prisons, beasts, racks, fires, torments, many deaths in one*; so that, unless there had been *divine authority enjoyning, power enabling*, and *special grace assisting*, the *Ordainers* in the Name of *Christ* sending, and so in conscience binding; together with gracious promises of a reward in Heaven, incouraging the *ordained*; doubtless, the glorious *Gospel* of *mans salvation*, had ere this been buried in oblivion; none had believed that report, nor heard of it, if none had dared to preach it; and none would of his own *good will*, have been so hardy, or prodigal of all *worldly interests, honor, liberty, safety, estate*, and *life*, as to adventure all *needlesly*, and *spontaneously*, on such a *message* to others, so unwonted, so unwelcome, so offensive to the ears and hearts of men, unless he had been conscious to a *special duty* laid upon him, by *divine authority*; which was always derived in that *holy* and *solemn Ordination*, which was the inauguration of Ministers to that *great* and *sacred Work*.

This indeed gave so great *confirmation* and *courage* to the *true* and *ordained Ministers* of the *Gospel*, that, *believing*, what they preached of a *crucified Saviour*; and knowing whose *work* it was, in whose *Name* they were *ordained*, by whose *power* they were *sent*,

Vera cruce digni qui crucifixum adorant. Insana religio. Cecil.

Exitiabilis superstitio. Tacit. Annal. l. 15.

παλλάδιον μωρίας (ὀλίγω δεῖν) ἀπάντα ἀνατρέπον. Julius Imp. ep. 7.

1 Cor. 2. 14.

Exitiabilis superstitio: Author ejus Christus, qui Tiberio imperante per procuratorem Pontium Pilatum supplicio affectus. Tac. l. 15. Annal.

Miranda, etiam pudenda credit christianus; cujus fides impudens esse debet. Tert. de Bapt.

Sacra sacrilegiis omnibus teriora. Cecil. de Christian.

Αἶρε τοὺς ἀθέους ζητείσθω Πολύκαρπος. Euseb. hist. l. 4. c. 14.

Else Christian Religion would have failed.

Multi barbarorum in Christum credunt sine charactere vel atramento scriptum habentes per Spiritum in cordibus suis salutem, & veterum traditionem diligenter custodientes, quam Apostoli tradiderunt iis quibus committebant ecclesias; cui ordinationi assentiunt multæ gentes. Iren. l. 4. c. 4.

to how *great ends* their *labors* were designed, even to *save souls*; they willingly bare the Cross of Christ, and counted it a *crown* and *honorary addition* to their *Ministry*, to be thought *worthy to suffer* for the Name of Christ; that what any of them wanted in the power of miracles, was made up in the wonder of their *patience*; when no *Armies*, no *State*, favored them, and both opposed them; when they had no temptations of getting a *better living* by preaching, than any other way; but rather losing of what they had; when they expected *few applauders* of their boldness and forwardness; many *persecutors* and *opposers* of their *consciencious endeavors* to do the *duty*, which Christ, by the Church, had laid on them; when they might not grow restive and lazy, and *knock off* when they pleased; but a *wo*, and a *necessity*, and an *heavy account*, to be given to the *great Pastor* of the Church, *Christ Jesus*, always sounded in their *ears*, and beat upon their *mindes*: These put them upon those *Heroick resolutions*, to endure all things for Christs sake, and the Churches sake, and the *good of those souls* committed to *their charge*. Nor did they *remit* their *care*, or slacken the conscience of their *duty*, in *preaching diligently* the *Gospel*, because of the *forwardness* and *seeming zeal* of those, that were *false Brethren* and *false Apostles*; who out of *envy*, or *spight*, or for *filthy lucre*, or any *vain-glory* among Christians, set up the *trade of preaching*, upon their own *stock of boldness*; without any *mission* from Christ, or those, to whom he had *delegated that power* to *ordain fit* and *able men*: Their seeming good will, and readiness to preach, did not free them from the brand of *false Apostles*, and *deceitful workers*; *Satans ministers*, and *messengers* sent to *buffet*, not to *build* the Church; *Wolves* in *sheeps clothing*, serving their *bellies*, and not the *Lord Christ*, or the Churches good; whose order and authority they despise: Nor can they be faithful to *Gods work*, unless they keep to his *word*; both, as to the *truths delivered*, and the *order prescribed*, and the *duties enjoyned*, and the *authority established*: Christ doth not onely provide food for his *family*; but *stewards* also, and *dispensers* of it, who may, and must see to give every one *their portion* in due season, rightly *dividing* the *Word of truth*; There is not onely *plenty*, but *order* and *government* in *Christs house*; nothing less becomes the *servants of Christ*, than this *sharking* and *scrambling way* of these *new men*, who will snatch and carve for themselves, and dispence to others, what, when, and how they list. It is justly to be feared, they are *theeves*, and come but to *steal* and *destroy*, who like not to *come in at Christs door*, but are thus *clambring* every where over the *wall*; and (confident of their numbers) dare to do it, not in the darkness of their *Night Conventicles*, but (as *Absaloms* incestuous rapes) at the *noon-day*, and in the eyes of this whole Church; to its great *grief* and *shame*, and to its

Acts 5. 41.

2 Tim. 2. 10. I endure all things for the elects sake, &c.

2 Cor. 11. & 12.

Phil. 1.

Tit. 1. 11.

1 Tim. 6. 5.

Rom. 16. 17. I beseech you Brethren mark them which cause divisions and offences, contrary to the doctrine which ye have learned, and avoid them. Vers. 18. For they that are such, serve not the Lord Jesus Christ, but their own belly, and by good words and fair speeches deceive the hearts of the simple.

1 Cor. 4. 1, 2.

John 10. 1, 2.

no little *danger*; These intruders appearing more *like plunderers* of the reformed Religion, than any way like to be humble able and faithfull Preachers; Nothing can portend good to the Church of Christ, that carrys besides gross defects such a *face of disorder*, violence, insolency and confusion; which, if these wayes of some men do not, many wise and godly Christians have lost their eyes.

12. *The weight of the work of the Ministry requires peculiar and appropriated workmen to it.*

7. Furthermore, One great mistake of our *Antiministeriall Levellers* is, from that *mean* and *ordinary* esteem, they have of the work, duty, and undertaking of a Minister; this makes them have so slight and indifferent thoughts of it, both as to the *ability* and *authority*; requiring very small measure of true *abilities*, and none at all of due *authority*; further, than any *presumer* of *his gifts*, will challenge to himself.

When as indeed, all *reason*, *Religion*, and holy *examples*, do *teach* us; That the *work of a* Minister of the Gospell is not meerly a *matter of lip labour*, of *voluble speech*, of confident *countenance*; making a shew, and flourish to others of that knowledge, reading, memory and elocution, which any man may have upon an ordinary account: There goes more to make a *work-man*, than to have good *materials* and tooles *amassed* together; To heap up these, or lay them forth to others view is not to build. To be arbitrarily, or occasionally, or impertinently, or charitably busie in exercising mens private gifts, as to Christian knowledge, is not presently, to do that *great and good work*, which the Apostle commends, which Christ enjoyns his Ministers, and which the *Church needs*. Every one that can handle the Hod, or the Mattock, or the Trowell, is not instantly an *Architect*, or may vye with *Vitruvius*. Nor can every knowing Christian, discharge that part of a *throughly furnished workman*, who needs not *to be ashamed*: as having materials, and Tools, and skill, and command.

See St. Chrysost. περὶ ἱερωσύνης, largely and eloquently setting forth what excellencies are required in a Minister above other men; says ὅσα πρὸς τὰ ἄλογα τῶν λογικῶν ἀνθρώπων διαφορὰ, as in a Shepheard above the Sheep, &c. 2 Tim. 2. 15.

There is a great difference between that *plausible cunning*, which *draws Desciples after mens selves*, and that *Ministeriall* conscience which makes *Disciples* to Christ; between the *setting up* among the *many popular Masters*, who love to hear themselves speak, and the *being sent* as *Embassadors*, to speak in the *name of Christ*; which is, not to get a *petty Magistery* and name among men; but to make known, as *they ought*, the holy *name* and mysteries of Jesus Christ: Nor is this, only to walk in the cool of the day; in the midst of an *Independent Paradise* (which other Ministers labours have planted, (where some elderly, better instructed, and wealthier Christians fancy they want nothing to compleat

Hoc habent hæretici artificium, plus persuadentes quam docent, cùm veritas docendo persuadet, non persuadendo docet. Tertul. adv. Vul. πανουργία. Acts 20 30. καπηλεύοντες τὸν λόγον τοῦ θεοῦ. 2 Cor. 2. 17. Who use the word of God as Hucksters do good ware, mixing it with bad to mend it the better. *Negotium illis in verbi administratione, non Ethnicos convertens, sed nostros evertendi; nostra suffodiunt, ut sua edificent.* Tertul. adv. Hær. c. 42.

them, but the *contentment* of an *imaginary Reign* and *Empire*; and are content to allow liberally to any Minister, that will assume them into a participation of *Church power*, that they may but think themselves *to rule*;) But it requires such an humble diligence, as is willing to *bear the heat and burthen* of the day; to contend with *younger ignorance*, and *elder obstinacy*, and aged *tetricalness*; not disdaining, nor nauseating the *cramb* of *Catechising*, to which principles few of the new *modelling Preachers* will decend: as loath to abate of those *high*-soring *notions*, and *seraphick speculations*, in which they please themselves, more, than any of their *hearers*; who seek to profit our souls, rather than vainly to applaud their *vainer teacher*; who thus new dressed and set up greatly despiseth his poor *neighbour Ministers pains*, serving only to breed up, as in a *nursery*, such plants, as he is to transplant to his congregationall Garden, and so to gather in due time the fruits of them to himself.

Vulgus quæ non intelligunt impensius miratur. Jerom.

No, the work of a *worthy Minister* is such, as must fit him, as well to stoop to lay the lowest *foundations*, in the youngest *Catechists*; as to set up the Crown and Corner stone of the highest Pinnacle in the *most advanced* Christians: He must know how to treat, both the *weak* and the strong, the ideot and the learned, the babes and simple, as well as the men grown and *well-instructed*; that scorns not the meanest, nor fears to do his duty to the *greatest* in the world; To which work there ought to be such an *adequation*, as to do every thing becomming so *high and heavenly a Master*; so holy and great a work, wherein the Apostle requires as to the doctrine and manners too *uncorruptness*, *gravity*, *sincerity*, *sound speech*, that cannot be condemned, *&c.* so that the Office and work of a Minister requires, not only *communicative* abilities for knowledge and utterance, but imports also *duty*, *conscience*, *care*, solicitousness, skill, fidelity, diligence, intentiveness, zeal, exactness, prudence and highest discretion, as in a most *weighty matter*, of infinite concernment; wherein the glory of God, the honour of our Saviour, and the good of mens souls is highly *engaged*: So that it is, not a *spontaneous curtesie*, or a pleasant *variety*, or a *plausible novelty*, or a *profitable* art, and trade or *mystery of living*; but a *serious custody committed*, a *precious charge* deposited, and a strict *account to be* returned, of the *Ministeriall* negotiation and function.

Οἱ ἀπηρτισμένοι χριστοπρεπῶς. Tit. 2. 7. 8.

De Sacerdote Chrysost. Σιμνὸς καὶ ἄτυφος, φοβερὸς καὶ προσηνὴς, ἀρχικὸς καὶ κοινωνικὸς, ταπεινὸς καὶ ἀδούλωτος, σφοδρὸς καὶ ἥμερος. περὶ ἱερωσ.

παρακαταθήκη. 1 Tim. 6. 20. 2 Tim. 1. 14. That good thing which was committed to thy trust, keep, *&c.* Heb. 13. 17. As those that must give an account for their souls. *Horribile effatum* (λόγον ἀποδώσοντες) *ministris non sine consternatione & animi deliquio audiendum.*

What is requisite in a Minister.

So that a Minister had need to have *the eye* and *illumination* of an *Angel*, the *heart* and compassion of *a Father*, the *tenderness* and indulgence of *a Mother*, the caution and courage of a *Commander*

der, the vigilancy of a *Watchman*, the patience of a *Shepheard*, the zeal of a *lover*, the diligence of a *woer*, the gallantry and honour of an *Embassador*, who as he gives no cause, so knows not how with patience to see his Master or Message affronted or neglected; The wisdom and discretion of a *Counsellor*; The constancy and resolution of a *Pilot*; whom no storm must drive from the Steerage, whom it becomes to be *drowned* with his hand on the helm.

ἐπισκοπεῖν ὅλον εἶναι ὀφθαλμὸν δεῖ, πάντα ὁρῶντα, μηδὲν περιεργοῦντα ὡς πολυόμματα ζῶα. Ezek. 1. 18. Pel. l. 1. Ep. 151.

Ἀνεμοταχείας ἐστιν ὁ διδασκάλικος λόγος καὶ ποικίλην ἐπιζητεῖ τὴν τῆς ἐπιστήμης οἰκονομίαν. Gr. Nis. de Cast.

For a true Minister who is enabled by God, approved by man, and so duly sent and ordeined by both, to the service of Christ in the Church, hath upon him, not only something of the honour and authority, but of the duty and care of Parents; and that right of primogeniture, which *from Christ* is derived to them; as from *the elder* among many *brethren*; which is *to teach*, instruct, provide for, direct and govern in the *things of God*, the younger succession of the family of Christ: Yea more, every true Minister hath part of the *work of God* assigned to him, having a *Deputation*, or *Lieutenancy* from Christ to fulfill what he hath graciously undertaken, (not as to *meritorious satisfaction* (which Christ alone hath perfected, but) as to *Ministeriall instruction* and pastorall government; teaching mankind, to know the will of God, how he is to be *served*, and how they may be saved, yea, and ruling them that are Christs with his Scepter; Furnished as the Ark with the Law, with *Manna*, and with *Aarons* rod, to convince men of sin, to comfort them with promises, and to keep them in holy bounds by just authority and Christian Discipline.

ἐμπειρίαν μεγίστην τὸ διδάσκειν vocat. Socrat in Pl. Apol. *Paternum est docendi munus.* Heb. 2. 12. I will declare thy name among my brethren, &c. 2 Cor. 6. 1. We therefore as workers together with (God and Christ,) &c. 2 Cor. 5. 18. All things are of God, (i. e.) ordered by him) who hath reconciled us to himself by Christ Jesus; and hath given to us the Ministry of reconciliation. V. 20. As though God did beseech you by us.

So that true Ministers stand as in Parents, so in *Gods and Christs stead*, as to the visible means and outward work of *divine institution*; which the Lord hath chosen to dispense *by such earthen vessels*; that, as they have some reflexions and marks of *divine authority*, and honour more than humane, upon them in their work and Commission, so they may have as they had need *more than* ordinary *divine assistance*, to carry them through the discharge of this work, *as it ought* to be done: In reference to which great and sacred imployment, the *Lord Christ*, fasted, and prayed a *whole night* in a mountain, the day before he chose, ordeined and sent his twelve *Apostles* to the *work of publike* Ministry among the Jews; yea and after they had enjoyed his holy society, and instruction for some years, yet before they were to go forth to the *Gentiles conversion*, (know-

2 Cor. 4. 7.

Luke 6. 12.

ing what difficulties they should encounter; what beasts, and men, and devils they were to contend withall; besides, how *strange and incredible a message* they went withall, to convert a *proud*, vain, luxuriant, covetous, and cruell world,) he would not have them go *from Jerusalem*, till they were endued *with power* from on high by the holy Spirit, their teacher and comforter.

> Acts 1.8.

> 13. *What opinion the antients had of the Ministry of the Gospel, and with what spirit they undertook it.*

8. And according to this solemn both *institution* and *preparation* of the first Ministers of the Gospell, which Christ sent (in whose power, and after whose patern, as neer as may be, all others ought to succeed in the Church) all holy, wise, able and humble Christians have alwaies looked, not without *horror*, *trembling*, and *amazement*, upon the Office and work of the Ministry, untill the pride and *presumption* of these times; Antiently the worthy Bishops and Ministers were, both before and after their *Ordination* to this Office, still asking this question, in their souls, *who is sufficient for these things*; and what shall I do (being a Minister) *to be saved*: still jealous, lest while they *Preach to others*, themselves *prove castaways*. However now *youthfull* confidences, or *rusticall boldness*, or vain-glorious *wantonness*, or ambitious ostentations, or covetous projects, or secular interests, or *friends* importunities, or *fortunes* necessities, and stimulating despairs, to live any other way; these (God knows) are too often the main motives, which put many men upon the work of the Ministry: Yet, Those *grand* and *eminent men of old*, whose gifts and graces far exceeded our modern tenuities, came not to this holy Ordination, nor undertook this service of God to the Church, either as *Bishops* or *Presbyters*, without *infinite reluctance*, grief, dread and astonishment; They had a *constant* horror of the worth and danger of mens souls; which only Christ *could redeem* with a *valuable price*; the losse of which, a whole world *cannot countervail*; also of the *terrors* of the Lord to slothfull and unfaithfull servants in that work; also of the strictness of accounts to be given at Christs *tribunall*; They had before their eyes, that *boundless Ocean* of business into which a Minister, once ordeined *lancheth forth*, and is engaged; to study, to preach, to pray, to fast, to weep, to compassionate, to watch-over, to visit, to reproove, to exhort, to comfort, to contend, with evill and unreasonable men, devils and powers of darkness: to take care of *young* and old, to temper himself to *novices*, *cathecumens*; to confirmed, to lapsed, to obstinate, to penitent, to ignorant and erronious, to hereticall *surlyness*, to schismaticall *peevishness*, to become all things to all men to gain some.

> 2 Cor. 2. 16. 1 Cor. 9. 27. *De propriâ anima negligens in alienâ esse non potest solicitus.* Jeron.

> Naz. Or. 29. Reproves that γλωσσαλγίαν: Importunate & aking tongues, that know neither how to speak, nor to be silent: Such Preachers he calls ἀδυνάμους σοφοὺς, θρασεῖς διαλόγους, τὴν τῶν ψυχῶν ἐπιστασίαν: After he shews how much care is to be used before and after the undertaking that holy Office. P. 48. 7. c. Eph. 6. 12. 1 Cor. 9. 22. ἐπίσκοπος ἄγαλμα πάσης φιλοσοφίας. Is. Pel.

The

The work indeed requires saith St. *Chrysostom*, a most ample and enlarged soul, lest any under our charge be ignorant, by our neglect; be misled by our errors, justly scandalized by us, and hardned against us; lest any *saving truth* be wasted or concealed, any *soul wounded*, any *conscience* or *faith shipwracked*; lest any *weaker faith* faint, any *stronger* fall; lest any be *tempted* and *seduced* by *Satan*, or his *Factors*: In fine, lest any *poor soul* should be damned by our default; which is by Christ committed to our charge, as Ministers of, and for Jesus Christ; whose work is to see, that the sufferings of Christ be not in vain; that the *soveraign salves* and *balms* of his blood, may be duly applied, to the benummed, to the tender, to the wounded consciences, to the broken, and bleeding, to the stony and hardned, to the fleshy and flinty hearts.

μεγάλης τὸ πρᾶγμα δεῖται ψυχῆς. *Crysost. in Act.* 3. λογ.

ὑπὸ μυρίων ὀμμάτων φρουρεῖται ὁ ἱερεύς· δεῖ αὐτὸν θεοπρεπῆ εἶναι, καὶ ἀμέλικτον, &c. Synes. ep. 105.

ἐὰν εἷς ἴδιος, ἀλλὰ κατηγορ... ἐστιν ἀνήρ. Id.

2 Cor. 11. 29. Who is weak, and I am not weak? who is offended, and I burn not?

This so prodigious a work, and more than humane undertaking, to be a *Minister* of the *Gospel*, either as a *Bishop*, or *Presbyter*, (for neither the difference, nor the distance, was great in point of the *main work*, either of *teaching* or *governing*; onely, the higher place, had the greater care, and the more *honor* drew with it the greater *burden* of *duty*) made those *holy men* of old, so loth and unwilling to yield themselves to the *desires*, *importunities*, and even *violencies* of those *Christians*, who looked upon them, as fit for so great a *work* in the *Church*; they said, *Nolo Episcopari*, in good earnest. Saint *Ambrose* was for his *learning*, *integrity*, *piety*, and *eloquence*, so esteemed in his *secular employment*, as a *Judge*; that the faithful people of *Millan* (otherways divided by the *Arrian* faction) thought none more fit to be their *Bishop*, and chief *Pastor*; to guide, by *teaching* and *governing them*, in *matters of Religion*. They in a maner forced him, from the *Tribunal*, to the *Throne*, or *Cathedral*, with *pious compulsions*, which to avoid, he fled by night, and after a nights wandring, found himself next morn at *Millan*: He put on the face of cruelty and bloodiness, invited loose and leud people to haunt his house; that he might seem unworthy of that *dignity*, and deter them from the *choice*: Which (he tells us) he suffered not without an *holy impatience*; complaining of the *injury* done him; and he would not have yielded, if he had not been perswaded, that the *impulse* and *motion* of the *people*, so *resolute*, so *zealous*, and so *unanimous*, was from God; whose pleasure was thereby signified to him; That leaving *secular affairs*, he had *work* for him to do in his *Church*; which he discharged with great diligence, courage, and fidelity, after he was *baptized*, *duly ordained* a *Presbyter*, and *consecrated* to be a *Bishop*; To whose *learned* and *holy eloquence*, the *Church* oweth, besides other excellent fruits, the happy *conversion* of Saint *Austine*.

ἔργον ἐργωδέστατον.

Ambr. off. l. 1. c. 1. *Ego invitus de tribunalibus atque administrationis infulis ad sacerdotium.* *Vita*, B. Ambrosii.

In like sort Saint *Jerome* tells us of *Nepotian*, That when his holy learning and life had so recommended him, that he was gene-

Nepotianus *eo dignior erat quo se clamabat indignum, populus quærebat, &c. Humilitate superabat invidiam*, Jer. ad Heliodorum. Ammonius *fugiens aurem dextram præcidit; cùm ad Episcopatum quærebatur, ut deformitate impediretur electio*, Zozom. l. 6. c. 32. Socrat. l. 4. c. 18. *Nihil in hac vita difficilius, laboriosius, periculosius Episcopi, aut Presbyteri, aut Diaconi officio; sed apud deum nihil beatius, si eo modo militetur quo imperator noster jubet: Hinc lacrymæ illæ quas ordinationis meæ tempore effundebam*, August. epist. 148. Greg. Nis. in vita Thaumat. *tells how*, Greg. Thaum. omni cura fugiebat τὴν τῆς ἱερωσύνης τιμὴν ὡς φορτίον ὑποβλέψαντες. *Naz. Orat.* 25. Tells how unwillingly he was brought to be a Bishop, which others hastned to so ambitiously.

rally desired to be made a *Minister* of the *Church*; he first hid himself; When he was found, they brought him to *Ordination*, as it were to *execution*, *weeping*, *deprecating*, and *deploring* with *unfeigned earnestness*; protesting how unfit, how unworthy he was, for that *great work*; whom nothing could have made more fit and worthy, than so great *humility*, with so *great holiness* and *ability*: Some (as *Ammonius*) did maim and deform themselves to avoid this *great undertaking*. Saint *Austine*, a man of incomparable abilities, professeth, That he esteems nothing more difficult, laborious and dangerous in this world, than the *office of a Bishop*, or *Presbyter*; though nothing be *more glorious* and *accepted* before God, if the work be discharged so, as we have in charge from our *chief commander* and *Bishop*, the *Lord Jesus Christ*. Hence (saith he) were those *tears*, which he could not forbear to shed plentifully on the day of his *Ordination*; which others wondred at then; and he after gives the world an account of them: O humble, holy, happy, well-placed *tears*, which watered on that occasion, one of the most devout, diligent and fruitful souls, that ever the *Church* of *Christ* enjoyed.

Μυρίων ἐπισκόπῳ πανταχόθεν ὀφθαλμῶν δεῖ. Chrysost. In act. 3. Ὁμ. Οὐκ οἴομαι εἶναι πολλοὺς ἐν τοῖς ἱερεῦσι τοὺς σωζομένους, ἀλλὰ πολλῷ πλείους τοὺς ἀπολλυμένους. Chrys. Ὁμ. 3. in 1. c. act. Ἔγω δὲ πολλάκις εἰς θανάτους ἀντὶ τῆς δὲ τῆς λειτουργίας εἱλόμην. Synes. ep. 11. *Thuanus* (*Anno* 1555.) tells of *Marcellus*, a wise and sober man, When the Scripture was read before him of the office of a Bishop, he with earnestness protested, He could hardly see how any man in the eminency of his place, could be intent to the salvation of his own soul.

Saint *Chrysostome* also (a great and glorious *star* of the *first magnitude* in the *Firmament* of the *Church*; who filled the *Orb* in which he was placed, and equalled by his *eloquent worth*, the *eminency* of the City (*Constantinople*) where he sate as *Bishop*) *passionately bemoans* his condition, and all of his *order*, as *Bishops*, and *Ministers* of the *Church*; professing, That he thinks the work, the danger, and the difficulties so great, that a *Bishop* and *Minister* had need have an *hundred hands*, and as many *eyes* to avoid scandals, and to dispatch the employment: So that he protesteth, That he cannot see, how many *Bishops* or *Ministers* can be saved; yea, and believes far more are damned, than saved. *Synesius* also professeth, Had he been aware of the *vastness* of the *work*, and *charge* of *souls*, he would have chosen *many deaths*, rather than have been a *Bishop*, or *Presbyter* in the *Church*; as he was, and a very worthy one too, from an eloquent and learned *Philosopher*. Thus, and to this tune, generally

all

all those *antient Bishops*, and most *eminent Ministers* of the *Church*; and this, not out of *restiveness*, *cowardise*, or want of *zeal*, *piety*, and *charity*, but meerly out of *unfeigned humility*; (as *Moses*, *Jeremiah*, *Isaiah*, *Ezekiel*, and others,) abasing themselves, out of the high esteem they had of the glory of Christ, the honor of his Religion, the dignity of his Ministry, and the preciousness of souls, for which, he had shed his *sacred blood*.

ὡς αἰδῶ τὸ Χρῦ καλεῖν κ ἀγῶνας καὶ ἄθλους πάντα τὸν καθ' ἱερωσύνην βίον. Greg. Nis. vita Thaum.

Quanto in præcipitio stant illi, qui tot mortibus sunt obnoxii, quot habent in tutela animas? Cleman. Spel.

9. Nor is the *work* (God knows) less or easier now, on our hands; nor the *burden* lighter; nor are our *arms* and *shoulders* stronger in these days, than in former times; that any *mens confidence* in undertaking, or forwardness in obtruding on that *calling*, should be now so great; when, indeed, we have (now) not onely *down-right ignorance*, and *blunter rusticity*, or *heathenish simplicity*, or *barbarous unbelief* to contend with; but also *schismatical curiosities*, *fanatical novelties*, *heretical subtilties*, *superstitious vanities*, *cruel hypocrisies*, *political profanenesses*, *spiritual wickednesses* to encounter. We are to deal, as *Ministers* even here in *England*, not with *raw Novices*, and *callow Christians*, or meer *strangers* to *Religious Mysteries*; but with such, as by much handling matters of Religion, are grown *callous men*, of *brawny hands*, *gross humors*, of *tough hearts*; such as think themselves fat, and so full fed with *Religious Notions*, that they are grown pursey, almost surfeted, and last their *appetite*; longing like *glutted* and *pampered Jews*, for any *novelties*, though it be for *Garlick*, and *Leeks*, and *Onyons*, amidst their superfluities of *Quails* and *Manna*: Nothing pleaseth their clogged stomacks, that is old, though never so true; nothing comes amiss, if it be but dressed up with *novelty*; old Christianity set on the *new block of faction*: O how welcome to many is a *new Church way*, a *new fashioned Ministry*, *new ordered Sacraments*, *new interpreted Scriptures*? With these wanton, proud, idle, lazy, coy, and scornful tempers, have we *Ministers* now to contest; with such *Sophisters*, as are ignorant, yet *proud* of their *knowledge*; need *teaching*, yet affect to be *teachers*; such as cast off all true *Ministry*, and *Church Orders*, and *Government*, when they most want them (as *Feaverish men* do clothes to make them sweat, when they kick them off.)

14. *The Work not now, easier, than it was, requires as able Ministers.*

Periculosissimus animo morbus est (ἀσιτία) spiritualis inappetentia, & σαλευμία, illa nauseabunda, quæ satietate in sacris laborat. Cameron.

Numb. 11. 5.

It is harder to deal with such mens arrogant, extravagant humors; with their various, subtil, and sublime fancies in Religion, (which are like the *running Gout*, every where painful, no where permanent; very *offensive*, though very *unfixed*) than with those *plainer simplicities*, and that *down-right profaneness*, which are in *Heathens*, and meer *ignorant ones*, who never took any *tincture* of *Christian*

Difficulties in the Work of the Ministry.

Christian Religion; whose ruder and open persecutions, were not more pestilent to the true Christian Ministry and Religion, than these craftier underminings are.

Nor do the Ministers of *England* so flatter themselves, that secular powers are so propitious to them, as not to finde more than ordinary cause to keep up the *dignity* and *authority* of their *Calling*, by all *internal sufficiencies*, and *external industry*, rather than trust to the *favors* and *benignities* of men, either great or small, few or many. *Gregory Thaumaturgus* when he was a Bishop of *Neocesarea* in *Pontus*, blesseth God, That when he came first to his charge, he found not above seventeen Christians; and when he departed from them, he left not in all his Diocess, so many *unbaptized*, or *unbelievers*: But the sad *task* of many excellent Ministers now is, after many years labors, to work upon the most rugged and ingrateful Christians, in many places, that ever were: Many grave men after many years pains, having merited, and expecting from their people, that Christian usage for love, and respect, which becomes both sides; the more they *preach*, and the better they *live*, and the more they love their people, the more peevish and froward they finde them: Like *hot irons*, they flie in the face of those that have heated them, and are daily forging them, both to *solidity* and *beauty* in *Religion*; these like *cross-grained pieces*, run with splinters into the hands and eyes of those that seek to polish them; they affect a *petulant piety*, and are taught by some, That much of their Religion consists in *despising* and *separating* from those Ministers, who have baptized and instructed them, and to whom the care of their souls is orderly committed.

Basil. Mag. lib. de Spir. S. c. 29. μεγάλης ἀρχιερωσύνης ἄξιον ὅτι τοσούτους καταλείπει τοὺς εἰδωλολάτρας ὅσους αὐτὸς χριστιανοὺς ὑπεδέξατο. Greg. Niss. περὶ θαυματέργου.

Nor is it onely, hence, that the *dignity of the Ministry* is wounded, and the *difficulties of the work* encreased, but even from our selves also, who profess to be Ministers here in *England*; The *Lord of the harvest* pardon our over hasty intrusions, our importune forwardness, our unfitness for the work, our idleness in it, our vaporings of it, our sinister aims, our crooked motions, our improving both our selves and others, more to private *Factions*, than to the *Catholike Faith*, or *Publick Peace*; to *popularity*, rather than to *piety*; to *pleasing*, rather than *profiting* of people; by which ways, it must be confessed, many of us, *Ministers*, have *miserably prostrated* the honor of this *sacred Function*; increased the *difficulties* of our *work*, laid *blocks* and *bars* in our ways; helped to *level* the *dignity* of the *Function* to *vulgar insolencies*; either *contemning* or *invading it*.

As in all times, so especially in these, *Ministers* of the *Gospel* had need to be *more than men*; above the *pitch of mortals*, little *lower than the Angels*; who are to *counter work* deep and deceitful workers;

workers; to *undermine* and *uncase* false Ministers; to *bear up*, and *recover* Christian and Reformed Religion, with it main *pillar*, and *support*, (the *true Ministry*) against those that seek to overthrow it. In the most serene and favorable times to the *Church* and the *Ministry*, a wise and gracious man should fear and tremble (though never so able, and by others recommended,) to undertake this *work*; so *sacred*, so *divine*, so *justly* to be avoided; If men looked not at *high*, *holy*, and *eternal designs*; yea, I should even think, the *best men* might well refuse the *charge* and *calling*, till *God* called thrice (as he did to *Samuel*,) till he even *chid*, or *threatned* them to the *work*, as he did *Moses*. For if in any undertaking in the world a Christian might be disobedient, or would be *deliberating*, and *demurring*; and ask oft of God and man, *Shall I, shall I run*, it ought to be in this: Let him that findes not *care* and *work* enough to look to his own soul, *covet rashly* to take charge of other mens; how sad is it to see loose and indifferent livers, forward, and earnest to be *Preachers*, and undertake a *Pastoral Charge*? The Lord forgive, what hath been thus hastily hudled, and inconsiderately entred upon by any of us Ministers; and grant us, that after *grace*, which may recompence, and as much as may be, expiate the *rashness* of the *admission* and *adventure*, by the *seriousness*, *diligence*, and *consciencousness* of the *performance*. Men, if they were well advised, and in good earnest, should rather need *spurs* and *goads* to be driven by others, than *bridles*, or *pikes* to keep them off from rushing into the *Ministry*.

1 Sam. 3. 8. Exod. 4. 14.

15. *Discouragements from the tenuity of maintenance.*

Nothing hath more *debased* this *holy calling*, and *discouraged able men* from it, than the *necessity*, here in *England*, in many places, to admit some mens *tenuity* and *meanness* into the Ministry and Livings; who had no other *motive*, but to obtain a *morsel of bread*, and scarce found that for their pains; For which necessity a *relief* was long ago hoped for, and expected, if not promised, from the *piety*, and *nobleness* of the *Parliaments* of *England*; who could not, but see, that in many, if not most parts, either the *Ministers abilities* and *pains* exceeded the *Benefice*; or the *starving tenuity* of the *Benefice*, like an *hungry* and *barren soyl*, eat up and consumed the *Ministers gifts* and *parts*; which at first were florid, and very hopeful, and so would have thrived, had they not been planted in a soyl that was rather a *dry nurse*, than a *kinde mother*.

In novercante solo satæ arbores quamvis generosiores & feraces cito sterilescunt. Varro. *Tenuitatem beneficiorum necessario sequitur ignorantia sacerdotum.* Bishop Jewel.

Nor was there then, or is there now, any way to avoid the mischief of admitting such *minute offerers* of their selves to the Ministry in places of so *minute maintenance*, unless the entertainment were enlarged; as is requisite in many *Livings*, where the *whole salary* is not so much, as the *interest* of the money, bestowed in breeding of a *Scholar* would *amount* to, which an able Minister cannot live

 upon,

upon, so as to do his *duty*; yet this fault of ordaining and instituting weak Ministers (which arose from the hardness of *Laymens* hearts) was better committed, than omitted by the *Ordainers*; for it was better, that such small *timber* (if as *strait* and *sound*, as can be had) be put in the *wall*, than the house in that place, lie *quite open*, and *decayed*; Better the *poor people* be taught in *some measure*, the *Mysteries* and *Truth of Religion*, than left wholly wilde and ignorant. I know, that as in a *building* it is not necessary that all *pieces* should be *great* and *massie timber*, less will serve in their place and proportion; yet the *principal parts* ought to be so *substantial*, that they might relieve the *weaker studs* and *rafters* of the burden; so that no danger might be to the whole *Fabrick* from their *feebleness*, so assisted: The state of the Church ought indeed to be so ordered, that there should be a *competency* for all, and a *competency* in all, *Ministers*; but in some there ought to be an *eminency*; as in *employment*, so in *entertainment*; upon whom the greatest *recumbency* of *Churches* may be laid; whose *learning*, *courage*, *gravity*, *tongue*, and *pen*, may be able to sustain the *weight* of *Religion*, in all *controversies* and *oppositions*; which *assertings* and *vindications* require, not onely *good will* and *courage*, but great *strength* and *dexterity*. The ablest Minister, if he well ponders what he hath to do, hath no cause to be *very forward*, nor should the meanest, that is *honest* and *congruous*, have cause to *despond*, or be *discouraged* in his *good endeavors*.

Great care ought to be had for Ordination of able Ministers, and for augmentation of their Means to competency.

To restore the *Reformed Christian Ministry* in this *Church*, to its *true honor*, there should be *greatest* care had in the *matter* of *ordination*; before which, antiently the Church had *solemn Fasting*, *Prayer*, and *Humiliation*; But in vain (as to many places, which all need able Ministers) will this care be, unless there be also some *necessary augmentation* of *Ministers* maintenance; As the *ablest men* should be invited to the *work*, so none *unable* should be admitted; and none, once *admitted*, should have cause by the *incompetency* of their condition to be *ashamed*; and by their *poverty*, contract *inabilities*; as Trees grow mossie, and unfruitful in *barren soyls*. Nor would this *pious munificence* be thought much by any *Christian Nation*, to which God hath been so *liberal* in his *earthly bounty*; if they did indeed value his *heavenly dispensations*, and the *necessity*, *work*, or *worth*, either of *true Ministers*, or of *poor mens souls*; whom *itinerant Preachers* cannot feed sufficiently, with a *bit* and a way; but they require *constant* and *resident Ministers* to make them *thrifty* and *well-liking*. I conclude this Paragraph, touching the *great work* of the *Ministry*, with that *Character* of an *able Minister*, which St. *Bernard* hath admirably set forth to *Eugenius*, the then Bishop of *Rome*, by which we may see, what sense was in those days (Four hundred and fifty years ago) of the duty of Ministers; and what kinde

kinde of ones, *holy men* then required in the *Church*; from whom, our *succession*, without any disparagement from mens personal faults, is derived.

Such (saith Saint *Bernard*) *are to be chosen, and ordained for Ministers of the Church, who are composed for their maners; approved for their sanctimony; ready to obey their Superiors, subject to Discipline; strict in their Censures; Catholike for their Faith; faithful in their Preaching; conform to the peace and unity of the Church; Who to Kings, may be as* John Baptist; *to* Egyptians, *as* Moses; *to Fornicators, as* Phineas; *to Idolaters, as* Elias; *to Covetous, as* Elisha; *to Lyars, as* Peter; *to Blasphemers, as* Paul; *to Symonaical and Sacrilegious Trafickers in the Church, as* Christ *to the Buyers and Sellers in the Temple. Such, as may not burthen, or despise the poor, but nourish and instruct them; not flatter, and fawn on the rich, but rather rouze and affright their proud security; not terrified by threats of Princes, but living and acting above them; not exhausting mens purses, but comforting their consciences, and filling their hungry souls with good things; who in every duty may trust more to their Prayers, than their Studies; to Gods grace, than their own gifts and industry. O* (saith he) *that I might in my days see the Church of Christ, set, and built on such Pillars! O that I might see the pure Spouse of Christ, committed to the care of such pure and faithful Guardians! Nothing would make me so securely happy.*

Tales eligendi sunt Ministri qui sunt compositi ad mores, probati ad sanctimoniam, parati ad obedientiam subjecti ad diciplinam, rigid ad censuram, Catholici ad fidem; fideles ad dispensationem, concordes ad pacem, conformes ad unitatem. Qui regibus Johannem *exhibeant*, Egyptiis Mosen, *fornicantibus* Phineam, Heliam *idolatris*, Helisæum *avaris*, Petrum *mentientibus*, Paulum *blasphemantibus*, Christum *negotiantibus. Qui vulgus non spernant sed doceant, non gravent sed foveant. Minas principum non paveant sed contemnant, qui marsupia non exhauriant sed corda reficiant. De omni re orationi plus fidant quàm industriæ suæ. O si videam in vita mea Ecclesiam talibus nixam columnis. O si Domini sponsam cernerem tantæ commissam fidei, tantæ creditam puritati; quid me beatius, quidve securius.* Bern. l.1. ad Eugenium.

Thus, this devout and holy man in his times, to whose pious and earnest desire, I could heartily say *Amen*, if I did but hope that ever the request might be heard, and granted in my time; but, though *all men be liers*, yet we have a *true God* to trust in.

16. *Private Liberty of gifts and publick Ministry, not inconsistent.*

As for that *Liberty* which some Christians plead, (not upon a *Socinian* or *fanatick* account, as against any *peculiar office*; and *power Ministerial*, but) onely in a fair and orderly way of *Christian charity*, and useful *conversation*; wherein private *believers soberly* and *wisely communicate* of those *gifts of knowledge* they have attained; not to the *subversion of faith* and *peace in the Church* or *Consciences*, but to the further *confirmation* of them; This, as it is no way *envied* or *denied* by any *good Ministers*; so far as God hath granted it, or the *charity* and *zeal* of any modest and humble Christian desires it; So there is no ground, either in *Reason* or *Religion* to be urged

 against

against the *peculiar Calling* and *Function* of the *Ministry*, from this *Christian Liberty* of *Charity*; any more, than there is cause to pull down any *mans dwelling house*, because there are some *sheds* and *pent-houses* leaning to it; which have their uses and conveniences in their kinde, and proportion, but not comparably to the *main mansion*; which hath far more strength, order, beauty, and usefulness: I shall afterward give a fuller account of that *Christian Liberty* in *Preaching* and *Prophecying*, which is by some *arrogantly* urged against the *Authoritative Ministry*, as any peculiar office and appointment of Christ.

Onely at present, I would endeavor to satisfie the sober and humble Christian, That the *Calling* of *the Ministry*, which is and ought in all Religious Reason, to be peculiar to some men, both in *abilities* and *ordination*, as well as in exercise of a *divine authority*, and *special power*, this (I say) doth no whit *quench* or *repress*, but rather *regulate* and *preserve* that true *Liberty*, which consists in private Christians *conferring*, *admonishing*, *informing*, and *strengthning*, one another in every *good word and work*; without any neglect, or undervaluing of the *Publick Ministry*, where it may be had. To which, as commonly all well-taught Christians ow (under God) the *light*, and *soundness* they have in *Religion*, so they know, That all *gifts* are bounded by the *Word of God*, which is the *measure* and *touchstone of grace*; that nothing is further from *grace*, than *unruly living*, and *disorderly walking*; that the *gravity of Religion* abhors all *uncomly motions*, and *rude extravagancies*; which are as far from *true piety* or *zeal*, as *mad-pranks* and *ravings* are from being heights or excesses of *reason*. *Private presumptions* (be mens abilities never so great) may not proudly and uncharitably *usurp* against *publick order*, *peace*, and *authority* in the *Civil State*; much less against that *divine polity*, which Christ hath established in his *holy Family*, the Church.

1 Thes. 5. 14. Warn them that are (ἀτάκτους) unruly, disorderly, out of their ranks and places, where God hath set them in his church. 2 Thes. 3. 6. We command you Brethren in the Name of our Lord Jesus Christ, that ye withdraw your selves from every brother, who walketh disorderly, and not after the tradition which he received from us. Tit. 1. 10, 11. There are many unruly and vain-talkers, &c. whose mouths must be stopped.

Ministers not less necessary for the Church, than Commanders are for an Army.

What wise Magistrate will allow it in a Subject? what discreet Commander (as *Clement* writing to the Factious *Corinthians* observes) will countenance that private and heady confidence in any Soldier, under pretence of valor, or hatred of the enemy, or zeal for the *Generals* honor, and Armies good, without any Order, Commission, or Command, to *engage* himself upon fighting the enemy, or commanding any part of the Army; to the violating of those *just and*

οὐ πάντες εἰσὶν ἔπαρχοι, οὐδὲ χιλίαρχοι, &c. ἀλλ' ἕκαστος ἐν τῷ ἰδίῳ τάγματι τὰ ἐπιτασσόμενα ὑπὸ τοῦ βασιλέως καὶ τῶν ἡγουμένων ἐπιτελεῖ, ὑποτασσέσθω ἕκαστος ἐν τῷ χαρίσματι αὐτοῦ. Clem. ep. ad Cor. p. 46.

necessary

necessary Rules of *Discipline*; in the exact observation whereof, the safety, strength, and honor of an Army, infinitely more consists, than in the *Thrasonick forwardness*, and *fool-hardiness* of any person in it, be he never so able or willing? which, *Manlius Torquatus* expressed, by that *severity* of putting his own son to death, for *fighting* without order from him his General, although he fought *successfully*: For wise men consider, it is not so necessary to fight, or to preach, as to do both *decently*, and in *order*; nor shall any man be *commended* or *crowned* for either, unless he do them *lawfully*: *Rashness* is no part of any mans *fortitude*, much less of his *Religion*; nor is *confidence* any sign of *true valor*; nor *boasting of courage*; neither is *confusion* any ingredient in *Christian charity*; nor *Faction* any support of the *Faith*; nor *disorderly walking* any fewel of those *holy flames*, which dwell in the *humble brests* of true Christians, and fill them with *commendable zeal*.

Livius, Dec. 1. lib. 8. *Disciplinam militarem qua stetit ad hanc diem Romana res solvisti, &c. Triste exemplum sed in posterum salubre, &c.*

2 Tim. 2. 5. If a man strive for mastery; yet he is not crowned, except he strive lawfully. *Secundum leges Athleticas.* Ἀγωνάκται, *Refractarii*: Disorderly Agitators. A Sect which *Clem. Alex.* tells of, στρ. 3. 320.

The Church of Christ is compared to a *City that is at unity in it self*, and to *an Army with Banners*: These *holy allusions* are so far argumentative, by way of *right reason*, and *religious proportions*, as to assure us, That neither the *strength* nor *beauty* of this holy City can be preserved, unless the *comliness*, *order*, and *exactness*, of those *gemmeous foundations* and *walls*, which Christ, and his holy Apostles have laid, and set up in *doctrine*, *holy institutions*, and *peculiar Ministry*, be observed and kept; which are not onely *guides* and *fences* for the Churches safety and direction; but also *limits* and *boundaries* to all mens extravagancy in Religion: Nor yet can the *majesty* of this *Heavenly Host*, the *Sacred Militia* of *Christs Church* on Earth, continue, either, as to its *safety* in it self, or its *terror* to its *enemies* round about, unless the *Standard-bearers*, the *Ministers*, whose office is to hold up the *Banner* of *Christs Cross*, against the wisdom, power, and malice of men and devils, be supported and maintained; for these are appointed by Christ, *the Captain-General of our Salvation*, to be the *directers* of the Churches motions; and as the *centers* of its peace, and order, in its several *bands* and *companies*; which are the *several Congregations*: Who, without *Ministers*, duly placed with *authority* among them, will soon be *as sheep without a shepherd*; or, as *soldiers*, are when the *standard-bearer* faileth, easily *scattered* and *destroyed*. And indeed, nothing seems more to reprove and confute, the *perverse disputings* of some men against the *setled order* and *calling of the Ministry*, (who pretend to Military Discipline and Orders) than this consideration: For they cannot, but in reason be *self-condemned*; since, if they have any *grains of Salt* in

Liberty must not expel Order out of the Church.

Psal. 122. 3.
Cant. 6. 3.
Rev. 21. 19.

Chrysost. in 1 Tim. hom. 5. ἀρχῆς δεῖν ἀνομίας, ἡ πόλεων, φυλάξων, ψυχῶν &c.

Heb. 2. 10. Ἀρχηγὸς τῆς σωτηρίας.

Isai. 10. 18. ἔχατε πάντων συγχύσεις ἐκ ἰστο αἰδόν τι, ἢ πλεονάσμος τῆς ἀταξίας. Naz.

them, they cannot, but daily see, a *necessity* of *exact order*, and *distinct power*, which must be observed among themselves as *soldiers*; without which, Armies will be but *heaps upon heaps*; *confused crouds* and *noises of men*; if any one, who fancies his own, or an others *sufficiencies*, shall presently *usurp* the power, and *intrude* into the office of Captain and Commander; whose work is not onely to use a few *good words* now and than, but to fight valiantly, and yet to keep both himself, and others in *good order*.

τάξις τὸ πᾶν συνέστησεν, ἐν νοητοῖς, ἐν αἰσθητοῖς, ἐν ἀέροις, ἐν ἀγγέλοις, ἐν πόλεσιν, ἐν πολεμίοις. Naz. Or. 26. οὐδεὶς οὐδὲν ἀκούει. Inter Cyclopes.

No less is order necessary to the Church in its Societies; over which able and fit Ministers duly placed, have, not onely the *work of Preaching*, lying on their Consciences, which requires more than *ordinary and vulgar abilities*; but, they have many other *great*, and *weighty affairs*, which they are to discharge, both publickly and privately; as *workmen* that need not to be ashamed; as those, that are *meet instruments*, and *workers* together with *God and Christ*, in the *great work* of *saving souls*; to which, if onely memory, and a voluble tongue, and an oratorious confidence, would have served, there needed not so *great preparations*, and *power of the Spirit* from on high, to come on the *Apostles*; which not onely furnished them with Matter what to say, and Languages wherein, but, with *just* and *full authority* to preach *Christs Gospel* in *Christs Name*; and to settle, a like *constant Authority*, *Order*, and *Power Ministerial* in all *Churches*, for *holy Administrations*; putting upon their *Successors*, whom they ordained in every place (as the spirit of *Moses* was put on the seventy Elders) of that *Spirit*; that is, of that same power Ministerial, which they had immediately from Christ. Nor was any one not *rightly ordained*, *antiently esteemed*, as any Minister of the Church, nor any thing he did valid; nor were any that adhered to such *disorderly walkers* and *impostors*, ever reckoned among *good Christians*, or as *sound Members* in the *Church*; As Saint *Cyprian*, most eloquently and zealously, writes concerning *Novatianus*, who usurped the office of a *Bishop* and *Pastor*, among some credulous and weak people; despising the *Ordination* of the *Church*. *How can he be counted a Bishop or Minister in the Church, who thus like a Mushroom grows up from himself? How can he have any office in the Church, who is not placed there by the officers in the Church; which hath ever had in it true Pastors, who by a successive Ordination, have received power to preside in the Church? He that sets up of his own new score, and succeeds none formerly ordained, is both an alien to, and an enemy of the peace and truth divine: Nor can that sheep*

Non tam spectandum quid agat quisque, quam quo ordine; nec tam quo animo, quam qua disciplina, Ep. Wint. Andrews.

Ordo postulat ut virtute eminentiores sint & loco superiores, qui habeant rationum ψυχῆς πρὸς τὸ σῶμα ἢ τῷ πρὸς τὴν ψυχήν. Naz. Or. 1.

V d. Clem. Ro. Epist. ad Corinth.

Numb. 11. 17.

Cypr. Epist. 76. De Baptisandis Novatianis, ad Magnum.

Novatianus in Ecclesia non est, nec Episcopus computari potest, qui Evangelica, & Apostolica autoritate contempta, nemini succedens à se ipso ortus est. Habere enim aut tenere Ecclesiam nullo modo potest, qui ordinatus in Ecclesia non est. Quomodo gregi Christi annumerari potest, qui legitimum non sequitur pastorem? quomodo pastor haberi debet, qui manente vero pastore, & in Ecclesia Dei ordinatione succedanea præsidente, nemini succedens, à seipso incipiens alienus sit, & dominicæ pacis & divinæ veritatis inimicus.

be

be reckoned, as one of Christs flock, who doth not follow a lawfully ordained Pastor. Thus Saint *Cyprian*, a Learned holy Bishop, and after a Martyr for Christ, testifies the sense of the Church, and all true Christians in his time, who flourished in the *third Century* after Christ.

I will onely adde one place more out of *Tertullian*, who lived before Saint *Cyprian*, in the end of the *second Century*, whom *Cyprian* usually called his Master, for the learning, warmth, force, and eloquence, which were in his works, till his defection. *Let these new Masters* (saith he) *and their Disciplies, set forth to us the Original of their Churches, the Catalogue and Succession of their Bishops and Ministers; so running upward without interruption; that it may appear their first Bishop or Presbyter had some Apostle, or some that persevered with the Apostle, for their predecessor and ordainer: For thus the true and Apostolically planted Churches do ever make their reckonings; as the Church of* Smyrna *had their first Bishop* (Polycarpus) *placed among them by St.* John *the Apostle: So the Church of* Rome *and* Antioch *had their Pastors, or Bishops, setled by the Apostle* Peter. Thus *Tertullian*, and with him *Irenæus*, and all the antients; who sought *to keep the unity of the Spirit*, and *the bond of peace, Eph. 4. 3.* The *purity* of *doctrine*, and *power* of *holy Discipline*, in the Church of Christ. These *holy men* never dreamed of *Self-ordainers*, or of *gifted*, yet *unordained Ministers*; nor did they own any Christians in Church Society, or Ecclesiastick Order, and holy Communion, where there was not an evident, distinct, and personally demonstrable Succession of *Bishops, Pastors*, and *Teachers*, in Ministerial Authority, so constituted by *holy Ordination*, lineally descended, and rightly derived from the *Apostolical Stem*, and the *Root, Jesus Christ.*

Tertul. lib. de Præscrip. adv. Hæreses. *Edant (Hæretici) origines Ecclesiarum suarum, evolvant ordinem Episcoporum suorum, ita per successiones ab initio decurrentium, ut primus ille Episcopus aliquem ex Apostolis, vel Apostolicis viris (qui tamen cum Apostolis perseveraverint) habuerit autorem & antecessorem: Hoc enim modo Ecclesiæ Apostolicæ census suos deferunt. Sicut* Smyrnæorum *Ecclesia habens* Polycarpum, à Johanne *Collocatum, refert; Sicut* Romanorum Clementem, à Petro *Ordinatum, &c. Traditionem itaque Apostolorum in toto mundo manifestatam in Ecclesia adest perspicere omnibus qui verè velint audire. Et habemus enumerare eos qui ab Apostolis instituti sunt Episcopi in Ecclesiis; & successores eorum usque ad nos. Quibus etiam ipsas Ecclesias remittebant, suum ipsorum locum Magisterii tradentes. Qui nihil tale cognoverunt neque docuerunt, quale ab his deliratur.* Irenæus, lib. 3. cap. 3. *De iis qui decedunt ab Apostolica Successione.*

17. Nor is this, so *divine an Institution*, so *solemn an Ordination*, so *sacred a Mission*, and so *clear* and *constant* a *Succession of Ministers*, (whose office it is to *bear witness* of the *Name of Christ*, in his love, and sufferings, and merits, to the end of the World, till the number of *Saints* be perfected; till the *work* of the *Ministry* is finished, and the *Body* of *Christ*, his Church, fully edified, *Eph. 4. 12.*) This, I say, is not of more concernment to the *glory of God*, (whose infinite and inestimable mercy is hereby set forth to mankinde,) or more conducing to the *honor of Christ*, in his wisdom, love, and care, for his

Peculiar Officers as Ministers, most necessary for the common peoples good, as to Religion.

his Church, than it is every way most necessary for the *common good* of those, whom the *Lord* is pleased to call to be *his people*, at any time, in any *Nation*, whatsoever; whose interest and benefit the *Lord Jesus Christ* far more considered (and so should all good Ministers do in their work,) than any particular ends, or advantages of their own; (Alas, the *divinest advancement* of *true Ministers* in this World, is their *faithful labor*; their *honor* must be their cares, and studies, and fears; their *crowns*, their sufferings and sorrows, persecutions, and perils, contempts, crosses, and deaths for Christs sake, and the Churches welfare:) But the peculiar benefit and advantage of the *Christian flock*, the *faithful people* of all sorts, is that which is most to be regarded; over whom the *Lord* hath made Ministers overseers; (not onely at the first plantation of the *Gospel*, as the *Socinians* say, but also in a *constant* and *clear succession* of *Publick Ministerial Authority*;) for this very purpose, That poor people may never be left as *sheep without a shepherd*; that they may not either wander up and down in the *wildernesses*, or *mountains* of their own fancies; or be led away by others seductions; or be beguiled by the devils wiles, and temptations; That they may hear, and believe, and persevere *stedfast* in the *Faith*; that they may neither be ignorant, nor erroneous, nor scattered and divided; that they may be preserved from *rustical simplicity*, *hypocritical formality*, *heretical pravity*, and *schismatical novelty* in matters of *Religion*; *that they may not perish* (or be left *naked*, *separated*, *scattered*, *idle*, and *rebellious*) *for want of vision*; thereby sinning against God, and their own souls. The pregnant significancy of that one word, which *Solomons* wisdom useth, hath these *swarms* or *spawnings* of several senses: All which variety shews, That the *state* of *common people* is never more desperate, than when their *Seers* fail; when their *Teachers* are *removed into corners*; when God sends them no *Preachers*, or *Prophets after his own heart*; when people are not onely without *light*, but put it out, quenching the *Lamps of the Sanctuary*, and *loving darkness more than light*; when they are given up to their own delusions, and others seductions; who blindly follow the *visions of their own hearts*, and the *Prophets* of their own sending, or the *Ministers* of their own ordaining; whom they shall have no cause to credit, esteem, love, or obey, as finding no competent gifts Ministerial in them, no Characters of divine Authority, or holy Succession, upon them.

People will easily be surprised when they have no *watchmen* to foresee, give warning, prevent, and encounter any dangers, of sins, errors, and temptations, which easily surprise the generality even of Christians; who are for the most part so busied, and incumbred, or so pleased and ensnared, or so burthened and oppressed with the secular and sensible things of this world, that they can hardly *watch*

1 Cor. 1. 21.

2 Cor. 1. 23, *&c.*

Princeps in prædicando, princeps in perpetiendo. Bern.

Mark 6. 34.

באין חזון יפרע עם Prov. 29. 18.

פרע signifies, *Perire, denudare, feriari, dissipare, rebellari, retrocedere.* Buxtorf.

Isai. 30. 20. Thy Teachers shall not be removed into a corner any more; but thine eyes shall see thy Teachers.

Ezek. 3. 17. Heb. 13. 17. They watch for their souls, *&c.*

one hour with Christ, no not in *his agony*; if they had not some *Ministers* divinely appointed, to put *them in remembrance*; to stir up their affections, to provoke them to piety, to prepare them for eternity, both instructing them in the *Faith*, and praying for them that their *Faith may not fail*. Nothing indeed is more *deplorable* and *desperate*, than the condition of mankinde, yea, and of any part of the *Church of Christ* would be, if the *Lord* had not commanded, and by a special providence continued an *holy constant succession* of the *Ministers* of the *Word* and *Sacraments*; who may be always, either *planting*, or *watering*, or *pruning*; and so, according to the *several proportions* of Christians, still preserving the *truth*, *life*, and *power of Religion*, so as it may descend to after ages. For there is no doubt, but without this *holy* and *happy Succession of Ministers*, either people would ever persist in their *original ignorance*, and *heathenish sottery*; or, although once planted with *piety*, yet they will *soon relapse* to *barbarity*, *Atheism*, and *unbelief*; or at best, content themselves with *idle formalities*, *spiritless superstitions*, *empty notions*, *mouldy traditions*, *lying legends*, *plausible fancies*, *novel inventions*, *vain imaginations*, or most *desperate errors*, and *damnable doctrines*; which is evident by the experience, as of former, so of these times; where few of those, that have cast off, and despised the *lawful*, and *true Ministry* of this *Church*, but either give over all *Religion*; or else think themselves capable, every night to dream a new and better way of *serving God*, and saving mens souls, than ever yet was used.

1 Cor. 1. 21. It pleased God by the foolishness of Preaching, to save them that believe.

18. This natural tendency to *Apostatize* from truth, to relapse to *profaneness*, to rest in *hypocrisie*, to run out to *extravagancies*, or to persist in *errors*, no people under Heaven are more subject to, than those of this *Nation*, *England*; whom, as God hath blest with a *land flowing with milk and honey*; so they have much of the *iron sinew*, and *stiffneckedness of the Jews*; for being full fed, they are also full of *high* and *quick spirits*, *various* and *vehement fancies*, finding out and running after many *fashions* and *inventions*. *Don Gundamor*, who had much studied the *English* temper, and knew how their pulse beat, both in Church and State, was wont to say, *He despaired not of those violent changes here in England*; which in no other Nation could be expected; who are generally content with their *customs*, and constant to their *principles*; whereas the *English* are always given to *change*, to admire *novelties*, and with most *inconsiderate violence* to pursue them: So that no *Nation* or *Church* under Heaven, have more need then, of constant, learned, able, and honest Ministers; who may shew them, guide, and keep them in the *good*, *right*, and *safe way* of *true Religion*; From which, none are more easily seduced, than those that have either a *sequacious softness*, and *credulity*

As all Christians subject to Errors and Apostacies, so none more than here in England.

Anglorum ingenia sunt aut varia & mobilia, superstitionibus & vaticiniis dedita; aut feroci quadam pertinacia aspera & contumaciter superba. Bodin. & Lansius. & Phil. Com.

lity toward other men, as divers of us have; or an *high conceit* and *confidence* of themselves; which people, much at ease, rich and high fed, (as many in *England*) are most subject to; Insomuch, that we see the *greatest disease*, as to Religion, now is, among us, not so much a *famine*, as a *surfet* of the *Word*; and knowledge, which hath here Hab. 2. 14. been *as the waters of the Sea*, disdains those shores of *order, office*, and *duty*, which the *Lord* hath set for its *bars and bounds* in his Church: Christians in many places, having had *great fulness*, are come to *great wantonness*; and the enemies of the Ministry, and Reformed Religion in this Church, are not such, as have been kept meager, and tame with emptiness, and ignorance; but such as have been *pricked with provender, high fed*, by an *able* and *constant Ministry*. These are grown to such *ferocious spirits*, like *pampered horses*, whom no ground will hold; daily neighing after *novelties*; rushing upon any *adventures*; and impatient to bear those Ministers any longer, by whose bounty they have been so liberally *nourished*, with all means of *knowledge, preaching, conferring*, and *writing*; These now affect *high racks*, and *empty mangers*; *subtilties* rather than *solidities*, and *novelties* more than *nourishment*; yea, they are become the *rivals* of their Ministers, and undertake like *Balaams* Beast to teach their Masters; not onely speaking with them, but against them; yea, seeking to cast them quite off, lifting up their heel against them, and trampling their *feeders* under their feet: Thus having either got the *bride* between their teeth, or having cast quite off their neck the reigns *of Order, Government*, and *Discipline in* Psal. 32. 9. *Religion*, they are become like *Horse and Mule* without *understanding*; without *gratitude, civility*, and *common humanity*; so far they are from *sober piety*: Running furiously without their guides, wantonly snuffing up the wind, and proudly lifting up themselves in their high crested opinions and presumptuous fancies of *notions, gifts, prophecyings*, and *inspirations*; Glorying in this *riotous liberty* and *mad frolicks* of *Religion*; which all wise, humble, and holy Christians know, are not more unworthy of, and uncomfortable to, all good Ministers (who taught them better) than they will be most dangerous, destructive, and damnable to those men themselves, who proudly affect those ruder and dangerous follies in the Church of Christ; who cannot (either they, or their posterity) be ever so safe, *as in Christs way*, at his finding, and under *his custody*; where, with holy and just restraints (becoming *Reason, Order*, and *Religion*) there are also the *most ingenuous liberties*, and the *most liberal fruitions*: Wandering prodigals in Religion, who forsake the order and regularity of their Fathers house, *which is full of bread*, will soon be reduced *to a morsel of bread*.

The greatest enemies of Ministers make them most necessary.

And we see already, such as have in their *pride and disdain* most forsaken

forsaken the *true Ministry*, are come by their *riotous courses*, to *feed on husks*; and from the *harlotry* of their wanton, and fine opinions, to *consort with swine*; having hired out, and enslaved themselves to all *rude,unjust*,and *profane designs*, or else wallowing in *filthy* and *sensual lusts*, which makes them sin against *Heaven and Earth*, and be no more worthy to be called *the sons of God*, or the *children of this Christian Reformed Church*. So that we evidently see, That those men *fight against God*, against *Christ Jesus*, against the *Reformed* and *Christian Religion*; against the *Word of God*, which is the standard of Religion; against the *Unity*, *Order*, and *Catholike conformity* of the *Church* of the *Christ* in all ages; against the *future Succession of Religion*; against their own *souls*; against their *posterity*; against the *common good* of all mankinde; and all such, as may want and enjoy the *inestimable blessing* of the *Gospel*, who ever fight against the *holy office*, *divine authority*, *necessary duty*, *sacred dignity*, and *constant succession*, of the *Evangelical Ministers*, and *Ministry*; without which the *Church of Christ*, like a *Field or Garden*, without diligent and daily *Husbandmen and Gardiners*, would, long ago, have *run to waste*; and been over-run with all maner of *evil weeds*, (which grow apace, even in the best Plantations;) if God in his *wisdom* and *mercy to mankinde*, and to *his Church*, had not appointed some men, as *his Ministers*, to take care from time to time, that the *field of the Church* be tilled in every place; that the *Garden* be weeded, and the *vineyard fenced*; and this especially for their sakes, who are the (πολλοὶ) most of men; whose *cares* and *burdens* of life, or whose *dulness* and *incapacity*, or whose *wants* and *weakness*, or whose lusts and passions, would never, either move them to, or continue them in any way, worthy the *name of true Religion*, if God had not sent and ordained (κήρυκας) *Cryers*, *Heralds*, and *Ambassadors*, to *summon*, *invite*, and by *pious importunity*, even *compel men* to come into the ways of true piety, and happiness; which, being not onely far above *sinful flesh and blood*, but quite contrary to them, had need have a *Ministry*, whose authority, for its rise, assistance, and succession, should be beyond what is of *humane original* and *derivation*; which who so seek to oppose, destroy, or alter, will certainly bring upon themselves, not onely the guilt of so high an insolence against *Christ*, and injury against this *Church*; but also, will stand accountable to *Gods justice*, for those many souls *damnation*, whom their *vanity* and *novelty* have perverted and destroyed, both in the *present age* and *after generations*, for want of *true Ministers*.

Luke 15.

1 Tim. 2. 7. *Præcones, vel Caduceatores.*

These *first weapons* then, which the *Adversaries* of the *peculiar Calling* of the *Ministry*, hoped to finde in the *Armony* of *Scripture*, or *Right Reason*, whereby to defend their *own intrusion*, and to offend

offend that *holy Function*, and *divinely instituted Succession*, are found (I think) to have, as little force in them to hurt the *Ministry*, or to help the *enemy*, as *Goliahs* Shield, Helmet, Sword, and Spear had, either to injure *David*, or secure himself; yea, (we see) those *smooth stones*, those *pregnant* and *piercing Authorities* of many clear and concurrent *Texts* of *Scripture*, both for *precept* and *example*, which I have produced, according to *right reasoning*, from *Jesus Christ*, and the *blessed Apostles*; To which, the *Catholike practice*, and *custom of all Churches* in after times, is as a *sling* directing them, more forcibly and firmly against the *brazen foreheads* of those *Anakims*, that oppose the Ministry; All these together, are sufficient to *prostrate* to the ground their *proud height*, and to put to flight that *uncircumcised party*, who have defied, and seek to destroy, the *holy Ordination of Evangelical Ministers*; whose poor and oppressed estate, although it may now seem, but as little *David*, with his *Scrip* and *Staff*, in the eyes of *self-exalting adversaries*, who despise and curse them in their hearts; yet these may finde them to come in the *Name* and *Power* of the *Lord*; sent by *Gods mission*, furnished with *Christs commission*, and appointed by the *Churches* due *Ordination*, to be *Leaders*, *Rulers*, and chief *Officers* in the *Church Militant*, under *His Excellency* the *Lord Jesus Christ*; who is the *Generalissimo*, chief *Captain*, and *Prince of our Salvation*; who having in former times delivered his Servants, the true and faithful Ministers, from the paws of the *Lions* and *the Bears*, (Heathenish force, and Heretical furies) will also deliver them out of the hands of these *uncircumcised Philistims*; who, having received from their Ministry, what ever honor and privilege, they can pretend to as Christians, yet now carry themselves, as if they were *aliens from the Israel of God*; and had never had relation to, or blessing from, this or any other true Church; where hath been a constant Ministry, not more *famous* for Learning and Industry, than *blessed* with all *Evangelical excellencies*, and *happy successes*: To which now, the *Lord* is pleased to adde this *crown of patience*, under great tribulations, and of perseverance in suffering much evil discouragement, where it hath deserved so well.

1 Sam. 17.

Heb. 2. 10. ἀρχηγὸς τῆς σωτηρίας.

CAVIL

CAVIL III.

Or Objection about Christian gifts, and exercising in common as Preachers or Prophets.

ALl impartiall spectators may hitherto behold the salvation of God; how the insolent opposers of the Ministeriall function, the men of *Gath*, are in their first encounter so deeply smitten and wounded, that they ly groveling on the ground: The remayning motions which they may seem to have, are but the *inordinate strokes* of hands and heels, the last *batteries*, and weak struglings, which attend impotent revenge and *exspiring malice*; It will be no hard matter, to set *my foot* upon their prostrate power; and to sever their Heads from their Shoulders (that they rise up no more) by the means of that *two edged* and *unparalleld Sword* of the Scriptures, rightly applyed; which hath both sharpness, weight, and brightness; the clearest reason, potentest conviction, and divinest Authority; with which they thought to arm themselves against the peculiar Office of the Ministry.

Inconditi morientium motus & invalidi exspirantium conatus. Sym.

Yet there are some *seconds* and *recruits* (who seem to have less fury and malice against the Ministry) who seeing the chief *Champion* of the Antiministeriall faction, thus *Levelled*, come in, either as to the spoyl, or rescue, (as *Ajax* to *Ulysses*) holding before them the shield of manifold Scriptures; Alleging, That notwithstanding there may be granted some peculiar Office and Institution of the *publike Ministry*; yet, as to the power *of preaching*, or liberty of prophecying, the promise is common to all believers, for *the powring out of the spirit upon all flesh, in the later dayes*: for the *Annointing* from above, which shall lead every believer *into all Truth*; so that they shall *not need* any man *should teach them*: being *all taught* of *God*. That the manifestation and *gifts of the spirit* are given to every one for the good of the Church; in teaching, exhorting, prophecying, *&c.* Which every one is *to covet*, and may communicate to others, for their conversion, or confirmation; as *Aquila* and *Priscilla* did to *Apollos*, and other Christians in *Primitive dispersions*; exercising and employing their talents received, if not as *Ministers* in Office, and ordeined, yet as *Prophets* and *gifted Brethren*; if not as Pastors, yet as Teachers; In like sort Christians, now, find their gifts of knowledge and utterance so great and good, that they cannot smother them, nor suffer them to be restrained and oppressed by the Ministers *encroachment* and *Monopoly*. Thus they, who would seem to be somewhat more civill and equanimous to the calling and Office of the Ministry.

Joel. 2.28. cited Acts 2.17.
1 Joh. 2.27.
Rom. 12.6.
1 Cor. 14.1.
1 Thes. 5.19, 20.
1 Cor. 12.7. 39.
Acts 18.26.
1 Pet. 4.11.

Answ. 1. *Gifts in others no prejudice to the Office of the Ministry; nor warrant to any man publike arrogancy.*

* Socinus lib. de Eccl.
* Osterod. Inst. c. 42.
* Smaltzius de Ord. Ecc.
* Radeccius de Eccl.
* Theoph. Nicolaides defens. Socin. c. 1.

My Answer first in generall is: That all these and the like small shot, which *Infaustus*, * *Socinus*, * *Osterodius*, * *Smaltzius*, * *Radeccius*, * *Nicolaides*, and others of the *revived Arians* have afforded these *Semiantiministeriall adversaries*, have been oft discharged, and received, without any hurt, as to the divinely established Office of the Ministry; Having been either satisfied with all *ingenuous concessions*, as far as *order*, *modesty*, and *charity* will carry them; or refuted with just *replyes*, against all vanity, arrogancy and confusion, by those learned men, who formerly or lately have given very sober, solid, and *liberall satisfaction* to any pleas urged, or scruples alleged out of Scripture; which will in no sort maintain idleness, vanity, pride, and confusion in the Church; under the *specious names* of liberty, gifts and prophecying; There are indeed many places exciting Christians to labour, to *abound* in every good gift *and work*; but yet as many to keep them within due order and holy bounds, becomming the honour of Religion.

Acts 14.23. When they had ordained them elders in every Church.
Acts 13.2. Separate to me *Paul* and *Barnabas*
1 Tim. 4.14. & 5. 22.
Acts 18.28.
Heb. 14.17.
2 Tim. 2. 4.
1 Thes. 5.12, 13.
1 Tim. 5.17.
1 Cor. 12.18, &c.
1 Cor. 14.32. V. 33. & 40.
Rom. 16 17.
2 Thes. 3. 6.
2 Tim. 4. 3.

All those (χαρίσματα) gifts were never more eminent and common in the Church of Christ, than in those times, when the Ministeriall power was by peculiar marks, ceremonies, and duties, distinctly and undoubtedly conferred on some *peculiar persons*; as, the *Apostles*, and 70. *Disciples*; on *Timothy*, *Titus*, and others, who were separated, and ordeined, by fasting, praying, examination and imposition of hands, to be Bishops or Presbyters in the respective Churches, as they came to be capable of setled order and Ministry. And notwithstanding the *extraordinary gifts of the Spirit*, which were then conferred upon many, not yet *ordeined Ministers*, we see, the Office and honour of the Ministry was never more clearly asserted, as *divine* (being set *over the flocks* by the Lord) so to be owned and esteemed, as distinct from *secular intanglements*, as an retire and compleat *imployment*, even for the best and ablest men, to which they should once ordeined *wholy give* themselves, and attend on it. Never was *order*, and peace, and *proportion* in the Church more enjoyned, and duly observed; never were *disorderly* and *unruly* walkers, false Apostles, *self-obtruders*, *house-creepers*, *heaps of teachers*, who caused divisions, more *severely* repressed, than in those Primitive times, when believers enjoyed most eminent gifts and graces *for some* ends: either in miracles, or toungs, or prophecying, (which was not that eminentest *sense of prophecying* (that is, *foretelling things* to come;) but *the opening* and *applying* the places of the Prophets, in the *old Testament* (which was then the only Scriptures the Church had; which St. *Peter* calls the *more sure word of Prophecy*) by which it might appear to the Church *more clearly*, that the crucified Jesus was the *Christ*, the promised, prefigured, and prophecyed *Messias*; so establishing the

Primitive prophecying, what.
1 Pet. 1. 19.
Prophetæ Scripturarum interpretes erant

the tradition and history of the new Testament (which concerned the Nativity, life, miracles, sufferings, death, resurrection, ascension, *&c.* of Christ,) by the places of the old; wherein oft times an Auditor among them *might have* that further *light* revealed to him, as to the fuller *sense* of any place, which another was handling; and this, but occasionally, not as a constant habit; only at present, it was beyond his naturall abilities, or endowments acquired by studies, *&c.* Nor was this (then an extraordinary gift, for the confirming and establishing of the new planted Church, or Christians in the faith) ever used, as it ought, but with great order, all gravity, charity, humility and peace among those, that were truly so enabled: And when any *vain pretenders* came up to abuse it; the Apostle requires, that there be a due *tryall*, and *subjection* of these *spirits of the Prophets* to the Prophets, who might wisely discern between true and false, between holy, wise, and excellent *inspirations*, (which were pertinent *interpretations*, or apt clearings of Scriptures,) and those *weak*, impudent, and *impertinent ostentations*, which were either very *false and foolish*, or *vulgar* and ordinary.

maximè propheticarum & obscurarum. Ambr. Theoph. Chrysost.

Prophetarum munus erat mysticum Scripturarum sensum ad salutem auditorum explanare. Erasm. in. 1 Cor. 14.

1 Cor. 14. 30. 1 Cor. 14. 29, *&c.*

2. *Of right interpreting and applying Scriptures.*

...Which, Secondly, is the most, that our *Antiministeriall adversaries*, who affect the name *of Prophets*, commonly amount too; while they handle the *Scriptures* (most what) with very *unwashen hands*; so brokenly, corruptly, rudely, rashly and perversly, as makes them not any way extraordinary Prophets, but *ordinary proclamers* of their own ignorance, shame, and impudence: who think they may take *liberty* in nothing more, than in abusing and wresting the holy Scriptures, which are sufficient to make any man of God perfect, both in gifts and graces, in abilities and in humility: And which should not be handled either privatly, or publikely, but with great humility, care, diligence, exactness and conscience; Since, as they were not of *private* and humane invention, so nor are they *of private interpretation*, after every mans sudden, unstable, and unlearned fancy; Who rashly singles out *texts* of Scripture here and there (as they do a *Deer* out of a Herd,) and runs them down, till they fall at the foot of his fancy or opinion; *torturing* and racking the places till they speak to his mind, and sense: Thus often times the Church of Christ hath seen men of proud and corrupt minds (as they say *Toads* of good Eggs hatch *Cockatrices*) from *some places of* Scripture ravished from their fellows, and *wrested* from the main *scope* and context, bring forth most *hereticall* and *monstrous productions*; contrary to those truths, which are most clearly set forth in the whole *tenour* or Analogy of the Scriptures, as their great design and main intent: Such those of old were, against the *divinity and humanity* of Christ; Against the holy Trinity; Against the grace of God; and of late against the Law, the Souls Immortality,

2 Cor. 2. 17.

2 Pet. 1. 20. 2 Pet. 3. 16.

Omnia adversus veritatem de ipsa veritate constructa sunt: operantibus æmulationem istam spiritibus erroris. Tertul. Apol. c. 47. *Dominici eloquii fures & violatores.* Aust

De Donatistis Retract. l. 21. *Falsa interpretatio Scripturæ est nervus Satanici regni.* Hilar.

mortality, good works, both the Sacraments, all holy duties as forms; Against any resurrection and judgment to come, against the very being of any Catholick Church, against the Scriptures themselves; And so now against any *Succession* or peculiar order of ordeined autoritative Ministers, to hold forth the Gospell of Christ, and true Religion to the world: So the Maniches from *Eph.* 2. 2. *By nature you are the Children of wrath*, argued Nature of man to be Evill, And from a principle of darkness and sin, coeternall with the good God. *Aust. Retract. l.* 15. *Apollinaris* and *Eutiches* argued from *the word was made flesh*, That Christ had not two distinct natures, but only one, the flesh turned into God. So *Arrius* against the Divinity, *Nestorius* against the Unity of the person of Christ. The *Anthropomorphites* urged Scripture for those humane shapes, which they grosly imagined to be in God, as in Man; because God speaking to man, speaks as man, not as he is in himself, but as he is most conceivable by us. In none of all which errors, those Patrons of them, any more than these (for liberty of opining and of prophecying as they list) will seem to want either *reason* or Scripture; which sometime they will call a dead letter; yea and killing too; Affirming that both it and the Ministry too are needless; that all are taught of God, by a *quickning Spirit* and a *Speciall unction*, &c.

1 Cor 3.22. 23. 2 Cor. 4. 15. Rom. 13. 8. Joh. 6. 27. Mat. 6. 25. 1 Pet. 3. 3. Tit. 1. 15. Mat. 23. 9. 1 Pet. 2. 9.

The same men can prophesy too if you let them alone, against all *civill property* and common equity and honesty, out of that place, *All things are yours, and you are Christs, and Christ is Gods*; Against borrowing, or at least *paying any* pecuniary debts; by *Ow no man any thing, but love*; Against all *honest* labour and diligence, by *Labour not for the meat that perisheth, Take no thought for to morrow*; Against *all modesty* and decency in cloaths, by that, *not of putting on of apparell*; Against all restraints of Laws and bounds of holiness in any thing, by that, *to the pure all things are pure*; *All things are lawfull for me*, 1 *Cor.* 6. 12. Against all *duty to Parents*, subjection to *Masters and Magistrates*, by *call no man Father, or Lord*: *be not ye the servants of men*, 1 *Cor.* 7. 23. by being *Gods freemen*; for, you are a *royall Priest-hood*, *ergo*, no peculiar Ministry; whereas that was said, to the Jews first, who had a peculiar

Exod. 19. 6.

Priest-hood, by which the whole Nation was blessed and honoured of God. Thus the devill, and his seducing instruments, never want *their lectures*, *quotations*, and *common places*, out of the Scriptures; When pride, poverty and liberty, once meet together to *prophecy* as they list, what mad work do they make, with *Scriptures*, Religion, conscience, and all order and Laws of Church or *civill societies*? As those false Prophets in *Germany*, not long ago did, and others after in *England* designed to have done, making the holy Scripture, which is the pure fountain of life, the very sink and receptacle of all heady opinions and sordid practises.

Muncer and *Phifer*. *Hacket* and *Arthington*.

Where

When as the *Holy Scriptures*, which are the *oracles of God* and hold forth his mind to the world in matters of Religion, are to be *understood* and interpreted (not by *minds leavened* with hereticall pride, or Schismaticall *peevishness*, or *captious* and criticall *moroseness*, or *Scepticall cavilings* and *janglings* (which commonly drive some other secular and *sinister end*, rather *than any thing* of true faith, good manners, and an holy life:) but, with all pious and cautious consideration, all humble diligence, and *ingenuous candor*; Which first regards, the *joynt Analogy*, the *concurrent tenor*, and that clear *proportion*, or *rule* of faith and holy life, in doctrine; both for *mysteries*, and *moralities*, which are evidently shining from many places, that *are Indisputable*; either for the clear Instructions in *morals*; or Institution in *mysteries*; or Imitation in Illustrious and commended examples for order and policy: All which are enough to make a man of God, and any Church of Christ, *perfect to salvation*.

Purissimum veritatis fontem in putidissimam errorum sentinam vertunt hæretici. Jeron. *S. Scripturæ locis multi abutuntur, ut si quis medicinalibus ferramentis se graviter vexet: quæ non ad vulnerandũ sed ad sanandũ sunt instituta.* Aust. Ep. 141. *Sensus Scripturæ expetit certæ interpretationis gubernaculum.* Tert. *Nulla vox divina adeo dissoluta est & diffusa, ut verba tantum defendantur, & ratio verborum non constituatur.* Tertul. de præs. ad Hær. Rom. 12. 6. 2 Tim. 3. 17.

And such light, *from the clear propotion*, and *concurrent harmony*, or constant tenour of Scriptures old and new hath this point of the peculiar *function of the Ministry Evangelicall*; both from the practise and precept of Christ, and his Apostles, and others after them; to which the use and judgement of all Churches do fully attest: In that tryall, approbation, benediction, *imposition of hands*, Ordination and solemn mission of some men in the Church to the *Office* and work of *the Ministry*, which is set forth in the New Testament: Against all which, *so full clear proofs, and so constant a light*, what ever can be urged, by *single* texts, or solitary and occasionall examples, out of Scripture, must needs be by these objecters either weakly, or wilfully mistaken in the phrase and manner of speaking; or else is *wrested* as St *Peter* tels us by *ignorant* and *unstable minds* from the *scope* and design of the Spirit of God in that place, (which is the measure of all right Interpretation:) Or else it only relates to something done by the rule of *occasionall prudence*; or speaks of some practise, which was only *temporary* not binding; or *miraculous*, and extraordinary; which cease, when the gift and occasion ceaseth; or it may be in some cases of *urgent necessity*, which might befall an Infant, planting, incompleat, *inorganicall Church*; either not fully *formed* and setled in the *due order*, or suddainly pressed and scattered with vehement *persecution*, and so forced from that order and exactness in outward Ministrations of the Church,

Nolunt agnoscere ea loca S. S. per quæ revincuntur: his nituntur quæ ex falso composuerunt, & quæ de ambiguitate ceperunt. Tertul. de præs. 2 Pet. 2. 16. *Tantum veritati obstruit adulter sensus quantum & corruptor Stilus.* Tert. de præs. ad Hær. c. 17. ὅπως λαβόντες τὰ λεγόμενα [illegible]. Epiph. h. 75. Acts 8. 4. They that were scattered abroad went every where Preaching the word.

which regard a sociall, publike, and common, more, than a solitary, and private professión of Religion, and which, in the Churches *setled condition*, they otherwaies duly and conscientiously observed, as *the will of God*. All which extraordinary cases are, in *all-wise mens judgement*, very far different and distant from that of this Church of *England*, unless it may seem under *some persecution*, by slanderous toungs, by false Brethren, and deceitfull workers, and disorderly walkers, the *troublers of our* Israel; whom the Apostle *Pauls* charity to this reformed Church, would (no doubt) have wished, that either *their mouths might be stopped*, or they *might be cut* off, and delivered with *Hymenæus, Philetus*, and *Alexander* the Copper-Smith, *to Satan*, that they might *learn not to blaspheme* the Scriptures, and the true Ministry, and this true Church, and in all these; the Gospell and name, with the Spirit and grace of Christ, all which have been manifested among us by the Ministers of this Church.

ut cresceret plebs & multiplicaretur, omnibus inter initia concessum est Evangelizare & Baptizare, & Scripturas in Ecclesia explanare. Ubi autem omnia loca circumplexa est Ecclesia conventicula constituta sunt, & rectores & cætera officia, &c. Ut nullus de clero auderet qui non ordinatus esset præsumere officium, quod sciret non sibi creditum, &c. Cœpit alio ordine & providentia gubernari Ecclesia. Com. in Eph. 4. Amb. ascridta. Tit. 1. 11. Gal. 5. 12. 1 Tim. 1. 20.

3. *Those and the like places answered in generall. The no validity of such captious disputings by Scripture, against Scripture.*

Truly I do not think that the so oft repeaters *of their Socinian Crambes*, The objectors of those and the like single places, or those temporary and occasionall practises in Scripture, by which men or women unordeined to be Ministers, did privately teach, or publikely prophesy, can be so weak and silly (many of them (for some of them are men only in malice, against *the Ministers*, but *children* in understanding;) as to believe, That there is any such weight or force in any of those objections, which their own reason and conscience (if not blinded with passion and prejudice against the Office of the Ministry,) will not tell them have very easy, *fair and full solutions*; Either first from the *extraordinariness* of the gifts, which were but *temporary*, and to which these men can with no face pretend, by any thing yet discovered by them, (Their zeal to disgrace and destroy the Ministry, by perverting and wresting the Scriptures, is no sign of their Apostolicall gifts, but of *their Satanicall or Schismaticall* malice;) Or secondly they are answered from the case of *the Church* in some places newly planted, or *persecuted* and scattered; Or thirdly, by the common exercises *of private Charity* among believers one to another; which all good Christians and Ministers allow still, and rejoyce in the *order, usefulness* and *modesty* of those charitable gifts, and Brotherly exercises, which may in their proper place (*being duly regulated*) as well consist with the divine authority and peculiar *eminency* of the Ministeriall function, as the *Moon* and *Stars* may be in the same firmament *with the Sun*; Although shining in a different time and orb, with different lustre, and to far less degrees of influence, yet to the same common end, the good of this inferior world.

Adulteria Scripturarum & expositionum mendacia. Tertul.

So

So that no wise and gracious Christian in reason can, or in conscience ought to sheath *those or other Scriptures* in Ministers bowels, which are rather *for their defence* and assistance, Shewing indeed the great use of a *constant* peculiar Ministry; to prevent the Churches desolations and such necessities of meaner supplyes: So far are they, from affording any ground, either wholy to give *a bill of divorce* to the setled Ministry (which by so many clear and pregnant texts is plain to be *divinely Instituted*;) or to encourage any Christians to entertain those proud and *spitefull Peninnahs* of pretenders to be *gifted* men; thereby to *grieve and vex* the Souls of the true and faithfull Ministers (as she did *Hannahs devout meekness*, with her malipert *insolency*) (1 Sam. 1.) It is no argument to perswade the Church therefore to cast out of Christs family *the Stewards* and dispensers *of holy mysteries*, which he hath appointed, because Christians have sometime in their enforced wandrings, been relieved by some strangers, or private and mutuall *Charity*; which may in such cases be *great*, though their gifts and provision be but moderate! However it were madness for Christians now where no necessity or disorder presseth, and when *neither gifts* are so good, nor Charity so great in any of *these new men*, to venture themselves upon their powers for supplyes; who (like the *foolish Virgins*) have too *little for themselves*, however they boast of their full Lamps and Oyl to spare. (*Multum differunt lex necessitatis & ordinis: quod ita fieri debet, & quod aliter fieri non potest.* Reg. Iu.)

Such small and feeble oppositions then, which (as *Tertullian* tels us) *either Hereticks or Schismaticks* are wont to bring from *broken and abused* Scriptures, for their novell opinions, their proud and pragmatick *confusions*, against the *antient and Catholick* sense, which the Church hath alwaies held forth by its practise, agreeable to the many clear and unquestionable places, do no more weaken the *divine authority* of those things which the Catholick Church upon lively grounds observeth (as it alwaies hath this of a constant ordeined Ministry) no more I say, than if *Dalilah* should have plucked two or three of *Sampsons* hairs, instead of cutting off his goodly locks and prodigious tresses. (Lib. de præsc. adv. Hære. *Proprium hoc est hæreticorum ex paucioribus Scripturæ locis plura intelligi velle.* Tert. ad Praxeam.) (Judges 16.) Nor may these false and flattering *Dalilahs* of our times, (who by cauponating Religion and handling the *Scriptures deceitfully*, seek to betray the strength, honour, and order of this reformed Church in *England*, under pretences of great kindness) think, that by twitching thus one or two hairs, the Ministers *strength* will fail them; or that the *Anti-ministeriall* Philistins shall presently be upon them, so as easily to prevail against the whole function of the setled Ministry; which being *divinely* instituted, and derived, will ever be *divinely assisted*: No, we find yet, (through the might of *Gods grace*, and the testimony of good *consciences*,) so great a strength and holy courage, in all (2 Cor. 2, 17.) (Mat. 28. 20.)

true and faithfull Ministers, as is abundantly able to assert themselves, their function, and the reformed Religion of this Church of *England*, against all these *Apollyons and Abaddons*; We are not so *dispirited*, nor *distressed*, but that we can still rowse up our selfs in the strength of God, and in the Spirit of Jesus Christ, and in the authority of our holy function; so, as easily to *break in-sunder* all such *withs and cords*, by which the *enemies*, not so much of our persons, as of our calling and Religion, hope *to afflict* us; so that these *uncircumcised in hearts* and lips, shall not safely touch us, or mock us. Only, as *Sampson* did *of the men of* Judah, we humbly crave of the secular powers, which are now over us, *that their hands may not be against us*, to fall upon us themselves; however they expose us, thus to contend with those men of *Ashdod* alone: Who came about us first *like Bees* with their importune stings, their vexatious disputings; But now they threaten to come upon us like *fat Buls of Basan* on every side, with their *horns* lifted up on high to destroy us; But the *Lord will* be *on our side*, so that we shall *not need greatly to fear* what these beasts of the people (these unreasonable men) can do unto us; Who will soon be extinguished, as fire *among the thorns*, when once the Lord shall arise to plead his own cause, not only by the *zeal*, and *patience*, and *constancy* of his servants the true Ministers; but also, by stirring up the *spirit of wisdom* in the hearts of all true Christians; who will soon be asham'd of that *levity*, contempt and confusion, which these mens vanity, or impiety, and hypocrisy, would fain bring upon them, and their posterity, in this great concernment of the set ed Ministry, and the true reformed Religion.

Judges 15.17.

Psal.118.12. *Et multitudine inimicorum & magnitudine pressus: & viribus & numero valentium.* Psal.22.12. Psal.68.30.

The evill designs of such captious disputers against the Ministry.

1 Sam. 5.

Rev. 9.7.

Mat. 7.10.

Zach. 4.12.

There are (no doubt) who of a long time have endeavoured and sought opportunity, when they might bring *with Carts and high shoos*, by the illiterate *rudeness* of the *seduced vulgar*, the *Ark of* our Reformed Church and Religion, into the house *of their misshapen* Dagon, which hath upper parts like a mans, but the lower *as a Fish*, the head adorned with Christian Religion, but the tayl deformed with superstition. They softly and fairly pretend *liberty* and improvement, with mens faces and womens hair as the *Locusts* which rose out of the *bottomless* pit) but they will end in the *Scorpious* tayl of *licentiousness*, superstition, and profaness; Such *Reformation* will soon prove *deformity*. They speak of *bread*, but it *will proove stones*, and Serpents instead of Fishes. Such manifestations of *private gifts* in wanton and presumptuous Spirits, will soon turn to the *quenching* and *resisting* of the true light and heat of *Gods Spirit*, whose purer flames are only fed with that *holy Oyl* which flows from the golden vessel of the Scriptures, divinely infused into them, and diffused into the humble hearts of all good Christians by

those

those pipes *of the Ministry*, which Christ hath appointed for that service: This *Anti-ministeriall Liberty*, which some seek thus to dress up, by an *adulterous* and wanton bravery, against the *calling of the Ministry*, is like the *woman which sits in the midst of the* Ephah *of wickedness*; upon the mouth of which God will (ere long) cast such *a talent of lead*, as shall cover and stop it up, by the just indignation and abhorrence of all good Christians, to see themselves, this Church, the Ministers of it, and the Reformed Religion so much wasted and abused, by such *prodigies of profaness* as some of them are: who speak nothing, but *proud*, and *perverse things*; full of *bold blasphemies*, and Anti christian confusions; under the colour of *gifts* and *Liberties of prophecying*; whereto as the wisdom and holy order set forth in Scripture give me countenance; so, in the next place, neither do these mens gifts, which they so boast and vapour of give any incouragement. Zach. 5. 7.

4. *The vanity and emptiness of these Anti-Ministerials as to their pretended gifts.*

For first no wise man doubts of those *mens emptiness, which their great noyse* and *sounding* sets forth every where: shewing they are *very full of themselves*; *puffed* up with their *own leven*; applauded also by some others, and blown up by people of their *own size*; who are as prone to flatter confident talkers, and undertakers, as Children are to fill *empty bladders* with wind; *Pint-pots* will cry up one anothers capacity and fulness, till they are set neer or compared and emptyed into *quart or gallon vessels*; 'Twill then appear, though they were soon full and ran over, yet they held but little, and are soon exhausted. These *Behemetick Preechers*, *Spagyrick-Illuminates*, *Familistick Prophets*, and *Seraphick Teachers*, who pretend to such strange Prerogatives of gifts, and new Lights, above all other Christians, yea and beyond the ablest Ministers; like frantick men alwaies bosting of their riches, strength, treasure, beauty, &c. amidst their sordid necessities, If a wise man come neer them, he shall find, that as to any true light of good learning, or sound Religion, they are *as dark and dusky*, as if they had been begotten in the Eclips of the Sun, and born in the last quarter of the Moon.

Vasa, quo inaniora eo sonantiora. Vulgus hominum, quæ non intelligunt impensius mirantur. Jeron.

Molesanorum Christianorum ut phreneticorum hominum & delirantium illud proprium est, Sibi semper adblandiri; de se suisque magna polliceri: jactabundi de Thesauris suis & divitiis, cum sint pauperimi; se reges somniant & ostentant, cum vincti, & cæsi, & laceri sint: vel uno hoc miserrimi quod sui ipsorum non misereantur. Erasmus. *Quartâ Lunâ nati plerunque moriones & Lunatici*: Cardan.

In good earnest, I wish I could find any just cause, by *their speech*, or Pamphlets, to set my hand to those ample *testimonials*, which these gifted men every where *give of themselves* and *their party*: I have *no envy at their parts*, nor ill will against any of *their persons*, nor have I suffered (or at least am not sensible of) any

 particular

particular injury from any of them: So that I can without any *passion* or *partiality* profess, that I never yet perceived any such *sparks of eminent gifts*, either in reason, or Religion, as renders them, either *envyable* or any way *considerable* in comparison of those Ministers whom they list to cry down, and disparage: Poor men, they are indeed *admirable*, (but not *Imitable*) for a kind of *chimicall Divinity*; which after much pains and puffing, *vapours into smoke*. They are rare for *odd expressions and phantastick phrases*, instead of the *antient Scripture forms of wholesome words*; Nothing is more wonderfull (*as monsters are*) than their *affected raptures*, wild speculations, and strange expressions: imagining that none sees their folly, because they shut their own eyes, and soar above the common mans capacity in specious nonsense: and calling those *glorious Truths*, which are sottish *vanities*, or *shamefull lyes*: What honest hearted Christian can bear the *filthy and unsavory expressions*, of some of these Anti-ministeriall Ranters, Shakers, and Seekers? their *metaphysicall mincings* of Blasphemy; their *ridlings* of Religion; their scurrilous *confounding* of the Incomprehensible *excellencies of God*, of the Lord Jesus Christ, and of the *Blessed Spirit*, with the nature of any creature never so mean and sordid, that to them its no wonder, if the *Egyptian* found *so many Gods in his Garden*, as he had Leeks and Onyons, or Frogs and Toads; Thus amusing their poor and silly auditors with high blasphemies, and most *obscure* extravagancies. Such of old were the rare speculations, inventions, and expressions of the *Valentinians*. Their *Buthi*, *Æones*, *Syzugiai*, *Pseudevangelia*, *Pleromata*, *conceptio spiritualis*, *umbra*, *κένωμα*, And a thousand such blasphemous whimsyes, which *Irenæus* tels of in his times. So that their *Dungeon-like Divinity* and *Mid-night Doctrines*, instead of *fair explications* of Truth by Scripture reasonings and the *demonstration of the Spirit* therein, are rather like *Hedge-hogs*, when they are handled, they wrap themselves up into such *prickly intricacies*; as makes them not *only useless*, *ugly*, and untractable; but hurtfull and scandalous to sober Christians and all true Religion; which these fellows dress up with their *foul fingers*, as Black-Smiths would do fine Ladys, sullying all they touch, while they would seem to adorn.

πολλὰ πραγματεύοντες, οὐδὲν πράττουσιν. Isoc.
Magno conatu nugas & nihil agunt.
Portentiloquia fanaticorum. Iræn.
Et sana & sanantia verba. 2 Tim. 4. 3.
ὑγιαινούσῃ διδαχῇ.
Felices gentes quibus hæc nascantur in hortis Numina. Juv.
Non credentium sed credulorum; non sanctorum sed insanorum; non illuminatorum sed delirantium Theologia. Iræn.

Certainly, If *spirituall gifts*, and *prophecying of old*, had been such *ordinary stuff*, such *raw* and rude *conceptions*, such short *thrums*, and broken ends *of Divinity*, such ridiculous and incoherent dreams, such senseless *and sorry confusions*, as some of these Familisticall fancies usually bring forth, either *extempore*, or *premeditated*; I do not believe the wisdom of the Apostle would have bid Christians either *covet it*, or *not despise it*. Both which precepts import, that such prophecyings as were of old, and are only fit to be used in

1 Cor. 14. 1. & 39.
1 Thes. 5. 20.

in the Church, had and ought to have such tokens of *excellency* and *worth* in it, for the edifying of Christians, as may induce wise and good Christians both to *esteem it*, and desire it; of which sort I think these *presumptuous Propheciers* find but a few, either to follow them or desire them, which is not the least cause of their *great envy* and *indignation* against those excellent Ministers, who so much stand in their light, as *far out-shining* them in all *reall abilities*, gifts and graces, they still retain the best and wisest of the people in some fair degree of order and discretion, which forbids them to choose *the figs of these new Enthusiasts*, which are very bad, before those of their *antient Ministers*, which are very good; between whom (indeed) nothing but extreme ignorance, or *ranting prophaneß* can make any comparison; Nor will their lowd (Εὕρηκα) bostings of rare discoveries, admirable inventions, and singular *manifestations*, salve their credit, or long serve their turn: For what are their rarities and novelties, but either *old Truths* in new *tearms*, *purposely translated by such brokers of religion*, out of the old forms of *sound words*? or else some *putrid errors*, long ago buried, which these (τυμβωρύχοι) searchers of the graves of old heretiques newly light upon, and take for some *rare hidden treasures*. Their splendid fancies like *chips of rotten wood* may shine for a while, and serve to amuse, or scare those silly souls who are still in the dark, *ever learning*, and *never comming*, (by the means of these Teachers) to the knowledge of the Truth; but they will never be esteemed as beams or sparks of divine light, untill all wise Christians have lost their eyes.

Merito contemnendi sunt isti nugivenduli Prophetæ qui Ministerii Evangelici contemptores fastuosissimi, nihil tamen ipsi proferunt præter nugas nugacissimas, & mera deliria. Zanch.

ἀλήθεια πᾶσα εὕρησίς ἐστι, μὴ ἐμπεσόντος πρότερον τῷ θείῳ βουλήματι. Chrysost.

καινοφωνίας βεβήλους. *Profanas vocum novitates affectant, qui antiquas doctrinarum veritates deserunt.* Aust.

In aliquibus splendor est de putredine. Verulam. 2 Tim. 3. 7.

5\. *The arrogancy and impudence of some pretenders to gifts against the true Ministers.*

I have many times been even astonished to hear, and read of the rudeness and incivilities of these Anti-ministeriall boasters: their *blustring* and crowding into Ministers Pulpits; their voluble and ratling *tongues*; their no *foreheads*, their lowd *clamors*; their active hands, their indefatigable agitations. I never wanted or wished any thing more in them, to make them *compleat Prophets*, and Preachers, but only *solidity*, *gravity*, *modesty*, *charity*, some *savour of learning* joyned with humility, and zeal with humanity; some methods of *intelligible reason*, and profitable *Scripture-Divinity*.

Sunt qui victum quæritant non sudore vultus sed impudentia frontis. Eras. de Monachis. *Ventosa & enormis ista loquacitas Religionis modestiam velut pestilenti quodam sydere afflat; nec veritatem ipsam minus quàm castiorem illam Eloquentiam, rebus sacris, & officiis divinis debitam & decoram corrumpit.* Verul.

Of all which they having so little, as amounts to nothing, yet I find they are alwaies *more than Conquerours* in all their adventures; If they do *but affront* a grave, sober, learned, and *godly Minister*,

(who

(who is fit to be *their father* in Instruction, and possibly hath been so, before they thus degenerated) if they dare (as what dare they not, when they go somtimes *like Wolves in heards*, from place to place, seeking what flocks, yea what *Shepheards* they may devour, seduce, or scatter?) If I say they dare oppose him in his own place with their impudent cavills, frivolous quæries, or scurrilous objections: If they can but interrupt him in his holy ministrations, or give him some astonishment to see such unwonted evill spirits *appear in the Church*; If at length they can by barbarous and *intollerable insolencies*, both of words and actions, disorder and hinder him in his *holy offices*, or at least sufficiently shew the rest of the amazed people, how safely they can contemn, and interrupt the *publick service* of God (which kind of *religious riot*, never was tolerated in any civill Nation under Heaven, or among any the *most barbarous*, that owned any *publick worship of their God*,) If the Minister (good man) *blush, and be ashamed*, or somthing disordered by them, and for them; If he in wisdom think fit to confute them *with silence*, not answering *such fools according to their folly*; as *Hezekiah* advis'd his servants to entertain the petulancy of rayling *Rabshakeh*: Or if he so far gratifies their importunities, and bears with their *rusticall manners*, and *confused janglings*, as to dispute with them, and by sober managing good arguments, without any passion, to drive them to apparent *nonplusses*, to all manner of confusions and contradictions; to a thousand absurdities, against all common principles of reason, against all *fundamentals* of Religion; against all Scripture evidences; against all *Maximes*, Logicall, Morall, Historicall and Theologicall; If his *froward opponents*, impatient to be so *soberly baffled*, are forced to quit all clear reason and Scripture proofs, retreating in vain, to their *new lights*, fond interpretations, and false glosses; to their *Seraphick whimseys*, and *Enthusiasticall dreams*, (which can save them no more now from shame, than *Baal* could his *self-wounding* and vainly *clamorous priests*) so that at length they fly to *down-right rayling* and threatning to scare the *good man* with the *next troopers* which they can get to appear with them; if at last, like *Wasps*, they are forced (by the godly Ministers learned gravity and constancy) to quit the place, and only leave their stings of reproaches behind them, being full of infinite malice, regret and despite for their confusion;

[illegible] Naz. Or. 26.

Apud omnes gentes illud invaluit ἀξίωμα, *Sacra publica non sunt temeranda. In hoc enim uniuscujusq; gentis hominisq; constat honos, quòd aliquem numini suo honorem deferunt.* Camer.

Pro. 26 4.

Isai. 36.21.

Ut flammæ frigida suffusa, sic & silentio nonnunquam gravissimè reprimuntur, & coercentur petulantiorū linguæ. Aust.

Perdes vocem in contentione, & nihil consequeris, nisi bilem de blasphematione. Tertul.

1 Kings 18.26

Their insolent boasting after their vain opposings of able Ministers.

Yet presently, after *this great Atchievement*, the *Trumpets* (or *rams horns rather*) must every where sound among the *Anti-ministeriall party*; The ([illegible]) *Triumphant songs* must be sung; Every where it must ring; that the *Walls of* Jericho *are faln*; Babylon *is stormed, Antichrist is plundred*; The *Pulpit guards are routed*. The *victory is cried up*; The *Triumph* must be adorned with colourable Narratives, bitter Invectives, lying Orations, and Philippick

decla-

declamations: signifying, what *glorious successes these doubty Champions had.* Lastly, the *poor Minister*, without any regard to his age, learning, worth, or credit, together *with his whole tribe and function*, must in a *fanatick pageantry* be led *captive*; In their *black coats*, and mourning habits, they must sadly follow *the Chariot* of these *invincible Heroes*; who like *Cæsar*, do but come, and see, and conquer any *true Minister* whatsoever, be he never so fortified with learning, prudence, experience, good credit and conscience; all these are but *stubble* to that fiery *spirit*, which is in these *holy Incendiaries*, who, like *Don Quixots*, or *Knights Errants*, have so many *Romances of religion* in their heads, strange fancies and inchanting opinions, that they never *want Windmills* and *Giants* to encounter; yea, and they never make *adventures* without glorious successes, and *unimaginable Miracles*; doing more wonderfull feats *with a Dwarf*, or a Squire, and an Enchantment, than ever the most *fortunate Generall* did, with the best disciplin'd Army of horse and foot. And in the heat of these *Rodomontadoes* of that credulous and cruell *Faction*, their disdain of Ministers ariseth so high, that they meditate nothing less, than to *sacrifice them* all to their just wrath and indignation; as *Elias* did *Baals* priests (for so they call the best of our Ministers) as if all the English world had lately been convinced, by these gifted men, of their former errors, and converted by *Miracles* and fire from heaven at the word of these rare Teachers, from listning to, or regarding any more, their true Ministers.

Et hoc proprium est eorum, qui de fide & Catholica Ecclesia minus recte sentiunt se suosq; sectatores & asseclas magni semper facere, omni grandiloquentia ornare, contra sentientes vilipendere, & summo dispectui habere. Hoc Gnostici, & Symoniani, & Manichei, & Novatiani, & Donatistæ olim, & omnes ubiq; heterodoxiæ novatores graviter agunt. Terr. *Quod deest meritis & sapientiæ, hoc clamore supplent & jactantia.*

1 Kings 18.

6.

The compare between the abilities of true Ministers, and these pretenders to be gifted men.

Thus is their ordinary *overvaluing of themselves*; thus their *scorn* of all others; thus their *implacable* anger against all able and *good Ministers*, which is therefore the more black and desperate, because it ariseth from *Envy*, and amounteth to *despair*, while they cruelly suspect, and somtimes smartly find, and sensibly feel the *reall abilities* of Ministers, both publickly appearing, and generally esteemed by all wise and good Christians, far beyond their *Phantasms*, their *frothy noyses*, and meer shews of being (as *Symon Magus* coveted to be esteemed) *some great one*; when he bewitched the people of *Samaria*, both great and small, so far as to think him the power of the great God. This makes them so touchy and impatient of *fair disputes*, of calm and sober Conferences, contenting themselves to be *blustering scorners*, and tumultuary opposers of those *excellent Ministers*, whom to compare to such *Zanys*, *Dwarfs* and *Pigmies*, (as to any true worth of men, or excellencie of Christians, or abilities and gifts for the Ministry) were to *honour* these, and to *disparage* those too much.

Insensissima est ira & minime placanda simultas quæ ab invidia ad desperationem procedit, & ideo odio habet quod alterius eminentiam assequi aut æmulari nequit. Lact. Λέγων εἶναί τινα ἑαυτὸν μέγαν. Οὗτός ἐστιν ἡ Δύναμις τοῦ Θεοῦ ἡ μεγάλη. Acts 8.9.

For what, I beseech you, (*O wise and excellent Christians* (for to you still I must appeal) are in *good earnest* those great gifts, and *rare abilities* which these later Donatists so much boast of against the *true and Ordeined Ministers of this Church?* Are they those grave, learned, and well digested-collections; or those judicious, sweet, and wholsome *Confections*; or those cordiall and spiritfull *distillations*, of divine and saving truths, diligently gathered (as Industrious Bees do their Honey) from *various readings*, by assiduous studies, frequent prayers, serious meditations, and well-made observations? Are they from search and understanding of the *Sacred Originals* of the *Divine Oracles*, or from much *converse* in elaborate *Commentaries* upon the Scriptures; from diligent reading of secular and *Ecclesiasticall Histories*; from good in-sight into all commendable *Authors* and *Sciences*? All which the studies and labours of holy and learned Ministers have competently or plentifully afforded them; and they have brought forth to the Churches of Christ, in all ages; and in no age or Church more liberally, than in this last age, and in this *Church of England*. By which Methods of wisdom attending *daily at her Posts and Gates*, true and able Ministers have filled, and are daily filling the *treasuries of their minds*, with excellent and wel-digested matters, *both old and new*, fitting themselves for *every good word and work*: All which *digestions of holy studies*, they seasonably, orderly, and discreetly bring forth with all the advantages (for the peoples profiting) of grave, clear, *Methodicall* and lively *Eloquence*, both in *Praying and Preaching*. These indeed have been, and still are, by Gods blessing, the *reall Ministeriall sufficiencies*, which the true Ministers of *England* have been, and still are blest withall; which *these* pretenders envy, despair of, despise, and would destroy.

Whence the reall abilities of true Ministers; and what.

Mat. 13.52. *Vetera legendo & meditando, nova invenire discimus.* Quint.

Because they know indeed (and so do the most and best of men) that their *short teddar* will by no artifice of clamour, rayling, and *Popular flatteries* ever stretch neer to *that proportion* which true Ministers have, no more, than the *Toad* in the fable, could swell it self to the *emulated Ox*. Alas, all the frippery of these *Brokers* and *bosters*, (who have nothing but a *Long-lane*, or *second-hand divinity*, which they so much hang out at their shop windows) extends to no more than a *plagiary* way of *filching* and *stealing* whole discourses, or taking some *Sermon notes*, from some able Ministers preaching, or writing; This good matter they miserably *prophane* and *deface*, with their evill *prefacings*, odd patchings, ragged mangings of it, and wild digressions from it, the better to conceal *their theft*; yet is this *laziness and theevery* the very best of their shifts; and among the most *veniall arts*, which are used by these *Wasps* and *Drones*, which now begin to grow *Hornets*, and hope to drive the true Ministers, as

The insufficiencies of the Anti-ministerials, and whence.

the

the *old Cananites, out of this good Land,* that they may inherit it; They have no other *staves* and *crutches* to lean their *lameness* upon, but only such as they have gathered out of the Ministers own *woods*, and now (like ungracious children) they beat with them both their own *Parents*, and the *Planters*.

Jos. 24. 12.

For, if at any time these *brazen orators* adventure to entertain their *leaden Auditors* (who like *Callow* birds gape wide, and are greedy to swallow any thing which is brought them,) with stuff of their own proper *mal-invention*, *un-preparation*, and dis-composure; Nothing is commonly more *weak* and flashy, (like whites of Eggs without salt,) Nothing more *loose*, *spungy*, *insinnewie*, and unsubstantiall, than what ariseth from no higher source than their own brains: their *sudden and shallow fancies*, which like *Rhewm* easily swims out of their lips, yea worse, many times nothing is more *pestilently* erroneous, and more *fanatically* confused; Even most *unwholsome*, and (to well-tasting Christians) most *unsavoury medlies* of *filthy falshoods*, desperate and *damnable doctrines*, tempered (as the Rats-bane of old Hereticks (which *Tertullian* tells of) was wont) with some *mixtures of Scripture Texts*, some *light inspersions of Truth*, to make them more *appetitious* and passable with their (at first it may be) somwhat *squeamish disciples*, who by little and little, *as Mithridates*, wonting themselves to nibble *and sip off* poysons, come to that confidence, that they venture to quaff up *any draughts*, into which their bolder *Mountebanks* evidently squeeze, and infuse the *venome* of most loathsome Creatures; such as have spit out their poyson, like the *Racovian Catechism*, and such like *primers of* the Devill, against Christ, and the holy Spirit; against the *grace of God*, the *Law*, the *Scriptures*; against the glorious Essence, goodness, and wisdom of *God*; against the Sabbath and Sacraments; against all *duties*, all distinctions of order, or office in the Church; against all restraints of *humane lawes*, against all holiness, *Morality*, and modesty in mens lives; The only Antidote which their wretched hearers have against all these, or the like poysons of souls, is no other, but their *custome* of drinking such horrid and *abominable liquors*, whose venom hath so *stupified* their *consciences*, that they *are past all feeling* and sense, of either sin, shame, or sorrow. Nor is there ever any of these *new Rabbies*, who can content himself with either the *orders of this Church*, or the Articles of Sound doctrines, or *Catechisticall foundations* and principles which it hath embraced and propounded, upon very *grave and good advise*, as most safe and necessary for Christians; They must ever have some *new fangle*, either of opinion, or practise, to make them *remarkable*.

Ferrea frontis Oratores, plumbei cerebri auditoribus delectantur.

Nihil proficit Congestio Scripturarum, nisi planè aut stomachi quis ineat eversionem aut cerebri. Tert. de Hæret.

Adjectionibus & detractionibus ad dispositionem instituti sui scripturas intervertit illorum pravitas. Cap. 17.

Ibid. Appian. in Bell. Mith.

Modestiora sunt errorum ac vitiorum initia, ex quibus tanquam ex minutis ovis ingentes non rarò enascuntur serpentes. Eras.

Consuetudo peccandi tollit peccandi sensum & conscientiam. Ber. Ephes. 4. 19. *De novitate nomen, & ab improbitate famam quærunt.* Tert.

7. *Gifts alone make not a Minister, nor furnish him with true Ministerial power and authority.*

But, if I should yield (which I cannot do with truth) or only suppose some of these men to have *even ordinary Apostolicall gifts*, (as they vainly and falsly pretend) yet even these would not make them beyond, or better than *fals Apostles*, unless they had the *call, mission and authority*, which *true Apostles* had immediatly from Christ, and which *false Apostles* untruly pretended to, who, though they taught the truth, yet with falsity pretended, they had seen the Lord Jesus, and were sent as other Apostles by him; Nor will those *common gifts* make them ordinary Prophets or Ministers in the Church, unless they have the *ordinary call and mission*, which Christ hath setled in the Church; A Serpent of gold, would not have brought those *healing effects*, which the *brasen* did, at Gods appointement *Gifts of knowledge* and utterance alone, are not *qualifications sufficient* for men to challenge the *right of Ordination* to publick Ministry; for the moralls and practiques of men, as well as their *intellectuals*, are much to be considered; the Priest might be able, and the Levite lusty for service, when they were unclean, and so unfit for the Temple. The levity, haughtiness, rudeness, boastings, and inconstancies *observable in* some mens looks, gesture, habit, and carriage (as St. *Ambrose* guessed at the mine and garb of two *Presbyters*, who afterward proved stark naught) makes them less fit to be ordained Ministers in the Church, than many, who have weaker gifts, but discover more prudence, gravity, meekness, humility, and diligence.

Autoritas Charismata præsupponit, at Charismata autoritatem non ponunt. Gerard. de Minist.

Qualis ordinatio talis successus. Luth.

1 Cor. 3. 3.

In actionibus tam sacris quā civilibus id validum quod legitimum, Reg. Ju.

A stock, and gifts, and parts, either naturall or acquired, though never so thrifty and spreading, is of it self, but *as a crabstock*, and can of it self bear no other than *sour fruits*, of Factions, Schisms, Emulations, and *carnall confusions* in the Church, till it is *grafted with holy ordination*, by that due ministeriall power, which *is in the Church*: As there are *formally*, or truly, no true *Sacraments*, where the same *Elements and words materially* are used, unless there be also a *right Minister* of holy things, who acts and consecrates not in any naturall or civill capacity as from his own mind, or other mens will, but by delegation and appointment from Christ; nor can there be *a right Minister*, or Officer from Christ (as I formerly proved) where there is not a right patent, divine power and commission *given in his Name by due ordination*; as it is but *treason and rebellion*, for the ablest States-man or Lawyer, to undertake and act the part of an *Embassadour* or *Judge*, *untill he be made such*, by those, in reference to whose will and work, such power and employment *only* can be conferred; That cannot be done in anothers name, which is not done by his consent, and according to his declared will. Men of the *greatest gifts*, if they are disorderly in the Church, are but as *Wens in the body*, the greater the worser, the more they swell beyond the modell and true proportion of the *bodies features*, the more

Quo meliores eo deteriores. Verulam. de Jesuitis.

defor-

deformity and inconvenience they bring to the whole body; nor hath any man any cause to boast of them; for it is not *the greatness, but fitness of parts*, which makes them handsome or useful to the whole; who knows not that *great wits and parts are oft-times great temptations*? as was said of *Origen*, whose frequent Preaching in the Church of *Alexandria*, before he was Ordeined Presbyter, gave great offence to grave and godly men, imputing his after errors and fall to his too great forwardness and presumption. The Serpent, which *was subtiller than other beasts*, is chosen by the Devill, as *a fit organe* for to convey his temptations: Proud and presumptuous gifts in men, are no better than those *inordinate excrescencies*, which exceed mens noses, or blind their eyes, or somtimes swell bigger than their heads; nor will their fate be better at last, than that of *the Giants was*, who presuming of his vast limbs, and the extraordinary number *of his fingers and toes*, (which were twenty four in all) yet there wanted not of *Davids worthies*, who slew him, when he defied the Church of God: If men be left to *measure themselves only by themselves*, (as most of these *overwise-men* do) which of them but is prone to think very *highly* of himself? and like the *Apes in the fable*, fancy they can build as brave Houses, and Cities, and Churches, as the ablest man, but when they come to the *Wood*, they have not so much as *Sawes*, or *Axes*, or any tools to begin the work withall?

Magnum ingenium magna tentatio. Vinc. Lyrin. de Origine, & Tertul. Gen. 3.

1 Chron. 20. 6

2 Cor. 10. 12.

But these *over-forward men* usually reply with great sadness and severity against Ministers *Monopolising* of the duty and office of *Preaching the Gospell*, That *Paul rejoyced if any preached Christ; though of envy and evill will, though not Ordeined, &c.* I answer, first, It doth not appear, but those men might have *due Ministeriall power*, to preach the Gospell; and yet through passion or faction they *abused* this power, *seeking their own things, and not the things of Christ.* Or secondly, It may be their preaching was, but *privat, domestique, and charitative Instruction or confirming of others, repeating* as the *Bereans*, *what they had learned of St. Paul*, or other Apostles, which is not denyed to any sober Christians, but only required to be kept within those bounds of *Order* and humility, so as it neither becomes *rivall* to, or opposer of, nor yet a *despiser*, and at last an abolisher of the office of the publique Ministry, which is the design of the presumptuous, and pretenders *against the Ministers*. Thirdly, If those whom the *Apostle* speaks of, were not *Preachers by office*, but only by their own little *motives* of applause or profit, or *Envy* and the like, they were moved to preach the Gospell of Christ, yet they did not like our modern *Intruders* and *Usurpers*, boast of *Extraordinary gifts* and call; nor did they deny, or seek to overthrow in others *the ordinary power and office of that Ministry*, which Christ and

Phil. 1. 18.

8. *Of St. Pauls rejoycing that any way Christ was preached.*

Phil. 2. 21.

Acts 17. 11.

and the Apostles had setled in the Church, and to which they pretended to have a zeal. Fourthly, at the worst, what ever they were, or did, regularly or irregularly, as to the point of *Preaching Christ crucified*, the Apostle so far rejoyced, not, as they were passionate, or *peevish, envious, disorderly, &c.* but so far, as *God restrained* them in any moderate bounds of truth-speaking. It was some joy to see a less degree of *mischief*, and scandal arise from their perverness and spite; That they did not *blaspheme* that Name, and preach another Gospell; or corrupt this in points of doctrine, with Jewish or Hereticall leaven; no less than they did with those *tinctutes of passions*, envy, and defects of Charity: A good Christian may rejoyce at any *preparation of men* to receive the Gospell, as in the *Indies*, tho they be first taught it, in much weakness and superstition; It is so far happy, in the worst of times and things, that there is no simple or *sincere evill, which hath not some mixture of good in it*, which it abuseth, else it could not be at all; and some extraction of good may be from it by the omnipotent wisdome of God, causing all things to work together for the good of his Church.

In omni malo est aliqua boni mixtura; Simpliciter enim & absolute malum esse non potest; Neque enim est malum pura negatio, sed debiti boni privatio, neque est cognoscibile nisi per bonum. Tho. Aq. 1. q. 14. *Non humanæ est imbecillitatis plena indagine cognoscere quâ ratione Deus mala fieri patiatur, quæ non incuriâ sed consilio permittuntur.* Salv. l. 1. Gub. *Mirandum non est quod mala exurgant, sed vigilandum est ne noceant, nec permitteret Deus exsurgere nisi sanctos per hujusmodi tentationes erudiri expediret.* Aust. Ep. 141.

Gods permissions not to be urged against his Precepts and Institutions.

But what sober Christian will urge *Gods permissions* against his Precepts and Institutions? The rule in the Word is still *right, constant, and divine*, though in the water of events, providence may seem crooked and irregular. Gods *toleration of evill*, of disorders, or *heresies in the Church*, doth not justifie them in the least kind against his Word, which forbids them. The Apostle was glad (and so may we be in evill times) *that things were no worse*, but he allows them *not to be so bad*; nor would he approve the doing of evill, or the envy and spightfulness in preaching, that *good might come thereby*; He only considered it in the event, as to *Gods disposing*, not in the agent or fact, as to mans perverting; A sober and wise man may make a good use of others madness and folly, as God doth of mans and devills malice. One may rejoyce, that there are some *poysonous creatures*, by which to make *Theriacas* and Antidotes; Many venomous beasts have the cure in them against *their own stings and poysons*.

Quæ permittit Deus non approbat in permisse praviter agente, quamvis approbet permissionem suam profundissimè & potentissimè sapientia quæ bona ex malo ducenda novit. Vid. Aust. Ep. 120. & Ep. 159. *In abdito est consilium Dei, quo malis bene utitur, mirificans bonitatis suæ omnipotentiam.* Rom. 3. 8. *Multa sunt in intentione operantis mala, quæ in eventu operis bona sunt.* Aquin. *Præscientia & præpotentia sua non rescindit Deus libertatem creaturæ quam instituerat.* Tertul. lib. 2. cont. Marcion. vid. Synes. ep. 57.

The

The same Apostle might rejoyce in the supposed (not decreed and absolute) *Necessity of Heresies* (*There must be heresies*;) that (as in these times) the *constancy* of judicious and sincere Christians may *be made manifest*. It is some ease that *Impostumes* break, whereby corrupt humors are let out and spent: possibly the *Apostle* might in some sense or notion *have rejoyced* in the *storm he* suffred, and the shipwrack, so far as it discovered Gods *extraordinary protection* to him, and for his sake, to those with him. And so may all his faithfull Servants the Ministers, have cause at last to rejoyce, when the Lord hath brought them and this Church to the fair haven, after this foul weather, which seeks to overwhelm them. But Christ is in the ship, and they have a good Pilot God, whose Spirit, with their own, bids them be of good chear. The Lord can and will save his that be godly, from so great a death. But such joyes are the serious and *sincere raptures* of very godly and wise men, far enough sequestred *from the flashes* of the world; which hardly ever discern in *Events*, what is *of God*, from *what is* of man; Good events, in which Gods over-powring is seen, are oft *consequentiall*, not *intentionall*, as to the second agents, and flow not from their *will* or *vertue*, but follow their work, through *Gods soveraign* over-ruling; who, as St. *Austin* sayes, would not *permit any* evill of sin to have been in, and from the *creatures pravity of free will*, and *infirmity of power*, if his infinite both power and goodness, had not known how to extract the good of his glory, out of the greatest evill.

And truly this good, we hope, *through the mercy of God*, both all true Ministers, and all true Christians in this Church of *England*, will reap, by this envy, contention, spitefull, unsincere and uncivill dealing of these *Anti-ministeriall Adversaries*, (who cry up their *new preaching*, and *prophesying wayes*, thereby *thinking to adde affliction* to those bonds and distresses which are upon Ministers in these dangerous and *difficult times*,) That this will make all *true Ministers* more study to be *able* for to walk worthy of, and alwayes to adorn that *holy profession*, and divine Ministration which they have upon them, that so they may *stop the mouths of gainsayers*, who lye in *wait for their halting*, and *rejoyce at their fallings*; Also it will breed in all *others that are serious, sound, and good Christians, a greater abhorrency* of these insolent and disorderly wayes in the Church, the root and fruits of which are carnall, not spirituall, pride, faction, strife, bitterness, confusion, scorn of religion, corruption of all true doctrine and holy manners, neglect and disuse of holy duties; prophaness and disposition to all superstitions, *licentiousness*, flatteries, and *lukewarmness*, as to the power of the true reformed Religion; As is most evident in those places, where these *New-pretenders* have most *intruded* themselves, and *extruded* the true and able Ministers.

1 Cor. 11. 19.

Plus est jucunditatis in sapientia Dei, quæ bona è malis extrahit, quàm in malis molestiæ. Lact. l. de Ira. *Respondet Epicuri quæst. cur Deus permisit mala, cum & potens sit, & bonus, Permisit malum ut emicaret bonum.*

Id. Acts 27.

Severa res est gaudium. Sen.

Cl. Alex. ϛρω. δ. τὸν θεὸν καταχρῆσθαι εἰς καλὸν τοῖς τῶν ἐναντίων τολμήμασιν.

The good which may come from this evill to true Ministers.

Phil. 1. 16.

Tit. 1. 9

Saluberrimus est malorum & inimicorum usus, quo illorum quadam ἀντιπαρασκευῇ, & meliores & vigilantiores reddamur. Erasm.

1 Cor. 3. 1.

Sad

Contempt of the Ministers of the Gospel, paves and strowes the Devils high-way to all impiety.

Sad experience will shortly teach all such as *love* this Church and *Reformed* religion, how much it concerned them to have endevoured great vindications, and by *civill Sanctions* of the honour of the *publike Ministry*; That there may be exact care in the *right authority for ordination*, and true antient succession, which conferrs the Divine power and office; as also *good incouragements*, and assistance in the due execution of it, that it may not be exposed to so many *affronts*, *reproaches*, and *disgraces*, of vile men, and insolent manners, who fear not, openly to contemn such a reformed Church, and its so famous Ministry, together with the whole Nation, and the Lawes of it, even in so high a nature and measure as this is, to vilifie their publike Religion, and to seek to extirpate the true Ministry of it.

Nulla magis illustrantur & confirmantur religionis Christianæ dogmata, quam quæ versutissima hæreticorum pravitas & deturpare & eradicare conabatur. Chamier.

Doctis medicis dant pretium medicastri, ut veris Theologis insulsi & impudentes Theologastri: Ipsi morbi minus noxii sunt quàm medici imperiti. Fernel.

As good Lawes oft rise by the *occasion of evill manners*, like Antidotes from Poysons; so *advantages* may at last accrew to the Reformed religion, and to the true Ministry of it, by *these oppositions*. Nothing makes the lustre of *truth* to shine more clear and welcome, than those *clowdings* and blasphemies, under which it may, for a time, be hidden and *Ecclipsed*; Nothing will make *able Physicians* more necessary and valued, than the swarms of such *ignorant Quacks*, as are of no valew, who are more *dangerous* than any *Plague* or *Epidemical disease*; Nor is the estate of any Church, as to Religion, more safe, by the multitudes of *preaching Mountebanks*, in stead of *True and able Ministers*. In stead of Propating the Gospell, they will every where so corrupt it with errors, so abase it with prejudices and scandals, so harden men against the power of it, by the *rottenness and hypocrisie* of their wayes, that there will be more need of *able and true Ministers* to recover and settle the honour of the true Christian religion in this Nation, than if it were now first to be converted from Paganism; For the Devils strongest holds are those, which are fashioned after the *platforms of religion*, and pretend to more than ordinary piety.

9. *The Character of Anti-ministerial pretenders to gifts.*

Μέγα τοῖς [illegible] Naz.

[illegible] Naz. Or. 1.

. . . So that when I consider the temper and form of this *Anti-ministeriall faction in England*, I find, that their heads by a *ricketly kind* of religion, are grown too heavy for their weak and overburthened limbs; Their self-conceit of their *extraordinary* gifts and abilities, presuming themselves to be able to do, what ever they fancy, makes them more than *ordinarily disabled*, as to any good word or work; Like *Narcissus*, they are so deluded with the flattering *Ecchos of their silly admirers*; and so taken with their own fashion, in such false glasses, that they are like *to doat*, till they die, and starve themselves, as to all *reall sufficiencies*, by the fond imagination of *how great gifts* they have, and their ignorance of how much (indeed) they want. Nothing more hinders *reall abilities*, than too *hasty presumptions* of them: If any of these *gloriosoes* have any

competent

competent gifts of knowledge, as to some things of *Religion*, yet (like the *Chickens* hatcht by the force of Ovens in the heat of *Camels-Dung*, as at *Aleppo*, *Damascus*, and other places in the East) they have commonly something in them, *monstrous*, *odd*, extravagant; either defective or superfluous in opinions, or practise; In intellectuals, or morals, or prudentials; Either vain or morose; light or tetricall; rude or proud; *popular* or *affectated*; Impatient of nothing so much as the bounds of that honest calling, in which God, and the Laws have placed them; Uusatisfied and ever quarrelling with that sober, peaceable, setled way of judicious and humble piety; which becomes good Christians, adorns the Gospell, and keeps up the honour of the Reformed Religion, and of this Church of *England*; which, these mens late *violent extravagancies*, and *disorderly walkings*, beyond and contrary to all holy rules of Religion, all modest bounds, of reason, Law, and common order among men and Christians, seek to make *weary*, *sick*, *and ashamed* of it self; when it shall see it self robbed and spoyled of all its *able Ministers*, Reverend Bishops, *learned Presbyters*, and orderly Professors, and only guarded by *a riotous and incomposed* rabble of such, whose ignorance, weakness and confusions will only serve to betray and destroy, the Reformed Religion; but never to defend it, against those many, malicious, crafty and well armed *adversaries*; who do but ly in wait for opportunities, to weaken, dishonour, disorder, and quite overthrow, both this and all other Reformed Churches.

Humanis oculis locata Religio. Crys. l. 9.

Ardeliones isti tepidos se suspicantur nisi inquieti sint, nec zelantes satis se credunt nisi omnia incendiis commiscentes & pulcherrima quæque Religionis in cineres redigentes. Gerard.

Phrænericus & immundus ignorantiæ Spiritus. Ire. l. 1. c. 13.

Qui custodiet ipsos custodes. Tutela intutissima.

Alas, these *gifted men*, who spread so large sayls, hang out such fair *streamers*, and seek to make so goodly a shew to the *vulgar simplicity*, as if they were strong built, *well rigid*, and richly *loaden vessels*, (fit to endure those *rough Seas* and storms, to which both the Truth and Ministry of the Gospell are frequently exposed;) are easily judged by all wise and truly learned Christians, to be but light keels, and flat bottomed Boats; by their *floting* so loftily; by their running so boldly over any *shelves and rocks* of opinion; by their putting into every small *creek of controversy*; which shews, they draw very little water; that they have not the due *ballast* of weighty knowledge and sound judgement; the want of which makes them so *fool hardy*, so apt to be tossed to and fro with *every wind of doctrine*; so prone to grow *Leaky* and foul, either *letting in under water*, cunningly and secretly, corrupt and brackish opinions, or *shipping* in above deck, openly and boldly, *whole Seas* of any *sinister* ends, and *worldly interests*, that are abroad in the storms and waves and confusions of *civill affairs*; from which the best

Ἀφροσύνης ἐστι τὸ κρίνειν κακῶς, τὸ βουλεύσασθαι κακῶς, τὸ χρῆσθαι κακῶς· τὸ ψευδῶς δοξάζειν, τὸ πάντα πλανῆσαι. Arist. de Virt. & vit.

Audacia est stupor quidam rationis cũ malitia voluntatis conjuncta. Aquin.

Eph. 4. 14. Heb. 13. 9.

πλὴν εἰ τῆς ἀμαθίας γένοιτο ἂν θαρραλεώτερον. Synes. Ep. 14. *Confidentia stultorum imperatrix prudentium scurra.* Sido. θράσος ἀμαθίας ἔκγονον. Naz. or. 26. *Temeritas inscitiæ filia.*

Christians study alwaies to keep themselves most free and unspotted.

Mat.23.5. *Confirmatur hypocrisis Pharisæi quando ampliantur Philacteria.* Chrys.

The *large Philacteries* of pretended *preaching gifts,* which some men so *Pharisaically* set forth to the vulgar view (who as St. *Jerom* saith, easily admire what they hardlyest understand) do not presently make them such *Rabbies,* and *teachers* in *Israel,* as they fancy and affect to be counted, where there is or may be had far better supplies of such able, and right *ordeined Ministers,* as the Church of *England* hath brought up. There are graces and gifts of the Spirit to be shewed in mens silence, as well as in their speaking; (as he that knew how to hold his peace put in his name among the famous Orators;) Yea if the case of this Church were so *desolate* as some pretend, and destitute of able and faithfull Ministers, (which blessed be God it yet is not) yet few of these *forward intruders* of themselves have such sober gifts, and well-grounded knowledge in the mysteries of Christian, and in the ordinary controversies of the *Reformed Religion,* as might supply the Church in its *cases of necessity*; wherein any Christians or Churches may possibly crave and have some relief, as to the *teaching, confirming,* or *comforting* part of the Ministry, from the larger and *golden rule of Charity*; Where Christian communion makes believers usefull to each other, not out of Office and speciall duty, but out of love, and that generall relation they have to each other; Which necessity thanks be to God is not yet the Case of this Church, nor shall ever need to be (by Gods blessing) if *Magistrates* and true *Ministers* would do the duties, which become them in their places: Though the Harvest be great, yet the Labourers are not few, which are of the *Lords sending,* if they may be suffered to do the Lords work: And if those *sturdy gleaners and pilferers* (who thrust themselves into others mens *fields and labours*) did not every where disturb and hinder them by their *sharking* and scrambling.

Mat.9.37.

10. *The Churches supplies in cases of necessity, When true Ministers cannot be enjoyed.*

Who doubts, or denyes, but in cases of reall, not feigned, affected, or imaginary *necessity,* when Christians are forcibly deprived of their true Pastors and Ministers, the Lord *Jesus Christ,* who hath speciall care of his Church, by the assistance of his Spirit, can turn *the water* of some *Lay-mens weaker gifts,* into *wine,* for the Instruction, confirmation, and consolation of scattered and *desolated Christians*; Although those teachers are not every way *exactly prepared,* nor fitted *for every work* of the Sanctuary? Rather than poor Christians, that hunger for the food of Heaven, should wholy want refreshing, *Ravens* shall feed them, as they did wildred and banished *Eliah*: A lay mans *barrell of meal and cruse of Oyl,* that is, his good skill and sound understanding in the *main fundamentals*

John 2. *Laude factam de necessitate virtutem; sed plus illam quã elegit libertas non indicit necessitas.* Ber. Ep. 113. 1 Kings 17. 6. 1 Kings 17.

of

of *faith*, and holy practise; Also in those gracious promises which God hath made to *upright hearts*; these may have *miraculous augmentations* and *effusions* to sustain a *widowed* Church and Orphan Christians in time of dearth: But we must not therefore suffer these *Acephalists*, these *circulators* and *beggars* to perswade us, that we are *famished* in our fathers house (where we see *servants are* wanton with fulness of Bread) meerly that they may *boast*, how they have made us to eat of *their mouldy scraps*, and drink of *their musty bottels*. In the *confusions of* a family, where violence overbears setled order, (removing both chief and inferior Officers;) those supplies are commendable, which the charity and discretion of any servants can afford one the other, yet without usurping any place and authority, which they have not, over others: But in a *setled* and *orderly* family, where there are *Stewards and Officers* appointed, it is a preposterous *charity* for every Servant to undertake to give to the Children, or Servants of the family, their portions. Precedents of extraordinary sustentation with Bread, Wine, and Oyl, either by *miracle* or *Charity*, are no warrant for any mens presumptions, rashness, and disorder, in *ordinary cases*, any more, than those fore-named examples should justify any man from *madness*, who presuming of extraordinary supplies, would cut up all *Vines*, or plant no *Olives*, or use no *tillage* and Husbandry, which are the wayes of Gods ordinary providence, both to exercise and reward mens honest and orderly industry. In like manner, where the Churches or societies of Christians greater or smaller are blessed with the enjoyment of those institutions and gifts which Christ hath appointed and bestowed for the joynt and publike good of his Church, in planting, preserving, and propagating true Religion with good order: (which ever was, and is to be carried on by the right Ministration of the word and Sacraments, and other holy Offices properly belonging to duly ordeined and authorised Ministers) there, *no pretended liberty*, or affected and self-made *necessity*, no right of *commonage* or levelling zeal, may violate *the bounds*, which Christ hath set, and the Churches *ever observed*; He that *breaks the hedges of* Religious order in the Church, the *Serpent* of an *evill conscience* shall bite him.

De Acephalis. Hos neque inter laicos neque inter clericos Religio detentat divina: mixtum genus est prolesque biformis. Isid. Hispa. de off. Ec. lib. 2. c. 3.

Prima est necessitas quam præcipientis Dei autoritas imponit; Secunda, quam permittentis providentia dispensat; Tertia quam deficientis in officio negligentia cogit, quam & peccatum esse & sui pænam cretlas. Bern. *Necessitas quod cogit defendit, modo absit malum morale.* Eccl. 10. 8.

II. *Of Christians Liberty to use their gifts.*

All true *Christian Liberties*, that is, such as are * comely, orderly and usefull, are by all godly and learned Ministers, allowed; and encouraged, in all faithfull people, of whatsoever calling, quality, and condition; *Masters* in their families; *Magistrates* on their Benches; *Commanders* amidst their Souldiers; *Princes* among their sub-

* *Libertas ut matrona, decora*

non est honesta si non sit. Gibeuf.
1 Kings 8.
Augustior Salomon in genua procumbens, quã in solio sedens: ornatior orans quam imperans. Jeron.

subjects, cannot appear, more to their honour and advantage within their places and callings, than, when, like *Salomon,* they shine with that wisdom, piety, and devotion, which becomes all true Christians, on all occasions; and may make them merit the honour of *Princes* and *Preachers* too in *Jerusalem*; which liberties and abilities, the humble piety of wise and modest Christians knows, how soberly and discreetly to use as to any occasion of private charity, or publike edification in their places; yet not insolently and unseasonably to abuse it: so, as to disparage, neglect, and usurp upon the *publike ordeined* Ministry. Every one may read and recite, and tell others of an Act or Proclamation, and help them to understand it; but only an Herald or Officer may publikely proclame it, in the name of him that grants it. Children or servants in any family may impart of their Provision and Bread to one another in charity and love: but this they do, not as Stewards and Officers, whose place is to give to every one their portion in due season. We read the *Bereans* were εὐγενέστεροι, More noble: Not for undertaking to Preach, but for industrious searching the certainty of the truth, duly Preached to them by the Apostles. Nothing is more generous and noble than orderly and Religious Industry. It were happy for all *good Ministers,* if there were every where more of those noble, *generous* and *industrious* Christians among their hearers, who like *the Bereans,* by often meditating, searching, repeating, mutuall conferring, applying, and (if need be) by further explaning, as they are able and have experience, of the word, duly Preached to them, would as it were *break the clods,* and *Harrow in the* good Seed, after the Ministers *Plowing and Sowing*: Yet still there is a large difference, between a true *Ministers* Preaching in Gods name to the *Judges at Assizes,* and *the Judges* reciting or applying some points of the Sermon, with wisdom and piety; so far as suites with the charge he gives; not as a Minister, but as a Christian Magistrate; whose Commission is only civill, to do civill Justice according to Law, and power given by man, between man and man; the other as a Minister is sacred; to reveale the *righteousness* of God in Christ, to men, for the eternall salvation of their souls.

Acts 17.11.

Spontanea voluntate non sacerdotali autoritate obtulerunt sacrificia, Abram, Isaac, Jacob. Isid. Hisp. l. 2. off. Eccl. c. 3.

But why any Christian should affect *in peaceable times,* and in a plentifull soyl, to have either any man that lists to imploy himself, or no Husbandmen or labourers at all in *Gods Field* and Vineyard, who by speciall care, skill, and authority should look to its right ordering and improvement most to the encrease of Gods glory, and the Churches benefit, I can yet see no reason; save only those *depths and devices of Satan*; which are hid under the arbitrary speciousness and wantoness of some poor *gifts,* the better to

cover

cover *those designs*, which the pride, malice, hypocrisy, and profaness of some mens hearts aym at; which are not hard to be discerned in many men, by that extreme *loathness*, and tenderness, which those *tumors*, and inflamed *swellings* of their gifts, and self *conceited sufficiencies* have, to be tried or touched, by the laying on of hands; that is in a due, exact, and orderly way of examination, approbation and Ordination; The fear is, lest if such pittifull *Prophets Spirits* should be *subject to the Prophets*, they should be found to have *more need* to be taught the mysteries, and principles of Religion, than any way fit to *teach others*, by a most *preposterous presumption*; whose foolish *hast* makes but the more *wast*, both of Peace and order, truth and charity in the Church.

Sophistæ verborum magis esse volentes quam discipuli veritatis. Irenæus de iis qui successionem Apostolicam deserunt. l. 3. c. 40.

1 Cor. 14. 32.

In docti præpropere docentes plerunque dedocenda docent; plus zizanii quam tritici seminantes; culturam Domini inficiunt magis quam perficiunt. Aust.

The greatest abillities of private Christians, being *orderly and humbly exercised*, are no way inconsistent with the *function of the Ministry*; they may be easily and wisely reconciled, however some men (whose interest lyes in our discords and divisions) would fain set them *at variance*; That Ministers should be *jealous* of their ablest hearers; and these emulous of their faithfullest Ministers. No hearers are more welcome *to able Ministers*, than such as are, in some kind, *fit to teach, reproove, admonish*, and *comfort* others: Nor are any men more humbly willing to be taught and guided in *the things* of God, by their true Ministers, than those who know how to use the gifts of knowledge, they attain, without despising the chiefest means by which they and others do attain it; which is, by *the publike Ministry* of the Church: This enables them to benefit others, in *charity*; but not to *bost* of their gifts in a factious vanity; or to give any grief, or disorder to the Ministers of the Church; who besides their labours in the *Pulpit*, have so furnished the Church with their writings from *the Press*, that, such Christians as can content themselves with safe and *easy humility*, rather than *laborious and dangerous pride*, may, upon all occasions, (I think) full as well, and for the most part, far better, *make use, in their families*, of those *excellent English Treatises, Sermons*, and *Commentaries*, which are judiciously set forth in all kinds of Divinity, than any way *pride* and *please* themselves in that small stock of their own gifts, either *ex tempore* or premeditated; which serious reading of those learned and holy Ministers works would do every way as well, and far better than this, which weak men *call prophecying*, that is, reciting (it may be by rote) some raw and jejune notions, and *disorderly meditations* of their own; which must needs come far short of *reading distinctly*, and considering seriously those excellent discourses, which learned and wise men have plentifully furnished them with, both with less pains, and more profit to

The use of excellent Books of Divinity Printed in English, far beyond most mens prophecying.

themselves, and others; I am sure with less hazard, of error, froth, and vanity, than what is incident to those self-Ostentations of gifts, which have more of the tongue, than heart or head; and oft-times resemble more the Player, than the Preacher.

12. *Animadversions on some passages in that Book called The Peoples Privilege and Duty as to prophecying, &c.*

So that the late published Patron of the *Peoples privilege and duty as to the matter of prophecying*, needed not to have added to his Book the *odious title of the Pulpits and Preachers encroachment*: For, if that Author will undertake to regulate the tryall and exercise of those gifts of *Lay people*, which he finds or fancies in them, within *such bounds* of reall and approved abilities, of humble, usefull, and seasonable exercising of them, without any Enter fering with, or diminution of the function, and authority of the true, and *ordained Ministry*, which is the aym he seems to propound, I wil undertake that no able and good Minister shall *forbid the* Banes, which he hath so publikely asked; Finding indeed no cause, why these two may not be lawfully joyned together, in a Christian and comfortable union, the *publike gifts* of Ministers, in a publike way of *divine Authority*; and *private gifts* of the faithfull, in a way of private *Christian Charity*: Nor ever did the Godly *Fathers* and *Ministers* of the Church encroach upon, put *away*, or give any *bill of Divorce* to the *humble* and usefully *gifted Christians* Liberty; Only, finding by experience, that (like *Dinah*) it is prone to gad abroad, run out through wantonness, pride, or weakness, to *much disorder*, vanity, and confusion (besides foolish and corrupt opinions,) and of late, to a petulancy, *contempt, and emulating* of the publike *Ordinance* of the Ministry, the wisdom *of the Church*, in all ages (for *ought* I can see) did think fit to keep it, within those safe and *privater* bounds of families, or at most within such friendly meetings, as are short of *publike solemn Church assemblys*: Nor was the modesty of any humble Christian ever grieved, that his abilities should be so wisely *restrained*; While yet, it had all *private freedom* and due encouragements; And in publike far better and more orderly supplies from Gods rich treasury, than from its own purse and penury.

Inconveniences attending that prophecying of the people on the Lords Day.

As for the publike use of *that Liberty and gifts* of *prophecying*, which that *Gentleman* so much crys up and magnifies; I do not think him so much a *puny in* discretion, but that he must needs see, it will be incumbred with many and hardly evitable *inconveniences*, so that it will be easy for a wise man to see the *Quare impedit*. For first, most good Christians are commonly well satisfied with those solemn publike exercises, and duties, *upon the Lords-Day*, as praying oft; reading oft; expounding the Scriptures; Catechising many times; and twise Preaching alwaies; besides the celebrating of one, or both Sacraments; All which are the *blessings*, which the bounty of God hath plentifully provided for Christian people, and powreth on them every Lords Day by the *Labours* of their faithfull and able Ministers; whom Christ and the order of the Church, have undoubtedly set over them in the way of Divine Authority; And to whom all serious Christians attend, as of duty and conscience; affording means *sufficient*, by Gods blessing on their devout *attentions*, judicious *understandings*, retentive *memorys*, fervent *affections*, and suitable conversations, *to save their souls*; For whom it were infinitely better, to have every where such a *Minister duly setled*, and competently maintained, by those Revenews, which are in all Law both divine and humane, due, as given for this service of God and the Church; than for Christians to be *fobbed* off, with new projects of Prophets, gifted Brethren, and modern *Itinerant inconstant and Mendicant Preachers*; which will amount to nothing but mischief; however they may make a shew for a while, as if there needed no constant resident Ministers, or other setled and ordeined Ministry; That so a way may be made to ignorance, superstition, Atheism and profaness, First; And in time, that sacred *Revenew* which is given to God, for the maintenance of his publike service and Ministry, may be turned to some secular uses, and come into private purses. It is most evident, that what *prophecying exercise* is by any gifted Brethren added (in publike) on the Lords Day to this *sufficiency of the* Ministry, will (for the most part) come very short of that weight, worth, and Authority, which usually is in the Ministers learned pains; So that, it will seem, but *as a Churl upon the Gentleman*; as tedious and nauseating, as *small Beer and Water*, after men *have drank well of the best Wine*; Or as the scraps of *coarse and plain Country fare*, after men have been filled with a feast of *marrow and fat things*.

Besides, this exercise of *prophecying*, which that Gentleman so pleads for, will hardly find any *convenient time*, or *temper* in Christians minds, on the Lords Day, either among or after the publike duties of the Ministry; It must needs seem, as *unseasonable*, flat, and *tedious*, as all *superfluities and excesses in matter* of Religion easily do, when they border never so little upon the *Nimiety* or *too much*: It is great wisdom to keep people short from a surfet of holy things; and to leave them with appetites, and give vacancy for digestion, rather than to *cram* and *cloy* them with matters *either of superfluity*, or *curiosity*; when indeed men do scarce with chearfulness and intention bear the holy duties of clear divine use, and most absolute *necessity*; In all which, *common people*, by this *superaddition* of a *prophecying exercise* on the Lords Day, will be but hindred

Cavenda vel maxime in sacris, ne sit satietas; Ne minimum devorando, fastidiosa sit regurgitatio cibi, Cui digerendo vacare debes, ut salubriter nutriare. Greg.

τίκτει γὰρ κόρος ὕβριν, Cl. 41. Strom. 6. Solonis dict. *κόρος τὸ πολλάκις*. Naz.

hindred from that profitable Meditation, and carefull *remembrance*, of what they have already plentifully heard from the Minister, *whose lips ought to preserve knowledge*, and on which the people ought *to wait*, as those that must give acconnt of their souls.

Inflantur potius ad morbos & vanitatem, quam superfluis ferculis nutriuntur ad sanitatem & vires. Ber. *Amarat nimietas quod poterat condire mensura.* Chrysost. p. 125. Pro. 27. 7. The full soul loathes the Hony comb. Mal. 2. 7. Heb. 13. 7.

It will then be neither convenient nor usefull (as it is not necessary,) to bring up *Prophesying* thus in the *rear of preaching*, as to the common peoples capacities or occasions; yea, rather it will be *to the injury* and hindrance both of Minister, and godly people, on the Lords day, unless you be sure to provide the people seldom any Minister; and none constantly resident; or else such *weak and short-winded Preachers*, that they may be sure to give time and room enough to these eager *Prophets*, and to be only *as foyls* to set off their fresh and more *glistring* gifts; or, as an *antepast* of coarser meats, to whet on the *appetite* for that more *delicate* fare, which *these prophets* will pretend to bring forth; we see already many of them stickle for *the Pulpits*, and *are smart rivals* against the Ablest Ministers, whom either small maintenance, or some factious and ingratefull people have almost quite dis-spirited; Upon whom the *Cryers* up, and admirers of these *new prophetick* gifts look, but as the *forlorn hope*, which is to make way all this while for the *main* body of those gifted prophets; Many of whom have so great an activity and *confidence* joyned with their *weakness*, that they had need be very *well-disciplined*, and kept carefully in their due *ranks and posts*, or else they will soon *rout* all order, and honour of Religion in this or any Church; Notwithstanding all *the good hopes*, all the *soft bespeakings* of esteem, and gentle insinuations for their acceptan for made by that *Charitable writer*, who hath so largely pleaded ce, them, at the common peoples bar; And who merited indeed, to have bestowed his pains so publikely, upon a subject that had a better title in the Scripture, and the Church, than this of peoples prophecying seems to have.

Ignorantiæ & imbecilitati proxima est Temeritas.

Besides this, (which I have alleged for inconvenient, superfluous, and so far *hurtfull*, as it is inconsistent with the ministers and peoples duty on the Lords day;) That *Gentleman* cannot but *consider*, how many *childish triflings* in discourses, how many *triviall skirmishes* in disputes, how many captious *bickerings* in words, how many uncomly *thwartings* are prone to arise (as in *Country cudgell-playing*) among *the vulgar*, be they never so godly; if you put them one pin above their pitch, they either crack or sound like strings over-strained, harshly and out of tune; although they may have good gifts

Tot erunt venena quot ingenia, tot pernicies quot & species, tot dolores quot colores, as *Tertul.* begins his *Scorpiacum*

yet as *Arelius* a Painter in *Julius Cæsars* time, who had good skill, in this corrupted his art, that when he was to paint any Goddeſs, he alwayes made them like ſome of his Miſtriſſes; ſo theſe are prone to adorn by their gifts, ſome error or odd opinion, and ſet it forth as a divine truth, and rare doctrine. Nor can you avoid (beſides erroneous and fond opinions) *envyings*, evill *ſurmiſings*, *jealouſies*, *unſatisfiedneß*, and *factious* bandings among the people, whoſe minds will ſoon be divided; ſome *liking*, others *diſliking*; ſome *admiring*, others *deſpiſing*; ſome *attending*, others abſenting from this *unwonted* uncouth exerciſe of Propheſying, which thus confuſed and abaſed will ſoon appear to *judicious* and ſober Chriſtians, a tedious and uſeleſs buſineſs (like Fidlers alwayes tuning, and never playing any good leſſon) and no way fit for a *Sabbath-dayes* ſanctification; when once the Country gaping, or the *gloß and novelty* of it is faded.

against the vanities and varietys of the *Gnoſticks*, who pretended to know more, and be more perfect than the Apoſtles. *Arelius flagitio corrupit artem, Deas dilectarū imagine pingens.* Plin. l. 35. 10.

So then, if the *Guardian* of the peoples Liberty, and privilege in Propheſying, can find any *other time* on the *week-dayes*, wherein to ſet up this exerciſe of *Lay-mens propheſying*, (that ſo people may not at all times come ſhort of that, *which he calls their duty*;) He muſt be ſure to provide Prophets of ſome *competent gifts*, beſides their diſcretion, elſe he will have much adoe to perſwade *people*, that *it is their duty* to neglect their weekly occaſions, and to loſe both their time and labour in attending ruſticall *impertinencies*, and ignorant *triflings* in religion, which (*of all things*) ſhould by wiſe men be avoyded among *the vulgar*, whoſe affections like the poor womans wort is oft very hot in the point of *Zeal*, when it is very ſmall in point of judgement, And is prone to run out from familiarity to contempt, from contempt, to down-right prophaneſs and Atheiſm in matters of Religion, when made cheap and vulgar: If he can indeed, furniſh out men, or women, (for they prophecied too 1 *Cor.* 11.15.) of *ſuch prophetick* gifts, as are worthy, to be eſteemed and encouraged by ſober and judicious Chriſtians, I ſhall promiſe him that I more willingly, and more conſtantly will be *their auditor*, (at convenient times and places,) when I hear they do, what becomes wiſe, humble, ſerious and modeſt Chriſtians, than moſt of theſe *pretenders* to be ſuch gifted men, and to have ſuch prophetick ſpirits, are *hearers* of *the true Miniſters* of this Church, be they never ſo able, either on the Lords day, or on any week-day *Lecture*; For, the firſt way, that many make to bring in their *Lay-prophets*, and *gifts*, is with *their feet*, trampling, *as it were*, upon the beſt *Miniſters*, and *their faithfulleſt pains*, while they ſcorn to ſtep out of dores to hear them, either Praying or Preaching, which pride and negligence, are not the leaſt of thoſe vertues, which recommend thoſe Prophets.

Of peoples prophecying on the week dayes.

τὸ γὰρ δημοσίᾳ φιλοσοφεῖν, μεγάλης ὀρέξεως τῶν θείων καταφρονήσεως. Syneſ. ep. 142. ex Lyſide Pythagoreo. Contempt of Religion riſeth from making holy things too triviall and common.

To

To be plain, the truth is, so much bran, filth, and dross of pride, popularity, schism, malipertness, and contempt of all men, that differ in any way form or opinion from them, and (of all Ministers above all) do hitherto generally appear in the face and manners of many of those (who more affect the name of *gifted men and Prophets*, than ever the *Pharisees did* the title & name of *Rabbi*,) that most sober and wise Christians suspect, they will hardly ever make such *Loaves*, as may be fit for *Shew-bread*, to be set up in *any publike place* of Gods house and Sanctuary ; If that Gentlemans piety, which seems tempered with much ingenuity, can *sift or boult out any good meal*, or *finer flowr*, that so they may be decent for Gods service, and the Churches use in any *publique way*, I know no man will hinder him from *baking, making, and distributing his bread* : But let them take heed, lest the Corn being *ground in such a new beaten mill*, it prove not full of *grit and gravell* ; which hath more offence, than either profit or pleasure in eating of it.

Mat.23.7.

13. *Of the private exercise of Christians gifts that are truly good.*

For the private *Exercise of his Prophets gifts* (which will now serve the turn) no man ever spake against it, further than it frequently carried it self unseemly, by neglect, separation, boasting against, contempt and opposition of far abler gifts in the publique Ministry, oft *undermining* and *shaking* those truths, that order, and holy way of life, wherein the peace of the Church, and the honour of true Religion consisted ; And even in this I conceive I have shewed to humble Christians a more excellent way ; Namely, *in using the learned helps* of other mens labours ; which are in every kind well composed; rather than to please themselves meerly *in the barrenness* and *rawness* of their own *inventions*, which yet they may add too, if need be, that so they may not seem to say nothing of themselves, or be forced to break for want of vent : If these so *cryed up gifted men*, be found meet to be made *publique teachers in the Church*, under the *name of Prophets* ; why may they not be ordained Ministers, in *a just and due way* ? There is like to be want enough of men of any competent parts, in the great decay and discouragement of such as are very learned and most able : If they are not fit for all offices of the Ministry, I wonder how they can have confidence enough to be publike Teachers in any kind; which work requires greater abilities and equall authoritie to any other holy Office; if they have any thing in them of modest and humble Christians, sure they would be more *swift to hear, and slow to teach*, as St. *James* adviseth.

James 1.19: *Tutior est in audiendo quàm loquendo celeritas. Non tam facile aures ac labra impingunt. Male au-*

As for those *Histrionick Players*, and vaporing Preachers (who with a *Theatricall impudence* in many places, seek to *fill the world*, with meer *noise and clamor* ; crying down all the *antient Ministry*, as Antichristian, and the Ministers as *no way called, sent, or authorised* by God or the Church, turning *all either into spirituall*, or *new prophetick gifts*,

gifts, to which they highly pretend) certainly, *their vanity* can move wiſe Chriſtians no more than thoſe *cheats* and *wanderers* do, who ſwear, they have found out, and can ſell you the *true Elixar*, the *Philoſophers ſtone*; which will turn baſer metals into gold, while yet (poor men) *their raggs*, ſords and beggery, ſufficiently confutes *their rare skill*, proclaming to all, but fools, their lying and *proud beggery*, which more needs anothers *charity*, than is any way able to relieve any mans *neceſſities*.

diendo ſolus ipſe laberis; male loquendo & alios tecum in ruinam pe(tra)bis. Pelarg. *Tenuitatis ſuæ maximè conſcii, maxima & mendaciſſima ſolent polliceri. Immodica enim oſtentatione levamen aliquod, remedium, & quaſi patrocinium, aliorum credulitatem prop:iæ mendicitati quærunt.* Eraſmus. *Mendacia mendicabula.*

Of the primitive prophetick gifts in the Church.

If this Gentleman be *in good earneſt, for a duty and office of prophecying*, (beſides, and not againſt, *the order of the Miniſtry*) let him *ſtudy* how to reſtore to us the reall and uſefull gifts of *primitive Prophets*, which may ſerve worthily to demonſtrate beyond what is already done by excellent Writers, *the true ſenſe of the Scriptures*, as to the great *myſteries of Jeſus Chriſt the Meſſias*; God forbid ſuch ſhou'd not have a *primitive uſe*, and eſteem in the Church : But let us not be abuſed with ſuch triflers, as ſhall either *darken* what others have well *explaned*, or ſhall only produce old protrite and ſtoln notions of other mens works, as if theſe were the rare and new fruits of their own *private prophetick gifts*; Poſſibly (with this Gentlemans *good leave*) the Church of Chriſt, neither *hath* now, nor *needs*, *any ſuch prophetick gifts*, as were primitive, and may truly be ſo called; No more than it doth *tongues, miracles, and healings*, which it had, and wanted too in thoſe firſt times and diſpenſations, when the Goſpell of Chriſt was ſtrange and new to the world, and to the Churches which were but newly planted or in planting; which now it is not, ſpecially in *England*, after the Church hath enjoyed thoſe *plentifull diffuſions of Evangelicall light* from Chriſt and the Stars in his right hand, for many *hundred* of years; ſo that *knowledge hath abounded, as the waters of the Sea*. It is very probable the Churches in ages ſucceeding the Apoſtles, gave over the *form of the exerciſe of propheſying*, when once they ſaw the (χάρισμα) or ſpeciall gift ceaſed; I remember no mention of this Prophecying among the publique officers duties or privileges of the Church; No *Councill*, no *Father*, that I find, regulates it, or *reckons upon it*; nor doth this Gentleman produce any one *teſtimony* for it, out of the Churches after-practice in Eccleſiaſtick Hiſtories and antient Records, which may beſt diſtinguiſh for us, what things *were of temporary*, what of *perpetuall uſe* in the Church. It is evident that all things that were *primitive* and *occaſionall*, are not therefore to be made *perpetuall*, or after *long ceſſation*, to be reſtored; many things uſed in the *infancy* and *minority* of ſome, or all Churches, have ſoon after

Chryſoſt. orat. 88. Gives reaſons why Miracles are now ceaſed in the Church. So *Iſid. Pel.* l. 4. *Ep.* 8.

Rev. 2.

Tacito omnium conſenſu per deſuetudinem abrogantur. Blond.

after been disposed, as the collections on the first day, 1 *Cor.*16. So the Ἀγάπαι, the *Agapæ*, or *love feasts*, 1 *Cor.*11.20. were by divers Councills forbidden, when they degenerated from the Primitive simplicity and purity; *Jude* 12. Spots in your feasts, feeding themselves without fear. So the *Holy Kisses*, or salutings, *Rom.*16.16. 1.*Thes.*5.26. The *common stock of goods*, *Acts* 4.32. publikely dedicated to the relief of the Church; in which the poorest believer had as much interest in what was given, though they contributed nothing, as he that gave most of his estate. So the anointing of the sick, *James* 5.14. So the Celebration of the Lords Supper every Lords day. The peoples *Amen*, 1 *Cor.*14.16. which *Jerom* sayes, was in his time, as a *Clap of Thunder*, such consent, lowdness and alacrity was in that voice of Christian Assemblies. The observation of the Jewish Sabbath, with the first day of the week; The abstinence from blood and things strangled, and the like.

Those collections for the poor on the Lords day, *Cyp.* calls *Gazophylacium*, and *Corbona.* *de Eleemos.* And St. *Chrysost:* endeavoured to restore them in *Constantinople.* See *Bero. Ann. Anno Christi* 44. In *Tertul.* time Christians abstained from blood. *Nec animalium sanguinem in esculentis habemus*, Apol. c. 9. yet in St. *Austins* time they did not abstain from blood, or things strangled. *Aust. cont. Faust. l.* 3. *c.* 13 Mat. 2, 20.

Nothing is more ridiculous in Religion, than (as some fond or fraudulent Papists do their exorcisings and shews of daily Miracles) to *continue the ordinary use* of all those things in the Church, which we read were practised in Primitive times, upon some *extraordinary account*, either of necessity or charity, or speciall gifts, *then only conferred*; Which, when they were at the *highest tide* among professors, yet were never wont to overflow the constant *banks* of the *divinely established* calling of the Ministry, but still were kept within those *modest, holy, and humble bounds*, which became the *Christian flocks*, toward those Guides, and Pastors, which were to be constantly over them *in the Lord*, with whom Christ promised to be, as by his Authority and blessing, so by his Spirit and assisting gifts, *to the end of the world*.

As for this Gentleman, whose devotion and charity hath raised him to so good hope and expectation, of finding or making fit *Prophets* among the common people; truly, if he can bring forth any Gentlemen, either *Lawyers* or others, of so pregnant parts, so *ready* in Scriptures, and of so good utterance, as in him appears; together with so much *gravity, candor, and equanimity*, as (for the most part) he expresses to the *Ministry*, as *a peculiar Calling*, and *divinely instituted office*, *such Prophets will be so far welcome, as they shall be usefull to the Church*. Both Ministers and others would be glad to see the *Inns of Court or Chancery* come in (like *Zilpah* and *Bilhad*) to supply the feared *barrenness* and decayes of *Rachel* and *Leah*, the *two Universities*, which were wont to be the fruitfull *Mothers*, and carefull *Nurses* of the true Prophets and Ministers; Nor would it be a less *acceptable wonder* to all true Christians and Ministers, to see such *Zenasses*, *devout Lawyers*, run cross to *Demas* his steps, and *forsa-*

Gen. 30.

2 Tim. 4.10.

forsaking this present world, to follow *after St. Paul*, than once it was *to see* Saul *also among the Prophets*. Men that can write & (I presume) speak too, after so serious and *Spiritual* a way, as that Author endevours, may merit as much freedom, and publique encouragement, as others vainly affect, and insolently usurp, under the pretence of *their prophesying gifts*; when indeed they are for the most part but meer pratings, very *weeds* and *trash*, the *soyl and load*, which may rend this *Gentlemans net*; but they are not those *good fish*, which he seeks to catch, not so much (it seems) for the *Churches necessities*, (which the constant Ministry may well, as it ought to supply (as *he confesses*,) but for its *Lenten dainties and varieties*, which blessed be God are not hitherto much wanted in any Church, and least of all in this, which hath hitherto enjoyed those *Manna and Quails*, which the Lord hath from heaven plentifully poured round about its tents, by the care and pains of the able, orderly and duly *Ordained Ministers*; If some places in this Church have wanted of that *large provision*, yet others have gathered so abundantly, and fed so *excessively*, that, while they *murmur*, they *surfet*; while they *complain*, their food comes out of their nostrils, as sometimes theirs did among the *ingratefull and wanton Jews*.

1 Sam. 19. 24. *Talis cum sis utinā noster esses.* Agesil. *ad* Farnabasum *inimicum, ac mobilem.*

Numb. 11. 20. *Satietas omnis sibi ipsi contumeliosa.* Aust.

14. *Answer to the Aspersions of pertinacy and superstition cast upon the Ministers in that book.*

These concessions then, of all able and true Ministers, being *so liberall* and friendly to all private uses, and to all gifts which are really fit to be publike, I cannot tell what that *great and dangerous pertinacy* is, with which that *Gentleman* (towards the *end of his book*) p. 78. charges so *gravely*, and threatens so *severely the Preachers in England*; as if all the fire of *Gods and mans wrath*, which hath faln on them, in these times, hath not made them so much, *as willing to part with, and be purged from their Babylonish superstitions, their popish opinions and practises*; *which (sayes he) they hold as fast, as their right hands, and right eyes*.

A very *sad reflexion*, if true, upon *All us that are, and must ever own our selves Christs Ministers*; And wherein this Gentleman had done more worthy of himself, if he had given *clear and particular instances*, than such *generall and obscure intimations*; which without sufficient proof, will seem no better, than those odious aspersions, and *vulgar calumnies*, with the *Anti-ministeriall Levellers*, to hide their own deformities, are wont to cast upon Ministers, and all men, *that differ from them*, and oppose their folly, out of principles of *higher reason*, and *sounder religion*, than that sort of people use to be acquainted withall; From the fauls and faylings, it may be, of some Ministers, but chiefly from the hatred and malice of those men, against *all true Ministers*, it's probable *this author*, may without any great *spirit of prophesying* foresee, and thus *solemnly* (as he doth from the *Tripos*) *foretell*, the great *sufferings*, which

Τοῖς ἑαυτῶν κακοῖς βοηθοῦσιν ἐξ ὧν ἄλλοις ἐπιφέρουσιν. Naz. Or. 20.

Κρείττονα εἶναι διαβολῶν ἀνθρώπινον βίον, τῶν χαλεπωτάτων ἐστὶν ἵνα μὴ καὶ ἀδύνατον εἴπω. Basil. in ep. 54.

Lingua maledica sanctos carpere solita est in solatium delinquentium. Ieron. ad Eust.

Ministers of learning, constancy, and honesty, are like to undergo, if God did not as well know how to restrain the pride and power of these men, as he doth behold the *rage and bitterness of them*, against all true Ministers; Not, *because they will not come out of Babylon*, as he phraseth it; but, because they will not so easily return (as many unwary souls do) to folly, and the principles of all confusion, to the *oppression* of all that truth and order, which the *wisdom* of our pious Progenitors hath observed for 1600. years, and transmitted to us, from the *hands of the blessed Apostles*, according to the rules of Scripture, and all religious reason.

Cum quis clericus ceciderit statim omnes tales esse, licet non manifestari possunt, jactitant profani, cum tamen si maritata aliqua adultera sit, non statim uxores suas projiciunt, nec matres suas tales esse dicunt. Aust.Ep.1.37. *Ideo à malis boni petuntur calumniis; εἰ μὲν γὰρ κακοὶ ἔλεγχον τοῦ ἑαυτῶν βίου τὴν τῶν ἀγαθῶν πολιτείαν ἡγοῦνται, καὶ διὰ τὸ ἐκείνους ἀπελάσαι τὴν οἰκείαν κακίαν περιστέλλειν οἴονται. Is. Pel. l.2.*

But what I beseech you is this sinfull *obstinacy* of the Ministers of *England*, for which this *Gentleman* hath such a *Sybilline rapture*, and more than *a prophetick horror*? Is it because their judgement is constant to the approbation of that due obedience and legall *conformity*, to which they formerly with good conscience subjected, as in matters of *extern right and decency in this Church*, wherein they *had a liberty* common with all Christians, (so far as they opposed not either sound doctrine in faith or holiness, and morality in manners) to conform themselves then in the use of them, as now they have liberty not to use them, while by force and terrour they are hindered; They being not of that nature of things *sacred*, for which a Christian is bound to kindle the fires of *Martyrdom*, nor of private contention against publique *Prohibition*,

Vid. Aug.Ep. 118. ad Jan. *contra præfractos illos qui superstitiosa timiditate consuetudini cujuslibet ecclesiæ repugnant, quæ nec fidei nec bonis moribus adversatur. Unaquæque provincia suo sensu abundet: pro more & consuetudine antiquâ: Consuetudines Ecclesiasticæ, quæ fidei non officiunt, observandæ, ut à majoribus traditæ sunt.* Jeron. ad Licinium. *Cavendum est, ne tempestate contentionis serenitas charitatis obnubiletur.* Aust. Ep. 86.

Is he angry, that *Preachers* do not all suddenly shipwrack their judgements, learning, and consciences upon every rock of *vulgar fury*, or fancy? that they are not presently *melted* with every popular gloing heat of seeming piety? and that they run not into every *mould*, which any faction hath formed for the advantages perhaps of secular interests? Is he displeased that they are not taken with, admire or adore every *Idoll of fanatick novelty*? that they seriously *try the modern spirits*, whether they be of *God* or no, and receive not every spirit? Is he grieved, that men of *learned and sober piety*, will not subject the *gravity of the Fathers*; the *wisdom* of the Councils; the acuteness of *the Schoolmen*; the fidelity of the Ecclesiastick Historians, together with the excellent learning and acurate judgements of the best modern Writers and Divines in all reformed Churches; yea, and

Id viri gravi prudentiæque dignissimum, non facile permutatis nec ad vulgi ἀρματοβλῆτα nutum, auramque leviter commoveri. Zanch. Orat. 1 Joh. 4. 1.

and the authority of the Scriptures themselves, in their most clear light and concurrent strength; that they will not prostrat all or any of these, to a company *of wretched Pamphlets*, fitter for *Cooks and Chandlers shops*, than for the reading of judicious and serious Christians; who have cause to look upon those *putrefactions of Pens and wits*, only as *Moths* and *Vermine* every where creeping up and down, and hoping (like *Ants*) only by their numbers to devour all antient Authors, and all good literature, that so they alone may survive, and satisfie the grosser palats of those who never relished any book so much as a Ballad or a Play, or a Romance, or some Seraphick raptures and pious nonsense? Is he scandalized, that we count not the *diseases* of Christians, health; their *putrefactions*, *perfections*; their *distractions*, raptures; their *ravings*, reason; their *dreams*, oracles; *baseness*, liberty; their *Chaos*, comlinesse? Is he jealous of us, because we rather study and profess solid truths, sober piety, good manners, and orderly government, which only become all true Christians, and Ministers above all? Is it our fault, that we endevour to Pray, Preach, Write, what we and others may understand; that we covet not to be *admired*, by not being understood; that we aim to do all things as becomes Men, Christians, and Ministers of the true Church of Christ, not after the *manner of plausible*, and easie fondness; which is afraid to *offend*, where there is power to hurt; that counts *greatness* as a badge of goodness, and success a sign of Sanctity; but rather with all just zeal, courage, and constancy, beseeming the *demonstrations* of the truth and Spirit of God, which never needed more to be asserted as to its divine power, and eternall honour, than in this pusillanimous and *frothy generation of vapourers*, who are the greatest enemies to, and betrayers of our Religion, as Christian, and as Reformed; whether they be *Gogs* or *Magogs*, open or secret; the one, or the many Antichrists; Papall or popular delusions? We hope this Gentleman is so good natured, that with all other excellent Christians he will forgive us those wrongs, by which we have been, and ever shall be piously injurious, and *faithfully offensive, as aiming not to please men, but God.*

Wherein then are we the *Preachers* of the good old way (One and all) meriters of such *fatall terrors*, as those words import, which like *Apocalyptick Revelations* are dark, but *dreadfull*; portending *God knows what sufferings* upon them all? If there be no men more *single-hearted*, none more open, candid, and ingenuous, than all good Ministers pray to be, who are no *Statists* or *Politicians*, but able and honest Preachers of the name of the only true God, and Jesus Christ, whom he hath sent, to shew Sinners the way of eternall life; If there be nothing more necessary, more usefull, less offensive, or burdensome, to any wise, sober, and godly minds, than their lives and labours are;

If

Prov. 26.23. Burning lips, and a wicked heart, are like a potsherd covered with silver dross.

Grande hoc & subtile artificium nescimus, vulgi ineptiis, & novitatibus assentiri; non enim tam blandi sumus hominum inimici. Ieron.

Sua dum pingunt vitia, nostras dedecorare student virtutes lenones vulgi. Erasm.

Blanda pernicies. Cyp. de Error.

Adulantiū non amantium vox est. Satis pii, modo divites estis, probi satis si prosperi, sancti & sapientes satis si læto & magnifico utuntur successu, fortia tantum & fulminantia venerantur numina. Bern.

1 Cor. 12.13.

If no men are more modest and moderate, in all their desires and designs, than learned, humble and diligent, (which are the *unpragmatick*) *Ministers*; what is the grief? why this complaint, *lamentation* and *burthen*, which this *Gentleman* takes up so prophetically against them, both as to their sin, and their suffering? unless men be *vexed*, that any worthy men are duly made Ministers, or that Ministers are but men; unless it offend, that they have food and raiment, which most of them *dearly earn*, and hardly get; unless they are impatient, as the Wolf was with *the Lamb*, that we breath in the same common ayr, or see the same Sun, or tread on the same Earth, or drink of the same stream; the troubling of which, is by the *troublers* of it, unjustly imputed to their innocency; who must therefore be accused, because violence hath a mind to destroy them; What is the *error*? what the *heresie*? what *the superstition*? what the *Popish opinion* or practise, which any of us *Ministers* so resolutely maintain?

1 King. 18. 17.

Sure this Gentleman is not to be thought of so low a *form of foundlings*, and *novices*, who *suspect* and dread every thing *as Popish*, which we hold, or act in common with the Pope or Papists; wholly to recede from any thing common with them, must divest us, not only of the main truths, duties, vertues, and grounds of our Religion as Christian; but we must cast off all, or most part of that, which denominates us either rationall or humane, both as to the nature and society of men: But, if we obstinatly retain any thing, either for opinion or practice, which may truly be branded with *the mark of the Beast*, as either erroneous or superstitious, beyond the bounds of Christian truth, or liberty, or decency: If either any generall Councill, or any Synod of this Church, since it were reformed; or any Parliament, and civill Convention of the Estates of this Nation have condemned what we *teach*, or practise, or opine; If any wise and learned man, not apparently *ingaged in faction or schism*, against the publique Constitution both in Church and State, did ever so much as accuse or convict us of any *such crimes*; In *Gods name* let us suffer what *He* thinks fit. If we have deserved it from men, it will be a mercy to be punished, and amended by them; If we have not, it will be an honour and crown to us, above all men, to suffer for *the testimony of Jesus Christ*, the honour of our function, and this Church, from *unreasonable*, and ungratefull men, who use Ministers as *their Oxen*, (but not in *the Apostles, or Gods sense*;) first exhausting and tyring them at hard labour, and then they destroy and devour them.

Prostracta est illa & superstitiosa timiditas, quæ à bonis abhorret quibus abutuntur mali. Aust.

Qualis affectatio in civilibus talis superstitio in divinis. Verulam.

Misericorditer plectitur qui ad emendationem ducitur. Aust.

1 Cor. 9. 9.

The appeal of all true and faithfull Ministers, as to their

But to *all excellent and impartiall Christians*, we may, and do as in the *presence of God appeal*; Is not this in some mens sense and censure, *the sin* of the ablest and best *Preachers*, (both for learning, piety and constancy) that they do not so easily yield to, or applaud *a Military or Mechanick religion?* that they are sorry to see so *goodly a part of the Catholike Church*, so stately *a pillar* of Gods house, as the Church of *England* lately was, so every day *hewing in pieces*, and mouldring to nothing, for want of due *order and government*, or seasonable and fit repairings? Is not this *the Crime*, that no learned and worthy Minister can own either the swords Soveraignty, or the peoples Liberty, to be the grand Arbitrators of piety, the disposers of mens consciences, the *Dictators* of all Christianity, the *interpreters* of all Scriptures, the *Determiners* of all Controversies; and this so absolute, as admits no *Conference* with, nor endevouring to convince, either Ministers or others, who are of different judgements?

integrity, far from this superstition charged on them.

Is it not their *trespass*, that true Ministers know too much? that they see too clearly? that they *examine things* too strictly? that they admit no latitudes of *Civill interests*, or *State policies*, and sinfull *necessities*, as dispensations of Gods *Morall Law*, and the rules of both common honesty and true piety? That they stand *valiantly* (many of them) and as becomes them, *in the gap*, against the insinuations and invasions of those *infamous heresies*, those *received errors*, those vile and *putrid novelties*, those *perfect madnesses*, those apparent blasphemies, confusions, and dissolute Liberties, which *threaten this reformed Church*, with a more sure inundation, than the *Sea* doth the *Low-Countriss*, if the banks and dams be not preserved? Is not this with some men the *unpardonable sin* of the *best Ministers*, that they do not crouch and flatter, and fawn on *every plausible error*, on every *powerfull novelty*, every *proud fancy*, and high imagination? that they *lick* not the *sores* of any mens consciences, or the *pollutions* of any mens hands with servile and *adulterate tongues*? That they do not cry up, or in any kind own for the gifts of the Spirit, those *passionate*, or melancholy, or cunning and affected motions and extravagancies, which some men *strongly fancy* to themselves, and weakly *demonstrate* to others; as to any thing like to sound reason, or Scripture religion? That they oppose these *Bells* and *Dragons* of *fanatick Divinity*, which the *Authors* of them will never be able to advance to any publike veneration, or reception, as spirituall, heavenly, and divine, among sober Christians in *England*, while such wise *Daniels* live; who have neither leisure, nor boldness so to mock God, and to play with *religion*; nor untill as *Ptolomy* did to magnifie the Image of *Diana*, to be (Διοπετὲς) faln from heaven, so they deal with able Ministers; when the best Statuaries had formed an Image of *Diana* to rare perfection, the King at one supper destroyed them all by the ruine of the house where they were, and after produced the Statue as faln from heaven. Or as *Herod* the *Idumæan* or *mungrill Jew* did with the antient *Records* and *Genealogies* of the stems of the Kings, and succession of the Priests, among the Jews, that so he might by

Multis in culpa est ut Socrati Athenis, τὸ ἀρεσκεῖν: pietatis, literaturæ, omnigenumq; virtutū eminentia, cujus individua comes est invidia, Melan.

Veritas nemini blanditur, neminem palpat, nullum seducit, a pertè omnibus denunciat, &c. Bern.

Suidas in Διοπετὲς.

Herodes primus ex alienigenis ex Judæorum ex ima plebe ortus, Ignobilitatis suæ conscius Genealogias Judaicas exussit, quantas potuit, ut sic facilius nobilitatem suam ementiatur. Euseb. hist. Eccl. l. 1. c. 7.

abolishing them, the better bring on his own title; So must these Antiministeriall adversaries, *first destroy* and cancell both common reason in mens souls, and the whole Canon of the Scriptures, which are the *durable oracles* of God, for the Churches directions, and a'l learned interpreters of them: *Torches* of *private* Spirits are ridiculous too be lighted up, while the *Sun* shines; unless it be for those who (having some mask or play to act) reproach the Noon-day Sun of to much splendor, and make to themselves and others an *artificiall* Night, which will better serve their turns: When all *light of* true reason, and Scriptures are extinguished in this Church and Nation or *much Eclipsed*; then, and not before, will *honest-hearted* Christians believe, that they have no *need of true Ministers*; or that those, they have hitherto had, have not been worthy the name of reformed; or have pertinaciously reteined any such Popish *opinions*, or *superstitions*, as are inconsistent with true piety.

Artificiosa sibi parant Lumina Histriones quâ melius ὑποκρίσεις suas obtegere & simulari possint: Lenocinantibus lucernis meridianum solem quasi de nimio splendore exprobrantes. Sydo.

Veritas loquendi grande præsagium mali. Lact.

And in this thing let the *Lord deal with us*, according to *the clearness* of our hands, and the uprightness of our hearts in his sight, either to deliver us into, or redeem us out of *the hands* of *violent* and *unreasonable* men; whose very *mercies* have proved cruell to poor Ministers; whose *pious constancy* is the greatest thorn in some mens sides. *But if our wayes please God he can make our very enemies at peace with us. Prov.* 16.7.

Psal. 18.24.

Διὰ τοῦτο μάλιστα ἀπεχθεῖς ἔχθροι ... ἀληθεύοντες καὶ ἀρεσκεύοντες οἱ ἐνδοκιμώτατοι. Is. Pel.

Wholy to remove the antient Ministry, as some men aym, under pretence of bringing up a *new nursery* of *gifted brethren*, and *Prophets* (which like *under-woods* are not so likely to thrive, while *Ministers*, like *goodly Timber* trees grow so high above them and over drop them,) will be *a work*, fully compleating those sad effects, which disorderly, unordeined, unsent, and unabled Teachers and false Prophets, *have already* begun to bring forth in this Church; And how can it ever be thought or hoped, that they will bring forth *better fruits*, either for the truth, honour, or power of the Reformed Religion; either for the Peace of Church, or State, unless there be a *speciall committee* appointed, for the regulating of *Prophets* and tryall of their gifts? in which none may be fitter (for learning, piety, and moderation) to be *Chayr-man*, than *that Author and zealous assertor of the peoples Liberty and Privilege*; who says he is not so much a friend to these new *Prophets*, as to be an utter enemy *to the function of the old Ministers*; though he would have Prophets planted, yet not Ministers *pulled* up *root and branch*; but only *pruned* from that, which he calls superstition: wherein his *Charity* to Ministers may perhaps make his censorious *severity* veniall. He that so much studies the Reformation of Ministers, we hope will not bring in such *Esopick* and deformed *Prophets*, as most of those, who have yet appeared, rather to scare men from, than to instruct good Christians in, true holyness and Religion.

Pag. 3.

It is evident enough, and too much, to all *true reformed* Christians, what wide *gaps*, that *generation of pretended Prophets*, and *gifted Brethren*, have already made, for the easy inrodes of what is truly Popery, *superstition*, or meer formality; All sorts also of corrupt opinions and Heresies; together with Idleness, barrenness, barbarity, Illiteratness, Ignorance, Atheism, and contempt of all true Reformed Religion, both in the *power*, and extern *form* order and profession of it: Many men (being prune) have learned easily to make little conscience of hearing, reverencing, or obeying the word of God, *Even from any true Ministers*, never so able and worthy; since they have learned to scorn, make sport of, and laugh at *these novell* and pittifull *pretenders* to Preaching and prophecying, of whose *insufficiency* and non-authority to Preach, and administer any holy mysteries *in Christs name*, common people being fully satisfyed; they are ready to dispute, and neglect, even that *divine Authority*, which is in the calling of true Ministers. 15.

The vanity and mischief of false and foolish Prophets.

What little or no good effects *the usurpers against, and opposers of the Ministry* of this Church can boast off, with truth, either as to speaking judiciously, or writing solidly, or walking exactly, so as tends any way to the advantages of piety, truth, charity, or peace in the Reformed Churches; or to the *honour and happiness* of this Nation, either converting, or establishing any *in truth* or holiness, I leave to the judgement of all considerate and wise Christians, whose prayers, sighs, tears, complaints, griefs and fears of *future darkness*, are in nothing more exercised, than in the present deplored aspect and almost desperate State of the Reformed Religion, in many places of Christendom, and in none more, than what is threatned in this *Church of England*: Fearing lest the *shadows of the evening being encreased*; and those *day stars*, which formerly shined in a learned successive and Authoritative Ministry, being darkned and Eclipsed; the *evening Wolves* should also encrease; and the Beasts of the Forrest multiply upon us; every one seeking for their prey; whom they may deceive and devour. Such as loathed Manna, were justly stung soon after with fiery Serpents. *Numb.* 21.6.

Jer. 6.4.

Jer. 5.6.

On the other side ask the looser and profaner Spirits, what *restrayning* power or *converting influence*, they feel from the *charmings* of these new-gifted *exorcists*, who undertake in the name of Christ (but indeed in their own name, and after their own fancies) to *call over*, and cast out the *devils of ignorance*, Atheism, unbelief, profaness, and hypocrisy, which are in mens hearts or lives; You may hear them with one voyce answering, as those did; *Jesus we know, and* Paul *we know*; *the learned and duly ordeined Ministers*, in a successive power from Christ, and his holy Apostles, we know, Acts 19.13.15.

 but

but who are you; ſelf flatterers, ſelf lovers, *ſelf ſenders*, *ſelf ſeekers*, *ſelf ordeiners*; nor is it to be expected, but that at laſt theſe *Sons of Sheva* will find *thoſe evill Spirits* in mens hearts, of pride, unbelief, Atheiſm, enmity againſt God, and all true holineſs, any whit milder or better natured than thoſe were; who contemning the bare ſound of the Name Jeſus, when deſtitute of the Authority from Jeſus; and mocking at the preſumption of thoſe *cenſurers*; flew upon them, *wounded, and expulſed* them: So *unſafe*, and in the end ſo thankleſs and comfortleſs an undertaking it is, to attempt this good work even of *caſting out devils* from men; where there is nothing but a *mock-power*; and no reall divine *Authority* to do it. The devils, which *felt torment at Chriſts preſence*, and were ſubject to the Apoſtles, whom Chriſt ſent, *falling down like lightning*, had the pleaſure *to beat* and *baffle* thoſe, who would chain them up, or caſt them out, without *divine Authority*. And no wonder if theſe *Eſtrick Birds*, who ſet forth their *ſoft and gay feathers*, having but little *bodies* and leſs *brains*, by wandring from their Neſts (their *ſhops*, and *looms*, and *flayls*, and *mills*, (the honeſt *ſtations*, and no way deſpicable *callings*, wherein God and man have ſet them; and from which they have no ſufficient call either from God or man to moove them) no wonder (I ſay) if they fall themſelves, and lead others into many *ſnares* and *divers temptations*; which they can hardly avoyd, being (in good earneſt,) moſt of them *very blind leaders of the blind*. Imagining as the Turks do of blind and *mad men*, that they have ſpeciall viſions, becauſe they want their eyes; and *extraordinary revelations*, becauſe they are deſtitute of common reaſon. Indeed it is feared that moſt of theſe mens Prophecying and Preaching, is either deſign to bring all confuſion on theſe Reformed Churches; or elſe meerly out of wantonneſs, in jeſt; as a kind of *recreation* and diverſion; but not as any buſineſs or matter of duty and conſcience; In one thing they are in good earneſt and moſt ſerious, that is to carry on their perfect contempt and malice againſt all true Miniſters.

Merito à Diabolis plectuntur, qui à Deo non mittuntur: Auſt.

Omnem præter Dei temnit Authoritatem Satanas, nec nomen Jeſus ſyllabarum ſono terret, ſed divina illa, quâ armantur poteſtas, qui in Chriſti nomine Miniſtrant. Ieron.

Mat. 8. 29. *Dæmones Chriſti præſentia cruciantur; ut malefici ad conſpectum judicis: Nondum enim judicis ſententia damnatos, propria condemnat & torquet conſcientia.* Pelarg.

Facile in laqueos Diaboli incidunt, qui à viâ Domini decedunt. Auſt.

Mat. 15. 14. *Cæcos à cæcis duci; non Major eſt in seducentibus arrogantia, quam in ſeductis inſania; in utriſquis ſummum periculum; nec minus dolendum quàm merito ridendum.* Auſt. *Geminæ plerunq; cæcitates concurrunt, ut qui non vident, quæ ſunt; videre videantur, quæ non ſunt.* Tertul. Apol.

16 Who ſees not, what *weakneſs* it is for ſober Chriſtians, after ſo great light of truth hath ſhined ſo long among them, to imagine, that ſuch a diſorderly Company of people, who for the moſt part by *ſecret ſtimulations* of pride, vain glory, envy, covetouſneſs, or ſome worſe Spirit; no leſs, than by *apparent over-weenings* of their *ſmall*, and at beſt but very *moderate* gifts; not tried or approved by any wiſe men; but only blown up by the *pitifull* applauſes of ſome ſilly men and women, who have with levity and unthankfulneſs

The weakneſs and ſin of Chriſtians to follow deluſions and forſake realities.

fulneſs

fulneſs forſook their true *guides and Paſtors*; and not *enduring ſound* doctrine, and holy order, deſerve for their *itching* ears to be condemned, to follow ſuch *heaps of Teachers*, ever learning, and never comming *to a ſound and ſetled knowledge of the Truth*? who ſees not (I ſay) what ſin it is, to follow, countenance or incourage ſuch *dangerous* and *diſorderly ſeducers*, and what weakneſs and meer folly it is, to imagin, that ſuch, as neither have skill to handle *trowell* or *ſword*, ſhould either *build* or *defend* our *Jeruſalem*? When they dayly pull down *better work*, than they can *erect*; And, what they ſeem *to build*, is of ſuch *unpoliſhed rubbidge*, ſuch rude, and rough-hewen ſtuff, with ſuch *intempered mortar*, that it is as *ſand without lime*; undigeſted, unprepared, uneven: neither for matter nor manner conſiderable; without rule, plumbline or levell; neither according to Scripture precept, nor the holy example, and Catholick practiſe of the Churches of Chriſt: So that the *gapings*, flaws, *ſwellings*, lowneſs, hollowneſs, uneveneſs, crookedneſs and weakneſs, (together with the dayly *mouldrings* of their Childiſh ſtructures) ſhew, what *wiſe builders* they are; and how fit to be made *publike Architects*, or *Maſter-builders* in this Church. Over whoſe Walls the crafty malice of *Jeſuitick* Foxes, and any other enemies, will eaſily go, and break them down, when ever they paſs: which makes many men ſuſpect, that theſe *Lay Preachers*, are but the *left hand* of *Babels builders*; fit inſtruments to divide, confound and deſtroy the Reformed Religion in theſe *Britiſh* Churches, and all thoſe who ſtudy to preſerve it. Which they only can, with any ſhew of reaſon, *effectually* do (by Gods bleſſing) who are *workmen*, that for their Authority and approved *skill*, as well as their good will and readineſs to build, need *not to be aſhamed*. Of whoſe *reall ſufficiencies*, *theſe new bunglers* are moſt impatient hearers and perfect haters; becauſe from thoſe Miniſters exactneſs, theſe mens bungling receives the ſevereſt reproaches and juſteſt oppoſitions.

Invidiæ ſtimulis motus Arrius contra Alex. ep. Alex. hæreſin occæpit. Theod. hiſt. l. 1. c. 2.

2 Tim. 4. 3.

Ædificant & ædificantur Hæretici in ruinam. Tertul.

Quale poteſt eſſe ædificium quod de ruinâ conſtruitur? Optat.

Neh. 4. 3.

Muros dum erigunt mores negligunt. Bern.

2 Tim. 2. 15.

A man may as well hope, that *hogs* by their *rootings*, and *moles* by their *caſtings*, will Plow and till his ground, as that ſuch Arbitrary, Caſuall, and contingent forwardneſs; or ſuch *inordinate activities* of poor, but *proudly gifted men*, will any way help on the great work of Chriſtian Religion, the propagating of the Goſpell, or the *Reformation* of hearts or Churches; which require indeed the greateſt *competency and compleatneſs*, both for gifts, learning, and due Authority, that can be had, both for the *Majeſty of Religion*, and for the *defence* of the *truth*; as alſo for the *binding* to diligence and exactneſs *the conſcience* of the *Miniſters*; no leſs, than for the *ſatisfaction* of other mens conſciences, in point of the *validity of Sacraments*, and other holy *Miniſtrations*; which have not

 any

any Physicall or naturall vertue, but a *mysticall* and Religious only, which depends upon *the relation* they have to the word and Spirit of the holy Institutor and Commander *Jesus Christ*. So that it is indeed a very *strange bewitchedness*, and depravedness in many mens appetites, that they should so cry up those *mush-room Prophets and Teachers*; who need more *sauce* to make them safe or savory, than their bodies are worth; (who are self-planted, soon started up in one night;) as if they were beyond all those former Goodly plants, for beauty, sweetness and wholesomness; which much *study*, care, learning, pains and prayers have planted *in the Church*: Or that Christians should so far flatter themselves that the *soyl here* in *England*, since it was *watered with civill bloud*, is so well natured and fruitfull, that there needs no such care and culture as was anciently used in the Garden of God, either in setting, watering, preparing, or transplanting those trees of the Ministry, which should be full of life; whose *leaves* should be for *the healing*, as well as their fruits *for the nourishing* of mens souls. So confident the devill seems to be of the *giddiness*, folly, negligence, and simplicity of these times, that he stirs up the *very thistles* (the most useless and most offensive burthens of the earth, which the foot of every vile beast is ready to crush and trample upon) to chalenge and contemn *the Cedars of Lebanon*; And he would fain perswade reformed Christians, to cut down and stub up those *goodly trees of the Lord*, which are *tall*, *strait*, and full of sap, as cumbring the ground; that those *sharp and sorry shrubs*, those dry and sapless *kexes*, may have the more room, and thrive the better; pretending that they will at easier rates and with less pains supply all the Churches occasions; when the Lord knows, and all excellent Christians see, by sad experience, that they are so far from that length, strength and straitness required in the *beams and pillars of the Temple*; that their *crooked* and *knotty shortness*, will scarce afford a pin, on which to hang the least vessell of the *Sanctuary*.

Rev. 22. 2. *Superseminationis satanæ.*

2 Kings. 14. 9.

17. *No design in the Author to grieve any good mans Spirit, or discourage his gifts*; 1 Joh. 4. 1.

Excellent Christians, *I protest before the Lord*, that I write not thus, out of any desire to *grieve*, *quench*, or *exasperate* any *mans Spirit*, in whom the wise and sanctifying graces, or *usefull gifts* of Gods Spirit do dwell in the least measure, with *truth and humility*; but only in the way of *trying the gifts and Spirits*, whether they be of God or no; if they be found, by the word of God, to be proud, foolish, evill, *unclean*, *unruly*; refusing to be bound with any bonds of good order and government, (such, as seems to have possessed some in this Church, who seek to *bewitch* others and to trouble all,) God forbid we should not all of us strive, by fasting, prayer preaching, writing, and all just *rebukes* of them, to cast them out, notwithstanding their *cryings*, tearings, and foamings.

Luke 9. 42.

It

It is far (I hope) from *my* Soul by any envy *or undervaluing* of any good Christians to damp the *Spirit of Christ in them*; I would have every one study *to improove* the talents he hath; and to be employed according to his *reall improovement*; of which no man being naturally proud and self flatterers is fit to *be judge* himself, but ought to be *subject* to the tryall and judgement of others; both as to that light and heat, knowledge and zeal, gifts and graces which any may *pretend* to, and wherein they may be really usefull to the publike, or any community of Christians; whose edifying in faith and love we have all cause, both in conscience and prudence dayly to nourish and increase *in Gods way*; which is an orderly, *peaceable, and blessed way*; wherein only either private Christians or Church societies can hope to *thrive* and *flourish*: I wish with *Moses all the Lords people were Prophets*; (Num. 11. 29.) Both able to give an account of their knowledge in the mysteries of Christ, and also to help on, in an *orderly* way, (as every wheel or pin doth in the motions *of a watch*) the great and weighty work of *saving souls*, which is the main end of the *Ministers* calling and pains. Better we Ministers be despised, than the Spirit of Christ in any *gracious heart* be justly *grieved*; or any good work of God in the *Church hindred*.

But we are well assured, by good experience, that none would be less *despisers*, or more *encouragers*, lovers, and zealous preservers of the true *Evangelicall Ministry*, and its *divine Authority*, than such men who have graces, with their gifts, and are both *able and humble*; none are more *slow to speak to* others in the name of Christ, (James 1. 19.) than they, who cannot hear others Preaching with due abilities and *authority*, without *fear and trembling*, as reverencing God, and the *Lord Jesus* Christ in their Ministers. There is no danger of *able parts*, where there are humble and *honest* hearts; no more, than we need fear the strength *of any part* in the body, will hurt, or offend the whole body, or disorder and violate any *other Member*, which is above it in place, in honour and in operation or function. Reason teacheth us, that the ability or strength of any part, in its place and proportion, doth not make it usurp the place, or execute the Office of any other *nobler part*: The measure of every part is the beauty and safety of *the whole*; (καὶ τὸ κάλλος, καὶ ἡ ἀσφάλεια τοῦ σώματος ἐν τῇ συμμετρίᾳ κεῖται. Arist.) which cannot in naturall, and ought not in Religious Bodies (which are Churches) be fitly disposed, but only in such a way, as God hath appointed for the daily forming, building and well-ordering of *his Church*, by such wisdom and Authority, as Christ established in it; Of which *the Apostles* and the Churches after them give us most evident testimony.

But to avoid destructive delusions.

But we must not be *deluded either with the devils* fulgurations and flashes, or his *transfigurations* and disguises; We must not forsake

forsake or stop up Gods *fountains* of *living waters*, by digging the devils ditches, and *wells*, which hold *no water*; nay we may not wash our hands at the *Devils Cistern*, to fit them for *Gods service*; Nor, may we take water from his troubled, muddy and poysonous streams, to water the *plants of Christs* Church; We may not *take strange fire* from Satans *Altar* to kindle the sacrifices *of God*. What need we *cut off Dogs necks*, and offer *swins bloud*, when we have so many *clean beasts*, which are appointed for *acceptable services?* that we shall not need any such vain *oblations*, which are but the *sacrifices of* fools, who consider *not that* they do evill, nor look to their *feet*, when they go to *the house of God*; being as ready to stumble and fall, and discover *their nakedness* and shame, as they are *forward* to ascend to the altar of the Lord, upon the *steps of pride* and presumption, which were forbidden to be made; The humble heart being alwaies most welcom to God; while others in vain arrogate to themselves power to perform those things which are not *required at their hands*. God hath said, *he will be sanctified of all those*, who *come nigh to him* in his *publike service*; which is done not only by that inward *sanctification* of the heart, by faith, fear, and reverence toward God, but also by that exact observation of such rules of order, power and Authority, which he hath set (who alone could do it) in the publike way of his worship and service before the Sons of men.

Luke 10.18. I saw Satan fall like lightning from Heaven.
2 Cor. 11.14. Satan himself is transformed into an Angel of light.
Isa. 1.13.
Eccl. 5.1.
Exod. 20.26.
Lev. 10.3.

We must not be such *Children in understanding*, as to allow all to be *gold which glisters*, when it will not endure the *Touch-stone* of Gods word, or the probation of the Churches judgment: We may not easily think, that *Gods Spirit*, in any private men, runs counter to that holy order and clear *Institution*, which the undoubted Spirit of God hath clearly set forth in the *Scriptures*, and which the Church in all ages hath observed in the way of an *ordeined authoritative Ministry*: All other, or later inventions may well be suspected to be but *Satans stratagems*, and devices. There may be so many *vermine crawling* in a dead body, as may make it seem to live and move, when yet there is no true *Spirit of* life, or Soul in it: So it is no wonder, if the various impulses, wherewith mens secret and corrupt lusts stir them, make some shew, as if diviner gifts and endowments agitated them, When indeed they have no other ayms or interests, than such, as *Judas Iscariot*, or *Symon Magus* might have; or those after Hereticks the Gnosticks, Maniches, and Montanists, *&c.* Who almost, that had any shew of gifts or parts, ever did mischief in the Church, without *great prefacings* of holy and good intentions, and pretensions of gifts and the Spirit of God? There may be gifted *Hypocrites*, *devout devils*, *angelized Satans*. Be mens gifts *never so*

Cainitæ Judæ proditoris Evangelium ostentabant, Ophitæ angelum in omni imunditie assistentem dicebant & invocabant. Hanc esse perfectionē aiebant sine tremore in tales abire operationes quas ne nominare fas est. Iren. l. 1. c. 35.
Nulla erroris secta jam contra Christi veritatē nisi nomine cooperta Christiano ad pugnandum prosilire audet. Aust. Ep. 56.

so commendable, if they want humility in themselves, and charity to others, which are the beauties of all endowments; if they are *puffed up*, seek themselves, walk *disorderly*, run unexamined, unappointed, unordained, in scandalous and undue wayes, they *are nothing*; either as to private comfort in themselves, or publick benefit to the Church; The presumption and disorder of their example doth more hurt (as the influence of some malignant stars in a *Constellation*) than the light of their gifts can do; they corrupt more than they either direct, or correct.

Miserrimis & instabilibus fabulis tantam elationem assumpserunt, ut meliores seipsos reliquis præsumpserunt. Irenæ. l. 1. c. 35. de Caynitis, Ophitis, Judæitis.

If any of these Prophets or gifted men be indeed so able, for the *work of the Ministry*, that religion may suffer no detriment by them, and people may have just cause to *esteem them highly for their work sake*, God forbid they should not have the *right hand of fellowship*, all incouragement from my self, and all that desire to walk as becomes the Gospell; when they are found, *upon just tryall*, fit to be *solemnly ordeined*, set apart, and sent forth *with due authority* to that holy service, in Gods name let them be sent forth with good speed. If they *disdain* this method of *Ministeriall office and power*, which hath been setled by Christ, and continued to this day in his Church (which no wise, humble, and truly able Christian, can with reason, modesty, or with conscience justly do) but they will needs *obtrude themselves* upon the Church, *and crowd in against the true Ministers*; they may indeed be, as *sounding Brass and tinckling Cimballs*, fit *rattles* for *Children*, or for the labouring *Moon*, or for a Country Morice-dance and May-pole, but they will never be as *Aarons Pomegranates and golden Bells*; usefull Ornaments to Gods Sanctuary in words or works; or any way becomming the Church of Jesus Christ; which is as the *woman clothed with the Sun*, the light of Truth, and the lustre of holy Order; And hath the *Moon under her feet*; not only all wordly vanities, and unjust interests, but also all humane *inventions* and *novelties*, which have their continuall variations, wainings, disorders, darknesses and deformities; whereas *Divine Institutions* are alwayes glorious by the *clear beams* of Scripture-precept, and the constant course of the Churches example: Both which have held their *Truth and Authority*, in the blackest nights of persecution, wherein no *untried* and *unordeined intruder*, was ever owned for a true *Minister of holy things* in any setled and incorrupted Church of Christ; No more than any man shall be accounted an Officer, or Souldier in an Army, who hath not either listed himself, or received his Commission. Order is that wholsomest ayr in which Religion lives best. There is no less *necessity* both in *Piety* and *Policy*, to preserve the Laws of holy order and discipline in the Church of Christ on Earth; which have the warrant and seal of his authority upon them, and are for the preservation of truth, peace, and honour in the Church; Since

Nec veritate sonori; nec charitate frugiferi. Greg.

Rev. 12.

H h we

we find by all experience of times, and most in our own, That the pride and presumption of *mens gifts and private spirits*, are no less wantonly active in matters of Religion, than in Civill and Military affairs.

Now, why any men *of piety, or in power*, professing the reformed Religion, should incline either to *connive at*, or to *countenance* any courses, which evidently tend to the shame, contempt, confusion, and extirpation of all true Religion, (as it stood in the profession *of the Church of England*, opposite to the gross errors, superstitions and prophanness of any, that are known and declared enemies to it) I can see no cause, unless it be *a supine negligence* in some, who, as they grow *greater*, so they are like *Gallioes, more careless in matters of Religion*, wholly intent to *State interests*; as if *States-men had no souls to save*, or no God to judge them; and were to give no account of that *power* and advantage they have, as well as that *charge* and *care* which lyes upon them to do all good they can to *mens souls* under their power; or else, there is some other interest secretly contrived, and cunningly carried on here, (as by open hostility in other parts,) amidst the dusk of our civill Commotions and troubles, by those *sons of Edom*, and *daughters of Babylon*, who have *evill will at our Sion*, and say of our *Jerusalem*, *Down with it, down with it*, raze it even to the foundations.

Acts 18.17.

Psa. 137.7.

Jude 9.

As it was for no good will, that the *Devil contended with Michael the Archangell, about the body of* Moses, minding rather to have it Idolized than *Embalmed*; No more is it from *any honest zeal*, or pious principle, that some men now so *earnestly stickle about* (and indeed) against the setled office, and *peculiar function of the Ministry*; either to have it in common, or none at all, with *any divine authority and commission*; whose first Anti-ministeriall batteries, which seemed to carry some shew of Scripture-strength I have hitherto resisted and repelled, not dashing or opposing Scripture against Scripture, but clearing its obscurer meaning in some few places, by that most evident and *concurrent Sense* which is manifestly held forth in many plain passages, and hath been constantly followed in the Churches of Christ, from the first setling of Christianity in the world *to this day*; As the Spirit of God in the Word cannot *contradict* it self in the main scope and design; so where any variation or difference in the letter may seem to be, It must be wisely reconciled, by discerning the different occasion, reason, or ground of things; sure we are, the pretended *gifts*; or dictates of privat spirits may in no sort be set up any way to *contradict* those testimonies and demonstrations of the Spirit, which are so evidently shining from the Scripture, as they are in none more than this of a peculiar function and holy ordination of the Evangelicall Ministry.

Sensus Scripturæ expetit certæ interpretationis gubernaculum. Tertul. de Pres. *Non verba tantum defendantur sed ratio verborum constituatur.* Id.

And

18. *Conclusion, and Transition.*

And here I might forbear to add trouble to you *O Excellent Christians*, or any readers, by any further enlarging of this Apology, whereby to vindicate the honour of the *divinely Instituted*, and *Ecclesiastically* derived Ministry of this Church; Since the holy Scripture is (as I have shewed) so *wholly, fully*, and *punctually*, for its peculiar Institution, and its constant succession to the end of the world, (whereto it is not denyed, but *private gifts* may come in with such assistance, as is humble, orderly, and edifying, but not as proud, invasive and abolishing; as *Hagar* they may do service in Christs family, but they must not grow insolent and malipert against *Sarah*.) What ever can be produced, in a matter of so high and religious a nature, as the Ministeriall office and authority is, beyond what the Scriptures (the only infallible rule) and the Churches constant practise (the most credible witness) do assure us, is for the most part but *as childish skirmishings with Reeds and Bulrushes, after combating with Pikes and Guns*; And I find indeed, that all after-Cavills of the Anti-ministeriall faction, arise, not much beyond *womanish janglings*, presumptuous boastings, and *uncomly bickerings*, for the most part; where, not religious reasonings, but peevish *Cavils*, and pertinacious *Calumnies*, like *black and ragged regiments* (impatient to see themselves so routed by the Scriptures potent convictions, and the Churches constant custome) do but *rally* themselves, as in *a case Perdue*, to see what can be done by *volleys of rayling* Rhetorick, and virulent *Calumniatings* against the Ministers of the Gospell in this Church; whose greatest fault is that which the devil finds with the best of men, that they are as *Job, upright*; not that there is any just fault to be found with their holy Calling, which hath nothing in it *irreligious*, or *unreasonable*; nothing immorall, or imprudent: nothing, but what is fully agreeing to all order, policy, decency, as following the best and *holyest Examples*, uses and customs of the Church, together with the *rules of Divine Institution*, and the ends of all true Religion, the glory of God, and the good of Mankind, both for souls and bodies, for temporall and eternall welfare, for internall peace of conscience, and externall tranquillity in Civill and Church Societies, both as men and Christians; All which the Ministeriall calling regards, and carries on as its holy design and work, which no other Calling doth; Not Magistrates, or Lawyers, or Physicians, or Tradesmen, or Souldiers, who do not think themselves to stand charged *in Christs Name*, with the care of mens souls, so as to make it their business to instruct, direct, and watch over them in the wayes of salvation.

Job. 1. *Culpam in beato Jobo non inveniens Satanæ malicia, ipsam innocentiam in crimen, & integritatem in calumnium invidiosè vertit.* Greg.

Lingua maledica sanctos carpere solet in solatium delinquentium. Ieron. ad Eust.

And for Ministers persons, such as are truly worthy to be counted such, their *failings* will not be found beyond what is incident to common infirmities, and *daily incursions* of frailties, inseparable from the best of men in this *mortall pilgrimage*; All which, the charity of humble Christians easily conceals, and willingly excuses, or pardons, when they consider how free and full a pardon of all sins, is from God by the Ministry, offered to every penitent and believing sinner: The grief and impotent despite, which the prophane, politick, and pragmatick enemies of the Ministry of this and all reformed Churches are transported with, ariseth from the like ground, as was in the hearts of *Tobias* and *Sanballat*, and that scornfull crue, against the *Jews*, that by *their means* this Church of God, as the Temple, is built, repayred, clensed, reformed; That by their valiant courage, learned skill, and vigilant Industry, the truth, faith, holy Ordinances, and good manners of this Reformed Church are asserted, vindicated, preserved, and restored from those ruines, rubbige, sords, and demolishings, by which erroneous, ambitious, covetous, and licentious minds seek to waste, infest and quite abolish the *Reformed Religion*, both in *England* and every where else.

Nehem. 4. *Solatium est malorum bonos Carpere.* Ieron. *ut improbi suo malo delectantur, ita invidi alieno bono torquentur.* Amb. Φθόνοι ταῖς ἀριστείαις ἀντιστρατεύεσθαι πέφυκεν. Amb.

In order to which grand design, the Anti-ministeriall Adversaries are not wanting, to bring all manner of *rayling accusations*, and indign Calumnies against both the Ministers and Ministry of this Church: Some of which, I think it a shame for me, by reciting of them, to *pollute*, either my Pen, or the purer *eyes* of those *readers*, who *excell in Civility*, as much as those evill Speakers do, in *insolency* and *scurrility*, both for carriage and language against the best Ministers in *England*. But it is no wonder if they give us *the gall and vinegar* of bitter reproaches *to drink*, when they intend shortly *to crucifie us*. All is less than was sayd, and done *to Christ himself*. It is part of our honour and blessing, to have men speak all *manner of evill* of us, if we can but make it appear to be, most *falsly* and and *injuriously*, as well as *most indignly* and *ungratefully*: Such manner of speaking becomes no mens mouths, but those, whose hearts abound with so much *malice* against the best Ministers; who ought to be the *best of men*, and generally are the *best of speakers*; In honour to whose many real and excellent gifts (becomming the dignity of their holy place and function) as also in charity to all others, chiefly those, who most despise and hate the Ministers of this Church, I shall endevour to let all men see in the following part of this Apology, the malice, futility, and falsity of those *evill speakings*, wherewith some men please themselves the more, because they think they please some others, whom they fancy to have a very evill eye, and an heavy hand toward such Ministers as most study to please God, and to preserve the Reformed religion in this Church of Christ.

στρεβλόλογοι καὶ σπερμολόγοι. Mat. 27. 34.

Mat. 5. 11.

CAVIL.

CAVIL *or* CALUMNY IV.

Against the Ministry of England *as Papal and Anti-Christian.*

THe fourth *Cavil* or *Calumny* then wherewith the office and function of the Ministers of *England* is battered and defamed, among the credulous, weak, and vulgar minds, is this; That if there be such a peculiar order and office of the Ministry established in Scripture by a *Divine Institution*, and so continued in the Church by a right Ordination, for some times of *Primitive purity*, to a holy succession; yet the present Station, Calling, and Authority of the Ministers of *England is apparently Antichristian*, as derived from *Episcopall Ordination*, and that descended from the *Papall* or *Roman authority*, which was but of late years abolished, as *that of Episcopie* they think now is, neither of them seeming to them to be of Christs appointment, or according to Scripture-rule and patern; So that if it be necessary to have peculiar Ministers by office, it is also necessary to cast off the former order and standing which is degenerated, and to begin upon some new account, which shall appear to be neerest to the pattern of *Divine Institution*, and primitive practise, how ever it may fail of a constant succession, for above these 1600. years from Christ; during all which time, it is evident indeed, that *Bishops have* had a *chief place* and influence in the Ordination of Ministers, and for 1000. the Pope hath chalenged something of Supremacy and Jurisdiction in these Western Churches, over all the Clergy, both Bishops and Presbyters; None of which are fit to serve in Gods house as Ministers, while they are not clensed from that leprosie, which they have contracted from the Pope and Prelates.

A Divine Institution in any institution of divine appointment See Butler's Analogy 1496 – note

Answ. I will first endevour to take off from the face *of our Ministry*, this scandalous visard of *the Papall authority*, which scares some people so very much, that they are afraid to medle with any thing that ever passed *the Popes fingers, except only the lands and revenews of the Clergy*; Having removed this veil or covering, which was sometime over these *Western Churches*, we shall easily see the face of the holy Ministry no less than of other *Christian Institutions* restored, without any *Disfiguration* or *Essentiall change*, by any such mask as might sometimes be upon it, through the *policy* and *folly* of many.

(1) *The Papal Usurpation no prejudice to the true Ministry of* England, *more than to all other Christian Institutions,*

It were a very *weak and injurious Concession*, no less prejudicial to the Reformed Churches, than pleasing to all the *Romish* party, if the

Pope

Pope could perswade us *Protestants*, and other Christians, to cast quite away, and utterly abhor what ever the *Papall usurpation* hath abused, or the Romish devotion hath used in matter of Christian religion; Sure then, we must seek for other *Apostles* and *Saints*, other *Scriptures* and *Sacraments*, another *Gospel* and *Messias*, than Jesus Christ, no less than *other Bishops and Ministers*; [For over all these, the *Popes of Rome have spread the skirts of their usurped authority*; their impure mixtures, their corrupt doctrines, and superstitious manners; Who as far as they *are Antichristian*, that is, go in any wayes contrary to *the holy rule*, and humble patern of Jesus Christ, yet might, yea and ought to *sit in the Temple of God*, as all *Antichristian spirits indeed do*, who cannot properly be, but where there is a *Profession of Christianity*: yet it doth not follow, that the Catholique Church, (against which the *gates of hell shall not prevail*, so as to extinguish *the name of Christ*) was either wholly ruined by *Antichristian superstructures*; or that the whole fabrick of it *must* be pulled down by us, and all parts of it made *Nehustan*, in stead of cleansing, repayring, and reforming, which is not a *novelty of invention*, but a sober restitution of all things in Religion, to the *primitive mode and pattern*, which is authorised and ordained by Christ; Who did no more himself as to the outward restoring of Religion and worship of God; Chalenging *Gods right* to his own House of prayer, when covetousness had made it *a den of theeves*. The *priesthood of old* failed not by reason of the *immoralities* of the Priests among the Jews; nor did the Didacticall or Teaching authority cease from *Moses his Chair* and succession, because the Scribes and Pharisees (who were men of corrupt doctrine, and hypocriticall manners) sate *therein*, and taught the Traditions and inventions of men mixt *with the commands of God*; No more did, or doth the Evangelicall Ministry and Sacraments cease, by reason of any Papall arrogatings, or other human additions.

ἃ δεῖ κἀθεχόμενον πᾶν πάντα ἡ βέβαιον. Ep. 67. *Plato.* All things handled by men, are subject to be stayied.

2 Thes. 2. 4.

Antichristus Christũ mentitur, & turpitudinem vitæ falso nominis honore convestit. Jerom. ad Geront.

Amara erat Ecclesia in nece martyrum, amarior in conflictu hæreticorum, amarissima in moribus domesticorum. Ber. S. 33. in Cant.

Petri Cathedrã occupat tanquam Leo paratus ad prædam bestia Apocalyptica cui datum est os loquens blasphemias, & bellum gerere cum sanctis. Ber. ep. 125. Mat. 21. 13.

Christus Templum Dei cauponibus & latronibus deturpatum non diruit aut penitus detestatur, sed purgamenta ista & fæces ejiciendo Dei domum in diviniorem usum asseruit: & hoc modo in pristinum honorem restituit. Chem.

Mat. 23. 2. Mat. 15. 6.

Therefore the wisdome and piety of the learned and godly *Reformers* of these Western Churches, especially *here in England*, contented themselves with *casting out* what ever corrupt doctrines, impure mixtures, vain customes, and superstitious fancies, the Papall vanitie and novelty had built upon those divine and antient foundations of *Christian religion*; which were layd by the Apostles, and *Primitive master-builders*, all over the world; Whose Canon the Scriptures; together with sound Doctrine, holy Ministry, comly Government, Sacramentall seals, and other Christian duties of prayer, fasting,

Inordinatio aliqua non invalidam reddit ordinationem, vitio relicto, rem ad legitimum modum revocarunt. Alsted. Suppl. Geiar. de Reform.

Luther owned no other call

ſting,*&c.* they reſtored with all gravity, moderation and exactneſs, with due regard both to the clear *ſenſe of Scriptures*, and the *Catholick practiſe of Churches, Conforming of all things*, either to the expreſs Precepts and Inſtitutions of the word of God, or to thoſe generall directions, which allow *liberty of Prudence*, and difference in matters *Circumſtantiall*; in all which the *Primitive Church* had gone before them. Herein they were not ſo *weak and heady*, as to be ſcandalized with, and inſolently to reject all things, that the Papall or Romiſh party had both received and retained in religious uſes from former and better times, either as Chriſtians, or Biſhops, or prudent men; for ſo they had very ſillily *deprived themſelves*, and all the Reformed Churches, of all thoſe Scriptures, Sacraments, holy duties, *Order, rites*, and good *cuſtoms*, which the Pope and Romiſh party had ſo long uſed, not as Popes, by any Antichriſtian policy, power and pride, but as they were Chriſtians, having received them *in a due ſucceſſion* at firſt, (though after much depraved) from thoſe *holy Predeceſſors*, which had been Martyrs and *Confeſſors* in that famous antient Roman Church.

of Ordination as a Miniſter, but that which he had, as he was made a Presbyter in the Romiſh communion. *Gerard.de Miniſterio.pag.70. Ab Epiſcopo ſuo ordinatus Lutherus.* anno 1507. *Nec aliam quæſivit ordinationem.* Gerard.147. *Multum differt inter cauſam & culpam, inter ſtatum & exceſſum.* Tert. l.1. adv. Marc. *Non negandum eſt bonum quod remanſit propter malum quod præceſſit.* Auſt. Ep.48.

(2) *How far neceſſary and ſafe to be ſeparated from the Romaniſts.*

No judicious *Proteſtant* or truly reformed Chriſtian, whoſe conſcience is guided by Science, and his reforming zeal tempered with true charity, either doth, or ought to recede farther from *Communion with the Roman Church*, than he ſees that hath receded *from the rule* of Chriſt, and the Apoſtolicall Precepts, or binding examples, expreſſed in the Scriptures, ſo far as concerns the true faith, in its Doctrines, Seals, and fruits of good works. In *matters of extern and prudentiall order*, every Church hath the ſame liberty which the Roman had, to uſe or refuſe ſuch ceremonials, as they thought fit, and to theſe every good Chriſtian may conform. In many things we neceſſarily have communion with *the Pope and Papiſts*, as in the nature and reaſon of men; In ſome things we ſafely may, as in rules and practiſes, politick, civill, juſt, and charitable, as Governours either Secular or Eccleſiaſtical; In many things we ought in conſcience and religion to have communion with them, ſo far as they profeſs the truths of Chriſtian religion, and hold any *fundamentals* of faith; And however they do by miſ-interpretation of Scriptures, or any *Antichriſtian additionals of falſe doctrines*, of impious or ſuperſtitious practiſes, ſeem to us rather to overthrow, or bury the good foundations, than rightly and orderly *to build* upon them. (for which ſuperſtructures and fallacious conſequences we recede from them, and diſpute with them;) yet we do not renounce all they hold, or do in common with us as Chriſtians.

Ad quamcunque Eccleſiam veneritis ejus morem ſervate, ſi pati ſcandalum aut facere nolitis. Aug. Ep. 86. reſponſum B. Ambroſii.

In the Lords Supper.

1 *Cor.*11,27. Whosoever shall eat this Bread.

28. So let him eat of that bread.

Solet res quæ significat ejus rei nomine quam significat nuncupari: hinc dictum est Petra erat Christus. Aust. Q. 57. in Levit.

For instance (it being not now a place to dispute them) We cannot own, as the Catholick sense of Christ, of the Scriptures, or the Primitive fathers, that sense which they in later times have given of the words in the Sacramental Consecration of the Lords Supper, by which they raise that strange doctrine of *Transubstantiation*, unknown to the first Fathers; And which seems to us 1. contrary to the way of Gods providence, both in naturall, and in religious things, which changeth not the substances and natures of things, but the relation and use of them, from naturall and common, to mysticall and holy; 2. Contrary also to the usuall sense of all *Scripture phrases*, and expressions of the like nature, where things are mystically related by religious institution, and so mutually denominated without essentiall changes; 3. Contrary to the common principles of right reason, 4. And contrary to the testimony of four senses, *sight, taste, smelling*, and *hearing*, which are the proper organes, by whose experience and verdict of things sensible, we judge in reason, what their nature is; 5. Contrary also to the way and end that Christ proposed, to strengthem a Christian receivers faith; which is not done, by what is more obscure and harder to be believed than the whole mysterie of *the Gospell*, as recorded to us in the Scripture.: There being nothing less imaginable, than that Christ gave his Disciples his *own very body*, each man to eat him *whole* and *entire*, and so ever after, when he was then at table with them, and is now by an Article of faith *believed to be as man in heaven*; These and the like strange fancies of men, which draw after them many great absurdities and contradictions, both in sense and reason, and the nature of things; being no way advantageous to the religious use, end, and comfort of the Sacrament, we reject, together with the consequentiall Idolatry of worshiping the bread: Also the *sacrilege* of detaining the Cup of the Lord from the people, we cannot allow, as being contrary both to the primitive practise of the Church, and to the express command of Christ in the Institution, which was after also revealed to St. *Paul* by Christ himself. Yet still we use and observe the Sacramentall Elements, with the same high estimation and veneration, which pious and purest *antiquity* ever did bear to that *Sacred mysterie*; how ever we forbear to use some of their expressions, whose Oratory occasioned in part the after error, which mistook that, as spoken of the Bread in its nature, which magnified it only in the Sacramentall use and mysterie, which is indeed very high; retaining both the Elements, words, and holy form, which Christ instituted, and Christians alwayes used, not so much disputing and determining the manner of Sacramentall union, as endevouring after those *graces*, which may make us worthy Communicants, and reall partakers of the Body and Blood of Jesus Christ, when we do receive that *dreadfull*, yet most

most *desirable* seal *of our Faith*, which consigns fuller to us, and confirms in us, those comforts, which as sinners we want, and may have most really and *only* from Christ; not by eating his flesh in a bodily and gross way with our mouths; but by receiving him by a true and lively faith into our souls, as he is set forth to us in the Scriptures to be God incarnate; the only Saviour of the world; of whose merit, death, passion, body and blood, we are by the same faith, (though in less degrees of strength,) really partakers, and nourished to eternall life, before we receive him in that Sacrament of the Lords Supper; yea though we never should have opportunity so to receive him; which is but the same object received by the same faith, to the same end, though in a different manner, and with different degrees.

Baptism.

So for *Baptism*; we retain the *substance* of that *holy Sacrament*, as we find it in the Scriptures, rejecting only those superfluous dresses (of Salt, Spittle, Oyl, Insufflation, and the like) which cumber and deform that duty and Ordinance, but they do not destroy it, nor do ever any Protestants, that are of any name or honour for Religion, re-baptise those, who were baptised in the *Roman* Church;

The *Apocryphall* additions of the Romish Church to the Canon of the Scriptures, we reject from being rules of faith (however we approve their excellent morals) And this we do upon the same grounds, that the Jewish Church of old, and the Primitive Christian for the most part ever did; yet we retain those books as oracles of God which we have received with and from the Romish Church, as of divine inspiration; according to that testimony which both the Jewish and Christian Churches fidelity, have given us of them.

Concil. Laodicenum omits only the Apocal. Apocrypha Books *Hieron. in Prolog. Galateo.* *Josephus l. 1. cont. Appio.* we (i.e. the Jews) have not infinite and different Books but only 22. which are justly called Divine. (τὰ δικαίως θεῖα πεπιστευμένα.) *Mosis* 5. *Prophet.* 13. *Psal.* 4. The rest from *Artaxerxes* to these times have not the like credit, because not a certain succession of Prophets.

Prayers in a language not vulgar.

The *unne*, dull, *spiritless*, and *formall* devotions, Liturgies and prayers used by the Romanists, in any tongue *unknown* to the most, and with so many *vain repetitions*, we refuse; yet still we retain the holy custom of Christians assembling in publike, and worshipping God by publike Liturgies, prayers and praises.

In somethings we hold nothing common with them, either in opinion or practise; as in the profitable fancy of purgatory; the popular fashion of worshipping Images or adoring God in and by *Images*; of oblations and prayers for the dead; of praying to Saints and Angels; of Auricular confession; of dispensing by Indulgences the merits, or supperogating righteousness of some Christians to others; Since in these and the like matters, which I only touch, it

τὸ τῶν πολλῶν μέρος καινὸν πάντων ἐστὶ τῶν μετεχόντων τῆς πίστεως ὁ γὰρ τὸ κτίσμα προσκυνῶν κἂν ἐν ὀνόματι Χριστοῦ τοῦτο ποιεῖ εἰδωλολάτρης ἐστὶ Χριστοῦ ὄνομα τῷ εἰδώλῳ θέμενος. Greg. Nis. de Placilla orat. Funeb. *Delinquens soli Deo cognitus de reatu nudare apud homines verecunda conscientia non cogitur.* Ser. 34. Chrysol. So Ber. s. 42. *Non expedit omnibus omnia innotescere quæ scimus de nobis.* in Cant.

To eat & drink : B: B: & B: of Xt truly to our Soul's health [illegible] partaken of His Merits · Passion · Death · Blood being not my work now to handle those controversies which have been so fully discussed by many learned men of this Church of *England*, whose works praise them ; We find no Scripture ground, either for precept or permission.

So likewise in the ambitious *claim of the Popes Infallible* judgement ; His universall *jurisdiction*, and *Supreme Authority* over all Churches and Councils ; We deny it, as un *usurpation* gotten by indulgences of some times and Princes ; also by the flatteries, frauds, cruelties, power and policies of *severall Popes* in their successions ; but not grounded on any Law, or right, either humane or divine ; neither by the Institution of God, nor by the consent of all Churches: Yet we deny not to *the Pope* such a *primacy* of place, or *priority* of order and precedency as is reasonable and just either in the *Roman* Diocess as a Bishop ; or in a *Councill*, as Bishop of that famous City.

In like manner for the sacred order and *function of the Ministry* ; we reject what ever imaginary power or will-worship is annexed to the *office* by humane superstition ; but we approve the antient form of Commission, and Divine Authority derived by them to Presbyters and Bishops, for Preaching the word, celebrating the Sacraments, reconciling penitents, use of the Keys in doctrine, or jurisdiction and Government ; Also of the continued power of Ordination, for a succession of Ministers in the Church. In all these and the like what ever we find to be *spurious issues*, of meer humane invention ; of *Scripture-less* opinions ; of groundless traditions, obtruded, as matters of Religion, upon the consciences of Christians; we use *that just* severity, which we think the Apostles and Primitive fathers would have done, to dash *these Babylonish brats against the stones* : yet still we redeem and preserve alive the legitimate succession, *the Sons of Sion* ; the *Israel of God* ; and justify *the Children of true wisdom and of the Heavenly Jerusalem*, that is, the divine and *truly religious* Institutions, upon Scripture grounds, although we find them to have been *led Captive*, and a long time deteined Prisoners by any unrighteousness, policy, superstition, tyranny, covetousness or ambition, in the Walls and Suburbs of *Babylon*: Though *tares* were sown among the good Seed in the Field of the Church, while men slept, yet we must not be such wasters, as to destroy the *Corn* with the *weeds* ; or to refuse both, because we like not one ; Though our Fathers ate *sour grapes* and our teeth were an edge, we must not therefore pull all our teeth out of our heads.

In the Roman Pontificall, The Bishop to be consecrated is charged after many Ceremonies and pompous modes, with this, as his office and duty, To judge, to interpret, to consecrate, to confer holy orders, to offer, to Baptize, and to confirm : after that the Consecrators laying the Bible on his shoulder, and their hands on his head, say these words, *Receive the holy Spirit* : *i. e.* the gifts and power to be a Bishop, or chief Pastor: to teach and rule in the Church. So the Presbyter is by the Bishop ordeyning and others with him imposing their hands on the head, enjoyned, To offer, to bless, to govern, to Preach and to Baptise, as becomes his place and Office. Mat. 13. 25.

Divine

Divine *institutions* are *incorruptible*; nor can any corruption of mens minds or matters cease on them, any more than * putrefaction on the Sun beams, when it shines on a Carkass or Dunghill: We may be corrupted, but holy Ordinances are like God alwaies the same, when restored to their Primitive Institution, which is their State of Integrity. Riches and honour are not unwelcom, though they descend to men from unworthy Ancestors; Nor should Religion so far as its title is good by the word of God, either in strickt precept and institution, or in prudence joyned with piety and decency. Good pictures will recover the beauty, when the soyl is washed off.

* τὰ θεῖα ἄφθαρτα. *Ut Aurum et gemmæ ita res Divinæ non corrumpuntur; quamvis opprimuntur; non vitiantur natura quum polluntur consuetudine. Non res ipsæ (ut nec veritas erroribus) sed nos malè utendo putrescimus.* Eras.

In a word, we retain the truth, faith, holy mysteries, Catholick orders, constant Ministry, and commendable manners, which the later Romanists have derived and continued from the first *famous Church* in that place; nor do we think it either conscience or prudence to deprive our selves of any *thing Divine*, though delivered to us by the less pure hands of men; or to cast away the provision which God sends us, though it be by Ravens; or to Anathematise all the Romish Church holds of saving Truths, because it hath in the Councill of *Trent* Anathematised some Truths.

The Bishops of *Rome* were alwaies *more cunning*, than to abrogate, or cast away those *essentials*, the main *foundations* and pillars of true Christian Religion, as *the word*, the *Sacraments*, the *Ministry*, and *Government* of the *Church*, on which they knew the *vast moles*, and over grown *superstructure* of the *Pontifician* pomp, profit, pride, reputation, policy and power, (through the *credulity*, of people, and *blind devotion* of most men, in these *Western Churches*) was built and sustained: Nor can any thing more contribute to the Popes depraved content, or repair his *particular interest*, in this Western world, than to see, any so *heady*, rash, *and mad Reformers*, as shall resolve to quarrell with, and to cast quite away, all those things of Christian Religion, which ever passed *through* the hands of the *Romish* Church; or any other never so erronious and superstitious; He well knows, how meager a *Sceleton*, how miserable a *shadow* Christian Religion must needs remain to those *furious* and *fanatick* Reformers; Being as much reduced to poverty and meer nothing in the very *essentials* of Christianity (both for Doctrine, Duties, Sacraments, Scriptures, order, and manners) as it would be in the matter of maintenance and Church Revenews; (where somemens *covetous and cruell Reformation* is resolved, if they may have their will, to leave nothing to maintain Religion, or its Ministry, but the meer scraps of *arbitrary* and *grudging contributions*;) Such will our Religion be, if we reject all, that was used by those, who abused many things; and we must after only adhere to the *beggary*

Ut in reficiendis domibus sic in moribus non destruenda omnia: sed repurganda: non diruenda sed reficienda. Ber. Ep. ad Abb.

Ἀντὶ θερμότερος, καὶ τῷ ζήσει τῷ πρίν ἑαυτοῦ πολλὰ μὲν κατορθοῦσι, τῶν δεόντων διαμαρτεῖν, καὶ πολλὰ δὲ διαμαρτεῖν ἐξ ἀγνοίας καὶ ἀμαθείας. Naz. Ep. Eudox.

gery of Seekers; attending new Instructions from Heaven, instead of following antient Christian and Catholick Institutions.

3. *Of Church Reformations; with moderation and charity.*

οὐδὲν δίκαιον φύεται χωρὶς τοῦ σωφρονεῖν. *Plato. de leg.* 3. Nothing is just but what was wisely moderated.

Certainly, *Church Reformations* in things Religious, should be carried on with all acurate strictness and rigor in clear *points of saving truths*, and in things of *divine Institution* so confessed by all; yet also, with much *charity*, candor, moderation and discretion toward any Christians in other things; wherein we must differ from them: Yet no further, than they seem to us to derogate from the truth and word of God; and so become detrimentall to mens souls. It is a commendable Schism, which separates the Corn from the chaff, and the Gold from the Dross; neither retaining both in a confusion, nor casting away both in a passion: In thus doing all things with *meekness of wisdom*, Christians may not only be able, upon sober and judicious grounds from Scripture, and the Catholick consent of the Fathers, to maintain what they do, as wise *Reformers* of abuses; but also the better invite others to embrace, and to approve our *just and well-tempered Reformation*; in the *unpassionate purity* whereof others will the easier see, as in a smooth and true Glass, their yet *remaining spots and deformities*.

Reformation of Churches is best done, not *by cutting off the* head of Religion, but by *taking off* those *masks* and *visards* which hide its face and beauty: Men will best see their errors, not by force pulling their eyes out of their heads, but by fairly taking away the *motes or beams* of prejudice, error and pertinacy, which are in their eyes, which hinder them, not from seeing at all, but from seeing so well, as we (in truth) think they may, and in charity wish they would.

1 Thess. 5. 21. Plato: τὸ μέτριον ἐστι μέσον ὑπερβολῆς καὶ ἐλλείψεως, moderation is the medium between the excess and defect: Neither taking nor refusing all, but trying all, and holding the good.

True Reformation free from Schism.

By this *shield of moderation* and charity, *proving all things* and *retaining what is good in all*, (with our pitty and prayers for any Christians, wherein we think they erre, as differing therefore from us, because from the rule which God hath set for his Church in things pertaining *to Divine worship*:) we justly defend our selves, in this, and other reformed Churches, (that are of the same temper and charity in their Reformations) from *the sin and scandall of Schism*; when we fairly and freely declare, that we separate no further from the Church of *Rome*, or any other particular Church, or Christian man, than we are by the word of God perswaded, that they *separate* from Christs holy rule, and from the custom and Doctrine of the *Catholick Church*; whose bounds and marks are the samenes of divine truths, and the unity of the Spirit, in Charity, which we retain to all Christians, as far as such, with whom, while we desire such communion, of *true faith*, *holy order*, and *obedience*, together with love, as they do with Christ, and all true Christians, we cannot in our own consciences, nor other mens censures, be esteemed

Schismaticks, as the Novatians and Donatists of old were; who so challenged the title of the Church to their factions, as to exclude all others, and refuse the offers and means of accord. As *Cyprian Ep.* 95. and *Aust. Ep.* 164. tell us.

To which brands of Schism we are then lyable only, when we recede, or separate from visible communion with any Church, without just and weighty cause shewn out of the word; or when we go further from them than there is just cause, and that too without charity; refusing the good which they have, while we withdraw from the evill we suspect: Which would be the case of the Church of *England* in this point of *immoderate Reformation*; if we should (as some would have us) therefore separate from all Scriptures, Sacraments, Ministry, Primitive Government, and order, because all these were retained, used, and after abused much, by the Roman Church and *Papall party*: we are bid to *come out of Babylon, Rev.* 18.4. but not to run out *of our wits*; to *act*, as Gods people, with meeknesse, moderation, and Charity, not with that fiercenesse, passion and cruelty which makes us as Sons of *Belial*, inordinatly run from *one Antichrist* to another.

Many Christians in the *Roman Church* may have in them *much of Antichrist* in some kinds, and so (God knows) may many others, in other kinds; either in Doctrine or manners; in endless innovations, and unsetled confusions; or in rigor and uncharitablenesse; All which may betray us, to what we seem most to abhor in Antichrist; for if nothing have more of Christ, than *Charity*, nothing can have more of Antichrist, than that *uncharitablenesse*, which many men nourish for zeal; mistaking a Cockatrice for a Dove; and a firy Serpent for a Phenix. Which may be, as Anti-Christian in *popular furies*, as in *papall tyrannies*; in confusions as in oppressions. It is strange how some men cry out against the *cruelty* of some Papists (which indeed hath been very *great*) when yet, they have the same Spirit of *destruction* in their own breast both against the Papists and others: longing for such a *Kingdom of Christ* (as they call it) and such a downfall of *Antichrist*, which shall consist in War, and Blood, and Massacres against and among all Christians, which are not of their mind and side. We think, that in *charity* we ought not to impute the faults and errors of *every Pope*, or *Doctor* of the Roman side, to all those of that profession; Nor ought we take those learned men among them alwaies at their worst; finding there is great difference between what they may hold in the heat of *publike* disputes, and what they opine and practise in a private way; nor are their death-bed *tenets* alwaies the same, with those of their Chayrs and *Pulpits*. Besides, many of the more devout and learned men among them, are now both in opini-

Uncharitablenesse is as Antichristian as error.

A Christianorū dissidiis venturus Antichristus occasionem accipiet. Naz. Orat. 14.

Qui Christi non est Antichristi est Jeron. Ep. 57. ad Damas.

So – The Bk are Turky which is a most stout Book.

ons and lives, much more modest holy and Reformed, than some were heretofore, whose Reformation in judgement or manners, in verity, purity, and charity we do really congratulate and joy in.

And, for the Body of the common people among the Romanists, many are ignorant of those disputes, wherein the mistaking is most dangerous; which if they do hold, yet it is under the perswasion and love of truth, retaining still the *foundation of Christ Crucified*, and hoping for salvation only by his merits; (as many now *profess* to do) and living in *no known* sin; but striving to lead an holy and charitable life in all things; Charity commands us to think, that in such, the mercy of God (accepting their sincere love to the truth, and their unfeigned obedience to what they know,) pardons particular errors which they know not to be such, & wherein no lust of pride, or covetousness, *&c.* either obstructs, or diverts them from the way of Truth; Though the *superstructures* may be many of *straw and stubble*, which shall perish, yet holding the *foundation* Christ crucified in a pure conscience, they shall *be saved in the day* of the Lord; Though the *vessell be leaky* in many places, yet by great care in steering, and frequent *pumping* (that is *true* faith and repentance) it may keep the *soul* from Shipwrack and drowning in perdition, which is *embarked* in the *bottom* of Christian Religion, and which *steers* alwaies by the compass of *conscience*, setting all the points of conscience, by the Chart or rules of *Scripture*; as neer as he can attain by his *teachers*, or his own *industry*.

Qui à seductis parentibus errorem acceperunt, quærunt autem cauta solicitudine veritatem, corrigi parati cum invenerint, hi nequaquam sunt inter hæreticos deputandi. Aust. Ep. 162.

1 Cor. 3. 12.

We are sorry for our *necessary differences* from the Romanists or others; which yet our consciences so far command us, as we think our selves enlightned by the word of God; contrary to which we cannot, and ought not to be forced actually to conform, or to comply with any men in things Religious: Yet have we no *lust of faction*, no delight in *separation*, no *bloody principles*, or tenets, against any *Christians* of any particular Church; desiring the same charity from them to us; which may, in lesser differences from each other, yet unite us to Christ, and to the *Catholick Church*, as true parts of it, though infirm, or diseased: This temper we should not despair of in the devouter and *humbler Romanists*; if they were not *daily enflamed*, by *politick Spirits* and violent *Bigots* among them, who will endure no Religion as Christian, which doth not kiss the *Popes Pantofle*, or hold his stirrop, or submit to that pride, flattery and tyranny, which some of them have affected; when indeed it ill becomes those, that chalenge a chief place in Christs Church, to be so vastly different from *the example* of the crucified Saviour of Christians.

Such talents then as have been *once divinely delivered* to the Roman (as to all other Christian Churches,) we have all aright to as-

beleivers

believers in private, and as Christians or Churches in publike communion and profession; nor can these Jewels be so embezeled, by being buried, or abused, but that we may safely take them up clear, and use them; together with those *other* which we have obteined, through the grace and bounty of our Lord and Master Jesus Christ; In whose name and right, we (as a part of his Catholick Church) received them first, and enjoy them now, *only Reformed*, according to what we first received of them; without any prejudice or diminution to their true and intrinsecall worth (which is divine) by reason of our *fellow servants* former, or present idle, imperious, impure or injurious use of them: We accept and use the *holy vessels*, which belong to the temple, and the Lord of the Church, without scruple, when they are graciously restored out of the profane hands of revelling *Balshazzers*; The remaining *silver censers* are holy, though the hand and fire were unholy which were applyed to them.

Ezra. 7.

Numb. 16.

4.

Our Ministry not from nor of the Pope.

Our Ministery then may be, and certainly is, very *good, holy*, and *divine*, as well as the Scriptures, and Sacraments, or other holy Ministrations, and duties are, when duly restored to their *primitive purity, order*, and authority; which go along with their right succession; notwithstanding they are derived to us through or by the *Romish Church*, or the Popes dispensation; yet do they not therefore descend from them, but only from Christ, the first institutor of his Church, and of this Ministry, with a perpetuall power of *succession*; Our Lord Jesus Christ, the gracious *Spouse* of the Church, as of every Soul, that truly believes and obeys (though with much unbelief and frailty,) disdains not to own *his relation* to any Church or Christians, though they are not *so faithfull* to him; though they lose their first love; yet they may *be still his*, by what still remains of soundness and outward profession; Yea and Christ will vouchsafe to admit us again to the communion and covenant of his love, even after *long wandrings*, and *unkind absences*, when ever we wash our selves, and return to him, from our disloyall adulteries and *pollutions*. He doth not utterly *divorce* any Church, when the substance and essentials of Religion (which are but *in a few things*) do remain, notwithstanding the many *meretricious* paints, and disguisings, which the wantoness of *humane inventions* may have put upon it; thereby disfiguring its *Primitive* beauty and simplicity. Mans vanity and arrogancy against God or men, doth no whit abrogate, either the right *which* Christ, or any Church and Christian posterity hath to the purity and power of his gifts and *institutions*, in the right way of his Ministry: All which may remain, with a

Possunt esse & pastores & Lupi alio respectu; Pastores in veritate quam profitentur, in potestate quā ritè obtinuerunt; Lupi in erroribus quos admiscent, in corruptelis morum, &c. ut Scribæ & Pharisæi in Cathedra Mosis panem veritatis proponebant sed non sine fermento errorum, officium distinguendum à persona, potestas à moribus. Gerard. *de Minist.* Rev. 2. 4. Jer. 3. 1. Thou hast played the harlot with thy lovers, yet return to me saith the Lord. Rev. 3. 2.

blessing

blessing in the *root* and Seed; though they be much pestered, overdropped, choked, and almost starved by *humane additions*, which keep them for some time from their full glory, vigor and extension.

Therefore the learned and godly Reformers of this *Christian Church* in *England*, did not dig any new *fountain of Ordination*, or *ministeriall power*; as some Romanists *calumniated* at first, and were afterward convinced of the contrary, by Master *Masons* learned defence of the Ministry of *England*, as to its right succession; but they only *cleared* that, which they saw was divine in the first broaching or *Institution* by Christ, and as in the purest derivation by *the Apostles*; however in time it became foul by *humane feculencies* and dregs as it passed, *rightly* (though not *purely*) through the hands of some Bishops and *Presbyters*) even to their dayes; Nor was ever any thing required by the best *Reformed Churches*, further to confirm and validate the *Authority* or *power Ministeriall*, which any had received, when he was first ordeined *Presbyter in the* Romish Church, but only this, to renounce, not his Baptism, but his *errors* and former *superstitions*; to profess the Reformed Truths of the Gospell, and accordingly to exercise that *Ministeriall* power, which he had received, truly, as to the *substance*, and duly, as to the *succession*; both as to the Office conferred, and the persons conferring it. Howsoever the *sword of the Ministry* had through the neglect of those, to whom it was committed, been suffered to *contract* the *rust of superstitions*, and to lose much of its beauty and *sharpness*; yet it was still that true and same *two-edged sword*, which came out of the mouth of Jesus Christ, *Rev.* 2. 12. the *first ordeiner* of a peculiar *setled Ministry* in his Church; Nor may it be broken or cast away, when it hath been rightly delivered; but only, cleared, whetted and furbished, from its *rust*, bluntness and dulness: That Pen, which now writes blottingly, might be well made at first, and will write fairly again, if once the hairs or blurs, which its *neb* hath contracted, be but *cleared* from it. It is still *Gods Field* and Husbandry with good Wheat in it, though the enemy hath, while men slept, *sowen many tares*; Bishops and Ministers reformed may *be Gods* true *labourers* and appointed Husbandmen, though they have some time *loytered*; as the Disciples were Christs, when their eyes were so *heavy to sleep*, that they could not *watch with* him that one *hour* of his most *horrid agony*.

Contaminarunt non sustulerunt Ministerium Ecclesiæ. Alsted.

Mat. 26. 40.

It were then but a *passionate* scuffling with mad men, a most impertinent disputing with unreasonable minds, further to argue about the *Popes usurped* or *abused Authority* in any kind over *Churches* or Bishops, or holy Ordinances and Ministry: For which he had as little *grounds* of Scripture or reason, as these *Anti-Ministeriall Objecters* have now, against this Church of *England*, and the

the function of the Ministry in it; against which, these *cunning cavillers* have not so much pretence to argue from the *Popes usurpation*, that our Ministry and Religion are all Antichristian; as they have both *Scripture, Reason*, and *Experience*, (besides the consent of all Reformed Churches) to conclude them to be *truly Christian*; if anger or envie, or covetousness had not blinded their *blood-shotten* eyes, they might easily see some of those *mighty works*, which have been wrought on mens Souls, by the *Ministry of England*, since the Reformation; and without this efficacious Ministry, I believe, neither these *Calumniators* had been so much Christian, as they pretend, nor so able spightfully to contend, with *shewes of Piety*, and *popular falacies* against the true Ministry of this Church, and the best Ministers, with whose *Heifer* they have plowed. Mat.11.28.

5. *Of the Popes pretended Supremacy in* England.

We know well, that not only the reformed Churches, but even the Gallican and Venetian (which keep communion with the Romish Church, and Papall party) besides the Greek, Asian, and African Churches, do generally oppose, and vehemently deny the Popes *abusive usurpations*, both in things Ecclesiasticall and Secular: And this upon most pregnant grounds; not only from Scripture, (whence nothing was ever fairly and pertinently urged, as some *places are fouly wrested*, and yet but little to the Popes advantage) but also from * *all Antiquity*, after that Churches were increased and setled, where the Fathers, and first famous generall Councills, make clearly to the Popes disadvantage, as to any power or jurisdiction in point of divine authority, which he claims beyond, or above other *Bishops and Presbyters*; further than the Roman Diocess first, and the Patriarchate afterward extended; which division and power for order sake was agreed unto by some *generall Councils*; where other four Patriarchs of *Jerusalem*, *Antioch*, *Constantinople*, and *Alexandria*, had also a limited, yet equall power in their respective Dioceses and Provinces, with the Bishop of *Rome*.

* *Cæteri Apostoli par consortium honoris & potestatis acceperunt, qui in toto orbe dispersi Evangelium prædicaverunt, quibusque decedentibus successerunt Episcopi.* Is. Hisp. l.2. off. Eccl. c.5. *Qui sunt constituti in toto mundo in sedibus Apostolorum, non ex genere carnis ut filii Aron, sed pro unius cujusque vita merito iis,* &c. Id. *ubicunque fuerit Episcopus, sive Romæ, sive Eugubii,* &c. *ejusdem est meriti, ejusdem est sacerdotii.* Jeron. ad Evagr. *Celebri urbi frigidum oppidulum opponit.* Eras. in verba Jeron. *Omnes Apostolorum successores sunt.* Id. Concil. Nicæn. 1. Gregory the Great oft protests against any Bishops or Patriarchs usurping and chalenging the title of *Universalis Episcopus aut Pastor*, as a token of Antichristian pride. *Concil. Hipponense. Anno* 393. *de primæ sedis Episcopo i.e. Romano.* [illegible] *Concil. Af. pag.* 119. & *pag.* 318. *can.* 123. They Excommunicated all that appealed beyond the Sea to other Province and Bishop. *Concil. Chalced. anno* 451. *Can.* 9. 11. 17. *Nec quisquam nostrum Episcopum se Episcoporum constituat,* &c. *Quando omnis habeat Episcopus pro licentia libertatis & potestatis suæ arbitrium proprium, ut nec judicari ab altero, nec judicare possit.* Cyp. tom. 2. in fine. *Hoc erant utique cæteri Apostoli quod fuit Petrus, pari consortio præditi & honoris & potestatis. Sed exordium ab unitate proficiscitur, primatus Petro datur, ut una Christi Ecclesia, & una Cathedra monstretur.* Cyp. *Episcopatus unus est cujus à singulis Episcopis in solidum pars tenetur.* Cypr. de uni. Eccl. & ep. 27.

Galf. monum. l.11.c.12. See Bishop *Godwin*, Successio of English Bishops. *Lucius rex in Anglia conversus ad fidem Christi, anno Christi 164.* Three Bishops out of *England*, *Eborius* of *York*, *Restitutus* of *London*, *Adolphius* of *Colchester*, were of the Councill of *Arles* in *France* eleven years before the *Nicane*, which was *anno* 330. See the Letter to *Austin* the Monk cited before, sent from the Clergy and Monk of *Bangor*. Sir *Hen. Spelman*, *Concil. Brit. pag.* 108. *ad. an.* 590. *Omnium provinciarum prima Britania publicitus Christi nomen recepit.* Sabel. Enn. 7 l 5. Beda l. 2. c. 2.

Nor had the Pope then for the first six hundred years after Christ any authority, scarce any name in these *British* Churches, which were undoubtedly converted by some Apostles or Apostolicall men; who left after *King Lucius* his time a famous and flourishing succession of Bishops, Presbyters, and Christians, long before any pretensions of the Pope over these *British* Churches: To which the *British* Bishops in *Wales* were strangers; nor would they own at that time, when *Austin* the Monk came from *Gregory* the Great; who sent hither more out of Christian charity than any Authority to convert the *Saxons*, who had by war and barbarity quite extinguished Christianity with all Bishops and Ministers out of *England*, and had forced the former holy Bishops and Ministers to fly into *Wales*, *Ireland*, and *Scotland*; from whence afterwards in a gratefull vicissitude the English (replanted) Churches received (for the most part) both their Conversion and establishment by a Succession of rightly Ordeined Bishops and Presbyters; for *Austin* the Monks Plantation and preaching extended not beyond *Kent*, *Surrey*, and the adjacent places; as Venerable *Bede* tells us; and our learned Country-man, Sir *Henry Spelman*.

The ambitious *Usurpation* and Antichristian *Tyranny* then of *the Papall power* and *supremacy* afterward, over Bishops and Ministers here in *England*, to which the title of *Christ*, St. *Peter*, or the *Catholick Churches establishment*, is *poorly begged*, and *falsly pretended*, we the Ministers of the Church of *England* ever did, and do, *as much abhor*, as any of these men can, who are so against the now *Reformed* and *established Ministry*, which we have vindicated from Papal and superstitious additaments, and asserted, or restored to it *Primitive* and *Scripturall* dignity, and divine authority, which it never *lost*; but only, not so *clearly discovered*, during the times of darkness and oppression. Our jealousie now is, lest the malice and activity of those, that now dispute, and act against our thus *reformed* and *prospered Ministry*, should prove ere long the *Popes best Engines*, and *factors*, that ever he had in this Church since the Reformation; if they can (as they have begun, and go on apace) but so far prepare the way for the *reintroduction of the Papall power*, and *Romish party*, as to cashier all the learned, reformed, and duly *Ordeined Ministers* in *England*, both as to their order, authority, and government: will not this Church in a *few more years of confusion*, and neglect, become, as a *fallow and unfenced field*, fit for the Papal subtilty and Romish activity, which he will plow *with an Ox and an Asse together*, the *lear-*

ned Jesuit, joyned to the *fanatick Donatist*; The *Seminary Priests with the gifted brethren*; *Friers predicant with Prophets mendicant?* So that no wise man, that loves the *Reformed religion* and the Church, can think others than that the hand of *Joab is in this matter. Achitophel is in Counsell with* Absalom. The *Conclave of* Rome is wanting to its interest, if it conspires strongly with this *Antiministeriall faction*; I should be glad to be as *Hushai* the *Archite*, a means to discover, blast, and bring to nought all *those desperat counsells and machinations*, which are layd by any against this reformed Church, and its true Ministry; The happy and seasonable defeat of which, by Gods blessing to this Church and Nation, I do yet hope may be such, as shall make all *Apostatising and ungratefull Politicians*, rather repent of their Apostacies, and see their folly, than follow the fate of that disloyall renegado, a traitor at once to his friend and sovereign.

In vitium ducit culpæ fuga si caret arte. Hor.

6\. *Reformation ought to reverence Antiquity.*

I confess I am not for such Reformations, as too *much suspect the prudence, or vilifie the piety of our forefathers*, therby to extoll some mens *after zeal* and skill. The errors and defects of the *Antients* joyned with their *charity* and *sincerity*, I believe were far more pardonable with God, than the late *furies and cruelties* of some men, pretending to mend those errors, and supply those defects. Not that it is safe for us to *return* to what we now see by *the word of God* to be an error; But we may in charity excuse their ignorance in some things of old; while yet we commend and imitate that wisdom, honesty, order, and gravity of religious profession which was in them, far beyond the *Modern transports* of some mens giddiness and levity, which toss them from *superstition abusing*, to superstition utterly refusing all those things which are not only *convenient* in Prudence, but necessary in Piety; as being stamped and established by divine *Institution*; such as this of the Evangelicall Ministry hath been proved to be. *Reformations* may bend so much from *the Pope*, on the right hand, till they meet him again on the left, forsaking that rectitude, uprightness, and stability of the *Mean*, in which only the truth and honour of Religion doth consist.

Mallem cum sanctis errare quàm cum sacrilegis rectè sentire.

Plato and *Aristotle* cõmend that ἐπιείκεια, Æquanimity and moderation in all things, though it be ἐλαττωτικὸς τοῦ κατὰ νόμον. *Eth. l. 2.*

Antichrist which some are taught more to fear in the name and in others, than to abhor in the thing and in themselves, is at both ends or *extremes* of Religion; as well that of prophaness, confusion, and defect on the one side, as that of *superstition* and excess on the other. We must love and entertain what ever we find of *Christs true Jewels*, and the Churches ornaments, amidst the *Counterfeits*, and *rags of Antichrist*; we must not slay any of Christs sheep, because it was gone astray, and is now found, but rather take it up, and bring it home, and rejoyce to have found it. Nor may we rend Christs garment in pieces, because it may be spotted, and soyled by

Luke 15.6.

mens hands, but rather *rinse* and *restore it* to its primitive purity. As *Christ redeemed* our Souls, so must we redeem his holy *Institutions* and ordinances, (as much as in us lyes) from the vain *Conversation of the world*; And then we may serve him in the holy wayes he hath appointed us without *fear of sin, Antichrist*, or *Superstition*, from which both our minds, and our devotions are happily freed.

1 Pet.1.18.

Every man hath cause to suspect *Antichrist in his own bosome*; As the kingdom of Christ, so the kingdome of Antichrist is within us chiefly. Certainly, it is far better for the Church and Christians to retain *what is Christs*, though in common with any Antichrists; than passionatly to cast away all that is Christs, under pretence of detesting Antichrist; men may fall *into sacrilege*, while they seem to *abhor Idols*; robbing the Church of what Gifts and dowry Christ hath given her; (among which, this of a *Constant and successive Ministry*, is a chief one in St. *Pauls* account) and this while blind and preposterous zeal thinks to strip the *whore of Babylon*, who dwells where ever division and confusion nestle in the Church, and to rifle *Antichrist* (who may roost in other places as well as *Rome*.) It is safer to be in Christs way, *though it be rugged*, and may have some inconveniencies through many infirmities, than to be in any other, which may seem fairer and smoother to us. As the *unclean spirit of grosse Idolatry and superstition*, may be cast out *for a fit*, so he may return to his house swept, and garnished with flowers, and shewes of piety, *bringing seven worse devils* of Atheism, Pride, Prophaness, and uncharitableness with him. It is the same *evil spirit*, which tears the Church by cruell Schisms, with that which casts it into the *fire of persecution*, and *water* of *Superstition*; There is alwayes hopes and means of salvation, when there is a *true Ministry though with many faults, yet of Christs sending, and the Churche's Ordaining*; but men may as justly despair of long enjoying the Gospels light, without a *due and setled Ministry*, as they may to have day long after the Sun is set, or Harvest in Winter. As graces and gifts internall, so the means and *Ministry externall*, are part of the *wings of that Sun of righteousness*, who shines no where in the world among Christians, without some *healing*, and saving vertue, severally manifested, as to the inward saving power, but alwayes in the *same way*, as to the constant outward Ministration, by which it is ordinarily dispensed: Papall *darknings*, or humane *Eclypsings*, are no warrant to abolish or exclude, that light of the Ministry, which Christ hath set up; Nor can we do *the Devil*, or any of his instruments a greater *greater pleasure, than quite to extinguish the lights of this Church*, in stead of snuffing and clearing them: Better to have dim *Lamps*, than none at all shining in the house of God.

Rom.2.22.
Eph.4.11.
Mat.12.44.
Mal.4.2.

But indeed the fault of the *English Ministry* with some men is, not

not that they lighted their Lamps at the *Popes taper*; but that they have, and do still *shine* so bright, as to offend both his, and all others eyes, who could not bear the splendor of the *English Churches* both *Ministry* and *Reformation*, wherein *Zeal according to knowledge*, and wisdome with sobriety, had at once purged away what was *vile*, and preserved what was *precious*, with great *moderation*; distinguishing between what was of *humane mixture*, superstition, or infirmity, and what was of *divine Institution*, *holy succession*, and *authority*. The same piety rejected the one, and retained the other.

Jer. 15. 19.

I conclude then, that the Papall encroachment, or Romish corruption, what ever it were, is no argument against the Divine authority, and constant office of the Reformed, and restored Ministry in *this Church*; It were a mad cruelty to knock our Fathers on the head, or to *cut their throats*, because they were diseased; and as they might, so they ought in all *piety* to be *healed*; How much more of perfect madness is it, for Christians to destroy their *Fathers*, who are now perfectly recovered, and in good health, only because they were sometime sick, or descended from infirm Progenitors?

7. *Extremes in Religion.*

It is easie for well-affected Christians to be *over-scrupulous*, and *over-righteous*, so to *over-act* in matters of Religion, as to *destroy themselves before their time*; like rude and *unwary* Combatants, who overthrow themselves, by *over-reaching* and overstriking at others beyond the measure of well-ordered and proportioned strength, which alwayes keeps it self strong enough to rule or command, and so to *preserve it self*. There is a secret *tide* of self-interest, prejudice, or passion, which imperceivably carries men *another way*, (much beside, or backward, or beyond what should be) when they think they steer with a *sure course*, and full gale to the *port of Reformation*, in which not only *sincerity* is required, but also great *discretion*, *judgement*, and *moderation*; Therefore *Reformation* is the work of learned, wise, grave, well tempered, and well experienced, as well as of godly and well-affected Christians; *Reformers* ought to be as skilfull, and sober *Physicians*, capable to distinguish between the strength of the disease, and the strength of nature; to preserve and foment the vitall spirits, though they quench the *feaverish flames*, and evacuate the vicious humours.

Eccl. 7. 16. πανταχοῦ κακὸν ἡ ἀμετρία, μάλιστα δὲ ἐν τοῖς ἱεροῖς. Naz. *Perit judicium cum res transit in affectum.* *Discretionis meta nulla superstitione, vel levitate vel spiritus quasi ferventione vehementia excedatur.* Ber. s. 20. Cant. *Fervor discretionem erigat discretio fervorem regat.* Id.

Vulgar Reformers.

Vulgar spirits are *rude and riotous Reformers*, which come only with their *Axes* and *Hammers*, without any Chissels, or finer tools; they are all for battering down, and breaking in pieces, nothing for *polishing* and cleansing. Hence it is, that they do no more, than pull down *Crosses*, and set up Weathercocks on Chutches, disposing Religion to perpetuall *vicissitudes* and *inconstancies*, which are most contrary to its nature. Like weighty *Pendants* once violently

Vid. Bishop *Davenant.* determin. 12. Against peoples reforming without the

lently swayed beyond the perpendicular *line and poyse*, they are a long time before they recover the *point of fixation* and consistency: Such are *popular*, *heady*, and *tumultuating Reformations*, usually carrying things at the first *impetus*, as much beyond the *medium* or centre of *true Religion*, as they were formerly, either really or imaginarily *deviated*; *Plebeian Constitutions*, are as subject to be *Paralitick*, as *Apoplectick*, to be ever *trembling* and *troubling* Religion in their *jealous furies*, as to be otherwhile *stupid* and *supine*, in their superstitious follyes; But once in motion, and throughly scared (as the *youth of Leeds* with Souldiers) with those *Panick terrors*, of superstition, irreligion, popery, heresie, *Antichrist*, and the like; they hardly keep, or recover themselves to any bounds, becomming sober men and *good Christians*.

Supreme Magistrates consent. *Necesse est verã religionem unica cum sit eandem semper esse.* Lact.

Sir *Kenelm Digby* relates the story in his book of Bodies.

Thence it is (as in many other excesses, and transports) that some men seek to pull down all *locall Churches*, because they may have been somtimes superstitiously abused; Possibly at the same rate, not one *place* of their Conventicle meetings should stand. So they would have all *Church-windows* either broken to let in *the cold and weather*, or quite stopped up, so as the light should be wholly shut out, because the Glasse was *somtime painted*. Such *immoderation* is just as if *Country-men* should not esteem, or use their fertile *Meadows*, because they are *somtime squallid* with inundations; or, as if they would suffer none to *sing* again, because some have sung *out of tune*; and break all *Instruments of Musick*, because they may be set to wanton ayres, and dittyes: Whereas (no doubt) in this, as in other *excellencies*, to which the ingenuous industry of Christians as men may attain, for *singing*, and *use of Musick*, either Orall or Organicall, in Consort or Solitary (which the sad severity and moroser humor of some men would utterly banish from all devout and pious uses, as if all *Musick* and *Musicall* instruments had been prophaned ever since the Dedication of *Nabuchadnezars* golden Image) even in this (I say) of Musick or melody, the great *Creator* may be glorified, both in privat and publick, either by the skilfull, or the attentive Christians, who have with *David* harmonious souls joyned to devout and *gracious hearts*, which like a good stomack digests all in Natures and Arts excellency to Piety. Like a modest Matron making a vertuous use of those ornaments and jewels, which either vice or vanity are prone to usurp and abuse.

Non usus rerum sed libido utentis in culpa est. Aust. doct. Christi.

Of Musick.

Dan. 3.7.

It is true, the *most blessed God* (whose transcendent perfections of wisdome, power, justice, mercy, love, &c. as so *many strings*, of infinite extension and accord, make up that *Holy harmony*, which is his own *eternall delectation*, as also the ravissant happiness of the blessed Angels, and souls of just men made perfect;) This God, I say, is not immediatly, and for it self delighted with-

any

any singing or melody of sense, any more than with other expressions of a reasonable soul, in Eloquence, Praying or Preaching; yet since the use of *Harmonious sounds* is a *gift*, which the *Creator* hath given to Man above all Creatures, and wherewith Man may be so pleased and exercised in the *use* of it, as thereby to be better dispoſed, and more affected, even to serve the Creator, either in more spirituall, holy, humble, calm affections, or in more flaming *Devotions*, and sweet *Meditations*, (which are the usuall effects of good and *grave Musick*, on sober and devout souls:) who, though they do not dwell and stay on this *ladder* of sensible melody, yet they may be still ascending and descending by the staves of it in fervency, charity, and humility to God, others, and themselves; I conceive no true Religion, but such as is flatted with vulgar fears, can forbid Christians, to make the best (*which is a religious use*) even of *Musick*; referring it, as all honest and comly things, to the highest end, *Gods glory*; And this, not only in reading or hearing *such Psalms* and *Hymns*, and *spirituall songs*, in which the divine truth of the matter, *affects the enlighened judgement*, and the *quieted conscience* with the neerest conformity to the holy minds and spirits of those sacred *Writers*, who have left us the matter so endited, though we have lost the *antient tunes* of their *holy Psalmodies*; but also in that *audible singing*, and *melodious delectation*, which is sensible in *good Musick*; and which hath a secret, sweet, and *heavenly vertue* to allay the passions of the soul, and to raise up our spirits to *Angelicall exaltations*, by which we may more *glorifie and praise God*, which is a part of our worship of him; And wherein the Spirit of God in *David*, and other holy men of the antient Church hath set us *allowable*, *commendable*, and imitable examples; Wherein the immusicall rusticity of some men of more *ferine spirits*, which no Harp can calm, or cause to depart from them, as *Sauls* did, must not *prejudice* the use, and liberty of those Christians, who are of more sweet and *harmonious* tempers, even in this particular gift and *excellency of Musick*; than which nothing hath a more sensible, and nothing a less *sensuall delectation*; So that if there be not Musick in Heaven, sure there is a kind of heaven in Musick; yet even in this so sweet and harmless a thing, we see that the immoderation and violence of Christians (which hath in it a vein of the old *Picts* and *Sythian* barbarity) is an enemy even to *Humanity*, as well as to *Divinity*, while it seeks to deprive men and Christians of one of the *divinest Ornaments*, most harmless contentments and indulgences, which in this world they can enjoy? I the rather insist in this most *innocent particular of singing* and *Musick*, because no instance can shew more those rude and unreasonable transports to which men are subject in what they call religious *Reformations*; If they do not carry all things

Μόνος τῶν ζώων ἄνθρωπος μετεχεκες, καὶ ἀριθμητικός, ὡς καὶ ὄργανον ἔμπνουν ἐστί. *Cl. Alex.* προτ. ἁπτέον μουσικῆς, εἰς κατακόσμησιν ἤθους· καὶ καταστολήν. *Cl. Al.* στρω. 6.

Vid. Basil. in Hom. 24. *de leg. gent. lib.*
1 Cor. 10. 31.
Col. 3. 16.

A corporalibus ad spirituales à mutabilibus numeris pervenitur ad immutabiles. Aust. l. 6. de Musica.

things with very *wise hearts*, and *wary hands*; that so the leaven of unnecessary rigors and severities may not make the *Mass* or *lump* of religion more sowr and heavy, than God in his Word hath required; who cannot be an enemy to the right and sanctified use of melody or Musick; since he commands *singing to his praises*, and loves a *cheerfull temper* in his service. Certainly Musick is of all sensible humane beauty the most *harmless* and divine; Nor did I ever see any reason, why it should be thought to deform us Christians, or be wholly excluded from making a part in the *beauty of holiness*.

Psal. 33. 2. 2 Cor. 9. 7.

No time or abuse doth prejudice Gods, or the Churches rights.

All wise and excellent Christians know this for certain, That mans *usurpation* is no prejudice to Gods dominion; nor do humane *traditions* vacate *divine Commands*, nor Antichrists *superstitions* cancell *Christs Institutions*; Vain superstructures of mans addition, neither demolish nor *rase* Gods *foundations*; men do not quit their rights to estates for anothers unjust intrusion; The *heady invasions* of one, or few, or many, upon the Churches rights and liberties, are no cause to make Christians remove the *antient Land-marks*, and *boundaries of true Ministry, due order, and prudent government*, which we find fixed by Christ, continued by the Apostles, and observed by the *Churches* obedience in all ages, although not without *tinctures* and blemishes of *humane Infirmities*. They are *sad Physicians*, and of no *valew*, who know not how to let their *Patients blood*, unless they *stab them* to the heart; Such are those *unhappy leeches*, who in stead of eating off, with *fit Corosives, the dead flesh of any part*, do lop off whole arms and legs. Some men are too *heavy for themselves*; and while they aim to go down the *Hill of reformation*, they suddenly conceive such an *impetuous motion*, as cannot stop it self, till it hath carried all before it, and at length dasheth it self in pieces. Much more folly it is quite to abolish the *use of holy things*, than to *tollerate some abuses with it*; True reforming is not *a starting quite out of the way*, as shy and skittish horses are wont to do, (when they boggle at what scares them, more than it can hurt them) with danger to themselves, and their riders too; not a flying to new *modes*, and exotick *fashions* of religion, and Churches and Ministers; but it is a sober and stayd restauration of these antient and venerable forms, which pious *Antiquity* in the Church of Christ, and the *antient of dayes*, in his *more sure Word*, hath expressed to us. 'Tis easie to pare off what one *great Antichrist*, or the many less have added; and to supply what they have by force or fraud detracted from that only complete *figure of Extern professional religion*, which Christ and his Apostles by him so have fashioned and deli-

Quamvis ritus ordinationis in Eccles. pontificia multis superstitionibus & inutilibus ceremoniis sit vitiatus, ex eo tamen ipsius ordinationis essentiæ nihil decedit; Distinguenda ordinantis infirmitas ab ordinatione, quæ fit totius Ecclesiæ nomine, distinguendum divinum ab humano, essentiale ab accidentali, pium & Christianum ab Antichristiano, fermentum a doctrina Pharisæorum. Gerard. de Minist. pag. 147.

Moderatio non tam virtus quam ductrix & imperatrix omnium virtutum. Auriga & ordinatrix affectuum. Ber. Cant. *Tolle hanc & virtus vitium erit. Nec abligurienda sunt mala cum bonis, nec eructanda bona cum malis.* Vetul. *Pravi effectus falsi sunt rerum æstimatores.*

vered,

vered; which is never well handled, no not by Reformers, unless Christians *have honest hearts, good heads, clear eyes;* and *pure hands*; when all these meet in any *undertakers to reform* the Church, I shall then hope they will seriously, sincerely and successfully do Christs and the Churches work, as generally men are prone and intent to do their own.

This then I may conclude, against all precipitant and blind zeal, which by popular arts seeks to bring an *odium* on all Ministers, and the Ministry of this Church, meerly by using the Name of the Pope, without giving any account to reason or religion of their Calumny; That there is no cause in reason, or religion, for any Christians to cast off the Ministry of *England*, as it stands Reformed, and so restored to its primitive Power and Authority, because of any *Succession* from, *relation* to, or communion with the Order and Clergy of the Roman Church and Bishop; no more cause, I say, than for these Anti-ministeriall Cavillers to pull out their eyes, because Papists do see with theirs; or to destroy themselves, because naturally descended from such parents as were in subjection to the *Bishop of Rome*, and in communion with that Church; we may as well refuse all leagues and treaties of humanity in common with Papists, as all Christianity; and all Christianity, as all antient lawfull Ministry; an holy Succession may descend, and Gods elect be derived from such as were true men, how ever vitious.

L I CAVIL.

CAVIL *or* CALUMNY V.

Against Ministers as Ordeined by Bishops in England.

I Have done with the *first part of this Cavill or Calumny*, which seeks to bandy the *Ministry of the Church of* England, *against the Papall and Romish wall*; that they may make it either rebound to a popular and *Independent side*; or else fall into the *hazard* of having no true *Christian Ministry at all*; from both which I shall in like sort endevour to rescue this our *holy Function* and Succession.

A second stroak therefore which I am to take, is made with great Artifice and popular cunning against the Ministry *of this Church, as it was derived and continued* by the hands of Bishops, *who were as Presidents, or chief Fathers in the work of Ordination among their Brethren and Sons (the Presbyters) or Ministers within their severall Diocesses*; *These Prelates or Bishops, the* Objectors protest highly against, *as being* not Plants of Christs planting; *whose Authority being lately pulled up by* power, *so that they seem to have no more* place or influence in this Church or Nation, *the* Presbyterie *also, and whole order of the* former Ministry (*they say*) *must necessarily also* fail and wither, *which were but branches, and* slips derived from the stem or root of Episcopall Ordination.

Thus we see in a few years, the *Anti-ministeriall* fury is *cudgelling*, even *Presbyters* themselves, with that staff which some of them put into *vulgar hands*, purposely to *beat their Fathers*, the grave and antient Bishops, and utterly to banish that *Venerable and Catholick Order*, or *Eminent Authority* of Episcopacy out of the Church; what the *Dove-like innocency* of those fierce and rigid Ministers *hearts* might be, as to their *godly intentions*, I know not; but I am sure they wanted that *wisdome of the Serpent*, which seeks above all to *preserve its head*; whence life, health, motion, and orderly direction, descending to other parts, do easily *repair* and heal, what ever lesser hurt or bruise may befall them,

It must needs be confessed, that as the *Events* have been very sad, so the *advantages* have been great, which the *Anti-ministeriall* party have gained, by the preposterous zeal of some *Anti-Episcopall spirits*, which transported them, not only beyond and against all bounds, or *rules* of Reason, Order, Scripture, Ecclesiasticall Custome, and Laws here in *England*, but even contrary to their own *former*, and some of their *present judgements*, touching Episcopall *Presidency*, which they never did, nor do yet hold to be *unlawfull* in the Church, how

how ever it might be attended with some *inconveniencies* and *mischiefs* too, not arising from the nature of that *Order*, and power, which is good, but from the *corruption* of those men that might manage it amiss. This makes many of these Ministers have now so *much work*, to take off that *leprosie* from their *own heads*, which they told the people had so much *infected the Bishops hands*; by the Imposition of which, they yet own their Ministeriall power, and holy Orders to have been *rightly derived* to them, in that *Ordination by Bishops*, which was used here in the *Church of England*, as in all antient Churches.

It is never too late to *rectifie*, and *repent* of, any mistakes and miscarriages incident to us, as poor sinfull mortals. Although Primitive *Episcopacy*, (which ever was as a *grand pillar* of the Churches Ministry, Order and Government,) hath been much shaken and thrust aside by mans power, or passion, to the great weakning and indangering of the whole Fabrick and Function of the Ministry, together with the peace and polity of *this Church*; yet wise men may possible see, after these thick *clouds and dust of dispute*, what *is of God in true Episcopacy*; yea, and they may be *perswaded* to preserve and restore, what is *necessary* and *comly* in it, however they pare off what is deformed, superfluous and *Combersome*; (in the behalf of which I am neither a pleader, nor an approver.)

It is now no time in *England* either to flatter, or fear the face of Episcopacy, or sinisterly to accept the persons of Bishops. There is nothing now can be *suspected* to move me to touch with respect those goodly *ruines* (from which the *glory* of riches and honour are now so far removed,) but only *matter of conscience*, and the *integrity of my judgement*; And therefore I here crave leave without offence to any, that are *truly godly* (either Ministers or others) who may differ from me in this point,) freely, yet as briefly as I can, to discover my judgement, touching this so *controverted* point of Episcopacy, in which from words men have faln to blows, and from wasting of ink, to the shedding of *blood*. I see that other men of different sense, daily take their freedom to vent themselves against all Bishops, and all Episcopacy; some of them so rudely and unsavorily, as if they hoped by their *evill breath*, to render that *venerable* name, and *order*, ever abhorred, and execrable, to Christian minds; which to learned and sober Christians ever was, and still is, as a sweet *Oyntment poured forth*; nor doth it lose of its divine and *antient fragrancy* by the *fractures of these times*, which have broken (it may be) not with devotion and love, so much as with hatred, and passion, that *Alabaster-box* of civill protection and Sanction, in which it was *here*, for many hundreds of years, happily *preserved* from vulgar insolency, and *Schismaticall contempt*. Why may not I presume to enjoy my *freedome* too, yet bounded with all modesty and sobriety, without any prejudice or reproach, reflecting upon the *Counsels*, or actions of any men *my Superiours*, whose power and practise, as to *secular mutations*, neither can, nor ought to have any *influence on mens opinions*, and consciences, further than *way* is made for them by the *Harbingers* of Reason and Religion, which are best set forth and discerned, in innate principles of Order and Polity; also in Scripture precepts and precedents; and lastly by the *Catholick Custome*, and *practise of the Church of Christ*.

Ans. In my answer therefore to this *Cavill* or *Calumny*, touching Bishops (which many Ministers are as afraid to *name*, or *own with honour*, as they are to call any holy man, either Apostle, Evangelist, Father or Martyr, by the title of *Saints*) my intent is not, largely to handle that late, severe, and *unkind Dispute* in *England* about Episcopacy or Prelacie; for this having been learnedly and fully done by others, would be, as *superfluous*, so extremely tedious both to the *Reader* and *my self*; Nor is it my purpose to justifie *all* that might be done or omitted by some *Bishops in their government*; But my design chiefly is, 1. to remove that *popular odium*, to allay that *Plebeian passion*, to rectifie those *unlearned prejudices*, and to take away those *unjust jealousies*, which are by some weak, and possibly well-meaning Christians, taken up, and daily urged against all Bishops, in a *Presidentiall eminencie among Presbyters*, or above other Ministers. 2. My next is, to justifie that *holy Ordination* and Ministeriall authority, which by the imposition of their hands chiefly was, with probation, prayer, and meet *Consecration*, duly conferred upon the Ministers of this Church, according to Scripture rule, and Ecclesiasticall custome in all setled Churches.

But before I handle the first thing proposed, I must seek to remove that prejudice which sticks deep in some ordinary minds against Bishops and their Authority, meerly arising from the *darkness*, and *sufferings of late so plentifully cast upon them*; if *arguments* and words could not, yet Arms and Swords have (they say) convinced Bishops, and subdued them, notwithstanding all their *learning*, their gravity, their piety, their protection, which they pleaded from the *Churches Catholick* custome, and the Lawes of this Church: The vulgar are prone to think those *wicked*, who are *unprosperous*, and accursed, who are punished.

Sed quid turba Remi? sequitur fortunam ut semper & odit damnatos. Juv.

Yet in true judgement of things, those great and many impressions of worldly *diminution*, and *supposed Miseries* made *upon Bishops*, are more just arguments against the innocency of their persons, place, and lawfull power, than *Jobs* afflictions were, which the Devil never urged against his integrity, but sought thereby to overthrow it, as God did prove and exercise it.

Job 1.

I

I believe there are too many that would be content there should be neither *Bishops* nor *Presbyters*, but such as are great sufferers; Nor yet any Word, or Sacrament, or holy *Ministrations*; nor any marks of Christianity in this, or any other Reformed Church: But the *measures of religious matters*, are never to be taken from the passions or prevalencies of men; nor from any secular decrees, or human acts, and *civill sanctions*. Godly and *famous Bishops* in eminency among, and above the Presbyters, were *many ages before any civill power* protected them, and so they may continue, if God will, in his true Church; even then when (as of old) most persecuted, and sought to be destroyed: *Worldly Counsells* and forces, which commonly are levelled to mens secular ends, and civill interests, signifie little or nothing indeed to a true Christians judgement or conscience in the *things of Christ* and true Religion; which must never be either refused, or accepted, according as they may be ushered in, or crowded out by *Civil Authority*. Christ doth not steer his Church by *that Compass*; Things the more divine and excellent, the more probable to be rejected by men of this world. At the *same* rate of *worldly frowns* and *disfavours*, Christians long ere this time, should have had nothing left them of *Scriptures*, *Sacraments*, *sound doctrine*, or holy *Ministrations*; All had been turned into *Heathenish* barbarity, *Hereticall errors*, or *Schismatical* confusions, if conscience to God, and *love* to Christ and his Church, had not preserved by the constancy and patience of Christian Bishops and Ministers, those holy things, which the wicked, wanton, and vain world, was never well pleased withall, and often persecuted, seeking to destroy both root and branch of Christianity: We are to regard not what is done by the few, or the many, the great or the small, but what in right reason, and due order, after the precepts and patterns of true Religion ought to be done in the Church.

ἐκεῖνο ὁμιλητέον τοῖς πολλοῖς ἀρέσκειν, ἐγὼ τοιοῦτος (*inquit Plato*) αὐτὸς ἀεὶ ἄλλα ὁ τῷ λόγῳ πείθομαι. *Cl. Al. sp. I.*

As for the *Government* of Bishops, so far as it referred to the chief power and office of *Ordeining* Ministers in a right succession for due supplies to this Church of *England*; Truly I am so far from condemning that Episcopall authority and practise, as unlawfull and Antichristian, after the rate *of popular* clamor, ignorance, passion and prejudice; That contrarily very learned, wise, and godly men have taught me to think and declare; That as the faults and presumptions of any Bishops, through any pride, ambition, and tyranny, or other personall immoralities, are very Antichristian, because most *Diametrally* contrary to the Precept and patern of our holy and humble Saviour Jesus Christ, whose place Bishops have alwayes as chief Pastors and Fathers among the Presbyters, since the *Apostles times*, eminently supplyed, in the *extern order* and Polity of the Church, So that above all men they ought to be most exactly conform

Episcopal power not Antichristian.

to the holy rule and example of Jesus Christ, both in doctrine and manners; So withall, they have taught me to esteem the Antient *and Catholick government of godly Bishops,* (as moderators and *Presidents* among the *Presbyters* in any Diocess or Precincts) in its just measure and constitution for power Paternall, duly exercised, such as was in the persecuting purest and Primitive times) to be as much, if not *more Christian,* than any other form and fashion of government can be; yea, far beyond any that hath not the charity to endure Catholick primitive and right Episcopacy, which truly I think to be most agreeable to right reason, and those principles of due order and polity among men, also no less suitable to the Scripture wisdome, both in its rules and paterns; to which was conform the Catholick and Primitive way of all Christian Churches, throughout all ages, and in all places of the world.

Episcopale officium maximè ornant & nobilitant gravitas morum, maturitas consiliorum, actuum honestas. Bern. Ep.28. *Cum honoris prærogativa etiam congrue merita requirimus.* Amb. de dig. Sa. *Ne sit honor sublimis, & vita deformis.* Id. Ἐπίσκοπον πρὸς ἓν μόνον βλέπειν δεῖ τὸ τῶν ἐκκλησιῶν ὠφελεῖν καὶ τὴν κοινὴν σωτηρίαν. Naz. or. 19. *Cogito me jam Episcopum principi pastorum de commissis ovibus rationem redditurum. Non Ecclesiasticis honoribus tempora ventosa transigere debere.* Aust. Ep. 203.

Which things very learned men, and friends to Presbytery joyned with Episcopacy have confessed both lately (as *Salmatius, Bochartus,* and *Blondellus*) and also formerly, as *Calvin, Beza, Moulin,* with many others: so far was ever any learned and unpassionate man from thinking Episcopacy unlawfull in the Church.

Blondel. Apol. pag. 177. 179. *Et in præfatione. Absit à me ut sinistrum de piissimæ illius antiquitatis consilio, & consensu, quæ Episcopalem ἐξοχὴν primum in Ecclesiam invexit mente quippiam suspicer.* So, *Ego Episcopos quodam modo Apostolorum locum in Ecclesia tenere largior: non munere divinitus instituto sed Libere ab Ecclesia collata illa ὑπεροχῇ* Blondel. test. Jeron. pag. 306.

Indeed, after all the hot *Canvasings,* and *bloody contentions,* which have wearied, and almost quite wasted the Estates, spirits, and lives of many learned men in this Church of *England,* as to the point of true Episcopacy, I freely profess that I cannot yet see, but that that antient and universall *form of government in due conjunction with Presbytery,* and with due regard to the faithfull people, is as much beyond all *other new invented fashions,* as the *Suns light* glory, and influence, is beyond that of the mutable and *many-faced Moon,* or any other *junctos* of *Stars* and *Planets,* however cast into *strange figurations,* or new *Schemes and Conjunctions,* by the various fancies of some Diviners and Astrologers.

Which free owning of my judgement, *in this point, may* serve to *blot out that Character* (*etiam ipse Presbyterianus*) added to my name, by the learned Pen of *Bochartus.* For although I own with all honour and love orderly *Presbytery,* and humble *Presbyters,* in the sense of the Scriptures, and in the use of all pious Antiquity, for *sacred and divine,* in their office and function (as the lesser Episco-

D. Bochartus, Epist. ad D. Morleium. Ἰσχὺς σύμβολον, καὶ ... Epist.

pacy

pacy, or inspectors over lesser flocks in the Church, yet not so, as abhorring and extirpating all order and presidency of Bishops among them, as if it were *Antichristian*, *wicked*, and *intollerable*; Nor do I think that *an headless*, or *many headed Presbytery* ought to be set up in the Church, as of necessity, and divine right; in this sense that *learned writer* himself, is no Presbyterian, nor ever had cause to judge me to be of that mind.

Τὸ ἱερὸν συνέδριον τῶν πρεσβυτέρων. *Bas. in Ep. 62. Eccles. Neocæs.* The holy consistory of Presbyters desires their chief or President to be among them.

I confess, after the example of the best times, and judgement of the most learned in all Churches, I alwayes wished such *moderation* on all sides, that a *Primitive Episcopacy* (which imported, the *Authority of one grave and worthy person*, chosen by the consent, and assisted by the presence, counsell, and *suffrages* of many Presbyters) might have been restored, or preserved in this Church; and this not out of any factious design, but for these weighty reasons, which prevail with me.

2. *Reasons for Episcopacy rather than other Government.*

Ignat. ad Antiochenos Bids the Presbyters feed the flock, till God shews who shall be their Bishop or Ruler. He salutes *Onesimus* the Bishop of *Ephesus*. *Ep. ad Ephes.* cited by *Euseb. l. 3. c. 35. Hist.* ἐν τῷ παλαιῷ πρεσβυτέρων ἡμῶν καὶ ἐπισκόπων [illegible] *Plat. Chil.*

1. For the *Reverence due from posterity, to the Venerable piety and wisdome of all Antiquity*; which alwayes *had President Bishops* in all *setled* and *compleated Churches*, together with the *Colleges* or *Fraternities* of Presbyters; yea, 'tis very likely, that before there were many Presbyters in one City, so as to make up a *Presbytery*, the Bishop and Deacons were all that *officiated* among those few Christians, which the Apostles left in that City; who afterward *increasing* to many Congregations, had so many *Presbyters*, Ordeined, placed, and governed by the *Eminency* of his vertue and authority, who was Bishop there, or Pastor before them, as in time, so some in speciall Authority and Office by Apostolicall appointment. And certainly in things that are not so clearly and punctually set down in express commands of Scripture, a *sober and modest regard* ought to be had

Ab Apostolis in Episcopatum constituti, Apostolici seminis traduces Episcopi. Tert. de Præs. c. 32. an. no 300. *Cornelius* Bishop of *Rome* sayes, the Church, committed to his charge had 46 Presbyters, and ought to have but one Bishop. *Euseb. hist. l. 6. c. 22.* *Vidimus nos Policarpum in prima nostra ætate, qui ab Apostolis non solum edoctus, sed & ab Apostolis in Asia, in ea quæ est Smyrnis Ecclesia institutus est Episcopus.* Irenæus, l. 3. c. 3. So in many places he testifies. *Lib. 4. ca. 43. & 45.* *Omnes hæretici posteriores sunt Episcopis, quibus Apostoli tradiderunt Ecclesias.* l. 5. c. 20. Cyprian. Ep. 67. *Adulteram Cathedram collocare, aut alium Episcopum facere, contra Apostolicæ institutionis unitatem, nec fas est nec licet.* The Generall Council of *Chalcedon* reckons 27. Bishops in *Ephesus* from *Timothy*. *Can. 11.* ἐπίσκοποι ἐκ προσώπων [illegible] *Con Chalced.* *Diotrephes* a factious Presbyter is branded by Saint *John*, for not enduring the preheminence of that Apostle. 3 Joh. 9. *Quod universalis tenuit Ecclesia, nec Conciliis institutum, sed semper retentum est, non nisi Autoritate Apostolica traditum Rectissimè creditur.* Aust. de Baptis. l. 4. c. 24. None among the Antients was against the Order and Presidency of Bishops, but *Aerius*, who was wholly an Arian; and upon envy and hatred against *Eustathius*, who was preferred before him in the Episcopall place which he sought, he urged *Parity* against Prelacy, contrary to the good order and peace of the Church. See St. *Austin. Hæres. c. 59. Epist. ba. 69*

in

in matters of externall polity and Church society to the patern of Primitive times; which could not follow so soon, and so universally any way, but from Apostolicall precept or direction; from which the Catholick Church could not suddainly erre in all places, being so far in those times from any passion or temptation either of covetousness or ambition, which had then no fewell from the favour of Princes, and as little sparks of ambition in the hearts of those holy men; who were in all the great and Mother Churches both ever owned and reverenced in antiquity, as Bishops, in a priority of place and presidency of authority, both by the *humble Presbyters*, and all the rest of the *faithfull* people. It is not among the things *comely* or *praise worthy*, *Phil.* 4.8. Either in charity, modesty, humility, or equity, for us in after and worse times, to cast upon all those holy Primitive Christians and famous Churches, either the suspition of a *generall Apostacy*, by a wilfull neglect, or universally *falling* away from that Apostolicall way; or a running *cross* to it: Neither may we think that all Churches *did lightly* and imprudently abuse *that occasionall liberty*, which might be left them in prudence; whereby further to establish what might seem the best for order and peace, as to the matter of Government: wherein if the Churches were free to choose, it is strange, they all agreed in this one way of Episcopall Government, All over the Christian world, till these later times. It becomes us, rather to be jealous of our *own weak and wanton passions*, and to return rather from our later *transports & popular wandrings*, to the neerest *conformities* with those first and best times; who universally had Bishops, either because they were so divinely commanded; or in holy wisdom they chose *that way*, as best; so far as there was left a Christian liberty of prudence, to those who were by the Apostles, set, as Pastors and Rulers over the severall *Churches*: and however the *name* at first was common to all Church Ministers, Apostles, and Presbyters, to be called Bishops; yet afterward, when the Apostles were deceased, their successors in the eminency of place, among the Presbyters, were called peculiarly Bishops.

Agnitio, vera est Apostolorum doctrina et antiquus Ecclesiæ status in universo mundo secundum successiones Episcoporum, quibus illi eam quæ in unoquoque loco est Ecclesiam tradiderunt. Iren. l. 4. c. 63.

Cyprian. l. 4. Ep. 9. *Omnes præpositi Apostolis vicaria ordinatione succedunt.*

Edant origines Ecclesiarum suarum, evolvant ordinem Episcoporum suorum, ita per successiones ab initio decurrentium ut primus ille Episcopus aliquem ex Apostolis vel Apostolicis viris habuerit autorem & antecessorem. Tertul. de præ. ad Hæ. c. 32.

So *contra Marcion. l. 4. Ordo Episcoporum ad originem recensus in Johannem stabit autorem.* *Con. Nic.* calls the precedency of the Bishop of *Jerusalem* ἔθος ἀρχαῖον, καὶ παράδοσις. An antient custom and tradition. *Can.* 7. It is not to be beleived that in *Tertul.* times any mistake in the Church cou'd be Catholick living 200. after Christ. When he tels us *Cathedræ Apostolorum adhuc suis locis præsidentur, apud quas ipsæ authenticæ eorum literæ recitantur*, ibid. c. 34. *Epiphan. Hær.* 75. Sayes its next to Hæresy to abrogate the holy order instituted by the Apostles, and used by all the Churches: it brings in Schism, scandalls, and confusions. *Toto orbe decretum. Jero. & à Marco Evangelista Presbyteri unum ex se electum in excelsiori gradu collocatum Episcopum nominabant.* Id. Ep. *ad Evag.* Theod. *in* 1 Tim. 3. *Eosdem olim vocabant Presbyteros et Episcopos, eos autem qui nunc vocantur Episcopi nominabant Apostolos ut Epaphrum, Titum, Timotheum, procedente autem tempore, Apostolatus nomen reliquerunt iis qui propriè erant Apostoli Domini: Episcopatus vero nomen imposuerunt iis, qui olim apellabantur Apostoli. Ecclesia non potest esse sine Episcopis; nec esse possunt Ministri, nec fideles.* Bellar. de Eccles.

Secondly,

Secondly, For the *avoyding of Scandall* giving to so many *Christian Churches*, remayning in all the world; who, for the *far major part*, are still governed by Bishops, in some respect distinct from and eminent above the Presbyters; It is not the work of *Christian prudence* or charity, to *widen differences*, between us and other Churches, Greek, Eastern, African, or Western; yea, we owe this *Charity* to the *Romanists*, and to our selves rather, who seem to have gained this great advantage against us, by the offence given them in utter *abolishing* the Antient and Catholick order and succession of Episcopacy; that they will less now esteem us Christians; or to be in any true Church; since they will not allow us any right and compleat Ordination of Ministers, and so no Sacraments, and no Christianity as to extern profession and administration *without Bishops*; yea, the best reformed Churches must needs be offended who approve such a Presidency of Bishops among Presbyters, where it is continued with the doctrinall Reformation; many enjoy Bishops stil as we did; No learned and godly men ever thought it cause enough to separate from any Church because it had Bishops. Such as have them not in a constant Presidency, yet count this no part of their Reformation; but rather deplore it, as a defect involuntary, pleading the Law of *necessity*, or some grand inconveniencies and difficulty to excuse thereby their inconformity, so far, to other Churches and to all Antiquity; yea the most learned and wise among their Presbyterians abroad, oft wish they had the honour and happiness of reformed and reforming Bishops. Nor ever did heretofore the most learned and godly people in *England*, Ministers or others, any more than the Princes, *Nobility*, and Gentry, generally desire the abolition of right Episcopacy; however now at last they had not either opportunity to plead for it, or such power and influence as to preserve it, against these inundations which God hath been pleased to suffer to overflow in this Church; But rocks are not presently removed, when over-flown: what is of God will stand, and out-live the deluge.

So the *Augustane* Cōfession. So *Luther* oft. Camerarius *in vita* Philippi. *Maximè optandum est, ut Episcoporū magna sit autoritas.* Melancton *Epist. ad* Lutherum & *ad* Bellaium *Ep.* Par. Bucer. *de animarum cura. A temporibus Apostolorū Episcopus à Presbyteris electus iisque impositus quemadmodum Jacobus Hierosolymitanus, Et de disciplina clericali, Episcopalem potestatem restituendam optat.* Calvin *Inst. l.* 4 *c.* 4. *S.* 2. Calvin. *Epist. ad* Sadoletum. & *Instit. l.* 14. *c.* 4. *S.* 2. Calv. *de necess. ref. Ecc. Nullo non Anathemate dignos fatear, si qui erunt qui non reverentur summaq; obedientia observent Hierarchiam in qua sic emineant Episcopi, ut Christo subesse non recusent, ab illo tanquam unico capite pendeant, ad ipsum referantur; ejus veritate colligati fraternam charitatem colant.* Beza in Apoca. 2. *τῷ ἀγγέλῳ* i.e. *προεστῶτι, quem nimirum oportuit imprimis de his rebus admoneri, ac per eum cæteros collegas, totamque adeo Ecclesiam.* Pet. Mar. loc. com. Zanchius, *Hoc minime improbari posse judicamus, ut unus inter multos Presbyteros præsit Epis.* conf. c. 5. th. 10. *Vedelius* notis in Igna. *Ex actis & Epistolis Apostolicis atque ex Eccl. historicis colligitur, ipsos Apostolos & eorum successores hunc ritum observasse, ut unus προεστὼς nomine Presbyterii Ministros legitimè ab Ecclesia electos per manuum impositionem & preces publicas ordinaret.* Gerard. de min. *p.* 372. Grotius *inter propriè dictas Aposto. traditiones esse asserit Episcopalem προστασίαν, & χειροτονίαν.* vot. pro pace. Peter du Moulin Epist. ad Episc. Winto. *Deodate* in his Epistle to the late Assembly. *Primis & beatis illis temporibus politeia Ecclesiæ admirabili Aristocratia mixta Epis. Presbyt. plebi sua jura tribuit.* Alsted. *de min.* So Gerardus *pag.* 232. *Retinendum Episcopalem ordinem asserit, Propter 8. rationes.* 1. *Varia dona dat Deus.* 2. *Exempla Apostolica; & Primitivæ Eccl. ἀξιώματα* 3 *propter εὐσχημοσύνην & εὐταξίαν Ecclesiæ.* 4 *Naturæ congruus est ordo, & rationi in omni cœtu.* 5. *Alit concordiam,* 6. *reprimit αὐθάδειαν & arrogantiam.* 7. *Nulli gravis ubi sit electione, & per suffragia Presbyterorum peragit officium.* 8. *Tollit Ἀναρχίαν Schisma & seditiones.*

Corepiscopi forbidden to ordain without the Bishops licence, by the Council of *Ancyra*, which was before the 1. *Nicene*.
So Concil. *Nicenum* owns and confirms the antient custom.
So Concil. *Arelat. c. 19.*
So Concil *Laod. c. 56.* *Presbyteri sine conscientia Episcoporum nihil faciant.*
Blondel. Test. Hier. *p. 255.*
So *Jerom, excepta ordinatione quid facit Episcopus quod Presbyter non facit.* Ad Evag.

Thirdly, I prefer a Primitive Episcopacy, as the best w... *of union*, and happy *satisfaction*, to all learned, wise, and good men; especially in that so shaken and disputed a point of *Ordination*, for the right succession and conferring of *power Ministeriall*: which the most learned and sober *Presbyterians* confess, not to be weakned by *Episcopall* Presidency; And very many, no less considerable men, for number, learning, and piety (as *Da. Blondell* among others) do think, the right *Ordination of Ministers* to be much more strengthened, adorned and compleated, where it passeth *through* the hands of the *Episcopall power* and order; if for no other reason, yet for this, that *it was the Apostolicall, Primitive*, and *universall* way, used in the Church, and by which the Authority and Office of the Ministry hath ever been, together *with Christianity*, derived to us from the Apostles times. Its evident, that the sudden and violent receding of many men from their former judgement and practise in this point, hath occasioned many *great* scandals, scruples and schisms, troubles and confusions, in matters both of Church and State; giving great advantages to all that list to cavil at, question, and *despise*, the Ordination, and Ministry of even those Presbyters (yea, their very Christianity, as to the outward form, order, and profession,) who so easily renounced, and eagerly cast quite away, that order and power, as unlawfull and un-Christian.

In schismatis remedium factum est, quod postea unus electus est qui cæteris præponeretur; ne unusquisque ad se trahens Christi Ecclesiam rumperet. Jeron, *ad Evag.* *Quod & Alexandriæ post Marcum Evangelistam factum est à Presbyteris; quomodo exercitus imperatorem faceret.* Cyprian. Ep. 55. *Non aliunde hæreses abortæ, aut nata schismata, quam inde quod sacerdoti Dei non obtemperatur.*

Triumphati magis quam victi sunt. Tac. de Germ.
Nehem. 11. 14. & 22.
Sciamus, traditiones Apostolicas sumptas de veteri Testamento: Quod Aron & filii ejus atque Levitæ fuerint in templo, hoc sibi Episcopi, & Presbyteri, & diaconi vendicent in Ecclesia. Jeron. *ad Eva.*

Fourthly, A right *Episcopacy* seems yet never to have had so free, full, and *fair an hearing*, as is requisite in so great a matter, so as to have been evicted to be against the Scriptures, as some pretended.

1. When as 'tis most evident, in most learned and godly mens judgements antient and modern, that it hath the *neerest resemblance* to that antient Patern at least, which God setled, the Government of his Church among the Jews; who had the heads of their Fathers, as Bishops; and rulers over their brethren, the *Priests and Levites, Numb.* 3. 24. Now 'tis manifest that our Lord Christ and the Apostles, had great regard to the *Judaick customs*, in *Christian Institutions*; As in the Baptising with water; In the use of the Bread, and Wine in the Lords Supper; In the Sabbatising on the Lords Day; and in the giving the power of the Keys to the Pastors and Teachers of the Church, to open and shut, to bind and loose; expressing thereby *Ministeriall* Authority: In all which there

there was some *like* or parallell precedents among the Jews, in making their Rabbins, and in celebrating holy mysteries, and governing those of *that Church* and Religion.

2. For, the *new* Testament, nothing either of precept or example seems against a right Episcopacy, commanding a parity, or forbidding order and subjection among Presbyters as well as other men: what Christ forbids his Apostles of exercising *dominion after the manner of Princes of the world*, excludes indeed, First from the twelve (who were (*pares in Apostolatu*) equally Apostles, and were not long to live in one society; but to lay the foundations of Religion in all the world, by a parity of power; coordinate, but not subordinate to any but Christ, who chose them) and proportionably, forbids all Bishops and Church-men, the secular *methods* of gaining or using any *Ecclesiasticall power and eminency* in the Church, as by ambition, force, usurpation, tyranny; by the sword, and severities, penally, inflicted on the Bodies, Estates, Liberties and lives of men; which was the way, of the world, but not of Christ, or his Ministers; yet these tyrannies which attend mens lusts and passions, as men, are as incident (besides factions and emulations) to the Presbyterian way, where some are alwaies heady and leaders, as to that *of a right* and regular Episcopacy, whereto Presbyters are joyned. The plain meaning of our Lord Jesus (who owned himself, as *chief* among his Apostles, yet condescended to *serve* them,) is; That, what ever *excellency* any Christian Minister or other had above others, in age, estate, parts, place, power, gifts, graces, or civill honors (for what hinders a Prince or Nobleman to be a Minister of the Gospell, and yet retain both his honour and estate temporall?) all these should be used and enjoyed without the *leaven of* pride, insolency, or oppression, and only be turned to greater advantages of *serving Christ*, and the Church, with all humble Industry; As Christ himself did; And after him the Apostles, who had undoubtedly as some order and precedency among themselves in the equality of their Apostolicall power; so also priority both of place, superiority of Church jurisdiction, and authority and power over *all other* Disciples and beleivers; And this not from any personall gifts temporary, and privileges so much, as from that wisdom and peaceable order, which Christ would have observed alwaies in

et ad Nepotianum.
So St. *Cyprian l. 3. Ep. 9. ad Rogatianum.*

Calvin. Inst. l. 4. c. 4. Sect. 2. Saith, Episcopall eminency is the best way to prevent Schisms, and to keep peace in the Church.

Luke 22. 26. But ye shall not be so: But he that is greatest among you let him be as the youngest, and he that is chief as he that doth serve.

Mat. 24. There may be a wise servant whom the Lord may set over his house. *Timothy* is taught how to behave himself in the Church as a Governour, no less than a Minister, or Teacher. 1 Tim. 3. 15. *Remis non scepter is gubernent Episcopi*: ὡς πόνον ϗ ἀγρυπνίαν: ἐκεῖνον τὰς [illegible] ἀρχὰς, ἵνα τιμηθῶμεν ϗ δοξασθῶμεν παρ' ἀνθρώπων. Chrysost. de Episc. Tom. 4. p. 627. τὴν δὲ ἐπισκοπὴν [illegible] [illegible] ἀλλ' ἐ τυραννικὴν δυναστείαν *vocat*. Is. pel. l. 2. not πρᾶγμα [illegible] as *Liban* to *Basil* says Bishops were, *&c. Basil. Ep.* 154.

his Church, after the Apostolicall example; By some of whom, as the antients tell us, Some Ministers *were clearly* constituted as Bishops, with an eminency of personall power over others, to ordein, censure, rebuke, silence, even Presbyters and Deacons.

D. Blondell confesseth p. 183. None can be dispensed with, as to the violating or neglect of that Church order and Government, which is prescribed to *Timothy* and *Titus*, which rule is of Divine right and perpetuall.

This is *undeniably* evident by Scripture in *Timothy* and *Titus*; The validity and authority of which examples were esteemed by Antiquity, and followed, as warrantable divine *precedents*, and obligatory examples to after ages, (in the like cases at least) for imitation; By preserving such an ordinary *succession* of power *in Bishops* among and above Presbyters; both in *ordination* and *jurisdiction*. Nor is this clear instance to be any way in reason, avoyded, by *saying*, that *Timothy* and *Titus were Evangelists*; (what ever that Office were in the Church (either temporary and personall; or common to other chief Ministers, and perpetually to succeed) for it makes nothing against a personall *superiority of power*, and authority in them over their respective Churches: which was to succeed to others in all reason, as well as *their Ministry* did; both these being alwaies necessary for the Church; and indeed their ordinary power as to Government, had no dependance on their being *Evangelists*; no more, than *their Preaching*, and other Ministeriall acts had; which we may not argue from these two persons, to be incompatible to any Ministers now; Unless they be *Evangelists*: For then, no Presbyters that are not Evangelists in their sense might study or Preach, in season, and out of season, rebuke, exhort, *&c.* or shew themselves *Workmen that need not to be* ashamed &c. Now if these acts and Offices of Ministry are derivable to other single persons in *a Ministeriall* way; why not also that Gubernative power too; which was from the Apostle signally committed to *Timothy* and *Titus*, and no where so expresly to any fraternity of Ministers, or Presbytery in common?

2 Tim. 2. 15. 1 Tim. 4. 13. 2 Tim. 4. 2.

After that rate of arguing, we may *conclude*, that none, but the *very chief Apostles*, might *feed the Lambs* and Sheep of Christ; because, that command was thrice given to *Peter*; who was reckoned among the chiefest of the Apostles; which Conclusions were as absurd, and ridiculous; (being by all the practise and sense of the Primitive Churches confuted,) as this; that the *power* of proving and ordeyning Presbyters, by laying on of hands, of receiving *accusations* against them, of *rebuking*, *censuring*, *excommunicating*, silencing and *restoring*, (all Acts *gubernative*) may not be *eminently* in any single person; unless they be Apostles or Evangelists; when as not only the use of such *order and power* is in all reason necessary for Church societies (no less, than for civill;) but *the succession* of it, in such sort as it began in them, to all times after, seems *clearly intimated*, by that vehement charge layd on

2 Cor. 11. 5. 12. 11. ὑπὲρ λίαν ἀπόστολοι. Joh. 21. 15. 1 Tim. 5. 19. 22. Tit. 1. 5.

Timothy

Timothy, to keep those *things unpartially and unblameably untill the comming of our Lord Jesus Christ.* Which *Timothy* in his infirm person could not do; but, in his care to *transmit the* holy patern to posterity, and to his successors; he might, as he was enjoyned, be said to do: For what is *once well done* in a regular publike way, is ever after done, as to the *permanency* of that vertue, which is in *a good and great example.*

1 Tim. 5. 21. 2 Tim. 4. 5.

τὰ μεγάλα παραδείγματα αἰώνιά ἐστιν ἀγάλματα, ὡς εἰκόνες ἔμψυχοι τῆς κατὰ θεὸν πολιτείας. Bas. M. ὡς ζωγράφοι, πάντα πρὸς τὸ παράδειγμα βλέπομεν: Id. *Perennis est & æterna præclari exemplaris virtus.* Jeron. *Quadratus Athenienſis Eccl. Episcopus Apostolorum Discipulus*, Jeron. Ep. ad Mag. St. *Jerom* tels us that St. *John* wrote his Gospell at the intreaty of the Bishops of *Asia. Catal. Script.* Eccl. c. 9. Rev. 2. Angels *i. e. Apostoli nuntii*: νομίζουσιν αὐτὸν ἄγγελον γίνεσθαι τῶν τοῦ θεοῦ προσταγμάτων οἱ Ἰουδαῖοι. Phot. Bibl. è Diod. Sic. *l.* 40. Austin. *Sub Angeli nomine Laudatur præpositus Ecclesiæ*, So *Beza*. Annot. The chief teacher in the Synagogue was called the Angell of the Congregation. *Ainsw.* in Deut. 31. 11. So Malachi. 2. 7. The Priests lips shall preserve knowledge, for he is the Angel or Messenger of the Lord of Hosts.

What other Churches did observe *after the* Apostles times, as to the manner of their Government, when they grew numerous, and spread to many Congregations and Presbyteries, we may easily be resolved both by the testimony and practise of all Antiquity: Fathers, Councils, Historians, who have registred the uninterrupted succession of Bishops, from the Apostles, both in the seven Asiatick Churches mentioned in the Revelation; whose * Angels were generally taken for their Presidents or Bishops; and some of Apostles then living; when as *Archippus, Evodius*, and *Onesimus*, and *Polycrates* were Bishops, *&c.* What after times observed, is evident to *this day* among all Christians; even those of the Eastern and *Abyssine* Church have *still their Bishops*: so the *Greek* and *Muscovitish* Churches; so the furthest *Asians*, which are thought to have been first converted by St. *Thomas*, (who furthest from believing, did the penance of travelling furthest, to Preach the Gospell in *India*) And I observe the *Fratres Bohemi* in their persecuted state and poverty for a long time, still retained a very happy and comly order of *Episcopall Government.*

Ordo Episcoporum ad originem recensus in Johannem stabit autorem. Tertul. *l.* 4. *c.* 5. *ad. Marcio.* So *Clem. Alex.* testifies that S. *John* made Bishops in *Asia.* *Ignatius Epist. ad Ephes.* but twelve years after the Revelation written. Dionysius. Polycarpus Placed by St. *John* for the Bishop of *Smyrna.* Iren. l. 3. c. 3. Before the Revelation. So the Epistle of the Smyrnenses justify of him calling him θαυμασιώτατος ἐπίσκοπος τῆς καθολικῆς ἐν Σμύρνῃ ἐκκλησίας. *Euseb. l.* 4. *Hist.* 116. *Anno* 1450. *Fratres Bohemi, lib. de fide & moribus eorum.*

Truly, I never found so much *light of* Scripture patern and precept, enjoyning any one, or more Presbyters to do all those works of power and jurisdiction; Nor ever did they without the presence of *an Apostle*, or some Apostolicall successor and Bishop, regularly ordein, excommunicate, silence, *&c.* so far as I can yet learn. There are but two texts that mention the Presbytery, (and but one which can be pretended for ruling Lay-Elders;) which yet these are not

 preceptive

preceptive or institutive, but meerly narrative and touching, without expressing any joynt power, Office, or Authority of Presbyters, with any President or Bishop: much less, without them and against them. Yea I read in St. *Judes* Epistles v. 8. *foul marks* put upon those in the Church, *that despise dominions, and speak evill of dignities*; Against whose proud and *seditious practises, a woe* is denounced,

Vers. 11. as against men, cruell like *Cain*, covetous like *Balaam*, ambitious as *Korah*, facticus disturbers of that order, which God hath set in his Church, (as well as in civill societies) after the mutinous

Numb. 16. 3. example of *Korah and his company*, who rose against *both Moses and Aaron*; parallel to whose evill manners and disorderly pra-

2 Pet. 2. 10. ctises, these men had not been, against whom St. *Jude* here, and St. *Peter* in his second Epistle so sharply inveighs (as *presumptuous, self-willed, despisers* of dignities, *&c.*) unless there had been some *eminencies* in the *Church Christian*, as well as was among the Jews, which these men were most bold to oppose and contemn;

Rom. 13.
1 Pet. 2. 13.

As for the *civill powers*, that then were in the world, humble Christians made conscience as God commanded them, to submit to them in *all honest* things. And those *hypocrites*, were no doubt *too wary*, to adventure any thing against them, whose power was terrible by the sword; But the Orders, Governments, Dignities and Dominions in the Church, were exposed by their weakness, to the scorn and affronts of any such proud and tumultuating Spirits; which cove-

Jud. 19. red *themselves* under the veil of Christian Religion, yea and pretensions of the Spirit too; the better to set off their Schisms, and separatings from that authority, *power*, and order, which God had by the Apostles setled in the Church, even in those times.

5 If there were not thus much of Scripture patern, and precept pleading fairly for a *right Episcopacy*; yet since there is nothing against it, in *Scripture*, or Reason, in Religion, or morals, yea and so much for it in common *reason*, true polity, and *almost necessitie* in Church societies, no less than in either families, Cities, armies, or any fraternities, and Corporations of men: No doubt the Lord of his Church hath not deprived or denyed *that liberty*, and benefit of *good order*, and rationall Government to his Church, which in all civill societies, may *lawfully be used*, according to wisdom and discretion; Truly, we may as well think it unlawfull, for one Minister to excell another, or many others, in age, parts, learning, prudence, gravity, and gubernative faculties: which if they may lawfully be had, and are found in some by the especiall gift of God, to so great differences from, and excellencies above, others; what Reason or Religion can forbid them to be accordingly used, and publikely employed in answerable differences of place and power for the Churches good? only Christ requires humility in priority, Ministry in their majority,

Ἐν πολιτείᾳ οὐδὲν ἀφόρμητον εἶναι δεῖ. Plato. de leg.
Nihil fit in rep. sine ordinis & regiminis custodia.
So *Lycurgus* ordered, *ut nullus in repub. ordo sine proprio esset Magisterio.*

rity, and service in their superiority, proportioned to their gifts and endowments, which God never gave in vain. Nor doth there eve want indeed a *plebs and vulgarity*, among many Presbyters, though honest and able men, some of whom are still young, and prone to be passionate, impudent, factious and schismaticall, whose folly is not yet decocted, nor youthfull heats abated, *&c.* For the good ordering of whom, beyond a *contemptible and heady parity*, a right *Episcopall presidency* may be as *usefull*, lawfull, and necessary; as a little Wine was for *Timothy*, in regard of his frequent infirmities 1 *Tim.* 5. 23. which St. *Jerom* every where owns, as the ground of the first constitution of Bishops after the Apostles. Nor can such a paternall *presidency* be injurious to others, If rightly ordered, in the due choosing and preferring of a *worthy* and *tryed person*; who cannot be said to be imperious, or to exercise *any* forbidden *dominion* over those, by whose suffrages and consent he is worthily placed in that power and place for the good of them all; which priority and eminency ought to be kept, within those bounds of Christian authority, which may *consist with Charity* and Humility. And after all this, we see by wofull *experience*, that the want of that right Episcopall Government, hath occasioned so many and great mischiefs, in this and other Churches; as do sufficiently shew the *use and worth* of it; which was alwaies the greatest conservator of the Churches peace and purity in the best and Primitive times.

Epist. ad Evagrium & adversus Luciferianos. *Ecclesiæ salus in summi sacerdotis* i. e. *Episcopi dignitate pendet, cui si non ex imia quædam & ab omnibus eminens datur potestas tot in Ecclesiis efficientur schismata quot sacerdotes. Propter Ecclesiæ honorem, quo salvo salva pax est.* Tertul. *de Bapt. Presbyteri & diacon jus habent Baptisandi non tamen sine Episcopi autoritate, &c.* Jerom. *Aliqui de Presbyteris, nec Evangelii nec loci sui memores, neque futurum Dei judicium, neque nunc sibi præpositum Episcopum cogitantes, quod nunquam omnino sub antecessoribus factum est, cum contumelia & contemptu præpositi sui totum sibi vindicant, quorum immoderata & abrupta præsumptio temeritate sua, & honorem martyrum, & confessorum pudorem, & universæ plebis tranquillitatem turbare conatur.* Thus *Cyprian* complains in his time, who was one of the meekest and humblest Bishops that ever were, of the Arrogancy of Presbyters acting without their Bishop, *Cyp. Ep.* 67. *Mutua at fœda sibi præstat errorum patrocinia errantium multitudo.* Cecil. in M. F. *Despit qui ad vulgi normam sapit.* Sen. [illegible] Cl. Al. [illegible] Naz. or. 24. *contra Arianos qui facile numeris gaudebant.*

If any Object the *vulgar prejudices* and *disaffections* in many mens minds, against any thing that is called Prelacy or like to Episcopacy, I answer, 1. The best observation to be made, as from the vote and sense of the (πολλῶν) most men, is this; what they most dislike and oppose, is most by wise men to be desired and approved; Its no rule for good men to walk by, in *matters of Religion*, above all. 2. I believe the generality of sober Christians in this Nation do so much see the misery of change, and the want of right Church

3. *Answer to vulgar unsatisfaction against Episcopacy.* [illegible] *Instar navis tempestatibus jactata est Episcopi anima:* [illegible] *&c.* Chrysost. in Act. Ap. hom. 3. Ethi.

Governm-

Government, that they are (both the most and best of them) rather desirous of a *restored* and regulated Episcopacy, than any other way, which hath been tryed in vain. 3. Neither headless *Presbytery*, nor scattered *Independency* are without many great dislikes already in the minds of many *good* Christians; who finding these remedies worse than the disease are prejudiced against them both. 1. For their novelty; being unheard of *in the Christian world*, for 1500. years, and the last of not above ten years standing in *England*; both brought in but abruptly, as rising from private mens interests, passions and policies; with which *Episcopall Government* did not well agree; Neither of them ever having had either *the vote* of any *generall* councill, or the practise of any considerable part of the Catholick Church. 2. Suspected they are by many, for their prevaling upon this Church, by a kind of force; against the consent of the *supreme Magistrate*, and this in *broken* and *bleeding* times; Planted not by Preaching and patience, but by the Sword, and watered with civill blood; Each driving their Chariot (as *Tullia* the wife of *Tarquinius Superbus* did) over their Fathers: As if they brought in (*Armatum Evangelium*) Christian Religion in compleat armor; and Christ marching, like *Alexander*, *Hannibal*, or *Cæsar*; when as Episcopacy was (*toto orbe decretum*) with wisdom, charity and peace, by consent of all Churches in all the world approved (as St. *Jerom* tels us,) and established even in those times, when persecution kept the Church most in purity, and unity with self, and when prayers and tears were the only arms used in the Church, to set up any part of the Kingdom of Christ; either in Doctrine or Discipline. 3. Because neither of those new ways, ever yet had such *plenary and peaceable approbation* (after due debate,) from the publike *reason, prudence and piety* of this nation, comparable to what the *Government by* Bishops, alwaies had, in all Parliaments and Synods for many hundreds of years, since we had any Princes or Parliaments Christian. 4. Neither of them, carry yet any promising face of more truth, peace, order and honour to the Christian reformed Religion, to this Church or Nation; nor yet of more *morall strictness* and holiness in mens lives; nor of more grace in *mens hearts*; nor of more love and union as to mens affections; yet in no degree so much as Episcopacy did, in the Primitive and best times; yea, and in these last times too, since the Reformation; for although it might have some sharp prickles with it; yet it bare *sweeter* and *fairer Roses*, than these last have done or are like to do, and with far less offense. 5. The same or worse *inconveniences*, which are by any objected against Episcopacy in its age and decays, discover themselves in the very *bud and infancy* of these new ways: As much pride, ambition, tyranny, vanity, incharitablenesse; more profaness,

Nobis nihil ex nostro arbitrio inducere licet, sed nec eligere quod aliquis ex suo arbitrio induxerit. Apostolos domini habemus autores, qui nec ipsi quidquam ex suo arbitrio quod inducerent elegerunt, sed acceptam à Christo disciplinam fideliter nationibus administrarunt. Tertul. de Præs. ad Hær. Livi Dec.1.l.1 Hieron, in Epist. ad Titum.

Prophaneſs, Atheiſm, Hereſie, Blaſphemy, Licentiouſneſs; far more faction, bitterneſs, vulgarity, deformity and confuſion; beſides the needleſs offence and ſcandall given to moſt Chriſtian Churches in all the world, who retain the government by Biſhops, being as antient as their being Chriſtians, and deſcended from the ſame origin, the Apoſtles, and Apoſtolicall men. 6. Neither of the new modes ever produced, either Precept or holy example, or any divine direction for them in any degree, ſo clearly, and ſo fully, as Epiſcopacy hath alwayes done; Nor yet have they produced any *promiſe from God*, that they ſhall be freed from thoſe inconveniencies, which were reall, or odiouſly objected againſt Epiſcopacy; and which may be incident in time to all things that are managed by men.

This government then by a fatherly preſident or chief Biſhop among *Presbyters*, ſeeming to have not equall, but far ſuperiour grounds, from *Scripture*, both as to the *Divine wiſdome*, ſo ordering the form of his antient Church among the Jews; alſo by the example, precept and direction evident from Chriſt Jeſus, and the holy Apoſtles in the *New Teſtament*; No wonder that many, yea far the moſt of godly and learned upright men, do rather approve a *Primitive and right Epiſcopacy*, than any other *new faſhion*, which is rather conform to ſecular intereſt, than to any thing of the Churches, or true religions advantages; eſpecially when 'tis evident, that Epiſcopacie hath the great and preponderating addition of the *Antient*, *ſole*, and *Univerſall government*, approved, and uſed by all the Churches of Chriſt, in the *pureſt* and moſt *impartiall* times; To which, neither of *the other*, can with any face pretend for themſelves; nor with any truth contradict; it being *averred* by all Antiquity, in the behalf of right and regular Epiſcopacy, which never *failed to ſucceed the Apoſtles authority and eminency*, either by their own immediate appointment in many places, even *while they yet lived*; or by the election and Votes of the Colleges and Fraternities of *Presbyters*, after the Apoſtles deceaſe, who ſtill choſe one man eminent, for his faith, piety, zeal, and holy gravity, to be duly conſecrated in power and place above them; *as a Father* among ſons; or an elder *Brother* among brethren; or as a *Maſter or Provoſt* in a College; or as a *Generall* in an Army; as St. *Jerom* himſelf tells us.

4. *The advantages of Epiſcopacy againſt any other.*

Auſt. Ep. 148. ad Valerium. Jeroni. ad Nepotianum. Ad Evagrium. Cryſoſt. hom. 3 in Act. *Apoſt.* τὴν ἐπισκοπὴν αὐτὸ λαβόντα εἴρηκε. τοῦτ' ἔστι, τὴν ἀρχὴν, τὴν ἱερωσύνην. ἀδελφοὶ ἐσμὲν, ἵνα δὲ καὶ ἐν ἀδελφοῖς ἵνα ἐπιτάττει, καὶ τοὺς ἄλλους πείθεσθαι. Cryſoſt. Hom. 3. in Acta.

If any man ask me then what kind *of Biſhop* I would have; I anſwer, Such an one for *Age*, as may be a *Father*; for wiſdome a *Senator*, for gravity a *Stoick*, for light an *Angel*, for innocency a *Saint*, for induſtry a *Labourer*, for conſtancy a *Confeſſor*, for zeal a *Martyr*,

Vid. Syneſ. *l.* 3. *Ep.* 216. Ἁπάσης φιλοσοφίας ἄγαλμα. de *Epiſ.* &c. *Vid.* Bern. ad

Eug.l.4. *Oportet te esse formam justitiæ, sanctimoniæ speculum, pietatis exemplar, veritatis assertorem, fidei defensorem, Christianorum ducem, amicum sponsæ, &c.*

Quod in aliis sacerdotibus deest per Antistitem suppleri debet Elotus. ad Aug. ep.

August. ad extremam senectutem impræter-missè prædicavit. Possid. *vita* Aug.

Et successores & incitatores Apostolorum.

Et zelum ac locum sortiti tam igitur ad curam quam alacres ad cathedram. Bern. ser. 77. Cant.

Martyr, for charity a *Brother*, for humility a *Servant* to all the faithfull Ministers and other Christians under his charge; I would have him venerable for those severall excellencies, which are most remarkable in the antient and most imitable Bishops; The devotion of St. *Gregory*; the indefatigableness of St. *Austin*; the courage of St. *Ambrose*; the learning of *Nazianzen*; the generosity of *Basil*; the Eloquence of *Chrysostom*; the gentleness of *Cyprian*; the holy flames of *Ignatius*; the invincible constancy of *Polycarp*; That so he may come neerest to the Apostolicall pattern, and resemble the most of any Christian, or Minister, the grace and *Glory of our Lord Jesus Christ*. I would have him (yet not I, but the vote of all pious Antiquity requires a Bishop) to be among men the *most morall*; among Christians the *most faithful*; among Preachers the most painful; among Orators the *most perswasive*; among Governours the *most* moderate; among *Devotionaries* the *most fervent*; among Professors the *most forward*; among Practisers the *most exact*; among sufferers the *most patient*; among perseverants the *most constant*: He should be as the *Holy of holyes* was both to the *inward court* of those that are truly sanctified and converted; and to the *outward court* of those that are called Christians, only in visible profession; I would have nothing in *Him*, that is justly to be blamed, or sinisterly suspected; And all things that are most deservedly commended by wise and sober Christians; I would have a Bishop of all men the most compleat, as having on him the greatest *care*, namely that of the Church, and of souls; And this in a more publike and eminent inspection; as one daily remembring the strictness of Gods *account*, and expecting either a most glorious *Crown*, or a most grievous *Curse* to all Eternity.

πατρικὴ κηδεμονία ἀλλ' ὁ τυραννικὴ αὐτονομία. *1 s. Pet.* 1, 2. Jerom ad Heliadorum. Naz. orat. lat. tom. 2. *Grandis dignitas sed grandis ruina si peccent.* Ieron. *Ut nihil Episcopo excellentius; sic nihil miserabilius si in crimine teneatur.* Amb. de dig. Sa.

Vid. Bern. Ep. 42. Vid. Amb. tom. 3. ep. 82.

Qualis eligendus sit Epis.

Quis ferat Eligi divitem ad sedem honoris Ecclesiastici, contempto paupere instructiore, & sanctiore. Aust. ep. 29

11. I would have him most *deserve*, and most able to use well, but yet least esteeming, coveting, or ambitionating the *riches*, *pomp*, *glory*, and *honour* of the world. One that knows how to own himself in *Persecution*, as well as in *Prosperity*, and dares to do his duty as a Bishop in both estates; I do not much consider the secular *Parade* and *Equipage*, further than as publike incouragements of *Merit*, as excitations to excell, as noble rewards of *Learning*, and as extern decencies or solemnities which do much set off, and *Embroider Authority* in the sight of the vulgar; I wish him duly *chosen* with judgement, *accepting* with modesty, *esteemed* with honour, reverenced with love; *Overseeing* with vigilance, *ruling* with joynt-Counsel, not *levelled* with younger *Preachers* and novices, nor too much exalted above the graver, and elder *Presbyters*; neither despised of the one,

one, nor despising of the other; I wish him an *honourable competency* (if it may be had) with his *eminency*; that he may have wherewith to exercise a *large heart*, and a *liberall hand*, which every where carry respect and conciliate love; If this cannot be had, yet I wish him that in true worth, which is denyed him in *wealth*. That his vertue and piety may still preserve the authority of his place; and this in the Order, Peace, and Dignity of the Church; That he may be the *Touchstone* of Truth, the *Loadstone* of Love, the *Standard* of Faith, the *Patern* of holiness; the *Pillar* of stability, and the *Center* of Unity in the Church.

Ut Episcopus non sit quod Libanius dixit πρᾶγμα δυσχεί-μενον, Res unde ægrè aliquid emolumenti emungatur. Basil. in ep. 154. *δυκίσμοιο θέ-μεθλα βὰν φέρε ἰμμαλόγιο.* Naz. Carm. 4. de Episc.

Nor are these to be esteemed, as *Characters* of an *Eutopian Prelate*, only to be had in the abstract of fancy and speculation; Many such Bishops have been antiently in the Church, and not a few, here in *England*, some still are such in their merits amidst their ruines and obscurings, and more might constantly and easily be supplied to the Churches good order, peace and honour; If Reason and not Passion, Religion and not Superstition, Judgement and not Prejudice, Calmness and not fierceness, Learning and not *Idiotism*, Gravity and not Giddiness, Wisdome and not Vulgarity, Prudence and not Precipitancy; impartiall Antiquity, and not interessed novelty may be the judge of *true Episcopacy*.

I think nothing further from a *true Bishop*, than *Idleness* set off with pomp, than *Ignorance* decked with solemnity, than *Pride* blazoned with power, than *Covetousness* guilded with *Empire*, than *Sordidness* smothered with state, than *Vanity* dressed up with great formalities. Bishops should not be like *blazing Comets* in their Diocesse, having more of distance, terror, and pernicious influence, than of light or Celestiall vertue; But rather, as *fixed Stars* of the prime magnitude, shining most usefully and remarkably in the Church, during this night of Christs *absence*, who is the only *Sun* for his light, and Spouse for his love to the Church; yet hath he appointed *some proxies* to woo for him, and *Messengers* to convey love tokens from him; among whom the holy Bishops of the Church were ever accounted as the chiefest Fathers next the Apostles, when they were indeed such as evill men most *feared*, good men most *loved*, Schismaticks most envied, and Hereticks most *hated*: *Right Episcopacy* is so great an advantage to the Churches happiness, and so unblamable in its due constitution and exercise, that it is no small blemish to any godly mans judgement, not to approve it, and nothing (as to *imprudence*) is I think more *blame-worthy*, than not to desire, esteem, love and honour it. Since such *Prelature* is as lawfull, as it is usefull; and it is as usefull, as either Reason or Religion; polity or piety can propound in any thing of that *nature*, which if not absolutely necessary, yet certainly most convenient for the Church, and commendable

Vid. Bern. ep. 28. & 152. & 42. ad Ep. Senonum.

Aug. ep. 203. *in Ecclesiasticis honoribus tempora ventosa transigere*, &c.

Amb. de dig. Sacerd. *Cum honoris prærogativa etiam congrui merita requirimus*, &c.

mendable in the Church (so far as it stands in a *visible Polity and society,*) being no way, either sinfull in it self, or contrary to any positive Law of God, any more than it is for Christians in civill government, to have Maiors in their Cities, Colonels in their Armies, Masters in their Colleges, Wardens in their Fraternities, Captains or Pilots in their Ships, or Fathers in their Families.

Nor is indeed the *venerable face* of true Episcopacy so deformed by some mens late *ridiculous* dresses and disguises; but that wise and learned men still see the many reverend and excellent *lineaments* of it, not only of pious and prime antiquity, but of beauty, order, symmetry, and benefit; such as flow from both humane and divine wisdome; if popular contempt and prejudices in some of the vulgar be any measure of things, or any argument against any thing in Religion, or in the Church of Christ; it will serve as well to vilifie and nullifie all Presbytery, and all *Ministry*, as all Episcopacy. Indeed neither of them can preserve their honor, use, and comliness, if they exceed their *proportions*, and either dash against, or incroach upon each other; contrary to those bounds and methods, which primitive wisdom observed between power and counsell, *Order and Authority, Community and Unity*. It is very probable, that a few years experience of the *want of good Bishops*, will so reconcile the minds of sober and impartiall Christians to them, that few will be against them, save only such, who think the best security for some of their estates to be the utter exploding, and perpetuall extirpation of Episcopacy; A thing which one *of the wisest of mortalls so much abhorred*, and for which he was able to give so good an account in Reason, Piety, and true Polity; that it appears to have been not pertinacy and interest, but judgement and conscience, that so long sustained that unhappy Controversie, which I have no mind to revive, but only (if possible) to reconcile, which is no hard matter where clear truths meet with moderate affections, and peaceable inclinations. For I find by the proportion of all Polity and Order; that if *Episcopall* eminency be not the main weight, and carriage of Ecclesiasticall government; yet it is as the *Axis* or *wheel* which puts the whole frame of Church society and communion into a fit order and aptitude for motion; especially in greater associations of Christians, which make the most firm and best constituted Churches.

In plebe nec veritas nec judicium; inter foedam potentium adulationem, & praeceps prostratorum odium, inanibus studiis & inconditis motibus omnia miscent. Tacit.

This being then the true figure of a learned, grave, godly and industrious Bishop, there need not more be sayd to redeem Episcopacy from prejudices; or to assert it against those triviall objections, which are not with truth and judgement, so much as with spight and partiality made against it.

Those *light touches* which are, by some men produced from the antient Writers in the Church, for the countenancing of the power

of

of Presbyteries without any Bishop and President, or for the *Independency* of power in Congregations, are indeed but *as the dust* of the balance, or *drops of a full bucket*, compared to those full and weighty testimonies, which they every where give, for the use of *Episcopacy*, unless men be allowed the confidence and liberty to *bastardise* the works of the Fathers as they list, and by a new purgatorian Index to antiquate all Records after 1500. years *legitimation*, by the consent of all Churches; as one lately hath endevoured to do, (a person indeed of great reading and learning, but in this not of equall candor and impartiality) who endevouring to find some foundation, whereon to build his Presbyterie, seeks to cast away as rubbidg and trash, all the Epistolary writings of holy *Ignatius*; who if he had wrote nothing, yet the *fame* of his piety, and sufferings made him sufficiently renowned in those Primitive times and after ages, both for a Bishop and a Martyr; his seat Episcopall being at *Antioch*, and his grave at *Rome*; But his writings being never so far questioned by Antiquity, as to reject those Epistles which we urge in this point of Episcopacy for genuine: and which are oft mentioned with honour, (and in part the very words) which we now read; so that it seems a passion and boldness *too servile to the cause*, which that learned man undertook; so to endevour at once to expunge those testimonies, and remains of *Ignatius*, which indeed are very weighty, and many, for the *distinction* of Bishops, Presbyters, and Deacons, even in the first century after Christ; which our learned and industrious Country-man Dr. *Hammond* hath lately, as (μέγας ὑπερμαχήσας) a valiant vindicator defended; not more to the honour of *Ignatius*, than of himself, whom providence hath chosen, and so enabled to be a Patron to so glorious a Martyr, and in so just a cause, as to redeem one of the first Fathers from that Presbyterian *Limbo*.

D. Blondell.

Ignatius called Θεοφόρος.

By *Euseb. Clem. Alex. Jerom.* & *Photii. bibl.* See the Lord Prim. of *Arm.* edition of *Ignatius*.

How *uncomly*, and *petulant* some other mens carriages have been, and are daily toward the antient *Fathers of the Church*, I need not tell, when 'tis too evident, how they put them oft on the *rack*, to make them speak, somthing in favour for either an Headlesse Presbyterie, or a confused Independency. Indeed, it is *a shame to see young men and novices*, so to make those antient, holy, and learned Writers to *scratch or blot* their own faces, with their own Pens, and to put out their Eyes *with their own stiles*; wringing, as it *were their noses*, till they *bleed a drop or two* for those new Modes and exotick formes of Church-government, which neither they, nor their forefathers even up to the Apostles times, ever saw or knew; And this tyrannie of quotations must be exercised upon the works of the Fathers, though never so much against the clear judgement and practise of those holy men, who were themselves, either eminent Bishops, as most of the Antients were, whose Works are extant, or humble and peaccable Presbyters, who universally owned and *submitted* to the authority of their Bishops; yea, some men have the forehead to urge a few obscurer passages in a few them against clear places, which are a hundred to one, wherein they express their own judgements, or the whole Churches practise in their times, to be without any dispute for *Episcopacy*, and Bishops with Presbyters as succeeding the Apostolicall eminencie in the ordinary power of Ordination and Church-government: Indeed, I have oft wondred, how men of *learning and piety*, had the confidence to cite *testimonies* even *out of Ignatius*, *Tertullian*, *Irenaus*, *Origen*, *Cyprian*, *Clemens* of *Alexandria*, *Ambrose*, *Austin*, and others in favour of a *Presbytery*, without and against a Bishop or President, when all of them, as all others of the Fathers are most clear, both in their own judgements, and as to the Churches Catholick practise (yea, and so is St. *Jerom* too) for the right use of regular Episcopacy, such as all sober men plead for and approve.

5. *Regulation of Episcopacy.*

Omni actu ad me perlato placuit contrahi presbyterium. Cornel. ep. Rom. ad Cyp. Epist. 46.

In the absence, sickness, or death of the Bishop, the Presbyters somtime governed the Church: So in *Cyprians* absence. *Epist.* 26. 30. 31. So *Theod. l.* 4. *c.* 22. when the Orthodox Bishop banished, the Presbyters, *Flavianus* and *Diodorus*, &c. guided the Church. So *anno* 1194. When the Turks prevailed over the

What ever the Fathers are brought in, as speaking for the Ministers rights in a joynt Presbyterie, or the peoples as for Independency, amount to no more, but either to repress the *arrogancy*, ambition, and tyranny of *some* Bishops, who in more favourable times usurped, or used their power against, or with neglect of the *Counsell* and *assistance of Presbyters* (which in all reason ought, and in Antiquity were ever joyned with the Bishop in weighty matters) or else when the insolence and scorn of some Ecclesiastick governours arose to the oppression of the *faithfull people*; To whom in Primitive times great regard *was had*, both by *Bishops* and *Presbyters*, in all publick transactions, which concerned their, and the Churches good government, that so all things might be done, with charity, good liking, and approbation of all Christians. This was not only very comly and convenient, but almost necessary in point of Christian prudence in those times, when Christians of all degrees were full of humility and Charity, kept short and low by persecution, and much depended upon the love and union between Pastor and people. Afterward indeed in times of peace and plenty, there oft appeared so much of levity, fury, and faction in the *common people*, that it was the wisdom of Governours to withdraw much of that liberty and indulgence, which formerly people enjoyed, but afterward abused to Sedition, Fury and Murthers in their tumultuary motions, and clamorous Elections. This is all that ever I observed from the *Antients*, in favour of the Presbyters power in common with Bishops, or of the faithfull people; Namely, that they would have (after the pattern of the Apostolike love, wisdome, and humility) all things of publike concernment, in the Church, to be so managed by *the chief Governour* or *Bishop*, as neither *Presbyters*, nor *People*, should think themselves

themselves neglected, wherein their suffrage, consent or approbation was fit to be had; but the one should be used as brethren, the other as sons; which temperance I greatly approve.

Greek Churches. *Balsamon* re's, they had no Bishops in many places a long time. *De Petro Apost.* ὅρα δὲ αὐτὸν μετὰ κοινῆς πάντα ποιοῦντα γνώμης, οὐδὲν αὐθεντικῶς, οὐδὲν ἀρχικῶς. *Crysost. hom.* 3. *in Act. Apost.* *Florentissimo illic clero tecum præsidenti.* Cypr. ep 55. ad Cornel. *Episcopus nullius causam audiat absq; præsentia Clericorum suorum alioquin irrita erit sententia Episcopi, nisi clericorum præsentia confirmetur.* Con. Carth. 4. can. 23.

It were endless and needless, to answer or excuse *personall Errors in Bishops*, or those *common inconveniences*, which are prone to attend all *Power* and *superiority* among men; For those are the fruits of *Power perverted*, of *Authority degenerating*, of *Governors ill governing themselves*, through personall errors and passions, or the corruptions and indulgencies of times; but they are not by any wise and impartiall man to be reckoned, as the genuine and proper effects, of that *order*, *government*, and *proportion*, which is in right Episcopacy (and which all reason, as well as Religion, allows to all sorts of men and Christians) no more than sickness is to be imputed, as a fault to health; or deformity to comliness: since both are incident in humane nature to the greatest strength or beauty. Yea, 'tis most certain, that there is nothing usefull, or commendable in any other way of governing the Church, in small parcells, or in greater bodies, which is not *inclusively*, *eminently*, and *consummatively* in a *well-ordered Episcopacy*; such as was not only in *primitive times*, but in our dayes; As all *Oeconomick vertues* are in a *good Father* or *Master*, and all politick excellencies are in an excellent Prince or Magistrate, which cannot be found in any other short of, and inferiour to those eminent relations; All other lower and incompleater forms are, as defective in point of advancing a common and publike good, as they come short of that main end, for with Episcopacy, as the Crown and perfectest degree of order was by *Apostolicall and primitive wisdome*, and piety, setled in the Church, which was to avoid Schisms; to preserve the Unity of the faith, and peace of the Churches; to keep good correspondencies by *Synods* and *Councills*; which could not be done by *multitudinous meetings*, which no place could hold, nor wise men manage to any order and decency; but all was easily effected by the conventions *of the chief heads and Fathers of the Churches*, the Bishops and Presbyters in any Province, Patriarchate, yea, and in all the world, which had commerce with the Roman Empire; where the chief overseers of the Flock, and representers of the Clergy met, and so were best able to give an account of the state of *the Church*, past and present, or to advise for the future welfare of it.

Bishops personal errors, no argument but of envy and malice against the office.

So that many wise men think it may be sayd of *Episcopall government* in its *right constitution and use*, as *Pius the second* said

Platina, in vita Pii. 2.

of

of the marriages of Clergy-men; He saw some reason why Marriage should be denied to them, (as, to the honour of their Order, and the redemption of them from secular cares, *&c.*) But he saw much more reason to allow them *that liberty*, which not only Nature, Reason, and Religion gives them, as well as any men, but even the honor of the Church required, to *avoyd the mischiefs and enormities*, which followed the contrary. And beyond all dispute, it appears after long dispute, that if it be not necessary by Divine prescript and direction to have such Bishops among the Clergy; yet there is no necessity made to appear against them, either in Reason or Scripture, Nor doth either Presbytery or Independency shew any so good title to divine right as Episcopacy doth, which includes the good of both those, and superads some thing of Order, Unity, and Excellency beyond them both, for the good of Presbyters and people too. Yea, I have known some Ministers of good repute for Learning and Piety, who were sometime *great sticklers* for the parity of Presbyterie; yet they have, since the mischiefs ensuing the change have confuted and *quenched* those former vain hopes, and excessive heats, confessed to me, That they see nothing in an Episcopall priority or *Presidency* unlawfull, as against Scripture or Religion, only it was thought by many godly men inconvenient; It may be so, but those men did not foresee the after inconveniences which grow greater by many degrees; So that I perceived that this long, hot, and bloody dispute, which seemed to hold forth the question and title of Divine right for Presbytery without a Bishop, was now referrable to the *judgement of Prudence*, rather than of Conscience; a matter of policie rather than piety.

Answer to what is urged in the Covenant against Episcopacy. *Tyrannicum Episcoporum regimen.*

This calmness at last abates much of that rigor, which some men *superstitiously urge*, and impose, *from the Covenant*, against Episcopacy in any kind or form; as if when *Scripture* and *Reason*, and *Antiquity*, and *Catholique* custome, are all for a right Episcopacy, it were of any force to be battered and Abolished by *the Covenant*; the sense of which, was sometime declared, to be only against the *Tyrannicall, abusive, and corrupt government of Bishops*, or those inconveniences which were conceived to be in the present Constitution, exercise, or use here in *England*, which one that had great influence in composing the Covenant, assured others was the meaning of the Composers; and the Covenants intent, was only to remove what was decayed in that antient Fabrick; and so preserve what was sound and good in it: The only lawfull and honest sense of this Covenant is sufficiently kept, if the former Constitution of Episcopacy in *England* be so reformed, as it easily may be, and in reason ought to be in what ever it needed alteration or amendment. However that Covenant being no infallible Oracle *dictated from heaven*; but a politique

Engine

Engine, continued and carried on by a company of poor, sinfull, and fallible men (upon whose heads we have lived to see that arrow fall, which they thought to shoot, only against the face of Episcopacy) all its words and senses are certainly to be brought to the rules of every mans place and calling, of a good conscience, of right reason, and of Scriptures; Nor may these, with all Antiquity, and the Fathers, *be forced to bow their sheafes*, and to do *homage* to that one *Sheaf* of humane *Combination*, and novell Erection, which holds forth, as nothing for *a headless Presbytery* or *Independency*; So, nothing of Reason, Scripture, or Conscience against *a right and primitive Episcopacy*; Against which to make a Covenant of extirpation, must needs be so much a sin, as it is against all reason and religion, to abjure the use of any thing which is lawfull, good and usefull; And if it be not necessary, as of Apostolike and divine Institution, if there be not Precept divine commanding, yet there is clear practise directing the Church that way of Episcopall government as best; which some men wel knowing, to have bin antiently approved and constantly followed by the *Catholike Church*; they used in the Covenant, *that art against Episcopacy, to soder Popery and Prelacy together*, thereby to bring the *greater odium on Episcopacy, implying that they were both intollerable and inseparable*; whereas in truth, there is nothing more ridiculously false and absurd, than to think the *Pope* to be the Father or Fountain of *Episcopacy*, or to affirm *Prelacy* to be Popery, as now the word is commonly understood to signifie Error joyned with pride, and superstition with tyranny. There were many godly Bishops, and holy Prelates in the primitive Churches, which were equal, or preceding, in time (as at *Antioch, Jerusalem, Alexandria, &c.*) to any *Bishop or Pope of Rome*; Many afterwards were equall to him in authority, as to their severall Provinces; Independent also, as to any derivation of power from the Bishop of *Rome*; As there are now many in the Christian world, and were in the English Church, both long before, and ever since the Reformation. Nor is the *Pope* by any wise men called Antichristian in any sense, as *he is a Bishop*, or Prelate of one Diocesse or Province; Nor was he ever thought to be so by *any judicious Protestant*; for then all Bishops in all the world, as Bishops, had ever *been Antichrists*; and then, the *whole Church of Christ*, from the Apostles times, must have had *no other government, ordination, or Ministry, but Antichristian*, which is a most *impudent and intollerable blaspheming of God, and the Lord Jesus*, and his blessed Spirit, and of the whole Church; As if, in stead of the *Spirit of Truth*, it had received only the spirit of Error and lying; in stead of Christs being *alwayes with it*, by the Ministeriall gifts of his Spirit, and the Apostles, and their Successors; only *Satan had presided in it by falsity and usurpation*; and, as if in stead of all *the ends of the Earth*

[Margin: 6. *Prelacy no Popery.* — *Episcopatus unus est cujus singulis in solidum pars tenetur.* Cyp. de un. Ecc. — Joh. 14. 16. — Mat. 28. 20. — Ps. 2. 6.]

O o

earth, given to Christ for his possession, in the way of an *Evangelicall kingdome and Ministry*, where truth and righteousness, charity and order, are his *Throne and Scepter*, all had been exposed to *Antichrists invasion,* that he might rule and reign in Christs stead.

It is upon other accounts than this, of *being a Bishop or Prelate* in a part of the Church, that the Pope is by many charged with the *odious character of Antichristian*, namely in reference to that ambition, pride, and usurpation, which by *fraud and force* the Bishops of *Rome* have obtained, and chalenge or exercise over all the world, and specially over *these Western Bishops* and Churches in later times; namely, since *Gregory* the greats dayes (who was an humble, devout, and holy Bishop; and had many pious martyrs, his Predecessors, as Popes or Fathers in that See of *Rome*, who abhorred the name of Universall Bishops, affirming they were Antichrist who ever arrogated that name of Universall Bishop;) Also for those gross abuses, errors, tyrannies, superstitions, and persecutions, which *many Popes* have made in the Churches of Christ, contrary to the word and example of Christ, and the Canons of *generall Councils*; From all which, we had *a Church and Ministry happily reformed*, even by the care and constancy of *many holy and learned men*, who were *Bishops and Martyrs in this Church of* England. As then we do not abhor to be men, or Christians, because *the Pope is a man*, and professeth to be a Christian; So neither may we *dislike Bishops*, because the Pope is one; nor Presbyters and Deacons, because there be *many of that title and office in the Church of* Rome.

Greg. in Epist. 32. Mauritio 600. years after Christ.

True Episcopacy may consist, without secular and civil advantages.

But in the last place, if primitive Episcopacy, and Apostolicall Bishops, now poor, and devested of all secular *power*, and *ornaments* of honour and estate, (and in this conform to their Predecessors in primitive and *persecuting times*) may not in reason of state with publick honour be restored, and established in this Church of *England*, yet it may be hoped, that the *Indulgence*, and liberty of times will give so much tolleration, That those whose judgements and consciences bind them either to be so ordeined Ministers, or to receive the comfort of divine Ministrations only from such as are in holy orders by the safe and antient way of Episcopall Ordination, may have and enjoy that liberty (without perturbing the publick peace) which both Presbyterians and Independents doe enjoy in their *new wayes*: For nothing will savour more of an imperious and impotent spirit (whose faith and charity are slaves to secular advantages and interests) than for those who have obtained liberty for their novelties, to deny the like *freedom* to other mens *Antiquity*, which hath the Ecclesiasticall practise and precedency of 1600. years; besides, the *preponderancy* of much reason, Scripture, and holy examples; All

which

which to force godly, grave, and learned men, Ministers or people, to renounce; or to comply with other wayes against their judgements; or else to deprive them of all *holy* orders, employments and ministrations in the Church, as Christians, cannot but be a most crying and self-condemning sin, in those men, who lately approved that antient and Catholick way, and after dissenting, at first desired, but a *modest tolleration.*

Since then the Pope, as *a Bishop, is not Antichristian*, as I have proved; neither can it be affirmed *with any sense or truth*, that either Episcopacy it self, or Bishops, Pastors and Governours in the Church are Antichristian; It will easily appear to sober Christians, how poor, popular, and passionate a calumny that is, which some *weak minds* please themselves to object against the Ministry of the Church of *England*, as if it were *Antichristian*, because the Ministers received their Ordination and Induction, both to the office and exercise of their Ministry, by the *hands and authority of Bishops*, with those Presbyters assistant who were present, which was the Universall practise of all Churches antiently in Ordeining Presbyters, and is at this day of most. This false and odious reproach of Antichristian Ministry, many Presbyters preposterously seek to wipe off from the face of their Ministry, as they are Presbyters, while yet with the same hand they make no scruple to besmear the faces of Bishops and Episcopacy; Not considering, that while they poorly gratifie the vulgar malice of some men against all Bishops, they still sharpen their spitefull objections against themselves as Presbyters.

7. *Bishops in* England *ordeining Presbyters, did but their duty, according to law.*

As then this solemn and holy *Ordination of Ministers by Bishops* here in *England*, by prayer, fasting, and imposition of hands, was *Antient* and *Catholick*, no way against Reason or Scripture; yea, most conform to both, in order to Gods glory, and the Churches welfare (which I have already demonstrated;) So, I am sure in so doing, Bishops did no more, than what their place, office, and duty required of them, here in *England*; according to the *Laws established*, both in Church and State; which had the consent of the whole Church and Nation, both *Presbyters and people*, as well as *Prince and Peers*: No wise man may blame that act, or exercise of government and authority in an other, which he was invested with, did enjoy, and acted in by *publick consent*, declared in the Laws, wherein each mans particular will is comprehended; nor may that be sayd to be a *private fault*, which is done in obedience to a *publick Law*; Bishops then, duly ordeyning Ministers in the Church of *England*, had the *approbation* of this Church and State, no less than of all *Antiquity*, and of all the Modern forein Churches, even those that have not Bishops, who yet ever commended and applauded that Venerable *Order*, here in *England*; As for Scripture which some pre-

Æquum est, ut quam feceris jusserisve legem, feras. Reg. Jur.

tend against Bishops, and for other wayes, I never read any place commanding any one or two, or more *Presbyters*, to ordein or govern in any Church *without a Bishop*; Nor do I find any place forbidding a Bishop to ordein, and rule among and with the Presbyters; According to that *appointment* of *Timothy* and *Titus*, which is of all most clear, for investing both Ordination and Church jurisdiction at that time eminently, (though perhaps not solely) *in one man*; and if that Constitution in the Churches of *Ephesus* and *Crete*, carry not a *Precept* or binding exemplarinesse with it to after-times, (which Antiquity judged, and followed *Universally*,) yet sure it *redeems* true Episcopacy sufficiently, and all good Bishops (in their right and moderate government of the Church, (especially in *this point of Ordeining Ministers*) from being *any way Antichristian*; to which we may be sure the blessed Apostle *Paul* would never have given any such countenance or patern, as that Jurisdiction and power given to *Timothy* and *Titus* must needs be: Nor are indeed the reproaches of popish and Antichristian, added by vulgar ignorance, or envy to Episcopacy, any other than *devillish*, *false*, and *detestable Calumnies*, invented by wicked men, to the reproach and blasphemy, not only of so many holy and *worthy Bishops* in all ages and Churches, as well as in *England*, but also of that *holy Spirit* of truth, and Ministeriall power which Christ gave to *the Apostles*, and they to *their chief successors the Bishops*; by whose learned piety and industry such mighty works have been done in *all ages, and in all parts of the Church*, and in none more, I think, than in this *Church of England*, chiefly since the Reformation of Religion, whereto godly and learned Bishops contributed the greatest humane assistance, by their preaching, writing, living and dying, as became holy Martyrs.

Can. 6. Concil. Nicæni.

8. *Primitive Customs, how far alterable in the Churches Polity.*

Consuetudo major non est veritate aut ratione. Cyp. Ep. 73.

Valeat consuetudo ubi non prævalet Scriptura aut ratio. Reg. Jur. *Præfracti est ingenii contra omnem consuetudinem disputare, morosi nimis pertinaciter adhærere.*

I am vehemently for the (ἔθη ἀρχαῖα) *antient and holy customs* of the Catholick Church, so far as they may be fitted to the state, and stature of any Christian societies; Not that I think all things of external Polity, discipline, and government, (by which Christians stand tyed in *relations publique* to one another) were at first so at once prescribed or perfected by Christ, or the B. Apostles, as might not admit after addition, variations, or completions in any Church, or Congregation Christian, according to those dictates of reason, and generall rules of Prudence, which are left to the liberty of Churches; by which so to preserve particular Churches, as not to offend the generall rules of order and charity, which bind them by conformity in the main, to take care of the *Catholick Communion*. We are not (I think) tyed so strictly to all the *precise paterns* of *primitive* and

Apostolicall

Apostolicall practise; which might well vary in the severall states, conditions, and *dimensions of the Church*. I read no command for Presbyters to choose a Bishop, or President among them, and in so not doing, they are defective, not as to the Precepts of Scripture; but to the rules of right reason; and the imitation of usefull example in primitive times; Nor do I find any Precept to one or more Presbyters to ordein others after them, who yet ought to take care both of their own being rightly Ordeined, and of after succession, according to that patern, Analogy, and proportion of holy order and government, which was at first wisely observed by the Apostles, and the after Ministers of the Church, either as Bishops or Presbyters. The same Coat would not *serve Christ*, a man grown, which did fit him, a *Child or Youth*; Only it is neither safe, comely, nor comfortable for any Christians, *wantonly*, and without great and urging reasons (next dore to necessity) to *recede from*, or to *cast off* the *antient* and most imitable Catholick customs of the Church: which truly is seldom done upon conscientious and reall necessities pressing, but most what upon factious humours, and for secular designs carried on under the colour of Church alterations. For how ever the alteration may at present please some mens activity and humour, whose turn it serves, yet it cannot *but infinitely scandalise*, grieve, and oppress, far more, and *better Christians*, who are of the old, yet good way.

1 *Cor.* 11. 16. If any man list to be contentious, we have no such Custom, nor the Churches of Christ.

In his rebus de quibus nihil certi statuit Scriptura, mos populi dei, vel instituta majorum pro lege tenenda sunt. Aug. Ep. 89. ad Cal.

χρόνῳ τὸ ἔθος βεβαιωθὲν, νομισθὲν νομός. *Naz. Or.* 34.

ἤρκεσεν τῷ ἐν ἔθει, καὶ μακρῷ χρόνῳ τετιμημένῳ μετάλλαξις. *Naz. Or.* 37.

Hence many wee see are at a loss now in *England*, how to justifie their past religion, shaken by changes, as if they had had no true Ministry, nor holy Ministrations and Sacraments hitherto; while some mens zeal without knowledge cries down Bishops, and *that whole government with the Ministry* for Antichristian; others are extremely *unsatisfied and solicitous* for the future succession, Not seeing any ground, for any Presbyters in this Church, so to challenge to themselves a sole divine power of Ordination and Jurisdiction, without any President Bishops: which was the antient way in *England*, ever since we *were Christians*, (as in all other Churches) And it is most sure, that *neither power of Ordination*, nor *Jurisdiction* was ever conferred by Bishops on any Presbyters here, either verbally or intentionally, as without and against Bishops; Nor did the Laws or Canons ever so mean, or speak; Nor was it (I believe) in any of the Presbyters own thoughts, that they received any such power to Ordein other Presbyters without a Bishop, when they were *Ordeined Ministers*. And sure, though acts of state, and civil Magistracy may *regulate the exercise*, yet they cannot *confer the holy power*, and order of a Presbyter or Bishop, on any man, which flows from a *spiritual head*, even Jesus Christ (as I have proved) and not from any *temporall Authority*; *Ordinances of Parliament* can hardly with justice or honour, batter or dismount the Canons of generall

Councils, the Catholick laws, or constant *Customes* of the Church. If it be supposed, that *the two Houses of Parliament* lately did but restore, and the *Presbyters resume* that power of Ordination, which was only due to them as such, and deteined *by Bishops usurpation from them*; It is very strange, they should never here, nor elsewhere have made claim to it, for 1600. years, in no ages past, till these last, broken, factious, tumultuary, and military times; If it were their right, only in common with, and subordinate to Bishops, they needed not then to complain, for they did, or might have enjoyed, as much joynt power, as was for their conveniency, and the Churches peace; The *eminent power* (at least for *Order sake*) was (even by their consents) lawfully placed in, *and exercised by the Bishops*; The levity and ambition of *ingrossing all to themselves* without and against Bishops hath almost lost all power both of Bishops and Presbyters too; since Presbytery alone, is but as *Pipe-staves*, full of cracks, warpings, and unevennesse, which will not easily hold the strong liquor of power and government, unlesse they *be well hooped about*, and handsomly kept in order by venerable and fatherly Episcopacy, which carried a greater face of majesty, and had those ampler and more august proportions which ought to be in government, beyond what can be hoped for, or in reason expected from the parity, and puerility of *Presbyters* in common: many of whom have more need *to be governed*, than they are any way *fit to bear* any great weight of government on their shoulders, however they may discharge some works of the Ministry very well.

Bona consuetudo, velut vinum generosum, vetustate valescit. Tert.

9. As it hath never yet been shewen any where; so it is least to be hoped for now in *England*, that any better fruits should arise from Presbyterie (thus beheaded, cropped, and curtayled of its crown Episcopacy) which it might not stil have (as formerly it hath) brought forth; If the honour and order of the highest branch, the Episcopall eminency, had been preserved with it: Not so as to *over-drop and oppress* all other boughs and branches, which are of the same root; but so, as to *adorn* them all; and to be most eminent in Christian graces, and Ministeriall gifts, no less than in *priority of place*, superiority of power, and amplitude of honour and estate: As many *Excellent Bishops*, both antient and modern were, against whose *incomparable worth*, while some *young and petty Presbyters* do scornfully declame, and *disgracefully* insult, they appear like so many *Jackdaws* perking on the top of *Pauls* steeple, or like living Dogs snarling at, and trampling upon dead Lions. Nor do indeed such *impotent tongues*, and miserable partialities of some men tuned to the most vulgar ears and humours, against all, even *good Bishops*; and against a right or regulated Episcopacy (such as was for the main and substance here in *England*) they do not in any sort become men that pretend to any true piety, learning, gravity, or civility.

Calm meditations between Episcopacy and Presbytery.

Petulantissima est insania paucorum malorum odio in bonos omnes debacchari.

I

I neither approve, nor excuse *the personall faults* of any particular Bishops, as to the exercise of their power and authority, which ought not in weighty matters to be managed without the presence, counsell, and suffrages of Presbyters, such as are fit for that assistance; The neglect of this St. *Ambrose*, and St. *Jerom*, and all sober men justly reprove, as unsafe for the Bishops, the Presbyters, and the whole Church, For in multitude of counsell is safety and honour too. *Rom*. 11.14. I am sure much good they might all have done, as *many of them did*, whom these touchy times were *not worthy of*; No wonder if the very best of them displeased some mens humours, who were impatient to be kept any longer in order; but, *like waters*, long pent up, they sweld to such *discontents*, as disdaining to pass the allowed bounds and floudgates of publick Lawes, they resolved to blow up and bear away the whole head and sluce of Government. Bishops had three Enemies to contend with, some Presbyters ambition, some Laymens covetousness, and their own Infirmities; And it may be Bishops faults had been less in some mens eyes, if their estates and honours had not been so great.

Hieron. *Communi concilio Præsbyterorum Ecclesiæ regebantur.* *Concilio Carthag*. 4. c. 3. *Nil faciat Episcopus*, &c. πρεσβύτεροι [illegible], not other (*Concil. Ancyran.*) assisted the Bishop in government.

I write not thus to reproach any of my Fathers or Brethren the Ministers, who begin many of them no doubt to be of my mind for moderate Episcopacy, if they have not alwayes been so; finding that the *fruit of the Summer*, doth not alwayes answer the blossoms of the Spring: cruell *frosts* may nip and blast those pregnant hopes of bettering, which men are prone secretly to nourish, whereby to excuse or justifie their desires of change and novelty. In which truly I never saw any thing of right reason or religion, produced for the extirpation of primitive Episcopacy. The main things that pressed upon it, were Forein power, domestick pride, the failings of some Bishops, the envious angers of some Presbyters, and the wonted inconstancy of the vulgar.

If any men, Ministers or others, are, as loth to *see and recant* their excesses and errors, as they were forward to run into them, but still resolve to keep *that partiall bias on their judgement*, which shall sway all their learning, and other excellent Ministeriall gifts against their own true interests, and this Church, with all reformed Religion, which consisted in due moderation and peace; I shall yet with my pity of their wilfulness or weakness, alwayes *love and reverence* what I see in them of Christ, and only wish that *temper and moderation from them*, which may most contribute in common to the vindication of the Order and Function of learned, grave, and peaceable ministers. This they may at last easily see, That every *soft gratification* of vulgar ignorance, envy, and inconstancy, set forth *with the forms of zeal*, and reformation, is usually returned with *vilifyings* and *diminutions* of their betters; who did vouchsafe *to*

flatter

flatter them, as if they indeed *feared them*. I wish a greater harmony, a sweet moderation and *Fraternal accord* among all true and *godly Ministers*, who dare to own, and do still adorn their office and calling: I should be glad to see the counsell and assistance of *well setled Presbyters*, crowned with the order and lustre of Episcopall presidency; which was antiently, as the Jewel wel set in a ring of Gold; or as a fair guard and handle to a good Sword, adding to its compleatness, comliness and usefulness. Alas the ordinary Ministers seem now *like younger brethren* (who sometimes lived handsomly under their Fathers, or elder Brothers care and inspection) so scattered and divided, that they are extremely weakned, and exposed to all injuries; yea, many of them like *Prodigall sons*, having riotously wasted their own and their Fathers portion, begin to consider what husks of popular favour they may feed on. So is *Insolency* the high way to *indigence*, and arrogancy soon knocks at the dore of contempt, Ministers must not wonder or repine at the measure they measured to others, wen offered to themselves.

Pro. 16. 18. Pride goes before destruction, and an haughty spirit before a fall.

Secundas habeat pœnitentiæ tabulas qui non habuit primas impeccantiæ. Amb.

I am far from reproaching any mens defeats or *Calamities*, wherein the Justice of divine vengeance is seen retaliating; I am glad if the occasioners *of our common shipwrack*, may have any fair planks, or rafters to save themselves, and the honour of their Ministry, either by recanting the *errors* of their *judgements*, or repenting the *transports* of their *manners*; If they retein their Antiepiscopall opinion with modesty and charity, yet I am not *disposed* to fly in any *godly mans* face, because he is not exactly like me, or to pull out his eyes, because they are not just of the colour of mine. I pray to be of that Christian temper for moderation and charity which can allow many latitudes of Prudence in extern things of religion, where no evident sins for their *immoralities*, nor evident errors against the fundamentals of Christianity, nor evident confusions of that charity and order which is necessary for the Churches peace, do appear. I wish that while Ministers or other Christians, differ in things of extern mode and order, they may all find and walk in *that holy way*, by which we may with one *shoulder of truth and charity*, carry on that great *work of saving Souls*, both our own, and those that hear us; that while we dispense saving truths to others, we may not for *want of humility and charity*, be cast-aways our selves. More of those *calming and moderating graces*, on all sides, had no doubt preserved both Bishops and Presbyters in their due place regard and honour; so that they should not have been put thus to *plead* for their Ordination and Ministry, or to play *this after game*, much to the hazard of their very Function, and succession of Ministeriall authority; The despising or abolishing of which threatens the annihilating of the very being of this reformed Church: in which the *right Ministry*, is

Multa toleramus quæ non probamus. Aust.

as

as *the Ark in* Israel, a *visible token of* Gods presence among Christians; And though the Philistins may, *for the sins of this* Church, take it captive, and *detein* it for a while, yet I believe, the Lord will bring it back again, with shame to his *enemies*, and joy to all *true Israelites*. 1 Sam 4. 1 Sam 6.

In the mean time this trouble and terror may be a means to amend the personall faults both of Bishops and Presbyters; which formerly might viciate, but they could not totally vacate, the Religion, reverence, and conscience, which is to be had of *Christs institution*, as to the Ministry; nor yet could they make voyd the honour of Religion, nor the authority, vertue, and efficacy of holy Ministrations; Where the persons duly ordeined did administer, and the holy things themselves were according to Scripture rightly administred, which alwaies remain holy, whatever is objected against *mens persons* administring; as sicknes, lamenes, or deformity deprive no man of the privileges of humane nature, nor his actions of reason nor his civill interest, of the benefit of the Laws. *Ely's* scandalous sons, unworthy indeed of, but yet rightly invested into the *Priests office*, did not take *away the* necessity, and sanctity of the services and sacrifices, much less of the *Priestly function*; which depended not on the *morality of the persons* administring, but on the *authority of the* Lord *commanding*; and the right investiture into the office. The miscarriages of Bishops or Ministers may take *away the beauty*, but not the being of Religious duties, or of that holy power, which they duly received; no more than lapses after Baptism, do unbaptise any Christian. No Christian thinks the series of Christs genealogy broken or blemished, corrupted or interrupted, stayned or maymed, by the *names of Tamar, Rahab*, and *Bathsheba*, which are links in that *holy chain*; which hath its *verity* in the history, but its *sanctity* from Christ, to whom it relates, as to the holy seed: So in the succession of *Ministeriall order* and authority, we dispute not by what personall vertues it was continued; but we are sure it hath been continued successively from Christ, and tends to him, as to the compleating of his second incarnation, in his body the Catholick visible Church; In which Christ is daily begotten and formed by the means of a right Ministry, and duly ordeined Ministers.

Personall faults of Bishops or Presbyters may viciate, but not vacate divine duties.

1 Sam. 2. 12.

10.

Of Ordination of Ministers.

Whether Bishops ordeined Presbyters, as *Prelates*, in a *superiority of* divine power and peculiar order, as succeeding the Apostolicall eminency (which antiquity for the most part thought,) looking on Episcopacy in ordination, *confirmation*, and jurisdi-

Where Bishops are Orthodox and may be had, Ordination cannot regularly be had without them *Ubi Episcopi desunt nec haberi possent, Orthodoxi Presbyteri in necessitate ordinare possunt.* Sarav. de grad. Mi. So Bishop *Downham* Con. in Apocal. Or by the Bishops authority delegated, as to the Chorepiscopi, who were but Presbyters, *Isid. Hispa. de Eccl. off.*

ction, not as the only, but as the highest branches of Church power lineally descended from the Apostolicall ordinary power of ruling, and governing the Church,) or whether they did those acts of power and authority only as chief by Ecclesiasticall right, in degree, and order of place *among the Presbyters*, as chosen or approved by them, and placed in a precedency of place, and *presidency* of action and inspection; but still of the same intrinsecall power and order Ministeriall, as to the first act or originall, I need not further gratify any mans curiosity in setting *down my opinion*.

> *Ego vero à Presbyteris solis administrata* χειροτονίαν *regularem, & ad Ecclesiasticarũ regularũ amussim factam non dixerim; Aut in ea institutum ab Ecclesia post Apostolorum transitum ordinem per omnia servare.* Blondel. test. Hierom. pag. 255. St. *Pauls* Epistle to *Tim.* and *Tit.*

This I am sure; What ever dirt and mire, *the restless* hearts of wicked men cast up against the calling of the Ministry in *England*, The Gospell, and the holy Institutions of it appointed by Christ to be dispensed to all the world, have never in any other way been derived to this long succession, save only by the *power of ordination*; which never was in ordinary cases believed or owned in the Church to be *valid* and effectuall, in any men, or from *any hands*, but those, who *were formerly* consecrated Bishops, or ordeined Ministers; Nor was this custom ever esteemed as the act of *any generall* Councill or Ecclesiasticall Canon; but it had both example, and precept, and constant succession from Christ to the Apostles; and from them to others, with a command of continuation; which was necessary for the Church, and ever most consciencioully observed in the Church; which never flourished better, than when the modesty, humility, and wisdom of *Presbyters*, joyning with and submitting to their Bishop (as fellows to the Master of a College) carried on that order, peace, and comly proportion in the Church (before all the world) that they were, in the first century, compared by *Ignatius* for their harmony to the strings well set, and *tuned on the Harp*; yea in an higher strain, he compares them to the *blessed accord between* the Father and the Son; Christ as man mediator and God; where in the sameness of the divine nature, yet *there is the* order and priority of relation.

> Ignat. Ep. ad Ephes. τὸ γὰρ ἀξιονόμαστον πρεσβυτέριον ἄξιον τοῦ θεοῦ οὕτως συνήρμοσται τῷ ἐπισκόπῳ ὡς χορδαὶ κιθάρᾳ. Epist. ad Smyrn. πάντες τῷ ἐπισκόπῳ ἀκολουθεῖτε ὡς ὁ Χριστὸς Ἰησοῦς τῷ πατρὶ, καὶ τῷ πρεσβυτερίῳ ὡς τοῖς ἀποστόλοις.

These were the antient pipes and conduicts of Ministeriall Ecclesiasticall power, which were first layd in the head and *fountain* Christ Jesus; after *branched* to all places by a continuall order and derivation of Ministeriall authority; Where the pipe is once broken, there the *stream of living waters* must needs fail: If any foulness flows, or obstructions have befaln these pipes of due ordination (as all that passeth through earthen vessels is prone to do, in time,) which Christ and his Apostles have layd to serve his Church with the living waters of grace and truth, and which have flowed these

sixteen

sixteen hundred years to the refreshing of infinite souls; yet we must not *cut them off*, nor quite stop them, or turn the waters another way; (as choosing, rather *Independent wells*, and broken Buckets,) but we ought to cleanse those pipes, and repayr those *conducts*, which only can hold, and convey that holy water (as the *vessels of the* Temple) restoring them to their Primitive use and integrity: Which, by Gods help is easily done, where pride, passion, policy, and worldly interests are really separated from those of Christ, his Church, and mens souls. Nothing were more happy, than to see this *sincerely done*; so that Christians would rather deny themselves, in profit and worldly advantages, than any way benefit or gain, by *Church Reformations*; than which, nothing is more sordid and more to be abhorred: contrary to the holy liberality of all good Christians in all times. If *Ananias* and *Saphira* were smitten for dissembling, how much more accursed are they who act all with a sacrilegious Spirit and hand, stripping and robbing the Church, instead of Reforming? I shall ever pray for just and liberall Reformations, while I live; mean time I rest satisfied in my conscience, That the ordination of Ministers, as it was in *England*, by a Bishop and Presbyters, as it hath the greatest regularity, so it hath the *greatest validity*, and admits the least dispute, as to the *right order* and succession of Ministeriall power.

As for the *Presbytery* and Presbyters, I think their *Ministry* very valid, and their authority very venerable, to all *true Christians*, especially in conjunction with their Bishop: Like *Tortesses* they were safest, while they keep under *that shell*; which some Presbyters having scornfully cast off as a burthen, striped themselves of *their shield* and *defence*, so that they are become very naked, feeble, and contemned creatures, whom the foot of pride and rusticity is prone to crush and trample upon on every side: That they have now no refuge or protection left, *but God*, and a *good conscience*; which are enough, if they do indeed enjoy them, though *with* poverty, and contempt from men.

θεοπρεπὲς πρεσβυτέριον. Ign. ad Ep. ἀξιονόμαστον πρεσβυτέριον. Id. ad Smyr. ὑπακούοντες τῷ ἐπισκόπῳ, καὶ τῷ πρεσβυτερίῳ, ἀπερισπάστῳ διανοίᾳ, Ign. ad Ep.

Thus I have, as well as I had leasure, vindicated the Ordination of Ministers, and that power which they have to administer holy things, in Christs name to this Church, to be *no way blameable*, but right and commendable; as derived by, and with the *hands of Bishops* and Presbyters; which is the *holy and Catholick way*, wherein only it is *ordinarily* to be obteined: if any men list to be contentious for other ways, my answer with St. *Paul* is again and again, neither we nor the Churches of Christ ever had *any other* custom, and with St. *Austin*, so Catholick a custom, so agreeable to reason and Scripture, could have no beginning but Christ and his holy Apostles.

1 Cor. 11. 16. *Aust. cont. Don. l.* 4.

11. *Of the peoples power in Ordination of Ministers*

There is yet one *Calumny* more against the *Ordination of our Ministers* in the Church of *England*; which pretends the *neglect among*

among us of what is by some thought most essentiall in making *a Minister*; that is, of the peoples right both in choosing and ordeining men to that office; the want of which, they say, makes our Ministry invalid.

Answ. For this pretended right of the people *no argument* is alleged, so strong, as that *of liberty*, which some have taken in these times, to separate themselves from *the ordinary Ministry* of this Church, and by a mutuall call of one an other to jugg themselves, *like Partridges*, into small *coveys*; which they call *bodies* or *Churches*, even before they have any Minister; which they resolve not to have, but of their *own* choosing, and ordeining; that they may be sure, (being a *creature* of their own) to have him after their own humour: flattering themselves, that they have a *plenary Church* power to all Offices and ends whatsoever. Although I have formerly given some generall account of the folly of this *imagination* in the vulgar; yet because it is a *Gangrene*, not easily cured, without oft lancing and opening, and hath far prevailed upon some *peoples minds*, who feed this opinion, with the venemous and vulgar *humours* of pride, self-loving, self-seeking, self-pleasing, self-flattering, and self-admiring; It is not a miss to give another stroak at *this high imagination*, which exalts it self against Christ, and the holy *order of his* Church; that the obstinacy of its arrogance and folly being pulld down, it may *be levelled* to that obedience, which becomes all Christian people.

People have no power Ministerial.

First, then, I must profess, that I never saw or heard any thing by any man, with any *shew of* Scripture, or reason, urged to proove this power of conferring the *holy order* and *authority of a Minister of Christ*, to be in the people, Either *eminently*, as an executioners power is in the supreme Judge; or *virtually*, as life is in the Suns beams; or *formally* and causally, as heat is in the fire; or *ordinatively*, preceptively, and derivatively, as the supreme Magistrates power is to some ends, and actions, in the meanest *Constable*, or *publike Officer*; So that it can be in them no other way, than, as *power may be* in *rebels hands*; or as *Korah* and his complices, if they had not been by God repressed, would have had liberty and authory, *from their own usurpation*, to make *Priests and Rulers* in stead of *Moses* and *Aaron*, whom the Lord had appointed.

Numb. 16. The Preface to *Korahs* rebellion, and confusion, is the peoples sanctity, v. 3.

Not by Scripture.

For Scripture, First it is evident in that (θεοκρατία) *divine patern* of polity and extern order of Religion in the Church of the Jews, we find that the wisdom of God leaves nothing of *holy concernments*, for *Priests* or Ministry, no nor the least sacrifice, offering, or ceremony, *to the peoples*, either ordering, or choosing; Nor is it likely, or any where appears, that the unchangeable wisdom of God in Christ, altering only *the manner* externall, and not the order, beauty, holiholyneſs, or the main end of the ſervice and Miniſtry Chriſtian (which his glory and his Churches good,) ſhould ſo much vary from the former exactneſs and warineſs, as *to venture* the order, beauty, and honour of Religion upon the rock of *vulgar rudeneſs*, ignorance, raſhneſs, headyneſs, ſtiff-neckednes; which formerly he ſo *much avoyded*, and which, not only the *tenderneſs of Christian Religion*, (which having many enemies, admits leaſt blemiſhes, and ſtudies moſt, what things *are comely*, as well as holy) but even *common reaſon*, and experience teacheth, all wiſe men to avoyd, as much as poſſible; Namely thoſe inconveniences and miſchiefs attending the weak heads and ſtrong hands of the vulgar, as in all things, ſo chiefly in thoſe which concern Religion. Who, that is wiſe, can be ignorant, that *the common* people, even *among believers and profeſſors*, are ſeldom or never qualified with thoſe gifts of knowledge, wiſdom, temper and diſcretion, which are neceſſary for all publike, and moſt, for *religious adminiſtrations*; where, not only the *credit*, but the *conſcience* of the Church is engaged, and ought to be very much conſidered, in order to the honour of Chriſt, and of his Church? It were a very blaſphemous reproach, I think, to the wiſdom of Chriſt, for any to imagine, that he had delegated the higheſt power of his Church to men *incompetent*; and *generally incapable*, without daily miracles.

Phil. 4. 8. τὸ γὰρ σεμνὸν καὶ τὸ δίκαιον ἐκπολὺ ἔκλ[illegible] ἀληθείας, ἀλλ' ἐξ ὧν ἂν ἕκαστοι δοκιμάζοι. Cl. Al. Strom. 5.

A multitudine abhorret maximè vera Philoſophia. Lact. Inſt. l. 3. c. 25. è Ciceron.

Vulgar heads, like many circles have ſo many circumferences that its impoſſible, to draw them to meet in one center. *Charron.*

Ubi major & hominum turba, major plerumq; eſt divinitatis injuria. Salv.

Beſides this, if they were ſuppoſable to have thoſe gifts, which were fit to try and judge rightly of a Miniſters ſufficiency; yet they cannot have power to authoriſe or ordein a Miniſter of Jeſus Chriſt; no more *than every* judicious man hath power to ſend an Embaſſador in his *Princes* name; or to make ſuch arbitrators and Judges; as he thinks fit *in other* mens buſineſs: This is a power only to be uſed and enjoyed by thoſe, to *whom it is given*, from him, who is *ſupreme*, as in the Church *Jeſus Chriſt* is: in whom the grand *power* of Ordination, which confers on man authority to diſpenſe holy myſteries in Chriſts name is originally ſeated, and from him derived and granted as a *grand Charter* or Commiſſion to his Apoſtles, firſt; and by them afterward exemplified and delivered to others, who being found fit for it, were aſſumed into, and inveſted with, the ſame delegated authority, as from Chriſt, and never given to the community of the people, at any time, or derivable from him in any degree of power Miniſteriall, be their gifts and graces never ſo good; Since this is a fruit of Chriſts wiſdom, munificence, and power toward his Church: an appointment full of holy order, and divine polity; *depending on* no private mens gifts or graces, but upon the good *will*, pleaſure, and power of *Jeſus* Chriſt himſelf, as he ſtands in the relations of *King*, *Prieſt*, and *Prophet* to his Church.

Now to whom Christ committed this great and sacred power, of ordeining a constant *succession of Ministers* in his name, and in what manner it was by them derived to others, I have already cleared (I hope) and other late-writers have done it too by Scripture, reason, and Ecclesiasticall *Catholick* Custom; In all which, it is evident, That the so much urged χειροτονία and χειροτονεῖν (which properly indeed signifies peoples *suffragating by stretching* forth of *hands* in publike and popular elections) is not to be urged by a *Criticall severity*, from the *Ethnick* sense of the word, to the *Churches* injury and confusion; Since the same word in sacred and Ecclesiasticall writings, as well as in others, is oft used in a sense which signifies nothing else but an *appointment* or *designation* made by any one or more to some speciall work and service, to which *God*, or *Christ Jesus*, or the Apostles, joyntly, or severally, or their *successors* the Bishops and Pastors of the Church in their severall precincts, are said, *to ordein*, or appoint, apart from any such *suffrage*, or autoritative influence of *the people*; Further than their sometimes *nominating* and *recommending* fit men to be *ordeined*, as *Acts* 6. 5. or else their comprobation and acceptance of those, who were by the Apostles, Elders, and Rulers of the Church ordeined, as Ministers over them; and this in Christs name; by a *divine authority*; which is for the peoples good, but not from them, as *a fountain*; nor *by them*, as any fit Pipes or Conduict, through which this *holy stream* of the Ministry, or the *pure waters* of the *Sanctuary* are to flow: So that I cannot look upon this late arrogant claim of the power of ordeining Ministers, as primarily belonging to the common people, or to other *Laymen*, as other than a fashion or opinion only befitting, and extremely resembling, those giddy, proud, and *preposterous fancies*, to which vulgar minds are subject (as *Tertullian* tels us) when once the reigns of Church *Discipline* are let loose; or some head-strong Schismaticks, get the bridle between their teeth: yea and it daily confutes it self; while the Authors and followers of it, are *continually* dividing and self confounding: So inconsistent is *error*, not only with *Truth* but with it self; easily mouldring with its own weight and weakness. And no wonder if the Lord prosper *not projects* arising from popular pride and presumption, and tending to the shame and confusion of true Religion: which no right reason, or order; no Scripture precept or patern; no Ecclesiasticall custom, or learned, and godly mans judgement, did ever allow, or can with any reason; as carrying with it all manner of *rusticall*, *unreasonable*, and *irreligious absurdities*; which are never wanting, where *vulgar passions* dwell, as infallibly they do, in the *meaner* sorts of men, pretend they to what *sanctity* they will; It will soon appear in how many and great defects they come short of that wisdom, gravity,

Pag. 143. &c. in the answer to the first Objection. See Dr. *Hammond* and Dr. *Tailor* of Ordination.

Porrexerunt manus, psephisma natum est. Tull.

Acts 14. 22.

Ordinationes earum quam temerariæ, tam inconstantes; Hodie Episcopus cras alius, hodie Presbyter qui cras laicus: Nam & laicis Sacerdotalia munera injungunt. Tertul. ad Hæret. c. 42.

Ad hæc opera blandi & submissi sunt. Cæterum nec suis præsidibus reverentiam exhibere noverunt. Id.

Ubi integra non est veritas, merito & talis est disciplina. Tertul.

vity, unpassionateness and impartiality, which *is necessary* to manage and order publike holy actions; and to confer a solemn Religious power to any in Christs name, to do Christs work, and in some sense to be in Christs stead. 2 Cor. 5. 20.

Best Christians are most modest.

Wise, humble, and truly *gracious Christians*, are of all men most remote from such bold and unsuitable *undertakings*; whereto having no call, from God, or the Church, they can never expect blessing on their adventures and rash endeavours: It satisfies them, that they have, as much influence in the ordeining and choosing of Ministers, as they are capable of, and is best for them and the Church: Yet, if it will please these Christians to fancy that they have some degree of power even in making their Ministers here in this Church, they may consider, that *neither Bishops* nor *Presbyters* in *England* made *any Ministers without the peoples* generall consent, expressed by those Laws and civill sanctions, which confirmed here, that divine order and constitution, which they saw *Christ had setled*, and the Church alwaies followed in ordeining lawfull Ministers, by that wisdom and authority which from the Apostles was derived in a constant succession of Bishops and Presbyters; who were for gifts of knowledge and judgement best able; and for lawfull power only able, by examination, benediction, and imposition of hands to consecrate any man a Minister, and confer the power of Holy Orders on him; who yet did, and doe this, as Delegates for the Church, but from Christ.

Ministers in England *ordeined with the peoples consent.*

If the power of choosing and ordeining Ministers were wholy left in Lay-mens hands, what a sorry choice (for the most part) would they make of the Man or Minister? how weakly would they examine his sufficiencies? how wildly would they *Institute* and *Ordein* him? what sad and slovenly hands would they impose on him? how soon would they *reject* and *disdain* those *Blocks* they had so hewen to be [th]eir *Mercuries*? and the *Idols* they had set up for their *Seers* and *Shepheards*, which many times can neither *see*, nor *hear*, nor rightly *understand* the *Mysteries* of *Religion*, nor the *Duties* of the *Ministeriall Function*? who sees not that *common people* are rather taken with a *familiar Rusticity* in a Minister, than with the best *learned abilities*; prefering, oft-times, a *confident Mechanick* to be their Teacher, before the *compleatest Divine* in a Country? They judge not what is *worthiest*, but what is *fittest* to their humours: rejoycing more in the *knack*, which they fancy, of Church *Power* and *Liberty*, (though it be to their prejudice) than in *what may really* advance their souls good, with *just Authority*; receiving more willingly one that comes in his own name, as gifted; or in their name, as chosen and ordeined by them, than if he comes in Christ name, and by that *right Ordination*, which hath alwaies been in the Church of Christ.

Vulgus vulgaria omnia impensius amat & amplectitur; Eminentiora & exortia potius admiratur quà amat; non raro odio & invidia & calumniis tanquam ostracismo suo prosequitur.

Certainly, *common people* may as well be their *own Preachers*, and

and Baptisers in course one after another; as *ordein* of themselves any one to be their Preacher; what hinders they may not all exercise that power, as Ministers, which they presume to give to another? which they cannot do, if they have not that power in themselves: and if they have all this power of the Keys as Stewards and Ministers of holy things, then 'tis not true that Christ hath given (τοὺς only *some*, but πάντας *all*) to be *Apostles*, *Pastors* and *Teachers*;

Ephes. 4. 11. 1 Cor. 12. 28. So that every part *in the* body may challenge to be *an eye*, and to have visuall power: which peice of *prophane confusion*, was never acted, or allowed in the Church, by any, that were worthy to be listed among *sober* Christians, or well-ordered Churches: who owned in all ages *their calling to be Christians*, and their gathering to the body of the Catholick Church (as parts and members) not to their own good nature, or preventive forwardness, making to themselves a Minister for Christ; but to those *true Ministers* pre-ordeined by the Church, and sent by Christ *to them*, while they sought *not after him*. These were in time, and order of nature, before the people, as spirituall Parents: by whose Ministry they were taught, Baptised, and made Christians; formed, guided, and governed in the things of God: so that the power of a Minister must needs flow from an *higher fountain*, Jesus Christ, and be conveyed by an *other Conduict* to the people, than *by the people*, Who can originally no more confer the power *of Ordination* to *Ministers*, than Children can give a *parentall* power, and authority to their Parents; or the vessels formed, can give a *formative* power and skill to the Potter.

12. *Peoples relation to their Ministers.*

The peoples *calling to themselves*, and electing a Minister, that is rightly ordeined; or accepting such an one, who is according to Laws both Civill and Ecclesiasticall sent among them, to *be their Minister*; is but a matter of *humane prudence* and *civill compact*, as to that particular place and people. An owning and acknowledging of that power, which he hath from Christ, by the hands of Church Rulers, to officiate, as a Minister of Christ for their good: It is not an induing with power, but meerly an *appropriating* of the exercise of his power *Ministeriall* to such a place, and such *a people*, for order and distinction sake; to avoyd *rambling*, and *confusion* in the Church; It is not any *conferring* of the Office, *function or habitude* of a Minister to any person, who is a Minister ordeined for the service of the *Catholick* Church, over all the world, wherever the *Gospell* may be Preached, the *Sacraments* administred, and other *holy offices* performed in a right and orderly way: Which *vast* power and authority, extending to all Nations,

Mat. 16. 15. and every *creature under Heaven*, capable of the Gospell, far exceeds any proportion of power, that can be imaginable, in any *handfull of private Christians* in one place, and can only be from the

Catholick

Catholick power of Christ, and that grand *Commission*, first given from Christ (to whom the *ends of the Earth belong*) to the *Order Ministeriall*, and by those of that Order *preserved* to this day, and never claimed in common, but by the irregularity, ignorance, or impudence of some few men, of *these last and perilous times.*

For how ever the *faithfull people*, in some places *during the times of primitive persecution* (which kept all sides more humble and holy) did oft-times express by their presence, their love and respect to their *Bishops and Presbyters*, by a *chearfull concurrence* with them in matters tending to the publique order and peace, and good government of the Church, so far as their discretion and modesty thought decent, and acceptable to their Governours and Pastors (In the Election of whom, they had something of approbative suffrages, *consent*, or *nomination*) yet did they never presume to challenge any *Power of Ordination*, to be in, or of themselves, but requested and obteined it, for those (whom they thus chose or approved) from the hands of such rulers in the Church, in whom the power Ministeriall was deposited, and *alwayes conserved.* It was enough for the *faithfull flock* to be *quietly present* at Ordination, to joyn in *prayer and fasting* with the Ordeiners, to attest the merit of those whom the Bishop with the Presbyters declared to be *Candidates*, or *Probationers*, and *Expectants* of the holy power of Ministry; which to confer, the common people have as much to do, as *Saul* or *Uzziah* had to *offer Sacrifice or Incense.*

Crysost. was accused for privately Ordeining. Ὅτι πολλὰς ἀμαρτ'εσε ἀνυ συνέδρης ἐχειροτόνησε. Phot. Bib. de Jo. Crysost.

Universus sexus & clerus à Sylvestro episc. ut Priscum & Theodorum ordinaret Diaconos proposuerunt. Con. Rom. 2. c.10. An:324.

Cornelius factus Epis. de Dei & Christi judicio, de cleri testimonio, & de plebis qui adsunt testimonio. Cypr. ep.52. *Sub populi assistentis conscientia fiebant ordinationes.* Cypr. l.1. ep.4. Ἀλλὰ μηδ' ἱερεὺς ἄνευ τῆς αὐτοῦ γνώμης πραττέτω τι, in Can. Apost. de epis.

What may be don in *cases extraordinary*, and of absolute necessity, or destitution, where Christians already baptised, and believing, cannot have a Minister *in a regular way*, I leave to *Gods direction*, and his *speciall dispensation*, who in *Cases extraordinary*, may extraordinarily manifest his pleasure. I am sure in the *hottest Persecution*, which *worried* and scattered the flock of Christ, when it was most innocent; the sheep neither chose, nor followed any other Shepheards, than those, which St. *Austin* calls most necessary for the Church, without which it cannot subsist, of whose *Ordination* and due authority they had assurance by constant Succession and according to the true *pattern in the Mount*; but they chose rather to supply the *necessitated absences of their true Ministers, Bishops, and Presbyters*, by prayer, fasting, meditation, reading, Christian conference, and mutuall exhortation, than to set up among themselves any Minister, by their own power, of popular *Ordination*; Yea (as the Jews would have done in the defect of holy and *Consecrated fire*)

In ordinandis Clericis fratres charissimi solemus vos ante consulere, & mores ac merita singulorũ communi consilio ponderare. Cyp lib.2. ep.5.

ἡ χειροτονία λαμβανέσθω μὴ γίνεσθαι· ἡ ἐκκλησίας ἐν τῷ ἐχέσθαι, ὡς ἐπεὶ παρόντων τῶν ἁγίων τὰς χειροτονίας γίνεσθαι. Theop. Alex.

Austin. ep. 180

ad Honoratum, Denies that Ministers may leave the flock destitute of *debitum & maximè necessarium Ministerium*, that Ministrie which is most due and necessary for their souls in times of danger and persecution, unless the office be supplied by some fit Ministers, while others by consent, or lot, fly to preserve a flock of Bishops and Ministers.

Christians rather contented themselves with the *Vote and desire, or purpose of Sacraments*, without the actuall perception of them, (or any other fruits proper to the Ministeriall function and power,) rather than *offer with strange and unholy fire*; where they could not have those Ministers, whose lips *had been touched with a coal from Gods altar*, that is ordeined by *a right Consecration*; which holy fire hath never yet been quite put out in the *Church of Christ*; nor *ever will be*, however some mens *petulancy* and presumption seeks to spit, or *piss* it out, by their irreligious, ingratefull, and contemptuous carriages against the office and due Succession of the Ministry.

Mat.28.19. Go therefore and teach all Nations, *&c.*
Joh.20.21. As my Father sent me, even so send I you.
Is.65.1.
Sub assistentiâ plebis conscientia, Cyp.

Humble and wise Christians willingly look back to the *Rock whence they were hewen*; and *the pit* whence they were digged: There they discern, That it was not the people, who made to themselves Ministers, but Ministers *sent* by Christ and the Apostles, every where made people Christians; They that sate in *darkness* had light brought to them, and were *found of God* by his messengers, as Shepheards sent to the lost sheep, *who sought not after God*; That the *holy succession of Ministeriall and Church power*, is indeed for the peoples good, and ought in some cases be carried with the peoples approbation, but it is not at all from the peoples pleasure, will, or vertue. That Jesus Christ, the Apostles, and all after Churches ever carried this Ministeriall and Church power in another way, distinct and apart from the people, yet most convenient for them, and most agreeable both to right reason, and to the order and honour of true *Christian religion*; which requires, that holy things be done *with all beautys of holiness*, by able and wise, and worthy men; to choose and appoint, or ordein whom, supposes as able at least, if not abler than they are, to *judge of them*; yet meer abilities as I have shewed will not serve neither, to give to others any commission as Ministers of holy things, unless the givers have first a grand *Commission*, or power of so doing, committed by others to them, which carries the strength of an originall divine Authority ascending to christ.

Which power, especially as to *Ordeining of fit Ministers*, being thus severed *from the people* for 1600. years, without any complaint made by the faithfull, or claim of right by reason or religion; there is no cause Christians should now listen to that fury, folly and faction, which would lay all in common: since nothing is brought by these Commoners to repeal the first divine enclosure of it, by the Institution of Christ, or to take away the prejudice of so many *Centuries* peaceable possession, as a peculiar to the Church Officers; those of the *Ministeriall Function*; In which there hath never been any

cessation.

cessation or interruption, as to legitimate succession, and constant Ordination.

Not that we deny (for any thing shall be granted to faithfull Christians, which is for their good) but that Christians of a *particular* parish or Congregation, may (if they have not otherwayes tyed themselves, and restrained things by Laws, with are the publiques, and so the *Peoples consent*; (as here for the most part in *England* it was) they may orderly choose, and desire such a man to be made a Minister or Bishop, and to be *over them in the Lord*, (as the people of *Millan* did St. *Ambrose*, yet a Lay-man and Magistrate;) Yet this is only so far, as first to *recommend him* to those, who have power to ordein him a Minister of the Catholick Church of Christ; next, to acknowledge that power and office Ministeriall to be rightly in him, as conferred to *him by just hands*. They may choose him, thus Ordeined, to exercise his Ministry and Office by particular care, mutuall relation, and joynt consent among them; But still this is as far from any such *αἵρεσις*, as some interpret it, as amounts to peoples giving *Ministeriall* power or Orders, as it is from Souldiers giving a Commission, when they only present by way of Commendation and Petition a worthy person to the Generall, or Commission officers to be made their Captain, which neither his worth, nor their willingness makes him to be without express Commission from the Generall under his hand and Seal. Nor is this any thing to the diminution of peoples rationall or religious liberties as Christians or men (which regulations and restraints they may not grudge to suffer, if Christ will have it so; as in this his will and command is most clear) but it is a fruit of *Christs wisdome*, and care for the faithfull peoples good, to avoyd infinite *inconveniences* and confusions, which constantly and unavoidably attend all things, that are transacted or touched almost by the common peoples *hands and heads*; who, though they mean and begin well, (as the Sea by modest lickings and slidings over the banks, which afterward its fury overbears with horrible inundations) yet are they never to be trusted with any thing, which a wise and good man would have well done.

People least able or fit to make or Ordein a Minister.

As then we see no Church power, especially as to Ordination and Ministry, is naturally in Christian people, who must be considered after their Ministers in time, and that order of nature which is between Effects and Causes, Children and Fathers, being first made Christians by Ministers whom they never Ordeined, nor so much as dreamt of or desired: So, nor can it in any reason be thought, by Christ afterward committed to them; least of all may they arrogate it to themselves, or involve it in any inferiour kind of civill and sociall power, which they may in some cases have; Since this power of sending

In causis fidei vel Ecclesiastici muneris eum judicare debere qui nec munere impar est, nec jure dissimilis, constantur assero. Dictum. Imperat. Valentini

& patris, quod Ambros. vehementer laudat, l.5. Ep.32.

sending and Ordeining Ministers to teach and rule the Church, is as far divided from that of peoples *choosing, approving, recommending*, or *accepting* one rightly ordeined, as the *waters above the firmament*, are from those beneath, in the Sea or Earth; what faithfull people may prudently do in private Church-matters, *within their sphere*, is rather a power *subjective*, obedientiall, and conformative (as that of the matter to the form) than *Mandatory, Operating*, and *Authoritative*; what they do discreetly, as to advise, chuse or agree with any Minister, is rather a common act of reason and polity as men, than proper to them as Christians in piety, and is so far commendable as they advise, chuse or agree in things of externall use, for their own good, yet no way troubling the Churches common welfare, order, and peace, nor *arrogating that spirituall and internall power Ministeriall*, either to make, or act as Ministers: which is from an higher principle, than Nature, Reason, or the will of man. People having no more power to Ordein, send, and Consecrate *true Ministers*, or Invest them in that Authority, than they had to *Anoint*, or *appoint the Messias*; and they may as well set up *a new Christ, and new Gospell*, as a new *Ministry*, and new *Ordination*; which Christ only hath once done, for all places and times, to the end of the world (at least as to ordinary cases, when right succession of power Ministerial may be had) and this without troubling, or interessing the common people in the business, to whom Ministers dispense not the peoples own; but the *grace of Christ*; of which among other gifts and graces as means, this is one; To give Apostles, *&c. Pastors* and *Teachers* to the Church; How can people primarily give power, to celebrate Mysteries, to Consecrate Elements, to confer Graces; which are so much above their thoughts, desires and merits? And who have no other way to order, regulate, and manage any of their Elections, undertakings, and affairs civill and secular, in what ever they pretend to have power, (which I think best, when it is least) but only that, of the *major part*, of *numbred voyces*, or by *the Pole*; If this doth not suffice to decide their affairs, then the more hands and *stronger party* (which is oft the worst) carries it, against the *other fewer and weaker*, which may be, and most-what are the *best and wisest*; Neither of which wayes of decisions (which are oft worse than that of *blind Lots and Chance*, (which many wise men rather chose, than *otherwaies* to determine matters by the uncertain and dangerous way of popular suffrages) can seem so *Infallible and divine*, as to induce a wise man to *acquiesce* in them, as Gods appointment; when very oft they come far short of those *rationall and morall proportions*, which a good man would require in judging of, and preferring alwayes, *the best and most deserving men*: sober men would never have matters of *Consequence* left to the most voyces of the vulgar, or

Joh.20.21. As my Father sent me, so send I you.

1 Pet. 4. 10. As good stewards of the manifold grace of God. *Eph. 4.11.* Christ gave some Apostles and Pastors, and Teachers. People may as well make Apostles as ordinary Pastors or Ministers, which are all from Christ.

or to their *Counter-scufflings* and *brutish contentions*, which oft shew that there is little of God in their heards and crowds, and clamors, more than may be in *storms and tempests*. As among the Cyclops where, [illegible].

How unlikely is it, that *Jesus Christ* should intrust these Plebs or people every where with power to chuse and ordein Ministers of his Church, in order to save souls? when the community have no other way in this Sacred concernment of mens souls, but such as they use in their most *trivial transactings* of humane affairs; As if it were all one power, which enables them to make a *Minister of Christs Church*, with that which makes a *Maior*, a *Bayliff*, or a *Constable*, in a Corporation. In those few experiments which the wisdome of this Church, or the lenity of some Patrons hath thought fit to give men of *Popular Elections* of their Minister, I have known, where a Parish rejecting a very able man offered them, have with great earnestness desired, and with as much greediness as the Whale did swallow *Jonah*, received a Minister of far less worth, who was of their own choise, yet within two or three years they have cast him out on dry land, and with *scorn* reproached and rejected him, who was so lately their delight and darling.

The greatest enemy of the Gospell of Christ, and of the reformed Religion would wish no *greater advantages* against true Religion, than to have the *Ordination*, choyce and appointment of Ministers left to *the Common people* in every place, which will soon be filled with as much ignorance, fury, faction, error and confusion, as either *Devills* or *Antichrists* would desire, whereby to make *Bethel Bethaven*, and to set up *Babylon* in the midst of *Jerusalem*; Yea, the peoples very *bare Election* of one rightly Ordeined to be their Minister, oft occasioneth very great *thoughts* of heart, and uncomfortable divisions, between both the people in their parties, and the Minister so chosen by some, but not by others; To prevent which inconveniences, and somtime mischiefs, the wisdome both of Church and State, had by consent of all estates, People, Peers, and Prince, setled that in a far quieter and safer way of *Presentations*, to the content of Patrons, Ministers, and all sober Christians.

I may then conclude, that as Bishops and Presbyters joyntly ordeining others to that holy Office, whereto themselves were *formerly Consecrated*, did as much, and no more than *was their duty* to Christ and the Church; So neither the *Pope of old*, had beyond his Diocess, nor *the People* now, have any thing to do with this *Ordinative power* which duly is in the Ministeriall order of the Church, by which an holy succession of *able, true, and faithfull Ministers*, Bishops and Presbyters, hath been continued in all Churches, and as yet is *in this Church*; What ever the Papall pride and usurpation as any *way eminently Antichristian*, in former or later times; or *Schis-*

matick and unruly people now, as the *many Antichrists*, in the Diametral distances of their errors, (being the two poles of *Church pride*, but not the axis of *Church power*,) have or do pretend, as if all Church power were in them, or from them ; it was and is all nothing else but vain shadows, and meer mistakes arising from the ignorance, darkness, connivence, *licentiousness* and *superstition* of times, and is no more *prejudiciall* to the true power of Ordeining Ministers, (which is from Christ only committed to *the order and fraternity of Pastors and Governours in every Church*, as hath been proved) than if some one or more, *cunning fellows*, should perswade *credulous and silly people*, whom they find or lead into the dark, or else blind them; that they were indeed *stark blind*, and had no power of themselves to see, or open their eyes, but must wholly be led by their guidance, without having any sight, or benefit of the Sun : These poor seduced men, have no more to do in point of relieving themselves, and confuting so *gross Impostors*, but only to open their eyes freely, and to use the light of that Sun, which they easily and clearly see shining over all the world; which is not more evident to sense, than this Truth is to judicious Christians, That the power of Ordeining Ministers hath alwayes, and only been in the Pastors, Bishops, and Guides of the Church, who both ruled well, and also laboured diligently in the Word and doctrine.

And since true Christians in this *Reformed Church of* England, both Ministers and people, have been so happy in this Church, as to be delivered from the *Romish superstitions*, and *Papall usurpations* ; they have now no cause to be less *cautious*, or more patient to be gulled, and deluded by *popular seductions*, lest the *second error* be worse than the first ; Inasmuch, as the furies and confusions of the vulgar are more dangerous than any errors *of Popes, or Bishops, or Presbyters*, are like to be; as *Earthquakes* are more dreadfull and pernicious than *Eclipses*, or the *Cloudings* of the lights of Heaven. The lights of the Church may *recover their lustre and vigour in due time*; nor do they ever shine so dark, but they afford a competent light, to shew the way to Heaven ; But *popular precipitancies*, and *licentious extravagancies of the vulgar*, are likest to overthrow all religion ; and *bury* all Christianity by Gothick and *Mahumetan methods*, in Atheism, Illiterateness, Confusion, and Barbarity ; For, as they have least *skill in them*, and no authority given them, to order and rule *Church affairs* ; so they have most passion, and unbridled violence in them : least able to distinguish between the abuse and use of things ; between gold and dross ; between what is of God, or of Man ; when once they have got power, and say that they know not Exod. 26. 1. what is *become of their Mosesses* ; their divinely appointed guides, their duly ordeined Bishops, and Ministers ; the first thing they

they do, is to *make themselves molten Images*, and contribute both their *Earings* and their *Ears*, their hearts and hands to those Calves, which they set us for *Tamuzzes*, or *Images* of jealousie and abominations, whereby to provoke the God of heaven to wrath; to reproach the honour of Christ, to affront the true Ministers, and to make the Reformed religion and this Church to become an hissing and astonishment to all round about. *A wise man of Spain sayd*, It is better in Church, as well as in places of Civill power and Judicature, to prefer corrupt men, than weak and foolish; The one is as a thief in a Vineyard, who will only take ripe grapes till he is satisfied; the other as an Asse which eats ripe and green, crops the Vines, treads down much with his heels, and when his belly is full, tumbles among them. Ezek. 8. 3.

13. *The vertue of holy Ordination.* Object.

But our *Antiministeriall Adversaries* are still ready *with scorn and laughter* to demand, What can Ministers, *either as Bishops or Presbyters*, confer more than other Christians, in the *point of Ordination*? What vertue or charm is there in *the imposing of their hands*, or in their prayers; by which to add to any mans ministeriall gifts and graces; or to invest any man in a way of *Church power*, more than is in any other Christians? whose *gifts and graces* may be equall, or exceeding, their *Infirmities far less*, than many Ministers are? What power can they have to give *the holy Ghost*, as they expresse in the form of Ordination? yea, whence do they challenge, as of right the Name of Clergy-men, as peculiar to their tribe and Calling; where as all the *Lords people are his lot, and his inheritance, and God is theirs*; Nor ought they contemptuously, as by way of diminution to be called *Lay-men*, or *the Laity*, Since they are all spiritually anointed, and chosen of God, to be Kings, Priests, and Prophets?

Answ. *Of the Laity and Clergy.*

Clem. Rom. ep. ad Cor. p. 53. Ὁ λαϊκὸς ἄνθρωπος τοῖς λαϊκοῖς προστάγμασι δέδεται. The Layman is bound up by Lay commands to keep his rank. *Igna. epist:* frequently. Tertul. *Hodiè*

I Answer to this last scruple first, as least, being not so much a beam, as a mote in some mens tender eyes, which like *Leahs*, are easily offended: As for the names then of *Clergy* and *Laity*, in which the *Nasuter Criticks* of this age, sent something of pride in the *Ecclesiasticks or Ministers*, and of despiciency toward the *faithfull people*, (who are to be animated, and flattered any way against the Ministry of the Church;) They may know that this distinction between the *Clergy* and *Laity*, hath been used in the Church, from the very first *Primitive times*, as the antient Fathers, Councils, and the Histories of the Churches both Greek and Latin do testifie; nor was the one ever intended or upbraided for a *badge of vanity* to the Ministry; nor the other imputed for a *brand of scorn to the people*; The piety and charity of those times were not at leisure, thus to (λογομαχεῖν) to stumble at straws. I am sure as they antiently were, so they still are usuall notes of difference in point of office and duty between Ministers,

nisters and people, not only in our ordinary Language; yea, in the exacter stile of *our Laws*, (which give both *reall* and *nominall* distinctions with the greatest authority;) Nor are they at all against the Scripture sense and meaning (if they be not just to its words,) since the *word of Christ* hath evidently placed as limits of office, so *Marks* and names of distinction between the one and the other, as *Pastor* and *Flock*, *Doctor* and *Disciple*, *Ruler* and *ruled*, &c. Yea, and we may easily gather from the Scripture dialect, that as the faithfull people are in generall (*Clerus*, *Ecclesia*) the lot or portion and heritage of the Lord; So the Ministers are *Clerus Ecclesiæ*; A lot, heritage and portion given by the Lord to the Church, and set apart, or Consecrated by the Church to the Lords speciall service; λειτουργούντων, *Acts* 13. to serve the Lord, and the Church, in holy publick ministrations, as the Apostles first did; into whose order *Mathias* was by Lot chosen to supply the place of *Judas Iscariot*, *Acts* 1. To which end Ministers in an holy Succession have ever been placed over the people in the name of Christ, by the power of his Holy Spirit; yet *Good Ministers* disdain not to be reckoned among Gods *People*, as children of the same *Spirituall Father*, and brethren in the same Family or houshold of Faith; nor will any *humble Christians*, (being not in holy orders,) affect to be *called Clergy men*, by a confusion of language; or disdain to be called Gods commons, or *Laymen*, which hath a sober, Christian, and charitable sense, in the dialect of those Christians, who know how to call and account their *true Bishops and Ministers*, as *Fathers*, *Instructers*, *Overseers*, and *Guides of the Church*, &c. These names then, or distinctive titles do but fairly follow (according to the use and nature of words) and decently express those things, which the mind of Christ in the Scripture, and all Custom or use of the Church have distinguished for order sake.

Presbyter qui cras Laicus. Laicis Sacerdotalia munera injungunt. De præ. ad hær. c. 42. & *sæpe alibi.* St. Cyprian often. So *Clemens* of *Alexand.* *Differentiam inter ordinem & plebem constituit Ecclesiæ autoritas, & honor, per ordinis consessum sanctificatus à Deo*, Tertul. de exh. ad Cast. c. λαϊκοῖς οὐκ ἐπιτρέπομεν ποιεῖν τι τῶν ἱερατικῶν. Const. Apost. l. 3. c. 10. ὡς δεῖν λαϊκὸς, ἐνιαύτου ἐν τῷ ἀμβῶνι. 1. Vid. Dr. Prideaux *Prælect.* *Consuetudo certissima loquendi magistra, utendumque planè sermone ut nummo cui publica est forma.* Quintil. Inst. l. 1. c. 6. *Sermo constat ratione, vetustate, authoritate, consuetudine.* Id. *Vetera verba majestas & religio quædam commendat.* Id.

The same supercriticall men will boggle at the words, *Trinity*, *Three Persons*, and *Sacraments*; which are not in the *letter*, but in the *sense*, and truth of the Scripture; And certainly no religion forbids us to adopt *convenient and compendious words*, to the Churches use, since we do safely translate the whole originall Scriptures to any ordinary languages, in which most Christians may best use them, not in the literall words, but in the Intellectuall sense or mind of God. A *strife about words*, and *syllabicall scruples*, fits only women or children, or peevish passionate men: As the Arrians of old, who caviled much at the words (ὁμοούσιος, and θεοτόκος) whose *syllables* were new, but their sense old, orthodox and sound, expressing the same divine

De verbis contendere non est curare quomodo error veritate vincatur sed quomodo tua dictio alterius dictioni præferatur. Aust. de doct. Christ. l. 4. c. 28. *Quid est contentiosius quam ubi constat de*

divine Nature in Christ the Son, with the Father; and that our *Emanuel*, who was born of the virgin *Mary*, was both God and Man; But this quarrel about names and words, is a very tedious impertinency to those Christians, whose serious piety studies only this, by apt and usuall words, to comprehend and express, *the truths and orders of Religion*; who are ready alwayes so to give to each other *the right hand* of Charity and Unity, as members of the same body, whose head is Christ; as yet to preserve that order and authority in the Church, which is divinely Instituted, and is as necessary for the Church, as it is for the body to have head, eyes, and mouth, distinct from other parts *of less honour*, yet not less *usefull in their place*. As for this pretended grievance then of these words, *Clergy* and *Laity*; We desire not to quarrell farther with our Adversaries, and we shall not need to dispute with others that are wise and humble, only we *pitty the simplicity of people*, who are thus easily cheated, and scared, by some sophistry, when they are told by their great scrupulosity, and censorian gravity, that words are as bad as Spels, that whatever tearms or Names, are not in the Scriptures, (as they have them translated) are not the speech of *Canaan*, but the language of the beast: Thus these severe Momusses; Thus the Antiministeriall factors for error, ignorance, and confusion. These are among the other small artifices used by those *miserable Rabbyes*, who to ingratiate with the vulgar, and lead *disciples after them*, are content to take away the antient marks of bounds, and known *distinction of names, between Minister and People*, that so people may take the greater confidence to cast quite away both the *name and thing*, the holy Ordination with all distinction of Office and Function Ministeriall in the Church; which if I can solidly maintain against *these underminers* of Religion, despisers of Ordination, and vastators of all true ministry, I doubt not, but I and others may still use these Names of Clergy and Laity without sin or scandall to any sober and good Christians.

re, certare de nomine. Aust. ep. 1. 74.

De verbis & syllabis intemperantius litigare solent, qui res ipsas & Ecclesiæ pacem negligunt. Sub λογομαχίας umbra φιλονικίαν & κακοτεχνίαν, suam occultare & dissimulare student; quod et Arrianorum pertinax astutia olim fecit. Amb. lib. de fide, & Jeron. de Arrian. Hyp.

Insignis est indolis in verbis verum amare non verba. Aust.

Sic vigeat humilitas ut non minuatur Authoritas. Aust.

1 Cor. 12. 23.

Error est honestius magnos in loquendo duces sequi. Quintil. Orat. Inst. l. 1. c. 6.

To the main therefore of the *Objection* which is made against 16
the vertue and efficacy of *Ordination*, by the Catholick and Antient way of Bishops and Presbyters, which they so slight, I answer; That at the same rate of prophane, and *Atheisticall reasonings*, they may as well dispute (as *Julian* would have done, and those *Scoffers daily do* (which are foretold should be *in the later dayes*) *What vertue is there in the water of Baptism*, more than any other, by which to regenerate a sinner, to wash away sins, to seal comforts, to confer grace, to represent the blood of Christ, of which a man may meditate every time he sees any water, or washeth his hands? Hence the mean esteem, and contempt indeed, with proud and presumptuous Catabaptists have against that holy Mysterie of Baptism,

Prophane minds prone to cavil at all holy mysteries, aswel as the Ordination of Ministers.

2 Pet. 3. 4.

which all Churches, in all ages, have used with reverence and comfort, according to Christs Institution, and the Apostolicall custome. So also the spirituall pride of those prophane Cavillers will argue, what efficacy can there be in *the Bread and Wine*, at the Lords Supper, more than in other of *the same Elements* at our ordinary Tables, and in every Tavern? What doth the form of Consecration, by the words of Christ and prayers add to them, or alter them? Nay, (since the *blasphemous boldness* of proud and wicked men, will count *nothing of outward form sacred*) no wonder if by the *same contradictive spirit*, they quarrel at not only the Humanity or flesh, but also the Majesty, and divinity of our Saviour Jesus Christ; and seeing the outward meanness, poverty, and ingloriousness of his life and death, many of them scarce own him for a *Saviour*, or for the true Messias; And no further than is agreeable to their Seraphick fancies; by which they labour (after the like fondness of some in antient times) to turn all the *solidity of Truth*, the *certainty of History*, and the *Sacredness of the mystery of Jesus Christ*, (*God manifested in the flesh*) into nothing but Familisticall whimseys, empty notions, and sublimity of nonsense; As if there were more light of Religion in their modern Meteors and gross illuminations, than in the Sun, Moon and Stars, in Scripture, Ministers, and Christians of old; whereas the same *holy and humble faith*, by which *true Christians* do believe Jesus to be the promised Messias, the Son of God, and only Saviour of the world, (notwithstanding all that blind Jews, or proud Gentiles object against him) doth also teach them, to receive with all *humble thankfulness*, and religious *reverence*, all those holy orders, duties, and Institutions, (in their plainess, poverty, and simplity) which Christ hath setled in his Church, and which the Church hath continued according to his word in all humble fidelity. Nor doth the meaness of *outward appearance*, or any naturall and civill disproportions which appear to humane sense or reasonings, any way prejudice, or weaken the faith, devotion, duty and obedience of those, *who live by faith*, and look with the *eye of faith*, and act with the *hand of faith*, in all those *holy offices and Ministrations*, which are grounded on the word of Christ.

Against whom *Irenæus* disputes.

Κρεῖσσον ἡμεῖς ἐν τοῖς λεγομένοις μετὰ τῆς ἀληθείας τῷ πτωχεύειν ἢ περιττεύοντι κομψεύειν, τῶν ῥητόρων διάκενα. Naz. Or. 23. *de Trinitatis Myst.*

τὸ φαινόμενον λιτὸν καὶ ἀκαλλώπιστον, τὸ δὲ κρυπτόμενον θαυμαστὸν καὶ ὑπερφυέστατον. Naz.

Heb. 11. 1. Faith is the evidence of things not seen, &c.

To judge of *Christian Mysteries or Ministries*, by common sense, or carnall reasonings, as *Sarah* did of the Promise, is to make Christian Religion most ridiculous, mean and *insignificant*, whose vertue and efficacy, as the faith of *Abraham*, depends not upon any *naturall*, *morall*, or *politique powers*, faculties, habits, abilities or actions, that are in, or flow from, *the persons* acting in them, and dispensing of them; nor the *Elementary* sensible natures of the things used in them; But meerly upon that *divine vertue*, and power of Christ Instituting such holy things, as duties to be done, to such a religious

Nemo judicet humano modo quod divino geritur sacramento, nemo mysteria cœlestia discutiat ratione humana. Crysso. S. 148.

Κρεῖσσον ἐστὶ τῆς διὰ τῶν λογισμῶν καταλήψεως ἡ πίστις. Bas. in ep. 43.

gious end, by such men, and means, in such a manner, and no other; and all this *in his Name*; that is, meerly as an Institution of *his divine power and wisdome*, and whence they have their *efficacy*, and also *authority*; not *indeed* among affected Novelists, curious speculatists, proud hypocrites, or contentious worldlings, but among humble, devout, and *true believers*, who are also doers of the will of God in all things, holy, just and morall, who *knowing* what belongs to the life *and obedience of Faith*, disdain not to submit themselves to any way and order, seem it never so *weak and simple*, that *Christ* hath appointed, to them and his Church; who alone can make *weak*, *foolish*, and *contemptible things to be powerfull* and *effectuall*, through the concurrence of his Spirit and grace, to those great and holy ends, for which they are by him Instituted in his Church.

τῆς θείας φύσεως καὶ τῆς θείας οἰκονομίας τρόπος ἀνέφικτόν τι ἔχουσιν. Just. Ma. de fid. *Tota ratio facti est potentia facientis.* Aust. Greg. Nis. *Vita Mosis. carnem agni licuit comedere,* ἐνεργῶς ἐσθίειν, *Ossa vero non confringenda credenda non curiosius discutienda sunt dei mysteria, &c.* 2.Cor.2. *In multis scientia Pauli à disputatione transit in stuporem, cujus tanta erit præsumptio, ut disserendo existimet aperienda potius quam silentio miranda?* Amb.voc.l.2. 1 Cor.1.27.

So that it is not any *Magick charm*, or *Enchantment*, as these *prophane minds scornfully deride*, which makes the common elements to become Sacraments, by that *solemn Consecration*, which is rightly performed by one, that is from Christ appointed *as a minister of holy things*. No more is it any *fantastick and imaginary power*, which of a *common man*, makes a *Minister of the Gospel, by due Ordination*; which is a *setting apart* of some fit and worthy men from the ordinary capacities, comon relations, and humane *affairs* of the world, either as naturall or civill, and *Consecrating* them by prayer, and imposition of hands, and power of the Spirit, to the peculiar service of Christ, and his Church, in *the holy Ministry*; And this not to be done by any one, that please themselves to be at once *both apes*, and *hypocrites in religion*, to act *a part*, and make a *Stage-play* of holy Ordination, by a *popular presumption*; but only by such as Christ hath fitted *with gifts*, and enabled with *power* of his Spirit, to *Consecrate and Ordein* a succession of Ministers to *the service of the Church*, being themselves formerly ordeined, and so invested *with that great and holy power of order*. So that it is the *powerfull Word and Spirit of Christ, as the King and Prophet of his Church*, which commands the duty, *establisheth the Order*, and gives the blessing, as in other, so in this of Ordination. In obedience to which, *true and excellent Christians*, willingly captivate all *their high imaginations*, and subdue every *thought*, which exalts it self against *the rule of faith*, the word of Christ, pulling down all *the strong holds of proud and humane reasonings*; Submitting to every holy *Ministration*, and true Minister in his office, *for Christs sake*; from whose grace, Spirit, and promise, they expect, and find that blessing, comfort, and inward peace, which is only to be had in Christs way; which depends meerly on *his divine will*

Pantomimi sunt in religione Hypocritæ; quo minus sancti sunt, eo magis simulant, παρεῖναι *studentes, non* εἶναι.

In ordinatione Deus est causa principalis, & homo instrumentalis; Deus vocat primario Ecclesia mediante, & declarante quem à Deo vocatum præsumit. Gerard.

2 Cor.10.5.

will and power, which changeth not the *nature of things*, but their relation, and use, to an higher and spirituall end; requiring *faith*, humility, reverence, obedience, and thankfulness in every believer or worshipper.

17. *Right Ordination Efficacious relatively and spiritually, not physically.*

Idem valet deputati ac deputantis autoritas, in quantum deputatur. Reg. jur.

So that although *Ordination of a Minister* to the peculiar service of Christ and the Church, by such as have the right and power by uninterrupted succession duly derived to them, and to be derived orderly from them in all ages, do not add to the *Naturall, Morall*, or *Spirituall* gifts and indowments of men, as they are *personall and inherent*, any more than the office of *Embassadour*, or *Judge*, or *Commander* doth, in *Civill*, or *Military* employments, confer any thing *to the inward abilities* of the man; yet, that honour and authority rightly derived to any one, invests him with a *relative*, yet *reall* power, qualification, and capacity of doing, or declaring the *will of another*, to the same validity, as if the *principall* himself did it; by whose *authority* alone any other is sent, and enabled to effect those things which none other can presume to perform without vanity, sin, and presumption, who hath not that *gift, power*, or *authority* consigned to him.

The right Ordination then of Ministers, in the way *of an holy succession* in the Church of Christ, hath in Religion, and among true Christians, these *holy* uses, and clear *advantages* peculiar to it.

1. *It confirms the truth of the Gospel.*
2 Cor. 8. 23.

Multi barbarorum in christū credunt sine charactere vel attramento: scriptam habentes in cordibus suis per spiritum salutem, et veterum traditionem diligentes custodientes, quam Apostoli tradiderunt iis, quibus committebant Ecclesias, cui ordinationi assentiunt multæ gentes, &c. Iren. l. 3. c. 4.

1. First, as to the main end, the *Glory of God, and the saving* of mens souls, (by their believing and obeying *this testimony* of all true Ministers, that Jesus Christ is *the only Saviour of the world*;) Nothing gives a more *clear and credible testimony to the glory and honour of Jesus Christ, and to truth of the Gospel*, than this uniform and constant *succession of Ministers*, by a peculiar *Ordination and authority even from Christ himself in person*, who at first began this Ministry, and sent some speciall men as his messengers to bear witness of *him in all the world*; that so men might believe, not only what is written in the word before it was, or as it *is now written*; but also as that glorious truth hath been thus testified every where, and in every age, by *chosen* and peculiar men, as a cloud of most credible witnesses, whom thousands at first did, and to this day, do hear *preaching*, and see them *Celebrating* the holy mysteries of Christs Gospell, who never had or used any written word, nor ever read it, and for the most part believed, before ever they *saw any part of the Bible* (which the constant Ministry of the Church, hath under God, hitherto preserved) chiefly upon the *testimony*, and tradition, or record of those, that were ever thought (and alwayes ought to be) most able and faithfull men, specially appointed, by Christ in his Church, as a perpetuall order, and succession of Witnesses, to testifie of him, and to minister in his Name to the end of the world; This *walking Gospel, and visi-*

ble

ble Ministry, consisting, *as it ought*, of wise, and worthy men, (who have good reputation, for their piety, learning, and fidelity,) running on to all generations, is as a continued *stream* from the blessed Apostles, who were the first witnesses immediatly appointed by Christ to hold forth his name and Gospell to the world. *Acts* 1.8. which, though never so far off in the decurrence of time from *the fountain*, yet still testifies and *assures* all wise men, that there is certainly a *divine fountain* of this ministeriall power, and so of Evangelicall mysteries and truth; which rose first from Christ, and which hath constantly run, as may appear by the enumeration, or induction of particular descents in all ages, in this *Channel* of the Apostles, and their successors, the Bishops and Presbyters *of the Church*; for the better planting, confirming, and propagating of the Gospell to all Nations and times; As a duty, charge, or office, *injoyned* by divine command to some men, and lying *ever as a calling on their consciences*; Hereby evidently declaring the *divine wisdom*, and Fatherly *care* of Christ, for the good instruction, and order of his Church, in his personall *absence*; In that he hath not left the Ministry of the Gospell, and his holy Institutions (which he would have alwaies continued for the gathering & edifying of his Church,) to a *loose* and *arbitrary* way, *among the rabble* and promiscuous heards of men; (which would soon have made *Evangelicall truths* seem but as *vagrant fables*, and generall, uncertain *rumors*; which run without any known and sure authority in the *common chat*, and arbitrary report of the vulgar; by which in a short time both the order, beauty, honour, purity and credit of Truth is easily lost among men;) This holy and successionall ordination of the Evangelicall Ministry gives great proof, and demonstration, as of Christs personall presence as chief Bishop and Minister of his Church; so of the fulfilling of Christs word, and the veracity of his promise, after his departure *to be with them* that were sent and went in his name, to the end of the world; That the *gates of hell* neither yet have, nor ever shall *prevail* against the Church: While it carefully preserves a right *succession*, holy order, and authority of true Ministers, the devill despairs of ever overthrowing *Christian Religion* in its reformed profession in any Country. Down with the order, and sacred power, and succession of the Ministry, and all will in a short time be his own.

Minister est verbum visibile, ambulans Evangelium.

Mat.28.

Mat.16,18.

2. It is also a *notable evidence* of the *Churches* care and fidelity in all ages; not only in the preservation of the *oracles of the word*, which it hath done, but also of a *constant holy Ministry* to teach and explain them; Also to celebrate those *holy mysteries* which are divinely annexed to the word, as seals to confirm the faith of Christians; And lastly to exercise that *wholsome discipline* for

2. Evidenceth the Churches care.

Agnitio vera est Apostolorum doctrina & an-

for terror or comfort, the power of which is chiefly in the Pastors and Rulers of the Church. As it is then for the honour of the wisdom of Christ in the originall, to have instituted such holy mysteries and such a Ministry, so it is for the honour of the *Church*, in the succession of all ages to have thus preserved them and it self, in that order which becomes *the family of Christ*; which had come far short of any well ordered family, if the Father and Master of it, Jesus Christ, had left every servant to *guess at his* duty, and all of them to *scramble* what part they list of *employment, aliment*, and enjoyment; but the Lord Christ, (as every wise Master doth) hath appointed, and his Church hath preserved to this day constant *Stewards*, and dispensers of *holy things in his house-hold*; whose duty tis to be faithfull to their Masters *profit*, and credit; to do their *duty*, and to *maintain* that place and *authority*, in which the Lord hath set them; nor is it any thing of a *pious easiness*, but an impious baseness, in them as Bishops and Ministers voluntarily to desert their station, and to suffer every one to usurp upon them, and to do what they list: Nor is any thing more intolerable, than the rudeness, riot, and impudence of those inferior servants, who pretending Christian liberty, and not induring *those officers* and Ministers whom the Master hath orderly placed over them; neither will they long indure the *Lord* or Master himself to rule over them; we read, *Mat.* 21. 38, They kill the Son, who first beat and shamefully intreated the servants which were sent.

tiquus Ecclesiæ status in universo mundo, & charactere corporis Christi secundum successiones Apostolorum: quibus illi eam quæ est in unoquoq; loco Ecclesiam tradiderunt: & Scripturarum sine fictione custodita tractatio plenissima, lectio sine falsatione & secundum Scripturas expositio legitima & diligens: sine periculo, & sine blasphemia. Irenæus. l. 4. c. 43. *In Ecclesia Catholica hactenus inviolabili observatione tenetur qua potissimum Catholici ab Hæreticis discriminantur, nimirum, ut cujusvis meriti atque præstantiæ vir fuerit non sua sponte prædicationis munus suscipiat; sed expectet donec ab Ecclesia mittatur, ab eaque sacris functionibus initietur, sicque initiatus prædicationi Evangelii mancipetur.* Baronius An. Anno Christi. 44.

But thirdly, *as to the persons* duly ordeined; This holy *Ordination* gives a reall divine power; which is necessarily *to be delegated* and derived from Christ, (since no man hath it, *in*, and *of himself*, or of *any will* of men) by which he is enabled to perform those duties, which Christ only hath injoyned in his word to be done, and to be thus done, by such men, and in such a manner, and no other, 1 *Tim.* 5. 22. *Lay hands suddainly on no man*, (i. e.) by way of Ordination: *Ergo*, no man is of that office, or hath that authority and power till ordeined, be his parts and gifts never so great and good. So 2 *Tim.* 2. 2. *These things commit to faithfull men (who may be able to teach others) ergo*, some peculiar Commission must be given to these, and to no other, to perform Ministeriall duties with authority. Such are those, of *making Disciples*, by *Preaching* the Gospell; by distinguishing from others; and also confirming, and uniting together among themselves in holy Communion, those Disciples, with the holy *seals of Baptism* and the *Lords*

Supper;

Supper; To edify, confirm, and preserve them by *teaching*, reprooving, praying for them, comforting, guiding, governing, *binding* and *loosing*, by the use of that *power* of the Keys, which is committed only to them, both in *doctrine* and *discipline*; doing all things toward penitents and impenitents, believers and unbelievers, not magisterially but ministerially, as from Christ, and for the Churches good; yet not precariously, and arbitrarily, or depending on mans pleasure, but *autoritatively* and conscienciously as doing the work of the Lord: knowing the power they have received of the Lord; the duties enjoyned them; the care required in them, the account to be exacted of them, as to the *Stewardship* of the souls solemnly *committed to their* care: which is done by that χάρισμα or *ministeriall gift of the holy Ghost*, which Christ gave to the Apostles. *John* 20.22. and by their hands, (as by St. *Pauls* to *Timothy*, 2 *Tim*.1. 6.14) to others, and so to a perpetuall succession.

Tit.2.15.

Iren.l.4.c.43. *Episcopatus successionem ab Apostolis habentes charisma veritatis certū acceperunt. ubi charismata domini posita sunt ibi discere oportet veritatem: apud quos est successio ab Apostolis, & sanum ac irreprobabile sermonis.* Cap. 45.

1 Tim.4.14.

18. *The holy Spirit given in right Ordination, how.*

For without this *gift or power of the holy Spirit of Truth*; whose property it is to lead the faithfull into all truth, no man is *truly* a Minister of holy things in the Church; So that it is a pittifull *piece of ignorance*, or putid *scurrility, and profaness*, for any that profess *Christianity*, much more for those that pretend to be *Ministers* in the Church, to slight, and expose to vulgar scorn, that passage used, as of *antient times* in all Churches, so in the Church of *Englands* manner of *ordeining* Ministers; *Receive ye the holy Spirit*: As if this were a meer *mockery*, and *insignificancy* in point of any sanctity conferred: When it is expressed to be meant (as it ever *was in the Church* understood) not of sanctifying graces, infused qualities, or habits of *inward holiness*, (which are immediatly from God, and not by man to be conferred; nor from man to be communicated to another; nor do they invest any one, that hath them, *in any Church office* or publick power over others (for then every holy man and woman should have this power:) but it is only meant of those *peculiar gifts*, or *powers of the* holy Spirit, which are properly *ministeriall* and *officiative*; as from Christ, and in his name: not by internall infusion, but by *externall* separation or *sanction*; *not enduing* with *grace*, but investing *in a new relation* and authority, distinct from the common Christians, duty, place, and officers of charity, *&c*. which are as parchment, wax, and writing, usefull in their kind; but not valid, as to any conveyance, till sealed, subscribed, delivered and witnessed, as the act and deed of the conveyer; who lawfully hereby confers to an other his right and power of acting, possessing, or enjoying, *&c*. So by a form of such Commission

Eph.4.8.

Commission or delegation, as Christ instituted, *that power* and ministeriall *gift of the holy Spirit* is continued, which was first committed to the Apostles by Christ; who only would do it: Nor can this power be understood so much for *extraordinary miracles*, (which were to cease;) as for that *ordinary Ministry*, which was to continue, as necessary for the Church in all ages: This power or gift of the Holy Ghost, as *ministeriall and officiating* in Christs name, as that of miracles, may be where there is no sanctifying grace; as was *in Judas*, and probably *in Demas*, and others; who might be *sheep*, as to their profession, and *shepheards*, as to their office, or *Episcopacy* (of which *Judas* had a part and fell from it) and *yet wolves*, as to the inward *habits and graces*. When the *Spirit of* Paul *was* joyned with the Corinthian Ministers and believers in excommunicating the *incestuous persons*; it was not the sanctifying Spirit or grace of the Apostle; but that *ministeriall power*, which he had eminently in and joyntly with the Church: The power and Spirit of Christ as it is given, so received in right Ordination, by *every true Minister*, that is worthily promoted; not *as to grace*, and inward vertue, of which man judgeth not; but as to *office and relative* power from Christ, in the publike service or Ministry to his Church. As every *officer civill*, or military that hath commission, acts, *in the Spirit*, name, and power of those, by whom authority is primarily derived to them. In this sense and to this use *the Spirit of Moses* was put on the 70. Elders. *Num.* 11.25. and *Elias on Elisha*. 2 *Kings* 11.9.

Acts 1.17.

1 Cor. 5.4. In the name of our Lord Jesus Christ, when ye are gathered together, and my Spirit with the power of our Lord Jesus Christ, &c.

3. Yea further, I doubt not; but the *solemn* and right *manner of Ordination by fasting*, prayer, and *imposition of hands*; (wherein the Spirit of the ordeiners, and the Christians present, with the ordeined, joyn together in his behalf to God,) is a very *great and effectuall* means, to indue the *ordeined*, in some sense, with an other Spirit; not only, as to power, but as to the increase of ministeriall gifts, which fit him to receive, and use that authority; yea, and for the *strengthning*, exciting, and *enlarging* those *sanctifying graces*, by which he is more fitted for, and prospered in, the work of the Ministry, than he was before; or any other can ordinarily be without this due Ordination; whereby his wisdom, humility, charity, zeal, devotion, industry, purity, exactness and constancy are increased so as are most requisite for the great work and office of a Minister.

Deus largitur gratiam: homo imponit manus. Sacerdos imponit supplicem dextram, & Deus benedic. potenti dextra. Episcopus initiat ordinem; & Deus tribuit dignitatem. Amb. de dign. Sacerd. c. 5.

4. It binds the *conscience of the ordeined*, more strictly to the duty and office, as to discharge it, so to endeavour, by all *holy means*, of study, prayer, conference, meditation, *&c.* to preserve, use, and augment those gifts, faculties, or graces, naturall, acquired, or infused, for the right discharge and fulfilling of his Ministry, to the

glory

glory of God, and the Churches welfare, both in true peace and holiness; Hence the great learning of *Origen* and admired gifts, were thought by some less prospered and blessed of God; because he presumed to do the work of a Minister before he was blessed, ordeined, and authorised by the Church.

D. Origine dicunt cum sine vocatione se ingessisse in officium docendi; inde factum est quid in tot errores prolapsus sit. Chem. de Ecclesia. *Res Dei ab homine dari non possunt.* Synod. Rom.

5. Due Ordination gives *comfort, countenance*, and divine courage to true Ministers, as the *anointing did to the Prophets of old*, and the solemn *mission of Christ* did to the *holy Apostles*, to Preach; not as *popular Scribes*, and *precarious Pharisies*, but as St. *John* the Divine having *authority* from Christ; whose Ministry (like *John* Baptists) is not from *men* on earth, (however transmitted by men) but from God in Heaven; In this confidence they can *rebuke with all authority*; With this conscience they cannot but *speak in the name of the Lord*; They do not fear the face of men, or devils, in Christs way; They forsake not, *as hirelings*, the flock, when the *Wolf* comes, as having no relation, or tye to the flock, which is not committed to those self intruders, but *usurped* by *force*, or *invaded by stealth*; True Pastors in time of generall (not personall persecution) dare not *leave their flock* destitute; but choose to be examples to them *of suffering* cheerfully for Christ; expecting Christs promise, and assistance in his way. The *righteous Minister* is as bold *as a Lion*; for he that walks uprightly in the Spirit and power, and way of Christ, *walks seemly*: But all *usurpers are cowards*, and are ready to insinuate, and crouch to all *wayes of mean* and vulgar *complyances*; giving the *Belfry leave* to *swallow up the* Church and Chancel too; Falsely and vilely flattering the people, as if ministeriall power *were in them* and *from them*; And this some do purely for *filthy lucre*; where there is a miserable dependance for maintenance upon peoples good *will*; and chiefly to prevent any question, or scrutiny, which may be made by some nimbler sophisters touching their precarious, usurped, and *beggarly authority* as Ministers, which is truly none; This keeps them justly so in aw, that those popular Preachers dare not use that just rigor, and severity, in cases of most apparent *crying sins* in people, which a true Minister having good conscience and good authority knows how seasonably, and discreetly, yet freely and effectually to use, not to his *own pomp*, Empire, or *advantage*; but to Christs glory, the *Churches* good, and the honour of Religion; though it be to his own detriment and danger, as St. *Chrysostom*, St. *Basil. Naz.* and other holy Bishops and Presbyters oft did.

Quomodo valebit secularis homo sacerdotis ministerium adimplere, cujus nec officium tenuit, nec disciplinam agnovit. If. Hisp. off. l. 2. c. 3.

Qui infideliter introivit quid ni infideliter agat, Bern.

Tit. 2. 15.

Acts 4. 20.

John 10. 12.

τὴν τοῦ Θεοῦ παρακαταθήκην τὸ ποίμνιον [illegible]. Gr. Niss. de Scop. Christia.

Aug. Ep. ad Honoratum, 2

Euseb. Hist. l. 6. c. 19. *Origen* Preached before he was ordeined Presbyter, before *Alexa*: Bishop of *Jerusalem*, and *Theod.* Bishop of *Cesaria*: for which *Demet.* Bishop of *Alexand.* reproves them: But they excuse it as a custom there, for probation of such as they found Idoneous for their learning and gifts. As common placing is in Colleges.

6. Right

6. Right Ordination preserves Order and Decorum in the Church and holy administrations; also it fortifies the function of a Minister with *due respect and decent regard*, even before men; so that neither the persons nor function and office of Ministers are *easily to be despised*, when publike Ordination is duly performed, with that solemnity, and holy manner, as was of old, in this and all true Churches, and which ought to be so still: It likewise conciliates in Christs name, and for his sake, much love, reverence, esteem, patience, and obedience, toward Ministers, in their places, and duty, from all true Christians; yea and it raiseth a just *veneration to duties*, thus rightly *celebrated* among the faithfull, by those, of whom Christ says, *He that receiveth you, receiveth me, and he that despiseth you, despiseth me, and him that sent me.*

Mat. 10.40.

Constantine the Great alwaies treated the Bishops and true Ministers of the Church, with all observance and pious respect. *Euseb. vita. Const. l. 1. c. 35.*

Mat. 10.14.

2. Tim. 4. 3.

This makes them *received in the name of Prophets*; as Apostles or Angels sent from God; valued by true Christians, as *their right eyes*; This makes Christ *sensible of their injuries* as his, and the very dust of their feet becomes *a dreadfull* witness *against wicked* and proud *rejecters of them*; who thinking them to be Ministers but *of courtesy or civility*, cannot regard them with conscience and duty; But imagine that they may, at the pleasure of any passion, lust, or secular design, *be mocked*, despised, degraded, cast off, and quite abolished: That so their liberty may prefer *a heap of teachers of their own raking* and making, before any of Christs sending, and the Churches ordeining: Such being most fit for their sinister ends, who *come in the peoples name*, and have no higher or nobler Spirit; acting all things in *their Levelled Ministry*, by the same irreverent, irregular, inconstant, rude, insolent, and uncomly *Spirit of popularity*; which is most prevalent in those, that are most enemies to and afraid of the true ministeriall power and due ordination; Those αὐτόκλητοι or δημόκλητοι creations of the people, when *men* list, are *easily rejected*, & cast off with scorn, yet without any sin and shame: yea they cannot be regarded, or followed, without neglect and affront of the true Ministry, and this not without *a great* sin; The devill is never pleased better, than with such *pragmatick Preachers*, and false Prophets; who do Satans work under Christs Livery; which is at once to invalidate, and overthrow as the true Ministry, so all conscience of true Religion; that so having by these *Nimrods hunted out*, and destroyed all the race of the antient holy order and succession, he may set *up the Babell* of his Kingdom. No Symptom of lapsing unto Atheism so great, as the despising of the Ministry; which *Eusebius* observes before the destruction of the Jews.

Cujus ordinatio despicitur ejus & prædicatio contemnitur. Ber.

Non Domini sed Dæmonis sunt hæc pascua, Hi pastores. Luther.

Alii non sunt recipiendi prædicatores quam quos Christus.

7. It gives *great satisfaction* to *the conscience of all* true believers and serious Christians, in point of duty discharged and comfort obteined by holy ministrations; of whose *validity and efficacy* they have then least scruples, when they are most assured of the autho-

rity

rity of the Minister performing them as *in Christs way*, so in his Name, wherein blessing is to be sought and only to be found; Hence also they expect the *graces of the duty*, when the *Ministration* is rightly done, *by those*, that are in Christs stead, as to the outward form, and presence, which none can *without a ly and hypocrisie pretend to*, but only true *Ordeined Ministers*; Others in their arrogant and impudent intrusions are *justly and easily despised*, and all duties they do; which are first questioned, then denyed, having no plea or pretence of authority *from Scripture*, *reason*, or from the custome and practise of the Church, whereby to perswade any *sober man to regard them any more*, than God did the *Oblations* of *Cain*, or *Corah*. Nothing is more abhorred to the God of order, than presumptions in piety, which disdain to serve God in his own way; Nor will their zeal cover their rudeness and disobedience, or excuse the ly, which pretends to speak, and go and run, and prophecy in Gods name when the Lord sent them not, *Jer.* 23.31,32. Therefore the antient *Greek Lyturgies* prayed in their *Ordination of Ministers*, and *Consecration of Bishops*, that God would bestow *on the Ordeined such* (χαρίσματα) *Ministeriall gifts*, that the holy Ministry might be unblemished, and unblamable, that thereby *a reverence might be preserved to holy offices*, and *holy officers too*, for the peoples stay, satisfaction and comfort.

instituit, qui primus Apostolos misit. Tertul. de præ. ad Hær. *Ostendant mihi ex qua autoritate prodierunt. Probent se novos Apostolos, & virtutes proferant & miracula.* Tert. Ib:d.

ἵνα ἦ ἄσπιλος καὶ ἀμώμητος ἱερωσύνη.

Joh. 10. 8. All that came before me were thieves: *i. e.* came without commission, in their own names.

In venientibus est præsumtio temeritatis, in Missis est obsequium servitutis. Jeron.

And whereas the *pleader for the peoples privilege, and duty to Prophecy*, *objects*, that *few people are ever assured of those Ministers* being duly ordeined, who daily preach *among them*, and administer holy things; It is true, every *Minister doth not*, every time he preacheth, shew the letters, or the Charter *of his Ordination*; Nor is it necessary, (but only at some times) If the discipline of the Church in this point were such, as it ought to be, in practise, and which was *in our Constitution*, *viz.* That none might presume to officiate (properly) *as a Minister*, in holy Administrations (beyond probationall preaching) but only such as were sufficiently known to be true Ministers *rightly Ordeined* in publique, under sufficient testimoniall; The strict care of this, would be a great means both to restore the lapsed *honour of the Ministry*, and to *establish many* shaken Christians in their faith.

Luther demanded of *Muncer* a fanatick Prophet what ordinary call or Mission he had; with which *Luther* contented himself. *In vita Lutheri.*

As right Ordination of the *Evangelicall* Ministry carrys with it the only acceptance from God, as a service and duty, for to others God will say, *Who required these things at your hands*? So it procures *unspeakable blessings* of Gods graces and gifts *upon the Churches of Christ*, and the *houshold of Faith*; more truth and soundness in the faith, more Union, Peace, Charity, Order, Constancy, *&c.* The

S 2 *flourishing*

flourishing of Aarons *rod*, Numb.17. both in blossomes and ripe fruit, sufficiently *testifies* (against these *envious murmurers* against Ordination) whom the Lord hath *chosen* and ordeined to serve him, as *Ministers of the Gospell.* Rom.4.10. How shall they preach unless they be sent? It's negative, They cannot rightly, lawfully, acceptably, succesfully, comfortably preach, unless duly sent in Gods way; nor can that place be meant only of the Apostles, as *F.Socinus* interprets it, since as Preaching and Ministry, so authority in them, and regard to them, is alwayes necessary for the Churches good. Never any Church or Christians were eminent for *sound knowledge, Orthodox profession*, or for *holiness of life*, in all charity and vertues, but only there, where true Ministry, and right Ordination was continued and incouraged. The more any Church or Christians are *defective*, or *neglective*, and loose in this, the more they are presently overgrown with ignorance, or Errors, or Superstition, or infinite Schismes, *prophane novelties*, and scandalous *licentiousness*; when every one that lists *makes himself or another*, a *Minister* in new and *Exotick wayes*; Such mock-Ministers are but as the *block*, that fell *among frogs*, nine dayes wonder; but afterward the Pageantry concludes in the prophane babblings, contempts, and confusions, justly and necessarily *following* such *mockeries and Impostures*; Nor are they attended with only contempt of those Pretenders, but also with *neglect and indifferency in some men*, as to all holy duties and ministry; which the miserable experience of many people in this Church *too much confirms at this day*: No men and women being more dark, unsavoury, disorderly, wasted, torn, wounded, and scattered *into factions and errors*, than those *deluded creatures*, whose first error makes way for all other, forsaking the *true light*, and salt of the world, and of the Church; the teaching, order, and guidance of their true and *faithfull Ministers*; After this they are easily abused *with twinkling snuffs, unsavory salt*, with *Wolves and thieves*, who come not in at the dore, when it is fairly open, but climb over, or *creep under the wall of government*, order, and discipline: that they *may steal*, destroy, and disperse the flock. *Out of you shall arise men, speaking perverse things* (*i.e.*) they rise of themselves by popular forwardness, and disorderly presumption, not from Christs and the Churches ordination. Hence they prove so grievous and mischievous to the Church. *Acts* 20.30. So that it is not only the Calamity and misery of poor Christians to be thus abused; but it draws them into many sinfull evils, and snares, while they forsake, or cast out and despise their *rightly Ordeined*, and duly *placed Ministers*, and *either follow and incourage such seducers*, as are very *destructive*, both to the Churches peace, and to mens souls, both in the present and after ages, or else fall to a neglect, indifferency, yea and abhorrency of all Religion.

Non fortunat Deus labores eorum qui non sunt ordinati & quanquam salutaria quædam afferant tamen non ædificant. Luther. tom.4. Gen. fol.9.

*Joh.*10.1.

The

The Order, Power, and Authority then by which *right Ordination* is conferred on the true Ministers of the Gospel, as was here in *England*, although they seem *to proud scorners*, to unstable minds, to ignorant and unbelievers, as frivolous, as the Gospel *seems foolishness*; yet to the humble eye of Faith, it appears as the *wisdome, holy order*, and commission of God, for the continuall teaching, well guiding, and edifying of the Church of God, by truth, and peace to Salvation. The blessed and great effects of which depend, as I have shewed, not upon any *naturall power*, or vertue, transfused from the *Ordeiners to the Ordeined*, but upon the *Word, Promise*, and *appointment of Christ*, sending them in this method of the Churches triall, approbation, and ordination; In which by the judgement and conscience of those who are of the same function (and so best able to examine and judge of gifts and abilities) the examined and approved is publickly authorised and declared to be such a Minister, as the Lord hath chosen to be sent, such as the *Spirit of Christ hath anointed and consecrated*, by meet gifts and graces, for the service of Christ, and the Church, in that great work of the Ministry: *One*, who is thus ordeined, the Church may (in any part of it) *comfortably receive*, and own in Christs name; *One*, who is partaker duly of the comfort of that promise from Christ, to be with his *true Ministers to the end of the world*; which could not be verified, as interpreters observe of the persons of *those then living*, and first sent by Christ (who were long since at rest in the Lord;) but of *their lawfull Successors*, rightly following them in the same office and power; without which they are not truly *their Successors in the Ministry*, and authority from Christ: No more than they can be Embassadors, Deputies, and Messengers *from or to any one*, from or to whom they have no *assignment* of any power, by letters, or other *way of commission*; which, when most legally and formally *done* by *deeds* and *instruments* of writing; yet these receive no naturall *change of their qualities*, nor is any *inherent vertue* conveyed to them, when they are made *instruments to testifie* the Will, and convey the power of any to another; but they have such a *change in relation* to their appointed use and end, as alters them from what they were before in *common and unlimited nature*.

20. *Summary Conclusion of the power and efficacy of right Ordination.*

Mat. 28.

Non sunt successores in officio qui ad officium accedunt alio modo quam institutum est. Reg. Jur.

The like is, as to religious ends and uses, where some men are specially ordeined to be Ministers, having all *their efficacy* and authority, as to that work, from the *will of Jesus Christ*, from whom alone such power is derivable, and that not in every way, which the vanity of men list; but in such as the Church hath constantly used, *according to the Scripture Canons and directions*; which are clear to *Timothy* and *Titus*, which are the great paterns, and evident commissions *for right Ordination*, and Succession to the Ministry, besides

ſides other places; Againſt the undoubted *Authority*, and pregnant teſtimony of which Epiſtles and Scriptures, joyned to the *Churches Catholick cuſtome*, it will not be eaſie for *any Noveliſt* to vacate and aboliſh *that holy Succeſſion and due Ordination*, which the true Miniſters of *England* have generally had in this Church, which in my own experience, I cannot but with all truth and thankfulneſs teſtifie, to the glory of God, to the honour of this Church, and thoſe reverend Biſhops, as Fathers of it, who not only with great decency and gravity, but with much conſcience and religious care, ordeined Miniſters, as very many, ſo very worthy. Nor on the other ſide will theſe Novellers eaſily *perſwade* judicious Chriſtians, That any *upſtarts*, and *pretenders* in any other way (which as it is poor and popular, ſo it comes very ſhort and unproportionate to what is required in, and of a Miniſter) can have the power and Authority of true Miniſters, having no right Ordination; to which no mans *pragmatick pride*, and ſelf-confidence, nor the oſtentation of his gifts to others by a voluble tongue, nor the admiration and deſire of his ſilly and flattering auditors, can contribute any thing, either as to the comfort of the one or the other; but much to the ſin and ſhame of them both, as *perverters of Chriſts order*, and the Churches peace; forſaking their own mercies while they follow *lying vanities*, which cannot profit them.

Habentes cum iis conſortium prædicationis habeant neceſſe eſt & conſortium damnationis. Tertul. de Hæret. auditoribus.
Jo. 2. 8.

17. *Yet meer form of Ordination, makes not an able Miniſter.*

Not that every man that is *Ordeined a Miniſter*, as to the meer outward form, in a right and orderly way, is preſently of the *eſſence* and *truth* of a Miniſter in *Chriſts eſteem*, or in the comfort of his own conſcience; The ordeined may be ſuch hypocrites (as *Simon Magus* was, when baptiſed) as have neither *reall abilities*, nor *honeſt purpoſes*, aiming at Gods glory, or the Churches good; but meerly at their own worldly ends, and baſe advantages; The *Ordeiners* alſo may be either *deceived* in the judgement of Charity, or *corrupted* by humane luſts and frailties, ſo as greatly to pervert and prophane this holy Inſtitution; No man hath further comfort of his being Ordeined a Miniſter, than he hath *reall gifts*, and *competent abilities*, together with an *holy and honeſt purpoſe of heart*, to *glorifie God*, in the diſcharge of that *holy office and power*, to which he is by the Church appointed; Nor can on the other ſide, the Ordeiners more highly offend in *piety* againſt God, and charity againſt the Church, than in a *ſuperficiall* and *negligent* way of ordeining Miniſters; which antiently was not done, but with ſolemn publick *faſting*, *prayer*, and great devotion. Indeed nothing ſhould be done in the Church of Chriſt with greater exactneſs, both for inward *ſincerity*, and outward holy *ſolemnity*, than this weighty and *fundamentall* work of carrying on the Miniſteriall power and authority in a fit and holy Succeſſion; Abuſes here are prone to creep in, the

τοὺς ὑπηρετοῦντας τῇ ἐκκλησίᾳ μετὰ πάσης ἀκριβείας δοκιμάζοντα παρεδέχετο ἡ παλαιὰ συνήθεια. Baz. M. ep. 187.
The antient cuſtom of the Church receives none to be Miniſters

Devill

Devill coveting nothing more, than to undermine, weaken, and overthrow this main Pillar on which the Church and house of God doth stand; Ministers either unworthily, or unduly Ordeined, are like sleight and ill built ships, which endanger the loss of themselves, and all those that are embarqued in them, and put to Sea with them; Miscarriages, in the matter of ordination of Ministers, are to the unspeakable detriment, and dishonour of Religion; as unskilfull, cowardly, or perfidious Officers are to Armies. I shall never hope to see the Church flourish, or truly reformed, untill this Point of *right Ordination* of Ministers be seriously considered of, and duly restored to its Pristine honour *and excellency*; when to Ordein Ministers for the service of the Church, was not to prefer men *to a Benefice*, so much, as to *recruit Christs regiments*, to *strengthen his forces*, to fortifie the Church and true Religion, with most *vigilant Watchmen*, and *valiant Champions*, whose care was on every side to defend the *Flocks of Christ*, against all enemies; which were to be as the Cloud or Pillar of fire, *both lights and guards to Christians*, upon all occasions; who made conscience to live with, to suffer with, yea and to *dy for the sheep*, as good Shepheards. Such men only are fit to be *Ordeined Ministers*, such Ministers ought to be prayed for, highly prised, and perserved in the Church, by all that desire to transmit any thing of true Religion to Posterity; nor was the Church of *England*, or yet is, destitute of such Ministers, both duly and worthily ordeined, to the service of Christ and this Church.

but upon strickt examination before they are ordeined. *Concil. Nic.* 1. and the *Concil. Carth.* 1. c 9. takes care that none be Ordeined Presbyters without due examination.

Oportet Ecclesiæ Epis. & ministrum Christi, esse formam justitiæ, sanctimoniæ speculum, pietatis exemplar, veritatis doctorem, fidei defensorem, Christianorum ducem, sponsi amicum, & cui ille irascitur, Deum sibi iratum non hominem sentiat. Bern. ad Eug. l. 4.

To abolish this order, or to usurp to undue hands, or to contemn this Sacred and right Ordination, which sends forth able Ministers in Christs way, can be no other, but a most *cruell* and detestable *sacrilege*, far worse than that of robbing the Church of its maintenance for such Ministers, both as preaching and ruling well (wich yet is a *sin of so deep a dy*, that no Niter can cleanse it, being seldome ever pardoned, because seldome repented of, so as to make a *just restitution*; without which, repentance is never true.) Yea, for any Laymen, in a *brutish violence*, and meerly by *Popular insolency*, to arrogate this power where it is not, or to *abrogate it* where truly it is, is a sin of a more heynous nature, than that of *Simon Magus* was, who had so much of *civility, justice, and good manners*, as to offer *money for a part of the miraculous and Ministeriall power*. It is indeed no other than a *Cyclopick fury*, and unwonted barbarity (ill becomming any sober or civilized Christians) thus *to wrest the keys of Gods house*, out of the hands of those *Stewards*, with whom the *great Master Christ* hath specially intrusted them, for the right Oeconomy, and dispensing of all holy Mysteries and Institutions; And when such rude and unruly fellows have thus insolenced these Officers of the Church, and bound their hands; how

Cyprian reproves Novatus, a factious Presbyter, *Quod Felicissimum satellitem suum, diaconum suum constituit, nec sciente nec permittente me; sola sua factione & ambitione.*

Acts 8. 18.

All undue Ordination is χειρονία ἄχειρε profanum detestandumq; ludibrium. Bas.

> *Ischyras* αὐτοχειροτόνητος, Self-ordeined, or only by *Koluthus* a Persbyter. Hence *Athanasius Apol.* 2. ποῦ ἐν πρεσβυτέροις ἐξετάσθη . πῶς κατεσκευάσθη, &c.
>
> Pro. 20. 23.

how comly will it be to see *the keyes of the kingdome of heaven*, managed, or committed, as it were, *to Boyes, to Pages and Laquies*? to weak, mean, mechanick, ignorant, dissolute, and riotous wretches, who not *conscious* to any true Ministeriall power, or just authority in the Church, can never *make conscience* of doing any holy Ministerial duty, to which they are *most unfit*; never caring how prodigall they are of the truth and honour of Religion; of their own, or other mens souls; It being *a sport to such proud and spitefull fools*, to do wickedly, to speak prophanely, and to live disorderly in the Church. And not content to commit a rape upon true Religion, and the *holy orders* of Christs Church, (as *Absalom* did on the house-top before the Sun, and all Israel) they will further in time justifie the *flagitiousness of their villanies*; as if *the zeal they had for true Religion*, provoked to such outrages these pestilent pandars for *errors and all licentiousness*, with their followers, who must presently all *turn preachers*, though never duly Ordeined, nor fit ever so to be; yea, their arrogancy makes them ordeiners too, of whom they please to set up to minister to their extravagant lusts and follies, which makes them many times much fitter for the stocks or cages, than for the pulpits. These will surely come at last as much short of the happy effects of *true Ministers*, as they are far from that holy power of right Ordination, which I have *proved to be from Christ and the Blessed Apostles*, rightly derived to us by the constant *Custome of this and all Churches*; and this not as a cypher, or meer formality; but, as of *sacred Institution*, so of reall and excellent efficacy, and divine vertue in the Church, where duly used and applyed. Which was that I had to prove against *the scurrillous objections* of those, that seek to despise and destroy the whole Function, Ordination, and divine authority of the Ministry of this Church.

Reader, the Reason why the Folios of this Book do not follow, is because the Copy (for Expedition) was divided to two Printers.

CAP. II.

Of speciall Gifts of the Spirit pretended beyond Ordinary Ministers.

ANother *great Calumny*, urged by their Adversaries against the true Ministers of the Church of *England*, (whose due and right Ordination I have vindicated to be as Divine, so both Necessary, and Efficacious) is as a *forked arrow*, sharpned with *Presumption* and *Prejudice*; On the one side an *high esteem* and confidence which they have of themselves; and a very *low despiciency* of all Ordained Ministers; on the other side, even in that which is the highest honour of Man or Minister; while these Anti-ministeriall Adversaries pretend, That the Ordained Ministers have *not the Spirit of Christ*; nor can or ever doe Pray, Preach, and administer holy things *by the Spirit*: which these *new Modellers* challenge in such a *plenary measure*, and power to themselves; that they *justifie their* want of ordinary abilities and endowments by *their needing* none: Excusing their not studying, or preparing for what they utter, by their being specially *Inspired*. Colouring over their well known idlenesse, ignorance, illiteratenesse, and emptinesse, by *the shews of speciall Illumination*, sudden Inspirations, and spirituall Enablements; Which they say they have far beyond any *Ordained Ministers*; And this by the Spirit of Christ, which is extraordinarily given to them; which suddenly leads them into all Truth, and enables them for all Duties and Ministeriall Offices: That this is their Call from God to Preach; and to usurp the places of all Ordained Ministers; whom they pretend, as far to exceed in Inspirations, as the Apostles did their former selves after once the power of that Spirit was come upon them.

3. Calumny or cavill. *That the Ministers of England have not the Spirit to which their Adversaries pretend highly.*

To this Calumny and Ostentation my first reply shall be; in all humble tendernesse to *beseech God*, to give me holy wisdome rightly to conceive of, and graciously to expresse my self touching the Spirit of God; that I may *not give any offence*; or occasion any grief, and mistake to any excellent Christians. I * know well that the Spirit of Christ is a thing of *pious curiosity*, and *holy delicacy*; That in what way soever it manifests it self to the Church,

Answ. 1. *Of the Spirit of God in men: how to be considered of.*

* 1 Cor. 10. 32.

* *Delicata res est Spiritus sanctus.* Tert.

 it

Flabat Spiritus & fluebant lacrymæ, ſuſpiria, preces. Bern.
Luk. 11. 13.
Ioh. 14. 17.

it is to be entertained in thoughts, words, and actions of Chriſtians, with all cautious tenderneſſe, and religious reverence; that ſo wee may neither conceive nor ſpeak any thing unbeſeeming its majeſty, and purity; nor *damping*, or afflictive to its *holy* influences, gifts, and breathings, on the *ſpirits of any true Chriſtians*; whoſe higheſt honor, happineſſe, and communion *with God*, and *Chriſt*, and *one another*, is *by the Spirit of Chriſt*. I know that its *motitions* and inſpirations are, as *moſt free*, (* blowing where it liſteth, (not where any man liſt to boaſt and pretend) ſo they are not ſo eaſily diſcerned *whence* they come, and whither they goe; ſave onely by accurate watchings, and ſober *obſervation*; where the ſureſt diſcoveries are made by thoſe *holy fruites* and effects, which are maniſeſt in the habits of grace, or *formations* of Chriſt in the new man of our hearts, or in the *works* of our lifes; which being done after a religious rule and way, are in the judgment of Charity to bee eſteemed as effects of Gods Spirit.

1 Ioh. 3. 24. Hereby we know that he abideth in us, by the Spirit which he hath given us. * Ioh. 3. 8.

Sunt quædam Spiritus ſancti circa nos diſpenſatoriæ viciſſitudines, quæ niſi vigilantiſſime obſerventur, nec præſentem glorifices nec abſentem deſideres. Bern. Cant. l. 17.

Rom. 8. 9.
Gal. 4. 6.
1 Theſſ. 4. 8.

Teſtimonium Spiritus ſancti præſentiæ præbent opera ſalutis & vitæ, quæ præſtare non poſſumus, niſi Spiritus Chriſti qui vivificet adeſſet. Ber. ſer. 2. S. An.

I am far from doubting or denying, that the *Spirit of Chriſt* dwels in the hearts of true Beleevers, by ſpeciall gifts of grace; beyond Natures ſphere; nor do I queſtion, but that the *Spirit of Chriſt* doth furniſh many men with *ſpeciall gifts* (above others) for the ſervice both of Churches and States, in the outward viſible way of Gods providence; as to *Bezaleel* and *Saul*: Nor yet do I deny but the Spirit of Chriſt may give *extraordinary abilities* (that is, beyond others, and beyond mens own ſelves, as to former common gifts and parts) for the good of the Church, in caſes where ordinary means are defective: Nor do I diſpute this holy and uſuall influence of Chriſts Spirit on Chriſtians, inlightning, opening, hatching, foſtring, calming, compoſing, and ſpecially comforting in particular caſes; alſo, quickning to duties, inabling in duties; yea ſometimes ſupporting with *heroicall impulſes* and aſſiſtances in conflicts, temptations, and ſufferings, from men and devils; alſo reviving in dejections, deſertions, darkneſſes, and exhauſtings of our owne ſpirits and common gifts: All this I willingly grant; and earneſtly deſire that I may have daily more experience of in my ſelfe, and from others: not onely for private comfort, but for *publique good* of the Church of Chriſt. I deſire highly to prize the happy priviledge of thoſe, that doe *truely enjoy* theſe inſpirations, and humbly uſe them. I wiſh all true Chriſtians a bleſſed increaſe daily in this

Omnia ſacra guſtata afferunt mortem, ſi non de Spiritu accipiunt condimentum; prorſus mors in olla, niſi Spiritus farinula dulcoretur: Abſque Spiritu & ſacramentum ſumitur ad judicium, & caro non prodeſt, & litera occidit, & fides mortua eſt. Ber. ſ. 33. Cant.

Cælum fit anima habitatio Dei facta: O quanta prærogativa, &c. Ber.

communica-

communion with God, and one another by *reall gifts of the Spirit*; which are beyond the *best improvements* of meer Nature; I know no other heaven here or hereafter, but *the reall and full inhabitation of Christs Spirit in our spirits*: that, of Naturall, Rationall, and Humane, they may become Spirituall, Gratious, and Divine: All that I fear, is, *wilfull hypocrisie*, and *weak delusions*; that which I most abhorre, is, *false and proud ostentations*; such as some men are prone to affect, and lowdly to boast of among credulous and simple people; to which there can hardly bee given so exact and punctuall answers and confutations, as both Reason and Religion afford to sober and wise Christians in all other Disputes.

Tepidorum & dissolutorum est nolle esse meliores. Solus Deus seipso melior esse non vult, quia non valet. Ber. ep. 91. ad Ab.

Certissimum est præsentiæ Spiritus testimonium amplioris gratiæ desiderium. Ber. ser. 2. And.

Portentiloquium hæreticorum. Irenæ.

For such *pretentions of Gods Spirit*, and of speciall Inspirations (with which the primitive Churches were pestered and abused, and by which the very Apostles were *affronted* and *opposed*) are as *meteors* and *comets*, so exalting themselves in *high notions*, above the *ordinary reach of Reason*, that they are not easily calculated by common accounts; they are Raptures and Enthusiasmes, by which cunning men seek to lose the eyes of spectators in clouds of *obscurities* and *uncertainties*: Like some *vaine* and *lunatick Christians*, who busie themselves more, how to interpret the *Revelation*, and to fulfill its *mysterious prophesies*, then to understand, beleeve, and obey the *holy truths* and *clear precepts* of the Gospell in all the other Scriptures: Holy, wise, sober, and humble Christians never boast, rarely tell of those *secrets of the Lord*, if ever they enjoy them: Vain, weak, and proud men doe often arrogate those *speciall inspirations* to themselves, as being least *discernible* or *confutable* by vulgar minds; who once *dazeled* with the *glisterings* and *flashes* of pretended Inspirations, think they may safely disregard, and not look so low as the *Scripture* oracles, and the *plain manifestations* of Christ by the Word, and his constant Ministry: Lead common people once into this maze; *wilder* their weak fancies in the Wood of those strange *speculations*, those unwonted notions, those pretty legerdemaines in Religion, which some men (as Juglers) study more, than any solid *trade of Piety*; they are hardly able to know (a long time) where they are, as to true Religion; or to find and owne any faire path of holy Truth, and Order, which might lead them out of that *Fooles paradise*, wherein some men take delight to lose themselves and others.

1 Ioh. 4. 1. Iude 19.

So the *Gnosticks*, *Montanists*, *Catharists* and others.

Quantum adest vera Spiritus sancti gratia, tantum abest omnis vana gloriola. Ber.

Psal. 25. 14. Rev. 2. 17. } καὶ τὰ ἄῤῥητα πρέποντα λανθάνειν βούλεται τοὺς ἀνθρώπους ὁ δίκαιος. *Cl. Al.* 51. 7.

2 Pet. 2. 18. When they speak great swelling words of vanity, they allure, &c.

2. *False and proud pretentions of the Spirit.*

* *Transgressor præcepti Dominici spurios sibi sociat Spiritus, & adærendo eis unus efficitur Dæmon.* Bern. Ser. Ben. Ab.

* The Fryers Mendicant pretended they had a fifth Gospell which they called the *Æternum Evangelium*; this they preached and defended, saying the old Gospels must be abolished and theirs received. *Mat. Paris. an.* 1154. *Naucleru. an.* 1254.

* Whose hypocriticall sanctity, *Guilielmus De Sancto Amore (vir & doctrina & pietate illustris)* opposed. Pope *Alex.* 4. caused their blasphemous book to be burnt. *Platina. Vit. Al.* 4.

The ordinary *Sophistry* and craft: when men want solid ground and *true Principles* of right Reason, Order, Law, and Justice, of Scripture Precept, and holy examples from Christ, or any truly gracious Christians, whereby to justifie their opinions, or practises, their * *retreat is*, (as Foxes when eagerly hunted) to hide and *earth* themselves in this, The spirit hath taught and dictated these things to them; or *impulsed* and *driven* them upon such and such ways; which are incongruous, uncomely, unwonted to, and inconsistent with, either the *Catholick Tenets*, or Examples, generally held forth in the *Church* of Christ, according to the plain sense and tenor of the Scriptures; * This is done with the same falsity, yet *gravity* and *confidence*, as *Mahomet* perswaded the credulous Vulgar (by the help of *Sergius* a Monk) that his *fits of Falling-sicknesse* and the device *of his Pigeon*, coming to his Ear where he had accustomed to feed it, were *Monitions* and *Inspirations*, which he had from God by his *Blessed Spirit*. * Just as weak and *confused Writers* of *Romances*, having not well laid the plot and design of their *Fancifull story*, are wont to relieve their over *venturous Knights*, with unexpected enchantments (ἀπὸ μηχανῆς:) which salve all inconveniences, superate all hyperbolies, and transcend all difficulties, as well as all rules of Reason or Providence: So many men defective in their *Intellectuall*, *Morall*, and gracious Principles of *true and sound Religion* (which all sober Christians own to be derived from, and directed only by the holy Scriptures, both in Faith and Manners) they presently *pretend the Spirit*, to be Patron of their most extravagant fancies and deeds; the Deviser *of their most incredible opinions*; the Dictator of their most *indemonstrable* dreams; which no *Jew*, or credulous *Greek*, or *Gypsy*, would ever beleive; nor any man, who were not willing to *depose his reason*, and to suffer a rash and fancifull credulity to *usurp* the *Throne* and *Soveraignty* of his Soul.

This, in *generall*, I may reply, to all those, that forsake ordinary Precepts, and follow *New Revelations*, or pretend the speciall motions *of the Spirit* against the constant Rules and Institutions of Christ *in the Word*; (and I may tell it upon grounds of far greater certainty both of Reason and Religion, than any of them can assure me or any man, that they have these speciall impulses and graces of the Spirit, beyond others who walk in the ordinary way of means, and received methods of Christian Religion.

1 Joh. 4. 1. *First discovery by the Word of God.* V. 3.

First, We are forbidden to *beleive every Spirit*; because the *Spirit of Antichrist* may *pretend to the* Spirit of Christ; we are commanded *to try the Spirits*, whether they be of God or no; we are told, that *every* spirit *which confesseth not that Christ is come in the flesh*

flesh, is *not of* God, but *is of that Spirit of* Antichrist, which is to come into the world; as Christ foretold, many *should come in his Name*, and say, *loe here is Christ, and there is Christ; But beleive them not:* What I pray doth more deny the coming of Christ in the flesh; (that is, by a visible way of the Ministry to his Church in his person, and in his succession) then to say, he is gone away again, without taking any Order, or leaving any Command or Institution, *for his Worship* and Service to be continued in the Church? by which his first coming might be made known, in *Preaching the Gospell*; and confirmed by the Seals of the Sacraments, to his Church? To say that Christ is so come now in the Spirit, *here and there*, by speciall Inspirations, that he never came in that other old way of the outward, and Ordained Ministry, of Word, and Sacraments; hath so much of the *spirit* of Antichrist, as it is against the evident testimony of the *Word* of Christ; against the *practice* and the *command* of the Apostles; and against the *Catholick* custome of the Church of Christ; which hath always thus set forth and witnessed the first coming of Christ, and must ever doe so till his coming again: Which second coming onely shall put a period to the Word, Sacraments, and that true Evangelicall Ministry, which now is by Christ Ordained in the Church: As the first coming of Christ, did to the Leviticall Priesthood and Ministry by Sacrifices, &c.

Mat. 24. 23.

2. We know, That, as the *Illuminating* Spirit of God *guideth* the *humble*, meek and industrious souls into *all saving necessary Truths*; so these *Truths* are confined to, and contained in the compasse of those, which are already once revealed to the Church by the Spirit in the Word of God; and which are by the Ministry of the Church dayly manifested, and in this way are sufficient to make the man of God perfect to salvation, 2 *Tim.* 3. 17. Which is that one anointing from Christ and the Father, which hath lead the Church *into all truth* by the sure Word which the Apostles taught and wrote: so that no Christians have need, that any man by any other spirit, or as from this Spirit, should teach them more or other as to salvation, 1 *Joh.* 2. 27. They that *gape* to heaven for the *Manna* of speciall Revelations, when they are not in the Wildernesse, but in the *Canaan* of Christs true Church, may easily starve themselves, or feed on the *wind* and *ashes* of fancifull presumptions, while they neglect, and despise the ordinary provisions, God hath made in his Church. It is clear, that whatsoever is said or done, *beyond* or *against this written Word of Christ*, and surest rule of the Church, is to be accounted no other, then apocryphal lying vanities, and *damnable hypocrisies*. * No *Spirit of Christ abstracts* any mans faith from the Word; or carries his practise against the Truth, Order, and holy

Joh. 16 13. Joh. 17. 17. Sanctifie them through thy truth, Thy Word is truth.

* *Hoc prius credimus, non esse ultra Scripturas quod credere debeamus. Nobis curiositate non opus est post Christum, nec inquisitione post Evangelium.* Tertul. de præ. ad. Hæ. c. 3.

ly Institution, which Christ hath setled in his Church: For it is most sure by all experience that the *holy Spirit* teacheth those Scripture saving-Truths, by the ordinary methods, and *orderly means*, which the Wisdom of the same Spirit in Christ, hath appointed to be used in the *Ministry of the Church*; which, who so *proudly* neglects, and so despiseth Christ in them, he may *tempt, grieve*, and *resist* the Spirit of God; but he will never find the comfort of the Spirit in his *unwarranted extravagancies*; which are but *silly delusions* and *baby-like novelties*, having nothing in them of Truth, Holinesse, or religious Excellency, beyond what was better known, believed, and expressed before in words and deeds, by a far better way; Christians ought never to turn such *children* and fools, as to think Religion is never well unless it be in some new *dresse* and fashion, of *unwonted expressions*, and strange administrations: we think that the *Spirit* of God teacheth all humble, constant, and exact obedience to the Word of God, *without any dispensation* to any men, at any time, in things of Morall duty, and Divine Constitution, or Order, according to the *severall relations* and religious capacities of Christians: no *reall sufficiency* of gifts or graces doth justifie any Christian in any disorderly and unruly course of acting, or exercising his supposed Inspirations in the Church; no more then they doe in the Civill Offices of State; Nor are these motions any thing of Gods speciall call in regard of the outward Order and Policy of the Church, where the ordinary way of Calling, Admitting, Ordaining, and sending forth right Ministers, may be had in the Church.

Ephes. 3.10.
Ephes. 4.12.

3.
The vanity of of their wayes compared to the Word.

Be these impulses of the Spirit never so great, yet they put no good Christian upon *idlenesse*, or *presumption*, so as not to use the ordinary means of study, hearing, reading, meditating, conferring, praying, and preparing, &c. Nor shall he either preserve, or increase, or profitably exercise any such gifts, without study, industry and preparatory pains; which are the means by which God blesseth men with that Wisdome, Truth, Order, and Utterance, which are necessary for the Churches good: The liberall effusions of some mens tongues; their warm, and tragicall expressions, (where there is something of Wit, Invention, Reading, Method, Memory, Elocution, &c. in the way of Naturall and acquired Endowments) alas these are no such *rare gifts*, and *speciall manifestations* of Gods Spirit, which these Anti-ministeriall men have so much cause to boast of; There may be high *mountains* of such gifts ordinary, and extraordinary, as in *Judas* the Traitor; which have no *dews of grace* falling on their barrennesse; Nor are these boasters of Inspirations manifested yet either as equall, or any way comparable to most *true Ministers* in any

sort

ſort, by any ſhewes of ſuch gifts; for the moſt of which they are beholding to Miniſters labours and ſtudies; with whoſe heifer theſe men make ſome ſhift to plough the crooked and unequall furrows of their Sermons and Pamphlets. A little *goes a great way* with theſe men, in their ſuppoſed Inſpirations; and where they cannot goe far on, they *goe round*, in *circling Tautologies*, ſnarled repetitions, intricate confuſions, which are ſtill but the ſame skains of thread, which other men have handſomely *ſpun* and *wound* up in better method and order; which theſe men have neither skill nor patience fairly to unfold; but pull out here a thread and there an end; which they *break* off abruptly, to the confounding of all true Methods of Divinity, and Order of ſound Knowledge.

The compoſedneſſe and gravity of true Religion (in Publique eſpecially) admits leaſt of *extravagancies* and *uncomelineſſe*; which diſſolve the bonds, or exceed thoſe bounds, by which Chriſt hath *fitly compacted* the Church together, in a ſociall way; giving every part, by a certain order and allowance (eſtabliſhed as the *Standard* in his Church,) that * meaſure and proportion, which is beſt for the whole: This place and calling every Chriſtian ought to own, and to attend; keeping within due bounds, till God enabling, and the Church ſo judging, and approving of his abilities, he be placed and imployed in ſome way of Publique ſervice, into which to crowd, and obtrude a mans ſelfe uncalled and unordained regularly by the Church, doth not argue ſuch great motions of the Spirit, (which like ſtrong liquor cannot be kept in any veſſell) but only evidenceth the *corrupt ſpirits*, the violent luſts, and the proud conceits which are in mens Hearts.

Hæretica conversatio quam futilis, terrena, humana! ſine gravitate, ſine autoritate, ſine diſciplina. Tertul. adv. Hær.

* Eph. 4. 16.

Certainly all Gifts, Graces and Influences of Gods Spirit in truly gracious and humble hearts, are in all Motions, Habits and Operations, as conform to the Scripture (which are the Canon of Truth, Peace and Order in the Church) as any *right line* is to that rule by which it is drawn; or as figures caſt in the ſame ſtamp and mould are exactly fitted to one another. The *Truth of the Word*, and *Graces of Gods Spirit* cannot be ſeparated, or oppoſed any more, than heat can be parted in the Sun from its light, or its beams croſſe one another in crooked and oblique angles.

It is no better, than a proud and Satanicall deluſion to fancy or boaſt, that the Holy Spirit of Chriſt dwels there, in ſpeciall Influences and Revelations, where the Word of Chriſt doth not *dwell richly in all wiſdome*, *Col.*

Auſtin. de Unit. Eccleſiæ. c. 16. *Non dicant ideo verum eſſe, quia illa vel iſta mirabilia fecit Donatus, vel Pontius, vel quilibet alius, aut quia ille frater noſter, vel illa ſoror noſtra tale viſum vigilans vidit, vel dormiens ſomniavit. Removeantur iſta vel figmenta mendacium hominum, vel portenta fallacium ſpiritum. Remotis iſtis Eccleſiam ſuam demonſtreat in canonicis ſanctorum librorum autoritatibus.*

Col.3.16. The *lodgings* of the Spirit are alwayes and onely furnished with the *Tapistry* of the Scriptures. Else all imaginary furniture of any private spirits, leaves the heart but *swept* and *garnished* with the *new brooms* of odd fancies, and fond opinions, to entertain with somewhat more *trim* and *composed dresse*, the unclean spirit; who loves to dwell thus in the *high places* of mens souls; and hereby seems to make the later end of those *filthy* or *silly dreamers* (in pride, vain-glory, hypocrisie, and lying against the Truth; blaspheming the true Spirit of Christ, contemning his holy and onely true Ministery, and Ordinances, and in all other licentious Apostasies) worse than their beginning was, in *ignorance*, errors and terrors; or in plain dealing sensualities, and downright prophanenesse; For it is *more tolerable to be without the Spirit of God*, than to lye against it, and blaspheme it, or oppose, and resist it, after some knowledge of the Truth. It had been better for such men *not to have known the way* of Christs Spirit in the Scriptures and the Church: It is far more veniall to erre for want of the Spirits guidance, and light, than to shut our eyes against it, and to impute our Errors, Dreams, and Darknesses to it; 'Tis better to have the heart *wholly barren*, than to lay our adulterous *bastards* to the Spirits charge; when they indeed are issues of nothing but Pride joined to Ignorance.

Iud.8.

Pope *Hildebrand, Cum & hæreticus & maleficus & sacrilegus esset, pro sacratissimo se ostentabat, & miranda quædam Magicis artibus patrabat; prunas subinde è manica excutiebat coram populo.* Car. Sigon. ad an. 1057. Avent. pag. 455. 470.

2 Pet. 2. 21.

4. *Like pretentions of old, confuted by mens practises.*

Nothing indeed is easier and cheaper, (at the World now goes) than for * vain and proud men to pretend to *speciall* Inspirations and Motions of Gods Spirit on them; as many *in the old times did*; who yet were sensuall, not having the *Spirit*: * So the *Gnosticks* called themselves (πνευματικοὶ) spiritual, men as well as knowing men; So the *Marcionites* and *Montanists* pretended, that their Master *Montanus* knew more *than the Apostles*; had more of the Comforter; was the Comforter it self, and told him, what Christ said, *his Disciples could not then bear*, Joh.16.12. The like lying fancies had the *Valentinians*, and *Circumcelliones*, and *Manichees*, who being idle-handed, grew idle-headed too, not caring what they said, nor what they did; for they fathered all on the Spirit. So the *Cathari*, and *Encratitæ*, calling themselves Chast and Pure; and (*Apostolici*) Apostolicall, and *above the Gospels*: both of old, and in * St. *Bernards* time; and in later times too, both in *Germany* and other places: rising to ostentation of *Prophesying*; speciall Inspirations; strange

* *Portentiloquium hæreticorum.*

* *Se spiritales esse asserebant Valentiniani: Demiurgum animalem: virginales Gnosticorum spiritus gloriabantur.* Iren. l. 1. & 3.

Austin. de Hæret.

Epiphan. l. 4. de Hær. c. 40.

* Sermo. 66. in Cantica.

Cerdom Apelles Marcionitæ privatas lecturas habuerunt, quas φανερώσεις, apellant, cujusdam Philamenæ puellæ, prophetissæ: & librum syllogismorum, quibus probare vult, quod omnia, quæ Moses scripserit, de Deo falsa sunt. Tertul. præ. ad. Hæ. c. 44.

ſtrange Revelations, ſhews of Miracles, and lying Wonders, fulfilling and interpreting of Prophecies, enthronings of Chriſt, &c. by which *ſtrong deluſions* they ſought to deceive the very Elect, if it had been poſſible; but they could never perſwade truly excellent, and choiſe Chriſtians, to *any belief of their forgegeries and follies*; ſince neither the temper of their ſpirits, nor their works, nor their words, were like the rules, marks, or fruits, of that holy and *unchangeable Spirit of Jeſus Chriſt*, ſet forth in his Word, and owned in the Church; But rather the effects of that *depraved ſpirit*; which is *moſt contrary to God*, and moſt inconſtant in it ſelf; which after all its fair *glozings* and *præfacings* of Purity, Gifts, and Inſpirations, is ſtill but * (*Borborites*) a *ſwiniſh* and *unclean* ſpirit, and differs as much from the Purity, Truth, Beauty, and Order of the true Spirit of Chriſt, which ſhines in the Word, as the moſt noiſome Jakes and filthy ſink doth from the moſt ſweet and *Cryſtall* fountain of everflowing waters.

Sleidan. Com. l. 4. *Cainitæ ἀναβατικὸν Παύλου confingebant, Epiph. Hæ.* 38. The *Cainites* pretended they had a book containing the *Raptures of Saint Paul*, what he then heard, &c.

* *Borboritæ*, ἄλογοι, *Cœnoli. Tertul.* and *Auſtin* call thoſe hereticks the *Gnoſticks*, *Cathariſts*, and others: who called themſelves *Apoſtolici, Pneumatici, Angelici, purgatores, electi.*

Πολλαχοῦ ἐνθουσιᾶν ἑαυτοῖς δοκοῦντες οὐ βακχεύουσιν, ἀλλὰ παίζουσιν. *Longinus.*

Manes the Father of the *Maniches* called himſelf an Apoſtle of Chriſt, the Comforter and Spirit: choſe twelve Diſciples, deſpiſed water Baptiſm, ſaid the Body was none of Gods work, but of ſome evill Genius; and his followers full of impure luſts and errours; yet ſaid they were called *Maniches* from flowing with Manna, (μάννα χέοντες.) They ſaid, the ſoul was the ſubſtance of God, to be purified: to that end they mixed the Euchariſticall bread with their ſeed, in obſcene pollutions and rapes, *ut iſto modo Dei ſubſtantia in homine purgetur.* Auſt. de Hæ.

5. True *Miniſters* find it hard, *having done all*, to obtain thoſe competent Miniſteriall gifts and graces of the Spirit, which are neceſſary to carry on that great work of their own and others Salvation to any decorum and comfort: which theſe *Glorioſoes* pretend as if they were bred and born to; or were ſuddenly, and at once endowed withall: few of theſe ever think they want the Spirit, if they have but confidence to *undertake* any *Miniſteriall work* and publique Office. Yea and the beſt Chriſtians, no leſſe than the ableſt Miniſters, find it hard in *truth* to obtain the *ſanctifying gracious influences of Gods Spirit*, by which with much diligence and prayer they are enabled to private duties; nor doe they find it ſo eaſie to fleſh and bloud to obey thoſe holy *directions* of the Spirit, or in conflicts *to take its part* againſt the fleſh; and to rejoice in the victories and prevalencies of the Spirit. Whoſe publique donations for the common good of Chriſtians, (*edifying them in truth and charity*) are chiefly manifeſted not onely by his ſervants the true *Miniſters*; but in the bleſſing of that very Order, Office, appointment, and *function* of

True fruits of the Spirit.

* *Venit & vadit prout vult, & nemo facile ſcit unde venit, aut quo vadat.* Ber.

Brevis mora, rara hora, mira ſubtilitate & ſuavitate divina ſuæ artis inceſſanter actitat in intimo noſtri. Idem.

Eph.4.8. & 11.

of the Ministry, both as instituted and continued so long time, by the wisdome and power of this *Spirit of Christ*. And by this great Gift of gifts, as by the Sunne in the Firmament, all others are ordinarily conveyed to private Christians, which chiefly consist, and are manifested in *true beleevers*, not in *quick strokes* of fancy, passionate *raptures*, strange *allusions*, and allegoricall *interpretations*, confused *obscurings* of Scriptures (which some men (with *Origen* make so much of:) but in bringing men from this childish *futility of Religion*, to a *manly seriousnesse*; which sets the heart soberly to attend, read, hear, study, and meditate on *the Word of God*; to prefer that *Jewell* before all the *hidden treasure* of their own or others Fairy fancies: to *assent* to the *saving Truths* both of Law and Gospell; zealously to love them, strictly to obey them; by hearty *repentance* for sins against God or man, *ingnuous confessions* of them, honest compensations for them, sincere amendment of them; hence it brings to a *quiescency*, and comfort in no way, but such, as is *conform* to the Word of Christ; burning with an *unfaigned* charity toward all men; most *fervently to the Churches service and welfare*: with an * *high esteem* of the *excellency of the knowledge of Jesus Christ*, his Institutions, and Ministry, his Word, and Spirit, and Grace; with a *gratefull value*, and *high respect* of those, by whose Ministry they have been called, baptized, taught, converted; and are still *guided* in the paths, light and breathings of the Spirit, to the hopes of salvation; the blessed expectation of which in Christs way raiseth them up many times to high, yet holy resolutions, to *deny themselves*, and *suffer* any thing for Christs sake, and the testimony of the Truth.

In veritate qua illuminaris, in virtute qua immutaris, in charitate qua inflammaris; serenata conscientia; subita & insolita mentis latitudine praesentem spiritum intellige, Ber.

* *In humili spiritu & pura mente spaciose habitat immensus Deus.*

* Phil.3.7.
1 Thes. 15. 12. 12, 13.
Heb, 13.17.

These, and such like (I conceive) are the best fruits of Gods Spirit; which are not the lesse excellent, because they are common: Gods children are not oft entertained with novelties, and never pleased with such new toyes, and ratles, or hobbey horses in Religion which some men bragge of. The *wandering clouds*, which some mens fancies exhale, of spirituall Motions and Manifestations, beyond plain and ordinary Christians, either for private comfort, or for publique benefit, are for the most part, without *water*, they *darken* but *moisten* not the Church, or the soul, they have so much of earthy or fiery exhalations in them, that they have little of the dew of heaven with them; Nor may they without great injury and high indignity be imputed to the Spirit of Christ: Nor doe such sorry flowers (which grow in *every dunghill*) adorn the *Garden* of God, the Soul, or the Church; nor justly *crown* any with the most honourable name of *holy* or *spirituall*: Which titles *vain men* much affect and boldly

Jude 12.

challenge;

challenge; ſober and humble Chriſtians do earneſtly deſire, and ſeriouſly endeavour to merit: Being an honour ſo farre above the naturall capacity of ſinfull mortality, that nothing, but a Divine bounty and ſupernaturall power can conferre the *Truth of that Beauty*, which is in holineſſe; and the right to that glory, which is in every True Saint: who are often hid, as *orient Pearles* in *rough ſhels*, in great plainneſſe, lowlineſſe and ſimplicity; which makes ſuch as are *truly Saints* and ſpirituall, as aſhamed to challenge the name, as they are afraid to come ſhort of the grace: Studying not applauſe and admiration from men, but the approbation of a ſincere and *good conſcience*; Him they look upon as the father of every good and perfect gift; the ſender of the *bleſſed Spirit*, by the *due Miniſtry of the Word*, into mens hearts; The *ſearcher alſo of all hearts*, and *tryer of the ſpirits* of men; far beyond what is ſet out in *paints* and outward *appearances* of extraordinary gifts *of the Spirit*; under which mask and diſguiſes *Achitophel*, and *Jehu*, and *Judas*, and *Simon Magus*, and the ſons of *Sheva*, and *Demas*, and the ſelf-made Propheteſſe *Jezebel*, and *Diotrephes*, all falſe Chriſts, falſe Prophets, and falſe Apoſtles, all true Antichriſts, and true Miniſters of Satan, grievous Wolves, *ſtudied to appear*; and did ſo for a while, till the Lord ſtirred up the Spirit of *diſcerning* in his true Miniſters and true Saints.

2 Cor. 1. 12.
Iam. 1. 17.

Heb. 4. 13.

6.
Reall power of the Spirit how diſcerned
2 Tim. 3. 5.

Which Spirit of Wiſdome teacheth us to meaſure and judge of *ſpirituall gifts*, and true holineſſe, not by bare and barren forms, but by the *power and practiſe of godlineſſe*: not by ſoft expreſſions, and gentle *inſinuations*, or melancholy *ſowreneſſe*, and ſeverer brows: not by *Ahabs* ſackcloth, or *Jehus* triumphs, or *Phariſaick* frownes: Not by bold *aſſertions*, lowd clamours, confident calumnies, precipitant zeal, audacious adventures, ſucceſſefull inſolencies: Not by heaps of Teachers, popular Sermonings, long Prayers, wreſted Scriptures, crowds of Quotations, high Notions, *Origenick* Allegorizings: Not by admired Novelties, *vulgar ſatisfactions*, ſplendid *ſhews* of Religion; empty *noiſes of Reformation*: Nor yet by *arrogant boaſtings*, uncharitable deſpiſings, confident preſumptions, haſty *aſſurances*, proud *perſwaſions*, pretended *Revelations*, fanatick *confuſions*: All theſe, either in affected Liberties, or Monaſtick rigors, oft bear up mens *fancie of the Spirit*, and ſanctitie, (like bladders) meerly by their *emptineſſe*: Nothing being more prone to diſpoſe a *vain mind*, to *fancy ſtrongly*, that it hath *Gods Spirit*, than the *not having* it indeed: *To make men preſume they are Saints, than

σκυθρωπoί. tetrico, aut triſti vultu. vultuoſi Phariſæi.

Simpliciſſima eſt ſpiritus ſancti virtus; ſine fuco, ſine fraude omnia agit: nulli gravis, piis ſuavis, omnibus utilis. Ber.

Nil tam metuit quam ne dubitare de aliqua re videretur: de Velleio.

Quomodo certiſſimi eſſe poſſunt, quum nihil certius eſt quam certos illos non eſſe de ſalute? Ber.

Certi non ſunt qui ſollicit non ſunt. Cyp.

Sola integra fides ſecura eſſe poteſt. Tertul. de Ba.

* 2 Tim. 3. 13. Deceiving and being deceived.

Splendore magis quam fervore delectantur hypocritæ. Ber. *Dum fallunt maxime falluntur.*

Hypocritæ sanctitatis tineæ: cui adhærere videntur vestimento pariter viciant; remedia in morbos, & sanctitatem in crimen vertunt. Chrysost.

* Luk.17.21.

Mark.13.22.

Comica deformitas, at nocumentum tragicum miserorum, religiosa delicta.

Cyp. Ep. 2. *Sleidan. Com.* l.4.

than the not serious considering what *true holinesse* is, and the way of the Spirit of Christ is: In its infallible rule, the Scripture; in its noblest pattern, Jesus Christ; in its foundation, Humility; in its beauty, Order and Symmetry; in its perfection, Sincerity; in its glory, Love and Charity; in its transcendent excellency, the Divine Nature. The *Devils Piracies* are made as much by the *frauds* and *fallacies* of hanging out *Gods colours*, the flags of the Spirit, and shews of holinesse, as by the *open defiances of persecution*, and *batteries of profanenesse*; Delusions in Religion, as *Dalilahs charms* on *Samson*, are oft stronger, than the *Philistins* force *against the Church*; Else our blessed Saviour would not have so carefully fore-warned and fore-armed his little flock, against those grand *Impostors*; whose deceit is no lesse than this, * *Loe here is Christ, and there is Christ*: As if he were no where in *England*, or in all the former Catholick Church; but only in the corners and Conventicles of new *Donatists*.

Loe here is Christ! a most *potent* and *plausible pretention* indeed, able by its native force, and mans *credulous frailty* to *deceive* even the *very Elect*; whom would it not move and tempt strongly to hear of a new Christ, in *New lights*, and new Gospels, new Church wayes, new Manifestations, new Ministry, and new Ministers; Yea to heare of a *Christ* without means, above means, beyond the Scriptures deadnesse, the old Sacramentall forms, the Ministeriall Keyes and Authority: Christ in the Spirit risen from the *grave of dead duties*; of expired Ordinances; and from the *Carkases of ancient Churches*; A Christ, who is already *come to judgement*; with whom his Saints are now risen, and dayly rising; seeing him not *as in a glasse* of means *darkly*, but by immediate *Visions*, glorious *Manifestations*, speciall *Inspirations*, plenary *Inhabitations*; thus sitting on *Thrones* and *Reigning* with *Christ* in his *Kingdom*?

Whom would *not these Trumpets awake*, and these alarms call forth? if we were not *forewarned by Christ*; and if we had not seen such follies formerly acted and *manifested to all the Christian world*; and sufficiently *confuted in all ages*; which never amounted to more than *Religious Tragedies*; for when the masks of *personated Prophets*, and *necessitous Saints*, and *hungry Enthusiasts*, and *idle Seraphicks*, were taken off, (which they put on either by the power or presumptions they had among the Vulgar) presently there appeared the *horns* of the *Beast*, in *pride*, *ambition*, *luxury*, *polygamy*, *cruelty*, *tyranny*, *confusion*; That those, who seemed to have come down from heaven in the *shews* of the *Spirit*, and *pretentions of Sanctity*, were but *Satans lightnings* falling down from heaven, and his most *abominable eructations* out of the bottomelesse pit.

If

If we other *poor Christians*, who still remain on the *other side of this Jordan*, (which those *Spiritosoes* pretend to have passed:) if wee, who creep on the ground, as worms and no men; who have dayly cause to *abhor our selves in dust and ashes*, who are forced dayly to *strengthen our faith*, to *renew our repentance*; to poure forth our souls oft in sighs, tears, prayers, with *broken hearts* and *contrite spirits*, contending with corruptions, wrestling with temptations; having enough to doe to fortifie our selves with the compleat *armour of Gods Word*, in Precepts, and Promises; and of his Spirit, in gracious habits, excitations to, and assistances in duties: Thus giving all diligence to make *our calling and election sure*: not counting our selves to have *comprehended*, but *pressing on to the mark* of the price of the high calling in Christ Jesus: Glorying in nothing but *in the crosse of Jesus Christ*, by which we are crucified to the honours, riches, policies, successes, flatteries, and glories of this inglorious world; yea to the Liberties, Religions, Devotions, Sanctities, new Churches, new Reformations, and new Ministers of this world; who forsaking the wayes of Christ, and the holy Apostles, and the ancient Churches, and the *true succession* of Ministers, and all Power; have *turned grace into wantonnesse, liberty into licentiousnesse, godlinesse into gain*; and very much embraced the present world; falling *down before Mammon*, and worshipping *the false gods* of this world. 2 Pet. 1. 10. Phil. 3. 14. Gal. 6. 14.

If we, who when we have *suffered much*, and *done something* in our endeavours and purposes of holinesse; yet find cause to cry out, *Wretched men that we are, who shall deliver us from this body of death!* if we could indeed *believe*, or find by *experience*, that the *exaltations*, and *Raptures* of these new pretenders to the Spirit, were more comfortable, than the *buffetings* of those good old Christians; That their *triumphs* in the world, were beyond the others *sufferings* from the world, that there were more of Christ in their *new Crowns of glory*, which they boast of, than in the others Crosses, which they patiently bare; If we could discern a more *self-denying Spirit*, a more *Christ-enjoying Sanctity*; That they were Saints, that is, Not *crucifiers of the world*; but *crucified to the world*: If we could see the *wounds of Christ* in these glorious apparitions; these *Christ-like phantasms*, (as *Antony* the Hermite required, when Satan appeared to him like Christ in glory) If that Purity, Chastity, Justice, Honesty, Contentednesse, Patience, Charity, Meeknesse, Humility, Peaceablenesse, Fidelity, Constancy and Orderlinesse, shined in them wherein those holy *men and women of old*, the Professors, Confessors and Martyrs, not getting but loosing Saints, imitated the holy Lord Jesus, and the most holy God, according to the lively characters of true holinesse, set *down in the Scriptures*: If we Rom. 7. 24. *Non credam esse Christum nisi vulnera videam crucifixi.* in vita Ant.

we saw such fruits of reall holinesse in their words, pens, and actions, in their Doctrines and duties, in their self-denials and Mortifications, in their meetings and Fraternities, in their Church Orders and Ministrations, as might convince us, that these pretenders to the Spirit, and despisers of the Ministers, have indeed more of that light, life and power of the holy Spirit of God, than either true Christians or godly Ministers formerly had, or now have in this, or *any other true Church of Christ*: How should we envy their *blessednesse* with an holy emulation? How should we, as Saint *John* to the Angell (whom it may be he *took for Jesus Christ*) be even ready *to fall at their feet*; to kisse their footsteps; to attend their directions; to imitate their examples; to partake of their raptures; to pry into their third heavens; to rise, ascend, reign and triumph, to enjoy the holy *Spirit* and *Christ*, and God with them, to all which they in word and fancy pretend?

Revel. 19. 10.

7. *Fallacies in this kind frequent among Enthusiasts.*

But the triple Crown of *meer titular* and verball *holinesse* (which is but *copper* gilded over) moves us not, further than to pity the sinner, and to scorn the pride: The *Gnosticks*, *Montanists*, *Catharists* of old, the later rude, and cruell *phanaticks* in *Germany* cryed (ἅγιος) *holy, holy, holy* to their parties and factions: As if there were *holy ambitions*, *holy seditions*, *holy covetousnesses*, *holy sacriledges*, *holy obscenities*, *holy cruelties*, *holy confusions* in the conversations of *true Christians* and spirituall men; Or *holy ignorances*, *holy errours*, *holy darknesses*, *holy heresies*, *holy schisms*, *holy hypocrisies* in their hearts and spirits: As if no duties, no Scriptures, no Sacraments, no Ministry, or Ministers, no Government, or Governours of the Church were heretofore holy, which were *primitively*, and universally, and constantly owned, and observed in the Church of Christ, as derived from him; As if *private fancies*, and *solitary dreams*, and single imaginations of weak and *silly men*, or women, were now holyer, or had more in them of the Spirit, than the publique *Oracles of the sure Word of God*; which the *Catholick Church* hath received from God by the hands of holy men; and by a constant succession of an holy Ministry hath delivered to us, with constancy and fidelity (as to the main:) however particular branches or members of this Church may have failed and withered. If these *Antiministeriall Novellists* have nothing whereby to set off their pretended gifts of the Spirit, and singular holinesse, but only novelty, fancy, and *uncertain* Inspirations, nothing to cry down all former holy ways of the Church, but this; that they are conform to all Antiquity and Scripture regulations; The least beam of whose glorious light alwayes either equalls, or far exceeds their new either superfluous, or dubious illuminations; Truly they

they must give all learned and godly Ministers together with all judicious and sober Christians leave, to passe by the *Idoll of their new dressed Spiritualty and Sanctity*, without *any admiration*, devotion or the least salutation: Nor can we at all consider *private spirits*, warped from, and bent against the *publique Spirit of Christ*, in the Scripture, in the practise of the Catholick Church; and in the most *eminent Christians*, both ancient and modern.

Potius vetera & tuta quam periculosa & nova sectemur. Tac.

We shall content our selves with that *plain* and *pristine* holynesse, and manifestations of the Spirit, which are expressed in the Word; deposited in the Church; preserved in an *holy Ministry*; exemplified in all true Christians: and most eminently in Jesus Christ and his Apostles, the great and famous Founders, Teachers and Establishers of holy Truths, holy Duties, holy Sacraments, holy Orders, and holy Ministry in the Church: And this with divine Power and Authority, not onely *personall*, but *successionall*; without which the instituted Service and Worship of Christ had ere this failed. These being ever since Christs time in all the world, imployed in Teaching, Gathering, Baptizing, Governing, Feeding, Preserving, and Perfecting the Body of Christ, which is his Church: We know not, and so we cannot desire, *other holinesse*, than that, by which we beleived the Truths, obeyed the Commands, feared the Threatnings, observed the Duties, preserved the Institutions, continued the Orders, reverenced the Embassadors, joyed in the Graces, hoped in the Promises; and were led conformably to Christ by that Spirit, which Jesus Christ had given to his Church, long before these *new coyners* had graven the stamps, or set up their Mints: We are glad, and blesse God, when we attain unfaignedly to that Spirit of Holynesse, which hears the Word of God with *fear and trembling*, from the mouth of those able and godly Ministers, which are the *Messengers* or Angels sent from Christ, by the Churches Ordination: Which teacheth us, to pray with *understanding*, constancy, fervently, and comelinesse; to receive the pledges of Gods love in Christ from their hands (duly consecrating the holy mysteries) with *reverence*, preparednesse, and thankfulnesse; That *holinesse*, which *loves* with sincerity, *gives* with cheerfulnesse, rejoyceth in well doing, suffers with patience, lives by Faith, acts by Charity; is holy with order, contentednesse and humility, without any fury, faction or confusion.

True holinesse and true Saints.

Sanctitas est scientia colendorum deorum. Tul. de Nat. D.

ἐπιστήμη τοῦ εὔχεσθαι καὶ τὸ θύειν τοῖς θεοῖς ἡ ὁσιότης. *Plato in Eutyp.*

That holinesse which hath nothing in it novell or præter-scripturall; nothing fancifull, verball, tumultuary, violent, schismaticall, disorderly, partiall, pernicious, or injurious to any; which chuseth to be a Martyr for Charity and Unity, as well as Verity, in the Church: rather suffering much than giving scandall or making a schism, according to the pious and excellent counsell

ὅσιον τὸ τοῖς θεοῖς προσφιλές, τὸ δὲ μὴ, ἀνόσιον. *Plat. Euryph. Sanctum est quod deo gratum.*

of

of *Dionysius* to *Novatus*. That holinesse which is old, as the *Ancient of dayes*, reall, rationall, *demonstrative* from the Word of God, and exemplified in the lives of former Saints: Which is meek, courteous, charitable, humble, just to all men, abounding with all righteousnesse, and the fruits of *righteousnesse*, *peace*, and *establishment*, both to private consciences, and publique Churches. That holinesse, which hath nothing in it supercilious, calumniating, defamatory, insolent, bitter or burthensome to any true Christians, true Churches, and true Ministers, which know how to reprove, what is amisse, without rejecting all that is well; to reform the crooked, without ruining what is right. That holinesse, which, as the Sun-beams is always like it self; like the *Father of spirituall light*; uniform and constant in all true Saints, in all ages, and in all administrations Divine, either immediate, or mediate; as to its rule, the Will and Word of God; as to its end, the glory of God, in Gods way; as to its Epitome, or sum, *the love of God*, and its neighbour; as to its *happy* fruits and effects, the good of mankinde, chiefly of the Church of Christ: These have ever been the same for kind, however differing in degrees, according to the measure which God hath given to his true Saints and servants; who never differed from God, or the Word, or one another, as they were holy and spirituall, however, as men and carnall in part, they had their *crookednesse*, unevennesses, and dissentings.

These are the fruits of Gods Spirit; this that *true Holinesse*, for which we pray, of which we dare not boast: These are the Saints, whose *shadows* we count *Soveraign*; whose presence a blessing; whose wayes unblameable; whose joyes unspeakable; whose works most imitable; whose conversation most amiable, heavenly and divine; who chuse rather to suffer, than any way to act in cases dubious, as to secular dissensions, which have much of the *Beast*, somewhat of the *Man*, and little of the *true Christian*: The worth of these Pearls is infinitely beyond some mens *counterfeit forgeries*, whose lustre is chiefly from worldly glory, and secular advantages; who out of *ashes* are melted up to the shining and brickleness of glasse, by the *fervour* of some spirits; who think it enough to *glister* with novelties, and to boast of *Inspirations*; fancying all is reformed, which is but changed, though much to the worse; who are forced to set off themselves by the foil of *severe censuring* of others; Fearing nothing so much as a true light; and those discoveries which are made of them by serious and judicious Christians; who judge not by mens *lips*, and *appearances*, but by their lives and practises, compared to the Word of God; For which, *true Ministers*, most eminently and impar-

Δεῖ γὰρ καὶ πᾶν ὁτιοῦν παθεῖν ὑπὲρ τοῦ μὴ διακόψαι τὴν ἐκκλησίαν τοῦ θεοῦ. καὶ ἦν οὐκ ἀδοξοτέρα ἡ ἕνεκεν τοῦ μὴ σχίσαι μαρτυρία τῆς ἕνεκεν τοῦ μὴ εἰδωλολατρῆσαι γενομένης. ἐκεῖ μὲν γὰρ ὑπὲρ μιᾶς τις τῆς ἑαυτοῦ ψυχῆς, ἐνταῦθα δὲ ὑπὲρ ὅλης τῆς ἐκκλησίας μαρτυρεῖ. *Dionys. Epist. Aurea. apud Euseb. l. 6. hist. c. 38.*

impartially holding forth to the discovery of all mens deformities, are of all men most abhorred by these pretenders; who at a true and full view will not onely not appear to other *such gifted* men, and spirituall, as they pretend; but they will be ashamed of their arrogance, and despite against those good Christians, and those true Ministers whom they have so much vilified and contemned.

8. *Vulgar mistakes of spirituall influences.*

The common mistake of proud, weak, or *fancifull* men, whose tongues are onely tipt with Sanctity, and the name of the Spirit, is this, That they know not indeed *of what Spirit* they are, as to Profession; Nor consider *of what Spirit* they ought to be, as to temper, if they will *be truly Christs Disciples*; Contenting themselves with light and *airy presumptions*, in stead of *serious* and *searching* examinations of truth: *comparing themselves with themselves*, they fancy they grow holyer, as they grow *bolder* in their opinions, or actions: Hence they are easily flattered into *high Imaginations*, and cheated with *strong Presumptions*; as if some common *gifts of knowledge*, some *Scepticall quicknesse*, some volubility of utterance, some Scripturall expressions, which they have attained beyond their former selves, or their equals, were rare, immediate, and speciall gifts of the Spirit. Then, because they should seem no body, if they carry their *small wares* in an *old pack*, * they *invent some* new fashion of *Religion*; or some modell of a Church-way, which they *strongly fancy*; after they have once brought forth their fancy to any *form and shape*, they are strangely *inamored* with it, all old figures never so uniform, Catholick, and comely, *seem deformed*, ugly, *Antichristian*: Then follows those quick emotions, and stirrings *upon their spirits*, which have the quicknings, only of *Self in them*; these are presently cryed up for motions, and * *manifestations*, and excitations, and impulses of Gods Spirit on them; then, they are easily moved to extraordinary heats, and irregular vehemencies, as counterfeit possessed are, by the looking on and *applauses of others*, whose sillinesse makes them gentle spectators, and *obsequious admirers* of any thing, that seems new to them, or is above them. Nothing troubles these *pretenders* so much, as if you look *too neer* and *too narrowly* on their practises. * Nothing angers them so much, as what they fear, may discover them: you must not ask them, where *are their miracles*, where their *Empire over Devils*; where their *languages*; where their *prophecies*; either as *predictions* of things to come, or as *interpretations* of obscure Prophecies in the Scripture, referring to Jesus Christ? These questions (though they are but *just* to be put, where *extraordinary Inspirations* are pretended)

Luk. 9.55.

Impudentiam pro pietate jactitant, quasi eo sanctiores essent quo verbosiores; Bern.

Ἀταλαίπωρος τοῖς πολλοῖς ἡ ζήτησις τῆς ἀληθείας καὶ ἐπὶ τὰ ἑτοῖμα μᾶλλον τρέπονται. *Thucid. hist. l.* 1.

Δυσθήρατος ἡ ἀλήθεια. *Bas. de Sp. s.*

* *Quos diabolus a veritatis via in veteri charitate detinere non potuit, novi itineris errore circumscribit, & decipit.* Cyp.

* φανερώσεις, The *Marcionites* had private lectures, which they called Manifestations or Illuminations; from a Propheresse, *Philumena. Tertul. præ. ad Hæ. c.* 44.

* *Impostoribus nihil est lumine inimicitius.*

are too hard for them: these pose them, and afflict them, when they are thus urged by Ministers, or any sober Christians; who expect no satisfactory answer, in any of those particulars, (which are the *proper effects and demonstrations of the Spirit*, in its *extraordinary motions*,) when indeed they observe in these *pretenders*, so little of *ordinary*, sound and saving knowledge; so nothing of that *meeknesse of wisdome*, which every true Christian, in whom the Spirit of Christ dwels, injoyes in some measure; so *utter desolation* of any thing, that may argue *any thing extraordinary and excellent*, which may justly own the *Spirit of Christ*, for its speciall Author and *infuser*. But quite contrary; grosse ignorance in many things; yet puffed up with intolerable pride, poysoned with errors, kindled with passions, sharpned with violence, delighting in furies, boasting in discords, schisms and confusions, either begun, or increased, or continued by the *restlesse agitations* of their fierce and unquiet spirits: whose *impetuous temper* is impatient of nothing so much, as true Christian patience; of Peace, Order, and charitable harmony in any part *of the Church of Christ*; There is nothing they can lesse endure, than able, learned, godly and resolute Ministers, in whom dwels (indeed) a far more excellent Spirit of God; full of wisdome, of power, of courage, full of Christ; who can and dare detect the deceits and juglings of these *vain mindes*: manifesting their folly, discovering their nakednesse, emptinesse, and nothingnesse in respect of any extraordinary Illuminations, or Inspirations of Gods holy Spirit in any way of Religion: After all the cry, and noise, and glorying of these *mens inspirings*, at the best, all amounts to no more, than the same Gospell, the same Duties, the same Sacraments, the same Jesus, the same God, who was with far more knowledge, purity, peace, love, zeal and constancy *owned*, served and honoured in this and other Churches, in that *ancient way and holy Ministry* which the Church ever used; which Christ instituted, and with which God was so well pleased, that he blessed it, as the means, to preach the Gospell, to *plant Religion*, to settle and govern the Church in first and after times, amidst all the persecutions and heresies that opposed it. This is the best of their Inspirings; the setting of some new glosse and fashion on Christian Religion, whose purity and simplicity like gold, cares not be thus painted over.

Magi & Augures nihil suis actibus successurum Iuliano affirmabant, nisi Athanasium primo velut omnium obstaculum sustulisset. Ruff. l. 1. c. 32. Hist. Ecc.

Gal. 1. 7.

But take these Inspired men in their *degenerations*, depravings and worstings of Religion, and you will easily see, how such *equivocall* generations and imperfect *mixtures*, and meer *monsters* of Religion, presently *putrifie* and pervert to error, faction, licentiousnesse, violence, rapine, civill oppressions, tyrannies, against all that applaud not, or approve not the *rarity* of their conceits

and

and inventions; which first kindle with *modest sparks*, as if they would enlighten, warm, and refine the Church, Religion, and Ministry; but after they have got to them *vulgar* fewell, they arise to such *dreadfull flames* and conflagrations, as threaten to consume all that was ever built before them: that so the goodly *Palaces* of ancient and true Religion being *demolished*, they may have a clearer ground, where on to set up the feeble cottages of their new framing and erecting. Poor men! thus once * puffed up with their tympanies of *self conceptions*, and getting into some *warmer Sun*, having once over-looked *their* first errors, they never after have leisure, patience, or humility to discern the *grosse* yet *secret distempers*, which are in their spirits; * the many distinctions, and disguises, and windings, by which worldly lusts, passions, and interests *slily creep in*, and concealedly worke in their hearts, even then most *securely*, (and so most dangerously) when under this *blind* of Gods Spirit; when the *Lord* shall be intitled to the whole plot and project of their follies and furies, both in its *softer beginnings* and its *rougher proceedings*.

Modestiora sunt errorum initia; & blandientia venena; Lactant.

* *Omnes tument, omnes scientiam pollicentur: ante sunt perfecti quam edocti.* Tertul. de Hæ. c. 41.

* Not raptures and gifts, but humility and charity give the greatest evidences and surest instances of Gods Spirit, and of salvation.

9. *Evidences of their folly.*

Of these fallacies in point of speciall Inspirings and motions of Gods Spirit, there are no surer detections than these: 1. That these so *moved and active spirits* do always finde lesse content, and pleasure in, have lesse zeal and contention for the *great things of God*, (which are Faith, Righteousnesse, Peace, and Holinesse) than they doe for their *little novelties* and *fancies*: 2. They finde lesse comfort and joy in themselves, to be kept within, and humbly to walk in those *holy bounds* of religious Truth and Order; (which the Word of God hath *clearly set* before them, and all holy Christians, and the purest Churches alwayes observed) than to be alwayes *busily disputing* for, and acting over those *petty parts* of their *scruples*, *novelties*, and *extravagancies*; Which have nothing in them but a *verminly nimblenesse* and subtlety, being bred out of the *putrefactions* of mens Brains, and the *corruptions* of the times, in matters of Religion; and are rather *pernicious*, than any way *profitable*, in comparison of the more sober strength, and usefulnesse of nobler creatures: Nor is it by gracious persons disputed, but that one *serious Christian* of the old stamp, one *able and faithfull Minister of the Church of England*, whom these so contemne and hate, hath heretofore done, and still doth more good, and gives greater *demonstrations* of the Spirit of Christ dwelling in him, with wisdom, gravity, learning, humility, diligence, peaceablenesse and charity, (by which many have been restrained or converted from sin: or established and confirmed in the ways of God) than whole *heaps* of these *novell Teachers*, and swarms of Inspired pretenders, who like *drones* do but seek to rob the *hives* and starve the

the Bees: who serve (in some fits) to *scratch itching* ears, to some tune of *pleasure, liberty, profit, novelty,* or *preferment*; but not to teach the ignorant, to settle the shaken, to compose the tossed, to heal the wounded, or to wound the ulcerated Consciences of any men to any *soundnesse of mind,* or true holinesse of manners.

Ædificantur in ruinam, illuminantur in cæciores tenebras.

Their Proselytes are rather *perverted*, than converted; made *theirs* by a *schismaticall* and *factious* adherence; rather than *Christs* by a *fiduciary* obedience; or the Churches by a charitable and humble communion; *Faction* and *confusion* and every *evill* work are the fruits of *pertinacious* and *pragmatick* ignorance, as *Union, Peace,* and *Charity,* are the *genuine effects* of sound knowledge and humble wisdome; In which wayes onely true Christians have ever judged the highest gifts and graces of Christs Spirit to be both derived and decerned. I am sure there is a vast difference between a wanton Fancy and a holy Spirit, between a glib Tongue and a gracious Heart. We may add to these discoveries of fallacious pretentions to the *Spirits speciall motions*; That, both in the first *broaching,* and after *drawings* forth of their new projects and inventions, the *authors* of them more *look to men, than to God*; how it may suit with *secular aimes,* and *politique interest's, private* or *publique,* than how it sorts with *Gods Word,* or the rule of Christ, or the Churches practise in purest times; or its *present distresses*; whose frame as to the main both for *Doctrine, Ministry,* and *Government,* hath alwayes been the same, both in times of persecution and of peace; when favoured and disfavoured by men; And such it ever was in *England,* and possibly it will be if it *out-live this storm*; I am sure these *Novelties* so much opposing this Church, and *true Ministers* in it, would never have so quickned by any inward *heat of Spirit,* if they did not presume that the *Sun did shine warm* on them; which yet is no infallible *sign of Gods blessing*; If these Antiministeriall adversaries, these now so *Inspired men,* (who join in their plots, and power, and activity, by which they either secretly undermine, by evill speaking and separating from the *publique Ministry*; or openly invade and arrogate the Office; or wholly deride and oppose the Function;) if they expected nothing but Winter and persecution, and such *measure* as they *mete*; I believe it would damp their spirits very much: They would then think it a part of *prudence* in a *Christian Spirit,* to *sleep in a whole skin*; by keeping themselves in that station, wherein God, and the Lawes both of Church and State have set them: As they *did very warily,* in those times, when there was just power *restraining* them in those due bounds, which then they thought became them best; and they would no doubt have thought so still, (for all the fullnesse of their spirits and ebul-

Abominanda religionis ludibria colentia temporum rationes, non leges Dei. Naz. or. Lat. *Hypocritarum pietas est temporum aucupium.* Cyp.

ebullition of their rarer gifts) if *strange indulgences* in matters of Religion, and Church Order, had not tempted them to *safe extravagancies*, and unpunished insolencies, chiefly against the Church, and Church men.

In other things, of *civill affairs*, where it is very likely their spirit prompts them, as much to be medling (because more is got by those activities:) they know how to *keep their spirits* in very good order; being over-awed with *evident danger*, attending any factious, seditious or tumultuary motions; None of these small *spirited men* (who are seldome *little in their own eyes*) are powerfully moved to usurp any place in the *Councell of State*; to arrogate the *office* and authority of an *Embassadour* or *publique Agent*; to set himself in the Seat of Justice *un-commissioned*; or to intrude into any place Military, or Civill, without a *Warrant* from other, than their own *forward spirits*; though their pride and ambition (* *like Absaloms*) *may fancy*, they could better dispatch businesse, doe exacter Justice, and speedier, than any in Authority; yet here, the *danger and penalty of intrusion cowes* their zeal, curbs their heady spirits, and *cuts their combes*: Nor are they often either so *valiant*, or so *fool hardy*, as to act by their pretended *impulses* in any way, but where they think there may be *safety*; which they now find (as *from many men*) in what ever they say, or doe, against the honour, order, and Ministry of this reformed Church of *England*: which they see hath not *many souldiers* to defend it; nor *advocates* to plead for it; nor *Patrons* to protect it. Wanton and petulant servants which were formerly but as the * *dogs of the flock*, will easily *insult over* the children of the family, when they see *them Orphanes*, and *exposed to injuries*: either wanting true * *Nursing Fathers* and Mothers, or these wanting that *tendernesse* toward them, which is hardly to be expected in *step-mothers*, and onely *titular* parents. It is no adventure for *timorous beasts* to goe over, where they find the fence trodden down, and the gap made wide; So, much more prevalent with *vain* and *proud* men are the *impressions of fear from men*, than those *from God*, whose commands and threatnings are attended with Omnipotent Justice, which is *slow paced*, but *sure*; Nor doe I doubt, but those subtle and *insolent enemies* against this Reformed Church and the Ministry of it, doe already * find the first strokes of Divine Vengeance in their own ingratefull breasts.

* 2 Sam. 15.3. *Nunquam defuit ambitioso preclara sui ipsius opinio, & summa de seipso expectatio.* Sym.

* Iob 30.1. *Insolentioris animi proprium est, calamitosam virtutem indigne tractare, dicteriis appetere; injuriis afficere; & de iis quæ immerita patitur maxime exprobrare.* Plin.

* Isa. 49.23.

* *Prima est hæc ultio, quod se Judice nemo nocens absolvitur.* Iuv. *Occultum quatienti animo tortore flagellum.* Id.

The further triall of these pretenders to the Spirit, I must leave to the *impartiality* of judicious Christians, in that experience which they have of the fruits which they bring forth. What truths of God have these *Antiministeriall adversaries* ever brought forth, or further cleared and illustrated, than was before?

 What

What weighty controversie or other question in Divinity, polemicall or practicall, have they learnedly and solidly stated? What part of obscurer Scripture have they well interpreted? What *body of Divinity* have they blest this Age withall, beyond what it formerly enjoyed in great variety and plenty? What cases of Conscience have they more cleared or better decided? Is either *Law* or *Gospell* beholding to them? yea rather; how have some men studied to make void the Law by immorall licentiousnesse? and the Gospell too, by such not *free* but rather profuse and prodigall *grace*, as excludes those holy conditions of repentance, and good workes, which the *Gospell* requires as necessary *concommitants* and *fruits* of true and lively Faith? What Scripture have they handled which they have not tortured, mangled, and broken the very bones of it? What controversie have they not more studied to pester and entangle? What *truth* have they not darkened with their cloudy *words* and senselesse *notions*, which they call glorious heights? What heresie have they not revived? What poysonous Error have they not tampered with? What sin and enormity have they not palliated, or excused, or applauded, as the effect, either of Christian liberty or necessity? How many simplier Christians Faith have they *subverted*? perswading them they never had Christ *rightly preached* to them; nor were in any *saving Church-way*, till these Inspired Teachers came to *direct* them; how to cast off and despise *their Ministers* and the whole Office of *the Ministry*.

Jam.2.17.

10. *How short they come of that Spirit which shews it self in true Ministers.*

Neither then the Word of God, nor right Reason, nor sober Sense will give testimony of any *speciall gifts of the Spirit* in these men, either in knowledge, or in wisdome, or in utterance, or in any grace or vertue; In all which they are nothing in regard of many Ministers and others, who as far excell them, as *gold* doth *brasse*, and *silver lead*; Nor are their fruits to the publique and to others, any way proportionable to their boasting against the Ministers: which is as far from truth, as it is from humility; if these may be measured and esteemed, not by *proud swelling words* of themselves; or by high scorns, and rude contempts of others; but by the *exactnesse* of holy walkings, and the fruitfulnesse of publique labours on the hearts or lives of others.

Hanc habet invidia in seipsa pœnam, aut non videre, aut nolle videre, aut maligne videre virtutem alienam, quam nescit imitari. Gerson.

Herein no *ignorance*, or *envy*, or *calumny* can be so *wilfully* or resolvedly blind, (but *onely in these men*) as not to see and acknowledge, That God hath *given witnesse* from heaven, against the crooked and *perverse* generation of these detractors from, and *destroyers of*, the honor of the *Ministry of England*; by the eminent Learning, Piety, Zeal, Industry, Fidelity, Charity, Patience, Constancy and vigilancy of many *centuries*, yea many *thousands* of able, and godly

godly Ministers, both in the *restauration*, and *preservation* of Truth, Purity, and Power of the Christian Reformed Religion in this Church; others have sought the *goods* of this Church, but these the good of it. I could here fill many Volumes (as many Ministers (both godly Bishops and Presbyters) in this Church, have done, by their acute, solid, devout, and most profitably pleasant writings) with the histories of *many* of their *lives*, (some of which are registred to posterity by commendable pens: others by tolerable ones, whose gratefull design is good; but their historique faculty far short of those merits, which they seek to eternize. How eminent have they been, as *Moses, in all good learning?* how indefatigable in their labours? how dear, usefull, and desireable to all good and excellent Christians in their lives and deaths? What Trophies they have not gained *over the adversaries* of our Christian and reformed Religion, by their Prayers, Sermons, and most incomparable Writings? No lesse have been their many and renowned Victories, which they have obtained over the very Devils; whom a long time they kept, as it *were in awe* and in a *chain*: How many sinners have been redeemed from his snares, and converted from the evill and errours of their wayes by their powerfull Ministry? How many *fiery darts* of Satan have they quenched? How many *weak hands* and *feeble knees* have they strengthened? How many *remorselesse soules* have they wounded; piercing between the *scales of Leviathan* by the two-edged sword of God in their mouths? How many *wounded Consciences* have they (like good *Samaritans*) healed with the balm of *Gilead*? How many doubting and despairing spirits have they revived and established? How many *mouthes* of *aliens* have they stopped, by the *unanswerable pregnancy* of the truths, which they have cleared and mightily maintained? In fine; before ever the *croaking Frogs* of *Egypt* spread over the land, and filled every place with their importune and insignificant noises, against the Ministers and Ministry of this Church; (seeking by their muttering clamours to contend with the *Nightingales*; and to silence the sweet singers of Israel;) how were the *excellent Ministers* of this Church, and the famous Ministry hereof, esteemed at home and abroad among the chiefest blessings, for use, and noblest beauties, for ornament, which this or any Nation and Church ever enjoyed? Being as the two *goodly pillars of Solomons Temple*, sustaining the burthen, and adding to the beauty of Religion; being *sacred Oracles* for holy direction, and great *examples* for vertuous imitation.

In what part of good learning have not some of the *Ministers* of *England* excelled, and some of *them* in all? What divine or humane truth have they not handled, cleared, and asserted? What controversie in Religion have they not rightly stated, fully disputed

puted, and solidly determined? What part of *practicall piety*, and Devotion have they not illustrated, and adorned in their Writings, with most sweet, suasive, and pathetick flowers of holy Oratory, mixed with truths, gathered out of the gardens of God, the *Scriptures*, and their own pure Consciences? What Scripture have they not commented upon, learnedly, methodically, clearly, and succinctly? Yea what Text (almost) in the whole Bible, *Old* or *New*, Law or Gospell, History or Prophesie, Psalmodicall, or Epistolicall, have not the Ministers of *England* preached and printed upon with *accuratenesse* and judgement? So that the *quintessence of the Sermons*, set forth by them in this Church, would in the judgement of the learned Lord *Verulam* make one of the most exact, and absolute Commentaries on the Bible, that ever was. It were endlesse to enumerate the *names*, the excellencies, the learned works, the holy fruits and blessed successes, which have attended the Ministers of this Church; whom one would have thought to have been set so above any such envy, and malice, and sacriledge, never any Reformed Christians would ever have so *maligned* and despised, as to have sought to destroy them and their function: Nor can I indeed in charity think, any doe so that are truly such.

The excellencies of the Antiministerials.

As for their bitter enemies and rivalls, these Inspirators, on the other side; I am ashamed to shame them so much, as I *must needs doe*, if I should shew the world their emptinesse, shallownesse, penury, meannesse, nothingnesse, as to Reason, Religion, Learning, common Sense, *pack-staffe* Oratory; How grosse, confused, raw, flat, insipid, affected they are in speaking or writing; how dark in doctrine; how disorderly in disputes; how impotent in perswasion; how impertinent in reproof; how unauthorative in all they say, and doe, as *Teachers*; What perfect Battologists they are; what circles they make, and rounds they dance in their Prayings and Sermonings; strong only in cavilling, and rayling, and calumniating against true and able *Ministers*: And for their writings, with which they have lately so crammed and abused the world; how little have they set out to any other purpose, save onely to wast a great deal of good paper; and to make the world beleive, they were *richly laden*, because they spread so *large sayles*? How doe their pamphlets cheat the well meaning buyers and readers with the *decoy of some very* specious and spirituall title; as if all were *Manna, and Aarons rod*, which were in their Arks; when there is nothing but such emblemes, for the most part, of *Mice* and *Emrods*, as the *Philistines* put into the Ark of God, as memorials of their sin, their shame, and punishment? What Reader may not *tear their books*, with turning the leaves to and

1 Sam. 6.4.

fro,

so, before ever he findes *acutenesse*, or solidity; learning, or piety; Truth, or Charity; Divinity, or Humanity; Spirituals, or Rationals; but onely antick fancies and affected words, strangely deforming *antient* and *true* Theology, in its morals, mysteries and holy speculations; How much better had they wrote nothing, than so much, to so little good purpose, to so evill an intent; onely to amuse the *simple reader*, with shews of rare notions; and by spiritlesse Prefacings, to lead on their ruder steleticks and declaimings against the Order, Government, Religion, *Ministers*, and *Ministry of the Church of England*; in which their scriblings they mixe so much *copperass* and *gall* with their ink, that they eat out all characters of Truth, Candor or Charity in their Papers, never affording them any word that may either savour of civility, as to ingenuous men; or of Justice, as to men of good learning and some merit; but all is written to deform them, their calling and Ministry, to expose them to vulgar scorns, to fit them for publique victims to the cruell malice of the enemies of the reformed Religion. Indeed against the Ministry and Ministers of *England* they chuse to write with *Aqua fortis* rather *than any ink*; and covet red ink rather than black, trusting more to their swords than their pens; nor doe they confide so much in their *Brains*, as their hands; their insolency being far beyond their inventions; which tempts them rather to pistoll Ministers by desperate Assasination, than to dispute with them in the *Schooles* or by the *Presse*.

Nor is this any envious or injurious diminution of these men, (who owe most of the good feathers they have to the preaching and writings of the Ministers of *England*, and not to any Inspirations;) but it's a just representation of their *ungratefull* vanity, and the Ministers reall worth, who have excelled, wherein soever these pretenders are most defective: And defective they are in all things, wherein able and true Ministers have most excelled. If this stroak of my pen seems any thing of *uncomely boasting*, they have compelled us to it, and so may the better excuse, and bear with this our folly; which is not yet such, by their provoking examples of vapouring and vanity, but that we know by Gods grace how to own, what ever is of God in any of them; and to ascribe what ever is good in Ministers, to the grace and bounty of God, who hath magnified his *power in their weaknesse*; And however *wee, now living, be Nothing*, yet our *excellent Predecessors*, by whom the honour of this holy function hath been rightly derived to us, have merited from us, and all good men this acknowledgement to the praise of Gods grace.

It is no detraction or injury to prefer the Ministers of England before these pretenders to Inspiration. 2 Cor. 12. 11.

Pro defensione famæ licita & honesta est laus propria. Reg. Jur.

Defensio est, non arrogantia, Amb. l. 118.

The blessings which have come to this Church and Nation by the true Ministers.

That the godly, able and faithfull Ministers in this Church of *England* have by Gods blessing been the great *restorers* and conservators *of good learning in this Nation*; the *liberall diffusers* of ingenuous education; the valiant *vindicators* of the reformed Religion; the *commenddable* examples of piety and vertue, in all kinds restraining, and reforming all sin, error, excesse, profanenesse, and superstition, by their good lives and doctrine; Teaching and encouraging all manner of holynesse, civility, candour, meeknesse, gravity, and charity, throughout the whole Nation; What noble, worshipfull, or ingenuous family hath not, or might not have, been bettered by them? (if they did not entertain them at illiberall rates, and ignoble distances: as too many used to doe, below the honour of their calling, and merit of their worth:) What City, or Country Village hath not been beautified, and blessed by them? Where ever such Ministers lived, as became the dignity of their place, and profession, there hath alwayes followed a *good sense* of piety, and a comely face both of Civility and Religion; And more might have been improved in every corner of the land, long ere this, if, what hath been oft vapoured and flourished, had been really performed; that is, the *setling* of a competent maintenance every *where* for a *competent* Minister. *Scandalous* livings *have been* no small cause of too *many* scandalous Ministers; whom *necessity* oft compelled to things uncomely, both for their society and support. Upon whose sores these *flesh-flyes*, the enemies of the Ministry, are alwayes lighting and biting; loth to see, or hear of, those *many incomparable Ministers*, who have been in many places of this Church, as Saint *Ambrose* was said to be in *Millain*, both the *ornament* of the City and *defence* of Religion: In stead of whom, some *new Jesuitick Modellers* would fain bring a company of *Locusts* and *Caterpillers* upon the face of the land, a sort of *illiterate* and unordained Teachers, who like *ambulatory Arabs*, or wandring *Scythians*, must every week or month change their quarters, as fast as they have *devoured silly widows houses*: These in a short time will not be much beyond *Cantors* and *Vagrants*; like rowling stones, neither getting mosse themselves, nor raising any building of piety, or sound knowledge in others; for the same small stock always serves their turn, in their severall gests and quarters. By this meanes (they hope) the *Church* and *State* in a short time will be spoiled of all those *fair flowers* of good Scholars and able *constant Ministers*, which were well rooted in learning, and plentifully watered with the *dew of heaven*, (the gifts and graces of Gods Spirit:) that so there may be *room enough*, for those *rank* and ill weeds to spread all over this *English* garden and field: under whose *specious covert* of spiritualty all sort of *venemous Serpents*

Cogit ad turpia necessitas. Non habet virtus inimicam præter paupertatem & invidiam. Eras.

Et ornamentum & munimentum urbis & Ecclesiæ, Ambrosius.

As the old *Circumcelliones*.

pents and *hurtfull beasts* may be hidden, till they are so multiplied, εὐάλωτον ἡ
that *through mutuall jealousies* and dissensions, they fall to tearing πονηρία ϗ
and devouring one another; for, however, like Serpents, wicked πανταχόθεν ἑ-
men may for a while twine together, yet their *different heads* will αὐτῇ περιπίπ-
soon find, wherewith to exercise *their stings* and teeth against each τουσα. Naz.
other; Impious mens confederacies are not friendship but faction and conspiracy. Nothing being more inconsistent, than ignorance, error, and impiety; which having no principles of union or order in them, can have nothing of firmnesse or stability among them.

I doubt not, but there are, (notwithstanding so many *bitter* 12.
spirits, and *rebellious children*, have become ungratefull Apostates, *The blessings*
against this Church and its worthy Ministery) thousands of ex- *which good*
cellent Christians, who have not bowed the *knee to these Baalims*: *Christians*
who have both cause and hearts to confesse, that the *feet of these* *owe to good*
messengers, the true Ministers of *England*, have brought *light* and *Ministers, un-*
peace to their soules; That their pious and constant labors have *der God.*
not been either so weak or unfruitfull, as might in any sort deserve, or justifie such hard recompenses, as these now are, with which a *foolish* and *unthankefull generation* seeks *to requite the Lord*, Deut. 32. 6.
and his faithfull servants, the true Ministers, whose names shall yet live among good Christians, with *durable honour*; and their Eccles. 7. 1.
memories shall be precious as sweet Ointments, when these *dead* (yet busie) *flies*, who seek to corrupt them, shall rot as dung on Eccles. 10. 1.
the face of the earth: Their *unsavory stench* is already come up, and hath greatly defiled many parts of this Church; being justly *offensive* to all wise, and good men in the present age; and for the future they will be memorable for nothing, but *illiterate impudence*, *ungratefull malice*, and *confused madnesse*, who like beasts were able to waste a fair field, and desolate a well reformed Church; but never to cultivate or plant any *thing like it*.

The field of this Church in many places, by the *blessed labours* of true and able husbandmen, was heretofore full of good corn; *the valleys and hils did laugh and sing*; poore and rich were happy in the great increases, with which the *Lord of the harvest* crowned the *labours* of his faithfull Ministers; before the enemy had such liberty to sow his tares, even at noon day; yea in many places to rout the *true labourers*, to leave many places desolate, and only to scatter that *self-sowing corn*, which is like to that which springs *on the house top, whereof the Mower shall never fill his hand*, Psal. 129. 7.
nor he that *bindeth up the sheaves his bosome*; Who sees not, that *one handfull* of that crop, which was formerly wont to be tilled by the *skilfull* and diligent hand of *true and able Ministers*, was, for its weighty soundnesse in knowledge, and modest fulnesse in humility, far more worth, than many *sheaves* and *cartloads* of these

burnt, and *blasted ears*; whose pride pretends in one night to grow to such eminent gifts of the Spirit, for preaching, as shall exceed all *the parts and studies of Ministers*; when it's evident to all, that will but *rub* them in their hands, that these *wild oats*, and *smutty ears*, by lifting up their heads so high, doe but proclaim their *emptinesse* and *lightnesse*.

And 'twere well, if they were onely such cockle, such *trash and light gear*; they now grow to sharp *thistles*, thornes mixed with true weed; which seeks to starve, choak, and pull down to the earth, all the hopes and joy of the true labourers; that rich crop of truth, order, piety, charity, and sincerity, which was *formerly* in great plenty, and still is, in good measure, on the ground: Yea thousands of Christians, in many places of this Nation, doe already grievously complain, of the *sad and desolate* estate, to which they are reduced for want of able and true Ministers, residing among them: crying out, that *a famine of the Word is* come upon them; and *leannesse is entred into their soules*: having none to sow the *immortall seed* of the Word, or to dispense the *bread of life* to them, but a *few straglers* now and then: of whose *calling and authority* to minister holy things, no wise man hath any confidence; and of whose *insufficiency* every way, all men have too much experience, where ever they obtrude themselves: That most Christians had rather (yea and better) want the Word and Sacraments, than receive them, *so defiled, so nullified*, by such unwashen, and unwarranted hands. For it is hardly to be *beleeved*, that those, who are so much *enemies to the spirit of Christ* in true Ministers (of which there hath been so great and good demonstrations, in gifts, lives, and successes) should either have, or come in the *power of the same Spirit*, which they so much *despise*, and blaspheme. Sure the *Kingdome of Christ is not divided against it self*; *but is uniform*, and constant; not depending on the various impulses of mens humours, fancies, and worldly interests, but established and governed by the most *sure Word*, and those holy rules, both for truth and order, therein contained: It is little sign of Christs *Spirit* in men, to *sow* those seeds of *errors* and divisions which holy men have been alwayes plucking up; or to build again that *Babell*, which so many godly *Ministers* have pulled down. But it becomes us Ministers not so much to dispute with these men about the Spirit, to which they so highly pretend; as to continue *to outdoe them* in the fruits of the Spirit, as our famous and blessed *forefathers* have done, and to leave the decision to the *Consciences* of true, and wise Christians, and to the *great Searcher* of mens hearts, and tryer of *mens spirits* and *workes*; who hath the *Spirit of burning*

Amos 8.11. Psal.106.15.

and

and refining; and who (if he hath not determined for the *superfluity* of wickednesse, and *ungratefull* wontannesse of this Nation, to lay us quite wast and desolate) will in his due time (after these *days of triall*) throughly *purge his floore*, and *weed his field*; even this, so *sadly havocked* and neglected Church; In which there are still some fruit, that have a blessing in them; and which we hope he will not destroy, who knows how to separate between *the pretious and the vile*. Isa. 4. 4. Mal. 3. 12. Isa. 65. 8.

13. Mean time Gods husbandmen, the *true and Ordained Ministers*, must have patience, (but not *slacken their* diligence) after the holy example of those *godly Bishops*, and Presbyters of the Church in the times of the *Arrian, Novatian, Donatistick*, and others prevalencies and persecutions. The fierce and *fiery spirit in the old hereticks* and schismaticks could least of all endure with temper and moderation, *those Bishops* and Ministers which were *soundest* in their judgements, faithfullest in their places, and holyest in their lives; * So that, not only they destroyed and drove away most of the orthodox Ministers, both Bishops and Presbyters, out of many Provinces in *Africa*, and so in *Asia*, as in *Europe*; but they sought with all fraud, and force to destroy, that *great Colosse* of Christian Religion, the most renowned Bishop of *Alexandria*, * *Athanasius*, who was the wonder and astonishment of all the world, for his learning, piety, and constancy: standing like an unshaken rock of *Truth* amidst the troubled Sea of *Arrian* Errors.

The patience and constancy of Ministers will best confute these pretenders.

* *Socrat. l. 1. c. 7. l. cap. 17. Can. African. Theod. l. 1. c. 12.*

* *Omnes quos factionis maculâ sciavit in Athanasium conspirabant.* Ruff. hist. l. 1. *Toto orbe profugus M. Athanasius sex annos in cisterna sine sole vixit.* Id.

If the hand of *Secular power* will not maintain the antient order of the true *Ministers of England*, in their Ministry, liberties, and lives, which we humbly crave and expect: * yet (we hope) the *Spirit of Christ*, and the power of *heaven*, will preserve us with good Consciences, amidst the trialls, losses, contempts, and deaths, which we may encounter: And however the * *Tail of the Dragon*, with many *windings* and insinuations, hath drawn after him *many stars from the heaven* of their formerly, (seemingly) sober, orderly, and *godly profession*, to the Earth of temporary successes, *worldly applauses, secular complyances*, and *irregular motions*, for vain glory, or for *filthy lucres* sake; yet *Christ* will still preserve * *in his right hand those stars*, which shine by his light, and are placed by his Name, Power, and Authority in the Firmament of his Church; * Although this may be the *houre of temptation*, which must come upon this Reformed Church, and the *power of darknesse*, which may for a time have leave, to deny, betray, set at naught, and *crucifie afresh the Lord of Glory*, in his true Ministers, and faithfull servants; yet good men may be confident, * that their bonds and scourges, their *revilings*, and *cruell mockings*, their being *sawn asunder* (between ignorance and error, schism and heresie, profanenesse and hypocrisie, superstition and licentiousnesse;) The very indignities, restraints

* *Ubicunque à perditis mala ista commissa sunt, ibi fervent ius, atque perfectius Christiana unitas profecit.* Aust. Ep. 50. de persec.

* Rev. 12. 4.

Rev. 2.

* *Brightman in Apoc.*

Rev. 3. 10.

* Heb. 11. 37.

Persecutio Christiani nominis in crementum. Lact.

Quanto magis premitur magis augetur. Id.

straints, injuries, and ruines of the godly Ministers, shall tend to the *honour, propagation*, and more glorious *restauration of the Reformed Religion*; which of later times hath wanted, nothing so much, whereby to set forth its primitive lustre and power, as the *constancy* and *patience* of the Ministers and Professours of it, in the point of comely suffering for the Truth. In which way the brightest beams *of the Spirit of Glory* are wont to appear. The base *cowardly* avoiding of sufferings, hath brought great reproaches upon many Ministers and other Christians; who (*Proteus-like*) by mean compliances, and palliations, suiting themselves to a *disorderly* and *variating world*, have much *eclipsed* and deformed the beauty and dignity of their holy Function, and Profession, both as Ministers, and as Christians.

Velut aurum, non verbis sed exiliis & carceribus probatur fides, & ad potioris metalli fulgorem resplendet. Ruff. Hist. l.2. c.6.

Crudelitas sectæ est illecebra; & semen est sanguis Christianorum. Tertul. Apol.

As it is far harder to *suffer persecution*, and to bear the *burning coales* of mens displeasure in *our bosomes*, than to make *long prayers*, or to preach soft and smooth Sermons; and to bandy *safe disputes* in the Sun shine of Peace, plenty, favour and prosperity: so more glory will then redound to God, and more honour to the Reformed Religion, from those sparkling rayes and effusions, of grace, which shall flow from *excellent Ministers*, when *they are red hot* in the forge of affliction, and hammered on the Anvile of the worlds malice, than ever did from those faint and weaker beams, by which they shined in the easie and ordinary formalities of Religion; Nor will any thing more assure them, and the uncharitable world, that they have *the Spirit of Christ in them of a Truth*, than when they shall find they have *holy and humble resolutions*, to suffer with Christ, and his Church, rather than *to reign with a wicked and irregular world*; whose Jesuitick *joys* will then be fulfilled, and crowned with garlands, when they shall see the learning, piety, order, government, and honour of that *Ministry*, (which sometime flourished to the great regret of all its enemies, in this reformed Church) utterly *prostrated*, vilified, impoverished and expulsed.

Piorum virtutes ut Aromata, quo magis conteruntur, eo frangrantius redolent. Ieron.

On the other side the spirituall joyes of *true and faithfull Ministers*, will be encreased by their being beaten, and evill intreated, and cast out of their Synagogues; by their being reproached, scorned, and wounded unjustly; not onely from their professed *enemies* of the *Romish* party; but even from those who were of *their own household*; who seemed to be their *familiar friends*: It is happier to have the least measure of Christs Spirit in *patience, truth*, and *power*; than to make the greatest boasts, and to enjoy the loudest vulgar applauses, which those *Chenaniahs* seem to affect and aim at; who dare now to *smite* every where the *true Prophets*, the plain dealing *Micaiahs*, on the mouth; designing to feed al the *true, able and faithfull Ministers* with the bread and *water of affliction*, because they

1 King. 22.

will not comply with, or yeeld to that novel, lying, proud and diſorderly ſpirit, with which their hearts and mouths are ſo filled with malice not onely againſt the Miniſtry, but againſt the proſperity of this and all other reformed Churches: which folly or fury they would have ſtyled and eſteemed to be in them, the *ſpeciall gifts* and *inſpirations of the Spirit of God.*

Proud and preſumptuous men doe not conſider, what is moſt true; * That the greateſt *blaſphemies* againſt Gods Spirit, and his Truth, are *oft coloured over* with greateſt *oſtentation of the Spirit*; as is evidently ſhewed both in former and later times; Many have a name to * *live by the Spirit*, and covet to be called ſpirituall, who are *dead in their luſts*, and *walk after the fleſh*. * They ſeem pure in their *own eyes*, and yet are not *waſhed from their filthineſſe*; Yea there is a generation, (O how lofty are their eyes!) yet are their *teeth ſwords*, and *their jaw teeth as knives*; Nothing is *more cruell, than ſupercilious hypocriſie*; * They were forward to crucifie Chriſt, who were *ſhy of* being defiled by entring into the Judgement Hall: They are moſt zealous to deſtroy the true Miniſters, yea the very function and ſucceſſion, who ſeem moſt devoted to be *Teachers*, *Prophets*, and *Preachers* of a new Spirit and form; Many ſeem *rich* in gifts and increaſed in *ſpirituall endowments*, thinking they need nothing of Chriſts true Miniſtry, when they know not that they are poore, and naked, and blind, and miſerable. There are (πο-νηρίαι πνευματικαὶ) ſpirituall wickedneſſes uſurpant in the high places of mens ſoules, as well as (σαρκικαὶ ρυπαρίαι) more ſordid and *ſwiniſh ſpirits*, that dwell in the lower region of mens luſts; It is expreſly ſtigmatized on the foreheads of ſome *pretenders to the Spirit*, (which was the glory of thoſe firſt and pureſt times) that they *are ſenſuall not having the Spirit*: Vain and proud ignorance (as we ſee in primitive *times*) is not onely content to be without the true, wiſe, humble and orderly *Spirit of God*, but they muſt alſo ſtudy to cover their follies, diſorders, and hypocriſies with the *ſhews of it*: as if it were not enough to ſin againſt its manifeſt *rules* and *examples* in the Word; which have alwayes been obſerved in the Church; unleſſe they impute alſo to it, their ſimplicities, fondneſſes, impudencies, filthy dreams, extravagancies, and confuſions: Counting it no ſhame to aſcribe thoſe unreaſonable and abſurd motions, ſpeeches and actions, to *Gods moſt wiſe and holy Spirit*; which any man of right reaſon and ſober ſenſe, or common ingenuity and modeſty, would be *aſhamed to owne.*

14.
Falſe pretentions to the Spirit.

* *Nulla erroris ſecta jam contra Chriſti veritatem niſi nomine coopertа Chriſtiano ad pugnandum prodire audet.* Auſt. Ep. 56.

* Revel. 3.1.

* Prov. 30 12.

* Ioh. 18.28.

Revel. 3.17.

Epheſ. 6.12.

Iude 19.

Irenæus: *l*. 3. *c*. 1. of the *Gnoſticks*, and *Valentinians*. *Gloriantur ſe emendatores eſſe Apoſtolorum: perfectam cognitionmen non habuiſſe Apoſtolos. cap.* 2. *Dicunt ſe non tantum Presbyteris ſed & Apoſtolis ſapientiores, ſinceram inveniſſe veritatem*: So the *Circumcelliones*, *Quæ non viderunt confingunt*; *opiniones ſuas habentes pro Deo*: *honores quos non habuerunt ſe habuiſſe proteſtantur*. Iſid. Hiſp. de off. Eccl. l. 3. c. 15.

Our

Our humble prayer is, that these new modellers, and pretenders to the Spirit may *learn not to blaspheme*; not to grieve, resist, and doe despite to *the Spirit of God*; which hath been, and still is evidently manifest *in the true Ministers of this Church*; and our earnest study shall be, that we may be truly endued with such gifts, graces, and fruits of the Spirit of Christ, that we may both speak, and doe, and suffer, as becomes *good Christians*, and true Ministers, after the example of holy men, and of our great *Master*, *Bishop*, and *Ordainer*, Jesus Christ: That (so the judicious Charity of those, that *excell* in vertue, wisdome, faith, and humility, may have cause to say the *Lord hath sent us in the power*, as well as in the order and office of the *Ministry*, to which we were rightly ordained: On the other side we fear, that the *great earthquakes* in the Church and darknesse *over the Reformed Religion*, (which may follow the true Ministers being set at naught and *crucified*, by the malice and wantonnesse of men) may in after times, give too much cause to those, that now neglect us, or afflict us, to say, as the *Centurion did of Christ*, Doubtlesse these were the messengers of the most high God; the true Ministers of Jesus Christ, and of his Gospell to this Church. Mat.27.54.

While we have any *liberty* and leave to *live* as Ministers, it will become us, not to be so discouraged by the impotent malice of any enemies, as to desert this holy calling, whereto the Lord by a *right ordination* in this Church hath *duly called us*; Not to look back to the world having once put our *hands to this plough*; to consider our *persecutors* no further than to pity them, and *pray for them*: notwithstanding all the injuries, and blasphemies, not against us so much, as *against God*; while they fear not to ascribe the great and good effects, which the Lord hath vouchsafed to work by his Ministers upon the hearts of thousands in *England*, to *Beelzebub*, *to the spirit of Antichrist*; or to any thing rather than to own the Spirit of Christ among us, which hee hath *promised* should ever be with his true and faithfull Ministers, in an holy succession of *authority*, and power, to *the end of the world*. Mat.12.24.

Scandalous inconstancy of Professors.

Indeed the greatest grief to the *Soules of all godly Ministers*; and which hath brought the greatest scandall and dehonestation on their Ministry, (next to some of their own grosse failings) is this; when the world sees so many of those, who seemed *to be baptized* with water, and with the Spirit; (to have been illuminated, and sanctified by their teaching; to have *tasted of the heavenly gift*, and the *powers of the world to come* (that is, of the authority and efficacy of the Evangelicall Ministry, which was to come after the *Leviticall* and *Aaronicall* order) Many who seemed to have rejoiced for many years, in those *burning and shining lights* of this Heb. 6.5.

Churches

Churches Ministers; to have (by their Ministry) been *well instructed*, reformed, washed, and escaped from the *pollutions of this world*, That (I say) some of these like *Jesuruns*, should thus *lift up the heel*, and thus kick against the Ministers and Ministry; like *Demasses*, thus to forsake them; like *Judasses* thus to *betray them*, whom lately they kissed and followed as Disciples; like *Swine* that they should thus *turn and revile* those, that *cast pearl* before them; returning to the wallowing in the mire and dirt of unjust, covetous, ambitious, erroneous, seditious, licentious, perjurious, malicious, and sacrilegious courses; No more now ashamed of their lusts, then those unclean beasts are of their *filthinesse* in the midst of the *fairest Sun-shine day*; and when they are neerest to the most *pure and Crystall streams*; But the light which they will not see in this their day shining on them, and discovering the frauds and evill of their wayes, they may after see in that darknesse, to which they are hastning, and to which they seem even of God to bee condemned.

But to conclude my answer in this particular, wherein the Antiministeriall adversaries pretend to such *spirituall gifts* and speciall calling, beyond the ordained and setled Ministry; if any *excellent Christians*, or any of those, that have either *wisdome* to discern, or power to dispose of things, to the advantage of this Church and State; if they doe in their *judgements* conceive, or in their *upright consciences*, laying aside all partialities, and obliquings to *worldly interest*, but meerly regarding the glory of God, the good of soules, and the honour of the reformed Religion, if they shall conclude that there is indeed more evidence, and power of Gods Spirit both in *gifts Ministeriall*, and in holy successes, in those men that stile themselves inspired men, *speciall Prophets*, and new *modelled Preachers*: if they be found to have more of *godly learning*, of sound wisdome, in the mysteries of Christ, of sincere piety, zeal and charity to the glory of God and mens soules good; if they are filled with *divine endowments*, for praying, preaching, duly exhibiting the holy Mysteries, for edifying the Church, for maintaining the truth of the reformed Religion, and the peace of this Church and Nation; if they have greater courage, constancy, industry, and conscience to carry on the *great worke of saving soules*; if they have more authority, from the word of Christ, from the Apostles practise, from the Catholick precedents of the Church of Christ, in all ages and places; by which to clear *their call* to the work of the Ministry, beyond what is produced for the ancient, and ordained Ministry of this *Church*; Truly we do not desire to be further injurious or hinderances to any mens soules: God forbid the *Ministers of the Church of England* should

15. *Conclusion and resignation of our Ministry, if, &c.*

be so *much lovers* or valuers of themselves, or envious to other mens excellencies, or enemies to your and the Churches welfare, as not *to be willing* to be *laid aside*, that these new mens more immediate and *greater sufficiencies*, *higher inspirations*, and *diviner authority*, may doe that work, to which we are found so *unsufficient*, defective and unworthy.

But if these pretenders to more spirituall prophecying, preaching and living, be by wise and godly men (who love not to mock God, or dally with matters of salvation and eternity, (which is the end of Religion) weighed *in the ballance of the sanctuary*; of the divine institution; of Christs mission; of the Apostles succession; of the primitive custome; and of the Catholick order in all ages and Churches; if the grounds of right reason, of good order, policy and government be duely considered, which require distinction in all societies, sacred and civill, and avoid confusion (most) in the things of God; if the judgement of the most learned, usefull, and holy men in all ages be pondered; if these new mens Spirits and gifts be throughly tryed by the *touchstone* of Gods Word; if their secular aims and warpings to the world be narrowly looked into; if the deformitie of their words and works be considered; if their simple or scandalous writings be duly examined; if the successes of their endeavours, and essays hitherto in many places, be seriously thought of, (which are evidently proved to be very sad and bad: little promoting either truth or peace; holinesse or comfort to any peoples souls; nor any prosperity and advancement to this Church, or any Christian reformed Religion;) if they be found in ignorance and weaknesse, or in factiousnesse and insolencies, or in pride and avarice, or in erroneousnesse, and licentiousnesse, so farre *too light*, that they are not so much, as *the dust of the ballance*, compared to the reall excellencies of those *true Ministers of this Church*, which have been, and still are, and may be in this Church, (if men be not all given over to lusts and strong delusions) God forbid any *excellent Christians* should be tempted by fear, or flattery, or any fallacy of *novelty*, *gain* or *liberty*, to desire or endeavour, or approve a change; which will be so shamefully and desperately pernicious both to themselves, and to their posterity.

BUt these *Antiministeriall adversaries*, who would fain impose upon the credulous world, with the pretentions of some speciall gifts and Inspirations of Gods Spirit (which are as yet no way discovered by them, in word or deed, as I have shewed) being conscious to themselves, that indeed they come short of those *common endowments*, by which the mindes of men, are oft much *improved*, through study and good learning: they seek to *oppose* and *decry* that in all Christians, and especially in Ministers, which they despair of themselves: So that not a dumb spirit, but a silly, prating, and illiterate one *possesses them*; which cryes out against all humane learning, and usefull Studies, as the divels did against Christ; *What have we to doe with thee?* Great calumnies and contempts are raised by these men, and their Disciples against all liberall Arts and Sciences, all skill in the tongues and histories; against all Books but the Bible, (and some of them can hardly dispense with that too, since they take all books to be of the same nature with those *conjuring Books* which were burnt, *Act.* 19. 19.) against the *Schooles* of the *Prophets*, and all *Vniversities*, as heathenish, Antichristian, marks of the *Beast*; as deformities, darknings, and impertinencies, where we have *Scripture light*; Also prejudiciall to that more *immediate divine* teaching, or Institution to which they pretend, and by which they say, they learn, and teach all *true Religion*; which they tell us is so sufficiently furnished, and fortified, as the *new Jerusalem*, with its own walls, *made of pretious stones*, (the impregnable *strength of truth*, and the *splendour of the Spirits gifts*) that it needs none of these *mudwalls* and *bulwarks* of earth, which men have cast up; Beautified enough with its own *native innocency* and glory, it desires not any of these *raggs*, and *additionall tatters of humane learning*; which (they say) hath so tossed and torn Religion with *infinite*, and *intricate disputes*, that the solidnesse and simplicity of *true Divinity* is almost quite lost, and confounded. Christ is almost oppressed by the *crouds*, and throngs of such as are called Rabbies and learned men: who may well spare their pains in the Church of Christ; where the Lord hath promised that *all shall be taught of God*, that his *Spirit* shall teach *them all things*, and lead *them into all truth*.

4. Calumny or Cavill. Against humane and secular learning in Ministers.

Matth. 8. 29.

Revel. 21.

Isai. 54. 13. Ioh. 14. 26. Ioh. 16. 13.

Answ. I see the *Devill* is never more *knave*, than when hee would seem to *turn fool*; How willing is he to have all men as ignorant, weak, and unlearned, as these *Objecters* are, that so none might discern his *snares*, and gins, of which *these Ignaro's* are to be his fetters; fain would he have all *Christians*, yea, and *Preachers* too, such **silly birds without heart*; that they might easily be *circumvented* by *his stratagems*, and catched with *his devices*; The better

Answ. 1. The craft and folly of this cavill against humane learning.

* Hos. 7. 11.

πολλοὶ καθάπερ οἱ παῖδες τὰ μορμολύκεια, ὅπως δεδίασι τὴν ἑλληνικὴν φιλοσοφίαν. Cl. Al. στρω. 6.

In subversione fidei nullum ab ignorantia remedium est. Saresb.

better to act *those Tragedies* which he intends against the *Reformed Churches*, he would have the windows shut up, and the light shut out; These are the *Fauxes* with dark lanthorns, to blow up all; and the *Judasses*, who are guides to them, that are to take Christ, with swords and staves; O how fain would some men, that the *Sun* were set, that their *glowormes* might shine; that the light of the house were extinguished; that so their sparkes might *appear*, which they have kindled to *themselves*, in their shining corners, and upon their *private hearths*.

Quærentibus quid in Scævola jam vulnerato esset accusaturus, respondit, quod totum corpore ferrum non receperat. Tul. orat. pro Sex. Ros.

Vero deficiente crimine laudem ipsam in vituperium vertit invidia. Tul.

Act. 18. 24. & 28.

Act. 26. 24.

Ier. 38. 11.

Truly this calumny against good learning, hath as much surprized me and my brethren the *Ministers of this Church*, as the accusation of *Fimbria* did question *Scævola*; who was impleaded by the other, for not receiving that *poynard* deeper into his brest, wherewith hee stabbed him, and intended to have *dispatched him*; The learned, and godly Ministers in *England*, never *thought* this would be *laid to their charge*, as a fault, the want of which had been a *foul shame*, and a just reproach to them: As the enjoyment of it was a great honour and advantage, both to them and to the *Reformed Religion*; They little suspected, that among Christians, *Apollos* should be forced to excuse his *eloquent* and *potent demonstrations*; or S. *Paul* his sober and sanctified learning, in which hee excelled, worthy of that famous City and University *Tarsus*, of which he had the honour to be free, and pleaded it as a priviledge, *Act.* 21. 39. Which learning made him not *so mad*, as those were who suspected, and accused him, that *much learning had made him mad*. And if humane learning be such *old clouts* and *rotten rags*, as these men of most *beggerly elements* pretend, (and wee confesse it is so, compared to, and destitute of, those *soul-saving Truths*, which are divinely revealed) yet there may be good use of them; if it be but to help the *Jeremies*, (the *Prophets and Ministers of the Lord*) out of those dungeons and mire, where otherwayes their enemies would have them ever to be lodged, both *sordidly*, and shamefully, and obscurely.

Μέγιστον τῷ ὄντι κτῆμα καὶ τιμιώτατον τῷ Θεῷ, τὴν ἐπιστήμην πρῶτον ἔργον ἡγεῖσθαι δεῖ, τὰ δὲ λοιπὰ ὡς δεύτερα καὶ τρίτα. *Just. in dialog. Tryph.*

Nothing (O *you excellent Christians*) is lesse necessary, than *to paint this Sun*, or polish this pearl, to set forth *to you* the use and necessity of good learning: of the benefit and blessing whereof in this Church *your selves* are so much partakers, and whereof you are so great *esteemers*, and *encouragers*; And nothing shews *good learning* more *necessary* to the *Church* and *true Religion*, both as Christian and reformed, than this; That the *Divel* by vain and fallacious instruments often hath, and still seeks to deprive them of that weapon, and defense, which he hath used with great strength, and cunning, for his chiefest arms; both offensive against the truths of religion; and defensive for his own most damnable doctrines and delusions.

What

What *havock* would he soon make of sound doctrine, as in former ages he endevoured, by those learned, and *subtill Sophisters*, his instruments, and *emissaries* on every side, if there were none on the *Truths side* able to encounter him, and his *agitators* in that *post of learning*! No wonder if the *Woolf* would have the *Flock* without *Mastives*, or these without *teeth*: it were much for his, little for the flocks ease and advantage. Although the *Divel* (*an old accuser*) must needs be a *cunning Orator* too, and be furnished with all the *swasive arts* of insinuation, which he fits to the *severall geniusses* of men and times; yet he never till of late in *Germany*, and now in *England* had confidence to make use of this place of Oratory, to perswade Christians to *burn all other Bookes*, that they might better study and understand the Bible; yea and the Bible too, that they might better understand the minde of God: Which is all one, as if the *Israelites* should have beene perswaded to have rid themselves of the *cumber of their swords, spears*, and *shields*, that so they might better defend themselves; or that they should have neither *file* nor *grindstone* to sharpen the naturall bluntnesse, or clear the *rustinesse* of their weapons; while yet the *Philistims* were all *well armed*, and dayly *preparing* to battell; Against whom there was no such warrant of a speciall divine protection, as to make the people of God presume, to neglect the use of those armes which art had prepared, and use had taught, how to imply. We see that *Jonathans* heroick motion carries him not upon that *successefull* and *great adventure*, without his *sword* and *armour-bearer*. Nor did *Davids* confidence in Gods protection, of which he had former experiences, when he was without any arms, against the *Lion* and *Bears*; nor yet the assurance he had, of the goodnesse of his cause; or of the pride and profanenesse of his enemy; none of these made him neglect to take, and use such armes, as he thought most convenient. The blinde and the lame (men of feeble and confused spirits; unlearned and unstable minds) which *are hated of Davids soule*, are ill assistants in *Davids* wars, against the *Jebusites*, who study to defend against him, or to surprise from him the City of *David*, or rather the City of God; which is the Metropolis where grace and truth doe dwell.

> *Crescenius* the heretick oft complained that Saint *Austin* was too full of his Logick and Syllogisms, when he could not answer his reasons.
>
> In the Emperour *Charls* 5. time: 1524.
>
> 1 Sam. 13.
>
> 1 Sam. 14. 13.
>
> 1 Sam. 17.
>
> 2 Sam. 5. 6.
> 2 Pet. 3.

2.

It is certain, that next to the primitive gifts of *miracles*, the gifts of humane learning have stood the Church of Christ in *most stead*. For ever since the Apostles and Ministers of Christ, assisted with extraordinary endowments of the Spirit, had by the *foolishnesse of preaching*, (as by *Davids* improbable weapons against *Goliahs compleat armature*) vanquished that old Idolatrous power of

> *Humane learning succeeded miraculous and extraordinary gifts.*

* *Nec miracula illa in nostra tempora durare permissa sunt; ne animus semper visibilia quæreret, & eorum consuetudine frigesceret quorum novitate flagravit.* Aust. de ver. Rel. c. 25.

of *heathenisme*, which prevailed in the world; and was long upheld by *shews of learning*, eloquence, and (in that way) *vaine philosophy*; The Church of Christ hath, ever since the cessation of those *Miraculous gifts*, (which attended onely the first conquests) made use of that very sword of that prostrated Gyant; *good learning*; both to *dispatch* him, and to *defend* it self; finding that both in humane and divine encounters, there is *none like to that*, if managed by a proportionate arm and strength.

Quantum ratio dat homini, tantum literatura rationi, religio literaturæ, & religioni gratia. Casaub.

Quantum a bestiis distamus, eo magis ad Deum appropinquamus. Sen.

* Languages unlock and open Truth.

Σκιὰ μὲν πραγμάτων λόγοι. Phal. Ep.

For, hereby the *mind*, and all *intellectuall* faculties of mens souls (which are the *noblest* and *divinest*) are more easily and fully *instructed*; more speedily *improved* in all the riches of wisdome and knowledge; which are part *of the glory*, and *Image of God* on mans nature. By this, which we call *good learning*, all *Truths*, both humane and divine, naturall, politick, morall and Theologicall; usefull either for *speculation*, or practise, are more clearly *extricated*, and unfolded out of the depths, darknesse, and *ambiguity* of words (which are but the *shadows of things*) by the * skill in Languages; which are the scabbards and shels, wherein wisdome is shut up. The inscription on Christs crosse is in three languages, *Hebrew*, *Greek* & *Latin*, *Luk.* 23. 38. Intimating as the divulging of the Gospel to many tongues and Nations; so that the mysterie of Christ crucified is not to be fully and exquisitely understood, without the keys of these three learned and principall languages; with which the Church hath flourished. Certainly it is not easie for unlearned men to consider how great use there is even of *Grammar*, which is the first and roughest file that good learning applyes to polish the minde with all; for much of the true sense even of the *holy Scriptures*, as well as of other Records, depends upon the true writing or Orthography, the exact derivation or etymology, and the regular Syntaxis or conjoining of words: yea that *Criticall* part of literature, which is the finest file or searse of Truth (wherein some mens wit and curiosity onely vapour, and soar high, like birds of large feathers, and small bodies) yet it is of excellent use, when by men of sober learning it is applyed to the service of religion; Many times much *Divinity* depends on small *particles*, rightly understood, upon one letter; upon such a mood, or tense, or case, and the like; many errors are engendred and nourished by *false translations*, and mistakes of words or letters; many truths are restored and established, by the true meaning of them, asserted upon good grounds, and just observations; which hath been done with great accuratenesse, by * men of incomparable excellency in this kinde these last hundred years; equall to, if not for the most part, beyond the exactnesse of the ancient Fathers or writers. Herein infinite observations of *humane writers* are happily made

* *Erasmus. Drusius. Hensius. Grotius. Salmasius. Fullerus. Lud. de Dieu,* and others.

made, and usefully applyed, as to the propriety of words and phrases used in the *sacred originalls* of the Word of God, so as thereby to attain their *genuine* and *emphatick sense*: also for the clearing of many passages and allusions which are in the Scriptures: referring to things naturall and historicall, in the manners, and customes of the nations. This once done, all Truths are by the methods and reasoning of Logick easily disintangled, and fairly vindicated from the *snarlings*, *sophisms*, and *fallacies*, with which error, ignorance or calumniating malice seek to obscure or disguise them, or therein to wrap up and cover themselves; *darkening wisdome by words without understanding*. After this they are by the same art handsomely *distributed*, and methodically *wound up* in severall clews and bottomes according to those *various Truths* which that excellent art hath spun out; That thus digested, they may again be brought forth unfolded and presented to others in that *order* and *beauty* of *eloquence* which * Rhetorick teacheth: By which truths have both an edge and lustre set on them, doe most *adorn* them, and *enforce* to the *quickest prevalencies* on mens mindes, and the firmest impressions on their passions and affections; that so their rationall vigour may hold out to mens actions; and extend to the ethicks or *morality* of civill conversation, which is the politure of mens hearts and hands; The softner and sweetner of violent passions, and rougher manners, to the candor and equity of polity and society: This civility was, and is the preface and forerunner of Religion, the great preparative to piety, the confines of Christianity, which never thrives untill barbarity be rooted up, and some learning with morality be sown and planted among men. Nor did Christian Religion ever extend its pavilion much further, than the tents of Learning and Civility had been pitched by the conquests and colonies of the *Greeks* and *Romans*.

Logick disposeth. *Qui logica carent materias lacerant, ut catuli panes*: Melan. Οἷον θριγκός ἐστιν ἡ διαλεκτική, ὡς μὴ καταπατεῖσθαι πρὸς τῶν σοφιστῶν τὴν ἀλήθειαν. *Cl. Al. Στρω. 6.*

* Rhetorick communicates to others. Ἀληθῶς φιλοσοφία τῶν παθῶν δέσποινα. *Naz. or. 23.*

Thus by this *golden circle*, and *crystall medium* of *true learning*, the short, dim, and weaker sight of our *reason*, (whose very light is become *dark* by sin, *bleared* with its own fancies, and almost *put out* by its grosser lusts and passions) may (as by the help of *perspective* or *optick glasses*) be mightily strengthened and extended, while it sees, as with the *united vigor* of the *many thousand* visuall rayes and eyes of those, who saw before us; That so those few *conjectures*, those dark and ambiguous *experiencies*, which any mans short sight and single life can afford him, may be ampliated, cleared, and confirmed by those many testimonies and historicall monuments, which others have left in their *learned writings*: which draw as it were, the lesser rivulets of *various observations*, from severall times, pens and places, to meet in one great and noble

Matth. 6. 23.

History. Ἡ δὲ φιλοσοφία παρασκευάζει τὴν ὁδὸν τῇ βασιλικωτάτῃ διδασκαλίᾳ. *Cl. Al. Στρω. 1.* παρασκευεῖ καὶ ὁδοποιεῖ τῇ θεολογίᾳ. *Id.*

noble current of true Religion, which is the wisest observer and devoutest admirer of what true learning most sets forth; the *providence*, justice, power, goodnesse, patience, and mercy of the *wise, great*, and holy God: the Creator, ruler, and preserver of all things, but chiefly the *regarder* of the sons of men.

Psal. 8.

God hath therefore blest his Church with *good learning*, that those *small stocks*, and portions of wisdome, which any mans private *patrimony* affords him, either by innate parts, or acquired experiments, (which, for the most part, would amount to no more, than the *furnishing* of a *portable pedlers pack*, with small-wares, toyes, and trinckets; fit to please children, ideots, and countrey people) may be improved by a *joint stock*, and united commerce of prudent observations; that so men might *drive* a great and publique *trade* of wisdome, to the *infinite inriching*, and adorning both of Church and State, both of Polity and Religion: These two being the *great luminaries* and *excellencies* of humane Nature; the one to *rule the* [*day* wherein wee stand related to God, in piety; the other to *rule the night*, wherein we are related to each other, by humanity, equity, charity, and bonds of civill society. Which *innate vertues and properties* of mans nature (*Reason*, and *Religion*) once neglected, and until'd, for want of that *culture*, which good learning, and that *sof ening*, which ingenuous education brings to the mind and manners of men; who sees not, by miserable experience, how mankinde runs out to *weeds*? whole nations *degenerate* to brutish barbarity: as among the *Tartars*, *Negroes*, and *Indians*?

Humanus sensus cum farcitur alieno invento cito attenuatur de proprio. Cassiod.

Barbarity succeeds the want of learning, as darknesse, the Suns absence.

Yea even among people, where some are *civilized* by literature and the profession of Christian religion, we finde, by daily experience, that the *unlearned sort* are either grosse, dull, and very *indocible*; or else they are rough, impolished and *insolent*, prone to a *rustick impudence*, and clownish *untractablenesse*; especially when they imagine they have (or dare arrogate to themselves) a power and liberty of speaking, and doing what they list; Nothing is sacred, nothing is civill among those, that carry all by ignorant confidence and *brutish strength*; we see in those of the *Antiministeriall faction*, that by want of learning (whereof they are generally guilty) men onely learn this *Indian* or *Turkish* quality, to hate, contemne and seek to destroy all good learning, which is nothing else, but the good husbandry and great *improvement of the reasonable soule* in it self to God and to others: Therefore the ambition of these *Ignoramusses*, is like the magick cunning of *Jannes* and *Jambres*; chiefly vented, and exercised, by a most impotent *pride*, and malice, in despising, and resisting those *Mosesses*, the true Ministers

Stolide feroces. Tac.

Scientia non habet inimicum praeter ignorantem.

2 Tim. 3. 8.

nisters of the Church: the *planters, preservers, reformers,* and *vindicators* and deliverers (under God) of true Religion; who have been, and are, (many of them) *eminently learned*: most of them, *competently*; so as at least to make a fair and ingenuous use of other mens more accurate and solid labours, who are their (συμμύςαι) brethren of the same holy function and Ministry; who have generally been in all ages and places, the *magazines*, or *storehouses* of all *good learning*; which I may affirm without any *envy*, or diminution, to those many *excellent Gentlemen* of this or other Nations, who have added to the honour of their birth, and other accomplishments of breeding, this most *eminent crown* and beauty of all, *Good learning.*

It is a *work* then fit for *Lucifer*, (so to contradict his name by his deeds) to *pretend light*, and *intend darknesse*; to cry up the spirit, which is easily done; that he may cry *down learning*, which is hardlyer attained, than the other is said: Who can wonder, if the *Philistines* would fain put out the *eyes* of our *Samsons*, (having once bound, and hampered them with poor and straightned conditions) that so they may lesse fear their strength, and safely *mock* them, and their reformed Religion: which never so thrived (after *miraculous gifts* were ceased) as when the forces and *glory of the Gentiles* came in to Christ; when Christianity was *graffed* on the old stock of heathen *learning* and philosophy; which now brings forth fruit, not after the old *crabbed sowrnesse*, but after the sweetnesse of the new Olive-cion, with which it is *headed*; yea we see, when Christian Religion ran out to much barbarity, illiterate ignorance, and superstition, for *many centuries*, till the last, (for want of the culture, and manuring of learning) it brought forth little *fair fruits*; but much of *Legendary fables*, lying wonders, religious *Romances*, stories of Chivalry in holy Warres and Errantries in Religion: The best effects were the Schoolemens cloistered curiosities and *intricate disputes*; who rather hewed and cut the *pillars of Christian Religion*, into small *chips* and shavings; than added much to the polishing and establishing of them; so intangling *Philosophy* with *Divinity*, as confounded both, much advanced neither; all excellent things, worthy to be known, being wrapped up in obscurity; or set forth in such *barbarous* and *fulsome Latin*, that they were like fair *Irish* bodies in *course*, and *ragged mantles*; And this, for want of that method and texture of learning, which might so card and sever each matter from other, as might give both *beauty* and distinctnesse to them.

3. *To cry downe good learning is only fit for Luciferians.*

Iudg. 16. 21.

Isa. 60. 11.

Rev. 21. 26.

Vid. Clem. Al. Στρω. 6. *Vult suum* γνωστικὸν τὸ σύμφορον τῇ ἀληθείᾳ ἐκ πάντων λαμβάνειν.

Which we see hath been done this last *hundred years* and more; In which so many men of admirable learning and industry have by

The advantages to religion by learning.

by the *help of printing* (with which the world is now rather surfeited than nourished) brought forth to their beauty, by an happy *regeneration*, so many of the *ancient writers*, both Christian and heathen; (which were formerly buried in obscure cloisters, and uselesse retirements, as in their graves; eaten with worms and covered with dust.) So that no *Sanhedrin* of the *Jews*; no *Senate* at *Athens*, or *Rome*; no Synod, or Councell of Christians were ever so, at once, compleated and furnished with *excellent men* in all kinds, as our Christian Libraries now every where are; In which there are attending on Christian Religion (which is as *the Kings daughter, all glorious within*) those *virgins*, which bee not *her fellows* so much, as her *handmaids*: who *clothe her* with *garments*; wrought with needle-work in *divers colours*; embroydered with the *sublimity* and *gravity* of *Plato*; with the *method* and *acutenesse* of *Aristotle*; with the morals and suavity of *Seneca* and *Plutarch* (who alone is a Library;) with the eloquence and oratory of *Demosthenes*, *Tully*, and *Quintilian*; with the florid language, and sober sense of *Xenophon*, *Cæsar*, *Livy*, *Tacitus*, and other excellent historians; with the various observations of the most learned *Varro* (whose life was spared in *civill dissensions* for his *incomparable learning*:) so of *Pliny*, *Ptolemy*, and other searchers into all curiosities of Nature and Art: Besides these, the very *goats hair*, and *badger skins* too, are made to serve the *Tabernacle* of the Lord; the *elegancies* of *Homer*, *Virgil*, and *other Poets*; (who are *magazines of fancy*, and *masters of wit*) are usefull: which way of expressing truth and religion in pathetick and poetick wayes of devotion the Spirit of God abhorreth not, as we see in some holy Poets who were writers of some part of the Scripture, as in *Job*, *Psalmes*, *Canticles*, *Lamentations*, and other places: where piety and poetry, truth and elegancy, Divinity and sacred curiosity, (in meeters and Acrostichs) meet together: Teaching us, *That God*, who is full of infinite varieties, and yet but one perfect simplicity, is to be seen, served, and praised, in *his severall gifts*, to any of which *Christian Religion* (which is of all religions the most *absolute*, perfect and comprehensive) can have no abhorrency; since they all *flow from God*, and return to him, through any wise and gracious heart; which as a *limbeck* or *hot still*, extracts somewhat *spirituall* out of every thing, of nature, art, experience, or history.

Psal. 45. 13.

Of *Plutarch* it is said: if all Authors were lost, he alone might supply.

Vivat Varro doctissimus Romanorum.

Exod. 37. 7.

Of *Virgil* it is said, if all Sciences were lost they might be found in him.

Grata de Deo fama in artibus sparsa.

From these *well stored quivers* of *humane learning* in all kindes, Christian Religion hath so furnished her self with excellent, and *sharp arrowes of all sorts*; that she easily makes *ready her bow*, and shoots against *the face of any adversaries* that dare provoke her; either in *Languages*, *Arts*, or *Sciences*; In Logick, Rhetorick, History

story, Antiquity; in *Philosophy*, naturall, morall, or politicall; In all which, by much conversing with, and contemplation of, those *ancient goodly pieces*, the Church of Christ hath, (as *Jacobs sheep* did by looking upon the *variegated rods*) brought forth answerable *parallels* of incomparable learning, in all kinds; So that *Pharaohs daughter*, matcht thus to *Solomon*, (the *learning* of the *heathens* joined to *Christian Religion*) may very well forget her *fathers house*; in stead of which (since the *King* of the *Church* hath delighted in her *beauty*) she hath brought forth children, which shee may make *Princes* in all the Provinces of good learning; which are become tributary to Christ, and subject to his Kingdome of righteousnesse and Scepter of truth.

Gen 30. 39. Psal.45. 10. Psal.45.6.

4. *Devils devises against Religion and Learning.*

But O how different, *many faced* and *crosse grained* are the *Devils engines*, methods and temptations! His first was to perswade by the speciousnesse of *increased* and diviner *wisdome*, * to eat of that *forbidden fruit* which the *tree of knowledge of good and evill* did bear; This was a pleasant bait, but *pernicious*; a golden, but poisonous and deadly arrow; Now the *duller devill* out of his almost exhausted quiver, produceth this iron headed, blunt, and rusty shaft; tempting Christians to abandon all *good literature*, and humane means of attaining knowledge both Divine and humane: And since he sped so well by this first temptation of *proud curiosity*, to be *like to Gods*, in eating what was forbidden; he despaires not to make us *now like beasts*; by perswading us to abstain from that *tree of knowledge*, which the Lord allowes us; and which his providence hath caused to flourish in the garden of his Church; and which doth not onely bear fair and excellent fruits, which are desirable to *make one wise to salvation*, but the very *leaves of good learning*, are for the healing of the Nations: Many *defects* are thereby supplyed in humane societies; many immoralities restrained; many diseases cured, as to the outward contagion, and covered as to the deformity; to all which, the nature of man is *other wayes* subject, and so exposed, that wee see in all ages, the barbarity of any people, either at first, or in the relapse, is chiefly imputable to the *want of good literature*; and that *civility*, which is as the *flowre* and *cream*, alwayes rising from learning; which onely *supples* the roughnesse, and brawny callousnesse, which grows by long ferity and rudenesse on mens mindes and manners; *Learning*, like the warmer beames of the approaching *Sun*, onely hath force to thaw, and melt that *frozen rigour of mens natures*; to adorn them with a sweet and florid beauty; to enrich them to a summers fertility: which without this, are ever *squallid*, and *oppressed* with a winters form, and horrid barrennesse, ever accompanying mankinde in the absence and destitution

* Gen.3.5. Revel.22.2.

Quod vomeres, rastra, aratra glebæ, hoc disciplinæ sunt animo. Varro.

Animi cultus est quidam humanitatis cibus. Tul. de fin. l. 5.

tution of learning: which mightily prepares mens hearts and minds for the seed of the Gospell, and for the harvest of true religion, which affords the best fruites of wisdom and tranquillity to the souls of men.

There is no doubt but Satan hath found himselfe, for these last hundred and fifty yeares, (since the happy *restauration of learning* first, and then of Religion) much *chained*, hampered, and galled by those excellent gifts of all sorts of *good learning* (which are as the string to the bow, and as feathers to the *arrowes* of Truth), wherewith God hath mightily fenced and adorned his Church, as he did in the 3, 4, 5, and 6 Centuries, after that *miraculous gifts* were quite ceased, or much abated; in which times the *Lord* stirred up *mighty men* of incomparable learning, to fight the *battailes* of the Lord, of his Truth, and of his Church, against *heathenish* and *hereticall* adversaries. Drive away *good learning* out of any Church and Nation by *famine*, starving it: or by *military insolency*, banishing it; the devill (no doubt) would be much more at his ease and liberty, as among *Indians* in barbarous idolatry; or *Turks* in ridiculous Mahometry; or among the *sillier* sort of *Papists* in saplesse superstitions; or among the wilder generation of *Enthusiasts* in their various fancies and most incongruous *dreams*; all which grossely erre, and covet to infect others through *ignorance* even in the matters of right Reason as well as Religion; and are destroyed for want of *sound* and *sober knowledge*; which is scarce attainable even in Religion (without a miracle) where either *people* despise, or *Teachers* are void of that assistance, which good learning affords.

Hos. 4. 6.

Which however thousands of good Christians, both men and women, have not had in the masse and bulk, yet they have enjoyed the spirits vertue and benefit of it (as it were more abstract and refined) by the studies, labours, instructions, and perswasions, which their *learned Ministers* have so prepared for them, and fitly derived to them; as they did in *England* both by preaching and by writing. The Devill would have lesse trouble to watch Christians in the Church, lest they should fly from his camp to Gods tents, if he could perswade them to put out their own eyes, and the eyes of their guides and Pastors too: or else, to shut up themselves into some blind corners; and confine the *Christian reformed Religion* to *obscure cels*, and silly *conventicles*; where, in stead of the *Suns fair light* of * true Reason, good Learning, and sound Religion; men should like Owls and Bats, and Mouls, onely howle, and chatter, and scratch one another in the dark. We know there are such kind of animals, which are ready to curse the day: and cannot abide the light, because their eyes are weak,

* *Suadet ne vescentium dentibus edentulus invideat; nec oculos caprearum talpa contemnat.* Hieron. *ad Magnum, de indoctis Christianis.*

weak, their workes are dark; and both mindes and manners are deformed.

The *despisers of good learning* are not onely *spitefull enemies* to the Christian reformed Religion (whose *perfection* disdaineth not to use those good *gifts*, which come from the * *Father of lights*, (any more than a *gracious soul* doth its eyes, and other senses of the body:) but they are also *silly abusers* and degraders even of *humane nature*; * whose *divine excellencie, Reason*, no man above the degree of *brutish stupidity, Bedlam madnesse*, or *divellish envy*, ever sought to deprave, or depresse: No doubt *such apes* knowing their own uncomely want of tailes, would be glad, if they could bring it in fashion, for all beasts to have none: and perswade them to cut off, (as burthens, and deformities) those *postern ornaments* and helms of the body, wherewith nature hath furnished the nobler, comelyer, and stronger creatures: But this mutilating of reason and deforming of Religion, by putting out the eyes, and cropping off the ears of Christians, and setting humanity it self into the stocks or pillory, is a greater undertaking (I think and hope) than ever such feeble, though nimble animals, with all their *apish tricks*, and mimicall grimasses, will be able to perswade, either all, or any beasts of the Forests, (unlesse it be the *silly asses*) to gratifie them withall.

5. *Despisers of learning are enemies to reason.*

* Iam 1. 17.

* Πάντες ἄνθρωποι τοῦ εἰδέναι ὀρέγονται φύσει. *Arist. Met. c. 1.*

λογικὸν τῆς ψυχῆς βρῶμα ἡ γνῶσις ἀληθής. *Cl. Al.* 5ρ. 5.

The *Lord of all the world*, the munificent donor of all blessings, who *gives liberally without envy or reproach*, hath *withheld no good thing* from his Church and people; and not only allows, but requires *us Christians*, devoutly to consecrate *all to his glory*; so as thankfully to adorn, even his Tabernacle, and Temple, with *those spoiles and tributes*, which we have taken from the *Egyptians*, and nations round about us: as *Moses, David*, and *Solomon* did; all three eminent for *learning* and *piety*: The *learning of the heathen* is now become a *circumcised Proselyte* to the Christian Religion; from *a captive alien*, it is *with shaved hair*, and pared nailes, (the pomp and peevishnesse of it being laid aside) admitted with *Hagar* into the holy family of the Church; as a pregnant handmaid to wait on Religion; though not as a *rivall* to be courted, and esteemed equall with *Sarah*. The severall parts of good learning, the Arts, and Sciences are, as those * *valiant ones about Solomons bed, vigilant guards*, and potent defenders of true Christian Religion.

Iam. 1. 5.

Ἐκ τῆς φιλοσοφίας ἀπαιδίζειν δεῖ τὸ χρειῶδες εἰς τὸν βίον. *Cl. Al.* 5ρω. 6.

Nostra sunt quæ in Philosophorum scriptis præstant: Deo vindicanda est omnis veritas. Amb. de Bon. M.

Decalvacam, illecebras crinium & ornamenta verborum cum emortuis unguibus seca. Hieron. ad Tam. *Spoliis Ægyptiis onusti & divites quamvis simus, tamen pascha nobis celebranda.* Aust. Doct. Christi. c. 39. * Cant. 3. 7. So *Naz. orat.* 19. Basil, hom. 24. *Ut rosas colligimus & spinas evitamus, &c. Ut fullones præparant pannum, & tinctores, &c. Quisquis bonus verusque est Christianus, Domini sui esse intelligat ubicunq; invenerit veritatem.* Aust. do. Christ. l. 2. c. 18 & cap. 39. *Quæ vera, quæ fidei nostræ accommoda dixerint philosophi, non solum non formidanda, sed ab iis tanquam injustis possessoribus vindicanda.* Id.

However it be true, That the *wisdome* of the world is folly, and all learning is barbarity, losse, and dung compared to, and separated from *the excellency of the knowledge of our Lord Jesus Christ*; yet nothing hinders, but that *Christian Ministers* may now (as *Christ* sometime did) ride upon *this Asses colt* to *Jerusalem*; Nothing is more comely than to see the wisest men offer their gold and frankincense and myrrh to Christ in his infancy: *Mat.* 3. We know, that, as an humble unbeleever cannot justly be counted either ignorant, or unlearned, if he be taught in all saving *necessary truths*; and * so, no man, never so much improved in secular knowledge, merits the name of learned, if he be ignorant of the *minde of God* in the mysteries of Jesus Christ; yet, *judicious beleevers*, can never be unthankfull despisers of those gifts of * good learning, in their *Teachers*, and *Ministers*, by whom they have received that benefit of instruction in true Religion; which, by their owne private industry, and simplicity, they could hardly, if ever, have attained: Although the *Mine of Scripture* be rich; yet unlearned men (as the most part of Christians are, in point of humane literature) cannot search it; nor work it; nor try, and refine it; unlesse they have the help of those, who have tooles and instruments, and vessels, and skill, fit for so rich and holy, yet hard and serious a work; wherein it is much easier for weake and * *unstable* mindes to fall into dark pits, and *damnable errors*; than of themselves, to attain and bring forth those saving truths, which onely can inrich the soul. Although the gifts of humane learning be not personally given to every Christian, yet they are so far necessary *for all*, as they are given to serve for the benefit of all; as every one in the flock enjoyes the blessings of those pastorall gifts and abilities, which are in the *Shepheard*; and every member of the body that light, which is in the *eye* for the use of all.

Dionysius dubitans, an legat hæreticorum libros, divinitus monebatur, ut omnes, qui ad manum venerint, legat; ut omnia melius expendere, refutare & magis abominari possit. Euseb. hi. Ecc. l. 7. c. 6.

* *Sine Christo sophia ipsa ratio, insania est. Sapientia omnis literata stultitia; Grammatica nugæ seriæ; Rhetorica inanis loquacitas; Logica profundum jurgium; Historia omnis, facetiores fabulæ; tota denique philosophia, δοξοσοφία speciosa & negotiosa ignorantia.*

* *Sic adhibeantur scientiæ seculares tanquam machinæ quædam, per quas structura charitatis assurgat, quæ maneat in æternum.* Aust. Ep. 119. ευσέβεια ἐστιν ὁσιότης γνωστική. Cl. Al.

* 2 Pet. 3.

6\. Learned defenders of Christian Religion necessary.

There needs not much learning to make a man in love with it, and covetous of more; It is a certain sign of very little, or none at all, where any man despiseth, or decryeth it in others. It never indeed, received opposition, but either by the *Gothick* barbarity of soldiers and oppressions of warre: or by the finer *spun* malice of such, as * *Julian the Apostate* was: who being both very learned, and very wicked, knew well, how *great advantages* learning afforded to the Christian religion, which he sometime

Sozomen l. 5. cap. 5.

* *Julian* in his Persick expedition wrote 7 books against Christ and Christian Religion; *Jeron. Epi. ad Magnum.*

professed,

professed; and afterward with most *cunning cruelty* persecuted; finding by experience, how potent, and irresistible the weapons of *Christian warfare* were, when skilfully managed by men of parts and learning: Such as those *Atlasses of Christian Religion* were before, and in, as also after his time; who equalled the most renowned heathens in all learning; (as well, as they exceeded them in true Religion) and in unspotted lifes: Such among others were *Justin*, a Philosopher and Martyr, *Tertullian*, *Ireneus*, *Cyprian*, *Origen*, (learned to a Miracle) So *Clemens* of *Alexandria*, *Eusebius*, *Epiphanius*; the three learned *Gregories*, *Naz.* *Niss.* *Thaumaturgus*: both the *Basils*, *Athanasius*, *Cyrill*, *Minutius Felix*, *Arnobius*, *Chrysostome*, *Jerome*, *Ambrose*, *Lactantius*, St. *Austin*, *Prosper*, *Hilarius*, *Prudentius*, and others, famous Bishops and Presbyters of most eminent learning, piety, and courage; who undertook the defence of Christian Religion, against the proud heathen, the pestilent hereticks, and the importune schismaticks of those dayes.

ὁ χθὲς προσκυνητὴς σήμερον ὑβριστής. *Naz.* στηλ. de *Juliano*. yesterday a professor, this day a blasphemer.

Josephus also a Iew, learned to a miracle, as *Jerom* saith, in the *Greek* monuments, defends against *Appion* the *Jewish* Church, which was the old stock, out of which the Christians are swarmed. *Hieron. Ep. ad Mag.* So *Philo* the *Jew*, very learned and an eloquent assertor of the *Jewish* religion. *G. Nissen in vita Thaum.* Διὰ ταύτης (φιλοσοφίας) ὁδηγήθη πρὸς τὴν τοῦ χριστιανισμοῦ κατανόησιν. *vit. Th.* *Miltiades*, *Hyppolitus*, *Apollonius*, *senator. Rom. doctiss. opuscula Christian. relig. contra Philosophos propugnabant.* *Titus Bostrensis*, *Amphilochius*, *Philosophorum sententiis suos libros refarciebant.* Id. Hieron. Ep. ad Magnum. So *Dionysius* Bishop of *Corinth*, and *Tacianus* who refuted the errors of *Origen*. Shewing *ex quibus fontibus philosophorum emanabant.* Hieron. So *Pantænus Stoicus doctiss. Christianus, in Indiam missus ut Brachmanis prædicaret.* Id.

Which made *Julian* the Apostate, elder brother to this *illiterate fraternity* (the despisers and destroyers of good learning) to become the *Ravilliak*, the *Faux* of his times, the prime Assasinator, and grand conspirator, who sought to stab and blow up all Christian Religion, by overthrowing all the *nurseries of learning*, and suppressing the Schooles of the Church: forbidding any *Christians children* to be educated in humane and ingenuous studies; which he saw were become as the outworks to the citadell of Christian Religion: (which sometime indeed needed not these humane guards and defences while the terrible and *miraculous gifts of the Spirit* were like a *pillar of fire*, and cloud, round about Christian Religion, during its wandring in the wildernesse of persecution, no more, than the * *Israelites* needed trenches for their *camp*, when the more immediate *presence of Gods salvation* was among them, beyond *all wals and bulworks*; or then * *Elias* wanted a troop of souldiers, when he was armed with *fire from heaven*, against the ruder Captaines and their fifties) Those *extraordinary dispensations* ceasing, when the Lord brought his Church to the *land of Canaan*; to a condition of worldly peace and tranquillity, through

Theodoret l. 3. cap. 8. *Propriis pennis configimur a Galilæis, inquit Julianus.* πολλὰ τὰ τῶν Γαλιλαίων καὶ παντοδαπὰ βιβλία. in *Bibliotheca Georgii Episcopi Alexand. quam Julianus sibi exacte conquiri jubet.* Epist. ad Porphyrium. 36.

* Exod. 13:21.

* 2 King. 1.

through the *Imperiall* ſavour and ſecular *protection*, under which *Halcyon dayes*, Chriſtians had liberty to attend thoſe improvements which are to be attained by ſtudy and learning in all manner of ingenuous, as well as religious, education.

But when the *Dragon* ſaw he could not by open *perſecuting* power deſtroy the * *woman and her child*; he then turned to other ſhifts; ſeeking by the flouds of *corrupt doctrin*, to poiſon thoſe *ſtreams*, which he could not ſtop: And ſo to furniſh out his *new modelled Militia*, with the better train and ammunition, he ſtirred up learned adverſaries againſt the Churches true and ancient faith; not only without, as * *Celſus*, *Porphyrie*, *Proclus*, *Symmachus*, and others; but even from within; as *Arius*, *Neſtorius*, *Apollinaris*, *Macedonius*, *Eutyches*, *Pelagius*, *Donatus*, and others, very many: This *maſter-piece* he carryed on with moſt powerfull ſuggeſtions, and ſucceſſes ſometimes; knowing well, what force *Error* hath, as well as *Truth*; when it is charged, and diſcharged with skill and learning. In ſo much, that he not onely *overthrew the Faith* of many *ordinary Chriſtians*; but robbed the true Church, in part, and turned at laſt upon the *Orthodox party*, thoſe *whole Canons*, great and incomparable pieces of all learning both *divine humane*; *Tertullian* and * *Origen*, (the converter of St. *Ambroſe*) who formerly had by their accurate and learned labours, both in preaching and writing, bravely aſſerted Chriſtianity; both by demoliſhing the *old remaining forts* of *heatheniſh Idolatry*, and prejudice; as alſo battering the new *riſing works* of hereſies and ſchiſms.

So that our moderate, illiterate *factors* for an *old crafty Dæmon*, doe not, or will not, conſider; that there ever hath been, ſtill are, and ever may be, *learned adverſaries* oppoſing or Apoſtatizing from the *true Chriſtian Religion*, both in its *fundamentalls*, and its *reformations*. There are very *learned Jeſuites*, and *other Papiſts*, of all orders; there are learned *Socinians*; renewed *Palagians*; revived *Arians*, and others, who want not learning; againſt whom the *learned Miniſters* of this and other reformed Churches, are often put upon *neceſſary*, though *uncomfortable*, and unhappy conteſts; Not for any malice, envy, or diſpleaſure againſt any of their perſons: (for learned men cannot but love and eſteem, whatever is good and excellent in others) but onely from *that Conſcience of Truth*, which the Miniſters of this and other reformed Churches doe conceive, upon *Scripture grounds*, and by the conſent of the *primitive* and pureſt *Churches* of Chriſt, they ought in all duty to God, to their own and other ſoules, yet with charity to their Adverſaries, to maintain; And, although the warre in Chriſtian Religion ought to be managed by learned men on all ſides, with all poſſible fairneſſe, candor, and civility, ſuch as the

* Revel. 12.

* *Origen* anſwered *Celſus*, and *Methodius*: *Euſebius* and *Apollinaris* wrote with great ſtrength and dexterity of learning againſt *Porphyrie*, who was one of the moſt eloquent in his time, and wrote againſt Chriſtian religion, 15. books, *Suidas*, & St. *Jerom.*

St. *Ambroſe* and *Prudentius* anſwered *Symmachus* his Oratory againſt Chriſtian Religion.

* *Vincent. Lyrin. lib.* 1. *Immortale Originis ingenium. Jeron. in Ep. ad Tit.*

In Origene adeo præclara, adeo ſingularia, adeo mira extiterunt, ut omnes pene multum longèque ſuperavit, Vin. Lyr. c. 23.

So of *Tertullian*, c. 24. *Quid illo doctius? quid in divinis atque humanis exercitatius? Apud Latinos noſtrorum omnium facile princeps, ut Origenes apud Græcos.*

the honour of the Christian name and profession requires; (for the more illiterate men are, the more rudely they bray and rail against one another) if it were a great sin to be supine and negligent in so great an engagement, which we think to be for Gods cause, the truth of Christ, and the good of soules: for which we ought to be *prudently vigilant* and *honorably valiant*: It would ill become us while we see the adverse partie *daily arming* themselves, with all possible *compleatnesse*, in languages, arts, and sciences, in Fathers, councels, and histories, for us to sit still in our *lazy*, and *unlearned ignorance*: expecting either *miraculous illuminations* and *assistances*, (as idle, vain, and proud mindes do) or else, most *inevitable ruine*, and certain overthrow of that truth and reformed Religion, which we professe to maintain; which in honour and conscience, besides the bonds of nature, humanity, and charity, we are bound to transmit to posterity (if not much improved by our diligence and studies) yet, at least, not sottishly impaired, to a just *impeachment of waste* against us, in this age, from those, that in after times may succeed us; who will have no great honour or happinesse by being heirs to our estates, lands, and dignities, if they be disinherited of all *good learning*, and that true reformed *Religion* which we have received from our learned and pious predecessors.

7. *The sad effects which must follow these illiterate projects.*

And this infallibly will be the *sad event*, and unhappy fate of the *succeeding generations* in *England*; if such *witlesse lack-latin Zelots* can prevail in their *absurd desires*, and most *fanatick endeavours*; who while they tell their *silly disciples*, (who are rather spectators than hearers of these mens *affected gesticulations*, and ill acted Oratory) That *Latin* and *Greek* are the *languages of the Beast*; that all books but the Bible, (and as much of that, as they take not to be for their turnes) are *Antichristian* and to be *destroyed*: Mean time the *common people* are not so much men and reasonable, as to consider the sad *metamorphosis* or change which already growes upon these *Ignorant Masters*, and their scholars; who like to *Lycaon*, *Io*, or *Actaeon*, begin to thrust forth their hornes and hoofs; and to shew their teeth, in their grosse errors, their rude, and savage manners; which are tokens evident and dreadfull enough of their brutised soules: That if the wiser, learneder, and powerfuller world among us in *England*, should, through basenesse, cowardise, and negligence, suffer this *illiterate and ferine faction* to increase and multiply, they will soon finde, by their violence, craft and cruelty, that these Islands will be more pestered and infamous for *wolves*, than ever they were in ancient times.

Sleidan. com. l. 10. An. 1524.

And what is it that these mens *brutish simplicity* would have?

 Namely

Namely this: That the *purer Religion* among the *Protestant and Reformed Churches*, should have no *learned Champions*, or able *defenders*; but onely such silly *Asinellos*, or *Massinellos*, who think it enough to trust to their rude and irrationall confidences; to their *hard heels*, and *harsher brayings*, for the defence of true *Religion*, whenas the *large and luculent* eares of these animals doe give so great advantage to any crafty error, or grosser heresie to get hold of them, that they will as easily be led to any *damnable opinion*, and desperate faction, as an *Oxe is to the slaughter*, and a *foole to the stocks*. For no men are more easily led *into any temptation*, than those, who presume to tempt God, by neglecting to use such due and proportionate means, as his wisdome in ordinary providence hath appointed, to attain those great and holy ends of *true Religion*.

Εὐάλωτον ἡ πονηρία καὶ πανταχόθεν ἑαυτῇ περιπίπτουσα. *Naz.*

In studiis tantum quisque probat, quantum se assequi posse sperat; de quibus desperant, ea despiciunt. Casaub. præf. in Ari.

In quantum ab ignorantia segregantur, in tantum contumacia agglutinantur. Tertul. de Pœn.

Yet we may see, how all *folly is ready to fall upon it self*; to confute its own principles; By *a rude unskilfulnesse* it sometime bandies the *ball* of contention against its own face: For these *great sticklers* against all good learning in Ministers, doe sufficiently shew, they have *fraud mixt with their follie*; like Foxes, they love not the grapes, while they cannot reach them; Their *despaire of learning* makes them despise it in others: Because it's *hardly possible* to have any degree of true learning, and not to oppose them; But, O how doe they seriously triumph and *superciliously rejoice*, when any man, that is but a *smatterer in learning*, or smels a little of the pen and inkhorn, (for other than such *novices, and dunces* never will so far shame themselves) appears for them, or seemes to leane, and adhere to them! how much more if he begins to stickle for their party and faction, being deceived with their *shewes of zeal*, and inspirations! O how doe they *prick up their ears*, and march then with greater courage and confidence, (as the Hares did, when they had got a *Fox* to lead them: in whom they thought was more strength, and cunning, than their own *fearfull feeblenesse* could be guilty of:) Even so these *bunglars in reason*, wresters of Scriptures, and hucksters of religion doe find fault with those *Tooles*, which they have no skil to use; and, like cowards, they quarrell with those weapons, as unlawfull, which they most fear, and can least resist. Which yet, could they once get into their hands, and abuse to their advantages, none would be more *imperiously cruell* and *insolent*; * For what would not these *Illiterate Furies* give to have indeed, *such an Inspiration*, as might in one night make them every way as learned and able in all points, as those *Ministers* and other men have been and still are, who dayly *pare* the ruder *nails*, and *muzzle* the *bolder jaws* of these degenerate and desperate men; who like *horse and mule*, being with-

* St. *Austin. de Doct. Christia*: tels of a servant among the *Barbarians*, who by three dayes prayers (*triduanis precibus*) obtained full knowledge in all humane learning: *ut librum quemlibet percurreret omnibus stupentibus.*

without understanding, are ready to fall upon those, that are fit to be their *Masters and rulers*, both in Church and State; who in stead of sound and healthfull learning have only the three distempers which Sir * *Francis Bacon* observed to be in most men; Fantasticknesse, Contention, and Curiosity, by imagination, altercation, and affectation.

Psal. 32.9.

* Sir *Francis Bacon L. Ver.* in his advancement of learning.

8. *Objection against learning as injurious to true Religion; the parent or nurse of errors.*

But the enemies of *good learning* tell us; That they discern so *many spots* and *black patches* in the face of this *fair Lady*, that they cannot esteem her a *modest Virgin*, or a grave and sober *Matron*; or any way fit company for true Christian Religion; but rather some *prostitute* of Impudicity, which is easily *courted* by every wanton spirit, and oft *impregnated* with grosse errors, which it either conceives and brings forth, or nourisheth and brings up; yea they have heard (for these men read but little, and understand lesse) that *great hereticks*, and enemies to true Religion have beene great Scholars: And even in the *bosome of the Church*, these *vermine* of heresies and schisms, have *crawled* most, since she put on and adorned herself (as some thought) with this *patcht* and beggerly *garment* of humane learning, which she took up in the *high way* of the Gentiles: *Arius* and his crew *wanted not learning*; nor * *Pelagius* Sophistry; nor *Donatus* eloquence, as St. *Austin* tels us; Nor those others of former or later dayes, who made the Van, or bring up the Rear of those *forces*, which the divel hath mustered and trained up against the purity and simplicity of the Gospel; Which (impediments rather than ornaments, as these men tell us, who presume to be better acquainted with the mind of religion, than any Ministers, or other able Christians) it doth now *utterly abhor*, and is ashamed of; yea and would fain quite cast away all those *glasses*, and *wimples*, and *crisping pins*, and *powders*, and *paints*, and *dressings*, and *curlings*, and strange *apparell*, which she had borrowed of humane learning; even as the *Jewish* women were weary of their *toyes* and *trinckets* which they had from the heathen; by which they provoked God against their vanity, pride, and folly.

* Aust. de Hæres. *Pelagii viri, ut audio, sancti, & non parvo provectu Christiani.* Aust. c. 3. de pec. mer. *Bonum & prædicandum virum.* Id. *Pelagii & discipulorum libri propter acrimoniam & facundiam leguntur a plurimis*, Id. Ep. 144.

Isai. 3.

Answ. Yet the benefit of learning is more than the danger.

Thus are these men ready with their *rude hands* to *undresse Divinity*; who, being *very blind and boisterous*, are not able to distinguish between pulling off the patches, or wiping away those spots and paints, which a fair face needs not; and the shaving off that *hair* which is given to Religion for an ornament and covering; Or the plucking out of those *eyes* indeed which it needs, not onely for beauty, but for direction. The learning of hereticks and schismaticks doth not so much deform the Church, and true Religion, as the learning of *Orthodox professors* adorns, and reformes it: which, as *fullers earth*, is the best means to take out those *kennel spots*, which noisome spirits, and *foul mouths* cast upon true Religion; There is the more need of wise and able *Physitians* to make wholesome Antidotes, and confections, by how much there are so many, whose malice is cunning (as the divels Empericks and empoisoners) to mixe pestilent drugs, and infusions with Religion.

1 Cor. 11. 19. There *must be heresies, and hereticks too*: not as necessary effects and consequents of learning, and religion, but rather from the *defects of them* in mens hearts and mindes. When men are not, either able rightly to understand, or not accurately to divide, or not exactly to distinguish, or not rationally to conclude, from *Scripture grounds*, and principles of truth; Or else, when they are prone grossely to mistake, and easily to yeeld to any semblances of truth, and fallacies of error, which are incident to credulous incautions, unstable, and unlearned soules, or to proud passionate and *heady men*, though never so learned. Hence follows their not onely *forsaking the right way*, and resolute persisting in their dangerous and damnable *mistakes* (as sheep gone astray, seldome ever returning of themselves to the *fold* and unity of the Church) but they would also draw others after them, that they may not seeme to erre alone; and by *numbers* at least, and *force* at last, carry on the evill opinions, which always tend to evill practises; unlesse the Lord had always furnished his Church with some learned and godly men; as able for *reduction*, as others were for *seduction*; as potent to *cure*, as others are to *infect*; whose learning defensive was more mighty than any offensive ever was: The flock of Christ was alwayes happily furnished with *Mastives*, whose teeth were as sharp, and strong, as the *Wolves*; With *Davids*, whose valour was always as great, as the ravening strength of *Bear* or *Lyon*; whom nothing else would have curbed and overawed; nor have (without miracle) been able to have preserved the flock of Christ from dayly scatterings and tearings.

So then in all right reason, either wholly remove *these offensive* enemies, and such weapons out of their heads and hands: or else give true Christian Religion leave to keep her *defensive Arms*, and those worthy men, who are able to use them; namely, the learned and godly professors, both Ministers and others of this, and other Churches; both Christian, and reformed: Whose learning, courage and honesty together, makes them *impregnable*: Whom otherwayes, even these *pitiful pygmies*, who now thus oppose them, would hope to be too hard for, if once matters of religion were reduced onely to tongues, and hands: for Ignorance makes men violent, and for want of reason to flye to force. * Possibly these *professors of ignorance, and rusticity*, may be lowder speakers, and bolder fighters, though

* τῇ δὲ ἀμαθίᾳ ἀκρασία, ἀναίδεια, ἐπιεικεστέροτης, ἀμνημοσύνη, εὐμετάβολον, καὶ βιαστικὸν παρακολουθεῖ. *Arist. Eth.*

though they be *weaker disputants*, and *flatter writers*: yea we commonly see, that *hereticall* pride, and *schismaticall* passion, (in men, that neither love the Truth, nor the peace of the Church) when worsted by arguments, fly to Arms; as the *Arians*, and *Donatists*, and *Novatians* did; when refusing fair disputations, which the Orthodox Bishops and Presbyters desired: offering (ἐπισκοπὴν καὶ εἰρηνικὴν τάξιν) *orderly*, and *peaceable disquisitions*, for the determining of differences, so that Christian union might follow; They presently ran furiously to *meere brutish and tumultuary violences*: Invading Churches by force; driving away the Orthodox and holy *Bishops and Presbyters*; who had not varied, nor would yeeld to change, that Faith, and holy order of Religion, and Ministry, which still remained in all the Christian Churches; as descended from the Apostles, and primitive Christians, and which had lately been confirmed, and declared by the first famous Councell of *Nice*, which consisted of 318 Bishops; besides other many learned assistants, holy Presbyters, and Deacons, together with some chief men of the laity; who were so all of a minde, that there were but 17 *dissenters* in the vote against *Arius*.

Vide Can. Afric. Concil. Carth. An. 410.

εἰς ἀπηνεῖς βίας; *ad immanes violentias.*

After the same *riotous fashion* also was that *ignorant* and *abominable rable* (as it's called) of the *Circumcelliones*, (a *subsection of the Donatists*) who were wont to ramble idly up and down, like squibs with fire and force, among the plain, and *pagane Christians* in the country; till (after great ostentations of piety, devotion, and zeale for *Martyrdome*, calling themselves * (*Duces Sanctorum*) *Captaines of the Saints*; and (ἀγωνιστικοὺς) contenders for the faith, they fell at length to *pilfering*, then to plundering, and wasting whole countreys, opposing in an hostile manner the Vicegerents *Pacelius* and *Macarius*; till at length they were by the Emperour himself * (*Honorius*) repressed and destroyed.

Βδελυκτὸν πλῆθος τῶν περισυναγαγόντων. Can. Afri. *Genus hominum agreste & famosissimæ audaciæ*: Aust. cont. Cresco. l. 3. c. 42. *Leniora latronum & prædonum facta quam Circumcellionum.* * St. *Aust. de Hæret.* *Optatus.* * *An. 348.*

That many men abuse *learning*, to abet errors; and religion, to colour *hypocrisie*; and the name *of the Spirit*, to indulge the *flesh*; and heaven, to carry on earthly designes, I make no question; nor will these *objecters*, I beleive; yet I doe not think their morosenesse is such, as presently to conclude, they must part with what they can well use, because they see others daily abuse good things, as health, beauty, strength, riches, preferment, meat, drink, cloathing, &c. all which oft nourish vanity, lusts, excesse; The aking of these mens heads, or teeth, makes them not willingly to lose them; no more may the *abuse of learning* take away the *use of it*; Wise men know, how to keep a mean between *starving* and *surfeiting*; between *drunkennesse* and *cutting up all vines*; condemning all men to drink nothing, but such *small stuffe*, as these *Antiministeriall* Teachers intend to *brew*, whereby to keep all Christians

ans as they pretend in a *sober simplicity*, which project is among their other *weak and silly conceptions*; For the *fumes* and *ventosities*, arising from ignorance, emptinesse, and want of good *sustenance*, may more trouble the brain with *giddy whimseyes* and *dizinesse*, than can ever be feared from *competent repletions*, unlesse men have very foul stomachs, or hot Livers: Wise men know to keep the mean between the riot, and the want of learning; There are, saith *Plato*, two diseases of the Soul of man (μανία καὶ ἀμαθία) madnesse and ignorance; Madnesse is from the abounding with pride and passion; Ignorance from the want of knowledge and instruction: Ignorance is but a tamer madnesse: mad men have lost their wits; and ignorant men never had them. Learning and Religion cure both. The highest and most *incurable* madnesse is, an *ungracious hatred* of learning, and an irreligious love of ignorance.

Plato in Timæo.

...We see by sad experience, That true Religion is as subject to be drowned by *inundations of barbarity*, and *deluges* of unlettered people, (fit to be followers of *Goths* and *Vandales*; or listed with *Jack Cade*, and *Wat Tylar*; or subjects to the titular *King of Sion*, *John of Leyden*) as it is to be *scorched* by the hotter beams of those *Phaethons*, who unskilfully manage the *chariot of the Sun*; that is, make an ill *use of good learning*: Which is as the *light of the world*; wherein Christian Religion is most honourably and most usefully enthroned, when it is guided aright: neither depressing reason too low, by fanatick novelties; nor exalting it too high, by intricate *subtilties*; but keeping the *middle way*, of the necessary, *plain*, and most *demonstrable verities* of Religion, which the Compasse of *right Reason* measures exactly by the scale of Scriptures.

Media tutissimus ibis, Ovid.

9. *Object. Many unlearned have been holy, &c.*

But these Objectors tell us, That many *holy and excellent Christians* of the common, and *unlettered* sort of men have been Worthies in grace and godlinesse; who never found any want of *Sauls* armour, those * great *incumqrances*, great *volumes*, nor those perplexed studies, in *pestred libraries*; That the * *poysons of opinions* are seldomer drunk, or pledged in these earthen vessels, than *in those of gold or silver*; That their simplicity was contented to enjoy, that one *book necessary*, *The Scriptures*: All other bookes they would have been contented, as these men now, to have them sacrificed to *Vulcan*, an heathen god, and meriting such heathenish oblations.

* Μέγα βιβλίον μέγα κακόν.

* *Nulla aconita bibuntur Fictilibus, tunc illa time, cum pocula sumas Gemmatas, &c.* Iuv.

Answ.

Answ. No doubt, but many very *good Christians* have been happily instructed, setled and preserved in faith and holinesse, who never were learned in any book, but that of the Scripture. * S. *Austin* tels, that *Anthony* the Hermite, who could not read, had all the

* L. 1. de Doctr. Christian. *S. Scripturas memoria tenuit & intellexit sine scientia literarum.*

Scrip-

Scriptures by heart, and understood them well; yea many, who never read any word in the Bible, yet have been blest, by the *Ministry of the Gospell*, to beleive and obey the truth of it; which is indeed the *life* of religion, and the *quintessence of all learning*. Yet it was the happinesse of those *honest Christians*, that they never met with such *pragmatick depravers* of all good order, piety and learning, and Ministry, as these now are; for certainly they had never learned from such, as these despisers of learning and Ministers are, either the *letter*, or the *true sense* of the Scriptures: which they attained by the learned labours of their *Ministers*, chiefly, both reading, translating, and interpreting and preaching the Scriptures to them. They were happily freed from such praters, whose pride and folly is *heavier than any lead*, or the sand of the Sea; whose *ungratefull humour* would have taught them first to have cast off all their *true Ministers* and Teachers; next, to despise them; and lastly, to destroy them, by a *most pious madnesse* and *spirituall ingratitude*. They are not only blind, but mad men, who wanting eyes themselves, would have all their guides see no more than they do, that so both might fall into the ditch. Whereas the humility of all sober Christians was ever such, as equalled their piety, exceeded their knowledge, and compensated their illiteratenesse: so as to be farre enough from thinking themselves equall to, or above the *first three*, their *lawfull Pastors and learned Ministers*, by whose faithfull endeavours, and studies, those saving truths, and holy mysteries, were prepared for them, and set before them: So that however they did indeed eat *clean food*; the *finest* of the *bread of life*; yet they could not, *but consider*, whose plowing, and sowing, and gathering; whose thrashing, and winnowing, and grinding; whose kneading, & *baking* had provided and prepared those *savory* and *wholesome victuals* for them, which their own blindnesse and feeblenesse, (like *Isaacks*) could never have *provided*, or catered for themselves: That they did alwayes *blesse those Ministers, and that God*, who sent such *Josephs* to provide, and distribute the food of heaven to his *otherwayes destitute*, and famished Church, which alwayes consisted for the most part of *that plebs*, or community of faithfull and poor Christians; who were alwayes happy in this; that, although they *had not provision of learning* in their own *storehouses* and cisternes; yet still they might have recourse to, and make use of their *Ministers fulnesse*, and store: whose lips ought to preserve knowledge, and to dispense it without envy or grudging: who rejoyced most, when their fountaines were most *flowing* forth to the *refreshing of poor soules*; The abilities of learned *Ministers* have alwayes been, like *Jacobs* and *Moses his strength*, a means to *rowl away the great stones*, which lie on the wels mouth (the Scriptures) which

Margin notes: Pro. 27. 3. — Gen. 29. 10. — Exod. 2. 17.

which are too heavy for ordinary *shoulders*, and to protect feebler Christians from insolent opposers. So that as the Eunuch asked, how he should understand, without an *Interpreter* to guide him.

Act. 8. 31.

Ministers are therefore set by Christ in his Church for *lights*, that each might enjoy them; as much, as if *each had* their *sufficiencies*: As the *meanest part* of the body hath as *much use* of the eye, as if it were an *eye itselfe*. That as it was in the *Israelites gathering Manna*, so it is in the Church of Christ, when setled and flourishing; He that *gathered much* had no *overplus*, and hee that gathered little, had no lack. So those honest Ideots, and Lay-Christians, (who have little or no learning, beyond that faith and plain knowledge of the *mysteries* of Christ and the *holy duties* belonging to a Christian) yet have no want of learning; And learned Ministers who have attained most eminent skill in all sorts of good learning, by Gods blessing on their studies, have no more than is needfull for their place and the Churches edification, or safety and preservation.

Exod. 16. 18.

10. *Wherein learning is necessary to Ministers.*

Si ad humana perdiscenda ista hominis vita brevis est, quid temporis sufficere potest ad intelligentiam divinam? Chrysol.

And much, I think, is needfull, to give a *right sense* of Scripture, from the originall proprieties or emphasis of words: To open the many *allusions* referring to *Judaick* rites and *Ethnick* customes in severall ages: To clear and unfold the Scriptures by *short paraphrases*, or larger Commentaries: To analyse severall passages so, as to reduce them to their proper place and order of reasoning wherein their force consists, (as the parts and joints of the body set in their due posture:) For the *method* of the reasoning, and the strength of the *argument*, or main scope in Scripture, is oft very different from the series, and order of the words in the Text; Many times the ambiguity of the words, the variety of stops, the incoherence and independence of the sense as to the letter, makes the method more obscure, and the meaning very intricate; yea the very text of Scriptures were in many copies of Bibles anciently (as in St. *Jeromes* time; and before him in *Origens*) *much altered*, by addition to, or detraction from the pure and authentick Scripture, untill those and other learned men, the Bishops and Ministers of the Church, with more accurate diligence reduced the Bible to its *purity*, and *integrity*; as much as is attainable by humane industry, or necessary to mans salvation; In these and the like cases I suppose, these objectors, who are very *simple* (but not with a dove-like *simplicity*) must needs confesse (unlesse they wholly trust to the *reed* of their *Enthusiasms*, which they have very little cause to doe) that there is a great need of *learned Criticks*: of *good Linguists*; of *methodicall Analysts*; *judicious Commentators*; *accurate distinguishers*; and *harmonious reconcilers*; that the truth, purity, and unity of the *sacred Oracles* may be preserved and vindicated, against

Jeronymus. In libris Jobi, & Danielis, & aliis.

Εὐθὺς ἐξ ἀρχῆς ἐπισκοπεῖν ἕκαστον τῶν μαθημάτων, καὶ συναρμόζειν τῷ τέλει προσῆκε. *Basil. in hom. 24. de Leg. Ethn.*

against Jews, Heathens, Atheists, Hereticks, and *capricious Enthusiasts*; who are ready to strike with contempt and passion, any part of Scripture, as uselesse, or corrupted; if it flow not as the *rock* with an easie sense and obvious interpretation to their weak and sudden capacities: They are instantly prone with an high *disdain* and *choler*, to prefer their most *impertinent imaginations*, sudden fancies and addle raptures.

Or, if they be ashamed of those, being too weak, grosse, and impudent to be vended at noon day, and in so faithfull a light as yet shines in this Church; then they are crying up the *book of the creatures*; and *God in them*; or they *applaud* some easier *morall heathens*; And I should think nothing should fit their fancies so well, as the *Turkish Alcoran*, or *Jewish Talmuds*, and *Cabals*; for these (if any thing can) have already out done them in toyes and *incredible fables*; which may save them the labour of further inventions. Swine will prefer the *filthiest puddle*, before the *fairest springs*: so will wanton proud and vain men take any light exception *against the Scripture*; which they hate the more perfectly, by how much they see it is a *most perfect rule*, and fully contrary to their proud, unjust and unruly passions: And however the *shell* of those holy and unparelleld writings, *the blessed Scriptures*, be in many places rugged and hard, so that every one cannot handle or break it; yet (blessed be God) others can; nor is the *kernell of saving Truth* lesse sweet and smooth, because it is not easily explained, but by the help of other mens better gifts; whom the Lord raiseth up, and fitteth for this very end, with variety of gifts, even in humane learning: Who (for the most part) have been of the *order of the Clergy*: although, in these later times (especially,) divers others, both *Nobility*, *Gentry*, and *Commoners*, have been as *excellent pioners*, who have by their private studies very chearfully, and industriously assisted, and helped the Churches chiefest Champions, and Leaders, *the Ministers*; who have not indeed, every one, those sharp *tools of steel*, which can work at the hardest places of this rock, and holy Mine, *the Scriptures*; yet have they generally such skill, and leisure, beyond the Vulgar, as enables them to try the *Ore*, to gather and refine the grains, to cast them into fit wedges or ingots of Gold: Truths reduced to some body, method or common place of Divinity. Thus assisted by their own and other studies, method, and industry, they are well able to make plain, yet learned and judicious Sermons; with pathetick homilies, fitted to the common peoples capacity, memory, and disposition: whom neither leisure, nor necessities of life, and the *hard labours* under the Sun, nor abilities of minde, would suffer or serve (*one of a thousand*) to attain to any competent measure of religious know-

2 Tim. 3. 16.

ledge; if holy and learned men, (Ministers of the Church) were not enabled by God, approved by the Church, and ordained by both, to that *constant service of the Ministry*, for the good of the *plainer Christians*; who enjoy, in every point of true doctrine, or solid Divinity, (which is as a *weighty* piece of gold stamped with the *clear testimony* of the Scripture, (as people doe in every piece of current money) the extract of the labour, and the result of the art of many mens *heads* and hands, who have thus fitted it for their ordinary use.

Besides this, when *common people* are once well stored, and inriched in their *honest plainnesse*, with competent and sound knowledge in Religion by the care and faithfulnesse of their able and honest Ministers; yet how easily would the *cheats of Religion*, delude and impose on these *poore Souls*, (these plain and single hearted Christians) abasing, or changing *counterfeit*, with truths; *cropt opinions*, and *round-headed tenets*, for full weight of Christian doctrines: Still *cogging* with *religious* * *dice*, and *cheating* with plausible fallacies, seemingly brought out of the Scripture; untill those *poore beleevers*, like the * bewitched *Galatians*, had lost all, or their most *part* of their *sound Religion*; yea, some of *these Impostors* doe not leave poore Christians, whom they have cousened with fair shews of the *Spirits revelations*, and new Gospels, so much faith, as to beleive the main *Articles of the Christian Faith*; or the Scriptures to be the Word of God; or, that there is any *true Church*, or any order and authority of *true Ministry*: And whither would not this *cousenage* and deceit of these hucksters proceed, even to overthrow *whole houses*, Parishes, and Churches, if there were not some learned and able Ministers in the Church; who are as Gods and the Churches publique Officers, to detect these jugglers, to discover these *deceitfull workers*, to set these cheats in the *pillory* of *publique* infamy; that they may *loose their Ears*; that is, their * *hearing* well; that credit and fame of gifts which they cover and *captate* among the Vulgar; and which they would enjoy, by reason of their many wiles, and artifices, by which they *ly in wait to deceive* with good words and fair speeches, (as the *Divels* setting Dogs) the well affected and *plain hearted* Christians, if they were not every *where routed*, and confounded by the Ministers of the Church, who are both *far abler* and *honester* men, and to whose charge the *flock of Christ*, in its severall divisions and places is committed; that they may take care it *suffer* no detriment either in truth, or in peace; in faith, or manners; in Doctrine, or in holy order. Thus then, although the soules, and faith of the meanest true Christians be *alike pretious* and dear to God, as the *most learned men's*, yet they are not *pieces* of the *same weight* for *gifts*; of the *same extension* for

* ἐν τῇ κυβείᾳ τῶν ἀνθρώπων, ἐν πανουργίᾳ πρὸς τὴν μεθοδείαν τῆς πλάνης. Ephes. 4. 14.

* Gal. 3. 1.

2 Cor. 2. 17. καπηλεύοντες τὸν λόγον.

2 Cor. 2. 17. ἐργάται δόλιοι.

* *Ut tandem male audiant, qui male & dicunt & agunt.*

Rom. 16. 18.

2 Pet. 1. 1.

for endowments; of the same *polishings* for studies; nor of the same *stamp* and *authority* for their calling and office; All which, as they are not to the essence of true grace, and religion; so they are much, to the lustre, power, beauty, order, usefulnesse and communicativenesse of those gifts, which goe with true Religion; and are by the *Lords munificence* bestowed on the Church and faithfull, for their well being, safety, and comfort, even in this world; besides their happinesse in another, which ought to be the grand design of all true Christians, both *Laymen* and *Churchmen*, both learned and unlearned, both Governours and governed.

But these Illiterato's further object with open mouth; That they are sure neither Christ nor his Apostles, had themselves, or commended to the Churches use, *humane learning*. 11. *Object. Christ and his Apostles had no humane Learning.*

Answ. My answer is; They *needed none*, *as humane*; that is acquired by ordinary education, or industry; being far above it, by those glorious and miraculous endowmen s of the *Spirit of wisedome*, which can easily shine in a moment through the *darkest lanterns*; (*men of the meanest parts* and *grossest capacities*.) So that those might as well dispense with the absence of all acquired humane learning, as he that hath the Suns light, needs not the Moon or Stars, or Candles; or he that had *Angels wings* and swiftnesse, would not want the legge of man, or beast to carry him: or he that is neer a *living* and *inexhaustible* spring, needs not labour to dig wels, as *Isaac* did: and so must we too, in the barren and dry land, where we live; which none but inhumane *Philistims* would stop up. This therefore of *Christ* and his *Apostles* is not more *peevishly*, than impertinently alledged by these men, in these times, against the use of *good learning* in the *Churches Ministers*; unlesse the reall experiences of these men *pretended Apostolicall gifts*, extraordinary *endowments*, and *immediate sufficiencies* from the Spirit of God, could justifie these allegations; either as fitted to them, as to the present *dispensations* of Christ to his Church; Although the Lord sometime gave his Church *water out of a rock*, and refreshed wearied *Samson* by a miraculous fountain, which suddenly sprung up in *Lehi* (not in the Jaw-bone, but in the place so called, from *Lehi*, (*i.e.*) the *Jaw-bone*, by which instrument he had obtained so great a victory; there where it continued afterward:) yet, I beleeve, these men will think it no argument to expect every day such *wonderfull emanations*; and neglecting all ordinary means, to expect from the *Jaw-bones* of Asses water, or drink to quench their thirst: I am sure this Church hath not yet found any such *flowings* forth, or refreshing from the mouths of these Objecters; whose lips never yet dropped like *Hermon*, so much as a *Dew* of sweet and wholesome

Gen. 26. 18.

Judg. 15. 19.

knowledge upon any place; and how should they? whose tongues are for *the most part set on fire*; and breathe out, with much terrour, nothing but ashes and cinders; like *Vesuvius* or *Etna*; whose eruptions are vastatious to all neere them.

Col. 2. 3. Matth. 12. 42. *unus verus & magnus est magister Christus, qui solus non didicit quod omnes doceret.* Amb. off. l. 1. Matth 5. 45. Mal. 4. 1 Cor. 1. 26. Luk. 2. 48.

As for our *blessed Lord Christ*; we know he was *filled with all the treasures of wisedome*, both divine and humane; for, being *greater than Solomon*, he could not come short of *Solomons wisdome* in any thing; who was in all his glory but a *Type* and *shadow* of Christ, and no way comparable to him: Our Saviours design, indeed, was, not as *Platos*, or *Aristotles*, to advance *naturall Philosophy*, meer morality, humane learning, and eloquence; (the beams of *which Sun*, by common providence, God had already made to shine by other wayes, on *the bad, as well as the good*; on the heathens as well as the Jews and Christians;) but *Christs intent* was, by word and deed, to set forth the *beams of the Sunne of righteousnesse*, the wisdome of the Father; the saving *mysteries of his Crosse*, and sufferings in order to mans improvement; not by humane learning, but by divine grace: And however our Blessed Saviour hath *crucified*, as it were, *the flesh*, and *pride* of humane learning, (as well as of riches, honour, and all worldly excellencies; which are infinitely short of the *knowledge and love of God in Christ*) yet he quickned and raised them all *by the Spirit*; which teacheth a *sanctified* and *gracious* use of them all *to his Church*, and true beleevers. Our Lord Jesus did not disdain to converse with the *learned Doctors*, and *Rabbies of his time*; among whom he *was found* after his parents had sought *him sorrowing*; because in vain, otherwhere; yet our *wanderers* and *seekers* are loth to *seek*; afraid to find, and disdain to *own Jesus Christ*, when they have found him among the *learned men*, and Ministers of this Church; lest in so doing, they should seem to confesse they had lost Christ, and true Religion, in their *illiterate Conventicles* and *ignorant presumptions*.

12. *The objecters may not argue from the Apostles gifts against learning now, since they have neither of them.*

As for the *blessed Apostles*, who were (θεοδίδακτοι) immediately taught of God, by conversing with the Son of God the Lord Jesus Christ, the Christian world well knowes their miraculous and extraordinary *fulnesse* of all gifts, and powers of the *Spirit*, both *habituall* and *occasionall*; so that they wanted neither any *language* nor *learning*, which was then necessary, to carry on the great work of preaching, and planting the Gospell: And no lesse doth the *wiser world* know the *emptinesse* and *ridiculous penury* of these (disputers against good learning) even as to the *common gifts* of sober reason, and judicious understanding; wherewith the blessing of heaven is now wont to crown onely the *prayers*, and *studies* of those, that attend on *Wisedoms gates* with all *humble industry*: whose great proficiencies these *poor men* envying, (as they

Δύσκολος ἡ τῆς ἀληθείας κτῆσις. Cl. Al. Pro. 1.

they have great cause) would fain perswade them to be as *much sluggards*, as themselves are; (who have neither *hunted*, nor *caught* any thing) by * *not roasting* what they have *taken in hunting*; that is, not to use those gifts of *learning* in all kindes, which Ministers have attained unto, by Gods blessing on their studies.

Contra bonas literas blaterant, εἰς ῥᾳθυμίας καὶ ὄκνου πρόσχημα. Chrysost. περ. ἱερ. εἰς ἀπολογίαν ἀμαθείας. Naz. or. 27.

* Pro. 12. 27.

As for that Primitive gift of Tongues, by which the Apostles at once *suddenly thawed*, and brake *that Ice*, which now *locks* and *seals* up to us the face of the *great deep* of Learning and Wisdome; so that they were instantly *Masters*, not onely to understand, but also to utter, the *mysteries* of Christ, (whereof they had partly an acquired, by Christs teaching, but for the most part, an *inspired knowledge*:) These *pitifull praters*, who would be counted Apostolicall, are so far from any *such gifts* of wisdome, or utterance, that they are scarse masters of their own *mother tongue*, neither knowing, for the most part, *what they say*, nor *whereof they affirm*; nor able with modesty, gravity, humility, or charity, either to use, or bridle *their tongues*; (which is an *Apostolicall* brand on them; shewing *that their Religion is but vain*;) And how can it be otherwayes, where sober speech, sound reason, common sense, and ordinary ingenuity, are as much wanting; as pride, contempt of others, intractable fiercenesse, and indocible ignorance doe abound? When their *great art* is, to *set off* to some popular shew and acceptance, their gifts and persons, by *proud swelling* words: sometimes *soring* in the height of *raptures*, and rare *speculations*, beyond *sobriety*; as if they were from sudden *inspirations*; when indeed they are nothing else but some odde ends of *metaphysicall* questions, and *devotionary contemplations*; which are every where found among the *Schoolmen*, and Monasticks; or in the *Platonists*, *Plotinus*, *Pimander*, and the like; to which Authours these men being strangers, yet drunk with their *own fancies*, sometimes they reel, and stumble upon such notions; which vainly *puffe them up in their fleshly mindes*; while they are still but *clouds without water*, carryed *with the tempests of passions*, and high *presumptions* above the plain, practicall and usefull truths of Religion; and indeed above the proportion and sphear of their own *gifts and parts*: Other whiles they seem as *Wels without water*, deep, but *dark* and dry, in their *profound follies* and profane niceties; as the *Manichees*, *Valentinians*, and others of old; by which they seek to confound, God *with the creatures*; good with *evill*; *Nature* with *Grace*; *Vice* with *Vertue*; *Law* with the *Gospell*; *Christ* with *Divels*; By all which rarities, *amazing* their *silly auditors*, they are no other but cunning Agitators for ignorance, atheism, profanenesse, hypocrisie, and superstition; that the life and power of the *Christian reformed Religion* may be wholly *baffled*, and despised together.

1 Tim. 1. 1.7.

Iames 1. 26.

2 Pet. 2. 18.

Col. 2. 18.

Iud. 12.

together with the Ministry of this Church: What can these *wretched men* expect, but the *blacknesse of darknesse for ever to be reserved for them* (without repentance) who study to cry downe all good studies, and learning; that they may the better eclipse all true and reformed Religion?

2 Pet. 2. 17.

Such *Pharisees* (for few of them *are good Scribes*) are like indeed to make excellent *Teachers of the Kingdome of heaven*, who are not able to bring forth any things, either *old or new*, having no *Treasure* of well digested knowledge, either divine or humane; but onely some of the *rubbidge*, of that *learning*, which they seeke to destroy; *pitifull rapsodies* of such *confused stuffe*, as they have scraped together; which becomes none but *bablers* and *pamphleters*; Which, whoever considers seriously, how much they have been a *shame*, and *bane* to true Religion, to the honour of this reformed Church, and to those *holy manners* which become sober, wise, and modest Christians, he would ever after love learning and learned *Ministers* the *better*, by how much he sees infinite cause to abhor the sordid and shamefull effects of *impudent ignorance*; which loves to *batten in its own soyl*; and refuseth to be cleansed: Such mouths full of errors, and foul with evill *speakings*, however the *Timothies* and *Tituses* of this Church cannot *now stop*, (as they ought to doe; if the exercise of that *just power* in the Church were not *obstructed*) yet they ought to *rebuke them sharply, and with all authority*.

Mat. 12. 35.

Tit. 1. 11. 2. 15.

And untill these *Seraphick despisers* of true, usefull and *sanctified learning* can (not boast and clamour among their Disciples, who are now grown *giddy* with too high notions and airy speculations, but till they can) evidently demonstrate to the wiser and soberer world; that they can *indeed perform*, what they pretend; that is, by immediate gifts, and unstudied enablings they can *solidly comprehend, soberly preach, methodically explain, clearly demonstrate*, the sacred mysteries of our Religion: also *resolve the difficulties*, *reconcile* the differences, and determine the doubts, or controversies arising out of the Word of God, or the points of Religion; so, as in some measure may tend to satisfie mens judgements, together with the scruples, and cases of their consciences: Till I say, these men can doe these in some *competent measure*, equall at least, if not beyond, what the *learned Ministers* of this Church have done, and dayly doe, by the blessing of God on their labors; they must give us leave still to follow our *studies*, with *humble prayers* and *diligent pains*; That so in stead of the *husks*, and *chaffe* of these mens *specious words*, and popular *insinuations*, (sadly deploring, and proudly despising those *excellent abilities*, which are in true Ministers, far above them) we may help to feed

poor

poor *hungry soules*; not with frothy vanity (wherewith these *proud Masters* send *their scholars* away, as puffed up and as empty as themselves) but with *good corn*, and that wholesome provision of sound knowledge and saving doctrine, wherewith the Lord is pleased to furnish us, in the honest, and ordinary way of his providence and blessing upon our industry: for we have now no *Manna* or *Quails* about our tents; which, while these men dream of, mean time exceeding *leannesse* is entred into their souls: And how can it otherwise be, than, that *sowing vanity*, and *visions of their own hearts*, they should *reap* other, than *wind*: and be satisfied, as they are extremely, (but most unhappily) with their *owne delusions*? Psal. 106. 15. Hos. 8. 7.

13. *Inspired holy men yet used their learned gifts.*

We doe not read that either *Moses*, or *Solomon*, or *Daniel*, or St. *Paul*, (first educated at * *Tarsis* a famous University; and after at the feet of *Gamaliel*) or Attick *Luke*, or eloquent *Apollos*, ever despised, or decryed, or disused those *acquired gifts* of humane learning; wherewith they were endued in the ordinary wayes of education; no not, when they were *extraordinarily inspired*: Their common gifts served them still in their *ordinary Ministry*; as to understanding, memory, utterance, or writing; by which they endevoured to set forth, *that Jesus was the Christ*, the promised *Messias*; So that in their arguments, disputes, reasonings, and allegations out of humane Authours; also in the style, phrase, and manner of their speaking, and writing, it might and may easily bee that the difference of Prophets, Evangelists, and Apostles naturall, acquired, or studied gifts, did still remain; when their *extraordinary* and infused might be *equall*; yet these did not equall them in their either more strict and *Logicall reasonings*, or their more *Oratorious expressions*; or more *elegant phrase* and proper language; which appear very different in those holy Writers and Penmen of the Scriptures, which had the same Spirit *directing* or *dictating*, as to the matter revealed to them; but they used their own ordinary abilities to expresse them by word, or pen, to others.

* *Tarsis celebris Ciliciæ Urbs, & Academia; ipsis Athenis, & Alexandriæ comparanda*, Strabo.

St. *Jeromes Epist. ad Mag.* answers that question, *Cur candorem Ecclesiæ Ethnicis sordibus polluamus*: and shews by the examples in holy Scripture and other holy writers, what holy use is to be made of the learning of heathens by Christians. See *Tom.* 2. *pag.* 331. St. *Paul* cites three testimonies out of heathen Poets, *Epimenides*, Κρῆτες ἀεὶ, *&c.* *Menander*, φθείρουσιν ἤθη, *&c.* *Aratus*, τοῦ μὲν γὰρ γένος ἐσμὲν, &c. So *Jannes* and *Jambres* out of *Jewish* Records and Talmuds. *Plures sine dubio legerat* B. Paulus *poetas, quam quos recitavit; & recitando aliquos, laudavit omnes, in quantum divinoris veritatis scintillas sæpius produnt*, Erasm.

And certainly when the Apostle *Paul* bids *Timothy* (as a grand and lasting pattern for all *Bishops* and Ministers of the Church, to *study*, to *meditate*, to give *himselfe wholly to those things*, that his *profiting may appear*, to stir up the *gift* that is in him, 1 Tim. 4. 13, 14. 15.

still

ſtill more fitting himſelfe to the work of the Miniſtry, (notwithſtanding he had ſome ſpeciall and extraordinary gifts) Sure the ſame Apoſtle gave *Timothy* no *example* of idleneſſe in himſelf; but both ſtudied and prayed; yea deſires the *prayers of others* for him, that he might (as an able Miniſter, and as a Maſter builder) *finiſh the courſe of his Miniſtry with joy*; This bleſſed Apoſtle needed not have been ſo ſolicitous for *the parchments*, which he left at *Troas*, if his memory had been alwayes ſupplyed with *miraculous aſſiſtance*; he needed not to have *committed any thing* to writing for his owne uſe. It is very probable that *thoſe parchments* were no *deeds*, for conveying any land or temporall eſtate; but rather ſome *Scheme* or draught of divine *Truths* and myſteries, *methodically digeſted*; which he had fitted for his own, and transferred to *the uſe of others*, as *Apollos*, or *Timothy*, or *Titus*: So little doth the *ſpeciall gifts* of the Spirit, in the Apoſtles or other holy men, juſtifie or plead for thoſe odde and *miſhapen figures* of thoſe *mens Divinity*, whether diſcovered by their tongues or hands; of whoſe deformity, and unpoliteneſſe, compared to the faſhion of all learned mens judicious, methodicall, and comely *writings*, and diſcourſes, theſe crafty men being conſcious, would have no *Sun*, or light of arts and learning ſhining among Chriſtians, by which their *ridiculous monſtroſity* might appear.

Ephes. 6. 18.
2 Tim. 4. 13.
1 Cor. 4. 6.

The ſame Apoſtle who bids us beware of *vain Philoſophy*, *and wiſdom falſly ſo called* (while it *oppoſed* the divine; or was preferred before the word and truth of God in Chriſt, which onely can attaine the end of all true wiſdome, to make a man happy to eternity) yet he could be no enemy to any part of true and uſefull Philoſophy; which is but the *knowledge of God in the creature*, of which he gives ſeverall touches, in his moſt divine writings; He commands us, no leſſe, to beware of * *falſe Teachers*, of *heaps of Teachers*; of *deceitfull workers*; of *unruly walkers*; of *unſtable and unlearned ſpirits*, who by *vaine bablings*, endleſſe janglings, high preſumptions, and *private interpretations*, wreſt the Scriptures, corrupt both religious Doctrine, ſound ſpeech, and *Chriſtian communication*: Such who are * *vainly puffed up in their fleſhly minde*; whoſe glory is to lead *Diſciples* after them; deſirous *to be* * *Teachers*, when they know not *what they ſay*, nor whereof *they affirme*; *Comparing themſelves with themſelves*; and abhorring all higher patterns, they can * *never be wiſe*, but in their own conceits, and there is * *little hope of them*.

2 Col. 1. 8.
1 Tim. 6. 20.
In tantum vana eſt quantum perverſa: felicitatis eſt doctrina; gentium Philoſophia. Tertul. l. de Anima.
* Rom. 1. 21.
2 Tim. 4. 3.
Imperitiſſima eſt ſcientia ſcire quid ſenſerint Philoſophi, & neſcire quid Chriſtus docuit. Auſt. Ep. 56.
Cum Philoſophiæ nidore purum veritatis aerem infuſcant. Tertul.

* Col. 2. 18. * 1 Tim. 1. 7. * 1 Cor. 10. 12. * Prov. 26. 9.

But

But O you, that *excell in learning or humility, or both*; I should fear to write too much for good learning, if I did not consider, that I write to those chiefly who can never think too much said, or wrote for it; because they know the many beauties and excellencies of it, both in reference to the glory of God, and the good of mankind, both for souls and bodies, their religious and secular concernments, their temporall and eternall interest.

16. *Monuments of learning how excellent and usefull.*

Indeed, no minde is able to conceive, but such as enjoy them, nor can any tongue expresse them, (since they *exceed the greatest eloquence* of those that most enjoy them) those bright, heavenly, and divine *beams of Reason and Religion*; which, with severall preparatory glories, shine from the daily reading of those *excellent writings*, and durable monuments of learned men in former ages; as rayes of light, falling from the *Sun*, on this inferiour world; breaking in upon all the *regions* of the soul: dissipating its *darknesse*; discovering its *disorders*, supplying its *defects*; filling it with the sweet and silent * pleasure of daily knowing something more excellent in the creature, or the Creator, which before it knew not: This secret and unspeakable contentment is more welcome to the *now improving soul*, than the beauty of a fair morning, which shows a *safe haven* to one, that hath suffered the *horrour* of blind and midnight tempests; more rejoicing the heart of a *true man*, than *liberty* and *light* doe him, that is redeemed from a *dungeon*.

Ægrescit ingenium, nisi fugi actione reparetur.

Cito expenduntur horrea, quæ assidua non fuerint adjectione fulcita: Thesaurus ipse facile profunditur, si nullis iterum pecuniis compleatur. Cassiod.

* *Jucundissima est vita indies sentire se fieri doctiorem.*

I should but *profane*, if I should too much unfold the *sacred and sweet mysteries of learning*, to an age that begins to *learn their letters backward*; to *love* onely the *hatred*, and *despising* of learning; that will not be able in the next generation to *read their Neck-verse*, as loth to have the benefit of their Book or Clergy. I know it is lost labour to read Lectures (if they were as splendid for their eloquence, as their subject) upon *Pearls* or *Pretious stones* to *Swine*, who had rather finde out one *corn* on a dunghil, and mousle up one *root* out of the earth, than have the *Gems* of both the *Indies*. These have deserved to be condemned to that illiterate folly, which they have chosen; to the ragges and *sordes*, which they affect to wear; to the blear eyes, which they so abhor to cure, that they rather covet to infect all others.

Illos suis moribus ulciscendos relinquamus.

But to men of more liberall, ingenuous and noble spirits, I know it cannot be unwelcome, to tell them, what *pure and refined contentment*, what *sweetnesse* and *honey* there is to be gathered, from those fair and never fading *flowers of learning*, which God hath made to grow in the field or garden of his Church; what

Vide Synesium de voluptate studiorum & præmio. τίς ἡδονὴ καθαρωτέρα; τίς ἀπα-θεστέρα; ... τῆς μᾶλλον ἀμόλυντος, τῆς ἐν λόγοις καὶ περὶ λόγους διατριβῆς; Synes.

life, what *joyes*, what *raptures*, what noble and holy *emulations* are oft raised up in that soul which dayly and seriously converses with *learned men* either alive or dead? How when all other *narrow Seas*, *Inland Meers*, or Mechanick *Lakes*, (wherein the soules of many men weary themselves with rowing to and fro, tossing up and down; seeking in them riches, strength, beauty, honor, liberty, applause, victory, *enlarged Empire*, &c. all which have their *envious bounds*, and presently discover their *dangerous shores*; (beset with losses, defeats, disgraces, poverty, weaknesse, deformities and a 1000 *deaths*:) Onely this *vast Ocean* of learning and Sea of knowledge is unlimited; always discovering *interminate extensions*, abounding in *varieties* of knowledge; *novelties* of wisdome, infinities of inventions; multitudes of wise sayings and sentences, (morall, politick, and divine;) which like stars are every where scattered & shining in that *Firmament*: Besides many noble *constellations* of excellent examples, provoking patterns, every where set forth, to excite the soul to some impatience of *emulation*: as the history of *Alexander the Great* did *Cæsar*; or the victories of *Miltiades* did *Themistocles*, which would not suffer *him to sleep*; All these, *embellished* with gallant resolutions, generous actions, rare events, sublime contemplations, soveraign comforts, and unflattering counsells; all which, are still *enriching* the unsatisfied soul with *treasures* and pleasures that never satiate, never perish: are ever * out of *envies*, *force*, or *fortunes* reach; as unseparable from us, as we are from our selves; For there are in this *Pacifique Sea* of Learning no *rocks*, but those of *error*; no *shelfes*, but those of *ignorance*; no *quick sands*, but those of our own fancies; no *pirates*, but those aboard us and within us; our own vitious lusts and passions; which onely doe threaten us, and onely can wrack us, or rob and hurt us; yea, and these are onely upon the *shores* and *keyes* of learning, where men first embarque; and where some lazy, or timorous, or proud, and sensuall spirits stay all their lives; but they are not in the *full Sea*, and vast extension of *Learnings boundlesse and bottomlesse Empire*; In which the humble, devout, and industrious soul once fully engaged, is every day more removed, and out of sight of the world: far from those fears, hopes, hazards, disorders, and discontents, which attend those, whose covetousnesse, or ambition, or passion, or lust still keepes them either on the shore of ignorance, or but on the borders of knowledge: who rather court Learning for a *Mistresse*, than wed her for a *Wife*.

From all which dangerous *remora's*, and shallower coasts, those onely are removed, as it were to another world, which is intellectuall, and divine, (having little common with beasts, nothing with

Τῷ ἀλλοτρίῳ θεοφοροῦνται πνεύματι ἐπιπνεόμενοι, ὡς οἱ φοιβαστικοὶ τῷ ἑτέρων μεγέθει συνενθουσιῶσι. *Longin. S. 11. de viris Doctis.*

Sueton. Iul. Cæs. *Conspecta Alexan. imagine ingemuit quasi suam pertæsus ignaviam.*

Solæ sunt sinceræ & tutæ studiorum & bonæ conscientiæ voluptates.

* ἔξω βέλους.

Liberaliora studia incipientibus aspera, progredientibus onerosa, proficientibus jucunda, perficientibus beata. Quintil.

with vain and wicked men) who being well advanced in all *good learning*, both divine and humane, begin at length to finde themselves differ from, and exceed themselves, (and all others who rest in their *illiterate simplicity and sordidnesse*) as much, *as light doth darknesse*; or the *Stars* in the Firmament do the *clods* and *molehils* in their fields: *Holy learning* always carrying that improvement, and contentment, which loves, and admires, and imitates, and so enjoyes all that virtuous prudence, and heavenly wisdom, which it sees to have been in those its *incomparable predecessors*, the *remaines* of whose soules are still extant; which otherwise would have seemed to have been of no nobler metall, than their bodies; and these, but levell to the dust of beasts, unlesse their *learned labours* had testified to the world, how they had lived as much above the *ordinary rate* of men, as these doe above the beasts; which most of men either serve; or, which is worse, *love more*, than their own souls. To these *Patrons* and *professours* of learning *we owe* our ingenuity, our courtesie, our civility: (for *morose* and *rustick learning*, which hath onely *rough-hewen* a *meere Scholar*, or moulded up a rude and rugged *Philosopher*, is as gold yet in the oar, or a jewell neither polished nor well set; having innate *worth*, but not that lustre it merits, and might well bear.) To *them* we owe our gratitude, our humanity, our rationall, and religious liberties, which redeem us from *being beasts, or divels*; Their care and labours have absolved us from the chains and bondage of blindenesse, barbarity, atheism, vulgar admirations, sensualitie, and irreligion; Gods providence having so tempered the various ingredients, and severall *doses*, which make up, from divers excellent hands, this admirable *Confection of good learning*; that it is a *Catholicon*, a soveraign for all distempers of minde, and disorders of the outward man: for misfortunes in estate; errours in understanding; pravities in will; violences of passions; corruptednesse in affections; troubles in conscience; immoralities of life, dejections of spirit; terrors, and encounters of death: And where *learned abilities* are rightly ordered, they apply, and communicate their virtues, with such *soft and oily insinuations*, seasonably and wisely fitted to every genius, capacity and occasion with gentlenesse, humility, charity, and discretion; that they heal any Patient that is willing without *hurting*, and cure without afflicting: Giving no cause of complaint to any, but such as are unwilling to be healed of their **shamefull* and *dangerous diseases*; who love *ignorant* and *flattering Mountebankes*, more than the most learned and *faithfull Physitians* of soules, which are the ablest and best Ministers; who cannot bee lesse necessary for the inward health of the minde, than these are

Eccles. 2. 13.

Βιβλία ἄφθαρτα τῶν νόων ἐντάφια, καὶ ἐπιτάφια αἰώνια. Stobæ.

Æterna sunt animorum monumenta Libri.

Enormis studiorum intentio solet plerumq; nec præ pedibus prospicere. Tertul. de An.

φυλακτικὸν σώματος ὑγεία, τῆς δὲ ψυχῆς παιδεία. Arist. Rhet. ad Alex. cap. 2.

** In morbis animi, velle mederi, & medicinæ & valetudinis pars est non minima.* Paris.

* τῆς ἀγνοίας ἐπίστασις τὸ πρῶτόν ἐστι μάθημα τῷ κατὰ λόγον βαδίζοντι. Cl. Al. Στρω. 5.

for the body, who are one ſort of thoſe, whom learning hath fitted for the common good. For I doe not think *Learning* and true ſtudy to be onely a *couch* to reſt a ſoft and wearied minde upon; or a *taraſſe* to pleaſe a wandering ſpirit, with ſome variable and pretty proſpects; or as a *Tower* for a proud ſoul to raiſe and magnifie it ſelf upon, as *Nebuchadnezzar* on his *Babel*; or as a *Fort* for a *contentious Sophiſter* to keep, in a diſputative war, and Logicall defiance againſt all the world; Nor is it as a *ſhop* for a covetous man to drive his trade, and get gain by the *brokage* of ſome ancient pieces: But it is as a *grand Magazine*, and Catholick *Storehouſe* of all divine and intellectuall excellencies, affording to all men, upon all occaſions, happy advantages, by which to glorifie the wiſe and *admirable Creator*, and alſo to furniſh both a mans ſelf & others with what may moſt conduce to his temporall and eternall felicity: Good learning is neither a *wanton Courtiſan*, onely for dalliance and pleaſure; nor yet a ſlave and drudge, entertained meerly for a ſordid and illiberall profit; but as a chaſt and *nobly ſpirited Wife*, for ſweet ſociety and legitimate productions, worthy of ſuch parents, a reaſonable Soul and good Literature, happily eſpouſed and marryed together. We oft ſee, that moderate mindes, with but a ſmall ſtock of learning well managed, attain to be maſters of great affaires, and become as uſefull, ſo very deſirable in humane ſocieties in practicall wayes: others of more ſpeculative retired and ſublime learning are not leſſe in * *magnitude*, but farther remote from ſublunary things, having that in their height, and neighbourhood to heaven, which they ſeem to want in their light and eradiations downward; In both, beſides the private contents they enjoy in the contemplations of reaſons, and Religions beauty (both which fair faces are beſt repreſented in the glaſſe of learning) they have a *kinde of Empire* and *Soveraignty* over all things, and all men, in all times, who appear at the tribunall of their judgements, fall under their cognizance, and ſtand to that cenſure they paſſe upon them, both in preſent and after ages, either for vice or vertue, honour or baſeneſſe, gallantry or villany; How ever Arms and Military power have carryed the * Kingdom and ſwayed the Scepter, which rules mens bodies; yet learning hath ever carried the Prieſtly ſervice, and in that a kinde of *ſoveraignty* over mens ſoules and conſciences; None being ever thought ſo fit by the light of nature, and all * Nations to teach the ſervice or diſpenſe the *Myſteries* of the moſt wiſe God, but thoſe that were eſteemed the *wiſeſt men*; leſt the folly and meanneſſe of the Prieſt or Miniſter ſhould prove the reproach of that Divinity which he ſerves.

* *In animis ſpeculativis obſcuritatem ſublimitas compenſat.* L. Ver.

* *Bonarum literarum potentes verè ſunt* αὐτοκράτορες, *nec in ſe ipſos tantum, ſed & in univerſum naturæ regnum jus quoddam ac dominium exercent, rerum hominumque omniumImperatores auguſtiſſimi,* Pro. 18. 1.

Rex ſacrorum Pontifex *apud* Rom. *dicebatur.*

* *Celebrandis Deorum myſteriis & optimi & ſapientiſſimi ſunt adhibendi viri, ne ſacrorum ſint opprobria ipſi ſacerdotes.* Tull.

I might adde, if any *colours* could expreſſe, or adde to this *intellectuall*

intellectuall beauty, (Learning;) what had we not lost of Reason and Religion; or what had we enjoyed (as men) of our *forefathers*, more than beasts doe of their *sires* and *dams*; if those had not left us the benefit of their piety and experience; the inheritance of their *wise observations*; the *issues* of their braines and pens? which farre exceed those of their *goods, lands*, and bodies; Since the *immortall remaines* of their mindes in piety, wisedome, honour, and vertue, teach us to *enjoy*, what otherwayes we, onely, should *have had* or *used*: and to *live*, where, else, wee should have *onely had a beeing*, and bare existence in the world, not many degrees above the *beasts*, who have all that is needfull for the body; but neither consider what they have, nor from whose bounty, nor to what end, nor within what bounds of *vertue*, all things are to be used.

Aliud est uti, aliud frui quæ habeas bona: cujuslibet illud est; hoc prudentis tantum. Amb.

Multum distat interesse, & vivere; valere, & sapere; pascere, & discere; Priora cum brutis communia; viris bonis propria sunt hæc posteriora. Sen.

These *excellencies* peculiar to *mankind*, above all creatures, we owe (beyond all dispute) to *those records of learning*, and piety left us, in all kindes, by our *famous predecessours*; and to the studious industry of those *sublimer spirits*, who have been impatient to suffer those inestimable *reliques* of our foresathers *Souls* to be devoured by *time and moths*, to be buried in dust and forgetfulnesse; who never thought it enough, for a *rationall and immortall soul* to fill its belly, to clothe its back, to satisfie its lusts, * to idolize an horse, to *dote* upon a *Dog*, or to court a *wanton Mistresse*? But disdaining all these low, sensuall, and momentary enjoyments, or debasements rather, (when excessive, chief or sole) of *their soules*; dayly are raised up by *generous, virtuous* and *religious excitations*, to advance their own and other mens both *mindes* and *manners*; And this, not onely during this transient, short and uncertain life among mortals; but further by erecting *living monuments* in *learned bookes*, they fortifie against *oblivion*; arm themselves against *mortality*; and counterruine the underminings of time; which is the *grave of all* * *Pyramides, Mausoles*, and those other like *monstrous structures* of grosser spirited men.

Δι' ὑπομνημάτων λιλῶν τοῖς ὕστερον ἀνθρώποις ὁ καλῶς συγγέγραφεν. *Cl. Al.*

* *Vita enervis & luxata nimis otio; quo non recreatur, sed evanescit virtus.* Val. Max.

Illud quam degener, & generoso viro indignum? Homo cum sis, brutis animalculis inservire, bruta colere, bruta deperire, brutum effictis omnibus & amore prosequi? mentem interea negligere, animam sempiternam & longè pretiosissimam prodigere, & inhumaniter perdere? Bern. *Ego me ex eorum esse numero profiteor, qui proficiendo scribunt, & scribendo proficiunt,* Aust. Ep. 7. *Qui voluptatibus dediti quasi in diem vivunt, vivendi causas quotidie finiunt; illis mors nunquam non acerba & immatura; Qui verò posteros cogitant, & immortale aliquid proferunt, memoriam sui scriptis extendentes: illis nulla mors repentina, nisi præclarum aliquod opus inchoatum abrumpat.* Plin. l. 5. Ep. 5.

Maxima pars ejus in memoriam & posteritatem prominet. Liv. l. 28. *Non potest quicquam humile & abjectum cogitare, qui scit de se semper loquendum.* Mamer. Paneg.

τὸ γράφειν, τίκτειν ἐστὶν ἐν δέλτοις ἀθάνατα, ἑαυτὸν τῷ χρόνῳ παρατιθεῖν. *Synes. de Insom.*

* *Insana substructiones.*

So that when the ages of learned men are undistinguishable in the *grave* from vulgar and plebeian dust, yet they still instruct, and doe good to mankinde, and glorifie the Creator by their soules and spirits, which are partly in heaven, and partly in their bookes; which have so much of *heaven* too, as they have more of sublimity, splendor, permanency and influence on the infe-riour world, than any other things, whereon men usually leave the impressions of their fading skill and momentary power.

Præclari scriptores non modo proximum tempus lucémque præsentem intueri satis credunt, sed omnem posteritatis memoriam spacium vitæ honestæ, & curriculum laudis existimant. Quintil.
Τὰ γραπτὰ αἰώνια. *Plato.*

So that these grosser *clods of earth, and lumps of mortality,* the *despisers of Learning,* are sure to dye and perish, as much as they merit, and desire; who neither use, nor leave, nor deserve any token or memoriall of *literate* industry; by which it may appeare, that either they or others ever lived, more than their *Oxe* and their *Asses* doe: who by how much lesse they are intellectuall, and not *improvers of their mindes;* by so much more they *degenerate* to *brutish sensualities,* and become wholly devoted to the beast of the man, the Body; which hath nothing on it remarkable, but this; that it is *married* to a rationall and immortall Soul; not to debase and oppresse it, but to serve it: Of those (*Borborite and Polysarkists*) *groveling, and indocible sensualists,* there can be no better account given at their death, then *may be of an hog;* That being most indocible, he wallowed at his ease, fed well, dyed very fat, and very unwillingly; worthy of the Epitaph on the Epicures Tomb,* That onely I injoyed which I did eat.

Βοὸς ἀγροίας βαθύς ἐστιν ὕπνος. Cl. Al. str. l. 2.
πηλὸς αἵματι μεμιγμένος. Sen. de Nerone.
Βιβλίον λήθης φάρμακον. Cl. Al.
In illiteratis & indoctis maximam partem hominis brutum occupat. Sen.
A pecudibus non sententia sed lingua discernit. Lact. de Epicu.
οὐ τὸ ζῆν περὶ πλείστου ποιητέον, ἀλλὰ τὸ εὖ ζῆν. *Plat. Crito.* *Tanquam pœniteret non pecudes natos.* Sen.
*Habui quod edi.

17. **Illiteratenesse no reproach or discouragement to humble Christians.**

Not that here I doe any way despise, or degrade those sober *good Christians* of either sex, whose education, parts, and way of life hath, and doth deny them the advantages of personall learning; such as is immediately acquired by the study of *excellent bookes:* For, first; true wisdome is the same *in all languages,* and may be obtained in conversation in part, as well as by reading; Next, they have by Gods providence, and indulgence to them, the blessing of many *learned mens directions,* (both Ministers and others) and the benefit of their *good example;* whom they have the more cause to love and value, by how much they see their own *defects;* which while they humbly and diligently supply by the *helps* which learned men afford them, they testifie, not onely to

Others, the *gratefull* ſenſe, and high eſteem they have of the labours of learned men, imparted to them; but alſo hereby they doe, as it were, *admit themſelves* into the *company* of learned men, and are *adopted* into the family, and fraternity of Learning; mutuall love, and charity ingrafting theſe *lovers* of learned men, into the ſame ſtock, of whoſe ſap, and virtue they are daily partakers; being diligent attenders upon thoſe whom God hath ſet over them, for this purpoſe; that they may be happily taught by them, as *children by their Fathers*: while the *ignorant pride* of others keeping them at a *ſurly*, and to themſelves moſt injurious, diſtance, they not onely injoy nothing of *learning in themſelves*, but by the neglect and diſeſteem of it in their *Miniſters*, are for ever condemned to their *ſilly beggery* and *ſupercilious folly*.

Μέτοχος ἀρετῆς ἐστιν ὁ τιμάζων αὐτήν. *Plato. de rep. dial.* 10.

The *wiſdome of God*, as in civill, ſo in Church *ſocieties* hath ſo tempered the different parts, as in the *naturall body*: where all members are uſefull in their kinde, but not all of *equall honour*, for the excellencie of their faculties and functions; yet the *diamonds of the eyes* cannot well want the *clay and pebles of the toes*: Nor are the nobler Organs of the *Senſes* ſo excellent or commendable in any thing, as in this, that they are uſefull and ſervient not to themſelves ſo much, as to thoſe leſſe beautifull, but not leſſe *neceſſary* parts of the body, for whoſe direction and good, Nature intended them: Neither *charitable learning*, nor *humble ignorance* will make any ſcornfull, or *envious ſchiſm* in a well formed body: whoſe beauty is the *variety* and *Symmetry* of parts. It were an *unnaturall barbarity* for the *eyes* to deny their light and guidance to the body, or for the lightleſſe parts to deſpiſe, envy, and ſeek to deſtroy thoſe *two great lights*, which the wiſe Creator hath ſet up in the *little world* of mans body. Such is the diſtemper and madneſſe of thoſe, who ſeek to *hoodwink with poverty*; to blind with contempt; to put out with *violence* the great *Luminaries*, both of Church and State, *Learned men* and *Miniſters*, who are the ordinary means by which true (both humane and divine, morall and myſterious) *knowledge* is imparted to the *common people*; without which neither hearts nor lives of men cannot be good; *Blinde affections* are no more acceptable to God, than *blind ſacrifices*, which were onely fit for *fooles*; However God workes grace by a more immediate, *divine influence* of his Spirit; yet it is by ſuch meanes rationally preparing, and diſpoſing, as he hath appointed in the Church; without the diligent and conſcientious uſe of which, it is as in vain to *boaſt of grace*, and the Spirit, as it is to expect the *heat* of the *Sun*, without its light; or to hope for *harveſt* without preceding ſummer.

1 Cor. 12.

Mal. 1. 16.

The

A plea for the nurseries of learning: the two famous Universities.

The *ignorant weaknesse* and *fiercer rudenesse* of those men, with whom I have chiefly in this *Apology*, and in this part of it to contend, may justifie this my so *large vindication* of learning; as necessary in other persons of publique influence, so *chiefly* in Ministers, whose *errors* or *rectitudes* are of the *highest concernment*, as conversant in *matters of God*, of *Soules*, and of *Eternity*. I should otherwise, be very jealous, that I had said too much in so clear a subject; (which needs as little, and deserves as much commendation, as the Sun in the Firmament) when I remember to how many men of *learned abilities* I make my addresse; of whose personall sufficiencies in this *kind of excellency*, as I have no cause to doubt, for I see some of them have undertaken the *publique honour* and protection of these (*Kiriath-sephers*) the sometime *famous and flourishing Universities of this English Nation*; The two *fair eyes* of this Church and State; and the *two greatest eye-sores* of these Antiministerial Levellers; which above all things as Ravens they aim to pluck out, or so to blind, that they shall not be of any use, either to Learning, or to the reformed Religion.

Josh. 15. 16. *Kiriath-sepher: Civitas librorum & literarum.*

But I presume, that *persons* of any true *worth*, Learning, Honour, Valour, or Religion, will never suffer these *goodly Garrisons*, citadels and magazines of all *good literature* to be plundered, slighted, or disbanded, either by military, or mechanick rudenesse: For besides the shame and infinite dishonour, which it would be before all *civilized Nations* under heaven, to doe, or suffer so great *insolence* and injury to be done, against them, and in them against the *publique good* and honour both of Church and State: It cannot but also be a *most crying sin before God*; if either we consider, that *sacrilegious barbarity*, which must in this be committed against (not the living onely in their rights, but even *against*) *the Dead*; the Monuments of *whose devout piety* and charity are there deposited; and by many learned men enjoyed, as in *unviolable Sanctuaries*; Or, if we duly weigh, in order to Gods glory, the many *great and publique blessings*, which by the bounty and providence of God have, from the benign light and influence of those *two great Constellations*, constantly and liberally flowed upon this Nation, to its unspeakable honour and advantages, both in Church and State: Which are so eminent, and so necessary, both to the well being of souls and bodies of men, in all degrees and estates; that no tongue, or pen can with gratitude enough to God acknowledge them: For take it from the highest, who sit upon *Thrones*, *judging the Tribes*, to the lowest, who *grind at the mill*: Neither Counsellours, nor Judges, nor Justices, nor *Commanders*, nor Lawyers, nor Physitians, nor Embassadors, nor publique Agents, nor any ingenuous imployment; nor the

Specimen est florentis reipub. ut disciplinæ professoribus præmia opulenta pendantur. Sym. 1. 73. *Literatura instrumentum est ad omnem humanam vitam necessarium.* Tertul. de Idol.

the meaneſt honeſt *mechanicks*, can diſpenſe with the want of thoſe *bleſſings*, of truth, order, peace, health, good laws and Religion, which from thoſe Seminaries of *good learning* are derived to, and enjoyed by all ſorts of men in this Nation.

Scipio liberalium ſtudiorum autor & admirator, & belli & pacis artibus ſerviit. Semper inter arma, aut ſtudia verſatus; & corpus periculis & animum diſciplinis exercuit, Vel. Pater. l. 1. *Non poteſt aliqua in mundo eſſe fortuna quam non augeat literarum glorioſa notitia,* Caſſiod. 10. 3.

It concerns no men to have *good learning* decryed, and the *Univerſities demoliſhed*, but only *juglers*, cheaters, and impoſtors, whoſe gaines are like to be *greateſt*, when their deceits are leaſt diſcernible for want of true light; * So *prodigious tongues* and pens were thoſe heretofore, and now, which by an unnaturall envy, brutiſh ignorance, barbarous malice, or ſordid covetouſneſſe, ſeek to deprive the *children of this Nation*, of ſuch full and fair breaſts, as theſe *Nurſes* afford; as if we were all deſigned to turn *Amazons*, and that fitting our ſelves for Arms onely, and not Arts, we muſt cut off, not onely one, but both our breaſts: Or as if the after generations were to ſuck not milk, but onely bloud; like the child which *Ariſtides* painted ſo lively, which ſearching for the breaſt, applyed it ſelf to the wound of its dying mother; which ſhee now dying ſeems to remove from the wound to the Breaſt.

Veritas luce & mora; falſa feſtinatione & tenebris valeſcunt, Tacit. An. 2.

* *Greenewood* and *Barrow* petitioned Q. *Elizabeth* (at B. M.) to diſſolve the Univerſities that their faſtidious ignorance might bee gratified with ſo great a diſhonour to this Nation, *Camden.*

* *Plin. Nat. hiſt.* l. 35. 10.

But, O you *nobler*, and better *educated Souls*, who therefore love *good learning*, becauſe you either have it, or enjoy the *bleſſings* of it, your *own*, and the publique honour are ſo intereſſed in this point, that no *ſober man* can ſuſpect, that any of you are of your ſelves ſo inclined, or can be brought by others *Turkiſh importunities* and *Barbarities*, to the leaſt thought of neglecting the preſervation of theſe two *incomparable Seminaries* of all good Learning, which have in former ages furniſhed both Church and State with ſo many excellent, both Magiſtrates, and Miniſters; which places for liberall *alimony*, for ſweet, and quiet *accommodations*, for copious, and rare *Libraries*, for ſtately *buildings*; and (which is the ſoule of Univerſities) for men of *eminent learning*, and piety, were not to be exceeded, *ſcarce paralleld* in all the world. To whoſe compleat felicity nothing can be wanting that either *friends* would moſt deſire, or *enemies* moſt *malign*, if ſuch *order*, *government*, and *good diſcipline* in point of moralls, and practiques be added, as beſt becomes learned and ingenuous men: whoſe greateſt honour is, to have *learning*, like gold, enamel'd with all the *beauties* of virtue, and embelliſhed with all the *ornaments* of true Religion;

Plato in Men. Παῖδας ἀνδρῶν ἀγαθῶν ἐγὼ μὲν νῦν τε παρακαλέσομαι καὶ ἐν λοιπῷ χρόνῳ ἀναμνήσω ὑμᾶς προθυμεῖσθαι εἶναι φρονιμωτάτους, καὶ ἀρίστους. I ſhall alwayes exhort the ſons of worthy men to be both very learned and very good.

* *Bonarum artium profeſſionem malis moribus corrumpunt Græci.* Curt. l. 8.

Sancta & fœcunda otio, Ber. ad Eug. *Nemo pictorum tam a ratione alienus fuit, ut armatas Musas unquam exhibere ausus fuerit. Certissimo argumento, vitam quæ Musis tribuitur placidam, facilem, tranquillamq; esse oportere.* Ælian. hist. var.

That the *sacred solitudes*, the *sweet vacancies*, the *happy leisures*, the *pleasant retirements*, the plenteous enjoyments, which by the *indulgence* of God, and the *munificence* of worthy men and women, they enjoy as Students, beyond the *most of mortals*; (whom either hard labour exhausts, or solicitous care distracts, or penurious servitude oppresseth) may not be abused, to the softer dalliances and idle entertainments of vicious *intemperancies* and disorders; when *those places* were intended by the *pious founders*, as *hives for Bees*, not as * *nests* for wasps and drones; receptacles and incouragements for virtuous industry, religious modesty, prudent integrity, and not for *Cretian Lazy-bellies*, cunning sophisters, and pragmatick wits, (which serve only to set a fairer glosse, and sharper edge on the basest errours, and the most debauched manners;) which ought, as ever in *conscience*, to be avoided, so then also in *policy*; when there are, as *many enemies* against the *Universities*, as there are evill eyes upon the *revenews*. Any plea will serve the design of *covetous and unlearned malice*, which seeks by pretending the dissolution of manners, laxation of government, and the shipracks of many ingenuous young men, sent to the *Universities*, to *justifie* those dayly and desperate calumnies used against them: That they are not onely *superfluous*, but also *noxious*; as uselesse, so hurtfull to the *Church and State*: Both which, some men will never thinke sufficiently blest, till they have made them, as *blinde as Beetles*, both in good learning, and true reformed Religion; that so the *English Nobility*, *Gentry*, and *ingenuous youth*, may either run out to utter *barbarity* in a short time, or else fall under the *culture* of those, who affect to be the *grand Masters*, and Catholick *Teachers* of all good learning, the *Jesuites*. The gravity of whose manners, and exactnesse, both of their *Literature*, and *Discipline* (wherewith they adorn that side, and party, which they are *listed* to maintain) is not to be so much imitated, as exceeded by our *Universities*; which are of the reformed party the most *Illustrious*; That so they may redeem themselves from those *jealousies* and reproaches, which either just severity or injurious calumnie, is prone to fasten upon them; and so merit both love, honour, and protection from all, that have any *true excellency* in this Nation.

* Δύο μὲν ἡμῖν ἐγνωρίζοντο ὁδοὶ, πρὸς ἱεροὺς οἴκους μόνον. *Naz. de Bas. m. & se ipso Athenis commorantibus; omnium semitarum præter quæ ad templa et scholas ducebant, nescii.* Orat. 20.

19\. *All worthy mindes subscribe to this plea and petition for the Universities.*

To this humble request, not onely *Divines*, and *Ministers* of *religious Mysteries*, which tend highly to the temporall and eternall welfare of mens soules; but all other *liberall faculties* (which exercise the man more than the beast; the head and minde, more than the hands and body,) will (I presume) most *readily subscribe*; Since, neither the learned Students, and honest practisers of the *Common Law*, (by which the boundaries of our estates, liberties, honours,

honours and lives are set and preserved *under God*) Nor those of the *Civill Law*; (in which are the *suffrages of all Nations*; the common sense, the generall Rules and rationall Maximes of mankinde; whereby all forain *treaties*, correspondencies, trafiques, and negotiations in war and peace, with enemies and friends, are *regulated* and *transacted*) Nor yet the *conscientious Physitians*, who study to preserve the *health*, strength, beauty and life of our bodies: None of these, any more, than the *Ministers* of the *Gospell*, can move or practise rationally, wisely, and conscientiously, in their *severall callings*, without those principles and foundations of humane learning, which are either generally preparatory, or peculiarly necessary to their *respective faculties*; upon whose stock, first planted, and watered in the *Universities*, those *scions* are commonly graffed, which either come to any flourishing, or good fruit in Church or State.

And certainly, if we generally dislike, and despise *pettifoggers* in the Common Law; meer *pragmatiques* in the Civil; and *quack-salvers* in Physick; there is no *reason* any sober Christians should desire or like *Theologasters*, meer praters and dunces in the *great science of Divinity*: *Ministers of the Gospell* should of all men be least *deprived* of, or defective in *good learning*, in as much as their work is of the *highest concernment*; nor is it without those *difficulties*, which may whet and exercise the most improved abilities, the most cautious studies, and the most conscientious diligence; All which are necessary ingredients to make up an able, and *worthy Minister*: What wise and sober Christian can think it fit to commit the *care of his soules welfare*, the *publique service* of his God, the *honour* of his Saviour, the *celebration* of holy mysteries, the *means* of grace, the comfort of his *conscience*, and the *conservation* of true Religion, together with the peace, order, and honour of the *Church* of Christ, while he lives, and when he dies; to commit (I say) all these to the custody, care, inspection, and managing of such men, whom he could not with reason, or without great shame in himself, and some from others, entrust with any publique commerce, trade, and negotiation; or with his private welfare in health, honour, estate, liberty, or life?

Ventosa loquacitas ut malignus imber sterilitatem magis quam fertilitatem terris infert. Bern.

Since all *divine and humane perfections* are in our *Lord Jesus Christ*; and from him every *good and perfect gift* is derived to the Church; nothing is more just and gratefull, than for Christians to use, improve, and return all those gifts, and indowments which our humane nature is capable of in this world, to the *glory of God*, and the *good of mankinde*; which, when they are *sanctified* both in the habit and use, are but *preventive* of, and *preparatory* to, those *eternall accomplishments*, which our soules expect in heaven;

which is that highest degree of happinesse which holy and humble learning studies to attain.

Nor can any wise man conceive, how either the *highest science*, which we call *Divinity*, or those other excellent ones, in *Humanity*, can ever be levelled to *vulgar* practises, and a *parity* of use among men; (which will prove an *Epidemicall disease*, like the scabs and botches of *Egypt*, when the *ashes* were scattered over the land) unlesse withall there could be a *levelling of mens reasons*, wits, capacities, and industries, as well as of their callings; or some law of *Ostracisme* made, by which it shall be forbidden for any man, to be *richer* and *healthfuller*, wiser, and learneder, more *holy*, or more *religious* than another.

Exod. 9. 10.

But these are *Cacotopian fancies*, which not the *profoundnesse of Plato*, but the *shallownesse* of *Thersites*, or *Dametas*, hath laid out to so vile, *wicked*, monstrous, and *ridiculous* formes; that no *good Christian*, who resolves not to banish all reason, and true Religion from himself and his posterity, can ever approve or follow, so, as to *wish to be of*, or ever to see such a *Commonwealth* of *Coxcombes* and Ideots, who by the want of all good learning both in *Magistrates*, and Ministers will soon learn, like *wild Arabs*, and *Scythians*, to rob, plunder, poyson, kill, deceive, and *damn* one another, growing as Mastive dogs, fiercer by dark keeping: Being *justly punished* by being given up to their *own hearts lusts*, to commit *all wickednesse with greedinesse*, for not *glorifying God* in the high esteem, and holy use of those *excellent* gifts, which by *good learning*, he confers upon humane Nature and societies; of all which in reference to the good both of *Church and State*, a gracious heart is never to seek, how to make a *gracious*, and thankful use either in himself or others.

Rom. 1. 24.

The 5. Cavil. Against Ministers incroachment upon the liberty of mens judgments and consciences.

BUt there are some, who ashamed to be reckoned among the *illiterate* crue (who despise and decry all good learning) and desirous to seeme *more moderate* and well *tempered* men, plead; That however *Learning* well used, may be very beneficiall both to Church and State, both in civill and religious regards; yet with God there is no * *acceptation of persons*: and in Christ Jesus *Greek and Barbarian*, the *learned* and the *Ideots* are all one; That God may dispense the beams of his Spirit in the light of Truth as well as in the heat of Love, how, and where, and to whom he will, yea, and oft *doth reveale his secret and hidden things*, not to the wise and *learned*, but to the babes and foolish: Therefore a *publique liberty*.

* Col. 3. 11.
Mat. 11. 25.

liberty at least, and fair *toleration* ought to be granted to any men, to opine, to teach, and accordingly to act, as they are inwardly perswaded and moved: And this without any such *tyrannous restraints*, as commonly *learned* men and Scholars, Ministers especially, have sought themselves and taught *Magistrates*, to lay upon both the judgement, conscience and practise of people, both in their first education, and after profession; studying to make all things in Religion, or manners, as *bastards*, and illegitimate, which have not their Certificate for their *ligitimation*; whereas the Spirit of God ought not to be so *strict laced*, stinted, and restrained; least of all *curbed*, and constrained, by any *prohibitions*, or impositions on mens judgements and consciences, which in matters of Religion are onely to be drawn with the *cords of a man*, such as mens reasons, or Scriptures, or the Spirits perswasion, may afford to every ones *capacity*, and not to tye them up by any *Creeds, Articles, Catechismes*, or *Injunctions* of Religion, much lesse by *penall* and *coercive Statutes*, which (like *Persian* sheep) carry tailes of injurious mulcts and penalties after them, that are heavier, then their bodies.

Answ. There is no *Jewell* which Swine delight more to *weare in their Snouts*, than this of *Liberty*; which how well it becomes such sordid and indocible cattel, those *excellent Christians* can best judge, who are worthy to enjoy so pretious a *token of Christs love* to his Church; as knowing best how to value it, and use it: I know well, that *true Christian Religion* ought not *to be made a snare*, or an *harrow*, or a *rack*, or an heavy yoak, or an *Egyptian bondage* to mens mindes and Consciences; this were to turn the *sweetest vine* into a *sharp bramble*, and the *figtree* into a *thorn*: Nor is there any thing which Christians should be more tender of (as the * *Ephesine* Fathers most piously admonish) than their own, and others *true liberties*, which Christ hath purchased with his *pretious bloud*; of which both Christian Magistrates, and chiefly Ministers, should be most exact keepers, and conscientious defenders; lest *piety* prove an *oppression*; and the *bracelets* or *ornaments* of Religion, become the *chains* of hypocrisie and *manacles* of *superstition*; binding such *heavy burthens* on mens consciences, which God hath not imposed

Answ. Of Christian Liberty.

Nil tam voluntarium quam religio; cogi non potest; longè diversa sunt carnificina est charitas, nec potest veritas cum vi; aut justitia cum crudelitate conjungi.

Defendenda est religio non occidendo, sed monendo; non sævitia, sed sapientia; non scelere, sed fide. Si animus aversus sit, jam sublata est, jam nulla religio, Lactant. li. Just. 5. c. 20.

Religionis non est cogere religionem, quæ sponte suscipi debet, non vi. Tertul. l. ad Scap.

So *Constantine the Great* would have no man compeld but perswaded to Religion. *Aliud est certamen pro religione sponte suscipere, aliud supplicii metu cogi,* Euseb. Eccl. l. 10. cap. 5.

* 1. *Concil. Eph. cap.* 8. ἵνα μὴ ἐν λειτουργίας προσχήματι ἐξουσίας κοσμικῆς τῦφος παρεισδύηται, μηδὲ λάθωμεν τὴν ἐλευθερίαν, κατὰ μικρὸν ἀπολέσαντες ἣν ἡμῖν ἐδωρήσατο τῷ ἰδίῳ αἵματι ὁ κύριος ἡμῶν Ἰησοῦς Χριστὸς ὁ πάντων ἐλευθερωτής.

wherein the *severer heights* and tyrannies of men are prone to usurp upon the ingenuous kingdome and gracious *dominion* of Christ, where none is a *subject*, but he that enjoyes that *free Spirit*, which *David* prayes to be established with; and none *is free* but he that willingly takes up *Christs yoak* and *burthen*, which are *light* and *easie*; but yet not loose or slack. For Jesus Christ having redeemed us from the greatest slavery, and spirituall bondage, hath indeed invested his Church with the *noblest immunities*, and governs it by the *divinest liberties*; which drawing is by the cords of *Gods love* to us, set forth in his Word; and binding us *with love* to God, and for his sake to one another, by so much includes all *true liberty*, as it wholly consists of love; whose very *life* and *essence* is *liberty*; It being impossible to command, consent, or to *compell love*; which is (αὐτοκρατῶς) the most *absolute Soveraigne* of it selfe, and under no Empire but that of God, who is *love*, and perfect *liberty*: And our *Liberty* is then truly Christian and divine (which onely is desirable, because onely true) when it is such, as Christ hath purchased for, and God hath revealed to his Church in his Word; with which men must seriously advise; and not with their own wanton and extravagant fancies; if they would bee informed what that *liberty* is, which onely becomes true Christians, who of all men have the least sinfull *licentiousnesse* indulged to them.

I finde there are no people more vehement *boasters* of, and sticklers for this, which they call *Christian liberty*, than those, who least understand it; most abuse it themselves, and are most impatient to allow it to others; if once they get such power as makes them able to oppresse, none are more *insolent*, or lesse tolerating those things, even in Religion, to others, for which they plead more of conscience, both as to Gods and mans Laws, than these objectors themselves can doe. Nor can any, the most modest plea, for *Christian liberty* be heard by those who were formerly so lowdly clamorous for the name, when indeed they did not either intend, or rightly understand what the thing is. It will be then a *work of Charity*; and an effect of that love, which I owe to these men for Christs sake, (in whom alone our liberties are founded, and conserved) to free them from that *captivity* of errors, and *bondage* of extravagant passions, wherewith they are oppressed and abused even in this great point of *Christian Liberty*; Then which as there is nothing, which sinfull men could lesse deserve, so nor is there any thing they can naturally lesse

Psal. 51. 12.

Matth. 11. 30.

Libera est apud Deum servitus, cum non necessitas sed charitas servit. Aust.

Quo sanctior quisq; eo solutior. Gibe.

Beata servitus quæ dominationem generat sempiternam. Chrys. l. 114.

Tertullian tels of the *Gnosticks* promiscuous lusts in their *Agapæ*: *Extincta lucerna in promiscuos amplexus ruunt. Hinc in Christianos ista infamia.* Scorpia: so Clem. Alex. *spω.* 3. So S. *Austin* of the *Gnosticks*, *Manichees* and others who held *nisi iniquissima quæq; operentur, Diaboli vim se non posse effugere: Hanc esse redemptionem, hanc vitam sine tremore.* So *Irenæus*, of the *Carpocratians* and others, that held nothing morally good or evill; all actions lawfull; onely they must beleive in Christ. *Sola humana opinione negotia mala & bona esse dicunt.* Lib. 1. c. 24.

rightly

rightly use, or more grossely mistake, and abuse. There is no Jewell, with which Christ hath endowed his Spouse the Church, and every true beleever, for which the Divel hath not some *counterfeit*; nor is there any, by which he *cheats* men more easily, and more to his advantage and the Churches detriment, than in the false figures and resemblances of *Christian liberty*. * For as no man naturally is willing to be curbed or restrained from any impulses of his lusts; so neither can hee easily learn that Paradox of true *Christian liberty*; which consists in the *severest restraints* from sin; and the exactest *conformities* to the will of God.

* *Liber est quisquis probus. Servire deo est bonis operibus & justitiam & libertatem conservare,* Lact.

You then, O *excellent Christians*, well understand with me; That as no *creatures*, Angels, or men, have that (αὐτουσία) self-subsistence; nor that (αὐτάρκεια) self-sufficiency, in and of themselves, which is peculiar to *God*; so neither have that (ἀνυπευθυνία) *unresponsiblenesse* to any other; nor that (ἀνυπεξούσιον) independence or absolute liberty in their will, which ownes no rule or measure of its motions, but its (εὐδοκία) own good-pleasure. For as Angels and men depend wholly upon God for our nature and being: so we must needs be subordinate to him, as our Authour, and responsible to him, as one *wiser*, *better*, *juster*, and stronger than our selves: Also *our will* * (wherein our rationall, and religious liberties are planted, and whence they spread or diffuse to all the motions and faculties under its Empire and command) hath its holy *limits* and bounds set to it by God, both as to the *Supream* end and highest good, which the wise God hath *proposed* in himself; and also as to those means, by which he hath revealed that end to us as attainable, either in piety, or charity; in private, or publique relations.

Compare with Hobbes

* εὐγενέστατος δεσμὸς εὐσέβεια. Nissen. *Religio est generosissimum animæ vinculum; quo ad Deum arctissime ligatur.* Aust.

This constant *tendency*, or intention to the Supream end, and those holy *regulations* (which in due and lawfull means, the wisdom of God hath prescribed) the more any creature, *Man* or *Angell* attaines, the more rationall, morall and *divine liberty* he enjoyes; and he is so much the more *freed* from those *shackles*, and impediments, which the chaines of darknesse and corruption, through ignorance of minde, and errour of understanding, or perversenesse of will, or excesse of passion, or violence of temptations, or depravednesse of customes, or delusion of examples, hamper and binde the soul withall, as the *wings of a bird* with birdlime; hindering its regard to the *Supream God*, which is the *glory of God*; and its exact applying to those means, which are proper for the attaining and enjoying of it. In the *fruition* of which the *true and eternall liberty* of the soul consists, (as the eyes in seeing most fully, and perfectly, its most desired object) and which it then en-

Βούλησίς ἐστιν ὄρεξις μετὰ λόγου. ὄρεξις εὔλογος. *Plat.* The will is a rationall desire or appetite of good.

joyes

joyes, when by the wisdome of the Word, and power of of Christ, being every way freed from sordid, sensuall, and sinfull intanglements, we onely *will* that which we know God would have us; and doe most willingly, what ever we so will, and know, as most conformable to his will.

Servire deo, est servitus, propter præcepti obedientiam; & libertas, propter recti licentiam. Aust. Ench. ad Lauren.

The will of God in his Word, the onely rule and measure of mans liberty.

Whose wise, blessed and unerring will, *revealed in his holy Word*, being rightly understood, is (now) the onely certaine and infallible rule; the sole *authentick Patent*, which any good Christian *will* regard, and follow, or alledge and plead in this point of *Christian Liberty*; either internall, or externall; private, or publique; solitary, or sociall; in thoughts, opinions, judgement, conscience, speech, action, or operation in any kind. Which the further it is from any error, transport, or licentiousnesse in a mans self, and from *any cloak of maliciousnesse* against others, the more it deserves to be counted and called *Christian freedom*.

1 Pet. 2. 16.

As a man freed from the distemper of *madnesse*, and rid of his *chains*, and got out of *Bedlam*, hath indeed, now, his *true liberty*, as a man; not to rave and speak, or doe such mad things, as he formerly did in his distraction; but to doe all things, as a *sober* man, who is master of his *wits* and understanding; and consequently under the most strict, yet *ingenuous restraints* of reason and religion; the *lawes* of modesty, humanity, honour, civility, charity, and society; from all which the *captivity* of his lunacy and madness unhappily freed him: But now the recovery of his right senses happily restores him to those duties and observances which become a man and a Christian: It is mercy, which redeems us from our native bondage to sin and wrath; and which sets us into the *gracious and glorious liberty of the sons of God*; which is to know, and love, and serve him, as he would have us: It is a *madnesse* for Christians, to think of, covet, or enjoy other *Liberty*, than such as the Saints in all ages attained, and such as the blessed *Angels* ever enjoyed; which the *Lord Jesus himself*, our great Liberator, both observed himself, and purchased for his Church; yea such as *God himselfe* is eternally blest with all; which is to be good, and to doe good without any *impediment*.

Ἀπὸ τῶν παθῶν ὥσπερ ἀπὸ πολλῶν δεσποτῶν καὶ μαινομένων ἐλεύθερος. *Plato. de rep.* 1.

Rom. 8 21.

Ἐλευθερία καὶ πλοῦτος ἡ τῆς ἐντολῆς τήρησις, πενία δὲ ἀληθὴς καὶ δουλεία ἡ τῆς ἐντολῆς παράβασις. *Naz. or.* 16.

Id liberrimum est quod minimè à summo bono impeditur, Gib.

2. *Of false liberty and true.*

It is the heavyest *chain* of the *Divels Tyranny*; and that in full bondage, which hath entered into mans soul; to imagine, that *our liberty* consists in thinking, or speaking, or doing, or omitting, what we list; without any regard to God or man, as if men were

were their own Masters, and had no Lord over them: To fancy, that all restraints *internall*, of modesty, fear, sense of honour, science of truth, or conscience of duty, in purity, piety or charity; also *externall*, of established order, good laws, just power, and government either in things civill, or sacred, are encroachments upon, and diminutions of *Christian Liberty*: The want of neglect of which limitens doth infallibly subject us to the basest, and most *infamous servitude*.

Ἀρετὴ ἀδέσποτον. *Plat. de Rep. dia.* 10. *Quo liberior eo miserior.* Ber. Ἐλευθερία ἐστιν ἡγεμονία βίου. *Plat.* Liberty is the right governing of our life.

Whereas, no doubt, the true *liberty* of any man is to be such, in his inward habits and propensities; also to doe such things most constantly, chearfully, and without sinfull impediments, which are most proper and advantagious to the nature and excellency of men: considered both in it self, and its relations; as it stands in reference to God its Creator, and its neighbour; when a Christian is free, to know, consider, meditate of, understand, remember, and beleeve what ever truths God hath revealed to him; yea, further when he is free to declare, and utter them in such an holy way, which charity, sobriety, order and gravity allow. It is no freedome for a man to think what he lists, in vain, erroneous or blasphemous thoughts; or to bolt out and vent all his raw, undigested, rash and rotten fancies, or irreligious opinions to others; He should set a **watch* over his thoughts, and lips with prayer, modesty, and humility; Trying and weighing all things, first with himself, by the Word, and the Spirit of God; or conferring so with others, as may have some *savour* of reason, and religion; an holy desire to learn, or teach in a regular, not a rude, insolent, and imperious way: the next liberty is, to doe those duties of piety and charity, publique and private, which God hath commanded every one, not onely in generall, but in such *restrictions* of place and calling wherein God hath set them.

ἡ κακία δουλοπρεπής, ἡ δὲ ἀρετὴ ἐλευθεροπρεπής. *Plat. Thedo.* Δικαιοσύνη ἐστιν ἕξις ἐν βίῳ νόμῳ ὑπήκοος. *Plato.* *Christiani vox est non ad placitum sed ad licitum.* * Psal. 141. 3.

It is also true liberty for a Christian upon good grounds to hope for, and expect that *reward* and crown, which God the *righteous Judge* hath promised to those that persevere in well doing; who in that way are free to enjoy all the comforts, priviledges, and Ordinances, which Christ hath instituted in an holy order and most regular way, for our private, or publique good; a Christian is free from the fears, terrours, judgements, curses and wrath of God; and from the *Laws rigour* or *condemnation*, upon his true faith, and unfaigned repentance: By which graces the beleiver being ingraffed into Christ, is free from the *observations of the ceremoniall law*, (which tended to Christ, and ended in him;) Also from the *politicall* or *civill* Law among the *Jews*, so far, as variation of times, and necessities of affairs require for the good of mankinde; yet without violating the principles of equity or charity in them; which

Rev. 2. 10. Rom. 2. 7. θεὸν θεραπεύων ἑαυτὸν θεραπεύει. *Clem. Al.* Rom. 8. 1.

which are *perpetually obligatories* upon morall grounds to all men: From the *morall law* also a Christian is so far free, as to its rigour and exactnesse of personall actuall obedience; the want of which in the least kinde is condemnative, in it self; but not so, as we are by *faith in Christ*; yet are we *not freed* from the approbation, and love of the morall law, as it is just and good; nor are we from a constant endevour to conform to its holinesse, not now as a *requisite* to the *justification* of a sinner, but as a fruit of that in our *sanctification*, which from faith and repentance brings forth love; and from love of God a stedfast purpose, and reall endevour to obey his holy *commands* in all things; which is our Evangelicall perfection, and highest *freedom* in this world; which is not wholly from sinning, but from a *wilfull sinning*. Also we *are free*, as to our purpose and new principle, from that *malice*, uncharitablenesse, from those envies, discontents, and worldly disorders in any kinde, as they have dominion over meer naturall and sinfull men: Being further free (that is willing, and content) to suffer what ever God is pleased to inflict upon us, for punishment, triall, or honor, in the way of testifying to his truth: we are also *free* from a *principle of love*, to yeeld ready obedience, as to God, so to man, for the *Lords sake*; what ever man in the name of God, and in Christs stead requires of us, in order to Gods glory, the peace, good example, and benefit of others, in any society, either as men or Christians.

Rom. 7. 16. Rom. 7. 23. Ioh. 8. 39. If the Son make you free, then shall you be free indeed. Rom. 6. 7. Rom. 13. 5. Heb. 13. 17.

3. *The liberty of Superiours and Inferiours.*

The grounds and rules of which externall *obedientaill freedome in civill and Church societies*, the Lord hath by *generall precepts* and directions expressed in his Word: leaving the particular circumstantiating, enacting, and applying of those *generals* to that *liberty* of wisdome, piety, and charity, which ought to be owned by *inferiors*, and exercised by *superiors*, as *governours* in *Church* or *State*; This Politick liberty admits of divers variations according to severall states, times, emergencies and occasions, to which Christians, as men, are subject in this world, wherein honest freedom may be used by such laws and restraints, as shall seem best for the publique welfare, to those in whom the power of giving laws to others doth reside; even in that just power and authority which God hath given to some over others, to rule them; to allow no such gubernative liberty to any men, is to deny that *indulgence* and authority which God hath granted, both to *Christian Magistrates*, and to Ministers, even to restrain in many things the private liberty of others, for the publique *good* and *order* of the community; nor may any man seditiously and factiously plead, or contend *for his private liberty* of speeches, or actions, further than consists with the peace, order, safety, and welfare of the publique; according to what is by *due authority* permitted, or forbidden: and however private thoughts of;

of discontent, mutiny, rebellion, and *cursing others*, fall not under humane cognizance and *judicature*; yet they as not *free*, as to the *tribunall of God* in a mans own *conscience*. Neither may publique *Authority*, (which hath freedome to rule; that is, to command, enjoin and exact externall obedience of others;) Nor may private liberty, (which is free to *obey in the Lord* the commands of Superiours, or else patiently *to abide* their censure;) neither the one, nor the other may turn this *liberty* to a cloak of *maliciousnesse* or *licentiousnesse*; Not the *one* to *tyranny* and oppression; beyond what piety, equity, order, and charity require; nor the other to make it any ground or occasion for factious and seditious perturbings of the publique order and peace: Nor may any party of men (though never so godly, and well affected) being in no place or authority, in Church or State, enabling them, carry on any design (though in its abstract consideration it be better, than what at present may be) by any violent, irregular and disorderly wayes, which are utterly *unwarrantable* in themselves, and no fruit of that Christian liberty, which Christ hath purchased for us; either inwardly, as to God and our consciences; or outwardly, as to Society and publique *relations* of men and Christians to one another; where every *relation imports a duty*; and every duty hath its bounds; beyond which, is not true and vertuous *liberty*, but inordinatenesse and excesse.

Eccles. 10, 20. *Nam scelus intra se tacitum qui cogitat ullum, Facti crimen habet.* Juv.

1 Pet. 2. 13. 20.

1 Pet. 2. 16.

Rom. 13. 5. Ἀνάγκη ὑποτάσσεσθαι, You must needes be subject, not only for wrath, but also for conscience sake.

Christian liberty and divine necessity may stand together; yea they are inseparable.

* *Relationes civiles mutuis officiis ligamur.* Reg. Jur.

Illud decitum quod legibus definitum, Reg. jur.

Yea and in some cases of *severer restraints*, by which Governors doe indeed trench upon those rationall or religious liberties, which God hath allowed to men and Christians; yet in these cases a true Christian onely wraps himself up in that *liberty of patience*, which knowes, when and how to suffer without injury to the publique tranquillity, or to his private peace of conscience: still keeping a * *meek and quiet spirit*, with the love, zeal, and profession of that, which he conceives to be the truth of God; these are the fruits of that * *free Spirit of Christ*, in Christians: which appeared most eminently in Christ; which makes us free to all things, but not to sin in thought, word, or deed: Looking upon sin as the great * *tyrant, usurper*, and *waster* of the true liberty of every man and Christian.

Prudenter aliquando & licita prohibentur, ne si permitterentur, eorum occasione ad illicita perveniatur. Reg. Jur.

Joh. 8. 30. Free indeed.

Libertas vere Christiana auferri aut extrinsecus spoliari nescit: quum non minus patiendo quam agendo exercetur. Aust.

* 1 Pet. 3. 4. * 2 Cor. 3. 17. * *Eo sumus liberiores quo a peccato immuniores.* Gibeuf.

It is then as farre from Christian liberty, as *sicknesse* is from health, *madnesse* or *drunkennesse* from sobriety, rottennesse from beauty,

4. *Divels Liberty.*

beauty, or *putrefaction* from perfection, for any Chriſtian to beleeve what he liſts, though it *be a lye*; or to *disbeleeve* and deny it, though it be a truth of God; to take up what opinions and wayes of religion he moſt fancies; and to refuſe, what ever he pleaſe to diſaffect, upon light, popular and untryed grounds; or openly to ſpeak and diſpute what ever he liſts, and publiquely to act, according as his private perſwaſions, paſſions, luſts, or intereſts, or other mens, tempt and carry him; wherein neither right reaſon, nor common order, nor publique peace, nor conſcience of duty, nor * *reverence of men*, nor *fear of God*, have any ſuch ſerious, and holy ties upon men, as are neceſſary for the common good; In which regard *private Chriſtians* are never ſo free, as to have *no yoake of Chriſt* upon them; no exerciſe of patience, ſelf-denyall, mortification, meekneſſe, charity, modeſty, and ſobriety, together with that comelineſſe and decorum, which beſeemes Religion and a Chriſtian ſpirit; beyond which the moſt *tranſporting zeal* may not expatiate: For that is no other than ſuch freedome, as *water* enjoyes, when it *overbears* and overflowes all its banks and bounds; or as *fire* ſeiſing on the *whole houſe*; Such as *drunken* men in their *roarings*, and *mad men* in their *ravings* contend for; ſuch as *wild beaſts*, and untamed Monſters ſtruggle for; yea ſuch, as the envious and malicious *divels* affect, and are moſt impatient not to enjoy: In whoſe *noſtrils and jawes* the mighty * *wiſdom* and goodneſſe of God (who is *Potentiſſimum & liberrimum agens* the fountain of all true rationall, morall, religious and divine freedome) hath his *booke* of *power*, and *bridle* of *terror*: not of love; Such are *thoſe liberties*, which thoſe (* *primogeniti Diaboli*) prime *birds of the Divels brood*, ſome *impudent Libertines* and *diſſolute wretches* now (as of old) aim at, who have caſt off all ſenſe of juſtice, order, ſhame, and humanity, while they clamour and act for *liberty*; that is, that their blaſphemies, profaneneſſes, impudicities, ſcurrilities, impudencies, and violences againſt all publique civill peace, as well as againſt all religion, order, and Miniſtry of the Church of *England*, may be *tolerated* if not *countenanced*; notwithſtanding they profeſſe to hold with us ſome common grounds of *Chriſtian Religion*, and ſtand reſponſible to civill duties and relations.

Libertas omni ſervitute ſervilior. Ber. Ep. 47.

Ὑποπεσεῖν καὶ παραχωρῆσαι τοῖς πάθεσιν ἐσχάτη δουλεία, τὸ δὲ κρατεῖν ἐλευθερία μόνη. *Cl. Al.* στρω. 2.

* 1 Pet. 2. 17.

Hæretica converſatio quam futilis, quam terrena, quam humana? ſine gravitate, ſine autoritate, ſine diſciplina; cujus penes nos curam lenocinium vocant: pacem cum omnibus miſcent, dum ad unius veritatis expugnationem conſpirant. Tertul. de præſ. ad. Hæ. c. 41.

Δεσπότης ἄγριος καὶ λυσσώδης τὸ ἀκόλαστον πάθος τῷ ἀνδραποδώδει λογισμῷ, οἷς ποιεῖ μάστιξι ταῖς ἡδοναῖς αἰκιζόμενος. *Gr. Niſ. v. M.*

* Ezek. 38. 4. Eſa. 37. 29.

* As St. *John* called *Cerinthus*, who was of this ſect of Libertines, *Irenæ.* l. 3. c. 3. *Congredere mecum ut te ad principem deducam: vox laſcivientium Gnoſticorum, Nicolaitarum & aliorum Hæret.* Iren. l. 1.

True Chriſtians ſhould be as fearfull to enjoy the *divels freedome*, (not which he hath, but which he *deſires*; that is, to *will*, and to doe whatever he liſts;) And as they ſhould be zealous for their own

own true, holy, and humble liberties, which lead them quietly to doe or suffer Gods will, in Gods way; so they should bee tender of encroaching upon those *publique liberties*, which are by right reason, order and Scripture granted to some men, as Magistrates and Ministers for the generall good of Christians. Men must not so please themselves in any thing they fancy of liberty, as to injure others; since no mans right can consist in the detriment, or damage of anothers rights or dues. As then no man rationally can think it a *liberty* denyed him, when he is forbid upon idle visits, to goe *to infected houses*; or being *infected* with the plague, to goe among others that are sound; or to drink poison and propine it to others; no more can any Christian religiously plead for a *liberty* to broach, and publish to others any *opinion* he pleaseth; or to *invade* any place and office, he hath a minde to; or to disturb others in their duties and power; or to contemne with publique insolence; or violently to innovate against established laws and orders in Church or State: much lesse hath he any freedome openly to blaspheme or disturb that religion, and way of devotion, wherein sober and good Christians worship God by that authority and order, which is setled in publique, according to their consciences and best judgements.

No mans liberty may be anothers injury.

Nullius emolumentum jure nescitur exalterius damno & injuria. Reg. Iur.

5\. *True Liberty and good government in Church and State agree well together.*

Here, neither Christian *Magistrates*, nor *Ministers* are to regard such pleas for *private Liberties*, as overthrow the publique order and peace; nor are they to regard those clamours against them and the Laws, as *persecuting*, when they doe but oppose and restrain such pernicious *exorbitancies*; nor are they in this infringers of the *peoples freedome*, but preservers of Liberties, which are bound up onely in the laws; nor are they *oppressours* of others mens consciences, but *dischargers* of their own duties, and consciences, which they bear to *Gods glory*, and the publique good; whereto as they stand highly related by their place and power, so they are highly accountable to God for them: And, if they should suffer arrogant ignorance to come to its full rudenesse, and extent, tumultuary *numbers* and brutish *power* will soon make good *private presumptions*; and cover over the most impotent lusts, passions, and ambitions of men, with the *pleas* and *outcryes* for Christian liberty: That is, that they may doe what they list; and no man else, what they should, in right reason and Religion, but onely what their proud fanatick pleasure will permit them; Thus oft by the *Engine of Liberty*, Christians are cast into

* *Leges sunt corporis politici nervi, sine quibus luxata & infirma fient omnia membra.* Verul.

Lex est libertatis conservatrix, civitatis anima. Marsf. Fic. *Est recte agendi norma. Dei vox. Hominum Lux.* H. Steph.

* ἡ ἄγαν ἐλευθερία ἔοικεν οὐκ εἰς ἄλλο τι ἢ εἰς ἄγαν δουλείαν. *Plato. Dial.* 8. *de Repub.* Too great liberty is but the dregs of licentiousnesse, and next to slavery. *De immanissimis Circumcellionum gregibus & Donatistarum, scripsit Tychonius; Quod volumus sanctum est: Quod sanctum est volumus: Catholicorum vox est.* Aust.

the greatest *Tyranny*, or Anarchy, which grow from imaginary or abused and corrupted freedomes; which, if not *suppressed* by an orderly and *just severity*, (which is the *greatest charity* to the publiq e) they grow from the lesser *fly-blowings* of secret opinions, private presumptions, and proud fancies, to become filthy *creepers* and noxious flyers abroad; (as the Frogs, Flies and Locusts of *Egypt*) to the great infection, and molestation of others; defiling and defacing all things, that are esteemed of publique religious order, beauty, peace, holynesse and true liberty.

Summa est in publicum charitas erga privatorum delicta severitas: Nec minor est in nimia lenitate severitas; Reg. Iur.

It is oft too late discerned (after *unhappy indulgences* and *cruell tendernesses* in this kinde) by all sober Christians; That it is not more the happinesse of mankinde, to have the *Sea restrained* by the bounds, which God in his *wonderfull providence* hath set to it, that it return not again to cover the earth; than this is, that he hath established by the light of Reason, and the commands of his *written Word* the *ordinances of Ministry* and *Magistracy* among Christian men; by which to *preserve* true Christian liberty in its sphear and due bounds of just laws, of sound doctrine, true beleeving, well doing, orderly obeying, and comely suffering; and withall, to keep out those enormous extravagancies which seek to overthrow both *Magistracy* and *Ministry*; which are the great *conservators* of Christians, in all honest and just freedomes; without which no men should enjoy any, while *violent* lusts and errours make way (by *levelling* all things) for their *thick*, and muddy *inundations*; which are the divels *spittings* in the face, and *vomitings* in the bosome of the true Christian, and reformed Religion; that so it might at once be both *ashamed* of it self, and loathsom to all others: Quite contrary to the that ancient *merited honour* of Christian Religion; which made *Christians of all men* the most strict, and severe livers; allowing so much the lesse or nothing of fleshly, worldly, and divellish liberties to themselves, by how much they most enjoyed a *spirituall*, gracious, and *divine liberty*, which no persecution or oppression took from them, any more, then it did their peace, truth, faith, and patience; these men alwayes *pleased themselves* in *denying themse ves* all things that were dishonest, injurious and uncomely; even so far as to abstain from the very appearance of evill; not onely in the conscience of a Christian, but even in the sight of heathens; Such as not only *Religion*, but common reason condemned. Nor did the Christians when multiplyed to numbers, and filling all places in the Empire, challenge by any force any liberty of Religion beyond what they had by civill favour of Magistrates; or that of their prayers, tears and patience, when persecuted and denyed civill liberties; as *Tertullian* tels in his apology: So wary they were of abusing their

Iob. 38. 11.
Psal. 104. 9.

Nec totam servitutem pati possunt homines, nec totam libertatem. Tacit. hist. l. 1.

The use of liberty among ancient Christians.

ἐλεύθερον τὸ ἄρχον ἑαυτοῦ. Plato.

Tit. 2. 12.
Divinissima est libertas sui abnegatio. D' Espenc.
1 Thes. 5. 22.

their liberty to any *insolency*, offence, injury, or *indignity* against any private person; much more against a *publique* and *common good* of either Church or State; the preservation of which, as to the *generall interests* of societies, wherein thousands are concerned, both in their soules and bodies welfare, is far more to be regarded, by wise, godly, and charitable men; than any *private pleas*, or pretensions for *Christian liberty*; especially when they look with an *evill eye*, and lift up an *offensive hand* against publique order, government, duties and institution: wherein are bound up, and contained that peace, piety, and religion which is enjoyed or professed by any Christians. 2 Cor. 10.32.

6. *False liberty destructive to the true.*

As then the best *governed families* and best *disciplined Armies* allow *no plea*, or practise of liberty to any *servants*, or *souldiers*, which are contrary to the rules and ends of right œconomicall or military discipline; which intends the common safety and welfare of families and Armies; So, neither may *Christian Religion* be thought to bring forth, or be forced to maintaine, that *Liberty* (as a legitimate issue of conscience) in its holy profession, and orderly ministrations; which is in all civill or secular dispensations esteemed, rejected and punished as a *turbulent and seditious bastard*: And which, being *but as Ishmael the son of a bondwoman*, is prone to *mock* and abuse the *Isaac* of true liberty, which is the *son of promise*, and is no way fit to be the heir, or to divide the Inheritance of Christian freedome; which is onely the portion of *holy, humble, sober*, and orderly Christians; for while some boast of, and challenge to themselves, and *promise* to others this false and *spurious Liberty*, they are still *servants to their lusts*, and in bondage to their *corruptions*; impatient of any restraints, but those of their own wils, interests and fancies; yea and this *Bastard Liberty*, like the *one base son of Gideon* (*Abimelech*) when once it can but *get power*, makes no conscience to destroy all the *lawfull heirs* of true religious liberty, which are possessed of truth, peace, charity, order, good government in any Church: yea and all civill justice too, and properties of goods and estates; which are presently thought by *licentious* men, inconsistent with their freedome, when once their powerfull lusts have set upon the heads of their *unruly designes*, the *Crown and title of Christian Liberty*. Which *disguise* the Divell fits to such a compleatnesse, that there is no error, no lust, no sin, no blasphemy, no villany, nor deformity in any mens opinions or practises so *horrid*, which hee doth not seek to colour over, or to cover with the *paint* and *palliatings of Christian liberty*.

Turbulenta hæreticorum audacia. Aust.

Gen. 21.9.

2 Pet. 2.19.

Iud. 9.5.

Coacta servitus miserabilis, sed affectata miserabilior. Ber. de Cons.

Which being a *pure* and *spotlesse Virgin*, (the highest beauty which a Christian can here be inamour'd of, and which he courts with

with all modesty, purity, and respect on earth, hoping to have the *full fruition* of it in heaven) disdains above all things to *be abused* by those bold and *filthy ravishers*, who like the inordinate *monsters of Gibeah*, will never think their *licentious* lusts satisfied, untill they have killed the *Levites concubine*: Destroying indeed all true *Christian liberty* (which is preserved onely by good order and government both in the Church and State) while they prostitute truths, duties, institutions, Ministry, and Magistracy to all manner of insolencies and confusion; as if Christians were never free enough, till they were without all sense of sin and shame; till they neither *feared God*, nor *reverenced man*; till they had broken all the bands of civill *justice*, and cast away the cords of all religious *discipline* from them; as the *Cainites*, *Judaites*, *Ophites*, *Adamites*, and others of old.

Judg. 19.

Assistentem in omni munditia Angelum dicebant & invocabant. Hanc esse aiebant perfectam operationem sine tremore in tales abire operationes quas ne nominare quidem fas est. Irenæ. l. 1. cap. 35. de *Cainitis*, *Judaitis*, *Ophitis*.

Which most *inordinate liberty* is no more to be enjoyed or desired by any good Christian, than that of the *Demoniack*: who being oft *bound with chaines* and *fetters*, yet brake them all, and was driven of the Devill into deserts, among the graves, often dashing him against the stones, and casting him into fire and water. Such will be the *sad fate* of every Christian Church and State, which either affects, or *tolerates* any such impious, fanatick, unlawfull, and unholy liberties; contrary to that purity, equity, order and decency; which is necessary to that religion which they professe as Christian. Therefore no wonder if the *Lord* by his word, and his true Ministers daily *rebukes* this *unclean spirit*; and seeks to cast out of this Church such an *untamable Divell*, which hath already got too much possession in many mens mindes; who are prone to *deifie* every *Diana*, as an image come *downe from heaven*, if it be but set up in the *silver-shrine* of this *popular goddesse Liberty*; which of all *puppetly Idols* lately consecrated to *vulgar adoration*, I can least of all *Idolize*: as that, which I see to have least of *divinity* or *humanity* in it: either as to piety, equity, purity, or charity.

Luk. 8. 29.

Act. 19. 27.

Yet is no man a more *unfained* servant and votary of that *true and divine Liberty*, which becomes Christians; which preserves truth, peace, order, and holinesse among men, both in private and publique regards, both in Church and State; and in this I wish all men my *rivalls* in the ambition and *sharers*, with me in the fruition; which will then be most, when we get our hearts *most freed* from that heavy *bondage*, wherewith errour, pride, passion, self-seeking, and the like cruell *task-masters* (under

der the great oppressing *Pharaoh*, the Divell) doe seek to enslave the soules, and consciences of men; by so much *the baser slavery*, by how much they fancy *their slavery to be liberty*: their freedom to sin, to be that *freedome* from sin, which Christ hath *purchased*: which dangerous mistake makes them *love* their *bondage*; to *bore their eares*; and to be most offended with those, who seek to shew them their *desperate errors* and *divellish thraldom*; which is the greatest *severity of divine vengeance* in this world upon men, by giving them over to Satan, or up to their own hearts lusts.

Ægypriaca est illa servitus sub jugo Pharaonis, Diaboli: fiunt lutea opera; terrena, sordida, dissolutaq; ab ipso dantur paleæ, i.e. leves & malæ cogitationes, quæ delectatione accenduntur, inde actione coquuntur lateres, & consuetudine indurantur. Ber. p. Ser. 34. *Extremæ est dementiæ in infima servitute & villissima captivitate de libertate gloriari; quasi cloacarum sordibus immersus, totus fœdus & inquinatus, de pigmentis tuis & fragrantia jactitares.* Erasm.

Yet this false and *damnable liberty* is by some men earnestly contended for, and imperiously claimed in the way of *publique toleration*; that they, or any men, may professe, as to Religion, what they list; being prone through pride and ignorance, to think that *no opinion* they hold, or practise *they* doe, is irreligious, profane, blasphemous, or intolerable; nor ought by any just severity or penalty bee restrained, or punished: Whereas Christians truly blessed with *tender Consciences*, and *meeknesse of wisdome*, are most willing to be kept within Christs bounds; and loathest to take *any liberty*, either in opinion or manners, beyond what in the truth of the Word, or in charity to the publique peace, and order is permitted: Humble knowledge makes Christians most *tractable*; yea and thankfull to those, either *Ministers* or Magistrates, whose love and fidelity to them, will least *tolerate* any error, or sin in them, without reproof, and just restraint.

7 *Some mens impudent demand of an intolerable toleration.*

Carpocratiani, & Valentiniani, et Gnostici, &c. portentosis quasq; libidines non licitas tantum statuebant, sed tanquam gradus aliquos quibus in cœlum ascendatur: Iren. l. 1.

Grata revigilantibus erit ea molestia, quæ non patitur errore, tanquam morifero somno & veternoso morbo, interire. Aust.

Others, whom *ignorance* makes proud, and pride erroneous, and both unruly; are ready to esteem all they hold or vent or dare to act, (especially under colour of religion, for in civill *affaires they are afraid* of the sword) to be so commendable, at least tolerable, that they merit, if not concurrence and approbation from all men, yet at least *connivence*, and toleration; nor may they be *touched*, or curbed by any authority in Church or State, (be their *extravagancies* never so pernicious and blasphemous) but presently they make huge outcryes of *persecution*; as if all were *persecutors*, who helped to * binde a mad man; or to put a roaring drunkard into the cage; which measure of healing them, is best both for them, and for others too; and is not to be used to any, but those

Tunc ei (phrenetico) utilissimus & misericordissimus, cum ei adversissimus & molestissimus videtur. Aust. Ep 48. de corre. Hæret.

 [that

that are truly such *disorderly* and *distempered spirits.*

I conceive it most clear and certain both in right Reason and true Religion, that the prudence, piety, and charity of Governors in Church and State ought to move in that middle way, between *tolerating* all differences, and none, in matters of Religion; wherein men are variously to be considered, according to that profession which they own, and make of Religion; Sure none are to be tolerated in blaspheming, or insolencing that *religion*, which is established by publique consent or laws, and which they professe in common with others; being in this *self-condemned* and without excuse; Nor are any of a *different beleif*, to what is *established*, to be *tolerated* in giving any factious and seditious scandals, against that Religion, which is by the wisdome, and piety of any Nation, and Church there setled, as sacred; being always presumed, that it is judged the *truest* and best: for no men can be supposed to binde themselves, and their posterity to any religion, which they *think false.*

ἀναπολόγητοι ἐ αὐτοκατάκειτοι. Rom. 2. 1. Tit. 3. 11.

Two wayes of just restraints in the Church. 1 Tim. 5. 20. Tit. 2. 15. Tit. 3. 10. 1 Cor. 5. 11.

There are two wayes of *coercive power* (established by God) over men, in matters of religion, either of the Word by Ecclesiasticall *admonitions*, reproofes and censures; which onely reach those in matters of error, or scandall, that are under the same form, beleif, and profession of Religion, (for these onely doe *consider* them): And where this *discipline* is (as in primitive times it was) *rightly dispensed* with gravity, wisdome, charity, and due *solemnity*, by wise and worthy men; it carries a great weight with it, being in the name and authority of Jesus Christ, and is of excellent use to the well being of the Church of Christ, to preserve the honour of Religion, and credit of Christianity. Nor is any thing of extern order, and *policy*, more worthy to be seriously considered and restored by Christians; which can never be done, till the right government of the Church be first setled; nor can this now be easily done, without the favour and concurrent authority of the Christian Magistrate; so far hath licentious *contempt*, and insolency prevailed against all ancient order, government, and discipline in the Church; even by the *Libertinism* of such, as would most be counted Christians. 2. A second way of animadversion or restraint of publique *disorders* in Religion, is by the power of the sword in the hand of the *Christian Magistrate*; who is to regard not onely the civill peace of subjects, but also that trust which lies on him, to *take care* for their *religious* interests, and their souls welfare, that they may be taught and preserved in the right way of *knowing* and *serving* God: The happyest condition of any Christians is, when both these *powers* are *wisely* and sweetly twisted together; so as the *Ministry* directs the *Magistracy by the Word*; and

1. By Church discipline.

And 2. Magistratick power.

Quanto plus potes in terrena republica, tanto plus impendens cœlesti civitati. Aust. Ep. c. 24.

and the *Magistracy* assists the *Ministry* by the *sword*: where the *censures of the Church* act by charity, and the censures of the Magistrate by a just severity; yet so, as neither *love* to the offender; nor *dislike* of the offence be wanting: That all be done to the edification, not to the destruction of the Church, or of any member of it, so farre as its welfare is consistent with the publique.

Neither civill, nor Church power among Christians should be as a *sharp* and *hard rock*, dashing presently all in pieces, that touch or strike at it in the least kinde, though never so modestly differing from the received Religion; nor yet ought they to be as *pillowes* and sponges, yeelding so *soft a reception* to every new opinion and practise, as to *invite all errours*, and novelties to a recumbency, or rest in their bosome; A Church, or Christian State, will soon be full of all *noisome vermine*, if they allow as a work of charity and liberty, every *sordid errour*, and *beggerly* opinion, publiquely to lodge, and nestle under their roof; yea and to *contend* for place, and crowd out that *Religion* which is established: Christian Magistrates should neither use the *sharp* rasor or two-edged sword of the *Spanish Inquisition*; which forceth with terror, either to deny, what men hold for truth; or to professe which that, they hold not; nor yet should they content themselves with the *wooden daggers* of *Amsterdam*; where civill authority excuses its *lukewarmnesse*, and gilds over its *tolerancy* of any Religion, with the benefit of trade and commerce. I doe not think it *Christian* to *extirpate Jews* or *Turkes*, much lesse any of Christian profession; but I think it both wisdome and charity, first, to endeavour by all fair means to convince all; And secondly, to restrain by just penalties, all those under civill subjection, (however of a different religion) from saying, or doing any thing publiquely scandalous to, and derogating from the honor, peace and order of that Religion, which is esteemed, and therefore setled, as the best and truest: As civill seditions and treasons are intolerable, so are *religions*; nor are such endeavours veniall, which by *printing blasphemous bookes* and divellish Libels seek to re ive old rotten errors and heresies; or to bring publique reproach, and scorn upon the *reformed Christian Religion* in this Church: no not although those *infamous pamphlets* were attended with *learned confutations*; since it's safer to forbid the use of *poysons* to the incautious people, than to permit them to drink them up, upon confidence of the virtue, which may be in the *antidotes* applyed; The nature of man is proner to imbibe *noxious* things, then to egest them: It is a tempting of God to tolerate evils and errours (which we may prevent) onely upon confidence of the remedies

Moderation differs from grosse toleration.

2 Tim. 2. 24.

we can apply. This is more like Mountebanks, than like good Magistrates or Ministers.

Christians must not be Scepticks in Religion. Ephes. 4. 14.

Since then, neither in right reason, and true policy of State, it is either becoming or safe, for *Christian Magistrates*, to have no *acknowledgment* of any face of Religion, so farre among their people and subjects as to establish, own and command it; nor is it any piety, for Christians, to be alwayes *scepticks* in Religion; ever *unsatisfied*, and unresolved, and unestablished in matters of Gods worship, and mans salvation, still *ravelling* the very grounds of Religion with *endlesse cavils* and *needlesse disputes*. Since the Word of God is neer and open to direct all men in the wayes of God; and since what is necessary to be beleived and obeyed in truth and holinesse, is of all parts in Scripture most plaine and easie; No doubt, but *Christian Magistrates* are *highly bound in Conscience* to God, and in charity to the good of their subjects, (to whom they must doe more good, then they are desired to doe by the *Vulgar*) to *establish* those things, as to the *extern order*, *Ministry*, *form* and *profession* of Religion, both in doctrine and duties, which they shall in their conscience judge and conclude, upon the best advice of learned and godly men, to be most *agreeable* to the will of God, as most clearly grounded on the Word in the generall tenor and analogy of it; and as most *fundamentally necessary* to be beleived and obeyed by all Christians; whereto the Catholick beleef and practise of all Churches (more or lesse agreeing) gives a great light and direction. Christians must not be alwayes tossing to and fro in religion, but come to an Anchor of fixation, as to the publique profession; else there will hardly be any civill peace preserved among men: who least endure, and soonest quarrell upon differences in Religion, each being prone to value his own, and contemn anothers.

Nulla res efficacius homines regit quam religio. Curt. l. 4.

Separatim nemo habessit Deos, neve novos: Tul. de leg. Rom.

Nihil ita facit ad dissidium ac de Deo dissensio. Naz. orat. 8.

These things of publique piety thus once setled by Scripture upon good advice, ought by all *swasive*, *rationall* and religious means to be made known by the *publique Ministry* to the people; for so Christ hath ordained, and the Church alwayes observed; to which Ministry (which I have proved to be of *Gods institution*, and so most worthy of mans best favour and encouragement) publique and orderly attendance, for time, place, and manner ought to bee enjoyned upon all under that power, for their necessary catechiand instruction; And this with some penalties inflicted upon idle, wilful and presumptuous neglects; when no *ground of conscience*, or other perswasion or reason is produced by those, that are not yet of years of discretion: if any of riper *years* and sober *understanding*

Solos credit habendos Quisq; Deos quos ipse colit. Iuv. Sat. 15. *Ægyptii cum diversi cultus Deos habebant, mutuis bellis se impetebant.* Diod. l. 42.

plead

plead a dissent, they ought in all charity and *humanity* be dealt with, by *religious reasonings*, and *meeknesse of wisdome*; if so be they may so be *brought to the knowledge of the truth*: But if either weaknesse of capacity, or wilfulnesse and obstinacy suffer them not to be convinced, and so to conform to the publique profession of Religion, I doe not think, that by *force*, and *severities* of punishment, they ought to be compelled to professe, or to do, that in Religion, of which they declare an *unsatisfaction* in judgment; yet may they, both in justice, and charity, be so tyed to their *good behaviour*, that they shall not, under great penalties, either rudely speak, write, or act against; or openly blaspheme, profane, and disturb; or contradict and contemn the Religion publiquely professed, and established.

> 2 Tim. 1. 25.
>
> What toleration becomes Christians.

And however the welfare of this publique is not so concerned, in what men *privately hold*, as to their judgement and opinion, (thoughts being as the *Embryos* of another *freer world*; yet when they come to be brought forth to publique notice in word or deed, they justly fall under the care, and censure both of the Magistrate to restrain them, as relating to the good of community; and of the Minister to reprove them, as his duty and authority is in the Church.

> *Facientis culpam obtinet, qui quod poterit corrigere negligit emendare.* Reg. Iur.

If in lesser things, which are but the *lace and fringe* of the holy vestment, the *verge* and *Suburbs* of Religion *established*, Christians doe so dispute and differ, as not to trench upon *fundamentall truths*, neither *blaspheming* the Majesty of God, or of the *Lord Jesus Christ*, or of the blessed Spirit; or the authority of the holy Scriptures; nor breaking the bounds of *clear morals*; nor violating the *order* of the holy Ministry of Christs Church, which *is the very hinge of all Christian Religion*; nor yet wantonly dissolving that bond of *Christian communion* in point of extern order, peace, and comely administrations of holy things: other private *differences* and dissentings, no doubt, may be *fairly tolerated*, as *exercises* of charity, and *disquisitions* of truth; wherein yet, even the *lesser*, as well as greater differences, (which arise in Religion) are far better to be publiquely and solemnly considered of, prudently and peaceably composed, (if possible) than negligently, and carelesly tolerated; as wounds and issues are better healed with speed, than tented to continued Ulcers, and Fistulas.

> *Ordo Evangeliti Ministerii est cardo Christianæ religionis.* Gerard.
>
> *Tolle Ministerium, & tolle Christum*; is one of the divels politick maximes.

I am confident, wise, humble and charitable Christians, in publique *eminency* of power, and piety, would not finde it so *hard a matter* (as it hath been made, through *roughnesse* of mens passions, and intractablenesse of their spirits, raised chiefly by other interests, carryed on, than that of Christ, true Religion, and poor people soules) if they would set to it in *Gods name*, to reconcile

> 8.
>
> *The mean between Tyranny and Tolerations.*

the many and greatest religious differences, which are among both *Christian* and *reformed Churches*; if they would *fairly separate*, what things are morall, clear and necessary in Religion, from what are but *prudentiall*, decent or *convenient*; and remove from both these, what ever is *passionate*, popular and superfluous, in any way, which weak men call, and count Religion; if the *many headed Hydra* of mens lusts, passions, and secular ends were once cut off, so that no *sacriledge*, or covetousnesse, or ambition, or popularity, or revenge should sowre, and leaven *reformation*; or obstruct any harmony and reconciliation; sure the *work* would not be so *Herculean*, but that sober Christians might be easily satisfied, and fairly lay down their *uncharitable* censures, and *damning distances*.

Instances in Church Government.

It is easie to instance, in that one point of *Church government*, as to the extern form; what unpassionate stander by sees not, but it might easily have been composed, in a way, full of order, counsell and fraternall consent, so that neither *Bishops* as fathers, nor *Presbyters* as brethren, nor *people* as sons of the Church, should have had any cause to *have* complained, or envyed, or differed? So in the election, triall, and ordination of Ministers, also in the use, and power of the *keyes*, and exercise of *Church discipline*; who in reason sees not; that, as these things concern the good of all degrees of the faithfull in the Church, so they might (as in St. *Cyprian's* and all primitive times) have beeen carried on in so sweet an order, and accord, as should have pleased and profited all; both the Ordainers and the ordained; with those, for whose sakes Ministers are ordained? So in the great and sacred *administration* of the mysterious, and venerable Sacraments, *especially* that of the *Lords Supper*; which concerns most Christians of years: how happily, and easily might competent knowledge, an holy profession of it, and an unblameable conversation be carried on, by both pastors and people, with Christian order, care and charity; so as to have satisfied all those, who make not Religion a *matter* of gain, revenge, State policy, or faction; but of conscience and duty, both to God, and their neighbour, and their own soules? which was the harmonious way of primitive Christians in *persecution*, when no *State factions* troubled the purer streams of that doctrine, government, and discipline which the *Churches* had received, from the *divine fountaines*; and had preserved sweet amidst the bitter streams, and great *stormes* of persecution; when no *interest* was on foot among Christians but that of Christ's, to *save soules*; which did easily keep together in humble, and honest hearts, piety, and humanity; zeale, and meeknesse; mens understandings, and affections; *constancy* in fundamentall truths, and *tolerancy* in lesser differences; That *Truth* and

* *ubi metus in deum, ibi gravitas honesta, & diligentia attonita, & cura solicita, & adlectio explorata, & communicatio deliberata, & promotio emerita, & subjectio religiosa, & apparitio devota, & professio modesta, & Ecclesia unita, & Dei omnia.* Tertul. ad Hær. c. 43.

Secular interests the pests of the Church.

and *Peace*, Order and Unity might kisse each other, and as twins *live* together, the foundations remain unviolable, while the superstructures might be varied as much as *hay and stubble* are from *gold and silver*; That the faith of Christians might not serve to begin or nourish feuds, nor Christians, (who are as lines drawn from severall points of faiths circumference, yet to the same center Christ Jesus) might ever crosse and *thwart* one another, to the breach of charity: but still *keep the unity of the Spirit*, in the bond of peace: The same Faith *invariable*, as once *delivered to the Saints*; yet with those *latitudes* of private charity, which Gods indulgence had allowed to true wisdome, and which an inoffensive liberty grants in many things to sober Christians.

1 Cor. 3. 12.

Ephes. 4. 3.

I doe not despair, but that such bloud may one day yet run in the veins of this Church of *England*, (which is now almost faint and swooning by the losse of much bloud, which civil wars and secular interests have let out) which may recover it to strength and beauty, both in doctrine and discipline: Yet will it never be the honour of those men to effect it, who trust onely to military force; or intend, either to set up any one violent faction, or a loose toleration in religion. It will be little lesse indeed than a miracle of *divine mercy* and Christian moderation, which must recover the spirit and life, the purity and peace of this Church.

9. *An excellent way for unity and peace in the Church.*

In the best *setled Church*, or State Christian, I conceive it were a happy and most convenient way for *calming*, and *composing* all differences rising in Religion, to have (as the Jews had their *Sanhedrin* or great Assembly) if we in *England* had some setled Synod or solemn Convocation, of pious, grave and learned men; before whom all *opinions* arising to any difference, from what is once setled, should be debated publiquely; deliberated of seriously, and charitably composed, if not definitively determined; that so the *main truths* may be preserved unshaken, which concern *faith and holinesse*, on which grounds *peace and charity* in every Church ought to be continued; So that none under great penalty should vent any doctrine in publique by preaching or printing, different from the received and established way, before he had acquainted that Consistory or *Councell* with it, and had from them received *approbation*; so that no man should be punishable for his error, what ever he produced before them; but might either *receive satisfaction from them; or only this charge and *restraint*, that he *keep his opinion to himselfe*, till God shew him the

Twise a year Synods were in primitive times appointed, where the Bishops and other chief Fathers of the Church met to consider of Doctrines and disputes in religion: ἀνακεινέτωσαν ἀλλήλοις τὰ δόγματα τῆς εὐσεβείας, κ τὰς ἐμπιπτούσας ἐκκλησιαστικὰς ἀντιλογίας διαλυέτωσαν. Can. Apoc 36. Which undoubtedly shew the practise and minde of the primitive times soon after the Apostles.

* Utili terrori doctrina salutaris adjungatur. Aust. Et deus ipse nos suaviter docet & salubriter terret.

truth.

truth; and that he presume not to divulge it, save onely in private conference to others, and that in a modest and peaceable manner.

In matters of judgement and opinion, (where no man is accountable for more than he can *understand*, and upon grounds of right reasoning either beleive or know) much *prudence*, *tendernesse* and *charity* is to be used; which will easily distinguish between *honest simplicity*, privately dissenting, upon *plausible grounds*; or *harmlesly erring*, without design; and that *turbulent pertinacy*, by which pride is resolved as a *dry nurse* to bring up by *hand*, at the charge and trouble of others, every novell and *spurious opinion*, which an *adulterous* or *wanton fancy* lists to bring forth, though there be no *milk for it in the breasts of Reason*, or Scripture rightly understood. The first is as *Joseph* out of his way, wandring and desiring to be directed; whom it is charity to reduce to the right way. The second is like sturdy Vagabonds, who are never out of their way; but seek to seduce others that they may rob or murther them; these ought to be justly punished and restrained. The first is as *cold water*, which may *dabble* and disorder one that fals into it; yea and may drown him too; but the other is as falling into *scalding hot water*; which pride soone boyles up to malice, and both to *publique trouble*; unlesse it be thus wisely prevented, before it have, *like fire*, a publique vent: for commonly *pertinacy* of men ariseth more from the love of *credit* and *applause*, which they think they have got, or may lose; or from some other advantage they aim at; than barely from any esteem they have of the opinions, wherein they innovate; which brats of mens brains not their beauty, but their propriety and relation commends to an eager maintaining; which in a publique debate by wise and impartiall men, of high credit and reputation for their learning, gravity, and integrity, will be so *blasted*, that they will hardly ever after thrive or spread.

Mallent semper errare quam semel errasse videri.

This, or the like care of Christian Magistrates, by way of rationall restraints, *charitable convictions*, and just *repressings* of all *factious* and *turbulent* innovations in Religion, (being full of wisedome, piety, charity, and just policy for the publique and private good of men) may not be taxed with the least suspicion of *tyranny*; nor may wise, and good men startle at the name and *outcry of persecution*; which some proud or *passionate opiniasters* may charge upon them; any more than good * *Physitians* or *Chirurgeons* should be moved from the Rules of their art and experiences, by the clamors and imputations of *cruelty*, from those that are *full of foolish pity*;

De Nerva dictum. Res insociabiles miscuit, Imperium & libertatem. Tacit.

Pati non est Christianæ justitiæ certum documentum: ut Donatistæ meritò repressi vociferabant. Aust. Ep. 163.

when

when they are forced to use *rougher Physick*, and such *severer medicines*, which the disease and health of the Patient doth necessarily require of them: unlesse they would *flatter the disease*, to destroy the man; or spare one part, to ruine the whole body. It is indeed an * *hating of our brother*, and partaking of his sin, and so a *persecuting of his soul*, to let him hunt the *divels suit*, without check, and to follow the trains of errour, by which he leades *men to perdition*; when it is in our way of *charity*, much more in our *place* and *authority* to endeavour to convert, or at least stop him so, as others may not be perverted by him; Good husbands will not forbear for their lowd crying to *ring and yoke* those *Swine*, which they see doe *root* up the pastures, break through the fences, and wast the corn; yet still they leave even *these beasts* freedom enough, to feed themselves, and live orderly, but not mischievously.

Math. 5. 10. Blessed are they that are persecuted; but it must be, for righteousnesse sake.

Steriles fugiendæ sunt passiones. Aust.

* Lev. 19. 17.

Non omnis qui parcit amicus est, nec omnis qui verberat inimicus: melius est cum severitate diligere, quam cum lenitate decipere. Aust. de coercendis Hæreticis, Ep. 48. vid. *Perperde non quid patearis sed quare, & quo modo.* Lact. Inst. l.

Although the *man* in every one is to be treated *humanely*, and the Christian Christianly, with all reason, and charity; (because the *Creator* is to be *reverenced in every creature*, and Christ in every Christian) yet the *Beast or Divell* (which may be even in regenerated men) must be used accordingly; that the *man may* be preserved, though the other be restrained: as we do, without injury, to those that are *mad*, or *dæmoniack*; to whom if sober men should allow *what liberty* they affect, cry out and strive for; it were to *proclaim* themselves to all the world the *madder* of the two. And none would have more cause to repent (when they *came* to themselves) of those indulgences, fondly granted them; which they (*poore men*) know not how to use, but to their own, and *others harm*. Indeed those men * *forfeit their private liberty* to the publique discretion, and power, who will not, or cannot use it, but to the publique detriment, and the injury of others; which to prevent or hinder is the *highest work of charity*. None but *sons of Belial*, that is, of such as will not indure *the yoke in Religion*, either in piety, purity, or charity, nor suffer others to enjoy the benefit of it in peace and order, can desire such a * *freedom*, as will not indure the Lord for their God, nor man for their Governour; who seek to break the *staves of beauty* and *of bonds* on their *Shepheards heads*; or to wrest the *keys* out of their hands; who *like wild asses* would be left to *feed in the wildernesse* of their own barren fancies, and to snuffe up *the winde* of their own or others vain opinions, till they are starved, and destroyed, rather than be kept in *good pasture*, with due limits.

Salute reparata tanto uberius gratias agunt, quanto minus sibi quemq; pepercisse sentiunt. Aust. Ep. 48. of the *Donatists* and *Circumcelliones* reduced by just punishments (*ab iniquieta sua tenacitate*) from their seditious rashnesse.

* *Sui juris esse non debet qui nisi in aliorum injurias vivere nescit.* Reg. Iur. * *Adeo libere esse volunt ut nec Deum habere volunt Dominum.* Aust.

There is a *damnable* and *damning Liberty*, a Toleration, which the *Divels* would enjoy; who would soone destroy all things, on which is any *Image of the Creators glory*; if the *sharp* curb and weighty chains of Gods omnipotency, were not upon them, both immediately, and mediately, through that wisdome, care, courage, and authority, which he gives to *Christian Magistrates and Ministers*, to resist, and to *bind up Satan*. If they then that are thus furnished by God, with *just power* in *Church* and *State*, should leave the things of God in matters of Religion (as *outwardly professed*) to *such liberties*, that all men may run which ways they please, of *ignorance, errour, atheism, prophanenesse, blasphemy*, being *seduced*, and *seducing* others; if they take no care, that *younger people* bee catechised, and others duly attend the publique duties of that religion, which is established, and which they still professe; if they should neither stop, nor restrain any man in any course of opinion, or practise, which he cals *Conscience*, without giving any account of Reason or Scripture for it to those *in Authority*; Certainly such an *intolerable Toleration*, letting every one doe, *what seemes right in their own eyes*, in the things of God, and onely to look *exactly to civill interests* and safety; is to make *Magistratick power*, which is *Gods Ordinance* for the good of mankinde, to concurre with the *malice of the Divels*, and that innate folly, vanity, and madnesse which is in mens hearts, to the ruine of simple multitudes; who cannot *sin*, or *miscarry* eternally, in such *sinfull liberties*, irreligions and tolerations, but at the *cost* and *charge* of the Magistrates souls; if they be Christian, and are perswaded of the truth of that Religion; as we read the *master* became a trespasser, or murtherer, and was put to death, who *knowingly* suffered his *petulant Ox* to enjoy such a *liberty*, as ended in the damage, or destruction of his *neighbours* goods, or life.

Ubi non est veritas, merito & talis est disciplina. Ter.

Judg. 21. 21.

Rom. 13.

Exod. 21. 29.

10. *Such Toleration is but a subtill persecution.*

A toleration of any thing as to publique profession among Christians under the notion of *Christian liberty*, is but the *divels finest*, and subtillest way of *persecution*; for he is as sure to gain by such *indulgences*, as *weeds* doe, by the husbandmans, or *Gardners* negligence or lothnesse to pluck them up, for *fear of hurting* the corn or good plants; which when they are fully discerned to be but weeds, as they are not *possibly* to be puld up by mans hand, as to the private errours and hypocrisies of mens hearts, which are to be left to the *great Judge and Searcher of hearts*; so nor may they *rashly* be pulled up by every one, that sees them, lest injury be done to the *good seed*; but yet they are not carelesly, and *sluggishly* to bee suffered to * *overgrow* and *choak* the good plants; As if nothing were true fixed and certaine in religion; nothing hereticall, corrupt, and damnable in opinion and do-

* The *Manichees* forbad to pull up any weeds out of a field or garden. Aust. de Mani. *Agrum spinis purgari nefas putant, quod plantæ sentiunt.*

ctrine; nothing immorall, unlawfull, and abominable in practise; nothing perverse, uncharitable, and uncomely in seditions, schisms and separations.

We read frequently the *zeal*, care and courage of Magistrates, Princes and Priests among the *Jews*, much commended for *reforming* Religion; restoring true wayes of piety; suppressing all *abuses in Religion*; Certainly it is not lesse a duty, nor lesse pleasing to God now, *among Christians*, to take all care that the name of *Christ be not blasphemed*; nor the way of truth perverted, or *evill spoken of*. We read also the Spirit of Christ *reproving* as a great sin and omission of duty, that *indifferency* in the Angels of the Churches of *Pergamus* and *Thyatira*; *tolerating* any thing, and condemning nothing; the one suffering those, that held the *doctrine of Balaam*, and the impure *Nicolaitans*, who taught all *libidinous impudicities* to be *free for Christians*: the other for *tolerating Jezebel*, under *the colour of a Prophetesse* to seduce the servants of God. The Apostle *Paul* commands some mens mouths should be stopped, who speak *perverse things* in the Church; wisheth those *cut off, that troubled them*: He gives over to Satan *Hymeneus* and *Philetus*, that they might *learn not to blaspheme*; Denounceth a grievous *curse* or *Anathema* to any that *should presume* to teach any other Doctrine than the Gospell; that *form of sound words* once delivered to the Church, which is *according to godlinesse*; He tels us that there is not onely a word, but a *rod*, or *power of coercion* left to the Church, and its lawfull Pastors or Ministers, for the *edification*, not for the *destruction* of the Church.

Hezekiah, 2 Chron. 29. *Josiah*, 2 Chron. 34. Rev. 2. 14. & 20. *Irenæ. l.* 1. Tit. 1. 11. Gal. 5. 12. 1 Tim. 1. 20. Gal. 1. 8. 1 Tim. 6. 3. 1 Cor. 4. 21.

And however this *power Ecclesiasticall*, which is from God, as that *other Magistratick*, be wholly severed and divided in their courses, while the Civill Magistrate is *unchristian*; yet when he embraceth the *profession of Christianity*, these two *branches* of power, (which flowed severall ways, yet from the same fountaine, God) doe so farre meet again, and unite their *amicable* streams, of Magistratick and Ministeriall, Civill and Church power, as not to * *confound* each other; nor yet to crosse, and stop one the other; but rather to increase, strengthen and preserve mutually each other; while the Minister of Christ *directs* the Magistrate, and the Christian * Magistrate *protects* the Minister; both of them, with a *single eye*, regarding that great end, for which God in his love to mankinde, and to his Church, hath established both these powers in *Christian Churches and Societies*; That neither the bodies, nor the soules of Christians should want that *good*, which God hath offered them in Christ; nor suffer those injuries in society, for the prevention or remedy of which, both *Magistracy* and *Ministry* are the *Ordinances* of God; for enjoying the benefit of both which *blessings*,

Magistratick and Ministeriall power when united.

Καισαροπαπία.

* As those of old that thought *Herod* to be the Messias. *Tert. de præs. ad Hæ. c.* 5.

* As *Eusebius* tels in *Constantine the Greats* time, who joined with the Bishops and Ministers of the Church in good government.

blessings, as every Christian hath a *sociall capacity*; so every lawfull Magistrate, and Minister hath according to their places, and proportions, a *publique duty*, and authority upon them, to see justice and holinesse, truth and peace, civill sanctions, and divine institutions, purely, and rightly dispensed to inferiours, for whose good they a·e of *God ordained.*

11. *In what case onely toleration of any thing in Religion were lawfull.* If there were indeed no rule of the *written Word of God*, which Christians owned as the *setled foundation* of Faith, the sure measure of doctrine, and guide of good manners in religion, both publiquely and privately; or if there were no *credible Tradition*, delivered by word of mouth, and parents examples, which men might imitate for the way of Religion, revealed to them by God; which was the way *before the flood*; but, every one were to *expect dayly*; either new *inspirations*; or to follow the *dictates* of his own private fancy and *reason*; Nothing then would be more *irreligious*, then to deny all freedom, publique, as well as private; nothing more just than to *tolerate* any thing of opinion, and speculation which any one counted his religion; yet even in that liberty, of *walking* and *wandering* in the dark, when no Sun of certain Revelation (divine) had shined on mankinde, the very *light of Nature taught men*, as among Heathens, that some things in point of practise, are never tolerable in any humane society. Rom. 1. 32. 2. 14.

But since the wisdome, and mercy of God hath given to mankinde, (which the Church alwayes injoyes) the *light of his holy Word*, and a constant order of Ministry to teach from it, the *wayes of God*, in truth, peace, and holinesse: not onely every Christian is bound to *use all religious* means, which God hath granted to settle his own judgement, and live accordingly in his private sphear, without any Scepticall itch, or lust of disputing alwayes in Religion. But both *Magistrate* and *Minister*, (whose severall duties are set forth, and different powers ordained over others, in Scripture, for a *sociall* and *publique good*) must take care to attain that good of a *setled Religion*, and preserve it in al ways of verity, equity and charity, which may all well consist with the exercise of *due authority*: Nor is it any *stinting* or *restraining* of the *Spirit* of God in any private Christian, to keep his *Spirit* within the bounds of the *Word of God*; wherein the things *revealed belong to us and our children*; Nor is it any restraint to the Spirit of God in the Scripture, to keep our opinions, and judgements, and practises within the bounds of *that holy faith*, and good order, which is most clearly set forth in the *concurrent sense* of the Scriptures, and explained by the *Confessions* of Faith, and practise of *holy Discipline*; which the *Creeds*, and *Councels*, and *customes* of the *Catholick* Church hold forth to them; Nor is it any *limiting*, or *binding up* of the Deut. 29. 29.

Spirit

Spirit of God in private men, for the Christian Magistrate and Minister, to use all publique means both for the *information, conviction*, and *conversion* of those under their charge, as to the inward man; and also of due *restraint* and *coercion*, as to the outward expressions in which they stand related to a publique and common good.

12. *What a Christian must doe in dissolute times.*

But if the *negligence of Governours* in Church and State, should at any time so *connive*, and *tolerate out of policy*, or fear, or other base passion; if through the *brokennesse*, and difficulties of times *the sons of Zeruiah* be too hard for Magistrates and good Ministers; so as the *vulgar* fury, corrupted by *factious*, and unruly spirits, are impatient of just *restraits*; but carry on all things against Laws and wiser mens desires to a *licentious Anarchy*, and *all confusions* in the outward face and publique Ministrations of Religion; yet must no good Christian think this any *dispensation* for any private errours in his judgment, or practise; he must be the more circumspect, and *exact* in his *station*, and duty as a Christian, when the publique course runs most to *confusion*: *tolerating least* in his own *conscience*, when most is tolerated by others: The love of God, and Christ, and of the truth of Religion; and the respect and reverence borne the order of the *Ministry* and to the Churches honour and peace; these must be to every good Christian the constant Law, and *severest discipline*; Teaching him to governe himself most strictly, when others affect *most a misgovernment*, or none at all in Religion; to act nothing immorally, rudely, and exorbitantly; to discharge all his relations, and duties with the more exactnesse; to bear with patience, (yet with sorrow) the *want of that publique good*, which he desires; No way to hinder the restoring of due order and authority to the Church, and honour to Religion; to pray for, counsell, and assist the recovery of it, according to the Scripture rules, right reason, and the custome of the best times.

In maxima rerum licentia, minima esse debet veri Christiani libertas, Gib. *Lex sibi severissima est pura conscientia & dei amor.* Ber.

And however the *vain and mad world* goes on wildly and giddily, as an *untamed heifer*; enduring no *yoke of Religion*, as to any publique order, Government, Discipline, or Ministry; yet must not a serious and well advised Christian delay to *guide his feet in the ways of truth*, and holinesse, nor neglect to work *out his salvation (in Gods way)* till publique distractions are composed: or delay to be good, till all turbulent and fanatick spirits *returne to their wits*; or till ancient publique order and Government in the Church be so settled, and Religion so fortified by civill sanctions, as it ought to be: for no man knowes, how long the *Apostle Paul* may *be in a storm*; or the *Church tossed* with schisms and factions, and secular interests, before it recover the haven of a happy setlednesse.

True Ministers and true piety most to be regarded in licentious times.

Therefore a Christian that makes it his work, not to *prate*, and *dispute*, and to *play* a part, or to gain, by the *name of Reformation and Religion*; but to *beleive* stedfastly, and obey constantly *that holy rule*; hath never more cause to *prize* and *adhere* to the *true Ministry*, and *Ministers* of Christ, than when he sees the greatest persecutions *lying* on the Church, either by violence, or toleration; by open force, or fraudulent liberty; which are (both) the *Divels Engines*, to batter, or undermine the Church of Christ: Never should holy *dispensations* be more earnestly desired and diligently attended from the hands of those Ministers in whom only is the right power, authority, and succession; than, when nothing is lesse tolerated among various and violent men, than a true Bishop and Minister, or a *right* ordained Ministry; which, of all things, is *to the divell* and evill men the most *intolerable*: Satan well knowes, that if he destroy the Sheepheards, the sheep will be scattered. When good Christians see the *abomination of desolation* set up; profanely *tolerating* any thing for *Religion*, allowing of any Mimicks for true Ministers, vulgar adoring of a *rotten Idol* of *licentiousnesse*, gilded over with the name of *Liberty*, when silencing true Ministers, and suppressing good learning, and crying up illiterate impudence, shall be thought a means to propagate the Gospell; Then let them that are seriously and soberly godly fly *to the Mountaines*, (to the true Ministers of the Church) from whom God hath appointed *salvation to descend to the beleeving souls*: Nor are they to regard what every bold and ignorant upstart boasteth and feigneth of *Inspirations*, liberties and blessed toleration; obtruding *himselfe* out of the promptnesse and pride of his own heart upon the credulous and silly vulgar (who love to be flattered to their ruine, and deceived to their destruction, but hate to be truly guided, and faithfully governed *to their safety*;) For all these *pretenses* of *Liberty*, *Toleration*, *Inspirations*, &c. are manifest to be but as the *divels silken halters*, by which he hopes to *strangle* the Christian and reformed Religion here and elsewhere: it may be (seemingly) and with more *gentlenesse*; but not with *lesse malice*, and cruelty to mens soules, than with those rougher *hempen cords of open persecution*.

Matth. 24 15.

Prope abest à crudelitate, nimia indulgentia & à persecutione enormis tolerantia; in tantum periculosa, quantum dissoluta. Melan.

From which, such sad toleration and rude Liberties are not very far; being but *new expressions* of Anarchy, and colours of *portending* confusion, or utter dissolutions of all Church order, peace and Government, into a cruell *licentiousnesse*, which is always tyrannous to true Religion: Nothing is more burdensome than some *mens levities*, nor more fulsome, and deformed, than their *Reformations*; nothing more uncharitable and untractable, than their liberties; nor more a *plague* and *death* to Religion, than, what

they

they call, *health and recovery*; when *vulgar* or *fanatick violence* binds so much the *staffe of discipline*, till it breaks; heady men *surfeit the flock* by *over-driving* it, and Wolves in sheeps cloathing, scatter and tear the sheep of Christ under pretence of letting them goe, whither *they list*; in stead of being true shepheards, fetching them home, and feeding them in *due bounds*, with good pasture: in which wholsome and safe bounds, both *Christian Magistrates*, and *true Ministers* should seek to feed the flock of Christ; not as *bare spectators* of their *wanderings* and *errours*, but as *enabled* and intrusted by God with a *coercive* power from Christ, for the Churches good: and where the Magistrate is negligent, there the Minister should be the more diligent in the place where Christ hath set him; who is the *great Shepheard of our souls*, beyond whose holy bounds for any Christians to affect any *Liberty*, is to *wear the divels livery*, while they are in *Christs service*. Few men complain of *want of freedome*, but they whose freedome would be their own and other mens *greatest bondage*: Nothing is *lesse desirable* to a good Christian, than to be *left to himselfe*: for men are then *neerest to be undone*, when they *may doe*, what they list; and least in safety, when they are their own keepers.

Sic vigilet tolerantia, ut non dormiat disciplina. Aust. l. 17. de verb. Ap.

ὁ ἀρχῶν ἀεὶ τῶν νόμων παταςεῦν. Thucyd.

Libera me a malo; hoc est, a me ipso. Ber.

The 6 Cavill. *Against the maintenance of the Ministry, as setled by* Law.

MY next *Calumniating Adversary*, against the Ministry of *England*, which I have to deal with and detect, is possessed with a *thirsty* and *covetous Spirit*; which would fain have *Liberty*, if not to speak, and act, what he list in Religion (without any restraint of Magistrate or Minister) yet at least to *pay* what he list to any *Minister*, since he is free to hear whom, and when he list, or none at all; he would not be tyed by any law to pay any thing to their support, although it be due to them, and a right which none else might challenge. He likes not *that setled maintenance*, which they challenge as due. This subtill and *frugall churl* of a Christian is a Jesuitick terrien, hath many wary fetches and windings against the Ministers of the Gospell in the reformed Churches; but none beyond this plot, that he hopes ere long to be too hard, or too cunning for them here in *England*: while under some specious, and politick pretention, he shall deprive them of all setled maintenance; and by so spoiling and distressing the Ministry, he shall be sure to pillage, and lay waste in a short time, all the *reformed Religion*, and face of any Church in *England*.

Answ. 1. *The vilenesse and sordidnesse of such spirits,*

This thirsty and covetous Divell is the eldest *son of Pluto*; *Beelzebubs Steward*; a perfect *hater* of the true God; a servant of *Mammon*; the

the very *ghost of Nabal*; a *child of darknesse*; an enemy to all *saving light*; so *deformedly* black, that he is ashamed to shew his face, but under the veil of religious, and reforming pretences; his *envious*

Matth. 26. 8

eyes, like Judasses, cannot endure to see any *costly effusions*, which the devout and liberall piety of former times have powred upon the *heads of Christ* and his *Ministers*; which some men would now

vers. 12.

make to be but an *Omen*, or presage, that their *death and buriall* is not *far off*; The envy and anger of these *Antiministeriall adversaries* is dayly and lowdly clamorous in *speech* and *pamphlets*; To *what purpose is this waste*; might not the *Glebes* and *Tythes* be sold, and better imployed? when there are so many *frugall undertakers*, who are able and willing to preach the *Gospell gratis*;

Joh. 12. 6.

Non nulli pari dolore commoda aliena ac suas injurias metiuntur. Tacit. hist. 1.

who would be no *burthen* to the *people*? Not *that Judas cared for the poore*, nor these for the people; but, *because he was a thief, &c.* What these envious objecters will be, time will best shew; at present their *eyes are evill*, because *other mens* have been good; and, as by an *ignorant confidence* they contradict the Apostles question, *Who is sufficient for these things?* so by a *sacrilegious ingrati-*

2 Cor. 2. 16.

tude they hasten to answer the Prophets question; or rather the

Mal. 3. 8.

Lords; *Will a man rob God?* Yes; these *projectors* for Atheism, Bar-

ὁ δεινὸς καὶ πάντολμος τῆς φιλοχρηματίας ἔρως. *Is Pel. l. 3. Ep. 24.*

barity and profanenesse, would fain perswade this whole Nation to join with their cruell and covetous design; to rob so many honest men, and able Ministers of that *maintenance*, which their learning and labours merit, which they have a right to as by law, so by the *possession* of *many hundred years*: that so they may at once *rob* this Church of the blessing of the true Christian reformed Religion; and rob God also of that honor and *holy service*, which both privately, and publiquely is done to him by *thousands* of his servants, the Ministers of this Church. It is no wonder, if those that *grudge at the cost* bestowed on Christ meditate to *betray him*; and had rather make a benefit or save something by his death, than see any thing bestowed on him while he lives, though it be by others bounty: For alas, what these men *grudge* at as given to Ministers, is little or nothing out of their own purses or estates: Nor is it given by them to Ministers any more than the *rent* they

Isai. 32. 5. 6.

justly pay to their Landlords. But what can *vile men* meditate save onely *vile things*?

Sacriledge against the light of Nature.

And indeed what can be more sordidly vile, or should bee more strange, and *lesse named*, among those that are called Christians, and reformed too; than such *degenerations* from the very *dictates* of nature, and the *common sense* of all *Nations*? Hath any

Jer. 2. 11.

nation *changed its gods*? And if they retained them, as Gods, did

Plato calls Sacriledge ἀνόσιον ἔργον καὶ πολιτοφθόρον. *De leg. c. 9.*

ever

ever any Nation rob,and ſpoil their gods; which yet *were not gods*? Ask among the heathen,and let them teach theſe unchriſtian ſpirits; was it not always eſteemed among men, as an act of piety, and *honor* and vertue, to *devote* any thing to the ſervice, and worſhip of their Gods; as a thankfull acknowledgement of that homage,they owed, and that dependence they had on the *divine bounty*? Was it not likewiſe counted in all times a moſt * *impudent* and *flagitious villany* to take take away any thing rightly dedicated to divine, and holy uſes? So far the *very light of nature* taught men to abhor ſuch *execrable theeveries*, and rapines, that it was by the * *Romanes* eſteemed as paricide, or murther of parents, worſe then Treaſon: a fighting againſt God. It was eſteemed an high ingratitude, not to devote and and dedicate ſomething; how much more to alien or take away from *Gods ſervice*, who is the giver of all?

ἱεροσυλεῖν, τρόπῳ καὶ νόμῳ λύ]ποντος ἔργον. *Polyb. l.* 6.

Facultates numini ſacratas nulla lex, nullus caſus facit caducas. Sym. m. V.

* Act. 19. 37.

* *Sacrum ſacróve commendatum, qui dempſerit, rapſeritve, paricida eſto.* Leg. 12. Tab. *Soli cum Diis ſacrilegi pugnant.* Curt. l. 7.

Now, why any Chriſtians ſhould take any ſuch liberty *againſt their God*, which the very *heathens abominated*; (and which the *primitive Chriſtians* never practiſed, but *contrarily dedicated* many great and rich things to the ſervice of God in his Church; which were called (*Patrimonium crucifixi, Donaria fidei, Anathemata Dominica, Depoſita pietatis,*) the pledges of piety, the bounty of beleevers, the donatives of love, (depoſited with Chriſt, a faithful repayer, no leſſe than an ampler deſerver of all things) I can ſee no cauſe, but onely that the divell, and evill men have more ſpite at our Religion in *England*, both as Chriſtian, and as reformed, than at any other, and therefore they envy any thing,that may be any means to continue, or incourage it. And ſince he could not keep us in *Idolatry*,he tempts us to *Sacriledge*: which the * Apoſtles queſtion clearly implyes to be a ſin equally or more abominable to God; The one robbing him of *his ſervice*, by a falſe worſhip; the other of the meanes dedicated to maintain his true ſervice and worſhip; Which was one of the deſperate projects of *Julian* againſt Chriſtian Religion; who tooke away the gifts and holy veſſels, which *Conſtantine the Great* had given to the Churches uſe, and Miniſters maintenance,with this ſcoffe; See in what goodly veſſels the *Nazaren* is ſerved!

Puniunt ſacrilegos Ethnici, cum ipſi de deorum poteſtate diffidunt. Lact. Juſt. l. 3. c. 4.

Sacrilegio proximum eſt crimen læſæ majeſtatis. Juſtini. Leg. Jul.

Tert. Apol.

Irenæus, l. 4. *cap.* 34.

Origen. in. Nume: cap. 18. *hom.* 11.

* Rom. 2. 22.

Theodoret. l. 3. *cap.* 6.

But the great *grievance* which theſe men cry out of, and hope will be very taking with tender *conſcienced covetouſneſſe*, is this; That the *Miniſters* of the *Goſpell ſhould have Tithes*; At theſe they are ſcandalized, as much as a *Jew* would be at eating of *Swines fleſh*; They are ſo afraid of *turning Jews* by paying *Tithes* to Miniſters, that they had rather *turn Turkes*, by taking quite away both Tithes and Miniſters: How well doth our *bleſſed Saviours ſeverity* fit theſe mens *hypocriſies*? while they ſtrain at the *gnat of Tithes*, and *ſwallow*

2. *Againſt maintenance of Miniſters by Tithes.*

Matth. 23. 24.

Ooo down

down the *Camels* of *rapine* and *Sacriledge*: they stumble at the *straws* of Tithes, and leap over the *beames* of *cruelty* and *unjustice*.

Tithes due by a civill right of Donation and Law cannot justly be taken away.

See Sir *Edward Coke*, on *Lit. Ten. l. 1. c. 9. Sect. 73.*

An. 850. King *Ethelwulp* with the Prelates and Princes in severall Provinces of all *England* (*gratuito consensu*) of their free will endowed the Church with the tithes of lands, goods, and chattels; *cum decimis terrarum, & bonorum aliorum sive catallorum, universam dotavit Ecclesiam, per suum Regium Chirographum.* Ingulph.

For if *God* had no right to require; or there were no word, commanding the *Tenths* to be devoted to his service, (who is *Lord* and *donor* of all:) or, if he had never *assigned this right*. (since himselfe needs nothing) to his *servants* the Ministers under the Gospell, (as he did most clearly under the Law:) yet sure the *Proprietors*, which were Princes, or Peers, or people of this land, (our *pious progenitors*) had a civill right to the *land* and the *fruits* thereof; which no Law of God ever forbad them to dedicate, as they had a mind, to the service of God, or any portion of it, as they pleased to the maintenance of the *Ministery* of the Gospell; Nay they (as all men) were incouraged, yea and commanded, to *honour God with their substance, Prov. 3. 9.* This they have often done, by the full and frequently renewed consent of all Estates in this Nation, for many hundred of years past; establishing by curses or Anathemas, and by civill laws the *dedication* of those Tithes, which are *Feudum Dei*, Gods fee, and his Ministers chiefest maintenance; So that, if these *Antidecimists* cannot think them sufficiently proved to be *Gods immediate gift* to his Ministers; yet they may easily see it is *mans gift to God*; that is, for the maintaining of his publique service, and Ministry of the Church: whereof the *donation* cannot but be, both in Reason and Religion, very lawfull; and so the enjoyment of them, at least in that tenure, very just; since it was done by the *right owners*, to a very right and good end: Nor doe I see how the alienation of them from that *holy use* can be lawfull, now, by the will of any men, since the title and *propriety is now in God*; though the use of the fruit be in in the Ministers of God, as his *Feodataries* and tenants, or homagers.

Qui augere voluerit nostram donationem, augeat omnipotens Deus dies ejus prosperos. Si quis verò mutare vel deminuere præsumpserit, noscat se ad Tribunal Christi redditurum rationem, nisi prius satisfactione emmendaverit. In lib. Abingd. *Quod divini juris est id nullius in bonis est*, Iust. In stit. l. 2. tit. 1. *Prov.* 20. 25. It is a snare to the man who devoureth that which is holy, and after vowes to make enquiry.

2. *Not honorably or piously.*

And if there could be a lawfull *resumption* by posterity, or an *abrogation* of the will of this Nation, in what it hath thus dedicated and given to God, if this could be done without a *crying sin of sacriledge*; yet doubtlesse the piety and honor of this Nation is still such in all worthy mention, that it would never be done by a *free Parliamentary and publique vote*: since, if all humanity and honour forbids any man to *resume* the gifts of charity, which hee hath once given to poore men, whereto they have *both mans and Gods right*, (as freely given to them for Gods sake by the lawfull owners) much more doth all *piety* and *religion* forbid

* *Nemo potest mutare consilium suum in alterius præjudicium.* Reg. Iuris.

forbid any men (νοσφίσασθαι to take away, or *subduce* by force or fraud, as *Ananias* and *Saphira* did) any thing, that is once by themselves (or others) dedicated to God: especially in such a way of service, which he requires in his Word; That is, for the maintenance of that order, government, and Ministry of holy things, which the Lord hath *appointed* in his Church. Which cannot be done without necessary subsidies of *life*, for Ministers, as men; And since a *power of demanding*, and *receiving maintenance* is in the true Ministers of the Gospell, in *Christs name*, (as the Apostle *Paul* proves; no doubt there is no lesse power in Christian people, of giving them, or rather *paying* them, as * a *due debt*, both in divine, and humane *equity*, either in occasionall, and moveable maintenance; or *fixed* and *perpetuall*.

Eusebius tels, that before the ruine of *Ierusalem* so impudent and violent were wicked men, that they took away the Tithes and benefit of the Altar from the Priests, so as many died for want, *Hist. Eccles. l 2. c. 20.*

* *Act.* 5 3.

Why hath Satan filled thy heart to ly to the Holy Ghost, and to keep back, (or defraud and purloin) part of the price of the land? * 1 Cor. 9 6, 7, 8, &c. Gal. 6.6.

The first was the way of *Ministers* and *Bishops alimony* in the *primitive unsetled*, and *persecuting times*; when Christians could not expect to be long masters of their own estates in lands; nor could they *endow* any Minister or Church with any part of them, to perpetuity; yet then in those hard and perilous times, we read in *Ecclesiasticall* stories, that the liberall *gifts* and *free-will offerings*, of all manner of good things, from the devout Laity to the then most deserving Clergy, amounted to more, than the after setled *means* by way of Tithes.

Ne invidia Clericis obveniat de possessionibus Ecclesiæ obtulit plebi B. Augustinus malle se ex collationibus vivere ut antiqui. Sed id Laici suscipere noluerunt. Poss. vit. Aust.

Which way of maintenance was as anciently, so generally setled in all Christians Churches after *Constantines* time, as well as in *England*: The benefit of which, as in all other things, thus given by *beleevers* to God (as a grateful acknowledgment, of his *dominion* over us, and all we have; of his *bounty*, conferring all upon us; of his *mercy*, vouchsafing to accept from us any portion of that, which *is his own*) returnes, indeed, to the *bosome of the givers*; and aimes, next the glorifying of God, at the spirituall and eternall good of their own souls; Nor can *God be unthankefull* to those, unto whom he gives the *grace* of being so *really thankefull* to himself, for what is done to the *Ministers* of Christ, is as done Christ himself; and what is done to Christ redounds to a mans own good: The divine munificence as

3. *Nor wisely.*

Am. Marcel. lib. 27. *De Damaso & Ursicino pro sede Episcopali ad cædem & sanguinem civium contendentibus: Hanc enim (inquit) adepti, futuri sunt ita securi, ut ditentur oblationibus matronarum; procedantq; vehiculis; circumspecte vestiti; epulis curantes profusis, adeo ut eorum convivia regales superent mensas.* *Primitias tempore regis Canuti contribuebant Ecclesiæ, quam contributionem. Semen Ecclesiæ*, Church seed, *appellabant*, Fleta, l. 1. c. 37. St. *Austin* complains in his time, *Majores nostri ideo copiis omnibus abundabant, quia deo Decimas dabant; & Cæsari censum reddebant. Modo autem quia discesserit devotio dei, accessit indictio fisci. Nolumus partiri cum Deo decimas, modo autem totum tollitur.* Aust. hom. 48.

the heavens alwayes returning with liberall showres and fruitfull dews upon us, what ever gratefull *exhalations* our devout humility (as the earth) sends up to him; either in *charity* to the poore, or in a *liberall requitall* to his Ministers: Neither of which are welcome objects to those *ravenous appetites*, who so much grudge that Tithes should by any title, though never so free gift, which is very just and good, be given to Ministers, and enjoyed by them; When once these hungry stomachs have satified themselves with the *flesh* of Ministers; the *Clergies maintenance*, or *Churches Patrimony*; who may doubt, but they will also *pick the bones* of all Colledges, Hospitals, and Almshouses? Nothing being sacred to a sacrilegious minde; nor unviolable to a violent and rapacious hand. Nor is it a hope so much to relieve their own *necessities*; but a kinde of *wanton cruelty*, which makes many of these *Evening Wolves*, so fierce and ravenous against the Ministers maintenance: Nay, many of them covet nothing more, than to see all the excellent *Ministers of England*, reduced to the same beggery, which the meanest of themselves now contend with all, or lately did; so little have most of them profited by their *over thrifty piety*: Nor are such *illiberall* souls ever to be *satisfied* with good things.

Sacrilegis nil sacrum. Hierocl.

** An. 587. Synodus Matisconensis de decimis leges renovavit: quas Christianorum congeries longis ante temporibus custodierat intemeratas. Can. 5.*

Synod. Moguntina sub Carol. M. an. 813. Can. 38. testatur, Imperatorem tributa remisisse, & eorum loco decimas Deo assignasse.

* τοῖς ἱεροσύλοις ἱερὸν οὐδὲν

3. *Against Tithes as Judaicall, &c.*

But Tithes are *Ceremoniall, Legall, Typicall, Judaicall*, and (which *visard* makes every *face ugly and terrible* to the vulgar) they are *Antichristian*.

Answ. 'Tis possible some simple *countrey people* may be *scared* to subscribe against Tithes with these *bugges words*; But sure, for these men, who pretend to *fright others*; I beleeve they have no more *reall horrour* upon them, to take *Tithes*, or more, of others, either as they pretend to be Preachers, or as they are Lay *Impropriators*; than the *conjurers* in *Lapland* have, who make many strange faces, and fearfull noises, as if they had raised, and espyed a *divell* in their circle; when all is to get but a little money of the *silly spectators*: The meaning of all this *great cry* against *Tithes* of Ministers is, to save a *little wool*, though the sheep be the *more scabby*; to spare some small matter, which some of these objecters (it may be) *yearly pay* to the Ministers, with much regret and murmuring: Yea, it is generally observed, that these *clamorers* who make the *greatest cry*, doe not yeeld the fairest *fleece*; nay most of them not one grain to the feeding, nor one lock to the *cloathing* of any Minister; nor indeed have they much wooll (for the most part) on their own backs, which makes them envy all that have. *Sheep* are silent under the *shearers hand*: but *dogs* are prone to bark and

and snarl at those that *feed them*: of whom the Apostle *Paul* bids the *Saints*, *Bishops*, and *Deacons* of *Philippi* to *beware*, as of *evill workers*; who are not content with the *circumcision* of Ministers maintenance, which hath been already too much made, by severer hands; but they aim at a *totall concision*; a taking all away. As for these *Repiners*, they are not so *guilty* of *paying Tithes*, as they would be of *receiving them*; 'Tis as much a *covetous*, as an *envious* spirit, which possesseth them: Yea, rather than fail of their designe against *Ministers*, they are not content with their own not *paying* any thing to Ministers, but they *repine*, that any men else should; whose gratitude and religion teacheth them to give to every man what is their due, especially to the Ministers of Christ, which they justly doe, as with a good will and chearfull minde, so with a good will, and with a far more judicious and upright conscience, both to God and man, than these covetous cavillers can possibly *carp*, or *grudge* against them; who, *poor men*, every day think they grow *leaner*, while they see or hear any Minister hath what they call a fat Benefice, or a *competent Living*: Although the *faithfull Lamp* spends its self, and all the Oil too, in the place, where hee receives it. Phil. 3. 2.

But these *murmurers* cannot digest the *Jewishnesse* of Tithes, and they are still fancying, and afraid some costly sacrifice must needes *goe along*, where ever *Tithes* are continued. *Of Tithes as Jewish.*

Answ. It may be, these men cannot *endure Tithes*, unlesse the *Jews* might enjoy them; who (although still *crucifying* Christ in their malice, hardnesse, and blasphemies, yet) these men seem far lesse averse from entertaining them with their fawning and flattering insinuations into their bosomes, than from maintaining or countenancing those Ministers who preach and beleeve in Jesus Christ *crucified*, as the onely *Messiah* and Saviour of the World; Nay these *Anti decimists* glory in two things, as *high tokens of their Sanctity*: one is, their endevours, first, to further the *conversion of the Jews*: the second is, to hasten the subversion of the office of the Christian Ministery: Nor doe the *Jews unwillingly* flatter them sometimes, as very great *factors* for them, when they see what rare *Jewish projects* they have common with them; against both the name and faith, the Church and Ministers of Jesus Christ; who had never so prevailed by his word against the *Jewish pertinacy*, and obstinacy, if he had not had an able, constant, faithfull and ordained Ministry; nor had this Ministry without *miracle* continued, if there had been no constant *maintenance*; which the more settled it is against covetous and ungratefull spirits, the more is the preaching of the Gospell, and its power likely to settle, in all *humane reason*; (Notwithstanding that the corrupt lusts of men are prone sometime to abuse peace and plenty, as *David* did his *leisure*, strength, and retirement;) One would think, that these men did forget, that the *Ministers* of the Gospell are men, as well as the *Jewish Priests* were, and that they have mouths given them not onely to feed others with the Word of life, but also themselves with bodily food, as the necessary *staffe of life*: Yea, they not onely may, but ought *to live of the Gospell*, as the Priests did *of the altars service*. Indeed the words and spirits of these *Calumniators* against Tithes and Ministers doe signifie, as if it would more trouble them, to see the knife of a Priest ready to *slay a beast*, than to see the *rudest fellow* of their faction ready to cut any *Ministers* throat in *England*.

Thou shalt not muzzle the mouth of the Oxe, &c. 1 *Cor*. 9. 9, 12. 13, 14, &c. The Oxe hath a mouth to feed himself as well as feet to tread out the corn for others.

But it is strange these men should now be so *squeamish*, as to Ministers *receiving of Tithes* (which were by the piety of our ancestors, given of old to them, or to *God* rather, for his service: And this not by Ministers perswasion, or importunity so much, as by the good will, and devotion of this *Christian Nation*) when themselves have alwayes so *good stomachs*, that they devour nothing more easily and *digest nothing* more chearfully, than these *sacred morsels*, when either they *fraudulently detain* them, or *injuriously* deny them to the Ministers; to whom in all justice and humane law, (it is clear) they belong; yet it is stiled by one of *this party* a *consciencious sincerity* in *many*, that refuse to pay them; Is it not rather a detestable *covetousnesse*, (which is *Idolatry*) that denyes, or defrauds any man of their due? is it not an abhorred sacriledge, that rob the Ministers of theirs? for which right or dues they have as much to shew (at least) as any man hath for any thing that is his, by the Laws of the land: Sure, we are but a very *base* and bad *Nation*, if many (as we are lately told by one) of the *very best* of the people, had rather in *conscience* and sincerity doe other men, and especially *Ministers* so great wrong (who must starve most of them with their families, or beg their bread having no other *livelyhood*, if they have not this) than pay, what is due to them, and so necessary for them; O *consciences* more thrifty, than tender; more *scraping*, than *sincere*; which have thus much of the *Jew* in them, that they make little or no conscience to cousen any, that are not of their own Tribe or faction; When did any of these *sincere men*, as he cals them, make *conscience* to pay their *Tithes* justly? or if not in that kinde, when did they make *conscience* to pay, as much, or more of *free* will to the Minister, as their Tithe came to? They might soon pull this thorn or scruple out of their consciences; if in stead of the tenth they would pay rather a sixth or seventh part, or any, that is not short of what the Law of man commands: so they shall bee sure, neither to savour of the *Jew*, nor of any injustice. But still we

Col. 3. 5.

Proposals of *H. R.*

O quam religiosa sunt avarorum delicta! Cyp.

Non statim religiosi sunt quia impune sacrilegi. Min. Fel. de Rom.

we may observe, when some men handle *Conscience*, their meaning is to lick their *own fingers*: But when, I pray, are these *sincere and best of men*, any whit *scrupulous*, or tender conscienced, in the point of their *possessing any Tithes* by an *Impropriate Lay-tenure*? When did any of them ever complain of them? when were they *surfeited*, or *over-charged* with them? Notwithstanding there is more *of the Pope* in an *Impropriation*, than in any thing else, about *Tithes*, for Tithes were generally so *Impropriated* by *his authority*; and are held in no other manner now, than as they were by the *Popes power* aliened *from the Rectory*, to some Monastery, or Religious house. *Statut. Hen. 8.*

So that as *Cato* merrily, yet severely said of the *Tuscane Sooth-sayers*, (who were least of all such, as their name sounds) Hee wondred they could forbear to *laugh* at one another, who so well knew each others juggling, and their own knavery; So may I reply to these *scrupulous Antidecimists*: Sure it is but their *sport and merriment*, thus to abuse *simple people*, with their *over-righteousnesse* or superfluity of malice rather, feigning a sense of that, as a *sin*, and *unlawfull* in *Ministers*; when *themselves practise* the *same thing* most willingly on very suspected grounds without any remorse, or scruple; as if they had an excellent good title from the *Pope*, and the Laws for Impropriate tithes (where the very end of peoples *paying Tithes* is frustrated; (which is their Institution and direction in the publique service of God;) And yet neither God nor man could give a good *title to Ministers* for receiving Tithes; who carry on that great *good end*, for which impiety and equity they were designed; which is to help on people in serving of God, and saving their soules; Such self-condemned, and unexcusable *cavillers* seeme in many things to be *children*, (as in peevishnesse, and inconstancy: in the most commendable quality (*innocence*) they are least like:) but I wonder they should be so much *babies*, and so weak in understanding, as to this point of Tithes, (unlesse, because they are too much men in *malice*) since this subject *about Tithes*, as the setled and best maintenance of the Ministry of the Gospell, hath been so clearly, fully, and learnedly explained, proved and asserted by all law, both *divine* and *humane*, by *many excellent pens*, not onely of Ministers, but of others; who may be thought more *impartiall* (as Gentlemen, and Lawyers.) both long since and of later times; But the way of these Antiministeriall men is to read no books, whose title they prejudge, nor to admit any truth to their partiall tribunall, but what is saving; (they mean, and so do I) to their purses.

Rom. 2. 1. Cui absolvi potest, qui nec sibi est innocens? Amb. off. l. 1. c. 12.

41 *Of the ancient right and use of Tithes.*

To refresh their memories therefore in so trite a subject; and stir up their duller consciences by a little account; I wonder how these *Scrupulosoes* can be ignorant, that Tithes were of *divine use* be-

fore

fore the *Jewish* constitutions: That they draw their *origin* either from the *common light* of Nature; or from that traditionall Theology, which was in the Patriarchs of old: which dictated, as a *Deity*, so a *Priesthood*, or Ministry to serve it; also a duty to consecrate, ordain, and maintain for that publique service some men, who should be fittest to attend it. Doe they not read that *Tithes* were paid by *Abraham* the father of the *faithfull to* * *Melchisedek* the *Type of Christ*? And why then should any *worshippers of Christ*, who are children of *faithfull Abraham* (by imitation of the same faith, which was in him, long before the Law of *Moses*) think it a *sin* or *error* in them, to pay *Tithes to Christ*, (the *Antitype*) by the hands of *his Ministers*; who are* *deputatively*, and *Ministerially himself*? whereas indeed it may rather seem a sin not to pay them; since we see Christ hath so good a title to them, who yet did not claime them when he lived, because the *Leviticall* Priesthood was yet standing; yet *Luk.* 8 3. divers that had been cured ministred to Christ and his family of their substance, and *Matth.* 10.10. he declares the Ministers right to be as good, as the labourers to his hire. If he that *receiveth* you, *receiveth* me, and he that *despiseth* you, *despiseth* mee; and he that giveth *to a Prophet* a cup of *cold water* in my name, *gives it to me*; if these be true, and Evangelicall; why is it not as true and *Evangelicall, He that payeth Tithes* to you, as my Ministers, *payes them to me?* Whether it be by *private* and *solitary*, or by publique and joint *gift* and *dedication*; Sure the highest right and *claim Paramount* must be eminently in Christ who is Lord of all, more then in *Melchisedeck*; and so either the obligation to pay them, or the lawfulnesse to accept them in Christs name, as a right to him; or as a free gift offered from beleevers to the honour and service of Christ, must needs be evident in all justice and religion; (As water is purest in the Fountain, and light clearest in the Sun, so is *Melchisedeks* right most in Christ:) Nay I think in good earnest, that a *Christian Jew* would hence draw an argument, (although he were of that *tribe of Levi*, to which Tithes were after commanded to be paid *among the Jews*) that he ought now to pay them to the *Christian Ministers*, or to Christ; as in relation to his service, and as an *agnition* of him to be *Lord and God*; since, even *Levi* in *Abrahams loins* paid Tithes to *Melchisedek*; that is, to the type and representer of Christ: *And since the Lord Jesus Christ is the perfection* and sum of the Priesthood and order of *Melchisedek*, he may justly claim what ever was typified; as a due or honour to be done to him; of which this is one; that he should receive Tithes who never dyeth, *Heb.* 7.8. & 15. So that this Evangelicall right of Christ, as those promises to *Abraham*, being before the Legall establishment, is not to be annulled by that law of the *Jews*, which was 400. years after.

Clem. Alex. στρ. 1. tels us that by the light of nature among the heathen (or by tradition) Tithes were consecrated to the Gods. So *Dionys. Halicar. l.* 1.

* Gen. 14.20. 41. Heb. 7. 4.

* Mat. 10 40, Ioh. 13. 20.

Heb. 7.4.8.9, &c.

Gal. 3. 17.

As to the intervenient appointment and after custom of paying Tithes, divinely setled by a positive Law among the *Jews*, (as the then onely Church of God) it carries not any *frown in its face* against *Christian Ministers* now *receiving Tithes*, or others paying them under the Gospell; if there were no Law of the Land devoting Tithes to God, and enjoyning the payment of them to Ministers as a rent charged upon lands, and estates; what sin could it be for any Christian (as many primitive Christians *spontan ously* did) to devote, set apart, and give *yearly the tenth* of all his *encrease* to the *Ministers* of the Gospell? Sure nothing of *right reason*, *Scripture*, or *true Religion*, (which onely should rule the conscience of any sober man) doth teach any Christian to abhor, what ever was instituted or practised among the *Jews*; if it be but after the law of *common equity*, gratitude, piety, or civility, toward God, or man; Else these *Antidecimists* must think they sinned, if they should but cover *their excrements*, which was once a law of cleanlinesse among the *Jews*; Deut. 23. 13. yea the example of God so *confirming* by a positive law, in that his ancient Church of the *Jews*, those *generall dictates* of nature, and the preceeding practise of *Abraham*, paying Tithes to *Melchisedek* as to the Priest of the most High God, and a type of Christ, according to grounds of common equity and naturall piety, or gratitude to God and man; This consideration I say should have the greater inducement to assure Christians; that, what is neither meerly *Typicall*, nor *Ceremoniall*, (as Tithes were never thought to be by any learned or wise men) but rather a thing of common *equity*, and piety; confirmed by a divine positive command, and the choice of God, this cannot but be as *acceptable* to God now, when *dedicated* (by the consent of any Christian people) to his *Evangelicall service*, and Ministry; as it was before either from the hand of *Abraham*, or his posterity: since it is no where forbidden in the Gospell, and by Gods wisdome hath been chosen as the *fittest proportion* under the Law.

Yea, and to those, that have not the *loosest*, but the *liberallest* consciences among Christians, it seems expressely recommended, after *that pattern*, Even so hath the Lord *ordained*, that *they that preach the Gospell, should live of the Gospell*; *Even so*, as they did, who *served at the Altar*; so far as the imitation can now hold; which though it cannot in the *Sacrifices*, yet it may in the *Tithes*, and in first fruits, and free-will offerings, which were frequently, and plentifully brought to the Bishops and Ministers of the *Churches* in primitive times, for their own support and the Deacons, with the poor; If the Tenth, or (*quantum*) *How much*, be not here expressed; yet it is *vehemently implyed*; Else the Apostle had proved nothing, nor given any directions, either for *Ministers* fitting support, or for

Cor. 9. 14. v. 13.

Christians *regulating* of their retributions; if he doth not command them to pay, at least a Tenth, sure he doth not condemn their paying a Tenth part, which they may freely doe, if there were no such divine right pleadable, as this indeed is to all Christians, whose covetousnesse doth not teach them to cavill against reason and Scripture too; However, this is the least, that we can make of that place; if in difficult *times*, (such as the *primitive* were) something were left to the gratitude, ingenuity, love, and *largenesse* of Christians hearts towards their Ministers, (wherein sometime they even exceeded their *power* and *estate* in *munificence*:) yet in quiet times, and in a plentifull land it may well be expected by God, (at least, it cannot be blameable) for any Nation, Church, or private Christian to *give*, and settle such a portion, as the Tenths of *the increase*, upon those that *serve the Lord*, and the Church in the Ministry of the Gospell. It is easily computed, that *Tithes* were not one *half* of the *Leviticall maintenance*; What reason can these men give (beyond their will and despite) why the *Christian Ministry* should fare worse, or have *lesse honour*, than the *Jewish*, since it is in many things, a *better Ministry*? 1. *Clearer* in the light of Doctrine, promises, and prophesies. 2. As *venerable* in the Mysteries. 3. Far more glorious in its chief *Minister* and Mediator, Jesus Christ, the Son of God; the other by servants. 4. Much *easier* in the burthen both of labour, ceremony and charges, to beleivers and worshippers; 5. Yet not lesse painfull to the Ministers, whose spirits are more exhausted by studies, preaching and other Ministeriall duties, than the *Jewish* Priests by more grosse and bodily labours. 6. Not lesse comfortable to devout and pious soules. 7. More universally diffused, as more convenient for all mankind; 8. And never esteemed lesse necessary to the Church, or lesse *acceptable* to God; save onely by *Atheists*, or Niggards; who had rather read that most blasphemous and no lesse irrationall than irreligious book, *De Tribus Impostoribus*, than the four Evangelists; valuing a cheap Alcoran before a costly Bible.

Heb. 7. 19. 22. Heb. 8. 6. Heb. 3. 5.

5. *Tithes not Popish or Antichristian.*

So then, I think I have with a very *soft* and sober fire, quite *decocted* the *Jew* out of *Tithes*, and with as much or more ease, will Antichrist, as *they call it*, or any dregs of Popery, evaporate out of them; Some mens teeth are so *set on edge* by too much *chewing of the Pope*, that they cannot bite, or taste any thing, but it relisheth of *Antichrist to them*; if the *Romish Church* and Bishops did ever use it: If any thing (as I have said) be suspicable for *Popish* or *Antichristian* in Tithes, sure it goes with the *Impropriations*; for if it were blameable to *alien Tithes* from the Ministry, and cure of souls, by annexing them to *Regular* and *Monastick uses*; and if it were not commendable to alien them from both, to *meer secular uses*; where they are usually expended

expended with more luxury and vanity, as with lesse piety and charity, sure the best way was to have kept them in their *originall design*; which was for the *maintenance of the Ministers*: Nor is the Popes trafiquing, or disposing of them, during his usurpation, here any *prejudice* to them, no more than a *blear* eye *eclipseth* the Sun by looking on it, or a foul hand abaseth a Jewell by touching it. That the Popes of *Rome* invented Tithes, is as true, as a learned *Rabbi* of these new wayes, (and a great Preacher too) once told me with most unhistoricall confidence; That *Pope Gregory the great* first invented *Infant baptism*; (which 'tis sure enough St. *Jerome* and St. *Austin*, *Cyprian* and others mention as a *Catholick custome* in their dayes, which was some hundred of yeares before *Gregory*; and they oft declare it to have been an antient, primitive and Apostolical practise; which no Father, no Bishop, no Councell, ever began; but was generally used, as we finde in St. *Cyprian*, from the first plantation of Christianity, and the making Disciples to Christ: Initiating them by water, as the *Jews* formerly had done Proselytes in their Church.) But this is onely in passant, to shew how great confidence attends grosse ignorance in these men; As to this of tithes, so farre as the Pope had to doe with them at any time, I have taken away the foolish scandall and vulgar prejudice, giving in *another place* sufficient account to all that are capable of sober truth; That nothing in Christian Religion, either in *Scriptures*, *Sacraments* and *doctrines*, or in the *order*, power, succession, government and maintenance of Ministers in the Church, are therefore *burnt with Antichristianism*, or with any thing which the *Vulgar* cals *Popery*, because the Pope set his foot sometime in them; For truely then our *Parliaments* (which are accounted sacred in their essence and honour) should be *Antichristian* too; for time was, when they did own the authority, yea and reconcile and submit themselves to the power of the Pope and *See of Rome*. If any men reply *Parliaments* have long agoe *purged* themselves of the Pope and Popery: Truely so have all things else in this Church, and *Tithes* among others, which these mens mouths so much water after; and sure such *squeamish stomachs*, as theirs, would never desire and digest them, (as they doe) if there were the *least grain of Antichrist* or Pope either in *Lay* or *Clergy* mens Tithes; for they vehemently pretend to have vomited up all, that *savours of the Pope* or Popery.

St. Aust. Ep. 28. B. *Cyprianus non aliquod novum decretum condens sed Ecclesiæ fidem firmissimam servans, corrigit eos, qui ante 8. diem puerulum non esse baptizandum putabant.*

Cypr. Ep. 59. ad Fidum, an. 250. *A baptismo post Christum prohiberi non debet infans recens natus, &c.*

But it's lost labour to seek further to pull this *prating worm* out of some mens *tongues*, when the root of it is in their *brains*; if they had but the tithe of common reason and sober sense, they would easily see, how little the Ministers of *England*, or any Christian Church of the like way is *beholden* to the Popes of *Rome*, in the matter of tithes; It had been better for us, that the Pope had never medled with them; which occasioned so many *Impropriations*, and these so many beggerly livings; which can hardly expect or make a rich and able Minister; if these men would really reform, they should promote the *restoring* (by some convenient way) those *Impropriate Tithes* to the Church; But their reformation is alwayes on the taking, not on the giving hand; like the footsteps to the Lions den, all are *towards*, none *frowards*. It's very probable, the Popes made little of their owne lands any where Tithable; if, when they saw the charity of *Christians grow cold*, and their *luxury*, in peacefull times, great, the Bishops of *Rome* perswaded others to settle the maintenance of the Ministery, and to provide for the *double honour* of the *Clergy*, by this *way of Tithes*, which might not be arbitrary, but legall, and certain; Truly it was one of the *most prudent*, and pious works, that ever any of the best Popes did for the Church; (And truly many of them were so wise and holy men, that they might in great part cover and expiate the lesser errours of others; if too much of secular pride, and humane passions had not afterward transported *them* beyond all bounds, becoming *Christian Prelates*) It were a madnesse, onely worthy of these *Antidecimists*, to abhorre to doe any thing, never so sober, which others (now become frantick, and disordered) sometime did in their *better moodes*.

6. *Of turning tithes into a Lay Channell for the ease of some tender consciences.*

But there is a late writer, who hath *projected*, how to *percolate* Tithes so through Lay hands in a *publique Exchequer*, or *Tith-office*, which will effectually purge away all that is *Jewish*, Antichristian, or uncircumcised in them; (as sure as a Monks cowle will recommend a *dead man* to heaven;) I am as solicitous for those officers danger, as *that writer* is for the *Ministers*; lest they prove *tithe-coveters*; when they shall have pregnant hopes, to make their *fees better*, for dispensing those *Tithe-pensions* to their poore pensioners and humble suppliants, than any one *Ministers* maintenance will be out of them; unlesse he be a *strange favorite* of that Court: I suppose *those Officers* for gathering, receiving, and distributing of Tithes in such pensions to the *remnant* of those poore *dependent*, and most patient Ministers, will be more sincere and *conscientious*, for a time, than to take any bribes, or rewards for *expedition*; But it is very probable they will not be men of such metall, as will never be corrupted: And O how sad a project will this be in a short time, if these Lay exactors should be more heavy and grievous, not onely to the poore Ministers, but also to the common people, in their rigorous exactions by troopers or *treble damages*, than ever Ministers were! How deplorable will it be, if these Lay exactors of Tithes should prove *sons of Belial* too, as well as *Elyes sons*; who found, I think, but little of the *peoples tithes*, in the sacrifices; So that, in this *odious reflexion*, that *writers pen* strikes

ſtrikes not ſo ſure, as the Prieſts *fleſh booke* did; and as unſeaſonably too: (which was indeed the ſin, ſerving themſelves of the peoples oblations before God;) while *that propoſer* hath no *tender* conſideration of any poor Miniſters condition: againſt *whoſe conſcience* it may be, as well as againſt his eaſe and profit (*very much*) to be deprived of what is his by a former and better Law; and after he hath laboured hard, then to ride and ſolicite, and pray and pay for his wages; Which of theſe envious *projectors* and ſupercilious diſtributers of other mens eſtates will kindle a fire, or open any door to a Miniſter of Chriſt for nothing? 1 Sam. 2. 14.

Nor doth *that Reformer of Tithes* lay to heart the *diſſatisfactions*, and ſcandall of many as wiſe and as godly mens conſciences as his precious ones are, who are (*ten for one*) perſwaded; that they ought, as by lawes of the Land, ſo in all *Religion* to God, and gratitude to their Miniſters, pay their Tithes *immediately*, and truly to them, which they had much rather doe, than have the beſt place, that any man can fancy in this new deſigned Office and *Exchequer* for tithes; Nor do I beleive a like project would pleaſe that great projector, if one ſhould take his *cloak* from his home, and make him ride ten, twenty or thirty miles to fetch it, every time he would *make uſe of it*. Certainly Tithes are by all equity and law; as much due to every Miniſter in his place, as the *coat*, which that *Propoſer* hath *on his back*. Nor is the *property* of things, onely to be conſidered; but the *proximity* alſo, and the *conveniency* of uſing and enjoying them; which the Law alſo *intends* to every man, in his goods: For my part I *like not*, either the *changing* of the *ſtream*, or of the channell of Tithes; becauſe it will but make it winde further off, or goe more about; and the new channell will lick up a great deale of the *old ſtream*, ſo that but little will come at laſt to the Miniſters Mill. The former courſe of paying them to the Miniſter immediately is much eaſier cleared, where ever any obſtructions or inconveniencies ſhall be found, either as to the Miniſters, or the people; How eaſily are far greater ſums dayly gathered in every pariſh, without any ſuits at Law or trouble, by the ordinary Officers, which may in this caſe eaſily be authoriſed to doe for Miniſters, as Church-wardens and Overſeers for the poor doe in their rates and cuſtomes. The *Viſion* of changing the way of Miniſters maintenance, or of making them receive Tithes by a *mediate* lay hand, hath a further State *myſtery* and politick meaning in it, than barely to *eaſe* the Miniſter and people of trouble; or to wipe off the ſully and ſmut of imaginary Popery, Jewiſhneſſe, or Antichriſtianity from Tithes; which may, through the hardneſſe of mens hearts, have ſomething inconvenient in them; but nothing, that I can ſee, evill or ſinfull, so as to give any tender conscience any offence, more than it would any honest man to pay his debts.

7. But Tithes are *too much* for the Ministers to receive?

Tithes are too much for the Ministers.

Answ. This indeed is the *thorn* I looked for in these *halting Christians*; Here it is that the *shooe* pincheth *envious avarice*: And why too much O you narrow soules? Their ordinary Arithmetick, at their fingers ends, tell them; that the *Ministers* are not the tenth man of the land, and why should they have the *tenth* part of the Increase? I answer, 1. What is freer than gift? and what wiser, than so *publique* and so ancient a gift, of a whole Church, and Nation Christian; which gave to God not according to the measure of these mens thirst, but of the largenesse of their own devout hearts, and as became the riches and honour of this Nation? The Laws of the land passed and conveyed Tithes to the Clergy and their successors for Gods service, even then when they were forbidden, for the most part, to *marry*; and enjoined to lead a single life: O how would the munificence of those times have burst these men with envy against the Clergy in their rich Celibacy; who repine to see them thus moderately provided for, when they are mostwhat charged with families, and many relations! 2. I may retort; No more are those *Lay men* the *tenth persons* in any Parish; who yet may have sometime the *Impropriate Tithes*, it may be, of ten parishes. 3. I adde, all worthy Bishop, and Ministers, that have any competency, are never such *unhospitable Nabals*, as to *eat* their morsell alone; many poore creatures are frequently relieved by them, and blesse God for them; after the example of Archbishop *Warram*, a most charitable and good man, who being sick, asked his Steward what money was in his treasure, and being answered there was none; he smiled, saying, It is well, it is time to go to God: *Erasmus* tels of that Prelates great liberality to the poor. 4. All, but envious eyes, see; that there is not one of ten among other men, but he hath either lands, or moneys, or some trade, and way of livelyhood, which the Ministers seldom have, being bred up wholly to their studies; nor is it fit they should have other cumbersome imployments, since that holy work will take up the *whole man*; if they study to be able and faithfull warriers, and not meerly popular and flourishing fencers:

2 Tim. 2. 4. No man going to war intangleth himself with the affaires of this life. 5. I might plead if not in equity, yet in pity; few Ministers in *England* now are single men; chusing rather to live among Gods cares and thornes, and the incumbrances of *honest* and *honourable* marriage; then either in *concubinary scandals*, or other wayes of luxury and lubricity; which are the divels cushions and featherbeds: Not, but that the godly and learned Ministers of

England

England doe highly honour that *Celibacy* or single life, which is indeed a redemption of the soul from *secular attendance* and cares (with *Martha*) to a *vacation* for God and his holy service, with *Mary*; we condemn not the ancient or modern devotion of any in this kind; when either distresse of times *inforce* it, or purpose of heart doth *chuse* it: Not as a *refuge* and easie *support* of life; but as an *exercise* of *penitence*, *mortification*, charity, devotion, and heavenly meditation; not upon presumptuous *confidence*, or friends *perswasion*, or fond superstition; but upon mature *deliberation*, humble *resolution*, and good experience of that *gift* obtained; which is able so to subject nature to the *Empire of grace*, the body to the soule, the flesh to the spirit, carnall and *sensuall imaginations*, to divine and spirituall * *contemplations*; repressing *innate flames* by holy fervencies, so as preserves the purity both of body and minde, together with the *title of virginity*; so that *votaries*, (not strict and presumptuous, or peremptory and absolute; but conditionate, upon humble, and modest *suppositions* of that *gift and mastery*, which * God only can give them over themselves, in order to an holy *Celibacy*) have yet power of that *Liberty*, in some cases, to be enjoyed, which the great and wise Creator hath allowed to humane infirmity: without any *reproach* either to *Himself*, (who is the *God of Nature*, as of Grace; of the *Body*, as of the *Soul*; of the *flesh*, as of the *Spirit*;) also without any uncomely or *dishonourable* reflexion upon any of his servants, who thankfully and holily use that his *divine indulgence*. We like the *golden chain of Celibacy*, when it is sincere; not *copper gilded* over, but *pure gold* throughout: when it is as an *ornament* or bracelet, which may be taken off, if need require; and not as *fetters* or manacles so strait, so heavy and so severely *sodered* on, as weak nature cannot bear, and true Religion doth not impose.

There have not been wanting many learned, holy and excellent *Bishops and Presbyters* in this Church of *England* since the reformation, who have glorified God, not in a *cloistered* and vowed, but yet in an unspotted and voluntary *Celibacy*; as others have in an *holy* and allowed *Matrimony*: Both of them abhorring those preposterous presumptions, rash affectations, necessitous snares, and rigid impositions of a single life, upon our selves or others; which make many votaries like *fair apples* splendid to the eye, but rotten at the core. We find that of *ten Virgins*, five were foolish. Flesh will *putrifie* in a close *cupboard* as well, as if it be abroad, unlesse it be throughly seasoned with salt. A Cloister is no security to chastity, unlesse there be such a *measure of grace*, as may keep from *secret pollutions*, no lesse then from publique *putrefactions*; wherein who so findes himself so frail and defective, that hee

Luk. 10. 41.

Βίος ἀσκητικός.

1 Cor. 7. 26.

Σύνδεσμος τῆς ἀνθρωπίνης πρὸς θεὸν οἰκειώτητος. Nili de Virg.

Non imperanda est virginitas, sed optanda; Quæ enim sunt supra nos, sunt in voto magis quam magisterio. Amb. de Virg.

* 1 Cor. 7. 7.

* Mat. 19. 11, 12.

Nil prodest carnem habere virginem, si mente nupseris. Jeron. ad Heliod.

Pura & perpetua virginitas est perseverans infantia. Cyp. de Bo. Pudic.

Matth. 25.

Non carnis solum sed & mentis integritas virginem facit. Amb.

1 Cor. 7. 39.

he cannot conquer and command himself; it is both wisdome and piety for him, or her, rather to chuse Gods *Purgatory of marriage*; than the *divels Paradise* of a Monastery: rather to sleep on Gods *bolster*, stuffed with thornes, or hard as *Jacobs* stone at *Bethel*, than to repose on the *divels pillow*, stuffed with doun; Fulnesse, ease and idlenesse breeding and nourishing infinite *swarms* of lusts, which may be hived up, as so many Drones, Wasps or Hornets, in those receptacles, which pious munificence intended only for *piety and purity*; not onely in the title, but truth of *Virginity*. Experience of later ages hath much abated the glory of *enforced Virginity*, and *vowed celibacy*; restoring to Christians, and to Ministers as well as *others*, the honour and liberty of *holy marriage*; which is by the * *Apostolicall oracle* asserted, as *honourable among all men*; and by *Scripturall Canons* granted to Bishops and Presbyters as well, as to any other Christians; and so used and taught in Primitive times: as *Clem. Alexandr.* telleth us. Against which, by a preposterous imitation of that *celibacy*, or single life, (to which the persecuting extremities of primitive times drave many holy men and women; that so the Gospel in its first planting and propagating should not want, (among other Miracles) this of holy mens and womens *chastity* and *severer virginity*, in desert cels and solitudes first, after that in Convents and Monastick societies) some mens after zeal and *emulations*, so superstitiously cryed up *virginity*, as injuriously to cry down the honour of *marriage*, especially among Churchmen.

* Heb. 13. 4. 1 Tim. 3. 2. 1 Tit. 1. 6. A bishop must be the husband of one wife.

Ναὶ μὴν καὶ τὸν τῆς μιᾶς γυναικὸς ἄνδρα πάνυ ἀποδέχεται ὁ Ἀπόστολος, κἂν πρεσβύτερος ᾖ, κἂν διάκονος, κἂν λαϊκὸς, ἀνεπιλήπτως γάμῳ χρώμενος. Cl. Al. στρ. l. 3. p. 329. Ed. Lugd. *Floruit cent. 2. olim discipulus Clem. Romani; quem Apost. Paulus salutavit.*

Which yet was not done, without much opposition, and remonstrance to the contrary, by many holy men, in those times; Among which, most remarkable was that of *Paphnutius*, a *Confessor*, and *worker of Miracles*; who had lost his right eye for Christs sake, whom *Constantine the Great* the more loved and reverenced for that glorious defect; He in the *Councell of Nice*, (where many holy men out of no ill minde, but thinking it would tend much to the honour of Christian Religion, to continue those *strictnesses* of *Virginity* in the Church, in the times (now) of peace and prosperity, which had so adorned it *in times of persecution*; that so it might not seem a matter of necessity compelling, but of devotion, choosing a single life) he *vehemently opposed* what was proposed touching making of Decrees and Canons against the *marriage* of the Clergy; shewing by Scripture and ancient practise, the *lawfulnesse* of marriage in Ministers of the Church; and the many not inconveniencies onely but *mischiefs* also which would follow such prohibitions;

Socrat. hist. eccl. l. 1. c. 8.

whose

whose holy and weighty reasons then swayed the Councell, that they made no such injunctions touching the Celibacy of the Clergy, which after times plentifully cast upon them, as so many chaines and snares; which proved no lesse to the dishonour and stain as of the Ecclesiasticall order, so of all Christianity, than the primitive freedome of virginity or marriage had advanced the honour of both.

Οὐ γάμος κακὸν ἀλλ' ἔννομον καὶ σύμμετρον ἀγαθόν. *Is. Pel. Ep. l. 3.*

In both conditions of life we think a pure and chast minde the best rule or measure; and a good conscience the highest crown or reward. We are not at all taken with gilded frames and titles of *celibacy and *virginity*, put to ill wrought and uncomely pictures of *vitiated* and *deformed chastity*; which is a double imparity, and of the divels deepest dye; when it is, but a colour and *artifice* of those that speak * *lies in hypocrisie*, forbidding both *meats* and *marriage*; Nor yet doe we any whit dispise or undervalue any excellent modern piece of * holy *Virginity*, wrought after those *primitive patterns*, and pristine *originals* of *sublime severities* in holy retirements; yet withall we give that due honor *which holy antiquity*, the blessed * Apostles, the sacred Scriptures, Christ and God himself have given *to marriage*; which hath also its divine beauty and comelinesse, however it be set in a plainer frame of more familiar conversation, domestick cares, and secular businesse.

ut Ecclesia, ita & fœmina virgo esse potest de castitate quæ mater est de prole. Amb. ad Mesal. de virg.

* Ἰησοῦς ἐκ παρθένου γενόμενος ἵνα καὶ γένεσιν τιμήσῃ καὶ παρθενίαν προτιμήσῃ. *Naz. or. 16.*

* Ὅσσον παρθενίη προφερεστέρη ἐστὶ γάμοιο, Τόσσον παρθενίης ἁγνὸς γάμος ἀμφιβίοιο. *Naz. Carm.* * Tim. 4. 3. πνευματικὴ ἐν σαρκὶ ζωή, οὐράνιον πολίτευμα ἐπὶ γῆς, τίμιον καὶ περιμάχητον κτῆμα, *Basil. M. ad Lap. Virg.* Ἀγγελικὴ πολιτεία, καὶ τῆς ἀναστάσεως προοίμιον. *Chrysp. Ep. 2. ad Olymp.* * 1 Cor. 7. 9.

That of St. *Jerom* (whose holy *heats* many times made his pen boil over) was an *hard saying*; *while I doe the duty of an husband*, I cannot discharge the duty of a Christian: St. *Austin* with more calmnesse and judgement, upon the words of the Apostle (*Hee that marrieth not doth better*, 1 Cor. 7. 38.) tels us, The meaning of the Apostle is, so to excite to higher *pitches of piety* in a single life, as not to condemn the lower fourm of *marriage*; And certainly St. *Jerom*, * who was so mighty a *champion* for *Virginity*, or single life, would never have so highly advanced that *above* and against first or second *marriage*, if he had lived to have seen how much the after *softnesse* and delicacy of *votaries* had degenerated from those *primitive strictnesse* and severities, which St. *Jerom* requires: Or, if he had calmly and charitably considered those *violent impulses* of nature, to which others may be as subject, as he confesseth himself to have been even in his eremeticall life; and yet furnished it may be, with farre lesse gift of *continency* to deny and overcome them, than that holy man had; who yet carried not the *Trophies* of his so much

Jeron. Contr. Jovinianum. *Quam diu impleo mariti officium, non impleo Christiani.* Aust. Ep. 89. *Ad majora sic excitat Apostolus, ut minora non damnet.*

* *Jeron. Epist. ad Furiam.*

* *Impossibile est innatum medullarum calorem in animum non incurrere, &c.* Ieron. *Illa sola virginitas Christi hostia, cujus nec carnem libido, nec mentem cogitatio maculavit.* Jeron. cont. Iovin.

magnified virginity, unviolated to his grave. Or, lastly, if he had lived to have seen, and heard the *fedities* and *abominable obscenities*, which afterward rendred many *Monasteries*, and *Nunneries*, as the *divels sinks*; *cages* of most *unclean birds*; and *channels* of all *impudicities*; rather than Gods *cabinets* of Jewels; or the Churches crystall *springs*; or the *Angels rivals*, and emulators; or the followers of Jesus Christ; As those his primitive servants in their persecuted and unspotted purity did, who chose purity with poverty, and chastity with *necessity* in any condition, married or unmarried, rather than *splendid sordes*, and *hypocriticall pretensions*; which the more they *mock God*, and delude the world, and *ensnare* unwary soules to *dreadfull inconveniencies*, the more they sear *mens consciences*, and damn *mens soules*; yea, and when those *dunghils* strowed over with the *roses and lilies* of chastity, and virginity, come to be turned, and discovered, who can expresse, or expiate the *infinite shame*, dehonestation, and infamy, which they bring to Christian Religion?

But this large *digression* by way of vindicating of the lawfulnesse and honor of Ministers marrying, (which a far more eloquent and polite pen of a learned Bishop hath formerly done beyond my praises) is so far *veniall*, as it was more necessary to plead for a setled and *competent maintenance* for them, now, when they enjoy the liberty, and bear the burthens of *married life*; To whom supplies far more, than that of Tithes, were granted then, when under the restraint of Celibacy; which yet was *shrewdly* blemished by *concubinary connivences*; which was the best of those evils, which much wasted the credit and honor of the rich and unmarried Clergy in those times.

The reverend Doctor *Hall*, Bishop of *Nor-*

To speak plain *English*, I suppose that those *objecters* and *projecters* against *Tithes*, and so against any setled *competent maintenance* of Ministers in this Church, (saving those impulses of covetousnesse, and temptations to envy, which are naturall in them) are set up, and animated, by such *Antidecimal proposals* and petitions to drive the Jesuites *nailes* home to the head: That they may urge for the more peevish, politick or superstitious Papists this sharp argument of *poverty*, indigence, beggery, or dependent necessity; which will be the *strongest* reason in the world against *Ministers marrying*; (Against which nothing from the minde of God in the Scriptures, or the practise and judgement of holy men in primitive, and purest times can be, with any colour of Truth, alleadged;) But the poverty of Ministers will, *beyond all the Sophistry of Bellarmine*, without any injunctions, or vows of Celibacy, either bring forth an *unmarryed*, because a *necessitous Clergy*; or else none at all, that shall be worthy (for learning, just confidence, and due authority)

thority) the name or place of a Minister, in this sometime so famous and flourishing a Church; whose honour even among its *enemies*, as well as friends, was not the least in this, That of all *reformed Churches* it had least *sharked* from the maintenance and honour of the Ministers; but maintained them in great part, worthy both of them, and it self. Alas what *hedge creeping* creatures will the Clergy of *England* soon come to be in the next *generation*; when nothing shall encourage the *parents*, or the children of any *wise and provident* men, either to fit them for, or to undertake such an office and calling, as will take up the whole man; and yet afford little or no maintenance; and that not setled, but *arbitrary*, and depending upon *Mechanick* or *feminine bounty*; where he that hath most *craft*, and can best *crowch or flatter*, shall have the *best living*; not according to his *merit*, but his *cunning*. This policy of *starving* the learned and married Clergy of this Church, (making this rich and plentifull land as those desolate and *inhospitable Islands* of old were, whither many *learned Bishops* and *Presbyters* were oft-times condemned and banished by the command of cruell persecutors) will soon make *roome* for the *Priests* and *Seminaries* of the *Romane* party; who will easily supply this Nation with a *better fed* and *better taught Clergy*, than ever these *hungry projecters* against Tithes will be able to afford; who, as they shall be lesse pinched with want, or debased to sordid shifts and complyings; so they will be far better stored with *learning* and al abilities, which may recommend and set forth the doctrins they teach, and the place or function they pretend to: Nor will it be the effect of their policy, in order to advance the *Papal Monarchy*, more than of their *piety* and *charity* rather to draw and confirm the people of this Nation to the *Romish* profession and subjection, (which hath much in it of learning, devotion and Catholick verity and order) rather then to suffer poor people to be led by blinde and base guides into all manner of ignorance, and extravagancy in Religion.

So then in all sober and impartiall reason, how can Tithes, as now they are pared, be or seem too much for the worke or charge of the Ministry? save that to *envy* and *avarice* all, that is anothers, seemes too much: Sure if these men had been *Lay Papists*, nothing would have converted them from Popery so much, as to have seen the rich lands, the *goodly revenews*, the plentifull tithes, oblations and donaries, which are there paid to their *Bishops* and *Churchmen*, without any grudging, yea with much *conscience*, by the *people*, (who in that point are very *commendable*, as in a matter of justice, gratitude and devotion; whose sincerity is never more tryed, than when it makes men *conquerers* of *covetous desires*;)

Invido omne alienum bonum nimium videtur. Tull.

Qqq 2 And

And truly, in this part of a *free and liberall spirit*, most Papists are far beyond these men, who make so great a stir with their *thrifty reformations*, who are still driving the bargain so hard, with God and their Ministers, even in those matters, which concern their soules, that all their piety cannot be worth *three half pence*, since they grudge, if their Religion cost them *one penny*; This wretched temper, as it is little to the honour, so little to the advantage of the reformed Religion; That men should be alwayes thus *sharking upon God*, and his Church, under shews of piety.

Triobolares Christiani.

8. And truly, I am strongly of *this heresie*, against all these *penurious reformers*; That nothing hath more *nipped*, and hindred the progresse of true, and *necessary reformations* in this western world, (as to matters of doctrine, discipline, and manners) or will occasion a greater relapse and Apostasie, than these *sacrilegious projects* and *covetous principles*, with which the Divell hath alwayes sought to blemish and deform, that which is called (and justly in some things) *reformation*. Many reformers are but kites, though they sore high, yet they have an eye to their prey beneath; some men still so propound and manage Church reformation, as if it could not take place in any Church, without *devouring all the lands* of the Church, and *beggering* all the *Church-men*; That to be *reformed*, never so well in *doctrine*, and manners, would not serve the turn; unlesse the *Clergy* suffer *those Lay cormorants* to devoure all; and to reduce the *State Ecclesiastick*, every where, from that dignity and plenty, (the *double honour*, with *which pious predecessours endowed them*) to beggerly and *shamefull dependences*; even upon those mens *courtesies*, from whom, (when they have truly hunted, and by learned paines gained a *just reformation* in points of doctrine and outward manner of religion) yet they shall as *Ministers* be then rewarded with nothing, but the very *garbage*, some poore and beggerly stipends: It is very probable, that the *wholesome waters* of true *Reformation* (which by the confession of many of the learned and *moderater Romanists*, was in many things of religion necessary among them) had been *willingly ere this drunk* by many of the *Romish party*; if this *Sacrilegious star* (which may well be called *wormwood*, although it seem to *burn as a lamp*) had not faln upon the *waters* of *Reformation*; of which many in *Germany*, and other places *have dyed*: because they were made bitter with such *sacrilegious and sordid infusions*; Reducing their reformed *Ministers* to such *necessitous* and *beggerly wayes* of life, that could be little to *their comfort*, or to the honor of their profession; and, no doubt, infinitely to the other mens prejudice and abhorrency of, what they so called, their *reformation*.

Covetous reformers the greatest hinderers of reformation.

1 Tim. 5. 19.

Revel. 8. 11.

Indeed it will be hard to perswade *wise and learned men* (how

ever

ever in other points of *controversie* they may be convinced, and willing to agree with the *Reformed Churches*) that they must without any other cause, but this, that they belong to *the Church*, presently forsake, and forfeit their lawfull and *goodly possessions* to some mens *unsatiable sacriledge*, who make *Church Reformation*, but the *Lay mens stalking horse* to get estates: Men doe naturally chuse to attend on *fat* and ointed *errors*, rather than on lean and starved *truths*: Nor doth any thing render the *Christian* and *reformed Religion* more *dreadfull* and deformed to the view of the ingenuous, and better bred world, than when it is set forth like the *Gorgon*, or *Medusaes head*, compassed with *sacrilegious Serpents*, and circled with the *stings of poverty* and contempt; threatning by poysonous bitings quite (at length) to destroy and devour all true piety: Then which, nothing is lesse *envious* of others enjoyments, or more *prodigally communicative* of its own: The word of Christ, bidding Christians sometimes, as *that young man, to forsake all and follow him*, doth not *oblige alwayes*; nor doth it become *these mens mouths*, who care not, who follow Christ, so as they may get the spoiles of *his naked followers*: Reforming Christians cannot sin more in themselves, and be a *greater temptation* to others, (hindring them *from due reforming*) than, when by their *covetous principles*, and cruell practises, they shall scare men from *true reformation*; and indeed from all *good opinion* of such mens religion; who in the peace and plenty of all other estates and degrees of men study to recommend piety to *Church men* onely, attended with *poverty* and contempt: As if Ministers could not be *godly*, except they were *beggerly*; nor worth the *hearing*, till they were not worth a *groat*: That they could never *trust* sufficiently in God, till they were brought to mean, and *shamefull dependences*, for their bread, upon the *shrunk* and *withered hands* of such men, as these *Antidecimists* are, which they are alwayes stretching out *against God* and his Prophets; Christ and his Ministers: Although piety be a Jewell to be taken up, where ever we finde it, though *in the dust of poverty*; and Christ is *beautifull*, when he is stripped: yet none, but *rude* and *barbarous* hands would *treat Christ* in such a manner, as exceeds their *wanton cruelty*, who crucified him; for when they **parted his garments among them*, they did not own him for their Saviour, or the Messias, as these *self-inriching reformers* pretend to doe.

Ita a natura facti sunt homines, ut pingues potius sectentur errores, quam macilentas veritates.

Matth. 19. 21.

Ministers ought to be by their liberality, as *Synes.* was called, Ἀλλότριον ἀγαθόν.

It was one of the scoffs of *Julian*, when he robbed the Churches and the Christians, He did it that the *Galilæans* might goe more expedite to heaven: ἵνα εἰς βασιλείαν τῶν οὐρανῶν εὐοδώτεροι πορεύωνται οἱ Γαλιλαῖοι.

*Matt. 27: 35.

O sad and sordid *soules*; O mean and *miserable reformers*; with whom the Ministers of this Church of *England* have now to plead, for their last morsell; that little remnant of their *Oile-*

and Meal; Charity forbids me to condemn you, and your *Sacrilegious faction* to be punished with your own manners and designes, which are most wretched, and unworthy the name of the *Christian profession*; which *above all Religions*, ever incouraged most the * *chearfull givers*, and abhorred rapacious *scrapers*; I might say to you, as * St. *Peter* did to *Simon Magus*, *Your money perish with you*; No, I rather wish your *Salvation*, (if possible) though it be without the restitution of, what you have already and intend further to rob Christ of, and his Church, and his Ministers; and his poor too: (for they had a good share in the *Churches revenues*;) Only I wish withall, that all the learned and godly Ministers of the Gospell in *England*, were in such a condition, as to *worldly competency*, that they *could preach the Gospell freely*; that so these repiners might hear them *gratis*, (as *most of them doe* when they vouchsafe to *hear them*) and so without *prejudice*, or grudging at the *maintenance* of Ministers in *point of Tithes*; That so, if it be possible, they may *repent*, and be *converted* from that *gall of bitternesse and bond of iniquity*, in which they are; It were happy if (as St. *Austin* offered to doe) all Ministers could release, that equitable, and Evangelicall power, which they have by Scripture; and that *legall right*, which the law of the land hath given them, to demand and receive Tithes, and other emoluments: That their *necessities* might not force them (having neglected all other wayes of getting, or improving estates, that they might fit themselves by their studies for this great work of the Ministry) either to take Tithes; or (which of all things is most *detestable* to men of any ingenuous spirits and learning) to depend upon *vulgar contributions*; which are so stuffed with pride *in the givers*, and contempt *toward the receivers*; so full of uncertainty; and so *certain high wayes* to basenesse, and beggery (as the genius of most men now is) that there are few *Mechaniques*, who would not disdain to be such Ministers; as must, when they have *done their work*, *beg* for their *wages*; and shall be sure to want them, unlesse they always abound in *sordid complyances* and *flatteries*, with the *vilest men*, and their vilest humours: For however people have now and then a *warm fit of giving* to their *Teachers*, yet it seldome lasts longer than the *heat* of some factious *design* or new fancy melts and thaws them: After that, they soon returne to that *frozennesse*, which is hardly *dissolved* by any mans warmest breathings, to some *few drops*, of incompetent, yet *insolent*, and supercilious *contributions*.

Magis aurum suspicere consueti, quam cælum. Min. Fæl.

Avari pænalibus cumulis oppressi. Cyp.

* Prov. 11.25. 2 Cor. 9.7. God loveth a chearful giver.

* Act. 8.20.

Ne invidia Clericis obveniat de possessionibus Ecclesiæ obtulit plebi Augustinus *malle se ex collationibus vivere ut antiqui. Sed Laici illud accipere noluerunt.* Possid. vita Aug. c. 23.

But I am afraid our distemper is *deeper*, and more subtilly dangerous to our *reformed Religion*, than we are aware of, in this point of Ministers maintenance; The burthen is not, That *Tithes are paid* (for that these projectors doe not intend to *quit* so (either to Land-

lords

lords or poor Tenants :) but that they are paid to the true and ordained Ministers, that thereby they are still continued, and incouraged in their Ministry; The grief is, that as they receive them, so every where they deserve them; The vexation of that is, that *Ministers* are not yet driven out of *their hives*; as Bees after all their labours; by the smoak of some such *sulphurous projects*: that so these *hungry Reformers*, and new *stamped Preachers* with their Jesuitick arts and insinuations may possesse their *honey*; The displeasure of some men is, that any Ministers, worthy of that name and calling; or that any thing of *good learning*, of *studious abilities*, of reall *gifts* and due authority, of the true *reformed Religion*, and piety, should still remain in this Church of *England*, which might hinder its return to the *Romish subjection*; of which those *wiser agents* despair not; when there shall be no better Ministers, than such, as either the vulgar *charity maintaines*, or the *vulgar choice* ordaines.

9. *Answer to the cavill of Ministers excesses.*

As for Ministers *superfluities and excesses*, which some men rather talk of with *envy*, than *prove with truth*; God knowes, few fishermen take fish now with *money* in their mouths, there are not many *golden cups* found in any of their *sacks mouths*; such as may tempt them to any *splendor* or *prodigality*; Alas, the most of them have scarce for *honest necessities*: Look to their poor widows and fatherlesse children, commonly their greatest portion is Gods mercy, and mans charity. And (to the *shame of this Nation*; so blest of God and Nature with abundance) many of them are by the *tenuity* of their *Benefices*, kept far enough from exercising that *hospitable largenesse*, which many of them have in the Theory and speculation, but cannot practise it; which is so commended by the Apostle *Paul*, and required in a Bishops *and Ministers way of living* among men; as having, not more a face of *humanity* with it, than of *Divinity*: (it being the *glory of God* to be *of a bountifull munificence and liberall goodnesse*) as carrying a *sweet savour* with it, making the Ministry of the Gospell, as a *fragrant ointment* poured out; much *recommending* the *Gospell* to men, when they can hear Christs Word, and tast of his *loaves* too; Besides, it gives a great advantage, and *usefull authority to Ministers* in the places, where they live; renders their counsels *more considerable*; their examples *more venerable*; their doctrine more acceptable, and more *credible*; for nothing more *justifies*, what we preach of *Gods bounty* and great *gifts in Christ*, to poor men; than, when they see religious men, and chiefly *Ministers*, most liberall of this *worlds goods*; as believing, they have *treasures laid up in heaven*; which * the poor hand mans (*which is Gods box*) carries thither: And indeed considering the great *numbers of poore* in many or most places of *England* now abounding; and

1 Tim. 3. 2. Tit. 1. 8. φιλόξενος. Iam. 1. 5. 17.

* *Manus pauperis gazophylacium Christi*, Chrysol. *Transmittitur in cœlum thesaurus bajulatore paupere.* Id.

the

the *retrenching* of most mens estates both in trade and house keeping, it were no more, than needed; if Ministers, (who are *constantly resident* among the poore) were able also, to be some *way relievers* of them, beyond *bare* and barren *words of godlinesse*; which signifie little to those, whose bellies have no eares when they are pinched with urgent and extream necessities.

Plus nostra religio vicatim insumit, quam vestra templatim. Ter. de Christianis Apol.

Quantiscunq; sumptibus constat, lucrum est pietatis nomine sumptus facere. Tertul. Apol. 38.

* *Quale affectatio in civilibus, tale superstitio in divinis.* Verul. *Religionis simia quo similior, eo deformior.*

* πενίας ἀκόλουθος δυσωπία. Stob.

Prov. 19. 4.

Qui mirantur opes, qui nulla exempla beati Pauperis esse putant. Iuven. Sat. 14.

Nothing should be lesse *illiberall, than true Christian Religion*; which sets forth the *highest bounty* of God to mankinde in giving Jesus Christ; Nor ever was any thing *lesse sordid*, than Christians in former times; the many *monuments*, here in *England*, of their *religious prodigalities*, and *devout excesses* to the Church and to pious uses, doe sufficiently testifie how far those Christians were from the *niggardize* and *Nabalism* of some men in these times; Then, they thought nothing too *much for Church men*; now nothing is too little: And truly it is a very foul shame that *superstition*, (which is but the * Mimick and Ape, or the wen and *excrescency of Religion*, an Hydropick holinesse, a nimiety of piety, an *overboyling devotion*, which at length quencheth it self) that this should put true *Reformation* to the blush: * *Poverty* is alwayes *attended with shame*, or impudence among the vulgar: and though it have *no cloak*, yet it needs one to cover its own *confusion*; and to keep it from *vulgar contempt*: O how *large hearted* and *liberall handed* in former times, and at present, in other Churches and Countries, is that Religion, which is *commendable* as it is Christian and liberall, however reformable as it is blameable for the *taints* of errour and superstition, which have, in many things, infected it! What hath more splendor, what more plenty, what more superfluity, than those that are of the *Roman* Clergy? who have more *vacancy* to their studies, devotion, and publique duties, than their Ecclesiasticks, or Church men, of all degrees? who have learned to use now those things, far better, than it may be former luxury and dissolution did; which occasioned, many worthy mens complaint of the *abuses* and *faults*; but not their envy at the *enjoyments*? The *moderation* of the *English Church* in this *part of Reformation* was at first very nobly commendable; and most worthy of the *generous piety of this Nation*; which did not deny or grudge *Church men* to have good and great *maintenance*, or honour, but only required that such means should still have *good Ministers*. They never applauded, as these new *Projecters* do, for a most heavenly Oracle, that voice which is faigned to have been offended with *Constantines* munificence to the Church; as if it had been poysoned when inriched: Nor did they thinke Religion *throughly reformed*, till it *was starved*; nor Ministers mended enough, till they were stark naked, or flead. Nor had heretofore the *common* and plain hearted people those *pestilent principles*,

Hodie venenum cecidit in Ecclesiam.

which

which now the *dregs* of men have here in *England taught* them; That an hundred pound a year is more *than any Minister can well spend* or *deserve*; It were good that these men would first try themselves that measure which they mete to Ministers. Certainly nothing is too little for *Church men*, if they lead *men to false gods*, or to a *false worship*; but nothing too much for them, if they teach men to serve the true God, in a true way.

Nor may these *poor spirited* men object against Ministers, the poverty of the *primitive Apostles*, Bishops and Presbyters; when the times, and the estates of Christians are now *much changed* from those *difficulties* and necessities, which then pressed upon all *sorts of Christians*; To be sure, if Christian people gave not then much of *their own estates* to their Ministers; yet, they never thought of taking away, what their *Ministers had*, as being *too much* for them; But, there is no doubt, that one *beam* of Christian love, bounty and respect, in after setled and plentifull times, (which were very pure and *primitive* too) was more *warm* and *comfortable* to their *Bishops* and *Presbyters*, than all the large *streaming tayles* of these modern *comets*, and *meteors of Reformation*; whose *malign* and *direfull aspect* against Ministers and all Church men, is no way recompensed by those *prodigious shews*, and pretensions of propagating the Gospell, or furnishing the world with *purer* and brighter *shinings*, than ever were in the Church; who shall be *lamps without oil*, and *shine without sustenance*: Ministers are *stars in Christs right hand*; but not in that sense, that they need no *fewell* to *nourish* them, in a naturall and civill life: Such *interpretations* of Scripture, and such *entertainment* of Ministers in the Church, will soon eclipse, or extinguish truth and charity, *honour* and *gratitude*, in the *reformed Churches*, and in all Christian professors; not onely to man, but even toward God, who as he hath ordained *Ministers to impart* to the people of their *spirituall things*, so also he hath commanded people to **communicate* to them; that are their * *true Pastors and Ministers*, *of all their temporall good things*: But it is in vain to urge Scriptures, to covetous hearers and *Sacrilegious* mockers of God and man: Nothing is more Apocrypha to those *misers*, than such texts, as command *honourable maintenance* for the Ministers of the Gospell; first recover the primitive bounty and charity of peoples hearts and hands to the Clergy, before you reduce the Clergy to primitive uncertainty.

10. *Answer to the poverty of the Primitive Clergy.*

Revel. 2.

* Rom. 15. 27.
* 1 Cor. 9. 11.
Gal. 6. 6. Let him that is taught in the Word communicate to him that teacheth in all good things. V. 7. Be not deceived, God is not mocked, &c.

But why doe not these *muck-worms* and no men (who would gnaw the very bones and carkases of Ministers) with the same teeth *bite* at other mens estates as well as Ministers, which are far greater every way; who yet doe lesse *service to the publique*, either to God or man, to Church or State, than the *able* and faithfull Ministers

 doe;

doe; since these *whining objectors* have such a pain and *wringing colick* in their *bowels* against Ministers having any setled competent and decent way of maintenance, why doe they not as well complain, that the *Captains*, *Commanders*, and *Military* officers, who draw *more immediately* from *the peoples* purses) have too much for their *pay*? why doe not these men propound, that there should be nothing but *parity, and poverty* among the souldiery? That they should depend on *peoples benevolence*, for their salary and pay? Yet they see that even to these *military* mens entertainment, the poore Ministers must pay; not a tenth, but of a *fifth* part of their small, hardly earned, and hardly *gotten meanes*, arising from their *ill paid tithes*: which are but the *wages* of their work; yet they are rated in taxes, as if their livings were their *inheritance*; when all is but for *life*, and to many of them not so good, as an ordinary *troopers* pay; few so ample, as an ordinary *Foot Captains*: And, as for higher Commanders, and Colonels, all men know, they have *Military Denaries*, and *armed Bishopricks*; enjoying much more, than is by some men thought fit for any *Bishop* and *Clergy man*; who (with their leaves, and without disparagement to any of those sons of thunder) had and have as much learning, true worth, and industry, to merit their *large entertainments* of the publique; and they had no lesse grace and true wisdom to use them, to the glory of God, and the benefit of others, than any of these, who are so much the favorites of *Bellona*, as to get what they merit, and to keep what they have gotten.

But these *Antidecimists* who seek to eat through the Bowels of their Mother the Church, dare *be bold* and shew their *teeth* onely against Ministers; and their maintenance by *Tithes*, (which may be easily proved as lawfull as any taxes are:) They know well, that the *souldiers frownes* and *swords* command their *pay*, and so are able to *curb* these mens *spitefull tongues and griping hands*: only they think they may safely *vent* their *passions and poison* against the despised, dejected, and *unarmed Ministers*; greatly crying out against their small salaries, which no doubt cost these men least, who speake loudest: who preferring, by a most *sinfull* and *brutish judgement*, the welfare of their bodies, before that of their soules, grudge to have any, so *good rewards* allowed to the Physitians of *mens soules*, as are *publiquely granted* to the * Physitians of mens bodies, in the Army. Yea, these men are so in love with their *spirituall diseases*, that they hate their *spirituall Physitians*: and had rather content themselves with any *cheap leaches*, or perish in their *feaverish ravings*, than be at any cost for cure, by learned and able Ministers.

* 20. s. *per diem*, is a Physitians pay.

Heu quam periculosus est iste morbus, quum & infirmitates suas amat, & medicos suos odio habet ægrotus.

But

11. *The Antidecimists pretended care of the Farmers and Ministers quiet.*

But these *Antidecimists* have a fit of *charity* upon them, which troubles them the more, because they are not wonted to it, in regard of other men; (for their charity not onely begins, but altogether stayes and ends at home;) O the *poor Farmers* (they say) finde it *heavy to pay Tithes*, to the Ministers! *Answ.* And will it not be as burthensome to them, when they shall pay them to *some Lay exactors*; who will be as rigorous to the full as ever *Ministers* were? But the husbandman is discouraged, and disabled in his tillage, and husbandry by paying the tenth of his *increase to the Ministers.* *Answ.* What? more now then when they shall be paid to other men that shall be in office, to *gather them*, or to *compound* for them? when did any countryman finde himself *poorer* at the years or lifes end, who made conscience to pay his *Tithes* to the *Minister*? which was ever thought by the *Jews*, (and is no errour I think among Christians) to be as a *hedge*, and *blessing* to the rest of that estate which a man hath; It's certain a Christian man enjoys the *remainder with more peace*, when he payes honestly that which is due to *another*; but chiefly to his Minister, who hath the title of the Law, and of God, and of personall merit, for his Tithes. And is it not a *profound project* meriting a publique reward, for a Christian to propound wayes for *plenty* of corn, and for a famine of the *Word*? So much it rules some mens Religion more to have a *good stomach*, than to keep a *good conscience*: for these, that would alien, or alter the right of Tithes from the Ministers; can make no scruple of any sacriledge, while they make no *bones* of violating the will of the dead, and that holy dedication, which hath been made to God, by this whole Nation, and so continued for many generations.

Massoreth sepes Legis. Divitiarum sepes Decimæ. Rab. Aquiba. Perk. Avoth.

Ditescimus in eo quod Deo donamus. Aust.

But they would not have Ministers *Tithe coveters.* *Answ.* No more would Ministers have such *projecters* coveters of Tithes or any thing else which belongs not to them. But I pray may not Ministers be as subject to the temptation of *covetousnesse*, when their Tithes shall be dispensed, as an *Almes* out of a *common basket*, by a Lay Office? (which is one of their rare and soveraign *antidotes* propounded to cure the Clergies *coveting*) I beleive their meanes will not be much more satisfactory to them by that project: Sure these *proposers* forget that covetousnesse is an * *inordinate* desire of another *mans goods*, or an excessive love of ones own; Honest men are not to be *odiously branded* with *coveting* that to which they have a right, both by *Gods* and *mans laws*: As for the trouble, and scandall of Ministers suing for their Tithes, and *persecuting*, as one calls it, their neighbours; the *proposer* might have far more handsomely *removed* that from people, than objected it to the Ministers; if he had with more *conscience* and *sincerity* exhorted people to *pay their*

* *Avaritia est inordinatus appetitus boni quod alteri debetur jure; aut inordinatus amor bonorum secularium, quæ ab ipso possidentur.* Less.

Tithes as they are due, *justly*, *chearfully*, and *conscientiously* to their Ministers; so as the laws of man (at least) command; which in *things* 1.Pet. 2. 13. *honest* become the Laws or *Ordinances of God*; But not a word of those exhortations to people, because nothing is like *to be got by them*: Although those had better become any Christian man, that pretends to a *publique piety*; or presumes of a capacity to advise a whole Nation; than to teach men first to *detain injuriously*; than to scruple wilfully or weakly the paying Tithes to Ministers; that is, to give to every man what is his due; which is the *rule* of common justice; and the best *project* in the world to preserve either Kingdomes, or Common-wealths in peace.

1 Tim. 3. 3. Tit. 1. 7. 'Tis very true, it becomes *Ministers* least of any men to be covetous or *contentious*; It is worthy of them to suffer *wrong*, rather than *revenge* it in many cases: But if they be by such *ingratefull* projections and *unjust temptations* put upon using the benefit of the Law, to obtain their own, the *persecution* is on the *Laymans* side; who is taught thus, rather to put forth his hand against the Minister, than to him his due in a fair way, in which payment the husbandman, Farmer, or owner of the land, hath no other merit, but onely this, of *quiet* and *honest* payment; for the Tenth of the *Increase* is neither bought nor sold, nor rented to any Landlord, or by any Farmer; God gives the increase; Nature the land; and the Law that *quantum* to the Minister; as *Gods portion*, and the *Churches rent*. Which if some *country Churles* refuse, or grudge to pay to their Minister; so, no doubt, many of them, would to pay their *Rents to their Landlords*, if they had but enough of *John of Leydens* spirits, and *Cripperdolins* principles to *animate* them, and *arm* them against paying, or owning any thing of *Landlords* title or dues; There are many *impure* and *unjust* men, who will soon style themselves *Saints* and the *meek of the earth*, if that be a good title to *claim* the *lands*; and to inherit other mens estates on the earth; as those *false Christs* and *Theudases* did endeavour in Sleid. com. l. 4. *Germany* to the ruine of themselves and thousands of others.

12. *Vindication and satisfaction of the honest Farmer in point of Tithes.*

But by the favour of the Antidecimists, and their *petitions*, which pretend to be so *bigge* with the names of *whole Counties*, and many *sincere godly people* in the countrey, *petitioning* against the *maintenance* of *Ministers* by *Tithes*, that they must needs come up to *London*, to lay their *great Bellies*, at the *Parliament-house dore*; I doe not beleive (because I never saw any ground, or had experience, to think so hardly and uncharitably of any *Country-men*, *Farmers* or others, that are either good Christians or honest men) that ever they did, or doe complain simply and absolutely against Tithes. Possibly they could wish, that some things about them were better ordered, for the *Ministers*, and their owne *greater ease*; which

which may be soon done, if the values of them were once brought to a just rate and *certainty*: and *Collectors* appointed, as in other Town-rates, to gather them in, according to the *compositions* made in money, or goods, by *way of distresse*; which may as conveniently be done in the *Ministers behalf*, as in any other way of collecting publique rates: And if Tithes have *sinned* in any thing; yet what have the *glebelands* of Ministers offended? yet there is as much ill will against them, as the other; though there be evill, indeed, in neither, to any men, but such, as call *good evill*, and *evill good*.

Furthermore to gratifie the plain *country man* and *Farmer with plain dealing*; (who hath the honour *above all men* in this Nation, to be the great supporters (by their *honest* labour, and love) of the *Ministry* and Religion in this *Church and Nation*) they may easily consider, with themselves, how they have no *reason in the world* to be against paying, and *maintaining* their *Ministers* by Tithes: For first, let them but take care, and pray to God for a good, able, and *true Minister*, and study to profit by his holy *labours*, they will never grudge him his *dues in Tithes*, or any thing else; for they will finde they have a good *penny worth for their Tithes* in the *blessing of God*, both on their soules and on their estates; if paying their Tithes were wholly their own *bounty* and gift. Which secondly, they may consider, is not so; but they are as a *rent charged* upon their lands, beyond what they pay to their *Landlords*; only the Minister hath some benefit by their labours, as they have of his. 3. They ought *seriously to consider*; that if Tithes were not by Law *assigned to the Ministers maintenance*, and paid to them, either they will return to the *Landlords*, in advance of their rents: or else be *confiscated* into some publique Exchequer; for the like, or the same, or other uses; But to be sure no *benefit* will flow to the *Farmers*, or countrey mans purse, by the *ebbing of Tithes* from the *Church* and *Ministers*.

As for the Landlords, Gentlemen, or others of estates, and revenews in land; I know many of them scruple their having any *Tithes* by the way of *Impropriations*; they never think they thrived the better for *them*; many of them if their fortunes other ways would bear it, would willingly give them, or at *easie rates* sell them again to the *Church-uses*; Some to their great honour have *freely restored them*; whom it grieved to see so many small Vicarages, and Livings, even ready to starve the painfull Ministers in them; So that I cannot think any true *English Gentleman*, that is a *good Christian*, would accept, or doth covet any such augmentation, which may be added *with a curse* to his *revenews*; by having the Ministers *portion* and *lot* cast into the lap of his inheritance, the benefit

of which cannot be great; but the mischief of it may be very great, to his estate, his *conscience* and *posterity*: And besides the sin; the shame, dishonour and uncomlinesse of such *acquisitions* cannot be little, when once Christians return to their *right wits*, from that popular madnesse, giddinesse and greedinesse which may reign for a time; who will not in sober senses think it most unworthy of *persons of honour*, learning and ingenuity, being *Christians*, and pretending to be more exactly *reformed*; that (these having other wayes fair, flourishing, and *blest estates*) should sell their owne, their families, their countries and their Churches honour and happinesse, (which consists in true *Religion*, and this depends on true and able *Ministers*; and these on competent and *constant maintenance*) as *Esau* did his birthright and blessing for a *messe of pottage*, for some small *sacrilegious additions*; which carry with them a *stain* to their names, a *moth* to their Estates, and a sting to their conscience? Such will be the accepting of Tithes, though freely *given them*, by those, who have no right to *alienate*, or dispose them, otherwayes than the will of the Donours, and piety of the Nation have *setled them* for maintenance of the *Ministry*. And alas, how little emolument will hence arise to splendid and *conspicuous estates*? Tithes like Mole-hils in an Evening Sun, cast long *shadows* from little heights; the noise may be great, the benefit will be little, and the comfort none, from *such morsels taken from the Altar*, to which there hangs *a coal of fire*, which may destroy even *Eagles nests*; and this with the greatest *justice* of divine vengeance; when Christians consider those *robberies* and *sacriledges*, tend, as to *Gods dishonour*, to the *reproach* of Christian reformed Religion, so to the unspeakable temporall detriment of any Church and Nation, besides the *inestimable* losse of many poore soules for ever; who will soon want *Ministers*, that are able and worthy, if there be no other means for them, beyond what can be expected in a *shamefull* and *precarious* way from arbitrary *benevolences*; which never yet failed to fail in a short time, as an *Egyptian* reed, all those that leaned upon them. Indeed, it is a *foul shame* for persons of honour professing Christianity to deal worse with their holy men, the *Ministers* of the true God and
Gen. 47.22. their onely Saviour; than *Pharaoh*, and the *Egyptians* did with their Priests; whose lands they would not buy into the Exchequer rents, no not in extream famine; but supplyed them freely with bread, and preserved to them and their successors the lands, dedicated as they thought to the service of their Gods; which piety that great and good favorite *Joseph* approved; nor doth any zeal for the true God tempt him to unseasonable exactions, *sacriledges* against the imaginary and reputed gods of the *Egyptians*.

And

And here, while I seriously consider the *many and great blessings* both of *mindes* and *fortunes*, which the bounty of God hath liberally bestowed on the *English Gentry*; I am so far from suspecting any such *sacrilegious* basenesse in them, as if they gaped to make a prey of the *Priests portion*, to *devoure* holy things, or to rob the Ministry of their maintenance; That I cannot, but here take occasion, rather to perswade those *true Gentlemen*, whose parts and piety, equall their honour and estates; that they would out of *zeal to the glory of God*, and love to their Saviour, and pity to this Church and Nation; come in, as the (*Triarii*) last assistance, and surest reliefe of the reformed Religion, and of the true Ministry of this Church; which is almost *overborn*, and oppressed, by the cunning and clownish clamours, and not by any true valour, worth or virtue, of their enemies: Nothing would be more worthy of that ancient honour, which the *Nobility* and *Gentry* of this Nation hath gained and enjoyed in all the world, than to see now the *Christian zeal and gallantry* of their spirits, therefore the more forward, to bear up the *dignity* of Christs holy Ministry, by how much they see so many set to oppose it, seeking by contempt to debase it; and by poverty to oppresse it: presuming, that the *present Ministers*, (though never so learned, godly and faithfull) once *over burthened* with *secular necessities*, will not long be able to assert the honour of *their calling*; nor will any after generation succeed to inherit their poverty and paines; but onely such, as shall further debase the *dignity* of the function.

An addresse to the Gentry of England in order to the honour of the Ministry.

As the Bohemian Nobility and Gentry did with great earnestnesse intercede for Jerom of Prague to the Councell of Constance: by their petion, subscribed with their names. An. 1415.

How glorious were it, for honourable and worthy gentlemen, like *Joseph* of *Arimathea* (whom good education and experience of true Religion have matured to *pious wisdome*, and sober zeal) now to own Jesus Christ, when the world is stripping, scourging, mocking, and crucifying of him; when he is so much *forsaken of those men*, whose feares dare not own him; or whose lusts aim to make a prey of him: Now to give the more honour and respect to the true *Ministery* of this Church, (by which they have beene baptized, and educated in Christian Religion); when they see so many vile and illiterate spirits, studying to debase the persons, striving to destroy the very function? This were worthy of a true gentleman, (whom vertue and grace more then birth and relations make such) to stand by *the forsaken*; to countenance the dejected; to pity the oppressed; and (at least) to *Petition* and intercede for the preservation of the true Ministry, and worthy Ministers; of whom they and the whole Nation have had so great and good experience.

Math. 27. 57. Joh. 19. 38. Mark. 15. 43. Luk. 23. 50. *Joseph of Arimathea*: A rich man: an honorable counsellour: a good man & a just: also a Disciple of Christ; &c. owned Christ dead, and begged his body of *Pilate*, &c.

I doe not think it seasonable, now, to invite *Gentlemen*, (where their estates and expenses may bear it), to follow those patterns of extraordinary *munificence*, which some of their rank have heretofore given them; by *restoring the Impropriate Tithes and alienated glebes* to the Church; either freely, or at an easie price; This were, now, to give *sacrilegious* rapine a greater temptation; which dayly gapes to devour all the remains of the *Churches Patrimony and Dowry*. To adde any bloud now to the *Churches veins*, were but more to provoke the thirst of greedy and unsatisfied *horseleeches* of this age; who cry *Give, give*, till they have quite exhausted the very life and spirits of all true Religion. This *motion and bounty* will be more seasonable in better times; when *Sacriledge* shall be accounted (*as it is*) a most damnable sin, and not a *trade*, or a fruit of zeal, or a flower of reformation; which by the Apostles arguing is a more *heynous sin*, than that of Idolatry, in as much as this owns a god, though false; this robs God, though true.

Prov. 30.15.

Rom. 2. 22.

I Cor. 12.31.

But behold, I shew *your noblenesse* a more *excellent way*: my ambition is to propound an *higher degree* of Christian glory to you, the *learned* and *religious Gentry*: which is to follow the steps of that noble *Prince, George Duke of Anhalt*; who disdained not having *Ministeriall gifts*, to *serve Christ* and the Church at *Marburg* in the work of the Ministry, taking upon him holy orders, in times of the greatest contradiction against the reformed Religion: and esteeming it greater *honour* to tread in *Christs* more immediate and narrowest *steps*, than to enjoy the more spacious pathes of secular *pleasures*, and State *imployments*; If you know the excellency of Christ; the vanity of this worlds glory; the *worth* of mens soules; the *weight* of that *Crown*, which is prepared for those, that *forsake all*, and *follow Christ*; you cannot think your selves *disparaged* by this my *humble motion* to you; Your estates will set a greater lustre now on you in the *eyes* of good people, than ever the great state, pomp, plenty, and dignities of former times set upon your predecessours; who of many of your families were Church men, and many of them very worthy ones: Where God hath given you *gifts*, fit for so sacred a service of him, and his Church, no man can propound to you a more *goodly province*, wherein gratefully to use them; or a more eminent way of *preferment*, wherewith to entertain your pious and commendable ambition; which is most worth the *pregnancy* of your parts, and *generousnesse* of your spirits; No *Cedar* is *too tall*, or *goodly* for the building of *Gods Temple*; Nor may it disdaine to descend from *Lebanon* to the holy hill of *Zion*: and no Jewell is too rich and glorious, for *Aarons breastplate*; nor for the foundations and wals of the *New Jerusalem*. The more *splendor* God hath set upon you, the more shall you reflect to his glory and the honor of that *Religion* you professe, by devoting your selves to *serve him*, and his distressed Church; in times, when labourers are few; and those

Phil. Melanct. & Camerarius: highly commend him for his piety and zeal: he died 1553.

Mat 19.28,29.

those much *overburthened*: If any religious way of life might be meritorious, this would be beyond the strictest votaries; in as much as it carries more paines and more benefit with it.

The advantages of an estate with the Ministry.

I have *seen* by the *experience of Gods bounty*, how great advantages an *estate* gives to any Minister; if God gives him grace and *wisedome* with it; How it addes to his *just confidence*, and courage in serving God, and *guiding* his people; how it *redeemes* him, not onely from vulgar *depreciatings*, mean *thoughts*, and worldly *solicitousnesse*; but also from the *temptation* of *flattery*, *popularity*, and that most sordid shamefull dependance on *others* frownes and favours; their *givings*, and *withdrawings*. I know how much it addes *boldnesse*, *credit*, and authority to a Ministers words, to his reproofs, comforts, monitions, and examples; As the expressions of those men, whom, not *necessity* of subsisting, but the *conscience* of doing good; the unfeigned love they have to Christ; the firm *beleif* they have of the Gospell; and the *value* they have of mens soules, put upon the work of preaching: Then will the country people think such *Ministers of the Gospell* to be in *good earnest*, when they see *hospitable relief* of the poor, both in health and sicknesse, both of their bodies and soules, goe along with the *Word preached*: whom many Sermons, and *good words* will not move; some charitable *good workes* seasonably applyed, as a hotter fire or warmer Sun, may soften, melt and convert; To all which, your plentifull, or at least, *competent estates*, piously and prudently managed, will give you *greater advantages*, than most of the *ordinary Ministers* can have; whom for the most part *necessity* drives into this *port* of the Ministry; and there keeps them so under *hatches*, or on the *Lee*, that they are *seldome* able to adventure upon any way, further, then their *country Congregation*, and obscurity afford them: who have onely this glory, of being *faithfull* in a little, and *bearing* poverty with *great patience*.

Sæpius emolliunt eleemosynarum dona, quos non commovent concionum verba. Adeo facta dictis sunt sonantiora, & ἐνεργητικώτερα.

Matth. 25. 21. *Non minor est de bene tolerata paupertate gloria, quam de bene collocatis divitiis.* Sen.

A few persons of your *rank* and *quality*, by some such *heroick* and *exemplary zeal*, (as so many brave *Christians of old against the Saracens*) would much confound the insolency of our *Antiministeriall Jannes* and *Jambres*: It would put the *divell* to new *shifts* and *inventions*; when he and they shall see the Lord stirring up in a way not usuall, the *spirits* of gentlemen, eminent for estates and relations; who *then chuse* to put their hands to the *Churches Oars*, and *helm*, when they see the *danger* greatest, and the *tempest blackest*. You, as *Hercules*, may come in to relieve *those Atlasses* of the faithfull *Bishops* and *Ministers*, who finde some mens *new heavens* too heavy for their shoulders; and their new earth an unstable foundation, to set their feet upon. Your learned *humility* cannot easily be *seduced* by *popular novelties* and *pretentions*, to climb over the wall; or

2 Tim. 3.

Joh. 10. 2.

 to

to break in upon the *Ministry* by new wayes, and *posternes* of facti-ous and fanatick presumptions; but will rather chuse (if God moves your hearts to his work) to keep your feet in his way; that you may come in by that ancient and *holy ordination*; whereever it may rightly be had in this Church; This will make not only

Joh. 10. 3. the *true sheep* of Christ; but the *true shepheards* also, glad to *hear your voice*; and to partake of those excellent gifts, which God hath given you; which study, prayer, and exercise will dayly increase upon you; It is great pity so many of your learned, and pious abilities should *lie idle*, or not have imployment worthy of them; especially when they are fitted for the Lords service, and the Lord hath need of *them*: *Doe not despise the calling*; *though* it be black, yet it is comely, as the curtaines of *Solomon*, though it be now forced to dwell in *Meseck*, and to have its habitation in the tents of *Kedar*: The first founder of our holy function, was a man of sorrowes, an outcast of men; in whom the world thought there was no form or comelinesse: Affliction hath reformed us by restoring Ministers to Christs image.

Which of you that hath the true sense, what it is to be a *good Christian*, and what honour it is to serve Christ in saving of souls,

Matth. 21. 2. but will at the first word, which *Christ sends*, *loose the Asse*, (which is tyed it may be to some small secular businesse, pleasure, or study) and let it be *brought to Christ*, being *fit for his service*; That so being strowed, and adorned with the richer ornaments wherewith your condition is cloathed; *Christ* may with the more conveniency and

vers. 7. decency *sit thereon*; and ride, as it were, in an extraordinary triumph to *Jerusalem*; and many may follow him with *Hosannas*:

vers. 9. Blessing you, that *come in the name of the Lord to save them*. The lesse *incouragements* you can now expect, as *Ministers of Christ*, from men; the greater will be *your honour*, the *sincerer* your comforts, and the ampler your *reward* from God; when the world shall see, that you honour the *work of the Ministry* for the work sake; and love Christ for himself, no lesse, than others doe, where that service is attended with *great revenues*, and dignities; There will shortly be need (more than enough) of some Ministers, who can undertake the *work*, and not want the *wages*; even the meanest minded men now begin to divert their studies, and education to another way rather than that of the Ministry: finding, that there they are like soonest to come a *ground*, and to dash against the *rocks of poverty and contempt*. A few of you (like *Davids* worthies) furnished with due and divine *authority* for the Ministery as well as *with gifts*; would mightily stand in the gap, repell, and confound

1 Chron. 27. the vanity and insolence of those, who are risen up to lay *wast* and desolate, this sometime so *famous* a Ministry and *flourishing Church*.

But

But this is onely an *occasionall digression* humbly offered to those *worthy Gentlemen*, who have parts, learning, piety and courage enough, to make them *dare* to be good, and to doe good, in so *high* and eminent a way, in the midst of a *degenerate* and *declining* age, which knows not how to prise the *Gospell of Salvation*, nor worthily to entertain the Ministry and Ministers of it.

The taking away Tithes will be a great burden to the people.

But to return to my former subject; it is most evident that these *projectors* against Tithes are no wayes friends to the *Farmers*, any more than to the *Gentlemen* and *Landlords*; for when Tithes are once taken away from Ministers, and being in Lay hands, are as easily cast into the *ballance* of secular businesse, (as other *Church lands* have lately been;) if then Christian people, *any where* would be desirous to have a true and able Minister (and cannot satisfie themselves with those *false Prophets*, and *unordained Preachers* which are so cheap:) truly they will finde a *new burthen* must then lye wholly on their estates and purses; to maintain their Ministers, while yet they must pay their Tithes other where.

These just considerations, and most undeniable reasons, have already made the honest *Yeomen* so wise, as in stead *of petitioning against Tithes*, to cry aloud, to all those *busie projectors*: 'Before you 'take away Tithes *from our Ministers*, first provide a better way 'for their *maintenance*; Exchange will *be no robbery*, if it be *no detriment*: (that is) such as shall be neither more *chargeable in a new 'way*; nor lesse comely and *honourable*; where a *legall right* may give 'claim against all impediments; else vile *dependences* on any mens 'favour, or good will, will abase both the calling, and *spirit*, and 'carriage of our Ministers, below what is *comely* for them, or 'willingly *seen* by us; who know, that in our true Ministers 'welfare the good of our own, and our childrens soules, under 'God, is bound up. Deprive not them of that *due* and *double honor*, 'which the *piety* and *gratitude* of this Nation hath *given to them*; 'lest you deprive us, and our posterity of the true *Christian*, and re'formed *Religion*; which we fear to be the aim of all those, that '*levell against Tithes* and Ministers; That so they may by a *Jesuitick* 'back blow, unperceived, strike through the loins of the *reformed 'Religion*, which hath been for many years happily among us, and 'this with more encrease of true saving *knowledge*, and *practise of 'piety* in one century of years, than was for many before; which 'blessing, next to God, we owe chiefly to our *able and faithfull 'Ministers*, who are not so *our servants* in the Lord, that they 'should be used as our *hinds*, or slaves; but rather (as they are 'called, and deserve to be reverenced) as our Spirituall *Fathers*, our '*guides* and *instructers* in the Lord.

Besides this, That I may wholly drown *this Wasps nest*, which

 makes

makes such a stir *in the countrey*, by their *stinging Petitions*, and buzzing projects against Tithes and Ministers; Let them know, That it becomes no men of honesty and ingenuity, thus to delude with specious pretences, the credulity of the *countrey Farmers*, who for the most part love their Ministers so well, and prise the *reformed Religion* so highly, and value so much their Saviour, Jesus Christ, his holy Institutions, and their own soules; that they would utterly abhorre the bottome of these repining *thoughts* and projects of these *murmurers* against their Ministers, if they did but discern them: Yea like *Zacheus*, many of them had rather part with *half their goods*, than starve or lose their Ministers, and their own soules too with their childrens and families: No, the *jolly plainnesse*, and *honest integrity* of the *English Yeoman*, is neither so lazy and idle, nor so sordid and illiberall, nor so cunning and hypocriticall, as these nimbler and *sprucer fellows* are: whose *quick-silver wits*, roving fancies, and fallacious *tongues*, aim at *new modelling* all things to their advantages; and hope with their *Jesuitick pretensions* and *fanatick leaven* to infect all sorts of men, both in City and Countrey: For their designe is, that all the worthy Ministers in *England* should be rather starved or beg their bread, than that they should come short of any such rare and little beneficiall projects as they have in their crownes: Hoping either to *buy* some *glebelands* and Tithes, or to farm some part of them, or to have some Office in a new erected Tithe Exchequer, which for a while affording some Ministers some small *pensions*, afterwards will serve for any secular occasions, that so Ministers being unprovided of means, the people may be left without any Ministers.

As for that *sting*, which is in the *tail* of these *projectors*, that by paying of *Tithes* to the Minister, the husbandman and farmer is disabled to pay *Taxes* to the State, whom it concernes more, to keep up and pay a *Souldiery* than a *Ministry*; My answer is, As the other objections savour of *hypocrisie*, and *self-interest*, so this of flattery; These *Polypusses* are so cunning, as to apply to the *surest rocks*, and turn themselves to any colour, which may be for their *safety*: But, are they such *wretches*, as to think, that nothing will suffice to *buy souldiers swords and pistols*, but onely Christs own food and rayment, which *must be sold*? It seems they had rather Christ should goe starved, naked in his Ministers, than themselves be ungarded; But we hope, that this is not the sense of any valiant, honest, or religious souldier; who knows how to be *content with his wages*, to doe *injury to no man*; least of all to the Ministers of Christ, whom they have not yet so learned of these men as to hate and despise, because they would destroy them, his

Luk. 3; 14.

Ministers:

Ministers: And sure no *souldier* can have any motive against the welfare of the *able* and *faithfull Ministers* of this Church; unlesse they fight against the *Protestant Religion*; and in stead of *Reformadoes*, turne *Renegadoes* to that Profession, in which they were brought up.

The *bottom and dregs* of some mens *agitations* against the setled maintenance of Ministers in this Church is, not so much to ease the people from *paying Tithes*, (which they shall be sure to doe, either by way of publique Exchequer, or to the private purse of Landlords, when these have bought them into *their revenue*;) the *project* is to have *no setled Ministry* in this reformed Church; For these Antidecimists know by their *countrey Logick*, which is not very good, (but there are Jesuites, who are excellent at it) That in a short time it will follow, No *setled competent* maintenance, no able or *worthy Minister* any where: But roome enough will be quickly made either for *Seminary* agitators, from *forain nurseries*; or for those *sorry pieces* of *motly predicants*, and *mungrill Ministers*, (*Centaures* in the Church, that are half *Laicks*, and half *Clericks*) who are indeed but the *by blowes* of the Clergy, uncalled, unordained, and commonly *unblest*; because false Prophets; either as to the *errours* of their *Doctrine*; or the arrogancy of their *authority*; whose *calling*, commission, and tenure, as Ministers, must chiefly depend upon *popularity*, *flattery*, and *beggery*: Such despicable *Mendicants*, as will in a short time make all ingenuous people weary of their *illiterate importunities*; and such *thread-bare* preachers even ashamed of themselves. *The aim of Antidecimists.*

This will certainly follow in a *Spanish projection*, by as necessary a consequence, as, *No Sun, no day*; no fewell, no fire; no oil in the lamps, no light in the house; no *pay*, *no souldier*; *no provender in the crib*, *no labour of the Oxen*: yea, and the utter vastation of the *reformed Religion*, as to the order, honor, and beauty of its *publique profession*, will as inevitably succeed, as the burning of the corn fields did, the running of the *fiery tailed Foxes* among them. Prov. 14:4. Judg. 15:3.

13. But the Antidecimists would have the Ministers of the Gospell follow other *honest trades*, taking upon them some *mechanick* or *mercenary* occupations, that so they might *earn their livings* other ways, and preach *gratis*; that is, for nothing; and at length as good as *nothing*, both for want of ability and authority; How would these men rejoyce to see men of learned parts, of noble mindes, and of ingenuous breeding, brought down to the levell of their *low form*; to shine no better, than their twinkling and *unsavory snuffes*; to be eminent in nothing beyond the *plebeian pitch*, and vulgar proportions: that so they might *spin* out their sermons at their *wheeles*; or weave them up at their *loomes*; or dig them out with *Of Ministers support by some mechanick trade.*

their *Spades*; weigh and measure them in their *Shops*; or stitch and cobble them up with their thimbles and lasts; or *thrash* them out with their *flayles*, and after preach them in some *barn* to their *dusty disciples*; who, the better to set off their odnesse and unwontednesse to their *silly Teachers*, must be taught (like crazy or *frantick men*) to fancy themselves into *some imaginary persecution*; as if in times of even too great *liberty*, they were thus driven with their new found *Pastors*, into *dens*, and *caves*, and *woods*, rather than vouchsafe to hear with the greatest ease, order, and decency the ablest *Ministers* of *England* in those places, which are dedicated to the *Churches* publique use and service. Indeed the *ruder way* of these mens exercising their *small endowments*, and discovering their *great idlenesse*, by *extemporary pratings*, may well enough consist with those mechanick imployments, to which they have been brought up; and from which this their *predicating* now and then, is but a *sport* and *recreation*; if it should not turne to some *account for profit*; But to such men, as make the Ministry of the *glorious Gospell*, to be their work and study, dayly to fit themselves for that *great* and *sacred dispensation*, of *saving Truths*, and *sublime mysteries*, it will appeare to be, alone, an *imployment*, so more than enough; that there will be little *vacancy* to *intangle* themselves in *secular* and inferiour businesse; which is casting down the stars of heaven, from their orbs and firmaments, to things terrene and sordid, which at best are but *losse and dung* in comparison of the *excellency* of that *knowledge of Jesus Christ*, which they determine above all things to know, and make known. If the *work of the Ministry*, (which is of so vast a latitude, and of so high concernment) require and takes up the *prime* and *flower* of the time, as well as the thoughts of the best and ablest men, that ever were conscientiously imployed in it, and all little enough; how sordid are those projects, which seek to divert Ministers by worldly necessities, to debase their minds below that *worthy office* and weighty work!

Nulla res bene exerceri potest ab homine alias occupato. Sen. de brev. vit.

1 Cor. 2. 2.

But *contempt* and *beggery* are the *double honour*, which these mens bounty and gratitude would give to those, that have and still do diligently *labour* in the *Word* and *Doctrine*: Either they own them not, as invested in any holy office and divine authority; or they would have them so *debased by poverty*, and vile dependency, that they might not be thought fit to be owned as such: while they are forced to intangle themselves contrary to the Apostles Canon, in the meanest affaires of life; hindering other poor men in their *manuall trades*: and receiving no other benefit of their learning and labours, but what comes in an arbitrary way from others, or is extorted by their most illiberall importunities: bringing down

2 Tim. 2. 4.

to

to the lowest step of disgrace the dignity of this holy function in this reformed Church; as if Ministers were to be nothing but an order of *mendicant Fryers*; these beg, when they need not; but those shall need, and beg, and have not: O how desirous are these *men* to have all true Ministers, like to Christ their Master; not *to have, whereto hide their heads*; while the *Foxes have holes*, and the *birds of the air have nests*; Such airy, light and *high flying fancies*, as these, (who like *seiled Pigeons*, the lesse they see, the higher they sore) doe dayly build their *nests on high*, and *feather* them very well: Yet they could be well content the *Apostle Paul*, (and all his successours, in the Ministry of the Gospell among the Gentils) should, either lie in the *tents* of their own making, or else with the *dogs of their flocks*, out of dores; while they *fatted*, and *anointed* may rest at ease, within the *curtaines of Solomon*, and dwell in *seiled houses*; to which some of them have hardly so good a *title*, as Ministers have to their *houses*, *glebes* and *Tithes*. Math. 8. 20.

Thus, *these Pharaohs*, dream of none, but *lean cattell* in the field of this Church; or, to *compleat the Vision*, they see the following *lean cattell*, which are now coming up, after the *former* (which were fat and wel favoured *devouring*) them up, as if they had not been; The new ill ordained, ill gifted, ill maintained, and every way *ill favoured Ministers*, will in short time (they hope) consume all those *learned*, *worthy*, able, rightly ordained, and sometime competently, if not honorably, entertained Ministers, which have been the *glory of this Church*, and Nation for many ages: These must now give way to *hungry*, necessitous, *crowching*, and *fawning pieces* of impudent ignorance; such as their Antidecimall Masters affect: as if they thought, that the more *thread-bare*, and *hunger-starved* Ministers were, and the lesse *wool* or *flesh* they had on their *backs*, the more *spirituall* they must needs be, the more *like Angels* or separate and *naked soules*; and the lesse *chargeable* they are, the more acceptable they will be to these patrons of *avarice* and *sacriledge*: Such are the noble, generous, and *blessed projects*, or proposals of these *Antidecimists*, than whom, a *meaner spirited* subject never exercised any ingenuous pen, nor more infested any Christian Church; nor (like gadflyes) more importunely disquieted learned, godly and true Ministers of the *blessed Gospell*. Gen. 41.

14. *Appeal to the liberall soules.*

O you *excellent spirited*, and *liberall hearted* Christians, to whose candour I must still *appeal*, as the great incourager and comforter (next God and a good conscience) of all faithfull and true Ministers, in these blustering encounters; Although we know, by too much experience, that there are many such *whining people*, *penurious protestants*, *triobolary Christians*; whose *beggerly soules* are prone to be leavened with the suggestions of these *Antidecimists*; (who

for

for the most part are *pitifull pieces* of ignorance, avarice, and sacrilegious envy; through whom, as through *vaults*, and *trunkes*, the divell *whispers* into common peoples eares, this *Infernall Oracle, Save your purses, though you damn your soules*) yet all worthy and true *Ministers*, who are *humbly conscious* to their endeavour, to deserve well of this Church of *England*, (of their own charges and all other good people) are still far from that *dejection*, or *despondency* into which their adversaries seek to cast them: For they still have frequent experiences of their peoples *unfeigned* love, respects, and chearfull kindenesse to them; whose generous piety oft seems to tell their *Ministers*, as *David did Araunah*, That they would be ashamed *to serve their God, of that which costs them nothing*. Notwithstanding they have many other publique pressures upon them, (which are of a far later *edition than Tithes*, and of a *greater print*) yet they cannot finde in their hearts the *least* grudging, at their paying Tithes to *their Ministers*; since they see no reason, why these, as *Christs Agents*, and *Gods Embassadours*, should not as well deserve, and enjoy a competent, and comely maintenance, as any *publique Officers*, either Civill, or Military: Who have more of power to exact, but not more of *right*, either humane or divine; nor yet more of merit, to require their *payes*, and *fees*; Yea, Ministers still dare to hope, that those in power have not any such *Nabalitick* and *churlish* humor, as to feast those that shear, and sometimes *flay the sheep*; while they starve the *Shepheards*: So great a confidence alwayes ariseth from the *conscience of well doing*.

2 Sam. 24. 24.

And whereas the *strongest insinuations* are made on the weaker mindes of the *common people*, by these *popular orators*, against the setled maintenance of *Ministers*, (as if the Vulgar shall save much by the shift:) I have before touched, and here again I *inculcate* it, to them, (because the *sharpest goades are pointed with profit*:) That when the old Ministers are spent or laid aside, and the former way of setled maintenance turned to another course, there is no doubt, but the new *projected Preachers*, what ever they be, (either like *mushroomes* growing up of themselves; or miscalled, and misplaced by the people) will finde their *stomachs* full as good, as their *gifts*; and their *digestion* full as strong, as their *elocution*; that when once they come to looke upon themselves, as any way setled and elected, or in any fashion ordained for Preachers, and Pastors, (or what ever *title* they please to *put* upon themselves) they will come quickly to plead and urge *Evangelicall precepts*, *divine right*, and *naturall equity*, for their maintenance; which first they will mutter, then *exact*, and *grudge*, *if they be not satisfied*, from their *ill fed* flocks, and *scabious Congregations*: And they will be prone to think, all is well in their *Churches and bodies*, if themselves be but well

fed,

fed, and *blithe*; though their poor peoples soules be starved, their mindes scattered, their consciences crazy; their diseases many; and neither skill, nor will in their *ill gifted teachers* to *heal* or *help them*: who are not likely to be very good at that *worke*, or cure; when from among the *lowest of the people* they mount to be *Ministers* for *a morsell of bread*, and from countrey Farriers will needs turn Physitians?

These men are rather of that sort, whose *mouths ought to be stopped* when they speak perverse things, for *filthy lucres* sake, as the Apostle *Paul* tels us: who was no enemy to the preaching of the Gospell: yet he approves not any *false intruders*, or *disorderly walkers*: Every simple and slight *Asse* is not fit to *tread out the corn*, but the ponderous and solemn Oxe; whose mouth *ought not to be muzzled*. Tit. 1. 11.

There are no doubt many *Jesuitick Geniusses*, in *England*, who like the *Ravens* would perswade the *Sheep* to starve their Shepheards, and to beat out their eyes and brains, pretending that so the flock may feed *the freer*, and the fatter; but hoping indeed, soon after, to *pluck* out the eyes of those weak and *silly animals*, and with more safety to make a prey of them. O how farre are some men in these days, who seek thus to pull out Ministers eyes from that *gratefull* and affectionate zeal of the *Galatians* to St. *Paul*; who were ready to pull out their *own right eyes* to doe him good; before they were foolishly *bewitched* by such enchanters who pretended new Gospels, so as to think him an enemy for telling *them the Truth!* O how lothe are vain and proud men to think, the *egges* of any opinions, which they have laid or *hatched*, to be *addle*; or their ways erroneous! if they doe but please themselves, it matters not how they displease God, and those worthy men, who have indeed deserved best of them. Gal. 4. 15. vers. 16.

15. *Hard measure offered to Ministers by some.*

Truly (O *you excellent* Christians) it would, and ought to be, a great *grief* and shame to the whole Order of the *Ministers* of *England*, if they had deserved no better of those Christians in this Church, (whom they have for many years *baptized*, taught, and nourished up in true religion) by all the *labours* of their love; then thus to have *a cup of cold water*, not given to them, but *taken from them* in the *name of Christs Ministers*. Here in they are forced to appeal to your humility, prudence, aud equanimity; whose *gratefull piety* hath oft expressed your love and value of their persons, profession and paines, far different from, (though now not sufficient to represse) the *petulancy* of these *kicking Jesuruns*, who in many places being *better fed, than taught*, despise *through much wantonnesse of the flesh*, the bread of heaven, *This Manna*; Studying nothing so much, as to make many *starveling Christians* and *lean Congregations*, through their *sacrilegious cruelty*, seeking to deprive the *true Ministers* Matth. 10. 42.

of their due maintenance; that so, they may deprive the poore people of their *true Ministers*; That the sins of this afflicted Nation, and self-desolating Church being *filled up*, they may bring by a *famine of bread upon the Ministers* a *famine of the Word*, and a *scarcity of Ministers*, upon the people; which is the (τὸ ζητούμενον) *Palladium*; the thing so much desired, by the enemies of this and all other reformed Churches.

We know well, and have alwayes found it by sad *experience*, that no *Adder is deafer*, and harder *to be charmed*, than *sacrilegious covetousnesse*; which, (laying one *ear to the earth*, listning to its gain; and stopping the other *with its tail*, that it may hear no noise or voice from heaven) easily eludes, and mocks all *sacred spels* of the best enchanters, *charm they never so wisely*: Indeed it is seldome seen, that any men either private or publique (for it's possible a Nation may be *guilty* of this sin) who gilded over their *holy thefts* with the *names of Religion* and *Reformation*, ever forbare the sin, or repented of it, or made due *restitution* after it: No *Harp* or hand of *David* can play so sweetly, as to make this *evill spirit* of sacriledge forsake *those Sauls*; whom it may possesse (though they be higher *by the head* than the *rest of the people*) as well as the lowest and meanest of the people: whose *necessities* may have greater temptation, and their consciences lesse *information* of the evill. Indeed no man is so base, and feeble, but he dares to adventure at this, *the robbing of God, of the Church, and the Ministers*; which is a *fellony* against the publique, and to every good Christians injury in the Church, or Nation. The reason of this boldnesse in some men is, because they finde, that although men of estates have quick *resentments* in their particular *concernments*, of private profit or honour; yet they have (for *the most part*) a *great coldnesse* and indifferency, as to those things, which concern the *Churches support*, or *Religions patrimony*; in *scrambling* for which, every man secretly hopes (unlesse he be of the more *honest and severe piety*) for some advantage. To be sure, these great sticklers against the Ministers maintenance by Tithes make no doubt, but they shall lick their *own fingers* well, if once they can but pull them from the Ministers; either they flatter themselves, (and I think very fondly) that as Tenants they shall save their *Tithes*, from both Minister and Landlord; or else as Landlords augment their rents; or buy some part of them; or, at worst, have some place in a *new office* of *gathering* and *distributing* of them.

Psal. 58. 5.

Patrimonium Crucifixi.

The great sense I have of that little, or no sense, which many men have of so publique a businesse, as that is, which concernes the setled support of Ministers; and in them of all *learning* and *religion* in this Nation; makes me sometimes prone to think it, al-

mosti

most a vain, unseasonable, and uncomely labour in me, or any other Ministers, (who pretend to something of more ingenuous spirits) thus to *plead*, and that publiquely, with any *earnestnesse* (which seems to draw somewhat of the dregs of *meannesse*) for their very bread: which, in the unequall *distributions* of humane affaires, we see is not *alwayes* to men of *worth* and *understanding*; Eccles. 9. 11. whom Christian principles and patterns teach to live *above earthly things*; to minde things, that are above; to learn to Col. 3. 1. want and to abound, to be *content in any condition*; And truly Phil. 4. 11. in this, the *Ministers of England*, (I think ought to have been prevented by *some other advocates*, than men of their *own coat*; As lately my worthy friend Mr. *Edward Waterhouse*, hath done in his Apology for learning and learned men: a work ; so honest and so seasonable, as well became the candor, piety, and ingenuity of a Gentleman and a Christian, who hath (the honour to have) made one of the first and bravest adventures in this kinde against these modern *English Saracens*. And possibly many good men have a good minde so to doe even publiquely; but they thinke it is (*conclamata res*) a *forlorne and desperate cause*, as may bee *offensive* and unacceptable: I almost think so too, if some men may have their will; and therefore the rather I have *been excited* to it: if it be displeasing to some, yea to many; yet I doe not think, it is so to the most, or the greatest part of Christians: I am sure it is not to the best of this Nation, of what condition soever they be; they cannot be so destitute of, and unaffected with, all reason, Religion, grounds of Conscience, rules of Prudence, considerations both of piety, honour, and *honest policy*: In all which they are related by their own interests to the good and *welfare* of their *true Ministers*. As *Socrates* when he was reproached for having no *preferment* in *Athens*, answered, It was enough for him to have *fitted* himselfe for preferment; It was *other mens work to bestow it on him*: So the studious learned, modest, and pious Ministers of *England*, might well have thought it enough for *them*, to have *merited* imployment, and decent entertainment; having with much paines, and study, and prayer furnished themselves for every *good word and work*, within the bounds of their calling; It seems hard thus to be put (many of them after many yeares sore labour and *travaile of their soules*) to plead for their *wages*, or livelyhood; yea and for their liberty, but to *worke*, *while it is day*, in the *Lords Vineyard*, of this Church; wherein Christ hath set and ordained them.

Although there be a generation lately sprung up of *degenerate* Christians, and *ungenerous English*; who would make this whole *Nation* like themselves, unworthy of the very *bones* of those excel-

Ingrata patria ne ossa quidem mea habes. Liv. an. ur. 566.

lent Ministers, which have lived here and merited so well of the publique (as *Scipio Africanus* said of his bones, when he died, banished by his ungratefull countrey, which *he had so preserved*) yet (we hope) neither the most, nor the best of men can be so stupid, as not to consider how much they are concerned in the continuance and incouragement of such Ministers among them; wherein no Nation or Church under heaven hath exceeded this. However Ministers be *earthen vessels*, and many have had both heretofore, and lately, great flawes and many *faylings*; yet they ought in this *Nation* to be still *highly regarded* if not for their learning, civility, ingenuity and good society (which is to be valued in any Nation that covets not to be *barbarous*) yet for *their work sake*; for that Gospell, that God, that *Saviour*, that *blessed Jesus* his sake, whom they truely teach; for the holy *Scriptures* sake, which they so frequently, and so fully explain; for those holy *Sacraments*, which they duely administer; both for the admission and augmentation, birth and nourishment of Christians in the Church of Christ; for the holy and good *counsels*, and spirituall *comforts* which they oft give; for the many wise stops and grave *restraints* to sin and error, which they frequently put; for the publique and *good examples*, which most of them afford, and all should, by their *place* and *calling*; These are cords of love enough to draw and binde all excellent Christians to them; these are places of Oratory sufficient to make even any *ordinary speaker* an eloquent and potent Orator in their behalf.

And for my owne part, having taken some serious view of the estate of this Church and the Ministers of it, both in reference to the present and after times; both as to that reall worth, which hath been, and still is in them; the excellent use of them; and the miserable want which will be of them; I cannot but at present, be extremely sensible of, and very much pity, those *sharp*, sad, and *unjust necessities*, which already have and must presse dayly more upon many worthy men of them, and their *families*, if some mens *envyous* and malicious *designes* take place: onely I hope *better things* of those, whose wisdome, piety and publique influence hath hitherto, under God, restrained those Fountaines of *the great deep*, from breaking in with all *sacrilegious violence* upon the whole Ministry: whose *wisdome*, *power*, or *counsell*, I doe not any way by this Apology seek to obstruct or prejudice, as to any thing that may be better *disposed of* to the advantage of true Religion and the Church of *England*; which are inseparable from a right and setled Ministry; nor can that be had without such *maintenance*, as is worthy of worthy men.

ὡς ἐπιλιπόντων εὐθύνης ζωῆς τῇ πενίᾳ θλίψει. Naz. or. 52.

If no men will be with us, but all *forsake* us, and some oppose us, as Ministers: yet we have one remedy, besides the *sympathy* and charity of you, O *excellent Christians*; which is, *patience* and *prayer*: * He that allowes us to pray for *our dayly bread*, and commands us to labour *honestly* for it, even in this function of the Ministry; he *teacheth* us to beleive, that he will either give it, or the grace to want it. There may be some good * *Obadiahs*, who will *feed the outed and impoverished Prophets of the Lord*, by *fifties* in *their caves*, and obscure retirements, as some have already done; and it may be good *Ministers* shall then speak lowdest, when their *mouths are stopped*; and be as well liking in all true grace and comforts of Religion with * *their pulse*, as those that feed dayly on *Kings provisions*.

17. *Good Ministers hopes in their desertions from men.*

* *Greg. Nis.* tels of St. *Ephraem*; Though he was very poor, yet he had a mine of rich prayers: Ἀληθῶς ὁ τοῦτο λόγος κλεῖ· θεοχάλκευτος, τοὺς θησαυροὺς οὐρανίους ἀνοίγων, καὶ τὰ δόντα χορηγῶν. *Gr. Nis. in vita S. Ephraem.*

* 1 King. 18. 4. * Dan. 1.

However, if we must be thus stripped and starved, to gratifie the lusts of some men; yet we hope for this mercy from God, and favour from man, that we shall not be forced to *desert our calling*; or to contract a *woe of not preaching the Gospell*, while we have abilities, though we preach (ἀδάπανον τὸ εὐαγγέλιον) though we have no publique incouragement: For why should all our studies and time be made unprofitable? It may be, we shall, by Gods help, redeem our former defects, by after *diligence* in the work of Christ: we may happily *work* and *war* the better, when we are more *expedite*, lighter armed, and lesse incumbred with envy and worldly impediments: We may (I hope) without presumption enjoy that liberty to preach the Gospel, which others now take to prate against it, and us; and it may be, people will hear, and profit better, when they see they have the Gospell at a *cheaper rate*: and will be more in love with the reformed Religion, when they shall see, how much better penny-worth they have of that, than of the *Romish superstition*; which is more *costly* by farre, yet lesse *comfortable* to a serious Christian: Though we be *made poore*, yet we may still *make many rich*; though we have *nothing*, yet we may *enjoy all things*; though we are are *troubled on every side*, yet we may not be *distressed*; though *perplexed*, yet not in *despaire*; though *persecuted* by men, yet not *forsaken* of God; though cast *down* and cast out, yet not destroyed, through the *grace* of God, which is sufficient for us; Many worthy Ministers may justly plead for their liberties, lives and livings, as those did with *Ishmael*, *Destroy us not*, for there are *treasures* of learning and saving knowledge with us. But it is better for them, to be *Christs Lazarusses*, and beggars, than

1 Cor. 9. 16.

Verba vertas in opera, nudam crucem nudus sequeres; expeditior & levior scandis scalam Jacobi. Ieron.

Pauper esse non potest, qui apud Deum dives est, Lact. Inst. l. 6. c. 12.

2 Cor. 6. 10.

Ier. 41. 8.

than the worlds *rich gluttons* and favorites: Yet it must needs be so; and so it will be, unlesse some *Michael* and his *Angels*, overcome this *greedy Apollyon*, this *sacrilegious Abaddon*, this penurious Divell, and his Angels, who prodigally *offers* Kingdomes to damne one soule, but grudgeth one *groat* to redeem many thousands.

Revel. 12. 7.

18. Nor will your noblenesse (*O excellent Christians*) interpret this, which I have wrote in behalf of the maintenance of Ministers, in this Church and Nation, to be any pleading for *Baal*, or *clamouring* like *Demetrius* and his complices in *his panick feares*, for his *silver shrines* and his *Diana*; where he considered more his *gain*, than his *Goddesse*: These are unjust and malicious *glosses*, which the enemies both of the *Ministry* and of *humanity*, are prone to put upon any, that plead *never so righteous a cause* with words of the greatest truth, justice, sobernesse, and moderation; those having a stinking breath themselves, think every mans unsavoury. But by the leave of such *latrant Orators*, and back-biters, I must tell them, what the wiser, and more Christian world well knows; that there is no cause, why *Ministers*, more than any other *order of men*, should neglect in fair and just wayes to obtain for, or preserve to, themselves, and their successours, those *worldly comforts*, and supports, which the providence of God and the *Christian munificence* of this Nation hath in the most free way of gift and by Law granted to them in Gods name, and for the service of Christ, and the honour of Religion; Other men are commended for their good husbandry, and honest care, to preserve their just estates; which tend not so much to the publique good, as the labours of Ministers doe: who may not in prudence, or conscience neglect those great, and publique *concernments* of Christ, and his Church, with which they are intrusted: Yea if they should have *an eye* to the reward, to their own just right and particular interests (which all other we see still have) yet it were no more than Law and Reason, all humanity and Christianity allow; unlesse they would be *worse than those Infidels*, that provide *not for their own families*; or be as bad, as those men, who to provide for themselves, and their families, care not to *rob*, and desolate even the Church and family of Christ: Ministers may be *wise*, yet *innocent*; provident, yet not *sordid*; diligent in things honest, yet not injurious to others: Nor is it any whit uncomely for *them*, to crave this justice or favour from any in power; That they may quietly injoy those publique *rewards* of their learning and labours, which are injurious to no man, merited in the esteem of all honest men; and therefore offensive to none, but envious eyes and evill mindes; Being the *fruit of the publique bounty*, wisdome, gratitude, and devotion of this *Christian Nation* to God, to Christ

Ministers just plea for their own, neither covetous, nor uncomely.

* Act. 19. 25.

1 Tim. 5 8.

and

and his Ministers; what they have a long time by law injoyed; what they are rightly possessed of; and what they have no way forfeited (unlesse other mens calumnies and cavils, their covetous projects and desires of novelty, be the *crime and fault* of Ministers:) And lastly, they doe intend with all *peaceablenesse, thankefulnesse*, and *usefulnesse* to use and enjoy, if God and man permit, so that no man shall have cause to repine at their enjoyments, who knowes how to make use of their gifts and labours.

The *shame* of pleading this *cause of Ministers maintenance* lies at their dore, who meditate, speak, and act so *vile* and *dishonest* things against them, as force them, thus to *vindicate* their just rights, against unjust projects: which seek by *falshood* and *violence* to take away, not only the *childrens*, but the *fathers bread* too, and to give it to *dogs*: who alwayes have sought to bring this reproach and *scandall* on this and other *reformed* Churches; that they still carry on, and serve *some covetous and sacrilegious design* with their reformations: When (God knowes) it is not the design, nor desire of any, that are *truly reformed* Christians, to *robb the Church*, and Churchmen of one *shoelatchet*; but rather to have added necessary *augmentations* to them: if they had not alwayes been hindered by the *covetousnesse* and envy of some *crosse faction*, who have longed to see the day, when with *Rabshakehs unclean spirit*, and foul *language*, they might see all the *reformed Clergy*, reduced to those *sordid necessities*; which I have as much *shame* to write, as these *Antiministeriall sticklers* have pleasure to wish it, and glory to speak it. Isai. 36. 12.

19. Our *comfort* in the worst of times and things is, That we *know in whom we have trusted*: not in these *Egyptian reeds*, which may faile us and pierce us, but *in the living God*; whom we have served though with *many frailties*, yet with *sincerity* and *godly simplicity*; We beleive he will not *fail* us, nor *forsake* us, though men, though Christians, though *reformers* doe; There is not a better sign of Gods love, than to be *persecuted for righteousnesse sake*; It is our honour, as St. *Jerom* wrote to St. *Austin*, that the divell and his fanatick factions do *unanimously* hate us, and malign us; for if they were for Christ, they could not *be against us*. And we finde by experience, that these *Antiministeriall agitators* have no such displeasure against any men, be they never so flagitious, or their estates never so *luxuriant*, as against the most orderly and deserving Ministers: So that it is their piety and pains, which *afflicts* their enemies, more than *their plenty*; And if they cannot strangle *Christ in the Cradle*, yet they hope to starve him in the Desart.

True Ministers comforts.
Multa quidem mala, sed varia solatia. Sal. l. 9.
Matth. 5.
Heb. 12.

Blessed be God, we see the *end*, and *bounds* of these mens power, and malice; They are *finite flesh*; and not *infinite Gods*; yea they are *proud flesh*, lately risen up, which God will *eat* off with *fitting*

corrosives

corrosives, if ever he heals this *Church and Nation*; These murmurers never set us on work, nor doe we depend on such unjust *masters* for our *wages*: Though they be not *converted* or gathered from their follies, factions and separations, yet our *reward* shall be from the Lord, who hath sent us, and whom we have served with *faithfull hearts*; as to our *temporary* subsistence, we hope wee shall never depend on these mens *injurious justice*, or *cruel mercies*; much lesse on their *envious alms*, and *supercilious charity*, who are our *enemies for the Gospels sake*, which we preach: And although we should not *be protected* in point of our civill rights from their despight and rage; yet as to the honour and vindication of our Ministry, and holy function, we must not give *place, no not for an houre*, to their *cavils* and *calumnies*: Yea we doe not despair, but that we may find so *much equity*, and pity in some mens hearts, in whose hands is power; that they will rather harken, and incline to the just *plea* of those labourers in *Christs harvest*, (who have borne the *heat* and *burthen of the day*, and who crave but liberty first to doe the work, to which Christ and the Church hath ordained them; and next, which is but a just and righteous thing, to *enjoy that reward*, which the *Law* hath assigned them) than to listen to the *envious suggestions*, or *injurious proposals*, of those *novell intruders* upon the Ministry, who have yet given not the least assurance to the wiser world, or any reformed Christians, that they in any thing *exceed*, or *equall* the true ancient Ministers of *England*; nor have they yet, by any demonstrations of modesty, ingenuity, sense of honour, or of shame, nor by any part of good learning, (which they decry and hate,) nor by any other usefull and commendable quality, redeemed themselves, from the most sordid passions, and saddest distempers of humane nature; nor yet reconciled themselves to any love and value of vertue, worth and *excellency* in others.

Isai. 49. 5. ὁ ἀνενδεὴς μετέχων ἀνενδεὴς εἴη ἄν. Cle. Al. στρω. 7. *Dei particeps nullius indigus.*

Gal. 2. 5.

We know well, that their *ignorances*, and *errours* are grosse in many things, both divine, and humane; (for how can they but erre excessively, who are very active, and for the most part both *bold* and *blind*?) Any piece of rustical ignorance & clownish confidence serves some mens turn to oppose any Minister withall, setting up their puppetly *Teraphims*, their deformed *Dagons*, their Images of jealousie, in the place and temple of the living God. Among their other errours, this, we hope, is none of their least; that they *fancy* and every where *proclaim*, that they have so *charmed* with their *philters* and *enchantments*, (which are Confections made up of *ignorance* and malice; pride and cruelty; covetousnesse and uncharitablenesse together, with a perfect disdain of all, that is rationall, learned or excellent) that with these charms they have so possessed many or most of those, in power, That they are resolved to root out, abase, and destroy all those Ministers, who are any way eminent in learning, courage and constancy, both for the honour of their *function*, and of the *reformed Religion*, and of this Church and Nation; We cannot think those in power to be so easily perswaded to be enemies to themselves and the publique, by being made enemies to true Ministers, without a cause: One of whose *serious and solid abilities*, is able to doe more good to Church and State in one year, than can be hoped from the whole *fraternity*, and faction of those *supercilious adversaries* of the Ministry, in as many ages, as a year hath dayes; For if wise men may guesse at the future, by what they already finde of them, they must conclude, that *like Fistulas and gangrened Ulcers*, the longer they prevail, the more desperate and incurable they will be, both to the Church and the State; every day bringing us neerer, either to old *Rome*, or the elder *Babylon*: to superstition, or confusion. For there is nothing almost in this Church of *England*, as to the extern order and profession of Religion, which some of these Antiministerials, and Antidecimists doe not contest against and study to overthrow.

20. *Answer to other lesse scruples.*

...Which makes me here a little *digresse*, (yet not from my maine design (which is to satisfie all excellent Christians and others, as to any thing by these men objectable against the Ministers and Ministry of the Church of *England*) by looking at some *lesser calumnies and cavils*, which they every where scatter among the common people, to alienate them from, or prejudice them against their *Ministers*: quarrelling against the places, where publiquely we meet to serve God, and many things used by us in our holy Ministrations; 1. As to the publique places where Christians meet and Ministers officiate, these supercriticall masters of words, and censors of all mens language and manners, but their owne, cannot indure the *impropriety*, and profanenesse (as they say) of calling those places *Churches*; This they scorn with very *severe smiles*, and *supercilious frownes*; so profound is their judgement, and so scrupulous their conscience, that they had rather pull down such publique and convenient places, than venture to be defiled, by coming into them, or once so much, as to call them *Churches*; they say they have far higher senses, and *definitions of a Church*, than will agree with piles of *wood* and *stones*.

Of publique places called Churches.

It was the work of *Diocletian* to burn all the books and destroy all the Churches of the Christians. *Euseb. hist. l.* 10.

Answ. We doubt not of their *deep Divinity*, touching a Church; which it may be, they will not dare yet to *define*; as not being well agreed, what a *Church is*, or what is the right matter and forme or way of a Church; Much broken and wrangling stuffe they have heaped up touching a Church; but scarse one stone is yet laid of the edifice. I have *otherwhere* endevoured to lead them out of the *labyrinth of their rubbidge*; who have disputed more about *constituting Church*, than ever they studied to be *lively* and *orderly* members, either of the highest sense of a Church, the mysticall body of Christ, (which is made up by faith and charity;) or of that *lower sense* of a sociall Church, which yet is most proper to us, and fals neerest under mans consideration; which consists of a *visible polity* of men on earth professing to beleive in the name of Jesus Christ; and partaking of those holy *Institutions*, which he hath appointed, both to gather and distinguish, to plant and propagate, to build and preserve, to guide and govern such an holy fraternity of *religious professors*, in such truth, order, and unity; as to have a professionall relation to Christ *the head*; and a communion of Charity with each other, as members of one body: which is that *Catholick Church all over the world* in its severall parts and branches: In these and some other the like ambiguities about a Church as greater or lesse they please themselves, spending much time to instruct their *silly auditors*, how much difference there is, between these Churches of Christ, which are *spirituall*, or *rationall*; and those *Steeple-houses*, which we other (weaker ones) call, *most absurdly* as they pretend, Churches.

O how devout a thing is ignorance! How *Saraphick* men, and women grow, by having no skill in any language but their own mother tongue, which yet in this is of our side; and being the rule of speech, every where justifies our calling those places Churches, by the authority of the best writers in humanity, law, history, or divinity. But that they say was an errour of speech which men sucked in with their milk: which to spend, and evaporate, these men are every day making issues in their auditours eares; that they may unlearn that *dangerous* errour, and scandalous word of calling the *meeting places, Churches*. I know *these Rabbies* scorne to be brought to their Grammars, or to any Etymologicall authours or makers of Dictionaries; (for these they reckon among the *cursed spawn of learned men*: and look on them as if they were *Negroes* of *Chams* posterity) yet I cannot but make a little stay here, that I may shew them the *way* to that *locall Church*; where some of them have not been, these many years, unlesse it be to make a *wrangling rate*: For however these be not the main Ulcers which I desire to cure; yet they are a strange *kinde of itch*, and scurfe of Religion, which makes many Christians oft scratch very unquietly and unhandsomely.

Church, *Kyrch*, or *Kerck*, *Sax.* *quasi Kuriack*, *i.e.* κυρίου οἶκος the Lords house.

It is very easie, and very true to tell them, that it is no more unproper, to call these places, where Christians as the Lords people publiquely meet to *worship the Lord*, *Churches*; than it was to call the *Synagogues* among the *Jews*, *the Houses of God*, for the building

Psal. 74. 8.
Psal. 83, 12.

building of which we read no precise *command from God*; which was but for *one house*: namely the *Temple at Jerusalem*. The *Saxon, Scottish, British*, and *Dutch* names, which are all from the *Greeke* (Κυριακὸς:) so the *Latin, Dominicum*, (as the *Lords Table*, and the *Lords day*) signifies no more than this; That such a place, time, or table, is set apart for the *Lords service*; or for the *Lords people*: Doth not *Joshua* say, *I and my house will serve the Lord*? meaning the *rationall family*, not the *materiall pile*; *Senate* and *City*, are used for both the persons, and the place; so is the *Parliament house* for both: These *Metonymies* are no *solœcismes*, but elegancies, and aptitudes of speech; and if they were lesse *proper*, yet sure, it is no sin for Christians to speak after the *vulgar* use, and common language. True Religion hath set no such *pedantique bounds*, as these *captious Criticks* would pretend; which scrupulosity of speaking is among the other *pedling superstitions* and popular trifles, which they pin on the sleeve of piety: Affecting to be knowne by such small differences of speech as their *Shiboleths* from other Christians: Indeed their great *penury* both of knowledge, and discretion makes them no more fit Masters to teach men, how to speak, or what to doe, then how to give; their learning, and their liberality are much alike.

These places called by the ancients *Ecclesia, Dei Domus*. *Tertul. de velan. Virg. Orig. in Psal.* 36. *Dominicum*. Aust. *Collectæ locus*, Cyp. Εὐκτήριον, Ναὸς τῆς τοῦ δεσπότου προσηγορίας ἠξίωται τὰ καθιερωμένα. *Euse. de laud. Const.* Ἐκ ὅλων κυρίου κυριακῶν ἠξίωνται ἐπωνυμίων. *Id. hist. l.* 9. c. 10. οἶκος ἐκκλησίας: Ἐκκλησιαστήριον. *Isi. Pel. l.* 2. *Ep.* 246.

2. As it is easie to help these *Infant-wits* over the straw of the name, *Church*, applyed to the place which they will needs make a stumbling block: so with as much *ease* we may relieve them, from that *rock of offence*, on which they dash, against the places we call *Churches*; in regard of their *dedication*, or *consecration* to sacred or religious uses: This they have onely heard; (it may be they never either saw or read it) yet they abominate the places for the report; counting them desecrated, and execrable.

21. *Of Churches as consecrated.*

This subject is learnedly and gravely handled (as all things he undertook) by the incomparable Mr. Hocker, *l.* 5. *Pol. Sec.* 14, 15, 16.

Here they may please to know, That wise men look upon that ancient custome among Christians of setting solemnly apart some place for the service of God, not as any *affixing inherent holinesse* to them, or deriving any *communicative*, or *virtuall holynesse* from them, but meerly a publique and solemn owning, appointing, and declaring those houses or places to be erected, and dedicated by *common consent* for those holy ends, uses, and duties, which Christians ought to intend, when they meet in those places; not

Vide *Hospin. de Templorum Origine*. *Quid lapides isti poterunt sanctitatis habere?* Ber. vid. Ser. 6. *Non locus hominem, sed homines locum sanctificant. Nemo se blandiatur de loco, qui sanctius dicitur*, Bern. 182.

for common, civill, profane, or uncomely affaires; which *appropriating* or *dedicating* is an act of right Reason, flowing from the light of Nature, and that common notion of *reverence* to be externally expressed to God, which is in all men, that *owne any God*: which right Reason is most agreeable to *true Religion*, and alwayes as servient to it, as Deacons, and Church-wardens ought to be to the Ministers in holy things; as both these, *Reason* and *Religion*, distinguish ends, duties and commands, which are divine, (as coming *from God*, or *relating to him*) so likewise they distinguish times, places, persons, actions, and other things, which are *separated* from *meere humane*, naturall, and civill uses, to such, as are (both preceptively, and intentionally) divine; that is, from God and for God: Nor can the God of order (who hath made the *beauty* of his works to consist, and to be evident in those *distinctions*, which he hath set upon every thing, both in the species and individuall) God (I say) cannot be *displeased* to see mankinde, (on whom is the *beauty of Reason*) or Christians, (on whom is the beauty of Religion) to use such order, distinction and decency in all things, which becomes them both as men and Christians; after the exam-
Math. 9.35. ples of the Apostles and Christ himself, who went about all the Cities and Villages, teaching in their Synagogues and preaching the Gospell of the Kingdome; which also befits and adorns Christians, as to extern profession (which is all, that appears of any mens devotion, or Religion to the eye of man) setting forth in comely sort that duty, relation, and service, which we publiquely professe to owe and pay to God, who abhors *sordidnesse* and *confusion*, as much as *profane vastators* love it.

Ægrotantium amicorum sordes toleramus, non item valentium, Sidon.

Necessity indeed admits no *curiosity* of place, nor affects any *elegancy*, but excuseth that, which, in plenty and freedome, is esteemed *sordidnesse*, and *sluttishnesse*; Religion requires externally no more, than God hath given of extern power and opportunity; where these are wanting, and by providence denyed, a *sick bed*, a *Barn*, a *Lyons den*, a *Dungeon*, a *Whales belly* is as a *Temple*, or *Church*, consecrated by the holy duties, which any devout soul, there performs to God: But as the Church of Christ, considered in its extern communion or profession, is visible; and *Christians* are exemplary to each other, and to the world; it is warrant enough for Christians to build, and to set apart to those publique holy duties, some *peculiar* places, upon Gods, and the Churches account; which grant we have in that great Charter and principle of Church policy (which, like a common
1 Cor. 14.40. rule, measures all things of extern, sociall Religion) *Let all things be done decently, and in order*; Both which fall, not properly under the judgement of Religion, but of Reason; not of Scripture, but of Nature; not of piety, but policy or society; nor need we other command

command to doe them, than the judgement, and consent, or custome of wise and holy men; which we have for this use *of locall Churches*, thus peculiarly applyed to holy services, ever since Christians had either ability to build them, or liberty to use them, which is at least 1400 years agoe.

If *humane*, or *Romish superstition* used, or affected, or opined any thing, in *consecrating Churches*, which is beyond true reason, and sound Religion, yet we do not think, that to be a *Leprosie* sticking so to the wals of the buildings, that they must be *scraped* all over, or *pulled down*, else they can't be *cleansed*; No: But, as *places* are not, any more than *times*, capable of any essentiall gratious, or inherent holynesse, (which is onely in *God*, *Angels*, or *Men*,) so neither are they capable of *inherent unholinesse*; The superstition is weak on either side, & weighs little; but the worst is on this side, to which these men so incline; which tends *more to profanenesse, supinenesse*, and *slovenlinesse* in the outward garb of Religion; which is not either so *Cynical*, or so *tetricall*, as these men would make it. What ever there is reall or imaginary, of *Superstition* in the places, or rather in mens fancies of them, who possibly *ascribe* too much to them, it will as easily recede, and quit them, when they come to be *consecrated* by the Churches reall performing of holy services, or publique religious duties in them; as *dreams* doe vanish, when one awakes; or as the dark *shadowes* of the night depart from bodies, when the Sun comes to shine on them, or into them; if these poore *objectors* mindes and spirits, could as soone be freed from those profane, superstitious and uncharitable tinctures, (with which they are, as with a *jaundise* deeply infected, against those places, and against those that use them, with the decency, becoming duties done to the Majesty of God, and in the presence of the Church of Christ) as those places (justly called Churches) may be freed from all misapprehensions, of their name, or their dedication; If the former were as easie, as the latter; both *locall* and *rationall*, *materiall* and *mentall* Churches, both *places* and *persons*, might long *stand* and *flourish*; Both which some *furies* of our times seek utterly to *break down*, and demolish, that there may be neither Christian Congregations, nor decent Communion in any publique place, beyond the beauty of a Barn or Stable.

Sacerdoti maxime convenit ornare Dei templum decore congruo. Amb. off. l. 1. c. 21.

Psal. 74. 6.

22. *Answer to other quarrels against Ministers publique duties.*

But these men have so much *tinder* and *Gunpowder* in them, against Ministers, that, whatever they enjoy, say, use, or doe in their function, be it never so *innocent* and *decent*, yet they kindle to some *offensive sparkes*, or *coales*, and *flames* against them: As if all the *Ministers* of this Church knew not what, to doe, as they should, till these new masters undertook to *School* and Catechise them.

If any Minister prayes publiquely with that *gravity*, *understanding*, and constancy, either for matter, words, or method, which best becomes a poore sinfull mortall on earth, when he speaks to the God of heaven; It is (they say), but a *form*, and a *stinting* of the Spirit: If they preach with judgement, weight, exactnesse, and *demonstration*, of truth, it is not *by the Spirit*; but of *study* and *learning*. If they *read* the Scripture, 'tis but *a dead letter*, and meer *lip-labour*: If they celebrate the *Sacraments* with that wisdome, reverence and decency which becomes those holy mysteries; they quarrell at *the place*, or time, or gesture, or company, or ceremonies used; Not considering that Ceremonies in Religion, are like hair, ornaments, though not essentials; and ought to be, neither too long, lest they hide and obscure it; nor too short, lest they leave it naked and deformed: Since the end and use of them is no more, but to set forth piety with the greater comelinesse and auguster majesty to men. If they name any *Apostle*, Evangelist, or other Christian of *undoubted sanctity*, with the Epithet of *Saint*, they are so scared with the thought of the *Popes canonizing Saints*, that they start at the very name so used: as if it were an *unsanctified* title; and not to be applyed to the memory of the just, *which is blessed*, but onely arrogated to some persons living; who frequently and ambitiously call themselves, and

2 Tim. 1. 13. their party, *The Saints*: If they use the ancient Doxology, giving glory to the Father, Son, and holy Ghost, which all Churches, Greek and Latin, did; the *Socinian* and *Arian* Ears of some men are highly offended at it: as if Christians must ask them leave to own the holy Trinity, and to give solemne publique glory to the Creator, Saviour, and sanctifying Comforter of the Church. If Ministers use those *wholesome forms of sound words*, which are fitted to the memories, and capacities of the meanest hearers; containing short *summaries* of things to be believed, practised, or prayed for; as in the *Creed*, the ten *Commandements*, and the *Lords Prayer*; Presently these men fancy them as the *recitation of some charmes*; and look on the Minister, as some *Exorcist*, confined to these *Articles of stinted* spels and formes: Yea so far hath the prejudices, affectations and ignorance of these men prevailed, against all Reason and Religion, in some places; that many Ministers (in other things) not unable, or unworthy men, *are carried away* with fear and popularity to comply with those mens *fondnesse* in a way of *dissimulation*; *Forbearing* to use publiquely at any time either the title of Saint due to holy men, or the *Lords Prayer*, and the *Decalogue*; which are both Scripturall Summaries, and commanded to be used. So also they lay aside the *Creed*, which is an Ecclesiasticall compendium taken

Vid. Voss. de Symbolis. out of the Scripture, and very ancient in the chief articles of it; containing the main foundations or *heads* of Christian Faith; nor

was

was any of these ever neglected, or not both frequently and devoutly used in the publique Liturgies or Services of sober Christians, either ancient or modern.

O how sowre and *spreading a leaven* is the *pride, passion*, and *superstition* of mens spirits which run after faction and novelties! that even *learned* and *grave* men should be, not so much *infected* with it in their judgements, as to be *swayed* and *byassed*, or over-awed by it, in their practise, contrary to *their judgements*; meerly, as St. *Peter with his dissimulation*, gratifying *these pretenders* to novelty *speciall sanctity*, by the not using of those divine and *wholesome forms of sound words*: in which neglect the presumed perfection of these *Antiministeriall men*, disdains to *condescend* to the infirmities of *novices*, and *weaklings* in religion, the babes in Christ, Those *Lambs*, which good *Shepheards*, must take speciall care of, as well as of their *stronger sheep*, feeding them with *milk*, (or *cibo præmanso*) the often repeated Catechisticall rudiments, and chewed principles of Religion, which are by the wisdome of God, and our Saviour, most fitly and compendiously set forth in the ten Commandements and the Lords Prayer, as to the main of things to be done or desired by a Christian; as also the summe of things necessary to be believed were anciently comprised in the Articles of the *Creed*, according to that wisdome of the Apostles or the primitive Fathers, which imitated those patterns, set by the Lord to his Church: That so the *Infants* or *younglings* of *Christs family* might not be *starved*, because they have not such teeth, as these mens *jaw-bones pretend* to; who (before they have well sucked in the first principles) are *gnawing bones*, or cracking kernels and *nuts*, exercising themselves, or vexing others, with odd questions, and *doubtfull disputations*; more troubled with *their Familisticall fancies*, about their own partaking *of the divine Nature*, their identity with Christ, and when and how it is; in what manner, and what measure they may be said to be God, and Christ, and the Spirit; than soberly establishing their mindes in the fundamentall points of things to be beleived, obeyed, and desired to the glory of God, and the honour of the Gospell.

Gal. 2.12.

Joh. 21: 15.

But I must leave these envious and unquiet Spirits to their censorious separations, wrangling themselves into vanities and errors; at length falling (like *Lucifer*) into the *blacknesse of darknesse*, to unjustice and cruelty; after that into grosser blasphemies and presumptions against God, Christ, and the holy Spirit: while they proudly affect, and presume to be not *like to the most High*; but the same with him; not in the beauties of *holinesse, grace*, and *godlinesse*, which are the *clear* (Image of God set forth) in the Word; but in the *glory and majesty of the divine Essence*; which is inscrutable; not to be communicated or comprehended, in its *superessentiall* being,

and

and superintellectuall perfection; no more than the vast and glorious body of the Sun, which is 160 times bigger than the earth, can be locally contained in the eye; to which yet it is by its beams in some kinde imparted and united. Such superfluity we see there is of folly, ignorance, weaknesse, pride and malice in *some spirits*: who, upon very *peevish* and perverse grounds, forsake our Christian *publique Assemblies* and duties celebrated in our Churches; (which are sanctified by the Word and prayer) scorning and condemning what we doe, upon the best grounds of Scripture and Reason; *separating* themselves from the true Ministry, and fellowship of the Church of *England*; as if they were most spirituall and refined; when yet they seem to be so grossely ignorant, so passionate, and some of them so sensuall, as is no argument of their having the Spirit of God, which is wise in all holinesse.

---

7. *Calumny.* Act. 24. 5. *Against Ministers as seditious and inconform to Civil government.*

BUt our Antiministeriall Adversaries object, as *Tertullus*, and the *Jews* did against St. *Paul*, that the *ordained Ministers* of the *former way, are pestilent fellows, stirrers up of the people*; *factious, turbulent, seditious*; not so *supple, conform*, and well affected to the present constitution of powers and publique affaires: So that it is not onely lawfull, but necessary, either to bring them to a plenary conformity, and subjection; or to *exautorate* and suppresse them, as to all publique influence in the Ministry: Thus doe these *Wasps* and *Hornets* buz up and down; who hope with their noise and *stings* ere long to drive all the ancient and true Ministers of God out of the land; or at least out of the service of the Church, that so they may be possessed *of the Hive*, though they *make no Honey*.

Answ. *Answ.* This Calumny is indeed of the *promising advantage* to the enemies of the *Ministers*, and their calling; and therefore it is with most cunning and earnestnesse every where levelled by some men against their persons, actions, and function; It is like the policy of *Julian* the Apostate, who to ensnare the Christians set the statues of the Emperours with the Idols of the Gods; That if Christians did civill reverence, as to the Emperours, they should be defamed as Idolaters; if not, they should be accused as despisers of the Emperours: And because I perswade my self, that all *excellent Christians*, how potent soever, can bear an *honest freedome*, and plainnesse, I shall onely, as to this *sharp and poysoned arrow*, oppose the *shield of plain dealing*; that in a matter so much concerning the

Naz. στηλ. 1.

the *satisfaction* of others, and *Ministers civill safety*, there may be no such *obscurities* as may harbour any *jealousies*.

1. *Some Ministers compliances.*

First of all, I need not tell *you*, what all the *English* world knows aboundantly; That there are *many Ministers* of very good abilities, who are not at all blameable in this particular; as to any *restivenesse* and *incompliancy* in *civill subjections*; they have sufficiently testified how Arts and ingenuous learning *soften* the spirits and manners of men; how they supple in them that *roughnesse* and *asperity*, which remains in others: how of *okes* it makes them become *willowes*; and in stead of hard wax, (which onely fire can tame) makes them gentle, as soft wax; so good natured, that they are not at all pertinacious of any former signatures, and stamps; either as civill, or sacred, made upon them: but readily and explicitely yeeld to any *formes* and *impressions*, though never so new and different; which the hand of power is pleased to make: And this, not only as to a passive sequaciousnesse, in the externall fashion of their civill conversation and profession; but as to those *internall characters* and *perswasions*, which their judgments have made upon their consciences. Nothing is more *tractable* and *malleable*, nothing more easily runs into any *State mould*, and receives any politick figure and mark, than many Ministers doe: whose judgements, or policy, or fears, or necessities have taught them how they may **serve the Lord, and the times too*; how to become *all things to all men*, in regard of things civill and extern; they have many *wholesome* and *prudent latitudes* of evasions, absolutions, *cautions* and *distinctions*, by which they unravell the cords of any *Oathes*, and untwist the bonds of any *Covenants*, or *Protestations*; They have in things meerly politick, as many distinctions, as would furnish any good Casuist, for the absolution of *entangled*, or the satisfaction of *grumbling consciences*; Thus furnished, no wonder if in *civill changes* which are fatall, and by them unavoidable, they can never be brought to *Baalams straits*; where an Angell should meet them with a *drawn sword*; and the Asse either fall under them, or *crush* them against the wall on either side.

* Rom. 12.11. Δουλεύοντες τῷ κυρίῳ. τῷ καιρῷ. *Beza* interp. *Domino servientes: ut* Chryso. Basil. &c. Erasmus, *Tempori servientes; i. e. Temporum incommodis sese accommodantes; patientia & charitate.*

Numb. 22.

utriusque fortunæ documento didicerunt, ne contumaciam cum pernicie mallent, quam securitatem cum obsequio. Tacit. hist. l. 4.

These Ministers acting according to their consciences cannot justly be blamed for any *refractarinesse*; many of whom are so much, every where, in any civill *conformities*, that you can hardly lose them in any State alterations, or labyrinths: nor doe they doubt but the Lord will be mercifull to them in this thing, which not private choice & inconstancy, but publique force and necessitie puts upon them. Charity commands to judge and hope, that these

 doe

doe all things, according to that light, and latitude, which is in their consciences, as to *things secular*: Wherein they conceive, that the *Providence of God*, which is as his *voice* teaching us by the *event of all* humane affaires what is his will, is a *sufficient absolution*, as to all *preceeding ties*, civill or sacred; which they look upon as obligatory onely in relation to power *Magistratick* publique, and effectuall, in what men, and in what manner soever they see it placed and exercised. Thus some learned men and Ministers plead it as a matter of not onely necessity and prudence, but also of justice and gratitude; that what ever power Christians are by providence cast under, and by that doe, in any order of justice, enjoy *civill protection*, there they should *pay* a *civill* and *peaceable subjection*, according to *Conscience* and *equity*; while they have the benefit of Lawes and government, they ought to yeeld obedience according to Law: and this not so much to the persons of men governing, who may be unworthy; but to the Ordinance of God, civill government, which is managed at present by them.

Mic. 6. 9.

2. *Others more pragmaticall and fierce.*

...2. There are indeed other Ministers, who are not only of *harder metall*, but of *hotter tempers*; of more cholerick constitutions, and *feaverish complexions*; who love to be moving in the *troubled waters* of secular affaires; who seem most impatient of any order, or publique rule, in which they have not some stroke, and influence, ready to undoe, what ever is done without them: Their breast is as full of turbulent and seditious spirits, as the *Cave of Æolus* is of windes, forgetting what *spirit* becomes the Ministers of the Gospell in all times; who, though they may denounce hell fire against all impenitent sinners, yet they may not kindle *civill flames of sedition*, or *imprecate revengefull fire from heaven* upon any men to destroy them. To the *misguided activity* of such Ministers some think the publique may owe much of its troubles; for whom the best Apology is their repentance, for any transports and excesses whereto they have been weakly or wilfully carryed beyond those bounds of *duty* and *gravity*, which as Ministers and subjects they ought to observe, both toward God and man; All that can be pleaded in any *veniality* for their folly and fury is, the * common *genius and generall distemper of times*, which slackening by civill dissensions the cords of humane lawes, and loosning the ties of wonted modesty and observance to *Superiours*, gave so great temptations, that many Ministers of more forward spirits, knew not how to resist them.

Luk. 9. 54.

* *Exeuntium omnem ingeniis medioeribus constantiam fatales regnorum & rerumpub: motus.* Ju. de pictur. l. 2. c. 13. *Plurimum refert in quæ cujusque virtus tempora inciderit.* Plin. l. nat.

Alas! who hath not sufficiently seen in our dayes by sad experiences, that even among *Ministers* there are not onely poor, *weak* and *credulous*, but also heady, turbulent and factious *men*; prone to affect any *miserable way of popularity*, and to debase their function and profession

profession to most *pragmatick impertinencies*, as in Ecclesiasticall, so also in Secular affaires; though their gifts be (other wayes above the ordinary size) very usefull and commendable, yet they retain much of the vulgar masse and leaven, and are subject to the same passions and common infirmities; yea no men are more prone to *rash indeavourings* and *bold activities*, by how much they have many *specious fancies*, and *pretty speculations*, suggested to them by those bookes they read: which to some men is a *kinde of Necromancy*, a *conversing with the dead*, and conjecturing by their counsels; So that some of them, *like Alchymists*, by their reading of *chymicall lights*, grow so possest of *their Elixars*, or *Philosophers stones*, as if it were within a stones cast of them; counting it a sinfull and *shamefull lazinesse*, for them to sit still, when they are tempted to such *goodly prizes*, as their notions and conceptions hold forth, in some way of reforming, or wholly changing the State of Religion and government of any Church; and in order to that they shake even the civill frame of things; to which they doe not think themselves longer bound in subjection, then they want a party strong enough for opposition; nor will they easily be perswaded that is the sin of Rebellion, which carries the face of Reformation: easily dispensing with obedience to man, where they pretend amendment before God. Want of experience in worldly affairs (which is hardly gained, within mens Study wals) oftentimes prompts warm spirited men, first easily to approve, then passionately to desire, afterwards weakly and unproportionably to agitate, those precipitant counsels and *specious designes*, which oft prove to the shame, and ruine of themselves, and their seduced party. Indeed few Ministers of more pragmatick heads, and *popular parts*, but think themselves fit to be (and take it ill, if they be not) *Counsellours of State*; Members of Synods, or moderators and determiners of all affaires both Ecclesiasticall and Civill; hardly acquiescing in any thing, as well setled either in *Church* or *State*, wherein regard is not had to their judgement, party, and *perswasion*; of which they are alwayes so very well perswaded, that, when they cry most down others as Churchmen from having any foot or hand in any civill businesses, themselves can presently step in *over head and ears*, so far implunged in State troubles and secular commotions, that they hardly ever get out of them with honour and safety, or with inward peace and comfort; Nor can they easily lick off that bloud, which may lye upon them, when they have no weapon left them but their tongues.

τοῖς νεκροῖς συγκεντίζεσθαι.

Studiis in umbra educatus, Sen.

Consilia callida & inhonesta, prima fronte læta, tractatu dura, eventu tristia, Tacit.

The truth is; *no men* are more *violently* and *superstitiously* devoted to their own fancies and opinions, than some Ministers are; none more *unfeigned Idolaters* of those little *Idols*, which their owne, or others imaginations have figured; and which they would fain set up, as Gods both in Church and State; To these, they preach it necessary that all Christians should bow down; that without *this mark* of conformity to their way none should either *buy or sell*: And when they have once so far flattered themselves in their own *well meaning projects*, that they proclaim *God*, and *Christ* to be engaged on their side; then they conclude, that *Hee* can by no means be so wanting to *his own glory*, as not to give all speedy and effectuall assistances to all their purposes and designes; which are verbally as much to his honour, as they would be really to their own advantages, if they should prevail and succeed: If they be defeated, both God, and all good Christians, (of a different minde from them) are prone to fall under their hard censures; and if they doe not charge *him foolishly*, yet they doe blame their brethren and betters, for want of *zeal to Christ*, and to what they list to call *his cause*: Such great counsails are oft agitated in the small conclaves of Clergy men: And what they blame in Cardinals abroad, or Bishops at home; themselves are eager to practise even beyond *Richelieu* himself: For they lay designes, not for one Church or Nation, but for the whole world.

Rev. 13. 17.

Isa. 55. 8. Ioh. 16. 2.

Forgetting, that *Gods thoughts are not as mans*; who may be never more mistaken, than when they think, they doe *God very good service* even by killing of others: Nor are, indeed, the thoughts of the wisest and most learned Ministers, or the humblest Christians, such as those (mens pragmatick projects are) who by easie perswasions, and *popular presumptions* do so much slight all *ancient wayes*, and Catholick customes of the Churches of Christ, which are the great seales of Religion, both evidencing and confirming those holy orders and institutions, which were appointed by Christ and his Apostles: Pretending to follow some new Scripture rules and patterns in things of *extern order*, and discipline; which can never by any sound interpretation of the places alledged be supposed, or proved to be either diverse from, or contrary to the universall way and use of the primitive Churches; who, without doubt, were as carefull to act in their outward order and government of the Church according to Apostolicall patterns, and traditionall institutions, which were first the rule of the Churches practise; as they were faithfull to preserve the *Canon of the Scriptures* which were after written, and to deliver them without variation or corruption to posterity. But *specious novelties* in Religion or Church forms once formed in some mens heads, are prone to move their hearts, with very quick excitations and zealous resolutions: Soon after, (like *salt rhewms*) they descend and fall upon their *lungs*, provoking them to continuall *coughs*; so that they cannot

be

be silent, or suppresse their desires of new things in Church and State; Then they are violently carried on to the spreading of their opinion, and way to others; who are easily made drunk with any *new wine*; At length they run giddily and rashly to some *rude precipice*; where if they go on, they are destroyed; if they retreat, it is not without shame from others, and regret in themselves: Together with after jealousies of State brought upon their *whole function*, or that *faction* at least; it being a case sufficiently known, that most men are so much *self-flatterers*, and *self-lovers*, that they are impatient of *any defeats*, ready to study and watch oportunities of revenge; when they see the children of *their brains*, which soon become the *darlings* of their devotion, to prove meer *abortions*; or to be violently dashed in pieces; when, indeed, they never had the due formations of Scripture, nor conceptions of Reason, nor productions of Prudence.

Hence, in Politicks, many times *sharp examples* have chastened severely the preposterous machinations and motions even of Churchmen and Ministers, when they forsake the ancient refuges of Christians, and Ministers (especially) which were *preaching* * *prayers*; and *tears*, and betake themselves to swords, and helmets, to plots and conspiracies. If those Ministers of hotter spirits doe not; yet others do finde themselves sufficiently taught that wiser *temper* and *modest* behaviour, which becomes *Ecclesiasticks* in all civill relations and affaires; especially if they carry any *face of change and novelty*, or have the least lineament of factious *non-conformities* to the established laws and customes in Church or State; wise men have sufficiently seen those miseries, obscurities, and disgraces, which (as black shadowes) have attended, even Churchmen, in that shame, and those defeats, by which God hath quenched the *rash heats*, and *over boylings* of their fancies, hopes, and activities.

* Δάκρυα μόνον ἔχουσι φάρμακον. Χριστιανοὶ κτ. τοὺς διώκοντας. Naz. στηλ. 1.

3. Some Ministers errors not imputable to all.

3. Therefore my answer to the main of this *Calumny* is, by way of *humble request to all excellent Christians*; that the *jealousies*, which some Ministers *weaknesse*, rashnesse, or folly may have occasioned, may not reflect upon the whole *function of the Ministry*; nor the sins and errours of any *mens persons* be imputed to *their profession*; as if it were among the *principles* of all *Ministers*, never *to rest quiet from civill combustions* till they have their wils: That Ministers may have many failings, is not denyed; if you would have them wholly without fault, you must have none of *humane* race and kinde; Not onely Gods exactnesse, but sober mens sight may easily discover *folly* in the *purest Angels of his Church*; many spots in the brightest *Moones*, and much *nebulousnesse* in the fairest *Stars*: Yet, God forbid, that any men of justice, honour, or conscience, should charge upon *all Ministers*, and the whole function, the

 disorders

disorders of some; when as there are many hundreds of grave, learned, wise, humble, meek and quiet spirited men, whose excellent vertues, graces, endowments, and publique merits, may more than enough, countervaile, and expiate the weaknesse, or extravagancies of their brethren; Ministers, as well as other men, (except those, whose opinions and fancies are so *died in graine*, that *their follies* will never depart from them) have learned many experiences both in *England* and *Scotland*; that an *over-charged*, or an *ill-discharged* zeal usually breaks it self in sunder; with infinite danger, not only to its authours, but to its abettors, assistants and spectators: And however, at first it might seem *levelled* against enemies, yet it makes the neerest friends and standers by, ever after *wary*, and afraid both of such *Guns*, and their *Gunners*; of such dangerous designes, and their designers. Nothing is more touchy and intractable, than matters of civill power and dominion, in which we have neither precept nor practise from Christ or his Apostles, for Ministers to engage themselves in any way of offense; which their wisedome avoided. They were thought of old, things fitter for the hands of *Cyclops*, who forged *Jupiters* thunderbolts, than for the Priests of the Gods.

Great and sad experiences (shewing how rough, and violent with bloud and ruine all *secular changes* are: how unsutable and unsafe to the *softer hands* of Ministers) these have added *wisdome to the wise*; and taught them very sober, and wholesome lessons, of all peaceable and due subjection, both to God; (who may *govern us by whom he pleaseth*) and to man, who cannot have power, but by *Gods permission*; which at the best and justest posture, is not to be envied so much, as pitied by prudent and holy men; who see it attended with so many cares, feares and horrours; infinite dangers and temptations; besides a kinde of necessity sometime in reason of State to doe things unjust and uncomfortable: at least to tolerate wayes that are neither pious nor charitable.

Psal. 75. 7.
Dan. 4. 17.

Habet aliquid ex iniquo omne magnum exemplum, quod contra singulos utilitate publica rependitur. Tacit. l. 14. An.
Liceat inter abruptam contumaciam, & deforme obsequium pergere iter ambitione & periculis vacuum. Tac. An. l. 4.

So that the humble, peaceable, and *discreet carriage* of all wise, and *worthy Ministers* (which only becomes them) may justly plead for *favour* and *protection* against this *calumny of pronenesse to sedition*, *faction*, or any illegall disturbance *in civill affaires*; even in all the unhappy troubles of the late yeares, the wisest and *best Ministers* have generally so behaved themselves, as shewed they had no other design, than to live a *quiet life in all godlinesse and honesty*; to serve the Lord Christ, and his Church, (peaceably if they might) in that station, where they were lawfully set; if they could not help in fair wayes to steer the ship as they desired, yet they did not seek to set it on fire, or split and overwhelm it: If in any thing relating to *publique variations* and *violent tossings*, they were not able to act *with a satisfied and good conscience*; yet they ever knew their duty, was humbly to bear with *silence*, and suffer with *patience* from the *hands of men*, the *will of God*; whose *judgements* they humbly adore, though dark, deep, and past *finding out*; If some mens dubiousnesse and *unsatisfiednesse* in any things (as they are the works of men, who may sin and erre) be to be blamed, (as it is not in any righteous judgement) yet it is withall, so far to be *pitied* and *pardoned*, by all that are true Christians, or civill men, as they see it accompanied with *commendable integrity*, *meeknesse*, and *harmlesse simplicity*; which onely becomes *these doves and serpents*, which Christ hath sent to teach his Church, both *wisdome* and *innocency*, to walk exactly and circumspectly in the slippery pathes of this world not onely by sound *doctrine*, but also by setled *examples*.

Χρὴ πρὸς θεὸν οὐκ ἐρίζειν. Pind.

Rom. 11. 33.

Mat. 10. 16.

Which excellent temper would prevent many troubles among Christians; and much *evill suspicion* against Ministers; who could not be justly offensive or suspected *to any in power*, if they saw them chiefly intentive to serve, and fearfull to offend God; always tender of good consciences, and of the honor of true Christian Religion; which was not wont to see *Ministers* with swords and pistols in their hands, but with their *Bibles* and *Liturgies*; not rough and targetted as the *Rhinoceroes*, but soft and gently clothed as the sheep and Shepherds of Christ. There is not indeed a more *portentous sight*, than to see *Galeatos Clericos*, *Ministers* armed with any other *helmet*, than that of Salvation; or *sword*, than that of the Spirit; or *shield*, than that of Faith; by which they will easily overcome the world, if once they have overcome themselves: whose courage will be as great in *praying*, *preaching*, and *suffering* with patience, meeknesse and constancy, as in *busling* and fighting; which becomes *Butchers* better than *Ministers*; to whom Christ long ago commanded in the *person of S. Peter* to put up *their swords*: nor was he ever heard to repeal that word; or to bid them draw *their swords*; no, not in *Christs cause*, that is meerly for matters of Religion, who hath Legions of Angels, Armies of truths, gifts and graces of the Spirit to defend himself, and his true interests in Religion withall: which are far *better* and fitter *weapons* in *Ministers warfare*, than such *swords and staves*, as they brought, who intended to *betray*, to take, and to *destroy* Christ. Let *secular powers* forcibly act (as becomes them) in the matters of Religion, so farre as they are asserted and established by Law, (whose proper attendant is *armed power*) It is enough for Ministers *zeal* to be with *Moses*, *Aaron*, and *Hur* in the *Mount praying*; when *Joshua*, in the justest quarrell, is *fighting with Amalek*; that is, the unprovoked and causelesse enemies of the Church. If at any time they counsel or

Mat. 26. 52.

2 Cor. 10. 4. The weapons of our warfare are not carnall.

Exod. 17.

act

act matters of life and death, they must be so clearly and indisputably just, and within the compasse of their duty and relation, as may every way become valiant men, humble Christians, and prudent Ministers.

Object. 4. Of the Engagement.

But to confute all that can be said for the *Ministers of England*, their adversaries are ready to object, that many of them scruple the *taking of the Engagement*; This they think is a *pill*, which will either choak their consciences, if they swallow it, or *purge them* out of their livings, if they doe not; For, contrary to all other Physick, this operates most strongly on those, that never *take it*.

Answ. Truly this is the onely tender part, the *undipped heel*, where (it may be) some of these *Achillesses*, able and good Ministers, may be hurt; In which I humbly crave leave without offence to the power, or prejudice to the wisdome of any men, to offer thus much in the behalf of peaceable Ministers. That,

1. It is not true of all: *many Ministers* have shewed, by their taking it, in such a sense of passivenesse under, and *non-activity*, against the present establishment, as is satisfactory to the Imposers, and inoffensive to their own consciences; what others would doe, if they could, with *inward peace*. And if there were no other excuse or Apology for these *peaceable*, and *painfull Ministers*, (who have not subscribed) but onely those *many pleas of Conscience*, which have been humbly tendred to publique view; these ought not to be unconsidered by such as professe to be *Christians*; who remember, how *cruell a thing* it is, to make mens *consciences passe*, as *Gideon* did the men of *Succoth*, or *David* the *Ammonites*, under *briars* and *thorns*, under *saws* and *harrows*; of either *sharp contradictions*, or *prickly distinctions*; unsafe *Salvoes*, which if they may seem *evasions* before men (in matter of Oathes lawfully taken) yet possibly, may not prove full absolutions before God, who hath oft severely exacted the *forfeitures* of perjury; as of *Saul* and *Zedekiah*. And how ever God in his providence may put suspensions of oathes, as to their actuall execution; yet they cannot find any absolution from the obligation which goes with inconditionate Oathes, so long as they are within our morall possibility of keeping them: How any man can swear or promise to be true and faithfull to two different interests, without being forsworne, or false and unfaithfull to the one or the other, seems a *Gordian* knot which onely the sword dissolves by cutting, not untying.

Perjurio maculare vitam suam magis timere debet quam finire Christianus. Aust. Ep. 224.
Judg 8.
2 Sam. 12. 31.
Σέβεσθαι ὅρκους, *Juramenta vereri religiosium.* Pythag. dict.
Mat. 5. 33.
2 Sam. 21.
Zach. 8. 17.
Jer. 34. 18.

And who can wonder, that seriously considers the *state of humane affaires*, (which are most fully represented in the glasse of our times, with as many variating faces, as the *Moon*) if some Ministers, (whom both grace and experience, age and manners have

have made *grave and calm*) are tender and *wary* of further *hampering their consciences* on any State cables: since they have seen that the former *threefold cords*, of Oathes, Protestation, and Covenant, could not resist those tides, and stormes, which have driven the whole Nation (as to extern events and affaires) from those grounds of fidelity and allegiance, both as to Civill, and Ecclesiasticall *obedience*, whereon they thought they had consciencioufly, safely and quietly cast *anchor* according to laws.

Jurandi facilitate in perjurium prolabimur, Aust.

Furthermore some mens *non-engaging* cannot be any great weakning to power, (however it may so seem to some mens jealousies and policies) since no mans *engaging* seems to be any great fortifying of it: For experience hath taught us how easily men are *absolved* from such publick ties, seem they never so strict: Nor is there any reason to think they will be stronger for the future, than they were in former times: *Publique security* doth not much consist in any *verball formalities*, but in that *efficacious power*, which men have by the sword; and which they exercise as long, as the *Lord of all the world is pleased* to execute his will, and *pleasure by any men.* Next to power, *publique authority* and *safety* riseth from the *satisfaction* of mens judgements, as to the justice of mens proceedings; winning respect and love by that equity in government and moderation, which is according to Laws setled and known: not by *arbitrarines* of will, and meer force; which as to the *principle* is tyrannous, be it never so tempered in the exercise. Under any such orderly Government, *wise Christians* and Ministers know, how with humility, peace, and patience, to *submit* as farre as is agreeable to piety, and necessary for the publique peace, no lesse than for their private safety. Last of all; Possibly those men whose interests made them most forward at first to goe in these *new and untrodden* wayes, found them not *so smooth*, (without any *rub* or *scruple*) in their own judgements and consciences; that they should greatly wonder, if others, (who are onely driven that way, without their choice, counsell or consent) doe fear, or finde something in it, which makes them *startle* or *stumble*. And truly, *in this point*, without any further arguing, (which is neither safe nor discreet as to publique resolutions of State, (in any private man) it must be *freely confessed*, that some Ministers (as well as other sober men) doe humbly cast themselves on the *mercy of God*, and the * *clemency* of those *in power*; hoping for such *toleration*, and *connivence* in this particular, as many did plead for, and injoy in their *former non-conformities*, which favour they may best deserve, because they will least *abuse it*: * Their quiet and godly carriage being as great security to Governours, as any oath can be from others: * Behaving themselves within those bounds of

Dan. 4. 17.

* *Novum imperium inchoantibus, utilis clementiæ fama.* Tacit. h. 4.

* Ἀνδρὸς καλοκαγαθοῦ βίος ὅρκος ἐστί. *Viri boni constans vita vim habet juramenti*, Cl. Al. στρω. 7.

of discretion, peaceablenesse, and *civill subjection*; which becomes them, and all truly wise and godly men in the many tossings, and changes, to which they are subjected, as other mortals, in this *mutable world*: In all which, if the strictnesse of *religion terrifies* any good

Zach. 8. 16, 7.

Christians *with the fear of any thing*, that lookes like false Oathes, or *perjury*, (one of the blackest stains, most indeleble spots and unpardonable sins of the soul) being a blaspheming, denying and defying of God: yet, certainly it allowes the most *conscientious* men, (whereever their worldly necessities and livelihoods force them to live under any *power*) such *latitudes* of honest and *peaceable subjection*, in things meerly civill and externall, as may not alwayes *force them* upon banishments, *prisons*, and *persecutions*; or else, evermore embroile them with *civill wars*, and *open hostilities*; even there where they cannot hope to *preserve themselves*, without a miracle. A wise and humble Christian is never far from his refuge; And when pursued or urged, beyond what he thinkes agreeable to a good conscience, he is not to seek for base and Foxes shifts, subtill windings, or sinfull coverts: He is alwayes ready either fairly to obey, or fairly to suffer: He needes not wiredraw his conscience, till it fits every State passage: if the way of the world be strait, yet Gods is still inlarged to him; if the worlds be large, yet he still keeps to Gods strictnesse. Certainly good men ought not too rashly to cast *away* that *just and fair protection*, which they enjoy under any *civill power*; (which, Christ tels us, no *man can have but from above, Joh. 19. 11.*) But rather with all *humble gratitude*, both to *give God the glory*; and man, that respect, which is due for any *favour*, and *indulgence* they have in worldly regards; which will ever seem least *heavy* to a good Christian; while there is no torture, rack or *tyranny* exercised upon *the conscience*; by forcing to declare or act there, wherein their judgments are not so fully satisfied, as to the point of approbation, or actual concurrence.

* Αρνησις εστι θεȣ ψευδορκία. *Naz. Car.* 158. Θεȣς ὁρκίȣς, *vocat. Thucid. l.* 1. *quos in fœderibus pangendis invocabant.*

Joh. 19. 11.

It is happy if at any time *truly conscientious Christians* can enjoy any fair quarter among *men of this world*; whose high and haughty spirits, if puffed up with successe, are hardly patient of Christs self-crucifying methods: It is wisdome in Ministers to merit, by humble and peaceable carriage according to a good conscience, all *moderation from secular powers*; who are more easily provoked against them than other men: Statesmen are often flatterers, seldom such reall friends to Jesus Christ, and his Church, as to deny themselves much for their sakes: Nor doe they usually much regard *those holy interests*, further than they are brought to a compliance with their designes: The *yoke of Christ* is commonly too *heavy* for the *iron sinews* of Conquerours necks; and his *gate too strait* for *triumphing Armies* to march through; with out much

stooping;

stooping and self-denyall; which is a hard lesson for those to learn, whose advantages are in their hands, unlesse grace be also in their hearts: It's alwayes seen that men of power *set up themselves* speedily and effectually, in places of honour, and profit: but to set up Christ and his Kingdome in any reall way of godlinesse and holy order (further than some verball, cheap, and popular gratification) is a work of *many ages*, and worthy of that pious and magnanimous spirit which was in *Constantine the Great*; whose Eagles wings served no lesse to protect the Church in peace and prosperity, than the Empire and his own person. *Great men* are generally shy of those *consciencious strictnesses* and self-diminutions, which true Religion requires; so that Ministers had need study to walk *inoffensively*, that they may catch men by *honest guile*: Laying aside all uncomely *rigour*, rude severities; and what ever may savour of either *scorn*, or *stubbornnesse*; using in civill affairs all fair submissions, which may consist with the peace of their consciences before God, and the honour of their profession before men; which is the purpose, and will be the practise of all truly wise and godly Ministers; who think it more honest and honorable to be open enemies, than false and feigned friends; to withdraw from, rather than abuse protection.

Victoria natura insolens est, & superba. Cic. pro. Mar.

2 Cor. 12. 16.

5. *The courage of Ministers in things properly religious and in their calling.*

But yet in matters properly religious, so far as *Ministers* are in Christs stead, and have the care and charge of true Religion, of the Church, and of the welfare of mens soules; Herein (O *you excellent Christians*) I know, you not only allow, but expect, that *all true Ministers* should be faithful to Gods glory, & the souls of them, * although they should *offend them*; That they ought to speak the truth *seasonably*, and wisely, though they *contract enemies*; that they must not by their * *pusillanimity*, and flattery prostrate the honour of true Religion, nor of their Ministry; which ceases not to be *Christs Jewell*, when it is for its splendor (which men cannot bear) *trodden under feet*. * They must still *looke stedfastly* to heaven, though men cast dust and ashes, stones and firebrands in *their faces upon the earth*. In this holy station and resolution, which is proper to them, as *Ministers of the truth of God*, I hope there are still many so * *valiant for the Truth*, so zealous for the glory of God, the name of Christ, and the honour of the reformed Religion; so *faithfull* also to mens souls, and their own integrity; that as they will not disdain to *serve even wicked Magistrates*, in Gods way, no more than * *John Baptist*

* *Non est dicentis præsumptio: ubi est jubentis domini autoritas*, Chrysost. l. 70.

* *Honestius est offendere quam odisse.* Tac. vit. Agr.

ἢ μὲν ἀλήθεια λόγων ἐστὶν εὐγένεια. *Syn. de Regno.* * Ἀποδυσάμενοι δὲ αἰσχύνην περιφανῶς ἐν τῷ τῆς ἀληθείας σταδίῳ γνησίως ἀγωνιζώμεθα, βραβεύοντος μὲν τοῦ ἁγίου λόγου, ἀγωνοθετοῦντος δὲ τοῦ τῶν ὅλων δεσπότου. *Cl. Al.* προτ. * Act. 7. 55. * Jer. 9. 3. *Non quid illi cupiant audire, sed quid nos deceat dicere considerandum, qui falsarum laudum irrisionibus decipi quam saluberrimis monitionibus salvari malint.* Al. l. 8. Or. * Mark. 6. 20.

did to preach to *Herod*) yet they would infinitely disdain to flatter them in any way, as *Gods*, or agreeable to true *Religion*, which is not so; or to *fear them* so, as to *betray* the cause of God; (which is alwayes pleading against the ignorance, or errour, or *violence*, or *hypocrisie*, or pride of the evill world) and to *sow pillowes under any mens Elbowes*, who may perhaps lean uneasily on the *skuls* and *bones* of those they *have unjustly slain*; or like *Ahabs* 400 *false Prophets*, to speak onely soft and *smooth* things to those men, whose hearts and *hands* are prone to harden by the use of armes both against piety, equity and charity: so that, at length, they may grow rough as *Esaus*, and red as *Edoms*; military passions and actions, especially in great and violent changes, *seldome keeping* within the bounds of that *justice* and *mercy* which Christian Religion constantly prescribes without respect of persons, to the strong, as well as the weak; to the *Conquerours*, as well as the *conquered*; *Successe* being for the most part, an *irresistible temptation* to men, by *power to gratifie* their lusts; and to think any thing necessary, and so *lawfull*, which is but safe and beneficiall: not regarding the exact rules of justice (in the Laws of God and man) which are *divine*, and immutable; by no advantages of gain, or honour to be warped or varied: The common places, Sermons and prayers of true Ministers must not be like some mens Almanacks, calculated just to the elevation of mens counsels, designes and successes, (wherein flattery would seem to be Prophetick and foretelling) but without respect of persons the same at all times to all men, as to the main rules and duties of holinesse.

Nudè cum nuda loquimur, non verenda retegimus, sed in verecunda refutamus, Ber. Ep. 43.

1 King. 20. 2. Isai. 30. 10.

Frustra de superatis hominibus gloriatur in faelix victoria, quae irae & superbiae succumbit. Ber. ad mil. Temp.

Although it be very *impertinent to dispute with power irresistible*, to *tax Cesar*, when he is able to *tax all the world*; or to quarrell at *his coin*, when he is master of ours; yet a wise *Minister* and Christian may *distinguish* between the publique power in men, and the private personall sins of men; A grave and constant spirited preacher of righteousnesse, will (as he should, in Gods way and Word) with all *religious freedome*, yet with all *civill respect* tell even the greatest *Princes*, and *Potentates* of their sins: as resolute *Eliah*, and honest *Micajah* did *Ahab*; as *Nathan* did *David*; as *Jeremiah* did the Princes and people too; as *John Baptist* did *Herod*; as St. *Stephen* did the *Jews*, and as St. *Ambrose* did *Theodosius* the Emperour; who for that Christian courage loved him the better; professing, that no man was worthy the honour of a Christian Bishop, or Minister, but he that knew how to own and use such pious and *resolute constancy*, as *he had done*; Yea what will you think of the freedome used by *Menis* Bishop of *Chalcedon* to *Julian* the Emperour, telling him that he was an *Atheist* and *Apostate*? Being blinde and led to the place where they were sacrificing, *Julian* with scorn asked him,

Non par est, ut deceptus splendore purpurae, ignores imbecillitatem corporis, quod hac tegitur. Amb. ad Theodos. Theod. l. 5. Eccles. hist. c. 17.

him, why the *Galilean* did not open his eyes; The old man answered he thanked God he wanted eyes to see so wicked a person. Sozom. l. 5. c. 4.

It is certain no men are better subjects in any time or under any State, than *such plain dealing Preachers*; although oft times none are lesse esteemed, by such men, who had rather enjoy the fruit of their *sins with peace*, than hear of them to *repentance*. But Ministers, who are *Gods Heralds*, must not consider, what voice pleaseth those to whom they are sent; but what he commands *that sends them*; It were better that hundreds of them were sequestred, plundered, imprisoned, banished, or burnt at *Stakes* in *Smithfield*, (after the example of many *holy Martyrs*) than that *their votes and suffrages* (as more sollemn parasites) should ever *flatter men*, either great or many, *in their sins*; or * call *evill good*, and *good evill*; or speak *good* of that, and blesse those whom they *think* * *God abhorreth*, who is as far from *approving*, as from commanding, any immorality, or injustice in any agents, (whom he suffers to act and doe great things in the world) when yet he so far approves *strange events*, as he permits them in his *unsearchable*, yet *alwayes most just wisdome*, which knows how to make good use of evill men and manners. God can make *Bathsheba* to be the *mother of a Solomon* whom he loved; when yet he never allowed the sin of * *David* or *Bathsheba* in their first coming together; the fruit of which the *Lord destroyed*. It justifies, as St. *Austin* saith, *Gods omnipotent goodnesse and wisdome*, but not mans impotent *passion* and folly; when he brings his glory, or his *Churches good* out of *their evill*.

Vitámque impendere vero, Nec propter vitam vivendi perdere causam. Juv.
Nihil turpius sanctis parasitis.
* Isai. 5. 20.
* Psal. 10. 3.
οὐ μὲν πρό γε τῆς ἀληθείας πιωητέα ἡμῖν ἡ ἀσφάλεια. Bas. M. de Sp. S. c. 21.
* 2 Sam. 12. 14.

Yet this *just and necessary freedome*, which Ministers of the Church in all duty to God, charity to men, and fidelity to their own souls, ought always, as they have fit occasion, to use, must not amount to bitter, *rude*, *importune*, and unseasonable *reproofes*; not to publique *raylings*, seditious reproaches, and popular *invectives* against any mens persons, or actions: * There must be *meekenesse with zeal*; humility with courage; modesty with freedom; gravity with constancy, and prudence with innocency.

Οὐδὲν ἂν εἴη τοῖς ἐλευθέροις μεῖζον ἀτύχημα τῆς στέρεσθαι τῆς παρρησίας. Demost.
* *Nobile plane ac generosum est vincendi genus, alios humilitate praeoccupare ut vincamus.* Sal. Ep. 5. χρῆ μιγνῦναι τῇ παρρησίᾳ τὴν πραότητα καὶ τῷ ἐλέγχῳ κεραννῦν τὴν ἀγάπην. *Isid. Pel. l. 4. ep. 139.*

If those, that are at any *time in Power*, doe not like, or will not protect and incourage *such Ministers* in all such religious freedom of speaking, as becomes the Word of God; if they presently make *those offenders for a word*; and looke on them, as enemies of their power, who only tell them and all men of those sins, which the Scripture *reproves*, *equally* in all men, and God will mightily *punish in the mighty*: If they resolve to *destroy all those Preachers*, Isai. 29. 21.

Impatientiam reprehensionis sequitur peccandi impudentia; unde impœnitentia, desperatio damnatio. Ber.

* *Mellei & saccharati doctores.*

* Rev. 10. 10.

Temperanda est reprehensio, ut non tam corrosores quam correctores videamur, emendare studentes non mordere. Ber. Ep. 78.

Veritas & dulcis est & amara: quando dulcis, pascit; quando amara, curat: & medicamen animo & pabulum. Aust. Ep. 210.

which are loth they *should be damned*; Truly such men deserve to have no Ministers, but those that are not worth *the having*; Teachers *after their own hearts*, and not *after Gods*; None are worthy the name of Christs Ministers, who *suffer Christians to sin securely*; others may heap up, and *feed on* * *sweet Teachers*, for a while, but they will finde them like * St. *Johns* book, in the belly, *bitter*, and *miserable comforters* in the end: None are so worthy of Christian *Magistrates protection*, as those that fear not to tell them *of their sins*; yet in a fair way too: Not in a *Cynicall severity*, but in a *Christian charity*; not so, as to diminish their power, (which * *is Gods, more than mans*) but vindicate true piety; What good Christian wil not be glad of *sanative wounds*, rather than * *poysonous kisses* to hear of those faults in a fair way, which he hath cause to be sorry, that ever he committed; and of which he must repent even to a restitution of injuries, or at least an agnition, if ever he have pardon? True Ministers are to consider, not what will *please* poore sinfull mortals, but what *will profit* mens soules; not what may *seeme good* to them, but what will *doe them good*; and however they may not transgresse the laws of *honour*, and *civility* by a *rudenesse of Religion*; yet they must take that * *liberty of speaking*, which the word of God *allowes*, and conscience requires, whether men will *hear, or forbear.*

* Prov. 27. 6. *Quantum odit peccatum tantum diliget fratrem, quem sentit peccati sui hostem.* Aust. Ep. 87. Ioh. 18. 37. For this end came I into the world that I should bear witnesse to the truth. *Sapienti grata sunt vulnere sanantia,* Ieron. * Ezek. 2. 5.

6. *Ministers quiet subjection merits protection.*

If then Christian Religion be not in *England* grown a meere fable, (as the Ministers of it, are too many, become a reproach and a by-word, a burden, and a song) If *modern policies* hath not *quite eat up* all that piety, which was sometime professed, in privater and obscurer stations: If *Mammon* hath not justled *God* out of the *throne of great* and strong mens hearts: If *Belial* have not deposed Christ: If the enjoyment or catching at the *shadowes* of temporall power and possessions, have not made men foolishly let goe the care to get and to hold fast eternall life. If Arms have not beaten away the graces of Gods Spirit; and fighting against Christians have not taught them to fight against God, and the checks of conscience: If the shedding of *mans bloud* have not taken away the sense and virtue of *Christs bloud*: If the *noise of warre*, and the cry of *the slain* have not *deafned* mens ears against the *voice of God*, and the cals of his Spirit: If the dreadfull and lamentable aspect of poore Christians supplicating in vain for life, and dying with horrour and anguish at the feet and before the eyes of their brethren, have not taken away the sight of charity and deprived men of the

light

light of Gods countenance in love and mercy: If there be any *tendernesse* of conscience, any sense of sin, any fear of God, any terrours from above, from beneath, or from within; if any belief of the *judgment to come*, and accounts to be given; if any thoughts of, and *ambitions* for a *better Kingdome*, than the earth can afford: No men will be more acceptable, even *to the greatest*, than those Ministers, *who know*, at once how to speak the truth, and yet to keep within the bounds, *both of Charity and civility*; Nor doth it follow (as the sophistry of some *Sycophants* would urge against true Ministers) that those will be most active to destroy or disturb the powers of this world, who are most faithfull to keep potentates soules *from damning*, in the world to come.

Nemo potest veraciter esse amicus hominis, nisi qui fuerit primitus veritatis. Aust. Ep. 52. *Charitas pie sævire, humiliter indignari, patienter irasci novit.* Ber. Ep. 2.

In these Christian bounds then of *peaceable* subjection, humility and holinesse, if the Ministers of *England*, which are able, discreet, and faithfull, might but obtain so much declared *favour*, and publique *countenance*, (which all *other fraternities* and professions have) as to be sure to enjoy their *callings*, *liberties*, and *properties*, which seem to be many times in great uncertainties, under the obedience and *protection* of the laws; as it would much incourage them in their *holy labours*, (which alwayes finde carnall opposition enough in mens hearts, and discouragement from their manners) so it would *redeem* them from those menaces, insolencies, and oppressions, of *unreasonable men*; who look upon them as *publique enemies* and *perdue*; because they thinke they have little of *publique* favour and incouragement: Ministers are so much men, that kind and *Christian usage* will, no doubt, much *win* upon them; The *Sunshine of favour* is likelyer to make the *morosest of them, lay off that coat of rigour and austerity*, which some (perhaps) affects to wear; than that *rough storm* and winde, wherewith they are dayly threatned, and by which many of them have been and are still *distressed*; which makes them *wrap* themselves up, as *Elias* in his *hairy mantle*, when they think their lives, and liberties, and livelihoods are sought after; and no *such protection* like to continue over them, as they thought in a Christian State and Church they might have both obtained and deserved, by their quiet and usefull conversation. As just *protection* invites *inferiors to due subjection*; so no men pay it more willingly than they, who besides *the iron chains of fear*, have the *softer cords of love*, and favour upon them: By how much (after many violent stormes and hard impressions) they are more tenderly used, the more is *respect* gained, and peaceable *inclinations* raised in men toward such as will needs govern them: The very best of whom are seldome so *mortified*, or heightned by *Religion*, as to forget they are men; or to be without their passions, discontents, and murmurings, joined with desires and endeavours to ease and relieve themselves;

selves; At least to change their *condition*, if they finde it Tyrannique and *Egyptian*; (that is, *unreasonable*, *arbitrary*, *injurious*, and oppressive: quite contrary to what is pretended, of *honest* and *just liberties*, both Christian and humane, civill and conscientious; which are, for every one to enjoy, as his private judgement of things, so what ever is his priviledge and property by Law; while he keeps within the practique obedience and compasse of the Law, whereto Governours, as well as governed, are bound, not onely in piety, but also in policy: Both tyranny and rebellion are their owne greatest Traitors: Magistrates seldome losing or hazarding their power, nor subjects their peace, but when they wander out of the plain *highway of Laws*; which are the *conservatories* both of Governours and governed. It is the least degree of justice, and short enough of any high favour, to permit, and protect worthy *Ministers* (with all other honest and peaceable men) as in doing their *duties*, so in *receiving* their *dues*: Yet this is as great a measure, as in these times, they dare either ask, or hope for; Immunities from any burthens, that lye heavy on them, Additions of honour or augmentations of estate, I think all wise Ministers despair of: Peace with a little as to this world, would be a great meanes, both to compose their studies, and to *strengthen* their hands in the *work of God*; Also to quench that fire, with which many mens tongues are inflamed against Ministers, their calling, persons and their maintenance; thinking they may both safely, and acceptably despise those, whom power *delights not to honour*; For whose ruine the malice of some *Antiministerian spirits* wisheth, as *many gallowses* and *gibbets* set up, as there are *Pulpits*.

Non diu stare potest potentia, quæ multorum malo exercetur. Sen. de Ira.

Dan. 3. 18.

But the Lord is able to deliver us: if not; yet, *be it known* to these violent and unreasonable men, that no learned, judicious and consciencious Ministers will *bow down* to worship that *papall*, or *popular* Image of *Anarchy* and *confusion*, which they seek to set up, as to the shame and ruine of this and all Reformed Churches, so infinitely to the detriment and dishonour of this Nation, as to its common welfare, in peace, plenty, or power, in good learning or true Religion. And however we are forced *for some time* to lye *among the pots*; yet shall we be as the *wings of a dove*; nor shall we want an *Ark*, whither to fly at last: where a *gracious hand* will receive us to *eternall rest*; when we shall retire to heaven, *wearied* with the troubles on earth, and finding no rest for *our souls*, amidst those *overflowing scourges*, which the just and *offended God* will certainly bring upon all such evill and unthankfull men, who love their power or profit more than their soules; and glory in despising those who professe to be *Noahs*, the Preachers onely of *righteousnesse* and of *repentance*; but no way the pragmatick plotters of troubles or seditious movers of civill perturbations. I

Hoc posteris dicite, Hominem Christo deditum posse mori, non posse superari. Ieron.

Psal. 68. 13.

Μηδὲν φοβερὸν ὅπου πατρὸς ἀγάπη· μηδὲν ἀλγεινὸν ὅπου Χριστοῦ δόξα. *Dictum juvenis inter tormenta; cum totum vulnus erat, & formam hominis, at non fidei amiserat.* Euseb. hist. l. 5. c. 1.

I Have now, *O you excellent and truely reformed Christians*, onely left a wary *super-politick*, and *over-cautious* spirit to encounter and dispell; which pleads *policy* against *piety*; and prefers outward *safety*, before inward *peace*: Being, as it pretends, lothe, yea and afraid to displease, deny or gainsay so great and powerfull, at least so active, bold and *pragmaticall* a party, as is by these Antiministeriall adversaries pretended to be, both among *military* men and others, *implacably ingaged* against, not onely the persons present standing, and maintenance of Ministers; but even the very calling, ordination, and function of the Ministry: which they are resolved to undermine by *calumnies*, or overthrow by force; either by fair or foul means: These Antiministeriall spirits must by all meanes be gratified; and by no means displeased; lest impatient of the repulses and elusions oft given to their many petitions and *essayes* against the Ministry they fly out to *greater disorders*, than either the Ministers or the Gospell, the reformed Religion, or Christ himself are worth: Better this *one function* of the Ministry, (though ancient, usefull and necessary to the Church; yea though holy and of divine institution, the greatest gift of God, next Jesus Christ, to the world) better this be destroyed, than a generation of violent spirits should get a head, and destroy both us and our Nation. Thus some men, whose feares are strong objecters against their judgements, and consciences; which cannot but acknowledg both of the Ministry and Ministers of *England*, that God is in them, and hath been with them of a Truth.

8. Cavill. Object. 1. It's not safe to plead for, or protect Ministers.

Answ. I see how *many Lyons* the base fears and *cowardise* of men are prone to fancy, to be in * *their way*, when they should undertake to maintain the *cause of God*, of Christ, and of true Religion, (which the cause of the Ministers *indeed*, is.) * Here the *shadows of mountaines* and * *fields of thistles* appeare *like armed men* to *timorous* and degenerous Christians; when yet all the *outward difficulties*, all the inward terrours, all the divels in hell cannot deter some men from *those adventures* wherein their worldly interest of profit, safety or honour are concerned; There oft-times necessities are first made, then they are prosecuted, after they are pleaded as grounds for excuse, at least, if not of *justification*, of actions lesse warrantable.

1. Mens cowardise in religious matters.
* Prov. 20. 13.
* Iudg. 9. 36.
* *Phil. de Com.*

If I thought (as truly I doe not) that this *ungratefull mutiny* of some men against the Ministry, and the mean *despondency* of others, (their cold and faint friends) were generall and *Epidemicall* among men of any considerablenes, for quality, number, and estate, that these did either oppose or *desert their Ministers*, I conceive it would admit of no better *confutation* and remedy, than for Ministers (with *Cesar*) to open our naked brests, and to offer them to the ponyards and swords, or pistols of those, that think it fit to *desert* us; and by a second hand to *destroy* us.

Sueton. in Jul. Cæs.

 If

Ministers yeeld to the sentence of the Nation.

If those that excell in any vertue, or in power, *doe indeed think* the Ministers and Ministry of *England* have deserved to be thus vilified and exploded, as the *filth* and *off-scouring* of all things: if in *reason of state* and *politick interest* it be found *therefore best*, because safest; that *Learning* must yeeld to illiteratenesse; *study* to temerity; *knowledge* to ignorance; *modesty* to impudence; *ingenuity* to rusticity; *order* to confusion; *gravity* to giddinesse; holy *eloquence* to vain blessings; *serious disputings* to rude and profane janglings; That the grave, learned, and venerable *Preachers* of the true Christian reformed Religion must give place to cunning and insolent *Factors* for all manner of errours, superstitions, and confusions; if this be *necessary*, or highly convenient for the publique good, they shall doe wisely, if not well, with all speed to stigmatize by *publique vote* and act, both the *Ministers* and their Ministry on the foreheads, as so many *vile persons*, whose craft hath hitherto *cheated* and abused the *English* world, in stead of seeking, and shewing men the true way to heaven; Nothing is more just, than to stop *such mouths*, whose *Oracles* are no better than those, which were silenced when Christ came into the world: Yea, quite to *abrogate* the function will be the shortest way whereby to satisfie the Antiministeriall malice: And to expiate the *sin* or folly at least of this Church and Nation; which self-displeased for entertaining them so long, and so liberally, shall now take but a just revenge in either *sterving* them, and their families to death, or condemning them to a *wandering beggery*; That so by such a *penall retaliation*, (as that Emperour commanded a *Cheater* to be *stifled* to death with smoak, because he vented only *smoak*) Ministers may want common *bread to live*, who have pretended to feed mens souls with *the bread of life*, and have in this onely deluded men; For coming now to be searched by the more accurate eyes of some new *Illuminates*, they are found, like the Priests and Temples of the *heathenish devotion*, to have in them, in stead of a *venerable deity*, nothing but the Images of *cats* or *crocodiles*, and the like despicable figures.

Fumum vendidisti, fumo pereas. Sueton. in Vespas.

If neither *God*, nor *good men* have any *further pleasure* in the *lifes*, *labours*, and *prosperity* of his servants *the Ministers of England*, against whom the *Shimei's* of these times are bold so loudly to cast forth their cursing and evill speeches; Let the *Lord do with us* as it seemeth *good in his eyes*; Loe, we are many of us in our *severall places* and *charges*, *yet residing*: (some are already scattered and ejected) most of us *almost beggered*, exhausted, weather-beaten, and shipwracked in stormes and tossings of these times. Some are even *weary of themselves*, filled with the dayly and *bitter reproaches* of their insolent adversaries; and even praying *with Elias*, It is enough, we are not better then *our Forefathers*, (thus persecuted they the godly Ministers,

2 Sam. 16.

1 King. 19. 4.

sters, the *Bishops*, the *Presbyters*, the *Apostles*, the Prophets of old;) fit our soules for thee, and take them to thee; that we may be delivered from so *injurious* and *unthankefull a generation*, whose aim is to destroy the true Prophets, and pull down all the *house of God* in the land.

Alas! we of *the Ministry* have no weapons or arms, no strong holds, or defenced Cities, besides our prayers, patience, and (as we hope) good consciences; it will be no hard work for a *few Doegs* to destroy all the *true Prophets and Ministers of the Lord in the land*: That so this great *Hecatomb*, so long desired, and expected, may be an *acceptable* sacrifice to the Jesuited Papists, and *pragmatick Separatists*, and all other malicious enemies of this reformed Church; and that true Religion, which the Ministers of this Church have professed and preached in many years. *Ministers unarmed innocency.* 1 Sam. 22. 17. *Non nobis tanti est vita, ut armis tuenda sit. Tiber. ad Senatum.* Tac. an. 6.

And this, not *upon light* and *unexamined presumptions*; not upon customary *traditions*, and the meer ducture of *education*; not upon *politick* principles, and civill *compliances*, with Princes or people; but upon serious *grounds*; as solid, and clear *demonstrations*, as can by right and impartiall reasonings, be gathered from the *Word of God*: and, (in cases of its obscuritie, or our own weaknesse) from that light, which the *consent and practise* of the *primitive*, and purest Churches of Christ hath held forth to us, in points of *Faith*, doctrine, and in all good orders or manners, becomming Christians; either in their private moralities, or their publique *decencies*. In this *integrity*, *innocency*, and *simplicity*, (which neither *men nor divels* can take from us) we are sure to be destroyed, if it must be so, and to be delivered from an ungratefull *generation of vipers*; who think it enough to destroy those, who have been a means of their being and life, as Christians; if our injuries and bloud could be silenced with us, yet the *very dust of our feet*, will be a testimony against such men at the last day of judgement: when it shall be more *tolerable*, for any Christian people under heaven, than *for these in England*; since among none clearer *truths* have been taught, or greater *workes* done, or better examples given; than have been here, by the *Ministers of this Church*. Matth. 3. 7. Matth. 10. 14.

Where hath there been under heaven more *frequent*, and more excellent *preaching*? where more frequent, and yet unaffected praying? where more judicious, pious and practicall writing? where more learned and industrious *searching* out of all divine truths? where more free and ingenuous declaring of them? so as nothing hath been withheld or smothered; where more devout, holy and *gracious living*? where more orderly, harmonious and charitable *agreeing*, than among those that were the best Bishops, the best Ministers, and the best Christians here in *England*? Adorned with *Ministers merit of this Nation.*

 these

these ribands, fillets and *garlands*, of *good words*, *good works*, and *good bookes*, must the Ministers of *England*, like *solemn victimes*, and piatory sacrifices, be destroyed? onely to gratifie, some mens petulancy, insolency, covetousnesse and cruelty, who list to be actors, or spectators in so *religious massacres*.

2. *Considerations touching the Ministers of England, humbly propounded.*

But O you *excellent Christians* of all ranks and proportions; If there be yet any ear of patience left free to hear the *Ministers plea and apology*; if *calumny* hath not obstructed all wayes of justice or charity; if slavish *feares* have not so imbased your *piety and zeal* for the Christian reformed Religion, that you dare not seem no not *to pity the Ministers of it*; if the *separations and brokennesse of Religion* (in our unhappy times) have not wholly blinded your eyes and baffled your judgements; so that you have lost all sight both of true Church and true Ministry here in *England*; I humbly desire, that before the true and ancient Ministers be cashiered, and quite destroyed, these things *may be considered*.

1. Whether it be a just proceeding to impute the *personall failings* of some men to the whole *function and profession*? whether, at that rate, all Judges, Magistrates, and Commanders may not be cryed down, as well as all Ministers? Since, where there are many, there are alwayes some, that are not very good. 2. Whether it be fitting to condemne and destroy any men in any of their rights, to which they pretend, either of *office or reward*, (and that by Laws, both divine and humane) without a fair and full hearing, what can be said for them? or whether any man would have such *measure meted* to themselves? 3. Whether *Pride* in some *Lay-men* of their gifts; Envy in others, against the welfare of the Ministers of Christ; *Covetousnesse* in others, as to their maintenance; *Profanenesse in others* against all holinesse; Ambition in others to begin or carry on some worldly ends and secular projects; *Licentiousnesse* in others, against all religious restraints; *Impatience* in others, to see *any govern* without or besides themselves; *Malice* and spite in others, against this, as all other reformed Churches; Hopes in others by our *confusions* to introduce their superstitious usurpations; *Whether I say these*, and the like inordinate lusts, and motions in mens hearts, as their severall interests lead and tempt them, may not be *great causes*, and influentiall occasions of these violent distempers, which break out thus against the generality of the *Ministers*, and the whole calling of the *Ministry* in this Church?

Yea, what if all odious *clamours*, and calumnies against them, and *their calling*, have no more of truth in them, than a *Jewell* hath of dirt in it when filth is cast upon it? (whose innate firmness preserves its inward and essentiall purity) What if nothing be wanting to the *innocency* and honour of the *Ministry* of this Church, but onely *patient*

tient, and impartiall Judges; pious *patrons*, and generous *protectours*? which was all St. *Paul wanted*, when he was accused of *many and grievous* crimes, by the cruell and *hard-hearted Jewes*; which were his Countrey men, and for whom he had that *heroick charity*, as to wish himself *Anathema from Christ*, that they might be saved; Whether ever any Ministers of learning, honesty and piety, (that had done so much for the religious welfare of any Christian Nation, as the able *Ministers of England* generally have done, for many ages;) were ever so rewarded by Christians? or whether ever it entred into the hearts of religious men, so to deal with *their Ministers*, as some now *meditate* and design?

It were good for men, how *metald and resolute* so ever they seem to be in carrying on their designs, to make some *pause* and *halt*, before they strike such a *stroak*, as may seem to *challenge Christ*, *and fight against God*: whose *stroakes* against men are heaviest, when they are least visible; and his *wounds sorest*, when men have the least sense of their *contending* against him. The perswasions and confidences of men may be great in their proceedings, (as was in *Saul persecuting*) when yet their zeale is but dashing against the *goades, or thornes*; and a meer *persecuting of Christ himselfe*; which will in the end pierce their own souls through with many errors. *Severissimè punit Deus cum pœnalis nutritur impunitas.* Aust. *Act. 26. 9. Act. 9. 4.

What if (notwithstanding many *personal failings* in Ministers as men) their function, calling, and Ministry be *the holy institution* and appointment of Jesus Christ; transmitted to these times, and this Church by a right order and uninterrupted succession, as to the *substance of the power*, and essence of the authority? (The talents or gifts were Christs, and from Christ, delivered to his Servants the Ministers of the Church: though some of them might be idle and *unfaithfull*; whose burying them in the earth, or wrapping them up in a napking at any time was no *wasting* or *imbezling* of the substance of them; nor any lessening of Christs right to them.)

3. *A summary of what makes for the function of the Ministry.*

And for this I have produced, not weak *opinions*; not light conjectures; not partiall customes; not bare prepossession; not uncertain tradition; not blind antiquity; not meer crowds or numbers of men; much lesse do I *solemnly alledge* my own *specious fancies*, *devout dreams*, uncertain guessings, *Seraphick dictates*, and magisteriall Enthusiasms; But 1. *evident grounds* out of the Word of God, for a divine Ordination, and institution at first. 2. *Scripture history* for succession, to four generations actually. 3. Promises and *precepts* for perpetuity of power Ministeriall, and assistance, which was derived by the solemn *ceremony* of the imposition of hands, by such only, as had been ordained; and so enabled with *successionall power*, till the coming of Christ. 4. This primitive root and divine plantation of the Ministeriall office and power, we finde oft con-

confirmed by *miraculous gifts*; besides the innocency, humility, simplicity, piety and charity of those *Apostles*, primitive *Bishops* and *Presbyters*, set forth in the *holinesse* of their lives; and the glorious successes of their Ministeriall labours; converting *thousands* by preaching the Gospell: and by their *Ministeriall power*, and authority planting Churches in all the then *known* and *reputed world*, oft crowning their doctrines and Ministry with Martyrdome. 5. After this I produce, what is undenyably alleadged, from authours of the *best credit*, (learned and godly men) famous in the Church, through all the first ages, shewing the *Catholick* and *uncontradicted* consent; the constant and uninterrupted succession by Bishops and Presbyters in every City, and Countrey; which all Christians in every true Church owned, received and reverenced, as men indued with such order and power Ministeriall, as was divine, supernaturall and sacred, as from Christ, and in his Name; though by man, as the means and conduit of it. This is made good to our dayes in the persons, and office of those *Ministers*, who were and are duely *ordained in this Church*. 6. Next I plead, (with the like *evident and undenyable demonstrations*) the *great abilities* in all sorts of ministeriall gifts; the use and advancement of all *good learning*; the *vindicating* of true Christian and reformed religion; the manifold discoveries of sound judgement, discreet zeal, holy industry, blamelesse constancy, and all other graces, wherein the Ministers of *England* have not been inferiour to the best, and most famous in any reformed Christian Church, and incomparably beyond any of their *defamatory adversaries*. 7. I add to these as *credentiall* Letters, the *testimonies* and *seales* which God hath given of his *grace* and *holy Spirit*, accompanying the Ministry in *England* upon the hearts of many thousands, both before and eminently since the Reformation; by which men have been converted to, and confirmed in *Faith*, *Repentance*, *Charity*, aud *holy life*; the tryall of which is most evident in that patience and constancy which many Ministers, as other Christians in this Church have oft shewen in the *sufferings*, which they have chosen, rather then they would sin agaist their Conscience, and that duty which they owed to God and man. 8. Last of all, if any humane consideration may hope for place in the neglect of so many divine; the *civill rights and priviledges*, which the piety of this Nation, and the Laws *of this Land*, have alwayes given to Ministers of the Gospell; by the fullest and freest consent of all Estates in Parliament: that they might never *want able Ministers*, nor these all *fitting support and incouragements*; These I say ought so far to be regarded by men of *justice*, *honour* and *conscience*, as not suddenly to break all those sacred sanctions, and laws asunder, by which their forefathers have bound them to God, to his Church and Ministers

nisters, for the perpetuall preservation of the true Christian Religion among them and their posterity.

Furthermore, if the godly Ministers of this Church of *England* (whom some men destine to as *certain destruction* and *extirpation*, as ever the *Agagite did the Jews*) if they be the *messengers of the most high God*; the *Prophets of the Lord*; the *Evangelicall Priests*; those, by whom *Salvation* hath been brought, and continued to this part of the *world*; If they have, (like the good *Vine and Figtree*) been serviceable to God and man, to Church and State; If they have laboured *more aboundantly*, and been blessed *more remarkably*, than any other under heaven; If they have preached *sound doctrine in season and out of season*; if they have *given full proof of their Ministry*, not handling the Word of God *deceitfully*; nor defrauding the Church of any Truth of God or divine Ordinance; If many of them have fought a *good fight*, and finished their course with joy, and great successe against sin, errour, superstition, and profanenesse; If they have snatched many *firebrands out of hell*; pulled many souls out of the *snares of the divell*; If they have fasted, and mourned, and watched, and prayed, and studyed, and taught, and lived to the honour of the Gospell, and the good of many soules; If they have *like Davids Worthies* stood in the gap against those *Anakims* and *Zanzummims*, who by *lying wonders*, *learned sophistries*, and accurate policies have, (to this day) from the first *reformation*, and coming *out of Egypt*, sought to bring us thither again; or else to destroy the very name of *Protestants*, and reformed Religion from *under heaven*; If almost *all good Christians*, (and not a few of these *renegadoes*, their ungratefull enemies) doe owe in respect of knowledge or grace, to the Ministers of *England*, as *Philemon to St. Paul*, even their *very selves*; If they have oft *in secret wept* over this sinfull Nation and wantonly wicked people; (as Christ did over *Jerusalem*) and as *Noah*, *Daniel*, and *Job*, oft *stood in the gap* to turne away the wrath of God from this *self-destroying Nation*; If, now, they have *no other thoughts*, or *practises*, but such as become the truth, and peace of that Gospell, which they preach, and that blessed example, which Christ hath set them; whom in all things they *desire to imitate*; in serving God, edifying the Church, doing good to all men, praying for their enemies, and paying all civill respects, which they owe to any men: If all true and faithfull Ministers, have done, and designe onely to doe, many *great and good works* in this Church and Nation; for which of these is it, that some men seek, and others with silence, suffer them to be stoned; as the *Jews threatned Christ*; and the inconstant *Lystrians acted on St. Paul*; who after *miracles wrought* by him among them, and high applauses *of him from them*, was after dragged, as a dead *dog*, out of

4. *The fruits of Ministers labours in England.*

Act. 14. 19. *of their City* by them; ſuppoſing *him to be dead.* If all true and worthy Miniſters being conſcious to their own Integrity, (a midſt their common infirmities) after their *eſcaping the late ſtormes,* (in which many periſhed) are eaſily able, without any diſorder to them, to
Act. 28. 5. ſhake off *thoſe Vipers,* which out of the fire *of ſome mens ſpirits* now *ſeiſe* upon them with *poyſonous calumnies* of *factious, covetous, ſeditious,* &c. If there be ſtill upon the true and able Miniſters of *England*, thoſe Characters of divine *Authority*; thoſe gifts of *the holy Ghoſt*, in all good underſtanding, knowledge, utterance, zeal, courage, induſtry and conſtancy, which fits them with power for that holy function; and carries them through it, with all fidelity and patience, not only to ſerve, but to ſuffer for the *Lord Jeſus* and his Church: If they have been *juſt Stewards*, and *faithfull diſpenſers* of the Myſteries of Chriſt to his houſhold this Church; how can they without infinite rudeneſſe, and unchriſtian inſolence be *ſhamefully uſed*, and driven out of their places and Offices? If they have been *ſpirituall fathers* to many ſoules, and as *tender mothers* to them; not diſdaining to bear with the manners of *childiſh Chriſtians*, in many places, (who turned their reſpect into peeviſhneſſe, and their love into ſcorn) how unnaturall will it be for Chriſtians to *become patricides*, murtherers of *their ſpirituall fathers*? to whom in ſome ſenſe they owe more, than to their naturall? If Miniſters be *Embaſſadors*, they ought not to be violated by the *Law of Nations*, (behaving themſelves, as becomes the honour of their *Embaſſy*, and *ſender*) how much more if *from God*, ſent *by Chriſt*, in his and his *Fathers Name*; and that with a *meſſage of Peace*, and reconciliation from *heaven* to poore ſinners? The greateſt and proudeſt of them, being but wormes meat, may not ſafely deſpiſe, injure, or turn away the leaſt of the ſervants and Meſſengers of our *Lord and Maſter Jeſus Chriſt*, which ſpeak *in his Name*, (that is, both his *Truth*, and by his *Authority*) which can be no where elſe (in any *ordinary Miniſtry*) but in thoſe, who are *duly ordained* in this holy *deſcent* and *ſucceſſion*.

[L]egatis vim aut [c]ontumeliam [i]nferre nefas. Reg. Iur. *Jus Legatorum cum hominum præſidio munitum, tum e[t]iam divino ju[r]e eſt vallatum.* [C]ic. de Aruſ. reſp.

If they have been *watchfull Shepheards* over their *ſeverall flocks*, for good and not for evill; how barbarous muſt it be for Sheep to turn Wolves, and devoure thoſe *Paſtors*, who have *fed them*, as *Jacob*
Gen. 31. 40. did *Labans flocks*, with all care and *diligence, day and night*, leading them by the *pureſt waters*, and in the *ſafeſt paſtures*? Nor is there now any more cauſe to change the wages of *theſe Shepheards* of ſoules (which is *alwayes like to be to their loſſe*) than *covetous Laban* had againſt *honeſt Jacob*.

If none other can *authoritatively*, and as of *Office and duty*, in the name and by the miſſion of Chriſt, bring the meſſages of peace, and reconciliation to ſinners; (which hath beſides the Word,

ſacred

sacred and *mysterious seales*; and other holy actions of power and authority to be performed by peculiar, fit and appointed Ministers) how *beautifull* ought *their feet* to be, and their steps welcome; which flow with truth and peace, grace and mercy? How farre should they be from being *trodden* under the feet of *proud*, *covetous* and envious men? who first casting dirt in their faces, after with much dust and clamour, seek to stir up, not onely the people, but the powers against them; as if they were *burthens of the earth*, not fit to live? *But wisdome is justified of her children.*

Rom. 10. 15.

Act. 21. 36.

Math. 11. 19.

5.

Ministers expect better things from good Christians.

I cannot be so injurious to my countrey and countreymen, as to think; that to *persons* of such worth, standing in such relations between God and man; invested with so holy authority; managing it with such divine power and efficacy; crowned with so great successes; recommended to all worthy Christians with so many publique merits, both to Church and State; (as the true and duely *ordained* Ministers of the Church of *England* are) either men of purity or of power, can be so *wanting* to, or so shrink from their duty to God, their love to Christ, their zeal for the reformed Religion, their care of their countrey, of their posterity, and of their owne soules; as not to dare to speak, or appear for them; or not to endeavour in all fair wayes to improve the interest they have in the publique, by which to preserve so many good and righteous persons (as to *mans tribunall*) from poverty, contempt, and ruine; yea to preserve themselves and their dearest relations from most irreligious infamy of ingratefull deserting and oppressing so deserving men.

Men cannot but be *unholy*, that can be so *unthankefull*: And if *Ingratitude* be in all other relations, and merits among men justly esteemed as the most *detestable disease* and *inhumane deformity* in the soul; shall it onely seem beauty, health, and a commendable quality, when it is offered by Christians to their Ministers? Such as may with equall *modesty*, and *truth* plead their own innocency, and protest against the *immanity* of their enemies malice? For setting aside the idlenesse and *pragmatick* vanity of some Ministers in later, and *more licentious times*, (whose either insufficiency, or lazynesse, or inordinate activity, or abject popularity, hath made them the staine and shame of their holy function; and whose *burthen* is too heavy for my pen to discharge them of) if we looke upon those learned, laborious, sober and venerable Ministers, who have been, and still are, *the glory and crown* of their function, of this Church and Nation, in their severall degrees and stations: *I may *lowdly proclaim* with *Samuel* this *protestation* in their behalf: Behold the * *Ministers of the Lord and of this Church*, (O you *unthankefull Christians and causlesse enemies*) witnesse against them *before the Lord* and before his people; *whose*

2 Tim. 3. 2.

* Godly Ministers not injurious but meritorious to the publique.

* 1 Sam. 12. 3.

whose Oxe or Asse have they taken? whom have they defrauded or oppressed? whose hurt or damage have they procured? whose good have not they studyed,and endeavoured? whose evill of sin or misery have they not pitied, and sought to relieve? what is the injury, for which so *desolating a vengeance* must passe upon them, and their whole function? What is the *blasphemy* against God or man, for 1 King. 21. which these *Naboths* must lose their lives, and *livelyhoods?* wherein have they deserved so ill of former or later ages; that they should be so used (*as Ahab commanded of Micaiah*; and the *Jews* did to *Jeremiah*) to be cast into prisons, into *sordid and obscure restraints*; or to be exposed to Mendicant liberty, for to be fed onely with the *bread and water* of affliction, if they can obtain so much? What necessary truth of God *have they detained* in unrighteousnesse? what *error* have they broached, revived, or maintained? what *superstition* have they nourished? what *licentiousnesse* in sin have they incouraged? what true Christian *liberty* (which alwayes containes it selfe in bounds of Gods and mans laws) have they denyed to, or defrauded the people of? unlesse all things of publique peace and extern order,in which the publique wisdom and consent of the Nation confined it self, them and all men in it, by laws, are to be called *superstition, tyranny* and oppression, in Ministers, more then all other men; who being under government, thought it their duty to sub- 1 Pet. 2. 13. mit *to every ordinance* of man, which did not crosse any *divine ordinance*; but kept within the bounds of that liberty, order and decency, which are left to the *wisdome of any* Christian Church and State; whereby to preserve the *honor of Religion*, and the order and peace of the publique.

Those jejune and *threadbare objections* oft used *against Ministers* in these things, (wherein there were but *obedientiall*, and *passive*; the activity lying in those, who had the power to enjoyne, and command them, which was done by all *Estates in Parliament*) have been so oft and fully answered, that all sober and wise Christians see the *weaknesse of reason*, and the *strength of passion* in them; as they are charged for faults on Ministers in their *respective obedience and conformity*; For which they were like to know *better grounds*, than any their enemies had against them: And being in all other main matters, very knowing and *consciencious* men, they are not in charity *to be suspected*, in those *lesser and extern matters*, to have sprung any *leak* of sinfull weaknesse, or to have made any *shipwrack* of a good conscience; Later events have much recommended former duties and laws, * shewing how weak, even Truth and Religion, are (as to *extern profession*) where (like loose and *scattered souldiers*) Beleevers or Professors are destitute of all *order* and just *discipline*.

* *Vires inordinatæ mole ruunt sua: Quo vehementiores, eo infirmiores; inque propriam ruinam valentissimæ.* Salust.

But

6. *Ministers in their weaknesses, yet superiour to their adversaries who cannot supply their roome.*

But if the Ministers of the Church of *England* had discovered many failings, as men compassed *about with infirmities*, which easily beset them, (for which they oft *mourned*; against which they were alwayes praying and striving) yet what is it wherein the pretended perfections of their presumptuous, and *implacable adversaries* doe excell the very weaknesses and defects of *Ministers?* yea wherein will the vapouring of any *new projectors* be able to repair the dammage or recompense the want, which *thousands* must have; (yea this whole Nation suffer) if by these mens *cruell designes*, they be deprived of the *blessing* of these, whom they please to count so weak, unworthy, and *contemptible Ministers?* Will those *old pieces*, or those *new Proteusses* (who pretend and fancy to be new stamped with the mark of popular ordination, (which is none of Christs, whose wisdome never committed any power of Ministry, and holy offices, or divine Ordination to the common people, as I have proved) who are betrayers, haters, and desertors of that true power and authority, which they formerly received in that just and *lawfull ordination*, (which was from *all antiquity* derived to this Church; from which no *mean and vulgar complyance* should have drawn any man of piety, learning, and honesty, to so great a schism, defection and *Apostasie*, from the Catholick rule and ancient practise:) will I say, these *new masters*, or those *heaps of Teachers*, which country people are prone to *raise up* to themselves, in their *fervent folly*, and zealous simplicity; will they furnish Church or State with *better and abler Ministers* in any kinde, with better learning, better doctrine, better preaching, better praying, better living, (then those former *Ministers* did in the midst of their *many infirmities?*

O miserandam sponsam talibus creditam Paranymphus! Ber. de Conf.

Prædatores non prædicatores, peculatores non speculatores, Raptores non Pastores, Id.

Jam. 3. 12.

Yea will not these new obtruders, with most impudent *foreheads* while they *looke you* in the face, *cheat* and *deceive you?* Will they not (while they *smile* upon you, with shews of *Gifts*, and *Spirit*, and *Prophets*, and speciall *calls*, and *extraordinary ordinations*) exchange *counterfeit* for true Jewels, brasse for gold, stones for bread, pebbles for pearls, dirt for diamonds, gloeworms for stars, candles full of theives and soil, for the *Sun?* In stead of the excellent and usefull worth, the divine and due authority of your learned and godly Ministers, you shall have either *confident ignorance*, or *fraudulent learning*, or *Jesuitick sophistry*, or *fanatick nonsense*, or *flattering errors*, or factious *semblances* of truth to *usher* in most *damnable doctrines* and most unchristian practises; Doe men gather *grapes of thornes*, or *figs of thistles?* Can these bitter fountaines send forth *sweet waters?* or *these burning* Etnas breath forth other than such sparkes and flames as their sulphureous spirits, and their hearts full of envy, and malice, and pride afford? which seek to darken the Sun of Truth at noon day; or to scorch up the fruits of holinesse; to infect the common air of Christian charity, order, and peace; in which true Christians delight to breath. When these *plagiaries* have destroyed, or driven away the fathers of Christs family, and Church; will they not either seduce and *steal away* the *children* to their own *erratick factions*; or even sell these *Orphanes* for a *pair of shoes* to *Cantors* and *Tom-a-bedlams*; committing, or rather casting away the soules of men to the *carelesse* care of those *sturdy vagrants*; whose minds are more unsetled than their eyes, or feet, or tongues; which are so far bent *against true Ministers*, as they are intent to their *booty and prey* from every quarter?

Will these (who seek to be the *maules* and hammers of the Ministers of this Church) either by their skill or power, wit or learning, prudence or policy, ever forge on the hard *anvils of their heads*; or bring forth out of the *rude moulds* of their inventions, any thing that shall be like a true *Minister of the Gospell?* Are there ordinarily any such *blocks* to be found among them, of which there is any hope, that they may *be shapen* to such *Mercuries*, as are the true *Gods Messengers?* Are there any such *tempting materials*, as any art and industry may promise to fit them up to such a *degree and pitch of competent Ministers*, as may direct the countrey plainnesse? and guide that *peevish* and *disputative madnesse*, which is among even the meanest people in every village? Will these *skippers* or *skullers*, ever furnish out *such Pilots*, as may safely steere the *ship of this Church*, in which the Truth of God, the honour of Christ, the reformed Religion, the happinesse of thousands of soules are embarqued, amidst the *rocks* of errours, *Syrens* of secular temptations, and *piracies* of strong enemies on every side? They say, that better *ships* are now built in *England* than ever were; and shall we be content with *worse Pilots?* lesse able Ministers in the Church? who are as the *Argonautæ*; bringers of the *golden fleece*; the riches, and righteousnesse of Christ the Lamb of God; the *treasures of heaven*; the true gold of *Ophir*; which hath been seven times tryed; in stead of which these *new trafiquers* intend to trade for nothing, but the *Apes and Peacocks*, toyes of new opinions: Shall *Noahs* Ark, the Churches purity, (which is the *Conservatory of Christs* little flock, of the *holy seed* of a Christian succession, both for fathers and children) be broken up or dashed in pieces against the rocks of *sacrilegious* envy and *policy*; for these Antiministerial projects will never be the mountaines of *Ararat*, on which the Church or true Religion may rest. Shall this Island, whose safety consists so much in the *guard of the Seas*, be lesse carefull to guard the coasts of the Church and the reformed Christian Religion? whose *narrow frete* or strait runs between the *rocks of Atheisme and Superstition*; of Parity and Profanenesse, of *Heresie and Schism*; of Tyranny and Tolerations.

ἡ εὐσέβεια ἐστι δεισιδαιμονίας καὶ ἀσεβείας μέσον. Isid. Pel. l. 4. Ep. 210.

Will

Will ever these new *dwindling Divines*, the *Propheticall pygmies* of this age, (which oppose the able Ministers and true Ministry of the Church of *England*) will they ever bring forth for the service of God, or for the maintenance of the true Christian reformed Religion, such a *race*, and *succession* of *mighty men*, of excellent Ministers, of incomparable Heroes, worthily renowned in their own, and after generations, whose *workes yet praise them in the gates*; of whom none, but evill *tongues*, can *speak evill*; such as this later age or century hath brought forth, to looke no further back to those excellent men of former and obscurer times? 'Can you expect *Crammers*, '*Latimers*, *Bradfords*, *Ridleys*, *Hoopers*, *Grindals*, *Whitgifts*, *Fletchers*, '*Sands*, *Elmers*, *Jewels*, *Kings*, *Abbots*, *Lakes*, *Bilsons*, *Babbingtons*, *Andrews*, *Feltons*, *Fields*, *Cowpers*, *Whites*, *Davenants*, *Potters*, *Prideauxes*, and '*Westfields*; with many others *now at rest in the Lord*, all *venerable* in *their Episcopall order* and eminency; as *fathers of the Church*; and as *elder brothers*, among their brethen, the other Ministers; whose humility disdained not to be *subject to those reverend Bishops*; although some of them might be equall to them in eminent gifts: 'Such as were *Gilpin*, *Fox*, *Knewtubbs*, *Perkins*, *Whitaker*, *Reinolds*, '*Willet*, *White*, *Richard Hooker*, *Umphry Overall*, *Greenham*, *Rogers*, '*Dent*, *Dod*, *Heron*, *Bifield*, *Smith*, *Bolton*, *Taylor*, *Hildersham*, *Crakanthorp*, *Donne*, *Stoughton*, *Ward*, *Holsworth*, *Shutes*, *Featly*, and Doctor *Sibs*: (which last fragrant name, I may not mention without speciall gratitude and honour due to the memory of that venerable Divine: not onely for the piety, learning, devotion and politenesse of his two *genuine writings*, (*The bruised Reed*, and *Soules conflict*) but also for that paternall love, care, and counsell, by which hee much oblieged mee to him in my younger yeares. Indeed that holy man I found altogether made up of sweetnesse and smoothnesse, *oil and honey*. As his actions, so his gifts and graces were set in a kinde of *Mosaick* work, admirable for that meeknesse and humility; which while they sought to conceal and shadow over his vertues, they gave the greatest lustre to them.

7. *Eminent Bishops and Presbyters of former days in the Church of England.*

Animi nil magnæ laudis egentes. Virg. Æn.

Besides these, there were an *innumerable company* of other *immortall Angels*; but yet *Ministring spirits* to this Church of *England*; who are now *made perfect*; and whom nothing would so probably afflict in heaven, as to see the *degenerate succession*, both of Ministers and Christians, now likely to follow in this age; Many of these and other *Worthies* of this function, in former times (as now) living and dying in *countrey obscurities*, were *buried in those sepulchers*, which they had made in the Gardens, (that is, those *Dioceses* or *Parishes*) which they had planted, or diligently watered; and disposed by pious industry to a pleasant, peaceable and happy fertility:

lity: Men, however different in some externall *lineaments* (as may be among Brethren) yet all of *excellent features*; and some of the *first three*, both in beauty and strength for piety, learning, judgement acutenesse, eloquence, depth, devotion, charity, gravity, industry, and a kinde of *Angelick majesty*; at once both *amiable and venerable*, both in their preaching, writing, and practice.

Ministers of the present age.
Nos ingentium exemplorum parvi imitatores. Sal. ad Agr.

These *great men* and *greater Ministers*, have indeed *left us* behinde them, a generation far inferiour to them, (for the most part) more feeble, and unable to work, or warr; having more enemies, enjoying lesse incouragements, (scarce any now considerable as to this world) bearing greater crosses, and heavier burthens every way, for charge, duty and reproach; who are oft forced to lay out in publique taxes a great part of that *little*, they have to buy themselves *bookes or bread*: Who have onely this *advantage* of our troublesome, envious and evill times; that we may learn to be more *humble* in our selves; more diligent in our *duties*; more charitable to others; and more *valiant* for the Truth: hoping, that while we have after the primitive pattern, nothing left to *glory in*, but *the Crosse of Jesus Christ*, both our afflictions and infirmities may prove *opportunities* to exercise, discover and increase the *graces of God* and true Ministeriall gifts in us, whose power can *perfect it selfe*, and us too in the midst of our infirmities, and support us under the many unjust oppressions, which threaten us. There are indeed yet left, through Gods mercy in the *field* or *forest* of this Church, and Nation, some *goodly old Trees*, both venerable Bishops, and worthy Presbyters, here and there: Some shrewdly *battered*, and strangely neglected; which yet retain something that is very goodly and gracefull, amidst their *battered tops* and shattered arms; being yet *stately monuments* or reliques of that former *benignity* which was in this *English* soil toward Churchmen and Ministers; many of whom grew to so *tall a procerity*, as of learning and worth, so of *wealth* and *honour*, in some degree answerable to their worth, and becoming that reall dignity which was in them; far more usefull and considerable by wise men, than any bare descent of titular honor. These I must be so civill to, as not to name any of them; that I may avoid suspicion either of *envy* or *flattery*; (two most detestable distempers in mens spirits, and full of malignity) Indeed I need not name some of them, for although they are left, as *cottages in a wildernesse*, and as *beacons on a hill*, yet they are still such *burning and shining lights*, as cannot be quite hid: Some of whose fame is in all the *reformed Churches*; and their eminency renowned in all the learned world; being indeed the *beauty and glory* of these *British Nations*; the *pillar and honor* of the *Protestant* party; the grand examples of *pious Prelacy*, learned humility, holy industry; the *great lights* of this Northern climate

climate; Which alone might serve to fulfill, what the *Cassiopeian flames* did portend, by that new star in the year, 1572. Shall this age be, not onely guilty spectators, but cruell actors in their distresses; whose necessities must needs be some *reproach* of the Nation; even a publique sin and shame, never to be expiated? Will it not be the *height of barbarity*, to compell such persons to *Bellisarius his Obolum?* After so many learned victories and triumphs, to force them to turn *their bookes into bread*; or to be their own *Cannibals*, to feed on their owne *bowels*, or to starve upon others *uncharitablenesse?* O how sad and sordid is it for such *learned worth* to be tryed with want, and such piety be exercised by penury! O prodigy of *covetous cruelty*, capable to astonish heaven and earth; which seekes to hide its wickednesse by its *enormity*; and to make its selfe incredible, by its *monstrosity and excesse*; men will think it a *fable*, which humanity (much more Christianity) should so much abhor to act, or suffer to be done, when it is in their power to help. O *Divine Providence*, which art indisputable, unsearchable, uneffable; how dost thou thus chuse *darknesse* for the garment of thy glorious lights; and *thick clouds* of obscurity, wherein to wrap up thy brightest beames among mankinde! Art thou preparing *Ravens* for such *Eliasses*; and working wonders for the nourishment of such *Prophets*? or shall their retirednesse, poverty and patience be thy greatest wonder, and their *Martyrdome* thy highest *miracle*, by which to convince and convert this crooked and adulterous generation? Truly, O excellent Christians, it is infinite pity, grief and shame, that so deserving vertues and most reverend years should be so much obscured and neglected, whose great learning and excellent gifts in all kindes, no men or Christians would despise, or not use and incourage, save onely such as are afraid, that either the true reformed Religion, or true Ministers should have any *lustre* put upon them, or so much as any competent livelyhood afforded to them, here; while forain Churches and Universities admire them, and would gladly entertain them.

Which wonder in heaven occasioned the learned studies of *Ticho Brahe*, and did, as he sayes, foretell extraordinary light of learning and Religion. *Tich. Brahe. Astro. Restitu.*

There are also some fair *Plantations of young and thrifty trees*, yet left, in this Church; whose *luxuriant* floridnesse wants nothing but a right *Church government*, to culture, prune, and order them; These, rightly planted out by due ordination, and preserved by wise discipline, would in time bear *store of good fruits*; if the *coldnesse and spewinesse* of the soil, and inclemency of the *English* climate (ever since our *Northern blasts*) did not make them *dwindle*, grow mossy, and shrubbed by popular and plebeian adherencies; or if a *violent hand* doe not pluck them up by the root, or so *bark* them round, and circumcise their *maintenance*; that no *fair fruit* can be expected from

from them, when there is *no sap* derived to them; who, if they were duly *ordered*, and incouraged, would still make the vain and erratick genius of this age see, That *true Religion* is to be preserved, and the *Kingdom of Christ* in mens hearts advanced, and the power of godlinesse maintained in Christians lifes, not by *new modes* and *fancifull fashion*, but by old truths, and the old Ministry; of whose line and measure, these *new pretenders* coming far short, they strive by their *calumniating activity* to supply their defects, after the same arts that the ungrateful sons of *Sophocles* did; who, that they might get their fathers estate (of whose *longævity* they were impatient) complained; that *hee doted*, and was past the use of those admired parts, which formerly had got him the love and applause of all *Athens*; beseeching the Magistracy, that they might make their father their pupill, and manage that estate for him, to which he was superannuated: The old man hearing of this practise of his unnaturall sons, made and publiquely recited the famous, and last of his Tragedies; which gave the people so great assurance of his still remaining reason and sufficiency, that they caused the former unjust grant to be revoked, and his unworthy sons worthily punished.

Oedipus Coloneus.

18. I must in like manner leave it to the judgement and conscience of all *excellent Christians*; whether there be *any compare*, betweene the gifts, labours, and successes of those goodly Trees, the true *Ministers*; (who have had the right power and succession derived to them from the *Apostolicall root*) and these *new shooters*, or *suckers*; who seek to *starve* the ancient trees, which so far exceed them, and over drop them; Are they not like *vines* and brambles, thorns and figtrees set together? Is not the comparison uncomely, and disparaging, not onely to *Christians judgements*, but to their *very religion?* Can the exchange passe without infinite losse, injury, and indignity, to all true Christians, of this, and all other reformed Churches? And therefore I shall presume such a *commutation* can never be desirable or acceptable to any, that are *soberly religious*, and truly consciencious; who have no *secular interest* wrapped up, under specious pretensions of piety.

The impertinency and insufficiency of the Antiministerial pretenders.

Wise and worthy Christians cannot but remember, and be extreamly sensible, of those *many great benefits*, which their forefathers themselves, and their countrey, have evidently received and enjoyed many years, by the labors of the *true Ministers* of this Church: equall or like to which, they cannot, with any probability, (nor by any experience yet had) expect, from the *sorry simplicity*, and *extravagant ignorance* of those *Antiministeriall adversaries*; who have as little *ability*, as *authority*, to carry on the great and holy *work*, of saving *soules*, either by dispelling ignorance, errours, or prejudices out of mens mindes; or by setling mens judgements in truth;

or

or satisfying mens consciences in doubts: (or by reforming mens manners in a way of due reproof, and discreet counsell; or by vindicating the reformed Religion against learned cunning and powerfull opposers; or by preserving any decency, order, and honor in the outward form and profession of Christian Religion, which will soon *deform* to all contrary effects, if other Ministry or Ministers be applyed, than such, as Christ hath instituted, and the Church alwayes ordained, and sent in Christs Name.

No man then can desire, or design the change of *this Ministry*, as to the *authority*, *order*, *rule*, and *succession*, who doth not also aime at the change of the whole *Ministration*, and work; Indeed those *rude and unchristian novelties*, which some men seeme to agitate; carry the aspect, not onely of Papists, and other *collaterall adversaries* against us as *reformed*; but of Jews, and Turks, and Heathens, such as would most *diametrally* oppose the name of any Christian Church; or, which is as bad or worse, they seeme to prepare the way for some *great Antichrists*, whose coming must be by *strong pretensions and presumptions* of some new wayes of *Ministry*, *Sanctity*, and *Piety*; 2 Thess. 2. 10, 11. in which are hidden the *strongest delusions*, most probable to overthrow the true Ministry and Churches of Christ, while they shall speciously cry up such *new wayes* of Ministry, and spirit, and gifts, and Churches; which neither we, nor our forefathers, nor primitive Christians, nor the Church Catholick, ever knew, or were acquainted with, either by Scripture precept, or any Churches practise; for however the best reformed Churches have restored many things to their pristine lustre, yet they innovate nothing as to Scripture grounds of doctrine, or Catholick order, succession and Institution.

19. *Addresse to men of the Military order.* As, then, those men are most the *souldiers friends*, who advise them, to keep to their *able and experienced commanders*; and not to venture their safety upon the *activity*, and *feates* of every *forward and nimble fencer*: So are they most friends to all good Christians, Magistrates, souldiers, or others in this Nation and Church, who perswade them (as *Clemens* did the *Corinthians*) to keep to their *ancient*, *able*, and *true Ministers*, of whom they have had so long, and so good experience; and although their persons be changeable by death, or other wayes of deprivation: yet ought the way and succession to be preserved, as to that *ordination*, triall, and mission, which is *Apostolicall*, and *universally practised* in the Church of Christ. *Clem. Ep. ad Cor.*

And since herein the *Allusion*, reason and proportion lies so fit, and equall between worthy *Ministers* and *able Commanders*, who have a *right Commission*; I cannot think, that any of the *military* order, who are persons of any worth, true honour, conscience,

 or

or *considerable* for piety, prudence, and Christian valour, (which *dares any thing, but sin*;) that any such *souldiers*, (I say) should be prone to kindle any discontents and mutinies, against the able and *true Ministers* of this Church. To whom (no doubt) they cannot but thankfully confesse; that, under God, they ow (for the most part) what ever *good learning*, *good breeding*, or *good conscience* they have: I am the further from suspecting so *unchristian*, and *unreasonable* a tempter in that sort of souldiers, because I know by *experience* that in all the troubles and shakings, which have been in these times, those of them who are sober and ingenuous men, have been both in publique, and in private very *loving*, *civill*, and *respective* to the true Ministers of this Church: so that those who glory in their *affronts*, contempts, and oppositions against the Ministers, doe but thereby *proclaim*, that they are the very *drosse* and ruder *dregs* of that *profession*; (for so it is like to be in *England*:) Nor can I think, that the irreligious motions, *unruly mutinies*, and inconsiderable menacings, of a few such unbred men, should either *over-sway* or *over-aw*, the sober *counsels*, and better *purposes* of those many better gentlemen, who sway either in *counsell* or in *power*.

Docti Ministri fortes milites dirigant; justi milites pios Ministros protegant. Illi veritate, hi virtute.

Whose protection, in all *peaceable*, *and good wayes*, why the *Ministers* of *England* should not as well deserve, hope for, and enjoy, as any other order, or rank of men, I see no reason; unlesse injuries, obloquies and indignities offered, by some of very mean *quality* and *condition* (for the most part) (and hitherto borne with that *Christian courage* and *patience*, which becomes grave and godly Ministers, should be argument enough to perswade all Christians to forsake them, and destroy them;) of whose safety, and welfare (no doubt) God himself, and the Lord Jesus Christ, are very sensible; as much concerned in their sufferings: Nor can I think but that those men, who are so *hardned* in their *malice* and *persecution* against the *Ministers*, and their holy function; doe oft hear a *voice* secretly calling *within them*; *O you Sauls, why doe you persecute mee in my servants the Ministers*; who preach my Word, in my Name, by my authority, and accompanied with my grace and spirit?

11. *In all Christian and true policy the true and ancient Ministery is to be preserved.*

Yea, not onely in all true Religion, and fear of God, which becomes true beleivers, but in all *reason*, and *policy of State*, it is, as necessary for those in places of power to protect the *true Ministers*, their divine calling and succession, as for these Ministers to be *protected* by them; and this, not onely in order to Gods glory, and the good of mens souls, their own and others; but for their own and the *publique peace*, safety, and honor before men; Nor is that promise, and obligation, (once given to the publique) to be forgotten, by which it was *assured*, that the *Levying of souldiers*, and raising of forces should be only as *scaffolds* to *build up learning*, piety, and

The Declaration of the two Houses, *An.* 41.

and the reformed Religion to higher heights, than formerly; and not as *scaling ladders*, to help to *storm*, *plunder*, and *impoverish the Church*; to *destroy* the Arsenals, and nurseries of good learning, or to pull down the main pillars both of learning and the Christian reformed Religion; which are the ancient *Ministry*, and succession of rightly *ordained Ministers*.

If those in *power and counsell* care not to help either in *preserving*, or *restoring* the true Ministers, and their calling, to their due honour, rights or incouragements: it will be thought rather a *want of will*, than of power, (of which the *British* world hath had great experience:) If they *would help*, but cannot; they must not think long to enjoy *that power*, which shall discover it self so *weak*, or so *pusillanimous*, as dares not own to be master of so pious, safe, and just purposes, as these are, to protect honest and godly men, in so holy, so usefull, and so necessary an imployment; as I have proved the Ministry to be. If they *can*, and *dare*; yet doe not; either *help will come another way*, by the gracious hand of God; whose terrours ought to be upon the highest mindes and loftiest looks: Or else we may fear the Lord hath, in *his fierce anger*, decreed to powre upon *highest and lowest*, root and branch in this Nation, the *vials of his sorest judgments*, and severest wrath, turning *our Sun into bloud*, and our *Moon into darknesse*; removing the *presence of his glory*, the Gospell, and the Ministry of it from us, and our unhappy posterity. Esther 4. 31.

However God shall please to deal with his *servants* the true and faithfull Ministers in this Church; yet it becomes them so far to be of *good courage*, as they have *him for their trust*, who *hath overcome the world*; who foretold *we should have trouble in the world*; but hath promised, we should *have that peace in him, which the world cannot give nor take away*; This comfort they have, that their *labours shall not be in vain in the Lord*: yea and for after times, *they may be assured*, That this bush of the *true Ministry* of the *Gospell in its due authority, divine ordination, and holy succession*, (wherein God hath so evidently appeared to his Church; and to none more clearly than to us in this age, and in this Church of *England*, shall never be consumed; however it may seem to be *set on fire*: Great tribulation threatens those, that will live *godly in this present world*; especially those, that contract more of the divels malice on them, by perswading many to live well; which is the work of true Ministers: whose labours are great; their *burdens* many; their *incouragement* small; and those greatly envyed: their *enemies* encreased on every side; their *comforters* few; their defense little or none, unlesse *God be on their side*; Which he will not fail to be, though all men *forsake them*, as they did St. *Paul*; And he alone is able to bear them up, amidst the *rough encounters* of these times, with that Christian

Ioh. 14. 27. 16. 33.

2 Tim. 3. 12.

* 2 Tim. 4. 16. *Verè magnum est habere fragilitatem hominis & securitatem Dei*, Seneca.

 patience

patience, courage and constancy, that becomes learned, and religious men; who know, *whom they have served*; in whom *they have beleived*; and may conclude, there are more *with them, then can be against them*; whose *upright soules*, and *generous consciences*, are, like *Elishas mountain*, full of *fiery charets and horsemen*; that is, devout flames of judicious zeal, which have upon them the *harnesse* of wisedome; and are managed with the reins, of Christian meeknesse and discretion; farre from those *politick presumptions*, and enormous confidences of some *Phaetons*, who never think they enlighten the *Church* enough, unlesse they set *Kingdomes and States* on fire, with wild and extravagant furies; who are far from being the *charets and horsmen of Israel*; for these, though they *are fiery*, yet they are *orderly*; and are patient of *government*, though they *excell* in *gifts*.

2 King. 6. 17.

12\. To such *Ministers* I here crave leave, as *Elihu* did, to make my addresse with *all humility and charity*, as to my *reverend Fathers*, and *beloved Brethren*; You, who have upon you the *marks* and *characters* of *right Ordination*, and true Ministeriall power; accompanyed with competent gifts, sanctified learning, devout industry, holy zeal, unblameable lives, and good consciences *toward God*, and *toward all men*; whose grand designe is to give *full proof* of those *Ministeriall gifts* and *endowments*, which you were, upon due triall, found to have, and to exercise that *divine authority*, which you solemnly, and rightly received; to discharge that *holy duty*, which in the Name of Christ, and by the power of *his Spirit*, was enjoyned you, in the day of your Ordination, by those, through whose hand the succession of that *Ministeriall authority* is derived from the Apostles: By all which, you were qualified and disposed, not to get a *good living or two*; but to cast into the Sea of the world, the *net* of the *Gospell at Christs word*, to gain soules to God, and Disciples to Jesus Christ; to teach and guide by sound doctrine, and holy discipline the flocks *committed* to you, in your severall places and proportions: Your earthly entertainment is from the *munificence* and *devotion of men*; but your *heavenly calling and authority to be Ministers*, is from Christ; *in whose Name* you doe all (as Ministers) and not in the *peoples*, whom some have taught to grow *tumultuous* against you, and *imperious* upon you: Neither your *work*, nor your chiefe *reward* depends upon men; It is the least of your comfort, or incouragement, that can *from thence* be expected, as nothing of your authority is from thence derived. *Levell* not your selves by *popular crowchings*, and *base compliances* in this high point of your *Ministeriall* power: It matters not much, how you be *levelled*, as to your *maintenance*, for which you chiefly do depend, not upon *envious men*, but upon a *bounteous God*; who will either give you *liberally* to enjoy.

Pathetick to true Ministers.

* Iob 32.

Minimum sit mercedis quod a seculo expectamus. Chrysol.

Ἀκριβ τῆς ἱερωσύνης ὁ Χριστός. *Chrys.*

joy all things, or contentedly to want them; The *withered hands* of these *Jeroboams* which are *stretched* out against you, may at your *prayers* be restored to the ancient fulnesse, and favour used toward the Prophets of the Lord in this land: If *bonds* and *imprisonment*, poverty and contempt attend you in this world, yet be of good *comfort*, Christ your *great Master* hath gone before you, and both by word and example, by his life and death hath called you *out of the world*; armed you against it, and set you above it; while *insolent dust* flies in your faces, and *proud wormes* fight against God in you, remember the *battail* is the Lords. The weapons of your warfare are *spirituall*, and of greatest proofe in sharpest *affliction*.

1 King. 13.

Ephes. 6. 12.

If you are to contend with *principalities and powers*, it must be, not by ill *language*, by railing and Satyrick invectives, by secret plottings, and practise, but by the primitive Ammunition of Patience and Prayers; by holy *perseverance* in your Ministry; such as becomes the spirit of the Gospell, in wisdom, learning, gravity; between the extreams of fear and flattery; with humble love and charity to all men: It becomes you (as *Vespasian* said of Emperours) to dye *upright in your spirituall armes* and harnesse, intent to your duty, fighting the *good fight* of faith, till you have finished *your course* with joy. In the midst of crosses, comforts grow best, as *Lilies among thornes*: The *clouds* of your *enemies* darts, poysonous opinions, corrupt doctrines, fraudulent dealings, sharp arrows of bitter speeches, *fiery trials* of persecuting menaces, your adversaries *cruell mockings*, and insultings, your friends prevaricatings with you, withdrawings from you, and *forsakings* of you; all these must onely (ἀναζωπυρεῖν) stir up the more to *quicker flames* of study, prayer, meditation, devotion, and holy resolution, those *many gifts and graces*, that learning, eloquence, and sufficiency, which are in you, as Christians, and as Ministers; wherein (to the praise of God) you are not *behind even the chiefest Ministers* in the Christian world. You are not now to expect *Prebendaries*, and Deaneries, and Bishopricks, as the *honorary* rewards and *incouragements* of your studies, pains and piety; This age could not bear your enjoying of them, though you used them never so well; It is your part to know, as well to *want them* as *to have them*; and in stead of those, to prepare for poverty, contempt, and imprisonment; you may be then at your *best*, when the evill world thinks you deserve no better; Never study by any mean ways to merit better of *sacrilegious spirits*; Be sure your *treasure* be *out of these mens reach*; It is your part to doe well, and worthy of your high calling: Leave it to God, how well you shall be *rewarded* here and hereafter: *Paul* never preached with greater authority, than

Sueton. Vespas. Vit. *Imperatorem stantem mori oportere, moriens dixit; inter manus sublevantium extinctus.*

Honoribus & divitiis carere posse magni est animi, at recte uti posse est maximi.

Act. 26. 29. Phil. 1. *in his chaines*; nor wrote with greater eloquence and majesty then when he styled himself, *a prisoner of Jesus Christ*; well doing will be reward enough, and a good conscience will be good chear at all times.

You cannot but observe, that your great *enemy the divell*, hath commanded, (as the King of *Syria* did) his *Legions of Hereticks*, Schismaticks, *Fanaticks*, erroneous, superstitious, idle, profane, licentious, and Atheisticall spirits, (who jointly *combate* against the truth of Christian and reformed Religion) that they should fight neither *against small*, nor great, but chiefly against the *reformed Ministers*, and the very *Ministry* it selfe of this Church.
1 King. 22. 34. Take heed that these smite you not, as those *did the King of Israel*, between the *joints of your harnesse*: between your *conscience* of duty to God, and your *civill complyance* for safety with men: between your love of Christ, and the love of your relations; between your fear to offend God, and your lothnesse to displease men; between your holding your livings, and keeping good consciences; between your *looking* to eternall necessities, and your *squinting* on temporall conveniencies.

Navigare necesse est, non item vivere, Appian. As *Pompey* said, when he set to *Sea in a storm*, against the advise of the timerous Pilot and Mariners; so I to you, It is *not necessary to live*, but it is *necessary to preach that Gospell*, which hath been
1 Cor. 9. 16. committed to your care: It is not necessary to be rich, and at ease, and in liberty, and in favour with men; but it is necessary to *witnesse to the Truth of God*, and to that office, authority and divine power of the Ministry of Christ in this Church, against a *crooked and perverse generation*; against the errours, pride, falsity, ignorance and hypocrisies which are in the world: What if Christ
Matth. 19. 22. cals us in this age to forsake all, and follow him? *Shall we goe away sorrowfull?* Truly the world will not treat you *much better*, when you have forsaken Christ to follow it: For, having once drawne you from your consciencious constancy, and judicious integrity, and pious reserves, it will the more *despise you*, and with the greater glory destroy you *as Ministers*: Our * *meat and drink* must be to do the will of our heavenly Father, as it was the Lord Christs, our great *sender and first ordainer*: Better we live *upon almes and beggery*, than thousands of soules be *starved* or *poysoned*, by those *hard fathers*, and terrible *step-mothers*, who intend to nurse Religion with bloud in stead of milk; and feed the Church of Christ after a *new Italian fashion*, commanding *stones* to be for *bread*, and giving it *Scorpions* in stead of fishes; mixtures of hemlock and Soules-bane, with some shews of *hearbs* of *grace*, of wholesome truths, and of spirituall gifts.

Age vero, qui relinquere omnia pro Christo disponis, te quoque inter relinquenda annumerare memento. Ber. de dil.

* Ioh. 4. 34.

Let the *envyous*, *penurious*, *sacrilegious*, and *ungratefull* world, see

that

that you followed *not Christ for the loaves*; Nor as *Judas*, therefore liked to be his Disciples, because you might *bear the bag*; Let no Scribes or Pharisees, Priests or Rulers outbid your value of Christ, or tempt you to betray him, and his *holy Ministry on you*; by any offers, unworthy of him, and you. Shew your skill and courage in the storm, wherein you are like, (for a time) *to be engaged*. Serener times made you carry *slacker sayles*, and a looser hand; now your eye must be more *fixed*, and your hand more strong and steddy, in steering according to *card* and *compasse*: the *Euroclydons* or violent windes of these *tempestuous times* will bring you sooner to your Haven: Hitherto you have (for the most part) appeared, but as *other men*; (busie, as *other ants*, on your molehils) conversing with the *beasts of the people*, in the valley of secular aimes, and affaires; now *God cals* you with *Moses up to the Mount*; and with Christ to a *transfiguration*, where you shall see the meeknesse, and charity of *Moses*, with the zeal, and *constancy of Elias* appearing with Christ; in which great *Emblemes* your duty, your honour, and your comfort will be evident; when you come to be *stoned with St. Stephen*, the *form of your countenance will be changed*, and you will then most fully see Christ, and most clearly be seen of men, as *the Angels of God*. Nothing hath lost and undone many of *us Ministers* so much, as our too great fear of losses and of being undone; our too great desires to *save our selves* by complying with *all variations, even in Religion*; nothing will save us so certainly, as our willingnesse to lose our lives, and livelihoods for *Christs sake*; and this, not now for one *great truth*, which is worth 1000 *lives*; but for the *pillar* and *ground* of all truths; the office and very *Institution* of the *true Ministry*, whose work is to hold forth, and publish the Truth of the Gospell to the *world in all ages*, by a right and *perpetuall succession*.

Piorum afflictio non est tam pœna criminis quam examen virtutis. Aust. de S. Iob.
Act. 27. 14.
τοιοῦτον ἀγαθὸν οἱ πειρασμοί, τοιοῦτον αἱ θλίψεις καλόν. *Chrys. st. in Act. ap. hom.* 3.
Matth. 17. 3.
Act. 6. 17.
C. 7. 56.

Despair not of Gods love to you: as *Philo* said to his countrymen the *Jews* at *Alexandria*, when he returned from the Emperour highly incensed against them: *Be of good courage*; it is a good *Omen*, that *God will doe us good*, since the *Emperour is so much against us*: Possibly you may (as St. *Paul*) be stoned, cast out, and *left for dead*, yet *revive again*; as is foretold of the witnesses. It may be your *latter end* shall be better, as *Jobs*, than your *beginning*; The experience of the sad effects, which attend *sacrilegious* cruelties against the *true Ministers*, and the want of such in every place, may in time provoke this Nation by a sense of its own, and of Gods honour, to more noble, and constant munificence, which is not so much a liberality as an *equity* to *able* and *faithfull Ministers*; It may be this Church, which hath so much forgot the *blessednesse* shee spake of, in having learned, able, and rightly ordained, and well governed

For Comfort.
Viro fideli magis inter ipsa flagella fidendum. Ber. Ep. 356.
Euseb. hist. l. 2. *cap.* 5.
* Act. 14. 19.
* Rev. 11. 11.
Gal. 4. 15.

Revel. 2. 4. verned Ministers, which seems to have forsaken *her first love* and honour to the Clergy, when Religion was (as in all times, preserved, so in these last) reformed, and vindicated by the labours, writings, lives, and sufferings of those excellent Bishops and Presbyters, who were heretofore justly dear and honoured to this Nation; so as no worthy minde envyed or repined at the honors and estates they enjoyed: Possibly it may *remember* from whence it is faln, and repent, and doe its first works: which were with piety, order, charity, true zeal, and liberality, without *grudging*, or murmuring against the honour or maintenance; much lesse the office, and function of the *Evangelicall Ministers*; whose pious wisdome casting off onely the additaments, and superstitious rags of mans invention, yet retained with all reverence and authority, the *essentiall institutions* of Jesus Christ; The disguised dress and attire, had no way *destroyed the being* and *right succession* of holy things: but only deformed it to a fashion, something different from their *primitive* majesty, beauty and simplicity; by putting on, what was *superfluous* rather, than pernicious.

But, if there should not be in our dayes so just and noble *recantations*, from this Church and Nation: yet, as Ministers of Christ it's fit for us to deserve it; we are reduced but to the primitive posture of those holy Bishops and Presbyters, who more sought to *gain men* to Christ, than honour and maintenance to themselves; Better we cease to be men, than cease to be Christs Bishops and Ministers: we must do our duties, till we dy; (having any opportunities) though we have no incouragements from men; our *lean, wasted,* and *famished carkasses* (such as St. *Chrysostome* saith the Apostle *Paul* carryed about the world, so much subdued by himself and *neglected*, as if he had not been *battered*, and persecuted enough by others) those will serve to be *Temples of the Holy Ghost*, and lively stones or pillars to the reformed Church of Christ, as well as if they had the *fatnesse of Monkes*, and the *obeseness of Abbots*; whose fulnesse you will lesse have cause to envy, when the pious industry of your poverty shall exceed the *lazy dulnesse*, and *uselesse fogginesse* of many of them amidst their plenty; (which no true reformed Christian grudges them, when they imploy in industry, humility, mortification, devotion and holy contemplation, as some of them doe; and thereby shew, that *plenty* is no enemy to *piety* in them;) Let us shew, that neither is *poverty* an enemy to *vertue* in us: Though the *Roman Clergy* rejoice at our penury; let not us repine at their *superfluity*, but wish them truth and holinesse, as ample, as their *revenues*; Above all, take heed, you doe not gratifie them, or any others, of *meaner spirits*, with any desertion or abasing of your *holy calling*, and *Ministry*, either in word, or in deed: Neither adopting a *spu-*

ὥσπερ γυμνῇ ψυχῇ τὴν οἰκουμένην περιπτάμενος. *Chrysost. de Paul.* τῶν τοῦ Χριστοῦ νομιμάτων ταμιεύς. *Is. Pel.*

rious

rious Ministry, of novell and popular *production*; nor giving over the consciencious exercise of that, which you have received here by an holy and right succession; your religious *constancy* in it will be the highest vindication of it, to be of no mean and *cravenly kinde*; which preacheth more out of duty and conscience to God, than from secular rewards from them.

Many of your *afflictions*, have been, still are, and are like to be as great, so of long continuance: Such, as to which God (no doubt) hath proportioned his gifts and graces in you, that so by this great *honorary of suffering*, as becomes you, both God may be glorified further in you; and you may be more sensibly *comforted*, and amply *crowned*, by him; your *losses* will turn to your greatest *gains*; and your *desertions* as from men, to your happiest *fruitions* of God. The highest and spring tides of grace usually follow the lowest ebbes of estate. Then are holy men at their best and most, when they seem least and nothing to man; as those stars whose obscurity is recompensed with their vicinity to heaven. Your *restraints* will be your *enlargements*; and your *silencings*, will proclaime the worlds *folly*, and unhappinesse, to deprive it self of your excellent gifts; and also set forth your *humility*, who know how to be *silent* with meeknesse and patience no lesse than to *speak* with wisedome and eloquence.

I should not need, nor would presume here, to make any particular addresse to those *reverened Bishops*, learned and godly *fathers* as yet surviving and almost forgotten in this *Church*; (whose worth I highly venerate; towards whose *dignity*, I never was, nor am either an *envious* diminisher, or an ambitious aspirer: whose *eminency* every way hath made good that abstract and *character*, which I formerly gave, of a true *Christian Bishop*) if I did not observe, how little they are for the most part considered by any ordinary minds, who generally admire the ornaments more, than the endowments of *vertue*; Vulgar spirits seldome salute any *Deity*, whose shrines and Temples are *ruined*: Few men have that gallantry of minde which *M. Petronius* expressed to *Julius Cæsar*, when he led *Cato* to prison, whom he with other Senators followed, out of the Senate, telling him: He had rather be with *Cato's vertue in a prison*, than with *Cæsars violence in a palace*: The worlds vanity is prone to judge those the greatest sinners, who are the greatest sufferers; whereas thousands perish eternally by their *prosperous successes*, few by their calamitous sufferings; The *methods* and *riddles* of divine dispensation and love are far different from *plebeian censures* and flatteries: God suffers his *Peters* to be winnowed, and his *Pauls* to be buffeted: yea he grindes in the sharpest *mils*, (as holy *Ignatius* desired) the corn he most esteemes; casting his *gold* into the hottest furnaces

*Μετὰ Κάτωνος ἐν τῷ οἰκήματι μᾶλλον, ἢ μετὰ σοῦ ἐνταῦθα εἶναι βούλομαι. *Xiphilin. in Pompeio.*

Absit ut hoc argumento religiosos putemus a Deo negligi, per quod confidimus plus amari, Sal. l. 1. Gub. de Aff.

furnaces, to make it at once more *pure* in it self, and more precious to himself: It is necessary (as * *Plato* saith) for the *divinest minds* to be *abstracted* from, and elevated above, and even dead unto the very best of things mundane and sensible; although good, lawfull and laudable; which a wiser than *Plato* tels us are to be accounted, by *Apostolick* and *Episcopall piety*, but * *as losse and dung in comparison of Jesus Christ*, which honour and treasure of your souls no envy, malice, fury or force can deprive you of.

* *Plato in Phædo.* Βιὸς κτ' τὸ νῦν; ἀφεςάναι ἀπὸ τῦ σώματος, καὶ πρὸς τὴν ψυχὴν τετςάφθαι.

* Phil. 3. 8.

This (no doubt) makes it seem not a *strange thing* to you, that the Lord hath thus dealt even with you; who have *suffered the losse of all things*, as to those publique, legall and temporary rewards of your studies, learning and labourers: while yet you were uncondemned for any sin, that ever I have heard of, committed either against the laws of God or man: only upon this account, because you were *Bishops* or *chief Presidents* in the order, government and care of this reformed Church; * according to the present Laws then in force, and agreeable (for the main) to the practise of all pious *Antiquity*. I need not put your *learned piety* in minde of that *voice from heaven*, which was audible to *blessed Polycarp* (a primitive Bishop and Martyr at *Smyrna*) when he was haled at fourescore years old to execution, (the tumultuous rable crying after him, αἶρε τοὺς ἀθέους, &c. Away with these wicked ones, &c.) But the celestiall eccho was (ἴσχυε καὶ ἀνδρίζου Πολύκαρπε) O *Polycarp* be of good courage, and quit thy self like a valiant man, a faithfull Christian, and worthy Bishop of the Church. None merit more to be preserved (many times) than they, whom vulgar fury and faction seeks to crucifie and destroy: Nor are any lesse meriting than those, who are by such easie *Idolaters* commonly adored. I well know, that there needs not greater *incitations* to constancy in vertue, or patience in afflictions (especially if for no evill doing) than those, which *innocency* suggests to good consciences; by which the grace of God hath (no doubt) enabled many of you to those (ἀριστεῖαι) great agonies and *victories of faith*, which you have (as *Job*) sustained in, and obtained over, the world, by your meeknesse, and, to such as observe it, admired patience; Enduring at once even from those of whom you had deserved, either as Brethren or Fathers, better things, so great *contradictions*, and so many *diminutions*; as not onely to have been *despised*, yea and by some contumeliously used in your persons, (*venerable* for *age*, *learning*, *piety* and *gravity*) but also to be quite *dejected* from that height, and utterly *ejected* from the enjoyment of those ancient places, to which both *high*

* See the judgment of Bishop *Cowper*: a learned and holy Bishop in *Scotland*: in his life written by himself.

* *Euseb. l. 4. hist. c. 14.*

honours

honours and *ample revenews* were anciently annexed; wherewith your selves were justly invested, and which your *predecessors* peaceably injoyed *many hundreds of years* past, in this Church and Nation: Herein you have excelled most of the ancient Bishops; who, although great and commendable sufferers, as *Martyrs* or *Confessors*; yet seldome from those, who were of the same *faith* and orrhodox profession; *Gregory Naz.* indeed was *stoned* and reviled when he came to *Constantinople*; and rejoyced to be so entertained, because they were of the *Arian faction*; enemies of Christs glory and godhead, which is the Churches greatest glory and comfort: In like sort divers godly and Orthodox Bishops were molested, banished, imprisoned and destroyed by *prevalent Hereticks* and *Schismaticks*, who yet ever set up Bishops of their own leaven and faction: For however men dared much against severall truths and fundamentall doctrines of Christianity; yet never till of later times did they rise to the boldnesse of denying and destroying the evident Catholick custome of the Churches government by Bishops as chief among the Presbyters: how ever single Tenets might be dark and disputable; yet this was so clear by universall practise and consent, that none ever gainsayed it, that were of any repute for learning or piety among the ancients. Your sufferings are the more strange and remarkable in this; that they are from those, who solemnly *protested* to maintain the *Protestant reformed Religion*, as it was *established in the Church of England*; in the extern order and policy of which, you then were, and had at all times been, chief *pillars* and *ornaments*.

Naz. orat. Lat.

In this so strange and sudden alteration, men soberly learned and *peaceably pious*, (and uncovetously Christian) doe still with all respect and reverence to you and your Order, consider; not onely that great and undenyable *justification*, which you have from the Lawes, wisdome and piety of this Church and State ever since they were Christians; as also from the Catholick and undoubted practise of all ancient Churches, blest every where with the excellent lives, learned labours, and glorious sufferings of many your *famous predecessors*; to whose care and fidelity the Church owes, for the most part, (under God) as the *lawfull succession* of Ministers, so the preservation of the Scriptures, of good learning, and of all holy *administrations*; But also they lay to heart that great humility, *moderation*, meeknesse, candor, and charity, most worthy of you, and most observable in you; By which you have been as sheep before the Shearers, not opening your mouths, yea you were, in order to publique peace, content so far to *gratifie your enemies*, and displease your friends, as in many things to have *been lessened*, in those rights and preheminences you had, according to the Laws and ancient customes of this Church and State; hereby hoping to have drawn others from their *exorbitancies*, to such a peaceable temperament, as might have been happy for us all.

Nor is it unobserved by wise men, how great a *justification* the providence of God hath soon given even to your order and office, (which some Ministers were so impatient not to root out) not onely by the preservation of it, and by it a constant Ministry and holy order in his Church every where for 1600 years, but also by that notable confutation and speedy defeat given to the vast hopes and violent projects of those (for other mens counsels and results upon a secular account I neither examine nor censure) Ministers, who being of your own tribe, were your *sharpest rivals* in a *Presbyterian excesse*: who have now as little cause to rejoice, in the so much endeavoured *extirpation* not of any Tyrannique, and Papall, but of all Presidentiall or Paternall *Episcopacy*; that they have great cause to repent, and be ashamed of those immoderate counsels and precipitant actions, which knew not how to distinguish between the failings of persons, and the benefit of order; between the rectitude of a Canon, or rule, and the crookednesse of depraved manners; which are incident to all sorts and degrees of men whatsoever, and to Presbyters no lesse than to Bishops: So that in such severities, which ruined at a dear and dangerous rate, what they might have repaired safely and easily, they shewed themselves neither good *Church-men*, nor wise *States-men*; neither very pious, nor greatly politick; For, by snuffing *Episcopacy* too close, they have almost extinguished *Presbytery*; and occasioned this *ruine*, threatning the order, honour, maintenance, and succession of the whole *function*, and calling of the *Evangelicall Ministry*; Their zeal not to leave an *hoof* in *Egypt* (as some violent spirits pretended) is probable to bring us *back again to Egypt*; or so lose us in the *wildernesse of Sin*, as few heads in after ages shall *enter into Canaan*: No wonder if the branches wither, when the root is wasted. It is comely in your *piety* and *gravity*, that you have not rejoiced in these so *sudden defeats*, and *speedy frustrations* of their so bitter and implacable *adversaries*; whose tongues (it seems) dividing, their building ceased and soon decayed: But rather you pitie these *confusions* incident to poor *mortals*; who so oft bruise themselves very sorely, by the fall and ruines which they maliciously, or unadvisedly bring upon others: as those violenter Presbyters have done even upon Presbytery it self, who in its due place and decent subordination is also an ancient, honorable and Catholick order of the Church of Christ, by their hasty demolishing of all moderate Episcopacy, where one Minister is preferred before another, agreeable to the eminency of his gifts and graces; the priority of his age; the rules of all right reason and order, which ownes any government in any society of men; The goodly height and orderly strength of which Prelacy was, not onely as the *root* for right derivation and succession, but also as the *shelter*, stay and protection (besides a great *beauty* and *ornament*) to the whole *Ministry*, of this and all Churches; yea and to the reformed Religion here as established; as not with lesse piety, so (without boasting) with as much (if not not more) *prudence* and *moderation*, as to the externe policy of it, as in any Church under heaven: The want of that *great benefit* and those *many blessings*, which the Churches of Christ, both in primitive and postern times, have enjoyed, by the *learning, wisdome, authority*, care, circumspection, and good example of excellent Bishops (whom no men will want more, than the commonalty of Presbyters) may in time (according to the usuall methods of *humane folly*, and *passions*, late and costly *repentings*) make men the more esteeme them, and desire their *just restauration*; The ancient *Persians* are reported, when their King dyed, to have allowed five dayes *interregnum*; during which time every man might doe what seemed good in his own eyes; That so by the experience of those five dayes *rudenesse*, riot, injuries and confusions; wherein rich and poore suffered, they might learn more to value the necessity and *benefit* of lawfull, orderly and setled *government*; *Want* doth oft reconcile men to those things, which long use hath made *nauseous*, and so offensive to them: when *wanton novelty* hath glutted and defiled it self with its *pudled waters*; possibly it may grow so *wise*, by an *after wit*, as (ashamed of it selfe) to returne to the *primitive springs*, and *purer fountaines*; where was both farre more clearnesse, and far wholesomer refreshings. Your charity forgiving and pitying your enemies, and your humility digesting your injuries and indignities offered you by any men, will invest you in more, than all you ever *enjoyed* or *lost*, as to reall comfort and gracious contentment; By how much you now have lesse to be envyed of *secular splendor*, the more you will be now, and in after ages admired for your meeknesse and contentednesse *in every estate*; *Primitive poverty* of Bishops will but polish and give lustre to your *Primitive piety*; Humane disgraces are oft the foils and whetstones of divine graces. The highest honour as of all good Christians, so chiefly of godly Bishops and Ministers, is not onely to **preach and rule*; but to suffer also as becomes the eminency of their places and graces; *Christ* is (for the most part) on the *suffering side*; and oftner to be found, not onely in the *Temple*, but in the furnace and wildernesse, than in *Courts* and *Palaces*.

Servil. de Mirand.

Carendo magis quam fruendo de bonis recte judicamus.

* καλὸν τὸ μὲν ἱερᾶν τι καλὸν, κρεῖττον δὲ τὸ προθύμως πάσχειν. *Is. Pel. l.* 2. 133. Ἐγγὺς θεοῦ πλήρης μαστίγων. *Cl. Al.* στρω. 2.

I may not (I hope I cannot) flatter any of you, so, as to tempt you to boast of your *Innocency*, to glory in your *merits*, or your *crosses* before God; His *exactnesse* findes *drosse* in the purest vessels, and defects in the weightiest *shekels* of the *Sanctuary*, shewing the most innocent and meritorious persons (as to men) so much of *sinfull infirmity* in themselves, as may both justifie *Gods inflictings*, and provoke the afflicted to true repentings; either for *any excesses*, to which they might be transported, as men; or *defects*, whereto they might be subject, as Bishops and chief Ministers in the Church of Christ; whose *holy industry* and *pious vigilancy* before God ought to be proportioned to those *eminencies*, which they enjoyed above others in the eye of the world; All that I aim at, in this *Paragraph*, is by this touch of *Christian sympathy*, to expresse a sense of duty, gratitude, honour and love, which I owe to God, and for his sake *to your Paternity*: Also to deprecate any offence, which I either really have, or may seem to have given any of you; To whose hands chiefly I owe, what I count my greatest honour, my being *duely ordained to be a Minister* of the glorious Gospell of Jesus Christ in this Church of *England*.

...You are still your selves, and not to be lessened by any mutations of men or times, while you possesse your learned and gracious soules in patience. Your *sufficiency* hath lost nothing while you enjoy *God* and your *Saviour* in faith and love; your *friends* in charity; your *enemies* in pity; your *honours* in knowing how to be * *abased*; and your Estates in knowing how to *want*, as *well as to abound*. You have by experience found the *Episcopall throne* and eminency to be, as * *Gregory Nazianzen* and *Nissen* call it, a *sublimity* fuller of envy and danger, than of *glory* and *dignity*; A *dreadfull Precipice*, hard in the *ascent*, laborious in the station, *hazardous* in the *descent*; of which *Chrysostome* expresseth so great an *horrour*, that he thinkes, few men fit for it, and few saved under it; the *charge* is so great, the *care* so exact, and the *account* so strict. * Nor doth he think it (προστασίαν, ἀλλὰ πόνον καὶ ἀγρυπνίαν) a *preheminency* so much, as *paines*; rather a burthen and *oppression*, than any *honour* or exaltation: And indeed to *great* and *excellent minds*, there was nothing in your *former height* and splendor, truly worthy of your *ambition* or others *emulation*, save onely the larger *opportunities* they afforded you, not of being better in your selves, but of doing more good to others. Of which *conveniencies* being now deprived, as you will have lesse to *account* for to God; so the *noblest revenge* you can take of the present age is, by patience under so *profuse afflictions*, by your prayers for your most unjust and *unplacable enemies*, by your *constancy* in studious industry and holy *gravity*, to let the world see, how impossible it is, for true

Ad cœlestia invitamur cum a seculo avellimur. Tertul. l. 3. advers. Marc.

* Phil. 4. 12.

* ὕψος ἐπίφθονον καὶ ἐπικίνδυνον. Naz. φορτίον δυσβάστακτον τὴν τῆς ἱερωσύνης φροντίδα. *Greg. Nis. de Greg. Thaum.*

* *Chrysost. in Act. hom. 3.*

Christian

Christian Bishops, not to be doing, or desiring good (while they live) to all men; and even to those, from whom they have suffered much evill *without a cause*.

Your *experienced piety* knows better, how to *act*, than I can write; as to true *contentment* in the world, *contempt* of the world, *triumphing* over the world, and *expectations* above the world; your *storms* and distresses, though (*decumani*) great and vast, cannot be long; And to be sure will never be beyond your Pilots skill, who looks on you as sufferers; if not for the fundamentall *saving Truths*, yet for the *comely order* and ancient *government* of his Church; Many of you are already in *prospect* of that fair and *happy haven* of eternall tranquillity: To which I beseech *our God*, and *Lord Jesus Christ*, the *chief Bishop* of his Church, safely to conduct you by the *wisdome* and power of his *Spirit*: As for your *fatherly solicitude* and Christian care of this Church and posterity, God will *relieve you*, by assuring you, that he hath so vigilant and tender care, as will cause all to work together for good; Nor shall the *insolency* of enemies, forain or domestick, who are pleased with your disgraces, and enriched with your spoiles, *alwayes triumph* in the ruines of the Bishops, Ministers, and this *Church* of *England*. Since then nothing is more apposite than the words of one of your own degree and order, *Gregory Nazianzen* (famous for his piety and learning, zeal and patience) I crave leave with all *pristine respects* to present you with that elegant and consolatory expression, which he useth to some godly Bishops whom the *Arian* fury had dethroned from their seats. Such of you (saith he) as are thrust from your *Episcopall* Chaires here on earth, yet are not *forsaken of God*: You shall enjoy surer *seates* in the *heavenly Cathedrall*, which is infinitely more high and happy: No good and wise man but prefers *holy obscurity*, before *pompous injury*. A minde exercised with such *gracious literature* as yours, will know better how to enjoy its *own wisdome*, and *others follies*; its own sufferings, and *other indignities*; than *vain men* can their seeming *plenty* and *prosperity*: *wise and holy men* draw good and *wholesome nourishment* out of *dinners of sowre hearbs*; while others turn to *poison* and surfeit their staled Oxen.

Οὐ τὸν θεὸν ἀπωλέσαν, οἱ τῶν θρόνων παραχωρήσαντες, ἀλλ' ἕξουσιν τὴν ἄνω καθέδραν, ἣ πολὺ τούτων ἐστὶν ὑψηλοτέρα καὶ ἀσφαλεστέρα. *Naz. orat.* 32.

* *Non minoris est gloriæ bene tolerata paupertas, quam magnæ opes innocenter partæ & modeste habitæ.* Tacit. An. l. 4.

I beseech you therefore *Reverend fathers* and *brethren* by the mercies of God, by the bowels of Christ, by your zeal for the truth, by your love of this reformed Church, and your Country; by your former experiences of your prospered labours; by your Christian victories of the many enemies over your order, profession and calling, who have hitherto only scolded, and railed at you, and

put

put rude affronts upon you, but neither lawfully fought you with the weapons of either Scripture, or Reason: I beseech *you* by the care and charity you have to your neighbours souls; by the necessity which lies *on you to preach the Gospell*, and administer holy things; by the *woe* which hangs over you, if you doe not, or draw back; by the compassion and tendernesse you have to posterity, that the reformed Religion may not be abolished, and all superstitious vanities, with fanatick profanenesse and confusions, prevaile in these sometime *fortunate* Islands;

I conjure you by your patience and perseverance hitherto under many trials, both in war and peace; (which may be to you the *sharpest war*) by the peace and joy you have had in the holy Ghost, and in well doing, and comely suffering; by your hopes of heaven, and the glory, which shall be revealed in you; by the coming again of *Christ your Master* and sender; by the Talents you have received; by the accounts you are to give; by the Crown you may expect; by all the thoughts of honor, vertue, grace, glory, immortality, eternity, which your precious soules and raised mindes are capable of; by all that is dear to you, and worthy of you as men, as Christians and as Ministers: by the obstinate pertinacy of your enemies in their malice against you: Never desert your station as Ministers of the Church of *England*; to quit and forsake your standing, as some have done, is to sacrifice your understanding to vulgar folly and senselesse importunities; cast not away your holy profession; betray not that due and *divine authority* you have by your holy ordination in this Church; wipe not off with your owne or the peoples unwashed hands that *sacred unction*, which is upon you, by your being duly *consecrated*, through the gifts, order, power, authority and appointment of the Spirit of Christ, to the office and work of the Ministry: Divert not your studies to any other more *gainefull*, safe, plausible, and honoured profession among men; whose dishonour it is to think any thing more worthy of their honour; as it is the honour of Ministers, to suffer dishonour upon that account; because they are Christs; whose wayes being lesse agreeable, no wonder if his message, and messengers be lesse acceptable to the world: Let not the *soft fleeces on any Wolves backs* deceive you; as if you might well spare your labours, when there are so many *spontaneous Preachers*: Be sure you *out-live them* in all wayes of true holinesse; you can easily (as you do) far *out-preach them* and *out-pray them*, both for truth, method, judgement, and Oratory: It is neither their learning, nor their conscience, nor their eloquence you have to contend with, but their ignorance, hypocrisie, and insolence: when these clouds shall thunder and lighten; when the

Si pertinacia in errore tantas habet vires, quantas in re bona haerere debet vastantia. Aust. Ep. 157.

they ſhall reſolve into **open violence*, and *oppreſſion*, (which is the laſt *reſult of errour*, if it attain to power) yet **fear not theſe*, that can plunder, ſequeſter, impriſon, baniſh and *kill you*; you have learned little in Chriſts ſchoole, if theſe be ſtill a terror to you; *Cannot you be content to be ſuch poore, deſpiſed and perſecuted *Preachers*, as Chriſt was? (you may be good Miniſters, when you are beggers; as ſome have been forced to be in theſe times) Are you aſhamed and afraid to be ſuch, as the Apoſtles were, * who forſook all and followed Chriſt in this work of the Miniſtry; Such, as were their **immediate ſucceſſours* for ſome hundred years; ſuch as your later *predeceſſors* were, thoſe holy and reforming Biſhops and Presbyters in the *Marian perſeoution*; * Such as the moſt of our brethren are now, or lately have been, or are likely to be in all the reformed Churches; Such as thoſe holy Biſhops and Presbyters were, before they met in the firſt *Nicene Councill*; * whither from their *introſpitable Iſlands* and deſerts, from their woods, caves, and deſolate cottages, from their priſons, racks and dungeons, they came forth with the marks of the *Lord Jeſus* on many off them, ſome * with an eye pulled out, others with an hand lopped off; with maimed legs, with ſhrunk ſinews, with ſtigmatized foreheads, and with knees made horney by continuall prayer, for thoſe that had ſo perſecuted and miſuſed them.

* *Errores jus in viribus computare ſolent.* Lactan.
*Mat. 10. 20.
Corona premit vulnera; palma ſanguinem obſcurat; plus victoriatum eſt quam injuriatum, Tertul. Scorp. c. 5.
* Mat. 19. 27.
Delicatus es ſi hic gaudere velis cum ſeculo, & poſtea regnare cum Chriſto. Jeron. ad Heſ.
* *In ea tempora incidimus in quibus firmare animum expediat conſtantibus exemplis.* Thraſ. moriens ap. Tacit. * Ἁπαξαπλῶς ἦν ἰδεῖν δῆμον μαρτύρων κατ' ταυτὸν συνηθροισμένων. *Theod. hiſt. de Syn. Nicæ.* * *Paphnutii effoſſum oculum ſæpe exoſculatus eſt Conſt. M.* Euſeb. in vit.

O *glorious ſpectacle*! O *venerable Councell*! O truely *Chriſtian Synod*, and *ſacred Aſſembly*; not of *Presbyters*, ſcorning and extirpating their *Biſhops*; but of Reverend Biſhops and humble Presbyters; all of them in their due order and holy ſubordination, renowned for their conſtancy in perſecution, and ſo moſt worthy to be Miniſters of the myſteries of Jeſus Chriſt! Shall we now be aſhamed (as a *more ſoft* and delicate generation) of their ſcars and maims? Have we ſo ſtriven for the *right and left hand in Chriſts Kingdome of Church Government*, as to forget to drink of Chriſts cup, and to abhor to be *baptized with his baptiſm*, which was not of water only, but of bloud? Are we aſhamed of Chriſts wounds, and thorns, and reeds; or of Saint *Pauls* chains; or Saint *Peters* priſon; or *Ignatius* his beaſts; or *Polycarps* torments; from whoſe body in the flames a ſweet odour diſperſed to the ſpectators? Doe we abhor to live, as *Cyprian* did, firſt baniſhed, then martyred? Or as great *Athanaſius*, ſixe years in a well without the light of the Sun, forſaken of friends and every where hunted by enemies? Or as *Chryſoſtome*, whoſe eloquent and learned courage exempted him not from much

Matth. 20. 22.
Euſeb. l. 4. c. 15.
Ruffin. l. 1. Eccleſ. hiſt. c. 14.

Martyres ad Cæli januam pœnarum gradibus ascendentes de equuleis & catastis scalas sibi fecerunt. Salv. l. 3. Gub.

trouble and banishment, where he dyed? You will want comforts, if you want trials and afflictions: Saint *John* had his glorious revelation in his exile; Those will be but probations, and increases of your graces and gifts too, which may be rusty with much ease; and warped by the *various turnings*, wherewith many Ministers think to *shift* off persecution, and to grinde with every winde.

* *Theodorus juvenis tristior ab equuleo depositus, inter cruciatus cantabat.* Ruffin. hist. l. 1. c. 30.

If you be indeed conscious to your selves of any *fraud* and *falsity*, of any sinister and unsincere way, by which your predecessours, and you after them, have either attained or maintained your *Ministry*, and function in this Church; if you know any thing *unreasonable, unscripturall, uncomely, immorall, irreligious*, or *superstitious*, in the way or work; in the means, manner, or end of your Ministry; if you are guilty of any thing different from, or contrary to the rule and *way of Christ*, his Churches good, his Fathers glory; dangerous to your own, or others mens soules; In Gods name, repent of your sin betimes, recant your learned folly, renounce your ancient standing; Doe this (as most worthy of you) heartily, ingenuously, publiquely, that by the *foyle* of your shame, the lustre of *Gods glory* may be more set off. Gratifie at length, (not now your enemies, but your friends, because your Monitors and reformers) the Papists, Socinians, Separatists, Brownists, Anabaptists, &c. with what they have so long and so earnestly desired, to such an impatience, as you see now threatens to *cudgell* you to a recantation of your Ministry, if you will not doe it by fair meanes and plausible allurements: O how joyfull and welcome news will it be at home and abroad, to hear, that you, as *Ministers of the Church of England*, have not onely helped to put down *Bishops*, and abolish *Episcopacy*; but you have, (to perfect your repentance, and to cumulate the courtesie) abjured your Office, renounced your standing, abdicated your calling, prostrated your Ministry at the feet of any, that list to kick at it, or tread upon it; and upon you too; as *Ecebelians*; as *unsavory salt*, that is *good for nothing*, unlesse it be new *boyled* in an *Independent Cauldron*, over a *Socinian Furnace*, with a popular fire! O hasten to remove your selves from that *rock of ages*, the Catholick ordination and succession, on which the Church and Ministry hath so long stood in all places, as a City on a hill, both in peace and persecutions: and levell your selves to *those smoother quick-sands*, which would fain levell you to themselves.

Calcate me salem insipidum. Euseb.

You will never be able to suffer what threatens you as Ministers of the old ſtanding and way, with chearfulneſſe and comfort; where your *conſtancy* is but *pertinacy*; as it is, unleſſe you have ſolid grounds, *ſound mindes*, and *ſincere hearts*; if you have any ſcruples, or thornes in your feet, your motions muſt needs be painfull, tedious and uncomely. When you are *converted*, help to redeem us, (the remnant of your poore *ſeduced brethren*) from our *errors* and *miſtakes*; from our miſts of ignorance, our chaines of darkneſſe; from our Catholick cuſtomes; from our Eccleſiaſticall Canons; from our hiſtoricall teſtimonies; from that holy ſucceſſion, that Apoſtolicall practiſe, that Scripture foundation, that divine inſtitution; by all which we fancy our ſelves both ſolidly built and ſtrongly ſupported; And this we have done in the ſimplicity of our ſouls, both we and our Forefathers for many generations; not onely ſince the laſt *reformed century*; but for a thouſand and half a thouſand yeares before, even ever ſince the Chriſtian Religion hath beene planted, propagated, and continued, by ſuch conſecrated Biſhops, and ſuch ordained *Miniſters* in all the world.

If you have found nothing of *God* goe along with your *Miniſtry*, either in your own breaſts, or your peoples hearts, or your Predeceſſors labours; if you are juſtly unſatisfied in that Ordination, and ſucceſſion, by which not only the *Miniſteriall authority*, but all Chriſtian priviledges and rites have been derived to you in this Church; if you never found it confirmed to you by Gods bleſſing on your owne, or others Miniſtry in your way; if you doe indeed finde a *brighter light*, a warmer heat, and a ſweeter influence from thoſe new *Parelii*, which of late have appeared in our sky, as rivals in brightneſſe to our old Sun, in number exceeding it; yea now threatning to eclipſe it, and utterly expell it out of its ancient orb and ſphear: if you really judge, that you have cauſe to * *blaſpheme*, or to ſpeak evill of thoſe *ſeemingly holy*, and reputedly *excellent Biſhops* and *Miniſters*, of this Church; as if they had hitherto been *lyars for God*, *deceivers for Chriſt*; *done evill, that good might come thereby*; if you judge, that you have cauſe to reproach, traduce, and deſpiſe all thoſe Chriſtians, (whoſe profeſſion, full of order, humilitie and holineſſe hath been the *crown and glory of this Church*, and the Miniſtrie of it) as if they had beene *ſilly ſoules*, whom Miniſters *ſmooth tongues* had onely deceived; If you can, or dare to *reprobate* all thoſe, both *godly Paſtors* and *people*; to annull their *Miniſtry*; to overthrow their *Faith*; to waſh off their *baptiſm*; to caſt out their *Sacraments*; to deſpiſe their *Sermons*; to laugh at their *prayers*; to cancell their *writings*; to deteſt their *examples*; to vilifie their *graces*, as *fancifull*, *hypocriticall*, *ſpurious*, *ſuppoſititious*, *ſuperſtitious*, *imaginary*, *unauthoritative*, *antichriſtian*.

Parelii are the ſeeming or mock-ſunnes which ſometime appear with the true Sun; as there did two here in *England*, *an.* 1640.

* Rom. 3.8. καθὼς βλασφημούμεθα, *&c.*

If you finde in your consciences good grounds for this boldnesse of censure; and consequently for a separation, profanation, and abnegation of your former way, both as Ministers, and as Christians, (for renounce one, and you must needs begin both; If you had no true Ministers, then you were no true Christians; and if no true Christians, you could be no true Ministers;) if so, follow by all meanes with speed your *later and diviner dictates*; please your selves in your *happy inconstancy*; hasten to disabuse the people of this Nation, whom so many *holy seducers*, the *Bishops* and *Ministers* of old have abused: O undeceive the miserable and onely nominall Christians of this age, before they perish in their errors and confidences of having true Ministers, and true Sacraments, true Christ, true Faith, true Repentance, &c. O deplore with bitter *lamentation*, the many poore creatures, both *Shepheards* and *Sheep*, who are gone down to the pit: death gnaweth upon them, while they dyed in so *zealous and dangerous errours*, in so fond a Faith, in so vain *hopes*, as mistooke the *gates* of *hell* for *heaven*; Antichrist for Christ among us: you may well blesse your selves in so *glorious a change*; and boast of your *gracious Apostasie*: Hasten to beget some new Church body, which may give you a *new call* and standing; which may rebaptize you, reordain you, and ere long invest you in such an office, power, and Ministry, as they and you shall think more valid, more authentick, more Christian, more comfortable; which hath surer footing, and better standing both in the favour of the times, and of God himself.

But if Scripture, and Reason, and consent of all holy learned men in this and other Churches; if Catholick custome, particular experiences, and holy successes; if divine testimony, clouds of witnesses, of blessed Ministers, and blessed people; of blessed Sermons, and blessed Sacraments; of blessed lives, and blessed deaths; of blessed Converts, and blessed perseverants in grace; if these be as *mighty bars*, crosse your consciences, which stop you either from a weak *retrogradation* to old Popery, or a wicked *precipitancy* to new vulgarity; if neither your judgement, nor your conscience can bear such a *rude revolt*, without great *violatings* of the one, and *woundings* of the other; if you dare not in a fit of popularity, so injure the dead, that are at *rest in the Lord*, so discourage the living and thriving Christians, so overthrow the Faith of many, so *blaspheme* the God, the Saviour and the Spirit of those holy men and women, living and dead, who have been called, and converted, and sanctified, and confirmed, and saved by that *Word of Power*, and those holy Ministrations, which your Fathers, and your Brethren, and your selves the Ministers of this Church have duly preached and administred, in that office, standing and authority,

where-

wherewith they were and you now are duly invested in this Church;

I beseech you, then, be *so valiant*, as to dare to be, and still to own your selves, as true *Ministers of Christ* in this Church, ordained by him, and for him: still seeking the things of Christ in the good old way of the ordained Ministry, while others seeke *their owne* in their *new models* and *fashions*. Doe not study to disguise your selves (no not outwardly) as if you were afraid *your coat* should discover your *calling*; or as if you pretended to have renounced it with your changed habit: you may preserve *white souls* under *black clothes*; as others may *black soules* under spendid colours: your sable colour, although very becoming the *gravity* of your calling in the best times, yet was never more decent than now, when (besides that you are *Ministers*) you have cause to be *mourners*: Adde not to the other *confusion of times*, this of your garments; nor gratifie them so far as a shoe-latchet in your clothes, whose aim is to levell and *confound* your *calling* with the *meanest of the people*: Although I placed heretofore no Religion in clothes and colours, yet now I almost think it piety to persevere in such a fashion, whose change would argue inconstancy, and so farre be irreligious, as it is acceptable to the erroneous, confirms them in their errours, and casts some shame upon the truth, both of our Ministry and our Church; In such a case a few graines of frankincense are not to be offered to any Idol. It was in ancient times thought an heavy punishment, for *a Presbyter to be deposed* from his degree and office, so as to be treated but as a *Layman*; O do not seek to desecrate, depose, or disguise your selves; hang not out the *flags* of your *motly Coats*, or pybald colours, as if you had taken from, or rendered up your *orders* to high shoes, and quitted that *distinction* you anciently have from the Vulgar; Since you did not ordain your selves, but were consecrated by the Word, and authority of Christ, through the hands of those who had received power to send you *in Christs Name, into Christs harvest*; why should you study or affect those mean palliations and miserable confusions, which are uncomely for men of holy gravity, learned constancy, and religious honour? Other men have dared much more in *worse adventures*, and *more unwarrantable undertakings*: You cannot adventure your many *talents of learning*, and ingenuous parts, your studies, labours, liberties, and lifes in a *safer way*, or on a *better account*; than in that ship where *Christ is imbarqued*, and so many pretious souls with him; you need no other *policy* entred to insure you, than this, that *you deal for Christ*, as *his Factours* for soules, and *Agents* for that *heavenly commerce* between God and sinners.

Therefore *hold fast* your profession, so, as neither to be ashamed of, nor a shame to your holy calling and Ministry; whose honor depends not on *factious fancy*, or *vulgar novelty*, but on *divine Institution*, and *Catholick succession*; Let the soules of men and the purity of Religion, be then *dearest* to us, when they are growne *cheapest* to others: Let our lives be strictest, when *liberty is made a cloak to licentiousnesse*; There will never need more true Ministers, than when every man shall be tolerated to be a Minister; that so *true ones* may be suppressed, and none but false incouraged: That the tyes of Duty and Conscience may lie upon none, either as Ministers, or hearers; as Pastor, or flock, to attend any holy publique worship and service of God: which is the high way to Atheism, superstition, confusion, any thing but the true Christian and reformed Religion. Abate not your *labours*, though men grudge, withdraw, and deny *your wages*; What can bee more glorious than to see you *contentedly poore* for Christs sake, and still continuing to make many rich; while you are exhausted and have nothing? imparting *things spirituall*, though you receive little or nothing of *things temporall*? this is after the pattern in the mount, after the example of *divine munificence*, where goodnesse is of free *grace*, and *not of the reward* or merit. Make any *honest shift* to live, but use no *base shifts* to leave your calling; Better your *tongues cleave to the roofe of your mouthes*, than you should renounce your *Ordination* and *Ministry*; or cease to preach in *that Name*, while you have power, liberty, and opportunity; Nothing will become us Ministers better, than *thread-bare coats*, if we can but keep *good consciences*: Nothing will be sweeter, than dry *morsels* and sowre hearbs, and a *cup of cold water*, (the *Prophets portion*) if we have *but inward peace*, and the love of Christ therewith.

2 Cor. 6. 10.

Prov. 15. 7.

It was articled against Saint *Chrysostome*, (when he was Bishop of *Constantinople*) by some of his envious enemies, as a matter of pomp and scandall, that he rode in the City *upon an Asse*, to ease his age. It will be lesse offence, when the world shall see *holy Bishops* and deserving *Presbyters* go on foot, and *asses riding* upon them; *Princes* (which Saint *Jerome* interprets *Bishops*) on *foot*, and servants on *horseback*; Though we be never so low, let us doe nothing below the dignity of our Ministry, which depends not on externall pomp, but inward power; the same faith, which shewes to a true beleiver, the *honour* and *excellency of Christ*, sets forth also the love and reverence due to his true Ministers of the Gospell; who are in Christs stead, when they are in *Christs work* and *way*, and need not doubt of Christs and all good Christians love to them.

Photius Biblioth. in Chrysost.

Psal. 45. 16.
Eccles. 10. 7.

An

An high point of wisdome, and piety would be in all *true Ministers*, of what degree soever, would be to take the advantage of this *Antiperistasis*; by the *snow and salt*, as it were, of *papall* and *popular ambition*, they should be the more congealed and compacted together into one body and fraternity: Having so many unjust enemies on every side, against every true Minister of this Church, whether *Bishop* or *Presbyter*; all prudence invites us to compose those *unkinde jealousies*, *breaches* and *disputes* which have been among us, because we own our selves, *as brethren*; among whom some may be elder in nature, or *superior* in *authority* without the *injury* of any: This subordination, if Scripture doe not precisely command, yet it exemplarily proposeth; Reason adviseth; and Religion alloweth; and certainly Christ cannot but approve; the more, because the pride of Papall *Antichrists* on one side, and the unrulinesse of *popular Antichrists* on the other side studies to overthrow it, and are the most impatient of it. I know some mens *folly* will not depart from them, though they be *brayed in a morter*: But sober men will think it time to bury (as * *Constantine the Great* burned) all unkinde disputes, breaches and jealousies, which have almost destroyed not onely the *Government*, but the very *Ministry* it self of this Church: No doubt, passions have darkened many of our judgements; earthly distempers have eclipsed our glory; secular and *carnall divisions* have battered our defenses, discovered our weaknesses, and invited these violent assaults from enemies round about; that none is so weak, as to despaire of his *malices* sufficiency to doe us Clergy men some mischief; the most tatling Gossips, the sillyest *shees*, who are *ever learning* and *never come to the knowledge of the truth*, undertake, not only to be *teachers*, but to *teach their teachers*, as *Tertullian* observed; yea and to Ordain their Ministers; such (no doubt) as they do deserve, having such Preachers for their greatest *punishments*.

For Verity.

* As *Constantine the Great*, burned all the bils of complaints exhibited by the Bishops and Churchmen, one against another. *Euseb. vit. Const.*

Privatæ simultates publicis utilitatibus condonandæ. Tac.

* *Salva fidei Regula de disciplina contendentibus suprema lex est Ecclesiæ pax.* Blondel.

ἡττηθῶμεν ἵνα νικῶμεν. Naz. or. 14. *Vincamur ut vincamus. de diffid. Christianorum.*

* *Clemens* in his Apostolike Epistle, advised any one to depart, if he findes for his sake the dissension is in the Church. *Ruffin. Eccles. hist. l. 1. c. 2.* *Discordiæ in unitatem trahant, & plagæ in remedia vertantur; unde metuit Ecclesia periculum, inde sumat augmentum.* Amb. voc. gen. l. 2. λύσις στάσεως ἔκγονον. *Naz. or. 13.* τῷ ζόφῳ τῆς στάσεως ἑαυτὸν ἐγκρύπτων ὁ δαίμων. *Naz.* *Ipsæ mulieres eorum quam procaces; quæ audeant docere: contendere, forsitan & tingere.* Tertul. præf. ad. Hær. cap. 41.

The kinde closing and Christian composing of passionate, and needlesse differences among learned, and *pious Ministers*, by mutuall condescending about matters of *sociall prudence*, order and government to be used in the Church, (which have chiefly (if not onely) brought so great misgovernment upon us, in *England*) would be a great and effectuall means to recover the happinesse of this Church, and the honour of the Ministry; which consists

Μαθωμεν ὑγιαίαν ἐξ ὧν νενοσήκαμεν. *Naz. or. 13.*

consists in an holy fraternity and godly harmony of love, no lesse than in truth of doctrine, and holynesse of manners; By our own leaks and rents we first let in these waters which have sunk us so low, that every wave rakes over us. No man, that is truly humble, wise, and holy, will be ashamed, to *retract* any *errour* and transport, whereof he hath been guilty, and of which he hath cause to be most ashamed; *Ingenuous offers* of *fraternall agreement*, and mutuall condescendings to each other had beene exceedingly worthy of the best Ministers both of the *Episcopall*, *Presbyterian* and *Independent* way, whose wisdome and humility might easily have reconciled and united the severall interests which they pretend to support, of Bishops, Presbyters, and Christian people. But who sees not that secular designes, and civill interests have too much *leavened* the dissensions of *many Ministers*, though in the conclusion they have not on any side much made up their cake by the match? while Church men, Bishops, and Presbyters, had no such *worldly concernments* to engage them, they had no such disputes, and mutinies, as to the *order* and *government* of the Church; which no *Councell*, no *particular Bishops*, nor *Presbyters*, no one Church or Congregation of Christians began of themselves; but all by *Catholick* and *undisputed* consent conformed themselves to *that order*, which the Apostles and Apostolicall men left in common to the *Churches* in every place, most sutable to their either beginning or increasing, to their setling, or their setlednesse.

Greg. Nazianzem offered himself to be *like Jonas* to the Church then troubled with sedition. *in vita Naz.*

Irenæus, l. 4. c. 43. & c. 45.

It is easie to see what Christ would have in the Church, as to extern order and policy, if *Christians* would look with a *single eye* at Christs ends. You may easily see how the worlds various interests, (which are as hardly commixt with Christ's, and true religion's, as oil with water) *serve themselves* with *Ministers tongues*, *pens*, and *active spirits*; who should rather serve the Lord Jesus and his Church, in *truth*, *simplicity*, *peace*, and *unity*; without any *adherences to secular policies*, parties, and studies of sides; by which sudden and *inconsiderate rowlings* to and fro, (as foolish and fearefull *passengers* in a *tottering boat*) some *Ministers* of *England* have welnigh *overturned* the Vessell of this *reformed Christian Church*, which might easily (as the most famous and flourishing Churches anciently were) have been uprightly *ballanced*, and *safely steered* by a just fitnesse and *proportion* of every one in their place, either for Ministry, or Government, and Discipline; where of old the *paternall presidency* of Bishops stood at the helm; the grave and industrious *Presbyters rowed*, as it were, at the *Oares*; and the *faithfull people*, as the *passengers kept all even*, by keeping themselves in *quietnesse*, *order*, and *due subjection*. Nor was it wont in primitive times, to be asked *of Princes*, *or people*, how they would have

have the Church governed, or by whom; who should *ordaine* Preachers; or who should preach the Gospell, administer the Sacraments, *confirm* the baptized, censure the scandalous, and receive the penitent; These were mysteries proper to Christian Religion, and intrusted to the *Pastors* of the Church, at first: also conserved by them in the midst of hot *persecutions* from secular *Magistrates*, without any variations, save onely such, as necessity of affaires and Christian prudence (yet in an orderly way) required and practised, as to some circumstantials: which was no more, than for a childe from his coats to come to *breeches*, or for the bark of a tree to increase, as the bulk and branches grow.

What humane *passion* then, and inconsideration hath any way wounded, *wisdome* and Christian compassion in Ministers of all sorts should seek to cure; The wounds of the Church will commonly *fester and gangrene*, if Ministers stay, till *Lay men* take them to heart; nor is the hand of any of them so proper as them, who have occasioned *most hurt*: we Ministers ought to be the *good Samaritans*, and by first healing the deformed scars of our own scandals; the boyling Ulcers of our own *passions*; the gaping *orifices* of our owne religious dissensions, our *influence* will be much more *soverain*, and *benign* to draw together, and heal up the *publique sores* of the Church, and reformed Religion; when we appear fit for so holy and good a work, it may be God will put it into the heart of those in *power*, to call us forth, and incourage us to *this happy* understanding.

O consider with your selves, how much the *men of this world* are wiser than you in their generations; you are commonly but the *beaters* of the bush for *the mighty Nimrods* of the world: what have Ministers got, yea what almost have you not lost (which wise men would have preserved) of credit, honour, comfort, or incouragement; while they helped to pull down the *Sion* of this Church? whose dust hath fallen into their own eyes, and besmeared their garments to a most *uncomely deformity*; Will you all leave this *Sion thus in her dust*, without any pity of her? is it better she should be ever desolated, than your *animosities* laid aside, and your *poore feuds* reconciled? Such *everlasting burnings* become not *mortall breasts*; least of all *heavenly hearts*, such as Ministers should have: Plead no longer such a zeal for Christ, as *over-layes* charity and humility; or such a desire for *Reformation*, which produceth so great *deformities*; It is not so much a charity, as a justice for *us Ministers* to advise, to weep, to pray for the *peace of our Jerusalem*; for from the Prophets in great part *evill* is gone out into all the land; our cold or our hot *fits*, our *luke-warmnesse*, or our negligence, or our timerousnesse, have cast this Church and many poore souls

Mortales cùm sumus immortalis non esse debent odia. Tantæne animis Cœlestibus iræ?

Jer. 23. 15.

into this *lingring distemper*; this almost incurable *Quartane*, which will never be cured, till we smell the *Rose of Sharon*; the sweet and celestiall temperament of Christs *fragrancies*; in all love and charity; in humility, meeknesse, kindnesse, forbearance, pity, and tendernesse to each other.

Not onely *all policy* and honest prudence then, as to the *recovery* of Ministers credit and reputation, but all *conscience* and piety, as to the requisites of Gods glory, and *charity*, as to the dangers and necessities of peoples soules, require now, such *double diligence* of us, all, as may compensate any former failings, and shew the world how necessary a *good*, worthy Ministers are; who every way fit those places, and fill those *orbs*, in which God and the Church have set them: It is high time for us to get beyond all *cold formalities, superficiall solemnities, popular complyings, covetous projects, secular ambitions*; *Penurious pains, slacker care*, and *indiligent tendance*, will not be sufficient to cure those *diseases*, we have now to contend withall; which are *ingenious* to avoid all cure, subtill to elude all skill, *cunning* to increase their *maladies*, cruell to spend their *infection*, and fierce to destroy their *Physitians*. Moderate and indifferent industry will hardly at any time convert sinners, and save soules; They are now like *harder metals*, which melt not but in such a degree of heat; Least of all now, when errour is adored for truth, sin and damnation it self are dressed up, and esteemed as a way to salvation: when *hel* it self is by some courted for heaven; and chains of darknesse counted liberty. (like those *Succubas* and *Empusas*, which some men are reported to have espoused and embraced for *beautifull wives*.)

Philostratus in vita Apollon. Thyanæi.

There needs, now, besides preaching gifts, and oratorious breath, that *vigor* of grace; that spirit of zeal; that fervency of charity; that humble constancy; that magnanimous meeknesse, which may make us *Ministers* unwearied in our studies, frequent and fervent in praying, oft in fasting, attentively watching, tenderly weeping, charitably visiting, solidly instructing, and diligently examining, &c. In all wise and meeke condescendings, even to bear with *mens infirmities*; to frustrate their passions; to receive their bullets and shot as upon *Wool-sacks*; to overcome their oppositions by something of a softer yeelding: still beseeching them and intreating them, to be reconciled to God in Jesus Christ, when they are to us irreconcilable. All obstructions of private peevishnesse, passion, hard speeches, haughty carriage, rough demeanor; all fashion of disdains, revenge, and secular contestations, must be removed as uncomely, uncomfortable, noxious: That people may see the *bloud* of Christ softning us; and the *bowels* of *Christ enlarging* us, as brethren, as *fathers*, or *mothers*, as tender and carefull Nurses in Christs family.

It

It is ever, and now most of all unseasonable (in so short and uncertain a *moment*, which is allowed us to preach, or *people* to hear, to learn, and to live in order to *eternity*) to exercise Christians in continuall *disputes*; to lead them in perplexed *pathes*, full of bryars and thornes; to wast their and our time in modern *impertinencies*; which will not profit a poore sinner, either living or dying. All times and paines is lost, which is not laid out in *Catechising*, *Preaching*, and *applying* sound, wholesome, healing, saving, *necessary truths*; which really mend both minde and manners: either *laying* the foundations in principles, or maintaining them in doctrines, or building proportionably upon them in practicks and comforts: where the *truths* of faith bear up the practise of an *holy life*; and an holy life adornes the Articles of true faith; where the Creed and the Decalogue goe together: That besides the *shewes of leaves in doctrines and opinions*; there may appear *goodly fruits* of purity, justice, mercy, charity, patience, peaceablenesse, civill obedience, self-denyall, which are grown so much out of fashion.

Alas! while poore people are amused with *novelties*, (as *Larks* with dasing glasses): or picking up *curiosities*; or gazing at *sublimities*; or dubious in *uncertainties*; or intangled with *subtilties*; as Deer in acorn time, they forget their food, grow lean and fall into divers *snares and temptations*; into many lusts and passions; yea into the grave and pit of destruction, whence there is no redemption. Many (as leaves from trees in Autumn) every day drop away: and dye in their *mazes* and *labyrinths* of Religion, by wearying themselves; in which they advance no more than *birds in a cage*, and *blinde horses in a mill*: whereas a true Christian should every day *grieve* to see himself nothing advanced in true holynesse, or solid knowledge: with grand steps he should be dayly going onward and upward, with ample progresses and mighty increases, of sound knowledge, indisputable verities, unquestionable practises, of ly duties and heavenly conversation: (these are the steps by which holy men and women have ascended to heaven, and conquered the difficulties of salvation) That thus al the world might blesse themselves to see the happy improvements of true Christians beyond other men; and the inestimable blessing of true and excellent Ministers paines among the silliest and worst of men in the dissolutest and worst of times.

Οἵη μὲν φύλλων γενεή, τοιήδε καὶ ἀνδρῶν. Hom.

O let not us then of the *Ministry stand still*, and look on our own, and the Churches miseries (as the Lepers, or *mothers did in sieges*) till their children and themselves *grew black with famine*: You that pretend to stand before the Lord of the whole world, and the King of his Church; you that bear the name of the most *compassionate Redeemer*, who shed *his bloud* for his Church, and laid *down his life* for his sheep; Doe you never hear in the sounding of *your own bowels* the tears, sighes, and fears, of *infinite good Christians*; nor the voice of this *English Sion*, lamenting and expecting pity, at least from *Ministers*? Is it worth thus much misery to root up *Episcopacy*, to set up *Presbytery*, and to undermine both with *Independency*? All which might be fairly composed into a *threefold cord of holy agreement*: such as was in primitive times, between Bishops, Presbyters, and people; whose passions have now ravelled out peace by *sad divisions*, and weakned Religion by uncharitable contentions: Though Parliaments, and Assemblies, and Armies, and people, should be *miserable comforters*, passing by without regard and remorse; yea though some be stripping the *wounded*, and robbing this desolated Church; yet doe not *you forsake her*, now she is smitten of God, and despised of men: Is it nothing to you (O you that are more *politicians, than Preachers*) that passe by? Stand and see, if there be *any sorrowes* like the sorrowes of this reformed Church of *England*, wherewith *the Lord hath afflicted her in the day of his fierce anger*; It concernes no men more than Ministers to succour her, which hath received these *wounds most-what in the house and by the hands of her friends*; O give *the Lord no rest*, untill he hath returned to this Church in mercy; if you can by counsels and prayers *reform* nothing in the publique, yet let nothing be unreformed in your private; if you must be laid aside, as to the peculiar office of Ministers, yet you may mourn and pray the *more in secret*; That the Lord would breath upon us, with a *Spirit of Truth and Peace*; of love and holy union; of order and humility; whereby none having any pride or ambition to govern, every one may be humbly disposed to be *governed*: For the great *crisis of all Ministers* distempers is in this; (not what Truths we shall beleive; what doctrine we shall preach; what holynesse we shall act; but) who shall govern? whether Bishops, or Presbyters, or people? yea the *Keyes* of some mens *pretended power* hangs so at the peoples girdle, that it is too neer the *apron-strings* even of mechanicks, and silly women.

Lamen. 1.12.

When a right temper of Christian humility and love shall be restored *to every part*, then will the *spirits of Religion* be recovered, and aptly diffused into every member of this Church; which *blessed temperament*, as Christian Churches enjoyed in their primitive, and florid strength; nor is it lesse necessary now, in their more aged, and so decayed, constitution; O let not after ages say, the Ministers of *England* were more *butchers*, then *Surgeons*: That they were *Physitians of no value*; neither curing themselves, nor others; If any of us have (not by malice so much as mistake) given stronger physick, and more graines of *violent drugs*, than the constitution of of this or any well reformed Church can well bear, let us not be lesse forward, to apply such *cordials*, *lenitives*, *antidotes*, and *restoratives*, of love, moderation, concession, and equanimous wisedome, as may recollect the dissipated and re-inforce the wasted spirits, which yet remain in this reformed Church, and the Ministry of it; On which the enemies round about doe already look with the greedy eyes of *ravens and vultures*, expecting when its languishing spirits shall be quite exhausted, and its fainting eyes quite closed; that so they may draw away the pillow, and remaining supports, of civill protection from under its head; and violently force it to give up the ghost: that the reformed Religion, and Ministry of this Church may be at length quite cast out, and buried with the *buriall of an Asse*; that neither the place of *reformed Bishops*, nor reformed *Presbyters*, nor reformed people, may know them any more in these *British* Islands.

In the last place therefore, I humbly crave leave to *remind those that act in highest places and power*, who are thought no slight or *shallow Statesmen*; That, if neither piety to God, nor conscience of their duty, while they undertake to govern, nor charity to mens soules both in present and after ages, nor zeal for the reformed Religion, move them as Christians; nor yet justice and common equity, to the encouragement and preservation of so many learned and godly men, the lawfull Ministers of this Church in their *legall rights*, and liberties; nor yet *common pity*, and *charity* to relieve so many pious men, and their families: If (I say) none of these should sway them, as men, or Christians, (the least of which should, and I hope greatly will) Yet worldy *policy and right reason of State* seems to advise the *preservation aud establishment* of the (so much shaken) *reformed Religion* here in *England*, which hath still deep root and impressions in the mindes and affections of the most, and best people in this Nation: Nor can this be done by more idoneous means, than by giving publique favour, incouragement, and establishment to the true and ancient Ministry, as to its main support; and to godly Ministers as its *headmost Professors*.

13. *Humble addresse to those in power in the behalf of Ministers.*

If it be not *absolutely necessary*; yet sure it is *very convenient*, in order to the quiet and satisfaction of mens mindes, (who generally think themselves most concerned in matters of Religion) either to confirm and restore to its pristine *honour*, *order*, and *stability*, the ancient *Ministry* of the Church of *England*; (which I have proved to be the onely true succession of *divine authority*) or else wholly to remove it; and to set Religion upon some other basis: For neither the reformed Religion, nor its Ministry, can either long, or safely, or comfortably stand in so *tottering and mouldering aposture*; like the wals of some great old fabrick, or *ruinous Cathedrall*, swelling out, and threatning to fall. It were better to take it down, than to hazard its dangerous breakings, and *precipitious tumblings*; *Scratches in Religion* doe soon fester, and easily turn to Gangrenes, which must either be *speedily healed*, or *discreetly cut off*.

It were high *proesumption* for one to advise, who professeth his ignorance, in State Policies: yet common prudence shewes, this to be the *high way*, and most *compendious passe to publique peace*. Namely, 1. *The setling of the reformed Religion in this Church of England*, and its publique Ministry, in comely government, competent maintenance, and holy succession. 2. The confirming, and if need be, explaining, or enlarging the Articles of the Church of *England*, in the *main fundamentals* of Religion, as Christian and reformed, both in things to be believed, and practised. 3. The restoring of that holy power and ancient exercise of *Discipline* to the Church, both in privater Congregations, and in publique associations: which may both carry on true knowledge, piety, and charity in Ministers and people: Also recover the *sacred Ordinances* of Christ, and publique duties of Religion to their primitive purity and dignity; which have been infinitely abased by *Laymens policies, Ministers negligences*, and vulgar *insolencies*; These would keep a fair course and form of Christian peace and holinesse in the publique, a midst *lesser differences*; and no lesse satisfie, than oblige every sober minded Christian; whose good examples have great influence on the *generality* of people.

But if the vulgar rudenesse, deformity, and inconsistency, be once taught, (by being tolerated) to *slight*, and *scorn their Ministers*, and in them all holy things, and true Religion; Either beleiving (as they are prone to doe) that their Ministers are not invested by any *due and divine authority* in that Office and Ministry, any more than themselves are; nor are assisted by any speciall grace and blessing from God; if they suspect that *civill Powers* doe set *Divines at nought*, and regard them no more, than as so *many pretenders, falsaries*, and *intruders*: How willingly will the mindes of common people, (whom nothing but *Conscience*, or the *Sword keepes in aw and order*) embrace any thing that makes towards *laxation* of duty to God, and observance to men? No water is more easily diffused, or more naturally strives, by its fluid nature to overbear, what ever bounds *pen* it up, or restrain it from wasting it self. Nor are such tempers slack, (where occasion tempts them) to revenge by *their riots*, all former restraints cast upon them, by any men, that sought to set limits, either of power, or piety to their lusts and passions.

πῶς φυλάξεις τοὺς ἀνθρωπίνους νόμους τοὺς θείους παρατρέχων; *Naz. Celeusio judici.* None can make conscience of humane laws, who disregards divine.

To

To avoid which rude and irreligious *extravagancies of common-people*, all * *wise Governours* have still countenanced the *publique exercises* of that Religion, which they owned and *established* as best; * Adding all civill reputation, favour, and authority to the use of it, and chiefly to those, who were its *prime professors* and *Ministers*; who were ever * *unviolable* in their publique officiatings; generally esteemed, as *sacred*, both for the protection they had from men, and the institution from divine power and wisdome; Which *policy* was not more wisely carryed in all false and feigned religions, than justly and most conscientiously to be observed, as it ever hath been by all worthy and noble minded Christians, (either *Princes* or *States*) in that, which we hold to be, and professe, as the onely true, Christian and reformed Religion: whose Oracles, Doctrines, institutes, offices, authority, and ministery have their originall, not *from man*, but from the onely wise and true God; who, first sent his Prophets, and servants; after that his Son (the Lord Jesus Christ) to be not onely a fulfiller and establesher, but also a *Preacher* of righteousnesse to mankinde; whose preaching, Prophetick, or *Ministeriall office*, (as to extern and visible administrations) the holy order and due succession of Ministers doe supply; and in the same power succeed by his speciall mission and appointment in the Church.

14. *Christian Ministers of all merit most publique protection and favour.*

* *Rex sacrificiis & Templis, & omni cultui Deorum & moribus & legibus praeerat*, Pomp. Læt. de mag. Rom.

Apud Ægyptios, ἀνάγκη τὸν τέλειον βασιλέα στρατηγὸν τ' ἀγαθὸν εἶναι καὶ δικαστὴν καὶ ἱερέα. Stob. in Reg. So *Plato: περὶ βασιλ.*

* Cæsar. Pel. Gal. l. 6. *Magno apud eos sunt honore Druides; Nam fere de omnibus controversiis publicis privatisque constituunt.* Plaut. Rudent. *Quis homo est tanta confidentia, Qui sacerdotem audeat violare? At magno cum malo suo fecit herclè.* Liv. dec. 1. l. 2. *Sacrificus Rex sacrorum dicebatur.* Constantine the *Great*, alwayes received the Orthodox and godly Bishops and Presbyters with all respect and veneration. *Euseb. in vita Const.* Ministry of the Gospell was called *Deificus ordo.* Amb. θεῖοι γεωργοί, *Clem. Al. sp.* 1. Μεσιτείαν θεοῦ καὶ ἀνθρώπων. *Naz. or.* 1. *Reverenda ipsis Angelicis spiritibus Ministeria*, Ber. *Columna Ecclesiæ, Id. Honor sacerdotii, firmamentum imperii.* Tacit. de Judæis, hist. 4.

Whose most *sacred Mysteries*, for infinite wisdome; for inestimable mercy; for unparalleld love; for holy precepts; for divine examples; for *precious promises*; for *ancient and undoubted Prophesies*; for exact *fulfillings*; for apt *institutions*; for sutable Ministry; for beautifull order; for blessed comfort; for sweet peace, and mutuall charity (which are, or ought to be) among the true professors of it, infinitely exceeds all the wisdome, designes, desires, and thoughts of all those, that ever pretended to any Philosophy, Religion, vertue, sanctity, or felicity. All which come far short, as of the inward *comfort* of mens consciences, so of that outward beauty, peace, and order, which doe most blesse humane societies; which *bonds of publick tranquillity*, all *true and unpragmatick Ministers* of the Gospell of peace, doe most effectually lay (in Christs Name) upon men; In which regard, of all ranks of men and orders, they deserve best of mankinde, where ever they live; while they keep within those Evangelicall bounds, that holy and humble temper, which becomes them; and which is proper *to the Spirit of the Gospell.* *Constantine the Great* writes: The greatest safety or danger to any State comes by Religion; if the reverence of it be weakned and honour abated, dangers attend: if by Lawes and authority it be setled and preserved, great blessings follow, &c. So that no men seem *more to fight* against their own peace, than those that suffer the ancient Ministry and true Ministers of Christ to be *destroyed*, or disregarded in any Christian Nation; which will be interpreted a *fighting against God*, and an *opposing Christ Jesus*; who as he is the onely *true rock*, on which the Church is to be built, as to internall comfort, and eternall happinesse; so he hath regulated it as to externall order, beauty, and harmony; and this not by every unskilfull hand, that hath a minde to be *mudling*; but by such, as he hath appointed to be tryed, approved, and rightly ordained to the work of *edifying* the Church in truth and love: This *Galilean* must overcome: Christ will no doubt *prove as a stumbling stone*; so a rock of *ruine and offence*, to all those that *dash against him*, in this Ordinance of his *holy Ministry*; which, though it seem small, and contemptible to those, that think themselves *Grandees*, (in power, and policy) yet as it was not *cut out by humane hands*, so it will be a *very burdensome stone to all*, that think to lift it out of the way, and lay it aside, from being an holy *function*, and divine institution.

Euseb. Eccl. hist. l. 10. c. 5.

Vicisti Galilae, vicisti. Julian dying cries.

1 Pet. 2. 6, 8.

15\. I think therefore (under favor) that it will be not the least point of *wisdome, and policy*, in those who by exercising magistratick power stand most accountable *to God and man*, for the support of the Ministry; to harken to, and follow that *grave counsell*; * *Take heed what you doe to these men*, who are the *true Ministers* of Jesus Christ, the messengers of the *most high God*, who *preach to you the way of salvation.* For if their function, mission, and *Ministry* be from Christ, (which I have proved, and those can hardly doubt, who are so much inlightned by Scripture, as some are, who may yet be *blinded* by *secular interests*) it *shall prevail*, though it be in the *way* of being persecuted: Humane malice may a while oppose; but it shall not quite blow out, quench or smother those burning and shining lights of the Church: Which it would doe with no lesse *detriment* to the Church, and State; than if it should extinguish the flame, light, and lustre of *the Sun in the Firmament*; * Nor are those *ordinances of heaven*, and that *Covenant* God hath made in Nature, more

The Ministers of Christ not safely to be injured.

* Act. 5. 35.

Greg. Naz. tels us that Saint *Basil the Great* was in so great reverence in the Church; ὡς ϗ ἀλλοτρίων ἀπὸ Θεοῦ νομίζειν παντὸς τὴν ἀπ' αὐτοῦ διάστασιν. They could not be friends with God who were at enmity with *Basil. orat.* 16.

* *Vide* Jer. 33. 20. which Prophesie is clear for a constant and immutable Ministry in the Church of Christ.

necessary

necessary, or lesse *durable*, than are these, of *holy Ministrations*, and Evangelicall Ministry, which God hath appointed for Christ in the Church; It is but little, and with far lesse comfort, that we see, *of God in the creature*; than what we see *of him in Christ*; nor are the beams *of the Sun so glorious*, or necessary, as these of the *Sun of righteousnesse*, which are diffused by his Ministers; which are *as his wings*, by which he hath moved into all parts of the earth, and his voice hath been heard to the ends of the world. Mal. 4. Rom. 10.18.

And truly the most judicious Christians, who are able to *discern the day of Gods visitation*, doe looke upon this *shaking and battery* made by some men, against the *publique office*, and authority of the Ministry of this reformed Church of *England*, to be nothing else, but the effects of those *counsels and plots*, which are always contriving by the *powers of darknesse*, and the gates of hell, against God, and Christ, against the *Orthodox Faith*, and *purest Churches*; And however they shall never prevail to destroy the true *Christian reformed Religion*, in all places; yet they may occasion its *ebbing*, and receding from a *negligent, wanton*, and ungratefull people, who love *Apostasies*, and *increase back-slidings*; as many in *England seeme* to doe: It may provoke the Lord to *transplant the Gospell to some other Nation*, which shall bring *forth better fruits*; and leave our *houses desolate*, who brought forth such *sowre grapes*, as these are, wherewith, after so many *hundred years*, some men now seek to *requite the Lord* and his faithfull Ministers in this Church; what can indeed be expected, but *some fatall Apostasie*, either to grosse superstition, or Atheistical liberty, or heathenish barbarity? which is *nigh at hand*, and even at the dore; when once the divine honour, and succession of the *Evangelicall Ministry* is outed, and overthrowne; for what else can follow, when people shall either have no *true Ministers*; or be taught to beleive that they need not any; and have no more cause to regard them that are such by profession, than so many *Mountebanks*; whom no man is bound in reason, honour, conscience, or civility to hear, obey, maintain, or reverence, as having no higher *mandate*, mission, or authority, than from their own mindes, or peoples humors?

Gildas de excid. Brit. deplores the sacrilegious injuries and neglect of holy men and holy duties before those miseries.

Isai. 1. 5.

Deut. 32. 6.

To prevent which *direfull* sin, shame, and mischief; to give some stay to the feares, and life *to the hopes* of thousands, besides (and better then) my selfe, I have taken this boldnesse upon me (by Gods direction and assistance, (as I trust) though *unknowne*, and not much *considerable* to the many *excellent Christians*, which are yet in this Church, and least of all *to those in power*, whom the matter most concerns) with all due respects, all Christian charity, and humility to present to the publique view of all those (whom this 16.

The preservation of the honour of the Ministry most worthy of all excellent Christians.

Ffff

this subject *of the Ministry* and *reformed Religion* doth concern) these most *sad and serious thoughts* of my heart, which are not busied about *Prophetick obscurities*, or *Apocalyptick uncertainties*; which may please melancholy fancies, and abuse curious readers: but about a matter most clear, from Scripture; most *necessary*, to the being of any true Church in this world; to the comfort of every true Christian; to the succession of Religion in after ages. None of which can be kept in any *way of Gods revealed will*, and ordinary providence, but onely by a right and *authoritative Ministry*; which carries a relation and bond of conscience with it, between Minister, and people; which cannot be had, unlesse we still keep to the pattern, which Christ hath set us, and the Church of Christ in all ages followed; without any *falsity*; though not wholly without some *infirmity*.

Nor is there any thing, wherein men of the *highest power and excellency* can shew themselves more worthy of the *name of Christians*, than in their endeavouring effectually to restore, and establish the *due authority* and *succession of the Ministry*; by being patrons, incouragers, and protectors of all able, and peaceable Ministers and their calling: Whose honour is Gods, and will redound to theirs, whom God shall so far blesse, as to make them instruments of so noble, and most Christian a work; But they had need to be *Herculesses*, men of most *divine vertue*, and *resolution*, that encounter the many headed hydras, and various monsters, which are at present set against the Ministry of this Church.

What ever *censures* any other actions of men may ly under (which God will judge) and of which they may have more cause at last to repent, than to boast) yet this (the *vindicating and establishing of the true Ministry and its authority*) they shall have of all things the *least cause* to repent of. Nor (I hope) will any worthy men give me (or any other Minister) cause to repent, that I *have presumed* to become an *humble suiter*, and a faithfull Monitor, in a matter of so great and so religious concernment; yea, peradventure I may find favour,
1 Sam. 25. 33. (which God can only *give in the eyes of men*) as *Abigail* did in *Davids*; who blessed God for her *seasonable* diverting of him from that *excesse of vengeance*, to which *immoderate passion* had tempted *him*; It is not safe to treat those as enemies, which are Gods friends, and *friends* to mens soules; It was an action onely fit for *Saul*, (whom God
1 Sam. 18. had *forsaken*) to destroy *the Priests of the Lord*, as enemies and traitors. If any consecrated *vessels of the Temple* should have soil, or *decayes* on them, yet none but *Nebuchadnezzars*, *Belshazzars*, or *Antiochusses* would quite break *them in pieces*, or melt them, and prophane them; No time can be too long, no counsell *too deliberate*,

before

before Christians put so severe a *purpose* in execution; or gratifie any *party* without hearing all sides; Nor should they, that disadvise from it upon sober, and good grounds, *be lesse acceptable* to men in power; than any of those, that prompt and incite to so *hardy and hazardous* an adventure.

This gives me some hope if not of *acceptance*, yet at least of *pardon*, for either that *prolixity* (for which none can doe greater penance than I have) or for that *plainnesse*, by which I may exercise any mans patience, who vouchsafes to read this my *Apologetick defense*: wherein I have not forgot, that, as it is written in a busie and pragmatick age, so possibly it may fall into the hands of some persons, whose imployments admit of *little leisure*, for such long discourses, or tedious addresses: But, as *others* in reading may be prone too much to remember their *momentaries*; so, I in writing have chiefly considered my *owne*, and others *eternities*. I have weighed with my self, how important a *businesse* God had laid in this upon my heart; and my heart upon my hand; The vehemency and *just zeal* for which, hath still dictated to my pen both *this spurre* and excuse; That in a Cause of so *great consequence*, it were not onely a *sin* for me to *say nothing*, but to say little; lest *shortnesse of speech* should detract from the worth of the matter; *Weak* shadowes would argue faint flames; either a dimnesse in that *light*, or a chilnesse in that heat, which ought to attend a businesse, which (to my judgement) seems of *infinite importance to present*, and future times; So precious a Jewell, as the true Ministry of the *glorious Gospell of Jesus Christ*, was not to be set with an unhandsome foil, or by a slight and perfunctory hand. I know *small fires* and *short puffes*, will not serve to make *great irons malleable*; No Divell is harder to be *unmufled* and detected, than that which conceals it self under *Angelick masks*, which some weak and credulous soules think a sin, to lift up, or to suspect. But we are not ignorant of *Satans devises*; No drosse, or masse of corruption is *more untamable*, and unseparable from mans nature than that of *sacrilegious enmity* against Christ, the Gospell, and the Ministry while they have any thing to lose.

17. *The Authors excuse for the prolixity of this Apologetick defense.*

2 Cor. 2. 11.

I am sure, what ever we or our *posterity* of this Nation may want, we cannot want Christ, or the true light of the Gospell, in its power and authority, without being a most *unhappy Nation*; To which, if the *preservation* of a learned, godly, and *authoritative Ministry* in a *due ordination and divine succession*, (such as was of late and still is, (though much wasted and weakned in *England*) be not thought necessary; truly no more will the Scriptures, nor the

the Sacraments, nor the peace of Conscience, nor the pardon of sin, nor the saving of soules ere long be *thought necessary*; No nor the *excellency of the knowledge of our Lord Jesus Christ*; whose Name and Worship will shortly be, either shamefully abused; scurrilously despised; (as now it is by many) yea and cleane forgotten, by the profane, stupid, sensuall, and Atheisticall hearts of men; unlesse there be some men, whose speciall calling and commission, from God and man, shall both enable and ordain them to *preach and administer holy things in Christs Name*; whose duty and conscience so commands them to serve God and his Church, that they cannot be silent, or *negligent* without sin.

18. *Mens pronenesse to Apostasie without a true Ministry.* To expect that arbitrary, and occasionall Preachers will doe the *work of Christ, and the Church*; is as vain, as to thinke, that passengers or travellers will build, and *plant*, and *sow*, *and fight* for men in their *civill occasions*; The men of this world, will finde many other imployments of *greater honour*, credit and content, than to *preach the Gospell*, with the crosse of poverty, and contempt upon them; (which is ever *crucifying* the world, and must expect to be *crucified* by the world;) It's rare to finde any generation of men that are truly *favourers* of Ministers, or the Gospel; therefore they are ever grudging at all cost laid out on Christs account, as lost and going *beside their Mill*, who had rather bee *savers*, than *saved by him*; Nor is the opinion, which sober men generally retain of the *excellency* and *necessity* of Christian Religion, in order to their salvation, sufficient to keep it up to a *constancy* and *succession*, without a true *powerfull* and *authoritative Ministry*: For we see that, although nothing concerns men more, than to *beleeve there is a God*, (the supreme good) of whose goodnesse, bounty, power, and protection we have every moment need, use and experience; and upon whose mercy our *sinfull mortality* can (onely) with any reason depend, both living and dying for our eternall welfare; yet many (yea most of men) are ready to run out to *Atheism*, and to live *without God in the world*, unlesse they have frequent and solemne remembrances, (besides their owne hearts) to put them in *minde in their dependance on, and duty to God*; In like manner, although nothing should be more welcome to mankinde, (because nothing more necessary) than the news of a *Saviour for sinners*; yet the *bitter root* of *unbeleif*, and many *sensuall distractions*, which are in mens hearts and lives, are prone to entertain nothing with lesse liking, than the hearing and obeying of this *holy Gospell*; though applyed to them in the best and winningest matters, that *humane abilities* can attaine: Nature and Reason teach there is a God, and no miracle was ever

To Atheism.

To Unbeleif.

wrought

wrought to convert Atheists; but the mystery of Salvation by Jesus Christ crucified is by no light of nature or reason attainable; and needed both miracles at the first planting, and a constant Ministry for the continuing of it in the world.

If then men be naturally so much *aliens from the life of God*, and so much *enemies to the crosse of Christ*; it is not like they will ever be so *good natured*, as seriously to undertake the constant *taske*, *care*, and *toile* of preaching to others; especially, when they *have no call to it*, but their owne, or others pleasure; no *conscience* of it, as a divine Office, and duty; no promise, or hope of divine assistance, or blessing in it; no thankes for it, or benefit by it, either from God or man: Alas, these *warm fits* and *gleames of novelty*, *curiosity*, *popularity*, *pride*, *wantonnesse*, *self-opinion*, and *self-seeking*; (which seem to be in some men, who count themselves *gifted*, *prophetick*, *specially cald*, and *inspired*) these will soon damp to *coldnesse* and deadnesse, when once either their design, which is bad; or their weaknesse, which is great; or their folly, which is grosse, shall be * *manifest to themselves*, and to others, as it is already to very many, good Christians; who finde, that all the *frolick* and *activity* of those men, is but helping forward the *pragmatick policies* of those, who study to ruine this, and all reformed Churches; For if once *true and able Ministers* be cryed down, cast out, and cut off as to *right succession*; the true Religion, as Christian, and reformed too, cannot (*without a miracle*) continue, but must needs be overrunne with *brutish ignorance*, damnable errours, and barbarous manners; which are already prevailed much in many places, partly for want of *able Ministers*, and partly by the *peoples supine neglect* of publique duties, and despising their true Ministers, under pretence of engraffing to *new bodies*, and adhering to new *gifted Teachers* and *Conventicles*; which we find breed up few or none in *knowledge*, or piety; but onely *transplant* proficients out of other mens labours, and nurseries: the mean time the *younger sort* generally runne out to ignorance, and the elder to what liberties they most affect; for want of that setled *Ministry*, order, and government, which ought in Religion, and reason of State to be both established and incouraged.

The valour of cowards, and the vertues of hypocrites are in the eyes of their Spectators.

* 2 Tim. 3. 9.

For my owne particular, I have obtained all I designed *by this defense*, if I may but put all *excellent Christians*, and those chiefly (whom it most concerns) in *minde* of that, which I thinke they cannot forget, or neglect without great *imprudence*, as well as sin: nor will any man be excuseable, who doth not with his best *endeavours promote it*. No private ends, or *sinister passion* of envy, covetousnesse, or ambition; no fear, or contempt of any men, hath 19.

The Authors integrity.

Animi directa simplicitas satis se ipsa commendat. Amb.

Satis habeo si res meæ nec mihi pudori, nec cuiquam oneri forent. Hortalus apud Tacit. An. 4.

Primum Ecclesia Dei jura, atque immunitates suas habeto, inter Leges Edgari.

hath any *ingrediency* in this piece, (however, in other things, no man is more prone to discover how *weak and sinfull a creature he is,* without Gods grace) I have nothing of *private interest,* for profit, or honor, to crave, or expect from great or good men; Indeed they have little or nothing left to tempt men with: I have more then I *can merit*, or well account for; yea I have enough; through the bounty of God, and the blessing of one (*to me*) *Inestimable Jewell*: whose *virtuous lustre* both beautifies and enricheth my life, to an *honorable competency*, and a most happy tranquillity, whose every way most over-meriting merits have deserved, as much as can be, to be consecrated by my pen to an eternity of gratitude and honour.

I have seen so *more than enough* of the *worlds vanity*, *madnesse*, and *misery*; that I doe not desire any thing more, than to spend the remainder of my life in a contented privacy to the glory of God, the *honour of this Church*, and the *welfare of posterity*; If I were offered the *choice of all wishes*, and the fulfilling of them in this world; I would *desire nothing*, next that justice which is the conservatrix of all civill peace and society, but this, That *such as are able*, would so far consider the honour of God, and the welfare of the Church of *England*; as to become *Patrons*, and incouragers of good learning, and the reformed Religion; and to this purpose, that they would establish that holy Discipline, right order, ancient government, and divine succession of able Ministers, which ought to be in the Church of Christ.

In reference to the *generall function*, and *fraternity* of whom, I cannot but intreat, and offer thus much at least as I have done, which cannot be to any good mans detriment, or the Publiques injury: For it is not a pleading for a *restitution of those honours, lands, jurisdictions,* and *dignities*, which were by pious donation, and devout lawes appropriated to that *profession*: I know how vain and unseasonable a motion it were to crave the restoring of honors, goods, and estates of those who are now almost reduced to petition for their liberties and lives. (It is nobler (since God will have it so) for *Clergy men to want those blessings with content*, than to enjoy them with so much envy and anger; as in this age seems inseparable from Bishops and Ministers in any worldly prosperity) Nor is it a challenging of those immunities, and *priviledges*, which the lawes *Imperiall*, and Nationall, every where *among Christians* indulged to the *Clergy*; we must learn to think it *freedom enough*, if we may have leave but to *preach and practise the Gospel of Jesus Christ*, which is our duty and dignity; we must esteeme it a great priviledge now to be but exempted from *vulgar rivalry* and mechanick insolency; which dares not onely to intrude into

Ministers

Ministers Pulpits, but to pull them out by unheard of outrages; not suffering the Church to be their Sanctuary. We claim not exemption from civill Magistrates *Court-censures*, and jurisdictions, (as was of *old in many cases*) our aim is so to doe all things, as shall feare no men to be *spectators*; nor our *enemies* to be our *judges*: Nor can we have so *full* and *desirable a revenge* on our enemies, as to doe well; who are never more sory, than to see any true Minister live *unblameably* and commendably. We dare not crave to be eased of *publique taxes*, either in whole, or in part; Notwithstanding (for the most part) our *charges* are great, our *livings* small, and but for life; yea and but the wages for *our war and worke*; (while we serve in a better Militia:) It matters not what our *secular burdens* be, so as we may make the Gospell any way lesse *burthensome, or more welcome to our hearears*: We urge not that *common liberty* which we have; and our *joint interest* in the publique civill welfare, as *men*; while yet we are made uncapable, and the onely men of any calling that are *excluded* from all publique votes, counsels, or influence; when yet any trade may invade our calling, and usurp our Ministry: It is well, if wee may be suffered to be of *Gods Counsel*; and permitted to acquaint others with it, in order *to their salvation*; our ambition is, so to live, that the diminutions, contempt, and poverty, cast *upon the Ministeriall* order (as to all secular priviledges or interests) may be no *disparagement to our function*, any more than it was to *Primitive* Bishops and Presbyters; who by their *constant patience and humility* gave *greatest Testimony* to the truth of the Gospell: whom their preaching moved not, their patience did. Yet, it will be little to the honour of this Nation, which as yet professeth the Christian Religion, to treat the Ministers of Christ after the rate, that *Diocletian*, or *Maximinus*, or *Julian* did; or as those *primitive persecutors*, either heathens, or *hereticks*; or as the Mahumetans at this day doe; under whom, it is a favour to *tolerate* any Christian Bishops, or Preachers, or Professors, among whom, even the remaining *Embers* of Christianity are almost raked up, and buried, under the oppressions, poverty and barbarity used against them and their Ministers. Nothing hath a *deeper* and *sharper* sense upon my soule, than when I see, not onely the great and heavy distresses, which already have, and will further fall on many, and most of my *betters and brethren*; (who as *learned*, *godly*, and *ingenuous* men, merit something at least of compassion;) but, chiefly, when, by *foresight of future times*, I consider, not without grief and horrour, the great decayes, if not *utter vastations*, of the *reformed Religion*; and of that true piety, (which

Quos prædicatio non potuit, illos vicit prædicantium patientia; quos documenta Evangelica non moverunt, de istis bene tolerata injuriæ tandem triumpharunt. Horn. de Eccl. prim. persec.

such hath heretofore so flourished in *England*) through the want of true, able and authoritative *Ministers*, all those inundations of ignorance, error, superstition, and confusion will certainly flow in, which all *good Christians* would most *deprecate* both from God and man; my own, and other *mens serious sense* of all which, I shall much grieve to finde either unacceptably, or unsuccessefully expressed in *this Apologetick defence*; which is humbly presented to the Christian candor, and submitted to the judgement of all those excellent Christians, whom it most concerns, and to whom it is directed; the least of whom I would not *willingly offend*.

** Fructus est laboris & finis operis placere melioribus.* Sym. Ep.

20. *Deprecation of offence.* *Non laudes sed laudanda quæro.*

Beseeching them in the *name of our Lord Jesus Christ*, to *accept in the spirit of meeknesse and love*, what I have written (I hope) as becomes a Christian, and a Minister of the Gospell in this reformed *Church of England*; Also to *cover* with the *vail of charity*, what ever *infirmities* may appeare, as in a frail and sinfull man; who knowing, that I had chiefly to contest with some men, that are *wise in their own conceit*, thought it a part of wisdome, in its season to *answer them*, according to their folly. (Prov. 26. 4.) And when I considered, that these *Antiministeriall spirits*, if they fear God, yet they seeme little to *reverence men*, either in the *hoary heads* of *pious antiquity* declaring its judgement in the writings of the Fathers, Canons of *Councels*, and histories of the Church; or in the *learned judgement* of those *excellent Authours* of *later edition*, (who are all against them) It hath made me the more sparing in so clear and confessed a cause, to cite their *infinite Testimonies*: My intent being, neither to make this *Apology* a *flag of ostentation*, for great reading: nor yet to *crowd up* and *smother* these men, *meerly with numbers of names and quotations*, (which is very easie) but rather to breath upon *them with the breath of life*, and to convince them with *Scripture*, and *right reason*; which may serve to meet with any in the ordinary rodes of rigid *Separatists*, *Papists*, and *Socinians*; as for *Seekers*, *Enthusiasts*, *Seraphicks*, and *Ranters*, they commonly fly like *Night-ravens* and *Scrichowles*, so much in obscurities, that I can hardly see them; though I oft hear their ominous *voices portending utter darknesse*, after their *evening fulgurations and flashes*: when I meet with any of these, I thought it my duty, and *honour* not to give them way; though indeed I know nothing probable to conquer such *obstinate* passions, to confute such *proud ignorance*, or to curb such *wanton liberties*, as these unruly spirits pretend to, but onely the hand of God in sicknesse, poverty, terrour, and improsperity: A little *winter* of affliction will easily kill all those *vermine* of opinions, which are bred in a *summers toleration*, through health, plenty, successes, preferments; and which seise at length the very heads and hearts of men.

If

If any Christian, *through meer simplicity*, and *honest credulity*, have erred; not daring to take the *hundred part* of that *confidence* to maintain Truth, or to assert worthy Ministers, and the right way of the reformed and Christian Religion, which others doe, to broach, and abet their desperate errors and calumnies: I hope I have (as my purpose is) offered to those *well meaning Soules*, in all plainnesse, and charity, what may redeem them from those *many false*, and *erratick fires*, which seek to seduce them, from their true Ministers, whom the light of right reason, and Scripture, and experience will shew them, are as much to be loved, honoured and esteemed, as ever *any Ministers of the Gospel* were to *any Christians* in any Church, since the Apostles time.

If any rude and *injurious detractors*, being over grown with *proud* and *presumptuous flesh*, instead of healing, rise to *insolent humors*, and *intolerable inflammations*, rayling, defaming, decrying, and speaking all manner of evill *falsely* against worthy Ministers, and their calling; being resolved, and having vowed, *as the forty men against Saint Paul*, quite to destroy them; The *corrasives* or *burnt alum* here and there *sprinkled* on the plaister of *this Apology* is purposely to meet with, and to *eat out that proud and dead flesh*, which may be in their corrupted minds and *benummed consciences*. The sober Christian must not think, that every one that makes a sowre face or wry mouth, or wincheth at this Apology, or passeth a severe, slight, or scurrilous answer upon it, or its author, is presently hurt or injured by me, or it, further than he whose bones are broken, is hurt by one that strives to set them; or he that hath ulcerated sores, is by him that seeks to search and heal them. These men I must needs offend as to their distemper: I did *designe it*; I ever shall offend them, if I will *defend this Truth*; It is my duty, and charity, by displeasing them, *to doe them good*: *Apoplectick diseases* are incurable, till *sense be restored*; some men are *benummed*, and *past feeling*; I cannot live, or dye in peace, if I should *hold my peace*, when *I ought to rebuke*, and *with all authority*, (because with *Truth and good conscience*; in *the name of Christ*, and of all *my brethren*) the *intolerable vanity*, ignorance, pride, arrogancy, and cruelty of those, who have set up themselves above, and against all those, that are the ordained, reformed, and faithfull *Ministers* of this, or any other Christian Church; In whom they list to finde nothing but *faults*, and *insufficiencies*; while they boast of their own rare *accomplishments*; which are no where to *be found*, but in their *proud swelling words*, by which they lie in wait to *deceive the simple and unstable soules*.

Act. 23. 14.

Ephes. 4. 19.

I could no longer bear their *insolent Pamphlets*, their *intolerable* 2 Pet. 2.18.

practises, their *uncharitable projects*, against the glory of Christ, and the happinesse of this reformed *Church*, and Nation; It grieved me to see so may *Shipwrackt soules*; so many *tossed* to and fro, who are floating to the *Romish coast*; so many *overthrown faiths*; so many willing and *affected Atheists*; so many *cavilling Sophisters*; so many *wasted comforts*; so many *scurrilous* and *ridiculous Saints*; so many *withered graces*; so many *seared consciences*; so many *sacrilegious Christians*; so many *causelesse triumphings*, of mean persons, over learned, grave, and godly Ministers; I was troubled to behold so many fears, yet so much *silence*, so many sighes and sorrows, yet so much dejection, and *oppression* of spirits, such *over awings*, in those men, whom it becomes in a spirituall warfare to encounter with beasts and *unreasonable* men, as being sure to *overcome* at last; Therefore (among others) I desire, this apology may be a monument of my perfect abhorrency and publique protestation against all evil counsels, and violent designes used against this reformed Church, its Religion, and Ministry: when posterity shall see the sad effects of some mens agitations. I expect no acceptance from any men further, than I may *doe them good*: Such as refuse to be *healed* by this application, probably their smart will provoke them to *petulant* replyes, which as I cannot expect from any sober, and serious Christian; so to the *wantonnesse* of others, who are wofull *wasters of paper and inke*, I shall never have leisure to attend; I have better imployment, whereto I humbly devote the short remnant of my pretious *moment*; even to the service of Christ, of this Church, and of all those *excellent Christians* in it; to whose favour this *sudden Apologetick* defence is humbly dedicated, in the *behalf of the Ministry of this Church of England*, by their humblest servant in the Lord

οὐ πάνυ ἡμῖν φροντιστέον ὅ, τι ἐροῦσιν οἱ πολλοὶ καὶ ἄδικοι, ἀλλ᾽ ὅ, τι ἂν ὁ δίκαιος κἀγαθὸς. Plato in Crito.

I. G.

FINIS.

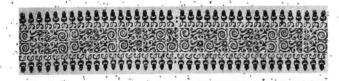

A Table of the chief heads handled in this Defense of the Ministery of the Church of ENGLAND.

Of

IV. *Objection.* The first Cavill or Calumny:

V. *Objection.* The second Cavill or Calumny:

The

Conclusion

A 2

IX. *Objection.* The sixth Cavill or Calumny :

X. *Ob-*

X. *Objection.* The seventh Calumny or Cavill:

XI. *Objection.* The eight Cavill or Calumny:

FINIS.

Christian Reader; these and some other Errata's have escaped the care used in Printing; and are, against the Authors and Printers will, left, as exercises of thy judgment and candor in reading and amending.

Errata in the Epistle.

pag. line. read. for.
p. l. r. f.

1. 12. r. distempers *for* enemies.
28. beyond *for* being
5. 30. motive *for* motion
6. 7. outvied *for* outvived

p. l.

10. 12. Prince *f.* Princesse
25. soon *for* far
21. 1. revolutions' *for* Revelations
24. 23. support *f.* wisdom
28. 4. *dele*, by esteem

p. l.

22. gentle *for* great
42. 7. their *for* the
8. setling *for* setting
43. 15. wantonly.

Errata in the Book.

pag. line. read. for. margent.
p. l. r. f. m.

3. *m.* explorant *for* explicant
5 *Non dii f. mordii*
9. 36. *r.* conscientiously
19. *m. putredo*
21. 19. *Add* so much as the law, &c.
25. 26. pathetick *for* politick
49. 23. formation *for* sumation
59. 25. piercing *for* pitifull
זביל *f.* לביל
62. m. *Reg. Jur. f. Reg. Jacob.*
107. r. בן f. בל
114. 23. peculiar *f.* popular
117. 43. body *for* badge
120. 41. *del.* men
123. 7. חחל *f.* ערה
223. 14. loosenes *f.* basenes
225. 28. adulatory *for* adulterate
233. 8. than their gifts can doe good.
237. The first Cavill.
236. m. *Stob.* f. *Amb.*
241. *m.* τὰ δίκαιως θεῖα πεπιστευκότα

p. l.

243. 10. their beauty
251. 6. *add* not strongly
260. m. *turba Remi.*
260. 41. *Add* no more just arguments
274. m *Imitatores f. incitatores*, -- *vigiles* for *igitur*
275. ω, κόσμοιο -- *congrua*
278. 3. *add* of them
279. 3. temperament *for* temperance
287. Prov. 11.14. *f.* Rom.
273 7. wrestling *f.* wresting
20. powerMinisteriall
378. m. *Artibus*
384. 22. Inspiratoes
388. 9. tine weed *for* true weed
r. shewing *for* shining
400. m. *cum non, &c.*
406. 8. beleever *for* unbeleever
493. 3. yet it were *for* if it were
430 1. ashes *for* ages
431. 36. *del.* not: *and read* can be good
440. 41. sinfull bondage
463. 2. bends *for* binds

p. l.

35 terrier
43. thrifty
466. men *for* mention
469. 25. *del.* with a good will and
470. 25. in piety *f.* impiety
477. 37. collections *for* customes
481. 12. impurity *for* imparity
492. 18. *ad.* give him
520. 93. *add* most promising, &c.
538. 7. *r.* vain babling *for* vain blessings
539. 37. fervent prayers
541. 21. terrors *for* errors
547. 11. *r.* odde pieces
549. 35. *r.* mortal Angels
575. *m.* unity *for* verity
2. *dele* would be
577. 24. undertaking *for* understanding
578. 18 spread *for* spend
584. 16. medling *f.* mudling
590. 5. mee *for* men
593. 25. Censure *f.* answer
594. 27. so many *f.* so may.

— f —

Gauden is himself the sole authority for his being the Author of Εικων Βασιλικη — The fact is that the king was the author himself — Gauden claimed authorship in order to obtain promotion — He was a turn coat and a time server. Having once preached against the King to please the Puritans

— So Dr Wordsworth in 1824

THE EASTWARD POSITION.

Sir,—Will you allow me to draw the attention of those interested (and who are not?) in the present proceedings at Lambeth to a work that not only proves much that Dr. Littledale has stated, but coming from a moderate Churchman will, perhaps, induce the prosecutors of the present day to look at their predecessors of the Reformation period. I mean the Rev. J. W. Haweis' Sketches of the Reformation Period, published by Mr. Pickering some 20 years ago. Here is a choice extract, in which the Eastward position comes in:—

"From the first hour they (the itinerant preachers) started on their missions to the East, when they gained their point, and won their suit against ceremonies, these men were the troublers of our Israel. About 1564, Archbishop Parker preferred one Richard Kechyn, a plain good man, to some living in the vicinity of Booking, charging him on his admission not to preach controversial sermons on the Divine counsels, but to follow the orders and rules appointed and established by the law, and make no variations, notwithstanding the endeavours others might use to persuade him to swerve from them. This admonition Kechyn punctually obeyed. The Litany he said in the body of the church, the service in the chancel, with his face towards the altar, but so as to be distinctly heard. He wore a square cap and surplice, and lightly touched the topic of Predestination in his discourses. On Rogation Week, too, he perambulated the parish bounds, read the appointed collects, and forbade not the poor to say Amen, nor to partake of the meal provided for those who formed the procession. This went on smoothly for a while, until a licensed preacher named Holland heard of his proceedings, and without delay hastened to

practice. 'Predestination,' he said, 'should and ought to be preached in every sermon, and in every place, before all congregations, as the only doctrine of salvation; and they that granted a truth in it, and would not have it everywhere preached, as well as they that denied it, were enemies to God and the eternal predestination.' The same sentence he pronounced on them who judged it—as Kechyn did—a high and secret mystery fitter for the schools and universities, where the auditories were learned, than discussion in a rural district. Having thus set the pastor to rights, he proceeded to the flock, haranguing on the enormity of those women who accompanied the processions in Rogation Week—an obscene derivation from the feast of Bacchus—and shamelessly said Amen to the curse on removers of a neighbour's landmark. This was, it may be supposed, a trial of patience. Kechyn, and many another like him, were exposed to this treatment from a man whose insufficiency might provoke the retort of Petruchio. But he was still more galled by a check from one who could claim some authority over him. The Dean of Bocking liked his regularity no better than the licensed preacher: his use of the surplice displeased that dignitary, and his mode of reading prayers: and he, with his brethren, were charged by the Dean at his visitation 'not to turn his face towards the high altar in service saying.' Kechyn at last could bear this system of contradiction no longer. He wrote to the archbishop's almoner that he was quite willing to disuse the surplice, to stop

High Altar

— And 1564 was a [illegible] [illegible] !!

January 14, 1876.]

Amens, etc., but earnestly requested a sight of the primate's articles, and an answer whether he should obey them or the annually varying injunctions of the dean. The conclusion is not given by Strype, but it is not needed to point the moral of the tale."

A series of choice bits from the book would be well worth extracting and reprinting.

G. W.

subject of crotchetty and impractical people might *mutatis mutandis* be read with profit by a section of High Churchmen.

From a conversation at the Lambeth Police Court on Wednesday it would appear that the Inland Revenue have, or have had, some idea of attempting to tax people who employ a lad for an hour or two in the morning to clean knives and boots as if they kept a man servant. It does the Government very little credit that its officers should have ventured even to dream of anything so harsh and absurd. If the scheme had succeeded, it would have struck a heavy blow at such institutions as Boys' Homes; and, moreover, it would have been a serious inconvenience to persons who, having manageable families, employ boys to do their more unpleasant household work, and dis-

[January 14, 1876.

up strife where it did not previously exist, and have invited parochial quarrels. For the most part the Acts are useless, as the chief religious bodies in competition are not in the habit of holding service at the grave, but in the house of the deceased; but where they are put in use, it is to make mischi...

High Altar

— and 1564 was a nonconformist !!

Lightning Source UK Ltd.
Milton Keynes UK
UKHW020254091022
410164UK00005B/221

9 781013 987519